The BLACK LIGHT and Fluorescent Art
The Social Stigma of "FLUOROPHOBIA"

Introduction: "Color and Art"

The First Discoveries of Fluorescence and Luminescence: "1500 B.C. - 1750: From China to Benjamin Franklin"

The First Fluorescent Paint: "Robert Switzer - "Day-Glo" Paint - 1933"

The Miracle of Fluorescence: "1930s - 1950s"

The Social Phenomenon Of Fluorescence: "The 1960s Movement"

The Greying of the Miraculous Fluorescent Rainbow: "Post 1960s - Social Stigma and Fluorophobia / "Alba" the Green Fluorescent Rabbit and Transgenic Fluorescent Animals" ("Qu'est-il arrive au miracle?")

Dedicated:
To my soulmate Michèle Delage. Also dedicated to the people who will live 100 years from now. Maybe they will have more Opened Minds and bigger eyes than most of the characters alive today.
Copyright, Nick Padalino, 2007-2017

© Nick Padalino, 2017
Published by Nick Padalino, Creator of "Electric Ladyland - the First Museum of Fluorescent Art"
www.electric-lady-land.com
All Photographs: © Nick Padalino, 2017

All rights reserved. No part of this book may be reproduced by any means in any form without written permission from the author Nick Padalino.

The BLACK LIGHT and FLUORESCENT ART
the Social Stigma of "FLUOROPHOBIA"

Introduction: "Color and Art" pg. 11

1. "Chromophobia"
2. The Parthenon's original vivid painted Colors
3. The Eiffel Tower's many different Colors
4. Coptic Art's restored Colors
5. The Sistine Chapel's restored Colors
6. "The Last Supper" restoration
7. The Colosseum's original Colors
8. Bourge Cathedral's original Colors
9. Le Corbusier - "Chromophobic" prototype
10. Ancient Rome's early Chromophobic Pliny the Elder
11. First published Chromophobic: Plato of ancient Greece
12. China's "Terracotta Army" originally painted with vivid Colors
13. Artist's lowest social standing: "Peynter-Steyner"
14. Renaissance 'war' of "Color versus Drawing"
15. Aristotle's "Chromophobia"
16. Goethe's "Theory of Colors:" Chromophobic handbook
17. "Chromophobia," David Batchelor (2000)
18. "Quest for Color," Cary Wolinsky, National Geographic magazine
19. "Men in Black," J. Harvey (1996)
20. "Color: The Story of Dyes and Pigments," Delamare and Furneau (1999)
21. Charles Blanc, "Grammar of Paintings and Engravings" (1867)
22. Le Corbusier's Chromophobic book "Purism" (1920)
23. Michel Eugene Chevreul (1786-1889)
24. Chevreul, "The Principles of Harmony and the Contrast of Colors" (1839)
25. 2,500 BC: first synthetic paint pigment, "Egyptian Blue"
26. "Color: A Natural History of the Palette," Victoria Finlay (2002)
27. "Fluorescent Mineral Society"
28. Electron Displacement - the Cause of Fluorescence
29. "Participatory Art"
30. Paul Gauguin (1848-1903): influence on Modern Artist
31. "Bright Earth - Art and the Invention of Color," Philip Ball (2001)
32. Faber Birren (1900-1988): Color author and expert
33. Sir Isaac Newton (1642-1727)
34. Tibetan holy "Kalachakra Sand Mandalas"
35. Buddhist "Thong drel:" 'Enlightenment through Looking'
36. American Indian Navaho Sand painters
37. Jackson Pollock (1912-1956): influence on Modern Art
38. 1999: Apple's "iBook" Color revival
39. "Green Fluorescent Protein" Movement of the Twentieth century
40. "Glo-Fish" invented and sold since 1997
41. Conclusion of "Fluorophobia" / Introduction to GFP Animals of the Twentieth century

The First Discoveries of Fluorescence and Luminescence: "1500 B.C. - 1750 - From China to Benjamin Franklin" pg. 50

42. 1852: Sir George Gabriel Stokes names "Fluorescence"
43. 1603: Vincenzo Casciarola discovers the "Bologna Stone"
44. 1777: Scheele discovers that Light produces chemical reaction in Silver chloride
45. 1800: Herschel discovers "Infra-red"
46. 1801: Ritter experiments with Silver chloride and discovers "Ultraviolet"
47. 1500-1000 BC: first documentation of Luminescence appears in China
48. 1000 BC: Japanese invent Phosphorescent paint
49. 550 BC: Greek philosopher Anaximenes writes about "Bioluminescence"
50. 350 BC: Aristotle writes about Bioluminescence
51. 200 BC: Indian "Mahabharata" contains verses on Bioluminescence
52. 102 BC: China Han dynasty has Phosphorescent gemstone
53. ±1 AD: Roman Titus Livius writes about Bioluminescence
54. 50 AD: Pliny the Elder hosts "Glow-in-the-Dark" Banquets in ancient Rome
55. Marcus Valerius Martialis (40-102 AD) writes about Bioluminescence
56. 618-904 AD: Chinese "Phosphorescent Pillow"
57. Stephen Batman (1537-1587) rewrites Bioluminescence book
58. Barthomaeus Angelicus (1190-1260) includes Bioluminescence in Encyclopedia
59. Conrad Gesner (1516-1565) writes first book on "Luminoscity"
60. 1565: Nicolas Monardes first documented observation of Fluorescence
61. 1603: Vincenzo Casciarola discovers the "Bologna Stone"
62. 1600s: "Bologna Phosphorus" sold by Casciarola is first Luminescent product
63. 1568: Cellini documents first natural phosphor - Diamond
64. Galileo (1564-1642) studies Bologna Stone
65. Nicola Zucchi (1586-1670) describes mechanics of Phosphorescence
66. 1640: Fortunius Licetus (1577-1657) writes about the Bologna Stone
67. Francis Bacon (1561-1626) writes about Bioluminescence and Triboluminescence
68. 1637: Rene Descartes (1596-1650) writes about Bioluminescence
69. Athanasius Kircher (1601-1680) first discovers Fluorescence in solution
70. 1704: Sir Isaac Newton writes about Bioluminescent wood
71. Robert Boyle (1627-1691): "The Father of Bioluminescence"
72. "Bioluminescent Bay," Puerto Rico
73. 1665: Robert Hooke (1635-1703) writes about Bioluminescent mechanics
74. 1669: Hennig Brand (1630-1710) discovers first chemical element - Phosphorus
75. Jacques Rohault (1818-72) writes about Bioluminescence
76. 1673: Christian Adolf Balduin (1632-82) produces a luminescent substance
77. 1868: Robert Plot (1640-96) 'discovers' Dinosaurs, writes about Bioluminescence
78. 1688: Pere Guy Tachard (1651-1712) documents Bioluminescence in book
79. 1692: Domenico Bottoni, Messina, Italian doctor lists Bioluminescent creatures
80. 1713: Jesuit Missionary Father Bourzes writes about Bioluminescence
81. 1718: Sir Isaac Newton writes on cause of Bioluminescence
82. Jean-Jacques Dortus de Mairan (1678-1771) writes about Bioluminescence
83. 1726: Charles Fracois de Cisterney du Fay (1698-1739) "Thermoluminescence"
84. 1728: Francesco Mario Zanotti does research on Bologna Stone
85. 1750: Dunot Hofmann first documents "Triboluminescence"
86. 1753: U.S. President Benjamin Franklin writes first correct explanation of Bioluminescence
87. Goethe (1749-1832) steals credit from unknown John Ritter for "Ultraviolet" discovery
88. 1833: Sir David Brewster does advanced research into Fluorescence
89. 1845: Sir John Herschel does further research into Fluorescence
90. April 28, 1852: Sir George Gabriel Stoke's (1819-1903) famous experiment with Fluorite that led to his naming of the phenomenon "Fluorescence"
91. Antoine, Edmond, and Henri Becquerel experiment with Fluorescence in late 1800s

The First Paint to Emit it's own Light: "Robert Switzer, "Day-Glo" Paint: 1933" pg. 67

92. February, 1903: Dr. Robert Wood (1868-1955) invents the Black Light Filter
93. "Fluorescence Viewing Box" Invented by Dr. Robert Wood
94. 1903: "Spark Box," Early Ultraviolet device invented
95. Franklin, New Jersey: "The Fluorescent Mineral Capital of the World"
96. 1915: First Ultraviolet bulb the "Argon Glow Lamp" sold to the public
97. 1912: Andrews perfects Fluorescent tubular lamps
98. "NICO Tubes:" First modern era Black lights in the 1920s
99. "Tilt-Lamp:" early Black lights of the 1920s
100. "Switzer Brothers" "Model 70" large 250 watt Black light
101. 1930s: "PurpleX" and other screw-in Black light bulbs produced
102. 1907: John Thompson Shannon creates first public Black light performances
103. 1924: Alexander Strobl creates Fluorescent Displays in New York City
104. 1935: "Box Office Magazine:" Alexander Strobl article on Black light
105. 1939: "Box Office Barometer:" list of Black light Theater companies
106. 1940: "Juggling Review Magazine:" article on Fluorescent Juggling
107. 1933: Nineteen year-old Robert Switzer Invents Fluorescent Paint in Berkley, California
108. "Black Art" is already a famous stage technique by 1933
109. 1934: Switzer brothers form "The Switzer Brother's Ultra-Violet Lab"
110. June, 1934: First official business of the Switzer brothers named "Fluor-S-Art"
111. late 1934: Second Switzer brother's business name is "Northern Lite Studios"
112. July, 1934: First Fluorescent paint sold to "Shell Oil Company"
113. 2009: "The Day-Glo Brothers" children's book by Chris Barton
114. August, 1934: First newspaper article on the Switzer brothers
115. October, 1934: First magazine article on Switzer brothers in "Scientific American"
117. 1934: Fluorescent "Fan Dances"
118. 1934-1935: Switzer brothers "Fluorescent Skeleton Ballet" with Delmar Gray
119. Aug. 24, 1935: "Box Office" magazine article with photo of "Fluorescent Skeleton Ballet"
120. 1935: Fluorescent "Invisible Laundry Marking" "Fantom Fast"
121. 1935: Joseph Switzer Invents new Fluorescent Lithography printing process
122. 1935: "U.S. Department of Justice" contact "Switzer Brothers" for "Invisible Fluorescent Ink"
123. 1935: Switzer brothers Invent "Fluorescent Fabric" for U.S. Military commission
124. 1935: "Conti-Glo" is fourth Switzer brother's business name, after move to Ohio
125. 1938: Switzer brothers invent "Fluorescent Metal Flaw Detection"
126. 1958: First time the "Switzer Brothers" sell Fluorescent Pigment

The Miracle of Fluorescence: "1930s - 1950s" pg. 88

127. "Grimes Ultra-Violet Cockpit Light" used in military planes during W.W.II
128. 1941: "General Motors" Annual Corporate Ball uses Black lights and "Day-Glo"
129. 1920s: "Radio City Music Hall," New York City, hosts "Fluorescent Skeleton Ballets"
130. 1940s-1970s: Black light with Fluorescent Colors and Fluorescent Minerals used in the CHURCH in the U.S.A. by Priests for Mass on the Alter(!)
131. "Blak-Ray" "Invisible Fluorescent Chalk Set:" "Use with Black Light for: "Church Groups"(!)
132. 1939: San Francisco's "World's Fair:" huge presence of the Black light
133. "The Kokoon Arts Klub," Cleveland, Ohio 1913-1956
134. "The Black Light Ball" in 1938 held by "The Kokoon Arts Klub," Cleveland, Ohio
135. William Byler patents the "Black Light Fluorescent lamp" in the mid-1930s
136. Dr. Richard Kuch patents the "Vapor Electric lamp" in 1904 in German
137. "Ultraviolet Radiation - It's Properties, Production, Measurement, and Applications," Luckiesh (1922)
138. "Quartz Mercury Arc Lamp" and "White Flame Arc"
139. 1922: Shortwave Ultraviolet 'Health Treatment Lamps'
140. 1928: "The Ultra-Violet rays," Dr. Lorand - 'Prevent Falling and Greying Hair'(!)
141. 1928: eighty-nine pages of "Shortwave Ultraviolet Miracle Cures"

142. 1930: "Ultra-Violet Light and Vitamin D in Nutrition," Blunt and Cowan
143. 1912: "Strahlentherapie" - first published paper on "Actinotherapy"
144. 1922: first English publication of "Actinotherapy"
145. Conclusion of 'Shortwave Ultraviolet Medical Treatment' nightmare era
146. 1904: "Quartz Mercury Vapour Lamp" invented by Kromeyer
147. Professor Niels Ryberg Finsen - The Founder of "Actinotherapy"
148. 1903: Finsen awarded the "Nobel Prize"(!) and dies 10 months later in a wheelchair at 42
150. Grim conclusion of Actinotherapy nightmare era
151. "Conti-Glo" "Black Light Beacon" (1941-1943)
152. 1941: Fluorescent Ice Skating Group in Ohio
153. 1941: police in Ohio begin work with the Black light and Fluorescence in "Criminology"
154. 1941: Fluorescent Movie Theater Carpeting
155. 1941: Fluorescent Juggling
156. 1941: Fluorescent Photography
157. 1941: Black light sports
158. 1941: two documented examples of Black lights and Fluorescent Colors used in Churches!
159. 1941: Fluorescent paint applications
160. 1941: "General Motors Corporation" "Annual Press Dinner" with Black lights
161. 1930s: Fluorescent "Depression Glass"
162. 1940s: "Alameda Theater" in Texas is a famous Fluorescent Black Light Movie theater
163. 1941: "General Motors" traveling Black light exhibition "Preview of Progress"
164. 1941: "Invisible Pass-Out Ink" used at paid entrances of amusement parks, etc.
165. 1942: Two Ohio Restaurants lit only by Black light and Fluorescent paintings
166. "Glow Walls" in Museums today were started in 1942
167. 1942: Fluorescent Black light "Instrument Panels"
168. 1942: Switzer brothers invent Fluorescent Material
169. Loie Fuller (1862-1928) is first "Luminescent Dancer"
170. Radium discovered by Curies in 1898
171. Loie Fuller invents "Radium Paint" for her "Luminescent Dancer" stage costumes
172. 1903: First Fluorescent mineral demonstration in London's Natural History Museum
173. 1904: "Radium Dances" in New York performances
174. 1907: "Skeleton Ballets" in San Francisco are the first public Black light shows
175. 1914: "Radium Craze" as another "Miracle Cure" using insane Radium products
176. "The Radium Girls" doomed watch-dial painters from New Jersey
177. Actinotherapy and Radium: the first causes of "Fluorophobia"
178. 1931: first Amusement park use of Black lights and Fluorescence
178. 1941-1942: "Conti-Glo" price list and product catalogue
179. 1942: Fluorescent paint applications
180. "Conti-Glo" 250 watt "Model 70" Black light for Museum collection
181. 1939: "Popular Science Magazine" publishes first article on Fluorescent minerals
182. "Ultraviolet Guide to Minerals," Sterling Gleason (1960)
183. 1939: Fluorescent mineral prospecting techniques
184. 1944-1950: "Ultra-Violet Products, Inc." "Mineralight Files"
185. 1944: Black light applications
186. 1944: Oil prospecting with Black light
187. 1944: Number 1 "Mineralight Files" on "Fluorochemistry" by DeMent
188. 1944: Number 2 "Mineralight Files," "Fluorochemistry in Petroleum Science"
189. 1944: Number 3 "Mineralight Files," "UV Light in Criminology"
190. 1945: Number 4 "Mineralight Files:" "Fluorescent Analysis with UV Rays"
191. 1944: Synthetic Phosphors (Fluorescent pigments)
192. 1944: Fluorescent Paint formulas
193. 1945: Number 5 "Mineralight File:" "Ultra-Violet Light as Aid to Education"
194. 1944: Fluorescent Black Light Church Sermons!
195. 1944: Fluorescent and Phosphorescent paint in theater and advertising
196. 1945: Number 6 "Mineralight News Bulletin:" "Fluorobiology"
197. 1945: Number 7 "Mineralight News Bulletin:" "Fluorescence in Food Science"

198. 1944: DeMent publishes "Food Stuff Listing"
199. 1945: DeMent publishes 64 Pages of "Luminescent Substances"
200. 1945: DeMent publishes 20,000 entries- "Handbook of Fluorescent Chemicals"
201. 1945: Number 8 "Mineralight News Bulletin," "Ultra-Violet Lights in Detection of Mercury"
202. 1945: Number 9 "Mineralight News Bulletin," "Ultra-Violet Light in Uranium Prospecting"
203. 1945: Number 10 "Mineralight News Bulletin," "Luminescence in Gem Science"
204. 1945: Number 11 "Mineralight News Bulletin," "Fluorochemistry in Dyestuffs, Textile Science"
205. 1947: Number 12 "Mineralight News Bulletin," "Ultra-Violet Fluorescence for Hobbyists"
206. 1945: "Numerous" Church Preachers had already used Black light in Church Sermons!
207. 1930s-1947: History of Fluorescent exhibitions in USA
208. 1940s: "Fluorescent Fire Places" and "Fluorescent Built-In Swimming Pools"
209. "Fluorescent Gems," DeMent (1947)
210. History of Fluorescent "Depression Glass'
211. 1950-1951: number 13 "Mineralight News Bulletin," last issue
212. 'The Practical Applications of Luminescence: Fluorescence-Phosphorescence-Black Light,' Maurice Deribere (France, 1938 and 1954)
213. Early 1900s French Ultraviolet instruments and lamps
214. Early 1900s Fluorescence Photography techniques
215. 1903: Kunz and Baskerville's monumental Fluorescent mineral examination
216. 1896: Edison uses X-Rays to examine 1,800 Fluorescent chemicals
217. 1903: First Fluorescent Mineral Demonstration, London, Natural History Museum
218. 1929: "Philadelphia Public Museum" - first Fluorescent mineral collection exhibit
219. 1938: Deribere discusses Fossil Fluorescence
220. 1941: "Luminescence of Meteorites"
221. 1938: "Applications of Fluorescent Minerals," Deribere
222. 1938: "Application of Black light in Tourist Caves," Deribere
223. 1938: Deribere - Fluorescence in advertising, theater, and household design
224. 1956: Deribere - Fluorescent paper and 'Luminescent Books'
225. 1954: Deribere - beginning of use of Ultraviolet in Art restoration
226. 1942: Deribere - Fluorescent highway pavement
227. 1938: Deribere - 'The Black Light at Home'
228. 1930s: Black light Window displays on the "Champs Elysees"(!)
229. 1954: Deribere - Fluorescent Billboards and Movie theaters in France
230. 1920s: Mercipinetti using Phosphorescent paint for Art in Paris
231. 1956: "General Electric" - "Black light - Lamps, Applications, Design Procedures"
232. 1915: "Argon Glow Lamps" first Ultraviolet lamp sold to the public
233. 1956: "G-E" - medical and military Black light applications
234. 1956: Black light 'Set Design'
235. John Plumer Ludlum biography: first Fine Artist to use Fluorescent Paint in 1945
236. June, 2009: Acquisition of original John Ludlum Fluorescent painting for Museum
237. 1983: Ludlum discusses effects of "Fluorophobia" in late interview

The Social Phenomenon Of Fluorescence: "The 1960s Movement" pg. 295

238. Impact of 1960s "Hippie Movement" on past generations
239. "Fantasy Lighting for After Dark using Blak-Ray," booklet (1960)
240. "The Road to Eleusis - Unveiling the Secrets of the Mysteries," Hofmann, Wasson, and Ruck (1978)
241. "Soma - The Divine Mushroom," R. Gordon Wasson (1968)
242. "Notes on Soma," Dr. Sampurnanand (1967)
243. "Mushrooms that Cause Strange Visions," "Life" magazine (1957)
244. Squandering of "The Miracles of Fluorescence"
245. "Ultraviolet Guide to Minerals," Sterling Gleason (1960) - "The Father of Fluorescent Mineral Collecting"
246. "GFP" "Green Fluorescent Protein" discovered in 1961 by Osamu Shimomura
247. 1993-1994: Martin Chalfie creates first two GFP life forms
248. 2007: "Red Fluorescent Protein" discovered in Moscow and begins a new era
249. Psychoactive drug experiments that Ken Kesey and Allen Ginsberg were initiated in were CIA programs

250. First Psychedelic "Day-Glo" School bus made by Kesey and the Merry Pranksters - "Furthur"
251. Merry Prankster Ken Babbs 'discovers' "Day-Glo" paint
252. "Electric Cool-Aid Acid Test," Tom Wolfe (1968)
253. "The Haight-Asbury - A History," Charles Perry (1984)
254. "Journey to the East," Hermann Hesse (1932) influences Merry Pranksters
255. "Steppenwolf," Hesse (1927) discusses early psychoactive experiments
256. Paul Klee is a member of Hesse's "Journey to the East" group
257. "Childhood's End," Arthur C. Clarke (1953) inspires Merry Pranksters
258. Merry Prankster "Mountain Girl" describes the Black light and Day-Glo paint at "AcidTests"
259. "Mountain Girl" remembers painting "Furthur" with Day-Glo paint
260. "Mountain Girl" remembers the "Black Light Corner" at the "Acid Tests"
261. "Psychedelic Drugs Reconsidered," Grinspoon and Bakalar (1979)
262. 1700s -1800s Nitrous Oxide users include Joseph Priestly, Humphrey Davy, and R. Southly
263. History of Mescaline use by Mexican Indians for 3,000 years
264. 1888: Lewis Lewin publishes first paper on Mescaline
265. 1896-1897: Arthur Heffter isolates pure Mescaline
266. 1919: Ernst Spath synthesizes Mescaline
267. early 1927: First book on Mescaline "Peyotl: La plant qui les fait yeux emerveilles"
268. 1953: Aldous Huxley takes Mescaline and writes "The Doors of Perception"
269. Aldous Huxley's masterpiece "Island" (1963)
270. Aldous Huxley and Humphrey Osmond correspond and coin the word "Psychedelic"
271. "The Road to Eleusis" (1978), first chapter by R. Gordon Wasson, Dr. Albert Hofmann
272. Dr. Albert Hofmann discovers L.S.D. in 1938, and later synthesizes Psilocybin in 1958
273. Dr. Albert Hofmann isolates psychoactive substance in 'Morning Glory' seeds
274. Dr. Albert Hofmann concludes that the ancient Greeks could have easily produced psychoactive drink for the Eleusian Mysteries
275. Richard E. Schutes, "Hallucinogenic Plants," (1976)
276. Cannabis - it's botanical history and use in modern times
277. 'Acid Art,' "Life" magazine (1966)
278. Marcel Duchamp, Visionary Artist (1887-1968)
279. "The Symbolism of Color," Faber Birren (1988)
280. Neuroplasticity
281. An Afternoon with Dr. Albert Hofmann, July 21, 1998
282. Turning on Dr. Albert Hofmann to Fluorescent Minerals
283. Dr. Albert Hofmann's first Fluorescent Mineral collection
284. Medical Marijuana legalized in the U.S.A., and featured on the front cover of "National Geographic" magazine (2016)
285. "Under the Influence, Plastic Arts and Psychotropics," exhibition in Paris (2013)
286. "The Day-Glo Designer's Guide," "Day-Glo" Corporation (1969)
287. Conclusion of 1960s Movement's intrinsic association with the Black Light and Fluorescence

The Greying of the Miraculous Fluorescent Rainbow: "Post 1960s - Social Stigma and Fluorophobia / "Alba" the Green Fluorescent Rabbit and Transgenic Fluorescent Animals" ("Qu'est-il arrive au miracle?") pg. 378

288. The jaded society of the Twenty-first Century: "Little Nicholas the four-year-old Camera Enthusiast"
289. "PRESS HERE," New book for Twenty-first Century children, Herve Tullet (2010)
290. Glow-In-The-Dark-Pets, "International Business Times" (2011)
291. "Glo-Fish," Transgenic Fluorescent aquarium pets for sale (from 1997)
292. Transgenic Bioluminescent Plants marketed (2013)
293. Dr. Craig Venter creates first synthetic Life (2010)
294. "Glow Genes - A Revolution in Biotechnology," Marc Zimmer, Ph.D. (2005)
295. Osamu Shimomura's Nobel Prize lecture (2008)
296. "Bioluminescence - Chemical Principles and Methods," Osamu Shimomura (2006)
297. Matrz and Lukyanov discover Red Fluorescent Protein (RFP) in Russia (2007)
298. Roger Tsien creates Fluorescent Protein in the full spectrum of Colors (2007)

299. Osamu Shimomura, Martin Chalfie, and Roger Tsien share Nobel Prize for Chemistry (2008)
300. Nearly absurd proposed applications during this 'GFP Craze' can be compared to the misguided Twentieth Century's 'Radium Craze' and "Actinotherapy" "Miracle Cures"
300a. June 23, 2015: "Green Fluorescent Protein" Transgenic "Mutant Lamb" is sold as Food to the French public(!!)
301. Marc Zimmer, Ph.D. discusses the first Transgenic Artist Eduardo Kac
302. "Signs of Life, Bio Art and Beyond," Edited by Eduardo Kac (2007)
303. "Green Light: Toward an Art of Evolution," George Gessert (2010)
304. Transgenic Art is 'justified' through comparison to human domestication of animals and plants
305. "The Eight Day, the Transgenic Art of Eduardo Kac," Britton and Collins (2003)
306. "Telepresence and Bio Art, Networking, Rabbits, and Robots," Eduardo Kac (2005)
307. Has Nature begun to defend itself against it's progressive destruction by Human beings?
308. "Jellyfish Invasion" causes closing of Nuclear plants (2011)
309. Worldwide "Bee Catastrophe" and disappearances reported (2010)
310. Phytoplankton, producing 50% of Earth's oxygen, is reported dying in large numbers (2003)
311. A short history of Fluorescent Art
312. Jonathan Borofsky's "Day-Go" Museum of Modern Art installation (1981)
313. Frank Stella's use of Fluorescent Color back to the early 1960s
314. Robert Mallary exhibits Fluorescent Mobiles in 1951, only six years after John Ludlum's first use of Fluorescent paint in Fine Art in 1945
315. James Rosenquist interviewed on his use of Fluorescent paint during the 1960s (2012)
316. Felix de Boeck, the first Artist in Belgium to use Fluorescent paint
317. Herb Aach claims to be the first Artist to have used Fluorescent Colors "successfully" (1970)
318. Pioneering Fluorescent Artist Richard Bowman (1950)
319. "Richard Bowman - Paintings and reflections, 1943-1961," San Francisco Museum of Art exhibition catalogue
320. Lucio Fontana was the second Artist to use Fluorescent paint in Fine Art (1948)
321. 'Spatial Environment in Black Light' by Lucio Fontana is the first "Environment" created in Art (1948-1949)
322. An introduction to the Fluorescent Artist who is the author of this book, and the first time this author saw Black lights and Fluorescence at the "New York World's Fair" (1964-1965)
323. The author's first Black light and experiments with Fluorescent paint (1969)
324. Finally leaving America, settling in Amsterdam, meeting Michèle and opening "Electric Lady" Fluorescent Art Gallery (1984-1987)
325. The creation of the Fluorescent "Participatory" Environment in "Electric Ladyland - the First Museum of Fluorescent Art" (1992-1999)
326. "Electric Ladyland - the First Museum of Fluorescent Art" visitor's guide
326a. "The First Fluorescent Minerals Collected in the Himalaya" (1998)
326b. "Fluorescent Mineral Artwork" from the 1950s in the Museum collection
327. "Thermal Expansion" Fluorescent and Phosphorescent painting series #1-447 (begun 1999)
328. "Creativatory Fluorescent and Phosphorescent Box" series (2011-2012)
329. Fluorescent painting series "Portrait and a Dream," and "Electron Displacement" (2012-2013)
330. "Oskar Fischinger (1900-1967): Experiments in Cinematic Abstraction"
331. Reflections on twenty-nine years of public contact and Fluorescent Art in "Electric Lady" Fluorescent Art Gallery
332. "Expressions in LIGHT: An introduction to fluorescent painting with Black Light," "Ultra-Violet Products, Inc."
333. Visions of the future possibilities of Colors, including "Smart Dust" and "Claytronics"
333a. The bottom line: "Fluorophobia" has literally produced the lasting durability of Fluorescent Colors and the Black light!

Introduction: "Color and Art"

Today in the world of 2016 - 113 years after Dr. Robert Wood invented the first Longwave Ultraviolet Filter and starred in rapt amazement at a Miracle he was beholding before his eyes through a small hole in a wooden box - and 113 years after the First Fluorescent Mineral Demonstration in the Natural History Museum of London in 1903 when people waited in line *for days* to witness something that had never been seen before: a rock creating and emitting it's own Light - today in 2016, after all the Miracles and Amazement of the past century-plus, this phenomenon of Fluorescence has been relegated and ultimately maligned to it's exclusive present-day use as an Entertainment Prop: Nightclubs, Discos, and, of course, "Black Light Posters" (man).

It may be contemplated: how could such a phenomenon - the invention of a paint - the first paint in the world to create and emit it's own Light through the Ultraviolet energy of a Black light - *How* could this truly amazing advent of the miraculous Twentieth century be reduced to the miserable level of being used only for mindless, spiritual-void displays in Nightclubs, paint on police cars and ambulances, clothes for maintenance men on the world's highways, and of course, Black Light Posters and Fluorescent backdrops for parties. The answer is quite simple for such a complicated question: Social Stigma, and the social phenomenon of the word I've created for this book: "FLUOROPHOBIA."

Go into the absolute bastion of Art today - The Museum of Modern Art in Manhattan - and you may search very hard, but it's very unlikely that you will find a single drop of Fluorescent paint - and the very suggestion of a "Black Light" being mounted on the ceiling of this most famous Modern Art institute on the planet, would most likely get you thrown out of the Museum!

This is pretty much the present-day attitude to what was once, before the 1960s, heralded as "The Future," today 50 years later is regarded as "the past." Imagine that Black lights had been used in Radio City Music Hall in New York City for "Skeleton Ballets" already in the 1920s, and had been initially used for the first "Ziegfeld Follies" in San Francisco way back in 1907 with very early 'Black lights' and Phosphorescent paint (which is an Asian invention from antiquity). Imagine also that Black lights and Fluorescent paint were used by "General Motors Corporation" in 1941 for their Annual Corporate "Press Dinner" complete with Dining Tables and table settings manufactured in totally Fluorescent Colors along with a circular chrome Black Light Dining Table Lamp fixture in the middle of each table designed exclusively for this purpose - What? What caused this great degeneration? It wasn't that the Fluorescent Colors emitting their own self-created Light through the energy of an Ultraviolet lamp did not live up to their expectations, but it was the way society, in all it's vast limitless wisdom, used this newly discovered pigment in such truly profound applications as Puppet Shows, Aircraft Carriers for the United States Military, Police cars, Emergency vehicles, Tow-trucks, and plastic Safety-Cones to indicate to their viewers a state of true spiritual enlightenment: "Highway Repair Ahead."

Even today, in 2016, when you go to the website of the most famous Fluorescent paint company in the World, "Day-Glo, Inc.," the same first Fluorescent paint company started over seventy years ago by Robert and Joe Switzer as "Fluor-S-Art," you can see that this world-famous Fluorescent paint company advises it's customers of similar "Applications" that Fluorescent paint can be used for: 'Haunted Houses, Outdoor Advertising, Temporary Markings, Signs, Goal Posts, Automotive, Theatrical, Safety, and Fun Houses.' Another large Fluorescent paint company on the internet is "Risk Reactor.com," selling a full line of Fluorescent paint and products. Their equally-celestial advise for "Applications" that Fluorescent paint can be used for includes such profound applications that they literally border on the surreal: 'Fishing Lures, Clock and Watch Dials, Exit Signs, Shoes, Caps, Aircraft and Automobile Dials and Instrument Panels, Firemen's Equipment, Traffic Signs, Fishing Equipment, Military Applications, Outdoor Path Marking, and Camping Equipment' - they forgot Skis.

The Human species, after all it's ego-announcement of higher understanding, and of late, the "New Age" movement, is, in the end, a very sluggish, primitive mammal - very slow to change, and has always been very opposed, throughout their evolution, to what lies outside their tiny circle of acceptance. This adversity not only to change, but also to any new phenomenon that challenge their minuscule realm of knowledge, combined with today's neoconservative outlook of the movement of the 1960s where Fluorescent Colors were first brought to the attention of the general public, and during that period these "Day-Glo" Colors became also intrinsically associated with the Hippie movement, these combined factors created the subject of this book: "Fluorophobia - the Social Stigma."

This condition of "Fluorophobia" is an extension of another related, but much older Social Stigma: "Chromophobia," a word created by Artist David Batchelor for his book of the same name from the year 2000. A fact that is not at all well known, and still today is greeted with signs of disbelief from almost all members of western society, is that one of the main pillars of Art, and, in fact, one of the most famous artifacts of the ancient world still in existence today - the Parthenon on the

Acropolis in Athens - was not always sterile White. Today's standard sterile White is the only accepted dignified Color that monuments of modern society can be: the Colors of the monuments of our 'Forefathers.' People were thankfully not always as sterile, antiseptic, and truly arrogant as they have been for the last two or three centuries. The Parthenon, all the temples on the Acropolis, and in fact, all the major temples in the ancient Greek society - the very model that today's western culture was fashioned and sculpted from - were *Brilliantly Painted!* The Parthenon and the ancient temples of Greece were painted, but do not get the wrong idea - these centers of government, society, and spirituality were not painted White, or Beige, or Tan, or Grey, as may be immediately imagined today, but brilliant Red and complementary Blue to create an effect on the most important buildings of the past that is, in today's standard, nearly impossible to imagine: vibrating brilliant raw Color used to move the human spirit and soul - on the actual Parthenon! Evidence of this fact can be seen on several statues and building sections that were buried in the Earth for millennia and did not completely fade in the sunlight. The clearest visual proof of this fact that I have seen myself are temple remnants in the National Archaeological Museum in Athens, where I photographed in 1984 an unearthed column section from a Temple still clearly Colored with it's faded original pigments. In the British Museum in London I also photographed in 1984 a section of a Greek temple with it's original brightly painted surface extremely faded, but visible to examination. Next to the original faded temple section, there is a replica of the same section of temple marble painted in it's original state of brilliant Red, Blue, and Gold patterning. This display showing the difference between the replica of the original brilliantly Colored section of a Greek temple next to the original piece of marble in it's present, nearly pure-White state, is nothing less than dramatic. My absolute favorite quote on this subject was in the 1800s when it was discovered that the Parthenon was not sterile White in it's former ancient glory but brilliantly painted with Color, Auguste Rodin, one of the greatest sculptors of the nineteenth century reacted with typical modern dismay and horror at this fact, and shouted 'I feel it in here,' as he pounded on his chest, 'that it was *Never Colored*!!' This is the archetypical reaction of a dignified member of recent past, and also of present modern western society. Even though most people today will still react in disbelief when hearing that the Parthenon and the temples of ancient Greece were brilliantly Colored, it is a fact of history. Over two millennia of very strong Greek sunlight has faded these once vividly-colored temples of ancient Greece to what could be called a "Snow-White:" virginal and pure for modern society's palette, but also embodying a quality that suits today's state of mind perfectly - like "Snow-White" herself, *Fictitious*.

In the study of "Chromophobia" it is unfortunate that the American Freemasons chose the appearance of the Nineteenth century Parthenon on the Acropolis in Athens to model the capital buildings of their new country after. White marble was chosen even though archaeologists at the time of the creation of the new capitol buildings in Washington, D.C. during the early Nineteenth century had already discovered and published that fact that the Parthenon and most of the other famous iconic buildings of ancient Greece were not in any way sterile White, but were painted with brilliant complementary 'vibrating' Colors. Not far from two hundred years after these initial archaeological discoveries, today in the Twenty-first century the average highly educated person still has no notion at all that the Parthenon was originally completed painted in what is referred to contemporarily as "Gaudy Colors" and in what is considered by modern "Chromophobic" civilized taste as primitive, tasteless, barbaric, or just plain-old childlike in the end. This is obviously because the modern 'advanced' - civilized even - citizen of the world, intrinsically egocentric in personality and in action, trying so hard to portray themselves as an advancement in the evolution of the species, is once again proved here to be almost as enlightened and spiritually awakened as the old expression that fits so perfectly with the Neo-Classical White House and Capital buildings in Washington, D.C.: "Monkey See, Monkey Do"(!)

During the nine years of writing this 'Black Light History,' there have been advances in technology which can only be described as exponential. New discoveries made through new techniques and advanced understanding. During this period between 2007 and 2016 definitive proof has been found on the statues from the Parthenon in Athens which is undeniable as well as digital. The largest collection of these statues from the Parthenon are not, as probably imagined, in Athens on the Acropolis, but in the British Museum in London. On these exquisite statues from the frieze on the Parthenon new studies have been made with Infrared cameras which prove well beyond the shadow of a doubt that these Parthenon statues were originally Colored with applications of vivid paint when they were made - Rodin could have pounded on his chest until his Nineteenth century ribcage collapsed, but these Parthenon statues, the Parthenon itself, and all of the temples of ancient Greece were not White, which is today the only acceptable Color to modern, prejudice, Chromophobic society, but vividly Colored.

Up until the present era archeologists knew for certain that the Parthenon had been painted, but what was not proved was whether the sculptures on the Parthenon had also been painted. Today in the British Museum through the use of Infrared Imaging, traces on the Parthenon sculptures themselves have been found of a pigment called "Egyptian Blue." Dr. Giovanni Verri working with a new technique of Infrared Imaging on the Parthenon sculptures in the British Museum has discovered astounding evidence of this "Egyptian Blue" pigment on the statue of "Iris," the Greek Goddess of the Rainbow. Broadcast in 2013 on "BBC's" "Who Were the Greeks," Dr. Verri demonstrates the use of Infrared Imaging and explains that the "Egyptian Blue" pigment used by the ancient Greeks to paint the Parthenon has a special property which allows it to first absorb visible light and then to reemit the visible light as Infrared light. This emitted Infrared light is very visible as a sparkling Bluish White light easily seen against the neutral Grey background of the rest of the statue not painted with "Egyptian Blue" pigment. Dr. Verri directs a beam of Infrared light at the "Iris" Parthenon statue and instantly it emits a vivid light on the belt of Iris that was originally "Egyptian Blue," and he explains that single particles of this pigment on Iris's belt are emitting this vivid light. It looks exactly as intense as when you put a Black light over Fluorescent pigment. Dr. Giovanni Verri's Infrared Imaging techniques have been called nothing less than a "revelation," and have revealed even patterns of "Egyptian Blue" pigment painted onto the Parthenon statues. As astounding as it could be to people who discover even the statues of the Parthenon were originally painted, they should not hastily jump to the wrong obvious conclusion which would be that this "Egyptian Blue" pigment was a dull, muted shade of Blue, because it was just the opposite - a bright "strong Blue," evidence of which can still be seen. When it was first conclusively acknowledged that the Parthenon and all other ancient Greek temples had been originally vividly painted, in the 1850s a sample of "Egyptian Blue" paint had been scrapped off an ancient Greek temple by Sir Charles Newton of the British Museum, who feared that he would not be believed back in England with the fact that not only the ancient Greek temples had been painted, but that the Colors used to paint the ancient Greek temples had been strong and bright. Evidence can also be easily revealed in the examination of Colors produced by the pigments the ancient Greeks used to paint their ancient temples, which include Gypsum found in the north of Greece and used to produce a pure White pigment, Realgar used to create a vivid Orange and coming from the Caucus Mountains, Ochre coming from Cyprus, Chrysocolla coming from Attica in central Greece creating an Aqua Blue-Green, Hematite creating a vivid Red and coming from an island in the Aegean Sea, an equally bright Red pigment created out of Cinnabar coming form Spain, and one of the most famous pigments in Art history: Aquamarine coming from Lapis Lazuli mined in Afghanistan. Again, these well-known pigments did not produce dull pastel shades of Blues, Oranges, and Reds, but are some of the identical pigments used for more than the last two-thousand years since the Parthenon of ancient Greece, and some are still used to produce vivid Color up until the present era.

On the other hand, the French are truly modern "Chromophobics." Not only was the 'Father' of "Chromophobia" Charles Blanc a distinguished citizen of France, but the actual iconic symbol of the country itself, "The Eiffel Tower" was not always the natty rusty "Eiffel Tower Brown" Color it is world famous for today. I always assumed that Robert Delaunay was using 'Artistic license' to paint the Eiffel Tower Red in his famous paintings of the icon of France from almost one hundred years ago, but in fact - get ready for it - The Eiffel Tower was painted bright Red as it's final Color when it was inaugurated in 1889 by Gustave Eiffel! "Venetian Red" was the actual name of the Color that the brand new Eiffel Tower was painted upon completion, to be more precise. But, bright "Venetian Red" was not the only Color the Eiffel Tower has been since it's completion in 1889, The bright "Venetian Red" paint job on the brand new Eiffel Tower was changed to bright Yellow in 1892, and then to a slightly more "Chromophobic" tone of Yellow/Grey in 1899, and following the example of modern "Chromophobia," the Eiffel Tower was painted for the fourth time in 1907 with a darker Red close to Maroon. This is the Color that Robert Delaunay was probably looking at when he created his famous painting "The Eiffel Tower" in 1909-1912 with it's bright Red rendering of the Tower, or perhaps he was recalling the Tower from his youth, in the 1880s when it was in fact bright Red. The Eiffel Tower remained the darker Red Maroon Color for forty-seven years, the longest time period of a paint Color on the Eiffel Tower since it's creation, and then in 1954 Color was revived and the Eiffel Tower was repainted in bright Red once again. The 1954 Red is described as the Color of Chinese wood, and although it was not the same bright Red as the inaugural Color, the 1954 Red was still a world better than today's Rusty Brown Color of the Eiffel Tower. This signatory Rusty Brown Color of the Eiffel Tower today was painted on in 1968, during the height of the "Psychedelic Movement," which France obviously was never really a part of. So in 1968 France decided that the Reds, Yellows, and even the Maroon Colors of the past were just that: 'of the past,' and the modern sober "Chromophobic" civilized dignified gentrified citizen of the world did not accept the decoration of Color anymore, but pragmatically styled edifices resembling rusted steel or raw quarried White marble was all that could be considered acceptable. Anything else was considered gaudy or excessively decorative - only the raw natural Color of the building material itself was acceptable anymore. The contemporary arrogant "Levitate above the stench of the primitive past" state-of-mind epitomized the change - most likely permanent - of the Reds and Yellows of the past century plus's Eiffel Tower to it's present statement since 1968 of three different shades of rusty Brown. The bottom level of the Eiffel Tower is painted in a dark rusty Brown, the middle section painted a medium shade of rusty Brown, and the top section of the Eiffel Tower is painted a light shade of, again, rusty Brown. This is to bring out the height and elevation of the Eiffel Tower, being lighter as it ascends towards the sky, but personally I think the first "Venetian Red" was a whole lot nicer. Another example of social conditioning is observable with these Color changes of the Eiffel Tower. My girlfriend Michèle was born in Paris, and although the Eiffel Tower was dark Red Maroon when she was born, and then was repainted a real Red, like the Color of Chinese wood when she was a young girl, and remained this Color Red until she was a grown woman, today she doesn't remember the Eiffel Tower as any other Color than the modern post-1968 rusty Brown. This is painful evidence of just how universal and complete the reach of the modern "Chromophobic" consciousness, and ramifications of this consciousness's assertion, has evolved and changed people's lives and even their awareness and memories.

Another similar example of the opinion of the present being wrong about the past can be seen in the "Coptic Art" from 'Coptic Egypt,' which is the period that began after Pharaonic ancient Egypt. This period has always been thought of as extremely dark with very muted Colors, but after half the restoration of the great "Red Monastery" in Sohag, Egypt is now complete, it is surprising to see that the opinion of muted Colors was wrong in relation to the newly revealed and restored original painted Colors. The "Red Monastery," which is about three hundred miles from Cairo, dates from about the Sixth or Seventh century. This period of Art history, including the Sixth and Seventh century, has been known to be not famous for it's use of brilliant Colors, in the same religious vein as Byzantine Christian Art, dark and very heavy. This was clearly presented in "The Art of Eternity" from the "BBC," in which the author Andrew Graham-Dixon stated that he was shocked above all by the 'explosion of Color' in the restored half of this "Red Monastery." What, for over half a millennia, has been traditionally seen as a dark heavy period in Art, was historically incorrect primarily because of the dirt and grime which had accumulated on the paintings over the centuries. Now, after the restoration of these Sixth and Seventh century Coptic Egyptian murals, it becomes clear that history's opinion was tainted by it's sight through centuries of dirt. After the grime is painstakingly removed through years of work, it is quite evident that the former idea of this grim, Colorless, austere period was wrong because after the restoration it proves that this period was 'a world filled with Color.'

This is not the first time that Art History has to be rewritten because of restoration through the removal of dirt and grime encrusted upon Paintings. Incredible as it may seem, the original impetus and movement, and even the original intent and Artistic direction or school that the Artist was rendering, may be almost completely lost and then actually altered, and sometimes even completely obscured and forgotten, under centuries of dirt and soot. This is a vivid example of how society views the past, and many times even alters history itself, because of it's modernistic arrogance and lack of any true perspective. The classic example of this point is something I've witnessed myself on my first Art journey to Europe in 1984. For centuries the history of Art has been taught with the school of "Mannerism," which included the amazing paintings of Caravaggio, following soon after the period of 1500-1510 known as the "Renaissance," but it was unknown where the inspiration for the vivid Colors of "Mannerism" came from. In the fall of 1984 I finally made it to my dream destination: the Sistine Chapel by Michelangelo in Rome. When I first arrived in Rome, the actual ceiling of The Sistine Chapel was just beginning to have it's four years of restoring scaffolding installed. The "Lunettes" by Michelangelo, and preliminary paintings of the Sistine Chapel were the first to have been restored, being right below the foot of the ceiling, and were on display freshly cleaned and revealed at the time I first arrived in Rome. The Colors were *Amazing*! I stood stunned looking at these beginnings of the Sistine Chapel ceiling - the "Lunettes" - like I was seeing Michelangelo's painting for the first time - brilliant vibrating complementary Colors - the robes looked Fluorescent! But, the restorers had intentionally left one piece of the front left of the Sistine Chapel "Lunettes" unrestored - in the original five hundred year old state - it actually looked as if someone had gone up the scaffolding and glued a piece of Black paper on the "Lunette." The difference was really hard to believe - and this was from the floor of the Sistine, not up close. The line between the freshly-restored "Lunettes" and the unrestored ceiling of the Sistine Chapel was clearly visibly, with brilliant Colors on the restored "Lunettes" juxtaposed with the extremely dark, dirty, blackened, as yet unrestored Sistine ceiling. Many Art magazines, like "Art News," had cover stories of this amazing restoration: 'The Rewriting of Art History!' No one knew where the inspiration for the Colors used in the school of Sixteenth century "Mannerism" had come from until the Sistine Chapel was cleaned. The ceiling of the Sistine Chapel, arguably the greatest piece of Art ever created by one person, is a total of 5,800 square feet and has over three hundred figures painted on it. This world masterpiece was begun, reluctantly, by Michelangelo Buonarroti when he was thirty three years old and took four years to complete, 1508-1512. This school of Sixteenth century "Mannerism" is the movement in Art that came after the high Renaissance of 1500-1510, when Artists began to paint scenes that were less inspired by naturalistic and classical ideals. The school of "Mannerism" is known for the alteration of the anatomy of the painted figures and the dramatization of the figures through the use of Color and light to add the emotions of the Artist into the painting, which had been done only in a subdued way by Artists up to that point in time. The origin of the bright, fresh Colors used by Artists of the school of "Mannerism" were a mystery until the Sistine Chapel ceiling was cleaned. One of the Artists of the school of "Mannerism" that best

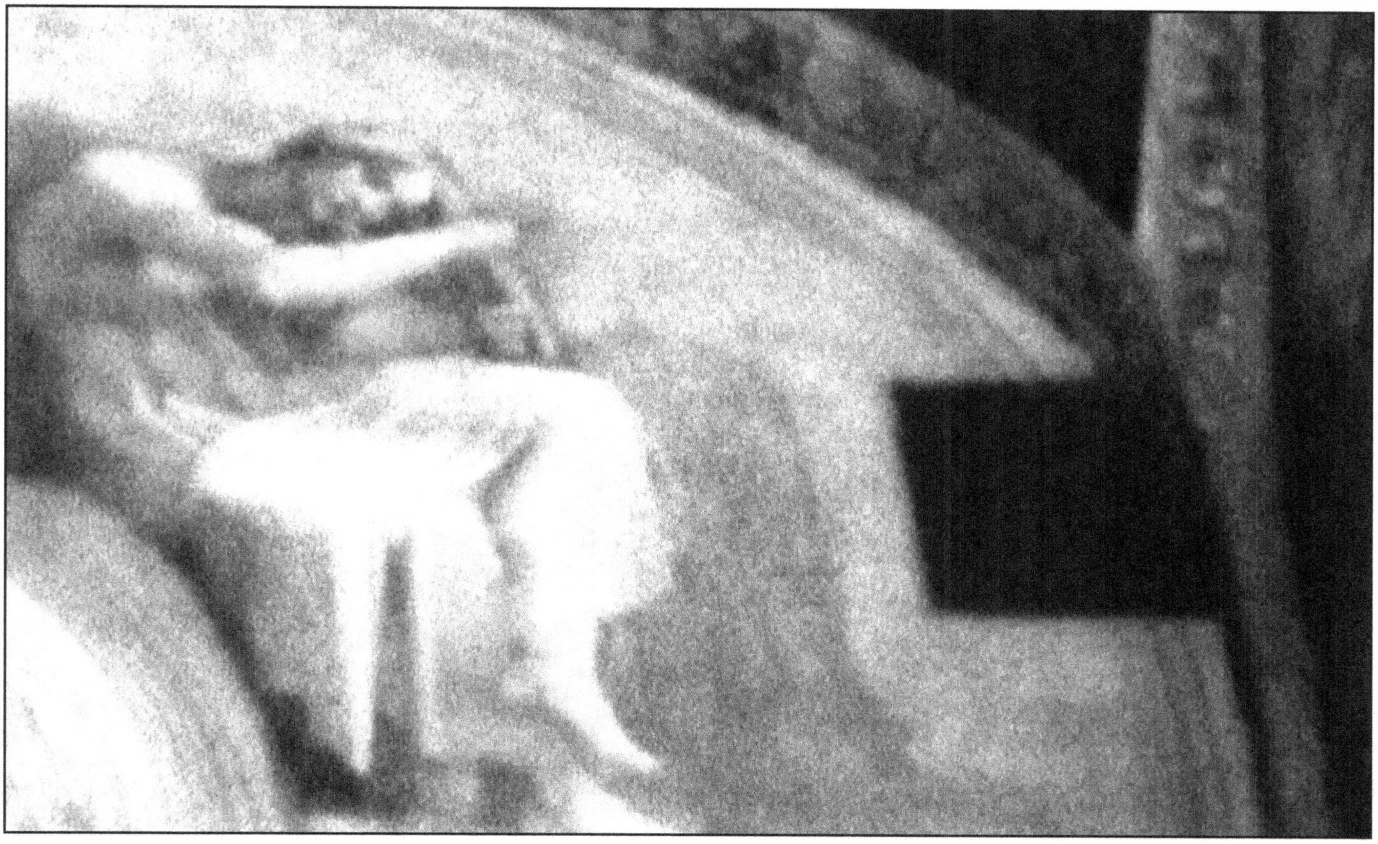

1984: The Sistine Chapel during restoration, showing a unrestored square Black section of Michelangelo's "Lunettes"

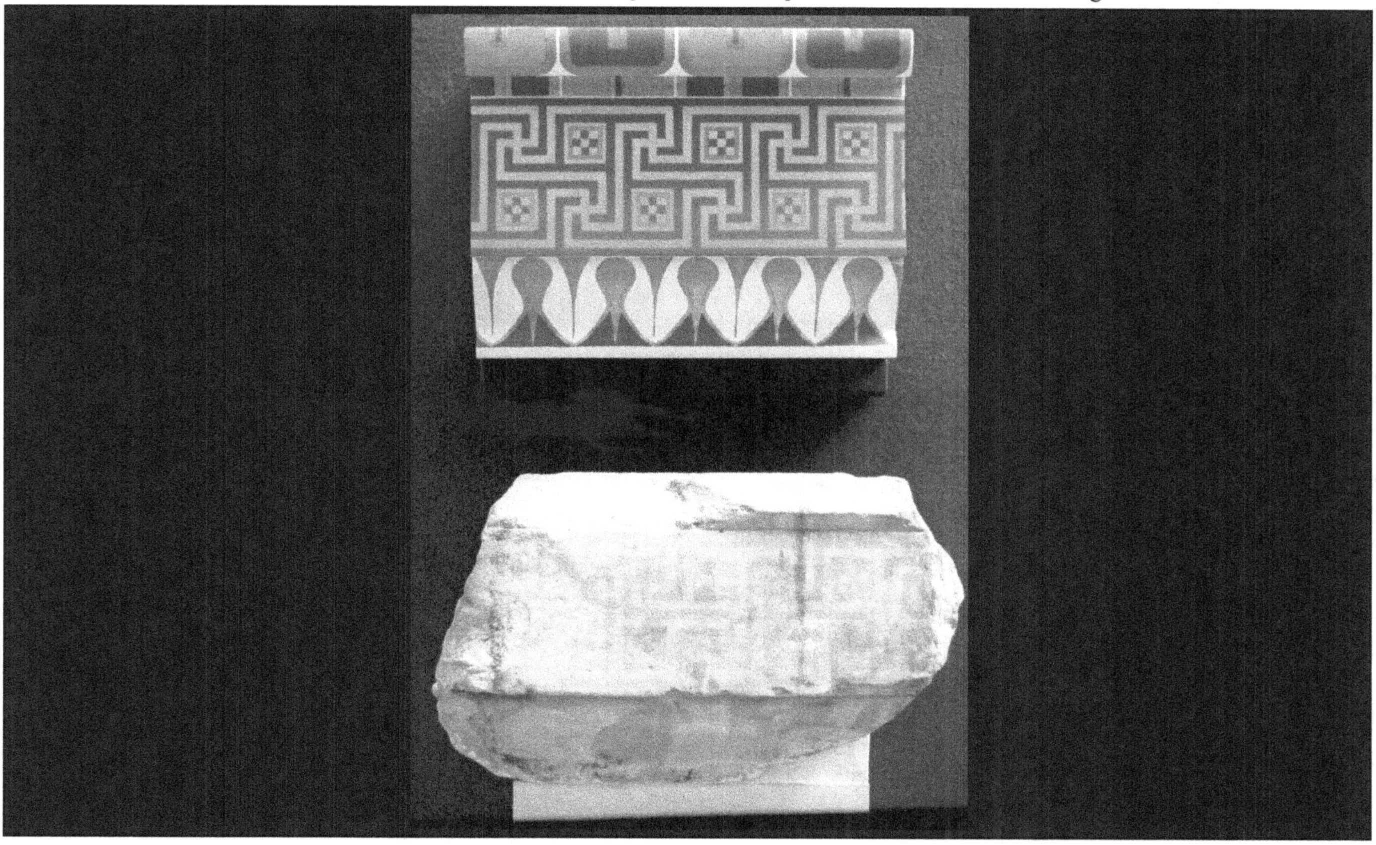

Ancient Greek fragment of a temple reveals it's original painted vivid Colors exemplifies the inspiration from Michelangelo's brilliant fresh Colors and distorted anatomical forms is Jacopo da Pontormo who painted "The Deposition" about 1528, sixteen years after the ceiling of the Sistine Chapel by Michelangelo had been completed. The freshness and brightness of the Colors throughout "The Deposition" are a radical departure from the dark, heavy Colors typical in painting for centuries before and after this brief period of time. The poses and especially the brilliant, pure Colors used in "The Deposition" immediately suggest the influence of Michelangelo's Sistine Chapel ceiling, most clearly on the center crouching figure supporting Christ. There is also something that is an interesting comparison, which happened in the same general period of time. "The Last Supper" by Leonardo da Vinci also was being restored for several years when I visited it in the fall of 1984. The interesting comparison is in the different kinds of praises the two masterpieces received after the restorations were complete. The difference between Leonardo and Michelangelo is easily seen through the hindsight of nearly half a millennia with quite a surprising technique: restoration. Leonardo originally was one of the great promoters of the elevation of the Artist's social standing during the Renaissance, especially through his use of mathematics and his stressing of the new Florentine doctrine of Drawing being more important than Colors in Art. After almost five hundred years both Leonardo's and Michelangelo's masterpieces were painstakingly restored. "The Sistine Chapel" and "The Last Supper" have both reappeared to us in a rebirth of their original splendor. Then, after studying the results of both of these restorations, the comments and articles began to become published, and the main comments about both of the restorations actually carried through from the Artist's original intentions, because the most amazing point about Michelangelo's restored painting was the Colors revealed, and by contrast, the point that was the most commented on about the restoration of Leonardo's painting was the detail - the 'Drawing.'

Michelangelo was the first Artist to truly inspire me was when I was a young boy and went to the New York World's Fair in 1964, where I went onto a moving walkway in the dark towards a brilliant light in the distance. This was the incomparable "Pieta" by Michelangelo, and I remember it today as clearly as the day I was there fifty-two years ago. Very fittingly, this inserted written section on Michelangelo will be one of the final additions to the nine years of writing this 'Black Light and Fluorescent Art history.' On June 21, 2016 (last week) to celebrate being together for thirty years, Michèle and I decided to go to what we've been talking about for as long as we've been together: the Sistine Chapel by Michelangelo. Since the thirteen year restoration had begun in 1980, when I first went to the Sistine Chapel in 1984 only the "Lunettes" had been completely cleaned, and the first two sections at the back of the Sistine ceiling had begun to be cleaned. Again, the photo I took in 1984 of the uncleaned portion of the last "Lunette" which had been cleaned, the "Amminadab Lunette," is a very good insight into the transformation of the entire Sistine Chapel. As I've written, the unrestored square section of the "Amminadab Lunette," closest to "The Last Judgment" on the left wall of the Sistine Chapel, in 1984 looked as though someone had intentionally put an opaque, totally Black piece of paper on the "Lunette." Today in 2016 this same 'Black' section on this "Lunette" is even more obvious and nearly unimaginable as the original unrestored condition that I saw the entire Sistine ceiling and "Last Judgement" in the first time. The fresh brilliant light and incredibly vivid Colors and Color vibrations that have been revealed beneath the centuries of dirt and grime make this unrestored section of the "Amminadab Lunette" I photographed in 1984 look quite literally unbelievable.

This time in 2016 I could get special entrance tickets so that we could get into the Sistine Chapel over an hour before the general public (which averages the unbearable 25,000 visitors a day) came pouring in, and I could have a long time to quietly and patiently examine the Sistine ceiling and "The Last Judgement," during which I discovered several more intentionally unrestored rectangular 'Black' areas left on both the front of the Sistine ceiling as well as on the top of "The Last Judgement." Now completely restored, immediately upon entering the Sistine Chapel (through the doorway under the "Last Judgement's" actual 'Pit of Hell') you look up at the incomparable Sistine Chapel ceiling and are overwhelmed by a brilliance and freshness of _Color_ which simply was not visible on my ten visits to the Sistine Chapel in 1984 when I stayed in Rome for two weeks the first time. Everything that has been written about and hailed back in 1993 for the conclusion of the Sistine Chapel's restoration was absolutely true - 'it's like you're seeing Michelangelo for the first time,' 'Art history will have to be rewritten because the influence for the vivid Colors of "Mannerism" were previously unknown.' The Sistine Chapel's restored Colors kept me in awe for hours, which are brighter and stronger than I ever imagined even after seeing the photographs of the restoration many times. What stands out in my memory is the transformation of the entire light in the Sistine Chapel - it is brilliant and the entire immense expanse of the Sistine ceiling and "The Last Judgment" look as though it has just been painted. The details of the musculature and drapery can clearly be seen from the floor now that they have been revealed again, and the brilliance of the precious Lapis Lazuli Blue pigment Michelangelo used in abundance on "The Last Judgement" is still overwhelming and transporting nearly five-hundred years later.

Of the entire Sistine Chapel, the specific areas of Colors I was the most fascinated by in 1984, are today in 2016 stupendous. There are two areas which shimmer in vibrating Colors and are rendered in a moire iridescence that Michelangelo painted about half way through the Sistine Chapel, and which are nearly facing each other on opposite sides of the Sistine walls. These exquisite vibrating complementary Color areas I'm referring to are the painted drapery of cloth worn by ancestors of Christ. "Rehoboam" on the left side of the Sistine ceiling in the second triangular section of the vault is painted by Michelangelo with such dazzling complementary Color combinations of shimmering Oranges turning magically into iridescent Greens, that it approaches the brightness of Fluorescence. On the exact opposite wall of the Sistine Chapel is the other extraordinary area of Color which, like "Rehoboam," approaches the Color intensity of Fluorescent Colors, and this is the "ASA - Jehoshaphat - Joram Lunette." The figure on the left of this "Lunette," "Jehoshaphat," is another of the ancestors of Christ portrayed by Michelangelo on these "Lunettes," which were the very first sections of the Sistine Chapel that Michelangelo began to paint, and "Jehoshaphat" is draped in Colors as shimmering and vibrating as "Rehoboam." In the transporting Colors of both "Rehoboam" and "Jehoshaphat" it is extraordinary that Michelangelo paints brilliant shimmering Oranges turning seamlessly into absolutely the opposite, complementary Color: brilliant shimmering iridescent Greens(!) The effect from the distance of the Sistine floor today is breathtaking, and has been inspirational to Artists across the many centuries since Michelangelo painted it - even to this Artist of the Twenty-first century who paints with Fluorescent Colors and Black lights. In "Michelangelo - The Complete Sculpture, Painting, Architecture" by William Wallace published in 1998, half a decade after the restoration of the Sistine Chapel was completed, the author is quite clear in stating that much of the discussion on the Sistine has been centered around Michelangelo's Colors. The 'brightness' of the Colors, the "cangiante" or 'changing' of Colors, and the "unexpected" juxtapositions of contrasting Colors are the controversies that, not surprisingly, this large book sold in the Vatican today explains as being what all the discussions were primarily excited by.

In actual fact the Greek Parthenon and ancient temples weren't the only buildings that were painted in past times, but they were the most famous. Another very famous building from the ancient world that had vivid Colors painted on all it's interior walls is also in Rome, the Colosseum. The interior walls of the entire Colosseum in Rome were not bare stone, as everyone sees today, but all the inner corridors were filled with paintings of the gladiators and fighters in the Colosseum portrayed in what "National Geographic" describes as 'Gaudy' Colors. This was done so that the inner corridors, where all the visitors walked, were not bare stone walls, but paintings of the celebrated gladiators. This also served the purpose of adding more light to the inner corridors of the Colosseum, where it is known that the 50,000-80,000 visitors could exit in only 30 minutes.

The cathedral in Bourge, France, where the citizens were apparently not always as "bourgeois" as they are regarded in modern times, has an amazing hugh relief sculpture of the Last Judgement on the entire facade of the church, which is almost completely uniform Grey stone now, but it was also completely painted when it was finished hundreds of years ago. Remnants of the pigment on the stone sculptures of this facade can still be just seen.

There is something else about the Bourge Cathedral, and in fact about most cathedrals around the world that is an example of the absolute hypocrisy that exists in the Western society. The inside of the cathedral of Bourge, when the Sun is shining, is ablaze with vivid Colors - reflected onto Grey columns, rows of chairs, walls, and all in vivid pure Colors that were intentionally used to lift the human spirit and transport worshippers in the cathedral to a state of heightened awareness enabling communication with God - What? Did you say that vivid pure Colors were used *intentionally* to lift and transport the spirit to a state of heightened awareness capable of communication with God? And it is further asked in amazement, 'where and on what were these brilliant transporting Colors used for - in of all places, cathedrals? "Stained Glass" is the answer accompanied by a quizzical look. Yes, everyone knows about the magnificent pieces of Art adorning most of the cathedrals in many countries of the world, know as "Stained Glass." These windows are made with dazzling pure Colors juxtaposed and crafted to bring forth the most vivid projected Colors possible. So, extremely brilliant Colors can be intentionally used to transport the spirit in Stained Glass windows around the world, but do not wear Yellow-Red clothes on a rainy day or you will upset scholars and Poets! Good for one purpose, but bad for all other purposes: talk about hypocritical. As the reader continues into this book, they will come across many vicious statements of "Chromophobia" penned by very famous authors throughout the history of civilization, and with this perspective it is quite evident how hypocritical the acceptance of society has been throughout time towards the use of Color. I wonder if Goethe, Charles Blanc, or even Le Corbusier had ever been inside "La Chapelle" in Paris and experienced instant transportation of the spirit while standing in front of immense ceiling-to-floor, wall-to-wall Colors dazzling with an unearthly brilliance - sparkling, shifting, illuminating, and vibrating. Colors used to spiritually transport the viewer in an area so vast it defines the word "overwhelming." I can relate with the personal experience of several enlightening visits to "La Chapelle" that it is something that cannot be imagined without physically experiencing the awe of these two complete walls of Color. No other Stained Glass in the world can compare to this Chapel. It is truly transporting. It can literally take your breath away. Standing before and immersed inside of these walls of pure Color, you can physically feel the Colors on you as warmth brought through the Stained Glass by the Sun; your mind wanders to a pure place where only Light, Colors, and Energy exist. Here the spirituality and the inherent transcendental power of Color is understood completely - by your mind, your body, and your soul. "La Chapelle" is most likely the largest display of Stained Glass in the world, even inspiring one of the Twentieth century's true visionaries Aldous Huxley, who wrote of his experience of standing before these immense walls of Color as an actual modern-day place of enlightenment. Underneath "La Chapelle" there is the original first Chapel that the upper Stained Glass chapel was built on top of. I remember being very surprised on my first visit to see this beautifully vaulted rounded lower chapel painted with my favorite Colors - a beautiful Blue ceiling (similar to modern Phthalocyanine Blue) with perfectly complementary bright Red stars painted on it. I had never seen a church painted with such Colors! As a final example, the largest and most famous "Rosetta" Stained Glass window in the world is the Chartres Cathedral in France. What is not famous at all about the Chartres Cathedral, and as a matter of fact is relatively unknown, is that the world famous Stained Glass windows of Chartres weren't the only source of vivid spiritually-transporting Colors in the Cathedral. The interior walls of this ancient Cathedral, today a standard uniform Grey stone, were originally painted in equally vivid spiritually-transporting Colors as the Cathedral's world famous Stained Glass. The entire interior of the Chartres Cathedral was painted first with a base coat of a burnt-Orange Color, then on top of the burnt-Orange base Color, the ribs of the ceiling vaults were painted bright combinations of the complimentary Colors Red and Green, with the numerous tremendous columns of the cathedral originally painted combinations of Blue and Gold. The impression of the entire interior would have been literally breathtaking to visitors coming into the cathedral centuries ago from their Color-void earthen huts. As John Gage has observed in "Color and Culture," the interior of many churches of the Medieval period were completely painted, leaving no areas of bare Grey stone (as we are all accustomed to seeing in churches today). As an example of a church from the Medieval time that is still vividly painted with most of it's original Colors from seven hundred years ago, the Church of San Francesco (St. Francis) in Assisi, Italy from the year 1300 has every surface painted in the entire interior of the church, with frescos of religious scenes, painted artificial structural elements, and intricate, vividly Colored patterns everywhere in the church's interior, leaving neither columns, walls, nor ceilings bare. Although not vividly Colored anymore, my photos from 1984 of the interior walls of the St. Francis of Assisi cathedral also reveal no original blank, unpainted surfaces.

    For living proof of vivid, brilliant, contrasting, pure Colors being used in the present day, including the rare combination of these vivid Colors being used on religious temples in the present day as these Colors had been used for centuries, if not millennia, in the west for spiritual enlightenment in churches, the Parthenon and most other ancient Greek temples, and countless other artifacts of the long-gone past that have returned to their native base spiritually-void "Color" of Grey (to match the spiritual quality of today's mass consciousness) - for proof of these brilliant spiritually-lifting Colors being used today, one only needs to leave our spiritually-void Grey western society and take a pilgrimage to India. In India the places of worship, called "Mandirs," are religious temples vividly painted with every contrasting vibrating Color combination known under the Sun. A pilgrimage to one of the holiest Mandirs in India will bring you also to one of the most brilliantly Colored temples in the world: Shri Badrinath at 10,248 feet elevation (3,110 meters) in the Himalaya, with it's vibrating Heavenly-Blue combined with Red, Orange, and Yellow Colors, is truly spiritually-transporting. Here in India the stigmatisms of the past millennia *do not exist!* Religion, God, and most of the rest of life itself, is seen, appreciated, and revered in India with enthusiasm and purity that cannot be paralleled in the west. There is a concept in Buddhism named "Tong Drel" in which a person receives blessing and enlightenment merely through the action of looking at a religious object or place of worship that has inherent transcending abilities. The very same belief is true of this Hinduist Mandir Shri Badrinath deep in the Himalaya of India. Hindus believe that just the mere sight of the Badrinath Temple frees a pilgrim from worldly bondage and brings them to the path of enlightenment. All that is frowned upon and viewed with repulsion in the west - all that our egotistical, consumer western society falsely make/believes it has risen above - is still thankfully intact in India, as it has been for countless thousands of years. All the west's long-gone communication with God that was possible through spiritually-transporting vivid Colors on the inside and outside of churches centuries ago all across Europe, is not "long-gone" in India, but still exists this very day. "Primitive" and "backwards" India has not lost it's spiritual path through the vast unlimited acquisition of wealth and the almighty "Lust for Comfort," but is very much still intact and alive today. The Grey uninspired, unenlightened existential western person is but a mere shadow of a human, when compared to any common person in India. The irreturnable distance the western person has intentionally and egotistically placed between themselves and any spiritually enlightening path in life, is as vast and unbridgeable as the distance they've placed between themselves and any spiritually-manifesting substances, such as pure, vivid, brilliant Colors covering the total insides and outsides of their holy places of worship. If let's say, the *Vatican* in

Rome wasn't intentionally left *unpainted*, with it's plain bare Marble left and considered as the finished outside appearance, but was painted with the same vibrating, vivid Colors of the Shri Badrinath Temple in India, catholics around the world would *Choke!*

So, how did the world change so radically and so dramatically that we now have the "White House" instead of the vividly painted Red and Blue Parthenon and the enlightening and spiritually-transporting "La Chapelle?" I think it is because of an ugly trait of human nature. In ancient times people lived in a nearly Colorless world - dirt, stone, or wood dwellings, naturally Colored materials for their clothes (Beige or Browns), and the few possessions they had were all made of natural products and rarely Colored. This created a life where Color was very rare and only seen when the occasion was auspicious, such as weddings or in the presence of royalty. In this Color-rarefied atmosphere of life, Colors had the power and ability to *transport* a person that saw them, and were intentionally used to that very purpose, such as in the Parthenon and in "La Chapelle" and countless other churches and temples. As time progressed, so did the production of Colors, culminating in a time when Color was everywhere, as provided by the advent of Industrial production. This all began to take place on a defining scale during the 1800s with the invention and production of many new Color pigments. During that period we see the building of "The White House," and the publications of books on Color Theory which were highly prejudicial of Color by very influential authors like Goethe and Charles Blanc, followed by the architect Le Corbusier. Bright pure Colors, after all the thousands of years of trials and tribulations to get them, when society finally had Color in mass, they typically began to view it as decadent - part of a world that was below them and past, when people were not as refined as these nouveau-civilized products of the birth of the Industrial Age thought they were at that time - when, in fact, that past world they were prejudicial against was in truth nearly Colorless and striving to achieve just what the modern person was throwing away(!) How typical. This will be discussed later in the book, but is concluded here by something Aldous Huxley wrote in a very powerful, but equally obscure book in 1959, "Brave New World Revisited." Discussing societies' reversal of feelings regarding their attitude towards the transporting abilities of Color, Huxley states, with a clarity of thought that he was famous for, that after Color was mass produced by the square mile and people became 'familiar' with Color in every facet of their everyday lives, they quickly became 'indifferent' to it. Let us not forget the absolutely infinite attention span of most human beings, and also their ability and desire to absorb all outside stimuli in a truly comprehensive manner. Trying to imagine the Color-rarefied lives that all people lived up until only about one hundred and fifty years ago is nearly impossible for our society with it's square light-years of Red and Orange linoleum! The only time these people long ago saw the Color Red was when they were rarely in the presence of a Bishop (who's robes were dyed with the extravagantly priced Red Cochineal bug's blood), or when they cut themselves.

As an example of society's outlook on Color, one of the most influential architects of the Twentieth century, Le Corbusier, who taught at the famous "Bauhaus Institute," states with obvious astounding arrogance (even for the Twentieth century) that pure vivid Color was only meant for people of a 'simple' race, such as a 'peasant,' and also for a 'savage." In his book "The Decorative Art of Today" from 1920, the title already belies a fathomless depth in Le Corbusier's attitude towards Art, just simply by using that truly profound word: 'Decorative.' Pure Color today is associated with such spiritual and enlightened states of higher awareness as Infantilism, Vulgarity, and Regression. States of Childhood and also states of heightened sexual eroticism are instantly associated with pure Color. I wonder if Le Corbusier had ever been to Rio de Janeiro in February to see the yearly world famous "Carnival" - he would have been so pleased, because before his eyes the three principle prerequisites that are prescribed for all people that actually use and enjoy pure bright Colors, would have been parading in front of him for nearly two days, twelve hours each day, from sunset until after sunrise:
1. He would have undoubtedly, being from Switzerland, associated all Brazilian people with his 1920 enlightened listing of people of a 'simple' race, a 'peasant,' or a 'savage.'
2. He would probably also have been horrified at the more than 2,000 nearly naked beautiful Brazilian women dancing manicly and parading in front of his face in every one of the Samba Schools that make up the days of the "Carnival." Here would have been Chromophobist's blatant heightened states of sexuality 'in the flesh.'
3. And, of course, this "Bauhaus Institute" professor would just as undoubtedly not missed the opportunity to lastly associate what was rolling before his eyes in Rio for two days and nights as an enormous example of his statement that these brilliant pure vulgar Colors were clearly never intended to have been used for making 'Great Art,' but here was proof of their limited use for what he was staring at: people who all come from the slums of Rio di Janeiro (the "Favela") acting like, at best, Clothes Dyers.

Another even more Colorful yearly human celebration would have, beyond the shadow of a doubt, given Le Corbusier an embolism: "Holi Festival" every spring (usually in March) all across the subcontinent of India. As the festival is in India, where there is arguably the most deeply religious society on Earth, this is naturally a celebration of the Gods. For one full day a high percentage of India's one billion plus inhabitants shower each other with pure brilliant Colors - head to toe! I remember being on a train with Michèle in northern India in the direction towards Nepal that day in 1988, and at every train station people had to quickly roll up all the windows of the train because Colors with water were being thrown even at the train as it pulled into each station. Not only do the Indians buy the brightest Colored powdered pigments to mix with water and throw on each other, but many of these powdered pigments they use in modern times are highly Fluorescent, being the brightest of all achievable Colors. Add this to the fact that the other ceremony that is combined with the throwing of Colors on each other on "Holi Festival" is the drinking of the holy "Bhang" and altering their consciousness with it's main ingredients of pulverized Marijuana and Mantras. Le Corbusier would have surely put his 'Stamp of Disapproval' on this religious festival, and used it as yet another example of people of a 'Simple' race, like a 'Peasant,' or a 'Savage' using bright pure Colors. So, if Le Corbusier had ever travelled to India on the Holi Festival he would have seen a second living, pulsing example of most of his prerequisites for people using and liking bright, pure Colors. In actuality, "Holi Festival" in India is a celebration of the Hindu God Krisha's feelings for his lover Radha. The famous throwing of Colors on each other during "Holi Festival" comes originally from the Krishna story where cowgirls shower Krishna and Radha with brightly Colored flower petals.

In the city where I live, there is a large neighborhood that has a world-famous name which is an extremely physical(!), graphic example of this sociological association of pure Color with heightened sexuality: "The Red Light District" in Amsterdam is where there are hundreds of prostitutes standing or sitting in various states of undress behind glass with a Red Light outside of each of these windows. Talk about society's association of heightened sexual excitement with bright Colors - this neighborhood is not called "The Beige Light Center" or even "The Green Light Center." A very ironic, and extremely curious twist on this story, and something that also makes a literal physical, graphic extention-bridge from "Chromophobia" to "Fluorophobia," is what began about fifteen or twenty years ago in "The Red Light District" in Amsterdam: the prostitutes started to slowly discover that their lingerie which they stand in their windows wearing is highly Fluorescent when they put a "Black Light" inside their "Red Light" windows(!) These prostitutes can be seen at night brilliantly Fluorescing in their underwear from the other side of the canals! Here we have an absolutely concrete proving point showing society's association first with the bright Color Red - "Chromophobia" - and next as a bridge to the natural extension "Fluorophobia:" the use of the "Black Light" in the prostitute's windows. The point also may be pondered: why Red and why the "Black Light"? The psychology behind this simple question could fill many volumes, each six times the thickness of this book. Obviously, the simple explanation of this particular example with prostitute's windows, would be to attract the attention of customers - but then, why Red and not Green or Yellow Lights? After working on Madison Avenue for six years as a Graphic Artist and Package Designer twenty-five years ago, I know the answer to this similarly simple question would also not only fill as many thick volumes as the last question, but this answer is also the main service sold for countless millions of dollars to industries by corporations called Consumer Research. "Campbell's Soup" the famous American soup company made more famous by Andy Warhol, began Coloring their soup cans Red in 1898, and since, many companies prefer their packages in Red because psychological studies claim that Red packages seem to be coming off the shelves and towards the shoppers.

It didn't stop with Color just being associated with heightened states of sexuality, but in Charles A. Riley's "Color Codes," Color gets a new, improved association with not only heightened states of sexuality, but even with homosexuality. Riley writes about the 'Colorful' passages of a composer's music brought out by the 'unnatural' or 'homosexual' aspect of his personality, while the 'White' or 'major' passages in the same piece of music are upheld by the 'normal' and 'heterosexual' side of the composer's personality. Charles A. Riley's mother sure gave him the correct first name.

This "Chromophobic" prejudicial view of society today did not start yesterday, but has it's roots extending way back to before even the Roman Empire - the first real empire that today's society is modeled on, with it's signature Imperialism and unjustified, overwhelming arrogance. The first modern writer on natural sciences, Pliny the Elder of the Roman Empire, 2000 years ago, already complained that strong raw Color was associated with decadent orientalism. But most probably the first writer on "Chromophobia" was Plato in ancient Greece. Plato had an attitude that was not wholly different from Le Corbusier and most other "Chromophobists," such as Charles Blanc, by writing that a painter was only a person that ground up and mixed different Colored 'Drugs.' After Plato, Aristotle went so far as to actually use the Greek word "Pharmakon" - "Drug" - for the word Color. Another true "Chromophobic" of the ancient world was Plotinus, who was a Greek philosopher living in Rome during the Third century. Plotinus, in his "Catalogue of Beauty" intentionally leaves Color out. This Classic(al) "Chromophobic" wrote eighteen hundred years ago that all of Color, including the light of the Sun, were not made up of different parts and symmetrically not beautiful, so all of Color and Sunlight itself was excluded from this idiot's "Catalogue of Beauty." A real student of Plato, with a teacher who considered only the "simple" Colors as beautiful, in regard, of course, to their similarity to the simple geometric forms of mathematics. In the ancient world, Color in painting represented only the decorative and embellishment of the fact, in short, what was regarded as the false. Aristotle wrote in "Poetics" that just the chalk outline of a portrait will always give more pleasure than the most beautiful of Colors applied to the drawing.

Pliny the Elder's "Chromophobic" account was written with a typically ancient Roman prejudice, stating that the painting of his day was too brightly Colored, and decadently not considered valuable if it wasn't covered in exotic expensive pigments. Pliny goes so far as to write in his "Natural History" that the Colors we see on the paintings of his day were not chosen by the Artist who painted the picture, but were rather chosen by the patron, which would then apply not to the taste of the painter, but to the taste of the patron, an ordinary citizen, of whom extravagance was a contemporary state of mind in First century Rome. A modernistic prejudice started perhaps with Pliny the Elder in the First century, when he placed the blame on the usage on the new exotic brilliant Colors on the Orientals. Pliny calls these brilliant new Colors "Indian Colors," while Petronius, Pliny's contemporary, was already writing that these brilliant exotic new Colors came from China and Arabia. The origin of this "Chromophobic" state of mind began in ancient Greece, which regarded itself as representative of modernistic clear-headed simplicity, while the Orient was relegated to the over-ornamentalized. Even the word "Color" itself in First century Greece was defined as 'decoration' and 'embellishment of an original structure in debate.'

Another relatively obscure "Chromophobist" was Philostratus, the ancient Greek novelist who lived from the Second to the Third century. This Philostratus wrote something bordering on the ridiculous: that Colors were not even needed in painting, because if the drawing was good, in Philostratus' opinion, even the brightest purest Colors could be rendered in Black and White(!) - Asshole. Furthermore, in Philostratus' opinion, the Colors used in cosmetics in his day were precisely the same Colors used in painting. Yet another obscure First century Greek "Chromophobist" was named Plutarch. In writing poetically beautiful, and at the same time viciously slanderous, Plutarch worded a passage like Goethe would eighteen centuries later - so sweetly that you would think that he had something nice to say, but also like Goethe, his sugar-sweet pen was dipped in bile. Essentially, what Plutarch wrote was that the most striking effect in Poetry was falseness, and this is what gave the most satisfaction to a poem, so, in relating it to painting, Plutarch concludes for us, very predictably, that Color is the most stimulating part of a piece of Art because it is lifelike by creating an illusion, similar to the falseness in the poem(!) Ancient critics considered Color as actually damaging to the piece of Art, and not even necessary. During the golden "Hellenistic" period - the highest period of ancient Greek Art - the emphasis was always placed on drawing, not on Color. This Hellenistic period even brought to us the first true "Conceptual Artists" who's opinions were that the most important part of the piece of Art was the mentally-formed concept, only, not the making or even the viewing of the Art, and it was also common procedure of the great master painters of the time to leave the actual mixing and painting of the Colors on a piece of Art to their apprentices.

Back to the subject of Roman Imperialism, look at the two most famous buildings in America today: "The White House" (can't imagine what Color it could be) and the Capitol Building in Washington, D.C. These are the models of Neo-Classicism that have not only come to falsely signify all great buildings of the ancient world, but also set the modern tone of unacceptance, which culminated in a Twentieth and Twenty-first century outward prejudice, and the maligning of the formerly enlightened state of pure Color. In 1800 the White House opened as the home for President John Adams. It was built by the "Freemasons" founders, who decided that the White House was to be a Neo-Classical building, so it must be White, like all the ancient classical Greek temples. These Freemasons went on the assumption that everyone else believed, that these ancient classical Greek temples were always as they appeared to their contemporary society. It wasn't until fifty years later, in the mid-Nineteenth century, that archaeologists began to realize that the Parthenon and all of the other classical buildings in Greece were not left bare White. Although the classically-modeled columns of the White House were stipulated by the Freemasons of America to be pure White, the original columns of the classical ancient Greek temples, which they were trying so hard to duplicate, were stripped with none other than Red and complementary Blue paints. The columns of ancient Greek temples and buildings were not White! A perfect example of how society can create something that is absolutely incorrect, but with such an unchallengeable state of supreme authority that it actually *changes* the truth. Just imagine if all the classical ancient temples of Greece had been made with Granite instead of White Marble before they were vividly painted: today in Washington, D.C. the President of the United States would be living in the *"Black House"!*

The fact, that is still shocking to most people in the Twenty-first century, that the Parthenon and temples of ancient Greece were originally brilliantly Colored and not sterile White is thoroughly discussed in John Gage's "Color and Culture - Practice and Meaning from Antiquity to Abstraction." Between 1800 and 1850 archaeologists across Europe and Scandinavia discovered the undeniable fact that Greek temples and sculpture had originally not been White, but brilliantly painted. The first written record of this discovery of the ancient Greek temples being originally brilliantly painted was in the Eighteenth century by Stuart and Revett who revealed that the Ionic Temple of Ilissus in Athens had originally been painted with bright Colors. The English scholar Sir William Gell in 1817 wrote perhaps the first "Chromophobic" account of these new discoveries in Greece, stating that he believed that no other nation had ever had more of a passion for "Gaudy" Colors than the ancient Greeks. After the discovery that the most famous ancient Greek temple, the Parthenon itself, had been completely painted with brilliant Colors, more evidence for this fact was unearthed. In 1862, the Mausoleum at Halicarnassus was excavated, and it was discovered that the sculpted frieze on the front of the Mausoleum by Scopas of the Fourth century B.C., had been brightly painted. These discoveries proved the former discoveries of the brilliant Colors used on the Parthenon to be quite true, because the remnants of paint discovered on this frieze on the Mausoleum at Hilicarnassus were bright vivid Colors, such as a Red pigment for the skin tones, and Ultramarine for the background of the frieze. An initial "Chromophobic" reaction to this indisputable fact was from Sir Isaac Newton, who wrote that he preferred the pure White classical sculpture of Pheidus over the newly discovered, brilliantly painted sculpture on the Mausoleum at Halicarnassus, which he considered to be less 'ethical.' Despite these undeniable unearthed archaeologically discovered facts of ancient Greek temples having been completed and clearly intended to remain brilliantly painted with pure Colors, the Neo-Classical architects of the Eighteenth century did not alter their designs, and subsequently, the White House in Washington, D.C. along with countless other building constructed from the Eighteenth century up until this very day, have been designed, and will remain, pure sterile White. This fact in itself belies an astounding arrogance, both amongst the architects of two hundred years ago, and continuing up until our present day, because the original intent of the Neo-Classical architects of the Eighteenth and Nineteenth centuries was to *copy* the ancient temples of Greece as closely as they could in their own new designs. Unfortunately, arrogance and prejudice have always been the true overriding forces of the human spirit, strong enough to actually change historical fact and archaeological evidence. It slightly reminds one of the pivotal point in "Animal Farm" by George Orwell when the 'Animal Commandments' are amended to read 'No Animal shall sleep in a bed - With Sheets!'

Although the arrogance of the Eighteenth and Nineteenth century architects was strong enough to alter and amend historical fact, it thankfully wasn't universal. There were several sculptors and painters of the period that did alter their Art after these historical discoveries of bright paint on the pure snow-White marble Greek temples. Lawrence Alma-Tadema, an English-Dutch painter in the 1860s completed a canvas depicting a very clear scene of the citizens of Athens examining the newly finished, brilliantly painted friezes of the Parthenon up close, while walking on hugh wooden scaffolding. Even a high member of the French Academy of Art, Ingres, altered his viewpoint to be more historically correct relating to the unearthed discoveries in Greece. Ingres painted two different versions of "Antiochus Strutonice," and it is apparent that the second version was greatly altered from the first because of these archaeological finds in Greece. In 1807, the first painting of "Antiochus Strutonice" by Ingres depicts a nearly monochromatic setting for the interior scene in an ancient Greek temple. The second version of this "Antiochus Strutonice" by Ingres in 1840, which I have studied in the Philadelphia Museum of Art, has changed dramatically, depicting the same classical Greek interior scene, but now brilliantly painted with bright Colors. Ingres scholars agree that he had learned of these new archaeological discoveries through the 1830 book "De Architecture polychrome chez les Grecs" ('The Multi-Colored Architecture from the Greeks') by J.I. Hittorff. It is quite evident the degree of influence this book had on Artists such as Ingres when seeing an 1843 illustration by J.I. Hittorff of a Greek temple painted in it's original intended Colors, which today would approach the intensity of the very word "psychedelic."

During this period of the mid to late Nineteenth century, a few Neo-Classical architects were altering the accepted pure White buildings by adding some Colors. Karl Friedrich Schinkel made plans for a new Royal Palace with a brilliantly painted interior to be built upon the Acropolis in Athens. In the same year, the multi-Colored painting of modern Neo-Classical buildings was put forth by Gottfried Semper. In 1846, Leo van Klenze made the painting "The Acropolis with the Preaching of St. Paul," in which the Parthenon on the Acropolis is brilliantly painted with pure Colors. Also in the 1840s, John Gibson, who is considered to be the last of the Neo-Classicists in England, took some small, but truly radical steps towards the acknowledgement of the facts that Classical ancient Greek sculpture and architecture had been painted. In 1846, Gibson exhibited a sculpted portrait of Queen Victoria that was lightly tinted with Colors, but in 1851-1856 Gibson created the sculpture that he is remembered for, his "Tinted Venus," shown at the "International Exhibition" in London in 1862. The sculpture was displayed to the public in a brightly painted Classically inspired setting by Owen Jones. One of the inscriptions on the brilliant setting would herald in the change of the mid-Nineteenth century's feelings towards Color, proclaiming to all that there was indeed neither beauty, youth, life nor health without Color! The sculpture "Tinted Venus" by John Gibson was "Tinted" as the title explains, not painted with bright Colors like the ancient Greek sculptures, but still a radical departure from millennia of pure snow-White sculptures up to that point in history. The Colors of Gibson's "Tinted Venus" were used mostly on her hair, lips, eyes, and gold ornaments, leaving the majority of the sculpture, the nude skin, only very palely tinted.

As final evidence of the ancient temples of Greece having originally been brightly Colored and not snow-White, in the late Nineteenth century, the remains of even Pre-Classical Greek period archaeological discoveries were unearthed in Mycanae and Knossos, which reveal the same remnants of pure Colors on the sculpture and the temples. This proves that not only were the Parthenon and the other temples of the Classical period of ancient Greece brilliantly Colored, but by the time of the Parthenon's construction, these multi-Color painted Greek temples were not new, but traditional, and had been the norm for centuries already in ancient Greece.

For the last example of ancient artifacts and monuments being in a brilliantly Colored state upon completion so many centuries ago, I will cite what is known as one of the greatest archaeological finds of all time: "The Terracotta Army" of China. This is an immense archaeological find, the scale being overwhelming even through photographs, but it's vast size doesn't compare to what is yet to be excavated, according to archaeologists. The first Emperor of China was named Qin - Qin Shi Huang Di - with the western area of China originally called Qin after it's ruler of three decades. At that time, there were seven independent states of China, and in 221 B.C. Qin conquered the other six states and united China into one country. The barbarians outside of this vast land heard of the Emperor Qin -pronounced "Chin"- and called the country "China." Qin ruled as the first Emperor of China for eleven years and was the literal founder of China as we still know it today. Qin built the first "Great Wall of China," built roads connecting the country together, and also created one unified Chinese written language enabling the whole country of China to communicate with each other. During his rule as first Emperor of China, Qin had an immense tomb complex built which was to be hidden underground in a hugh area of "Xi' an" in central China. The work force that built this complex was just as tremendous with an estimated 700,000 members. New estimates by Chinese archaeologists consider the total buried funerary complex in "Xi' an" to be as large as sixty square kilometers. Presently, only a very small amount of the total archaeological site has been excavated and is exhibited in the immense "Qin Shi Huang Terracotta Warriors and Horses Museum." The Funerary Temple Mount inside a small mountain that dominates the otherwise flat landscape of "The Terracotta Army" terrain, is supposed to be the most extravagant, originally including actual rivers of liquid Mercury representing The Yellow River and The Yangtze in China, that were made by some mechanical process to flow into a huge Mercury ocean. Evidence for this has been found in recent years by images created by measured sound waves and through the discovery that the ground in the center of this small mountain has up to one hundred times the amount of Mercury in the dirt than is normally detected in dirt from the surrounding areas. "The Terracotta Army" was discovered by a peasant in 1974 while digging for a well in this area of "Xi' an." Looking into the well hole, the peasant saw a head looking up at him from the underground. After five years of restoration of the countless fragments of broken Terracotta found at the archaeological site, the first reconstructed figures of this Third century B.C. "Terracotta Army" went on public display in 1979. Today, two million people a year visit "The Terracotta Army" exhibit halls in Xi' an, China. From an ariel viewpoint, the Museum building that houses "The Terracotta Army" display, with it's seven thousand Terracotta Soldiers, looks as big as an airport hanger for 747s.

Now, for over thirty years mass-produced, seen on the front cover of "National Geographic" magazine and many other publications in languages around the world, television documentaries, and even the Internet, everyone, including the present day replica producers and retailers, have the same conception as with the Parthenon and temples of ancient Greece and countless other archaeological examples that have yet to be discovered (or rediscovered) - that they were always as we presently see them in their bare, Colorless state. On the statues being presently restored by a German archaeological team, the discovery was made that all these thousands of statues were originally dyed or painted with full Colors! This German team has also discovered a way of preserving the discovered pigments on the figures of "The Terracotta Army." This immense "Terracotta Army," presently numbering over seven thousand restored Terracotta life-sized statues were not Earth-Colored Tan as we see them today, but the entire Army of these Terracotta warriors were brightly Colored. Remnants of a 'Flesh'-Colored pigment can be seen on the faces and hands of the recently restored statues done by the German archaeologists. The intricate armour covering the soldier's torsos have certain plates Colored with a Red that is still bright today, but the Color of the majority of the armour is a vivid and very rare Purple called "Han Purple." This "Han Purple" is a pigment that has been used in China for over 2,000 years, first synthesized by Chinese Alchemists from Barium Copper Silicates. It was used in large Imperial projects and pottery, most famously on "The Terracotta Army." These brightly painted warriors of "The Terracotta Army" of China also wore clothing and armour still bearing the remnants of the Colors Yellow, Blue, and Pink pigments. When seeing a photograph of this immense "Terracotta Army" in it's natural Earth-Colored state today we are awed, but seeing a retouched image of this tremendous Army brightly Colored in comparison, the original awe-inspiring photograph suddenly looks dead, and immediately it is revealed, once again, the inherent transporting ability of Colors. The figures look lifelike, animated, and inspiring - a world of difference from the mud-Colored soldiers we are left with today. By the way, as can probably be imagined, there are no immediate plans by the Chinese to repaint or redye in bright Colors the seven thousand soldiers of "The Terracotta Army."

In 2016 on a "BBC" series dedicated to the Renaissance it's show's presenter immaculately clarifies the story of the Color which originally covered the ancient sculptures that directly inspired Renaissance sculptors including Michelangelo. As the presenter explains, the sculptures of ancient Greek and Roman periods were being unearthed during the era of the Renaissance in Italy, which at that time greatly influenced sculptors such as Michelangelo. When the incomparable "Belvedere Torso" was dug up during Michelangelo's life he famously critiqued it as having been created by a 'sculptor who was more wise than nature.' As the presenter shows the sparkling snow-White slab of Carrara marble he is holding in both hands while standing in the huge quarry it was removed from, he explains the obvious, being that when the sculptures from ancient Rome and Greece were being dug up during the Renaissance they were pure White, and in this bleached state they were "fundamentally misleading." Although the ancient sculptures were pure White when dug up after many centuries in the ground, these sculptures were not pure White and bleached when they were buried. It is clearly stated that these exquisite ancient Greek and Roman sculptures were "never White," and that these iconic sculptures are distinguished as having been originally "highly Colored" with the presenter even using the contemporary compliment "Gaudy" to describe the Colors which covered these ancient sculptures. In conclusion the obvious is once again considered, being that White marble lasts much longer than the Colors of paint (especially when underground for centuries). When these originally Colorful ancient iconic Greek and Roman sculptures were dug up they were only Colorless and pure White as we still know them today, and in that condition they went on to also 'mislead our entire civilization.' Michelangelo and all of modern civilization since that time - up until the present day - was falsely inspired by a "mythic White" ancient world that had never existed in reality, but has only existed in our presumptuous imaginations. 'I feel it here in my heart that they were always White!'

Today, in the first decade of the Twenty-first century, fifty full centuries after the first synthetic pigment was invented by the ancient Egyptians "iryt hsbd" (artificial Lapis Lazuli), and now with a list of manufactured Colors that is 9,000 pages long and fills nine volumes of the "Color Index International," the pigment produced in the absolute largest quantity today is White - yes, *White!*

One subject not mentioned yet, the subject that includes "Chromophobia" as a stipulating factor of it's curriculum, is Photography. "Black and White" is the absolute foundation of photography, unaltered from it's conception. University photography classes teach in plain English that using Color in photography is something like 'cheating.' Classical and contemporary photography was and is produced, and presented in Museum across the world almost exclusively in Black and White, only. It is taught that only with Black and White photography can you achieve the true tones and values of nature and the world around us. Very true if you are completely *Color Blind*. It is taught that only with Black and White photography do you emphasize the subject without the "distraction" of Colors. In this way photography tried to elevate itself to the very level of Analytical and Synthetic Cubism. A Brazilian Photographer was being interviewed about his Black and White photographs of San Paulo. He very clearly stated his opinion that his photographs were only Black and White to accent the drama and existentialism of daily life in San Paulo, but if he had taken the same pictures in Color, he continued, the same dramatic photographs would have looked "Postcard-y." Here we have the absolute epitome of "Chromophobia:" the general inability of people to appreciate, or even realize, the inherent transporting spiritual powers of Color, and so viewed upon as distracting the average creator and viewer is left with something that is much more palatable for their abilities, desires, and the lives they live through: Colorless, Spiritually-void, and drained of the natural powers and mysticism that surrounds us all. Again, what a pity.

After considering in perspective all these produced prejudices and created Social Stigmas surrounding the world of pure Color, it becomes clear the dismissal and disregard of society when confronted with the brightest Colors ever invented: Fluorescent Colors! Society equated even the normal pigments of bright pure Red, Orange, and Blue with a regression to a childlike state, or to equally dignified states of madness, sexual excitement, or savagery - in short, all that is beneath, or under, or inferior, or even degrading to the precious modern decree of "normality." In other words, society states, in far too many words, that today if you like - or God forbid even *use* - such unbridled pure Color there is, at best, something wrong with you, or even at worse, that you could be considered to be mentally and/or sexually dangerous. This is the perverse degree that society has brought us to: equating what was once thought of as enlightened, or even representing a state of heightened awareness or knowledge, to now being regarded as something childish, and to a major degree, something to be disregarded and relegated to children's toys, signs of madness, or degrees of abnormality in society. Another point to examine is just *why* children and 'uncivilized' cultures and peoples have always been listed as the few members of the known world that will still accept and even enjoy bright pure Colors. The intention of this classification is to obviously link the acceptance and enjoyment of pure Color to a mentality that is still undeveloped, and can therefore not compare to the fully developed civilized serious mentality that, through it's gained and learned sobriety not only naturally looses any contact with Color, but intentionally discards their former acceptance and enjoyment of pure Color as readily and insistently as they discard their childhood toys. This explains only part of the question - the part that could be called the 'political' aspect of the question. The 'physiological' aspect of the question runs much deeper. Another point in common between children and 'uncivilized' societies and 'savages' is that they do not have University degrees. A baby, before learning to talk, read, write, and calculate, is in a state of super-perception. All their senses, including their eyes, are as wide open as they will ever be. Before the lessons in language, logic, and ego begin, the brain has no reason to alter itself before the onslaught of the personality. But, as the lessons begin, all this raw input of stimuli must be regulated, relegated, and generally reduced, until we achieve the parent's goal: to become acceptable, competent, productive, serious, sober, "Chromophobic" members of a mass culture of seven-and-a-half billion sentient beings that individually condition themselves to purposefully use a mere percentage of their brain, only. And, obviously, that part of the brain does not like Color.

In this charged state of modernism and gentrification, a state that has come to regard bright raw Color as signs of all that is unacceptable in society, or abnormal even, on this stage of the Twentieth century enters the brightest, rawest, and most shocking Colors ever seen or invented by humanity: Fluorescent pigments! In hindsight, it is perfectly lucid to see that these Fluorescent pigments could never have been accepted by the society of the late Twentieth century, even if the 1960s revolution had never happened. "Qu'est-il arrive au miracle?"

What happened to the Miracle becomes very clear when seen with the hindsight of exactly forty years. In 2007, forty years after "The Summer of Love" - 1967 - when the world became aware, through the media, of a revolution taking place in Western culture known as the Hippie Movement - it is all too clear what precisely created the Social Stigma of "Fluorophobia." The underlying theme of the 1960s Hippie Movement wasn't just the superficial differences of wild dress and long hair, that the media immediately stressed and capitalized on, as usual, but something much deeper - the very factor that wrought horror into the minds of established middle-aged society: Consciousness expansion through the use of psychedelic drugs. Here we have, in a precise condensed form, the very root of the prejudice and general negativity that the entire movement of the 1960s has since been viewed in. This prejudice and social stigma also did not begin yesterday - this feeling of established society began simultaneously with the movement's conception. Just the difference of the movement's exterior - the hair and the wild fashion - was already too much a radical departure from 'normality' for society to accept. But this was nothing compared to the interior of the movement - consciousness expansion through the use of underground psychedelic drugs, the most famous and strongest of these drugs being L.S.D. Now in a movement of heightened awareness and perception, Fluorescent Colors emitting their own vivid light through the energy exchange of an invisible Ultraviolet source became the very identifying Colors of the 1960s Movement. Here is the absolute strongest factor that caused the Social Stigma of "Fluorophobia" that has existed for the last fifty years. Although the outward obvious difference of the Fluorescent Colors with their nocturnal "Black Lights" created initially a portion of the Social Stigma of "Fluorophobia," the 'killing blow' for Fluorescent pigments was society's intrinsic bonding of these 'out-of-the-world' Colors with the 'out-of-this-world' so-called "Drug Culture" of the 1960s. Having said this, many drugs, including psychedelic drugs, were no strangers to some very influential Artists over the last one hundred years. The Morphine use of Gauguin is well enough documented, but much less documented is the early Mescaline use by very famous Artists. Cezanne's father complained of his son leaving his study of law and Aix en Provence to live in Paris and become an Artist who 'smokes drugs.' In the late 1920s a German chemist Karl Beringer synthesized Mescaline from the Peyote Cactus. Karl Beringer was a friend of Carl Jung and Hermann Hesse, who's experiments were documented in Hesse's world-famous novel "Steppenwolf" (1927). Karl Beringer wrote "Der Meskalin Rauch" ('The Mescaline Experience') in 1927. A very influential, but much less well known novel by Hermann Hesse is "Journey to the East" where there is a proto-hippie society of thinkers and Artists on a spiritual journey towards the East. One of the members of this society in the book is Hermann Hesse's friend Paul Klee. Joan Miro was also similarly inspired, immediately apparent in his early landscapes that continue underground to the subterranean world of roots, etc., and probably some of the earliest (and best) psychedelic self-portraits ever painted. Robert and Sonia Delaunay's Paintings of Light itself, finally moving into the realm of pure Color and abstraction, are also documented as being very early experimenters. "Cubism" is obvious.

There is yet another reason for the Social Stigma of "Fluorophobia," and the word is applied here with the full meaning of it's Latin root: Fear. As if the reasons like "Chromophobia," and the association with the 1960s Movement were not enough, there is also a physical, not just emotional, reason for the Social Stigma of "Fluorophobia." Starting in the late 1800s, and continuing well up into the 1940s, Ultraviolet was used in medicine as a misguided 'Miracle-Cure.' Ultraviolet Medical treatment, which was called "Actinotherapy," used a much stronger Ultraviolet energy than the Longwave Ultraviolet energy that comes out of "Black Lights," the most common source of Ultraviolet that almost everyone has seen in clubs and on posters. The "Black Light" produces harmless Longwave Ultraviolet energy that is just outside the Visible Spectrum of all the Colors we see. This harmless Longwave Ultraviolet energy comes through the Ozone Layer and is essential for life on Earth, including Photosynthesis. The Ultraviolet energy that was used in the beginning of the last century as a 'Miracle-Cure' in Medicine was not harmless Longwave Ultraviolet, like from "Black Lights," but much stronger, dangerous Shortwave Ultraviolet energy, which does not come through the Ozone Layer, never reaches the surface of the Earth, and *Does Not* come out of "Black Lights." This, in fact, is what the Ozone Layer is at the top of the Earth's atmosphere for, to prevent harmful Shortwave Ultraviolet energy from reaching the surface of the Earth. At an altitude of fifteen miles (twenty-four kilometers) there is a fragile layer of Ozone an eight-of-an-inch thick, only, (3 millimeters) that does not allow the dangerous Shortwave Ultraviolet energy through to the Earth's surface. Again, Longwave Ultraviolet energy comes directly through the Ozone Layer and is contained in sunlight reaching the surface of the Earth. The Ozone Layer is actually created by the strongest of all Ultraviolet energy coming from the Sun, called "Extreme Ultraviolet," or "Vacuum Ultraviolet." Extreme Ultraviolet, Shortwave Ultraviolet, Middlewave Ultraviolet, and harmless Longwave Ultraviolet are all created inside the Sun and travel trough space to the Earth. The "Extreme Ultraviolet" collides with Oxygen molecules in the Earth's upper atmosphere, frees one atom of Oxygen from these molecules, then recombines with the freed Oxygen atom to form "Ozone." Hence, the magic of Nature is displayed in all it's complexity here: the Ultraviolet traveling through space from the Sun *creates* it's own filter for itself, so the harmful components of this Ultraviolet energy don't reach the Earth's surface.

In the early part of the Twentieth century, the "Alpine Sun Lamp" by "Hanovia," and many similar lamps sold by other companies were using Shortwave Ultraviolet energy as a 'Miracle-Cure' because logic at the time suggested that if you go out in the Sun and the Ultraviolet energy is what makes you healthy, then lamps should be created that could give people the most Ultraviolet possible to make them the most 'Healthy'(!) What was not learned up until the mid to late 1940s was that there are different kind of Ultraviolet energies, and not all of them are harmless. First, the Visible spectrum - all the Colors we can see - is from about 770 nanometers being Red, to 400 nm. which is Violet. Longwave Ultraviolet is right next to the visible spectrum, is harmless, very weak, and comes directly through the Ozone Layer, with a wavelength of 350-400 nanometers. Next is Middlewave Ultraviolet energy that is the Ultraviolet that gives us suntan and has a wavelength of 300-350 nanometers. The third general classification of Ultraviolet is the Shortwave Ultraviolet energy that was used in the early part of the Twentieth century as the 'Miracle-Cure.' This Shortwave Ultraviolet has a wavelength of 250-300 nanometers, and is dangerous for living things. All Ultraviolet energy below 310 nanometers causes sun Burn, not suntan, and is very dangerous for long exposures, also creating Vitamin D activity. The skin tans between 320 and 400 nanometers to protect against deeper penetration of U.V. rays from the Sun. Sun burn happens with Ultraviolet between 290 and 310 nanometers, so all suntan lotions are really "U.V. Filters," containing a filter for Ultraviolet energy below 310 nanometers, which will make the skin burn, not just tan. The third most popular 'question' or statement that too many visitors to "Electric Lady" Art Gallery since 1987 have 'asked' is: "These Black Lights are dangerous, right?" This statement comes from the general public's memory - stigma, actually - of these 'Miracle-Cure' U.V. treatments that went on for many decades in many parts of western society. These Shortwave Ultraviolet Medical 'Miracle-Cure' lamps were also manufactured for many decades by many different companies, with too many of them being made. The most famous of all these U.V. treatment devices being the lamp I mentioned before, the "Alpine Sun Lamp" from the American and English firm "Hanovia," but these lamps were manufactured by many different companies including "Sperti," "General Electric," "Ultra-Violet Products, Inc.," and even the ever-popular "Sears-Roebucks, Inc." So, as can be imagined, these lamps entered into many different facets of society, especially in the United States and across Europe. These 'Miracle-Cure' Shortwave Ultraviolet Medical Treatment kits were not only dangerous to use, but they also look like something out of a Frankenstein movie, with glass attachments that were used to put harmful Shortwave Ultraviolet energy into the ears, nose, mouth, and every other imaginable orifice of the human body. Something else that must be explained about the outrageous claims made by the manufacturers of these Shortwave Ultraviolet 'Miracle-Cure' Medical Treatment lamps - they did not just claim to make you Healthy, but they made unbelievable claims as the selling-points for their 'Miracle-Cure' lamps, such as the claim from the mid-1930s Shortwave Ultraviolet Medical Treatment lamp on display in "Electric Ladyland - the First Museum of Fluorescent Art," to "Grow Your Hair Back"(!) for bald men. In the Museum there is also a flip-chart on the wall that displays much obscure information about Ultraviolet energy, such as it's fundamental use in creating the first Television sets in the late 1920s, "Common Items that are Fluorescent" including Green Peppers, Cucumbers, Tomatoes, Eggs, Teeth, Fingernails, etc., and also six advertisements for these 'Miracle-Cure' Shortwave Medical Treatment lamps which are from 1923 up until the early 1940s. These never fail to make Museum visitors laugh, with their truly impossible claims, such as an advertisement from 1928 claiming that these Shortwave U.V. lamps could "Cure Rickets in children's legs"(!) These retro advertisements are about 'dated' today as "Coca-Cola" advertisements from the same period proclaiming that Cocaine-containing Coca leaves were inside the soda. These Ads claimed not just to 'Grow Hair Back' and 'Cure Rickets,' but a list of 'Miracle-Cures' that were supposedly attainable with these lamps long enough to fill a complete paragraph in almost all these advertisements. In the Museum collection there are many of these original 'Miracle-Cure' advertisements, and also very old books on "Actinotherapy." In one of these books on Actinotherapy from 1927 by Russell and Russell, with a title that typifies the horror a person today reading it would react with: "Ultraviolet Radiation and Actinotherapy," there are Black and White photographs from "Westminster Hospital" in London showing daily treatments given to babies under massive Shortwave Ultraviolet lamps, which went on for years.

As now can be understood, making people sick with what was claimed as a 'Miracle-Cure' did not exactly put Ultraviolet close to people's hearts sixty years ago, or increase society's love for these Ultraviolet lamps. The most famous high-society Shortwave Ultraviolet Medical Treatment center was created by Dr. Kellogg in the United States, where the richest members of American society would travel to Michigan to get these 'Miracle' treatments. Most people today do not remember Dr. Kellogg for his 'Miracle-Cure' Shortwave Ultraviolet Medical Treatments, but for his "Corn Flakes!"

Today Ultraviolet is still used in medicine, but only harmless Longwave Ultraviolet, like the Black light, in Dermatology and for various very interesting applications in medical tracing. Middlewave Ultraviolet is also used in Medicine today for skin treatments including Psoriasis. The biggest use of Harmful Shortwave Ultraviolet today does, in fact, make people Healthy, finally, when it is used for purifying drinking water inexpensively in countries such as Africa. As well, Shortwave Ultraviolet lamps are used in most "Koi" fish ponds, also to purify the water. Shortwave Ultraviolet is very important in the study of astronomy, where it is used when photographing celestial bodies in many different wavelengths of light and for many other applications, and in mineralogy where it is used for identifying elements in minerals, and for fascinating Fluorescent mineral displays behind glass, which Shortwave Ultraviolet does not penetrate.

Something else to put into prolonged perspective when contemplating such atrocious 'Miracle-Cure' contraptions of Short-wave Ultraviolet Medical Treatments from seventy-five years ago: how will people of the future look upon our present-day 'Miracle' contraptions that all of contemporary society is so proud and smug about today? This is a question in the Museum, after I explain the 'Miracle-Cure' Shortwave Ultraviolet Medical Treatment kit on display, that has been asked by a few of only the sharpest of visitors. My answer is: 'How many times a day, or even an hour, do you put this little marvel of high-tech radioactivity about one inch away from your brain and your eyes - this 'Miracle' of the end of the industrious glorious Twentieth century that shoots invisible rays off into the edge of space to orbiting satellites and then also 'Miraculously' receives invisible rays back from the edge of space = all one inch from your brain and eyes, this 'Miracle' called a "portable telephone?"' This is not to say that the Portable telephone will be the only Horror from our arrogant "We've Done it All" present monetary-based spiritually-void early Twenty-first century society. The list is so long it would take another book just to contain it. Think about it the next time you save time by using your Microwave Oven to heat up your dinner, or when you see a news report about Transgenic Fluorescent Animals.

Another point that must also be put into it's proper perspective today, and will surely be greeted in today's Twenty-first century state-of-mind with the same degree of utter disbelief as telling people that the Parthenon and all the ancient Greek temples were not always sterile White, but entirely painted with vivid complementary Colors: Artists were not always regarded by society as they are today - celebrities, famous, powerfully influential, and even possibly immensely wealthy- don't tell Jeff Koons or Damien Hirst! If you travel back in time just the span of ten human life times, you would see the opinion of society towards Artists as something that the majority of people today would find hard to even imagine. Before the great Renaissance of 1500-1510, and even lasting up until the early Seventeenth century in England, Artists were some of the lowest members of established society and they were called a "Peynter-Steyner" (Painter-Stainer) or even just "Daubers." The first name obviously comes from the centuries-old low caste clothes dyers (Stainers). Artists were originally associated with alchemy and even early chemistry because of the means of getting the actual pigments used to create the Colors in their paints. Before the Renaissance the Artist was only, at best, an elevated 'Craftsman' and their skills that were admired were only the physical ability to do their job mixing and producing pigments, and making their 'pictures.' All the traits that Artists are valued and known for today weren't even considered before the 1500s, such as creativity and aesthetics. In the Middle Ages, painting was regarded only as a craft, like making furniture, and likewise, painters were only regarded as craftsmen, like woodworkers. This classification equated painting and painters as a factor of society that did only lowly manual labour. The Renaissance Artist finally raised the social standing of their profession to the level of a 'Liberal Art' through the use of mathematics. In the 1500s the four main subjects taught at the few Universities that were already established were Astronomy, Literature, Music, and Mathematics. Here we have the cause for the change that occurred during this period, which took almost five hundred years to reverse itself: the Artist purposefully distancing themselves from the lowly association of producing and grinding pigments in a dark Alchemist's laboratory. This also produced some of the earliest real tangible social prejudices against Color, and thus "Chromophobia." The Artists of Renaissance Florence were intent on raising their social status to the same level as respected scholars such as Mathematicians or Astronomers, so they distanced themselves not only physically from the smokey alchemy labs grinding pigments into Artist's Colors, but also distanced themselves spiritually from this Medieval association by separating themselves from Color itself. Renaissance Artists in Florence stressed that the most important part of Art was Drawing ("Disegno"), not painting with Color ("Colore"), in an attempt to alter society's outlook on their profession by disassociating themselves from the Medieval stigma of the "Peynter-Steyner" who's job had only to do with the Coloring of existing objects, not with the creation of objects by drawing them.

To restate this fact that is hard to believe today, during the Middle Ages painters and sculptors had been regarded by society as nothing more than craftsmen, in the same social standing as a carpenter or a baker. The contemporary social standing of the Artist as a genius, as a person detached and elevated above the common social standing of a craftsman like a bread baker, did not occur until the Renaissance. The Artist as an educated man of learning gradually became the outlook of society, and many Artists during this period of the early Renaissance learned in two different methods, one being the studying of texts on aesthetics, and the other being the studying of classical sculpture and architecture. To directly study classical sculpture and architecture, Artists travelled to Rome, where there was the most sculpture and architecture from the past classical period. Two of the earliest Artists from Florence to relocate themselves to Rome during the pre-Renaissance were Donatello, as well as Brunelleschi, who had just lost the competition for the bronze doors of the Baptistery of Florence to Lorenzo Ghiberti. Manetti, a contemporary writer of the period wrote probably the first and earliest description of the "Bohemian Artist," about these two Artists Donatello and Brunelleschi. Manetti writes that neither Donatello or Brunelleschi had a normal life with the common worries of a wife or children. More foretelling of the future vision of the bohemian Artist was Manetti's description of these two Artists as being unconcerned with what they ate or drank, and also being not concerned about how they dressed themselves or with the lifestyle they lived, as long a they had the essential materials needed by themselves to be able to create their Artwork. Many Artists of this period who had travelled to Rome to study the sculpture and architecture of the Classical period, returned to their homes with many artifacts of the Classical period they had collected. Donatello brought back to Florence a large collection of ancient coins and gems from Rome, and Lorenzo Ghiberti brought back to Florence Art objects he had collected in Rome. Some of the Florentine Artists went so far with associating themselves to the Classical period that they produced works they tried to convince people as being Classical period antiques, such a Michelangelo's very early Cupid sculpture and small religious statues now in the cathedrals of Bologna and Sienna, and also Leon Battista Alberti who wrote a comedy which he convinced people was actually written by a Classical Roman author. In the period leading up to the Renaissance, the painter Giotto had a large influence on contemporary Artists, with his inclusions in the painting of a sense of real three-dimensional space and actual communication between the painted figures. What must be understood here is that the Artists who were the most influenced by the Classical world were Artists who were already opposed to the doctrines of Medieval Art. During the high Renaissance several original Hellenistic Greek statues were discovered in the vicinity of Rome, which greatly inspired Artists, including both Michelangelo and Raphael. The hugh "Laocoon" marble and the "Belvedere Torso" of the Hellenistic Greek period greatly influenced both the painting and sculpture of Michelangelo. Of the "Belvedere Torso," Michelangelo said that 'the Sculptor was wiser than nature itself.' The "Belvedere Apollo" was also an ancient Hellenistic Greek sculpture used for at least three pieces of Art by Raphael during the high Renaissance. Another point to be understood is that the Artists of the Renaissance, such as Michelangelo, Raphael, and Donatello did not produce Art that just copied the feelings of the ancient Greeks and Romans, but went beyond the Classical sculptures into a realm where they could express their own feelings about God and life. Donatello's sculptures became less classical after his sojourn to Rome, and Michelangelo's figures became less naturalistic, defying classical rules of anatomy. Although these famous Artists of the Renaissance were profoundly inspired and influenced by the 'pagan' Art of ancient Rome and Greece, the majority of the Art they themselves created were deeply Christian religious. One of the only Renaissance Artists who created paintings that were not religious and Christian-based, was Piero di Cosimo, who dared to paint scenes of primitive lifestyles. Here we have a rebel Artist who dared, nearly four hundred years before Vincent van Gogh, to document on canvas scenes of common life and what his contemporaries could have called poverty. The difference between the reception of painting of common poor life by Piero di Cosimo, and the baroque exuberance of the standard religious paintings done by his fellow Artists of the Renaissance would be nearly impossible to imagine with the passage of four centuries. The Renaissance biographer Vasari describes Piero di Cosimo as an eccentric and a loner. Piero di Cosimo was the first Artist to be described as a true "Bohemian Artist," in the same light that Paul Gauguin and Vincent van Gogh were 'first' described in the 1880s. Vasari describes Piero di Cosimo as being constantly shut up in his atelier, not allowing anyone to see him paint, and living the lifestyle of a wild animal rather than that of a man. Vasari goes on to describe Piero di Cosimo as a dirty, unkept person who's only food was hard-boiled eggs, and to complete this description, Vasari informs us that di Cosimo only cooked these hard-boiled eggs when it was necessary to build a fire to prepare his painting materials, such a varnish or glues. The only other Renaissance Artist that Vasari describes similarly, such as being a loner, poor, strange, and moody was di Cosimo's contemporary Uccello. These two Artists of the Renaissance were atypical of their contemporaries, who created their Artwork in workshops, or even before the Renaissance, in Craft guilds.

The first real call for change in the social outlook of an Artist's standing was in the 1430s by Cennino Cennini, who wrote the "Book on Art." Cennini's book was a call for his fellow Artists to raise their social standings and change the outlook of general society towards themselves. Cennini goes so far as to list the changes an Artist should have made to promote this social change, such as living the regulated life style of a scholar studying science or theology, which would include eating and drinking a normal amount of light food and light wine at least two times a day, and another point was stressed: not to spend too much time or energy on women. Another large influence on this changing of the social attitude towards Artists were the writings of the ancient Romans Pliny the Elder and Vitruvius. These writings taught Artists of the late Fifteenth century and early Renaissance studying classical Roman works, that their fellow Artists, who had lived during the time of ancient Rome, had been respected as intellectually gifted individuals, not as craftsmen. Artists of the pre-Renaissance, such a Ghiberti and Cennini began to consciously associate the practices of painting, sculpture, and architecture to subjects of the universities including the Liberal Arts of poetry and mathematics. Their argument was that since the Liberal Arts of mathematics and poetry began from the formation of a theory, then the creation of Art should too begin from the formation of a theory. Leonardo da Vinci was the outspoken leader of this particular school of thought, comparing an Artist who creates without scientific theory to a sailor without a compass or rudder. During the Renaissance the relentless actions of Artists like Leonardo da Vinci had their desired effects, being that society began to regard Artists as individuals of intellect and status, but at the same time the different types of Artists struggled amongst themselves over which of their professions had a higher social acceptance. Leonardo stated that painters were more socially acceptable than sculptors, because painters could work at ease, like gentlemen, while sculptors did heavy physical work with sweat pouring down their faces, like a common laborer. Leonardo's opinion began to take precedence during the Renaissance, with his stressing of the tremendous Artistic output of a painter compared to a sculptor, and even going to the lengths of portraying a painter as a gentleman because he could create his Art to the accompaniment of music, as Leonardo himself did, which the sculptor could not because of the amount of noise his brute physical sculpting produced. One Renaissance sculptor who was a contemporary of Benvenuto Cellini was Baccio Bandinelli, who suffered so much from the sculptor's second-class position behind the painter, that in an attempt to raise social outlook, he decided to call his sculpture workshop an "Academy," borrowing the term from gatherings of literary intellectuals.

The 'war' between the status of the painter versus the status of the sculptor made definite progress in raising society's outlook on the social standing of the Artist and the Arts. The publication of Federico Zuccari's treatise in 1607 is what could be called the 'crescendo' of this movement that started in the mid fourteen hundreds, with it's peak in the high Renaissance spearheaded by the doctrines, writings, and teachings of Leonardo di Vinci, who stressed that "Disegno" (Drawing) was the most important part of Art, not "Colore" (Color). The painter Federico Zuccari published this treatise in 1607 bringing the logical culminating conclusion to this movement with Zuccari stating that "Disegno" (drawing) was actually only just below Theology in importance, the proof for Zuccari being his claim that the word "disegno" originated in the phrase "segno di Dio," meaning 'a sign from God.' From here Zuccari states what Leonardo had already written, being that the genius of the Artist lies in their creation, where their genius allows them also to create, like God. Leonardo di Vinci wrote similar statements decades before Zuccari's 1607 publication where he stated that painters had 'divine power' through their knowledge, which had literally transformed their minds into likenesses of 'the divine mind.' Leonardo da Vinci lead the movement of this new social outlook of the Artist being the possessors of divine knowledge through their acts of creation, being separate and above the common person, and even towards today's standard social attitude of the Artist as a unique social individual because of their eccentric creative genius. By the mid-fifteen hundreds, after the high Renaissance, there was nothing left of the concept of the Artist being just a common craftsman, akin to a carpenter or a baker, but the attitude of society had changed so dramatically that the Artist was even, on occasion, elevated to the state of nobility. One of the main events that definitively changed society's outlook towards Artists was the formation of an Academy of Artists in the 1560s by the powerful Cosimo de Medici of Florence. This Academy of Artists was lead by an aging Michelangelo, then in his eighties, and would include the influential Artists Cellini, Titian, and Tintoretto. The main achievements of this Academy of Artists were the raising of society's outlook of Artists above the common craftsmen, to a point of near-divinity, and also the founding of the new attitude that the sketches and preliminary work of Artists should be kept and treasured as pieces of Art as well, and not discarded as had been the tradition up until that point in time. The culmination of the movement and it's ideals came with the tomb of Michelangelo in Florence in 1564. The extravagant tomb combines the three Arts that were considered divine by that time, painting, sculpture, and architecture, represented by the use of Fresco, a sculpted bust of Michelangelo, and the design of the Sarcophagus itself, creating more than just a tomb to commemorate Michelangelo's death, but a literal stone monument of the triumph of "Art" over "Craft." These maneuvers to raise the social standing of the Artist above the lowly craftsman all had their desired calculated effect, and by the time of one of the true 'modern Artists,' Turner, it was clear that the Artist was regarded as a visionary. In Turner's day there was a common practice known as "Varnishing Day," which is about a well-known and applicable today as "Actinotherapy," and would also duly shock almost any Artist or gallery director worldwide. "Varnishing Day" was a big event that was held on the opening day of an Artist's exhibition, and would unbelievably entail the Artist himself literally painting the final master touches onto their painting and finally varnishing the painting "live" in front of the gathered, waiting public audience in the Art gallery!

Clearly the initial sociological stigma had it's roots in the free-association of Color itself representing something to distance yourself purposefully from, if you wanted to be regarded as a person with any kind of social standing. Here we are witnessing the probable birth of true "Chromophobia." Prenatal "Chromophobia" - "Chromophobia" in the womb - would have to be represented by Plato, and then by Aristotle in ancient Greece more than 2,000 years ago. Aristotle wrote in his "Poetics" a formula that was copied nearly verbatim by the Florentine Artists of the Renaissance, stating with typical Aristotelian authority that Drawing in Black represented 'Thought' in Art, but Color in Art not only entailed no thought, but it could even go so far as to actually degrade the quality of the Art (the drawing). He stated that a drawing in just Black would always give more 'pleasure' than a combination of all the most beautiful Colors in the world. A Classic(al) "Protochromophobic!" In fact, this identical prejudice has been kept in very good health much later on down the line by half a millennia of Art Historians and writers since the Florentine painters of the Renaissance. Many centuries ago, during the "Tang dynasty" in China (618-907), Daoists were reacting to a Confucian world, and believed that only the use of Black in painting was able to represent something created by the intellect, and not the use of Color which would only represent something created by the mere eye. True "Chromophobists" of the highest order. During this "Tang dynasty" the belief was that true Artists should have to use only Black to convey the deepest inner meanings of nature and Art, while the use of Color was considered totally vulgar, commercial, and not to the taste or choice of the elite of society. Already in China so many centuries ago this social stigma of "Chromophobia" was well established and intricately defined by the elite of society. These Chinese would have been shocked at what Goethe and Le Corbusier had to say about their lack of refinement and culture reflected by their Color choices through history. In extreme contrast, and as a vivid example of the vast degree to which society can shift opinion, during the "Qing dynasty" a thousand years after the "Tang dynasty" in China, the Color was Yellow. Qianlong Emperor (1711-1799) was the fourth Emperor of the "Qing dynasty," ruling for one of the longest periods in Chinese history, 1735-1796, and had incredibly strict rules concerning Color. The Qianlong Emperor's clothing was pure Yellow silk embroidered with Golden thread, and he was the only person that was allowed to wear this Color. The law stated that Yellow was the most noble Color in all of China and it decreed that anyone besides the Emperor that was caught wearing the Color Yellow would be punished by decapitation. The law was so strict that the Crown-Prince was the only person that was allowed to wear even Orange. This is similar to the punishment of death that was carried out in ancient Rome if anyone but the Emperor was caught wearing "Tyrian" Purple. Whereas the dazzling Yellow Color of the robes of Qianlong Emperor of China most likely were made from the pollen of countless thousands of Crocus stigmas, the "Royal Purple" or "Imperial Purple" Color of the robes of the ancient Roman Emperors were made by the Phoenicians in the city of Tyre with countless millions of small "Murex brandaris" sea snails, incidentally, which can still be seen as "Murex Hill" in present-day Lebanon. The amount of sea snails that was necessary to make but a single Roman toga Purple was a staggering 12,000 "Murex brandaris," which produced the needed one and four-tenths gram, only, and is the reason that there is the one hundred yard (meter) by fifty yard "Murex Hill" still in existence 2,000 years later.

The first Color-Theory book I ever read in the mid-1970s in college was through the advice of my Color-Theory professor Bruce Rigby (who's class made such a profound impact on me that I still remember his name after forty years): "Theory of Colors" by Goethe, the first edition having been published in 1810. This was the single reference suggested by professor Rigby to read. The only book I have ever seen with a more detailed published observation of Color than Goethe's is M.E. Chevreul's "The Principles of Harmony and Contrast of Colors" from 1839. In "Theory of Colors" there are complete chapters dealing with only the Color of shadows, to give an example of Goethe's degree of depth. But, two centuries before Le Corbusier, and many years before Charles Blanc, Goethe wrote the Prototype of modern "Chromophobia" in this "Theory of Colors," that would be closely copied and followed implicitly by all future Chromophobics up until our present day, and most likely, into the near future. Goethe lists a cast of social-misfits and mental deficients that would echo in all Chromophobic volumes for the next two hundred years: the savages, the uncivilized societies, the uneducated, and of course the children, will always choose, and actually generally prefer pure vivid Colors. He also restates his point, in case we didn't understand it's subtlety, by further stating that 'refined' people of society do not wear clothes dyed with vivid Colors, and also these 'refined' members of society do not even own objects that are brightly Colored. As a logical conclusion, Goethe states that the 'refined' sector of society's ultimate choice will be to arrive in a time when they actually 'banish' vivid pure Color. There are more passages in Goethe's "Theory of Colors" where he states further examples of his own personal prototypical "Chromophobia." The last section of his book (Part VI) deals with none other than the way that Color effects our 'Morals' - for *46 pages!* In this section he lists the Colors, beginning with Yellow, and divides his 'moral' comments into twelve different Colored parts. Only six pages into this section he begins, again with a highly prejudicial pen, to list just what kind of people could possible like the Color Yellow-Red. He first lists men that could easily wear the same description if they were "Neanderthal," being physically strong, having no patience (like a child), and of course having no education - this is the type of 'men' he lists as the kind of person that would like Yellow-Red. That's not all: he writes that the use of Yellow-Red is world-famous for being used by 'Savages.' And of course, the now-famous trio of society's pure vivid Color lovers (David Batchelor also coined the name "Chromophilia" in his book "Chromophobia") would hardly fair complete without the addition, once again by Goethe in 1810, of the stigma of "Infantilism" to join with the other members of Goethe's 'caste' of what he describes as being nearly-retarded, savage, and practically cavemen! Goethe tells us that if you leave children alone with Colors, they will always use Orange and Red the most. In a different section on Red-Yellow (not to be confused with the section on Yellow-Red), Goethe goes so far as to clearly and intentionally associate nationalism to Colors, as well. Being German, Goethe does not miss the opportunity to state very clearly that the Germans and English prefer leather that was dyed pale Yellow, while the more 'active' French dye their leather Yellow-Red, obviously alluding to Goethe's opinion that the German and English were more culturally refined and further from the 'savage' than the French(!) For Goethe's grand nationalistic Color conclusion, he states that the Germans and English have a 'sedate' country, relating his opinion to the point that these two countries prefer clothing of Earth-Colors, or Yellow together with Blue, but again, France was not a 'sedate' country and Goethe explains this by accompanying his opinion with the point that the French love - of course - brilliant Colors, hence, proving to Goethe that the German and English were far more refined and superior to the French - wait until you hear what he had to say about the Spanish and the Italians! Of course he associates Red with the Italians and Spanish in southern most Europe, and goes on to word a passage so poetically, that you would nearly be deceived into thinking that he had something nice to say, but in reality, Goethe viciously states that nations like Italy and Spain have no dignity as of yet, but getting some dignity is their 'aim.' Goethe tells us of personal experience with Yellow-Red, being that it was even unbearable for men of education that he knew to see someone dressed in Yellow-Red on a cloudy day. Can you imagine this moron! Goethe would have loved the physiological Color testing that has gone on for over half a century now. Tests have claimed that Human beings, a well as many animals, respond to seeing the Color Red on a physical level with accelerated Heart rates and by releasing Adrenaline into the bloodstream. Studies in the U.S. have stated that men react the strongest to Reds with Yellow added (Red/Orange), and women react the strongest to Reds with Blue added (Magenta). In an excellent article "Quest for Color" by Cary Wolinsky in "National Geographic" magazine, there is a curious point made about German preference for Color in relation to food. For many years egg producers are feeding some of their chickens Marigolds and Paprika to produce a select number of eggs sold only to Germany, where the preference is for a darker egg yolk of a Yellow/Red, not the natural plain Yellow. On the combined subjects of chickens and Red, in the U.S.A., 100,000 chickens have been fitted with Red contact lenses for a study. The chickens will kill each other by pecking if they see the Red of blood, so with the Red contact lenses they cannot see Red, reducing the rate of 'chicken murders' dramatically.

In the section of Goethe's "Theory of Color" on the history of these 'Morals' of Color, once again Goethe doesn't hesitate to list the following group of literal "Pillars of society," such as: people who live in the woods, societies that are uncivilized, and for sure no list of "Chromophilias" would be complete without the greatly refined highly educated children. These are the members of society that Goethe lists being attracted to Colors in their brightest state, especially Yellow-Red, but also in any combination. Again Goethe informs us that Germans wear Blue, while Green is also worn in Germany outside the cities, but in strong contrast, Goethe states that people in southern Europe dress in 'cheap' silk dyed with very bright Colors. Goethe then lightly cloaks his highly derogatory, sexist, nationalistic, and intentionally prejudicial next list of a further abridged 'caste' of socially-inferior, morally indecent, uneducated, savage - childish even - Color lovers that would repeat itself over and over again for the next two hundred years as generations of "Chromophobics" referred back to Goethe's famous 1810 treatise on Color: first the 'Female' is associated with the love of Color (man's oldest, brainless trick in the book), next the 'uncivilized societies' are added represented by ancient Rome, and finally the example of the dignity and refinement of the 'Chinese' is portrayed by stating the fact that the Emperor wore the ultimate Colors that Goethe would have regarded as proclaiming uneducated and uncultured - Orange with Red, while his religious ministers also wore the equally undignified Lemon-Yellow. Curiously, in the very next paragraph Goethe, possibly feeling he was a little heavy-handed in the preceding paragraphs, allows the possibility to exist of another reason or two, that are nearly comical (and highly lame), for 'Refined' people to dislike brilliant Colors, not only because they aren't people that live in the woods, uncivilized, uneducated, savage, Chinese, children, women, or even nearly-retarded, but possibly because:

1. Their eyesight is weak(!)
2. Perhaps the 'refined' people just can't make up their minds which Color to wear, so they end up only wearing Black and White
3. There is mostly cloudy skies in northern climates, so slowly people of the north would 'banish' Color.

The part of this book that is really disturbing is the "Introduction" to my 1970s edition, which was written by Deane B. Judd in 1969. In this sixteen page Introduction, it is stated not just once, but two times that Goethe was 'unprejudiced' in the way he wrote about Colors in this "Theory of Color." This claim is even repeated, for a third time, on the back cover of the book. If writing that people who enjoy pure bright Colors are:

1. Savages,
2. People who live in the woods,
3. Uncivilized,
4. Uneducated,
5. Unrefined,
6. Uncultured,
7. Cavemen,
8. Childish,
9. Female,
10. or even Chinese,

is 'Unprejudiced' what in the hell could possibly be called *Prejudiced*?

Goethe would have been very pleased to read "Men in Black" by J. Harvey, in which the title is quite clear as to the shade of the book. Harvey echoes Goethe while stating that in some Oriental and European cultures refinement and distinction is achieved by separating yourself from Color itself. In the Renaissance, wealth and nobility was portrayed by wearing Black clothing. After the Renaissance, this doctrine spread all over the civilized world in Europe culminating in a present day commonly accepted formal dress-code of Black, only. In this Black formal atmosphere, it is clear why the 'new' Art using brilliant Colors, beginning with the Impressionists, was considered by the ignorant, prejudiced general public to be vulgar. The Neo-Impressionists including Gauguin, Van Gogh, Cezanne, and Seurat tried to show the public that pure saturated primary Color was not only intended for and used by children and primitive people, but was acceptable amongst adult educated Europeans as well - imagine that! These new acceptances and the general embracing of pure Color coincided and was inspired by the discoveries and production of many new synthetic Colors in the 1800s.

Goethe, it seems, also wasn't the only German who held these highly prejudicial viewpoints with regards to 'Nationalistic Chromophobia.' In the little gem of a book "Colors: The Story of Dyes and Pigments" by Francois Delamare and Bernard Furneau, there is a Color reproduction of a 1929 poster by Muller Kludt advertising German pigments and paints. Don't get the wrong idea, this poster is also as 'unprejudiced' as Goethe was. The main subject matter of this 1929 German poster is a Black woman with a bright Pink head-dress and a native shawl of bright Blue with a bright Red tie around the waist. She is wearing hugh tropical earrings, and the Sun is baking down behind her. She is also pouring a virtual waterfall of vivid Red paint from one bright Yellow pot to another, and next to her is another pot of brilliant Yellow paint. Let us not be too hasty to jump to conclusions here though, this poster is as 'unprejudiced' as Goethe was - the woman in the poster really looks German.

One textbook classic "Chromophobic" was an Art historian of the Nineteenth century named Charles Blanc - who surely was born to love Colors with such a name - and wrote the book "Grammar of Painting and Engraving," published in 1867. In this book he writes something that could almost be a xerox of the Florentine Painter's credo from the Renaissance, stating that an Artist must learn to draw through much hard work, but on the other hand, an Artist is already born as a Colorist which is so simple that it does not need to be learned. He also curiously employs a nearly stone age mentality to try and convince us that he has risen above the stench of the Nineteenth century by utilizing the oldest, and again brainless, trick in the book: fusing "Drawing" with the masculine side of Art, and relegating "Color" to the feminine side of Art. This idiot Charles

Blanc went so far as to unforgivably relate Color to many other sides of society that have historically always received infinite respect from western societies, like the Chinese for example, who Blanc actually demeans for being better Colorists than Western Artists by personally translating these viewpoints into his idea, which stated that this was proof of the Western Artist's superiority to the Asian Artists because the Asian Artists had supposedly allowed the lower part of nature to take over by being great Colorists! What a mentality. He writes about Color being not only unimportant and clearly secondary to the most important part of Art, drawing, but he also goes so far as to state that Color is detrimental to, and can cause the actual "Fall" of Art! This typical, nearly prototypical, arrogant nouveau-civilized Nineteenth century intellectual writes with such pride, conceit, and profound authority that he almost convinces the reader that he knew what he was writing about. Charles Blanc educates us lowly forms with his enlightened visions of all of life on Earth, and all Art also, by putting forth the proposition in writing that 'Intelligent Life' can communicate by a language of sounds, such as words, but - and here is the profound Blanc part - 'Unintelligent Life' - inorganics - can only communicate through Color(!) Blanc gets cosmic here and writes about Sapphires or Emeralds communicating to us through Color, so he can come to the conclusion, with signatory arrogance and the same high 'risen-above-the-grime' profundity, that hence, Color is a characteristic of the 'Lower Forms of Life.' This Charles Blanc could literally have been the biological father of Le Corbusier! What is completely astounding to me personally, is that this same classic Chromophobic Color-hater Charles Blanc, along with his 1867 "Grammar of Painting and Engraving" was the Color theorist who first turned on the Impressionists! During the late 2009 once-in-a-lifetime exhibition "The Letters of Vincent Van Gogh" in the Van Gogh Museum in Amsterdam the actual "Grammar of Painting and Engraving" book was on display in a glass case opened to the page with Blanc's Color Wheel, and was described as the source of knowledge on the subject of Color theory and Complementary Colors for Vincent Van Gogh and many painters of the Impressionist/Neo-Impressionist schools. For Seurat, and other Neo-Impressionists who were "Colorists," the 1839 "Principles of Harmony and Contrast of Colors" by Eugene Chevreul would prove much more important, which Chevreul's book is still considered today, whereas Blanc's book has rightfully been forgotten.

    A very graphic example of the viewpoint of modern society is in a book by this typical member of the Twentieth century elitist group of Architects, who are also now honored as 'Artists,' the prejudice and supremely arrogant Le Corbusier, who taught at the absolute elitist institute itself, the "Bauhaus Institute" in Germany. In his 1920 book "Purism," that he co-authored with A. Ozenfant, Le Corbusier states that Color chemistry will have no effect on great Art, and furthermore, he immortalizes the "Peynter-Steyner" stigma by associating the pure Colors that come out of a paint tube with the Clothes dyers, thank you very much. If you have ever seen a piece of 'Art,' and I use that word loosely here, 'produced,' and I use the word very intentionally here instead of the correct word "created," by the prophet Le Corbusier, you can immediately see exactly where he was coming from. Spiritually devoid and feelingless are words that immediately come to my mind when I think of the oeuvre of Le Corbusier. Not only was the 'Art' that Le Corbusier produced spiritual void, but his written manifestos on Art theory were no bargain either, being even more spiritually void. Le Corbusier and Ozenfant went so far as to divide all of Color into three 'scales,' like controllable notated written music. The 'Major scale' for Le Corbusier was made up of the following Colors: Ochre Yellow, Red, Earth Colors, White, Black, and Ultramarine Blue, with Le Corbusier relating them to strength, stability, and balance, and also relating them to all the great paintings of all the great periods of Art. The next 'Dynamic scale' was: Citroen Yellow, Orange, Vermillion, and all other related disturbing Colors. The last scale Le Corbusier called the 'Transitional scale' and listed: the Madders [Reds], Emerald Green, and the 'Lake' Colors [such as "Crimson Lake," the favorite bright Red of the Impressionists], which he wrote were not even usable to make Art. Of all the prophetic statements of Le Corbusier, the one bit of philosophy he should never be forgiven for is his derogatory criticism of Cezanne - yes, Cezanne! This was the ugly little statement by Le Corbusier where he writes with unprecedented arrogance stating the "Error" of Cezanne, identified by this architect, was his fascination with Color, and especially the new bright synthetic Colors developed in the Nineteenth century which, according to the prophet Le Corbusier, should have been left to only the lowly Cloth Dyers! What! Just what kind of imbecile would criticize Cezanne? And furthermore, what kind of imbecile would criticize Cezanne's choice of Colors? Let us look a little closer and examine this Swiss prophet a bit. First of all, this egotist's name wasn't even Le Corbusier, but Charles-Edouard Jeanneret (another Charles!), which doesn't sound at all like the name of a 'prophet,' so Le Corbusier was his 'stage name.' In one hundred years from now, Le Corbusier will be as well remembered and as famous as the architect who built "The Leaning Tower of Pisa," while Cezanne, one of the most pivotal and influential Artists of the entire Impressionist and Neo-Impressionists periods, whom Le Corbusier criticized in writing, will be held in the same high respect one hundred years from now as are Artists of the past like Michelangelo and Leonardo da Vinci. Over the past months of writing and rewriting this "Introduction" I have been forced to read and reread all the vicious slandering "Color-Debunking" of this *dried-apple* of a man, and several times, in anger, I nearly removed a piece of the "Common Items that are Fluorescent" display in the Museum which

I give daily demonstrations on. This display includes three paper money notes to demonstrate the invisible Fluorescent security ink that is used on many things that the reader has in their own pocket, such as credit cards, drivers licenses, and money ("Common Items"). Two notes in the display are pre-Euro Belgian and French notes, and the third is the Swiss note with the picture of Le Corbusier on it. I even went so far as to check the other day how I attached it to the black linen base of the display years ago, then with the clear intention of removing it, because first of all I didn't like looking at his face anymore every day, but the real reason was to remove the presence of this "Super-Chromophobic" from "the First Museum of Fluorescent Art!" This morning at about 9:30 AM, baking in the early Sun, I understood that Le Corbusier's presence can <u>Never</u> be removed from "the First Museum of Fluorescent Art" because, as I realized laughing out loud with the company of only a sweet chirping Mesange next to me - did you ever hear of <u>Karma</u>? In simple terms, this is something like his punishment - serving time for the spiritual crimes of:

1. Equating pure Colors to the mentalities of only savages, peasants, and simple races,
2. For criticizing Cezanne and 'educating' us by revealing Cezanne's "Error," and,
3. Above-and-beyond all else, for not only stating that this very "Error" of Cezanne was his choice to use pure bright Colors, but also for stating that these pure bright Colors should only be used by Clothes Dyers!

A very surprising, and at the same time amusing point was made by David Batchelor in "Chromophobia," a point most people never noticed probably because of the volume and the fore-granted honorable respect that Le Corbusier has been given - one of the 'fathers' of contemporary architecture - *but* every one of Le Corbusier's buildings except for one were *Colored!* In the end, this man who spoke in such ugly terms about the divinity of not only Color itself, but even the people who like Color, he himself only made one building that was White in his entire architectural career! As so many times when examining the mental workings of manic personalities, they don't only do what they said was not to be done, but they do it so much. The building that is considered Le Corbusier's masterpiece was the "Pavillon de l'Esprit Nouveau" (Pavilion of the New Spirit) that was built in 1920, the same year that he wrote "The Decorative Arts of Today" in which he states definitively that Colors are only for people of a 'simple' race, like a 'peasant,' or a 'savage,' but yet with astounding hypocrisy then Le Corbusier makes the "Pavillon de l'Esprit Nouveau" in none other than - get ready for it - Ten different Colors! The ten 'official' Le Corbusier Colors used to adorn this masterpiece were White, Black, light Grey, dark Grey, Yellow Ochre, pale Yellow Ochre, Burnt Sienna, dark Burnt Sienna, and light Blue. Not exactly Day-Glo Colors, but in the end Le Corbusier's masterpiece, as well as each and every building he ever designed, spare but one, were *Not White*. It would be hard to conceive the degree of mental horror and physical disgust the prophet Le Corbusier would have experienced if he had ever visited a tropical country like Venezuela or Mexico, who's inhabitants would easily have been considered by Le Corbusier to have fulfilled every one of his ten prerequisites of people who love Color: 1. Savages, 2. People who live in the woods, 3. Uncivilized, 4. Uneducated, 5. Unrefined, 6. Uncultured, 7. Cavemen, 8. Childish, 9. Women - all valid to him except for his tenth prerequisite, being Chinese! Now for "Mr. Day-Glo" himself - Le Corbusier - the Colors of the buildings and houses in Venezuela and Mexico would have probably killed him. For the modern "Father of Architecture" who's designed buildings were mostly White with some piss-Colored highlights, the intensely vivid Colors of the houses and buildings in the homelands of these people would have proved fatal. In Venezuela the houses are the brightest and most vivid contrasting beautiful Colors of any architecture I have ever seen, Mexico only coming close with it's vivid architecture. To top it off, in public places in Venezuela the entire trunks of living trees are sometimes also painted with vivid Colors, like all the buildings and houses! Several other localities are famous for their brilliantly Colored houses painted in pure pigments, such as Cape town, South Africa, and Burana Island in the Lagoon of Venice, where all the houses are vividly painted for fishermen returning home to recognize easily which house was theirs. In La Boca, a neighborhood of Buenos Aires, Argentina, the houses are also beautifully painted with brilliant pure Colors. The residents were so poor that sailors that lived there would take left-over paint from the boats to paint their houses. Another very unique fact about Color also is found in Buenos Aires, with the capital building being completely painted in an off-Red matt Color. This off-Red paint coating the Buenos Aires capital building was made with Bull's Blood, which not only gives it an odd Color, but also waterproofs the limestone it is constructed out of. A locality that Le Corbusier would have definitely not felt at home in was Curacao in Nederland Antilles, where a law was passed by the governor long ago which stipulated that all houses had to be painted any Color but White, because in the bright sun White gave him a headache. These Color codes went very far, especially in China, where during the Ming Dynasty during the 1300s the Colors of the roofs making up the many buildings of the "Forbidden City" were strictly regulated by governing status. Color was very important to the Chinese and during this Ming Dynasty the Colors Gold and Yellow were forbidden to be used by anyone except the Emperor, including the Color of the roofs of the buildings. Yellow or Gold roofed buildings immediately indicated that it was owned by the Emperor.

The Colors Blue and Green represented revival and youth, so the buildings with Green roofs in the "Forbidden City" were exclusively owned by the younger princes of the new generation.

So, in the end, imagine Le Corbusier's *Mortal Despair* in knowing that he has always, since the day of it's opening, been a part of the permanent display in "Electric Ladyland - the First Museum of Fluorescent Art." A second proof of Le Corbusier's Karma is the fact I realized, after over eight years, at 2:30 AM this morning photographing in the Museum and glancing down into the display case of "Common Items that are Fluorescent:" Not only has Le Corbusier's face been on permanent display in "the First Museum of Fluorescent Art" since opening day, but for that entire period of tenure Le Corbusier has been right next - vis-à-vis - to the former French Franc portraying his very favorite Artist whom he bestowed with limitless praise: Paul Cezanne! By distancing himself so completely from the very roots of Art, Le Corbusier is not even an Artist to me anymore, but in my mind, he has regressed himself back through a half millennia of time and returned to his rightful status as a lowly "Craftsman" - a celebrated and decorated builder, only.

Of all the books on Color Theory, the one that is probably the most important in modern times for Art is "The Principles of Harmony and Contrast of Colors" published by Michel Eugene Chevreul in 1839. This is also probably the most thorough written account of Color perception ever made, with a little over 1000 numbered paragraphs by Chevreul dealing with incredibly minute changes in Color perception. In one section there are over one hundred experiments for the reader to perform, such as placing a Colored piece of paper over one eye and then looking at a nearly infinite amount of different Colored pieces of paper to perceive the extremely subtle changes that occur in human perception when confronted with such juxtapositions. In this monumental two-volume 742 page treatise on Color there is *not one* word written with the prejudice which prevails in almost all other Color Theory books before and after Chevreul. After over 700 pages, Chevreul adds his first personal opinion on Colors, writing with true innocence that he found the delight a person experiences with vivid Colors similar to tasting good food and drink(!) Nothing about mental deficients, savages, children, or perverts in this dignified book that is an essential study for anyone interested in Color, even today in the Twenty-first century. Faber Birren compares, in the 1981 Edition's Introduction to Chevreul's book, the difference between the Color Theory books by Goethe and Chevreul, stating that Goethe did not have objective viewpoints, and that his views were very prejudiced. He compares Goethe the poet to the methodical mind of Chevreul the scientist, and rightly concludes that Chevreul is the "Father" of modern Color Theory. Birren also plainly states that all Color Theory books written since Chevreul's employ his Harmony of Colors, and furthermore, that his book "The Principles of Harmony and Contrast of Colors" has become so much an accepted part of Color education that Chevreul is most often not even credited as it's creator any more.

Michel Eugene Chevreul was born in 1786 in Angers, France, and lived to be one hundred and three years old. He published hundreds of books and articles during his lifetime, had an international reputation, and received awards and honors from Scientific Societies around the world. In 1824, King Louis XVIII appointed Chevreul as "Director of Dyes" for the French Royale "Manufacture Imperiale des Gobelins" which was the state controlled manufacturer of Tapestries, upholstery, and drapery fabrics internationally famous since Louis XIV. In January 1836 and January 1838 Chevreul gave eight public lectures on Contrasts of Colors at the Gobelins Museum, which became the basis for his book, "De la loi du Contraste Simultane des Couleurs" of 1839, which, together with Newton's "Opticks" and Goethe's "Farbenlehre" formulate the most important works on Color in history. It was a magnificent book with two volumes, the first text volume being 742 pages, and the second volume was the 9 1/2 x 12 3/4" (24 x 32.5 cm.) "Atlas" with forty Color plates, some of which folded out to twenty nine inches (73.5 cm.)! The importance of the book was shown by how fast it was translated into other languages. Only one year later, in 1840, the German translation was published, and then in 1854 the English publication was published, followed by a Philadelphia publication 1869-1873. At the time Newton's "Opticks" was the only other book on Color to be published for so many editions, and also for a period of over twenty-five years. After Newton's "Opticks" and Goethe's "Theory of Color" the main Color Theory books following Chevreul were Charles Blanc's "Grammaire des artys du dessin" of 1867, which dealt with Chevreul's theories giving a thorough examination of Optical Mixture of Colors. Also in 1867, Herman von Helmholtz published "Handbuch der Physiologischen Optik" which explained complementaries, Colored shadows, after images, and additive mixture of Colors. In 1879 Ogden Nicholas Rood's "Modern Chromatics" was published. Rood was an American painter and a physicist with his book giving a lot of inspiration to the Neo-Impressionists, especially to Camille Pissarro. Being an Artist as well as a physicist, his book was the first to examine the Human nature of Color perception, not just it's physical nature. David Sutter wrote articles for "L'Art" in 1880 pointing out that there should be a union between the worlds of Art and Science, and two other books to inspire the Neo-Impressionists were the 1885 editions of "The Scientific Esthetic" and "Education of the Spirit of Color" by Charles Henry. Later, in 1915, American Albert Munsell published the important "Atlas of the Munsell Color System."

Faber Birren sums up the immense contribution of M.E. Chevreul in his Introduction to "The Principles of Harmony and Contrast of Colors," stating that with Impressionism and Neo-Impressionism, the use of new Color Theory initiated the many principles of Contrasts of Colors used by these Artists that gave way to a new way of looking at Art, in which Color would ultimately become the subject matter itself. Chevreul wrote another influential book on Color Theory at the age of seventy-eight, in 1864, entitled "On Colors and their Applications to the Industrial Arts." On the occasion of Chevreul's one-hundredth birthday, he was honored in many countries of the world, and when asked how a man lived to be one hundred years old, he truthfully replied 'Work is one of the essential conditions for a centenary life.' Finally, after almost half a millennia, the time came when Color would once again replace Drawing as the most important part of the creation of Art. Chevreul's Principles of Color would herald in one of the most exciting periods of Art History, a period in which Art was lead away from it's self-imposed five hundred year old 'charade-for-social-status' which glorified Drawing as the most important aspect of Art, and was guided back to the Color and to the Light.

I can tell you, through personal experience, what it as like for an Art student studying in America in the 1970s. From 1975-1980 I was in College and graduated with degrees in "Fine Arts/Painting," and "Advertising Design." Throughout these five years of college, when I took five different Art courses each semester, such a "Color Theory," "Painting," "Sculpture," "Printmaking," "Photography," etc., can you believe that never once was it mentioned, or God forbid taught, about how Artists worked or how paint was produced through the alchemy of pigment production before the period of the "Impressionists." The absolute single mention of the notion that it was not always as it was in the 1970s for Artists, was the single historical fact taught in "Art history" of how the world changed and made possible the 'Painting from nature' that was the essence of "Impressionism:" the invention of the 'Collapsable Tin Tube' to store paint inside of. There was no lesson taught, or any interest in, what happened *before* this collapsable tin tube for holding paint was invented. In all fairness, it was not just the choice of the Artist to distance themselves from the physical labor and the socially-deemed lowly job of pigment grinding to produce their own paints, but another reason exists for over a century that completely changed not only the way an Artist works and actually creates their Art, but also the way that they thought and lived their lives. The invention of the collapsable tin tube to store paint in was very important, but then even more important was the invention and discovery of many new sources of Colors to make pigments from, especially the synthetic pigments that began to be produced in the 1800s. Before the invention of the collapsable tin tube to store paint in by American painter John Goffe Rand in 1841, Artists for centuries had stored their paint in such a complicated way that it would shock Artists of today. Sections of Pig Bladder, that's correct - *Pig Bladder* - were cut into squares, and a small portion of wet paint was stored in these small sections of pig bladder which were 'sealed' by tying up the top with a string. When the Artist wanted to use the paint stored in these little pig bladder containers, they would put a hole into it with a pin and squeeze the Paint out. As can probably be easily imagined, this was not quite as efficient as a collapsable tin tube. These pig bladder paint containers had to be made by hand, of course, and these packages, as can also be easily imagined, were not exactly hermetic, so the paint dried out very fast inside these pig bladder sections, causing a lot of waste of their precious paints. Much more influential to the change that took place in the working methods and lives of Artists was the invention and discovery of completely new paints, starting in the late Eighteenth century. For thousands of years Artists had to be very close to the availability and production of their paints. The Alchemists and early Chemists were almost as important to the creation of a painting as the actual Artist who painted it, and there existed a close tie between the two. Today an Artist goes into an Art store and casually selects any Color of the entire gradated spectrum that they want by simply lifting a sparkling metal tube covered with a shinny full-Color printed label, which itself was designed by a Graphic Artist/ Package designer on Madison Avenue, and then they pay for it and go back to their studios to paint with it. No pigment to find and buy, no pigment to spend many hours grinding in to fine powder - in short no work to make their Color. No work to make their paints means several things: first, of course, more time to paint, only, and not be bothered by actually grinding and making the paint. And second, of course, no work to produce their own paints means, also, no knowledge, or interest even, of the entire process of Where, How, and Why the paint they are using was produced. Thousands of years of experiments, trial and error, inventions and discoveries to create handmade paint, is about as relevant now to a contemporary Artist as Wilbur and Orville Wright are to the Director of "KLM." Don't get the wrong idea, this is not what is called "Lost Knowledge," but it enters another modernized, digitized, gentrified realm called "Thrown-Away Knowledge."

The first synthetically produced pigment was created by the ancient Egyptians in about 2500 B.C. and is known as "Egyptian Blue." It's original Egyptian name was "iryt hsbd," which translates as iryt (artificial) hsbd (Lapis Lazuli), and was the reason for their quest for synthesizing pigment in the first place. True "Ultramarine" pigment has always been some of the most expensive paint pigment in the world. It is made from Lapis Lazuli mined in northern Afghanistan since ancient times. To produce Blue "Ultramarine" powdered pigment from these rocks of Lapis Lazuli is almost as much of an Art as the actual painting done with the pigment itself. The complicated process involves separating the pure blue pigment inside the Lapis Lazuli from all the other minerals it is made of. When the Romans imported this pigment from Egypt it was first called "Alexandrian Blue," and then later called "Egyptian Blue." During the Renaissance this Ultramarine pigment was called "Oltramarino" meaning 'beyond the seas.' The ancient Egyptians also made another synthetic Blue pigment that was a darker Blue than "iryt hsbd." This darker Blue synthetic pigment was made by tinting Green with Cobalt, and this original synthetic darker Blue Pigment is what many centuries later became known as "Delft Blue," which is still used in Holland today to paint the world famous "Blue Delft" glassware.

    Some of the ingredients that make up most of the paint produced before the Eighteenth century would shock and may even disgust a contemporary Artist. The most famous and expensive Red in the world was made from Bug's Blood obtained from a parasite that lives on a Cactus plant. The fortune and power of the country of Spain was built on bug's blood, as Spain held the world monopoly on this pigment. To get an idea of what a market this "Cochineal" bug's blood was, between 1575 and 1600, Spain shipped over fifty tons per year from the Americas, where the bugs were cultivated, to Spain, where they were sold as some of the most expensive pigment that could be bought, known in English as the famous paint Color "Carmine." Another Color and more shocks: "Indian Yellow" pigment produced in India from the late nineteenth century until the very early Twentieth century, and sold by "Windsor and Newton" paint company in England, was made from Cow's Urine. This brilliantly Colored Cow's urine was then dried and sold as the paint pigment named "Piuri" in India and "Indian Yellow" in the west. The cows in a town called Monghyrin in the state of Bihar in India were fed on a forced diet of Mango leaves only, which then produced a brilliant Yellow Color in their Urine. This also caused the cows to be sick and die early, and in India where the cows are holy animals, this was unacceptable and was stopped by laws passed in 1908. Probably the very biggest of shocks having to do with paint pigment production is not from one of the bright pure Colors we all know, but from two of the so-called 'non-Colors' Brown and Black. In the Seventeenth century, "Bone Black" was supposed to have been made from Human Corpses. In fact, "Bone Black" was made from livestock bones, not Human, but another 'non-Color' *was* made from human corpses: Brown. The recipes went so far for this morbid Brown pigment as to stipulate that the human corpse had to have Red hair, and had to have died not by disease! Another Brown pigment was called "Egyptian Brown," but this name was changed from the original name "Mummy," which obviously told of the actual ingredient of the Brown "Mummy" pigment: ground up ancient mummified bodies from Egypt, of course. Not only are these examples of how gruesome paint production could get before the late Eighteenth century, but some of the paint pigments were also dangerous or even deadly, having been produced with Mercury, Lead, and Arsenic, just to mention a few of the toxic ingredients used. These facts and recipes also did not bring the Artist any closer to the production of their own Colors in a general movement that sought to change the image of the "painter" from one of a lowly 'craftsman' to one of refinement and high class. It is now known that one of the most famous warriors of modern times, Napoleon, most likely was finally defeated and laid in his grave not by a soldier or another warrior, but by his Wallpaper! The wallpaper in Napoleon's final retreat island bedroom was all the rage in fashion at the time because of a particular Green pigment that was very attractive to the period's taste. The only real problem was that this wallpaper's Green pigment was based on Arsenic, and Napoleon's bedroom in the "Longwood House" on the island of St. Helena was naturally a moist place, allowing the Arsenic in the wallpaper's pigment to become deadly through it's release into the air caused by the room's high humidity, and in the end resulting in the final conquest of a former Emperor. Victoria Finlay in "Color: A Natural History of the Palette," explains this in depth, going so far as to list references of an original incontestable existing sample of this poisonous wallpaper from Napoleon's final retreat bedroom. The Green pigment in Napoleon's deadly wallpaper was "Scheele's Green" which was a very healthy Copper Arsenite chemical mixture discovered by Carl Wilhelm Scheele in 1775. Napoleon was only fifty one when he died in his poison bedroom on St. Helena, and in 1960 it was even discovered that a sample of Napoleon's hair contained very high levels of Arsenic.

    Besides all the toxic chemicals and elements used to make pigment through the ages, occasionally indigenous people have used much healthier natural products to create Colors with. In India since the beginning of documentation four natural vegetable dyes have been used to paint, including the Red cabbage which creates a beautiful Violet to Red dye, Rhododendron leaves which can be used to produce bright Green dye, Turmeric spice to create bright Yellow, and finally Curry powder is used to make an Orange-Yellow dye.

    For Art students in the 1970s, "Impressionism" was the intended and taught 'Birth of Art.' Very few was taught of what happened before the "Impressionists." For Art students of my generation, all the history of Art before the 1870s was not taught or even considered important - only a thin one hundred years was taught in the course entitled "Art History"! Sure they mentioned Michelangelo, da Vinci, Rembrandt, and other major Artists of the past, but my actual Art history textbook, which is still printed as one of the most popular textbooks on Art history: Arnason, "History of Modern Art," began with Modern Art, period. On the first page there is one of the very few reproductions of a piece of Art from before 1870, "The Death of Socrates" by Jacque Louis David, which is only reproduced in this Art history book because scholars of the 1970s taught that it was considered one of the first pieces of Modern Art because of the composition of the painting. Jacque Louis David paints the figures in the scene as if they are on a stage, not with the classical 'Renaissance Window' in the painting, which had stipulated that the scene was a slice or picture of a real historical event that had happened in a real historical place. Just this simple design departure was enough to signify a dramatic change in the intent of the Artist. Here we have not a mechanical reproduction that produced an actual two-dimensional *replica* of an event or person, just like a camera would eventually do, but something that was never dared or ventured before: the Artist interpreting a scene, event, or person in their own way and - Horrors! - including their opinion in a painting by altering the authentic historical scene or subject intentionally to produce their own personal version, or much more famously, "Impression." This is what I was taught in the 1970s in Art school: the Artist as celebrity, and sociologically as a changer of the world. No mention of the "Peynter-Steyner" in Art school in the 1970s, this I can state with personal experience. So for Art students of the 1970s, there was, out of a 30,000 - 40,000 year period that Art has been documented as being created, only a mere 100 years of this vast period actually taught - that calculates to a comprehensive 0.0025% of Art History. It is probably not that the professors did not know what had happened before the "Impressionists" in the 1870s, but they obviously had absolutely zero interest for it. These were the professors of the new elitist group of Artists of the 1970s, who would not only distance themselves from lowly pigment grinding and their former titles of "Peynter-Steyner," but more efficiently and more complete, they wouldn't even teach that these essential Art trades and titles had ever existed! After going to Art school for five years and graduating with a degree in none other than "Fine Art/Painting," it is hard to believe that the first time I ever heard that painters stored their paint in sections of tied pig bladders was when I was almost fifty years old and read the exquisite book that should be required reading for every Art student, "Color: A Natural History of the Palette" by Victoria Finlay. The entire history of Art before 1870, and especially the entire history of Paint and Pigment production, was completely ignored - not taught or mentioned. In hindsight, thirty odd years later, I feel absolutely cheated as a painter that this history was never taught to me because it was regarded as being not important for an Artist to learn(!) 5,000 years of even synthetic pigment production, going back to the ancient Egyptian's "Egypt Blue" was swept under the carpet of the university, along with it all the insight and knowledge, and especially the sense of identity, was erased the absolute simplest way: by not teaching it in the first place. These severe politics/editing have almost a flavor of Art fascism. It is all too clear now *why* they taught *what* they taught. It was an extension, but quite the same in the end as the intentional change of the Artists of the Renaissance era when Florentine Artists began to stress that 'Disegno" - Drawing - not Painting with Colors - "Colore" - was the most important part of Art. By doing this they intentionally distanced themselves from the lowly "Peynter-Steyner" of Medieval times, and artificially created a new world image of themselves as members of the elitist group of high society, in the same class as Astronomers and Mathematicians. What they did in the 1970s, when I was in Art school, was, in my opinion through personal experience, nearly to the point of being "Orwellian." Having never taught the basic trades and physical history of Art in reality before the 1870s, they not only intentionally distanced themselves from the 5,000 years of Art history when this new elitist group had been amongst the lowest caste of society, but for all intended purposes they eradicated the entire 5,000 year struggle and history - the Identity of the painter - the simplest, most humanly efficient way: by *Not teaching* it had ever happened in the first place! In hindsight my memories belie an almost 'New-order' ring to them. Changing public opinion and knowledge intentionally to artificially create a new world view of yourself. It was so complete, so intentional, and so extremely efficiently executed it could have been a military maneuver.

    Finally, my qualifications for writing this small book "Fluorophobia - the Social Stigma" are most likely unsurpassed. I have been an Artist all my life, since before starting grade school, and bought my first Black light in 1969. In 1987 I opened "Electric Lady" Art Gallery with Michèle Delage in Amsterdam, where we have exhibited to the public our Fluorescent Artwork under Black lights for the last twenty-nine years. In 1999 we opened "Electric Ladyland - the First Museum of Fluorescent Art" downstairs from the Gallery, where for the last seventeen years personal tours and Fluorescent demonstrations have been given to over 50,000 Museum visitors. Having used regular Colors and ordinary paints up until 1969 when I bought my first Black light, I was fascinated with the intensity and amount of Color coming from the Fluorescent "Poster Paint" under my small 18 watt Black light. When you paint with Fluorescent paint, you can immediately see that something extraordinary is happening before your eyes, something that seems to defy explanation. As a matter of fact, the explanation of the cause of Fluorescence eluded me until I joined the "Fluorescent Mineral Society" in the early 1990s and bought some of the few booklets and the one book that together comprised the total contemporary 'Library' of Fluorescent minerals in the early 1990s. The extraordinary reason behind this fascinating phenomenon will be explained later in the book, but for now the simplest explanation is that invisible Ultraviolet energy from a Black light goes into the atoms of something that is Fluorescent, like

Fluorescent paint, and this causes an energy exchange to occur, resulting in the Fluorescent paint itself giving off the Colors. The Light - Colors - are coming out of the Fluorescent paint itself, not out of the Black light. This is called "Emitted light" and it is miraculous to observe. What we see all around us every day of our lives is much different and is called "Reflected light," which means that that the Light we see is coming out of a light source, like a light bulb, and reflecting part of the spectrum of Light off a surface and into our eyes. Simply, with Fluorescence the Light - Colors - are coming out of the Fluorescent paint, not out of the Black light. This accounts for the unbelievable brightness of Fluorescent Colors, and this is what makes these Fluorescent Colors incomparable to any other Colors.

On April 19, 1987, Michèle Delage and I opened "Electric Lady" Art Gallery in Amsterdam which would exhibit our Fluorescent Artwork to the public. On April 19, 1999, after seven years of work, we opened "Electric Ladyland - the First Museum of Fluorescent Art" downstairs from the Art Gallery. In this unique Museum there is a large room-sized Fluorescent "Participatory" Environment that the visitors enter physically and then participate in the Creation of Art. This is what I call "Participatory Art." "Participatory Art" occurs when the visitor *takes part* in the Creation of a piece of Art, and is, for the duration of their visit, *a part* of the piece of Art. This is vastly different from most forms of conventional contemporary Art where the visitor is merely a viewer, and as such, is not a Participator in any way. So, for twenty-nine years by now I have seen on a daily basis, quite literally, an infinite amount of varying degrees of the Social Stigma of "Fluorophobia." What must be explained here is that by far the majority of visitors to "Electric Lady" Art Gallery, and in fact, even to "Electric Ladyland - the First Museum of Fluorescent Art," are not exactly Art historians, let's say, or even people that regularly visit Art galleries and have a slight interest and knowledge of Art, but a good portion of the visitors, viewing hundreds of pieces of Fluorescent Artwork under a dozen Black lights throughout the gallery, are tourists. These are not always the most passionate people that you can meet, with regards to their deep, indivisible viewpoints on Art, especially when confronted with Art they have never seen before. The two most common unforgettable quotes I have heard countless times by visitors who, I would assume, are amongst the most enlightened of all visitors to the Art gallery are, "Is that a Fish Tank?" and the ever popular "Wow, back to the 60's, man!" I have to admit the first quote bothers me more, but I'm not that crazy about the second one either. In "Electric Lady" Art Gallery, the brightest pieces of Art, out of literally hundreds of pieces of Fluorescent Art on display, are five Fluorescent environments that are built into wooden boxes and have either one or two Black lights installed in each sculpture box. I made these from 1990 to 1992, and they were 'maquettes' for the Fluorescent "Participatory" Environment I built in the Museum between 1992 and 1999. These five sculpture boxes are extremely bright and usually what grabs the attention of anyone entering, or even just looking into the Art Gallery. Now what must be explained here is that these five sculptures, "Mind-Arising Box #1" to "Mind-Arising Box #5" are admittedly all rectangular, I also admit that they do have a piece of acrylic glass in front of each of them, and they are also brilliantly lit with Fluorescent Colored forms = Viola: "Fish Tank!" Out of all the 312 infinite choices in their weak little minds to choose from to relate to this unknown entity before them, the only common denominator of their vast consciousness is: "Can you put a fish in there?" The basic predator/animal instinct is to reduce any outside stimuli to something palatable - something to eat. The very basic of intellect, nearly Reptilian in my personal viewpoint, and many times even entering the realm of the Insect kingdom. As another separate, less volatile, example of pure public outlook on Fluorescent Art, the young Dutch mailman for my Art Gallery and Museum in Amsterdam one day comes in to give me my mail. He glances around himself with a quizzical look on his face, then gestures with his arm, as if to encompass all of the hundreds of Fluorescent Artworks on the four walls of the Gallery beneath a dozen Black lights, and asks, "All these Fluorescent things under these Black lights - you call this *Art* too?!?" In the year 2000, a year after opening "Electric Ladyland - the First Museum of Fluorescent Art" I received a telephone call one afternoon from a man who immediately begins with the proclamation: "Hello Nick, you're now talking to the Number One World Expert on Fluorescence! My name is Rolf and I have a Black light company in Germany." I try to reply as gently as possible to this claim/phone call: "So being the Number One World Expert on Fluorescence, then you must have a really Incredible collection of Fluorescent Minerals." There was a moment of absolute silence on the phone, and then the "Number One World Expert on Fluorescence" replied in utter shock: *"Minerals FLUORESCE???"*

One further point that does not make logical sense to me is that in almost all of the contemporary books written around the world on Colors, numerous Artists that are famous for their use of Color are dealt with extensively, but almost universally, they exclude arguably the most influential and famous Color painter: Paul Gauguin! In the 382 page "Bright Earth - Art and the Invention of Color" by Philip Ball from 2001, many Artists are discussed at length, such a Yves Klein, Matisse, Kandinsky, Rothko, Titian, Van Dyck, Veronese, Tintoretto, Rubens, Rembrandt, Turner, Delacroix, Monet, Van Gogh, and Cezanne, but Gauguin is given just passing references, like footnotes. The most obvious exclusion of Paul Gauguin in "Bright Earth" is in the sixty-six full-Color glossy painting reproduction sections of the book. 'Plate 1' is by the contemporary English-Indian

Artist Anish Kapoor, who also has another piece of his Art reproduced in 'Plate 48.' There are two plates of Titian paintings, and even two plates by that 'master of brilliant Colors' Van Dyck, two 'Plates' are taken by regional English landscape painter William Hunt, two plates also from Monet, a Renoir plate, a "La Grande Jatte" plate by Seurat, and then last, the page of plates for the Impressionist 'Greatest Hits' which starts off correctly with the top 'Plate' of these being a Cezanne Provence landscape, and the bottom 'Plate' being "The Night Cafe" by Van Gogh. On this final page, the third 'Plate' in my opinion should have been "Day of the Gods" by Paul Gauguin, one of the undisputed all time masterpieces of Color. But to add true insult to injury, of all the paintings that Mr. Ball chooses to print in this third plate it is none other than the "The Talisman" by Paul Serusier which is also described by Mr. Ball as being the 'impulsive' sketch which inspired the Nabis school to bright Colors. What is particularly galling here is the fact that not only is Gauguin barely discussed in this large book on Color history, and not only is there not one painting by Paul Gauguin reproduced in the sixty-six possible 'Plates,' but on the final Impressionist page of three Color plates, Philip Ball decided to print this "Talisman" painting by Paul Serusier that is commonly known to Gauguin scholars as having been composed by Gauguin for his young disciple Serusier who was painting by his side in Brittany, and furthermore it is also common knowledge amongst Art historians and Gauguin scholars, that Gauguin himself took the brushes out of his young disciple's undecided hands and proceeded to entirely Paint the rough structure of this famous painting "The Talisman" attributed to Paul Serusier, on it's small cigar-box top. Likewise in the book "Chromophobia" Gauguin is mentioned just one time in between discussions of Yves Klein and other Artists, also seemingly odd for a book written about Color and Art. Even in the new edition of the superb M.E. Chevreul "The Principles of harmony and Contrast of Colors" published in 1967 and 1981 with the Introduction and Notes by Faber Birren, Gauguin is again given footnote mention. The back cover of the 1981 edition states that Faber Birren was at that time the authority on Color, also being a Government and Industrial Color Consultant. He had written over twenty books including "Color Perception in Art," " Creative Color," "Principles of Color," "History of Color in Painting," and "The Textile Colorist." But this author, in the last Introduction section to M.E. Chevreul's book, "M.E. Chevreul - His Influence," doesn't mention Gauguin throughout his paragraphs of ten selected painters going from Ingres to Robert Delaunay. Three pages before the end Gauguin is listed after Van Gogh and Cezanne, in parenthesis, as a 'Postimpressionist.' Even though it is well known that Gauguin disliked the 'scientific' approach to Art that many of his contemporary Artists, such a Seurat, were practicing through their theoretical studies of Chevreul and others, this was still an Introduction dealing with the use of Color in Art changing everything - changing Art itself - so Gauguin most definitely should have been included, because he was absolutely pivotal in this movement. Almost systematically, every major contemporary book on Color, Color Theory, Color and Art, etc. either leaves Paul Gauguin out completely, or just gives him a footnote or two. Without realizing it, and surely without acknowledging it, all these contemporary writers on Color Theory have just given Paul Gauguin a 'backhanded' high complement through their obvious exclusions. Even after over one hundred years, Gauguin's Art is *still* too Colorful, powerful, raw, unique, and 'savage' to fit with the taste of contemporary Twenty-first century Art critics and writers. Gauguin has inspired generations of Artists in much further realms than he's usually credited for, not just with his Artwork, but also with the exuberant life he is world famous for having lived. More than anything else, Gauguin has inspired Artists with his lifestyle, spiritual dreaming, fantasizing Colors, passion, devotion to Art, drama, and state-of-mind. Gauguin went to the other side of the Earth to seek infinity, meaning in life, the unknown - 'magic' in a word - to fire his mind and Art in a way that was literally impossible if he had stayed "home" in Europe where he was born. Leaving Gauguin so obviously out of their books on Color in Art, reminds me of the story John Lennon used to tell about his Aunt Mimi who brought him up like a son (his late mother Julia's sister Mary Elizabeth 'Mimi' Smith). John said that his Aunt Mimi would have these books in her house on wild people like Vincent Van Gogh, but... 'Don't you bring one of those crazy Artist types into my house!!' she would tell John when he brought over an Artist friend, as well.

    This first modern master of Color, Paul Gauguin, describes the spirituality of Color very deeply, as well as definitively, in his 1896-1898 manuscript "Diverses Choses" ('Various Things'). After Gauguin 'points out and then explains' Color as being "living matter," the "Soul" of Color is next acknowledged, through means of "intelligence" and the "heart," to allow our imaginations "to soar," and this "Soul" of Color then becomes the 'new opening' of a "door" leading into not only "mystery," but more precisely stated by Gauguin as "the infinite."

    As in so many other numberless examples, the arrogance of modern western society has tinted history with it's self-declared supremacy. In science classrooms and universities throughout the western world, for hundreds of years it has been taught that Sir Isaac Newton discovered the world-changing fact that sunlight is composed of all the Colors of the spectrum. This has been taught as one of the most important discoveries ever made, and Isaac Newton has since been respected as a Father of Science - then you travel to India. The fact that the Sun's light is composed of all the Colors of the spectrum has been taught in India for over 1,500 years (maybe Newton's great great great Grandfather was from Mumbai). In India 1,500 years ago it was a time when a great ruler unified the north of India, and was named the "Chandra Gupta Period." This was a time of amazing progress in technology and astronomy. The first produced Iron was in India around 400 A.D., centuries before the Chinese developed the "first Iron," and 1400 years before the "Industrial Age" with Iron production in the western world. Today in New Delhi you can see this first marvel of the "Iron Age" in the form of a thirty-five foot (eleven meter) tall 6,000 kilo column made of pure "Forged" Iron, known commonly as the "Iron Pillar of Delhi." Chandra Gupta scientists also pioneered the use of the number "0," which is half of the entire "Hypertext" of the "Binary System" of numbers that every computer on the Earth runs on in today's world. But the most astounding discoveries of the Chandra Gupta period were by a scientist named Aryabhata (476-550). *Before 550 A.D.* Aryabhata proved that the Earth orbited around the Sun, not that the Sun orbited around the Earth which would still be believed in all of the western world for more than another *one thousand one hundred years*! Aryabhata also measured the circumference of the Earth almost precisely before 550 A.D. as well, again more than 1100 years before western scientists would attempt such an inconceivable "unprecedented" feat. Aryabhata calculated the circumference of the Earth to be 24,835 miles, which is only 0.2% smaller than it's actual 24,902 miles. Aryabhata also calculated the length of one day, a "sidereal day," as being 23 hours 56 minutes and 4.10 seconds before 550 A.D., and the precise length of one day is 23 hours 56 minutes and 4.091 seconds, which makes Aryabhata only 9 thousandths of a second off! His calculations for the length of a year on Earth, a "sidereal year" were 365 days 6 hours 12 minutes 30 seconds, which is only a 3 minute and 20 second error for the actual length of a year. Aryabhata was the first in the line of brilliant Mathematicians and Astronomers in the Classical Age of Mathematicians in India, and one of the first people to use Algebra. The Mathematician's standard "Pi" (3.1416) was proved irrational in Europe in 1761, but Aryabhata proved "Pi" to be irrational in writing before 550 A.D. In the field of Trigonometry, Aryabhata gave the area of the triangle in his lifetime a well. In his writings he also stated that the Moon shines by the reflected sunlight, and he explains the eclipses of the Sun and Moon, even beginning to chart these celestial events. Perhaps what is the absolute hardest for western Astronomers to swallow with their western superiority complex, is that before 550 A.D., a thousand years before the Renaissance in Europe, and at a time when the mighty America was only woods that were inhabited by symbiotic indigenous natives, and Europe, where culture "originated," was nothing more than a collection of tiny muddy Medieval villages, the Astronomers in India during the Chandra Gupta Period before 550 A.D., were already measuring the age of the cosmos in Billions of years! This did not happen in the west until well into the Twentieth century with the advent of the Radio Telescope age = Fifteen Centuries later. Not only that, but unlike the 'civilized' western Christian-based ideological consciousness, the population of India was not traumatized by the discovered fact that the universe was billions of years old, and being a spiritually-based highly religious country where enlightenment is the most sought after, highest attainable state you can achieve in this life, not your 'estimated profit' or the closing balance of your almighty bank account, the fact that the universe was billions of years old was totally and undramatically accepted as a natural fact. To complete the deflation of the western scientist's ego, on the Quantum level even, the earliest reference to the building block of all matter, the Atom, was in the Sixth century BC, literally thousands of years before the western scientists "discovered" Atoms, and was also discovered in - of course - India! Not only was the Atom discovered in the Sixth century BC in India, but in the Fourth century BC - 2,400 years ago - the Greeks were already calling these particles "Atoms" (indivisible). The discovery of the fact that the Earth revolves around the Sun and is not the center of the universe began with Heraclides, who wrote that the Earth turns on an axis. About 300 BC Aristocris combined the theory of Heraclides' with his own discovery, and announced that not only did the Earth revolve on an axis, but that the Earth was not the center of the universe, and in fact revolved around the Sun with the Moon. He also discovered that Solar Eclipses are not caused by demons or gods, but are chance events caused by the Moon passing in front of the Sun. Aristocris discovered that the Sun was the center of our Solar system and that all the stars we see are actually other Suns out in space. In 1609 - nineteen-hundred years later - Galileo proved that Aristocris had been absolutely correct.

In Indian Astrology the Sun God "Surya" is a ruler of eight cosmic bodies. Each of these eight cosmic bodies brings one Color to Earth, and it is taught that this is a powerful force in a person's Astrological destiny. To Hindus every one of the Colors is respected as a power of nature and every one of the Colors individually effects their lives. When studying Hinduism and learning about the energy levels and Colors of the Chakras, for example, Color is both defined and experienced to a degree that has few parallels in western culture. In November, 2005 I could sit amongst Tibetan Monks while they created a Holy Sand Mandala for five days. It was in a small room in a Buddhist Center in Amsterdam, so I could sit very close to the monks while they created this amazing holy mandala. The first morning, before they started, I could talk to one of the monks and ask some questions. He told me that originally the Colored sand they use to make the holy mandalas was made from precious gemstones like Lapis Lazuli and Turquoise, but now the Colored sand is made in a way that is know in painting terms as a "Lake." Traditionally, paint is made with pigments that are crushed and ground very smoothly, and then this powdered pigment

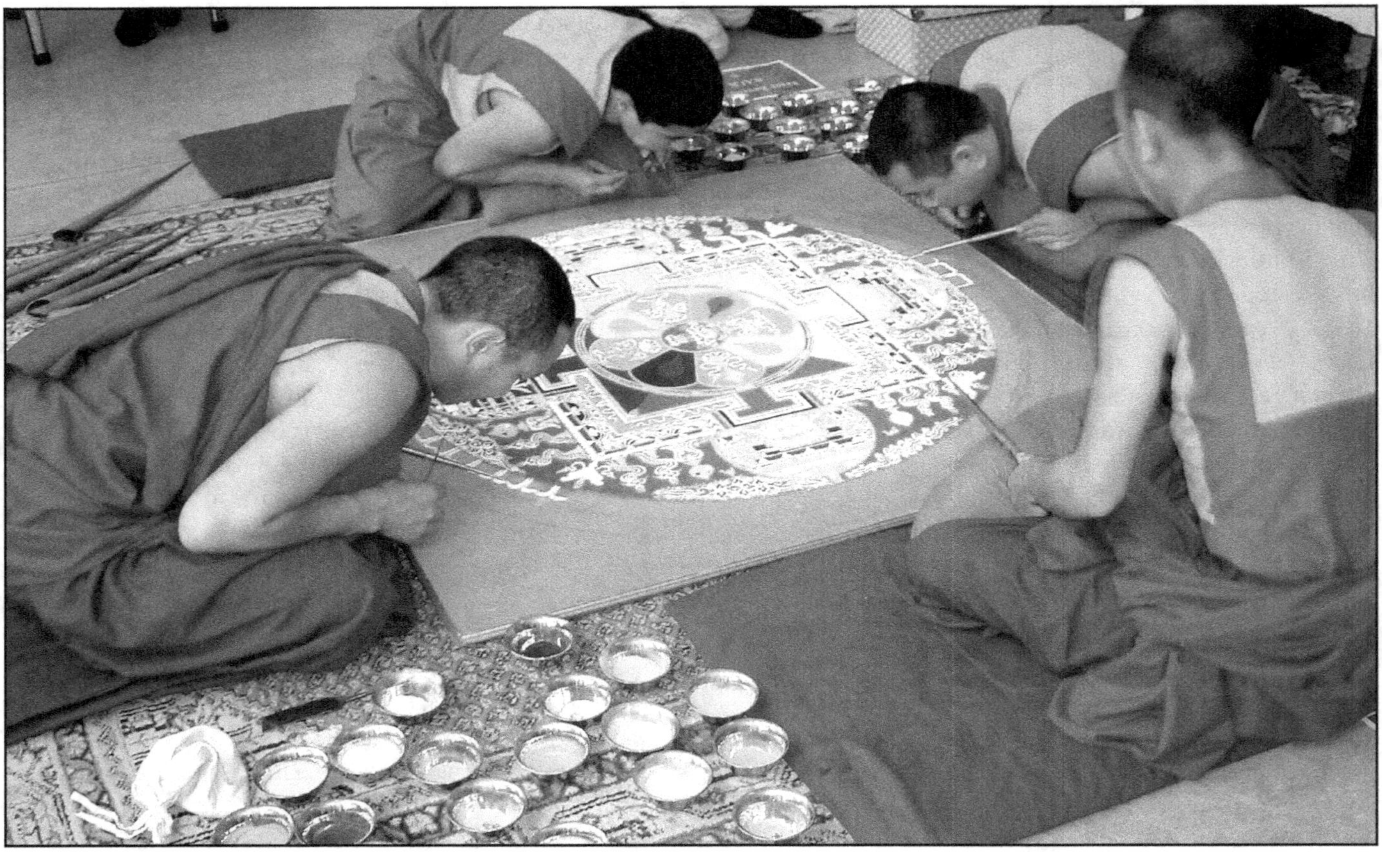

Tibetan Monks create a "Kalachakra Sand Mandala," Amsterdam, 2005

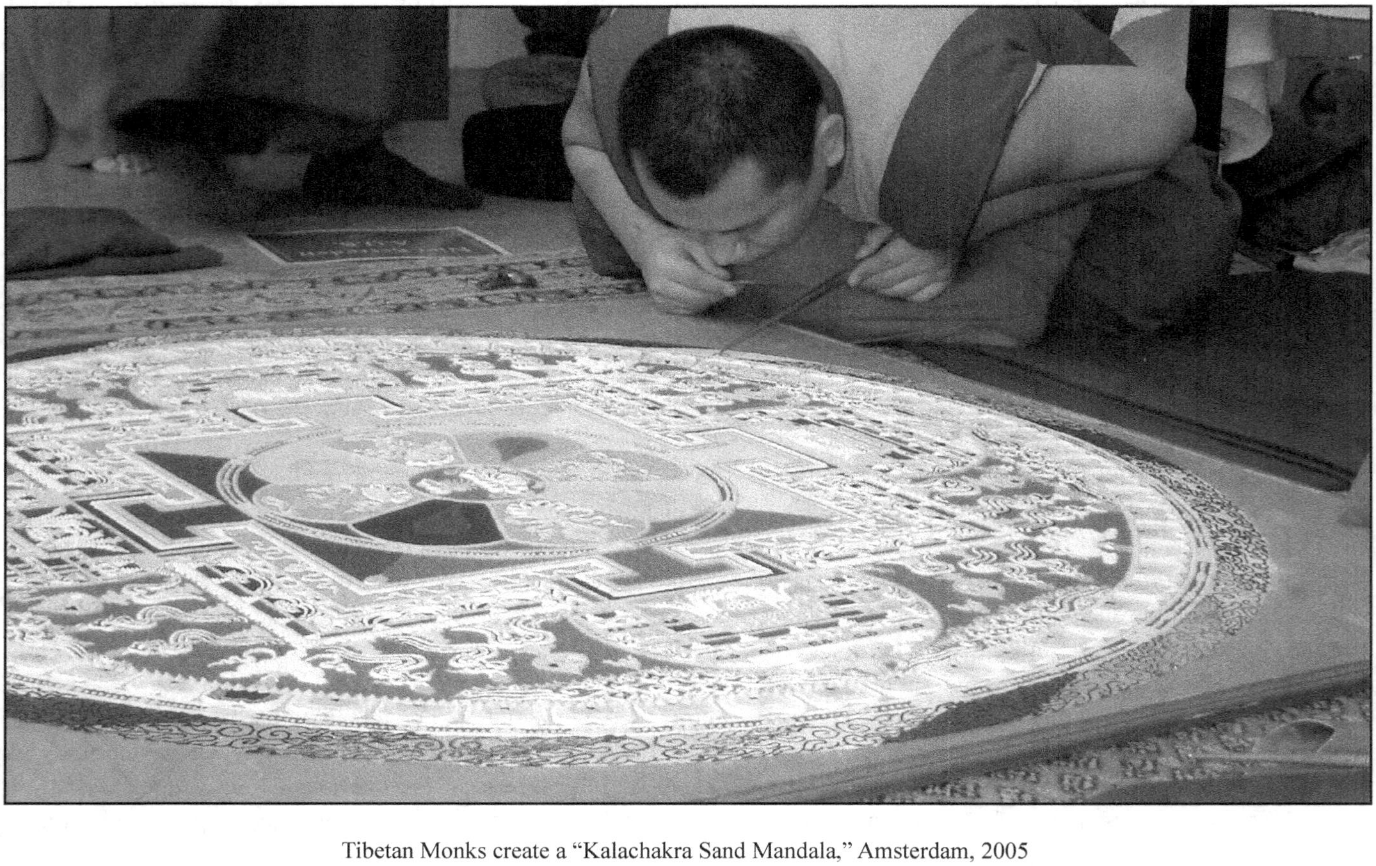

Tibetan Monks create a "Kalachakra Sand Mandala," Amsterdam, 2005

is mixed with a "vehicle" (something to 'drive' the paint) like oil, or in modern times acrylic mediums. "Lake" paints are made in a much different manner. These "lake" pigments cannot be powdered, but are more like a liquid dye, so this pigment/dye is attached to microscopic particles as a dye. These dyed microscopic particles are then used as the pigment, and are what the "lake" paint's Colors are made from. Any Impressionist student knows of the preferred Red paint of that period: "Crimson Lake." This is the same method that the Tibetan Monks use to make their Colored sand for the holy mandala today. The intent and the spiritual communication that these Tibetan monks had with the creation of this holy mandala is something that I've rarely seen. Before the monks begin the creation of the holy mandala every day, there is a pooja - a prayer session - for about fifteen minutes which is a real sensory experience, complete with very strong horns, cymbals, and extremely deep monk voices. The eight Tibetan monks sit on all four sides of the mandala to mark the four directions for the prayer session, and then four monks, one sitting in each of the directions, will create the holy mandala. Something happened here that I will never forget. There is an event that is occurring in the morning while the monks are making the prayer ceremony that goes way beyond what you see. Since the holy mandala is made on the floor, the outlines are put onto a large piece of wood which is on the floor. But there is a big problem here: by the Buddhist rules, it is not allowed to sit upon the holy mandala. But it is not possible to create the holy mandala without sitting upon it. So, the problem is solved in a typically Buddhist manner. During the morning prayer session with the horns, cymbals, and singing, the Tibetan monks are in meditation and they are visualizing the lines of the mandala and the actual holy mandala itself rising up off the wood and being levitated several inches above it. So for the duration of their work, the Tibetan monks are not breaking any religious rules, because to them, they are sitting on the wood, not the holy mandala which is suspended in mid-air above the wood!

The history of this Tibetan "Kalachakra Sand Mandala" is exquisitely recorded by Barry Bryant in his book "The Wheel of Time - Sand Mandala." The Dali Lama, after his exile from Tibet caused by the Chinese invasion in 1959, broke with tradition and through his commitment to world peace and by his decision to clarify misconceptions, the "Kalachakra Sand Mandala" was constructed by four monks from the Namgyal Monastery in India as a cultural offering at the Museum of Natural History in New York City during July and August, 1988. At this first major western Kalachakra Sand Mandala creation, that was held in New York City, a total of 50,000 museum visitors would watch, day by day, as the four monks created the Holy Sand mandala. The main reason for the Dali Lama's decision to bring the Kalachakra Sand Mandala to the west was because in Tibet since 1959 when it was attacked, invaded, and very nearly decimated by the People's Republic of China, the whole of Tibetan Buddhism has been intentionally pushed to the brink of extinction by the Chinese. Most people have just no idea of the extent of the Chinese destruction and murder in Tibet half a century ago. In 1872, the country of Tibet was enormous. On an official map from the United States Library of Congress from 1872, the country of Tibet was the entire western half of today's China! If you draw a line straight up from Vietnam, the country on the left, stretching thousands of miles all the way to it's western border, which included Kashmir, was Tibet - equal in size to China. From 1872 until 1959 Tibet was reduced by the Chinese to a tiny country above India, similar in size to Nepal. Then in 1959 during the so-called "Cultural Revolution" which should have been more truthfully called the "Cultural-Destruction," the Chinese invaded Tibet, destroyed most of the 8,000 monasteries in Tibet, tortured and killed most of the countless thousands of holy Tibetan Monks, and in the end, *Eradicated* the ancient holy country of Tibet. Today there is *No country* on the world map above India and to the west of Nepal - only the vast space of China, stretching from what was formerly the western borders of Tibet above Afghanistan and Kashmir, all the way to Peking. It should never be forgotten what the "Religion is Poison" Chinese did to the Tibetans, and definitively, it should never be forgiven. But, since it happened on the other side of the world to defenseless holy people, the western world took very few notice of the devastation the Chinese were unleashing on Tibet, and absolutely no action. Imagine if China would have done precisely the same to a western country in Europe in 1959 - It would have been more well-known than "The Holocaust." My father fought from 1950 to 1952 in "The Korean War" which was America's way of trying to defend the western-minded South Koreans from the Chinese-minded north Koreans who were Communist and very related to China. Then it may be pondered: "What about in 1959 when the Chinese launched the invasion on Tibet as had happened on southern Korea?" - I don't remember "The Tibetan War" after "The Korean War." Why did no one defend the Tibetans and Tibet? As the definitive final killing blow from the Chinese to the Tibetans and Tibet, for the 2008 Olympics in Beijing, an express train line has been built directly connecting the capitol of China to the 'Hidden City' of Lhasa, the capitol of the former country of Tibet where the first "skyscraper" in the world was built millennia ago. And talk about Karma - almost precisely on the Fifty year anniversary of China's decimation of Tibet, the Beijing Olympics opened during the Summer of 2008. Needless to say, *Anyone* before the 2008 Beijing Olympics who did not already know about what the Chinese did to the Tibetans in 1959 now knows. Everything that the Chinese tried to suppress and lie about for forty-nine years was completely thrown into the faces of the Chinese - with the whole world watching on television

The Tibetan monks that created the Kalachakra Sand Mandala in Amsterdam in November, 2005 were from the "Gaden" Monastery of Tibetan Buddhism built in 1409. This used to be a very important monastery of Tibetan Buddhism before it was destroyed along with 8,000 other monasteries in 1959 by the Chinese invaders. To give an isolated example of how devastating the invasion of the Chinese was in 1959, in just this one Gaden Monastery alone there were 7,000 monks in 1959, and in 2005 there were but a regrouped 169. The first day of this "Kalachakra Sand Mandala" ceremony in Amsterdam, I could talk with one of the monks and ask him some questions about the Holy Sand Mandala. The actual design of this large "Kalachakra Sand Mandala" is a flattened, two-dimensional representation of the five-story palace of the Buddhist deity Kalachakra. To make this holy mandala, four monks begin by rubbing the top 'ribs' of a brass cylindrical funnel-shaped instrument called a "Chakpu." There are five different Chakpus for each monk to choose from, each numbered one to five with corresponding different sized openings to allow more or less Colored sand to flow out of the Chakpu. The monks run a small steel rod over the 'ribs' on the top of the Chakpu, and through this created vibration, the Colored sand flows out of the front opening of the Chakpu. The faster the Chakpu is rubbed, the greater the vibration, and the greater the amount of Colored sand flowing out. There are fourteen different small pots of Colored sand used to make these holy "Kalachakra Sand Mandalas:" White and Black, and then the Blue, Red, Yellow, and Green sands each have three different shades of dark, medium, and light. All of these Colors and shades of sand also have two different pots each: one pot of rough grains for 'background' work where the Colors are applied relatively quickly, and another pot of very fine particles for details and for drawing the initial forms. It was a truly enlightening experience that I will never forget, and that I will always be thankful to have been in attendance of.

As a perfect example of the heights that can be reached solely through the act of the viewing of an Image, there is a Buddhist concept that exemplifies the very state of enlightenment that can be achieved by simply looking at an image that is made with this transcendental ability. In the Kingdom of Bhutan, there is a five story tall Buddhist Tapestry, the largest in the world. The tapestry is called a "Thongdrel" and is only shown one day a year before daybreak, so that the Sun won't damage the tapestry. "Thongdrels" are comprised of two silk layers, one being the Painting or tapestry itself, and the outer silk layer is a Yellow drape that protects the painting or tapestry, similar to a Tibetan "Thangka" paintings. Only once a year, at the highlight of the "Tsechus" festival this immense holy tapestry is viewed. This "Thongdrel" is not allowed to be touched by the direct rays of the Sun, so it is unfurled at 3:00 in the morning and rolled back up at 7:30 A.M. As the sunrise comes, the crowd of 2,000 Buddhists surges forward towards the "Thongdrel" to be blessed. "Thongdrel" to Buddhists literally means 'Liberation by Sight,' and it is believed that just by being in the presence of the "Thongdrel" brings spiritual liberation. The belief is that just *looking* at this hugh "Thongdrel" tapestry brings Enlightenment.

The American Indian "Sand Painters" are another group of Artists that use Colored sands for centuries to create a deeply spiritual Art, and I was fortunate enough to witness an American Indian Navaho Sand Painting ceremony in Paris in 1996. From February 22 - March 31, 1996, American Navajo Indians created a Sand Painting at the "Parc et grand halle de La Villette" in Paris. This exhibition consisted of gallery space with Navajo sand paintings on display, and a large hall where the American Navajo Indians created Sand Paintings. The creation of the Sand Painting by the Navajos was done in a highly charged state. The large hall was filled with people who were quiet and following every motion of the Navajo Sand painters intently. The hall was dark except for a raised center platform where the Navajo Indians were creating the Sand Painting, which was brilliantly lit and stood out as a focal point. My lasting impression is from the Navajo Indians themselves who were creating the Sand painting. Although it was in Paris, and the hall was jammed with people starring at them, the Navajos making the Sand Painting appeared to be absolutely detached from their physical surroundings and looked as if they were making the Sand Painting under the Sun in the desert of the American southwest by themselves. It was a timeless transporting experience in that hall, with the timelessness achieved by the transcendental consciousness of the Navajo Sand Painters everyone was intensely studying in front of them. After the ceremony of the Sand Painting was finished, Michèle and I could talk to one of the Navajos, who was an Indian woman about sixty years old. She spoke and also appeared as if she was in her home of the deserts of the American southwest. She told us that not only was this Sand Painting exhibition in Paris the first time she had ever left America, but it was actually the first time she had ever left the Indian reservation where she was born! These Sand Paintings that are made by the Navajos of the American southwest are created on the ground and are made for Healing purposes only. The Navajos believe that these Sand Paintings are living beings who inhabit the Sand Painting to heal. There are over 1,000 different Sand Paintings used by the Navajo Medicine Men for healing, with the Colored sands being prepared from natural sources. The White sand is crushed "Gypsum," Yellow Ochre, Red Sandstone, Black Charcoal, and even a mixture of Gypsum and charcoal producing Blue sand. Red and White sand makes Pink sand, and Brown sand is made by mixing Black and Red. For other Colors the Navajos use flower pollen, corn meal, and powdered tree bark or root. To make the Sand

Paintings, the Colored sand is put into the hand and then precisely poured from the hand onto the Sand Painting. There is no instrument to flow the Colored sand onto the Sand Painting, such as the Chakpu that is used by the Buddhist monks to create the holy Sand Mandala.

A real Healing ceremony with these Sand Paintings would involve the Medicine man chanting while the Sand Painting is being created so that the Holy beings or "Yeibicheii" could come into the Sand Painting. During the healing ceremony, the Medicine man would ask the patient to sit upon the Sand Painting so that the channelled "Yeibicheii" that have entered the Sand Painting would absorb the illness and take it away. After the healing ceremony is complete, the Sand Painting is considered toxic since it absorbed the patient's illness, so it must be destroyed before the sunset. The creation of the Sand Painting, the healing ceremony, and the Sand Painting's destruction must all be done between the sunrise and the sunset, only. Here we can see a similarity with the creation of the Sand Mandalas by the Tibetan monks, which must also be brushed up into a container after days of it's creation, and then poured into a river so it can mix with the celestial waters and all waters of the world. The permanence of the created piece is never considered by the Navajo Sand Painters, or the Tibetan monks, and the very permanence of a piece would not only destroy itself, but also the spiritual energies it has created. Here we can see as much a difference in the way of looking at a created visual image, as in the intent of the creator of the piece of visual imagery. The work is done in a humble, religious attitude, void of ego, towards a goal that has nothing to do with personal gain in any way. The creation of visual imagery that is transcendental in a true sense, being created in a state of consciousness that is rarely experienced in western culture by Artists - or anybody, for that matter.

The two visual Artists to have inspired me the most in my life are Jackson Pollock and Paul Gauguin. Growing up in New York the greatest inspiration and direction for my Art took place in front of Jackson Pollock's "One: Number 31, 1950" in the 1970s "Museum of Modern Art" and realizing that it was an entire *Environment* to be entered. Before 1980, when the original Museum of Modern Art was all but destroyed for the new architectural design incorporating the office tower, Jackson Pollock's "One: Number 31, 1950" was just able to be fit into it's exhibition space. The ceiling of the MOMA was about a full yard (meter) lower than the post-1980 new building's ceilings. What this did was to create a very intimate space in which the huge mural was just able to be fit into. These close quarters enabled me to envision the continuation of his painting onto the ceiling and onto both left and right walls - a true environment that looked as if it could be physically entered into. There are only two existing recorded interviews of Jackson Pollock speaking about his Art, and in one of the interviews he speaks with definite uncertainty about the direction he was going in and wondering about. He's speaking about the great 'drip' "Action paintings" he made during the late 1940s and early 1950s, and he was trying to explain them in his interview. He said that these paintings are becoming something else 'like a wall.....a wall painting'(!) The word he was possibly searching for to define these huge paintings was a word that was not yet commonly used in the realm of Art in the early 1950s: "Environment." He realized that these huge expanses of canvas - these large cosmological areas of drips of paint - were no longer just paintings, but something else - something further - a full "wall" - an area of 'space' that could be visually and spiritually entered - an Environment. In the last years of her life in the early 1980s Pollock's wife Lee Krasner was videotaped in an interview speaking precisely about this period. Lee Krasner remembered Jackson taking her into his studio to show her his drip paintings and he asked her not if they were "good paintings" or if they were "bad paintings," but he asked her if she thought that these drip paintings were even "Paintings." Again, I clearly remember being changed for life while in front of the huge canvas by Jackson Pollock in the old MOMA in the late 1970s tripping, while the Painting became an Environment - a space - an area that the viewer could enter, that was quite separate and quite different from the simple experience of just looking at a painting on a wall, as was traditional, and, in fact, still is quite traditional today in 2016. In what was probably the greatest of all Jackson Pollock exhibitions, the MOMA show from November, 1998 until February, 1999, in which even a reconstruction of Jackson Pollock's studio/barn on Long Island was presented, a CD was sold which contained this pair of the only Pollock spoken interviews known to still exist. A small selection of these spoken words by Jackson Pollock will be given for a glimpse of this true pivotal Artist. Pollock, an Artist known to be a relatively quiet person of few words, defined a "Modern Artist" perfectly in just a single sentence, stating that 'it seemed to him' that a "Modern Artist" 'works and expresses' the "Inner world" by 'working with Time and Space' to "Express" 'their feelings,' 'rather than illustrating them.' Pollock continues, further explaining that the "Modern artist" 'expresses Energy and Motion,' as well as "Inner forces." Defining the inner dynamics of "Modern Art," Jackson Pollock also clearly explained that 'it seemed to him' that a "Modern Painter" could not "express" 'the age of the radio, atom bomb, and the airplane' in past "old forms" 'from the Renaissance or any cultures of the past.' Again clearly and lucidly defining "Modern Art" Pollock continues, stating that "each age" will find their "own techniques." About the core of "Modern Art," Jackson Pollock explains in interview that to himself the "important part" in "Modern Art" was the "Unconscious," and that he also felt that "unconscious drives" 'meant alot while viewing a painting.' In conclusion, the Artist further explains that "Technique" was only "the means" for creating a "statement." After what seems like Pollock's reply to a question asked by the interviewer, the Artist's opinion was that he thought that the viewers of his paintings shouldn't look "For," but should look "Passively" at his abstract creations. Jackson Pollock adds that the viewers of his paintings should also try and "receive" what the Artwork had "to offer." The single most important sentence of Jackson Pollock for the current Artist writing this book begins with Jackson Pollock telling very hesitantly that he had a "general notion" of what he was "about," and of "the results" on his huge Abstract Expressionist paintings, continuing on with a statement in which Pollock explains that "the direction" his painting was "taking here" was "away from" the traditional "easel" and becoming "some form..." - and then Pollock hesitates, trying to find words - calling this new "direction" of his monumental Art the creation of "some kind" of a "Wall....." - and then after a short silence - ".....Wall Painting." Quite naturally five-second segments of these prophetic interviews with Jackson Pollock are heard on the collage CD which is constantly played in "Electric Ladyland - the First Museum of Fluorescent Art" every day since it opened.

After the new MOMA building was opened in the early 1980s, again, the ceilings were all higher and Jackson Pollock's paintings were rightfully displayed in four full rooms, but the intimacy was completely gone. This bit of lost intimacy is *Nothing* compared to the atrocity of the brand new MOMA with the "Atrium" 'designer' building that opened on November 20, 2004! A full quarter of the MOMA world famous permanent collection that I have been looking at for over thirty years is gone! The immense, absolutely empty "Atrium," which was built so museum visitors could discuss truly profound subjects of Art such as "Where do you want to eat lunch?" or the ever-popular "Harold, my feet hurt!" has taken up a quarter of the total exhibition space for Art in the museum! Since I was a teenager I have stood for ages and got divine inspiration from a very famous painting in the museum collection that was even highlighted in the post-1980 building by hanging it at the entrance of the painting collection: "The City Rises" (1910) by Umberto Boccioni. Now after about six hours of searching for this painting, and after having paid my extravagant $20.00 entrance fee and visited the MOMA that December, 2004, I decided to go and ask a museum guard in the "Atrium" where they had "The City Rises" displayed. What a mistake. This museum guard, about thirty years old, looked at me like I was a piece of trash and actually turned his face away from me when I asked about the location of "The City Rises" by Boccioni. Not to be one not to insist I walked directly into his turned face, which he had deliberately turned away from me, and directly asked him again where "The City Rises" by Umberto Boccioni was in the museum. This guard gives me the most disgusted face imaginable and dismisses me with a wave of his hand and the prophetic answer, "I never heard of that painting!" What has also been lost forever is the final half hour celebration of each day in the former MOMA, where the sunset coincided with a crowd of the most inspired museum visitors sitting in near-meditation in the intimate space containing Monet's huge "Waterlilly" walls of canvases. As these daily gatherings of enraptured MOMA visitors sat in front of Monet's visionary "Waterlilly" paintings during the final half hour of each MOMA day, there was a complete wall of floor to ceiling windows behind them in which the tinted sunset and skyline of Manhattan was also seen. These same spiritually-transporting "Waterlilly" paintings by Monet have now been hung in this New Jersey stylized "Shopping Mall-like" "Atrium" of the new MOMA, where they have been degraded by the new MOMA's architecture, and appear something like insignificant postage stamp-sized Blue canvases in a hall of idiots talking about every known subject except Art, all with their backs turned to Monet's formerly mesmerizing paintings. What has been lost is far more than 'obvious,' and closer to 'painful.' Thankfully not all museums cater to idiots, and not all museums change their designs to suit these idiots so that they can increase their profits. As a perfect example of this, the other major museum in Manhattan is The Metropolitan Museum of Art. While I was growing up, it always bothered me that a large room - "The Greek Sculpture Court" in the MET was used for an exclusive restaurant for museum visitors. It was not always that way, because originally this "Greek Sculpture Court" was an exhibition hall which replicated the size of the Parthenon on the Acropolis in Athens. Then it was decided to 'cater' to the public and turn this large Greek Sculpture exhibition space into a restaurant. In December, 2005 on my annual visit to the MET, I was delighted - the restaurant had been permanently Closed! The decision was made to destroy the large public restaurant and return the space to it's former splendor with a Greek Sculpture Court - not gentrified fourteen dollar mozzarella and tomatoes sandwiches with a sprig of basil! The Metropolitan Museum of Art has intentionally taken the exact opposite direction that The Museum of Modern Art took in 2004 by constructing it's empty "Atrium" that lowered the learning experience of seeing Art in a museum to a common everyday routine of talking to your friends in the Shopping Mall. To my former favorite museum in the world, the MOMA, I do not return. It's a little like the directors of the MOMA asked a famous Shopping Mall architect from New Jersey to work in collaboration with Walt Disney and combine their ideas into making a 'Tourist Museum.' The feelings in the museum are extremely "Shopping Mall-like" with a carnival atmosphere paraded about by tourists - very seldom did I see anyone vaguely resembling an Artist, or, for that matter, very seldom did I see anyone at all actually looking at the paintings. They have managed to reduce Art to a "too-palatable" level, similar to what many critics have spoken about in the last decade, that the building itself became more attractive to the "vulgar herd" than the Artwork that it was built to display and protect. As for what is on display in the MOMA (excluding "The City Rises" by Boccioni), in the tremendous room of "Recent Acquisitions" there was a crowd gathered in front of a hugh African sparkle-painting. The crowd was gathered around this hugh sparkle painting which was leaning against the wall, not hung on it, and in the center of the painting was a hugh protrusion that was also encrusted in sparkles. The painting also was leaning on the wall propped up on two Brown-Black forms, the same as the protruding form in the center of the painting. Going closer, I read the label on the wall and finally realized what all the crowd was so interested in - the Brown-Black protrusion in the center of the painting and the two similar forms holding the painting up against the wall were made of - get ready for it - Elephant Shit! Another "Recent Acquisition" was from a Swiss Artist (naturally) and consisted of a big robust metal frame that was filled behind a piece of plexiglas with old chocolate. They made the MOMA a Yuppieized version of the original MOMA. Very cold feelings - my sister thought the picture on the front cover of the MOMA booklet was a hospital. No feelings at all to do with Art or creativity, it is a space that common people can meet in between exclusive, expensive luncheons and talk about everything in the world except Art. I felt betrayed, and for the first time in my life, I felt like I wasn't welcome in the MOMA. Thousands of baby carriages and thousands of fat asses. The Temple of Modern Art in the world reduced to an "Art Amusement Park." They simply went too far and reduced the experience of possible enlightenment down to a common, boring afternoon of 'entertainment' - for one-and-all - a family affair - as enlightening as a veritable trip to the Shopping Mall! How sad and how disappointing to see all these years of Love and work and human desire put into a blender and reduced to a palatable pulp. A potpourri of the "Greatest Hits" of Art. A foul-tasting, mixed-up pulp of Modern Art, which after my seven and a half hour drink from this vessel, has left me with painful indigestion that will last me the rest of my life.

Something that has not left us since the change of the millennia almost a decade ago is "Chromophobia." In about 1999, "Apple" computers made their big comeback by introducing and selling millions of their new "iBook." The selling point behind this line of extremely successful, "Apple"-rejuvenating "iBook" was that it came in about eight vivid Colors, with six of the standard Colors "Apple" produced also fittingly named after fruits: "Blueberry Blue," "Tangerine Orange," etc. All the Colors were bright and pure, including two limited-edition models, one being Fluorescent Green, and the other was a 'Flower-Power' 60's revival pattern. This was the very identifying point of these "iBooks" - their very vivid Colors, unprecedented in the Computer industry. Just seven short years later, in 2006 I bought a second "iBook" from "Apple," but this time there was no trouble to choose which Color I wanted the computer in - it was only sold in White, like every other computer of the entire "Apple" line is. If you want to place a special order, this new "Apple" "iBook" was also available in the equally vivid Color of Black. Talk about a dramatic change.

So, in conclusion, the four most important factors that gave birth to the Social Stigma of "Fluorophobia" were the true 'Hallmarks' of the Twentieth century's society (and countless century's societies before them): Ignorance, Fear, Hatred, and Prejudice, which, unfortunately, have also not left us as the millennia changed over ten years ago, but may have even increased. As a concluding example of the narrow-minded prejudicial embarrassingly primitive consciousness of "modern man" with infinite profound limitless knowledge and perspective, not to mention a hell of an ego to match, on the fifth of September, 1906, in a hotel room near Trieste a man in a final fit of mortal despair hung himself. He had been ostracized by the entire scientific community of the world as an "Irreligious materialist." Imagine the degree of despair that would cause a scientist to tread a rope around their neck and then throw themselves to their own death. Who was this monster and what was his horrid crime that caused the entire scientific community to banish him? His name was Ludwig Boltzmann and this "Irreligious Materialist's" unforgivable crime that he was ostracized by the entire world of scientists for, was giving the proof of the *Atom!* The scientific community in 1906 considered the study of atoms a waste of time because you couldn't see them(!) The best part, and the part that is so sordidly medieval-human in it's irony, is that this poor genius who discovered the proof for something that is the literal building block of all future science - the Atom - was proved absolutely, irrefutably correct in a small paper published by Albert Einstein in 1905 - one year before Ludwig Boltzmann hung himself, but Boltzmann had never been informed. Nice ending for the person who turned the Western world onto the Atom. On the first page of this "Introduction" is mentioned the adversity to change and the adversity to new phenomenon that challenge the minuscule realm of society's knowledge. This is what was being referred to. Read "Anthem" by Ayn Rand.

And finally - last-but-not-least, let's say - the "here-and-now" contemporary horror creating a new, improved - digital, even - Social Stigma of Fluorescence in yet new generations, and at the very same time confirming the old fears and social stigma held by all other generations: flashing across T.V. screens and front pages of newspapers at the dawn of the Twenty-first century - "Alba" the Genetically-Altered Fluorescent Green Rabbit!! Yes, a living animal that Fluoresces brilliant Green from head to toe, and not only that, but the Rabbit appeared as a normal White albino Rabbit when the Black light was turned off.

Now "Alba" the Fluorescent Green Transgenic Rabbit was not the first Genetically-Altered completely new form of life man-made in creation, but it certainly was, and is, the most well known. The fact that "Alba" was created not as a scientific experiment, as would be immediately imagined, but solely for the purpose as a piece of "Art," infuriated almost everyone except Eduardo Kac, the Brazilian "Transgenic Artist" or "Bioartist" who commissioned this "GFP Bunny" ("Green Fluorescent Protein") in the year 2000. Now the manipulation of life as we knew it with the DNA of the "Aequorea victoria" Jellyfish is unquestionably the stuff of nightmares and horror movies, at least, and the Black light clearly has nothing to do with this contemporary insanity except for it's use to show it off, but, what do people remember? "Those poor Fluorescent animals under the Black light!" The picture they see is the lasting memory: the Fluorescent Green Bunny under the Black light and the undeniable mental link it forms with the inherent fear of modern life and technology - and here we have the *mother* of all fears concerning modern day technology - the creation of genetically altered virtual monsters, thank you very much. But do not get the wrong idea - it did not start or end with the Fluorescent Green Transgenic Rabbit "Alba," but goes back to 1993 with the first life genetically manipulated with "GFP," which was the simple Intestinal Bacteria "E. coli," and then the Flatworm, both of which were engineered to Fluoresce Green under Black lights, by their "creator" Martin Chalfie of Columbia University in New York City. Following this, the first (of course) commercially available Fluorescent animal for sale were the "Nightpearls" in 1997, first in Taiwan, where they were invented, and also China, and then in the United States (except California) starting in 2004, sold by a Texan company as "Glo-fish." This is a genetically altered 'Zebra Fish' that will glow like Fluorescent paint in Red, Green, or Yellow when you put a Black light over the aquarium. These "Glo-fish" went down to $5.00 each in the U.S. and have sold many millions there to date. As of December, 2009, the "Glo-fish" are sold in major pet stores in the New York area for $5.99, and were not hard for me to find to photograph in a store. Another living animal under the Black light, and another horror to instill the Social Stigma of Fluorophobia: the very reasonable fear of releasing genetically-transmuted Fluorescent living animals into nature! The genetically altered fish corporation assures us that we should not be alarmed, because (and this is the best part) the Transgenic Fluorescent aquarium fish cannot live in cold water(!) What the hell happens if you flush one of these Transgenic fish down the toilet in Florida? There's not exactly Arctic water temperatures there. We are assured, once again, by the genetically altered fish corporation that these Fluorescent fish are all sold sterile. Another "fact" the genetically altered Fluorescent fish corporation informs us of is that there is 'No Change' at all in the behavior of these Transgenic fish - the only difference is the Fluorescent Color of the fish. Then a study that can be found on the Internet was made of these Transgenic Fluorescent fish, and the results are downright horrific enough to be the story line of a 1950s Monster movie: Transgenic Fluorescent Red 'Zebra Fish' were put in an aquarium with normal, non-Genetically Altered 'Zebra Fish,' identical in every way except for their inability to Fluoresce Red. The Transgenic and normal 'Zebra Fish' were studied closely while cohabiting the same aquarium, and there really seemed to be no difference between these Transgenic and normal 'Zebra Fish.' But, then the experimenters decided to cut off the fish's food supply and virtually starve the 'Zebra Fish' to see if the behavior would change. Did it change! When the Transgenic and normal 'Zebra Fish' were starved, the Transgenic Fluorescent Red 'Zebra Fish' *Ate* the normal 'Zebra Fish' alive! They became cannibals - talk about '*No Behavioral Change*'!! The Transgenic Red Fluorescent 'Zebra Fish' ate the normal 'Zebra Fish,' but not the other Transgenic Fluorescent Red 'Zebra Fish,' because instead of behaving like the non-Fluorescent 'Zebra Fish' were the same species as themselves, the genetically altered Fluorescent 'Zebra Fish' behaves like it is a different species. Continuing along at a rapid pace, next, in 1998 comes the "GFP" Mice, which was the actual first Fluorescent "GFP" mammal. Next came the star - "Alba" the "GFP Bunny" in 2000. The first year of the Twenty-first century was something of a 'bumper crop' for the creation of genetically altered Fluorescent animals, beginning with "Alba's" birth in February, 2000, then came the first Transgenic "GFP" primate - "ANDi" the Green Fluorescent Monkey, who was named after the procedure that invented him, "inserted DNA," turned backwards. Thankfully, as the created Transgenic Fluorescent animals get closer to Human Beings, the results become poorer. "ANDi" the "GFP" Monkey doesn't Fluoresced at all, but just carries the bioluminescent "GFP" gene, and his two stillborn female siblings were Green Fluorescent only in the hair and the toe nails. Also in the year 2000, the Fluorescent Silkworm and another Transgenic life-form for sale: the first Bioluminescent Orchid which glows-in-the-dark Green. It was auctioned as the only Bioluminescent Flower in the world in the year 2000 with a very low starting bid of $200,000. In 2001, while doing research for the government production of "GFP" Marijuana (!) for legal Hemp plant identification, the first "GFP" Flower was created, a Fluorescent Green Daisy, in Italy of all places. In 2002 the first Green Fluorescent "GFP" Chicks were hatched, but it didn't compare to the photos of full grown brilliantly Fluorescent Green Pigs from Taiwan in 2006 - 2006 was the "Year of the Pig" in Chinese astrology. They've even bred four generations of piglets that retain the Fluorescent gene! In 2007 the first animals to Fluoresce brilliant Red instead of Green were created, the Red Fluorescent Frog (first made transparent at the Hiroshima University), by using the discovered "RFP" ("Red Fluorescent Protein") instead of "GFP," which was discovered in Moscow in a 'Sea Anemone' by Sergey A. Lukyanov in 2007. What got a lot of attention well up until the present day, is the absolutely gorgeous 2007 creation of the Fluorescent Red Cat. This is a White long-hair Angora cat that is Fluorescent Red only in the skin, not the hair, so the beautiful cat appears to softly glow a Red just around the eyes, the nose, and the ears under the Black Light. This is not all. The list is larger than what I have included here, with such "Side-Show" attractions as Red Fluorescent Sheep, and even a Housefly that Fluoresces Yellow, making it an easy target with a Black light and a Fly-swatter. In 2010 they created a Green Fluorescing Beagle as well as an Orange Fluorescing Beagle.

The degree of negative impact that these extremely starling thirteen living Fluorescent Black light-reactive creatures I've listed have made the last thirteen years on the Social Stigma of "Fluorophobia" is incalculable.

Vincent Van Gogh said that 'the Painters in the future' will be "Colorists" that the world 'had never seen before.'

Paul Gauguin went one step further than his younger friend Van Gogh,
and in 1899 in his paradise Tahiti, defined "Color" as a "vibration" 'just like music' and more importantly, clearly stated that Color has the ability "to attain" the most "elusive" and the most "universal" of nature's "inner Force."

1. The First Discoveries of Fluorescence and Luminescence: "1500 B.C. - 1750 - From China to Benjamin Franklin

The history of Fluorescence is usually thought of as a relatively contemporary discovery of the Twentieth century or possibly dating back slightly earlier, but the observation and study of Fluorescence was started centuries ago, along with the observation and study of Phosphorescence and Bioluminescence which goes back thousands of years. Very few people are aware of the fact that there were already "Glow-in-the-Dark" Banquets in ancient Rome! In the majority of literature on the phenomenon of Fluorescence, Sir George Gabriel Stokes, an English professor, is usually credited as the "Discoverer of Fluorescence" in the year 1852. The year is correct, but the facts are wrong. Sir George Gabriel Stokes did name the phenomenon of Fluorescence in 1852 after the mineral which he was studying the effects of sunlight upon - Fluorite - which emitted Blue light when excited by a single beam of sunlight in a darkened room, but he was not, by far, the first person to discover or study the phenomenon of Fluorescence. More concise writings on the history of Fluorescence cite the discovery of Fluorescence in 1603 by a shoemaker and Alchemist living in Bologna named Vincenzo Casciarola. Although Vincenzo Casciarola discovered the "Bologna Stone" and sold the first inorganic luminous substances in western culture, which was "calcined" powdered Barite from the area of Bologna, this shoemaker and Alchemist from the sixteen hundreds was also not the first person to discover Fluorescence, Phosphorescence, or Bioluminescence. The person who did discover Ultraviolet energy, not Fluorescence, but the invisible Ultraviolet energy that comes out of a Black light (and the Sun) which creates Fluorescence, was a very obscure scientist named Johann Wilhelm Ritter. Fittingly, this man who discovered the Black light's energy was a real character - he was a brilliant scientist who made many discoveries and even inventions, but at the same time he had a very eccentric personality, delving into the Occult and in the end dying at the young age of thirty-four. John Ritter was born in 1776 in Chojnow, Poland (then Germany) and began working as a Pharmacist's apprentice between 1791 and 1795. After he inherited money, he could finally go to the University of Jena in 1796 and pursue his dream to study science. In the next seven years of his short life, Johann Ritter would make two discoveries and two inventions that would each change the world, and which are still being used today in many fields of science and in everyday life a well. Shortly after beginning to study at the University of Jena in 1796, in 1798 he discovered "Electroplating" which jewelry and computers would not exist today without, and then in 1801 he made his most famous discovery: Ultraviolet. As a pioneer in the field of scientific electrochemistry Johann Ritter invented the first "Dry Cell Battery" in 1802, and the next year in 1803 he invented the first "Storage Battery." That's the invention of Electroplating at twenty-two years old, the discovery of the Ultraviolet spectrum at twenty-five years old, and the invention of the Battery at twenty-seven!

As a prelude to the discovery of the Ultraviolet spectrum by Johann Ritter in 1801, for decades scientists had been experimenting with different rays of the spectrum of sunlight. Between 1775 and 1777 the natural philosophers Landriani and Rochon discovered that different temperatures were produced by the different Colors of a projected spectrum of sunlight through a prism, and in 1777 Scheele discovered that light produces a chemical reaction in Silver chloride. In 1800 finally the first invisible energy was discovered by Herschel: Infrared heat energy that is beyond the last Color of the visible spectrum, Red. Influenced by his beliefs and philosophical views of Romanticism and Naturphilosophie, Ritter believed in the polarity of all nature and concluded that there must be another source of invisible energy beyond the opposite Violet end of the spectrum to Infrared. In 1801 Johann Ritter was experimenting with the light sensitive Silver chloride, which was discovered by Scheele in 1777 to turn from a Colorless substance to Black after being exposed to light. What physically happens is that the Silver chloride is destroyed by light and turns Black, and what this eventually resulted in was the literal birth of Photography. What Johann Ritter did with this Silver chloride in 1801 was to experiment with the reaction time of the Silver chloride to each of the separate Colors of the spectrum. At this time period is was already thought amongst scientists that Blue light caused greater chemical changes than Red light, and Ritter proved through this experiment with the Silver chloride that the Blue light indeed did break down the Silver chloride faster than the Red light. But, when Johann Ritter put the Silver chloride into the dark end of the spectrum beyond Violet - the opposite invisible end of the spectrum to where Herschel had discovered invisible Infrared energy, Ritter was *amazed!* The time it took for the break down of the Silver chloride in the invisible Ultraviolet portion of the spectrum beyond the Violet was by far much faster than the times it took for the Silver chloride to break down in any of the visible Colors. This result proved that not only was there invisible energy beyond the Violet end of the spectrum, but that this invisible energy was even more powerful than the visible spectrum of light. Johann Ritter originally called this invisible energy "Chemical Rays," but soon after through the much more famous studies of the much more famous Goethe, and other scientists, the energy became known as "Ultra-Violet." Only in the last fifty or sixty years has this energy been known as "Ultraviolet."

What must be presented here is the stolen credit given to the famous German writer Goethe over the last two hundred years for being the first scientist to discover Ultraviolet energy by using primitive photography salts and experimenting with sunlight through a prism(!), when the unknown, unpopular, and unrespected twenty-three year old German Jena University student Johann Ritter actually discovered Ultraviolet energy nine full years before Goethe published his "discovery." How nice. In every book that I have on Fluorescence, and on Fluorescent minerals, there is one person, and one person only that is credited as the first scientist to discover that there is invisible Ultraviolet energy that lies outside the visible spectrum beyond Violet: Goethe. The famous quote by Goethe from 1810 that I know by heart is written in every one of these books as well: 'Beyond the Violet barely any light could be seen, but the phosphors then gave off a vivid glow.' The 'phosphors' that Goethe is talking about are the 'primitive photography salts' (also quoted in all Goethe references) that Johann Ritter had used to discover Ultraviolet energy in 1801, Silver chloride. By revealing the true facts, it can be seen that Johann Ritter was the true discoverer of Ultraviolet, along with the method, reasoning, and eccentric state of mind that Ritter possessed is what was necessary to discover the invisible Ultraviolet energy, which is the 'polarity' in nature that Ritter was conscious of and searching for after the discovery of Infrared energy. This reasoning was way beyond the classic straight mind of the famous Goethe. It just didn't seem right to me that a person that was so prejudiced, and ultraconservative in regard to his published opinions, beliefs, and theories of Color, could at the same time have had such an open inquisitive mind and the degree of insight needed to make such an esthetic discovery of a cosmological force of nature. He didn't.

In this chapter on "The First Discoveries of Fluorescence and Luminescence" there will be many phenomenon of Luminosity listed in the quest that eventually led to the discovery of Fluorescence itself, most inclusive being Phosphorescence, Bioluminescence, and Chemiluminescence.

The facts to research are not that crystal clear, but it is apparent that about 1500-1000 B.C., almost two thousand years before Vincenzo Casciarola was born, in China the first written references on the phenomenon of Luminescence are found. These ancient texts introduce Bioluminescence through the first recorded descriptions of the self-illuminating insects 'Fireflies' and 'Glow Worms.' In "A History of Luminescence - From the Earliest Times until 1900," considered a 'bible' of luminescence written by E. Newton Harvey in 1957, there are very precise references to what is probably the first recorded historic writing on the subject of luminescence. Harvey states that around 1,500 - 1,000 B.C. the first description of a Firefly and a Glow worm was documented in China in "The Thirteen Classics." In one of "The Thirteen Classics" called the "Shih Ching," meaning the "Book of Odes" there is a sentence "i-yao hsiao-hsing" which can be translated as 'The light of the Glow Worm is all around' and 'Glowing on and off are Fireflies.' From 400-100 B.C. another Chinese book the "Li-Chi," meaning "Notes on Ancient Rites," has in Book four "Yiieh Ling," which describes the third month of the summer, and has a description of the Firefly stated as being created out of rotten grasses.

The second occurrence of important documented luminescence comes in the form of Phosphorescence, know commonly as "Glow-in-the-Dark." It seems nobody agrees on the year, but about 1000 B.C. there was in Japan a magic painting made in which an ox appeared each evening at Sunset and continued to glow with it's own light into the night. The Chinese Emperor heard of this magic ox painting and had it sent to China where he demonstrated the Phosphorescent ox to his Royal Court. The legend goes that one of the Emperor's priests discovered what made the magic ox appear on the painting in the dark, his explanation being that the ox had been painted with a special paint that contained "calcined" oyster shells (oyster shells heated to a very high temperature, just below the point of melting or fusing, for a long period) which became Phosphorescent through this process of calcination, and would make the ox glow-in-the-dark after sunset every night. There are several references to this occurrence with the magic Phosphorescent ox painting in China, but the date that is cited by these references is extremely different, two references citing 1000 B.C., and two references citing the same occurrence in 980 A.D., nearly two thousand years later. There is also no agreement on the references citing the date of the Invention of Phosphorescent paint, but some references also date this invention in China during the Sung Dynasty, which lasted from 960-1279 A.D., and some references state that Phosphorescent paint was invented in Japan.

The next written reference on the phenomenon of luminosity comes from Anaximenes of Miletus about the year 550 B.C., who was an ancient Greek pre-Socratic natural philosopher. Anaximenes was the first person to describe Bioluminescence by writing that while he was rowing a boat at night, light was emitted by the sea when it was struck with an oar. This was undoubtedly the signaling of tiny Bioluminescent sea-creatures, most likely the Bioluminescent sea plankton "Dinoflagellate." Anaximenes of Miletus was born around the sixty-third Olympiad (528-524 B.C.) in the ancient Greek city of Miletus, which is now in Asia Minor and part of Turkey. Anaximenes was a student of the philosopher Anaximander, and like most of the Greek philosophers of his time, Anaximenes was involved in trying to describe the natural world. Anaximenes wrote descriptions of how he believed the universe began and also wrote on astronomy and meteorology, but he is most famous for proposing that air is the fundamental element of the universe, and that when air is compressed it can take the forms of water and earth. Anaximenes believed that air was the substance that everything else was made of, even the Gods and the soul. He wrote that when air is dissolved it becomes fire, when it is compressed it becomes water, when it is condensed beyond water it becomes earth, and when furthest compressed it becomes stone. Anaximander and his student Anaximenes of Miletus were amongst the first philosophers to explain the workings of the universe as being independently sufficient, in other words, without need of, or having been created or influenced by the Gods. This was a very advanced modernistic viewpoint, which we would later call "Science." Anaximenes was also the first Greek to clearly differentiate between the planets and the stars.

Two hundred years later, another important written account of luminosity comes also from ancient Greece, and was written by one of the most famous of all the Greek philosophers, Aristotle. About 350 B.C., Aristotle wrote that he thought that 'lightning was similar to when the sea is seen to shine after being struck by a rod,' similar to Anaximenes of Miletus' description of his sightings of most likely the Bioluminescent sea plankton "Dinoflagellate." Aristotle appears to be one of the first philosophers to document "cold light." This "cold light" had been written about before by the Chinese and Anaximenes of Miletus, but Aristotle was most likely the first to recognize it in dead fish, fungi, and the Bioluminescent secretions of the 'Cuttlefish.'

In India around the year 200 B.C., the longest poem every written, the "Mahabharata" which contains 220,000 verses, contains a Sanskrit word "kyadyota" meaning Firefly or Glow worm. This religious Hinduist poem the "Mahabharata" contains several verses in which Fireflies or Glow worms are described. In "A History of Luminescence" a verse from the "Mahabharata" is described as comparing a God to the light of a Firefly at night in the rain.

Another more recent written record of luminosity occurs back in China again. There are many Chinese books and poems that describe a Phosphorescent natural Pearl called alternatively a 'night-shining jewel' or a 'Moonlight Pearl.' In the Sixth century appears one of the first written accounts in the "Tung ming ki," which states that the Emperor Wu of the Han Dynasty had by the year 102 B.C. a White gem which was highly Phosphorescent and looked as if it was giving off the light of the Moon, which Emperor Wu called a 'Moon-reflecting gem.'

There is a historian of ancient Rome named Titus Livius, also known as Livy, who lived from 59 B.C. to 17 A.D. He wrote an enormous history of Rome that covers the Roman Empire for 770 years and is a gigantic one hundred and forty-two volumes long, called "Ab Urbe" ('From the Founding of the City.') He also wrote about Bioluminescence, comparing the light in the sea to fire. Livy documented that the sea looked like it was on fire, and there were 'fires' all along the shore line as the water hit the sand.

A very Colorful character of history also documented luminosity, Pliny the Elder of ancient Rome (23-79 A.D.) who died while investigation the volcanic eruption of Vesuvius at Pompeii. Pliny the Elder discovered a Clam which squirted Bioluminescent light-emitting liquid that made the entire mouth luminous when eaten, and he began a trend for "Glow-in-the-Dark" Banquets in *First century Rome!* This Bioluminescent Clam discovered by Pliny the Elder would squirt Phosphorescent Green slime when frightened, resulting in anyone eating these Clams ending up with Phosphorescent Green glowing lips! These Bioluminescent Clams are described by Pliny the Elder in his ninth book of "Historia Naturalis," in which he states that the Clams "shine" by "themselves" in a "dark night." Of the "Glow-in-the-Dark" banquets of First century Rome, Pliny writes that these Clams would "shine" in "men's mouths" as they ate them, as well as on their "hands" when they held these clams, and even if a drop of the Clam fell on the floor, it would also shine Bioluminescent Green.

Besides eating this Bioluminescent Clam and ending up with Bioluminescent Green 'shining' lips, Pliny also documented the fact that a Bioluminescent 'shining' paste - or Make-up - could be easily made by mixing water, honey, flour, and the Bioluminescent part of the clam. The luminescent Make-up would not only Glow-in-the-dark, but it could be dried and stored, and even after a year when mixed together with water it would again luminesce. Like Murex snails, which Phoenitian "Tyrian" Purple dye for royalty was made from in antiquity, this Bioluminescent clam discovered by Pliny the Elder in ancient Rome was also collected to the point of near-extinction.

Pliny the Elder documented the Bioluminescence of the Jellyfish and the Glowworm before anyone else, as well as being the first person documented to use this Bioluminescence for a practical purpose. Pliny writes about the Bioluminescence of the Clam, Fungi, Snails, Jellyfish, Glowworms, and "Lantern fish," stating that the Bioluminescence of Glowworms in the dark looked like 'sparkles of fire.' The Bioluminescent Jellyfish discovered by Pliny the Elder is the Purple "Pulmo marinus," commonly known as the "Sea lung," and after using the Bioluminescent Clam to create "Glow-in-the-Dark" banquets in First century Rome, Pliny the Elder found the practical application for this Purple Bioluminescent Jellyfish as well. Instructions by Pliny are documented to about 50 AD, and instruct a person to "rub" the "Pulmo marinus" Jellyfish on wood, and that this piece of wood would then look as if "on fire," and could be used to walk in the dark, much the same as a burning torch. Pliny the

Elder's most prophetic documentation is the possible application of Bioluminescence to be "effectual in medicine" and for making "antidotes." Two-thousand years after Pliny the Elder documented these prophetic medial applications for Bioluminescent creatures, Osamu Shimomura discovered Green Fluorescent Protein - "GFP" - in the Bioluminescent Jellyfish "Aequorea aequorea," commonly known as "Aequorea victoria," a relative of Pliny's "Pulmo marinus" Jellyfish. This "GFP" would revolutionize medical and scientific research at the dawn of the Twenty-first century. This Bioluminescent phenomenon, described as early as 550 B.C. by Anaximenes of Miletus, later by Aristotle, and then by Pliny the Elder, is a physical process by which visible light is emitted by an organism as a result of a chemical reaction. Bioluminescence will be further described in this book, but for now, it occurs most commonly in insects, fish, squid, sea cacti, sea pansies, clams, shrimp, and jellyfish. The Bioluminescent abilities of these creatures are not the same, nor are the uses of their Bioluminescence. The Bioluminescent emitted light most often has one of three functions, being defense, finding food, or attracting mates.

Marcus Valerius Martialis, also known a Martial, was a First century Roman poet who lived from 40-102 A.D. He wrote about life in the Roman empire, documenting both it's amazements and horrors. Martialis was the author of twelve books of Epigrams, a style of writing which he is also considered creator of, that were published between 86-103 A.D. in Rome. Bioluminescence was a subject that Martialis also wrote of, reporting that the bright light of Bioluminescence in the ocean could still be seen even as one wave splashed on top of another one.

During the Tang Dynasty in China (618-904 A.D.) there are two more very early written accounts of luminosity. Tang Ming Huang was Emperor of the Tang Dynasty, and during this rule, Madame Haoguo had built the "Hall of Conjugative Joy." The famous item in this Hall was a Phosphorescent Pillow, which illuminated the Hall so brightly at night that candles were not needed. Also during the Tang Dynasty, there was a famous drinking cup made of Phosphorescent Jade, which originally belonged to an important drinking set from Jiuquan, Gansu Province. Jiuquan City was an important town on the Old Silk Road, and even today this is still a Chinese tourist destination, where cups of Phosphorescent Jade have always been regarded as being the very best for drinking wine and liquor. During the Zhou Dynasty, a drinking set made of Phosphorescent Jade was given to the monarch from the western regions of China as a tribute, to give an idea of how valuable that they were regarded by the Chinese culture.

In Fifteenth and Sixteenth century Europe, books were published containing references to Bioluminescent animals that were rewritten from ancient texts which had been published during the Middle Ages. One author of that period who is described in "A History of Luminosity" has a very amusing name: Stephen Batman (1537-1587), who published a book that was taken from the encyclopedia of Batholomaeus Angelicus who lived from 1190 to 1260, and who had written about Bioluminescent animals. In 1555 the first book completely devoted to the phenomenon of luminescence was published by Conrad Gesner, who lived from 1516-1565. This small book was published in Zurich in 1555 and had a very large title: "A short commentary on rare and marvelous plants that are called lunar either because they shine at night or for other reasons; and also on other things that shine in darkness." In this first published book on luminosity, Conrad Gesner writes about the Bioluminescent light of dead fish, rotten wood, "pygolampides" which Gesner calls Glow Worms, small sea creatures, Fireflies, and a small caterpillar-like worm.

After the Renaissance in Europe, the first observation of true Fluorescence actually happened. Up until this point in history the ancient Chinese, Greeks, and Romans had observed and recorded the luminescent phenomenon of Bioluminescence and Phosphorescence, but in 1565 the first observation of Fluorescence in solution was recorded by the Spanish physician and botanist Nicolas Monardes (1493-1588). The experiment that Monardes carried out produced a Blue tint in a vessel of clear, Colorless water containing the wood "lignum nephriticum" when it was excited with sunlight. This wood "lignum nephriticum" was used as a medicine during that time period for treating kidney disease. By 1570 it was also known that the Blue Color emitted was produced by the sunlight reacting with the solution of an extract of "Lignum nephriticum" or "Lignum peregrinum," but that this Blue light disappeared if the solution was acid-based and not just water. In 1615 the same Blue emission of light was produced by a Colorless solution containing water and chestnut rind, "Aesculos hippocastanum," which we know today is originating from what is called "Aesculin Fluorescence."

After many important recorded documentations of Fluorescence, Phosphorescence, or Bioluminescence, comes the person who is most often cited in books as the first person to "Discover Fluorescence," Vincenzo Casciarola (or Cascariola) of Bologna, Italy. Vincenzo Casciarola was a shoemaker and alchemist living in Bologna, who was undoubtedly more interested in alchemy than shoemaking. In 1603, in one of his many attempts to find the legendary "Philosopher's Stone," he "calcined" (heated to a high temperature for a long time, but below the melting or fusing point) powdered Barite (which is Barium sulphate and is known as a 'heavy spar') that he had collected on the slopes of Monte Paterno near Bologna. This simple preparation produced an impure Barium Sulphide, which glowed in the dark a Reddish Color after it was exposed to sunlight, and became famous as the "Bologna Stone." Alchemists considered this material that Casciarola had discovered as magical, and named it "Lapis lunaris" or "Moon stone" because like the Moon, it gave off light in the dark that it had received from the Sun. This was most likely the first inorganic luminous substance to be sold in the west, and it was marketed as "Bologna Phosphorus" which was basically calcined Barium Phosphate. This first synthetic glowing inorganic material that Casciarola sold as "Bologna Phosphorus," and made by heating together Barium Sulphate and coal, would Phosphoresce with a Reddish light after sunset, and it could be recharged in the sunlight every day, so that every night it would re-emit Reddish light. The way Vincenzo Casciarola discovered this "Bologna Phosphorus" was by trying to extract precious metals from the mineral Barite that he was melting near his house, which was a basic method of alchemy. This Barium Sulphate heated with coal, became calcined, and after this calcination with carbon and exposure to daylight, the substance glowed in the dark with a Reddish light. These "Bologna stones" alternatively named "Moon stones" were called a "phosphor," coming from the Greek word meaning "light bearer," and they are most probably the first inorganic artificial "phosphors" to be produced. In "Cold Light - Creatures, Discoveries, and Inventions That Glow" by Anita Sitarski it is documented that Casciarola was known to mix egg or water with his powdered Barite and shaped it into animal forms, which would also glow-in-the-dark after calcination.

Cellini, in 1568, documented the first known natural phosphor, Diamond, which most often Fluoresces in the Sun, and then when brought into a darkened room the Diamond Phosphoresces. This is what made alchemists consider Diamonds magical substances, and this is also, in the end, what made these tiny pieces of sparkling carbon crystals so valuable and to be considered the ultimate gemstone a person could possess, even up until today. The definition of a "Phosphor" is a substance that is capable of Phosphorescence (glowing-in-the-dark). The name of the element Phosphorus also comes from the Greek word "Phosphorous" meaning "light bearer," and was discovered in 1669 by a German alchemist Hennig Brand while experimenting with Urine.

The discovery of the "Bologna stone" or "Litheo phosphorus" by Vincenzo Casciarola in 1603 attracted the interest of many scientists and alchemists, including Galileo (1564-1642). Galileo and other scientists of the era stated after studying the "Bologna stone" that a "phosphor" can not emit luminescence unless it has been first exposed to natural light, realizing that this meant that light itself would have to be stored somehow within the "Bologna stone" before emission. Fifty years after it's discovery by Casciarola, the Italian mathematician Zucchi began to describe the mechanics of Phosphorescence scientifically by stating that the brilliant sunlight that the "Bologna stone" was exposed to during the day was not just absorbed and then reemitted in the dark in an unchanged form, like water being absorbed by a sponge, but that the sunlight absorbed into the "Bologna stone" during the day reacted with the Barium phosphate, and that when the White light absorbed during the day was emitted at night, it was obviously different light because it was even a different Color: Reddish. Originally when Casciarola discovered this "Bologna stone" it was simply called a 'Light Sponge,' which incorrectly effected the way it was thought of, in particular to the German poet Goethe. Further experimentation with Vincenzo Casciarola's discovery lead to the idea that the "Bologna stone" is not like a 'Light Sponge,' because, for example, when the stone was excited by a Blue light, it then reemitted Red light, not the same Blue light. Also becoming apparent was the fact that there occurred a slight delay in the emission of light from the "Bologna stone," indicating that the light was not just being absorbed as White light and being reemitted back out unchanged and instantaneously. This delay of light emission from the "Bologna stone" is now called "Phosphorescence." We know today that this "Bologna stone" contained Barium sulphate with traces of Bismuth and Manganese, as well as alkaline Earth metals. All of these listed traces in the Barium sulphate are well known activators of Fluorescent minerals, with Manganese in particular being very interesting with regards to this "Bologna stone," because Manganese is the most well known "activator" of Red Fluorescing minerals, the best example being so-called 'Mangano Calcite' which even incorporates it's Manganese trace into the common name of the mineral itself. These "activators" are usually impurities in the mineral which occur in very tiny amounts, like one part per thousands, being the reason why they are called traces, and these traces are what absorb the Ultraviolet energy and reemit it as Visible light, through what is termed in the study of Fluorescent minerals as "Impurity Activation." It is now also clear that the "Bologna stone" was not a 'light sponge,' but that the absorbed daylight and heating caused an electron movement in the atoms of the "activator," and this is what produced the Reddish light during the night. The quantum mechanics of Fluorescence are different from the quantum mechanics of Phosphorescence. Mineral Fluorescence occurs when a mineral containing certain impurities in the correct amounts is excited by an Ultraviolet energy, including the Sun. This invisible Ultraviolet energy causes "Electron displacement," also called a "Quantum jump," which means it causes an electron in the activator atoms to move to a higher orbit, because it now has more energy from the Ultraviolet. In this higher orbit, the electron moves through sub-orbits, and in this way looses a tiny fraction of the newly gained energy. For the atom to rebalance itself, the electron then jumps back to it's original orbit, and in this process the extra energy is emitted from the atom as visible light. The essential part to realize here is the tiny amount of energy lost in the electron's movement through the sub-orbits, because if this did not happen, the same invisible Ultraviolet energy that went into the atom would also be reemitted as invisible Ultraviolet energy, and not visible light - Colors. A little less energy is released by the atom which causes it to be Visible light, not the higher energy Ultraviolet. The grand difference between Fluorescence and Phosphorescence is that with Phosphorescence the electron that receives extra energy from the Ultraviolet does not simply jump up to a higher orbit in it's atom, but it jumps out of it's atom completely. The freed electron now wanders through what is called the crystal lattice, and in this crystal lattice there are occasional 'defects' - missing atoms for example, that can be visualized as 'traps' or 'holes' that the electron wandering through the "Crystal lattice" can 'fall into.' When this happens it may take seconds, minutes, hours, or even days, months, or years to come back out of the 'trap,' hence the delayed time of Phosphorescence, proving definitively that the "Bologna stone" was much more complicated than the initially described light sponge.

For two centuries after it's 1603 discovery by Vincenzo Casciarola. the "Bologna stone" was studied by scientists and alchemists, exemplified by a book written in 1640 by Fortunius Licetus (1577-1657) who was the professor of Philosophy at the University of Bologna. The book about Vincenzo Casciarola and his discovery of the "Bologna stone" in 1603 was entitled "Lithophosphorus Sive de Lapide Bononiensi." In his book Fortunius Licetus tells us that Vincenzo Casciarola was a humble honest man who was fascinated by chemistry, and had been born in Bologna. Quoting also from "Pharmacopea Spagirica" by the Bolognan chemist Petrus Poterius Andagauensis, we are told by Licetus that Vincenzo Casciarola abandoned his job as a shoemaker to full-time pursue the alchemist's dream of transforming simple rocks into Gold. Casciarola took a stone that he called "solar" to Scipione Begatello, who was known for his alchemist's trait of transformation, because Casciarola believed it was perfect for the transformation into Gold judging by it's content of Sulphur and it's heavy weight. Licetus tells us that after Casciarola made much work on the stone, it did not become the "Philosopher's stone" (Pluto of Aristophanes) but it became the "Luciferous Stone," which although the stone did not become Gold, could absorb and emit the Gold light of the Sun. Vincenzo Casciarola also told Antonio Magino of his discovery of the "Bologna stone," and Magino, being the professor of Mathematics at the University of Bologna, gave gifts of prepared "Bologna stone" to several scholars.

In 1625, only twenty-two years after Casciarola had discovered the "Bologna stone," the secret detailed receipt of it's production was published by Pierre Potier (Poterius) who was the physician to the King of France, and who had obtained the secret receipt while he had lived in Bologna. This published secret receipt for Vincenzo Casciarola's "Bologna stone" was later printed in the excellent and rare book "A History of Luminescence" by E. Newton Harvey, which is, again, almost 700 pages long and was recognized as the most complete history of Luminescence ever written and the 'bible' of Bioluminescence. Only recently, in 2006, "Bioluminescence - Chemical Principles and Methods" by Osamu Shimomura, the eighty year old Japanese scientist who discovered "Green Fluorescent Protein" in 1962, was published. "Bioluminescence - Chemical Principles and Methods" contains the most complete listing of Bioluminescent creatures ever published, including every known form of Bioluminescent life on Earth, and is an essential source of knowledge for all students of luminosity. Poterius' account of Casciarola's secret receipt informs the reader that the "Bologna stone" can be prepared in two different ways, depending on the desired results. The first recipe instructs the user to grind the Barite stone to a very fine powder, then to bring the Barite to the point of "calcination." The second recipe is the same, except that the ground Barite powder is next formed into 'cakes' with either water or egg-white. After this, the 'cakes' are dried, then put into layers with coal in a furnace and calcined for four to five hours. Then the oven is cooled, and the 'cakes' are taken out. If the 'cakes' are not heated enough the whole heating process is repeated up to three times. We are also instructed that the best stones to use for this are pieces of shining and pure Barite. Poterius tells us that after the process is completed, portions of this Phosphorescent substance are formed in little boxes (pyxidiculum) which "Shine wonderfully" when it's dark. The production of the first receipt is the same, but when not formed into 'cakes' with water or egg-white, it is named "Lixnium" and although it is prepared the same way, once the powder is calcined and dried, it "produces a sulphurous, fetid, sharp, and biting salt." This is extremely interesting, because today, four hundred years later, some of the Phosphorescent pigments that I make my paint with are precisely the same: Fetid smelling, Sulfurous, sharp, and biting enough to make your eyes tear! Even today, only some of the most recently produced Phosphorescent pigments are not still made with Sulphur, such as the extravagantly-priced Phosphorescent pigments I also use containing Strontium or Europium. Casciarola would be proud to know that we are still using something like what he called his "Lapis solaris" 500 years later.

Francis Bacon (1561-1626) in 1605 was delving into the mysteries of many different forms of Luminescence. Bacon not only reports about his observations of different forms of luminosity, but begins to investigate the causes of these lights. First Bacon describes sugar giving off light, and also observes that it gives off this light only while it is being scrapped, which we now call "Triboluminescence." Next Bacon writes about the sea ("salt water") and tells that it will also shine with light, then likewise he observes that this only happens when the sea is turbulent, which we know today was probably the Bioluminescent light of tiny sea creatures named "Ostracods," or the microscopic sea plankton "Dinoflagellate." Then he observes that Glowworms also have their own Bioluminescent light and reports that the Glowworms produce their light not only during their life, but even a little after their death. Twentieth century research has proved Bacon absolutely correct, showing that the oxygen needed for the Bioluminescent flashing is carried to the Glowworm's light organ by a network of air tubes on either side of the light organs, so that if enough oxygen reaches the light organ it can continue to give off light even after death. It is possible that female Fireflies can still emit light several hours after they are dead, and they have the ability to also control the light organs on their bodies by flashing only a portion of her lights independently of each other when disturbed, or flashing her entire lights when answering a male's flash during mating. Francis Bacon's most detailed analysis is of the putrefied scales of fish, which he observed to glow-in-the-dark, through what we know today as Bioluminescent bacteria, and he concluded that only these Bioluminescent putrefied scales of the fish are the same as Bioluminescent dead wood, which we also know today has it's glow due to Bioluminescent bacteria, proving Bacon's insight four hundred years ago absolutely correct.

Rene Descartes (1596-1650) was a famous French philosopher, mathematician, writer, and scientist. He is called the "Father of Modern Philosophy" and is most well remembered in this vein, but he is also less well remembered as the "Father of Modern Mathematics." His name in Latin is Cartesius, and he is the person who the "Cartesian coordinate system," used in geometry and algebra, is named after. Descartes also founded analytical geometry, but he is today remembered mostly for his three word philosophical phrase "Cogito ergo sum" 'I think, therefore I am.' Descartes believed and was the first person in the west to write that the universe could be described physically through motion and matter, also writing that he believed that everything in nature could be explained through mathematics and science. In 1637, Rene Descartes documented Bioluminescence, as well, by recording that when he hit sea water, he believed that the motion of hitting the sea water would 'generate sparks' like the sparks that are generated by hitting a piece of flint-stone.

The Bioluminescent glow from wood was experimented upon by several scientists at the end of the Seventeenth and beginning of the Eighteenth centuries. The luminescence would be studied with the wood in a solution of water. The German Jesuit priest Athanasius Kircher (1602-1680), who is recognized as one of the first to discover Fluorescence in solution was examining these luminescent properties of aqueous extracts of wood and recorded in 1646, in his book "Ars Magna Lucis et Umbrae," that he believed the observed Color of the luminescence of the wood extracts would depend on the intensity of the light in the room. Kircher documented that he had found that the Color of the emitted luminescence from the wood extract would be different and was effected by the angle that you would look at it from. He believed that Yellow light would be emitted by 'transmitted' light on the extract, and Blue light when 'reflected' light was upon the extract. Some very notable scientists disagreed with these findings from Kircher, including Robert Boyle who in 1664 wrote about his disagreement, and also Sir Isaac Newton and Robert Hook in 1678 disagree with these findings of the extracts of wood by Athanasius Kircher. In 1704, Isaac Newton (1643-1727) wrote a treatise on Optics and stated that the extract of wood "Liugnum nephrticum" showed different Colors, which was caused by the angle of the light that excited the solution. Newton reports that if the Sun is exciting the solution through 'transparency' the produced Color is Yellow, and if the Sun excites the solution 'laterally,' the produced Color is Blue, which is very similar to Athanasius Kircher's findings of 1646. This was the identical wood "Lignum nephriticum" that Nicolas Monardes had used for his experiments on luminosity one hundred years before in 1565. In Kircher's book of 1646, there is a very interesting passage in which he also wrote about an application for Fireflies to be used to light the interior of houses at night!

Going back to Vincenzo Casciarola's "Bologna Stone," by 1666 the formula for making the Phosphorescent "Bologna Stone" had apparently been lost already. This is confirmed by John Evelyn (1620-1706) who was one of the first Englishmen to have seen the "Bologna Stone" Phosphoresce, even reporting on the use of different Colors of light to excite the stone's Phosphorescence, but Evelyn did not take a piece of "Bologna stone" back to England, because as is written in the "Philosophical Transactions of the Royal Society" in 1666, the formula to make the "Bologna Stone" had already been lost in just over 60 years. A Mathematics professor at the University of Rome named Nicola Zucchi (1586-1670) made one of the most significant contributions of the era to the study of the phenomenon of Phosphorescence, which he did through the study of this "Bologna stone." In Nicola Zucchi's book "Optica Philosophia" of 1652, he describes experiments and observations of the "Bologna stone" such as the fact that the Phosphorescence of the stone became stronger when the stone was exposed to stronger light, and that the Color of the light emitted by the stone was always Red, regardless if the exciting light source was White light or if the excited White light had been passed through Red, Yellow, or Green filters. Zucchi came to the conclusion from these observations that the exciting light is not just absorbed, like the popular 'light-sponge' theory of the time, but that the exciting light 'excites and unites' with 'substances contained in the stone.'

Although Nicolas Monardes and Athanasius Kircher are recognized to have discovered Fluorescence in solution, it was Robert Boyle, who in the 1660's was the first person to analyze and document the internal mechanics of the phenomenon of Fluorescence displayed in organic solutions, like wood. Robert Boyle went beyond the previous scientists in their experiments with the luminosity of extracts of wood in solution, by producing a Fluorescent solution through many experiments with these extracts of wood in solution. Boyle believed that this Fluorescent solution he produced was the 'Essential salt' contained in the wood that caused the fascinating and mysterious luminous glow in the wood. This was most likely the first concentrated Fluorescent extract ever produced. Robert Boyle (1627-1691) is known for his experiments with luminosity, but he is more famous as the "Father of Bioluminescence." Boyle carried out many experiments with Bioluminescence on wood, human flesh, fish, and other creatures, such a Glowworms. In Robert Boyle's day, Firefly lights were believed to be the spirits of the dead, and dead trees emitting Bioluminescent light through bacteria were thought to be magic. In 1672, English scientist Robert Boyle wrote a letter to The Royal Society, the most influential scientists of his day, on the subject of Bioluminescence. He reported to these scientists that his cook had run into his laboratory petrified of the ghosts that were all lit up in the cellar of his house. His cook was so perturbed that Boyle himself went into the cellar to investigate the source of his cook's hysteria. Boyle wrote that it was indeed true: the entire cellar was aglow, but there was not a candle lit anywhere. Boyle writes that the lit up cellar came from a single source of light - a dead chicken hanging from the ceiling gave off the 'blue-green' light. Boyle writes further to The Royal Society that although he is known for experimenting with creatures that 'make their own light,' he had never seen anything as intense as this light. Immediately experimenting with the dead chicken, Boyle discovered that same evening some of the very foundations of Bioluminescence, which is what he is most well remembered for. His reported findings were contained in five statements, two of which are inconsequential, such as the direction and speed of the wind, and also what time the Moon rose that night, but the other three discoveries from Boyle that night are still the fundamental principles of all Bioluminescence. Robert Boyle proceeded to experiment with the dead chicken and his findings included the very important fact that the Bioluminescent light gave off no heat, which would later be termed, and is still known in science today as "cold light." Boyle also reports that when he poured wine on part of the chicken, that part of the chicken gave off less light. Boyle's third postulation after studying the Bioluminescent glowing dead chicken was perhaps his most important of all. Even though the element Oxygen had not been identified yet in the 1600s, Boyle wondered what would happen if the dead chicken had all the air removed from around it. Boyle reports that when he covered part of the chicken to keep air from it, the Bioluminescent glow was extinguished: no air = no glow. Robert Boyle then concludes his letter to The Royal Society with a startling fact. After he had finished his experiments on the Bioluminescent glowing dead chicken, Boyle instructed his absolutely horrified cook to make the dead chicken for his dinner that night! Boyle's last report in his letter was that *'the bird was delicious'*!

Even though the Bioluminescent bacteria that was responsible for making the dead chicken glow was never discovered during Boyle's lifetime, nor the Oxygen which he had also concluded caused a definite effect on the Bioluminescence, Boyle was a real scientist and he made discoveries without even having to know the causes of his discoveries. He put luminescent wood and Glowworms under large glass jars, pumped out all of the air creating a vacuum, and discovered that all of these creatures that emit Bioluminescent light are not able to emit light without air. When Boyle let the air back into the glass jars, the Glowworm and luminescent wood lit up once again. In this primitive 1600s experiment, Robert Boyle became the first person to prove that Oxygen is a necessary element for Bioluminescence.

This incredible story of Boyle and 'the bird was delicious' was expanded upon in "Cold Light - Creatures, Discoveries, and Inventions That Glow" by Anita Sitarski, with the added facts that Boyle's Bioluminescent chicken had been sitting on his pantry shelf for a week after it was purchased. This chicken was glowing with about twenty areas of Greenish Blue bacteria Bioluminescence, and Boyle later wrote that when he picked up the glowing dead chicken even brighter Bioluminescent glowing was produced, which was described by Robert Boyle as a "splendid show." This "Glowing Chicken" of Robert Boyle made such an impression on Dr. Bruce Applegate and Nathan Bright of Perdue University that they themselves covered a dead chicken with the identical Bioluminescent bacteria which had colonized themselves on Boyle's chicken centuries ago, and took photographs in the daylight, and then in the dark with the Greenish Blue Bioluminescent glow of the chicken very visible. These two photos printed in "Cold Light" reveal a very clear Green Blue light being emitted from the entire dead chicken in various intensities, making the Bioluminescent photo appear to be an X-ray or a ghost image. It's no wonder that Robert Boyle's cook was so petrified! Another well-known fact about this Bioluminescent bacteria is that in the 1860s during the Civil War in America, doctors reported on soldiers who's wounds were also glowing with this Greenish Blue bacteria, and even determined that these Bioluminescent glowing wounds healed better than wounds that did not glow. It is believed that the Bioluminescent bacteria in these soldier's glowing wounds were responsible for removing dead tissue and the spread of infection.

The word "Bioluminescent" comes from the Greek word "Bio" translated as "Life," and the Latin word "Luminescence" meaning "Light," which together means "Living Light," or 'Light produced by a Living thing.' As all light is the result of some kind of energy released, like fire for instance, Bioluminescence is a "cold light" produced by members of all three forms of life on Earth: animals, plants, and bacteria, lichens, and fungi through their natural energies, including "metabolic energy" where animals are concerned. Amongst the most well known are rotting wood, some shrimp, squid, clams, sharks, flashlight fish, jellyfish, bacteria, some mushrooms, fungi, and toadstools, which give off their own Bioluminescent light. The most well known Bioluminescent creature is by far the 'Firefly.' Like most Bioluminescent creatures, these Fireflies prefer warm climates, are relatively unknown in cold areas of the world, and like most Bioluminescent land creatures as well, these Fireflies also produce their most dazzling displays when the darkest phase of the Moon is occurring, so they will be signaling their flash when it is the darkest and their displays will be the most visible. Although Antarctica is the only continent without any Fireflies, they are most commonly found in warm climates. In northern Europe, for example where I live in Amsterdam, the Dutch have never seen a Firefly. Fireflies and Glowworms are the earliest described form of luminescence, documented by the Chinese over 3,000 years ago, possibly coming from an ancient Chinese encyclopedia written by a student of Confucius. About 100 B.C. the Chinese later classified these Fireflies as winged insects with fire in their bodies. The Firefly is also used in many potions of Japanese folk medicine, and in the Thirteenth century Fireflies were crushed, mixed with a tincture of roses and used as a medical treatment for the ear in Arabia. When early pioneers returned to northern Europe from the "New World" they would tell of natives that would catch and release Fireflies in their huts, to light them at night, or tie them around their ankles to light the way in the forests at night. In First century Rome, Pliny the Elder incorrectly wrote that the Firefly's light is controlled by it's wings and that the Firefly will only light up when it spreads it's wings. The Firefly's light does not come out of their wings, but, out of the lower one-third of it's body. Fireflies without wings, like some European female species, and also the larval stage of all Fireflies are called Glow Worms, but the only real 'Glow Worms' known in the world are in New Zealand and the eastern part of Australia, suspended from cave ceilings, such as Waitomo Cave in New Zealand. The Glow Worms in Waitomo Cave in New Zealand are "Arachnocampa luminosa," and these are the only species that are truly Glow Worms. Fireflies in the end are neither flies nor worms, but are classified as a beetle, because they have four wings, not two like flies. The Yellow-Orange light that the Fireflies produce is for mating. In the United States, east of the Mississippi, only, every June to July countless fireflies come out for one to two hours about dusk and flash their Bioluminescent light. As many as one hundred species of Fireflies will be present at once, with each species having it's own personal flashing pattern that must be answered precisely by the female's flash, who waits in the brush. A common North American Firefly is named "Photuris pennsylvanica," and the female is a real monster. She imitates the flashes of another species, then when a male lands near her to mate, she pounces on him, killing and devouring him. The most common Firefly that I've seen every summer growing up, is the "Photinus pyralis" which is the common North American Firefly that is found on the east coast of the United States. The male "Photinus pyralsi" flies and flashes his light for exactly half a second, every five seconds. The female must wait exactly two seconds before flashing her response, and most of the time it is only virgin females which glow, because once a female has mated she rarely flashes her lights again. It must be remembered that these insects don't live twenty years. A female Firefly rarely lives past ten nights of glowing, and she usually outlives the males by three days. David Attenborough, host of the best television program I've ever seen on Bioluminescence, "Nature's Neons" on the "BBC" in the 1990s, commented rather cryptically that a Firefly with a bad sense of timing is doomed to a life of celibacy. Concerning the Fireflies of south east Asia, particularly in Thailand, the species "Pteroptyx malaccae" put on one of the most dazzling displays of any Fireflies in the world. Thousands of male "Pteroptyx malaccae" gather in a single tree and then begin to flash in synchronicity. The unbelievably bright entire flashing trees can be seen by female Fireflies for over half a mile (close to a kilometer) away, attracting countless females. This technique of thousands of Fireflies gathering in the same tree and then flashing their Bioluminescent lights in synchronicity has also in recent times been documented occurring in several localities across the world from Thailand to the United States' southern state of Tennessee. The Firefly belongs to the general family of beetles known as the "Lampyridae" with the worldwide numbers of different species of Fireflies being over two thousand. Fireflies similar to today's species have been found as old as thirty-million years in fossilized rock, showing that the species of Firefly fossils found in the Americas are very different from the fossilized Fireflies that were found in Europe and Asia, most likely meaning that were separated a very long time ago. Today the biggest concentration of Fireflies is in the tropics in South America, but have been found in areas across the world. Surprisingly, two Museum visitors a couple of years ago told me occasionally they even see Fireflies during the summer in Finland, which is the coldest climate I've ever heard of Fireflies living in. The actual anatomy of the Firefly's light organ is very interesting. Although it appears very bright in nature at night, the light of the Firefly is very small and you would need four hundred Fireflies to equal the brightness of just one candle. The female has the most complicated light organs, which take up about a third of it's body. Out of the eight segments the female Firefly's body consists of, the sixth and seventh body segments contain large luminous bands, while the eight segment just has a luminous spot on either side. The two spots on the eighth band were the first which developed in the larva and were glowing even when the Firefly was an egg. The large luminous bands on the sixth and seventh segments of the female's body were formed only after the larva had reached maturity. Each light organ on the Firefly is made up of three layers, and act very similar to the glass lens, light bulb, and mirrored reflector in a manufactured light. On the outside, the first layer of each light organ is made of a transparent strong skin (like the glass lens of the lamp), then underneath this transparent tough skin, there is a second layer which is the layer that gives off the Bioluminescent light and is made up of light-emitting cells (like the light bulb in the lamp). The bottom and third layer of the Firefly's light organs is like the back mirrored reflector in a manufactured lamp, and is made up of very special cells which are composed of crystals of Uric acid which reflect the produced light from the second layer through the first layer - the glass lens - and out of the Firefly. When a Firefly is turned over during the daytime, when it isn't flashing, the light organ is a pale grayish-beige Color - this is the Color of the Uric crystals in the third reflector layer of the Firefly's light being visible underneath the two transparent layers above them.

  Another very famous land creature that gives off a Bioluminescent glow is the "Glowworm." Although some species of female Fireflies and Firefly larva are called Glowworms, the real 'Glowworms' live in New Zealand on the ceilings of caves, and also in eastern Australia in bushes as well. When entering "Waitomo Cave" in New Zealand, the visitor is struck with a dazzling sight of thousands of "stars' on the ceiling of the cave. These "stars" are actually the pupae, or the larval stage, of the life of a "Fungus Gnat." These inch long (1.7 cm.) Glowworms live in a tube of mucous they produce stuck to the ceiling of the cave, and they also produce long sticky threads that they hang down from the ceiling, sometimes as many as seventy sticky threads per Glowworm. When other insects see the many Bluish-White lights from the Glowworms on the ceiling of the cave, they fly up to what they may consider the way out of the cave - the night sky all lit up with stars - then they become entangled in the sticky threads hanging from the ceiling. When the insect gets caught in the sticky treads on the ceiling it struggles to free itself, which causes vibrations in the treads that are sensed by the very sensitive Glowworm, who proceeds to reel in the sticky thread ensnaring the insect and feeds on it. Visitors must be careful in the "Waitomo Caves," because even a cough or a whisper is enough to scare the Glowworms and cause them to extinguish their lights. A visitor to the Museum told me that during the tour on the water in Waitomo Caves, the tour guide asks visitors 'Do you want to see the stars go out?' and then slaps a rubber inner-tube people float in onto the water and instantaneously all the Glowworms become frightened and immediately turn off all of their lights. Over the past seventeen years in the Museum I have heard alot from Australian visitors about Glowworms migrating from their native New Zealand and being found in Hazelbrook, Australia, south of Sydney in Apollo Bay and in the Blue Mountains. This is the southeast of Australia, closest to New Zealand. There is also a "Glowworm Tunnel" outside of Sydney in the Blue Mountains, which is an abandoned old railroad tunnel that Glowworms have colonized, and they have made such a spectacular Bioluminescent display that I even heard about it on the other side of the world in Amsterdam.

  Another relatively obscure Bioluminescent insect called a 'Railroad worm' ("Phrixothrix") lives in South and Central America and is called "el farrocarril," Spanish for 'railroad.' These creatures which look like a cross between a caterpillar and a worm have a spectacular display, with two bright Red 'headlights' on the front of their body, then eleven pairs of Greenish-Yellow lights along the sides of their body, which gives their signatory display of a railroad train with two bright Red 'headlights' at the front of the train, along with twenty-two Greenish-Yellow train 'windows' along their sides.

  Although the most well known Bioluminescent creatures live on the land, like Fireflies and Glowworms, the greatest amount of Bioluminescent creatures on Earth live in the oceans of the world. To give an idea of the amount of species which that could encompass, it is estimated that over ninety percent of all sea creatures that live beneath one hundred meters (300 feet) have some sort of Bioluminescent self-glow. Most well known Bioluminescent creatures of the seas are also the creatures that live on or near the surface, and therefor are the creatures we most often encounter. The Color difference is very noticeable from the land to the sea. Most Bioluminescent land creatures glow with a Greenish glow, which is the easiest Color to see at night on land, and most Bioluminescent creatures of the sea glow with a Bluish color which is the Color which penetrates water the easiest. Amongst all the Bioluminescent sea creatures, probably the most well known are the tiny microscopic Phytoplankton "Dinoflagellate." The most famous place to encounter these brilliant "Dinoflagellates" is in the Caribbean Sea on the southwest of Puerto Rico, in Vieques, called originally by locals "Bahia Fosforescente," meaning "Phosphorescent Bay." Since about ten years ago I've begun to hear from visitors in the Museum that in Puerto Rico they have finally realized their obvious mistake, and the Puerto Ricans have properly renamed the bay "Bio Bay," or more complete, "Bioluminescent Bay." The original name of this world famous bay in Vieques is a little less romantic: "Mosquito Bay." These Dinoflagellates which live in their countless numbers in "Bioluminescent Bay,' emit a chemical from their bodies when disturbed called Luciferin, that mixes with oxygen and produces a dazzling Blue light. They are not fish or animals, but are just one-celled plants - Phytoplankton. These Dinoflagellates live around the world mostly in, again, warm climates, but as visitors have also told me in the Museum over the past seventeen years, Dinoflagellates lighting up the ocean water have been seen very occasionally as far north as Ireland, Holland, and even one visitor remembers seeing these lights in the water one time many years ago in Finland! Incidentally, these microscopic Dinoflagellates are the only living creatures on Earth that can be seen from space, because when the wind blows and stirs up the water in Puerto Rico's "Bioluminescent Bay," countless billions of Dinoflagellates light up, which in turn lights up the entire south west bay of Puerto Rico! These microscopic plankton may have been responsible for changing world history. The 'barn fires' that Christopher Columbus saw and thought were built by the natives, which in turn caused him to change his plans of landing on the mainland of America and instead turn around and land on the islands of the West Indies, were almost undoubtedly the lights of Caribbean Dinoflagellates! This is just one example of the ways that Dinoflagellates communicate, with the belief today that the very first communication on Earth could have been created by these Bioluminescent bacteria and Phytoplankton such as Dinoflagellates.

The reason "Bio Bay" or "Bioluminescent Bay" in Vieques, Puerto Rico is the most famous and intense display of Bioluminescence known in the world is because of several natural reasons. "Bioluminescent Bay" is a lagoon surrounded by Red Mangroves, which will only grow in the tropics, and the roots of these Red Mangroves release a compound called a "Tannin," which is part of the bark and fruit of some plants (commonly known as the agent that "tans" leather), being a high source of Vitamin B12, and this B12 is one of the most important foods for the Dinoflagellates. The Red Mangrove leaves, when they fall into the water of "Bio Bay," also provide other nutrients to the Dinoflagellates. There are different factors which make "Bio Bay" a perfect place for Dinoflagellates to live, such as a relatively pollution-free environment, enough forest cover around the bay to hold back sediment from washing into the bay during rains, as well as the physical depth and size of the bay. "Bio Bay" is deep enough and large enough to stay cool during the day, but warmer than the surrounding ocean temperature. Another necessary factor is a small connection with the ocean that does not cause large tidal exchanges of water, but is just enough to maintain a cool water temperature as well as avoid stagnation. These microscopic creatures are very sensitive, and even the motors of boats and sun-creme on swimmers can adversely effect the Dinoflagellates. When all the conditions are as perfect as they are in "Bioluminescent Bay," these Dinoflagellate "Pyrodinium bahamense" can flourish in nearly countless amounts, averaging over 700,000 Dinoflagellate in a single gallon (3.8 ltr.) of "Bioluminescent Bay" water. Dinoflagellates are a one-celled plankton that uses photosynthesis to live, like other plants, and are only about one five-hundredth of an inch long. The burst of light that each Dinoflagellate emits is amazingly a hundred times the size of the Dinoflagellate body itself. This natural phenomenon is so spectacular that once a year in "Bioluminescent Bay" in Vieques, Puerto Rico a "Bioluminescent Festival" is held at night, when everyone dresses in White and swims with the Bioluminescent seawater filled with Dinoflagellates. What is not well known is that there are all together three different "Bioluminescent Bays" in Puerto Rico, the 'second' famous "Bioluminescent Bay" is called "Laguna Grande," being located in the northeast of Puerto Rico in Fajardo. The third "Bioluminescent Bay" is in La Parguera, Lajas also in the southwest of Puerto Rico, with less amount of Dinoflagellates in the water than the other two localities.

Another visitor to the Museum from Ecuador told me a fascinating Bioluminescent story about ten years ago. Supposedly the rarest display of sea Bioluminescence occurs in Ecuador only an average of one time every fifteen years, and is called the "Crimson Tide." A man about twenty-five years old told me about this extremely rare event in Ecuador that is so important it changed the culture of the people of the country. He told me that one night only, on average about once every fifteen years only, the sea comes rolling onto the shore and emits not common Blue or even Green light, but brilliant pure Red light. The Blue or Greenish-Blue lights are a very common occurrence in the hot water of Ecuador, but this Red Bioluminescence is an extremely rare and auspicious event. He told me that he has only seen it once during his life, and his father has only seen it twice, and that it is the most well known amongst the fishermen who live along the sea shores. What he told me last let me understand the profound effect this Red Bioluminescence once every fifteen years in Ecuador has had on the people that live in that country. Originally, the sea in Ecuador was named "Le mare" which is masculine, but it was renamed "La mare" which is feminine, because this Red Bioluminescent tide once every fifteen years is seen by the people of Ecuador as the menstruation of the sea.

Among the countless species of Bioluminescent sea creatures, the larger known ones are fish, clams, squids, and some shrimp. These creatures, along with the chemical causes of this phenomenon of Bioluminescence were explored by Raphael Dubois who carried on with Robert Boyle's findings two hundred years later in the late eighteen hundreds.

Another important person that documented luminescence was Robert Hooke (1635-1703) of England. In 1655 Robert Boyle hired Robert Hooke to construct the Boylean air pump. In 1660 Hooke discovered his "Law of Elasticity" which described the dynamics of the force of stretching solid materials, such as wood. Hooke's "Law of Elasticity" concludes that the force applied to a solid body is in proportion to the actual stretching of that solid body. These were the first documented studies of material "stress." Five years later, in 1665, Hooke writes very influentially that he believes that the cause behind the mysterious lights of Bioluminescence lies in the 'Internal vibrations' of the light-emitting material itself. Nine years later, in May, 1676, there was a very popular play amongst the upper-class of London named "The Virtuoso" written by playwright Thomas Shadwell. The play was a caricature of the alchemists of the day, but the main character Sir Nicholas Gimcrack was intended to resemble the most famous alchemist in London at that time, Robert Hooke, who was in reality the "Curator of Experiments" for The Royal Society of London. The sarcasm went so far in the play that it portrayed Robert Hooke (Gimcrack) reading his Bible by the Bioluminescent light of a rotten leg of pork(!) Robert Hooke himself went to see the play, and by all written accounts he was *not* amused.

The next important historical documentation of Luminescence was made by an alchemist who made a major discovery that Robert Boyle was to profit handsomely from, and that Boyle even attempted to lay claim to the actual discovery of. Hennig Brand (1630-1710) was an alchemist from Hamburg that is recognized as the first scientist to discover a chemical element. The year was 1669 and Hennig Brand, who was also known as Dr. Teutonicus, was trying to transmute simple substances into the precious metal Gold, like most alchemists were doing at that time. The simple known substance Brand was experimenting on was a common substance used in Alchemy, the beginnings of chemistry, and also had the same Color as Gold: human Urine. Hennig Brand filled a tub with human Urine and let it turn putrid after many days. He then boiled the putrefied Urine until it reduced to a paste, and proceeded to then intensely heat this paste. As the paste was heated to an extreme degree, vapors from the heated paste were collected in a container holding water, which caused the vapors to condense. This is the point where Brand should have collected from the water his condensed precious Gold, but instead what was condensed in the water was a waxy White substance. To counter his disappointment, Brand found that when it became dark this White waxy substance glowed with it's own light. The White waxy substance that Brand had produced was the first chemical element discovered by a scientist: Phosphorus, which is the letter "P" in the table of Elements, and was named from the Greek word meaning 'bearer of light.' Before this time, only the heavy metal and non-metal elements were known, such as Gold and Sulphur. What Hennig Brand had done in his experiment first, was to produce ammonium sodium hydrogen-phosphate by reducing the human Urine, and next he produced sodium phosphate by heating the produced paste. When this paste was heated with charcoal, which is Carbon, it produced two separate substances: sodium pyrophosphate, and the discovery of the element which glowed in the dark, Phosphorus. This newly discovered element Phosphorus was first called "Brand's phosphor" by the public, but Brand himself called the substance "Miraculous Light" and "Cold Fire." The emitted light from Phosphorus is not termed "Phosphorescence," but "Chemiluminescence" because the light produced is through a chemical reaction of the element Phosphorus mixing with humid Oxygen. Brand tried to keep his receipt a secret, but made the mistake of selling the secret receipt to a German chemist Johann Daniel Krafft, who proceeded to travel around Europe showing his magic substance that glowed in the dark. Krafft even showed his substance in London, where it was seen by Robert Boyle. The secret Urine receipt of Brand's was spread around Europe and Phosphorus was made in Sweden in 1678 by Johann Kunckel, and next in London in 1680 by Robert Boyle. Boyle even managed to improve the receipt of Brand's by using sand. Then Robert Boyle began to make something which would become a world-wide market up until this present day. Boyle coated the tips of small pieces of wood and created the world's first "Match" in 1680. Boyle called this substance "icy noctiluca," meaning 'cold light,' and eventually the element Phosphorus became known as "English Phosphorus" or even "Boyle's Phosphorus," typically robbing Hennig Brand of not only the hugh profits made through the production and sales of this substance, but even the credit as it's discoverer. Incidentally, the most common matches today in northern Europe are still made in Sweden.

In 1670, Jacques Rohault (1618-1672), who was a French philosopher and mathematician wrote about his experiments with luminosity in the form of Bioluminescence. In very early attempts to understand these lights glowing in the water, Rohault determined that during the hot summer season, the waves of the sea would emit much more light - 'Sparks' - than during other seasons, and summarized that the first two 'elements' were acting upon the agitated sea water's salt, and through this reaction, the emitted light was produced. Jacques Rohault also experimented with and concluded correctly that stagnant water will not produce emitted light by any forced means. Jacques Rohault, a friend of Rene Descartes and also teacher of Descartes' natural philosophy, made famous experiments weighing air and magnetism, but his own masterpiece "Traite de physique" of 1671 was the most widely used textbook on natural philosophy of it's time.

Before 1675, possibly in 1673, Christian Adolf Balduin (1632-1682) produced another luminous substance, as had Vincenzo Casciarola in 1603, and Hennig Brand in 1669. Balduin was a magistrate in Saxony, as well as an alchemist, and he named the substance "Hermetic phosphorus," which he made by first producing Calcium nitrate and then drying it. The dried Calcium nitrate was impure, probably containing Sulphur through his mixture of chalk and Nitric acid, and was also Phosphorescent like Casciarola's "Bologna stone," continuing to glow with light in the dark. The substance became known as "Balduin's phosphorus" or "Phosphorus Balduini." His book "Aurum superius et inferius auroe superius et inferius hermeticum" printed in both Amsterdam and Frankfurt in 1675, contains descriptions of his Phosphorescent substance in the chapter "Phosphorus hermeticus, sive magnes luminaris." Balduin describes his procedure of making a solution of chalk in Nitric acid and distilling it until it was dry. He discovered that when the Calcium nitrate was overheated it turned into a Yellow substance that was Phosphorescent. Balduin documented his discovery and sent this documentation together with a sample of his "Phosphorus Balduini" to The Royal Society in 1676. For his discovery Balduin was elected as a Fellow of The Royal Society.

Robert Plot (1640-1696) was the first Professor of Chemistry at the University of Oxford, and the first keeper of the Oxford Ashmolean Museum. Plot is best remembered as the first person to document the finding of a Dinosaur bone. In his "Natural History of Oxfordshire," he described the fossilized femur of a 'giant,' which we now know to be the dinosaur "Megalosaurus." Plot writes, in 1676, that the fossilized bone was found in Cornwall, and in his opinion it was similar to the thigh bone of an animal or a human, but the bone was nearly two feet (65 cm) around, and weighed almost twenty pounds (9 kilos). Robert Plot's opinion on the matter was that the bone was real, but had probably been the fossilized bone of an elephant that had been brought to England in ancient times by the Romans. Even though Plot became first keeper of the Ashmolean Museum at the University of Oxford where the tremendous bone he discovered was housed, it was not well kept, and unfortunately has now been lost to time. Robert Plot did not only document the finding of the first Dinosaur bone, but also claimed that he "discovered" Dinosaurs with this famous find. True of many "discoveries," the ancient Greeks had knowledge of Dinosaur bones and documented this knowledge 2,000 years before Robert Plot "discovered" Dinosaur bones in the Seventeenth century. Ten years later, in 1686, Robert Plot wrote of his observations of Bioluminescence, stating that he believed that the Bioluminescent light emitted by sea water was similar to rotten fish or rotten wood. Robert Plot believed that the light given off by salt water of the sea, rotten fish, and rotten wood, all derived form the same source, simply the act of the three materials giving off their moisture, not the effect of putrefaction. Robert Plot was again in the light in 2009, when his statue as the first director of the Natural History Museum in London was removed from the grand entrance stairway to the museum, and was replaced by a much more important scientist who really did change the world, and also someone whom Robert Plot personally detested and even publicly abused: Charles Darwin.

Pere Guy Tachard (1651-1712) was a Jesuit priest who is remembered for a fascinating book describing Siam (Thailand) during the late Seventeenth century. In Paris in 1686 Tachard published "Voyage de Siam des Peres Jesuites Neons par le Roi aux Indes et a la Chine," an account of his visit to the royal city of Siam which was Ayutthaya on the central plains. Ayutthaya was a magnificent city by the Seventeenth century and in the book by Pere Guy Tachard he describes the immense wealth and power of the royal city in detail, including the amazing amount of jewels and gold. Two years after this famous description of Siam was published in Paris, in 1688 Pere Guy Tachard published the English edition in London, entitled "A Relation of the Voyage to Siam by six Jesuits sent by the French King to the Indies and China in 1685." In this account of their voyage to the east, Tachard documents his theory of Bioluminescent light in ocean water, believing that the lights seen in 'violent' sea water in the dark were 'caused' by the Sun's heat, which during the day filled the ocean with 'fiery and luminous spirits' that would 'reunite' after dark to be emitted by the ocean when it became rough.

Domenico Bottoni was a very famous doctor of the Seventeenth century in Italy. Bottoni (or Bottone) became a professor of medicine in Messina at a young age and was so famous that he became the physician of the Viceroy. During his lifetime he had some books published on medicine, but he is most remembered for a book he left in manuscript form, unpublished at the time of his death on natural history and earthquakes. The book was published in 1692 and is divided into three parts, the first part "De igne in genere" describing historical writings on fire. The second part of Bottoni's book is "De ignibus coelestibus" and describes fires that produce light without heat in which he discusses the Firefly, and the third section of his book was "De ignibus terrestribus" concerned with fires inside the Earth, especially Mount Aetna and Mount Vesuvius. The second part of Bottoni's book, describing what would later be called "Cold Light" is the most important here, because in this section Bottoni describes the luminescence of water, fish, rotting wood, glowworms, fireflies, earthworms, inorganic phosphors, skin, hair, the Aurora Borealis, and more. The mechanics behind all of these various states of natural luminosity Bottoni lists is, in his opinion, motion only. Bottoni writes that the light of Fireflies, the ocean, fish, and rotting wood, were all produced by motion alone. Some of what Bottoni wrote boarders on the ridiculous today, such as the reason that Fireflies light up at night when trapped in a bottle is that the air that is contained in the 'tubes and bladder' of the Firefly is set into 'quick motion' by the sunlight during the day and remains that way at night. Athanasius Kircher in 1646 wrote that he believed Fireflies got their light from nature to see and to be seen, but Bottoni was very opposed to this opinion and believed that nature's Bioluminescence was absolutely the same as the naturalistic action of motion and the creation of sparks, only.

In 1713 a Jesuit Missionary to the east Indies named Father Bourzes wrote a letter concerning Bioluminescence to Father Estienne Souciet. It is published in the "Philisiphical Transactions (1683-1775)" Vol. 28 of 1713 as "A Letter from Father Bourzes to Father Estienne Souciet, concerning the Luminous Appearance Observable in the Wake of Ships in the Indian Seas, Taken from the ninth volume of Letters of the Missionary Jesuits."

In 1665 Robert Hooke wrote that he believed 'internal vibrations' were the cause of Bioluminescence. In 1718, one of the most famous and influential scientists in history, Sir Isaac Newton (1642-1727), wrote a paper that was in agreement with Hooke's idea of 'internal vibrations' being the cause of Bioluminescence. Sir Isaac Newton believed that the light emitted by luminous 'bodies' was caused by 'agitation.' Newton considers the 'agitation' and 'vital motion' produced through the actions of 'heat,' 'friction,' 'putrefaction,' and raging 'sea-water' to be the motion or agitation needed to vibrate the particles of the luminous bodies into an emission of light. Isaac Newton is famous for his pioneering work with the prism and for his discovery that the Colors of the prism are the constituents of White light itself. Similar to his interpretation of Bioluminescence being caused by the agitation of 'particles' of the luminous bodies, Newton was also the first to state that all light was made up of 'particles.'

Before 1731 a 'brilliance surrounding a star' was discovered by a French Geophysicist named Jean-Jacques Dortus de Mairan (1678-1771). Charles Messier and William Herschel also catalogued this star cluster forty years later, and Messier assigned his number "M-43" to what's now called an "Open Star Cluster." This "Messier 43" is the companion galaxy to the great Orion Nebula "M-42." J.J.D. de Mairan is known for his work done with the Aurora Borealis, and this discovery of "M-43" which was first published in Paris in 1733 as "Physical and historical treatise of the Aurora Borealis, M. De Mairan. Series of the Memoirs of the Royal Academy of Sciences, for the year 1731." J.J.D. de Mairan is also remembered for his discoveries in biology, in 1729 starting the field of biology that is known today as "Circadian Biology" and was involved with the 'internal clocks' of organisms through de Mairan performing experiments with daily leaf movements of plants. In 1717 J.J.D. de Mairan wrote a thesis in which he publishes his understanding of Bioluminescence, including descriptions of the luminous jellyfish "Pulmon marine." J.J.D. de Mairan describes the cause of luminescence as a result of Sulphur being moved and separated from it's ordinary positions in nature.

Another form of luminescence that was studied during this period of time is "Thermoluminescence," which is a luminescent phenomenon in which heat acts as the activating element that is the force needed to release energy from a mineral or substance in the form of visible light. In "Fluorescent Light and It's Applications" by H.C. Dake and Jack DeMent from 1941 it is stated that probably the earliest investigations into Thermoluminescence were performed in 1726 by Du Fay, who documented that Green Fluorite, Quartz, and Calcite emit brilliant light when warmed up gently. Charles Francois de Cisternay du Fay (1698-1739) was a French chemist who is best known for his discovery of the 'negative' and 'positive' electrical charges, which he called "Vitreous" and "Resinous."

In 1728 the study of the "Bologna stone" began again, and Francesco Maria Zanotti led a group of scientists on the study of Phosphorus. Zanotti's group, along with the assistance of Bolognian naturalist and mathematician Count Luigi Ferdinando Marsigli, repeated the experiments of Zucchi from seventy-five years before with a little more flair. Zanotti concluded that the "Bologna stone" did not act merely as a 'Light-sponge,' as was generally believed, and proved this by conducting experiments such as putting two pieces of "Bologna stone" in the same room and exciting one of the pieces with the refracted Blue Color of a beam of sunlight projected through a prism, while the other piece was excited with the refracted Red Color through the prism. This experiment proved definitively that the "Bologna stone" was not a mere 'Light-sponge' because both of the pieces of "Bologna stone" Phosphoresced the same Red Color in the dark.

Another Luminescent phenomenon is "Triboluminescence," in which the mineral or substance must be physically rubbed or crushed to create visible light. This is perhaps the oldest known form of produced luminescence, discovered countless millennia ago by rubbing sticks or stones together to create sparks for fire. In "Fluorescent Light and It's Applications" by Dake and DeMent of 1941, it is documented that probably the first experiments with the Triboluminescent properties of the Fluorescent mineral "Sphalerite" were performed in 1750 by Donat Hofmann, who wrote that this mineral gave off visible light when it was crushed or broken.

Another surprising inclusion in this list of the many "Discoverers" of Fluorescence, including Bioluminescence, is a famous American President Benjamin Franklin (1706-1790). The iconic picture of Benjamin Franklin's experiment with electricity holding a line to his kite and metal key in a lightning storm is known by all school children in the U.S.A., but his studies of Bioluminescence are relatively unknown. Benjamin Franklin first believed that the 'source of lightning' was the ocean, and that lightning and the Bioluminescent lights seen in the ocean were caused by 'friction' between the particles of salt and water, which produced an 'electric fire.' In 1750 Franklin further experimented with ocean water and found that it would eventually loose it's luminescence in a bottle when shaken. Franklin also discovered that by adding sea salt to water, it would not luminesce when shaken, so he discarded his former incorrect theory of friction and salt water. In 1753 Benjamin Franklin wrote to John Bowduin, and in this correspondence Franklin proposed a cause of Bioluminescence that was actually the first *correct* explanation of Bioluminescence in history. Before Franklin, alchemists and scientists had published hypothesizes on the cause of Bioluminescence ranging from mildly bizarre to downright absurd, including the ever-popular sea salt on fire, sparks created by sea salt collisions, friction between the Earth and it's atmosphere, vulcanism, flashing of small broken ice particles, phosphorus, 'light-sponges,' and even animal putrefaction. Benjamin Franklin was the first person to realize that these Bioluminescent lights were created by 'extremely small animalcule' that were, in effect, invisible according to Franklin's description which stated innocently that these 'animalcule' would not be visible even with the 'best glasses.' The most well known and probably the most abundant Bioluminescent sea-creatures in the world are Dinoflagellates, and Benjamin Franklin was the first person to correctly conclude that the lights in the ocean were created by tiny living animals. Dinoflagellates are plants, not animals, because they are sea-plankton, but none the less they are microscopic living creatures in sea water and flash with a Bioluminescent Blue light that is much larger than their actual bodies. So after many centuries of incorrect hypothesizes, Benjamin Franklin had the insight to realize that neither electricity, fire, nor the Sun created these mysterious lights at night in the ocean, but that the light was in reality created by a living creature too small to see with the eye.

Since the vast majority of writings on the History of Fluorescence begin the timeline with Sir George Gabriel Stokes, the English scientist who named the phenomenon of Fluorescence in 1852 after intensely Fluorescent English specimens of the mineral "Fluorite," I decided to alternatively document here the most obscure and rarely documented period of Fluorescent and luminescent history which ends one hundred years before Sir George Stokes named Fluorescence. Having stated this, I also realize that no book covering the History of Fluorescence would be complete without the inclusion of Goethe and Sir George Stokes, so in short, to bring closure to this timeline, I will briefly include the essential History of Fluorescence that German scientist Johann Ritter began with his discovery of Ultraviolet in 1801 (who's credit was stolen by German philosopher Goethe), and with Sir George Stokes naming of the phenomenon of Fluorescence in 1852.

In early scientific enquiries into Fluorescence, between 1790 and 1810, the spectrum was studied by the German philosopher Goethe (1749-1832) who wrote of the phenomenon of Fluorescence without the same prejudice his writings on Color are biased with. Goethe is credited today as being the first person to record the fact that Invisible Ultraviolet energy can produce Visible Light, which we now know as the phenomenon of Fluorescence, but again, this is stolen credit. Goethe wrote that he passed a ray of sunlight through a prism, and then through this projected spectrum he moved primitive photography salts. The primitive photography salts gave little or no reaction as he moved them from Color to Color through the projected visible spectrum, but when he moved the photography salts outside of the visible spectrum of Colors and into the darkness just to the left of the Color Violet, he was amazed that these primitive photography salts gave off a 'vivid glow!' His historic conclusion was written after twenty years of study on the subject: "beyond violet" 'where hardly any color is seen, the primitive phosphor produced' "vivid brilliance..." Again, as was stated at the beginning of this chapter, this world famous experiment of Goethe's is the same experiment made by a young unknown, uncredited scientist - coincidentally, also from Germany - Johann Wilhelm Ritter (1776-1810) who discovered Ultraviolet energy in 1801 - nine full years before Goethe wrote his famous 'first' writings on Fluorescence in which he describes the experiment that Ritter made in 1801, and in which he essentially *steals* the experiment, credit, and discovery of Ultraviolet energy from the young, unknown, unaccepted Johann Ritter. Typical. It is no coincidence that Goethe's recorded period of the study of Ultraviolet ended with his historic announcement - in 1810 - the very same year that Johann Ritter died. In further retrospect, this Goethe may have been an ancient relative of the German man who created the "Gerstmann Museum" in Franklin, New Jersey, Ewald Gerstmann, and who typically stole the credit of the discovery of the mineral "Gerstmannite" from the unknown, disliked, unrespected nearly deaf ex-Franklin miner Nick Zippco, who truly did discover it. Ewald Gerstmann even typically named the mineral after himself: "Gerstmannite." I was to personally find out that this 'method of operation' was very common with the questionable characters of Franklin, New Jersey "The Fluorescent Mineral Capitol of the World," as well as with members of the "Fluorescent Mineral Society."

More advanced modern research into Fluorescence began in 1833 with Sir David Brewster (1781-1868), inventor of the Kaleidoscope, who passed a beam of Sunlight concentrated by a lens through an alcohol solution of Chlorophyl contained in a glass pot. The Color of the light after it left the solution was the same Green Color as the solution, but the Color of the line it made through the solution was bight Red. Assuming the phenomenon was caused by solid particles held in suspension by the liquid, Brewster called the phenomenon "Internal Dispersion." He also obtained similar results with Fluorite and other substances. Through these early experiments by Sir David Brewster in the early 1800s, Fluorescence first became known to the modern scientific world.

Twelve years later in 1845, Sir John Herschel (1815-1879) found that when a solution of Quinine bisulphate with a small amount of Sulphuric acid was viewed in a beam of Sunlight, the solution remained Colorless. except for the thin layer at the top of the solution which emitted a beautiful Sky-Blue light. Because of this top layer in the solution of brilliant Sky-Blue light, Herschel named the phenomenon "Epipolic Dispersion" (surface dispersion).

After the ground breaking experiments of Brewster and Herschel, in 1852 Sir George Gabriel Stokes (1819-1903) came to the conclusion that the facts observed through the previous two researchers could have the same cause, the only difference being the effect produced by the medium that the rays passed through. First Stokes thought it could be caused by polarization, but soon he realized it could be due to the change of the "refrangibility" (refraction) of light. To test this, Stokes projected a beam of sunlight into a darkened room, then he placed a prism into the beam of sunlight and produced the spectrum into which he began to move a solution of Quinine bisulphate through, Color-by-Color. No change occurred until he reached about the middle of the Color Violet, when a Bluish light began to appear, as if the solution of Quinine bisulphate at that point of the spectrum became self-luminous. The Blue Color became more intense as the Quinine Bisulphate was moved further into the Violet light and continued to emit Blue light until the solution of Quinine bisulphate was moved far past the Violet and into the dark. This experiment demonstrated to Stokes that by passing light through a particular medium, "certain invisible rays" which belong to the Color Violet have their refraction changed so dramatically that these "invisible rays" become Visible Light - Colors.

For his most famous experiment, the study of the Fluorescence of the mineral Fluorite in 1852, which effects had first been scientifically recorded in 1824, Stokes again projected a ray of sunlight into a darkened room. For this experiment he placed into the beam of sunlight not a jar containing a solution of Quinine bisulphate, but a clear, Colorless English specimen of the mineral Fluorite, which is the Fluorspar mineral Calcium fluoride. When the beam of Sunlight entered the crystal of Fluorite, the clear Colorless Fluorite emitted a brilliant Blue light. By 1852, the name for Fluorescence was "True Inner Dispersion" which Stokes disliked, and because of the fact that the Fluorite crystal displayed the phenomenon so intensely, he suggested the name "Fluorescence." Sir George Stokes was far from the first person to discover Fluorescence, but he was the person to name the phenomenon.

In "Aglow in the Dark" by Vincent Pieribone and David F. Gruber the experiments of Sir George Gabriel Stokes are explained in detail. As a mathematics professor in Cambridge University, Stokes made an Optics laboratory in his house. The method of experimentation used for the historic experiments Stokes performed involving sunlight's reaction on 'Quinine Bisulfate,' later on the prism, and inclusively his famous studies on the Fluorescent mineral Fluorite, were described in his one hundred page paper of 1852, "On the change of the Refrangibility of Light." This paper by Stokes is described by E. Newton Harvey in "A History of Luminescence" as amongst the 'most complete' in the entire physics history, and this came from a man who wrote the largest, most complete book on luminescence ever published at that time, a full six hundred and ninety-two pages. In this paper, Stokes described his understanding that the Fluorspar (Fluorite) crystal that he had placed in the ray of sunlight through his window shutter was actually emitting light, which was properly termed at the time "True Internal Dispersion," and was definitely different from just the mere scattering of light, like smoke in the air, which was termed "False Internal Dispersion." In this 1852 paper Stokes used the term "Dispersive Reflection" in an attempt to make the name of this new phenomenon more understandable, but finally Stokes wrote that he disliked all these complicated names used in the 1800s, so he decided to coin a word "Fluorescence," derived form the brilliant display of the phenomenon displayed by the mineral Fluorite, with regards to the similar use of the word "Opalescence" describing the optical property of the Opal. In this 1852 paper Stokes also described the "spark" as a source of Ultraviolet energy, and in doing so predated by fifty-one years the technology of the first Ultraviolet producing contraption called a "Spark Box."

For Sir George Stokes famous experiments with the Ultraviolet components of sunlight effecting solid and liquid objects, Stokes sawed a four inch hole (10 cm) in a window shutter of his dark room, which he commented that the hole could have been 'still larger' to be better. Next Stokes screwed a small shelf 'blackened on top' to the window shutter, directly underneath the four inch hole, which Stokes designed to hold the items to be examined in the sunlight passing through this shutter hole. Stokes added in his paper that the only other scientific equipment that was needed to perform experiments using this rudimentary ingenious design were a few pieces of 'colored glasses,' a small White porcelain 'tablet,' an 'ordinary prism,' and one or two jars to hold fluids. Through his studies of optical properties, Stokes also answered a question that had been asked since time began: "Why is the sky Blue?" In his paper "Dynamical Theory of Diffraction," Stokes described for the first time that the Color of the sky is Blue because as light moves through the atmosphere of the Earth the longer wavelengths of light including Red, Orange, and Yellow pass straight through the air, but the shorter wavelengths of light including Blue are absorbed by molecules of gas in the atmosphere and scattered in all different directions, hence when we look up at the sky we see the Color of the Blue light which has been scattered.

In the optics laboratory in his house, Stokes made a discovery that changed the understanding of science on April 28, 1852. Experimenting with Quinine bisulphate and sunlight through the four inch hole he had made in his window shutter, Stokes first put a piece of Red stained glass over the hole in his shutters and concluded that only Red Color passed through the Red glass because the stained glass absorbs most of the Colors and only lets through the light that is the Color of the glass. On April 28, 1852, Stokes Stokes experimented with a Blue colored piece of glass over his shutter hole, which projected Blue light into the darkened room. Next Stokes took a glass of Yellow-Colored solution of "Quinone," which is a plant chemical that is Fluorescent, and placed it into the beam of Blue colored light - and it shockingly created a Yellow glow in the Quinone solution! These are the seldom published small details of the famous experiments of Sir George Stokes that led to his naming of the phenomenon "Fluorescence" in 1852.

During this time period the Becquerel family in France made much progress in the field of Fluorescence as well, going back to the late 1800s. Antoine Becquerel and his son Edmond measured the spectrum of Fluorescent light emitted by minerals under different wavelengths. Edmond also discovered "Activators," realizing that a tiny amount (one part per four-thousand) of an impurity Manganese was the cause of the Red Fluorescence of the mineral Calcite, and he later invented the "Phosphoroscope" to measure duration of Phosphorescence. Again, this was all achieved without the modern aids of electricity or lights. Edmond Becquerel's son Henri is credited with the discovery of Radioactivity which he observed and documented after placing a specimen of the mineral Uranium on an unexposed photography plate.

An extremely rare (and just as obscure) publication from 1896 has references to very early experiments with Black light and Black light photography: "The London, Edinburgh and Dublin Philosophical magazine and journal of Science" from Taylor and Francis. In the thirtieth section "Intelligence and Miscellaneous articles" of this rare publication from 115 years ago there is an article named clearly "BLACK LIGHT" written by M. Gustave Le Bon. Le Bon writes about very early ("recent") Black light experiments with photography employing the use of the primitive Cathode ray, which Le Bon refers to as "Light" having "Kathodic origin." This was apparently the first time "Black Light" was used as a term in print: 1896 by M. Gustave Le Bon, a French sociologist. In this 1896 "Philosophical magazine and journal of Science," Le Bon wrote that "Black" invisible light which passed through a steel plated box from an oil lamp could expose a photographic plate completely. Admittedly alot of his conclusions were bizarre at best, including his belief that humans could look through walls if the eye was constructed different than it is, because 'opacity only exists for human eyes, not light,' but Le Bon did introduce the term "Black light" through this 1896 publication.

This point in time, the late 1800s, before the dawn of the Twentieth century, is the starting point for many well-documented studies of the history of Fluorescence, and precisely for this reason I will end this timeline here. The subject of this chapter is "The First Discoveries of Fluorescence and Luminescence - 1,500 B.C.- 1750: From China to Benjamin Franklin" and was intended to bring light to the 'Pre-History' of Fluorescence, the period before Sir George Stokes famously named the phenomenon in 1852.

2. The First Paint to Emit it's own Light: "Robert Switzer, "Day-Glo" Paint: 1933

The prior chapter dealt with the 'Classical' history of the phenomenon of Fluorescence, but here begins the 'Contemporary' history - the modern era of the history of Fluorescence. Dr. Robert Wood (1868-1955), an American physicist, began the modern era of Fluorescence by inventing the Ultraviolet Filter, and should today be credited with the uncredited invention of the Black light (the "invention" of the Black light has been credited by 'Internet scholars' to the man who did not invent the Black light, but did patent the Black light in 1935, William Byler). Dr. Robert Wood announced the invention of the Ultraviolet Filter in February, 1903, and this filter was made with Nitroso-aniline, which Dr. Wood went on to improve upon by adding the dye Uranine, because his first filter also allowed visible Blue light through as well as the invisible Longwave Ultraviolet. Dr. Wood again improved the Longwave Ultraviolet filter he had invented by using a new glass mixture of Barium Sodium Silicate with nine percent Oxidized Nickel. Today over 110 years later the Longwave Ultraviolet filter and even the Black light itself is sometimes still referred to as "Wood's Glass." This filter allowed Fluorescence to be seen through a small hole when a box with "Wood's Glass" fitted into it's top was put out into the Sun. The "Wood's Glass" Ultraviolet filter blocked out all rays of light and energy from the Sun except the Longwave Ultraviolet energy that comes through the Ozone layer and reaches the surface of the Earth. This allowed Fluorescence to be observed in a mineral, or other Fluorescent substances, when the box fitted with a light-tight Ultraviolet filter was put out into the Sun. This is one of the first Ultraviolet devices, which was created by Dr. Wood around 1903 and is known as the "Ultraviolet Viewing Box." In the 1938 French first edition of "Les Applications Practiques de la Luminescence" by Maurice Deribere there is an illustration of a model of this 'Longwave Ultraviolet Filter Instrument' that was also manufactured in France and was named "La Callophane." This French Ultraviolet Instrument is explained as being a small device that could be used with sunlight or with any other source of Ultraviolet energy. The illustration shows a man with a wooden triangular three-dimensional instrument that he is looking into, and which is completely covering the front of his face. It is explained that the full hinge on the front of the instrument allowed the unfolding of the device, which became a triangular structure with a base inside and a 'Woods' Longwave Ultraviolet filter built into the top of this small device. Judging from the illustration, it appears that the instrument was designed to view into with both eyes. What "La Callophane" looked like, in short, was large triangular wooden binoculars.

Dr. Robert Wood also became the first person to publish Infrared photographs he had taken on experimental film in 1910, and he was also the first person to publish photographs of Fluorescence in October, 1910. The first photograph ever taken in the Black light was a self-portrait of Dr. Wood's highly Fluorescent Teeth and Eyes! The technique Dr. Wood first developed for photography of the Fluorescence of his face and hands was the utilization of an Ultraviolet filter on the light source, as well as a Yellow-Colored "Barrier" Filter on the camera lens itself to block Ultraviolet from entering the lens of the camera and fogging the film. This photographic setup, almost one hundred years later, is precisely the same technique that I use to photograph Fluorescent minerals in the Twenty-first century, and would be nothing less than a revelation to most photographers today, including the Brooklyn based photographer who published a pure Violet-Red "Ultraviolet Photograph" of a Parrot in National Geographic magazine in 2011, while leading many millions of readers to believe that this is what a Parrot looks like while Fluorescing under harmless Longwave Ultraviolet energy contained in sunlight that reaches the surface of the Earth. This photographer also hams it up by *covering his eyes* while taking this incorrect photograph, again misleading millions of readers with the *incorrect* fact 'that Longwave Ultraviolet is harmful.' After being a member of "National Geographic" since the 1960s, I wrote a long letter including true, scientifically-accurate photographs of Fluorescing birds to the magazine, but not surprisingly never received an answer back.

Next, an early mechanical device for producing Ultraviolet energy was also produced in 1903 and was called a "Spark Box" or "Iron Arc." The "Iron Arc" lamp had been invented in the late 1800s already as an early experimental medical therapy lamp which will be discussed later. The "Spark Box" was a clumsy device that consisted of a wooden box with a generator inside of it capable of producing 9,000 volts of electricity. This 9,000 volts of electricity was passed through a tiny gap between two iron bolts in a small round unit at the front of the Spark Box, which proceeded to create a massive spark that contained many different wavelengths of energy, including Ultraviolet. When a Fluorescent mineral was placed underneath the massive spark of the unit, a slight amount of Fluorescence could be observed. This Spark Box was produced for the purpose of mineral identification in northern New Jersey, "The Fluorescent Mineral Capital of the World," where mining went on from 1852 until 1986 for Zinc, most famously the Zinc ore "Willemite" which Fluoresces brilliant Green when under an Ultraviolet lamp. In the late 1990s I personally have seen in operation, photographed, and placed a super-rare Fluorescent mineral under the spark of possibly the last still functioning Spark Box, which is in a private collection in Manhattan. During the decades following 1903, the technology of Ultraviolet production advanced rapidly with numerous new inventions leading to what is

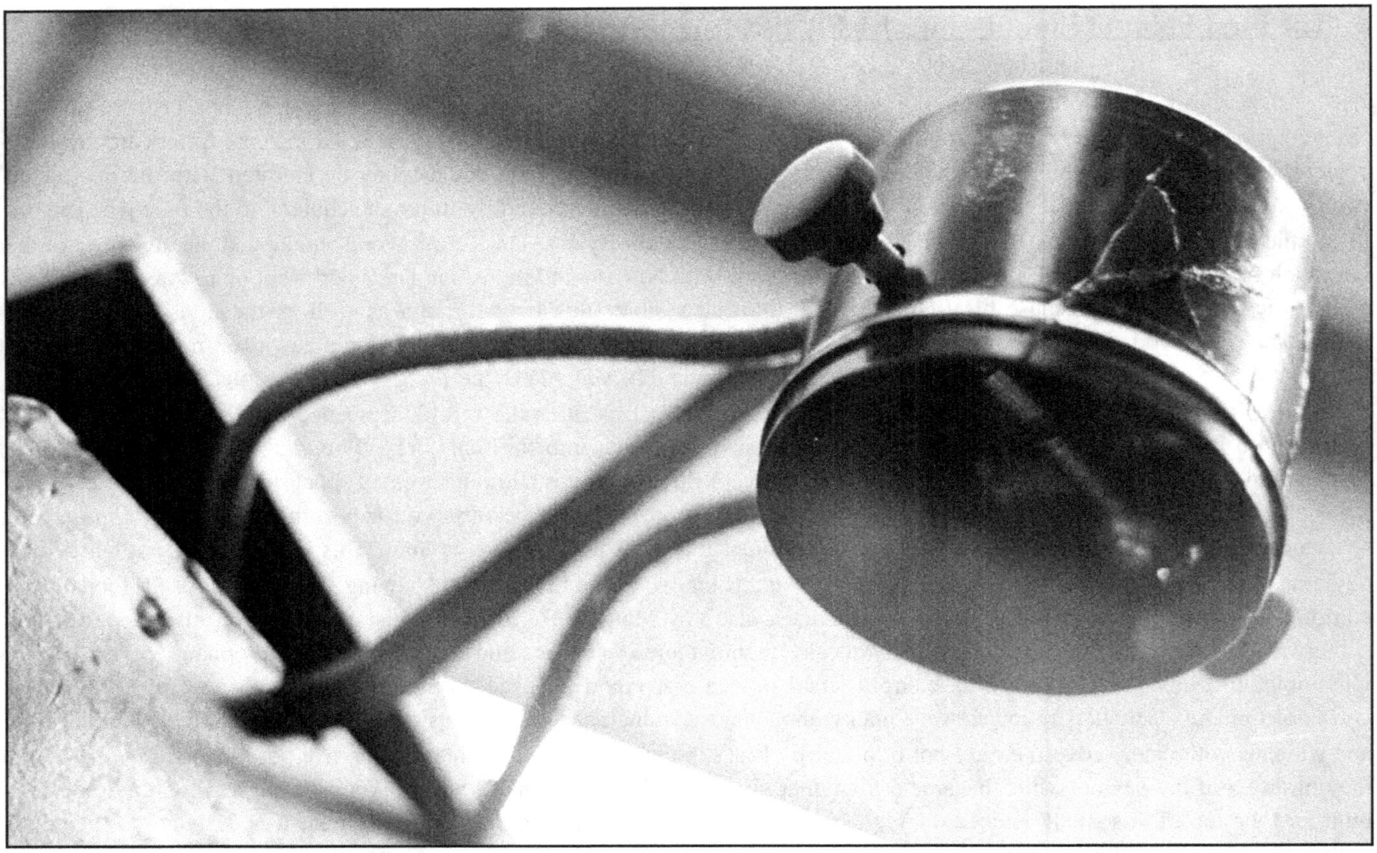

1903: The "Spark Box" or "Iron Arc Lamp," one of the first Ultraviolet-producing mechanical device (close-up)

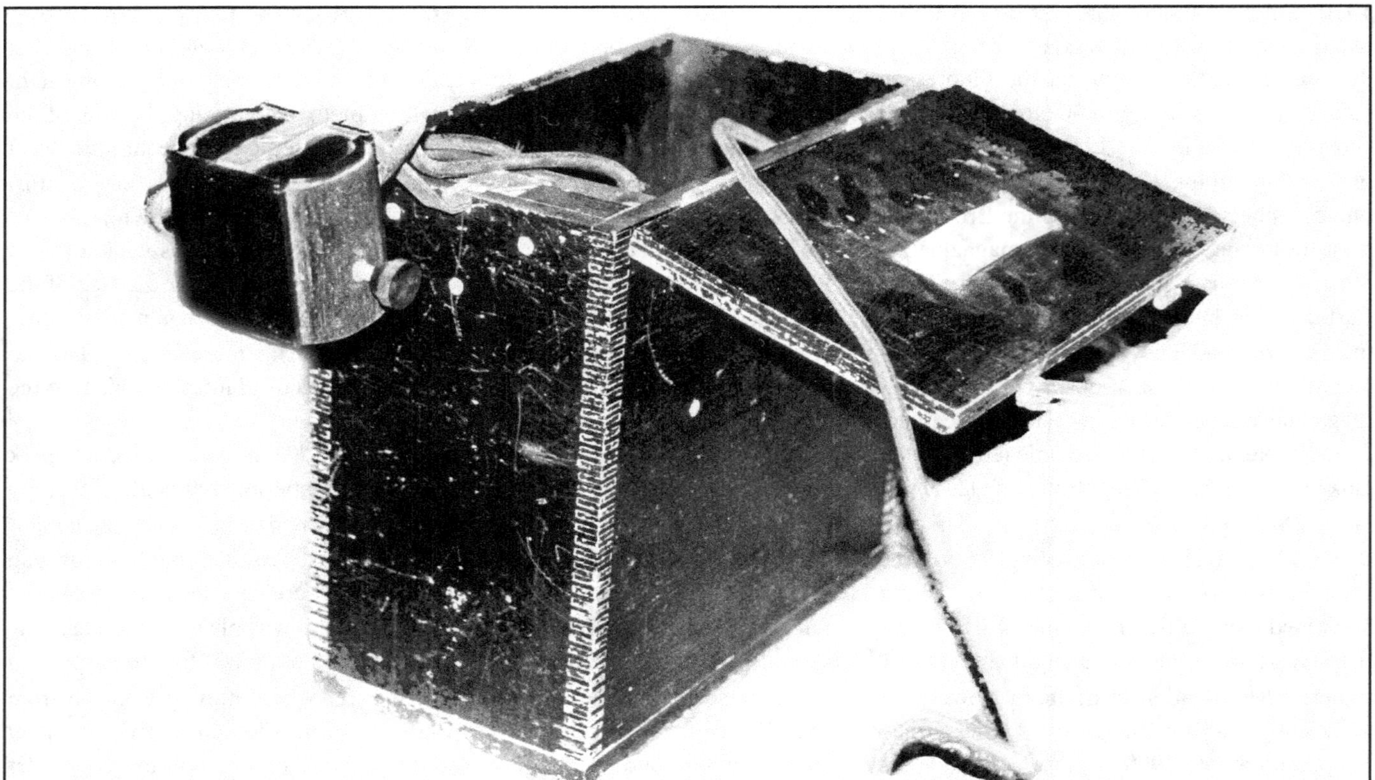

1903: The "Spark Box" or "Iron Arc Lamp," one of the first Ultraviolet-producing mechanical device

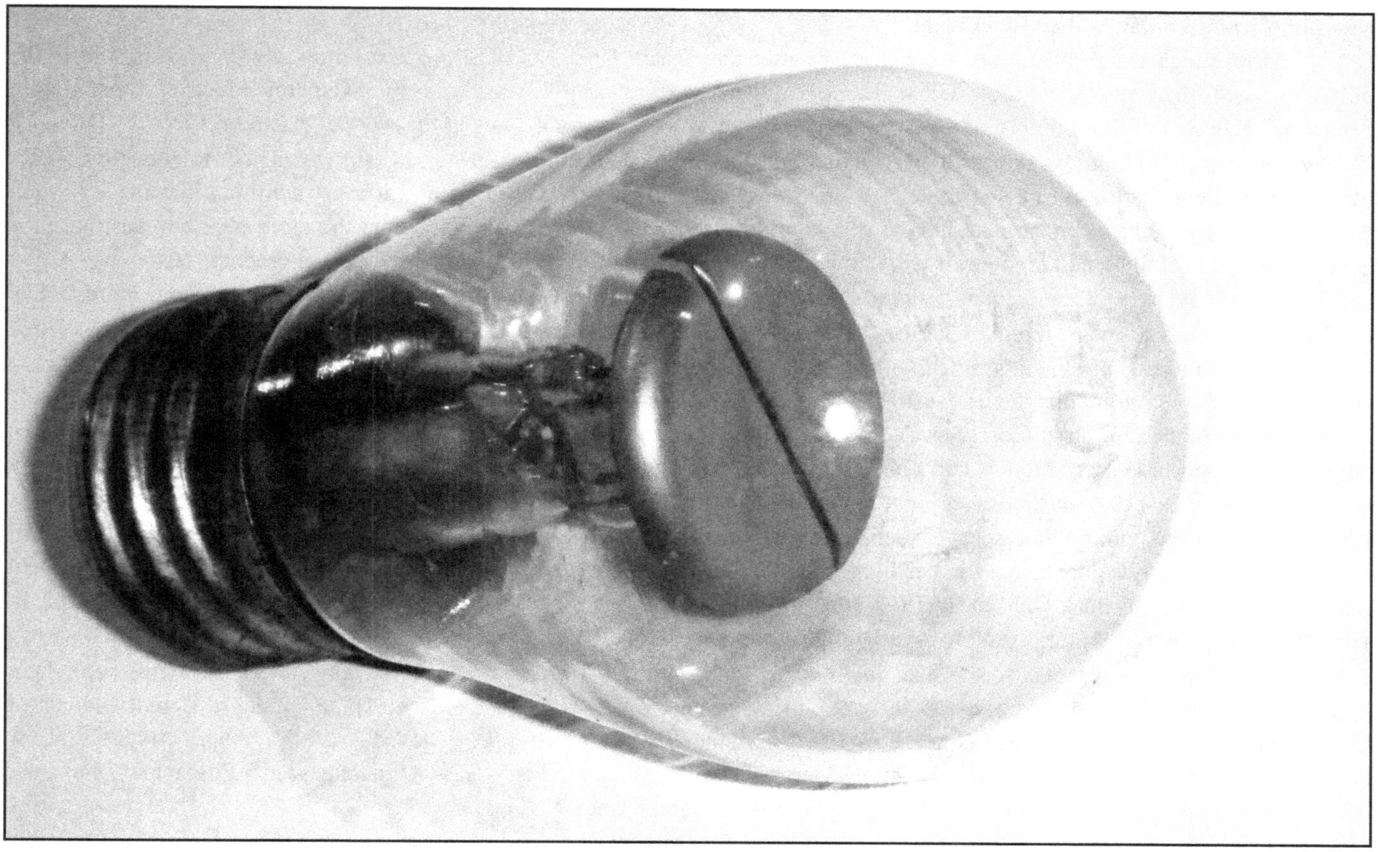

1915: The "Argon Bulb" or "Argon Glow Lamp" was the first Ultraviolet lamp sold to the public

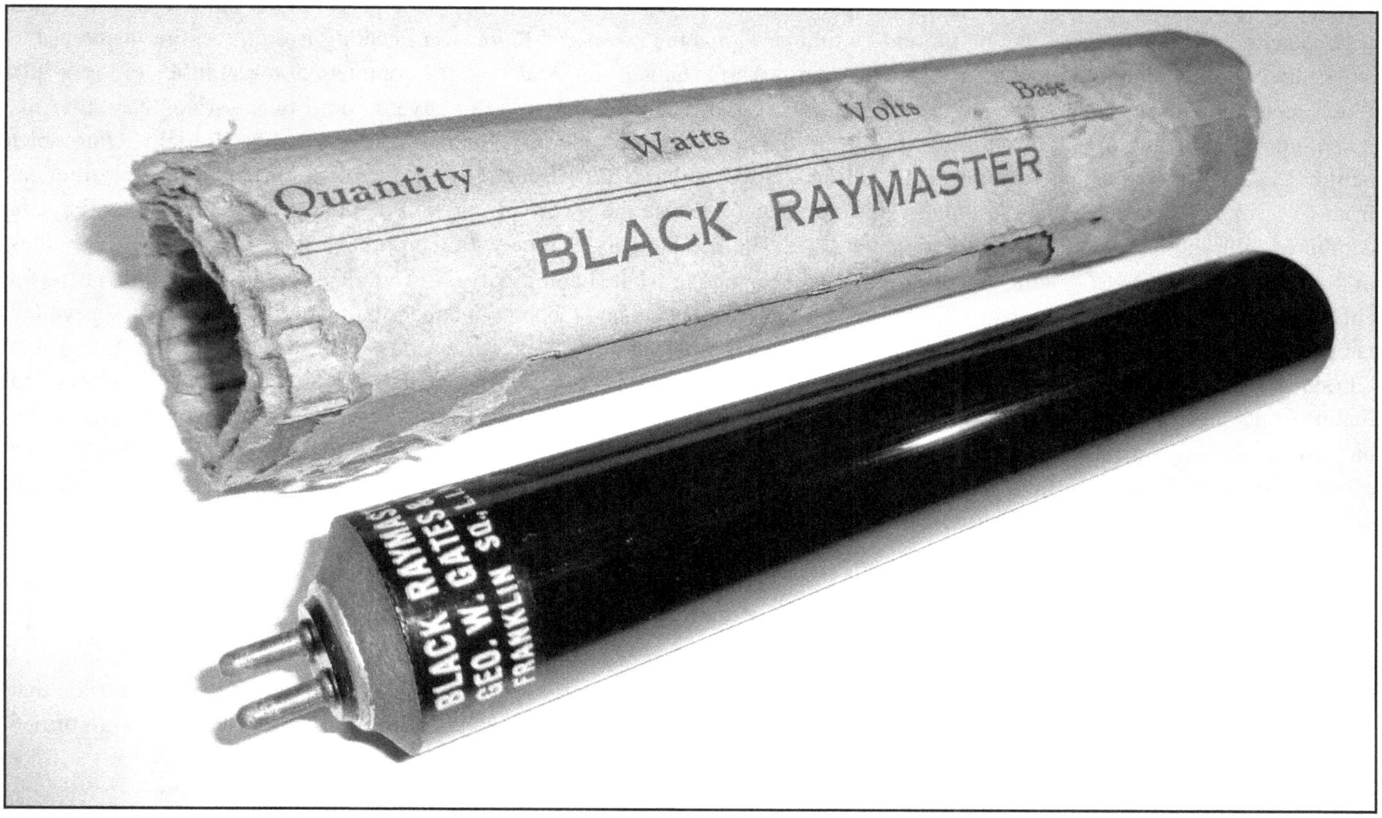

1920s - 1930s: The "NICO Tube" was the first common tubular "Black light" or "Wood's Lamp"

commonly known today as the "Black light."

After much experimentation, a dozen years after the "Spark Box," in 1915 the first Ultraviolet lamp was sold to the public, known then as an "Argon Glow Lamp." This 'Argon Bulb' was sold by "General Electric Vapor Lamp Company" (GEVL) of San Francisco, today one of the biggest electrical companies in the world: "General Electric" ("G.E."). This was a small bulb that was only two and a half watts and produced a Purple glow and Longwave Ultraviolet energy. After years of searching there are three of these 'Argon Bulbs' in the Museum collection and it must admitted that these 'Argon Bulbs' were convenient, compact, and have a very long life (these three bulbs still work), but the main problem was that they gave off only a pitifully small amount of two and a half watts of Longwave Ultraviolet energy, so in practical terms the 'Argon Bulb' must be held very close (6 inches/10 cm.) from the Fluorescent substance to be able to observe just a dim Fluorescence. In a "Popular Science" magazine in 1939, there is a photograph of a 'Fluorescent Museum' which consisted of a tiny box filled with pieces of Fluorescent minerals, fitted with a total of six 'Argon Bulbs' that were mounted only about 3-4 inches (7-10 cm.) above the Fluorescent minerals themselves. The "Argon Glow Lamp" was too weak and had to be held extremely close to the Fluorescent substance for any Fluorescence to be observed. The first real "Black Lights" were produced in the 1920s, after the perfecting of the Fluorescent tubular lamp in 1912 by W.S. Andrews. In "Fluorescent Light and It's Applications" of 1941 by H.C. Dake and Jack DeMent, there is a photograph of this early Fluorescent tubular lamp made in 1912, which was called an 'Early Vacuum Tube with a Fluorescent Screen,' and appears as a thick clear glass tube with two small Black ends sealing it off. Before Andrew's early 'Fluorescent tubular light' there had been much experimentation for over eighty years. In "Fluorescent Gems and Minerals" by Jack DeMent in 1949, there is a short history of the earliest days of the Fluorescent tubular lamp. In 1835 Wheatstone was the first person to create a light source by passing an electrical charge through Mercury vapor. Between 1852 and 1867 several patents were issued in England for 'Enclosed Mercury Vapor Arc' lamps. These lamps were later improved by the addition of electrodes made of solid metal and also Mercury. DeMent explains many different sources of Ultraviolet energy in his book, including the "Spark Box," the "Open Arc" and the "Closed Arc," the "Vapor Arc," the "Low Pressure Mercury Arc," the "High Pressure Mercury Arc," "Incandescent Gas," "Incandescent Filament," the Sun, "Corpuscular Radiation," "Cathode Ray Tubes," "Ultraviolet Lights," and "X-Rays."

The only similarity with this early 1912 Andrews Fluorescent lamp and the standard Fluorescent lamps used today is pretty much the tubular glass. The method that W.S. Andrews created this early Fluorescent lamp was to powder the Fluorescent material to be used in the lamp and then to coat it on a metal cylinder inside the glass tubular lamp. The difference with today's Fluorescent lamps is that in modern tubular lamps the powdered Fluorescent coating is on the entire inside of the glass tube, not just on a metal cylinder inside the lamp. Unfortunately for Andrews, the commercial possibilities of the White Fluorescent tubular lamp, which is standard lighting across the planet today, did not develop until twenty-five years after his invention. This technology, however, was the key to the original and modern production of Black lights. Initially, Ultraviolet lamps - "Black lights" - which were also called "Blacklights" at that time, were made by fitting dark Purple Ultraviolet filters in front of "Iron-arc" lamps, but these units were impractical because they were heavy, hot, and had a very short operating life combined with the fact that they were very expensive. The break through came with the production of the first "NICO" tubes in the 1920s. These "NICO" lamps were similar in appearance to what is commonly known today as a "Black lights." It was a cold cathode tubular Fluorescent lamp that was produced with Nickel and Cobalt contained in the tubular glass, which gave the lamp it's name "NICO." This "NICO" Black Light blocked out almost all energy emitted from the lamp except Longwave Ultraviolet, and gave the lamp it's signatory 'Black' Color when turned off. The very first "NICO" tubes were a contraption that most people couldn't imagine today, called a "Tilt-Lamp." Although the "Argon Glow Lamps" used Argon gas inside the bulb to cause the reaction which produces only Ultraviolet energy and has no need for a filter, these new "NICO" lamps used Mercury gas inside the lamp tube which allowed them to be much more powerful, but Mercury gas produces many different wavelengths which gave need for the Black "NICO" Filter. The problem with the first "NICO" lamps called "Tilt-Lamps" was that these lamps were manufactured with liquid Mercury instead of Mercury gas, which would be used in all future "NICO" lamps and "Black lights." Liquid Mercury in the long tubular lamp meant that when you plugged in the lamp only half the lamp lit up. The reason these lamps were called "Tilt-Lamps" was because you had to physically *tilt* the lamp so that the unlit half of the lamp was towards the floor which allowed the liquid Mercury inside the lamp to physically flow down the inside of the tubular lamp and then the unlit half of the lamp also lit up. It doesn't take much imagination to come to the conclusion that these lamps were nearly impossible to use in Fluorescent displays. Every time the numerous "NICO Tilt-Lamps" were turned on in a Fluorescent display, each and every one of the lamps would have to be turned on and physically tilted towards the floor for these lamps to completely light up! Soon after this, realizing these "NICO Tilt-Lamp's" impracticality, Mercury gas was substituted for the liquid Mercury, and since then there is no need for tilting your "Black light" to light it up(!) These first real

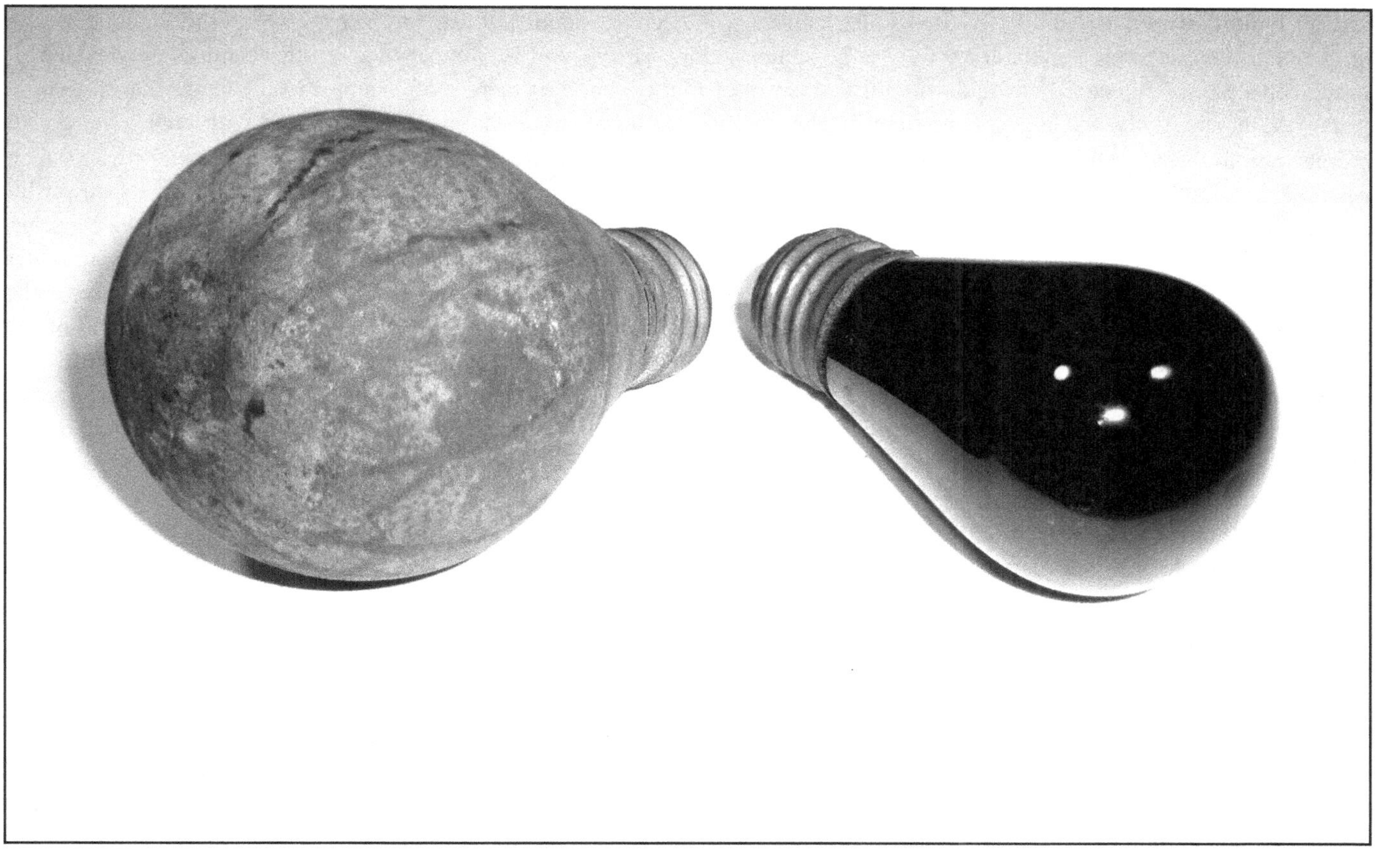

1930s: Early "Black light" bulbs also called "PurpleX" and "The Magic Wonder Lamp"

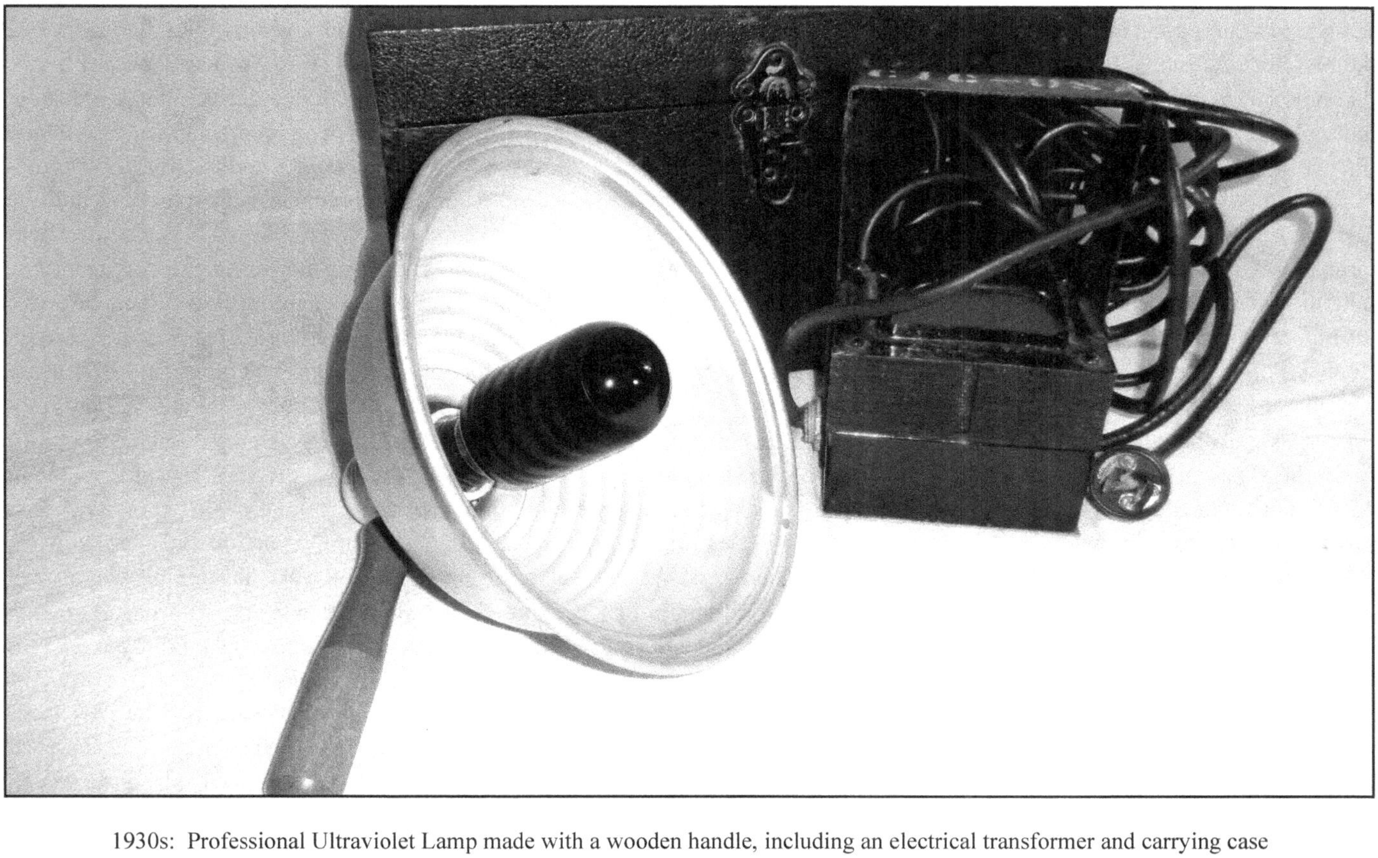

1930s: Professional Ultraviolet Lamp made with a wooden handle, including an electrical transformer and carrying case

"NICO Lamps" were very similar to today's Black lights with Mercury vapor in them and being very cool to the touch. The problem with these lamps was that they were large, clumsy, slow starting, and very expensive, so other lamps were developed. In the collection of "Electric Ladyland - the First Museum of Fluorescent Art" there is an example of the lamps that were used in the 1930s and 1940s for large Fluorescent displays as well as installations like in Movie theaters with hugh Fluorescent murals, and in theaters all over America and Europe, including the famous "Radio City Music Hall" in New York City which held Black light "Skeleton Ballets" in the 1920s! These Ultraviolet lamps were much more compact and extremely powerful, but they operated at such a scalding temperature that they created fire hazards in public displays. The lamp in the Museum collection is a perfect example of these limitations, being a "Switzer Brothers, Inc." "Model 70" 250 watt flood lamp unit that was manufactured in the late 1930s and 1940s, and was used in hugh displays. The lamp is about two feet tall (65 cm), weighs almost twenty-five pounds (11 kilos) and has a tremendous bulb in it that causes the 1930s complete iron construction of the lamp to become hot enough to fry an egg on (or burn the skin off your fingers). Obviously these created alot of problems when concealed in small spaces to hide the lighting unit itself, such as fires. These hugh lamps were extremely powerful and great sources of produced Ultraviolet for Fluorescent installations, but high operating temperature was a draw back that could not be overcome. As the "NICO" tubes progressed, they became smaller and much less expensive, so the uses of the heavy, very powerful, and extremely dangerous lamps faded out and were replaced by what is still used and called today "Black lights." In the Museum collection are also three normal screw-in bulbs that were produced in the 1930s and called exotic names such as: "PurpleX," "The Magic Wonder Lamp," and even "Black Lights," but as with similar screw-in bulbs called "Black Lights" of the 1960s and 1970s, incandescent bulbs produce almost no Ultraviolet, so the filter of the screw-in so-called "Black lights" emits almost only visible Violet light, and very little invisible Ultraviolet energy. This is the reason why those screw-in "Black lights" create such a Purple haze, because they are emitting visible Violet light, which does indeed cause sensitive synthetic Fluorescent paint and posters to Fluoresce, but with no comparison to the intensity of Fluorescence emitted by Fluorescent paints and inks under tubular Black lights which emit ninety-seven percent of their energy as invisible Longwave Ultraviolet energy, and only three percent as visible Violet or Blue-Purple light. This historical background of Black lights is included here to give a perspective of the Ultraviolet situation at the time when the first Fluorescent paint was invented and used in the first public displays.

Regarding the actual invention of Fluorescent paint, I have personally heard many undocumented claims in the last twenty-nine years running "Electric Lady" Art Gallery, and even more claims in the last seventeen years operating "Electric Ladyland - the First Museum of Fluorescent Art." The earliest claim was that Dr. Robert Wood invented both the Longwave Ultraviolet filter and Fluorescent paint in 1896. Tracking down and buying the book "Doctor Wood Modern Wizard of the Laboratory" of 1941, and even the 1941 "Time" magazine with Dr. Wood on the cover, there is not one documented word about not only Dr. Wood inventing Fluorescent paint in 1896, but about Fluorescent paint at all. The only documentation of Dr. Wood inventing the Ultraviolet filter states February, 1903 as the date, also. Next, in telephone conversations and letters from Thomas S. Warren, who founded "Ultra-Violet Products, Inc." in California in 1932, and whom I had contact with from 1993 until he died in 1999, Mr. Warren told me that: "Mr. Shannon, founder of "Shannon Luminous materials, Inc." made what was probably the first Fluorescent paints in the 1920s and 1930s. These paints were Longwave U.V. Fluorescent paints - something like today's Fluorescent paints. Around the same time, a man in New York and a woman in Chicago developed their own line of Fluorescent paints." After years of researching and searching in general, I also have found that these facts were not correct. John ("Pop") Thompson Shannon was working with developing Fluorescence for the first Ziegfeld Follies in 1907, using Carbon-arc Black lights, and in 1912 he joined "Keese Engineering Company" which he later made "Shannon Luminous Materials, Inc.," but the fact of the matter is that he did not invent Fluorescent paint. In fact, Johnny Shannon, as he was known when he was with the "General Electric Vapor Lamp, Inc." company in the early 1930s, became the very first distributor of "Northern Light Studios" Fluorescent paint made by the "Switzer Brothers" who later became the "Day-Glo" company. Bob Switzer worked together with Johnny Shannon in 1934 in Los Angeles to produce a Fluorescent "Pygmalion-Galatea" show for the Beverly Hills Chamber of commerce. The man Thomas S. Warren was referring to in New York developing Fluorescent paints in the 1920s was most likely Alexander Strobl, the founder of "Stroblite Company" in New York, who began making Fluorescent displays in 1924. What must be clarified at this point is that Robert Switzer, founder of the "Day-Glo" company is credited as inventing the first Fluorescent paint, not Phosphorescent paint. Phosphorescent paint ("glow-in-the-dark") was invented over 1,000 years ago in most probably Japan. This Phosphorescent paint is the paint that was used by Alexander Strobl in New York going back to 1924, and also by Johnny Shannon going all the way back to 1907 for the first Ziegfeld Follies. In the "Boxoffice" magazine of Aug. 24, 1935, there is an article by Alexander Strobl called "Spectacular Effects with Invisible U.V. Lighting" which contains two photos of a "Skeleton Ballet" being performed at Radio City Music Hall in New

York, which was comprised of thirty female dancers dressed in Black costumes with Phosphorescent skeletons painted on them, performing on a darkened stage under Black lights. In an even more obscure magazine "Boxoffice Barometer" of 1939, there is a small advertisement for "Stroblite Co." that reads simply "Luminous Colors that Glow in the Dark. Sensational Costumes and Scenic Effects." In this magazine is also the section "The Modern Theatre" with a directory of services and merchandise for theaters in 1939. At that date there were only three listings under the professional directory section "Black Light Murals:" "Stroblite Co." of New York, "Switzer Brothers, Inc." in Ohio, and "Ultra-Violet Products, Inc." of California. By 1940 the number of companies that were listed as dealers of "Black light equipment and materials" had increased, documented in a very obscure trade publication Bert Hensen's "Juggling Reviews" of Oakland, California on Feb. 11, 1940. According to this "Juggling Reviews," by early 1940 the Black light companies were: "Black Light Products" in Chicago, "Montandon Magic" in Oklahoma, "New Jersey Zinc Co." with a New York office, "Switzer Brothers" in Cleveland, Ohio, and "Stroblite Co." in New York City.

The person that is credited with the actual Invention of Fluorescent Paint in many books and publications, on a voluminous amounts of websites, and also by "The New York Times," is Robert Switzer, the teenager who mixed up his first batch of Fluorescent paint in 1933. Like so many profound discoveries, the invention of Fluorescent paint by Robert C. Switzer in 1933 was the end result of a serious accident and a life changing event. "The Story of Switzer Brothers Day-Glo" by Liesa Bing in 1991 is the only publication that fully documents the invention and history of Fluorescent paint in a comprehensive and scholarly fashion. This book, as well as all future books or documentations of the Switzer Brothers Fluorescent paint history, must be indebted to Liesa Bing's book "The Story of Switzer Brothers Day-Glo."

Emmet and Maude Switzer had four children born in Fromberg, Montana. Their first child was a daughter, followed by three sons, Robert born in 1914 and Joseph born in 1915. Fred was the youngest child. In 1930 the family moved to California with thoughts of the education of their young children. In 1931 Emmet Switzer, who was a pharmacist, bought a Pharmacy in Berkley, California.

In 1932 Robert Switzer graduated from Berkley High School and with a Scarfe Scholarship he began to study medicine at the University of California. As a pre-med student, at the age of nineteen in 1933 during the middle of the great Depression in America, Robert Switzer needed the best paying job he could find, because of his studies in pre-med and also because his family needed money with business not being the best in his father's Pharmacy. Turning down offered jobs paying just ten cents an hour, the young pre-med student Robert Switzer found a sampling job with the "Heinz Company" (the famous ketchup) quality control lab paying twenty-five cents an hour. For his quality control job with "Heinz," he had to sample incoming shipments of their products. Robert Switzer would open up train freight cars, and then climb up on top of a high load of bottled products to sample them. On August 16, 1933, Switzer was found unconscious and seriously injured beneath collapsed wooden crates that had contained a full load of bottled "Heinz" products. Still a teenager at age nineteen, Robert Switzer was rushed to the hospital and had both a scull fracture and internal bleeding that were severe, along with the additional brain damage and extreme memory loss, double vision, his left eye wasn't coordinated with his right eye anymore, and to make matters worse, Robert Switzer's left optic nerve was severed partially. Robert Switzer remembered waking up in the hospital and looking in the mirror at his very swollen eyes which he described looking like tomatoes. For the young man's treatment, the doctors prescribed convalescing in the dark for a period of half a year.

Into the story now enters Joe Switzer, Robert's brother who was a year younger and had graduated high school a year after Robert, celebrated as an 'accomplished Magician' having already performed magic acts in front of school, church, and other public audiences with his own stage name "Kleeland the Magician." Studying famous magicians, Joe became interested in "Black Art" which were magic tricks performed on a dark stage utilizing Phosphorescent "Glow-in-the-dark" stage props to amaze audiences and had been famous for decades already in 1933. During Robert Switzer's six month convalescence in the dark, Joe and his father built a darkroom in the basement where Robert could experiment in photography techniques and also with "Black Lights" and different Fluorescent substances. Joe had found information on early "Black Lights" and had bought dark Purple "Ultra-Violet" Filters that could be mounted in front of a powerful iron-arc lamp, producing strong Longwave Ultraviolet emission that would greatly improve the illusions in the dark during a magic show. Then the two Switzer brothers built their first portable Black light, and made an experiment that is most commonly stated as the 'Discovery of Fluorescent Paint' by the Switzer brothers. Robert and Joe Switzer, who were still teenagers at this point, brought their first portable Black light into their father's Pharmacy and discovered many Fluorescent chemicals, including "Murine" eye wash that could be used on plain paper which would cause it to Fluoresce a strong Yellow-White. Next, Robert and Joe inspected chemical store rooms in San Francisco and in the University of California, discovering several naturally Fluorescent organic compounds vividly Fluorescing under their portable Black light. They used these natural Fluorescent dyes to produce their first primitive

Fluorescent paints by adding them together with alcohol solutions of White shellac. Adding Colorless hydrocarbons like Anthracenes to the paint mixture produced the Switzer brother's first "Invisible" White, Blue, and Green paints. "Invisible" Fluorescent paints react with vivid emission of Colors only when placed under a Black light. When they are not under a Black light they are Colorless, Beige or White, hence the name "Invisible." These facts are presented as the invention of Fluorescent paint by many sources, including "The Robert and Patricia Switzer Foundation" website and the book "The Story of Switzer Magic Day-Glo" by Liesa Bing.

During the six months of convalescing in the dark, Robert Switzer also began experimenting with the "Black Light" that he had constructed with his brother Joe the magician. In 1933 Fluorescent Minerals had already been identified under different sources of Ultraviolet for almost thirty years at that point, and Robert Switzer studied these Fluorescent minerals in his basement "darkroom" under the "Black Light." According to different sources, including "The Guardian" (an English newspaper) and several internet reference sources, Robert Switzer mixed up his first batch of Fluorescent paint by crushing up Fluorescent minerals to use as a Fluorescent pigment, and then he proceeded to mix these pulverized Fluorescent minerals with wood varnish and "Murine" eyedrops in the Family Bathtub(!) Eventually, the experiments in two different fields of Fluorescence the Switzer brothers carried out in their father's Pharmacy and other chemical laboratories discovering Fluorescent natural compounds, and in Robert's 'darkroom' in the basement examining Fluorescent minerals under their "Black Light," led to the vividly Fluorescing 'Daylight' Fluorescent paints still in production today, made with "Synthetic phosphors" used as their powdered pigments. The chemical formulas of the naturally Fluorescent compounds the Switzer brothers initially discovered in their father's Pharmacy, and of the natural Fluorescent minerals, were synthetically produced and the Switzer brothers were eventually able to produce very brilliant Fluorescent paints made with Synthetic Phosphors as their pigments.

With the vast resources of $1.75, in early 1934 Robert and Joe Switzer formed "The Switzer Brothers Ultra Violet Laboratory" in the family kitchen. The very first use of these Fluorescent paints and other Fluorescent materials that Robert and Joe had been developing was on a model Stagecoach for a national contest run by the "Fisher Body" Company. Robert made this Fluorescent Stagecoach with the help of his brother Joe, and together they decorated the model with different Fluorescent materials that would vividly Fluoresce under Black lights, including proof of their early creative genius through the use of melted petroleum jelly used on the Stagecoach windows to make them Fluoresce a brilliant Blue-White. On January 15, 1934 Joe Switzer put in writing his first idea for the company, which was to use the Black light and Fluorescent Colors in 'Advertising displays.' The two brother's first venture was to try and persuade a car dealership on Lake Merritt in Oakland, California to paint one of their new, expensive cars completely with Fluorescent paint(!) to display in their showroom under Black lights to their customers, but the owner did not agree. At that point the Switzer brothers thought that they were the first to have the idea of using Black lights and Fluorescent Colors in the fields of advertising and entertainment, but doing research in the University of California's library, they soon found out that others had the same ideas with Fluorescence in advertising and entertainment years before them, such a "Stroblite Company" in New York which began using Fluorescence in advertising and stage production back in 1924, and even earlier, Johnny Shannon, eventual founder of "Shannon Luminous Products, Inc.," had worked with developing Fluorescence for the first Ziegfeld Follies in 1907 using early carbon-arc "Black Lights." These very first companies and developers designed stage effects and advertising displays incorporating early "Black Light" carbon-arc lamps with relatively common Phosphorescent paint, discovered in antiquity, that will "Glow-in-the-dark" as well as Fluoresce when put under a Black light. The big difference was that the Switzer brothers had invented an entire range of Colors of Fluorescent paint that would Fluoresce under a Black light, not just Phosphorescent Greenish or Bluish, which was all that was existing up until the Switzer brother's invention.

In June, 1934, Robert and Joe Switzer formed their first official business on the investments of $170.00 by Robert and $50.00 by Joe, and which they named "Fluor-S-Art Co." The Black lights that were used for the company's first displays were large, fragile, expensive 50 inch (127 cm) "NICO" (Nickel Cobalt glass) cold cathode mercury vapor discharge tubes, similar to contemporary Black lights, that the brothers bought from "General Electric Vapor Lamp Co." (GEVL) of San Francisco, and then rented to their customers for the installations of 1934 and 1935. Already in 1934 the Switzer brother's company first name was changed to "Northern-Lite Studios" after they began working with Delmar Gray, the owner of Art and display studios in San Francisco. Delmar Gray, who began working with the Switzer brothers in May, 1934, was already known in San Francisco for his displays, especially animated displays. With "Northern-Lite Studios" modestly housed in part of Delmar Gray's commercial Art shop, Delmar designed and built the displays for the company, being a master at Fluorescent painting on velvet murals. Delmar Gray's technique was very advanced for these first Fluorescent displays and public installations, initially painting just the tips of the pile of dark velvet with White paint, and then applying Fluorescent paint to just these White tips of the dark velvet. During 1934 and 1935, Delmar Gray designed, built, and also painted the public displays installed by

"Northern-Lite Studios," but by July, 1934, the limitations for public displays of Fluorescent paint and Black lights became very apparent. Delmar Gray had great success with a sales demonstration in a dark studio room and succeeded in selling this design to one of the biggest department stores in San Francisco, but after it was installed in the store front window, the light from the street all but obscured the breath taking Fluorescent display the department store owners had been shown in the dark. With this initial failure, "Northern-Lite Studios" realized very quickly that much designing, planning, and adjustment to the final display would be needed for each and every Fluorescent Black light display and installation they were commissioned for. The custom designing of each installation was going to take alot of planning and time, and the Switzer brothers realized from the start that they could not charge the customers for the extensive design and engineering work necessary for each successful store window display, so they devised a plan to offset the cost of unpaid designing and engineering, by charging unheard of prices for their Fluorescent Paint, which were in 1934 and 1935 considered "exorbitant" even. A small pint (.47 liter) of paint was so high priced at $10.00 in the mid-1930s, that customers even asked if the pure element Radium was used to make the paint! To give an idea of what $10.00 was worth in 1934, for the same amount of money that one pint (.47 liter) of "Northern-Lite Studios" Fluorescent paint sold for, a person could have bought over a quarter of an ounce of *Gold,* which in 1934 was less than $40.00 an ounce. With the very high price of their Fluorescent paint combined with just as exorbitant prices for their Fluorescent coating of display props, materials, and clothing used in the commissioned public store front displays, the cost of their time designing each display, such a Shading devices necessary to block out street light in store front installations, was then compensated for. The company also sold Fluorescent paint itself, and the very first sale of Fluorescent paint by "Northern-Lite studios" was in July, 1934 to Shell Oil Company. In 1934 "Northern-Lite Studios" sold four different kinds of Fluorescent paints, including invisible Blue and Green translucent lacquers, opaque enamels, Artist Oil Colors, and sun resistant Fluorescent paint. Robert and Joe Switzer's "Ultra Violet Laboratory" was then housed in the laundry room and one-car garage of their parent's house(!) and their only pieces of 'professional' equipment was their mother's blender, their mother's kitchen utensils, and their father's large mortar and pestle for essential powder grinding. To complete this first homespun "Ultra Violet laboratory," the Switzer brothers also used a shed in the backyard to mount samples of their Fluorescent paints in continuous sunlight for determining fading degree, and for a drying space for their Fluorescent coated material and paper. During the writing of this book, in 2009 the first commercially published book on the "Switzer Brothers" was printed, a children's book entitled "The Day-Glo Brothers - The True Story of Bob and Joe Switzer's Bright Ideas and Brand New Colors" by Chris Barton. This book is printed with full "Day-Glo" Fluorescent Inks and is highly Fluorescent under a Black light, with a detail revealed by the author, who was in the very envious position of having full access to the Switzer archives for the writing of his book, that during this period which the teenagers Bob and Joe Switzer were using their mother's new electric kitchen blender for mixing up Fluorescent paints in total secrecy, their mother baked them a special surprise Fluorescent 'Angel Cake,' made of course with her new electric kitchen blender that she had used - before the two brothers could clean all the Fluorescent paint out of the blender!

In this early history of the Switzer Brothers Fluorescent legacy, what happened in August, 1934 is legendary. As already noted, Robert Switzer's younger brother Joe was an amateur magician in high school and he was also the impetus of Robert's initial exploration of the Black light during his six months of recovery from his accident. Joe was already including in his magic performances a very early stage technique known as "Black Art" which was a magic illusion created to be performed in the dark with Phosphorescent stage props, or with Black and White painted objects that appeared to disappear when presented on a similarly-Colored background. By 1934, Joe was a member of the Pacific Coast Magician's Association, and had told the president of the association about the Fluorescent magic illusion he had developed with the Black light. Replacing another magician during the August, 1934 Oakland Magician's Convention, Joe Switzer dazzled the audience with his "Headless Balinese Dancer." Written accounts of this 1934 performance of the "Headless Balinese Dancer" by Joe Switzer "Kleeland the Magician" sound very exotic, even by today's standards over seventy years later. The performance began on a dark stage, and in a flash of light a Balinese dancer begins an exotic dance accompanied by similarly exotic music. In a startling finale, the female Balinese dancer raises her head off her shoulders with her brilliantly painted hands and long fingernails, then continues to dance until her headless body falls to the floor to be followed around the stage by just her head! The prize of "Outstanding Effect" for this August, 1934 magician's Convention was won by Joe Switzer for this "Headless Balinese Dancer" performance, and the very first article about their company was published in the "Oakland Tribune." The success of this "Headless Balinese Dancer" illusion took the joint efforts of all the Switzer family and Delmar Gray and his wife. The Balinese costume was constructed with hundreds of pieces of their highly Fluorescent coated papers, and the Balinese dancer's head was made and painted by Delmar Gray and his wife. Being business men, the entire "Headless Balinese Dancer" magic illusion was packaged and offered for sale with a price of $75.00. This "Headless Balinese Dancer" illusion was performed several times after the August, 1934 Magician's Convention, and for the later performances there were also wild additions, such as a Fluorescent sword to cut the Balinese dancer's head off, and Red Fluorescent "blood" to squirt out of the Balinese dancer's body.

The first magazine article about the "Switzer Brothers" and "Northern-Lite Studios" was in the October, 1934 issue of "Scientific American." Towards the back of the October, 1934 Scientific American there is this small article entitled "Midnight Paintings" in the section of the magazine called "The Scientific American Digest." The contributing editors of this magazine section were Alexander Klemin, head of the Daniel Guggenheim School of Aeronautics at N.Y.U., and A.E. Buchanan, Jr. of Lehigh University, with this issue containing small stories of the new developments in science in 1934, such as 'Bathysphere's New Quartz Window,' the prophetic 'Overweight Men are Healthier and Stronger,' and very early discoveries of the presently studied "Dark Matter" in Astronomy entitled 'Is "Empty" Space really Empty?' This first magazine article 'Midnight Paintings' for the "Switzer Brothers Ultra Violet Laboratory" is about one-third of a page and is printed with a Black and White photograph of a "Switzer Brothers" wall painting composed of a landscape with large trees in the foreground and a village with a church spire in the background. The article begins with the statement that 'Fluorescent Paint is becoming popular,' and describes Fluorescent paint being used in stage performances of 'Fan Dances' whose fans Fluoresce under Black lights while the dancers themselves are invisible in the dark. The article continues with a short explanation of the phenomenon of Fluorescence in regard to paintings and murals, and describes the light emitted by this Fluorescent paint as 'weird' and 'unearthly,' comparing it to Phosphorescence. The Fluorescent wall painting illustrated in the magazine is credited to "The Switzer Brothers Ultra Violet Laboratories" of Berkley, California, and is described as a painting which is a White surface in daylight, but at night under Black lights, the White wall disappears and a glowing landscape appears in soft Green. In this October, 1934 article, the uses for Fluorescent paint are listed as stage costumes and stage scenery, painting pictures, and advertisements, with the reader being advised that the Fluorescent paints are available in different Colors. A simple, accurate explanation of the physics closes the article, comparing Fluorescence to Phosphorescence and correctly concluding with the statement that both are forms of luminosity.

Towards the end of 1934, the "Switzer Brothers" installed their first successful indoor display for another San Francisco department store "Hale Brothers." Joe Switzer had sold the concept of a Fluorescent Christmas installation in the 'Fairyland' display of the department store's toy department. The Fluorescent Christmas display was installed for eight weeks including Christmas, 1934, and was the "Switzer Brother's" first success with a public exhibit. The Christmas installations must have been fabulous, including Fluorescent ice caves and caverns along with a Fluorescent Aurora Borealis. Fluorescent waterfalls and a small lake, all made with Fluorescent liquids, were continuously flowing in the installation, made complete with many Eskimos and other animated objects such as seals and dog sleds all vividly Fluorescent having been painted with "Northern-Lite" Fluorescent paints. The center of this very large Fluorescent installation, which comprised hundreds of square feet, was naturally a Fluorescent Santa Claus sitting on his throne. To make this large installation successfully Fluorescent, six large 50 inch (127 cm) NICO tubular Black light lamps were mounted above the display.

The "Switzer Brothers" "Northern-Lite Studios" second major sale was to the biggest theatre of it's time in San Francisco, the famous "Warfield Theater." Delmar Gray made Black costumes painted with Fluorescent skeletons on the front and back of the costumes for twelve women in a chorus line, and together with Black lights over a darkened stage, "The Skeleton Ballet" was re-born. For years after this, the "Switzer Brothers" "Northern-Lite Studios" Fluorescent paints were used on stages all over America, including Radio City Music Hall in New York City. Again, the August 24, 1935 issue of the magazine "Boxoffice" features a full page story "Spectacular Effects with Invisible U.V. Lighting" written by Alexander Strobl, founder of "Stroblite Co.:" in New York. The article by Alexander Strobl contains two photographs of the 1927 "Skeleton Ballet" being performed at Radio City Music Hall in New York, and reveals that the Radio City Music Hall "Skeleton Ballet" was longer, with thirty dancers, than the first "Skeleton Ballet" painted by Delmar Gray which featured only a dozen dancers. The design of the skeleton costumes written about and photographed in this "Boxoffice" magazine issue is also different from Delmar Gray's original design in San Francisco, because in Radio City Music hall only the front of the costumes of the dancers were painted with a Fluorescent skeleton, while the back of the costume was left only Black, so if a dancer turned their back to the audience during the performance, it would look like the dancer disappeared. This is so long ago that this stage effect was still called "Black Art" in the "Boxoffice" article, in reference to very early magician's stage illusions incorporating Phosphorescence and other optical illusions on a darkened stage. Again, this "Black Art" is precisely what Joseph Switzer as an amateur teenage magician was interested in when he got his brother Robert excited about it, who was recovering in the dark for six months after his terrible accident.

The "Skeleton Ballet" in San Francisco was a success for the "Switzer Brothers" company "Northern-Lite

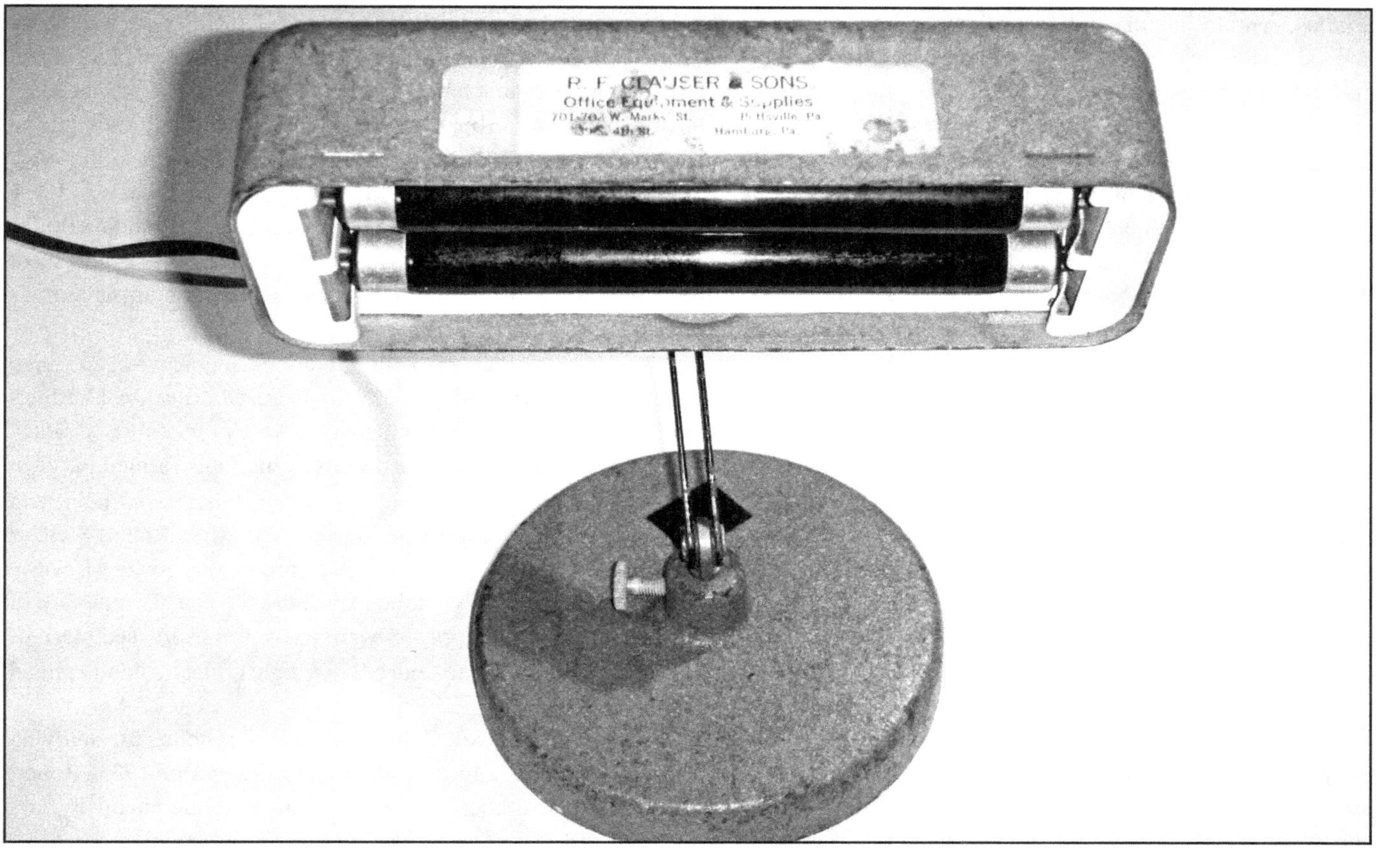

1930s "Stroblite" double-tube Black light with stand

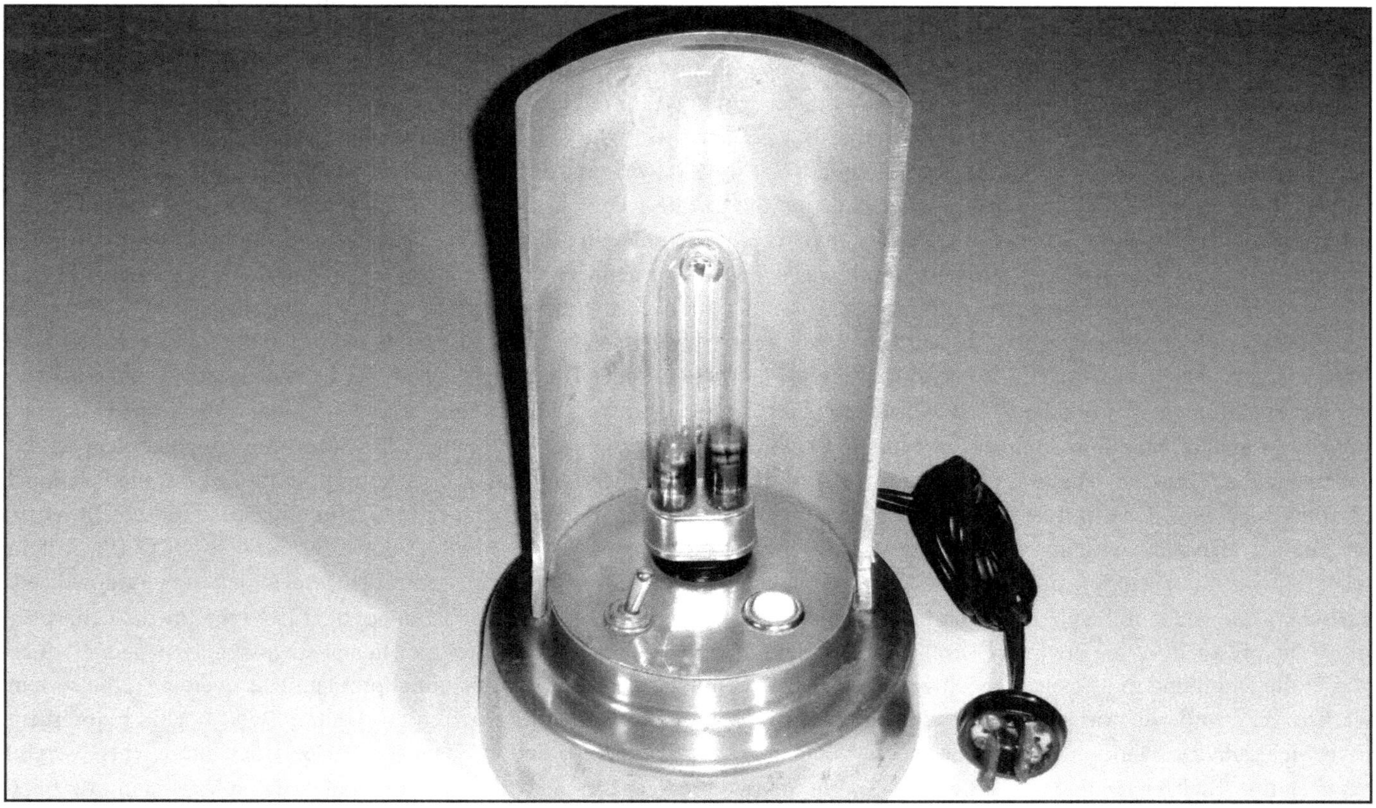

1930s Ultraviolet Germinology Lamp, "Bishop & Whalen Ultra-Violet Ray Equipment Co. Limited," Vancouver, B.C.

Studios," enthralling the audience with a darkened stage and twelve women dressed in Black costumes dancing with a skeleton painted in Fluorescent paint on both the front and the back of the Black costumes. To insure the intensity of the Fluorescent performance, an ingenious device was used, which consisted of a moving boom that had three large NICO Black lights attached to it. The Black light-equipped boom was hidden from the audience by a backdrop, and Robert and Joe Switzer rode on the U.V.-equipped boom during the first shows to be sure the U.V. lamps were in the best spot on the stage to cause the most brilliant Fluorescence of the Skeleton costumes as possible. The first San Francisco "Skeleton Ballet" ran for a week and was very successful. Delmar Gray paid the "Switzer Brothers" $15.00 for their half of the NICO Black lights rental and $60.00 for the Fluorescent paint used on the costumes, and this "Warfield Theater" in San Francisco went on to make other Fluorescent Black light shows (actually all the way up until it closed in the late 1970s, most well remembered being the many infamous "Grateful Dead" concerts).

In 1934, the "Switzer Brothers" "Northern-Lite Studios" became associated with Johnny Shannon who was then working in Hollywood with the "General Electric Vapor Lamp Company." Johnny Shannon, who had used "Black Art" effects way back to 1907 in the first Ziegfeld Follies which is recognized as the first public performance in which experimental Black light was used for special visual effects, in 1934 became the "Switzer Brothers" first "Distributor," and later formed his own company in California "Shannon Luminous Products, Inc." which is still a very large company selling Fluorescent paint and products today in the Twenty-first century. In 1934 Johnny Shannon was interested in stage illusions and when Robert Switzer was in Los Angeles, Johnny Shannon worked with him to create a Fluorescent Pygmalion-Galatea production for the Beverly Hills Chamber of commerce. The spectacular performance began with the sculptor Pygmalion finishing the marble sculpture of Galatea in normal stage White light, then the stage became dark and the sculptor's prayers were answered as his sculpture of Galatea came alive and danced around the darkened stage with a Fluorescent costume under Black lights, planned and created by both Robert and Joe Switzer.

In January, 1935, Robert Switzer decided to return to the University of California on his scholarship studying chemistry and medicine that had been interrupted by his accident during the summer of 1933. By the end of 1935, Robert Switzer realized that the severe accident had damaged his memory and concentration to a point where studying chemistry in a university wasn't possible without the combined help of his mother and sister, so he decided to leave school to continue developing the "Northern-Lite" Company that he had started with his brother. While at school, during the summer of 1935, Robert Switzer had worked with quality control at the Union Oil Company. While working with this Union Oil Company he was permitted to inspect the petroleum products and chemical derivatives in Union Oil's research storerooms for Fluorescent substances. What Robert Switzer found in the storeroom of this research laboratory were ingredients that would lead to the future "Switzer Brothers" production of Invisible Fluorescent Dyes for textiles.

1935 also brought the "Switzer Brothers" a contract with the "National Marking Machine Company" for a new development, "Invisible Laundry Marking." Leonard S. Smith Jr. was president of the "National Marking Machine Company" and had read the article in "Scientific American" about the "Switzer Brothers" "Midnight Paintings" and was interested to use the Black light technology for marking laundry invisibly. When meeting the Switzer brothers in his hotel room for the first time to sign a contract with his company, Smith was shocked that neither of the brothers was twenty-one years old yet. Joe Switzer went to work in Cincinnati on the inks they would use for the invisible laundry marking, and during the same period Joe also worked on developing Fluorescent Lithography inks in Cleveland. For the invisible laundry inks, Joe developed three Colors of ink that were invisible in daylight, highly Fluorescent under Black lights, and were not effected by the washing, drying, and ironing of the laundry on which they were to be marked. Joe Switzer began working with Leonard Smith's Invisible Laundry Marking Company in March, 1935, where a lab was set up for the Ultraviolet research, complete with a chemist and a professor. The first venture into this Invisible Laundry Marking was a disaster, after Smith had installed National Marking Machines in several large Cincinnati laundries. The marking machines first printed large invisible Fluorescent letters on laundry, then after washing, drying, and ironing, the laundry was easily sorted under powerful 50 inch NICO Black light tubes. Everything started off very good, but soon laundry marked with the invisible Fluorescent ink was returned and customers demanded to be paid for their laundered clothes that had Brown stains visible in daylight from the Invisible marking Ink. The president of the company Leonard Smith, had to reimburse many customers for their Brown-stained laundry, which was in the end found to be caused by only one particular washing product. After this initial problem was overcome, the system worked very well and was marketed as "Fanthom-Fast," setting up in laundries across the United States. This Fluorescent Invisible Laundry Marking business was very commercially successful, and by January, 1936, when arguments erupted between the "Switzer Brothers" and Leonard Smith, the two brothers had made over $1,200, which was a large sum of money for the era. During the time of Smith's Invisible Laundry marking contract, the two Switzer brothers learned much about

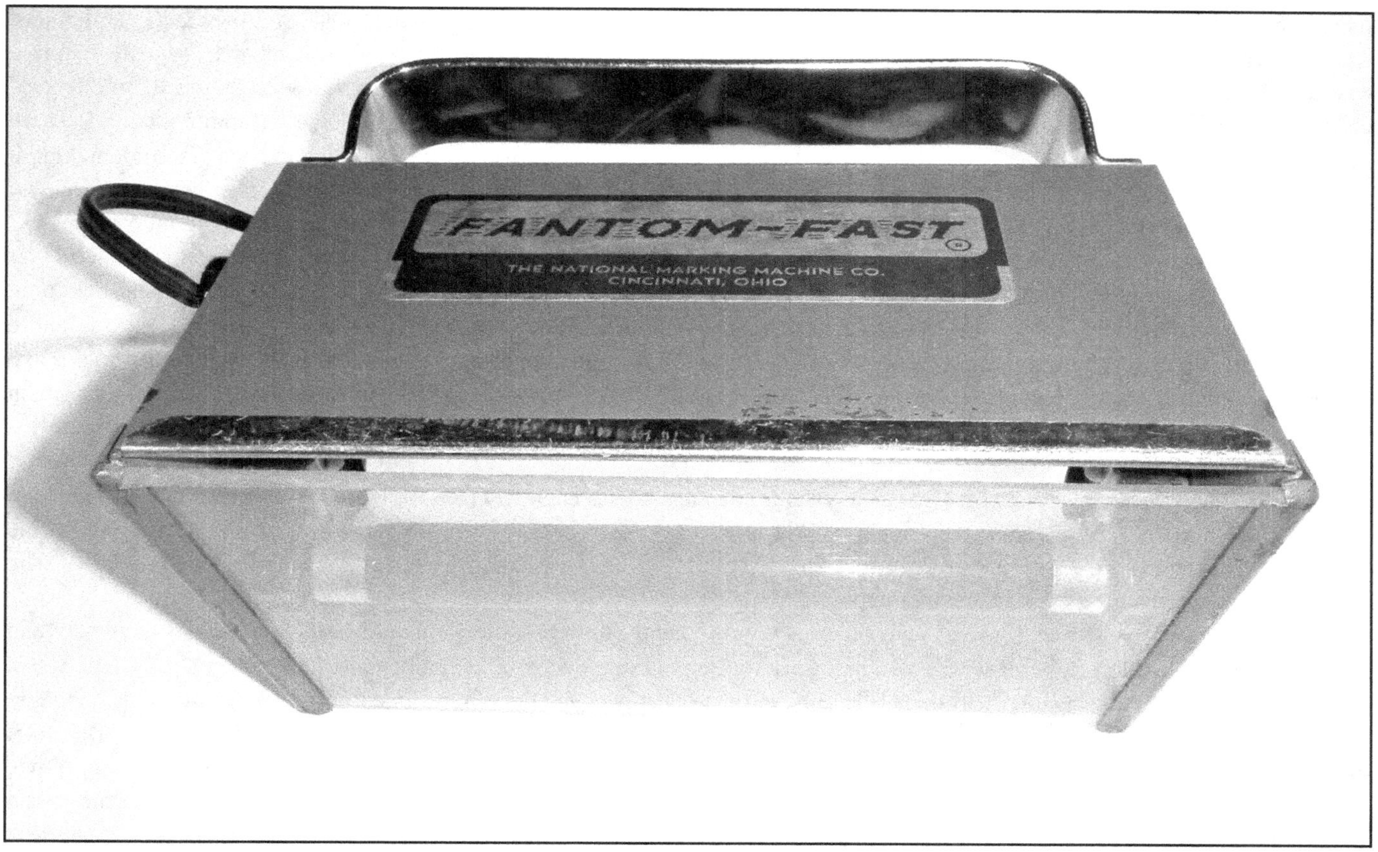

1930s-1940s "FANTOM-FAST" Invisible Laundry-Marking Black light, "The National Marking Machine Co.," Ohio

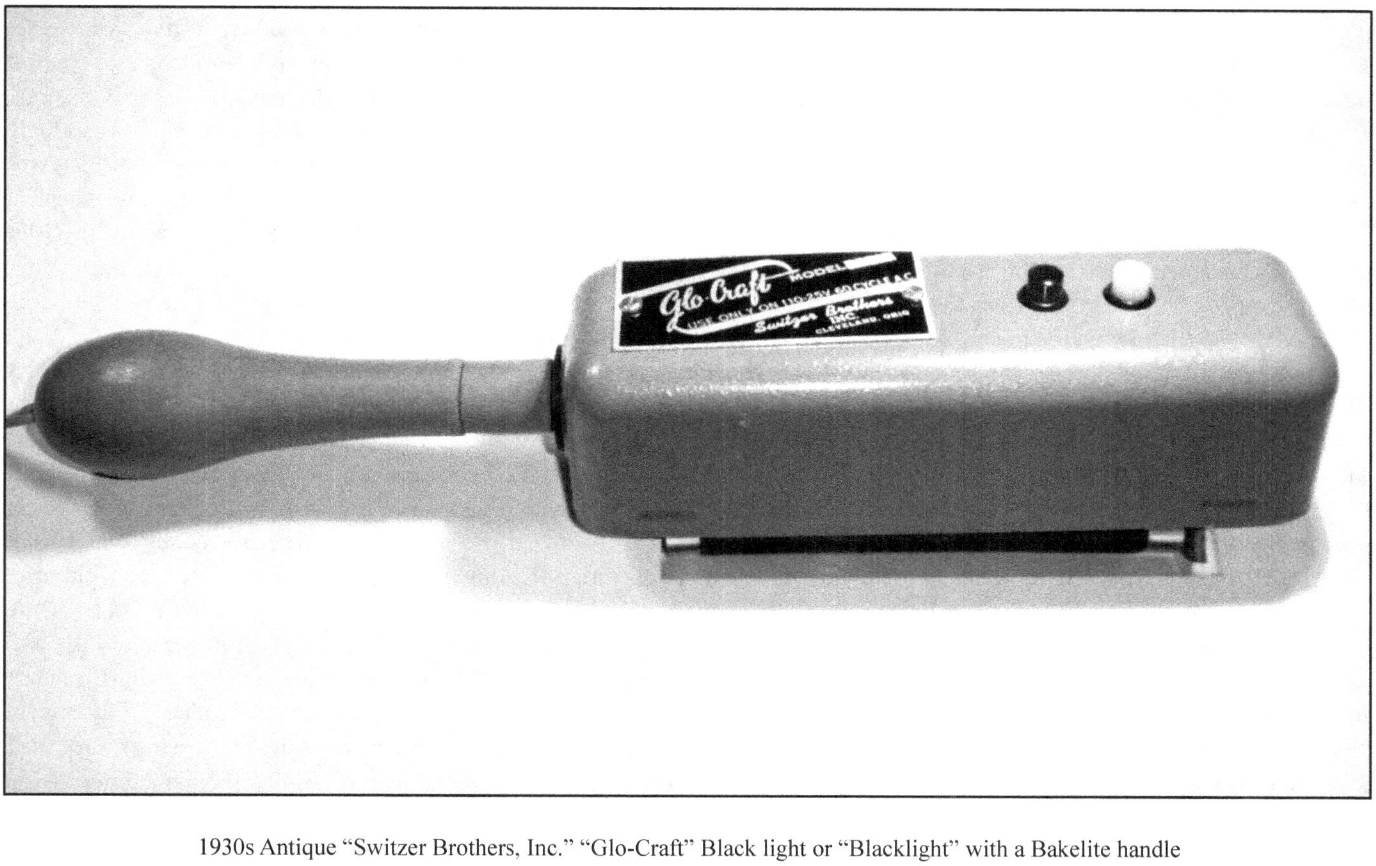

1930s Antique "Switzer Brothers, Inc." "Glo-Craft" Black light or "Blacklight" with a Bakelite handle

patenting and legal processes of protecting their inventions, so by the time that the agreement with Smith ended in arguments, the two brothers knew alot about the business side pertaining to contracts and patents. Eventually the Invisible Laundry Marking industry completely collapsed because clothing manufacturers began dying their material with "Optical Brighteners" causing the clothes to Fluoresce in sunlight and appear "Whiter-than-White," known today as "Daylight Fluorescence." These items of clothing made with optical brighteners would completely Fluoresce under Black lights (like today's T-shirts), making it impossible to read Fluorescent invisible laundry markings on the laundered clothing. In the Museum collection is an extremely rare Black light unit from this "Fantom-Fast" Invisible Fluorescent Laundry Marking history. The lamp is about 5 inches (13 cm.) tall and 5 inches deep, made out of metal and triangular shaped with the large side down, which contains the small tubular four watt Black light in this unit. This "Fantom-Fast" Black light in the Museum looks to be a portable metal hand-held unit, with a chrome handle at the top. The four watt Black light is backed by a curved metal reflector encompassing the entire bottom of the lamp. Although the unit is well designed, the Black light tubular lamp is protected by a sheet of thick clear plastic, which unfortunately cuts the emission of the Black light. The most noticeable feature of the small institutional-Green Black light unit is it's logo printed in bright Red on a reflective sticker put on both sides of the lamp. The Red logo is nearly a prehistoric design, absolutely immediately recognizable as being from before the 1950s era. "FANTOM-FAST" is printed in Red italicized hand-drawn letters which are all curved at the edges, with each letter of the logo having horizontal lines behind them to 'illustrate' motion or movement, not-so-subtly referring to the "FAST" of "FANTOM-FAST." In plain English, the "Fantom-Five" logo is grotesque and nearly a caricature of the 1930s or 1940s era. Beneath this wonderful logo is printed "The National Marking Machine Co. Cincinnati, Ohio."

During 1935 the "Switzer Brothers" ventures with Leonard Smith and the National Marking Machines Company had started, and in June, 1935 Robert Switzer also met Carl Moellmann, the owner of "Continental Lithography, Co." which was a company connected with Warner Brothers Pictures. In 1921 Carl Moellmann resigned form his position at "Morgan Lithography" in Cleveland to form his own company in the same city, which he named "Continental Lithography." By 1935, the "Continental Lithography Company" was already the largest firm for the printing of movie posters for the growing movie industry, including Warner Brothers. The movie posters were produced by lithography and were used to advertise movies in theatre displays and on billboards. Joseph Switzer got a commission for a movie theatre 'Lobby display' in Cleveland's biggest Warner Brothers theatre "The Hippodrome." Robert Switzer and Delmar Gray designed and built an extravagant display for "The Hippodrome" movie theatre, accommodating very large 40 x 60 inch (102 x 152 cm) Continental Lithography movie posters under Black lights. "Continental Lithography" owner Carl Moellmann had not signed a contract for the extravagant Fluorescent movie theatre 'Lobby display' that had been created by the "Switzer Brothers" company "Northern-Lite," and it took one month for him to agree to purchase the display. The "Switzer Brothers" charged "Continental Lithography" $381.00 for the Fluorescent Movie Theatre Poster display, which was an astronomical amount in those days, and which reportedly caused Carl Moellmann to complain for years to come. This large extravagant Fluorescent Movie Theatre Poster display was very popular with public opinion, and subsequently was shipped off to be displayed in different Warner Brothers movie theaters in New York and other cities. This commission for Fluorescent Movie posters with "Continental Lithography," a sister company of Warner Brothers, is the job that almost every source of reference on the "Switzer Brothers" and their eventually-named company "Day-Glo" states as their 'first job.' This Carl Moellmann was one of the co-founders of a very avant-garde group of Ohio Artists known as the "Kokoon Klub," who will be discussed at length in this book.

After the great success the Fluorescent Movie Theatre Poster display made for "Continental Lithography" by Robert Switzer and Delmar Gray, "Continental" became interested in developing Fluorescent inks for lithography. All of the inks that "Continental Lithography" were using were at the time were manufactured by the Cleveland firm "Forbes Ink Co." and Carl Moellmann paid for research conducted by Dick Forbes towards the production of successful Fluorescent lithography inks. Dick Forbes proceeded to hire Joe Switzer and made all printing machinery available to Joe in hopes of new Fluorescent lithography inks being developed. Joe's creativity paid off when he invented a whole new way of making Fluorescent lithographic posters. By mixing water into the oil-based printing operation, Joe invented a printing procedure that could print posters in any Fluorescent Color on a lithographic direct rotary press. This lead to the very first patented product of the "Switzer Brothers," with Joe Switzer's name and an application date of January 8, 1936, "Fluorescent Lithography Ink" was awarded a patent on April 4, 1939. In 1935 the U.S. Department of Justice made their first inquiries to the "Switzer Brothers" for Fluorescent Invisible Inks, which would eventually lead to the U.S. military using the "Switzer Brothers" Fluorescent paints, dyes and many other Fluorescent products extensively during the Second world war. Another "Switzer Brothers" invention of 1935 would be used in hugh amounts by the U.S. military during the Second world war, Fluorescent Fabrics. Even before the Second world war, in northern Africa allied troops were being bombed by their own allied bombers, but were then

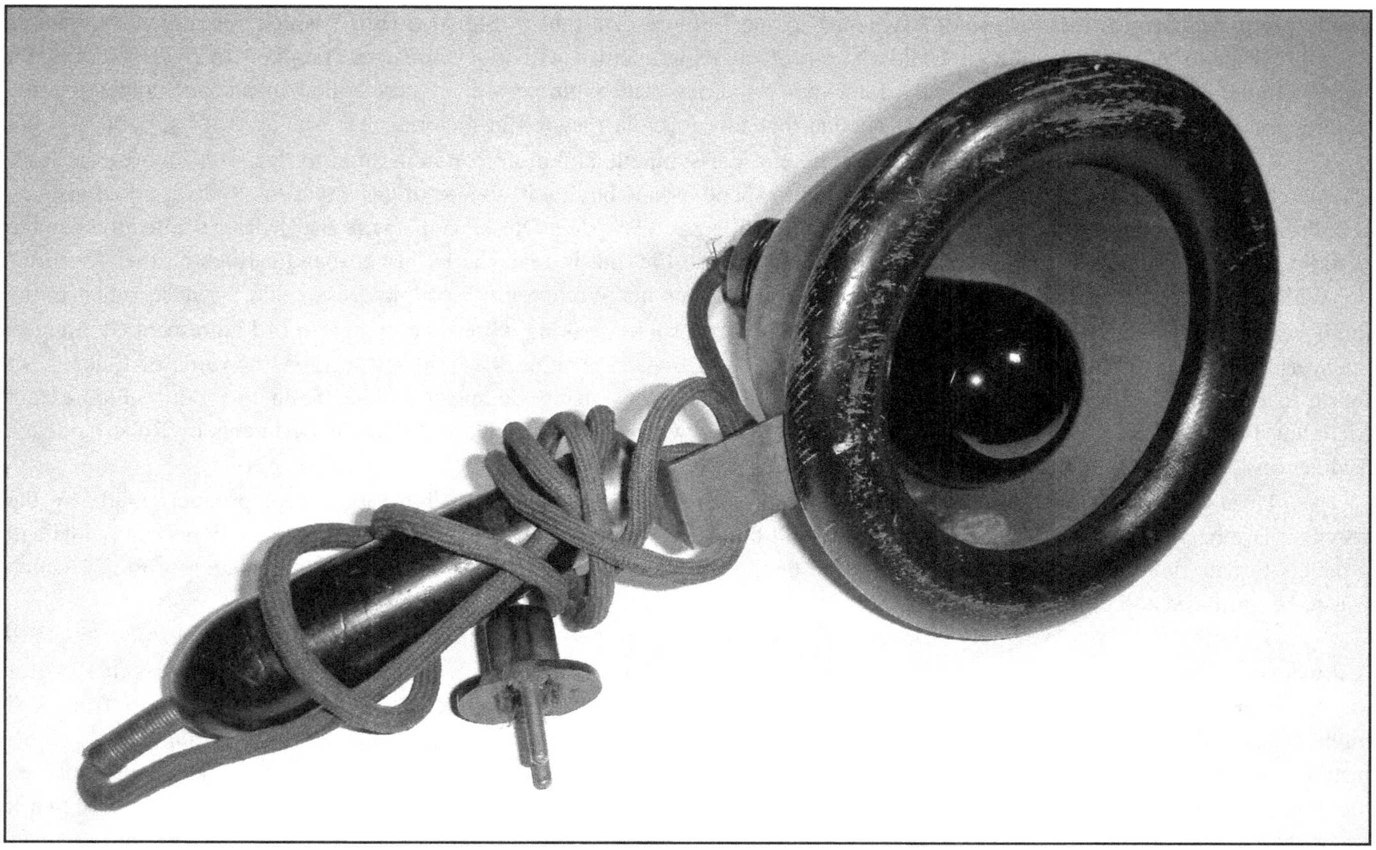

1930s Czechoslovakian Ultraviolet Medical Lamp with wooden handle and wooden lamp flange

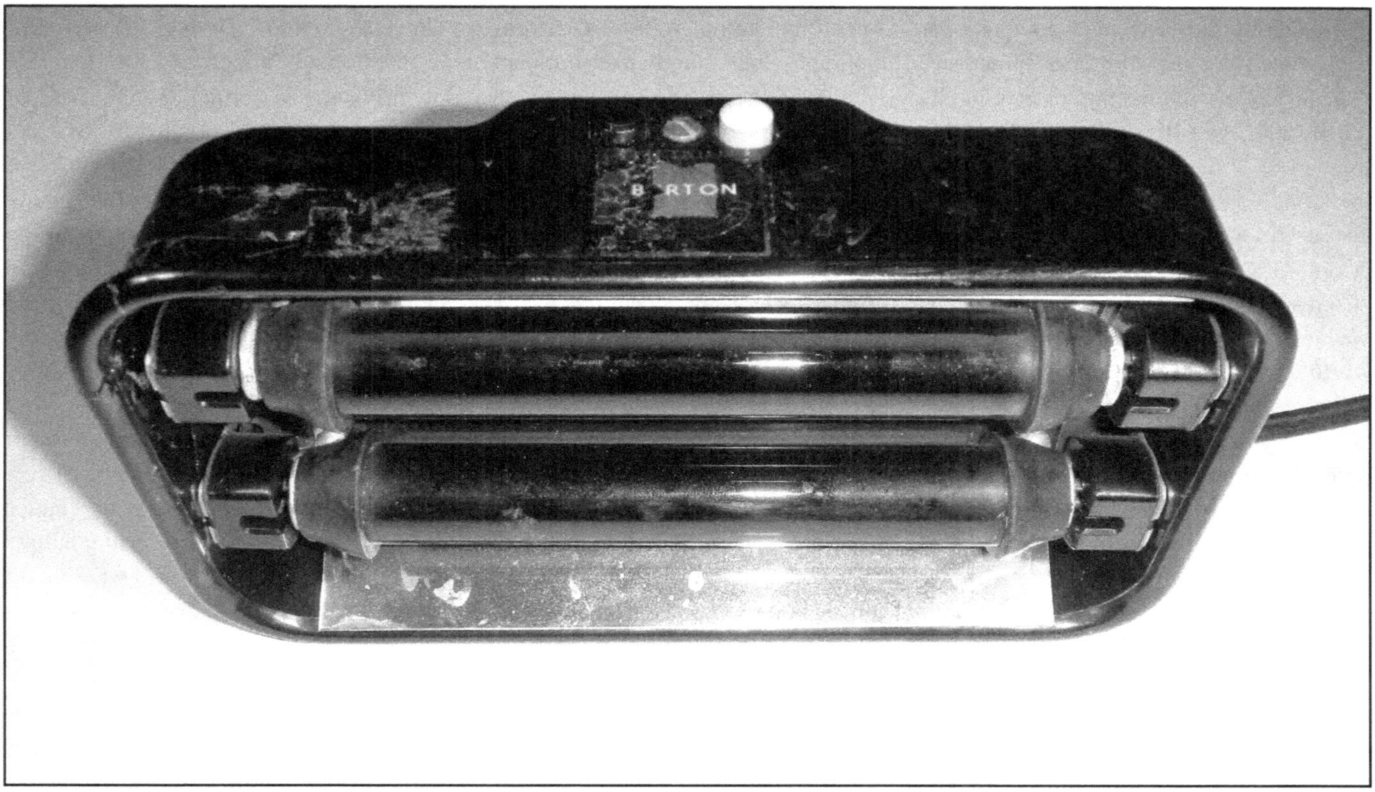

1930s-1940s "Burton" Bakelite Ultraviolet Medical Lamp ("Burton" still produces a similar Ultraviolet Medical Lamp in 2016)

finally protected by the military's use of "Switzer Brothers" Fluorescent fabric "Signal Boards," which could identify them as friendly troops to the allied bombers. The Switzer brothers experimented with alot of different products to create Fluorescent fabric for the U.S. Military commission. First experimenting with Chinese silk, it was boiled in alcohol containing the Fluorescent dye Rhodamine and also white shellac, but this formula resulted in material that was as stiff as wood and not usable. Then the Switzer brothers decided to try the cheaper synthetic and more common Satin to dye with Fluorescent inks. The two brothers had no Satin fabric, and didn't want to spend money buying it, so legend has it that Joe Switzer asked his new wife, who he had just married in 1936, to "borrow" her White Satin Wedding Dress. Bob's wife Pat Switzer wanted to keep the Wedding dress to traditionally hand down to a daughter later in life, but instead she let her husband and his brother "borrow" the White Satin Wedding dress. Needless to say - Pat never saw her White Satin Wedding dress again, because, again in the family bathtub, the two Switzer brothers dyed it with Fluorescent Inks, making it the very first piece of Fluorescent Clothing in the world! During the approaching Second world war, "The Switzer Brothers" would sell millions of yards of Fluorescent fabric to the U.S. military for visual signaling. All this technology using Cellulose Acetate Satin to produce Fluorescent Signaling fabric for the U.S. Military during the Second world war were the results of the first experiments by Robert and Joe Switzer on Joe's wife's Wedding dress.

During the mid 1930s Spiritualists conducting seances began to use Invisible Fluorescent products made by the "Switzer Brothers" to conjure up 'communication' with the dead, resulting in one of the oddest uses of Fluorescent paints and products to date, with the singular exception of the thankfully obscure "VISIBALM" "Fluorescent Embalming Fluid" which was to be produced and utilized a few years later.

The year 1935 was extremely productive for the "Switzer Brothers," being the year that their young business began to really develop into something important. A nightclub named "The Club Trouville" was one of the biggest successes of 1935 for the "Switzer Brothers." Robert and Joe Switzer, along with Delmar Gray, convinced the owner of "The Club Trouville" nightclub to make the whole nightclub exclusively lit by Black lights and Fluorescence. The entire nightclub had Black lights installed along with Fluorescent coatings on every part of the nightclub, including not only the dance floor and stage, but even the dining tables and actual walls of "The Club Trouville." The club opened in October, 1935, and was such a success that it can still be read about seventy years later in several antique articles documenting the history of the Black light.

All these new business opportunities in 1935, foremost with "Continental Lithography Co." of Ohio who successfully began to market their Fluorescent Movie posters to movie companies including Warner Brothers, caused the "Switzer Brothers" to change the name of their company, and to move the company form California to Cleveland, Ohio. During this period of time, experimenting with even Fluorescent lithography Inks, the Switzer brothers made an extremely important invention with their discovery of a method of making "Daylight" Fluorescent pigments which also glow brilliantly in normal daylight without the presence of a Black light, and which are the same type of Fluorescent pigments still in common production today. Starting in 1934 as "Fluor-S-Art Co.," then moving on to the names "Switzer Brothers" and "Northern-Lite Studios" in 1935, in 1936 the name of the company became "Conti-Glo" after working together with "Continental Lithography Co.," and after having also used the full company name for a short period. By 1939 the name of the company was "Glo-Craft," but throughout the "Conti-Glo" and "Glo-Craft" periods, on the information panel of Ultraviolet lighting units, beneath the company name brand "Conti-Glo" or "Glo-Craft," the panel would also include manufactured by "The Switzer Brothers." This name for their business "The Switzer Brothers, Inc." would not become their company's official name until 1946, and the name that the whole world knows the company as, "Day-Glo" would not be officially the company's name until 1965: "Day-Glo Color Corporation."

The early fame for "The Switzer Brothers" came through the U.S. military's extensive use of their Fluorescent products during the Second world war. Fluorescent paint was used not only on Aircraft carriers to help pilots landing at sea, which was an advantage that no other military force had, but on the actual aircraft itself, ranging from small areas of the fighter planes being coated with Fluorescent paints to avoid midair collisions, to entire aircraft being painted with Fluorescent paint for high visibility. Not only was Fluorescent paint used on the outside of the military aircraft during the Second world war, but on the inside as well for "Black-Out" conditions during bombing raids. One of the most powerful bombers used during the Second world war was the hugh B-17, also known as the "Flying Fortress." Part of the standard control panel instruments on the B-17 was a very specialized piece of equipment - a Black light - made by "Grimes Mfd. Co.," which was also based in Ohio. The name of this piece of equipment is an "Ultraviolet Cockpit Light," which is impressed into the bottom of the original 1940s lamp in the Museum collection. This "Ultraviolet Cockpit Light" has an Ultraviolet filter on the front of the small lamp that can be turned by hand to convert a regular White light lamp into a Black light. On bombing missions during the Second world war, all the lights in the aircraft would be extinguished for "Black Out" bombing missions, which wouldn't allow the bomber to

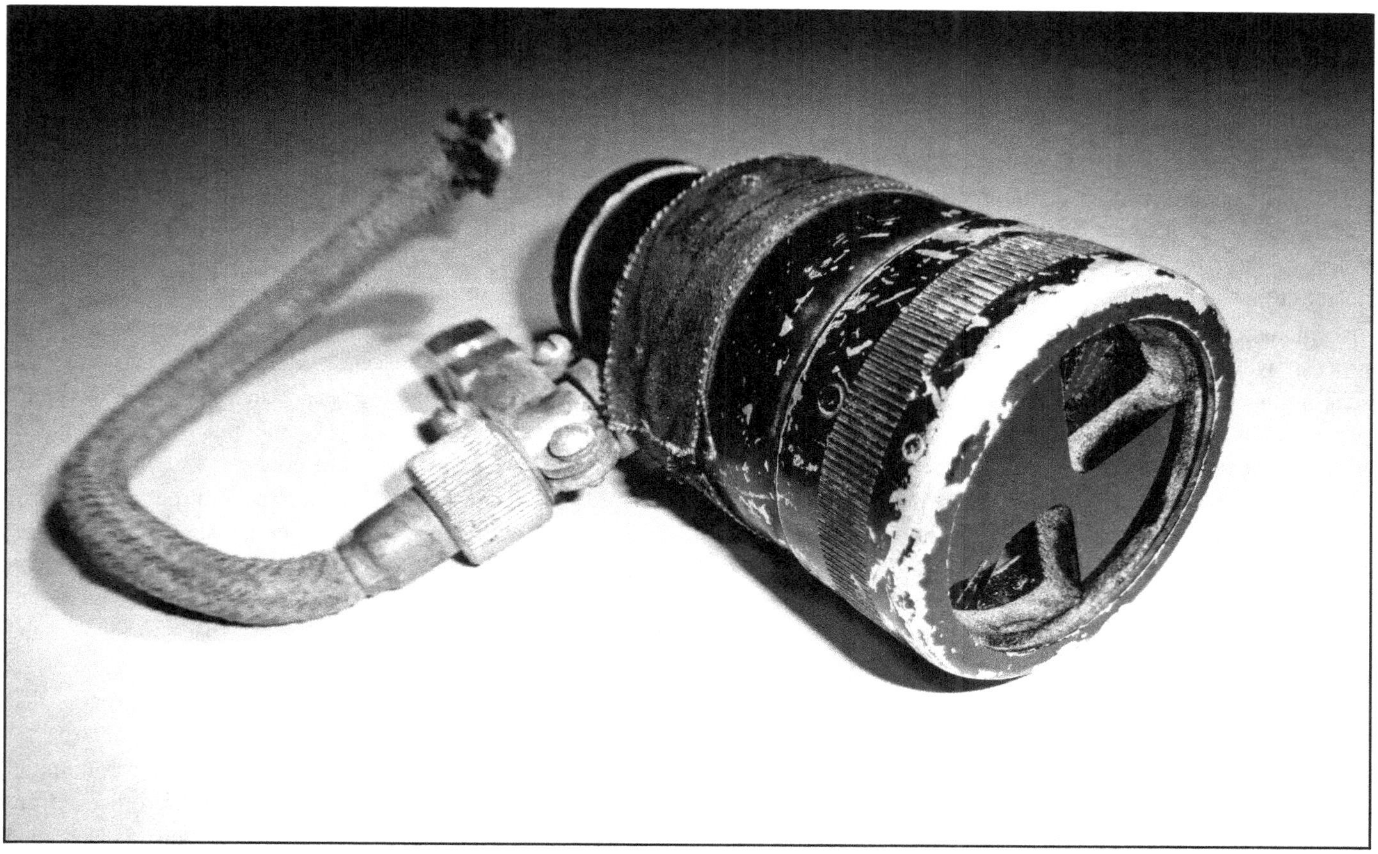

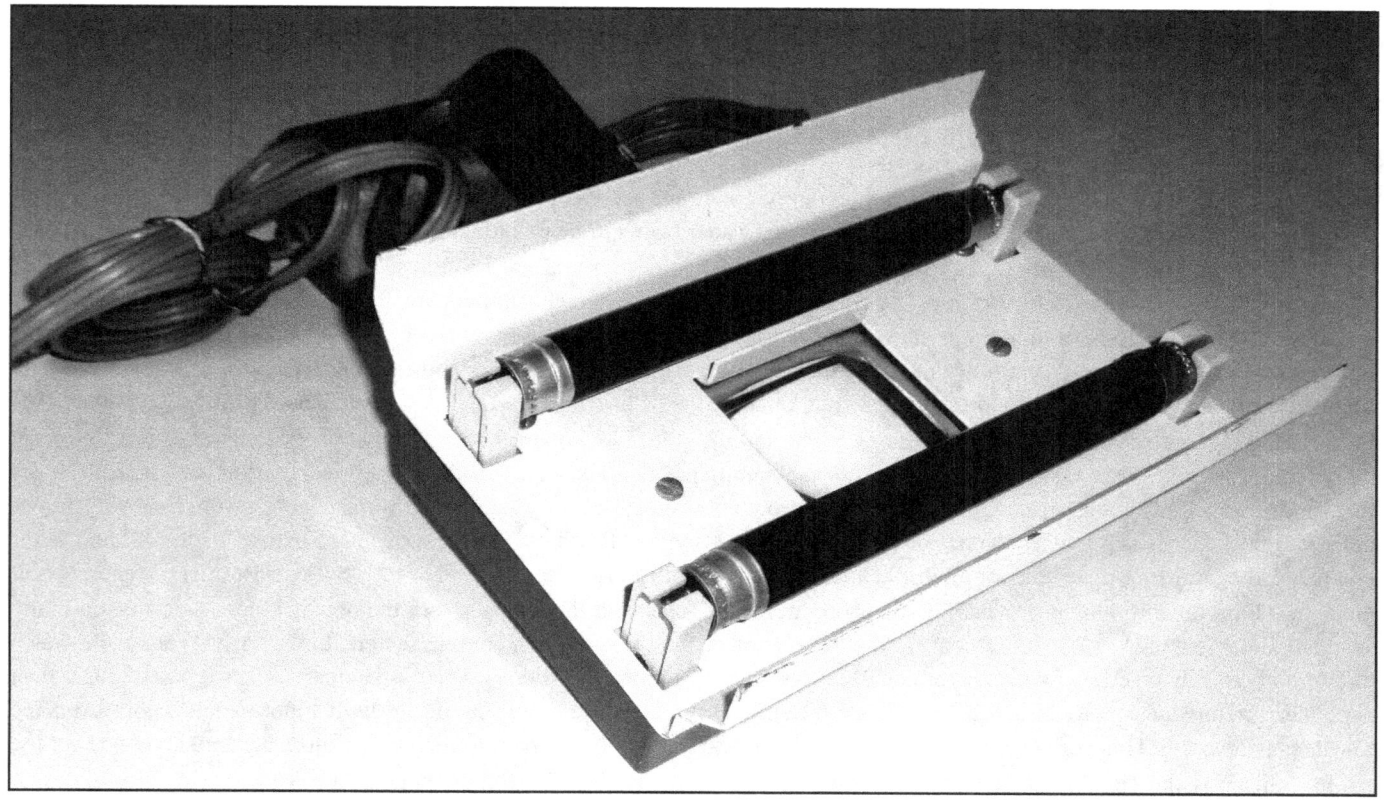

1940s World War Two "Grimes Ultraviolet Cockpit Light" from the dashboard of a "B-17" Second World War Bomber

1930s-1940s "Hampton Mfg." Ultraviolet "Metal Stress Detector" with a central magnifing glass for metal inspection

be seen at night by enemy troops on the ground. The "Grimes Ultraviolet Cockpit Light" would be turned on and then all the bombing charts, which were likewise printed exclusively in bright Fluorescent White-Blue inks on Black board (and are ultra-rare today), could be easily read by the crew members through their "Grimes" Black light on the dashboard, without dangerously giving away their position in the night sky.

Another use of the Black light and another "Switzer Brothers" invention for the Second world war, which became important even after the end of the war and is still used today for metal production in industries all over the world, is Fluorescent "Metal Stress" Flaw Detection. This all began in 1938 with an article in a Cleveland newspaper reporting many wheel castings for Ford Automobile that were flawed. Robert (Bob) Switzer began experimenting on Fluorescent metal flaw detection in the basement of his house with a gas burner, and in the process of inventing Fluorescent metal flaw detection, he also managed to ruin his wife's laundry equipment. From his basement laboratory Robert Switzer invented the "Zyglo" process, which was a simple procedure involving the injection of high penetrating Fluorescent dye into metal parts, and also soaking the metal parts in the Fluorescent dye. Tiny cracks known as "Metal Stress" were then easily detected when the metal part was observed under a Black light. The invisible tiny cracks in the metal would be clearly visible under a Black light as brilliant Blue-White 'spider-webs' of cracks. In 1938 Metal Flaw Detection was already being done by a company named "Magnaflex," but this couldn't compare with the much more advanced detection of Metal Stress cracks through the use of Fluorescent dyes and the Black light, the system which Bob Switzer named "Magnaglo." In a demonstration of his new Fluorescent metal flaw detection he called "Magnaglo," Bob Switzer used a piece of metal from the owner of "Magnaflex" Dr. De Forest, and proceeded to shock "Magnaflex's" owner when he displayed in clear view under a Black light twice the amount of cracks in the metal that were detectable while using only the "Magnaflex" method. Another big drawback to the original "Magnaflex" procedure for detecting Metal Stress cracks was that their technology worked through magnetics, and was absolutely useless on much of the new material being used to build aircraft: Aluminum. The "Magnaflex" process that involved magnetics and X-ray only managed to find the big cracks in Aluminum aircraft parts, but "Zyglo," which was the name finally used for the "Switzer Brothers" Fluorescent metal flaw detection, found countless tiny cracks in the Aluminum parts, and proved itself vastly superior to the "Magnaflex" process. Problems now arose for the "Switzer Brothers" from contracts they had signed with Carl Moellmann of "Continental Lithography," who was greedy by all accounts, and claimed total ownership of all processes invented by the "Switzer Brothers." This all changed after the end of the Second world war, when military use of "Magnaflex" and "Zyglo" Metal Flaw Detection was finished. With "Magnaflex" producing negative sales after the end of the war, Carl Moellmann's businesses were in grave trouble, and this is how he was forced to give back all that he had taken from the "Switzer Brothers," including the contract with "Magnaflex." After this experience with "Continental Lithography" and Carl Moellmann was behind them, Robert and Joe Switzer had learned many lessons, and to protect their business and inventions, they officially changed the name of the company in 1946 to a name that would clearly state the owner's rights: the "Switzer Brothers." After the Second world war, Fluorescent paint was again used in advertising, on highway billboards, and for attracting customers in gas stations, such as ESSO, Gulf, and Atlantic, where Fluorescent paint was used on gas pumps, buildings, and signs. Fluorescent Paper began to be manufactured by the "Switzer Brothers," initiating use in cards, catalogues, and packaging. The very first package design that used Fluorescent Ink was for the "Chesterfield" Cigarette Christmas carton(!) of 1956. The trade magazine advertisement announcing the world's first packaging use of Fluorescent ink is printed in Fluorescent ink and is on display under a Black light in "Electric Ladyland - the First Museum of Fluorescent Art." The long-past era of this first Fluorescent package and it's advertising is painfully apparent when seeing the Fluorescent package of "Chesterfield Cigarettes" marketed as the "Christmas Carton"(!) with an actual printed Christmas gift-label on the cigarette carton to write both the recipient and the gift-giver's names on. A few short years later came one of the most famous uses of "Day-Glo" Colors in history - the common Soap box. In 1959 the "Tide" soap carton was made with the full Fluorescent Red-Orange package that is still in production half a century later. Within a few years almost every major detergent package in stores was printed or produced using "Switzer Brothers" Fluorescent inks, before "Colgate" and other companies began using these inks on their packages as well. For the first time, in 1958, the "Switzer Brothers" began to sell the actual Fluorescent pigment for making their products, like paint and ink, and through the use of Fluorescent inks in many soap and detergent packages, Fluorescent Colors became more well known in the public sector. In the early 1960s there was a hugh boom of Fluorescent "Switzer Brothers" Plastics used to produce millions of "Hula Hoops." "Turtle Wax" car polish containers, detergent packages, and many "Proctor Gamble" products were now produced with Fluorescent Colors from the "Switzer Brothers." This period of the late 1950s and very early 1960s was when Fluorescent Colors became known to all the world - this was the fruition of more than two decades of work by the "Switzer Brothers," when everything from bumper stickers for political candidates were printed by the millions with Fluorescent ink, and the application that has come to epitomize the use of "Day-Glo" Color today - half a century later - the 'Safety Cone' on the world's highways, as well as school crossing guards and countless road worker's "High-Visibility" Day-Glo vests, etc., etc., etc. This was all just a few short years before the literal explosion of "Day-Glo" Colors which most famously occurred in the mid to late 1960s during the Psychedelic Revolution, but this use of the "Switzer Brothers" Fluorescent Colors, the first Fluorescent Paint in the world on banal, common, mindless factors of society, like 'Safety Cones' on highways for example - in combination with the past early history of Fluorescent paint used as a "Wartime Paint" during the Second world war, *caused* the great degeneration and demystification of "Day-Glo" Colors, and also inevitably caused such banal applications to become forged in people's consciousness. Let's not forget one of the most memorable banal uses of Day-Glo Colors: Fluorescent Yellow Golf balls, and Fluorescent Yellow Tennis balls. Unfortunately, as previously stated in this book, the use of the first Fluorescent Paint in the world for banal everyday commodities did not start yesterday, or even way back in the 1960s. As evidence of the profound applications suggested for this new miracle technology, in the 1942 book "Fluorescent Chemicals and Their Applications" by Jack DeMent and H.C. Dake the following list is as long as it is banal, and which includes all the new 1930s-1940s applications for the Black light and a number of new DeMent suggestions. The ever-popular indoor and outdoor 'Bulletin Boards,' ornamental work, and a new suggestion of Fluorescent outdoor landscaping. The uses in theatre are listed as Fluorescent carpeting, Fluorescent murals, Fluorescent stage props and special effects, and for one of the first uses of the Black light and Fluorescent Colors, Fluorescent Movie posters. Next are listed another of the "Switzer Brothers" early very successful ventures of Fluorescent nightclubs, cocktail lounges and bars, which the author suggests applications of Fluorescent table settings, Fluorescent carpeting, Fluorescent waitresses (!) complete with Fluorescent make-up, Fluorescent murals, ceilings, and menus. For simple applications with Fluorescent paints, dyes, or inks the authors suggest Fluorescent Christmas displays, toys, gifts, games, cards, paper, catalogues and advertising presentations. One of the obscure, and hard to imagine applications presented in the 1942 "Fluorescent Chemicals and Their Applications" is Fluorescent sand painting to be used for 'group functions,' parties, meetings and picnics, advising that alot of the Fluorescent effects that could be attained with this sand painting couldn't be made by nature. The Fluorescent sand painting is also advised for baby's nurseries and diverse landscaping work. Another of the early successes of the young "Switzer Brothers" is another of the applications suggested in the book, Fluorescent laundry marking, in which clothes brought to the laundry were marked with Invisible Fluorescent ink for identification in sorting the washed clothes. More applications straight from the "Switzer Brothers" are listed as Fluorescent rope with rope manufacturers including one Fluorescent thread amongst all the other threads that make up their manufactured rope for later identification, as well a Fluorescent Pass-Out Checks at parties, dances, fraternity and social meetings. The common 1930s-1940s application of Fluorescent Store Window displays using Fluorescent advertising slogans and products for sale is also listed as well as the diverse 'physics' lectures, the exposure of quack physics, and for use in the *Church!* Next DeMent and Dake list the famous 1941 "Switzer Brothers" Criminology application of the Black light and Fluorescent Invisible marking and tracing powders, suggesting to coat the invisible Fluorescent powders on money, paper, tools, sales merchandise, and 'persons'! Moving to the nearly-obscure, the authors continue on with their five page list of Fluorescent applications and suggest making Fluorescent candleholders, signs, toys, and lecture pointer sticks with the famous Fluorescent wood Black Locust which has a vivid Yellow uncommon Fluorescent Color. The authors go on to even suggest using Turmeric as a natural plant pigment which also Fluoresces Yellow to stain the wood for a Yellow daytime Color as well. The next profound application for Fluorescent Color and Black lights in this 1942 book is the most outrageous of the lot, suggesting to mark Fluorescent ink on Babies, so that there would be no mix-up in which baby belonged to which mother! The authors pleasantly console the readers to the fact that these Fluorescent inks that would be stamped on the back or the sole of the foot of the babies would be harmless and could even be used as evidence in a court room by simply placing a Black light over the baby. The exciting subjects of classroom demonstrations and stamp collecting are next explored by the authors, with healthy 1940s advice including bringing Uranium minerals into the classroom to show the school children. If the reader thinks that was bad, it's nothing compared to the next grizzly World-war two era applications of these miracles, as the authors write about the new unique use of Fluorescent artificial teeth. Now I have written elsewhere in his book about the experiences with people that have a false tooth or teeth in the Black light, and how odd it looks, but this is truly better than the alternative that is suggested in this book of almost seventy years ago, because the details of these 'new' Fluorescent artificial teeth are given by the authors and they are hair-raising. To make the artificial teeth Fluoresce, and look like natural teeth under Black lights, the artificial teeth were manufactured with - wait for it - 'Uranium phosphors!' If that wasn't enough to make the reader cringe, the next related medical application is maybe even worse: Fluorescent Artificial Eyeballs also made with 'Uranium phosphors' so they would Fluoresce like natural eyeballs! Those poor people. An 'invention' of the authors Dake and DeMent is next suggested, which is the invisible Fluorescent Tattooing of Social security numbers, addresses and names of people who suffer from Epilepsy or Diabetes as a 'warning code.'

Finally, after half a chapter of Fluorescent applications, the authors use the forbidden word "Art." But don't get the hopes up, because the suggestions that the authors have generously written concerning the uses in Art for Fluorescent Color and Black lights do not include starting an Artistic revolution and changing the world by the advent of a new age of Fluorescent Art, but the ultra-banal suggestion of using Fluorescent pigments to dust on the human body so that muscle definition on a model could be more easily rendered. That's it. Swiftly moving to Theatrical gimmicks and Magician tricks, the unnecessary advice is included by the authors that Fluorescent chemicals should never be *eaten!* To close the lengthy section of cosmic, world-changing, mind-expanding Fluorescent Applications, Dake and DeMent discuss Fluorescent dyes for manufacturing of marbleized plaster of Paris, plastic, cement, or wood, and finally the 'Grandfather' of the ever-popular contemporary Fluorescent Icon, the Fluorescent Highway Safety-Cone: Fluorescent Yellow Highway dividing line paint! I must admit that this wasn't the worse idea that these two nuts had, and the subject will be expanded later in this book.

As testament to the banal applications the original "Day-Glo" paint was marketed for, an original can of "Neon Red" "Day-Glo" "All Purpose Fluorescent Paint" is in the Museum collection. Since both the company names, "Switzer Brothers" along the bottom of the can's Fluorescent "Neon Red" and Black wraparound label, as well as the "Day-Glo" logo (with "First Name" printed above and "in Fluorescent Color" printed below "Day-Glo") across the center of the can's label (in no less than four different type fonts), the date of this original can of "Day-Glo" paint is most likely from the 1960s when the "Switzer Brothers" officially changed the name of their company to "Day-Glo." This small metal paint can holding just a "1/4 pint" of still liquid "Neon Red" "Day-Glo" oil paint has "Caution: Combustible" written across the top front of it's Fluorescent label, as well as first indications of it's banal suggested applications for this unique Fluorescent paint through the two small drawings on each side of the front of it's label. Left of the "Day-Glo" logo are the two drawings of a child's bicycle and of two garden tools. Right of the "Day-Glo" logo are the drawings of a sign for house numbers along with a child's wagon. On the back of this antique can of 1960's "Day-Glo" paint's label is a printed list of "Applications," which once again clearly reveal the banal and truly lame consciousness possessed by these Switzer brothers who invented Fluorescent paint: 'House Numbers, Fire Extinguishers, Mailboxes, Water Skis or Buoys, Driveway Markers, Fishing Lures, Bicycles or Toys, Boats or Trailers, Tools or Models, Fuse Boxes, and Water or Gas Valves.' These are the eleven nearly celestial, and virtually surreal suggested "Applications" for the first Colors ever invented which possess the unprecedented ability to absorb invisible Ultraviolet energy and to then reemit this invisible Ultraviolet energy as the brightest Colors ever seen - Fluorescent Colors. Did anybody see the word "Art" mentioned on this can of "Day-Glo" paint anywhere?

In the end these banal applications for the new miracle of the Black light and Fluorescent pigments typify the social attitude and truly infinite perspective that almost all people had for this amazing phenomenon since the period of the 1940s, as exemplified by the attitude of the "Switzer Brothers" who invented Fluorescent paint in 1933, and by this 1942 Dake and DeMent book. In painful truth this social attitude towards Fluorescent Colors hasn't changed even today in 2016, almost three-quarters of a century later, and agonizingly will exist undoubtedly extending into at least the foreseeable future.

Much like Dr. Robert Wood, who was the inventor of the Black light Ultraviolet Filter in 1903 and as such was essentially the uncredited inventor of the "Black light," the pioneer of Fluorescence Alexander Strobl has been for the most part also uncredited for being "First in Fluorescent U.V. Color Effects...Since 1924." Already publishing photographs for his article "Spectacular Effects with Invisible U.V. Lighting" in a New York magazine "Boxoffice" of August 24, 1935 introducing the first professional public performances of Black light "Skeleton Ballets" in Radio City Music Hall, New York City in 1927, Strobl founded the very first company for "Fluorescent UV Color effects ... Since 1924." To put this into perspective, the inventor of Fluorescent "Day-Glo" Paint, Robert Switzer was just ten years old when Alexander Strobl started his first company for "Fluorescent UV Color effects ... Since 1924," and Switzer then went on to invent Fluorescent "Day-Glo" Paint in 1933, which was nine years after Alexander Strobl began his first company for "Fluorescent UV Color effects ... Since 1924." Robert Switzer founded, along with his brother Joseph, thier first company "Fluor-S-Art, Inc." in 1934, ten full years after Alexander Strobl's first Fluorescent company. Another pioneer of Fluorescent manufacturing still famous today was Thomas S. Warren, who founded "Ultra-Violet Products, Inc." in 1932, which was, again, eight years after Alexander Strobl founded his first company for "Fluorescent UV Color effects ... Since 1924" as well.

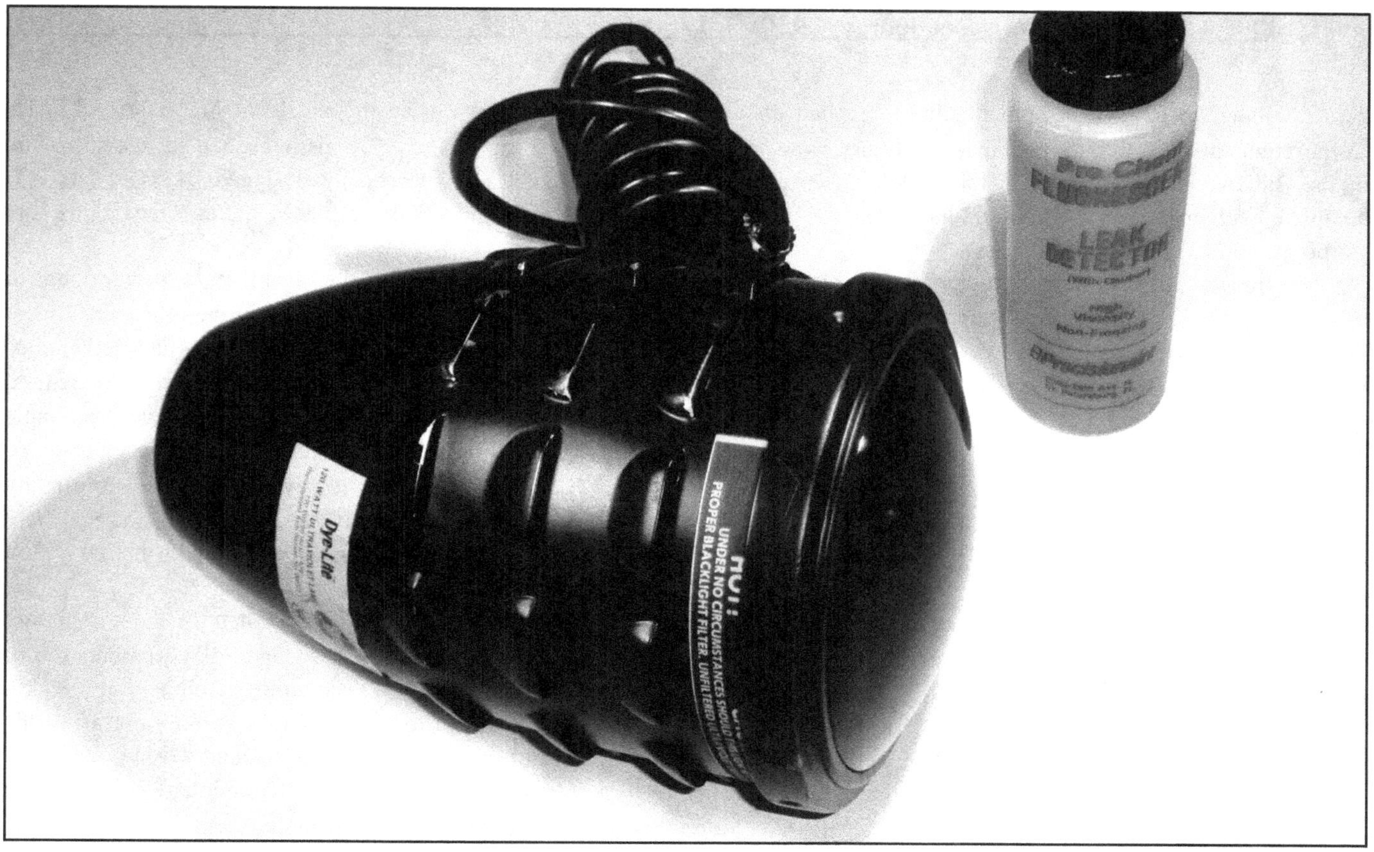

1940s-1950s "Dye-Lite" 120 watt Ultraviolet Leak Detection Lamp with Fluorescent "Leak Detector"

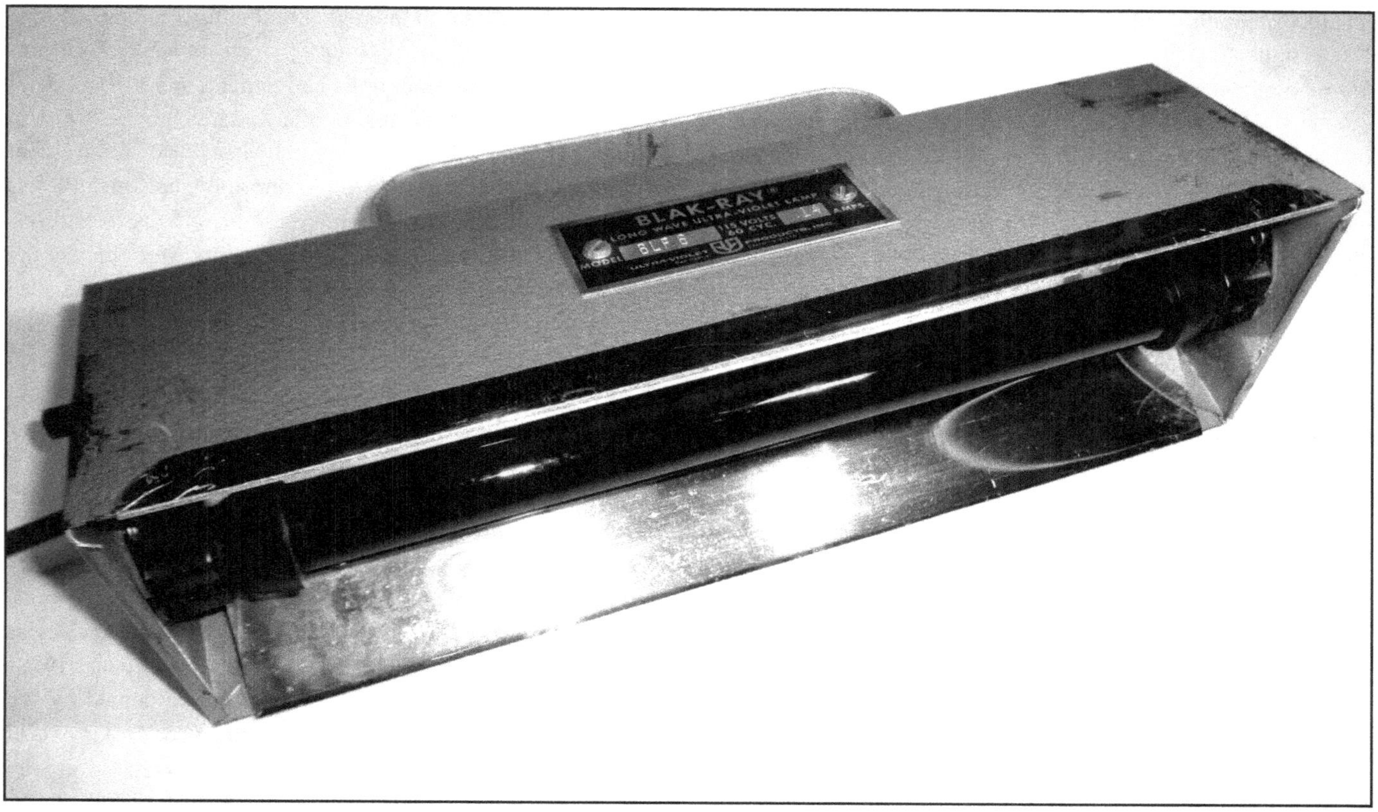

1930s-1940s "Ultra-Violet Products, Inc." "Blak-Ray" "BLF 6" "Long Wave Ultra-Violet Lamp"

3. The Miracle of Fluorescence: "1930s - 1950s"

Imagine, for just a moment, that there had once upon a time been a day when the President of "General Motors Corporation" decided that for the General Motors Annual Corporate Ball, which would host 550 distinguished guests, the theme of the Ball would incorporate, in the middle of every one of the dining tables, a specifically designed **BLACK LIGHT,** complete with matching brilliantly Fluorescent table cloths, napkins, menus, and all other pieces of the General Motors Corporate Annual Ball's dinner table setting!

Imagine, for just another moment, that there had once upon a time been an era when the most popular performance in "Radio City Music Hall" in New York City was a **BLACK LIGHT** "Skeleton Ballet," and that in one of the biggest and most famous department stores in New York City, "Bloomingdales," their huge window displays on the street level had tremendous **BLACK LIGHTS** installed in them for their Fluorescent Window displays(?) Black lights and Fluorescent paint in General Motors Annual Corporate Ball - And "Radio City Music Hall," - And "Bloomingdales?!" "Impossible" is a very probable comment audible from almost every reader on this page in this book. But "Impossible" these three facts of history presented here are not. In this chapter "The Miracle of Fluorescence: 1930s - 1950s" there will be listed events and facts from many decades ago that today, in our present gentrified, neo-conservative, very nearly neo-fascist fully "Fluorophobic" society, these actual historic facts will undoubtedly be met with intense shock, also disbelief, and very possibly even with hatred. Bon appetite.

Imagine, for yet another unimaginable moment, that there had once upon a time been an era when the most important and famous American Fighter Aircraft and Bombers of the Second world war were equipped, as standard instrumentation of their cockpit control panels, with a **BLACK LIGHT** - What! In the Second world war two very famous Bombers of the U.S. Air force were the B-17, also known as "The Flying Fortress," and the B-25. Two of the most famous Fighter aircraft of the U.S. Air force during the Second world war were the P-38 and P-51. All four of these historical U.S. Second world war aircraft had as standard equipment a "Grimes Manufacturing Company" "Ultraviolet Cockpit Light." This "Ultraviolet Cockpit Light" was manufactured in Urbana, Ohio by "Grimes Mfg. Co.," founded by Warren Grimes in 1933, who had started out in 1925 by developing lighting for the early Ford Tri-Motor aircraft. The "Ultraviolet Cockpit Light" was manufactured for the U.S. Air force as standard equipment in B-17 Bombers and other Fighter aircraft for "Black Out" bombing runs at night over enemy territory. Not only did the B-17's and other Fighter aircraft have a standard Black light in their cockpit, but to go along with the Black light all bombing charts were printed with Fluorescent White ink on Black board to easily read under the "Grimes Ultraviolet Cockpit Light" mounted on the instrumentation panel. These small Black light units had either a spiral Black wire or a dark Grey material-encased wire attached to them, which allowed the units to be hand held or attached to a bracket while in operation. The "Grimes Mfg. Co." "Ultraviolet Cockpit Light" in the "Electric Ladyland - the First Museum of Fluorescent Art" collection is a small unit, being only a three inch (8 cm) long round lamp painted Black with a one and a half inch (4 cm) radius lamp front. The front of the lamp has two hourglass shaped Black light filters with a White bulb behind the two filters, so with the two filters aligned the unit would act as a regular White light, but when the front Black light filters were rotated, the two hourglass shaped Black light filters would create a complete Black light filter allowing no visible White light to be seen from the "Grimes Ultraviolet Cockpit Light," and resulting in only invisible Ultraviolet energy being emitted. It seems that there were different models of this "Grimes Ultraviolet Cockpit Light" manufactured for uses in different aircraft, because I have seen photos of an identical unit with a solid Black light filter fitted to the front of the light, not a Black light filter that could be rotated allowing for either White light or Black light. In other photos of this "Grimes Ultraviolet Cockpit Light" there is also the instrument panel bracket that the lamp was attached to, which is a round fixture that is screwed into place, and has a square metal bracket that sticks out of it, into which the square metal bracket of the same size attached to the lamp would fit. There is also a screw on the bottom of the bracket to secure the lamp into it's fixture. One photo of this lamp also shows a very old fashioned metal beaded pull-cord to turn the lamp on and off. To complete the equipment needed in the cockpit of the B-17 and other "Ultraviolet Cockpit Light" equipped U.S. Fighter aircraft of the Second world war for "Black Out" bombing runs, UV-visible pencils and Fluorescent Slide Rules such as the "E-6B" were also issued. The "E-6B" Flight Computer is a circular slide rule used in aviation that was developed in the late 1930s in the United States by a Naval officer. By the mid to late 1930s this is the slide rule Flight Computer used in both the American and British Air Force, which was then also copied by the Germans and Japanese for their Air Forces. Over 400,000 "E-6B were manufactured for the American Air Force during World war two, almost all manufactured from a Fluorescent plastic that is very bright and easy to read under a "Grimes Ultraviolet Cockpit Light." All the lights would be extinguished in the B-17, B-25, P-38, and P-51 during "Black Out" bombing raids, except for the small "Grimes Ultraviolet Cockpit Light," so that from the ground the huge four engine B-17 "Flying Fortress"

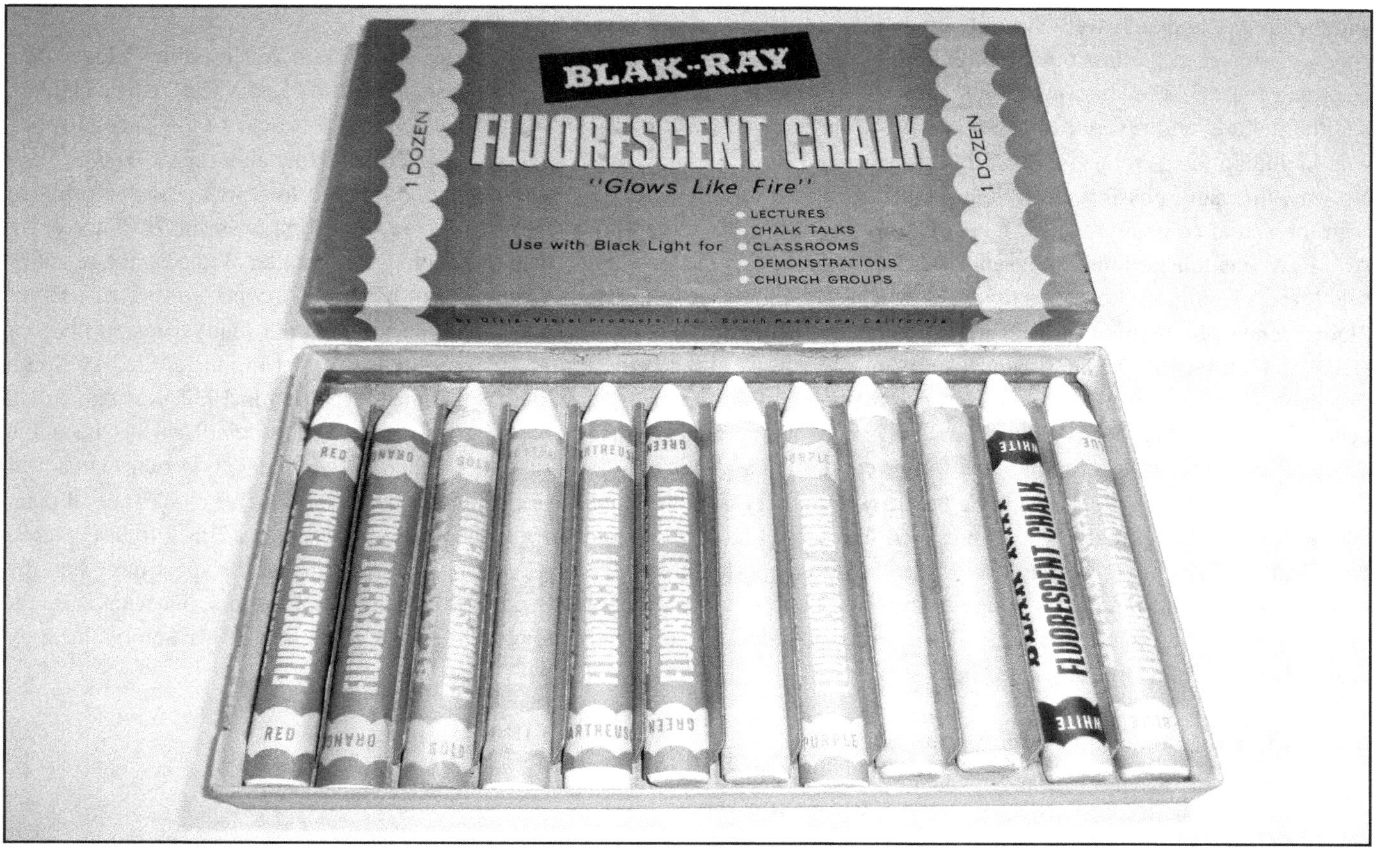

1953 "Blak-Ray" "Invisible Fluorescent Chalk Set," "Ultra-Violet Products, Inc.," San Gabriel, California

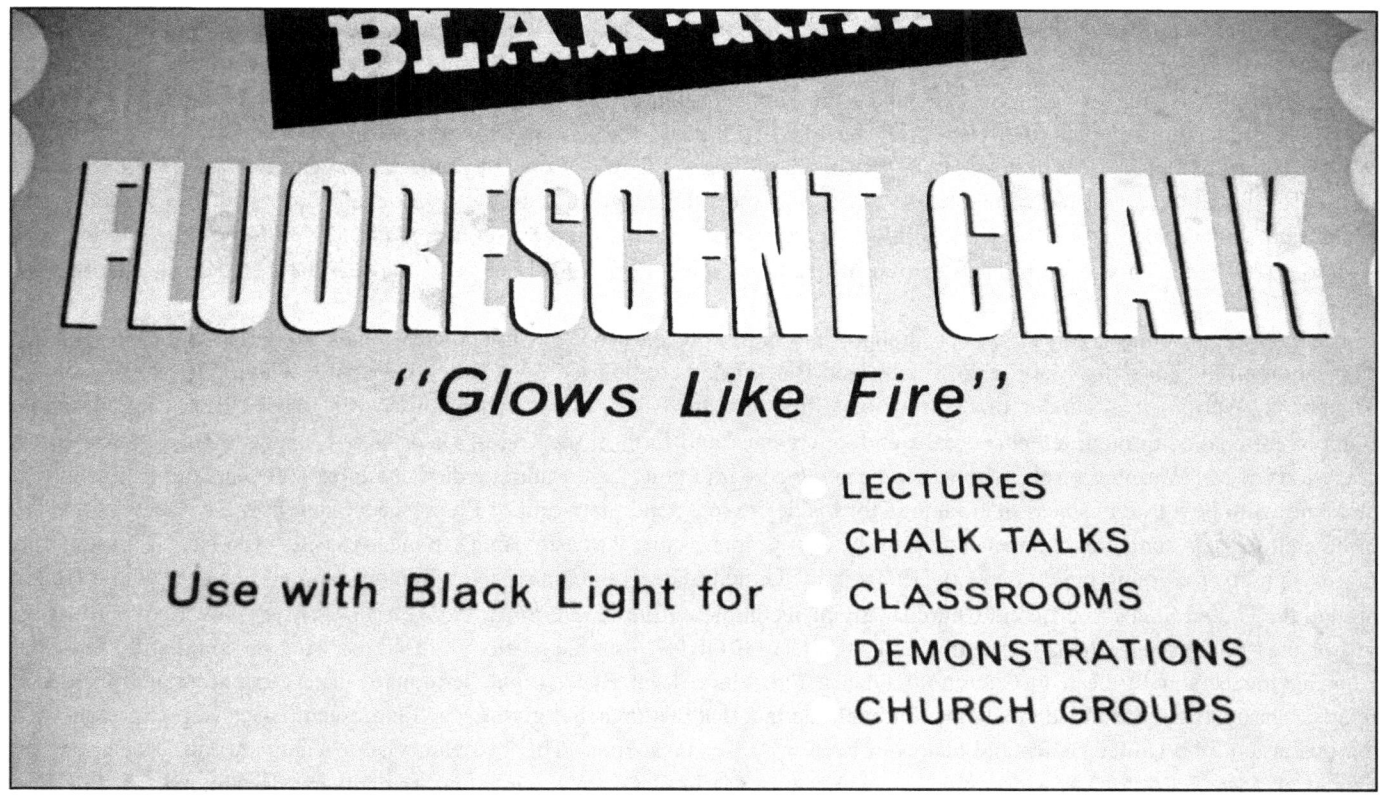

"Use With Black Light for: <u>CHURCH GROUPS</u>" (!!) (1953)

and the other war planes were virtually invisible.

I have, in the last three paragraphs, so far managed to blaspheme the American Corporate World (who's bigger than General Motors?), the largest and most famous of the Entertainment Industry (who hasn't heard of "Radio City Music Hall"?), and the historic and revered Military Forces of the Second world war (actually, all the four major forces of the Second world war, including the Americans, English, Germans, and Japanese).   So what's left to blasphemer? How about the *CHURCH?!* - No way, this can't possibly be serious - suggesting that Religion and the Church had a sordid and forgotten past that mingled with the actual company of the Devil <u>BLACK LIGHT</u>?! Everyday in "Electric Ladyland - the First Museum of Fluorescent Art" I give demonstrations to Museum visitors, and amongst the fascinating displays demonstrated under White light and Black Light are "Common Items that are Fluorescent," Fluorescent minerals, Fluorescent Mineral Artwork, and Artifacts of Fluorescence. Something that never fails to amaze visitors (and many times causes them to laugh out loud) is a small box of "Blak-Ray" 'Invisible' "Fluorescent Chalk" manufactured in the early to mid-1950s by "Ultra-Violet Products, Inc." of South Pasadena, California (it was so long ago that the name of this company, founded by Thomas S. Warren in 1932, was still called "Ultra-Violet Products, Inc." during an era when "Ultra-Violet" was the correct word, not "Ultraviolet" as has been the accepted correct spelling for the last forty years).   This 'Invisible' "Fluorescent Chalk" set contains "1 Dozen" chalks of different Fluorescent Colors, including the truly retro, very controversial Color name "Flesh." These twelve chalks are all plain White Color in the normal daylight, but burst into vivid Fluorescent Colors of the whole spectrum when a Black light is placed over them, giving their signatory "Invisible" reaction, and then even Phosphoresce in all the Colors of the spectrum when the Black light is turned off. This change from plain White to vivid Colors is in itself astonishing to all visitors, but what is by far much more amazing to visitors today in the current cultural conservative state of "Fluorophobia" is what is written on the sixty year old cover of the "Fluorescent Chalk" set:

Use with Black Light for • LECTURES
- CHALK TALKS
- CLASSROOMS
- DEMONSTRATIONS
- ***<u>CHURCH GROUPS</u>*** (!!)

To prove how *outrageous* a claim it was, that "Fluorescent Chalk" and Black lights were suggested in the 1950s to be used for <u>CHURCH GROUPS</u>, in the "Rick Steves - Amsterdam, Bruges, Brussels" major Tourist Guide printed in the United States, under the listing for "Electric Ladyland - the First Museum of Fluorescent Art," Rick Steves (who has himself visited the Museum incognito) writes 'that visitors can see the first historic fluorescent crayon made in San Francisco from the 1950s. Wow.' The label reads "use with black light for church groups." "Wow." Now out of the six sentences that Rick Steves wrote in the Tourist Guide about his comprehensive Museum tour, the suggestion on the small chalk box about Fluorescence and Black lights being used in a CHURCH, of all the places, made such an impact on him that it is a full one-third of his entire review.   This has been written in each edition of his Tour Guide since 2003, and is still in the 2016 edition of Rick Steves' guide.

To be absolutely honest, even I thought it was hilarious when I got this ancient chalk box years ago and read the suggestion on the cover for Fluorescent Chalks and Black Lights to be used by "Church Groups!!" Having personally known Thomas S. Warren, the founder of "Ultra-Violet Products, Inc." in 1932 which manufactured these "Blak-Ray" Invisible Fluorescent chalks, through telephone calls and letters back and forth in the mid to late 1990s, I always thought it was just a crazy idea of Mr. Warren himself, who was very involved with Fluorescence until he died at almost 100 years old, and who was also known to be a true business man famous for his desire to extend the world of Fluorescence into as many facets of society as he could. But - something happened in the Museum years ago that was astonishing to me. A visitor who has clear memories of growing up as a young boy in the early 1960s in the United States, remembers a very famous Church Preacher who travelled around the United States to different Churches giving a complete *Fluorescent Black Light Sermon*! After showing this Museum visitor the "Fluorescent Chalk" set with the "CHURCH GROUPS" user suggestion, he told me what he could still remember from having personally been in Church attendance for "Fluorescent Black Light Sermons."   The facts he related to me, in relative clarity, truly astounded me, beginning with the fact that this Preacher giving his "Fluorescent Black Light Sermon" was famous around the United States and had even been in "Life" magazine. This Museum visitor's name is Jake Kenn., and he visited on May 5, 2005. Growing up as a young boy in Marietta, Georgia, Mr. Kenn. remembers the "Fluorescent Preacher Hofmann" while attending Church on Sunday, and he told me that it was an unforgettable experience, with the priest using

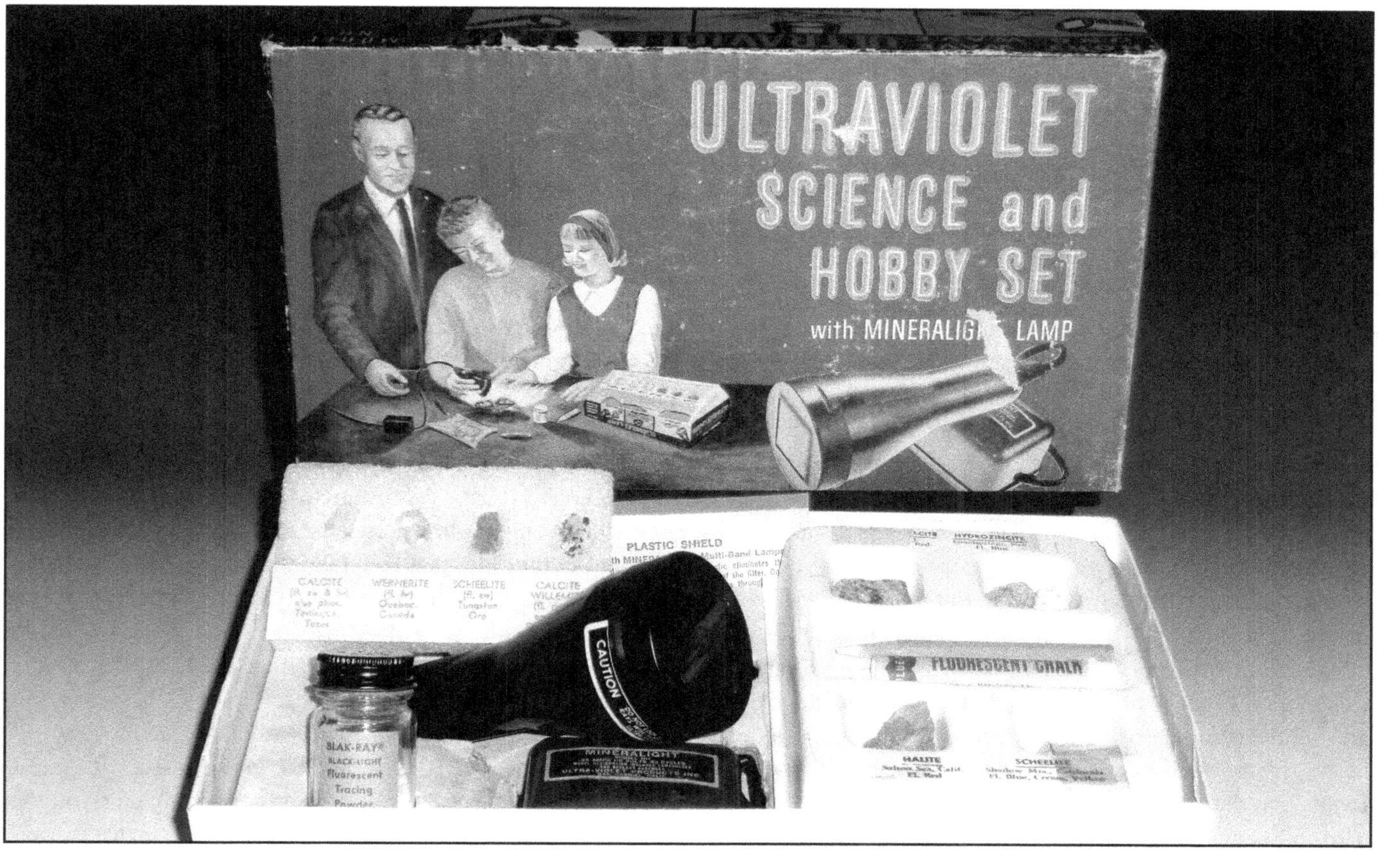

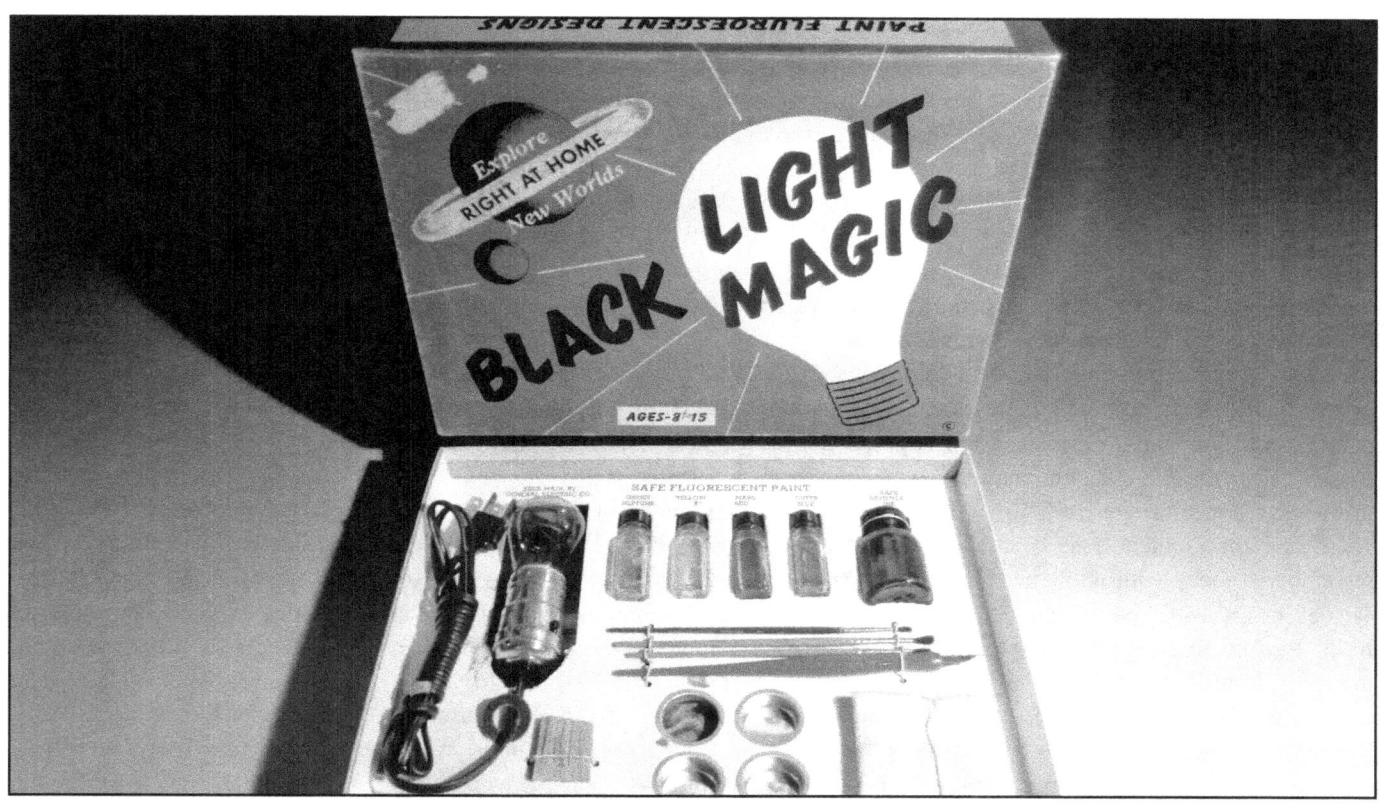

1950s "ULTRAVIOLET SCIENCE and HOBBY SET - with MINERALITE LAMP," "Ultraviolet Products, Inc."

1952 "BLACK LIGHT MAGIC" Set "For Ages 8-15" "Explore New Worlds - RIGHT AT HOME," Stroward, Inc.

Fluorescent paint and Black lights throughout the Sermon, keeping the Church congregation enraptured. Particular details Mr. Kenn. still remembers are fascinating, such as the "Fluorescent Preacher Hofmann" routinely as part of his Church Sermon giving Fluorescent mineral demonstrations with Black lights on the Alter (!) while talking about their relation with God. This truly unique and visionary Preacher would also make invisible Fluorescent paintings and show them on the Alter with the Black light, while different religious images would appear through the use of the invisible Fluorescent paint during the Sermon at certain passages. Mr. Kenn. was very excited while telling me this story in the Museum, and remembered it well from the mid-1960s in Georgia. What Mr. Kenn. was really astonished to see also in the Museum was a 1950s-1960s "Mineralight Ultraviolet Lamp" "Science and Hobby Set" on display in the Artifacts of Fluorescence display case. This "Science and Hobby Set" is precisely the set that this Museum visitor won many years ago as a boy in a contest held by the same "Fluorescent Preacher Hofmann," in which the child who could memorize the most Bible scriptures won this Ultraviolet Mineralight Set! The last time Mr. Kenn. remembers seeing the "Fluorescent Preacher Hofmann" was about 1980 in a Church near Atlanta, Georgia. The "Fluorescent Preacher Hofmann" had become famous in the years that had passed as he had travelled around America giving Fluorescent Black Light Church Sermons. By the time that Mr. Kenn. experienced his first Fluorescent Sermon as a boy, in the mid-1960s, the "Fluorescent Preacher Hofmann" was already well known, and had been making the Fluorescent Black Light Church Sermons for some years by that time. The last Fluorescent Black Light Church Sermon of the "Fluorescent Preacher Hofmann" that Mr. Kenn. was in attendance of was about 1980 - and for this particular Armageddon Sermon there was a six foot (1.9 meter) inflated Fluorescent globe of the Earth on the Church Alter that the "Fluorescent Preacher Hofmann" would make an extremely dramatic, unforgettable ending with, having all the lights dimmed in the Church and only a strong Black light on. This visitor still clearly remembered the climax of the Fluorescent Armageddon Sermon, where the "Fluorescent Preacher Hofmann" used the large inflated Fluorescent globe of the Earth in the Black light, which, as the Destruction of the World happened in this Armageddon Sermon, he exploded this inflated Fluorescent Earth globe with a pin, leaving the entire petrified Church congregation in absolute darkness(!) This "Fluorescent Preacher Hofmann" could very well be the famous Preacher who inspired the contemporarily hysterical listing "CHURCH GROUPS" to be "used with Black Lights" on the box of the set of Invisible "Fluorescent Chalks" on display in the Museum. Another astounding story on this hard-to-believe subject of historic Black Light Church Sermons was told to me in the Museum by another visitor in 2011. Drey Sam. was born in 1952, and lived in the extremely rural community of Pender, Nebraska. He told me an incredible story which happened to him when he was about sixteen or seventeen years old during the late 1960s. Pender, Nebraska is a remote community which consisted of only about 1,200 residents in the 1960s and the unbelievable incident which Mr. Drey Sam. was in attendance of occurred in what he described as "one of the smaller churches of the town." Mr. Sam. told and wrote down for me this story with a relatively clear memory of the event: "In 1968 or 1969 (or maybe 1967) I saw a traveling Evangelist in Pender, Nebraska on an Omaha Indian Reservation who did a mass showing various religious scenes in Fluorescent chalk, with his own portable Black light in the darkness of the church(!) This church preacher then asked people to come up to the alter and dedicate themselves to Jesus (which I didn't do). It was so striking that I remember it to this day."

This chapter "The Miracle of Fluorescence: "1930s-1950s" is meant to provide an insight with documented historical perspective into a state of mind and public opinion that today seems nearly impossible to believe. But imagine, one more time, that there had once upon a time existed a very high regard and public opinion towards Black lights and Fluorescent paint. One of the most important events that exemplifies the high public regard that Black lights and Fluorescent paint had in society was the 1939 World's Fair "Golden Gate International Exposition" in San Francisco. This was no ordinary World's Fair, but an event of colossal proportions even by today's standard, that began by constructing the biggest man-made island in the world at that time to house the historic event. The proportions can be better understood when realizing that in 1939 $50,000,000 was spent on this "Golden Gate International Exposition," which wasn't just a World's Fair, but also a celebration of the completion of the two largest bridges in the world at the time, the San Francisco-Oakland Bay Bridge, which opened on November 11, 1936, and the Golden Gate Bridge which had recently opened on May 27, 1937. This magnificent exhibition is still remembered today with it's famed "Treasure Island" which took one and a half years to construct in the San Francisco Bay. This event was truly spectacular, hosting live concerts by Judy Garland, Bing Crosby, Count Basie, Benny Goodman, and even Irving Berlin who sang his new song "God Bless America." Johnny Weissmuller -and even Jane- were live at the event, and to top it off, Charlie Chan made a movie there from April 17 to May 13, 1939: "Charlie Chan at Treasure Island." There were exhibits from thirty-six countries, immense exhibition areas housing $20,000,000 worth of Art treasures, including the "Birth of Venus" by Botticelli, and a mural was painted live by Diego Rivera as visitors to the World's Fair watched. To give an idea of the importance of the event and to make the point clear that this was a Pacific World's Fair, at the exact moment that the Sun rose in Bombay, which would mark the absolute start of the "Opening Day," a radio signal was sent all the way across the

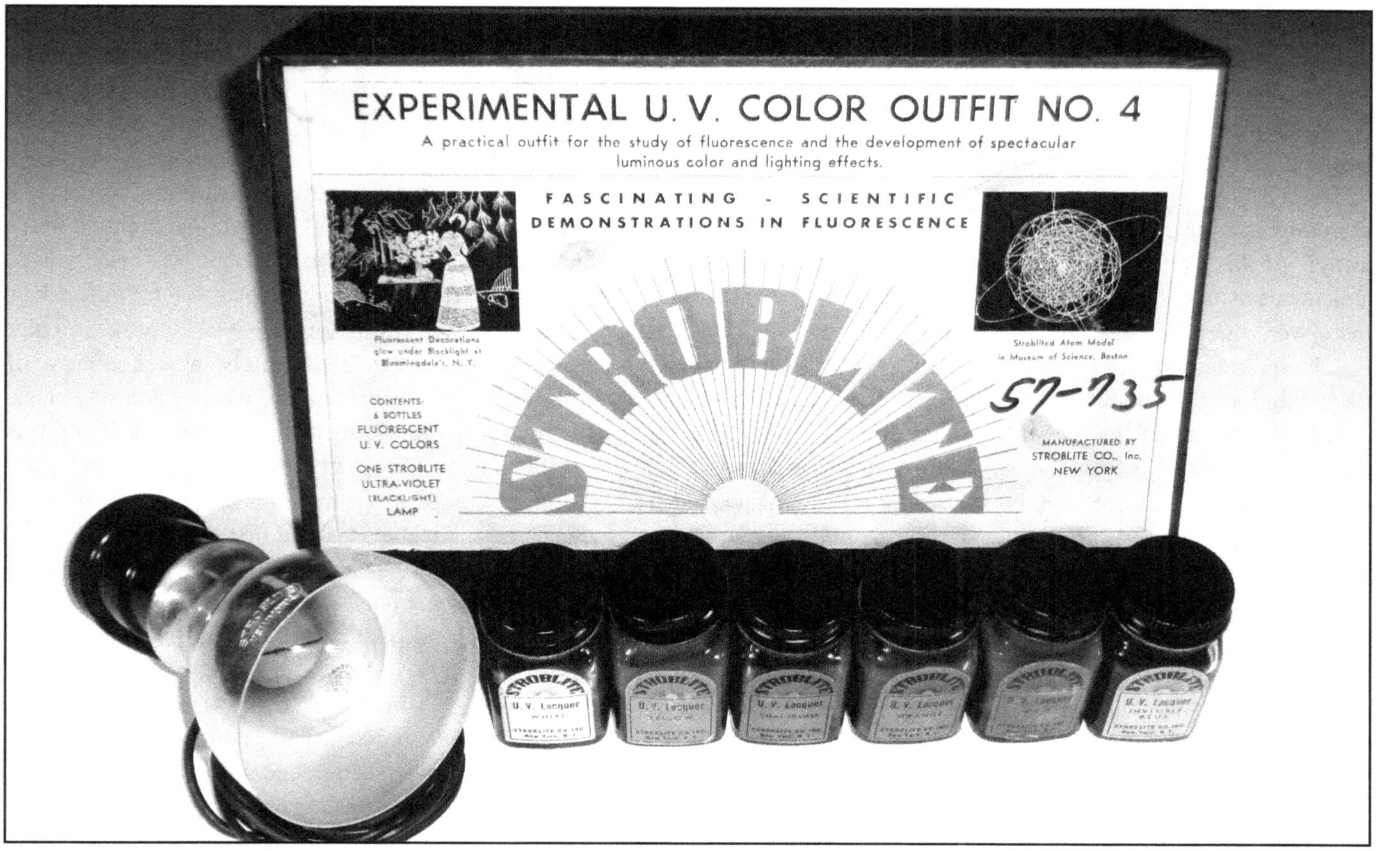

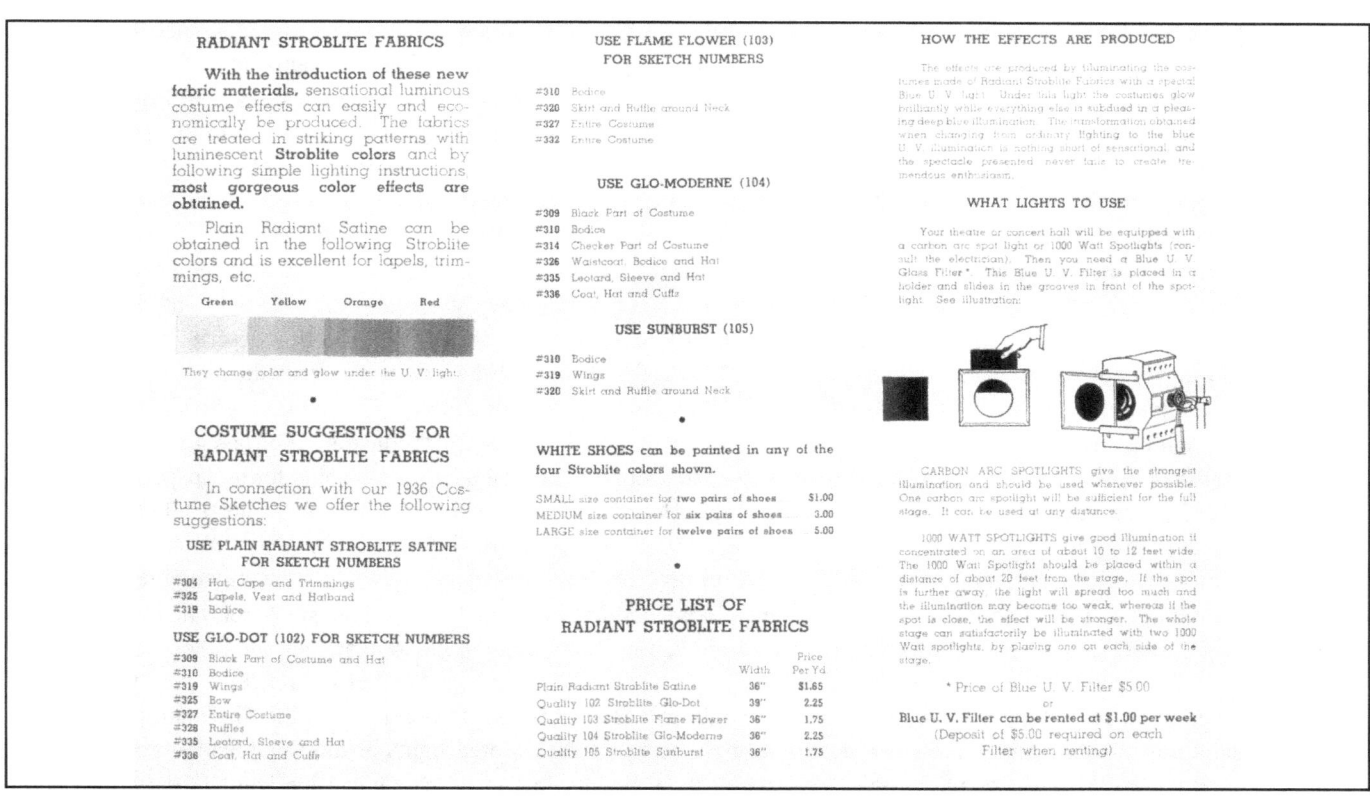

1930s-1940s "EXPERIMENTAL U.V. COLOR OUTFIT NO.4," "Stroblite Co., Inc.," New York

1936 Fluorescent "RADIANT STROBLITE FABRICS" brochure, "Stroblite Co., Inc."

Pacific Ocean to "Treasure Island" and at exactly 10:30 PM San Francisco time February 18, 1939, the brilliant, unprecedented amount of lighting was turned on, illuminating the entire island. One of the main exhibition features of this 1939 San Francisco World's Fair "Golden Gate International Exposition" was the lighting and Colors. The budget of $1,500,000 for outdoor lighting done by "General Electric Co." for the exposition was unheard of at the time. On "Treasure Island" there was the four-hundred foot (123 meters) "Tower of the Sun" which was illuminated by two dozen enormous searchlights that were each a yard (meter) wide. The "Official Guide Book" of the "Golden Gate International Exposition" explains that these twenty-four searchlights were eight different Colors and generated 1.44 billion candlepower of light that could be seen one hundred miles away! At this 1939 World's Fair the major new lighting innovation of the Black light and Fluorescent paint was widely used and stands as one of the highlights of the entire event itself. The "Official Guide Book" also tells us that in the World's Fair there were three hundred "ultra-violet mercury" or "black light lamps" used to create effects on Invisible Fluorescent paint which would burst into vividly Fluorescent statues, sculptures, and murals, being documented as having been used in many of the exhibitions throughout the entire World's Fair. This description in the "Official Guide Book" to the World's Fair continues, explaining that all of the Artwork produced at the World's Fair with the Invisible Fluorescent paint under Black lights was startling and looked as if the Fluorescent Artwork was suspended off the wall in a Phosphorescent glow. This is very likely the first Invisible Fluorescent paint being sold by the "Switzer Brothers," who, as discussed in the previous chapter, had invented Fluorescent paint in 1933 in Berkley, California in their family home as teenagers, and had created the first company to sell this new, amazing paint. The 1934 "Midnight Painting" article in "Scientific American" magazine about the "Switzer Brothers" "Northern-Lite Color Laboratory" described the effects of their early Invisible Fluorescent paint murals very similarly. There is a WPA sponsored writing project that describes just how extravagant and truly ahead of it's time the entire design of the "Golden Gate International Exposition" was. The entire conscious design of the whole of "Treasure Island's" use of Colors represented the first intentional large scale public application of "Chromotherapy," which uses Color itself as the health treatment (and has again become very popular in the last twenty years of the 'New Age' movement). To project the Colors of the World's Fair in this planned application of "Chromotherapy," during the daytime the tremendous amount of flowers throughout the fair, including an unimaginable twenty-five full acres of the 'Ice plant' known as 'Magic Carpet,' together with Colored walls created the Color Therapy, but during the night was the real show with "fluorescent tubes" and the new "black light" together with "ultra-violet floods" and many other designs of lighting, which created the historic lasting image of the "Golden Gate International Exposition" itself. There is an excellent full Color photograph of this "Magic Carpet" display of 'Ice plants' in the book "The San Francisco Fair - Treasure Island 1939-1940," which proves it was in fact an incredible display with an unimaginable amount of flowers in bloom. The Color photo's caption in this book explains that this natural flower "Magic Carpet" designed by Horticulturist Julius L. Girod was an amazing twenty-five acres, which spread out from both sides of the "Elephant Towers," which were carved to represent "Cubist Elephants" at the entrance to the Fair. In this same book of 1989 edited by Carpenter and Totah, there is a personal memory of a regular exhibition featuring a Black light performance in this 1939 San Francisco World's Fair, by one of the performers. One of the swimmers in the "Aquacade" exhibition in the Fair named Sol DeGuarda wrote of memories in this "Aquacade" show performing along with Ester Williams, particularly one routine performance named the "Blue Danube," during which all the swimmers in the show wore Fluorescent caps and gloves. As these swimmers began the performance the spot lights would be on, and as they swam into the pool the lights would go off and Black lights would be turned on, just showing their brilliant Fluorescent caps and gloves. The best description of the Black light and Fluorescent Phosphorescent paint's usage in the 1939 San Francisco World's Fair comes from the most reliable source, my crumbling original copy of the "Official Guide Book of the Golden Gate International Exhibition on San Francisco Bay" printed in 1939, with a cover price of twenty-five cents. Just a glance at the cover Color illustration of this guide immediately informs the reader of it's era, with it's massive Art-Deco stylized sculpture, as well as it's cloth spine for this paperback. At the back of this 1939 guide there is the section "Night Lighting - How it's Done," with a description of the 10,000 floodlights, 2,400 Fluorescent tube lights of Blue, Pink, Green, and Gold, 130 searchlights, and 300 "ultra-violet" or "black lights" hidden in the trees, shrubs, and trenches from the eye, which were all used on Treasure Island. New Colors were obtained by mixing Pink Fluorescent tubes and Blue floodlights to create Mauve light, and lighting with "graded intensity" from the base to the top of the buildings. "Black lights" were projected onto "invisible luminescent paints" applied to statues and murals of the "Court of the Seven Seas" to create "tinted pictures" which have a "phosphorescent glow." Another reference to this "Court of the Seven Seas" exhibition is in the 1939 "Treasure Island - Night and Day" postcard fold-out souvenir. The main picture, even used on the cover of this postcard fold-out souvenir, is a night scene of the Colored lights of this "Golden Gate International Exhibition," and in this immense "Court of the Seven Seas" the brilliant glow of Black Light Blue and Violet-Purples is the entire foreground of the picture.

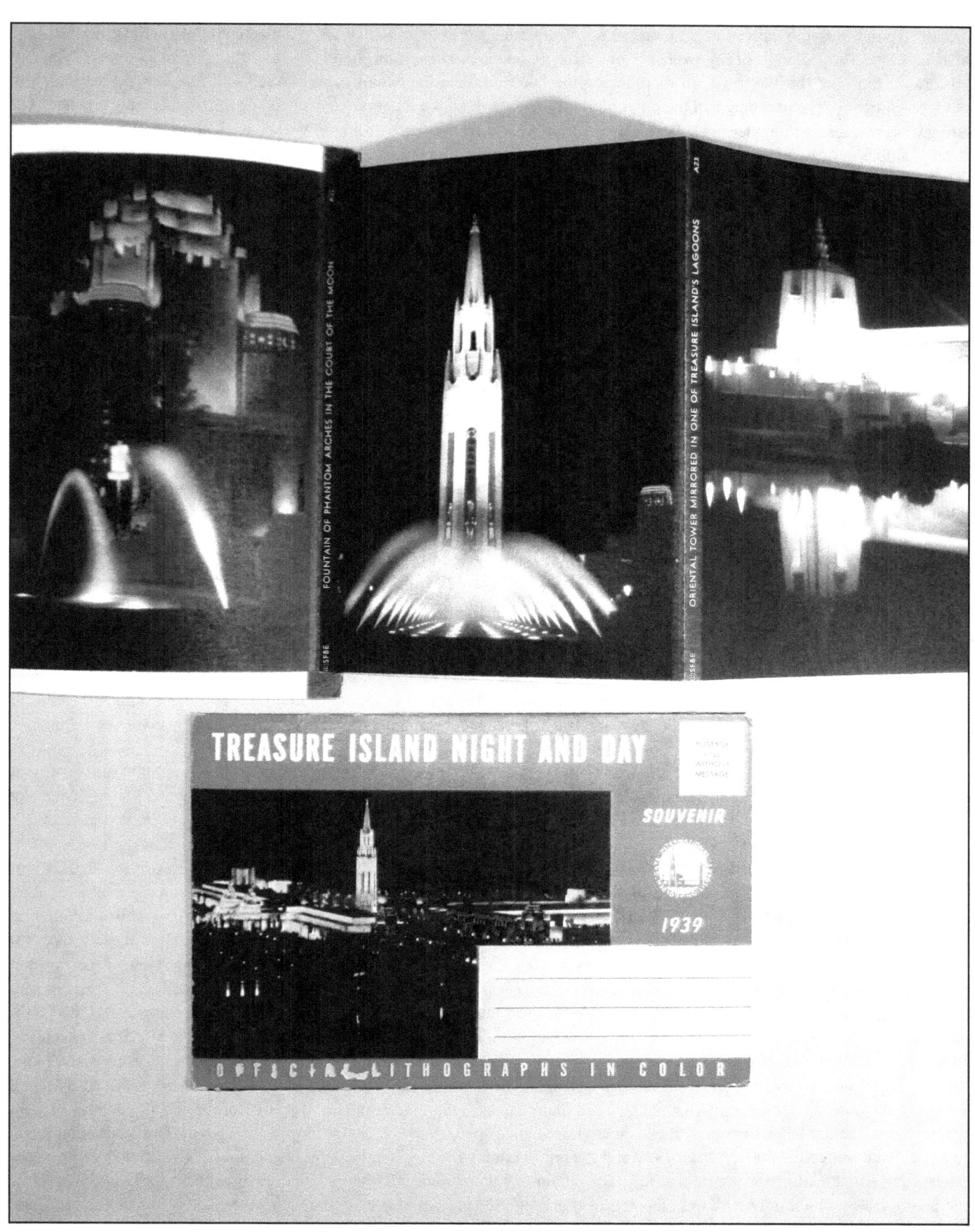

1939 San Francisco World's Fair "Golden Gate International Exposition" "Treasure Island - Night and Day" fold-out souvenir

In the Museum collection is an original postcard from the second half of the "Golden Gate International Exposition" held in 1940. The Color postcard (with it's place for a "one cent stamp" on the back) is of the "Railroad Express Agency Historic Exhibit" of the World's Fair, reproducing the two murals in the exhibit, one of 1839 with the new railroad and the obvious portrayal of a 'past era,' and the other mural of 1940 with all the modern icons including the airplane, the Golden Gate Bridge, skyscrapers, and modern vehicles. The description of these two murals in the World's Fair on the back of the postcard is an example of how important and widespread the use of Black Lights and Fluorescent paint was at the 1939 World's Fair "Golden Gate International Exposition:"

> "RAILROAD EXPRESS AGENCY
> An outstanding example of the use of fluorescent
> paint and black light in depicting a "Century of
> Service" in vacationland at the Golden Gate
> International Exposition."

A very clear photograph of the San Francisco Golden Gate Exhibition of 1939, showing the extraordinary amount of lighting visible at dusk is in "Fluorescent Chemicals and Their Applications" by Jack DeMent and H.C. Dake from 1942. The photo validates the huge amount of lighting and the copious amount of produced light that caused the entire exhibition to be brilliant. The photo's caption reads that there was a 'wide use of Fluorescent paints and Ultraviolet light flood lamps,' credited to "General Electric Company."

In the Museum collection is this 1939 treasure Island fold-out postcard souvenir. This "Official View Folder, Golden Gate International Exhibition, San Francisco - 1939" is especially valuable for it's documented photographs of "Treasure Island - Night and Day," which show the wide use of the Black light and Fluorescent paint in the event. Sixteen "Original Lithographs in Color" fold out of this full-Color postcard souvenir, with one side of the postcards having a daylight scene of the major attractions of the Exhibition, and the other eight cards on the flip side of this postcard set have the night scene of the same attractions. The lighting and Colors of this Exhibition were nothing less than spectacular, and although the cards are not glossy, the Colors were reproduced well through lithography. Inside this postcard fold-out there is a description of the San Francisco Exhibition, explaining that Treasure Island is beautiful during the day, but at night it becomes an 'enchanted island of Color and light.' 'The magic "black light" on luminescent murals' is explained in the text to create an 'experience entirely new.' These "magic" Colors of this Exhibition can also be seen in another collection of postcards reproduced from the originals, "The 1939 San Francisco World's Fair in Postcards" by Herbert Rolfes, as well as many other publications, since this was such a famous event.

At the same time as the San Francisco 1939 World's Fair Golden Gate International Exhibition, 3,000 miles away in New York the World's Fair was also being held. Though not as famous for the massive use of Black light and Fluorescence like in the San Francisco World's fair, there was the presence of this "new" technology in the New York World's Fair as well. Alexander Strobl, founder of "Stroblite...First in Fluorescent Effects from 1924" directed the painting of "Democracy 2039" in this 1939 New York World's Fair with his full line of Fluorescent "Stroblite" paint. One or two rare photos of this extravagant display can be found on the internet and in "National Building Museum" books. These rare photos show a massive public Fluorescent display in the '39 New York World's Fair that people would walk around on circular walkways. This huge circular public display looks about fifty yards (meters) across and the photo shows the presence of a few visitors on these walkways, who look just tiny in this massive display. The circular walkways surround a huge Fluorescent Black light view of the world in 2039, a century after the Worlds Fair, displaying a very organized circular city layout along with roads, lakes, rivers, and surrounding countryside. This "Democracy 2039" was even built on a curved surface to duplicate the curvature of the Earth, and must have been spectacular in the dark under Black lights. On the internet, facts are revealed that "the effect" was achieved in this "Democracy 2039" by Alexander Strobl using paint that reacts to "Ultra-Violet lights" which came from Black lights that were presumably mounted under the circular balconies above the display. It is also revealed that many of the "roads" were not painted, so only the "main arteries" Fluoresced under Black light. Descriptions of this Fluorescent 1939 display explain that the huge circular balconies which the visitors viewed the display from above also physically rotated. The description refers to an original printed photograph from 1939 and the information written on the back of this photo, which stated it was a staged photograph which had been "very difficult." The author of this internet information from 2010 explains that the difficulty of the photograph was not only with the Fluorescent Black light effect, but also was compounded by taking the exposure "while moving." Twenty-five years later the current author experienced these unforgettable moving walkways in the 1964 New York

World's Fair's Vatican Pavilion, in front of Michelangelo's "Pieta." White light and Black light photographs of the "Democracy 2039" display can be found on the website "worldsfaircommunity.org"

The July 3, 1939 World's Fair issue of "Life" magazine has a cover photo of most likely the first woman's two-piece bathing suit, of course in Black and White. Opening up this 1939 World's Fair "Life" magazine, the first page sets the date with a full page advertisement for "Plymouth" automobiles announcing the new Plymouth "Coupes" starting at just $645, and the expensive Plymouth "Sedan" priced starting at $685(!) More startling than this ad is the half-page ad in this "Life" magazine for "Kellogg's ALL-BRAN" The "Natural Laxative Cereal" with the headline offer for this "Laxative Cereal" enticing customers to "Join the Regulars"(!) This cartoon-style "Kellogg's" ad from 1939 looks about as old as the Colosseum in Rome! Last in the retro shocks is a living portrait of Matisse at seventy years old.

This July 3, 1939 "Life" magazine has the feature story on the 1939 World's Fair in New York which contains photos of amazing displays from seventy-seven years ago, such as the "General Electric" "Steinmetz Hall" with twelve minute shows of real Lightning produced by ten million volts of electricity before live audiences(!) This 1939 World's Fair was held in Flushing Meadows, Queens, New York, the same location that the 1964 World's Fair occupied, and there is a night photo of the "Parachute Jump" which was moved after the World's Fair and still functions for the past seven decades in Coney Island. 'The most recent' addition added to what "Life" called the 'amusement area' and the 'girl shows' was Salvador Dali's "Dream of Venus" which contained a "Wet tank" with girls swimming through Dali surreal landscapes, as well as a "Dry tank" with a sleeping Venus in a thirty-six foot bed. These interior displays and the exterior structure of the "Dream of Venus" pavilion consist of prototypical Dali Art.

Although unfortunately there is not a photograph of "Democracy 2039" in this sixteen page article on the 1939 World's Fair, the reason this "Life" magazine is in the Museum collection is because of the "Science" section article 'Black Light Used For Black-Outs.' The subtitle of the article informs the reader that this "New Ultraviolet lamp" 'would enable traffic in England to move during air-raids in the dark.' This two page article has eight excellent photographs to give examples of this 'Black Light Effect' used on England's roads already in 1939 for "two years." Clearly explained that England was training it's citizens to react in "enemy air-raids," and that their main defense was to plunge entire cities or country sides into darkness - a state of alarm named "Black-Out" - during this Second world war era. The main problem was explained as the inability to drive in the dark, so an "Oxford physical chemist" Allen V. Rhead introduced the method of using Black lights and luminous paints. The short three paragraphs of text explains that Black light is an invisible part of the spectrum called "ultraviolet" or "short waves." It is further explained that "inventor" Allen V. Rhead along with the "co-inventor" John Evans introduced an "ultraviolet ray" portable lamp that can be mounted on any "motor vehicle." This portable Black light for vehicles in England used early "Mercury-arc" technology and was attached to any vehicle battery. Dramatically explained, it is stated in this 1939 article that Rhead's Black light Mercury-arc lamp would throw 'a beam of invisible ultraviolet' that caused road markers that were "specifically painted," to "gleam" in the dark. It is also explained that although one lit match can be seen a mile away, the emitted light of Fluorescent paint under Black lights is only visible for a mere five-hundred feet (165 m). This is incorrectly called "reflected" light of the "black-light maximum" in this article, but it is correctly stated that this would make it impossible to see from "enemy aircraft" above. It is next stated that the "Fluorescent Powders" used to make paint, plastic, rubber or varnish react under Black lights are "Chemist Rhead's" secrets. Rhead produced a variety of Colors of these "Fluorescent Powders" and suggested to use Fluorescent White for "curb-sides" of streets, traffic lights in Fluorescent Blue, first-aid stations in Fluorescent Yellow, and for hospitals Fluorescent Red. Allen V. Rhead of Oxford also suggested using "Black-light Sets" inside of hospitals and factories, as well as use by "ambulance squads."

The first three very clear Black and White photos of this "Black Light" article show the comparison between a "Daylight" photo of an English street intersection, a "Night" photo of the same spot with "ordinary headlights," and the third photo of the same intersection under only the Black light mounted on a car and the emitted Fluorescent Colors of street markings. The curbs were painted in Fluorescent White, trees are painted with Fluorescent paint about two yards up from the bottom, and to complete the effect Fluorescent paint was used for the lines on the street. The caption explains that it only cost about twenty-five cents a mile to 'process' roads with Fluorescent paints for "Black-Outs." Two small Black and White photos of the "Oxford Boathouse Wall" are next in the article, one in the daylight and the other under Black light. "A.R.P" painted in "almost pure" Fluorescent pigment apparently stood for "Air Raid Precautions." The last three photos in this "Life" magazine from over seventy years ago are of Rhead in his Oxford laboratory testing a "Mercury-vapor bulb" (while smoking a pipe). The photo's caption explains that although this lamp gave off five percent visible light, the additional filter cut the visible light from the lamp to zero. The next photo is of a "street cleaning truck" of Oxford that is so old it looks like something out of a "Laurel and Hardy" movie. This simply ancient-looking vehicle is equipped with one "black-light headlamp" next to the normal headlights, which is explained to be a "Mercury arc bulb" fitted with a "black-glass filter." The final photo shows the mechanical setup of the Black light, with a transformer and an inverter under the hood next to the engine. The reader is also told the price for this "Black-Light" "Black-Out" vehicle set was an extravagant $50.00 in 1939, but it would become cheaper, and the article closes with the information that the "Government" was studying plans to make this "Black-Light" "compulsory" for all vehicles.

Just three weeks later in the July 24, 1939 issue of "Life" magazine, also in the Museum collection, a letter was printed by Alexander Strobl himself, who was involved in the 1939 World's Fair Fluorescent "Democracy 2039" display. This letter from Strobl was more important to the history of the Black light than the entire article in the July third issue of "Life" just discussed. The letter from Strobl is headlined "Black Light" and begins with this Black light pioneer Alexander Strobl, the Hungarian chemist who immigrated to New York, praising the recent attention that the Black light was getting, which Strobl called the "neglected member" from the family of "sun-radiation." Strobl next states quite clearly that he was extremely disappointed once more because an American invention was presented to the American public through "Life" magazine as a "European discovery." Strobl states clearly the historical facts that "Fluorescent Colors" of "all forms," including 'paints, liquids, powders, varnishes, and make-ups' were being used in America already "over a decade," and that "ultra-violet lamps" which were portable and consisted of "mercury-arc bulbs" had also been used in America for "some years" already. Strobl states in the letter to "Life" that the "Black Light" manufactured "First" was made in America in 1932 by "Westinghouse" at his own "instigation." This obviously predates the claim of the "Black light" being invented by American William H. Byler in 1935 which will be discussed further. Alexander Strobl further clarifies the fact that European experimentation with the Black light began just "several years" before and was begun by a "European lighting engineer" that was given all the information on Black lights and also "effects" of "fluorescent lighting" by "General Electric Company" and Strobl himself.

Concerning the 1939 New York World's Fair, Strobl writes that over fourteen different World's Fair exhibits used Black lights and Strobl's "Fluorescent Paints." To further illustrate the misplaced credit to Europe concerning the invention of Black lights and Fluorescent paint, Strobl continues his letter to "Life" with the fact that the very subject of the 'European invention' of Black lights being used on roads was presently in an exhibition in the New York World's Fair "General Motors" "Futurama" exhibit, with Black lights and Fluorescent paint illuminating "roads of tomorrow," as well as eliminating the dangerous glare of road lights and headlights. Strobl also explains that in the "Perisphere" his exhibit "Democracy 2039" was painted with his "Stroblite" Fluorescent Colors, and thus able to present a "night effect" of what a city could look like from above, lit only with the "black light."

In all fairness Alexander Strobl closes the "Life" letter with his opinion that "proper credit" is due to Mr. Rhead for presenting an important 'practical use' of the Black light, even though he was not the first inventor of either the Black light or Fluorescent Colors.

In contemporary times many self-proclaimed "authorities" of the internet have now credited the "Invention of the Black Light" to an obscure scientist originally from Missouri named either William H. Byler or William F. Byler, depending on which 'authorities' website you read, clearly exemplifying the inability of these 'authorities' to even get Byler's *name* correct! Logic would suggest that if these 'authorities' of the internet couldn't even get his name correct - than what else can you believe or trust from these "internet scholars?" What, typically, these "internet scholars" got correct is expanded upon and inflated to the point that it becomes not only incorrect, but goes so far as to effectively change history for the large - and rapidly expanding - portion of society that believe everything that they read on the internet is unquestionably correct.

In "Summer 2009," the website of the "University of Central Missouri's" "Today" web publication introduced - much to their own credit obviously - the article stating that William F. (or H.) Byler was "Inventor" of the "Black Light." Byler graduated from the University of Central Missouri with degrees in chemistry and physics in 1927, and later earned his masters and doctoral degrees from the University of Missouri. This web publication is entitled "Central Yesterday" 'Remembers William Byler "Blacklight" Inventor,' and even manages to spell "Black light" incorrectly. This web article can be found on the net in a second, and goes on to give credit to William F. Byler as the lone creator - as well as the "Inventor" - of the Black light. In typical self-made authority style, a fact is discovered and then with complete arrogance - and incomplete knowledge - the fact is grandly expanded upon without the slightest interest in the actual history produced or originated by the single fact they have discovered. What I am referring to is the fact that William Byler applied and received the first Patent for the Black light either in 1939 or in 1935 - depending on which article you read. This "Today" UCM internet article states that Byler became a research scientist for "General Electric Corporation" in 1937, which just happens to be around the date that Alexander Strobl wrote in "Life" magazine that "General Electric" and himself supplied all the needed knowledge to produce Black lights and Fluorescence Colors to the Europeans for the first time to initiate production abroad. Byler went on to become director of research at the healthy "U.S. Radium Corps." in 1939, developing Fluorescent and Phosphorescent chemical applications. The UCM article gives credit to Byler for several patents, including the patent issued to him 'after 1939' for the Black light.

Several other "internet scholar" articles crediting William H. (or F.) Byler with the Invention of the Black light can be found on the website "e-How," which needs no introduction with such a name. Two articles are published by this website that I am referring to, one asking who was the "Inventor" of the Black light, and the other asking what is the Black light "History." When reading these two articles I found far more mistakes and incorrect history than knowledge itself. The Invention of the Black light is of course credited to William H. Byler in 1935, before working for the "General Electric Corp." for two years and before becoming director of research for the "U.S. Radium Corporation" for thirty-two years. The Black light "History" article right next to this article on the same website states that in the 1930s William H. Byler worked for the "General Electric Company" laboratories in Schenectady, New York and then developed the Black light in 1935. This article also goes on to state that the first Black light manufactured with "Byler's Invention" was called the "Wood's lamp" crediting the Black light Filter invention of 1903 to Robert William Wood. This article continues and goes on to give credit to Byler for the suggestion of using Black lights to "illuminate instrument panels." Even a book written in French in 1938 by Maurice Deribere 'Uses and Applications of the Black light' got the facts more correct than this "e-How" internet article of the Twenty-first century. This "e-How" authority writing about the Black light "History" goes on to also credit the 'Invention of Fluorescent Paint' to John Thompson Shannon in the 1940s. Again, a decade before the 1940s - in 1933 - Robert Switzer Invented Fluorescent Paint in Berkley, California. John Thompson Shannon did create the first public performance in 1907 using experimental Black lights and Phosphorescent paint (invented 1,000 years ago in Asia) in the "Warfield Theater" in San Francisco, but Shannon did not "Invent" anything.

So, typifying a Twenty-first century conclusion which generally contains much more ego than historical fact, here has been presented three different internet articles written by different 'authorities.' One of the three articles gives credit to Byler for the Black light "Invention" after 1937 or 1939, and the other two articles credit Byler for Inventing the Black light in 1935. One of the three articles credits Byler with the first idea of using Black lights in instrument panels of planes in the 1940s, which had already been published in French on the other side of the Atlantic Ocean in 1938. Another of the three articles credits John Thompson Shannon as the "Inventor" of Fluorescent paint in the 1940s, also a decade after Fluorescent paint was actually invented in 1933, and not by Shannon, but by Robert Switzer. With such credentials, what the hell can be believed from these 'authorities?' These facts, not esoteric in any way, are not open to an individual's interpretation, but are hard historical facts which are dated and documented nearly one hundred years ago. Like many other extremely complicated technological inventions, including the "Television," there is no single "Inventor," but a series of profound inventions by many different scientists and researchers which are all used in tandem to create the final invention, such as the "television," the "automobile," the "Black light," and the "computer" as examples. Going by this erroneous information's method of operation, typical of the internet, it would then have to be logically concluded that the "U.S. Radium Corporation" *Discovered Radium* - <u>Not</u> Marie and Pierre Curie, because the "U.S. Radium Corporation" was the first to Patent "Radium," not the humble, extraordinarily intelligent, greed-less visionaries Marie and Pierre Curie(!) There is a reason that the television and the Black light have never before been credited to a single "Inventor," and the reason is because there was no single "Inventor." But, again, all of that past clarity is now being fogged over and stained with excrement by the pure arrogance and the enormously inflated and self-created egos of Twenty-first century "Internet scholars." What evolution - you don't have to even study to become a "scholar" any more, just buy a God-damned computer for $500! Back to 1939 when people had to actually physically go to a university, sit in classes looking and listening to a Human being called a "teacher" - not at a plastic screen - and had to "study" and "learn" - true "facts" were revealed by true "authorities" - people who intimately knew what they were talking about and teaching because they had spent a good portion of their lives - decades - only concentrating on the subject and learning as much as possible about the subject - not false self-created "authorities" who spent $500 on a computer, maybe have never read one entire book in their whole lives, and have also spent an extravagant fifteen full minutes looking up other similar self-deitized contemporary "authorities" and then incorrectly - and as quickly as possible - have copied the already incorrect information off the internet, and then have written other related articles about other 'passing interests' such as "The Price of Rice in China."

In the Museum collection is an original postcard sent from Switzerland to William Byler of the "U.S. Radium Company" from the 1950s, as well as the original 1939 "Official Guide Book" of the "New York World's Fair" - "The World of Tomorrow." The front cover design and lettering of this 1939 "Guide Book" immediately give the impression of the first "Superman" comics of the same era with the title "Official Guide Book" hand-lettered in 'shadow-type' - with about a mile of shadow behind each letter. The design on the front cover contains the two most important elements of the 1939 New York World's Fair - it's logo, and it's "Theme Center" for what was called "The World of Tomorrow:" the pointed "Trylon" and the circular "Perisphere," which contained the Fluorescent "Democracy 2039" exhibit under Black lights. After no mention of Black lights, which were a major part of the theme of the World's Fair going on at the same time in San Francisco, there is a six page article "Democracy - the Theme Center." Again no mention of the Black lights in this "Official Guide Book," not even in the six page article on "Democracy" itself. There are three Black and White Artist's renditions in the section on "Democracy," the first of which is of the interior of the 200 foot (65 m) wide, eighteen story tall Perisphere which housed "Democracy" and which was designed by industrial designer Henry Dreyfuss. Not a single word about Fluorescent paint, the powerful Black lights mounted above the exhibit, or even about Alexander Strobl. "Building the World of Tomorrow" was the theme of the show "Democracy 2039," and it is described that there were two circular "viewing platforms" surrounding "Democracy" which appeared to be "suspended in space" and revolved around the display "in opposite directions." The only single indication of "Democracy" having Black lights and Fluorescent paint for this 1939 World's Fair is an oblique reference using the term "luminous world" to describe "Democracy." In only two other photographs in the 1939 "Guide Book" does it look apparent that Black light and Fluorescent paint were used. Almost every photo in this 1939 Guide was taken during the daylight hours, but the "Hall of Communications" was photographed both in daylight and at night, with a massive 160 foot tall (23 meter) entrance and was described as a "wonderland" of both "Light and Color," and looks identical to Fluorescent paint emitting brilliant Color under Black lights. One other photo in this 1939 World's Fair Tour Guide apparently was taken at night under Black lights with Fluorescent paint - the massive, vivid, and cheerful display "Retreat of Death." To realistically date this time period, this exhibit describes the "New York City Cancer Committee" still using "Radium" to treat malignancy! Finally, the most dated photo in the entire 'Tour Guide' - the display in the "Transportation" section of the World's Fair described as being a "dramatic visualization" representing "swift travel" over a "long distance" by a "Rocket ship(!)" The photo of this display looks the closest to "Flash Gordon" in the book: in front of a room-sized map of the world there is a 'Frankenstein laboratory' with a giant "death ray" shooting out of it. Today it looks just plain ridiculous.

Another large-format book very surprisingly without a photograph of the "Democracy" Fluorescent display is a book printed specifically on "The 1939 New York World's Fair - Trylon and Perisphere" by Cohen, Heller, and Chwast. In this lavish publication filled with very large Color photographs of the "Trylon and Perishere," which was the symbol of the New York 1939 World's Fair as well as the exhibition that housed the Fluorescent Black lit "Democracy 2039" display painted by Fluorescent pioneer Alexander Strobl, there is but a single partial Black and White photo of Fair visitors viewing this magnificent Fluorescent display in normal White light. Not only is this single photo of Fluorescent "Democracy 2039" in the White light, not the Black light, but the photo is even mislabeled and under the section on the "General Motor's" "Futurama" exhibit. This mislabeled partial photo shows Fair visitors on a circular balcony overlooking the vast miniature city of a Fluorescent Black lit future "Democracy 2039" from individual booths on cushioned chairs with a curving glass wall in front of them. For my Christmas trip back to America in 2013 I met the girlfriend of my cousin Anthony, who's father is eighty-nine and went to this 1939 New York World's Fair when he was fifteen years old. This clear man still has fond memories of the Fair, and was so happy to meet someone still interested in something that happened seventy-four years ago that I gave him this "Trylon and Perishere" book.

In 1964 and 1965 I personally went to the New York World's Fair in Flushing Meadows, Queens as a boy, and although it was an unforgettable event that I still treasure lucidly until today, with life changing exhibitions that were so important to me that they even inspired some of the Fluorescent "Participatory" Environment I built in the Museum, such as "Futurama" by G.M. with cars that you drove into the 'future,' and even Michelangelo's "Pieta" which had never moved from Rome since the night he snuck into the Vatican nearly five hundred years before - But I remember seeing only once, and I repeat: *Only Once* a Fluorescent Black Light display in the entire 1964 New York World's Fair, which was in my favorite exhibition, "G.M.'s" "Futurama." I don't readily recall at the New York World's Fair any 'startling murals that looked as they were off the wall in a Phosphorescent glow painted with Invisible Fluorescent paint' either, to tell the truth. And this was in the middle of the 1960s, two and a half decades after the "Golden Gate Exposition"! As an example of the mystical and esoteric nature of the 1964 World's Fair in New York, comparable with the use of "Chromotherapy" in 1939 in San Francisco, there was, in all fairness, "The Formica House" built completely out of the housewife's dream, the new "Formica(!)" With hindsight, it is really quite a shame that the New York World's Fair didn't have 300 Black lights and Fluorescent paint all over the place like in 1939's San Francisco "World's Fair," because the 1964 World' Fair in New York was the event that Ken Kesey and the Merry Pranksters had driven all across America in the first "Day-Glo" psychedelic iconic school bus to visit, as documented so well in "The Electric Kool-Aid Acid Test" by Tom Wolfe.

The "Kokoon Arts Klub" Cleveland, Ohio, 1911-1956

The "Kokoon Arts Klub" was formed in 1911 by commercial Artists working at the Otis Lithography Company in Cleveland, Ohio, and with their beginning something like in an abandoned tailor's shop, this Artist's group was founded with the intent of exploring the "New Art." Their documented intent was printed in 1931 as their "Narrative and Roster," and states that the butterfly cocoon was the inspiration, as this miracle of nature transmutes itself, and from a crawling caterpillar emerges a soaring, beautiful butterfly.

What did emerge was an outrageous group of modern Artists who went so far to stretch the limits of acceptance during the 1920s and 1930s that they managed to even have one of their annual "Bal-Masques" cancelled by the mayor of Cleveland! Beginning in 1913 the Kokoon Arts Klub held an annual "Bal-Masque" of which posters, costumes, and other artifacts are in museum collections today. In 2011 for the one-hundredth anniversary of the Artist's club formation, a book was published "Out of the Kokoon: Festival of Modern Art and dance, 1911-1938" by Henry Adams, as well as public exhibitions held in Cleveland to celebrate the event between 2009 and 2011. This book by Adams is the catalog of the exhibition in Cleveland Public Library's Fine Art and Special Collections department presented from August 1 to December 31, 2011, which included vibrant costumes and posters from the Kokoon Klub, and was entitled "The Kokoon Arts Klub: Cleveland Revels!" Many of the historical details, as well as the social perspective of the era in Cleveland, are found in the Adams catalogue.

The reason for including the "Kokoon Arts Klub" in this history of the Black light is mainly because of their pioneering 1938 "Black Light Ball" in Cleveland, Ohio, which was just five years after Fluorescent paint was invented and only three years after the Black light had been patented. Similar to the coming chapter on the 1960s Movement, this wild group of Artists in Cleveland represents very early proponents to the Black light and Fluorescent paint, before prejudice, stigmatism, and ultimately rejection became part of the Black light's aura - in fact during an era when almost nobody had ever heard of Fluorescent paints or Black lights. The "Kokoon Arts Klub" members were easily comparable to another group of limit-testing and limit-breaking characters who would become known as "Hippies" three full decades after the "Kokoon's" final party "The Black Light Ball" of 1938, and for this reason both of their movements will be examined in detail to reveal what factors of society were drawn to and adopted this new unearthly technology which revealed totally mysterious, unseen emissions of the brightest Colors ever created.

The "Kokoon Arts Klub" was formed a century ago by Ohio Artist Carl Moellmann and by the Artist William Sommer, who had both come from the J. Ottman Lithographic Company in New York to the Otis Lithographic Company in Cleveland. In the 1920s and 1930s Cleveland was the capital of Movie poster printing in both the U.S. and the world, as well as having printing contracts with both "Time" and "Life" magazines. Cleveland was an industrial city on the banks of Lake Erie and was also situated one full day's ride closer to the movie capital California than New York. In 1908 the Otis Lithography Company in Cleveland got a huge contract to print Movie posters for the entire industry, and by the late 1920s Cleveland had the capacity to produce half a billion movie posters a year. This huge industry needed Artists, who would hand-draw the movie posters with crayons on lithographic stone. Otis Lithographic Company needed more skilled quick Artists for their huge productions, and in 1908 they hired two of the most experienced poster Artists from J. Ottman Lithographic Company in New York: Carl Moellmann and William Sommer. Carl Moellmann originally grew up in Cincinnati, Ohio, and then while working at J. Ottman Lithographic Company in New York he became manager after his friend William Sommer declined the job and recommended him. During this period Moellmann studied drawing and painting from the famous Artist Robert Henri and became close friends with other members of New York's "Ash Can School," which was a rebel urban Art group led by Henri. The "Ash Can School" held an exhibition "The Eight" at the Macbeth Gallery in 1908, which was the first American Art scandal of the Twentieth century and which has been regarded as the beginning of Modern Art in America. After working at the Otis Lithography Company in Cleveland, with financial backing from his friends, Moellmann opened up his own rival printing business in Cleveland: "Continental Lithography," which would be the company the "Switzer Brothers" would be invited to Ohio to become associated with, and in turn would temporarily rename their company to "Conti-Glo."

The two founding Artists Carl Moellmann as president and William Sommer as vice-president would fashion the ideas of the "Kokoon Arts Klub" after the avant-garde "Kit Kat Club" in New York which was a meeting place for Artists and writers who were interested and involved in new forms of Art beyond traditional and academic, and was a club which was already famous for being notorious. Some references state that Carl Moellmann had been a member of New York's "Kit Kat Club." In reality, the first "Kit Cat Club" was in London during the early 1700s and was a tavern owned by Christopher Catling which was famous for it's mutton pie "Kit-Kats." Upper-class literary and political leaders comprised the members of this "Kit Cat Club," who were amongst the first dignitaries who's portraits were made in a new size in 1735; a size which came about because of the ceilings of the "Kit Cat Club," which were so low that portraits had to be painted half-length. More well known is the "Kit Kat Club" in New York formed by illustrators and newspaper Artists during the beginning of the Twentieth century. This was the club that inspired the Kokoon Klub's formation, and which the Kokoon Klub's activities were modeled after, including the "Kit-Kat Club's" live model drawing events held in their studio on Fourteenth Street in New York City and the group exhibitions and auctions in this space, as well as an annual Ball. What is detailed in the Adams catalogue is that the founding of the "Kokoon Artists Klub" in 1911 was a direct result of the first Art controversy of the Twentieth century in 1910 in Cleveland, when Cleveland Artist Abel Warshawsky returned from France with revolutionary and shocking canvases he had painted with a palette knife using pure brilliant Colors, producing landscapes which were similar to Gauguin. Warshawsky was asked by young Artists in Cleveland to take charge of a painting class several times a week, and amongst these young Artists was William Sommer. After a short time because of the commercialism in Cleveland Warshawsky returned to Paris, but it is remembered today that the 1910 exhibition of Warshawsky was the "seminal event" in the formation of the "Kokoon Artists Klub" the next year in 1911. The "Kokoon Arts Klub" of Cleveland began with thirteen members, of which eleven members had German roots.

Legend has come to be told that the Kokoon Arts Klub was started in an abandoned tailor's shop, but this is clarified in Henry Adam's book, which explains that the Kokoon Arts Klub was founded in August, 1911 as announced in the "Cleveland Town Topics." Bylaws limited the membership to thirty, but at it's peak the membership was over sixty. For it's formation in 1911 there were only thirteen members who met two times a week at the back of a Mrs. Allen's house in a rented room which was situated behind a tailor's shop. There was only a pot-bellied stove for heat and freezing models would have just a "large wardrobe" (cabinet) to change their clothes in.

Carl Moellmann, the cofounder of the Kokoon Artist Klub in 1911, was a very important person in the history of the Black light and Fluorescence by having been an influence in the history of the "Switzer Brothers" who invented Fluorescent Paint in 1933. After Carl Moellmann formed his own printing company in Ohio, "Continental Lithography," the Switzer brothers moved from Berkeley, California to Ohio where they established their company in association with Carl Moellmann's "Continental Lithography," and again, temporarily renamed their Fluorescent company "Conti-Glo" in the 1930s.

Just how outrageous the Kokoon Arts Klub was is a little hard to truly comprehend today, over one hundred years after the Klub's formation, but the height of their fame and notoriety came from their annual "Bal-Masques" (Masked Balls) which went on for decades, and which are most famous during the 1920s and 30's which was the peak of the Kokoon Arts Klub, culminating in their "Twenty-fifth Silver Jubilee Anniversary Bal-Masque" of 1938: "The Black Light Ball." Through Black and White photographs of the members of the Kokoon Klub during the 1920s and 1930s dressed - or undressed - in their Bal-Masque costumes, it becomes immediately apparent just how outrageous these Cleveland Artists a hundred years ago were! At least half of the photographs of the women members of the Kokoon Klub in their "Bal-Masque" costumes are shocking when realized that the images came from the 20's and 30's, with photos that could be from a Trance party in Goa or Ibiza today - breasts completely visible through transparent, or lack of, tops. What must be remembered is that during the 1920s and 30's women's fashion had just begun to expose the ankle at the bottom of her yard long dress. Some members of the Kokoon Klub for the 1938 "Black Light Ball" came dressed solely in Fluorescent Cold-creme! Today it seems possibly a little tame, but the outrage of showing up at a public Masked Ball in Ohio in the 1930s completely or even partially nude was unthinkable at the time. The nudity or partial nudity of these Kokoon Klub members and their invited Bal-Masque guests was only part of the scandal they caused, because just their acceptance and involvement in the "New Art" of the early Twentieth century was already outrageous enough for the average citizen at that time.

Most references a century after the Kokoon Klub's formation, including "The Encyclopedia of Cleveland History," state that based on the Klub's inspiration from the avant-garde New York Kit Kat Club, their purpose was to open or introduce to the public the "New Art" of the early Twentieth century. Although the club originally excluded women in their membership, the images that are the most shocking and modern today are the nude or semi-nude portraits of these women members in the 1920s and 30s. For years the Kokoon Arts Klub was located next to a former tailor's shop, but in 1921 the club relocated to a large venue also in Cleveland. The artifacts that remain today are largely from the most famous, and in some ways infamous, annual event of the Kokoon Klub, their Bal-Masque which in all documentation sounds about as outrageous as could be possibly imagined for the early Twentieth century. Twice a year the Kokoon Klub also held public Art exhibitions of their member's Artwork, which by all accounts were generally "controversial" at least. To give an idea of the public reaction to the Kokoon Arts Klub's public Art exhibitions, in 1914 the "Cleveland Leader" newspaper headline announced that "The Biggest Laugh" of Cleveland that week wasn't in theater, 'But in an Art Gallery.' The poster for this "Exhibition of Modern Art under the Auspices of the Kokoon Arts Klub at the Taylor Galleries, 1914" is printed in Adams' catalogue. The Artist for this poster was William Sommer, and the antiquated image is of a woman embracing a huge electric light bulb - which was the new invention of the future, and which was to be exhibited in just a few months at the Electrical Exposition of Cleveland. Despite typical negative reaction to the Kokoon Arts Klub's public Art exhibitions, in 1916 the Cleveland Museum of Art opened and then in 1919 the juried competition of local Artists began in the museum, which was subsequently won by Kokoon Klub Artists for years to come.

In the early years the Kokoon Klub also exhibited as the "Secessionist Group" (inspired by both the "Vienna Secession" as well as the "Photo-Secession Gallery" of Alfred Stieglitz in New York), and even as the "Cleveland Independents." Grace Kelly, the Art columnist for the "Plain Dealer" began her career in 1911, the same year as the Kokoon Arts Klub's formation, with an article in which Warshawsky and his Impressionist students are labelled directly as "freaks" who 'slap on paint' with a "deliberate intention" for merely "attracting attention." Inspired by Warshawsky's paintings and Art classes in which he taught radical Color juxtaposition, in March 1911 seven "Cleveland Modernists," including Warshawsky, Carl Moellmann, William Sommer and others who would start the Kokoon Arts Klub that coming August, exhibited their work together. The "Cleveland Leader" newspaper reported that this "Secessionist exhibition" was "no place" for anyone who had a "weak heart." Blame for the radical Art in this 1911 exhibition was placed on Robert Henri and his 'school of the east,' who remained a hero figure to these "Secessionist/Kokoon Klub" Artists. A local German-language newspaper went so far as to attribute the "startling features" of many of the pieces of Art in Kokoon Klub exhibitions to the "bad influence" of master Cezanne! The year later in February, 1912 the second Secessionist exhibition was held, which was after the Kokoon Arts Klub had been formed that past August. Every Artist in the exhibition was a Kokoon Klub member, and newspapers called the show "one gorgeous riot," reporting that these Artists painted 'just as they liked' without copying past masters, which gave them their name "Secessionists." Rembrandt, Raphael, and Mr. Color himself Van Dyck are all mentioned in obvious contrast, with accusations of influence flying towards Matisse, 'Luminists,' Pointillism, and the Post-Impressionists. By 1913 the reviews for the third "Secessionists exhibition" began to acknowledge the "Post-Impressionists" which was what they labelled the exhibiting revolutionary Kokoon Arts Klub Artists, whom's Art was defended for it's "new, vital expression" of Color and line, it's inspiration through "savage arts" and 'oriental psychology,' as well as it's purpose of creating Art not for Art's sake, but Art "for life's sake" as Nietzsche had taught.

Cleveland Artists who were members of the Kokoon Arts Klub had also brought knowledge of "radical ultramodern art" back to Cleveland from their travels. William Zorach travelled to Paris in 1910 and returned to Cleveland in 1911 with stories of the new painting by Picasso and Matisse. August Biehle travelled to Munich in 1910 and returned to Cleveland in 1912 with inspiration from the "Blue Rider" group with it's first non-objective Artist Kandinsky. Finally the Armory Show of 1913 which opened in New York and then travelled to Chicago and Boston, revealed to Cleveland Artists the extent of "Ultramodern Art." Included in the Armory Show was Van Gogh, the Post-Impressionists, Cubism, Fauvism, Futurism, and German Expressionism, but nothing was as controversial as the "most discussed" painting in the exhibition, Marcel Duchamp's "Nude Descending a Staircase." In Adam's catalogue the reproduced paintings of "Secessionist/Kokoon Klub" members all are immediately recognizable as being inspired by masters of the late 1800s and early 1900s, such as Warshawsky's 1909 "Bridge of Vernon" immediately reminding the viewer of Gauguin's vibrant Colors as well as even his brush strokes inspired by Cezanne. Vernon is where the train stops for the walk over this "Bride of Vernon" to visit Claude Monet, who was still creating masterpieces until 1926 in Giverny with his water-lily pool (which is now a museum) just a few kilometers away. William Zorach's 1913 "Maine Harbor" is very close to Matisse's landscapes of the same period in which blank canvas makes up a large portion of the image. William Sommer's 1912 "The watchtower" is as close to Vincent Van Gogh's "Church at Auvers" of 1890 as Warshawsky's paintings are to the paintings of Paul Gauguin, and Sommer's "The Three Graces" of 1916 and "Dancing Nudes" of 1917 are obviously inspired by Matisse's work of that period, particularly Matisse's large "Dance." In 1912 August Biehle turned the Kokoon Klub Artists onto the totally abstract painting of the first non-objective Artist Wassily Kandinsky and the "Blue Rider" group from his travels to Munich, and by 1935 Biehle's work approaches the visionary painting of Robert Delaunay and his style of Dynamism. After the Armory Show "broke the ice" for Modern Art in 1913, where in New York alone 175,000 visitors had attended, a "follow-up exhibition" "straight from Paris" of Cubist paintings went to five different cities in the U.S., including Cleveland. Reactions in the Cleveland press were typical of society a century ago when confronted with Cubism (and has changed little in the ensuing century), including labeling Cubism as "sheer tomfoolery," it's Artists 'imitative monkeys,' and it's intention "mass mystification" and "metaphysical."

The Armory Show had it's strongest influence of attending Kokoon Klub members on William Sommer, who had travelled to New York to see it. In Henry Adam's book William Sommer is stated as being the Kokoon Arts Klub's "unquestionable leader," being one of the oldest members, a cofounder, and an Artist all his life, Sommer was interviewed at that time and is documented as saying that the Armory Show made him a "convert" to the Modern Art and that he didn't "begin to live" until he experienced the Armory Show.

Although the early Kokoon Arts Klub exhibitions received harsh and abrasive reviews in the early years of 1911-1913, the feeling did not change or progress through the passing of a decade. In 1925 the Kokoon Klub's public Art exhibition's paintings were proclaimed in a newspaper article as "abortions" and in 1927 as "monstrosities." The Art exhibitions of the Kokoon Arts Klub were always held in the "Kokoon Klubhouse's" main room, and always had a "large female nude" prominently displayed in the show as a way of announcing the Klub's "bohemian spirit." The annual exhibition would display about fifty Artworks made by about twenty Kokoon Klub members.

Since the ridiculed Art auctions and exhibitions of the Kokoon Arts Klub members not surprisingly made almost no money, in 1913 the Kokoon Klub planned a Masked Ball at the Elks Club to raise funds. Although Artistic bohemian masked balls had already been staged in New York, it had never been done in Cleveland before. Due to their already outrageous reputation, getting a permit for a bohemian Arts ball featuring "outrageous costumes" splashed with Color was only achieved because the Cleveland mayor was also a painter and an "art enthusiast." In "Out of the Kokoon" a friend of William Sommer's described the very first Kokoon Arts Klub's "Bal-Masque" of 1913, explaining that a "giant cocoon" was carried through the crowd of the party by 'four huge Negroes who were almost naked.' After a girl floated out of the cocoon dressed only in "butterfly wings," there were "twenty naked" Kokoon members dancing 'painted like Indians.' It must be remembered that this was during the era of the First world war! The next day Cleveland's shock was complete, with all the newspapers reporting the "capital B" of Bohemia was now "located in Cleveland." Even though the Kokoon Klub managed to raise every eyebrow in Cleveland with their first masked Ball, they also managed financially to raise nothing, and in fact to loose $1.00 when the receipts of the "fundraiser" were counted. What this 1913 first Bal-Masque did do for the Kokoon Klub was make them famous all over Cleveland and to make them realize that they should make their party an annual major event of the Klub. By the third Bal-Masque many Clevelanders had heard about the ball and the Klub raised enough money to rent a different clubhouse. Several events led to the Bal-Masque becoming the major spectacle of the Kokoon Arts Klub, including the opening of the Cleveland Museum of Art just a few years after the first Bal-Masque, which in turn led to less interest in the Klub's public Art exhibitions. During the same year, in 1916 the Kokoon life-drawing classes also seemed to become less attended after instructor William Sommer moved from Cleveland to the suburbs, as well as automobiles becoming more common which could transport Artists anywhere they wanted to draw.

The Kokoon Arts Klub's Bal-Masques quickly became the most famous event of the year in Cleveland, being held annually in January or February, and always scheduled for Friday nights, not Saturday, so the parties could carry on all night without breaking any laws (on Sunday morning). Henry Adams explains in his book that in the early times every year's Masked Ball would begin with a naked model on stage, and that it usually was the Kokoon Klub's favorite model Marie "Mayme" Nichols. For one year's Bal-Masque costumed Kokooners carried in a coffin accompanied with "Copin's funeral march." Out of the coffin then popped Mayme Nichols dancing dressed only in butterfly wings. Another year's Bal-Masque began with Mayme Nichols being chased around the ball after jumping out of the cocoon that Robin Hood with his Merry Men had carried in. William Sommer began one year's "Pygmalion" Masked Ball with a large sketch pad, and as he was drawing a figure on it, Mayme Nichols "stark naked" jumped through the piece of paper and started dancing for the audience! After the undoubtedly shocking "opening skit," the dancing began at the Bal-Masques, which also featured separate acts such as shadow plays, songs, or dances performed by Kokoon members. The Bal-Masque's highlight was the midnight guest's promenade of their unique Colorful costumes: the "Grand Pagent."

As the Kokoon Arts Klub's Bal-Masques grew in attendance, the "drab venues" they rented for the annual event also changed into luxurious Cleveland hotels and even the Masonic Hall. By 1922 the Masked Ball had one thousand crazies inside, and it is well documented that there were also crowds of people turned away at the door who had literally begged entrance. At it's peak the 1925 Bal-Masque was attended by 1,800 people, and every year until the onslaught of the Depression in the 1930s the attendance continued to grow.

What has also been documented many times was the importance of the "Kostumes" made and worn by the Bal-Masque's attending guests. There was a Kokoon Klub Bal-Masque Costume Committee manning the door rejecting any guest's entrance because of ordinary costumes, or rented costumes, or any costume that did not fit the standard of the Kokoon Klub's "Costume Committee." So, at the entrance to all Bal-Masques members of the Costume Committee would not allow invited guests into the ball if their costumes were not relative to the annual theme of the party, or even if their costumes weren't "historically accurate." The typical costumes of clowns, tramps, and dominoes were forbidden entrance to the ball, as were any kind of rented costumes. It wasn't just that you were invited and then showed up in a party costume to these Kokoon Arts Klub annual Masked Balls, but was stipulated that the invited guests were expected to research, design and create their yearly costumes through the costume sketches presented by Klub members for inspiration, as well as through the lessons for making "abstract costumes" given also by Klub members. Combining the sketches of costume designs with the lessons given by Klub members to invited guests for making their costumes, the guests also had available materials in the Cleveland Public Library set aside for their inspiration. This was the very advanced theme of the annual Bal-Masques, that presented the concept which was 'introduced' and popularized years later, in which the audience participates and is directly involved in the event, as well as being an intrinsic part of the event itself. A photo of the three nuts making up the 1925 Costume Committee is in Henry Adam's catalogue, and even though it's an old Black and White picture, it is obvious that the Colors on these three character's costumes must have been nearly Fluorescent (not to mention a headdress approaching a yard tall on Kokoon Artist Joseph Jicha in this photo). The Costume Committee was not to be taken lightly, with printed notices stating that the decision of the Committee at the door of the Bal-Masques was "final." The best that rejected costumed guests and guests without costumes could hope for was being relegated to the "Ball Room Balcony" where there was no dancing. Besides being judged for your costume/creation at the entrance door by the Costume Committee, there were also prizes awarded by this committee for the costumes which were the "most exceptional." A "recognition badge" was awarded to the guests wearing the best costumes, and these chosen best-costumed guests would receive either a cloth or plaster badge, as well as an invitation to the costume party which was members-only held later each year at the Kokoon Klubhouse. For a glimpse into the past, the Cleveland newspapers every year printed photos and lists of the most outlandish costumes at these Bal-Masques. For the 1918 Bal-Masque held in the Hotel Winston, it was reported by papers that guests turned up in costumes which were from 'the Bible, opera, nature, literature, famous paintings, and even the rag bag.' Cleveland papers also reported on the costumes for the 1922 Bal-Masque which included a "Cubist King Tut," Carl Moellmann dressed as a Totem pole, a hot water bottle costume, Ali Baba along with his forty thieves, and even a skyscraper costume. Costumes for the 1925 Bal-Masque consisted of just a "rug" for one man, another dressed as a "Roman senator," and to complete the scene there was also "Potiphar's wife."

In Henry Adams' "Out of the Kokoon" the shocking effect of nudity in the 1920s era at public Masked Balls is tactfully labelled as "Konserving Kloth." From the very first Bal-Masque starting with Miss Mayme Nichols dressed in either just butterfly wings or a topless dress with hand-painted butterfly wings (depending on the reference), the annual event followed in these steps each year, and was described as nothing less than "shocking."

What is left today from the Bal-Masques of the Kokoon Arts Klub are the costumes in museum collections, as well as Color posters for this annual scandal of Cleveland, and unfortunately only Black and White photographs. Reproduced in Color in the "Out of the Kokoon" cataloge is Mary Biehle's dress for the "Bal Bizarre" in 1930, which is a beautiful modern design, in no way reminiscent of the 1930s era, with a Black background and areas done in the technique of Indonesian "Batik" which are lighter than the base Color and look similar to this wax technique. These lighter areas of Mary Biehle's 1930 Bal Masque dress are filled in with hand-painted vibrant Red, Blue, and Gold areas of what looks to be paint containing glitter. The headdress of Esther Rose Kaplan for the 1931 "Bal Papillon" is also reproduced in Adams' catalogue, which is now in the Kent State University Library collection, and is very large - about a yard (meter) tall - shinning in Silver. Across the center are two V-shapped stripes of vibrant Violet and Orange-Red, creating the reference to this piece as a "buckram headress." What must be stressed here is plainly stated in all documentation of Kokoon Bal Masques, that the costumes of both the members and the guests were extremely important, and in a real sense was a very early form of "Interactive Art" - or even "Participatory Art" - where the visitor or guest becomes an integral part of the piece of Art itself. This was stressed and was prepared for by the numerous instructions available for guests from Kokoon members on costume design each year, along with a special "Costume night" held each year weeks before the Bal Masques. Sketches of costumes would be mounted in the Kokoon Klubhouse to inspire and instruct guests in their own costume creations, with partial nudity, Italian Futurism, and Cubism being very important design elements. A precious part of the "Out of the Kokoon" catalogue are the large number of photographs of guests and members dressed in their Bal-Masque costumes throughout the years. What is also clearly explained was the importance of body makeup used for the Bal-Masques. Before the annual Masked Balls there was a lecture and demonstration on body makeup presented by theater makeup specialist Murray Bliss Butler. A Black and White photo of Kokoon Artist Edwin Sommer along with his wife Juliet at the 1926 Bal-Masque could easily be mistaken today for an image from Haight Ashbury in 1966 during the peak of the Hippie Movement (besides the lack of hair on Edwin Sommer). Sommer has on a wildly painted top hat which must be over a yard (meter) tall, a tunic with what looks like mirrored decorations of Rajasthan design also made popular during the Hippie Movement, as well as beads hanging to his waist and pants painted similarly to his huge top hat. His wife Juliet next to him in the photo has what looks like a rope or mop wig on and a skirt that is as short as what Twiggy wore in 1966 as well. There is a photo of Carl Moellmann and his large family dressed for the 1924 Kokoon Klub Bal-Masque, in which the cofounder is forty-five years old and dressed in a Black tuxedo with a Kokoon Arts Klub logo hanging as a pendant. Moellmann's wife and the other six members of his family are not so conservatively dressed though, all in their Bal-Masque costumes, including an ornate clown, an Arabian princess, and Napoleon himself! Again, in almost all of the photos of the Kokoon members or guests of the Bal-Masques, the women look very modern, close to images of a wild party today, but the men with their Black-rimmed round "spectacles," Charlie Chaplin mustaches, and overall attitude almost always look like they're from a century ago. What is noteworthy as well is that there are no fat people in any photographs of these 1920s and 1930s crazies, standing as another contrast to today.

For an example of the themes of these annual parties, for one Bal-Masque the highlight was Congo dancers performing while painted completely Blue. As for the costumes the Kokooners designed and wore to the Bal-Masques, the daughter of one of the famous presidents of the Kokoon Arts Klub, Philip Kaplan and his wife Esther Rose, preserved many of her parent's Bal-Masque costumes, which were presented at the one-hundred year anniversary exhibition in the Cleveland Public Library and Kent State University. These preserved costumes look very contemporary today, with brilliant Colors and provocative designs, not at all what would be first imagined from the 1920s and 30s. In another Black and White photograph from the 1929 Bal-Masque, which was entitled "Le Bal Dynamique," Edris Eckhardt and other members of the Kokoon Arts Klub are in full party costumes, with two men wearing shinny clothing topped with headdresses that look like Cubist paintings, along with makeup, next to two women with loose hair, one of which has a grass skirt standing next to another with a costume which exposed much more of her body than the bathing suits of 1929. Another Black and White of Kokoon members in Bal-Masque costumes shows a man dressed like a Roman soldier looking at a man dressed in something like a Nineteenth century military uniform who is flanked by two women, one of which wears a swan helmet, and both of which are dressed in string-bikinis. But these costumes would be tame compared to costumes worn to the Twenty-fifth Anniversary Silver Jubilee "Black Light Ball" of 1938, for which some invited guests showed up at the Bal-Masque, again, dressed solely in Fluorescent cold-creme.

Although the Kokoon Arts Klub is documented as existing between 1911 and 1956, and that the height of their influence and fame was during the 1920s and 30's, the last "Bal-Masque" was held in 1946, but the great Depression, the Second world war, and the general aging of it's original members eventually took it's toll as the years advanced, not to mention that the "shock" of the "New Art" gradually wore off and was eventually considered mainstream by society. By the time of their twenty-fifth Anniversary "Black Light Ball" in 1938, Cubism and the "New Art" that the Kokoon Arts Klub was formed to make people aware of were about as "Shocking new" as computers and the Internet are to people today in 2016. What is left a century later from these outrageous Kokoon Klub "Bal-Masques" are posters and other printed Artwork form the Bal-Masques, and Black and White photographs which can at least convey the general feeling or intent of these notorious annual events.

For the 1915 Bal-Masque the theme was the contemporary Art movement "Futurism," which was led by Italian Artist Umburto Boccioni, and from photographs of the costume designs and newspaper articles it is apparent that for this 1915 Masked Ball a change took place regarding guest's costumes, which for the first few Masked Balls had largely consisted of gypsy costumes and costumes based on "theater characters." For the 1915 "Futurist Night," held a few weeks after the Bal-Masque, the costumes of guests were being created as pieces of Art, with very modern designs and Colors which were "strikingly brilliant." The newspaper "Town Topic" documented the "Futurist Night" and also described costumes of the Bal-Masque guests made of "screeching colors" and of startling artistic "effects" including 'Post Impressionism, Cubism, and Futurism.' In all the newspaper articles documenting the annual Bal-Masques of the Kokoon Arts Klub, the description that is constant is the extravagant "Color" used on not only member's and guest's costumes, but for the entire decoration. In one newspaper article the "great Russian colorist" Bakst is credited with some of the Bal-Masque costume's inspiration. For the "Futurist Night," it was reported that Mayme Nichols was presented as a stark naked monochrome "Bare Possibility," and that the guests were dressed in a "superabundance" of all Colors of the spectrum.

During the best years of the Kokoon Arts Klub, for every Bal-Masque a contest was held for the designed "Invitational Poster," and a two-hundred dollar prize was awarded to the winning Artist. These posters were "Invitational Posters" which were folded into quarters and mailed to invited guests weeks before the ball. The entrance ticket design for each year's Bal-Masque was the second-place winner's Artwork, and the mailing envelope for the invitational posters was then printed with the third-place Artist's work. From 1924 to 1926, and for the Twentieth Anniversary in 1931, illustrated "Souvenir programs" were also produced.

The 1917 Bal-Masque's Invitational Poster is the first Kokoon party poster still in existence, which was William Sommer's design for the "Fifth Annual Bal-Masque" of January 19, 1917. This lithograph which measures forty-six by thirty-one inches (117 x 79 cm) has stated on it that "All" must wear costumes and that the entrance was five dollars, as well as containing a short poem. Sommer's poster is of a loosely-painted clown-costumed upright bass player with four barelegged girls dancing to the music behind him. There is an existing photo of cofounder Carl Moellmann dressed at this 1917 Bal-Masque as the "fiddler" of this poster, along with his wife Marie and three other costumed girls dancing as the "Polliwog Quartet."

The 1918 Bal Masque was held in the Hotel Winston and according to local newspapers was reported to have visitors in costumes which were from everything including 'the Bible' and the 'rag bag.' The Bal-Masque invitational poster for this Sixth Annual event was painted by Michael DeSantis. This long thin poster by DeSantis has a very painterly design of what is described in "Out of the Kokoon" as a 'scantily-dressed couple dancing in a large vaulted space,' similar to a venue's interior during a Bal-Masque. As Adams points out, the 1917 and 1918 early Bal-Masque posters are created in a style which relates to an intimate and Artistic audience present during the first years of the Kokoon Arts Klub's Bal-Masques. As the audience multiplied over the coming years the style of the invitational posters also changed. In a Black and White photo of DeSantis and a guest in full Bal-Masque costumes for the 1922 ball, including DeSantis' headdress which gives the impression of him having long hair, this couple look like they could have stepped out of one of Ken Kesey and Merry Prankster's "Acid Tests" a full forty-four years later, dressed in full psychedelic clothing.

Even more rare than the Kokoon Arts Klub annual Bal-Masque invitational posters, and finely reproduced in "Out of the Kokoon" is the Artwork for the actual paper entrance tickets to the ball, as well as the accompanying envelope that the posters were mailed to guests in. To this Artist, the Artwork that came in second place was closer to fine Art, not immediately recognizable as sensationalist, and not consisting of a heavy and obvious sexual undertone; being in contrast to the first place Artwork used for the posters which was much closer to illustrations than to fine Art. This viewpoint is most likely shared with the author of "Out of the Kokoon," because the front cover of his exhibition catalogue has the second-place winner of the poster contest for the "Thirteenth Annual Bal-Masque of the Kokoon Arts Klub" in 1926, which was Edwin Sommer's painting of a fully clothed and wildly dressed couple dancing on the clouds with rays of light shooting all around them. The first place winner for that 1926 Bal-Masque invitational poster was Joseph Jicha with a gouache of the nude deity Agni and the Greenish female spirit of the carnival who has a Red mask and a topless bathing suit, and is immediately recognizable as a commercial poster illustration, not a painting like Sommer's second-place Artwork.

The second-place design printed for the "Tenth Annual Bal-Masque of the Kokoon Arts Klub" of 1922 was made by Ray Parmelee and is a dark, mysterious painting containing a clown and a Yellow tutu party girl in a circle at the bottom of the Black entrance ticket, and out of the clown emerges a huge peacock feather which fills two-thirds of the entire image. Again, reported in Cleveland newspapers were the costumes for the 1922 Bal-Masque which featured a "Cubist King Tut," Carl Moellmann dressed as a Totem pole, a hot water battle costume, "Ali Baba" along with his forty thieves, and the skyscraper costume.

Joseph Jicha created Bal-Masque invitational posters for five years in a row from 1924 until he left Cleveland for a job in Chicago in 1928. This is the defining "Art deco characteristic" of the Bal-Masque posters, and what Adams refers to as the "Kokoon Klub look." The "Eleventh Annual Bal-Masque of the Kokoon Arts Klub" invitational poster from 1924 by Joseph Jicha is described in "Out of the Kokoon" as a "strange carnival" and a "dance-floor world" with a red-haired woman wearing a surgical mask who has "claw-like fingers" and acts as a marionette manipulating manicly-dancing Bal-Masque guests with her left hand. The manically-dancing group also gives the impression of a cauldron filled with a boiling mixture, but upon close inspection it can be seen that the large Redheaded girl who is the 'Spirit of Carnival' is literally pouring the steaming contents of a Black pot with a handle and thus creating the bubbling mass of dancers/stew. The reason for this 1924 poster being very subdued and not a shocking sexual image is most likely because the preceding Bal-Masque of 1923 had been cancelled by the mayor of Cleveland!

The 1925 "Twelfth Annual Kokoon Arts Klub Bal-Masque" invitational poster by Joseph Jicha is a simple design with a couple dancing dynamically with exaggerated leg-lengths and with two spot lights illuminating their stage on an otherwise Black background. The entrance ticket design for this 1925 Bal-Masque is a beautiful painting by Edwin G. Sommer that first appears to be a majestic landscape of snow-capped mountains, but on closer inspection becomes a couple dancing in full Bal-Masque costumes. There is a feeling of Japanese inspiration particularly in this 1925 ticket, which is amongst the finest pieces of Art of any of the Kokoon Arts Klub printed pieces through the years, with the headdress on the woman being very reminiscent of Esther Rose Kaplan's preserved headdress from the 1931 Bal-Masque. In contrast to the 1924 souvenir booklet of the Bal-Masque, the 1925 edition was drawn by William Sommer's second son Edwin G. Sommer, who created a very modern design in Black on a Green-Blue stock. The image is similar to the invitational poster of 1925 done by Edwin Sommer as well, with a very stylized couple dancing together in an image which gives the first impression of mountains in a landscape.

The modern design of the couple in an abstract background creates a picture which would not be dated in any way if printed today.

The Thirteen Annual Kokoon Arts Klub Bal-Masque invitational poster of 1926 is a watercolor printed by lithography and was also done by Joseph Jicha with it's theme "Thirteenth descent: Deity Agni - Son of Fire - with the Spirit of Carnival thru Myriad of Color." In this poster by Jicha, which is the most reproduced of the six Bal-Masque posters he designed, the Artist paints himself as the "Deity Agni" ("Agni" means "fire" in Hindi), and his wife Jerry as the topless "Spirit of Carnival" descending from heaven down to the dance floor through "Cycles of Color." Although the Colors Jicha used are brilliant, the general dynamics and imagery still retains the feelings of a picture of the Art Deco period. In "Out of the Kokoon" the "God of Fire" is described as having Orange hair resembling flames, with the bottom half of his legs also giving the impression of holy ashes from the Agni in India, which are very important to Hindus as well. The entrance ticket for this 1926 Bal-Masque is one of the most famous of all Artwork printed by the Kokoon Artists, used as the cover of the catalogue and the poster for the exhibition of the Klub's one-hundredth anniversary held in Cleveland, the Edwin G. Sommer painting of a wildly dressed couple dancing on the clouds with spotlights shooting off into the heavens all around them. The souvenir book for this 1926 Bal-Masque presents a very valuable illustration of what a Kokoon Bal-Masque must have looked like. The August Biehle Artwork is a dated image of a crowded party scene containing a central nearly-nude couple ecstatically dancing surrounded by Bal-Masque characters in top hats, wearing huge feathers, etc. - in other words a typical annual party of the Kokoon Arts Klub. Printed on White stock, this 1926 souvenir book was produced with not just Black ink, but with the addition of a grey tone. In the air suspended above the wild crowd of Bal-Masques crazies is a transparent cocoon with the magical transformation of a butterfly taking place inside of it.

The 1927 "Fourteenth Annual Bal-Masque" invitational poster was also painted by Joseph Jicha and is a watercolor of the god 'Midas: Whatever he touches turns to Gold' printed as a lithograph. This poster is described in the exhibition catalogue as Midas who doubles as a chrysalis of a butterfly, holding a wand and descending from a golden-starred heaven while touching dancers of the Bal-Masque who are then instantly transformed into Gold. The entrance ticket to this 1927 Golden Bal-Masque was drawn by August Biehle and is an extraordinarily detailed ink drawing which is an extremely modern image and very reminiscent of graphic Artwork done forty years later during the 1960s.

The "Bal Des Arts" "Fifteen Annual Bal-Masque" of the Kokoon Arts Klub in 1928 had for it's poster the last of Jicha's six posters in a row, which was a light watercolor interpreted in the exhibition catalogue as the "duality" of Bal-Masques, and which was simultaneously a descent into physical pleasure and an ascent towards the spiritual and pure realm of abstract life and Art. This was the theme of 1928's Bal-Masque: "Abstraction." This 1928 poster is by far the most typical Art Deco image of the Bal-Masque posters of the period, featuring two Jicha extended figures one of which gives the impression of a god with lightning bolts coming out from his head, while touching and giving life to a dark figure emerging from the flames. The entrance ticket for the 1928 "Bal Des Arts" was painted by David Samson and is a cubist figure which looks more like a commercial illustration than any other entrance ticket of the Kokoon Klub. The cubist figure is an Artist holding a palette in two of his hands while two more of his cubed hands and arms straddle this four legged, three-headed Artist.

The "Sixteenth Annual Bal-Masque" of the Kokoon Klub in 1929 was called the "Bal Dynamique" and it's invitational poster done by Rolf Stoll finally begins to leave the Art Deco Jicha influence behind and move into the future, with four nude or nearly-nude figures in very dynamic poses. In 1929 technology changed for printing and much finer, more accurate images which were closer reproductions of the original Artwork were produced. In the classic lithography technique, the painting is made by an Artist and then redrawn onto lithography stone by skilled lithographic craftsmen for printing, which would undoubtedly vary from the original Artwork. In 1929 when Jicha left Cleveland for Chicago, the printing had advanced to produce "photolithography" which, as the name suggests, allowed the Artist's original painting to be photographed and reproduced intact, not redrawn by a craftsman. This new printing technology was how the Rolf Stoll "Bal Dynamique" poster was printed, and it's superior printing technique is apparent when compared to former lithographic Kokoon posters next to their respective original Artworks. The angular way that Rolf Stoll's figures are fit into the picture plane of both this 1929 poster as well as the next poster by Stoll for the 1930 "Bal Bizarre," is attributed in "Out of the Kokoon" to a "compositional system" of Jay Hambridge known as "dynamic symmetry" popular during that era. The entrance ticket to this 1929 Bal Dynamique was created by Joseph Garramone, and features a man with a large headdress dancing dynamically with a topless woman which fills the image.

The last Kokoon Arts Klub Bal-Masque invitational poster that retains some of the Art Deco stylized figures and exaggerated dynamism was for the 1930 "Seventeenth Annual" event entitled "Bal Bizarre." Similar to Stoll's 1929 poster, exaggerated figures awkwardly fill the space with "Bizarre" dynamic poses once again in Stoll's 1930 poster. A woman completely nude except for a piece of cloth and a wild geometric headdress fills the entire area of the lithograph, with a Black male dancer in shorts and a multi-Colored headdress also in a dynamic pose behind the nude woman accompanies her, holding onto a large Green piece of material which forms the background of the poster. With the same advanced "photolithography" printing technology, Rolf Stoll's watercolor was accurately reproduced on this 1930 "Bal Bizarre" poster. The entrance ticket for this "Bal Bizarre" of 1930 was done by August Biehle and is a very complicated painting with six or more figures interwound into a frenzy of movements. A Buddha-like figure top-center with a third eye, sitting in the meditation position, along with a central figure below who is turning in a cubist gyration with the top half of the body in a frontal view, and with the bottom half of the body completely reversed as seen from behind.

Finally in 1931 for the "Eighteenth Annual Bal-Masque of the Kokoon Arts Klub" entitled "Bal Papillon" (butterfly), the invitational poster painted by James Harley Minter enters the true modern age, and definitively leaves the Art Deco imagery behind. A nearly abstracted large female nude figure with a butterfly head and surreal butterfly wings dominates the poster. The butterfly/woman hands are holding marionette strings leading and giving animation to a couple in a dynamic dancing pose, who have on few articles of geometrically shaped rainbow-Colored clothing. The design as well as the execution of the Artwork by Minter retains no residue of the heavy Art Deco movement, which is immediately evident in all of the 1920s Kokoon Klub's posters. This 1931 "Bal Papillon" Artwork was so far from the typical Bal-Masque posters of the Kokoon Arts Klub that it was used for the Opening invitation of the May 14 - July 31, 2010 exhibition in the Cleveland Artists Foundation at the Beck Center for the Arts: "The Kokoon Arts Club: Cleveland Revels!" The reported highlight of this 1931 "Bal Papillon" was a show of thirteen girls wearing Black tights performing the "Butterfly dance."

In the early 1930s the effects of the Great depression caused by the stock market crash of 1930 would begun to be felt by all people in America, and this Depression was also the killing blow to the Kokoon Arts Klub and it's Artists. In 1929 the estimate of the Kokoon's Bal Dynamique's attendance was between two and three-thousand, and by 1930s Bal Bizarre the number of guests were only slightly less. But, by 1931 during the first full year of the Depression the Bal-Masque had so few guests that it lost money. In 1932 Joseph Jicha returned to Cleveland after the Chicago advertising agency he worked for went out of business, and for 1932's Bal-Masque which was for members only, Jicha created his last Kokoon poster of a Indonesian Black shadow puppet dancing with a nude White woman. This February, 1932 "Members Masque" was the "Nineteenth Annual Bal-Masque" and the Artwork by Jicha is atypical of all the other Bal-Masque posters, giving the impression of a Brown chalk sketch, not a painting, gouache, or watercolor similar to other Bal-Masque Kokoon posters.

The invitational poster announcing the "Twentieth Annual Kokoon Arts Klub Bal-Masque" of February, 1933 is just as inoffensive and atypically non-shocking as the 1932 poster. This 1933 Twentieth Anniversary Bal-Masque was entitled the "Once in a Blue Moon" "Kokoon Arts Klub Balmasquette," and is dominated by a very lightly Colored and inoffensively stylized nude couple in a swirl of stars being swept off to the Moon upside-down into space. This 1933 "Balmasquette" was much smaller, being held in the Kokoon Klubhouse rather than renting an expensive hall. There were only one-hundred couples invited and the entrance was halved to five dollars. This invitational poster was printed in just Blue and Black being cheaper to produce than a full-Color poster, similar to Jicha's 1932 poster, and the size was also much smaller at nineteen by fourteen inches (48 x 36 cm.). The Artist of this poster is not even known.

After two Bal-Masque annual invitational posters of 1932 and 1933 being stylized and relatively inoffensive compared to most other Kokoon Arts Klub posters, the February 24, 1934 "Bal Risqué" poster is one of the most outwardly sexual images of any of their posters through the years. In what gives the first impression as the front cover illustration of a "Pulp magazine" of the same time period, six young women dressed only in bikini bottoms dance together in front of five simply lecherous-faced men framing the image. A king, sultan, wizard, a Shakespearian type of character, and a Twentieth century man surround the six mostly naked young girls dancing, and all five of these typical through-the-ages men have lecherous grins on their faces and give the general idea that they are drooling. In references this Bal-Masque "Bal Risqué" poster's Artwork is listed as being made by an unknown Artist.

The next Bal-Masque annual party of the Kokoon Arts Klub was called the "Bal Artistique" and held in March, 1935 in the Trianon Ballroom in Cleveland. The Artist for this 1935 invitational poster was Auguste Leysens, and the Artwork gives the impression immediately of being a painting, not an illustration like the 1934 "Bal Risqué" poster with the topless girls illustrated. The entire center of this 1935 poster is a painting of a girl dancing dressed in just a native grass skirt, and with her fire Red hair loose and flying. Behind this painted lady, who would look undated if presented today, there are a few members of the ball including a mandolin player to her left who has a Green and Blue face and the wildest head of hair imaginable, looking something like a Yellow burst of flames. To this topless dancer's right there are two people attending the ball, a man dressed like Shakespeare, and a woman with a wild headdress on. For this "Bal Artistique" a burlesque dancer from New York,

Miss Faith Bacon, was hired to do a nude fan dance, but the times had definitively changed, as well as the subdued attire and feelings of the people over the prior twenty years plus of the Bal-Masques. Besides this, Kokoon Artists Michael DeSantis and Ray Parmelee had both just died, and original Kokoon Klub members were now in their fifties or sixties.

In 1936 there was no Bal-Masque of the Kokoon Arts Klub, being only the second time the party was cancelled since 1923, when it had been cancelled by the mayor of Cleveland.

Rightfully labelled as the best of the Kokoon Bal-Masque late period invitational posters, the painting for the 1937 "Twenty-fourth Anniversary Bal-Masque" was done by Auguste Biehle and is described as a woman inspired by the "Ballet Russe" which was an important influence to Kokoon Artists, but her typical pose as well as her clothing are closer to classical representations of Hindu Goddesses in India. The central dancer's face in this poster also has Indian features, especially her eyes, and on her forehead is a stylized third-eye of Hinduism. Across the center of the poster diagonally a line of Kokoon Bal-Masque dancing costumed crazies are having a ball.

What originally began the writing of this section on the wild "Kokoon Arts Klub" was the Bal-Masque they had in 1938 - "The Black Light Ball!" This was only five years after Robert Switzer had invented Fluorescent paint in 1933, and it is a unique example of society's and Artist's opinions of Fluorescent paint and also of the "Black Light" which had only just been patented three years earlier in 1935. What is a little surprising about this 1938 "Silver Jubilee Ball" named "The Black Light Ball," besides guests showing up dressed in just Fluorescent cold-creme, is the poster from the event. After seeing the vibrant, seething sexually-explicit posters that have been preserved from the Bal-Masques of the 1920s and 1930s, "The Black Light Ball's" poster from 1938 is much more sedate - nearly static compared to the dynamic illustrations making up the majority of the former posters. The dancing naked girls explicitly making up the subject matter of almost all former Kokoon Arts Klub annual Masked Ball's posters are gone. What is left is quite surprising for the imagined culmination of twenty-five years of crazy Kokoon Arts Klub's Bal-Masques, and gives the initial impression of an ancient Greek sculpted 'frieze.' A flat-Colored illustration, which appears to be a gouache, in which the figures are portrayed in static 'motion' on a beach. It is such a departure from the sexually vibrant images of almost all of the Kokoon Klub's former Bal-Masque posters, that even the nudity of almost all of these nine figures in the poster goes unnoticed. The nine figures in the 1938 poster are not only flatly painted, but also illustrated in a style similar to cartoons, with Black outlines and no tonality or modeling in any way. First of all, the entire background of the poster illustration is a uniform flat Grey which makes up a full two-thirds of the image. In this Grey 'sky' is the White-lettered title: "Silver Jubilee Ball '38," which is so subtle that it nearly disappears at a distance. The bottom one-third of the poster contains the illustrated beach scene in which a Chinese figure dressed in full ceremonial clothing is sitting. In front of this Chinese figure there is a nude girl reclining, rendered in such a flat Color and static pose that she looks more like a statue than a woman. The four figures to the left of the central Chinaman, as well as the three figure to his right, look like they are having a tug-of-war over the central nude girl/statue. The first figure to the left of the nude girl/statue is a fully clothed girl with her hair illustrated exactly like "Little Orphan Annie" cartoons - Black with true Blue highlights. The three figures tugging behind "Orphan Annie" have wild headdresses, and are almost nude, but rendered again in a very bland, cartoon-like style. Similarly, the three figures to the right of the central Chinese man are just as static and flat, including a pitch Black half-nude man and two half-nude dancers also wearing wild headdresses. Not only are the figures rendered in a non-offensive flat cartoon-like style, but even further than that, the majority of these topless girls in the illustration are painted with their arms in front of their breasts, hiding their nudity.

It is obvious that twenty-five years of aging had passed since the initial young energy which began the Kokoon Arts Klub's parties in 1913. What would be imagined to be the wildest and most outrageous poster - for their Twenty-Fifth Anniversary - was in fact one of the most sedate and bland of all the Kokoon Klub's posters. Another departure from the full illustrated posters of all the previous Bal-Masques is the design of this 1938 "Black Light Ball's" poster. The bottom half of the poster, only, is the actual poster announcing the Bal-Masque. The top half of the poster is divided in two and upside-down from the bottom poster, designed in this manner to fold up into a quarter-page booklet. The 'cover' of the booklet is done in very dated typefaces and has an illustration of a girl's face with her eye looking at a round ball containing the logo of the "Kokoon Arts Klub" and the announcement: "25th Anniversary Silver Jubilee." The headline in Red reads "The Kokoon Artists Present Black Light Costume Bal Masque." Another difference with this 1938 poster is the lack of an 'invitation line' which was filled in and mailed to the invited guest. This makes this 1938 poster possibly a general advertising poster, not an "Invitational poster" like former Bal-Masques.

This 1938 last Bal-Masque poster of the Kokoon Arts Klub is also described by Henry Adams as having "ugly draftsmanship" and being "crudely drawn." The unknown Artist of this poster loosely put into a bland scene one 'Chinese mandarin, an African prince, an Ethiopian executioner, a "flapper," dancers and a nude,' in such a detached manner that they appear like individual 'stickers' applied next to each other on a board. The entrance ticket to this 1938 "Black Light Ball" was quite different than the bland poster, and was drawn by August Biehle. The top half of the ticket had two detachable tickets for a free "Bal-Supper" in the ball's venue the "Hotel Carter Rain-Bow Room." The Biehle drawing is of an exotic female dancer wearing huge butterfly wings stepping through an open stage curtain. Party goers smiling heads, only, are suspended in the darkness around the dancer, serving as a preview of the enormous Fluorescent Rainbow painting which would be shown under black lights at this "Black Light Ball," and which would contain hidden faces seen only when the U.V. lamps were turned on. Henry Adams takes a stance typical of today's general society and denounces the use of the Black light and Fluorescent paint for the 1938 Kokoon Arts Klub "Black Light Ball" as a mere "gimmick" for their last "comeback." What must be put into perspective here is that a mere five years before this Kokoon Arts Klub "Black Light Ball" in March, 1938, Robert Switzer as a teenager had just *invented* Fluorescent paint. What Adams offhandedly refers to in 2011 as a mere "gimmick" with jaded hindsight of seven decades, was in 1938 for this "Black Light Ball" a new invention of cutting-edge technology - most people had never heard of a Black light in 1938, so the effect must have been on people at this "Black Light Ball" something closer to a "miracle" - than what is today, typically, reduced and described as a mere "gimmick."

The details of this 1938 "Back Light Ball" reveal just how miraculous the event must have been, with an eighty-five foot long (23 meter) mural painted by Kokoon Artists of a gigantic Rainbow (the ball was held in Cleveland's Hotel Carter's "Rain-bow Room"). Using the Invisible Fluorescent paint invented by the Switzer brothers in 1933 which reacted only when the black lights were turned on, the mural was an eighty-five foot long rainbow in the normal White light, but when the lights were turned off and the Black lights turned on, the rainbow turned into a full crowd of the faces of all nations of the world, vividly glowing in different Colors of Invisible Fluorescent paint.

At "The Black Light Ball's" climax a showgirl from New York, Leeanova Scotti, did a performance wearing nothing but butterfly wings, but unforeseen by the use of invisible ultraviolet black lights, only her butterfly wings Fluoresced, and Scotti's naked body was in the dark(!) It is easy to understand that this Silver Jubilee Twenty-Fifth "Black Light Ball" of 1938 lacked the energy and enthusiasm of the 1920s Bal-Masques, when realizing that original members formed the Kokoon Arts Klub twenty-seven years earlier were old by the time of the Twenty-Fifth Jubilee. At the time of the 1938 "Black Light Ball" the two founders of the Kokoon Klub were Carl Moellmann at the age of fifty-nine, and William Sommer who was seventy-one. When they formed the Klub they had been only thirty-two and forty-four, making Moellmann nearly twice his age as when the Kokoons began. As the cruel hand of faith would have it, this author was given pure painful perspective of what he was writing about when "Electric Lady" Art Gallery had it's twenty-fifth Anniversary on April 19, 2012, during the writing of this section on the Kokoon Arts Klub and their Twenty-Fifth Anniversary "Black Light Ball."

"Kokoon Arts Klub" "Black Light Ball" Press Release (1938)

One of the most precious artifacts of this Kokoon Arts Klub 1938 "Black Light Ball" is the typed letter intended "For General Release" announcing this Bal-Masque. Undated, but obviously before their March, 1938 "Black Light Ball," the headline of this 'Press Release' announces that the "Theme" of "The Black Light Ball" will be a "Pageantry of Light!" This single-page press release from early 1938 begins by stating that 'One of the startling and most interesting effects known today by modern science' will be extensively used by Kokoon Artists for their March "Black Light Ball." 'Artists of the Kokoon Club are painting now a huge eighty-five foot long mural that will completely, mysteriously, and spectacularly change during the Black Light Ball.' It is further explained in this press release of early 1938 that the huge mural will be a "luminous Rainbow," which will 'flood the ballroom with invisible black light causing hundreds of figures of all nationalities to mysteriously appear, flashing in colors which are brilliant and glowing.' This press release continues, and announces with the enthusiasm of 1938 that "The romance" of the "Black Light" will continue with the costumes of both members and guests, which will become "radiant" and have "fiery Colors" under Black lights. This single-page press release from the "Kokoon Arts Klub" ends with the statement that 'although the Black light causes the glow of the mural,' what makes this "attraction" possible is the 'recent development of luminous Color which is beyond the scope of other Colors' because it reacts - "glows" - under Black lights. This press release ends with the information that "Black light effects" could be seen any evening before the ball in the Kokoon clubhouse.

A second 'Press Release' also headlined "For Immediate Release" was scanned as well for this author by an archivist of Kent State University, and is two pages long. The title of this press release is 'Kokoon Artists Paint with Light' for their "25th Bal Masque." This press release begins with a short history of the Kokoon Arts Klub, stating that it was formed by "ambitious young artists" twenty-five years ago for 'promoting community interest of modern art,' and that for the "first time" in their initial 1913 Kokoon Ball, the Kokoon Artists inspired guests to create costumes which could "express the individual." The Kokoon Balls were also created in this 'modern art spirit' by covering 'light fixtures, ceilings, and walls with bright Colors.' The fact that these Kokoon Balls benefited the community of Cleveland is given, along with credit to the Kokoon Klub for introducing Cleveland to modern Art, in preview of their newest "startling innovation:" a "Black Light Ball." It is explained in the text that "Black Light" was a new type of "lighting" which 'energizes "Conti-Glo," a luminescent new medium.' With enviable 1938 enthusiasm, this press release explains that "Conti-Glo" luminescent paint now allowed Kokoon Artists 'to keep up with advances of science' during this "age of light." 'Artists now paint with light' was hailed in 1938 as a "New age of Art." This new miraculous Black light effect on Fluorescent paint was accurately, beautifully, and poetically explained over seventy years ago as being painted 'by Artists capable of breaking open neon lights and pouring this liquid light into their paint pots'(!) This press release ends with a statement that the Black light "miracle of science" was the key to the Kokoon Club's "progressiveness."

Another rare artifact scanned for this author from the Kent State archives is an original Cleveland newspaper article from before the 1938 "Black Light Ball" containing three photographs. The headline of this small 1938 article announces that "Black Light" will 'Decorate Arts Ball.' Three photos of examples of Fluorescent costumes under Black lights for the "Black Light Ball" are printed with this 1938 article, but comparing these three photos to the original un-retouched photos from the Kokoon Klub, the female model's nipples and pubic hair have been censured by being painted over with White for printing in the newspaper. Even with their painted over private parts, these photos could, again, be from a wild party today. The text explains that these three photos are 'examples' of the "new luminescent medium," the Black light's "startling effects," which will be used at the annual ball of the Kokoon Arts Club that coming Saturday night. It is foretold that at the coming "Black Light Ball" there would be costumes which would be 'turned into a flash of brilliant glowing colors' by being treated with new luminous paint. The short article informs the reader that Kokoon Artists were painting a huge eighty-five foot mural that "will change completely" when seen at the "Black Light Ball" under the "invisible black light."

By far the most important scan made for me by the Kent State Archive is a press release from "Conti-Glo," the company that the Switzer Brothers formed in association with Carl Moellmann's "Continental Lithography Corp." in Cleveland. If only one statement could represent "The Golden Age of Fluorescence" and all that it embodied, such as the infinite possibilities made available through the new scientific invention of the invisible Black light and it's Fluorescent paint which reacted in such an unforeseen way as if it was alchemy - or even magic - then this is the statement. This was decades before the 1960s Movement - in fact before most of the Hippies were even born - and nearly half a century before this "alchemy" - or even "miracle" - was rejected, neglected, and relegated to what the author of "Out of the Kokoon" labels typically as a mindless "gimmick." Any different approach that strays from 'normal' in the mind of the simple person who views life and it's content through their own filter of banality, is calculated within this banal mind containing only the very limited parameters available to these folks. There is a very famous recorded interview with Jimi Hendrix in 1967 at the beginning of his rise to fame, and an interviewer, not unlike most people at that time asks Jimi about his "gimmicks" such as playing the guitar with his teeth, behind his head, and other unseen 'abnormalities' to this simple-minded common journalist. Jimi had a similar reaction for this simpleton, speaking in a condescending tone and informing the journalist that all of life could be seen as a "gimmick" if the observer was shallow enough and non dimensional. Again, these simple idiot's reactions do not stem from the failings of what they so rapidly and completely condemn, but rather stem from the lack of knowledge and insight they embody, in other words, from their own "Mirror of Self-Reflection" which reveals an infinity of ignorance. Before prejudice and familiarity led to indifference and in general a very hollow jaded arrogance, which could be a very fitting description of society in general for the last three decades at least, people were not only still dreaming but also possessed infinite enthusiasm towards achieving these dreams. Before most of society put these infinite dreams up their noses - or directly into their bank accounts - documents were thankfully left which contrast dramatically to this jaded gentrified era of the ego we are presently immersed in, and one of those old, forgotten documents is this "Press Release" declaring the Black light and Fluorescent paint as "A New Medium" to be used during this new "Age of Light." With great perspective and vision this press release begins with the fact that 'all civilizations in every age searched for it's own medium in a quest to express it's own culture and era.' The examples are given of the Egyptians choosing eternal granite for it's 'permanence,' the Greeks choose sparkling White marble for it's 'refined beauty,' and the Gothic era chose "soft stone" to rapidly erect their temples with. Oil painting is next examined in this press release's timeline, as a representative of the Renaissance and all the heights and peaks achieved during that enlightened era. It is explained that the "luscious color surfaces" produced by Oil paint was the defining characteristic that led Artists to choose this medium during the Renaissance era. It is further explained that since the Renaissance, for five-hundred years, Artists have developed this innovation of oil paint in 'attempts to get Color to reflect light.' But, during "the last century" Artists had the desire to 'expand' this search towards the dream of creating Art which is 'animated and contains the brilliancy of light itself.' It is plainly stated next that Artists witnessed scientific advancement in their field of Color and light, but that these Artists were confined to the very limited parameters of their "age-old medium," oil paint.

The text of this press release next states that 'many startling discoveries have been made by science in the uses of light and color' and that 'finally a medium was discovered which Artists have been long searching for: CONTI-GLO - a new luminescent medium' which "modernizes" 'the old-fashioned vehicle of the Artist through the latest advances of chemistry and physics.' The new invention of "Conti-Glo" Fluorescent paint is explained as "unique" and containing the property of 'having both a normal appearance under ordinary light and easy handling like normal pigment paint.' 'This Fluorescent paint will glow with brilliant flashing Colors which have a radiance that has never been formerly attained, when exposed in the dark to Black Light which is filtered, harmless ultra-violet.' 'After the Black Light is turned off CONTI-GLO Fluorescent paint's glow instantaneously ceases.' 'CONTI-GLO mixed with paint which is ordinary non-luminescent creates the opportunity for changing a scene completely just by turning on either the Mazda White light or the Black Light.' It is further explained that 'under the Black Light the parts of the Artwork painted with CONTI-GLO Fluorescent paint luminesce and glow in vivid Colors, but the painting's areas that have been painted with ordinary Colors are just Grey or Black under Black Lights.' 'This luminescent revolutionary Color gives the chance to the Artist now to keep in stride with this modern age's advances in light.' 'Now the Artist can paint with an actual Source of Light and easily can attain great brilliancy in Color without using the former unsuccessful and artificial techniques in an attempt to simulate light.' This "Conti-Glo" Fluorescent paint was sold in "regular artist tubes" and also as a lacquer, a watercolor, and "costume dips," and is explained 'can blend or be mixed with ordinary artist's oil paints.' 'By using both CONTI-GLO Fluorescent Artist oil paint and regular oil paints, the Artist can produce a "dual" painting which consists of two different paintings on one canvas.' 'The Artist can change the painting, and display entirely different scenes by simply turning on the Mazda White light or the Black Light, and in this way create paintings which are forcefully dynamic and animated - not static.'

The title of the next section of this press release from way back in the non-stigmatized "Golden Age of Fluorescence" 1930s is enough to make any gentrified Twenty-first century Art historian - or Artist - spit a vein, boldly stating the fact that the new invention of Fluorescent paint in combination with the emitted light of Fluorescence caused when this Fluorescent paint is put under a Black light was the crowing achievement in the entire Human History of Art: 'The CLIMAX to the IMPRESSIONIST'S SEARCH'(!)

Now if prejudice, tradition, ignorance, and lack of perspective are examined - especially *tradition* which the old-fashioned Art world is still even today pickled in, exemplified by the number of Artists today in the Twenty-first century who *Do Not* paint on that ancient traditional surface: Canvas - if these were all magically removed, and if the cobwebs were also magically removed from the eyes of these same traditional Art historians, Art critics, and even Artists themselves in the present, it is not only logical but entirely *obvious* that Fluorescent Paint - which creates and emits light - is indeed the crowning achievement and truly embodies this vein-splitting title of the next section in this 1930s press release: 'The CLIMAX to the IMPRESSIONIST'S SEARCH'(!) In unprecedented boldness the facts of this incredulous statement are bolstered by the further incredulous example of none other than Eugene Delacroix's visionary quest to 'simulate light's radiance' by arranging different pigments juxtaposed, and in this way 'intensifying' and increasing the Color's brilliance. The combination of brush strokes and Color juxtaposition, beginning with Delacroix, are the defining changes in techniques which led to the 'new school of Art - Impressionism' as stated in this press release. It is explained further that 'later attempts to pitch the intensities of their Colors higher led to the Impressionist's paintings becoming bleached and White.' This is concluded in the press release as the "limitations" of the Impressionist's quest towards a new Art, a brilliance which has been bleached of it's intense pure Colors.

Again - logically and void of stigmatism - this press release's conclusion is that 'today's Artist no longer needs to depend on Reflected light to bring out the brilliance from a painting's surface, because with the new invention of Fluorescent Paint the Artist can now apply this new luminous paint which actually emits light - gives off light - from the painting's surface.' This again logical, non-stigmatized and scientific conclusion introduced to the public over seventy years ago, is that Fluorescent paint and Black lights - far from being a mere "gimmick" - literally give an Artist the new technique of *"painting with light."* In this early era of the last century it was clear to see that the Twentieth century's "medium" in painting, "moving pictures," advertising, and architecture was "Light," and also this new technique of "painting with light" would enable Artists to reach "unlimited realms."

The next section of this "Conti-Glo" 1930s press release announces in it's headline that 'Fluorescent Paint Increases the Scope of even the New Art.' The examples of Artist's attempts of the early Twentieth century 'to transform, change moods, and express action' over the "past 50 years," including the new "Sur-realism," exhausted the traditional techniques at their disposal, but the new technology of Fluorescent paint under White light and then under Black lights, gave the new possibility 'to create "dual roles" in a painting.' It is further detailed in this press release that "Conti-Glo" Fluorescent paint also reflects "Mazda" (White light), but in addition to this common property, the 'second spectacular property' of Fluorescent paint is the "ability to radiate" 'brilliant Colors glowing in darkness under the newly developed, inexpensive Black light,'

If any one point could be singled out as the defining point which caused Fluorescent paint and Black lights to never be accepted by Fine Art - right up until the present day - it is the following market attempts and the hard-sell advertisement techniques which not only group Fine Artists unacceptably with 'Mural painters, Stage designers,' and especially 'Commercial artists,' but also introduce to the Art world the new "gimmick" of 'Changing Paintings' or even what was labelled "X-ray Scenes," in which one painting under normal White light completely changed into another painting when put under a Black light. This is what the first Artist credited with using Fluorescent paint in Fine Art made famous in the 1940s: John Ludlum. "Who?" - exactly - John Ludlum's Fluorescent masterpiece sold in 1973 as the most expensive painting ever sold by a living Artist - including Picasso who was still alive at that time - and, again, in chorus: "Who?" A formerly world-famous Artist who's name is difficult to even find on the internet forty years later! He helped to create, and in the end suffered intensely from, this "Social Stigma of Fluorophobia" in it's peak during the past half century, especially after it's inextricable association with the 1960s Movement and it's embracement by popular culture at that time. This 1930s press release in itself both introduces, and begins to give birth to, this dream of the common person which would also help greatly to stigmatize the new technology indefinitely; the dream of 'paintings changing from day to night,' or changing from 'landscapes to city skylines,' "phantom views," "X-ray Scenes," figures changing costumes, and even 'floral scenes being transformed into brilliant undersea views.' These endeavors are stated in this press release as all being "easily obtained" with this new Fluorescent paint under Black lights. With the gained hindsight of three-quarters of a century, it is easily understandable how this hard-sell purely commercial Madison Avenue mentality introducing the new "gimmick" of paintings changing 'from day to night,' etc. could easily have disgusted Artists and caused them to immediately reject what had the sound of only an aesthetically-void advertising campaign "gimmick." After having contact with Thomas S. Warren, who founded "Ultra-Violet Products, Inc." in 1932, and his clan, and after having personal experience of their questionable spiritually-void and creatively dead abilities, it is much easier to understand the feelings of Artists towards these pretentious, money-minded common businessmen who have as much innate knowledge and intimate feelings for Art as a blind man has for Colors.

"Conti-Glo" Fluorescent paint is next assured to the public in this 1930s press release that it is superior to "old types" of luminous or phosphorescent paints previously available, as well as being "harmless" (there was still the remnants of the Radium craze in the air at this time), and finally 'incomparable to pale old-fashioned Colors.'

If the Fine Artist wasn't already disgusted from the hard-sell attitude of this press release's sales pitch, then the final part of the release would have achieved that goal. The reader is explained that 'regardless of which "ism" the Artist was a "disciple" of,' the "*craftsmen*" of Fine Arts was now able to achieve 'enhanced beauty in their paintings with Colors they could never obtain before, thanks to this new scientific aid.' Furthermore, the "Sur-realist" Artist could now 'further develop with radiant light' the "Unusual effects" they render. Again stressing "the sudden changes" a painting could make, such as "day to night," when the "Mazda" White light was turned off and the "Black Light" was turned on, and also that these "amazing startling" effects are promoted as 'shapes transforming themselves and becoming figures, Colors becoming different and taking on different hues which could allegorically change meanings.'

The final part of this press release gives identification to the killing blow to Fine Artist's acceptance of this new Fluorescent paint and Black lights, when the "Interior Decorator" is intimately associated with the "Fine Artist." It is graphically stated that these "Interior Decorators" would be "artfully successful" by using this new miraculous Fluorescent paint and Black lights for 'drapes, walls, ceilings, furniture, and even murals.' It is advertised that "miraculous" changes to decorated interior designs could now be achieved when the "Mazda" White lights were turned off and Black lights which were "small and compact" hidden in 'vases, niches, or grillwork' were magically turned on. If the Fine Artist wasn't totally disgusted and turned off yet, in this very same paragraph of this press release, which begins with the "Interior Decorator" in the first sentence, ends with the last sentence associating the Fine "Artist" - the painter - with the "Interior Decorator" and further claims they are both the same craftsmen. It is also advised that Artists could now "produce fantasies" with glowing Colors cheaply through their use of new 'small, powerful and inexpensive black lights.'

Next paragraph in this paper, next killing blow to Fine Artists, which manifests itself in the form of the next Artist/ craftsman: the "Scenic designer" for "stage decorations." It is explained that 'unusual decorations and transformations' were now possible on the stage set by using "Conti-Glo" Fluorescent paint, such as "scenery and dimensions" completely changing, or 'creating the illusions of great depth or height.' Even an example is given of psychological roles, actor's features and their costumes, in the running production "Strange Interlude," being changed through the use of "Conti-Glo" by a "clever" stage director.

If the first full three typed pages weren't enough to totally disgust Fine Artists for the newly invented Fluorescent paint and Black lights in this 1930s press release of "Conti-Glo," the final paragraph would bring not only the press release to a definitive conclusion, but also the opinion and decision of the Fine Artist would be indefinitely concluded after three pages of being associated with, and included in, every "craftsman" occupation from the common carpenter to the commercial Artist, to the mural painter, to the Stage designer - and even the crowning achievement of this press release - the epitome: the "Interior Decorator!" Having associated with and having included together the Fine Artist with these artisans or craftsmen, this final concluding paragraph cements this detestable relationship and association with 'Artists of all fields,' including lithography craftsmen, and for the *grand finale* - 'Window display designers and Advertising Billboard designers!' 'Artists of all fields for their general advancement should acquaint themselves with the new perfected luminescent Colors which were specifically designed for general usage.' 'Conti-Glo has been used for printing successful lithographs and for future commercial window displays as well as advertising billboard designs.' The final concluding statement of this press release is the offer to "the clever artist" of nothing less than a "type" of art 'that is new - with an unlimited field and tremendous possibilities' for this advertised "Painting with Light."

It is not necessary to even close the eyes, because merely by squinting, the image of an Artistically-void, greasy, bespectacled, suit and tied greedy Madison Avenue advertising executive can be immediately visualized and even easily projected into place at their seedy little desk on the fourteen floor of some miserable office building instructing their secretary to type these prophecies - all with a vision-quest and a truly Artistic objective of filling their bottomless pockets with filthy paper. The undeniable karma of this bunch is that by trying to make the most money possible - by including and associating all Fine Artists with Interior Decorators, Stage, Window, and even Billboard designers - instead of just the Fine Artist - the same Artistically-void greedy businessmen with nothing more on their palettes than "estimated profit" - actually *caused* the Fine Artist to immediately, indelibly, and quite indefinitely reject what was marketed to them, to quote Henry Adams again, as a mere "gimmick."

'The Fluorescent Paint Business of Robert and Joseph Switzer,' "Advertising Age," (1953)

A final scanned gem from the Kent State Archive for this author is the October 26, 1953 article from "Advertising Age" of the Fluorescent Paint business of Joe and Bob Switzer with it's handwritten notes by Kokoon Arts Klub president Philip Kaplan on it's first page, begins with the statement that the Switzer Brothers began as "magicians," but that their emphasis was still on "Fluorescent research." This 1953 article on the inventors of Fluorescent paint was collected by Philip Kaplan fifteen full years after the Twenty-fifth Anniversary " Black Light Ball" and just three years before the Kokoon Arts Klub disbanded in 1956 with only twenty-five aged members left. On the first page of this 1953 Switzer Brothers article Philip Kaplan wrote: "Note - I played an important part in the development of Day-Glo. Used it at Kokoon Costume Bal etc. Sold orders..." Next to this Philip Kaplan also wrote "Note - I helped develop the product in Cleveland in 1936-1938..." This article concludes both the large amount of scans made for this author by the Kent State Archive, and also the "Golden Age of Fluorescence" which began with the 1930s - the age of endless possibilities, the invention of Fluorescent Paint, the Kokoon Arts Klub's 1938 "Black Light Ball."

The Switzer brother's article from 1953 begins unsurprisingly not with Fine Art, or painting, but with the mass-produced first 1953 magazine cover printed with "Fire Red" Fluorescent ink: "McCall's." The conclusion of this event, which marked the first "general household" magazine to be printed with Fluorescent "Letterpress ink" from "Day-Glo," was that this was the "largest audience" to ever see the Switzer Brother's "Optic-catching" Fluorescent Colors. Not only did this new "Day-Glo" Fluorescent "Letterpress ink" light up the front cover of the banal household "McCall's" magazine in 1953, but it also was used to reproduce an "atomic blast" on a full "five-color" cover for "Popular Science" magazine in May, 1953, as well as being used on the next two covers of that magazine. It seems that the first use in magazines for Fluorescent ink was inside the December, 1952 issue of "Town and Country" magazine for a picture of a "Christmas tree," according to this article, using the first "gravure ink" from Day-Glo developed under F. H. Levey, Inc., and that this Fluorescent "letterpress ink" for magazine printing was developed by the "Interchemical Corp." licensed by the Switzer Brothers. At the time of this article's printing there was already planned the next November, 1953 issue of "McCall's" with another Day-Glo front cover. Joseph Switzer is introduced first as the 'younger brother' and as the "research man" of the Switzer brothers. The Switzer brother's laboratory is described as having "complete equipment" consisting of everything from "Spectrophotometers" to obscure "Launderometers" which tested their Fluorescent Colors for 'washability, lightfastness, and brightness.'

This new "Letterpress ink" produced for the Switzer brothers by "Interchemical" had already in 1953 been used in thirty-four countries 'on everything from billboards to toys - even on guided missiles.' Another ink developed by "Interchemical" for Day-Glo during that early period was "Aniline ink" used on "flexographic presses." This was used particularly for packaging of products to be sold inside stores on shelves, due to it's limitation of rapidly fading in sunlight.

The story is retold in this 1953 article of the 'dream of two schoolboys' which became the "Switzer enterprise." 'Some say these Day-Glo Fluorescent Colors invented by the Switzer brothers brightened "drab spots" more than any invention besides "Edison's lamp."' It is told in this article that "scores of patents" were owned for these Fluorescent Colors by the Switzer brothers, and that although they 'only started their business using just an egg-beater and an amateur magician's set,' in 1953 more than four-thousand companies are licensed to use Day-Glo Fluorescent Colors in a "dozen industrial fields," including 'magazines, beach balls, theater, displays for point of sale, and even golf balls.' As far as their roles as president and vice-president, Robert (Bob) Switzer who is credited with the invention of Fluorescent Paint in 1933 is in this article explained to be two years older than Joe Switzer, and as Joe is involved in the technical development of the Colors, Bob takes charge of the administration of running their business. The Switzer brothers decided not to become "big manufacturers," but instead operate a "pilot plant" in Cleveland, Ohio and license out the manufacturing to many other companies. It is explained that all the business of Day-Glo is done only from a two-story building in Cleveland with just sixty employees. The involvement before the Second world war with Carl Moellmann is briefly stated as the two brothers being "pay-check workers" for "Continental Lithography, Corp." before selling "millions of yards" of Fluorescent Signal Cloth for both World war two and the Korean war. During this early period the story is told of how Joseph Switzer and his wife with their first baby lived in half of a rented room, and in the other half of this rented room, behind a partitioning curtain, worked the Switzer brother's *chemist* developing Fluorescent inventions.

By 1953, the year of this article, the Day-Glo plant was producing "tons of pigment" around the clock, mostly dry powdered Fluorescent pigment for "licensees" such as the huge paint manufacturer "Sherwin-Williams, Co." Besides using this Fluorescent pigment to produce banal "Sherwin-Williams" house paints, the just-as-miraculous uses for this Fluorescent pigment are also listed in this '53 article as 'raincoats, shower curtains, and hunting jackets'(!) Besides these spiritual, and truly Artistic applications for Day-Glo pigments, the use of "Zyglo" and "Magnaglo" metal-stress detection in industrial plants is also added.

The killing blow to Fluorescent Color (not even to mention the obtrusive additive and necessary accessory the Black light) was brought about through, again, not the failings of Fluorescent Colors or Black lights themselves, but by the pure greed, lack of sensitivity, and also a lack of understanding or interest in non-profitable applications of Fluorescent Colors including Art, of the Switzer brothers themselves and all other like-minded solely business orientated American entrepreneurs. Fine Artists being associated with, and considered nothing more than the list of craftsmen, such as "Interior Designers" that the Switzer brothers are writing about in this 1953 article *was* what caused the rejection of Fluorescent Colors in Fine Art. It only needs a few centuries of perspective, and knowledge of history, to see this. During the 1500s Leonardo Da Vinci fought like mad to get the Artist - who was considered up to that time in history, again, nothing more than a craftsman, and was even referred to as a "peynter/steyner" (painter/stainer of cloth) - to disassociate themselves with Color, and all that Color was associated with, such as the filthy grinding of substances into pigment which was nearly like old-world alchemy. Leonardo fought to bring the "peynter/steyner" out of the dark low social standing of the clothes dyer by disassociating the Fine Artist with not only Color, but any work to be considered a physical craft, including even marble sculpting, five-hundred years ago - half a millennia - so any association with craftsmen, such as Billboard designers, or even the epitome: the Interior Decorator, was very much similar to considering the most respected world-class master chef in Paris equal to, and associated with "McDonalds"! In the same way that the finest French chef and "McDonalds" both 'cook food,' the Fine Artist and the Interior Decorator both 'use Color,' non? Not only are the factors of "Chromophobia" here to deal with, but even a more ancient and much more sensitive issue: "social standing." To the average brain-dead greedy businessman cloth dying and painting on canvas both use Color, the same way that a master Parisian chef and "McDonalds" both make food. The Switzer brothers considering the Interior Designer to be equal to the Fine Artist was no less offensive to Artists than being considered a "peynter/steyner" five-hundred years ago. Period. Again, the pure greed to sell as much "product" as humanly possible is what indelibly stained Fluorescent Color in Fine Arts, and this occurred years before the 1960s Movement.

If the Switzer brothers associating Fine Arts with Interior Decorating was not enough to disgust Artists, more than half of this article associates Artists with "Advertising!" The second half of this 1953 article comes right to the point: 'Switzer sales promotion as well as advertising' was always the top priority. It was explained that advertising executives were 'hopping all over Canada and the U.S.' "plugging" Fluorescent Colors not to Artists, obviously, but to 'sales and advertising firms.' "Day-Glo's" own advertising was reported in this article to be "six figures' and the company even published the "Day-Glo Herald," with it's editor being a newspaper and public relations executive. Moving further and further away from "Art," this article continues by listing fourteen different manufacturing companies from America to South Africa producing Fluorescent Colors under license by the Switzer brothers, and needless to say these were not Fine Art companies, but more like "Sherwin-Williams" the large house paint company, and other industrial firms. The closest it comes to Art in this list of industries under license from the Switzer brothers is the "American Crayon Co."(!)

The Switzer brother's true Colors come out in this last half of their article, in which the majority of the direction they were leading their Fluorescent paint company in was their very first idea for their 1933 invention: Advertising. The success story is listed in this 1953 article as supplying "Day-Glo" Colors to eight of the "major oil companies" for both 'outdoor and point of sale advertising,' including "Esso Standard Oil." The list of non-Artistic industries associated with and using "Day-Glo" Fluorescent Colors continues with Firestone Tires, Ford, Chevrolet, Mercury, Buick, Oldsmobile, Pontiac, and even Nash. This purely aesthetic list of companies using "Day-Glo" Colors continues to include "Home Appliances" and the RCA, Zenith, and Motorola corporations, as well as Budweiser beer, Westinghouse, Heinz ketchup, Canada Dry, Western Union, and TWA.

The final part of this 1953 "Advertising Age" article on the Switzer brothers and their Day-Glo paint retells their early history, starting with the day in 1933 that Bob began mimeographing advertisements for the Fluorescent paint mixed up "by Joe" in the Berkeley kitchen of their mother. Curiously it is Joseph Switzer the younger brother, not Robert in the article credited with mixing up the first Fluorescent paint. This is exactly how the credit was also changed in the 1969 "Day-Glo Designers Guide" when the Switzer brother's history was retold. In almost all references Robert Switzer is credited with inventing Fluorescent paint in 1933, not his younger brother Joseph. The "New York Times" 1997 obituary of Robert Switzer plainly states "Bob" as the inventor of Fluorescent paint, as well as the website "Robert and Patricia Switzer Foundation." A list of references that states Robert Switzer as the inventor of Fluorescent paint in 1933 is very long, but the short list of references that claim Robert's younger brother Joseph invented Fluorescent paint in 1933 is limited and oddly includes the 1969 "Day-Glo Designers Guide" published by the Switzer brothers, and this 1953 article in "Advertising News" containing personal interviews with both the Switzer brothers. Perhaps it was an attempt by Robert to give equal credit to his younger brother Joseph, since they had built their entire corporation from literally nothing together. It is further clarified in this 1953 article that "Black Fluorescence" had been known by chemists for close to a century, but that it was Joe Switzer at seventeen as an amateur magician that started the Day-Glo history by his inspiration while sitting in his father's Berkeley drug store when he read a "Popular Science" magazine article about making a home-made magic "black light." In this 1953 article from "Advertising Age" the credit goes totally to Joseph Switzer, not Robert Switzer, for first: exploring his father's drug store that night - alone - with a "home-made" black light, second: for discovering several drugs that night in his father's drug store that glowed under his black light, third: mixing these Fluorescent drugs with shellac and inventing Fluorescent paint, fourth: staging the first black light magic shows in high school, and finally for fifth: also the first sales of Day-Glo paint to San Francisco and Oakland "night club" entertainers. Only after a couple of months into this chronology is Robert Switzer mentioned for the first time, with the "real debut" of the Switzer brothers at "The Pacific Coast Assoc. of Magicians" Oakland convention with their infamous "Headless Balinese Dancer" Fluorescent act.

In this article the history of Fluorescent Paint continues with the story of how the two brothers "abducted" the kitchen blender of their mother and also took over the garage producing "glowing goo." Bob sent "direct mail" pieces out and their first real orders began from magicians and from night clubs, as well as theaters. The story is included of their first time being cheated by a 'spiritualist' who magically disappeared while still owing the Switzer brothers "30 bucks" from glowing ink he ordered to write "spirit messages." An important documentation is contained in this article of the Switzer brothers selling Fluorescent paints as well as Fluorescent varnishes for 'decorating sizable areas' of the Golden Gate Exposition in San Francisco in 1939 and also the New York World's Fair of the same year. Listed amongst their early achievements in the article is Sally Rand, who had a glowing "G-string" made for her, and the "Invisible Laundry Marking Ink" which was their first introduction to the "National Marking Machine" in Cincinnati, Ohio. The brothers are said to have gone "Jalopying" to Ohio from California and there earned their first patents for "Zyglo" and "Magnaglo" metal-stress detection. Still struggling the two young brothers developed Fluorescent printing inks which were then used by the U.S. military in World war two for the printing of 'Fluorescent maps, bombing manuals, and charts' which would glow under Black lights while still retaining the cover of darkness. The article includes the important Fluorescent "Fabric marking" and their invention of "Daylight" Fluorescent Colors which would 'glow in the daylight with four times the brightness of ordinary colors.' This 1953 Switzer brothers article in "Advertising Age" ends with the fact that what was important to them was their solid business policies, and that they believe that they were founding what they called a new industry.

Before William Byler patented the "Black light" fluorescent tubular lamp in the mid-1930s, and just a year after the Longwave Ultraviolet filter was invented by Dr. Robert Woods also in America, a German physicist Dr. Richard Kuch (1860-1915) is today credited with the invention of the Ultraviolet high-pressure lamp in 1904 while working for "Heraeus" in Hanau, Germany. Similar to the claims of 'Inventing the Black light' by William Byler, who was the first person to patent the black light in the mid-1930s, Richard Kuch was not the first person to invent the "Vapor Electric Lamp," but he was the first person to patent it in 1904. In "The History of Medicine" by D. D. Banerjee it is clearly stated that the "invention" of "mercury vapor lamps" was made by Leo Arons in 1896, by Cooper Hewitt who invented the "quartz lamp" in 1901, and by the man who is documented in many books on "Actinotherapy" as being the person who invented the Shortwave Ultraviolet Quartz Mercury vapor health treatment lamp in 1904: Kromayer. Dr. Richard Kuch went on to become managing director of "Heraeus" from 1909 to 1915 as a partner with the two Haraeus brothers. This German company, which is still in existence today in Hanau, Germany as a global corporation, is also still involved with the manufacturing of Ultraviolet and Infrared lighting technology, as well as the original business of the company, the smelting of precious metals. This "Heraeus" corporation began three-hundred years ago in Hanau, near Frankfurt, as the Heraeus family bought the "Unicorn Pharmacy." In 1856 Wilhelm Carl Heraeus developed a new technique for the melting of Platinum. After taking over his father's pharmacy in 1851, Platinum was very popular for jewelry design but was difficult to work with because of it's hardness and it's extremely high melting point which left jewelers no choice but to forge Platinum while White-hot. Wilhelm Carl Heraeus found a solution to this problem by melting two kilos of Platinum in a "oxyhydrogen" gas flame, and by doing so gave birth to the "first German Platinum melting house." By the end of the Nineteenth century the Heraeus company was melting and processing about a ton of Platinum per year. The two Heraeus brothers developed the company they took over from their father, continuing to research new smelting techniques, and hired an old school friend Dr. Richard Kuch who was a physicist and chemist. From 1889 Richard Kuch had his first commission from Wilhelm and Heinrich Heraeus for researching photo paper made of Platinum. The Platinum photo paper could not be realized, but Kuch showed such abilities as a research scientist that the brothers made Kuch head of scientific research in their business. Richard Kuch's first patent was in 1891 and involved the gilding of sheet Platinum. Three years later Kuch applied for a U.S. patent that was issued to him in 1905 for the "Vapor Electric Lamp." By 1899 Kuch had already made a major discovery in the development of a new process for creating bubble-free Quartz glass of high purity. Dr. Kuch made this bubble-free Quartz glass from "rock crystal" which he melted with an "oxyhydrogen" blow pipe, which was a medical and scientific breakthrough. Dr. Richard Kuch is today credited with the invention of the first industrial Quartz glass Ultraviolet lamp in 1904, and then in 1906 Heraeus established Quartz lamp manufacturing in cooperation with the "AEG" company. Kuch's revolutionary new technique of making bubble-free Quartz glass of high purity in industrial quantities was achieved by melting rock crystal at around two-thousand degees celcius with the "oxyhydrogen" gas flames. This led to further research by Kuch and in 1904 to his patenting of the Mercury vapor Quartz glass lamp. This Mercury vapor Quartz glass lamp was used in the light therapy Shortwave UV "Actinotherapy" health treatment craze of the first half of the Twentieth century, as well as an artificial suntanning lamp back to 1911.

This first industrial Quarz glass high-pressure UV lamp of Dr. Richard Kuch in 1904 went on to become the "Original Hanau Hohensonne" artificial Sun lamp in 1911, and was part of the first artificial tanning 'Suntan Salon' industry, which is still a major industry a century later. In 1930 "Heraeus" developed a small household Ultraviolet "Hohensonne" Sun lamp, which was a very popular UV 'Tanning lamp.' In the early 1950s "Heraeus" designed the first Infrared emitter, and in 1973 the Quartz lamp manufacturing shared with AEG since 1906 was taken over by "Heraeus." Continuing it's research and development in Ultraviolet, started over a century ago in the company by Dr. Kuch in 1904, in 1992 an independent subsidiary is formed named "Heraeus Noblelight," from the British manufacturer of UV curing lamps, and "Amba" becomes part of "Heraeus" as the corporation extended it's operations into Asia and became a worldwide group.

"Ultraviolet Radiation - It's Properties, Production, Measurement, and Applications" M. Luckiesh, 1922

First, for a glimpse into the very early Ultraviolet history during the time period just before the 1930s-1940s "Miracle of Fluorescence" era, a very early and rare hardcover edition of "Ultraviolet Radiation - It's Properties, Production, Measurement, and Applications" by M. Luckiesh from way back in 1922 is in the Museum collection, and this antique book offers a peek into that era. "Ultraviolet Radiation" is a technical book, written during an era when the applications of

Ultraviolet were just being discovered, before "The Miracle of Fluorescence" era that would begin shortly. To give a general feeling for the age of this book, in the "Preface" written by M. Luckiesh on March 22, 1922, the first sentence contains the words "six score years" sounding like the Gettysburg Address. This book is so old that on the last page there is a printed advertisement for the publishing company, and the two pages previous to the ad contain descriptions of the eight previous books by the author, an example being the hardcover 1916 edition of "Light and Shade and Their Applications," 135 illustrations, 277 pages, for just $3.00.

The "Preface" by M. Luckiesh details the author's purpose for writing the book "Ultraviolet Radiation" in 1922, being that at the time there were many sources of Ultraviolet energy being discovered and created, and with this increase was bringing also newly discovered applications for this Ultraviolet, but that the limited literature on the subject of Ultraviolet which already existed was very "confusing" and was not scientific, void of studies with investigations into the "Spectral character" of this Ultraviolet, which Luckiesh includes many illustrated examples of in this book. The introduction to the book concentrates on the chemical applications of Ultraviolet, and how these applications helped create Photography, which was also still in it's relative youth in 1922.

On the discovery of Ultraviolet by Ritter in 1801, M. Luckiesh adds the background event of Scheele's 1777 experiment of projecting the visible spectrum into Silver chloride, which caused both the release of Chlorine gas and the production of pure Silver in the invisible area of the spectrum outside of visible Violet, in the area known in 1922 as the 'region of the violet rays.' Scheele had, in effect, discovered Ultraviolet but he didn't realize it himself, and it was Ritter in 1801 who realized the invisible energy just outside of visible Violet to be Ultraviolet energy. Infrared energy was discovered by W. Herschel in 1800 and just the next year in 1801 Ritter discovered Ultraviolet. M. Luckiesh describes the advanced work and discoveries of the effects of Ultraviolet energy and of visible light on Silver salts, concentrating on their effect upon Silver chloride. Gay Lussac and Thenard were experimenting on the different effects of light on Chlorine and Hydrogen by 1809, in 1815 Planche documented his experiments on the effects of light upon different metallic salts, and soon after there was established a "Photo-chemical Absorption Law" by Grotthus. "The Father of Color Theory," Eugene Chevreul was the first person to describe a very important photochemical effect in 1837, when he documented his observations on the bleaching (fading) of vegetable dyes by the action of sunlight, air, and moisture. All of these discoveries of the early 1800s by Scheele, Ritter, and a host of other scientists were the foundations needed for Niepce and Daguerre to produce the first practical Photography process in 1830.

This very early 1922 book "Ultraviolet Radiation" by M. Luckiesh also has several Black and White full page photographs, including some of the most well known sources of Ultraviolet energy at that time. A very valuable 1922 list of different sources of "Ultraviolet Radiation" is printed in this book and presents many Ultraviolet sources that are completely unknown today, along with their relative strengths (measured in "Ultraviolet Ergs" per second, per square cm., per foot candle): Quartz Arc (Opal glass), Graetzin gas lamp, Carbon (gem) filament bulb, Copper-Hewitt Hg. tube (glass), Sunlight, Acetylene torch, 100 watt Tungsten bulb, Nernst lamp, Magnetite Arc (glass), Magnetite Arc (Quartz), Quartz Arc (old), Quartz Arc (new), and the most powerful of them all, the Carbon Arc (Quartz). The strengths of only the last two apparatuses of this list were rated as being really powerful, comparing the weakness of the first apparatus listed being the Quartz Arc (Opal glass) with a strength of 4.3 "Ultraviolet Ergs," to the 87.6 and 91.0 "Ultraviolet Ergs" listed for the Quartz Arc (new) and the Carbon Arc (Quartz) apparatuses.

The first photograph of these ancient Ultraviolet apparatuses in Luckiesh's book is of a "White Flame Arc," which consists of two bullet-shaped metallic objects producing a brilliant White flame between them. The caption informs the reader that the White Flame Arc was a strong "Near" Ultraviolet energy source, similar to sunlight (Longwave Ultraviolet). The next full page photograph printed in this 1922 book is the nattiest looking 'Black light' that could be imagined, which was called a "Quartz Mercury Arc." Honestly, this Ultraviolet 'lamp' (if it could be called such a thing) today would remind a person of an outdoor Gas Cooking grill! This Medieval-looking contraption's caption calls it a "Quartz Mercury Arc" and the photo shows an open cross section of this grotesque lamp/machine to point out the Quartz Arc that is concealed inside two halves of iron box-like housings. Complete with loose wires everywhere, these two sections housing the Quartz Arc are mounted to the top half of a vertical iron pole. The bottom of the iron pole has the most antique electrical apparatus that can be imagined attached to it, complete with more loose wires. As I've explained, these neither looked like, or were called "Ultraviolet lamps," but were referred to as "Ultraviolet apparatus." Such an Ultraviolet apparatus was used to clean water - the monstrous machine that is next photographed in Luckiesh's book, the "Quartz Mercury-Arc Water-Sterilizer." The photo of this "Recirculating Drinking Water System" of a large factory that had the Quartz Mercury-Arc Water Sterilizer incorporated into it's design looks like a photograph of the Titanic's engine room! This really huge, ugly factory machine from ninety years ago is a very good example of technology that is still used today - Shortwave Ultraviolet Water Purification for not only people, but also for most large fish tanks and fish ponds all over the world. Since the Shortwave Ultraviolet energy is a "Germicidal lamp," it kills germs instantly as the water rushes past the Shortwave source in these examples

Of course in 1922 during the height of the 'Shortwave Ultraviolet Miracle Cure' era there is not only a full page photograph of a half-naked woman being assisted by a nun-like nurse under a simply tremendous 'Shortwave Ultraviolet Health-Treatment Lamp,' but there is an entire chapter named "Effects Upon Living Matter" devoted to that ill-advised 'Miracle Cure' era in Luckiesh's book. Like I often tell visitors in the Museum, idiots back then used to drink Radium also!

But all the prehistoric photos in this 1922 book that I've described couldn't prepare for the shock of the photo of what could be barely even called a 'machine,' described as a "Dye-Testing" apparatus that used a "White Flame Arc." This most primitive looking machine makes the other antique machines in this book look nearly high-tech! The 'White Flame Arc Dye Tester' consisted of a forty inch (101.5 cm.) barrel standing upright with an open top, and large triangular wooden braces on either of it's sides supporting the barrel, and a Frankenstein-laboratory device mounted above it. There is literally "chicken wire" held in place by two cheap metal clamps between the barrel and the Frankenstein device. This Frankenstein device looks like an ancient gas lantern from the 1800s with many curled wires attached to the very top of it and running up towards the ceiling(!) In total contrast, the last photo in this 1922 book has an apparatus that looks nearly like the inside of a computer compared to the Frankenstein barrel in the previous photo, and which is a picture of a very large "Blue-Printing" machine that printed with the "Carbon Arc." This was a very complicated machine that had six large mechanical heads inside a large metal housing that were attached to six curved glass containers which most likely housed the Carbons arcs.

In this book Luckiesh has presented a wide variety of Ultraviolet apparatuses that were already manufactured and in public use by 1922, ranging from primitive machines that are hard to imagine anymore, to sophisticated complex machinery. The peek into the far past of the history of Ultraviolet energy is what makes this book by Luckiesh a very valuable source of lost history from the beginning of the Twentieth century.

"The Ultra-Violet Rays - Their Action on Internal and Nervous Diseases and Use in Preventing Loss of Hair Color and Falling of the Hair"   Dr. Arnold Lorand (M.D. Vienna), Physician at Carlsbad Springs, Czecho-Slovakia, Author of "Old Age Deferred," "Health Through Rational Diet," Philadelphia, 1928

The second sentence of this book already begins by informing the reader that a good portion of the book would center on the subject of "Falling Hair" and it's turning to Grey with ageing. Dr. Lorand explains that since the causes are "Essentially internal," then the treatment of baldness must also be "internal," which the good doctor considers 'Ultra-violet Ray Therapy' to be, as well. To prove his point Dr. Arnold Lorand explains that he personally had a bald head for many years, but that after sitting under the Shortwave Ultraviolet "Quartz light" Treatment lamp "Several hundred" times for a period of *seven years* (!) the doctor had "at last succeeded in growing a modest crop of hair." The good doctor concedes that if he had been younger than in his 50's, he was sure that he could have grown all his hair back with these "Ultra-violet rays." After confessing to having treated a 'large number' of patients suffering from various nervous and chronic internal diseases with Shortwave "Ultra-violet rays," the doctor also adds his advice for the effects of natural sunlight.

Just the titles of some of the chapters in Dr. Lorand's book are nearly hysterical when reading them today, ninety years after they were published. It is explained in Chapter four that the condition of the Endocrine Glands could be improved by "Ultra-violet rays," as well as Chapter five's "Reduction of High Blood Pressure" through the Shortwave "Quartz Light," and - wait for it - the 'Treatment of Obesity' (!) by the Shortwave "Ultra-violet Rays." Part one of Dr. Lorand's book discusses Shortwave "Ultra-violet ray" treatment for 'Gall-stones, ulcers of the stomach, and enlargement of the liver' in Chapter seven, treatment of 'Neurasthenia and Impotence' in Chapter eight, and even treatment for 'Old Age' with Shortwave U.V. in Chapter nine. 'Part two' is entirely devoted to "The Treatment of Falling Hair by the Ultra-violet Rays" for a grand total of *eighty-nine pages* with Chapter nineteen named 'Stimulating the Growth of Hair by the Quartz Light.' 'Part three' concludes this Dr. Lorand book of 1928 with it's miraculous 'Treatment by the Quartz Light for Greying Hair.'

Dr. Lorand's explanations and justifications for Shortwave "Ultra-violet ray" Quartz Light Treatment being used as the new "Miracle Cure-All" of the early 1900s, are today lost in archaic thought and analysis, such a Lorand's comparison between the high frequency vibrations of "Ultra-violet Rays," which the author believes to be connected to their therapeutic properties, and the rapid motion of clear rushing streams which are also highly vibrating and contain, through the effects of these vibrations, much less bacteria than still water. Dr. Lorand continues on, trying to convince the 1928 reader that the sunlight in California and Switzerland was more therapeutic than the sunlight in other parts of the world, and also that the Color of the sky

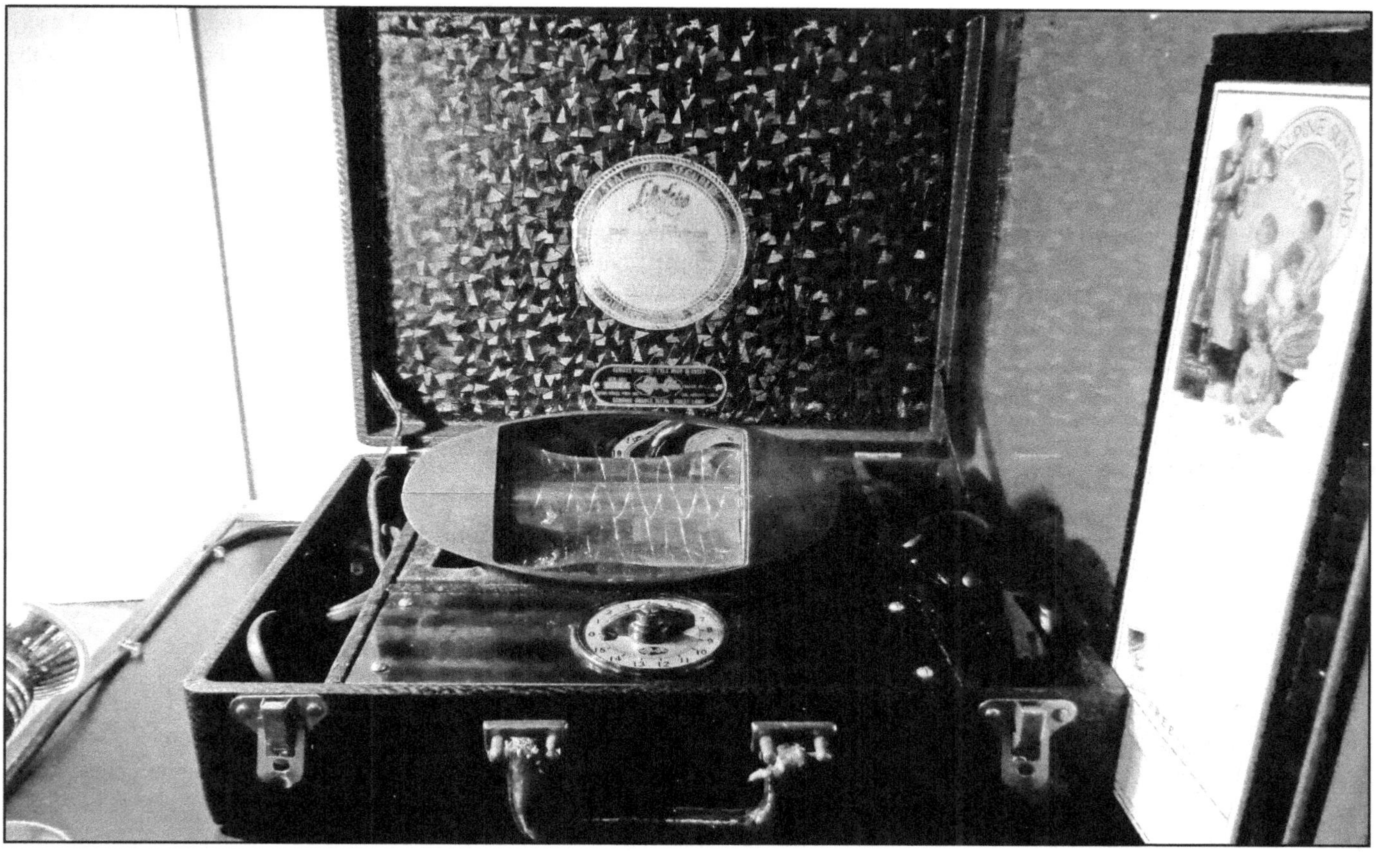

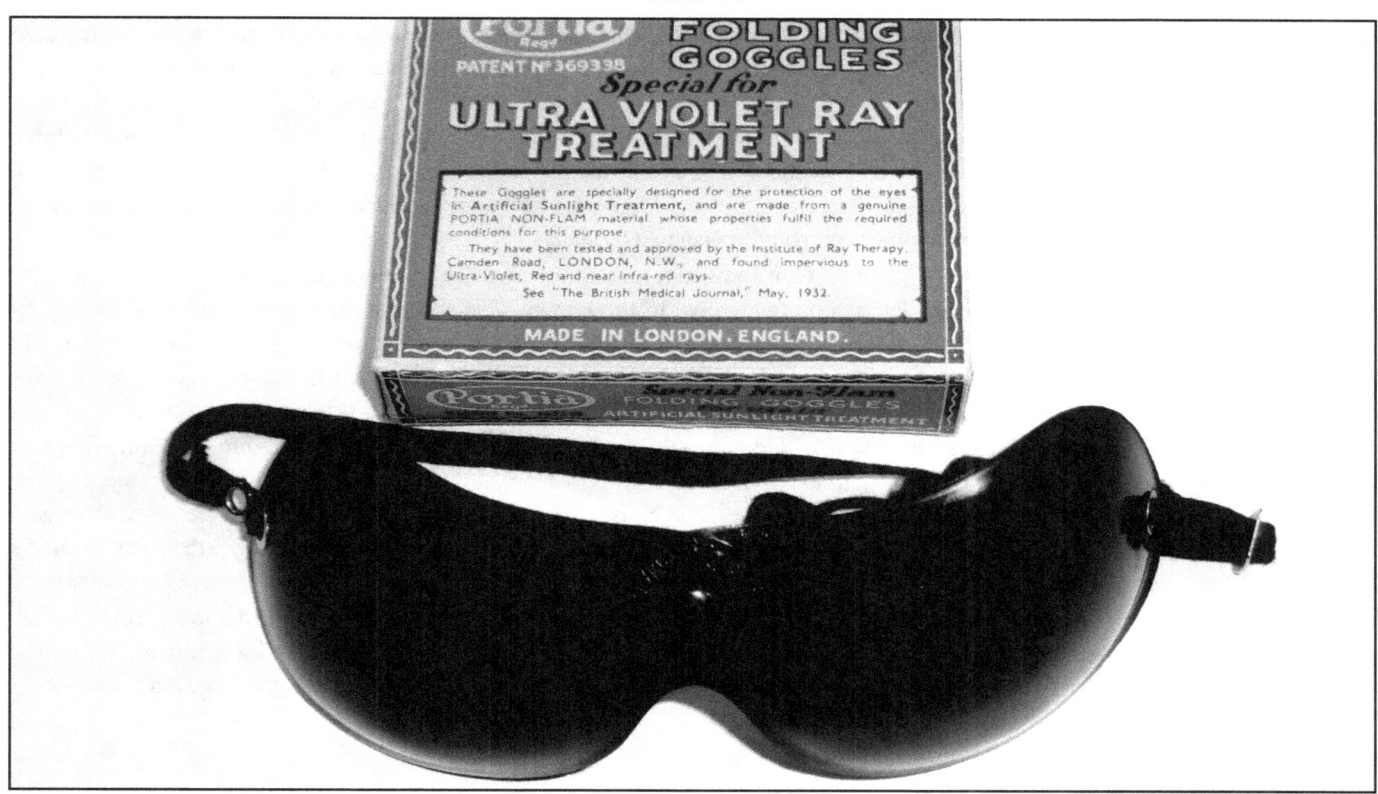

1920s-1930s "Actinotherapy" Shortwave Ultraviolet "Miracle-Cure" Lamp: "Life-Lite" "Genuine Ultra-Violet Rays Lamp," Los Angeles, California

1920s-1930s "Actinotherapy Goggles - Special for Ultra Violet Ray Treatment," "Portia/Solport Brothers Ltd.," London

is just as important to indicate good "health-dispensing rays," because, according to Dr. Lorand a deep Blue sky indicated a sky filled with "Chemical Rays." Finally on page twenty of Dr. Lorand's book the name of the "Ultra-violet rays" emitted by the Quartz therapy lamp is given as "External Short-Waved Rays." As further proof of Dr. Lorand's archaic logic presented in his 1928 book "The Ultra-Violet Rays," after the doctor explains that it was proved that a human skull is penetrated by the "Ultra-violet Rays," he concludes that this should lead the way to curing diseases in deep internal organs, such as "tuberculous kidneys." Probably the most completely incorrect statement in Dr. Lorand's book (besides the entire 213 pages of the book dealing with the "Ultra-violet Ray's" 'Growing Your Hair Back' and 'Preventing your Hair from Turning Grey') is the statement in which Dr. Lorand quotes Rollier, who was absolutely incorrect when he stated that the 'outer rays' of "Ultra-violet," which he defined as 'very Short-waved and very active' (today known as "Shortwave Ultraviolet" energy) would actually *Turn into* the 'inner rays' that were 'long-waved and of milder action' (today called "Longwave Ultraviolet" energy) after the "Ultra-violet" entered the human body(?) The author goes on to state that in his belief the Color of the Blue blood of deep-sea Lobsters is to counteract the effect of "Ultra-violet Rays" from the Sun. In the "Ultraviolet Artifacts" display case in the Museum I have an "Ultra-Violet Products, Inc." Shortwave Ultraviolet Health Treatment Lamp on display, with an advertisement from 1928 next to it announcing the headline that 'Shortwave Ultraviolet would Cure Rickets'(!) Here in Dr. Lorand's 1928 book is one of the actual sources of that misguided knowledge, as the doctor explains in depth the use for the Shortwave Ultraviolet "Quartz Light" for treatment in the cure of Rickets. Dr. Lorand states that this Shortwave Ultraviolet Rickets cure was discovered in 1921 by Huldschinsky and after articles were published on the subject other doctors were convinced and began to also use Shortwave Ultraviolet Lamps in misguided attempts to cure Rickets.

For an archaic history of an antique technique, Dr. Lorand states that the reason Quartz was used to create the early Shortwave "Quartz Lights" was that Quartz is transparent to Shortwave Ultraviolet and passes right through clear Quartz, while common glass absorbs ninety percent of Shortwave Ultraviolet. Today in 2016, ninety-three years later, the Shortwave Ultraviolet lamps and filters manufactured throughout the world still are produced using fused Quartz crystals. The doctor explains that the Quartz was made into a tube and that a column of Mercury was heated to the point of incandescence inside this Quartz tube, which in turn created the Shortwave Ultraviolet energy of the lamp, reported as being a brilliant Green-Blue light. Dr. Lorand reports in his 1928 book that Kromayer was the first person to produce a "Quartz lamp" for Shortwave Medical Treatment, and that this first "Quartz lamp" consisted of a small lamp with a hole through which the Shortwave Ultraviolet energy was released. The problem with this Kromayer "Quartz lamp" was that it could only be used on small areas of the body, not over entire areas of the body. The first Shortwave Ultraviolet Health Treatment Lamp that was manufactured with the ability to treat large areas of the body is stated by Dr. Lorand as being in Elster, by a man named Bach. Bach developed a "Quartz lamp" that had a large tube of Quartz surrounded by a curved half globe of a metallic reflector, which would reflect the concentration of Shortwave Ultraviolet rays onto the patient. This "Quartz lamp" was called the "Alpine Sun," remembered now as the "Alpine Sunlamp," and this was the most popular Shortwave Ultraviolet Health Treatment Lamp, manufactured by the "Hanovia Company" in Newark, New Jersey, as well as in England by the "British Hanovia Quartz Lamp Company" in Slough, and also by another company in Hanau, Germany.

For a rudimentary explanation of the effects of the dangerous Shortwave Ultraviolet energy on the skin, Dr. Lorand assures the reader that Shortwave Ultraviolet 'is not dangerous' to the human skin and that the sunburn that was caused by sitting under these Shortwave U.V. treatment lamps, "Erythema," usually lasted for a couple of days, before disappearing, and that this sunburn was caused by blood rushing to the skin exposed to the Quartz lamp, which indicated to the good doctor "better Local Nutrition"(!) Doctor Lorand continues to explain cheerfully that after all the skin of the face was repeatedly exposed to strong Shortwave Ultraviolet energy, it would simply *peel off*, and that the new skin formed underneath would be created by the body to have not only a better complexion cosmetically, but also that this new face skin would be created by the body to be void of any imperfections. What a bunch of true-Blue Nuts! Dr. Lorand supports all of his theories by the restated point that this miraculous Shortwave Quartz lamp could grow back an entire new head of Hair on a man that was formerly considered "chave comme un genou" (bald as the knee). To further improve the Shortwave Ultraviolet Quartz lamp treatment another 'Miracle Lamp' called a "Sollux Lamp" could be used together with the "Alpine Sun Quartz lamp." This "Sollux Lamp" is explained as producing no Ultraviolet, but by being a very strong electric lamp it produced a brilliant White light along with much heat. These two monstrous lamps would be positioned with the unfortunate patient between them.

"Ultra-Violet Light and Vitamin D in Nutrition," Katherine Blunt and Ruth Cowan, 1930

To give an idea of how little was known about Vitamin D, and most Vitamins in general, this book "Ultra-Violet Light and Vitamin D in Nutrition" in the Museum collection was written in 1930 and published through "The University of Chicago Home Economics Series." Besides encapsulating proof of the ignorance of the 1930s era, especially in areas of Shortwave Ultraviolet "Actinotherapy," this book contains the most disturbing photographs of how far "Actinotherapy" went eighty years ago. Several of the Black and White photographs in this book are so visually disturbing that I decided to not present them in the "Fluorescence" wall flip-chart mounted in the Museum.

The "Forward" of this 1930 book has the authors explaining that if enough Vitamin D is not received by human or animal bodies they would be doomed to contracting "Rickets," and that before the miraculous new invention of the Shortwave Ultraviolet lamp used in "Actinotherapy," the only produced source of Vitamin D was the dreaded "Cod Liver Oil" known at that time as "bottled Sunshine"(!) The point for writing the book is stated by the authors as the summarizing of the recent research that had been done on Vitamin D and the effects of Ultraviolet energy, in regards to the Calcium and Phosphorus of the body. Morris Fishbein, the Editor of the "Journal of the American Medical Association" in 1930 writes in the "Forward" that without Vitamin D a child will develop Rickets, their ribs and teeth will not be strong, and their stomachs will be "Distended." Mr. Fishbein also states in this "Forward" that Vitamin D had been first identified in 1923, only seven years before the book's publication. This limited knowledge of Vitamin D, especially pertaining to it's effect on the human body when too much Vitamin D is produced, is absolutely obvious to a contemporary reader, with an example being the contents of the eighth chapter of this 1930 book. "Distribution of Vitamin D" is the title of this eighth chapter, and the entire known Vitamin D resource at that time consisted of cod liver oil, other fish oils, egg yolk, cow's milk and butter, as well as human milk, with the full length of the chapter being just twelve pages long. In fact, any part of this 1930 book "Ultra-violet Light and Vitamin D in Nutrition" is startling when opened up today. Page one of the book already manages to offend not only women, but even Jewish, Russian, and Japanese immigrants. Moving swiftly along, page two explains experiments on laboratory animals, and by the third page we are already exploring the wonderful world of "controlled experiments on children"(!) The authors explain that the improved heights and weights of women, Jewish, Russian, and Japanese immigrants, and even laboratory rats was totally due to the increased knowledge of bone growth, coming from the discovery of Vitamin D in the early 1920s.

The very beginning of this doomed Shortwave Ultraviolet Medical Treatment "Actinotherapy" era is stated as being credited to an Englishman named Mellanby who began by doing almost four-hundred experiments on puppies, which he published in 1918 and 1919. First the good Dr. Mellanby starved the puppies and fed them poor diets to deliberately cause them to contract Rickets, which he proved by the "X-ray photographs" he made of the puppy's bones. This 'harmless' experiment continued by administering cod liver oil to some of the puppies, who were cured of the Rickets, butter fat to other puppies which were less effectively cured of their laboratory-induced Rickets, and finally lard, cotton seed, and olive oil failed to cure other puppies' Rickets. This all came to a conclusion when American researchers led by McCollum at the John Hopkins University realized that "fat-soluble, growth promoting Vitamin A" was in fact the active "Antiachitic vitamine." The two photographs accompanying this text are the first two shockers of the book, being one of the very healthy puppies of Dr. Mellanby who was cured from it's induced Rickets by cod liver oil in 'Fig. 1,' but in 'Fig. 2' right next to it, there is a pitiful puppy that had only grown to half it's size and had terribly bent and malformed legs due to it's thirteen weeks on the Dr. Mellanby Rickets diet.

For the actual beginning of the Shortwave Ultraviolet lamp's use in Medical Treatment, the source is given in this 1930 book as having been in Germany from just after the First world war - but this is quite incorrect. The authors state that in 1919 and 1920 in Berlin, Huldschinsky found a very large percentage of older children having Rickets, and he did his initial research at the "Oscar-Helene Home for Crippled Children." The majority of Huldschinsky's experimental subjects were the ripe age of just three to five years old, were terribly deformed, and all had Rickets. Huldschinsky had the brilliant idea of giving these very young children, who were also very sick, "radiations" from dangerous Shortwave Ultraviolet Quartz Mercury lamps to cure their Rickets! This work of the German doctor was published, along with his experiments at the "Public Welfare center" in Berlin, in the September 1928 "British Journal of Actinotherapy." In 1921, only a year after Huldschinsky's experiments in Germany, Hess and Unger in New York City proved that Sunlight alone could cure infantile Rickets, and also Rickets in rats. It seems that the dangerous Shortwave Ultraviolet Treatment won out over natural harmless Sunlight because of the research done in 1924 by Steenbock in the University of Wisconsin, which proved that foods that contain no trace of Vitamin D could miraculously "develop it on irradiation with Ultraviolet"(!) The discovered "miracle" of the Shortwave Ultraviolet lamp was that it actually *created* Vitamin D! Very good - but the ignorance of this 'age of innocence' was in the fact that when Vitamin D production gets carried away, and too much Vitamin D is produced, for example under these Shortwave Ultraviolet Treatment lamps, it develops into very healthy Skin Cancer. This is the underlying deadly theme of the whole ignorant movement of the Shortwave Ultraviolet "Actinotherapy" of the 1920s-1940s, knowing that Vitamin D, which was found to be produced by Shortwave Ultraviolet lamps, was the cure for Rickets, so if Ultraviolet could cure the disease, the method developed used the most amount of this Ultraviolet energy, which was produced not by harmless Longwave Ultraviolet "Blacklights," but by the dangerous Shortwave Ultraviolet Quartz Mercury lamps. As is well known today, 'more' is not always 'better.' In regards to the morbid photos of the two puppies, Mellanby didn't stop there, with a photo of his huge doomed Rat colony, photos of two female Rat X-rays, once again with induced Rickets, and also with two photos of six week old chickens, one that had been raised in darkness and a much larger "specimen" that had been raised in sunlight.

After much discussion about not only the types of window glass that would allow Ultraviolet energy from sunlight to pass into buildings, and even a long explanation of the transparency to Ultraviolet energy of the different types of clothing material worn, it is admitted by the authors in this 1930 nightmarish book that 'other possible dangers are not well understood' concerning the widespread use of the Shortwave Ultraviolet Medical Treatment lamps in 1930, and even that at the time using 'artificial Ultraviolet Rays' was still 'very uncertain in many of it's aspects.' At this point in the antique book, on page 105, start the simply horrible photographs of Shortwave Ultraviolet Medical Treatment on children eighty years ago. The first of these 1930 nightmare photos looks like an image from a 1950's horror movie, with six little boys naked except for their diapers, crutches, and Shortwave Ultraviolet Protective Goggles lined up on a metal platform waiting to enter the interior of "the Ultraviolet-ray apparatus," which was a room-sized Ultraviolet cabinet that was entered by the crippled children who were then moved along it's irradiated interior on a "moving platform." This "Ultraviolet-ray apparatus" at the Spaulding school is partially visible in the photo, revealing it's size, which looks to be about twice the height of the nurse, who was also wearing safety goggles to lead the crippled children through a curtain and into the machine, which was at least fifteen feet (4.5 m) long.

The next Black and White photograph in this antique book is probably the most disturbing Shortwave Ultraviolet Treatment image I have ever seen, being part of the section of the book "Experiment in the University Co-operative Nursery School." This photograph was taken on the inside of the "Ultraviolet-ray apparatus" in the Spaulding school, and reveals the chamber to be quite tall and wide, with walls angled at their tops and bottoms, and with very large Shortwave Ultraviolet lamps positioned close together about halfway up the side walls to a height that is precisely the face level of the crippled child in diapers and protective goggles, who is sitting in an antique wooden wheelchair on the floor's moving platform. Simply harrowing.

"Actinotherapy Technique." Hanovia edition - An outline of indications and methods for the use of modern light therapy." 1933

This small book was published by the "Hanovia" Shortwave Ultraviolet Therapy Lamp Company in 1933, with a Forward by Sir Henry Gauvain who was an important English doctor and surgeon. The Introduction of this small book is written by the "Hanovia" company and it is explained that although there were nearly one thousand books and papers published by 1933 on the subject of "Actinotherapy" - Shortwave Ultraviolet Lamp Health Treatment - this book was printed as a 'Handbook' to doctors working with "Actinotherapy" on their patients. The book is divided into two parts, the Introduction presenting a short history of the use of Shortwave Ultraviolet "Actinotherapy," while the second part contains the working "Actinotherapy" Handbook which presents physical ailments that this Shortwave Ultraviolet Therapy was misguidedly thought to cure. It is quite clearly stated that this "Actinotherapy" Handbook was published as a working reference tool for doctors, and the actual 1933 copy of this book in the Museum collection has a stamp of the original book's owner on the first page: "J. Gordon Wilson, M.D." It is stated in the book's Introduction that this doctor's "Actinotherapy" Handbook was published as a parallel source of reference to the "Hanovia" company's physiotherapeutic publication "The Quartz Lamp," which was printed in both Newark, New Jersey and Slough, England.

In the first chapter of this doctor's reference guide for "Actinotherapy" it is clearly stated that the only part of the human body that was "very sensitive" to "short ultra-violet rays" were the eyes, and for this reason thick protective glasses or goggles were worn by patients undergoing "Actinotherapy" under powerful Shortwave Ultraviolet lamps. The reference list at the end of the book's first chapter reveals just how early Shortwave Ultraviolet Health Treatment had been written about, with the first reference being in German, which was published way back in 1912 by F. Bering and H. Meyer as "Strahlentherapie" and covered the early subject of 'Photo-Chemical Measurement' of 'Actinic Output,' and another reference that is listed covering the subject of the Mercury-Arc Lamps that was also entitled "Strahlentherapie" by Johannsen in 1915. Of the two full

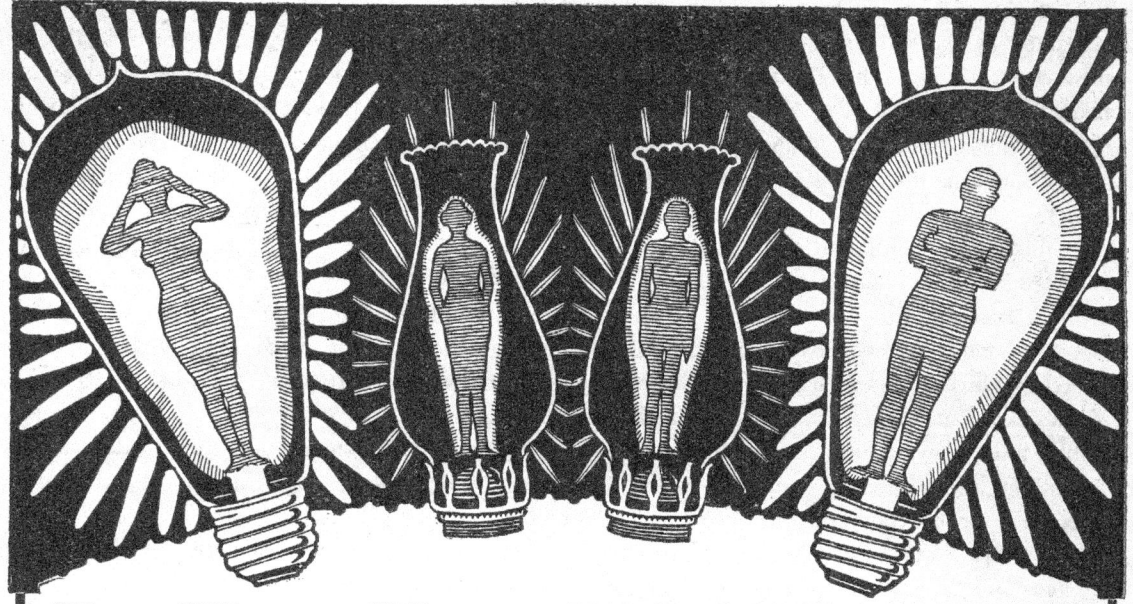

1922 "Actinotherapy" Shotwave Ultraviolet "Miracle-Cure" advertisement, "Vi-Rex Electric Co.," Chicago, U.S.A.

pages of early "Actinotherapy" published references in this book, the earliest published English language reference is from 1921 and was printed by the "American Journal of Electrotherapeutics" in October, 1921. Quite honestly, while reading through this miserable little book that is eighty years old, it occurs to the contemporary reader that this book has more the feeling of a medical handbook out of a "Flash Gordon" movie, or even a medical handbook from the Medieval times. It is stated in this "Hanovia" edition of "Actinotherapy Technique" that the "bactericidal action" of "Actinic rays" was first documented in 1877, and that the "Cure of Rickets" by "Actinotherapy" had been an established medical treatment by 1919. This all came to form an established branch of medicine termed "Actinotherapy" after research had been done in several countries and Vitamin D had been identified.

Even though Vitamin D had been identified in the 1920s, by the writing of this book in 1933 it is clearly admitted by the author that there was very little known about Vitamin D; not the function of the Vitamin in the body, or even where it originates from. This makes it very easy to understand why the eventual danger of increased activity and production in the skin, caused directly by this "Actinotherapy" treatment of sitting under harmful Shortwave Ultraviolet lamps, and which could eventually turn into skin cancer, was not known or even considered during this 'age of innocence.' The authors, who were mostly doctors, blissfully unaware of the immanent detrimental bodily harm they were advising their readers to cause, continue on cheerfully explaining the "Penetration of the Skin," "Effects on the Blood," the Metabolism, and the general physiological effects. The references for this chapter of the book reveal that the first publication describing the "Skin Effects" of Shortwave Ultraviolet "Actinotherapy" was in 1922 by K. W. Hausser and W. Vahle, with again the German title "Strahlentherapie." Other very early references cited at the back of this 1933 book are "Ultra-Violet Rays in Modern Dermatology" by R Bernstein of 1918, the German "Therapeutische Montatsheft" by H. Heusner of 1918. "The Chemical Action of Ultra-violet Rays" of 1925 by C. Ellis and A.A. Wells, "Light Treatment in Surgery" by O. Bernhard of 1926, and "Clinical Application of Sunlight and Artificial Radiation, including their physiological and experimental aspects, with special references to Tuberculosis" by E. Mayer in 1926.

The second part of this 1933 Doctor's Handbook on Shortwave Ultraviolet "Actinotherapy" consists of a huge list of symptoms that could be treated with this harmful technology, which continues on for *one hundred and five pages!* Everything from "Psoriasis" to "Syphilis," without forgetting "Baldness" or "Rickets," could be cured with the new miracle of the Shortwave Ultraviolet "Actinotherapy!" Let me state very clearly one more time:
1. The harmful Shortwave Ultraviolet energy created by these "Actinotherapy" lamps <u>Does Not</u> come out of "Black lights."
2. Shortwave Ultraviolet energy does not come through the Ozone layer, does not reach the surface of the Earth (except in areas where the Ozone layer has been destroyed) and does cause skin cancer through prolonged exposure to the skin.

The detrimental, and even possibly fatal effects on the human body caused directly by this Shortwave Ultraviolet "Actinotherapy" from the late Nineteenth century up until the 1940s has left it's indelible mark permanently on society's mind, by creating one of the first sociological nightmares that would establish the title of this book "The Social Stigma of "Fluorophobia." The cause of this stigma is very clearly revealed by investigating the intimate details of the directions of this miserable little book of 1933, complete with the only photograph of the book, a nightmare of an image displaying all of the twenty-eight different "Applicators" made for the Shortwave Ultraviolet Treatment unit named the "Kromayer Lamp." Now, to make people today cringe, it must be explained that this "Kromayer Lamp" was specifically designed to "Irradiate" the "membranes which line orifices" of the body(!) As a hair-raising example, there were no less than three different phallic-shaped "Kromayer Lamp Applicators" to enable a doctor to "Irradiate" harmful cancer-causing Shortwave Ultraviolet energy to the inside walls of the vagina. Not to stop there, another of the twenty-eight "Applicators" was designed specifically to shoot Shortwave Ultraviolet energy directly into the empty sockets of extracted teeth.

"Ultra-Violet Radiation and Actinotherapy." Dr. Elenor H. Russell and Dr. W. Kerr Russell, 1927

The last book I will refer to in this nightmare movement of the Shortwave Ultraviolet "Miracle" Health Treatment era is one of the oldest books in the Museum collection, and this book with the already healthy title of "Ultra-Violet Radiation and Actinotherapy" contains by far the most illustrations of any book from the 1920s I've come across. This 1927 book published in Edinburgh was written by Dr. Russell and Dr. Russell and is filled with 168 Black and White photographs, some of which are images that are nothing less than haunting. To once again give an idea of the era that this nightmare book was written in, the first sentence of the Forward by Sir Oliver Lodge informs the reader that "ether and matter" were at that time "attracting more attention." To give historical credit to the movement of that era of Shortwave Ultraviolet Health Treatment, the authors begin their book by quoting doctors from history who first practiced Sun treatment, going all the way back to the Father of Medicine, the Greek Hippocrates who lived on the island of Cos about 460-370 B.C. and was the first doctor to practice "Heliotherapy."

The first historical chapter includes the discovery of "Ultra-violet" energy by Ritter in 1801, who passed sunlight through a prism and recorded the fact that in the dark area of the spectrum "beyond the Violet" there was energy that turned his Silver Chloride Black. Ritter's discovery came after hundreds of years of experiments by scientists such as Christian Huygens who is credited as formulating the "Wave Theory" of light in 1678, Dufay who discovered in 1733 that two kinds of electricity existed, and Faure who was apparently the first person in modern times to use solar rays in medicine by treating skin ulcers with sunlight. Faure's method became known and this lead to other doctors focusing the Sun's rays on open skin wounds. In 1777 Scheele discovered the Sun's ability to darken primitive Silver Salts, in 1779 Ingenhouse discovered that the light of the Sun is what creates Photosynthesis not it's heat, and during that same year Bertrand published "The Influence of Light on Living Organisms." Just prior to Ritter's discovery of "Ultra-violet" in 1801, Volta announced his creation of the "Voltaic Battery" in 1799, and in 1800 Sir William Herschel discovered the energy that is contained in the opposite side of the spectrum from Ultraviolet: "Infra-Red." In 1802 Sir Humphry Davy created the first "Electric Arc," which was the first artificially produced source of Ultraviolet energy, and which was used to begin this era of Shortwave Ultraviolet Medical Treatment. In 1815 Fraunhofer discovered that lines contained in the spectrum could be used to identify different elements, and in 1820 Grotthus wrote the Law of Photo-Chemical Absorption. That same year Hans Christian Oersted discovered Magnetic Fields, and eleven years later Faraday used this magnetic force to create the first electrical dynamos. The authors document the monumental 'first' photographs by Daguerre in 1835, and then a very early example of Health Treatment using the Sun, which is termed in their book "Heliotherapy." In 1845 Bunsen created the modern Spectroscope and in 1862 Foucault and Fizeau found the speed of light. Three years later Maxwell discovered that light is composed of 'Electro-magnetic vibrations," and was the person who started an actual revolution in society by his experiments that led to the development of the Light Bulb. No history of light (no matter what Color it is) would be complete without the story of James Clerk Maxwell (1831-1879). In 1831, the year that Maxwell was born, Michael Faraday showed that if a magnet is waved it will effect electrical current, which was a big discovery in it's day, and which eventually fascinated James Clerk Maxwell years later. As a young man Maxwell was fascinated in very bizarre projects, such as trying to formulate an equation of the possible pattern that paper arbitrarily falling would create, and then invented the "Light Polarizer" out of a wooden box with two mirrors and a crystal from Iceland (commonly known today as "Rhombohedral Calcite" or 'Optical Calcite'). Being a natural born scientist, Maxwell put pieces of glass into a fire and made them Red hot, than next plunged them into ice cold water. When viewing these pieces of glass through his "Light Polarizer" Maxwell was fascinated by the beautiful Colored patterns of the stress lines he had created with his hot-cold experiments. The patterns were so beautiful and fascinating to Maxwell that he made a series of watercolors of them that are still in existence. The point that captivated Maxwell was that apparently physical forces could effect the way light was seen, and even the Colors of light that were seen. Besides all the other incredible discoveries made by Maxwell in the 1800s, he is also credited with the achievement of taking the very first Color photograph. This was early in his career, and also a full thirty years before anyone else took Color photographs. In his most important work later on in his life Maxwell would prove that very strong electrical fields that were created by magnets would also effect light as well. One of the many accomplishments that Maxwell is famous for in science is that he came up with four equations that would alter science forever, because they proved that Light, Electricity, and Magnetism have something to do with each other, and that they could perhaps be even the same form of energy, which he proceeded to call an "Electromagnetic Wave." Maxwell correctly concluded that if light is an electromagnetic wave, then the different Colors of the light of the spectrum must correspond to different electromagnetic waves vibrating at different frequencies. This he realized as the way to harness electromagnetic energy, through which electricity could be harnessed as well. This all led to Maxwell inventing a Light bulb in the 1860s that literally changed the world. At the time, in London the first electric lights were in use, which were called "Arc Lighting" and worked through the simple technology of creating light through sparks, which, however, was noisy, inefficient, and unstable, but was better than the smelly, dangerous gas lighting that had been in common use up to that point in time. Maxwell realized that to create a Light bulb, the solution was to use incandescence, not sparks, and create a 'glowing' light. Also to keep the glowing light burning without burning out too fast, the bulb would have to be made in a vacuum, and would also need a long lasting filament to glow. Maxwell first experimented with paper, and then other materials to be carbonized and then utilized as a filament, but all materials burned out too fast. Maxwell then made the first real Light bulb filament by carbonizing cotton, which proved to be fairly resistant in it's transformed carbonized state. Maxwell, however, is not the person famous for inventing the Incandescent Light bulb, but another British scientist originally from Scotland named Joseph Swan (1828-1914). In 1850 Swan began experimenting on a filament Light bulb using a vacuum in glass and paper filaments, and by 1860 he had a working Light bulb that he could partially patent, which looked like a Lemon with a point on it's top, and which glowed Reddish. In 1875, after Maxwell's discoveries, Swan returned to his work on the Light bulb and this time he used a cotton filament, just as Maxwell had been able to prove worked very well. Swan applied for and received the British patent for an Electrical Light Bulb in 1878, which he demonstrated in 1879 at the Sunderland Technical Collage to the Newcastle Chemical Society. The new Electric Light Bulb was a sensation in England, and Swan installed working light bulbs around the country, his own house "Underhill" on Kells Lane in Low Fell, Gateshead being the first home in the world to have an operational Electric Light Bulb installed in it. "The Swan Electric Light Company" was founded by Swan in 1881. The first house to be completely lit by Electric Light bulbs was not Swan's however, but a rich associate of Swan's named Lord Armstrong who owned a huge estate named "Cragside," in Northumberland, England. The estate had it's own lake and a river which was used to drive a Siemens dynamo to create the first hydroelectric power station in the world. This electricity was initially used to power one Arc Lamp installed in "Cragside" in 1878, and was then used to power the Electric Light Bulbs of Swan's to light the mansion. In 1880 Armstong's estate "Cragside" became the first house in the world to be completely lit by Electric Light Bulbs. More than forty electric Light bulbs were installed in "Cragside" with an estimated power, unheard of in it's day, equalling over one thousand candles.   In 1879, a year after Swan, Thomas Alva Edison (1847-1931) also invented an incandescent Electric Light Bulb in New Jersey. The two men had a healthy collaboration and Swan merged with Edison's company, forming the "Edison and Swan United Company," which became known as the "Ediswan" company and were selling Electric Light Bulbs with this name from 1881. This was the name of the company until the 1892 merger when the company was finally named the "Edison General Electric." The difference between Swan and Edison was that Edison had the ambition and desire to light up not just his own country, but the entire world. Edison went on to design every component for the first large scale public Electrical Supply Company in existence, which is still in existence today, over a century later, and is still named "Con Edison." In 1897, another extremely important scientific discovery was made that was the direct result of trying to discover the actual technology of light, and this discovery was made by another British scientist who was named Sir Joseph John Thomson (1856-1940). In the "Cambridge Center of Research on Vacuum Tubes" J.J. Thomson invented his own Cathode Ray Tube. Then by utilizing magnets to deflect light projected into his Cathode Ray Tube, Thomson was the first person to prove the existence of a smaller particle than the Atom, which became known as the "Electron." In his experiments with his Cathode Ray Tube, Thomson found that he could deflect light rays by nothing more than an electrical field, not just by a magnetic field, which was already known. J.J. Thomson then had the astounding proof that light must be therefore made up of *Both* waves and particles, which he called "Corpuscles."   These "Corpuscles" became known as "Electrons," the name suggested by George Johnstone Stoney in 1894 before the particle was definitively discovered and proved by Thomson. In 1906 Thomson was awarded the Nobel Prize in Physics for his discovery of the Electron, and in 1937 his son also won the Nobel Prize for proving that Electrons have a wavelike nature.

Back to this Shortwave Ultraviolet nightmare era, in 1877 Downes and Blunt documented the proof of what would spark the Shortwave Ultraviolet Health Treatment era, stating that light is capable of being "Bactericidal." In 1889 another scientific discovery that lead to Shortwave Ultraviolet Health Treatment was made by Widmark, who proved that it was the "Ultra-violet rays" in sunlight which caused Erythema (Sunburn). In 1893 Finsen published early experiments he had made on the "Physiological action" of light, making him the first person to announce a "Light" unit that could be used on the treatment of tuberculosis of the skin: the "Finsen Light."   Following the monumental discoveries of X-Ray by Roentgen in 1895, Radioactivity by Becquerel in 1896, Electrons by Sir J.J. Thomson in 1897, and the other "wonder" named Radium by the Curies, the authors state that in 1902 "Bernhard of Samaden" used sunlight as the Medical Treatment for "Tuberculous lesions" and wounds. This is the first photograph in the book, a portrait of "Oscar Bernhard, M.D., St. Moritz" who appears as a very common looking Greying country doctor. The second photo in the book is of "Augustus Rollier, M.D., Leysin" who is credited with the distinction of having been the doctor who opened his first clinic in Leysin, which is in the Vaudois Alps in Switzerland, where he treated tuberculosis with the brilliant Alpine sunshine. Then comes the discovery that literally created the Shortwave Ultraviolet Medical Treatment era, the "Quartz Mercury Vapour Lamp" by Kromayer in 1904. The third photo in this 1927 book is of a Medical Superintendent of the Finsen Institute of Copenhagen, a Doctor Axel Rein, who is infamous for being the first doctor to use harmful Shortwave Ultraviolet energy as a Medical "Miracle" Cure, and began in 1913 using a "Carbon-Arc bath treatment" (sounds healthy already). In 1918 another nut named Huldschinsky was the first person to make the outrageous claim that harmful Shortwave Ultraviolet 'rays' could cure Rickets. The last historical dates are within the 1927 publishing date of the book itself, being the December, 1924 founding of the healthy "Sunlight League" which preached that sunlight was the elixir of life and it should be used as a "Tonic" because it was now discovered in the 1920s to be "nature's universal disinfectant." The last entry is the March, 1926 publication of the monthly magazine "The British Journal of Actinotherapy."

The second full half of the historical chapter of this 1927 book "Ultra-Violet Radiation and Actinotherapy" is dedicated to the character named "Professor Niels Ryberg Finsen" who was considered someone of a God-like status in 1927, because he was credited as being the founder of "Modern Actinotherapy." Proving it's divine effects, he died at the ripe old age of forty-two years old. There is not one, but two portraits of this Danish Avatar of doom, who was born in 1861 and died in 1904. When he was fifteen his father sent him to school in the bitter climate of Iceland(!) In 1882 he was studying medicine in another bitter climate - Copenhagen - when he realized that in the room of his friend he could work much better and longer then in his own room, because his friend's room was flooded with sunlight. The "eureka" moment for Finsen was the rare cosmic occurrence of a cat laying in the Sun. This sage recorded another rare completely unknown fact, being that when the shadow came, the cat moved back into the Sun(!) In 1890 Finsen finished medical school, and then in 1892 he began experimenting with sunlight in Ribe. The experiments he performed in 1892 are nearly laughable today, and are so simplistic that they were probably laughable at the time he originally performed them as well. He first painted an area of two inches (5 cm.) of his arm with opaque Black "Indian Ink" and then exposed his arm to strong sunlight for three hours. A few hours later this mental giant washed the Black Ink off his arm, and to his total amazement (!) the skin that was painted Black was not Sunburned, but all the rest of his arm was. Two days later he had another flash of divine insight and decided to put his arm in the Sun again, resulting in the White area that had been painted Black turning Red, but almost no noticeable reaction on the rest of the arm that had been Red two days before. This genius then answered an age-old profound question: why the "Negro" is Black and people living in northern countries are so White(!) These obvious answers to age-old questions are what brought this Finsen fame, and through this "research" he created what he called a "Red Room" to treat victims of Smallpox. This first genius idea of Finsen's was to put Red plastic in the windows of the "Red Room" to treat Smallpox, but the only problem was that there was no Smallpox in Denmark. Not to be put off experimenting, when the disease broke out in Bergen, Norway in 1893 Finsen had published "The Harmful Influence of Chemical rays on the Animal Organism" which stated that bacteria lives in darkness and is killed by sunlight. First experimenting on different animals, Finsen made a box that had a top composed of Red, Yellow, Blue, and Green glass. When Earthworms were put into the box they all went under the Red glass, when Butterflies were put in they all flew around under the Blue glass, and Salamander eggs were observed to have the most "movements" under the Blue glass. This led Finsen to the conclusion that light must have a "chemical effect" on life that could be either destructive or developmental. This experiment led Finsen to his concept of "Light Baths" in which the cold "chemical rays" of light were thought to be more beneficial to health treatment than the heat of the Sun. This advanced into Finsen experimenting on light and led to his concentrating sunlight first with glass lenses, then with Quartz lenses. The heating effect of the sunlight was removed by passing the Sunlight also through water, and then Finsen had further insight to remove even the Red and Yellow rays of sunlight by adding Methylene Blue dye to it. After initially experimenting his ideas on the Ear of his wife(!) which he discovered would absorb more sunlight when the blood was physically pressed out of the tissue, another divine flash of insight came to this sage, namely that the sunlight was not so reliable or even strong in Denmark. This realization of Finsen caused him to experiment on artificial sources of Ultraviolet energy, namely "Arc Lamps" which produced, very unfortunately, deadly Shortwave Ultraviolet energy, not harmless beneficial Longwave Ultraviolet energy that is in fact present in all sunlight that passes through the Ozone layer and that reaches the Earth's surface. In November, 1895 Finsen began his first experiments on a skin disease known during that period as "Lupus of the face." Mr. Hansen, manager of the Copenhagen Electricity Works, where Finsen was allowed to set up his experiments, had a friend who had been suffering from this disease for eight years, so this unfortunate man, Mr. Morgensen became Finsen's first "guinea pig." From November, 1895 to March, 1896 Finsen put his patient under a primitive Shortwave Ultraviolet "Arc Lamp" and in the end he claimed to have completely cured the Lupus. This simple experiment on the 'cured' engineer Mr. Morgensen literally started a revolution. By October, 1896, with the help of the mayor of Copenhagen, "Finsen's Medical Light Institute" was founded with it's goal of making "Practical Use" out of Light rays for medical treatment. In exchange for free "Electric current" for his institute, fifteen patients were treated from the municipal hospital in the first five months of it's operation. This number jumped to seventy-three by the following year, and the authors cheerfully report that by the writing of their book in 1927 the number was two hundred patients per day. After publishing a paper on "The Use of Concentrated Chemical Light Rays in Medicine" in December, 1896, even Queen Alexandra and King Edward began to visit the Finsen Light Institute. By August 12, 1901 a huge building was opened in Copenhagen known as the "Finsen Medical Light Institute" through a Danish grant of twelve thousand pounds. In 1903 they unbelievably gave the *"Nobel Prize"* to this Finsen(!) Proving how miraculously beneficial his Shortwave Ultraviolet Medical Treatment was, the very next summer, in 1904, Finsen was literally unable to walk and was pushed around in a wheel chair by his wife. Ten months after the Nobel Prize had been awarded to Finsen for his 'amazing' discoveries, he himself dropped dead at Forty-two! By the time of this 1927 book's writing, a large new hospital had been opened on Strand Boulevard in Copenhagen and together with the "Radium Institute" on it's grounds, not to mention the "Light Baths" building for treating internal diseases with Shortwave Ultraviolet, this area condemned more people to horrible deaths than most prisons.

As an example of how little was known during this era of Miracle Medical Treatments incorporating such deadly technology as Shortwave Ultraviolet energy and even drinking Radium, the "Quartz Light Spectrum" is an illustration in this 1927 book and quite clearly it is stated that only "Chemical rays" (Ultraviolet), X-Rays, and Gamma rays were known outside of the Violet end of the Visible Spectrum, and only "Heat Waves" (Infra-Red) and "Hertzian waves" were known outside of the Red end of the Visible Spectrum.

The proof for the proverbial saying 'a picture is worth a thousand words' is contained in the first four portraits of 1927 book, beginning with the image of a simple looking country doctor Oscar Bernhard, the second portrait is the only one that actually looks like an intelligent person, Dr. Augustus Rollier, the third portrait of Dr. Alex Rein looks like a stuffed animal straight from the Taxidermist's office, and the fourth portrait of the "Father of Actinotherapy" Professor Niels Ryberg Finsen looks like an escaped convict.

Within this limited knowledge of the "Electro-Magnetic Spectrum" there was enough potential to base a separate 'Health Therapy' for each of the known sections of this spectrum. "Hertzian waves" were used for "High Frequency Diathermy," "Infra-Red Rays" were used for "Thermotherapy" and "Calorotherapy," and "Visible Rays" were used for "Phototherapy." Now comes the very dangerous part - using the high energy portion of the spectrum "beyond Violet" for health treatments. By the publication of this 1927 book some of the most "advanced" new "Miracle" health treatments in practice were also some of the deadliest most misguided attempts at medicine in human history, starting with the 'star' of the book, and what the actual title of the book is, "Actinotherapy," which energy is most noticeably called just "Ultra-Violet Rays" (without any knowledge of the differences between "Longwave" Ultraviolet, "Middlewave" Ultraviolet, "Shortwave," or even "Extreme" Ultraviolet energy). The next very healthy medical treatment used in 1927 was called "Roentgen Therapy" with Roentgen's X-Rays, and finally, probably the most famous of all the "Miracle Cures" that the nightmare past had conjured up to doom people to horrible deaths: "Radium Therapy" cheerfully using extremely 'healthy' Gamma Rays - all in the name of medicine!

As stated before, this 1927 book has the huge amount of one hundred and sixty-five Black and White photographs printed in it, and many of these photos are just as nightmarish as the text that they accompany. In the early chapter on "Natural Ultra-Violet Radiation" there are photographs of "Children Patients" playing in the bright Sun of the Alpine snow landscape of Dr. Rollier's Clinic, naked except for diapers, shoes, and a hat. Another photo is of these diapered "Children Patients" playing on the beach of Hayling Island. The next photo is of the "Sun Gallery" of Leysin, showing the medical treatment for "Pott's disease," which was to line up ten little girls about ten years old and to put each of them on a bed in the Alpine Sun, laying on their stomachs completely naked. From here the photos become more and more droll, beginning with the "Solarium" of Lord Mayor Treloar's Cripple Hospital in Alton, which has displayed in the photo seven crippled children in what look like elevated coffins on high legs out in the direct sunlight. Similarly, a photo is printed that was published in "Modern Science" and shows four young boys in their underwear ice-skating for Dr. Rollier's "Natural Sunshine Cure" in his clinic located in the Vaudois Alps in Leysin. Moving swiftly from the logical to the deadly, the following chapter introduces the "Actinotherapy" nightmare era with "Carbon Tungsten and Iron Arc Lamps." The first photo of this chapter has a curved apparatus containing two "Quartz globes" with "Tungsten filaments" that would be placed directly over a bedridden patient(!) The more advanced (and deadlier) Shortwave Ultraviolet Arc Lamps in use during the height of this "Actinotherapy" era continue to be documented in the book for the next seventy-eight pages, with photographs that are unforgettable. In keeping with the heroes of the "Actinotherapy" movement, the first Shortwave "Ultra-Violet Carbon-Arc Lamp" is credited to Professor Finsen, which he created for the treatment of "Lupus" in 1893, known as the world-renowned "Finsen Light." A diagram of the "Finsen Light" is accompanied by the gruesome explanation of it's use, which was for a nurse to hold the device by it's four handles and to press it into the part the body that needed treatment, which would effectively drain the blood from the skin at that point for the designed purpose of enabling a greater amount of Shortwave Ultraviolet rays to penetrate the patient's skin. The text explains that four patients could be treated with each "Finsen Light" simultaneously, and that in the "Light Institute" of Copenhagen there were seven of these lamps in continuous use(!) The photographs of the different Shortwave Ultraviolet Arc lamps used at the Finsen Institute continue on for many pages, and progressively get more and more ominous in appearance, with intended Shortwave Ultraviolet treatments that stagger the imagination today, such as "Schanz's" special Carbon-Arc lamps for treatment of the Eye. The sixty-five separate pictures of these lamps starting with the "Finsen Light" of 1893, continues up until the 1927 publication date of the book, and contain grizzly contraptions that make the machinery in Frankenstein's laboratory look like children's toys. A photo of Shortwave Ultraviolet Scalp Treatment in the author's medical practice has a huge lamp suspended above a female patient's head, and the reader is told that the lamp contained a "Kelvin, Bottomley, and Baird Atmospheric Burner." Sounds very healthy. The following photo has a naked child laying down on the two author's "Treatment Couch" with not one, but two huge Shortwave lamps above, which the caption explains could be fixed at only three to six inches (8-15 cm) from the child's body. An especially monstrous looking contraption is the subject of the following photograph, and it shows a woman with a huge Shortwave Ultraviolet unit shooting deadly rays *up her nose* in a "treatment" for Hay Fever! Logic would suggest that it is better to sneeze. More horror photos follow, with the very next page showing a young girl about ten years old completely naked laying on a bed under a tremendous Shortwave Ultraviolet lamp unit that looks to be about a full yard (meter) across. In almost all of these photos there is a board on an adjustable metal stand that is positioned in front of the young patient's face, because at least they realized the Shortwave U.V. was dangerous for the eyes - but only the eyes. As far as the skin, there were too many instruments produced during that period that were designed to measure the exposure of Shortwave Ultraviolet on the skin of the patient, including the early "Dr. Keller's Erythema Dosimeter," "Levy-West Ultra-Violet Pastilles," "Pouillet's Pyrheliometer," "Ruben's Thermopile," "Langley's Bolometer," "Furs004tenau's Actinometer," the "Beck Ultra-Violet Spectroscope," and the truly ominous looking "Ultra-Violet Radiation" measurement apparatus of "Griffith and Taylor's." The photos and list continues with the modern looking "Muller Ultra-Violet Spectroscope," the prehistoric looking "K.B.B. Microscope Illuminent Lamp," and the antique looking "Hanovia Analytic Lamp" which was a Shortwave Ultraviolet examination box fitted with a curtain in front of it.

To cite the lack of knowledge that this deadly Shortwave Ultraviolet Health Treatment movement had at it's disposal, the chapter on "Biological Effects" is enough to make the hair stand upon a modern reader's neck. After many experiments had been made, and many photographs had been taken, the authors remained baffled by the fact that when they put plant seedlings just sprouted from the ground under a Shortwave lamp they die! The actual realization and bafflement are captured in a concluding sentence in which the authors admit that "even short exposure" to Shortwave Ultraviolet radiation through an unfiltered Mercury Vapor Lamp was "detrimental" to the growth of plants. Just the opposite opinion was true of the exposure of this Shortwave "Ultra-Violet Radiation" on humans, they thought, just as curiously concluding on the very next page that for people, the body's "whole metabolism" is "quickened" and the patient's health and vitality are improved(!) Continuing on with the great 'benefits' of Shortwave Ultraviolet Health Treatment, the authors also come to the conclusion that "Ultra-Violet rays" form antibodies in the patient's blood, raising the body's immunity, and also have very beneficial results when used directly on opened "lesions." The "Miracle" of the Shortwave Ultraviolet lamp is extended to even curing "Diarrhoea" and "Broncitis" in children suffering from Rickets, and being a cure for "Herpes zoster."

The remainder of this 429 page 1927 nightmare book is just as misguided and misinforming as the first part of the book, preaching that this dangerous cancer-causing Shortwave Ultraviolet energy that never reaches the surface of the Earth by not being able to pass through the Ozone layer (which was also completely unknown in 1927), could be used as a "Miracle Cure" to 'Grow Your Hair Back,' and 'Cure Rickets' and just about every known ailment a person can be afflicted with. The photos that accompany this "killer" history are just as deeply disturbing as the text they buttress. "Fig. 104" is a beauty of a photo, in which not one, but two completely naked infants are laying on a bed with an enormous Shortwave Ultraviolet Treatment Lamp suspended over them both. This 'speciality' lamp was designed by both the authors of this 1927 book and it was even a "Hewittic Air-Cooled Mercury Vapour Lamp" with a "Magnetic Tilting Device" running off a "Counterweighted Chain" and two "Cog-Wheel Pulleys." Needless to say these two infants did not live to be one hundred years old. One of the funkiest photos in the whole book follows the two infants photo, and this looks precisely like a torture scene from a cheap horror movie, in which a Nurse with Black protective glasses on has a tremendous metal Shortwave Ultraviolet Lamp, complete with the author's "Suspension Housing" that is attached to the ceiling, put *up a patient's nose!* With a cord attached around the patient's neck to hold it in place, this horror machine was specifically manufactured in the 1920s for the specific purpose of "Simultaneous Irradiation of Both Nostrils"(!) The very next page of this gruesome volume has the very next nightmare. Two more babies, maybe a two year old and a three year old girl under another design of a suspended humongous Shortwave Treatment Lamp. "Fig, 108" could surely bring tears to a sensitive person's eyes: *eight* very young children, each about four or five years old, are all completely naked lying together on a bed under a monstrous looking Shortwave Ultraviolet contraption that is fitted with eight separate Shortwave Lamps - one for each little girl. There is also a photo of the "Safety Goggles" worn by patients of "Actinotherapy," and these "Wellsworth Hardy" Goggles could be used with three separate types of lenses, as well as being made with "Condensite" which reportedly did not conduct heat or electricity. The next photo is so stunning I have it mounted in the "Fluorescence" Wall chart in the Museum for the last decade, and shows a scene from something like hell. Five completely naked infants are in a metal child's playpen in the middle of a room with safety goggles on, and in one corner of the room, about 2 meters away from the playpen there is an enormous Shortwave Ultraviolet Treatment lamp standing about five feet (1.5 m) off the floor on a ominous looking base. In the other corner of this same room there is not one, but two more just as enormous Shortwave Ultraviolet Treatment Lamps on just as ominous looking ancient metal bases - *all* pointing directly at the five naked babies! Not only were these three Shortwave lamps positioned to point directly at the five naked babies in the metal playpen, but under this playpen, inscribed in the floor of the room are unbelievably three "Dosage Circles" that indicate precisely where the most intense concentration of Shortwave Ultraviolet Radiation would be, so the playpen could be positioned directly over this 'ground-zero' position! The very next page has a little girl, maybe eight to ten years old, naked on a bed, with not one but two huge Shortwave Ultraviolet Treatment lamps again suspended directly over her young exposed naked body. It is proudly proclaimed in the caption of the photo that this deadly set-up was used by both the authors! "Fig. 113" reminds me of the Van Gogh painting housed in Russia of the prison yard with the prisoners walking in a tiny enclosed circle, but this photo is not of prisoners, but completely naked young children - ten of them - walking in a circle in front of four huge Shortwave Ultraviolet Treatment Lamps on pedestals. This horror chamber also has the circles inscribed in the floor, like in the playpen photo, and this photo caption points out that the 'ground zero' circles put on the floor were in fact called *"Dosage Circles!"* Opposite this photo is another of the photos I've presented in the Museum since 1999: six very young diapered children with safety goggles playing around a medieval-looking huge Shortwave Ultraviolet contraption, with a begoggled nurse in Westminster Hospital in London. The last of the horrific photos in this 1927 horror volume is one of the worse I have ever seen, and portrays a completely naked little girl, about six to eight years old between "Simultaneous Irradiation" of two "hospital type" "Saidman Carbon Arc Lamps." This little naked girl sits between two huge machines, about seven to eight feet tall each (2.1-2.4 m) that have chains and pulleys in contraptions that defy the imagination. Towards the end of this 1927 book are some of the most disturbing photos, including a special horror machine used at the famous "Finsen Institute" in Copenhagen, to shoot Shortwave Ultraviolet into the Eyes! There are even special scissor-like instruments photographed for turning a patient's eyelids inside-out for this special Shortwave Ultraviolet treatment.

No book of this era would have been complete without photographic evidence of the Shortwave Ultraviolet Treatment Lamps curing Baldness (!) and in "Fig. 148," two photos prove this with "undeniable" evidence. Very obviously, this misguided, uniformed era of "Actinotherapy" did not cure too many people of any diseases or sicknesses, and if patients were exposed to these "health" lamps for too long a period, it would be very likely that they would develop skin cancer. Again, this energy has <u>Nothing</u> to do with "Black lights" which produce only harmless Longwave Ultraviolet, and the horror created around the world by this Shortwave Ultraviolet Health Treatment movement can still be heard today, over a hundred years after it began, because a portion of society still "remembers" this era when asking "the Black light is dangerous, isn't it?"

It must be obvious to anyone reading the previous section on the nightmare "Actinotherapy" Shortwave Ultraviolet "Miracle Cure" era, how the deserved stigma that arose in society due to this horror movement could have easily bled into the public's opinion of the Longwave Ultraviolet Black light. Both have a Blue glow, both are called "Ultraviolet" energy - even if they are completely different Ultraviolet energies. The fact is that the Black light did not just become stigmatized by it's intrinsic association with the 1960s Hippie movement, but that the Black light began to be stigmatized by society before almost every single reader of this book was even *born*, and in fact before there were even Black lights! Beginning in 1893 with "Finsen's Light," this Shortwave Ultraviolet Medical Treatment era is in actuality the very first stigma for the Black light, even earlier than the more famous "Radium Miracle Cure" era that began shortly after it's discovery by the Curie's in 1896. Every major discovery had/has it's obligatory idiotic reaction by a society that is plainly of the same mental capacity as their reactions. When Roentgen discovered X-Rays in roughly the same era there was such a public outcry with ridiculous articles and comics in many publications that society went so far as to create "X-Ray Pants" for sale so people couldn't see through their clothes!

"Conti-Glo" "Black Light Beacon" 1941-1943

To give an idea of just how important and respected the Black light and Fluorescent paint were during the era of the 1930s-1950s, in the Museum collection are three extremely rare editions of a monthly publication called "Black Light Beacon" from May, 1941 (Vol. 1 no. 3), Sept./Oct., 1941 (Vol. 1, no. 6), and January, 1942 (Vol. 2, no. 1). This "Black Light Beacon" was published by the "Conti-Glo" Division of Continental Lithography Corp., Cleveland, Ohio, which was the name that the "Switzer Brothers" were using during their association with Continental Lithography Corp. Each issue of this "Black Light Beacon" has examples on every page of major uses of Black lights and Fluorescent paint throughout America at that time. Some of these historically-outrageous ideas and claims of the three issues of "Black Light Beacon" from 1941 and 1942 will be examined, with reportages and examples of Black lights and Fluorescent Colors being used by factors of society that today

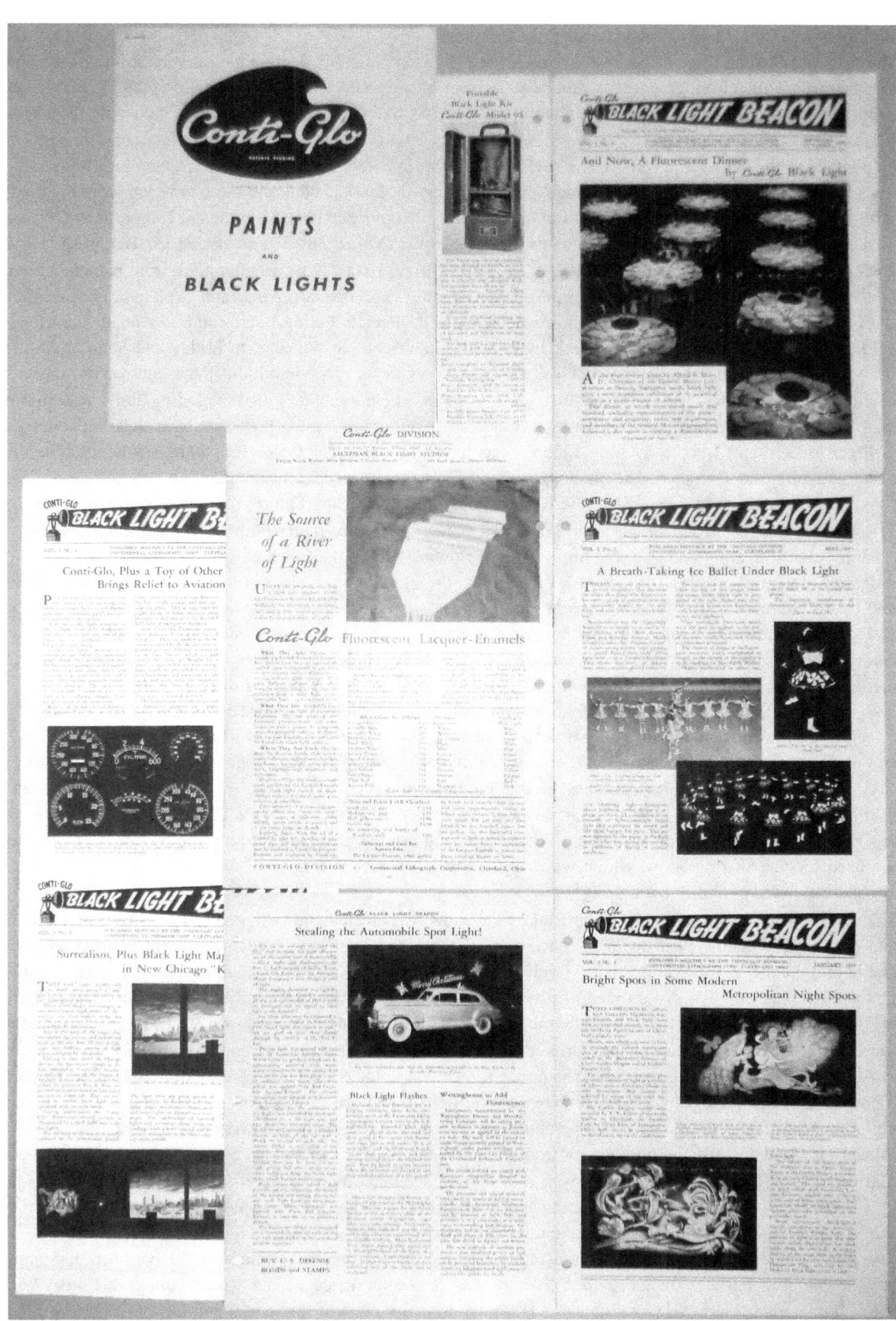

1941-1942 Collection of "Conti-Glo BLACK LIGHT BEACON," "Conti-Glo Corporation," Cleveland, Ohio

would seem impossible to believe, or even consider.

The front pages of all three issues of the "Black Light Beacon" in the collection have a very striking logo, immediately recognizable as retro. This retro logo consists of a large 1930s/1940s era Black light unit (the "Model 70" 250 watt Black light spotlight from the late 1930s and 1940s manufactured by the "Switzer Brothers" company, which was at that time called "Conti-Glo") with "Conti-Glo" written in a curve above the lamp. Out of the Black light in the logo comes a page-wide ray of Black light, containing the White title "BLACK LIGHT BEACON" in a very funky early 1940s hand made type font. The logo is printed as a high contrast Black and White image, making it very dramatic, and at the same time immediately readable as an antique logo. On the first of the issues in the Museum collection, "Copyright 1941, Continental Lithography Corp." is printed right below the logo, and in a horizontal band as a header to the issue, "Vol. 1, No. 3" and "PUBLISHED MONTHLY BY THE CONTINENTAL LITHOGRAPHY CORP., CLEVELAND, O." "May, 1941." The article on the front page is a reportage of a 'Black Light Ice Ballet,' and is accompanied by three photographs. The opening paragraph explains that the only phrase to describe the effects of the Black lights and Fluorescent Colors is 'Breath-Taking,' and continues on to describe a 'breath-taking' Ice Skating Performance done under Black lights with Fluorescent costumes. On Friday and Saturday, March 21 and 22, 1941, the "Precision Group" of sixteen women skaters put on a spectacular White light/Black light performance, being part of the Cleveland Skating Club's "Book Revue." This front page article explains how the skating show was first performed under normal White lights, and then went into a total 'blackout.' Under very powerful Black light units all sixteen women of this 1941 "Precision Group" were incredibly Fluorescent, having Fluorescent Colors on their hair-bows, "Skating shoes," gloves, skirts, and bikini-style tops. The three photographs on the front page accompanying this article are surprisingly proficient for sixty-eight years ago, especially the two Black light photos of the Fluorescing "Precision Group" of the skaters. The article explains that the group of performing skaters under the Black lights with only the Fluorescent parts of their costumes visible was captivating and gave the impression of flowing 'liquid light,' which was reported by the local newspapers as the highlight of the entire evening. It is next explained that the Fluorescent Colors of the sixteen "Precision Group" skaters were created by the use of "Conti-Glo" Fluorescent Satin, which was invented by the Switzer brothers for the U.S. military in the 1930s. To give an idea of how old and truly antique this article is, credit is given to the man who did the lighting direction for the Skating show by indicating that he was working the control "telephones," which were also painted with "Conti-Glo" lacquer enamels, making them highly Fluorescent and easily readable under the lighting director's Black light. But, that's not all - this was the 1940s when Black light and Fluorescent Colors were "New Age" - "The Future!" Besides the Fluorescent skaters, a very large Fluorescent mural of a pair of Fluorescent skaters was on the wall above the orchestra, and even the lighting for the director's table was well thought out. The director's table was at the edge of the ice, so the lighting had to be designed as to not interfere with the darkness of the Fluorescent revue of skaters, so all the cue-sheets and director's instructions had "Conti-Glo S-195" invisible Green powder applied to them and were easily read by the director under a "Conti-Glo" Black light desk lamp on his table. What's amazing are the details describing the tremendous amount of Black light energy used for the Skating show, which was supplied by no less than a *dozen* 250 watt "Conti-Glo Model 70" Black Light spotlights suspended over the skating ring!

So now we have seen how a spectacular Black light show was created and designed in 1941 - over sixty-five years ago - with attention to every detail, even down to the design of the Ultraviolet lamp and Fluorescent instruction sheets on the director's table at the edge of the skating ring. Twelve Black light units of 250 watts each comes to a total of 3,000 watts of Black light for the ice show. To give an idea of how strong that is, it would take eighty-three of the standard large 36 watt Black lights that are in common use today to equal the power used for the 1941 Skating show. The two Black light photographs on the cover of this "Black Light Beacon" are printed in Black and White, but are extremely vivid and prove that the display had to be a Black light extravaganza, worthy of the praise it received in the Cleveland, Ohio newspapers after the performance. These two photos of the Black light performance are very proficient, and prove how extreme the intensity of Black light used for the Ice skating performance must have been (even if they were heavily retouched) - every detail of the Fluorescent costumes of the Ice skaters is vivid, even in the photograph from the audience showing all sixteen Skaters in performance together. Not only was the Black light/Fluorescence technology and design on such an advanced level that any production in today's world over sixty-five years later would be very proud to have accomplished, but the Black and White photographs of the performance as well are of a quality that is also unsurpassed (and rarely attained) in today's world.

Now for a grandiose comparison, demonstrating in three-dimensional real time what I have been complaining about for the last one hundred pages. In December, 2008 I was in the audience of the world famous "Holiday" Ice skating performance in Amsterdam. Now this skating show is known in many parts of the world, and has been performing in Europe for decades. In fact, this Ice skating show started in the 1940s in Cleveland, Ohio, and it still incorporates a Black Light/

Fluorescence performance in part of the show, so it is even possible that this world famous Skating show had it's beginnings with the Cleveland, Ohio "Precision Group" of these sixteen women on the cover of this May, 1941 "Black Light Beacon." So, logic would suggest that after over 65 years of practice and continuous public performances around America and Europe, the Black light/Fluorescence section of the Skating performance would be *at least as good* as it was almost seven decades ago, but honest to God, in 2008 the Black light/Fluorescence section of this Skating performance was just *Shit!* It was such a poorly-planned design that the Fluorescence of the twenty or thirty performing Skaters was barely noticeable because it was extremely dim - What?!? 67 years later?! Yes, and we were sitting in good seats in the third row - in the front. After almost seventy years it was obvious that this was a poorly-designed 'throw away' section of the two hour Skating extravaganza. In 1941 there were twelve 250 watt state of the art Black light spotlights suspended over the ice skating ring, producing enough longwave Black light Ultraviolet energy to practically cause something on the Moon to Fluoresce, but almost seventy years later, in all their infinite wisdom, the lighting designers of this 2008 Ice spectacle made the design, very probably, with their *eyes closed*. Suspended above the Ice skating ring for the 2008 performance I saw in Amsterdam, were not twelve 250 watt state of the art Black light units, but about eight units that looked like hugh cotton lamps, being 10-15 feet tall (3-5 meters) with circular hoops inside to maintain the form, and very intelligently completely covered with highly Fluorescent White material. Then comes the 'high-tech' design element of fixing the Black lights inside these large White material cocoons, so that when the Black lights were turned on inside the cotton cocoons, the effect was that they caused the White material covering of the lamp units themselves to Fluoresce intensely, but as Black light has a hard time going through a Fluorescent material, and is mostly consumed by the action of causing the material cocoons themselves to Fluoresce, you could barely see the Skaters! How nice. Also, as the material was so highly Fluorescent, no indication of what type or how many Black lights used for the performance was visible, but I strongly doubt it was anywhere remotely near eighty-three. Today in the Computer/Internet/Digital Age, four decades after going to the Moon, the design and effect of the Black Light/Fluorescence section of this formerly 'Breath-Taking' show was *pitiful*, in the full meaning of the word. For about ten minutes barely-visible Skaters performed on the ice while the audience looked up to the ceiling above the skating ring at the intensely Fluorescent Blue-White lighting units, while listening to pseudo-psychedelic background music, the whole performance managing, in the end, to produce a 'one-tenth baked' version of it's intended 1960s inspired theme 'Magical Mystery Tour.' Truthfully it looked as if the lighting designers not only had no idea at all about the technology and effects of Black light and Fluorescence, but that they also did not even test the design in any way what so ever to see that it worked before the show began.

    Page two of this "Black Light Beacon" has another reportage that would seem on the verge of unbelievable today, documenting the use of "Conti-Glo" Fluorescent paint and Black lights in a 'New Ohio Theatre.' This is a reportage of the new "Boulevard Theatre" in Columbus, Ohio that had just opened. This theatre had a large auditorium seating about a thousand people, and the main theme of the design of the theatre was 'Color.' There are two photographs contained in the article, one of the interior of the large auditorium in the theatre in the White light, and the other photograph is in the Black light showing the large Fluorescent murals that lined the left and right walls of the theatre. Eight large Fluorescent murals, four on each side wall, lined the "Boulevard Theatre's" auditorium, as well as eight Fluorescent ceiling murals, each above one of the eight wall murals. Each Fluorescent mural was very large, measuring eight by twenty-two feet (2.5 x 6.7 m) and was painted on canvas using highly Fluorescent "Conti-Glo" lacquer enamels. The eight large Fluorescent murals lining both sides of the auditorium of the "Boulevard Theatre" in Columbus, Ohio portray stylized flower bouquets painted in a very 'curious' way - the way to try to explain their designs is by imagining a Gauguin or Rousseau painting mixed together with a piece of Art from ancient Rome(!) The engineering design of the theatre's Fluorescent murals and Black light units was as well thought out and as well executed as the Ice Ballet of the 'Precision Group's' Skating performance on the previous page, complete with three-dimensional large flower pots on the walls that each Fluorescent flower bouquet appeared to be growing out of. Now these large constructed flower pots at the base of each of the eight Fluorescent bouquets were designed to contain and conceal two separate powerful "Conti-Glo" 100 watt Black lights. A "Model 96" 100 watt flood lamp was used for each of the Fluorescent wall murals, and a "Model 99" 100 watt spot light was pointed straight up at the ceiling for each of the smaller ceiling murals above each wall mural. As with the reportage of the Ice Ballet on the first page, the photograph of the Fluorescent effect of the theatre wall and ceiling murals is Black and White and extremely proficient, capturing what must have been a truly spectacular display in this 1940s theatre. The article on this Columbus, Ohio theatre explains that the intensity of light emitted by these eight large Fluorescent murals on the two side walls of the theatre, together with the eight Fluorescent ceiling murals above each wall mural was enough, together with the light of the movie screen itself, to provide all the light needed in the movie theatre while the movie was playing, eliminating the need for White lights in the theatre during the projection of the movie, which is very visually disturbing to the viewers - like in all movie theaters all over the world today.

At the bottom of page two is a small article about the head of a U.S. school who wanted special ink for school report cards and records that were always being changed secretly by the students. "Conti-Glo" Horizon Blue Writing Ink was the product recommended to the head of this U.S. school, because it appeared as regular Blue ink in the White light, but when examined under a Black light, the grades that were secretly changed by students on their report cards using pens that matched the daylight color, are instantly revealed as 'forgeries.' The head of this U.S. school was also informed that "Conti-Glo" sold Invisible Writing Ink as well, which only appears on a page when a Black light is turned on.

Next page of this 1941 "Black Light Beacon," next unbelievable Fluorescence revelation. Page three's main article is another use of Black light and Fluorescent Colors that would seem very improbable today - Black lights and Fluorescent Colors used for the entire display in a Sales Convention. The product being displayed at this Fluorescent sales Convention was a typical 1940s idea, 'The Iron Fireman Robot Furnace' for buildings. The two vivid Black and White photographs in the article show the sales convention display, and the actual "Iron Fireman" furnace, all highly Fluorescent having been coated with "Conti-Glo" Fluorescent lacquer-enamels, including large banners, decorations, and the product itself. At the top of the page are three other small articles, one announcing that a well known "Ultra-Violet" lighting specialist of "G.E." who many "Conti-Glo" customers had worked with had just transferred to a new job: 'Defense Lighting' for the U.S. military (this was 1941). The remaining two small articles are announcements from the "Conti-Glo" company itself, informing customers that their expert advisory and engineering departments would help and advise them with any Fluorescent/Black light project they were planning, and also announcing a service from "Conti-Glo" which would coat any articles of clothing or stage costumes with Fluorescent "Conti-Glo" Colors. The small reportage lists several of the Fluorescent items they've recently coated for customers, including the Cleveland Skating Club revue's Fluorescent socks and gloves, Fluorescent Orchestra suits for Nick Stuart's Orchestra performing in Biloxi, Mississippi at the Biloxi Beach Hotel, Fluorescent Bandstands for the famous Sammy Kaye Orchestra, a well as Blue Baron's Orchestra's Fluorescent coats. The small article concludes with a short list of examples of Fluorescent props, costumes, umbrellas, and other items that "Conti-Glo" had recently coated with Fluorescent Colors for theatrical performances.

The next page is a full-page advertisement from "Conti-Glo" displaying their two most powerful Black light flood lamps that were used in large Fluorescent public displays and performances all over America. The largest Black light unit produced by "Conti-Glo" at that time was the unit in the top photograph of this advertisement: the large "Model 70" portable 250 watt Black light used in theaters and very large public displays, such as the Ice Skating show on the front cover of this magazine. In 2008 I was able to locate and buy an original 70 year old "Conti-Glo" "Model 70" 250 watt Black light unit for the Museum, which is still in operating condition with a foot-long original bulb in it that looks like part of a science experiment. I can personally attest to the "Model 70" unit's large, heavy, brutal design. The first impression today of this tremendous unit is immediately a feeling of something from the Second world war, like an instrument off of a battleship or something - even the 'Battleship Grey' Color is the same. This 250 watt "Model 70" Black light is a little over twenty-five pounds (12 kilos), twenty inches tall (50 cm) and had an astounding price of $59.50 in 1941, which was equivalent to the price of *an ounce and a half of Gold*! The other Black light unit photographed is the "Model 80" 250 watt flood lamp designed for permanent installations, consisting of a large lamp unit with a separate electrical transformer for mounting these units inside of walls and other places in public displays. There was also available from "Conti-Glo" the "Model 72" and "Model 82" listed in the advertisement as 250 watt spot lights, and the "Model 86" and "Model 87" which are described as 250 watt 'flush-mounting' Black light flood lamp units for Fluorescent theatre carpeting, as a given example.

Page five has a very interesting article about a famous Fluorescent Mural painter named Oscar Glas of the Belgian Art Studios in New York City who was well known for his use of the 'new' upcoming medium for applying Fluorescent paint to: Velvet(!) The article starts off with an explanation that velours are the new upcoming material preferred by Artists to paint Fluorescent murals onto. The velour material itself is described in this 1941 article as 'ultra-modern.' The article continues on to describe the two large Fluorescent murals painted by Mr. Glas on velour for the "Essex Theatre" in Port Henry, New York, and is complete with two very clear Black and White photographs of the vivid Fluorescent murals. Explained in the article is the technique used at the time for painting Fluorescent lacquer-enamels onto velour, suggesting that short-pile White or light Colored velour is the easiest to paint on, enabling the use of brushes or spay-guns, and advises that the dark Colors of the murals be made by just painting on non-Fluorescent paint. Concluding the article is the advice to Artists who want to paint Fluorescent Colors on dark velours, and is the same advice I give to people almost seventy years later: Paint the dark area of the velour to be coated with Fluorescent Colors with White paint first, because whatever is under the relatively transparent Fluorescent Colors optically mixes with them and can easily change the Color. A visitor to the Museum during 2007 who was from Oregon told me about another small alternative museum in Portland called "Velveteria," which is a Museum of Velvet

Paintings. In this "Velveteria" there is a room for modern Fluorescent velvet paintings under Black lights, but unfortunately the couple who run the museum don't mention the Fluorescent velvet paintings from the 1940s era in interviews on their website and don't seem to be aware that there were Fluorescent velvet paintings being created back then, so consequently the collection starts about 1970. On a link from the "Velveteria" website there is information about the Artist who is supposedly the person who started the movement of velvet painting in America, Edgar Leeteg, who was known as the "American Gauguin." Edgar Leeteg was originally from California, and painted in Tahiti from 1933 until 1953, where he made thousands of Black velvet paintings, which were brought back from Hawaii and which eventually reached the United States and Mexico.

At the bottom of page five is another of the famous applications for the Black light - the use of Fluorescence and Black lights in Criminology by the police. The small article is a reportage of the Annual Clinic and Banquet of Crime Clinic, Inc. that was held in the Cleveland Hotel on March 15, 1941 and was attended by about eight hundred people. Cleveland, Ohio police officers demonstrated their used of the "Conti-Glo" Black lights and Fluorescent Colors for use in criminology. For the Police demonstration a "Conti-Glo" "Model 91" Black light unit was used together with Invisible Writing Ink and Invisible Fluorescent Powder, proving what a valuable tool that the Black light and Fluorescent Colors had become for police investigations already.

The next Black Light/Fluorescence 'Believe-it-or-not' articles await the reader of this 1941 "Conti-Glo Black Light Beacon" on the next page. Page six has a half page article at the top, followed by five small articles below it. The top article is a good example of how many facets of society were touched by and adjusted, and many times improved upon, by the enthusiastic momentum created by an era of discovery and newly-invented knowledge. A very dramatic contrast to the present gentrified "We've done it all" and of course "We know it all" Yuppified "Fuck Art, let's dance" contemporary era. Like Moe Howard of "The Three Stooges" used to say, 'They're Temperamental: ninety percent Temper, and ten percent Mental!' A precious very definitive example of this contemporary 'forget the miserable past' state of mind is graphically illustrated very often in the Museum. For over the last two decades in "Electric Lady" Art Gallery under five hundred watts of Black lights, and even more evident in the Museum under one thousand watts of Black lights, when a visitor with False Teeth smiles in the dark under Black lights, it looks like they had their teeth knocked out! This is because the false teeth or tooth appear Black due to the fact that they are non- Fluorescent, compared to the famous vivid natural Fluorescence of the teeth. The teeth are the most Fluorescent part of the exterior of the human body, but the body fluid semen is even brighter under a Black light. By the way, not only human teeth are highly Fluorescent, but the teeth of cats that walk into the Gallery are just as vivid under the Black lights. Since even fossilized shark teeth are Fluorescent, I would assume that if not all teeth, then the teeth of most species are Fluorescent. There is a small impurity of a mineral Apatite (!) in the human tooth which is the "Activator" of the Fluorescence. So, for the last three decades, at least, most false teeth have been made of non-Fluorescent synthetic materials, with zero regard to how they will compare to the rest of the naturally Fluorescing teeth a person has in their mouth. In the eclectic, sometimes bizarre Museum collection is documentation and advertisements form the dental field in the 1940s and 1950s pertaining to the new product of "Fluorescent False Teeth," such as matching the true Color and natural reactions to light of all the other natural teeth - now that's a good idea! There were charts and sets of false teeth manufactured in many different shades of White, as well as many different intensities of Fluorescence, so a patient could have a very close match for their false teeth to the rest of their original teeth. Again, this is not 'Lost knowledge,' or even 'Forgotten knowledge,' but it is clearly in the realm of that pitiful state of 'Thrown Away knowledge.'

This top article on page six of this "Black Light Beacon" is another similar example of the examination and adjustments, followed by improvements, to minute parts of life half a century ago or more. The article is about the Color of roast beef on display in butcher's shops under new Fluorescent tube lamps, compared to the former well-known Color of the displayed meat under normal incandescent light bulbs. The problem investigated in this article is the cool light with a Bluish glow that comes out of Fluorescent tube lamps makes roast beef in a butchers shop looks pale and not nearly as nice as people were used to under the warmer light of incandescent light bulbs, hence the customers thought the roast beef was not healthy anymore. "Conti-Glo" had a simple, very efficient solution, of course, "Conti-Glo" No. 2626 Red Color Corrective Lacquer was developed with the intention of spraying this paint onto the 'reflectors' behind the Fluorescent tube lamps. This added the missing Red tint to the wavelength of White light emitted from the new butchers lamps, and hence brought the 'blush' back to the displayed roast beef, making it look 'healthy' again. Tests had also been made to ensure the Red "No. 2626" paint would be the same Color after half a year's use. The technical side of this lighting adjustment is explained next, informing the reader that the new early 1940s Fluorescent tube lamps (we don't even get the name right today, commonly referring to these lamps as 'Neon lights') emit more cool White light towards the Violet, Blue, Green, and Yellow end of the spectrum, and therefore less warm White light towards the Orange and Red end of the spectrum, thus roast beef and other meats under Fluorescent tube lamps look Bluish, closer to the Color of rotten meat than healthy Red meat. We are informed in the article that Red filters had been tried on the tube lamps, but abandoned because they reduced the amount of emitted light form the lamps. The reader is also informed that this Red "No. 2626" was being used on the reflectors of Fluorescent tube lamps in restaurants and bakeries as well, so as to not only make the food look good, but also to make the customer's complexions look more natural and healthy. This was an age when the newly invented Fluorescent White light tube lamps were in big style, and being installed everywhere - even to eat under in restaurants - it must have looked like India today in those restaurants of yesteryear!

The five remaining articles at the bottom of this page of the "Black Light Beacon," and the three articles on the last page of this monthly publication from May, 1941, are something like 'current events' or 'Black Light News' for this 1940s Black light 'Age of Invention.' The first small article addresses an idea that can be found published in a large amount of literature and advertising continuing for decades after the late 1930s: Fluorescent Carpeting in dark public places, like Movie theaters for example, which is activated by Black lights. The article explains that such a large amount of "Black Light Beacon" readers have inquired about Fluorescent carpeting that "Conti-Glo" had published an information and instruction manual specifically on the subject of "Conti-Glo" Black lights and Fluorescent carpeting. This booklet is explained to be a manual covering all aspects of Fluorescent carpeting activated by Black lights, including a history of the Fluorescent phenomenon, technical help for design and installation of the Fluorescent carpeting and the Black light units, along with detailed instructions, Black light photographs of Fluorescent carpeting, and even design plans for the Black light units installed which would create a floor covering which emits it's own gentle light through the use of these specialized Black light units designed exclusively for use with Fluorescent carpeting.

The second small 'Black Light News' article is another of the few applications for the Black light from 1941 that can still be seen in use today: Fluorescent Juggling. The article tells of a juggler who made a big hit at the time by disappearing in the darkness of the stage while White, then Red, and finally Blue Fluorescent juggling balls appeared in mid air out of the darkness. This juggler, possibly the first Fluorescent juggler in an endless list that continues up until the present day, ended his 1941 astounding juggling performance with a Fluorescent American flag being lowered behind him on the stage as the orchestra played "America." Again, this was 1941.

Another small instructional article for "Black Light Beacon" readers that is not only still relevant today, but could in reality give needed instructions again - 'a refresher course' - to photographers attempting to photograph Fluorescence today. This article is a good example of the degree of refinement, understanding, and knowledge that went into the initial Black Light movement of the late 1930s and 1940s. The subject of the article is something that alot of people are still wondering and experimenting about almost seventy years later: "Black light Photography." The article starts off with a very surprising explanation which I strongly doubt would exist in a contemporary article on the same subject, informing the reader that technically the photographs taken of Fluorescent objects under a Black light are not literally photographed by 'Black light,' but by the light emitted by the Fluorescent objects which have been excited by the invisible Ultraviolet energy of the Black light. The small article concludes with the very advanced advice of using a special filter for the camera lens, so Ultraviolet Black light energy will not enter the lens and effect the film [the Ultraviolet energy actually 'fogs' the film]. Amazing. Can it be imagined, that over a half a century later, the largest article that can be found on the internet (the subject is rarely found in printed publications, with the notable exclusion of the excellent "Kodak" booklet from decades ago on Infrared and Fluorescence-Ultraviolet Photography) which covers the subject of photographing under Black Lights - Ultraviolet lamps - is an article stretching many pages on the website of the "Fluorescent Mineral Society" and is an article which leaves out this most essential of advice for photographing Fluorescence. This essential advice of using a 'special Filter' for photographing Fluorescence under Black light Ultraviolet lamps is not included as instructions in this modern article, but just treated like a footnote. This confusing, misleading modern article on Black light Ultraviolet Photography of Fluorescent minerals is a prototypical example of the present day's arrogance, and destruction of the important knowledge it has reaped. Imagine that the most important instruction for Black light Fluorescence Photography is included in a tiny 1941 article that stretches an enormous three whole sentences long, but is only included in an article stretching over five pages and written over half a century later - as a passing mention - informing the reader that this accomplished Belgian Black light Ultraviolet/Fluorescence photographer had heard about "Kodak" 'Wratten Ultraviolet Barrier Filters' being used for Fluorescence photography, but he had to admit that he had never actually tried them(!) What progress. Dr. Robert Wood, the first person to photograph Fluorescence in 1915, already realized that a Filter was needed on the lens of his camera to not allow the Ultraviolet energy into it and effect the film. When viewing photographs of Fluorescent minerals under Ultraviolet lamps taken by the author of this modern article it is quite obvious that he has never used an 'Ultraviolet Barrier Filter' on his camera, having as much stray Ultraviolet and ambient light on the background of the photographs as on the Fluorescent mineral subjects themselves.

The last of the small articles on this page of the "Black Light Beacon" is, again, another example of Black light technology being used today having it's infancy in the 1930s-1940s era: Criminology. This short article is about a women's hospital that was not receiving the money that it's customers were sending through the mail. "Conti-Glo" "Invisible Green Powder" was used to dust onto the money that the police sent purposefully to the women's hospital. Then the employees of the hospital had their hands inspected under a Black light, and the hospital's telephone operator's hands had bright Green streaks on them, conclusively proving her as the thief.

The final page of this monthly publication from 1941 "Black Light Beacon" has another article similar to the Ice Ballet Black Light performance on the front page. The Black light performance reported about on this last page is from the 'Open House' of Cleveland's Woodland Recreation Center. A class of young women made up the Fluorescent performance, and came onto the stage in a total "Blackout," and then under powerful Black lights they had vividly Fluorescent elements on their "Conti-Glo" coated stage outfits. The class of young girls all had Fluorescent bows in their hair, Fluorescent bows on their shoes, Fluorescent stripes down both sides of their pants, and Fluorescent buttons on their tops while they whirled their Fluorescent batons. Next, Fluorescent Volleyball and Fluorescent Badminton were played in total 'Blackout' with all elements of both the games having been coated with "Conti-Glo" Fluorescent products. The article reported that the audience was crazy for this simple performance by the gym class of young girls under Black lights, and informs the reader of the high intensity of Black light used on the stage during the girls' performance that night. The very proficient photograph shows a dozen highly Fluorescent costumes outlined with brilliant highlights used in the girls' performance in Cleveland, and we are told in the article that six "Model 70" 250 watt Black lights were suspended over the small stage with only twelve girls performing on it - that's 'only' one thousand five hundred watts of Black Light! I am positive that the amount of Black light energy used on this small stage in Cleveland in 1941 with only a twelve girl gym class performing on it was *several times* the amount of Black light energy used for the pitiful Black light performance on the tremendous ice-skating ring for the world famous 'Ice Capades' show I was in attendance of December, 2008! The article concludes with the simple details of how the girl's costumes were made Fluorescent, including the coating of their batons with "Conti-Glo" lacquer Fluorescent paint, and the use of "Conti-Glo" Fluorescent Satins for making the girl's hair and shoe bows, as well as the stripes and buttons on their costumes.

The last page of this "Conti-Glo" "Black Light Beacon" is very valuable because it is a full page advertisement for "Conti-Glo" Lacquer Enamel Fluorescent paints. On the top of the page is a Black and White photograph of a machine producing Florescent paint. The photograph is very effective, showing the machine in almost total darkness as the background, while a brilliant 'River of Light' made of "Conti-Glo" Fluorescent paint flows through the dark machine. In typical 1940s style the reader is told in the first sentence of advertisement that a Black light emits 'life-giving' energy which will also cause the "Conti-Glo" Fluorescent paints to glow vividly. The reader is first informed that these paints were Fluorescent lacquer oil paints which could be applied to any Colored base without the need for coating the base with a light Color such a White, as is once again a required procedure with almost all of today's Fluorescent acrylic paints. Next this "Conti-Glo" Fluorescent lacquer enamel paint's intensity of Fluorescence under Black lights is compared to inferior 'old fashioned' dim Phosphorescent luminous paints. The part of this advertisement that is the most dated is the section listing 'Uses' of this Fluorescent paint, which is divided into the four categories of Decoration, Display, Entertainment, and Sales. Pertaining to the area of 'Decoration,' the reader is suggested to use Fluorescent paint not only on their homes, but also in ballrooms, restaurants, clubs, theaters, hotels, and even the contemporary shocker - *the Church!* The ideas for the Sales and Display headings are similar, promoting the use of Black light and Fluorescent paint in sales presentations and store displays. For Entertainment the reader is informed of Black light and Fluorescent paint uses in the additional public sectors of schools, stage performances, and unbelievably, twice in the same advertisement: *the Church!*

The final instruction part of this full page advertisement advises the user how to apply the "Conti-Glo" Fluorescent paint. The reader is informed that these Fluorescent paints can be applied by air-brush, traditional hand brush, or the third, very amusing method, of 'Dipping' objects directly into the paint to coat them. What is very amusing and incredibly ironic about the technique of 'Dipping' being an instructional use for applying Fluorescent paint in 1941, is the similarity with the famous 'Dipping' technique with Fluorescent paint used by Ken Kesey and the Merry Pranksters decades later during the Psychedelic era, and continuing up to the present day by Kesey's son Zane. Those characters on their way across America in 1964 during the famous 'Bus-Trip' made a Fluorescent Oil Paint 'Dipping' Session outside in nature - in a *Lake*(!) When Ken Kesey left his body in November, 2001 (two months after 9/11 and the same month as George Harrison) his entire coffin was "Dipped," using a huge milk vat at his family Dairy farm in Oregon as the "dipping" container.

The 1941 advertisement closes with a list of "Fluorescent Enamel Lacquer Colors" sold in 1941 by "Conti-Glo," and is helpfully divided into several columns, first giving the name of the Fluorescent paint, next the Color of the paint's appearance in daylight, and finally the Color of the 'Light Emitted' by the Fluorescent paint under Black lights. Today such an eloquent, accurate, detailed description of Colors of 'Light Emitted' by the Fluorescent paint under Black lights will not be found on any website, sales brochure, or on any Fluorescent or Phosphorescent paint lists from any Fluorescent paint manufacturing company in the world. The twelve Colors listed by "Conti-Glo" of their Fluorescent paints for sale in 1941 are extremely interesting because five of these twelve Fluorescent paint Color's names are still in use over seventy years later by the current world famous incarnation of the "Conti-Glo" company, "Day-Glo" Corporation, still in Cleveland, Ohio where the "Switzer Brothers" established in the 1930s. The twelve Colors of Fluorescent lacquer enamel paints in this 1941 advertisement include the 'Invisible' Fluorescent paints that were White and light Creme-Colored in daylight, but Fluoresced Blue/White and Green under Black lights. Amazingly, several of the Color's names are instantly recognizable to this author almost seven decades later, because the modern "Day-Glo" Corporation still produces Fluorescent paint and Fluorescent pigment with these five identical names in the Twenty-first century. Probably the most shocking part of this whole 1941 Fluorescent paint advertisement (besides the double listing of the 'Church' for uses of Black lights and Fluorescent paint) is the Price List!

The second issue of "Conti-Glo" "Black Light Beacon" in the Museum collection is from September/October 1941, and is "Vol. 1 No. 6." The cover story from this 1941 magazine is one of the most unbelievable reportages this author has ever come across concerning the use of Black light and Florescent Colors: a Black Light "Press Dinner" for *"General Motors Corporation"* in 1941, where five hundred dignified guests were seated for dinner at specially designed Black Light Dinner Tables complete with Fluorescent menus, napkins, and all the other table elements - this is not a joke! There is a large high quality photograph that fills three-quarters of the front page of this 1941 "Black Light Beacon," showing a partial photograph of the Fluorescent Black Light Dinner of General Motors Corporation in which eleven of the dinner tables can be seen, each table seating nine guests, and each table equipped with a large UFO-shaped chrome Black light fixture directly in the center of the Dinner table. The details in the article written about this General Motors Corporation Fluorescent Press Dinner are just as surprising as the photograph itself. The chairman of General Motors Corporation in 1941 was Alfred P. Sloan, Jr., and on September 10, 1941 the General Motors Corporation held this Black Light Fluorescent Press Dinner in Detroit, Michigan ("Motor-City") which included almost five hundred distinguished dinner guests including members of General Motors Corporation, members of the United States military (this was 1941), and press members from radio, magazines, and the newspapers. This Fluorescent Black Light Press Dinner's theme was no less a serious matter, and was meant to exemplify the effort and contribution that General Motors Corporation was making for the U.S. military during the Second world war era in 1941. The actual point of the Fluorescent Black Light Press Dinner given by General Motors Corporation was to demonstrate the Black light's use as a U.S. military weapon. This five hundred guest Press Dinner itself was the culmination of a full day presenting the war effort of General Motors Corporation, involving all phases of their 1941 production, from the assembly line to the testing of the finished vehicles. The theme of this General Motors Corporation Black Light Press Dinner was War Defense for the U.S. military forces of the Second world war, made perfectly clear by the appearance of a tremendous Fluorescent American flag at the closing of the evening. The General Motors Black Light Florescent Press Dinner for the U.S. military and members of the press was composed of no less than fifty specially designed Black Light Dinner Tables, each seating nine invited guests. Each of these fifty Dinner Tables was designed to be a complete self-contained Fluorescent light source as the entire Press Dinner was held in the dark, which was termed 'Blackout' during the Second world war era. The center of each of the fifty Dinner Tables was equipped with a Black light unit designed exclusively for it's intended use on a Dinner Table. This Dinner Table Black Light unit designed and manufactured by "Conti-Glo" was made with the intention of being the center highlight of the Dinner Table as well as it's light source, with it's shinny circular chrome construction including three old fashioned candle holders on top of the unit for traditionalists. This specifically designed Black Light Dinner Table unit looks about one and a half feet tall (45 cm) and is shaped like a chrome UFO with a diameter about equal to it's height. The top circular chrome section of the Dinner Table Black Light unit contained a "Conti-Glo" "EH-4" circular Black light, and was above it's small circular base containing the Black light's electrical components, which was fitted with a chrome grating. The Florescent Black Light Press Dinner is described in this article as being completely designed for Black light and Fluorescence, and for this 'Blackout' Dinner. Each one of the fifty circular Dinner Tables for this General Motors Corporation 'Blackout' Dinner had this specially designed circular Black light at it's center, and was equipped with Fluorescent features which produced it's own light to be able to eat by. Each table had nine guest dinner settings, which included Fluorescent dinner glasses, napkins, and specially designed Fluorescent dinner menus that were covered in clear plastic on which the names of the speakers at this Defense 'Blackout' Black Light Dinner were printed in invisible Fluorescent ink and only visible during the dinner when the Black Lights were turned on in the center of each dinner table. The table cloth was vivid Fluorescent Blue and served as the main light source for each dinner table. The fifty tables seating almost five hundred General Motors Corporation guests were made complete with a Fluorescent ashtray for each guest and a highly Fluorescent specially designed flower bouquet graced each of the Black Light Dinner Tables for this unprecedented and obviously never-repeated General Motors Corporation Black Light event. Can any reader imagine General Motors Corporation today hosting a BLACK LIGHT Press Dinner? So here we have in one source, documentation with photographs of the Black light and Fluorescent Colors used by both General Motors Corporation and the U.S. military War Defense department simultaneously.

Turning the page of this September/October 1941 "Black Light Beacon" the reader finds a full page advertisement for creating your own Black Light Dinner. Two very clear photographs are on the top half of the advertisement, the large photo of the Black Light Dinner Table set-up in the dark, presenting the dinner table itself with it's highly Fluorescent table cloth and almost all Fluorescent implements of the dinner itself, such as the napkins and drinking glasses. The caption for this Black Light Dinner Table photo informs the potential customer that this is how their Dinner Table will look in their house or restaurant in the dark and the package that is being sold in this "Conti-Glo" advertisement is the "Conti-Glo" Fluorescent Dinner Table package 'No. 1.' The second smaller insert photo is a daylight view showing a close up of the Fluorescent Dinner Table's center chrome circular specially designed Black light unit. This Black light unit is briefly explained in the text of the advertisement to be polished 'chrome steel' and it's appearance is compared to Silver, as traditionally was used for table settings. The reader is informed that the Ultraviolet energy used by the Dinner Table Black Light unit is harmless Longwave Ultraviolet energy, as is in all common Black lights. There are also three candle holders added at the top of this cylindrical chrome unit for the tradition of a candlelit dinner not being forgotten. As explained, this Dinner Table Black Light unit looked like a chrome flying saucer suspended by small posts above a smaller cylindrical base for the electrical components of the Black light, which is itself covered with a chrome grating for heat dissipation. The total unit looks about a foot and a half (45 cm) high and wide judging from the photographs, and is surrounded by a specially designed circular bouquet of Fluorescent flowers whose both petals and leaves are described as being Fluorescent and transparent. The description of this Black Light Dinner Table package 'No. 1' ends with a paragraph about the most Fluorescent feature of the Fluorescent dinner table, the highly Fluorescent table cloth made with "Conti-Glo" Fluorescent Satin developed for the U.S. Military during the 1930s. This Black Light Dinner table Setting 'No.1' was sold as a complete package by "Conti-Glo," similar to how the "Switzer Brothers" had packaged their first Magician's Black Light Stage Kit at the beginning of their careers only a few short years before in the mid 1930s. This advertisement lists eight components that the Black Light Dinner Table Kit 'No. 1' would have consisted of, including the most important feature, the circular chrome Black Light Dinner Table unit with an 'EH-4' circular "Conti-Glo" mercury Black light. Next, the most Fluorescent and light producing feature of the Fluorescent Dinner Table, the "Conti-Glo" Fluorescent Satin Table Cloth. This Fluorescent table cloth was eighty inches square (2 meters) and the table cloth was Invisible Blue Fluorescent, meaning that it was ordinary White in daylight, but under the Black light it Fluoresced a vivid Blue. Six Fluorescent wine glasses, two of each of three different Fluorescent Colors are main features for each place setting for this Black Light Dinner Table kit, along with six Fluorescent napkins, also two of each of three different Fluorescent Colors to match the wine glasses, and three Florescent ash trays in three different Fluorescent Colors. The center circular chrome Black light unit was wreathed with a circular multi-Colored Fluorescent bouquet at it's base, completing this Fluorescent Black Light Dinner Table package 'No. 1,' which was being offered for sale for the very large sum of $150.00! Once again, this price of $150.00 was equal in 1941 to nearly four ounces of *Gold!*

With information and hindsight, I can now understand why I have heard several times over the last ten years of giving personal tours in the Museum, of a Restaurant in Ohio many years before the 1960s that was completely lit by just Black lights, allowing the diners in the restaurant to eat by just the emitted light of the Fluorescent table setting and the Fluorescent paintings on the restaurant walls. I have to admit that what always amazed me when hearing these old memories of this Fluorescent Black Light Restaurant was it's location in Ohio, not San Francisco or New York City as I would have first imagined, but this was before I knew that the "Conti-Glo" company, later becoming the famous "Day-Glo" corporation, was started in Cleveland, Ohio. Something that is very odd to this author seven decades later, is the use of non-Fluorescent traditional dinner plates in the 1941 Black Light Fluorescent Dinner Table package, instead of the extremely Fluorescent 1930s Green "Depression glass" that is so well known as a "Common Item that is Fluorescent" in the Twenty-first century, and has been for sale as Fluorescent Black light glass on the internet for years. I would assume that the highly Fluorescent quality of (only) the Green "Depression glass" had not yet been discovered at that point in 1941, or it would surely have been included in the package. Originally named "Uranium Glass" until the 1950s when this glass was being thrown away because of the fear induced by it's name, the name was changed years after it was produced to it's current incarnation of "Depression glass" (because it was made during the era of the 'Great Depression' in America). Of the five different Colors of "Depression glass" originally manufactured, Green is the only Color that Fluoresces, through the impurity named "Uranyl" in the glass that was included in the manufacturing process. "Uranyl" is a mixture of Oxygen with Uranium that produces a molecule that is as weakly radioactive as old Color T.V. sets, but the name "Uranium glass" was originally coined in a time when Uranium was considered something good - like nuclear fusion, for that matter - although this name was enough to induce great fear when heard by the general public later in the 1950s era, after the recent horrors of the Atom bomb and after Nils Boer had definitively stopped writing musicals about Atomic energy. The era of 1941 was already a time when nuclear Uranium stories and plans were being explored for mass destruction weapons to be used in the Second world war, and this may have already tainted the public's taste and opinion towards Uranium and things nuclear, so this may have been the reason for the "Depression glass" not being included in this Fluorescent Dinner Table package, or may have been a contributing factor in it's exclusion in the package.

The next reportage in this time-warping "Black Light Beacon" is another one of the examples of the widespread use and positive public opinion regarding Black lights and Fluorescent paint in the 'Miracle Era' of the Black light during the 1930s and 1940s: Movie theaters. The last issue of "Black Light Beacon" resurrected in the previous pages reported on a smaller local Movie theatre in Cleveland, but the Florescent Black Light Movie Theatre in this issue was a large major theatre just built in San Carlos, California called the "Carlos Theatre." In the article the owner of the theatre is stated as 'Fox West Coast,' possibly going on to become "Twentieth Century Fox" one of the largest movie production corporations in the world today. This "Carlos Theatre" opened January 10, 1941, only nine months before the publication of this "Black Light Beacon." We are told that San Carlos is a small wealthy community just outside of San Francisco, and that this large theatre cost $150,000, again quite a sum in 1941. The Black and White very clear half page photograph at the top of the article shows the ceiling and curved walls at the back of the "Carlos Theatre," which were covered with gigantic painted Fluorescent ornamental floral designs on what must have been the entire space above the audience's heads. The photograph is of the back of the theatre which had the largest and most elaborate of these painted Fluorescent decorations since it was furthest away from the Movie screen at the front of the theatre. The photo reveals that this "Carlos Theatre" must have been quite large, with forty-five seats in each row of the audience, it must have held between one and two thousand bedazzled movie goers. The Fluorescent Murals on the walls and ceiling of this "Carlos Theatre" had become so well known in only a little over half a year, that on mornings of the weekend the manager of the theatre gave tours of just the theatre itself without a movie running. The article informs the reader that the Fluorescent paintings on the theatre walls and ceiling were made by 'Vogue Studios' in San Francisco, and the Black light design and installation was done by 'Keese Engineering Company' which was run by the "Switzer Brothers" first Fluorescent paint distributor in the mid-1930s, Johnny Shannon, who was in this magazine article stated as the current distributor of "Conti-Glo" products on the West coast. Mr. John T. Shannon, as he is referred to in this "Black Light Beacon," was one of the first people to have used Luminous paint and Black lights, having dazzled the audiences of the first "Ziegfeld Theatre" in San Francisco in 1907 with "Black Art" pioneering Fluorescent stage shows. Today, "Shannon Luminous Paint, Incorporated" is still a major company producing Fluorescent paint, remaining in California.

The description of the Fluorescent murals in this "Carlos Theatre" sound extravagant, made with the intention of awing the theatre goer, again with the largest and brightest of the Fluorescent paintings towards the back of the theatre and getting smaller and less distracting towards the front of the theatre where the movie screen was. The huge Fluorescent murals in this theatre were designed with geometric swirls and vaguely represent plants, flowers and ferns, but the overall impression when seeing the photograph today is a typical 1940s style. The entire design of the wall and ceiling Fluorescent murals stressed the point of three dimensional "tromp l'oeil," making the painted Fluorescent floral patterns look as though they were constructed in plaster. The explanation for the painting procedure of this extravagant Fluorescent Black light Movie theatre reveals the degree of thought, planning, and experience of the designers and Artists of these murals. First the walls and ceiling of this theatre were prepared with 'acoustic' plaster, and next it was painted with White 'casein' paint. The areas of wall and ceiling that were in between the Fluorescent floral designs were painted with a light Tan Color, which had been chosen because of it's non-Fluorescent reaction under Black lights. The three dimensional effect of the wall and ceiling Fluorescent murals are clearly proficient, as illustrated in the photograph, and were accomplished by spraying different shades of Grey 'casein' paint first to render the shadowed areas of the tromp l'oeil design, and next the "Conti-Glo" Fluorescent paint was sprayed on to complete the murals, which created a dramatic three dimensional effect in the dark under Black lights. The Colors of Fluorescent "Conti-Glo" lacquer enamel paint used in these "Carlos Theatre" murals were 'Invisible' Green, 'Invisible' Blue, 'Fire Orange,' and a custom shade of dark Red. The article continues on to explain the Black light design of this theatre which must have created an exceptionally vivid display of Fluorescence, accomplished by no less than eighteen theatre Black light units, nine on each side wall of the theatre! These very powerful Black light flood lamps were built into the walls of the theatre with plaster ornaments concealing them. But that wasn't all the Black lights that were used. The Fluorescent murals on the two side walls of the theatre were "black lighted" by use of additional Black light theatre units built into the ceiling itself, as well.

The details of such an extravagant carefully planned and expertly designed Fluorescent Black light installation reveal, once again, the superior, advanced production of Fluorescent Black light displays which were much more spectacular and advanced than anything that is accomplished today in the Twenty-first century, seventy years later.

This famous "Carlos Theater" in California was created with Fluorescent paint under Black lights, and is credited to the "Vogue Studios" of San Francisco, but another Artist is still known today for his magnificent "Tower Theater" Fluorescent murals from the same general time period in Fresno, California. Anthony B. Heinsbergen (1895-1981) was born in Holland, and emigrating to the United States, received his first commission to paint a movie theater in 1924. He is still remembered today for his Fluorescent ceiling mural 'Leda and the Swan' of this "Tower Theater" in Fresno, which must have been a simply breathtaking display of Fluorescent murals and sculptures under a documented multitude of Black lights! The Black light was designed for these "Tower Theater" Fluorescent murals by R.H. McCullough and Walter Bantau. It is also documented that Heinsbergen's assistants, the two brothers Frank and Tom Bouman installed the "Tower Theater" murals, and to ensure their intense display, the two brothers reportedly finished the Fluorescent murals in the "Tower Theater" at night under just Black lights. According to the website Historicfresno.org, the first movie theater to use Black lights and Fluorescent paint in it's design was the "Academy Theater" of 1939 designed by architect S. Charles Lee in Inglewood, California, with this "Tower Theater" in Fresno being the second movie theater to have Fluorescent murals and Black lights installed.

One of the very rare internet presentations of such projects from seventy years ago is a scholarly overview of one of these Black Light Fluorescent Movie Theaters of the 1940s and the 1950s, which was being restored by the Smithsonian Institute of Washington, D.C. in 2003. The "Alameda Theatre" in San Antonio, Texas was another Movie theatre like the "Carlos Theatre" in this "Black Light Beacon" article, which was designed to be lit solely by huge Fluorescent murals painted onto the side walls of the theatre. As the Smithsonian Institute itself puts it, these Fluorescent "Black Light" Movie Theatre Murals were part of a 'dramatic trend' in Movie theatre interiors during the 1940s and the beginning of the 1950s. The information given on this web page of the Smithsonian Institute's "Smithsonian Center for Materials Research and Education" restoration of this historic theatre from 1949 is extremely detailed, including microscopic photographs of cross-sections of the layers of paints that these Fluorescent murals are made of. The two very large Fluorescent murals in the "Alameda Theatre" are highly Fluorescent, even in contemporary photographs of the sixty year old paintings. Both are based on the theme of San Antonio, Texas' Mexican heritage, the large Fluorescent mural on the left wall of the Movie theatre is called 'Saga of the Seven Flags' and vibrantly depicts cowboys, Mexican and American buildings, as well as warplanes in the sky above. The Fluorescent mural on the opposite wall (the 'western wall') of the theatre depicts ships from Spain sailing towards an Aztec temple while a highly Fluorescent Cortez rides his horse in the middle of the scene. A rare 1948 photograph of the Artist Frank Lackner who painted these Fluorescent Black light murals is on the Smithsonian's web page, standing on scaffolding that itself looks like coming from antiquity, and smiling in a completely White painting outfit. He is pointing to the mural and holding what looks exactly like a large old-style can of Spray-paint in his other hand. Since there are no paint stains of any kind on his completely White painting outfit (paint stains are very typical of painting by hand with a brush) and since the "Black Light Beacon " article on the "Carlos Theatre" in San Carlos, California seven or eight years earlier had been completely painted by spraying the paint onto the Fluorescent murals, the large old-styled can of Spray-paint in Frank Lackner's hand could have been the method he used for painting both of the "Alameda Theatre" Fluorescent murals. Perhaps his right hand may be holding a brush, and the can in left hand might be a can of normal liquid paint which is just in an odd-shaped can, so the Fluorescent murals could have been painted by Frank Lackner in the traditional method with a brush, but the small digitalized web picture even when blown up to six hundred percent is not clear enough to correctly infer.

Typically, today when you log onto "cinematreasures.org" a webpage about the historic "Alameda Theatre" there is a photograph of the neon-clad *exterior* of the theatre. In the four paragraph detailed explanation of this historic contemporarily unique Black Light Fluorescent Movie Theatre, the reader is informed of many facts which include: news that the award for the most outstanding Movie theatre in the United States was given to the "Alameda Theatre" in 1949, the history of the theatre which opened on March 9, 1949 in San Antonio, Texas as one of the last of the 'Grand movie palaces' built in America and which was the largest Movie theatre ever dedicated to Spanish speaking movies and performing Arts, the details of the 1,050 pieces of neon lighting making up the front of the Movie theatre's eighty-six foot (26 meter) marquee, and various other facts - and then - buried in the center of the text block there is one incorrect sentence misinforming readers of the 'phosphorescent' Black light murals!

Typically, again, is a "PBS" Television news clip found on the internet, "The News Hour" with Jim Lerer from May 30, 2007, announcing the opening of the "Museo Alameda" which is what the "Alameda Theatre" has now become. The news report is about this Hispanic American theatre's cultural importance and heritage, but during this five minute report, the

Fluorescent Black Light Murals are show on both sides of the theatre's interior - without Black lights and with all the White lights on in the theatre, and for sure, also without any mention by the Museum's Director of the Fluorescent murals or Black lights any more, just the facts about these murals representing the Hispanic American's heritage and cultural past. As can be easily imagined, the murals look miserable in this News reportage seen by multitudes of viewers, and the large water-damaged areas in the 'east' mural are clearly visible and look terrible - these same water-damaged spots that are nearly invisible in the correct Black light viewing of the mural, obviously as intended by Smithsonian restorers(!) The restoration by the Smithsonian Institute of the "Alameda Theatre" in Texas from 1949 is the only attempt this author knows of to preserve a piece of theater history of the extraordinary era of the "Miracle of Fluorescence" that occurred between the 1930s and the early 1950s.

The next surprising reportage of Black light and Fluorescent paint in this "Black Light Beacon" comes from, once again quite unbelievably, "General Motors Corporation!" Not only did "General Motors Corporation" have the Black Light Press Dinner with five hundred distinguished guests eating in 'Blackout' with just a Black light in the center of each highly Fluorescent Dinner Table in 1941, but the world famous corporation also mounted a Traveling Exhibition of patriotic Second world war Fluorescent Black light paintings called "Preview of Progress." This traveling exhibition by "General Motors Corporation" was totally centered around the mobility of the United States to protect and defend itself in the time of war, and consisted of five very large public murals painted exclusively with "Conti-Glo" Fluorescent paint. The article describes the Fluorescent murals as being material mounted on panels of Aluminum, and also reveals the name of the Artist, Russell Au Werter from Detroit. The traveling exhibition was displayed as part of a lecture that was given by the director of the exhibition Mr. E.L. Foss, in which the five large Fluorescent murals are shown in only the White light one by one going in step with the lecture. The first Fluorescent mural shown was entitled 'Men' and portrays the theme of men mobilized for war defense through the actions and labors of engineers, draftsmen, and workers in the fields of telephone, telegraph, and television. The second Fluorescent mural presented to the audience during the lecture was called 'Methods' and is mostly a collage of imagery depicting machinery at work producing war time implements including electronics, steel, glass, and the newly developed technology in 1941 'Plastic moulding.' Having roughly the same dimensions as the first two panels, the third panel is also a large vertical rectangle, in which is depicted 'Materials' of a mobilized nation going to war, with the subject matter of the Fluorescent mural including farming, oil, rubber, metal, fabrics, wood, and again the newly developed plastics (what is commonly referred to today as 'Bakelite').

These three Fluorescent "Preview of Progress" Murals were meant to be seen one after another and then together, first in the White light and then in the Black light. After these first three vertical format Fluorescent murals were shown to the audience, two horizontal format Fluorescent murals even larger than the first three murals were presented. These two very large Fluorescent murals were meant to explain separate themes, one in the White light presentation, and another in the Black lights Fluorescing. The first of these two highlighted murals seen by the audience has very subtly written across the entire bottom of the painting 'STRENGTH AMERICA' with a machine gear in the center and a man standing on the gear equipped with all types of research tools including engineering triangles and chemical flasks. At the bottom of this mural are stripes and at the top are stars, but the main part of the mural consists of three boxes on the left of the mural and three boxes on the right, each box with a theme that was painted inside which was designed to change from the White light presentation into a different scene when the Black lights were turned on. The White light - Black light change in imagery for these six boxes on the Fluorescent mural included telephone lines in the White light becoming antennas on battleships in the Black light, an electrical power station becomes a B-17 bomber in the Black light, a pleasure car becomes an army truck, tractor tires turn into tires for war planes, oil drums Fluorescing on top of a White light image of the production of oil, and other themes just as jovial as these. This large horizontal Fluorescent mural was called 'Strength of America,' but the last of the five murals was the largest of them all, depicting a map of the whole United States, and across the bottom of the outline map there are designers and workers at war factories on the left, an elegant contemporary mansion in the center, and on the right Mr. and Mrs. America with their child in front of a modern metropolis complete with a 'new' 1941 car in the foreground of a cityscape. This Fluorescent mural served as the climax to the war time lecture presented by "General Motors Corporation" that was entitled 'Who Serves Progress Serves America.' The main center imagery inside the map of the U.S. is a pioneer settler of America wearing a Davy Crockett buckskin fringed jacket and standing in front of a covered wagon while holding a rifle (could have never guessed he was American). When the Black lights were tuned on, the center image of the Pioneer turned into a Fluorescent Statue of Liberty, and the Conestoga covered wagon being pulled by a team of farm ox in the White light turns into Fluorescent engineers developing war materials such a chemicals and iron. The article closes by informing the reader about the two powerful "Conti-Glo" Black light units used on the five paneled traveling exhibition '"Preview of Progress."

The next article in this "Black Light Beacon" is another historic first, reporting on the very first use of "Conti-Glo" Fluorescent paint used in the Movies. The article reports that the first distributor of "Switzer Brothers" Fluorescent paint in the mid-1930s, Mr. John T. Shannon of the Keese Engineering Company (which would eventually turn into "Shannon Luminous Products, Inc.," still in existence today) was working with a major movie studio on the West Coast developing movie backgrounds painted for the first time with "Conti-Glo" Fluorescent paint. The first Fluorescent scenery background panel used in the movies was a Japanese nightscape with a Japanese house in front of a bay where the moving searchlights of two battleships scan across the night sky (sounds wonderful). The article tells the reader that these Japanese Fluorescent background movie scenery murals were for the movie version of an old opera, and that another movie studio was in the process of using Fluorescent paints in their productions for the first time as well. In Chris Burton's 2009 children's book "The Day-Glo Brothers," there is an illustration of the first Fluorescent Movie Posters printed by the Switzer Brothers, with a picture of an Asian woman standing in front of a harbor, with the name of the movie in the illustrated poster being "The Lamps of China." At this time, on June 8, 1935, there was a major American movie released in Black and White named "Oil for the Lamps of China," which may be the full name of the movie that the Switzer Brothers printed this first Fluorescent movie poster for. It's possible that the first time a movie audience ever saw the use of Fluorescent paint and pigments in a major 'Moving Picture' was in the "Wizard of Oz" released on August 25, 1939. The extremely brilliant Red Color of the cloud created by the disappearance of the Wicked Witch of the West in the first Color scene of the movie when Dorothy's house falls on the Wicked Witch's sister, and also used atop the house in the scene in the woods when the Wicked Witch once again disappears in a cloud of very vivid Colored Red smoke after throwing fire balls at the Scarecrow, both these clouds of brilliant Red look precisely like Fluorescent powdered pigment. There are several other scenes in the "Wizard of Oz" in which Fluorescent paint and pigments have most likely been used, including the scene where the Wicked Witch has Dorothy trapped in the castle tower, and her wand and other details of the scene looks exactly like Orange/Red Fluorescent paint. This "Black Light Beacon" is reporting about the first time "Conti-Glo" Fluorescent paint was used to create full scenery in the form of background paintings, but in the "Wizard of Oz" the Fluorescent paint and pigment that was most likely used was for mere "props," making special effects. I have never found any sort of documentation about Fluorescent pigment or paint being used in the "Wizard of Oz," but the date of the movie production is right in the middle of the era of "The Miracle of Fluorescence," and visually the Color and the brilliance of the Color of the powder and the paint used in several scenes of the movie lead me to believe it must be Fluorescent powdered pigments and Fluorescent paint, most likely "Conti-Glo" because 1939 was only six years after Robert Switzer had invented Fluorescent paint. Two more small articles are on the double page spread under the "General Motors Corporation" 'Previews of Progress' article. The first small article informs customers of the three new "Conti-Glo" Display and Demonstration offices in America. In New York City on the famous 'Forty-second Street' a new office was opened in which customers could get a demonstration of both the Black lights and the Fluorescence of "Conti-Glo" paint. The next pair of Demonstration and Display offices opened were the 'Saltzman Black Light Studios' in Chicago and Detroit, which the reader was informed were the exclusive distributors of "Conti-Glo" products in the midwest states for "civilian uses." The last two offices "Conti-Glo" opened in 1941, during the biggest increase and demand for their products (which were made exclusively for the United States military forces during World war two) that the company would ever have - except for just the opposite period of the 1960s Psychedelic Movement when the world found out about "Day-Glo" Colors. These last two Display and Demonstration offices opened by "Conti-Glo" in 1941 covered the American south, with new offices 'Black Light Research, Inc.' in Florida and Cuba, again, distributors of "Conti-Glo" standard products for "civilian" uses is the literal bottom line of this small article. The underlying theme of the entire Black light technology and all products made with Fluorescent pigments, including paint and fabrics, during this 1941 era was clearly centered on the United States military defense for the Second world war, with any 'civilian' uses of the "Conti-Glo" products being very much secondary. The "Smithsonian Institute" website detailing the restoration of the historic Black light Fluorescent "Alameda Theatre" in San Antonio, Texas, which was discussed on the previous pages of the present chapter, includes several extremely rare photographs including the front cover of a full magazine printed by "Conti-Glo" for the uses of their Fluorescent products in the military during the Second world war. Illustrated on the cover of this magazine are battleships, war planes and bombers, tanks and soldiers, making it instantly recognizable as 'war time.'

Another very ingenious use of Black lights and Fluorescent pigments during this era of 1941 is another ingenious use of Black lights and Fluorescent pigments that was abandoned many decades ago: Fluorescent Carpeting in the darkened environment of Movie theaters was a major new use of the technology during this era. The next page of this "Conti-Glo Black Light Beacon" has a photograph and article highlighting the new use of the Fluorescent carpeting technology. The article is about the reportage in a magazine 'Show Parade of all Hawaii' where the reader was informed about the new technology of

Black lights and Fluorescent carpeting being used in the isles of the 'Waikiki Theatre' in Honolulu, Hawaii. This technology is described as creating a 'magic carpet' through the use of hidden Black lights and Fluorescent carpeting in the isles of the darkened Movie theatre, so the effect of walking on 'Moonbeams' is reported in this "Black Light Beacon." The original article in the 'Show Parade of all of Hawaii' described the effect as being in no way an interference in the viewing of the movie in the darkness of the theatre. The clear photograph credited to von Hawn-Young Company portrays a smiling usherette walking down the 'Moonbeam' Fluorescent carpeting under hidden Black lights in an aisle of the 'Waikiki Theatre' in Honolulu, wearing a uniform made of "Conti-Glo" Fluorescent satins. Very obviously with the absence of such "good ideas," today we can clearly see yet another use of the Black light and Fluorescent Colors that was abandoned half a century ago.

A very efficient use of the Black Light and Fluorescence from the 1940s that has not been abandoned up until the present time is in the field of Criminology. In this 1941 "Black Light Beacon" there are two articles dealing with the newly developed field of Black light and Fluorescent pigments used by police in many different fields of Criminology. The small article presented first in this magazine is documenting the use of Black light and Fluorescence used in criminology during it's infancy. A local story is told in the article about teenagers in Cleveland making false alarms to the Fire department. The police dusted the Fire alarms in Cleveland with "Conti-Glo" Invisible Green Powder and when the next false alarm went off, the police examined suspects hands with a Black light and the guilty teenager's hands were brilliant Fluorescent Green. The small article ends with a sentence suggesting uses for the "Conti-Glo" Invisible Fluorescent Green Powder, including identifying thieves and burglars, and then advancing to 'wartime' sabotage and international spies.

The full page article follows which is a confirmation of the infancy of Black light and Fluorescence used as a Criminology tool in 1941 at the time of this trade magazine's publication. The opening introductory paragraph states quite clearly that the Second world war's defense forces extensive use of the Black light and Fluorescence had greatly excited the general public about the use of this unseen phenomenon of Fluorescence. The Black light used with Invisible Fluorescent powders had an obvious use outside the military in the public sector of police enforcement. This full page article begins with the first example of the use of "Conti-Glo" Invisible Fluorescent Green Powder in the apprehension of both criminals in the public sector and also against sabotage in the Military. The "Conti-Glo" invisible Green powder used in criminology is described as being invisible in daylight, but under a Black light for interrogation the invisible powder Fluoresces a vivid Green. Examples on where to use this Fluorescent invisible Green powder fill a full paragraph and include machines and tools in a production plant, valuable documents, records and files, military blueprints, maps, and secret charts. The ability of this Fluorescent invisible Green powder is detailed within the article, explaining that the Fluorescent powder will stick to the hands and subsequently will be smeared on the clothes of the criminal when they touch themselves with their hands, but this powder will be invisible and undetectable in daylight. The possibilities of using the Black light in a criminal court is discussed next in this article, offering the possibilities of photographing evidence under a Black light and then using printed photographs as convincing evidence in the courtroom. Added to the applications of the Black light in criminology is the field of forgery. The fact that anything that is erased on a piece of paper will alter the paper itself and be easily seen under a Black light is presented in this article, and gives examples of bank checks and business records. The fact that a typewriter's ribbon's ink varies in Fluorescence from one manufacturer to another is also described in this article as another application in criminal investigations. The last examples of the Black light's new use in this field of criminology are cited as detection of the Fluorescence of writing inks used to forge financial papers, and also the James Bond-like Invisible Writing Inks that can be used to detect, again, saboteurs. Closing this full page article on the new field of Black light use in criminology is a suggestion for the new "Conti-Glo" 'Model 94' Portable Black light unit in a box to be used in this new field. This "Conti-Glo" new Portable Black light 'Model 94' is advertised on the following page of these "Black Light Beacon," and includes a photograph. This portable Black light unit was a full kit in a Black box with a handle, looking like an old-fashioned small traveling trunk, and was a completely independent unit with a twenty-five foot (8 meter) wire. The applications for the portable Black light unit listed in the ad include non-military applications such as the field of entertainment, for school lectures, criminology, and field laboratory examination. This 'Model 94' 1941 Portable Black light unit consisted of a tall rectangular trunk-like box having the bottom quarter containing the electrical transformer sealed, while the top opened area had a section with the electrical wire rolled up next to the largest section of the box holding the 100 watt Black light lamp and it's folding metal mounting bracket. The price of this Portable 100 watt Black light kit, including a two ounce container of Invisible Green Powder and a one and a quarter ounce container of Invisible Writing Ink was $49.75 (one and a quarter ounces of Gold in 1941). This portable Black unit was offered for $49.00 with sixteen ounces of 'Pass-Out Check Ink,' and the unit was sold by itself for $45.00. The prices for the Invisible Detection Powders were $7.50 for two ounces of Invisible Green Powder, and $1.00 for one and a quarter ounces of Ink for 'Pass-Out' checking. Next to the advertisement for this Portable Black Light unit 'Model 94,' is another ad for the same

100 watt Black light lamp as the portable unit, but this 'Model 96' is for a permanent wall mounting. The intended use for this unit 'Model 96' was for it to be mounted above the exit door for paying customers, or employees that were marked with Fluorescent ink for identification under this Black light unit. The ad also mentions that this Black light could be used for other effects besides security, and states the price as $29.75. The last article in this "Black Light Beacon" explained the new use of Black lights and Invisible Pass-Out Check Ink for marking paid customers' hands with Fluorescent ink when they leave an arena, ballroom, or resort, and then easily scanning their hand under a Black light unit (Portable Black light unit 'Model 94' is suggested) when they return to the venue after the intermission. This is another of the rare uses still alive today from the original age of "The Miracle of the Black Light," being one of the most well known uses of the Black light today in general public. The Portable Black light "Conti-Glo" 'Model 94' has further applications described in this article, including lighting for stage shows and dance halls, interior decoration, and public lectures. The small article closes, again, with the criminology application of the 'Model 94' with Invisible Green Powder used for apprehending criminals and for detecting sabotage.

This September/October, 1941 issue of "Conti-Glo Black Light Beacon," from the first to the last page was concentrated on the U.S. Military War Defense use of the Black light and Fluorescence, with almost each and every article and advertisement concentrated, or at least mentioning, the military or defense use in detecting sabotage.

In the last of the three extremely rare issues of the trade magazine "Conti-Glo Black Light Beacon," which is from January, 1942 and is 'Vol. 2 No. 1,' finally there is an article about *Art!* After the last issue of "Black Light Beacon" that was saturated with articles concentrated solely on the Second world war and the U.S. military's use of the Black light and Fluorescence for the war, it is a pleasant relief to see this front page article with two photographs reporting about the use of Black lights and Fluorescent paint for making Art - imagine that - and without one sentence about the Second world war.

This front page 1941 article is detailing some very rare facts that I've heard about several times over the past twenty-nine years of talking to visitors in "Electric Lady" Art gallery, and in the last seventeen years of giving tours to visitors of the Museum. As I've mentioned before briefly, the story about a mystical Restaurant in Ohio, of all places, where all the lighting in the Restaurant were Black lights, and where the illumination for the Dinner Tables came solely from the emitted light of the Colors of the Fluorescent Paintings on the walls of the Restaurant has been told to me several times by visitors over the years, and it made a deep impression on me. It was one of my very early notions that the Black light and Fluorescent Colors were very popular in a time period before the famous 1960s, and that the Black light and Fluorescent Colors were used in serious sectors of the public, like restaurants for instance, which would seem on the verge of hilarious in today's world.

The full page article on the front cover of this "Black Light Beacon" is a reportage on not one, but two different Restaurants in Cleveland, Ohio in January, 1942, that were opened for business and featured Fluorescent paintings under Black lights as the primary lighting design for both these restaurants. "Chin's Golden Dragon" and "Freddie's Paradise Cafe" were the names of these two restaurants in Cleveland where "Conti-Glo" Fluorescent paint and Black lights were used to create Fluorescent murals. The general description of Art made with Fluorescent paint under Black lights is written with an awareness and observance that obviously escaped the Director of the Museum of Modern Art in New York City, and nearly every other museum director on the planet, for that matter. The effect of the emitted light of the Fluorescent paintings under Black lights is eloquently described in this simple magazine as comparable to the translucent light coming through the Stained glass windows of cathedrals, and the fact is given that the emission of light from Fluorescent paint under Black lights combined with it's translucence and three-dimensionality cannot be achieved by an Artist without the use of this new Fluorescent paint.

In "Chin's Victory Room" in the Cleveland Restaurant "Chin's Golden Dragon" the reader is told that there were large Fluorescent murals created with "Conti-Glo" Fluorescent paints that were made by R.R. Elliott of Cleveland's Gallo Studios, and that the subject matter of the Fluorescent mural photographed in this article is originally inspired by an ancient Chinese painting motif of 'Victory.' The Black and White photograph of the "Chin's Golden Dragon" Fluorescent mural of 'Victory' that was installed on the wall behind the orchestra portrays what appears to be a Chinese goddess in the center of the mural on a throne, with a pair of huge peacocks and stylized clouds in the foreground. These "Chin's Golden Dragon" Fluorescent murals were painted on Black velvet with "Conti-Glo" Fluorescent lacquer enamel paint over a base layer of White 'casein' paint. What is just as amazing as the use of a Fluorescent mural under Black lights in a popular restaurant, are the details of the incredible amount of Black light that was used on these Fluorescent murals, creating a breath taking effect that is unparalleled with today's typical use of a few Black light 36 watt Fluorescent tube lamps, only, mounted on a ceiling. As a comparison, today if a restaurant had a large Fluorescent mural on the wall, there would be two 36 watt Black lights mounted above the mural on the ceiling, without any facure board or any attempt (or idea) to conceal the two Black lights, which would be permanently glowing a Purple-Blue light very distractingly above the mural - a total of 72 watts of Black light. In 'Chin's Golden Dragon' the 'Victory' Fluorescent mural in 1942 had two 'Model 99' Black light spotlights of 100 watts each just for this one Fluorescent mural. The effect of 200 watts on one Fluorescent mural must have been extraordinary. The general regression of using convenient, cheap, safe, weak Black light tubular lamps instead of intensive professional Black light units in public displays did not help in the universal loss of fascination, interest, and even knowledge over the past seventy years.

"Freddie's Paradise Cafe" was the name of the other Fluorescent Restaurant in Cleveland in 1942, and the description of this venue makes it sound even more extravagant than "Chin's Golden Dragon." The fact is documented in this "Black Light Beacon" proving what I have heard over the last two decades in the Gallery, and in the Museum, of a restaurant in Ohio where the customers ate dinner solely by the emitted light of Fluorescent paintings on the walls of the restaurant above their dining tables - "Freddie's Paradise Cafe" was the actual restaurant! The reader is informed in 1942 that in "Freddie's Paradise Cafe" no less than seven large Fluorescent murals under Black lights were mounted on the walls of the restaurant and that the light emitted by these Fluorescent murals on the walls of the restaurant were all the lights that were needed for diners in the restaurant to eat under. Victor Kosa of Youngstown, Ohio was the Artist who painted the seven Fluorescent murals in "Freddie's Paradise Cafe" and a photograph of one of the murals is included with this article, depicting a very typical underwater aquarium scene, still a popular overused motif with Fluorescent paint today.

The details of the amount of Black light energy used on the seven Fluorescent wall murals in "Freddie's Paradise Cafe" are not written in the article, but judging by the amount of Black light used on the large Fluorescent flag (6 x 9 feet - approximately 2 x 3 meters) unfolded for the finale of the show on stage at "Freddie's," the amount must have been sufficiently breath taking. Only this six by nine foot (2x3 meters) unfolded Fluorescent flag had two 250 watt 'Model 70' Black lights! It must have been as bright as the Sun. Not only was this 1942 time period the era of "The Miracle of Fluorescence" when people's interest and fascination were absolutely inflamed by this new phenomenon of the Black light and Fluorescent Colors, but in this era before the decadence present over the last four decades was formed, Black light and Fluorescence was used on a scale, with such an intensity, and with a degree of knowledge and designing that today is nearly impossible to even imagine, unfortunately.

An exquisite photograph on the next page of this January, 1942 "Conti-Glo" "Black Light Beacon" shows the interior of a Restaurant in Los Angeles that was prodigiously Fluorescent, with what looks like an immense three dimensional diorama of a Fluorescent jungle display that was installed into one full wall of the restaurant. This photograph is valuable because it shows the setting, and even more importantly the scale of the restaurant with dining tables in front of what must have been a truly enormous Fluorescent jungle setting. Judging from the sizes of the ten or more dining tables in front of this Fluorescent jungle installation, the dimensions of the full jungle diorama cut into the wall of this Los Angeles restaurant were a minimum of approximately five yards (meters) tall by nine yards wide. That is a surface area of four hundred square feet. From the Black and White photograph of 1942, which is quite clear, it is stated in the photo's caption that this was an 'illustration' from an original photograph (meaning it was highly retouched with the new tool in the 1940s called an air-brush), the dimensions and design of this immense Fluorescent jungle scene in "Clifton's Cafeteria" in Los Angeles are possible to approximate. Having created literally thousands of Fluorescent paintings, Fluorescent sculpture boxes, and the Fluorescent "Participatory" Environment that is entered by Museum visitors, to my eye it appears that this four hundred square foot opening for the Fluorescent jungle diorama was cut into the wall of the restaurant with the bottom of the diorama being about five feet (1.5 meters) off the floor - face level if standing directly in front of the immense space - this is clear because the three dimensional thickness of the bottom wall forms an extremely bright shelf at the bottom of the Jungle scene. In the bottom left corner of this immense Fluorescent diorama is a huge bunch of Fluorescent flowers that must have been close to ten feet (3 meters) tall, and create the foreground of the three dimensional Fluorescent jungle diorama that spills out into the restaurant. From the photograph it looks as if there were some three dimensional Fluorescent jungle plants inside the front space of the diorama to create a middle-ground in front of what must have been a huge Fluorescent mural of a painted jungle scene. With the exaggerated perspective created when working with Black lights and Fluorescent paint, this entire huge jungle diorama installation could have achieved an extremely three dimensional tromp l'oeil effect within a mere space of only a three foot (1 meter) empty area between the front facure wall and the back flat Fluorescent mural. This would also have allowed enough space in the 'pit' behind the front facure wall in which several large and extremely powerful 250 watt "Conti-Glo" 'Model 70' Portable Black Light units could have been concealed. It must have been a staggering installation. The photograph of this "Clifton's Cafeteria" in Los Angeles is also precious because it shows that the amount of light coming off of the huge Fluorescent mural jungle installation was clearly enough light to make the dining tables and chairs visible in the photograph, thus there would have been clearly enough light for the diners to eat their meals only by the emitted Fluorescent light coming off of the Fluorescent mural itself. Inside the restaurant's dining area, left and right of the dining tables and chairs are also two very tall and very vivid three dimensional palm trees. These two Fluorescent palm trees seen in the photograph look to be also a tremendous size, about five yards (meters) tall, and so highly Fluorescent that they nearly appear to be made out of Neon lighting. Unfortunately in existence fifteen years before my birth, I dream about seeing one time just a Color photograph of such a magnificent Fluorescent installation like this from all those years ago.   Since the first commercial Color film was manufactured in 1907 by the Lumiere Brothers in France, which was called the "Autochrome plate," and then the first multilayered Color film, the famous "Kodak" "Kodachrome" was introduced as Color slide film in 1936, which was widely available and was the first Color film that became commercially successful, during the era of these photographs printed in the "Black Light Beacon," such as "Freddie's Paradise Cafe," "Chins Golden Dragon," and the "General Motors Corporation" Fluorescent Black Light Corporate Dinner, it is at least possible that there could have been Color photographs originally taken, and that these Color photographs from seventy years ago are still in existence somewhere.   In "Fluorescent Light and It's Applications" of 1941 by Dake and DeMent it is written that in 1939 C.W. Jarrett made accurate Color photographs of a display of Fluorescent minerals using the new Kodachrome film, a pair of Wratten 2-E Ultraviolet Barrier Filters, and exposure times between five and fifteen minutes. For early examples of the general quality of Color photographs of Fluorescence, in the rare 1956 soft cover book "Rocks and Minerals - Radioactive and fluorescent minerals Ores and metals, gems, and meteorites, etc." by Richard M. Pearl there are fifteen photographs of Fluorescent minerals printed on the front and back covers, as well as in a glossy section of the book. In all fairness, the quality of the photographs reproduced in the book are mediocre at best. It is hard to determine if the fault is in the original photographs or in the Color printing of the book, or both, but most of the Color photographs are washed out and don't convey the true vivid experience of the brilliant Colors of Fluorescent minerals under Ultraviolet lamps.   Only a few of the fifteen Color photographs are correct exposures and have the saturated Colors of Fluorescent minerals, including a nice shot of a large Franklin, New Jersey Red Calcite, Green Willemite, and non-Fluorescent Black Franklinite bolder next to a carved sphere of the same minerals. This photograph is printed on the front cover of the book and also in the Color photograph section inside the book, and it is apparent that the quality of the paper stock used in the inside Color section of the book was very inferior to the Cover stock, because the Color photograph of the Franklin minerals is much more defined, and printed with more saturated Colors on the cover than in the inside section. All the fifteen Color photographs are credited to "Ultra-Violet Products, Inc.," the company owned by Thomas S. Warren, who at that time was supposedly the owner of the largest collection of Franklin, New Jersey Fluorescent minerals in the world. Mr. Warren's collection is partially visible in the last Color photograph in Richard M. Pearl's book, and it shows both the scope and the size of this collection. What is very helpful in this early book is the fact that there are three different photographs of Fluorescent minerals also taken in ordinary White light to demonstrate the unbelievable difference, as these Colorful rocks reveal their plain Grey shades.

At the top of this page in this 1942 "Black Light Beacon" is an article of the invention of a new product that has continued to fascinate people up until the present day in the Twenty-first century (how rare is that!) Something that has become very popular again in children's museums around America in the last ten or twenty years is an installation known as a "Glow Wall" or "Glowing Silhouette Wall," also known by kids as a "Shadow Wall" or just a "Silhouette Wall." This is simply an entire Phosphorescent Green wall in front of which kids stand, then a White light flashes (or a Black light if the installation is really good), and when the child moves away from the wall and they see their Black silhouette against a full glowing Green wall, which will surely provide infinite infantile amusement to endless museum visitors for decades to come. It is such a popular phenomenon that in the digital 2009 Spring Newsletter of a large company that I buy Phosphorescent pigments from, "Glow, Inc.," an entire reportage was published about the present "Glow Wall" popularity and the new "Glow Wall" Phosphorescent paint being manufactured by "Glow, Inc." to resist finger prints and other damaged to the paint caused by children touching it all the time(!) In "Fluorescent Chemicals and Their Applications" by Jack DeMent and H.C. Dake from 1942 there is a photograph of a "Glow Wall" from seventy years ago, which was then simply referred to as a "Phosphorescent Screen." The Black and White photo shows a man standing up shaking hands with his own full body Phosphorescent image on a wall sized Phosphorescent screen, and is credited to "General Electric Research Laboratories." As usual in 1942, this new product was not designed or manufactured for the creation of "Glow Walls," or with the amusement of children in mind, but for the very serious opposite matter of the Second world war. The article in the "Black Light Beacon" describes a horrific scene of an entire city being in a total 'Blackout' during the wartime, and offers a safe solution for people to be able to see something around themselves in this total 'Blackout' situation using the new "Conti-Glo" Phosphorescent 'P-10' sheets of plastic. Designed for emergency use in a total 'Blackout' wartime nightmare, this flexible Phosphorescent 'P-10' from "Conti-Glo" came in rolls and was sold by the yard (meter). Described as having an off-White Color in the daylight, this Phosphorescent plastic was also sold in sheets and was manufactured with a fabric base to resist damage and with the ability to cut this Phosphorescent sheeting into any size or symbol that was needed. The article closes also with very clear wartime intentions for this 'P-10' Phosphorescent plastic product with "Conti-Glo" offering a new brochure for use of their new product to see during wartime 'Blackouts,' and provides a sample of this 'P-10' with the brochure. The last paragraph of this article illustrates just how important the use of Black lights with Fluorescent and Phosphorescent products manufactured by "Conti-Glo" were during the Second world war, offering another separate publication of "Black Light Beacon" printed exclusively as defense issues, and available only upon request from a military company and only upon proof of the requesting customer's official military defense identification. What a difference from "Glow Walls!"

On a much lighter side, the two remaining small articles on this page of the "Black Light Beacon" are about the subject of new uses for Black lights and Fluorescent Colors: Criminology and Juggling (not together). The first article is about a Sorority club in a Columbus, Ohio college in which all the girls were having money stolen from their rooms. The Columbus, Ohio police were called and they contacted the Cleveland, Ohio police who had been using Black light and Fluorescent criminology technology already for some years at that point. The Cleveland police marked a dollar bill with "Conti-Glo" Fluorescent Invisible Green Powder and after the dollar bill disappeared, the Police inspected all the girl's closets until one girl's closet full of clothes was found to contain streaks of Fluorescent Green under the Black light.

The remaining article about Fluorescent Juggling is interesting because of some of the facts it reveals, such as the ready-use of "Conti-Glo" Fluorescent Lacquer Enamel Paints for spraying, indicating that this paint might have also been available in spray cans, like suspected in the photograph of Frank Lackner, the Artist who painted the huge Fluorescent murals in the "Alameda Theatre" in San Antonio, Texas in 1948. This article starts - in 1942 - stating that Black light and Fluorescent Colors are 'not new' for their use in the field of entertainment, but the Hollywood distributor of "Conti-Glo" products, "Keese Engineering Company" run by the Fluorescent pioneer Mr. Joseph Shannon, recently helped in a new application of Black lights and Fluorescent paint in entertainment: Juggling. The small article explains that a juggler from the circus came to "Keese Engineering Company" and 'sprayed' all his juggling equipment with "Conti-Glo" Fluorescent Lacquer Enamel Paints, and when the juggler performed all the White lights were turned off, creating an effect of the juggler's act under Black lights that was breath taking.

On the following page of this "Black Light Beacon" is another cheerful article about living during wartime in a city experiencing a state of 'Blackout.' The reportage is about the innovative idea they had at the Fairmount Hotel in San Francisco during this 1941-1942 Second world war period. Not to stop hotel visitors from going into the swimming pool of the Fairmount Hotel at night during 'Blackout,' the hotel installed large Black light units around the swimming pool, and all the visitors in the pool wore Fluorescent caps, gloves, and socks, so while swimming in total 'Blackout' the swimmers could be easily seen by lifeguards around the hotel pool, which also illuminated the area of the swimming pool itself through the light created by their specialized Fluorescent swimming accessories.

Another small article about the use of Black light and Fluorescence for Criminology follows on this page, but this time it was concerned not with paper money, but with coins. The story about antique dimes disappearing form the Philadelphia Mint is told in a paragraph, and the thief was caught when Fluorescent Dimes began appearing in the area where an employee of the Philadelphia Mint lived. This was done by a special formulated Fluorescent medium to be used specifically on metal, an example of which I have in the Museum collection from around the same general time period of the 1940s or 1950s, which is an entire Criminology Kit for Police use made by "Fargo International." This antique Fluorescent Criminology Kit is in a double sided box complete with a portable Black light, a fountain pen and different sized application brushes, a spray can of Fluorescent Marker to be applied to floor surfaces, and six bottles of different Fluorescent Tracers. Five of the bottles contain Invisible Fluorescent Tracing Powders, and one of the jars contains Invisible Fluorescent Tracing Gel to be used specifically to mark metallic objects, including coins, with an Invisible Fluorescent tracer making them immediately identifiable when inspected under a Black light, just like in this reportage of antique metallic dimes disappearing from the Philadelphia Mint.

The large article on this page of the "Black Light Beacon" included a photograph of another nearly impossible-to-believe use of Black light and Fluorescent paint. A "Conti-Glo" dealer of Dallas, Texas named the Roy C. Company finally achieved what the Switzer Brothers tried to do almost ten years before, at the very beginning of their careers in the mid-1930s: painting a brand new car in a showroom with Fluorescent paint and displaying it under Black lights. The car was a brand new Dodge of the Alexander Motor Company in Dallas, and although the photograph showing the completely painted highly Fluorescent 1942 Dodge reveals that the Fluorescent effect achieved under Black lights was spectacular, the car itself is an image that is so incongruous with the idea of "Day-Glo" paint and Black lights, that it is impossible to fit together with today's notion of the phenomenon of Fluorescence. The image is as hard to believe as the suggestion "Use the Black Light for: CHURCH GROUPS" on that box of 1950s Invisible Fluorescent Chalks! Most of the other photographs accompanying the other articles in these three rare issues of the "Black Light Beacon" from 1941 and 1942 are all images of Fluorescent displays

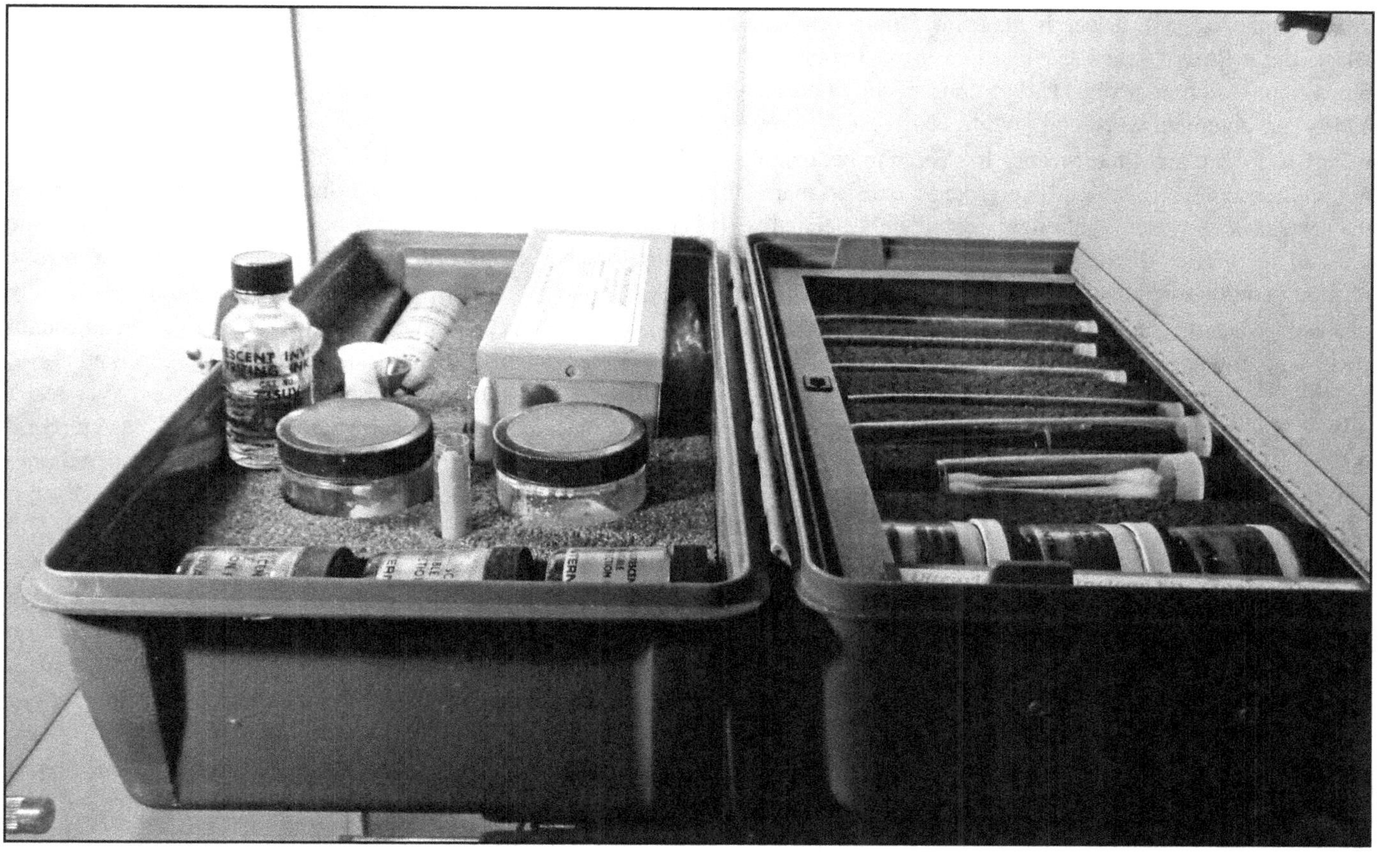

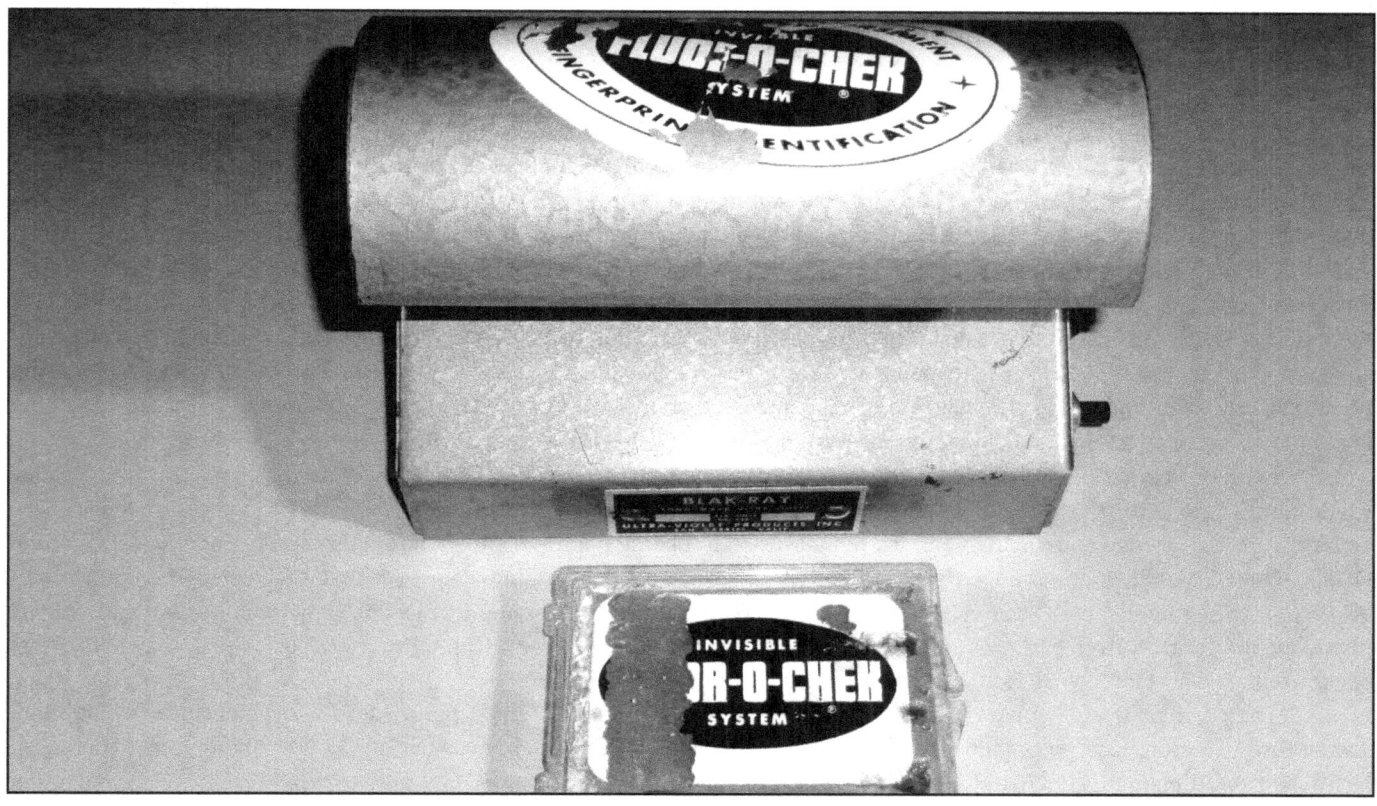

1940s-1950s "Ultraviolet Criminology Kit," "Fargo International," New Oxford, Pennsylvania

1940s Invisible Fluorescent Fingerprinting Ultraviolet Unit and Ink Pad, "FLUOR-O-CHEK Invisible System" "Product Endorsement Fingerprinting Identification," "Blak-Ray Long Wave Ultra-Violet," "Ultra-Violet Products, Inc." California

or performances under Black lights using Fluorescent Colors, such as the Ice Skating Show, the "General Motors Corporation" Black Light Press Dinner, the interiors of restaurants with Fluorescent paintings on the walls under Black lights, and other photographs of similar objects, but none of the photographs is as 'dated' as this photograph of a natty old Al Capone-styled 1940s car, complete with total 'White walls' on the tires. The car is just the opposite of what the general public's notion of what Black light and Fluorescence has come to be, namely a 'Cool' space-age design - the beginning of a New Age and a new era with designs, ideals, and Fluorescent Colors to match the high aspiration of those charged times. But, this photograph of the 1942 Dodge under Black lights completely painted with Fluorescent Colors is something nearly inconceivable. 'All the Kings Horses and All the King's Men could never put them back together again' - this is the broadened effect behind the phenomenon that is the subtitle of this book: "FLUOROPHOBIA - the Social Stigma." Stigmatizing something so indelibly that even when a person has the reasoning and benefit of knowledge that such an era had existed at all, even this person cannot fuse together this gained knowledge with such unbelievable photographs of images from almost seventy years ago. Having had a brilliant "Buccaneer Red" 1977 "Trans-Am" with a huge eagle on it's hood custom made for me when I was twenty years old, and having still today, over thirty years later taste for car design in general, especially of this 1942 Dodge monster is nearly is complete with antique split front in one full piece yet), wheel hubs extended first cars with the wheels and car body chrome to sink a Battleship, and finally as 'cool' today in the Twenty-first century completely "Day-Glo" painted World war 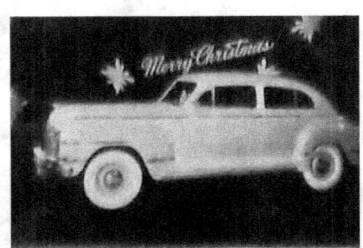 on the other side of the world, a sculptural Art cars like Lamborghini, the photograph painful! This old miserable clunker of a car windows (they couldn't make a windshield off the side of the car (a remnant from the being separate), 'wing-windows,' enough complete 'White wall' tires that look about as "Spats!" If the reader could imagine a two battleship under Black lights, or Franklin Delano Roosevelt, in his wheelchair, dressed in completely Fluorescent clothing and turning slowly on a rotating pedestal under massive Black lights with his signatory pipe in his mouth(!), then this same reader could probably imagine this grotesque photograph of the 1942 Fluorescent Dodge under Black lights!

The details of this 1942 Fluorescent Dodge display written in the article are fascinating because, one more time, they reveal the careful design, planning, and final execution of such a project from the middle of the Second world war era. The new Dodge 'automobile' was sprayed twice with "Conti-Glo" Invisible Green Watercolor, which the reader is informed can be completely removed with nothing more than warm water. The Red details of the car were first painted with White Watercolor, then a layer of 'Neon Red' "Conti-Glo" Fluorescent Lacquer Enamel was applied over the White watercolor, and finally all the chrome of the Dodge was painted with invisible transparent Blue lacquer, so essentially this new expensive Dodge 'automobile' could be returned to it's original, for sure non-Fluorescent Colors, and be sold after the display was finished. Under the Black lights it must have been an incredible combination of a completely Fluorescent Green car with complementary Red Fluorescent trim together with Fluorescent Blue highlights of chrome complete from the front to the back of the car. It doesn't mention how the 'snazzy' complete 'White walls' of the tires were coated with Fluorescent Color, but we can assume it was with White Fluorescent paint. If so this would have been a very timely Fluorescent 'Red, White, and Blue' - and Green - Dodge (sounds like the 1960s Broadway play "Hair.") As usual, again in the 1940s, the Black lights used to activate the Fluorescent Dodge display were nothing less than intensive. It is told in the article that there was a powerful 250 watt "Conti-Glo" 'Model 70' Potable Black Light mounted directly in front of the Fluorescent Dodge, with two 'Model 91' 100 watt Portable Black Light units, one on each side of the Dodge, creating what must have been an incredibly vivid Fluorescent car under 450 watts of Black lights! The design of this Fluorescent Dodge showroom display was also exceptional, having timers and 'flashers' on the normal White lights of the automobile showroom, so they would be on for fifteen seconds, then they would turn off for forty-five seconds displaying the spectacular Black light effect to be seen on this Fluorescent Dodge. The entire Fluorescent Dodge under massive Black lights was on a rotating platform, slowly turning in the automobile showroom in Dallas, with Black velvet draping totally covering the background of the car (and also blocking out any showroom's 'spill' of White lights from behind the Black velvet drapery). To complete the 1942 Fluorescent Dodge showroom display under Black lights, on the Black velvet background "Merry Christmas" and stylized Fluorescent flowers (also looking like stars) were painted with "Conti-Glo" 'Neon Red' Fluorescent Lacquer Enamel Paint.

The last remaining small article on this page of the January, 1942 "Black Light Beacon" documents the beginning of another use of Fluorescent paint that is as well known today as Fluorescent Highway Safety Cones: Fluorescent coating of Instrument Panel components, like the Fluorescent end of the speedometer pointer in your car's dashboard, for example. In 1942 "Westinghouse Electric and Manufacturing Company" began to use "Conti-Glo" Fluorescent paint to coat the indicators on dials of instrument panels, and this continues on the indicators of instrument panels of automobiles, military and civilian aircraft, and almost every type of instrument panel made since that time and up until the present moment. The article informs the reader that the Fluorescent coatings on these components of instrument panels by "Westinghouse" were to the standards of the U.S. Air Force. These Fluorescent instrument panel indicators were designed specifically for the purpose, and resisted fading, moisture, heat, and scratching. The article informs us that the details of numbers or symbols coated with Fluorescent paint makes them stand out very sharp and extremely bright. This article closes with a 1940s-1950s nightmare, relating the facts to the reader that the machine application of this paint on instrument panels was much more efficient than painting the instrument panels by 'Hand' with 'Radio-Active' paints! This nightmare scenario was another nail-in-the-proverbial-coffin for Black lights and Fluorescence: "Radium Paint" used, most famously, on watch dials and numbers in the early part of the Twentieth century, up until all of the women employees painting these watches with Radium paint, without gloves or knowledge of Radium's Radioactive danger, not to mention putting the tip of the Radium paint coated brush in their mouths to sharpen the point, all these women began to die! It is now documented that the greatest percentage of workers fatality of any employment known were these poor uniformed women that painted watch dials with Radium paint. Was about as good an idea as "Actinotherapy." More on the "Radium Girls" when discussing Marie Curie and the "First Luminous Dancer" Loie Fuller.

The back cover of this "Black Light Beacon" is a full page advertisement with four photographs of one of the Switzer Brother's inventions commissioned for the U.S. military for use during the Second world war: Fluorescent Satin. The article and photographs do not center around the military's use of this product, but the 'civilian' use of Fluorescent satin for stage performances. The four photographs at the top of the page are of a female dancer dressed up in full 1940s regalia, complete with the oversized jewelry and large feathers coming out of her hair, giving the general impression of Greta Garbo, or even Marlene Dietrich. The four photographs are numbered and a full caption explains each of the photos. The first photo shows the female dancer Francita pose-dancing in the full 1940s stage costume made with "Conti-Glo" Fluorescent satin in the White light, and then in the second photo the lights are turned off and the full Fluorescent effects of this satin is displayed on another female dancer who is this time sitting in a totally Fluorescent dinner gown, made complete with a large Fluorescent bracelet and even larger Fluorescent flower in her hair. The third photo is of Niki Lou Norman, a female dancer spinning in a very shinny Fluorescent satin gown that looks as ornate as a wedding gown in the Black light, and in her hair is also a Fluorescent flower. The last photograph is of a female drum majorette in a Fluorescent costume that is so vivid that no other features, including her face, can even dimly be made out in the photo. The Fluorescent boots, dress, top, wrist bands, majorette hat, and of course the spinning baton, are all vivid in this photograph. Photographs one and three are combination photos, utilizing the Black light and also some White light, creating an image in which features like the dancer's faces can also be seen. The second and fourth photos are just in the Black light, because outside of the Fluorescent features of the two dancer's costumes, no details can be even dimly seen, such as the two dancer's faces or arms.

The six paragraphs of text accompanying these four photographs of female dancers wearing different Fluorescent satin stage costumes begin with suggestions for uses of this new Fluorescent satin, including dinner gowns, stage costumes, drapes, or for use in Fluorescent displays. This "Conti-Glo" Fluorescent satin is described as beautiful in both the White light, having Daylight Fluorescence (meaning the Colors were similar to what everyone knows today as being vivid in either the White light or the Black light) and then of course when the lights were turned off and only the Black lights were on these Fluorescent satins, they were extremely brilliant. The suggestion is also written in the text for cutting out symbols, like of course in 1942 'stars and stripes,' but also signs or flowers, and then adhering them to other Fluorescent satin or non-Fluorescent material to create spectacular effects under a Black light suitable for decorations or clothing design. These vivid Fluorescent satins that the Switzer Brothers had invented and were first used by the U.S. military for 'Signal Panels' and other high-visibility safety equipment, were made in seven different Fluorescent Colors in 1942. Again, some of the Fluorescent Color's names are familiar to "Day-Glo" paint users over seventy years later, but a few of the names were true World war two names, like 'Flag' Red and 'Flag' Blue obviously. Still on the "Day-Glo" website can be found the Fluorescent Colors sold as 'Saturn' Green, 'Arc' Yellow, and 'Neon' Red, identical to the names given to "Conti-Glo" Fluorescent satins presented in this article, and also their full line of Fluorescent paints in 1942 as well. The other two Colors this Fluorescent satin was sold in were the Blue and White Invisible Colors, being only vividly Colored under Black lights, and in the daylight gowns made with either of these two invisible White or Blue satins would appear as normal White dinner gowns.

The text also states that these Fluorescent satins were the brightest of all the "Conti-Glo" Fluorescent product line, even brighter than their Fluorescent paint! The quality of these Fluorescent satins is next compared to 'old fashioned' Fluorescent materials made in the 'past' (five years or so, only). It is explained that this 'old fashioned' Fluorescent material was simply painted with Fluorescent Colors and then dried stiff, not suitable for making into stage costumes or clothing like the new generation of these "Conti-Glo" Fluorescent satins which were very soft and unchanged from traditional luxurious non-Fluorescent satins. The perspective customer is also informed that these Fluorescent satins can be dry cleaned many times and are also resistant to fading in the sunlight. These seven Colors of "Conti-Glo" Fluorescent satins were sold by the yard for $3.95 (ten yards would have cost more than a full ounce of Gold) and were slightly wider than a yard at thirty-nine inches.

Amazingly, the very day I began to write this description of the Fluorescent satin dancer's costumes article in the "Black Light Beacon" from 1942, a beautiful girl named Erika had travelled all the way from Italy to Amsterdam to visit "Electric Ladyland - the First Museum of Fluorescent Art" after writing her college thesis on the phenomenon of Fluorescence and having included many photographs in her thesis from the Museum's website in a portion of her thesis about the Museum. In her thesis she has included a large section on Fluorescent Dance and Fluorescent Stage performance, such as in the famous "Black Light Theatre" in Prague that has been performing for the last thirty years, and a photograph of the very first Luminescent Dancer Loie Fuller.

Marie Louise Fuller was born in the American state of Illinois in 1862 and began her very early career as a child actress, later as a "Skirt Dancer" in burlesque, vaudeville, and even circus shows. Fuller became first well known in America with her "Serpentine Dance" in 1891, but she felt that her American audience still thought of her as an actress, and therefore had not as much respect for her as an innovative dancer creating a new Art form as Fuller expected. The reception that Fuller got in Paris on her first European tour proved to her that in Paris she could be respected as a modern dancer without any memories or preconceptions of her former career as an actress. Loie Fuller became famous in Paris almost immediately and was a regular performer at the Paris "Folies Bergère" with her image printed many times on the famous "Folies Bergère" posters. These historic posters show Loie Fuller performing her dance creation of swirling many yards of material into the air with the combination of different luminous effects which she was the inventor of, including dancing on a glass stage with a multitude of spotlights concealed in the stage floor designed and patented by Fuller. For these extravagant performances on the glass stage floor, with a carpet of spotlights concealed underneath which illuminated her swirling material from below, Loie Fuller had up to thirty electricians working the large number of lights below the glass stage. Loie Fuller had already begun this new modern dance performance during her early vaudeville years in America, and had also patented the mechanical equipment for the projection of light upon her material dance costumes. In the early 1890s Fuller had found something that would change her life - and the dance form - for ever. In a costume box Fuller found a very thin silk skirt that was nearly translucent and wore it for a dance performance in which she began moving the translucent silk material around herself. The audience was captivated and began to call out what they thought she was representing such as a Butterfly, Orchid, and Spirit. The acts that she perfected and became world famous for in Paris represented already many years of work for Fuller, who had started this new dance Art performance by twirling yards of the material her stage costumes were made of into the air above her head and moving these swirling masses of spot lit material with long hand 'wands' made of aluminum or bamboo already in America during her vaudeville performances. During these famous unique dances, Loie Fuller herself remained nearly motionless, but she was twirling yards of material with her hand wands, creating the impressions of performing butterflies or flowers on the stage. These stage performances involved the diligent work of dozens of electricians who were operating the many floor mounted spotlights designed and patented by Fuller, which were covered with unique Colored glass filters that were also invented by Fuller using her secret chemical dyes. The very famous Loie Fuller performance of "Fire Dance" combined all of her early inventions, including a glass stage and a glass platform for her to perform on, which was lit from below by spotlights that were covered with Rose and Vermillion Colored filters, creating the effect of Loie Fuller in her swirling dress appearing to be a dancing flame of more than ten feet (3.2 meters) tall.

For her "Skirt Dance," Fuller had invented, designed, and even patented the new elements of her costume designs, including hand wands made of fabric, glass stage floors, and stage mirrors. She kept the chemical dyes she developed for creating the Colored glass filters she used on her stage spotlights a professional top secret. Loie Fuller's huge stage dresses were all a plain White silk, intentionally, so the many Colors of her designed stage lighting could play on the plain palette of her White costume, creating the effect of swirling light and Colors. Through performances such as these, Loie Fuller became associated with the Art Nouveau and Symbolist Art movements in Paris, and she knew many famous Artists and scientists at that time, such as Toulouse Lautrec who had painted her portrait at least twice, the pioneering movie makers Auguste and Louis Lumière who had filmed her "Serpentine Dance" in 1896, Auguste Rodin, Jules Cheret, Stephane Marllarme who had renamed her "Loie" in Paris, and perhaps most importantly Marie Curie and her husband Pierre, who would give Loie Fuller ideas of using the Curie's discovery of the new magic light-emitting element "Radium" to paint her costumes with and create an unprecedented stage effect for her dances.

The pure element Radium was discovered by Pierre and Marie Curie in 1898 after years of work which was begun by Marie Curie through studying the work of Henri Becquerel's discovery of some sort of radiation coming out of Uranium salts. For her Doctoral thesis Marie decided to work with these 'Uranium Rays'. After meeting and marrying Pierre Curie, he abandoned his research on crystals and joined Marie in her work. First they isolated a part of the Uranium mineral Pitchblende that was about four-hundred times as powerful as Uranium itself and they named it Polonium in honor of Marie Curie's birthplace Poland. The physical work of reducing by hand tons of Pitchblende into it's constituent forms was monumental, and resulted in the production of a "Residue" of Uranium, which Loie Fuller later wrote looked like a reddish lumpy powder, and then further reducing this Uranium "Residue" through many chemical processes to arrive at the pure state of the element Radium. After years of work Marie Curie had reduced by hand eight tons of Pitchblende to obtain one single 'decigram' (a tenth of a gram, only) of an element they discovered that was even more radioactive than Polonium: "Radium." In December, 1898 Marie and Pierre Curie announced the discovery of the new element Radium and became celebrities in a very short time because of this. For many years Radium became the new Miracle discovery - the Future - and was used for products and in ways that would make a person today *squeal!*

After the news about the discovery of Radium spread to all parts of society and became well known, Loie Fuller wrote to Marie Curie and asked her if she could get some Radium to create a unique dance costume that Fuller envisioned as having Blue glowing Radium-painted Butterfly wings which she would fly away with on stage. Marie Curie refused to give Radium to Loie Fuller and warned her that it was not meant to be used for such applications as clothing worn on the body because of the unknown properties of the element. Not being one to take no for an answer, Loie Fuller went in person to the Curie's house on the Boulevard Kellermann in Paris and gave them a private dance performance, in which she lit her body and dress with electric spotlights covered with Blue filters made of cellophane to create an example for the Curies of what a Radium dance costume could look like. Loie Fuller and her lighting team spent one day preparing the Dining room of the Curies for the Dance performance, and that night the Curies invited a few friends over and had a private Loie Fuller performance. She became friends with Marie and Pierre Curie, introduced them to famous Artists including Rodin, and was a friend as well with their daughter Irène later. Through this friendship Loie Fuller finally obtained a Radium substance from Marie Curie. Loie Fuller began experimenting with this Radium substance and Phosphorescent salts in her Latin Quarter laboratory in Paris, and during her most famous experiment to make Radium paint for applying to her dance costumes, in her laboratory full of assistants the experiment exploded! Loie Fuller wrote that after the explosion in her laboratory which could have killed her and her assistants, all of them were completely startled and looked around at each other only to discover each and every one of them had all of their eyelashes and eyebrows completely burned off! Not only were their eyelashes, eyebrows, and clothing destroyed, but the Phosphorescent stage dress Loie Fuller was making the experiment on had 'disappeared in smoke!' Loie Fuller later wrote of the explosion in her laboratory, saying that it had made a 'great sensation' in the surrounding neighborhood of her laboratory (!) causing her Parisian neighbors to call her a 'Witch!' The details of Loie Fuller's laboratory explosion are given in "Electric Salome: Loie Fuller's Performance of Modernism" by Garelick, where it is explained that in Loie Fuller's unpublished notebooks she wrote "My Laboratory" in which Fuller herself detailed the explosion. Loie Fuller wrote that after she met Thomas Edison who had stopped experimenting with Phosphorescent 'salts' because of the health risks to his employees, she continued working with these dangerous substances in her experiments trying to invent Radium paint for her dance costumes. Loie Fuller describes "her house" blowing up in Paris while experimenting with burning magnesium in an attempt to "illuminate" sulphur and calcium 'salts.' These exploding experiments on the way to inventing Radium paint not only lost Fuller some hair and eyebrows, but not surprisingly also lost her the insurance policy on her house in Paris as well! In "Electric Salome" Loie Fuller's laboratory assistants who also were part of her exploding experiments and singed eyebrows are described as being her young dance students, several of whom years later would develop cancer after their work with Fuller on Radium. Even after Loie Fuller died in 1928, Gabrielle Bloch who was her companion, still experimented with these dangerous luminous 'salts' and went on to produce in Paris the "Ballets in Black Light." To give an idea of the intensity and the degree of damage that was done by this explosion of Radium and Phosphorescent salts in Loie Fuller's laboratory, Fuller later recalled that all of her hair never even grew back again after the Phosphorescent radioactive explosion! To further give an idea of the character of this unique and definitively eccentric woman Loie Fuller, she added to the story of her hair never completely having grown back after the Phosphorescent explosion in her laboratory, that in fact she 'did not care'! Finally, after living through explosions in the face and permanent loss of hair, Loie Fuller invented Radium Paint in 1904 from Pitchblende residue and created her famous "Danse du Radium" - "Radium Dance!" Other luminous performances of Loie Fuller that must have been magnificent followed, and were entitled "Danse ultraviolette" and "Danse phosphorescente."

The first self-luminous stage dress Loie Fuller made with the use of Marie and Pierre Curie's newly discovered "Radium" caused nothing less than a rage and a fashion in itself during that time period. The stage costumes that Loie Fuller created with the self-luminous Radium paint she invented must have been really spectacular. The intensity of Radium is nearly unimaginable for most people - this stuff is not bright like a "Glow Stick," but close to the brilliance of a Welder's torch or burning Magnesium. In June, 1903, in the London Natural History Museum the first Fluorescent mineral demonstration in history was held in which a single show operator invited one viewer at a time into a dark booth to behold the unforeseen wonders of Radium and Fluorescent minerals. The show was such a phenomenon, that people waited in line *for days* to see a tiny gram of Radium and a few pieces of rocks that gave off their own Colors, keeping in mind that this occurred in London, where the weather is not exactly like Hawaii. King George the Fifth of England attended the historic exhibition and was given a demonstration in which five huge thick metal British Pound coins were stacked together, and through all five of these obviously opaque coins the light from one gram of Radium could be seen! There is a Black and White photograph of a Loie Fuller dancer kneeling in a Radium dance costume which gives a little idea of the intensity of light that must have been emitted from her Radium dresses. The Radium dance dress is so extremely bright that about three-quarters of the dress is completely overexposed and totally White in the photo. In her right hand she is holding something that is so incredibly bright that you can't even make out the shape of the object - it's just like a ball of pure light. The amount of light coming out of the Radium stage costume is enough to light her face for the photograph and to overexpose most of the Radium dress to such a degree that in the photo it appears as plain White light.

Even though Loie Fuller had patented many of her inventions she used for her stage performances, one hundred years ago these laws were rarely followed and her famous act was copied very quickly. Already in 1904, the same year that Loie Fuller invented her Radium paint and performed her self-luminous debut "Dance du radium," another musical opened on Broadway in New York City, across the Atlantic Ocean called "Piff, Paff, Pouf," in which a "Radium Dance" was performed by dancing girls dressed in luminous stage outfits jumping a luminous jump-rope. This was followed shortly by the first use of luminescent stage costumes under the new invention of the "Blacklight" in the first "Skeleton Ballet" on stage for the first of Florenz Ziegfeld's "Ziegfeld's Folies" in 1907 in the Warfield Theatre in San Francisco.

As an example of how extraordinary and inspiring Loie Fuller's performances were, one of the famous dancers who helped form the school of modern dance in the Twentieth century was Isadora Duncan, who not only saw Loie Fuller perform in Paris, but was also trained by her as well. In her memoirs Isadora Duncan wrote of Loie Fuller's dance performance, telling of how Loie Fuller turned into multi-Colored shinning Orchids, to shimmering underwater Sea Flowers, and then to a spiral Lily before their very eyes on the stage. Duncan compared Loie Fuller's performance to the magic of Merlin, calling her dance a sorcery of flowing forms. The impact and the influence that Loie Fuller had on the modern dance form through the inspirational performances beheld by dancers such as Isadora Duncan and Ruth St. Denis is well documented.

The documentation by the New York Times in a small article published on February 5, 1911 is a perfect example of both how famous Loie Fuller was at that time, and of the magnificent brilliance the Radium stage dress that Loie Fuller made and performed in for her historic dances had. The headline of the article is 'The New Luminous Dance,' and underneath the headline in bold letters is written 'The Dancer Loie Fuller Invented a New Dress that Lights Up a Whole Theatre.' The article was written on January 28, 1911 and starts with the announcement that the Dancer Loie Fuller invented the "Luminous Dance," and that she was at that time in London giving lectures on the newly discovered element "Radium," as well as giving demonstrations on the luminous dress she made through her experiments with Radium and Phosphorescent salts. The article amazingly states that Loie Fuller's Luminous Radium Dress on stage emitted enough light for anybody in the audience to read a newspaper by without straining their eyes at all. The reporter states that the light emitted from Loie Fuller's Radium Dress was in fact enough to light up an entire Theatre! The article explains that the Color of the light emitted from the Radium dress was first a dark Violet, then it turned to Blue, and finally becomes a brilliant White light. Loie Fuller also curiously states in the article that she thought that Radium could not be used on stage for scenery or backdrops, and also gives credit to the scientist she studied Radium with M. Janin, as well as to her friend Madame Curie who discovered Radium with her husband Pierre in 1898. The article ends informing the reader that Loie Fuller had a laboratory in the Latin Quarter of Paris for doing research on Radium and Phosphorescent salts, in which she invented the Radium paint for her dresses.

The lecture on Radium that Loie Fuller was giving in London in 1911 which was reported on in this previously presented article from The New York Times is still existing in a form. For the lecture Loie Fuller wrote twenty-nine pages of script that is still preserved today. Some of the statements and ideals and ideas that Loie Fuller presented on the then 'Wonder Substance' Radium in 1911, today are sometimes amusing, and sometimes come close to 'hair-raising.' Loie Fuller began the twenty-nine pages of notes for the Radium lecture with statements about science being the uncovering of nature's facts, and how supernatural things are all eventually proved to be just natural events, and this true Twentieth century woman even claims the end of superstition. She believed the most supernatural thing during that time to be the new Telegraph without wires, in fact. The main portion of the lecture was on the element Radium itself, and Fuller begins by listing the names for Radium in 1911 as being 'Radioactive Matter, Earth Salts, Illuminate Crystals, or Reduced Pitch Blend.' The lecture continued with a full description of the incredible process that Marie and Pierre Curie used to discover Radium in the Pitchblende. Loie Fuller describes the reduced residue of Pitchblende looking like a lumpy Reddish powder, and relates the fact that it took eight tons of hand-reduced Pitchblende to obtain less than one single gram of Radium. Fuller also explains the procedures of Marie Curie with an example of how Curie would leave a solution in a glass for Radium experiments, and the next day the glass itself had changed Color to dark Violet. Fuller next explains that in the daylight Radium looks like table salt, and her description of Radium in the dark is not exactly poetic, comparing the glowing light of the element to 'dead fish' and the Color of 'dead Phosphorescence,' what is termed today "Bioluminescence." Fuller calls the Radium marvelous and states that it is something that begins to unlock the laws of the universe. In the course of the lecture the questions are presented: where does the light of Radium come from, and where does the heat of Radium come from, and both questions are answered quite truthfully, very tellingly stating that 'nobody knew.' Loie Fuller's lecture notes continue on to call Radium a natural magic, representative of those times of "Radium Magic," and again later in the lecture asks what is Radium, with the same deadly answer 'I don't know.' Towards the end of these Radium lecture notes, Loie Fuller makes a comprehensive comparison between the 'old' energy source of "Electricity," and the 'new age' energy source "Radium." Loie Fuller's comparisons begin with the facts that Radium is a soft light without rays and that Electricity was just the opposite, then continues on to rave about the superiority of using Radium over Electricity, such as Radium is a constant steady light while Electricity was unsteady and vibrating, Radium permeated objects while Electrical lights just lit up the outside of objects, Radium is a light that never goes out and Electricity 'always' goes out, and that Radium is a light that is caused by 'nobody knows what,' while old fashioned Electricity was a light that was caused by 'everybody knows what.' Loie Fuller states that electricity was a great power but that Radium is a greater power, and that electricity is caused by the building up of something while Radium is produced by the breaking up of 'everything.' Fuller ends the comparisons with the statement that electricity must be applied to something to get it's effect, while Radium's effect happens spontaneously, and perhaps the most horrific of all her comparisons, where she states that Electrical lights are 'ruinous' to the eyes, but that Radium was just the 'reverse!' Loie Fuller concludes with her predictable opinion that Phosphorescent light was 'marvelous.'

To put these statements and the Radium lecture by Loie Fuller in a proper perspective, in 1911 the "Radium Craze" was in full swing - Radium was the "Miracle Cure" - the "Future" (sounds familiar) with everybody desperate to get a tiny bit of the new Radioactive element in any orifice of their bodies (and no orifices were excluded). It all started with newspaper articles from 1903 that proclaimed this new miracle drug Radium could do everything including the absurd claims of curing the insane, preventing dogs from getting Rabies, getting chickens to lay already hard-boiled eggs(!), and to tell the sex of unborn babies. The first Doctor to claim Radium as a "Miracle Cure" was not surprisingly a Doctor from New York City, a Dr. William J. Morton who called his new 'Miracle Cure' "Liquid Sunshine!" Between 1903 and 1904 the claims of Radium reached ridiculous levels, with newspaper articles claiming it would *"Make a Blind Girl See"* (August 24, 1903 Newark, New Jersey newspaper), that Radium was a "Substitute for Gas, Electricity, and a Positive Cure for Every Disease," and even *"Turning a Negro White"* with the Magic Rays of Radium, the "New Mystery of Science." During the "Radium Craze" there were a multitude of deadly consumer products made with the exclusive selling point of all these new products being the fact (or sometimes fallacy) that the products all contained this new "Wonder Cure" Radium! There were products that would shock the hell out of anybody today who was told about them, such as the outrageously healthy "Radium Toothpaste," and the even healthier "Radium Ice-cream," "Radium Tea," and even - what else - "Radium Health Tonics!" There were "Radium Razor Blades," "Radium Face Creme" - think about it, the women rubbed highly Radioactive, deadly Radium into their faces every day! The Timewarp Nightmare list continues with more outrageously 'healthy' products like "Radium Bath Salts," "Radium Lipstick," and even companies that outright stole the Curie's name with "Curie Hair Tonic" that was guaranteed to - of course - *'Grow Your Hair Back!'* (you probably lost more hair with this stuff than even with the Shortwave U.V. Medical Treatment Lamps made famous around the same time). Another illegal use of the Curie's name was by a doctor who called himself "Alfred Curie" and sold "Curie Tho-Radin" which was advertised by a photograph of a blond woman with this "Curie Tho-Radin" Skin Creme on, who's face is glowing in a beautiful Blue light! There was also the outrageously deadly "X-Radium Heater" that was a Pot Heater for *Food!* In the Museum collection is a photograph of this advertisement from the 1930s which includes a horrible picture of a mother with her baby in a highchair and another small child, all at the dinner table, dressed in some funky-looking 1930s clothes, and in the middle of the dinner table is the steaming pot of food that is being kept warm through the Radium that was advertised as being contained in the small metal round "X-Radium Heater" under the pot of food on the dinner table. The headline reads: "A little marvel of comfort and economy wanted in every home." The price of this "X-Radium Heater" to heat the pot of food on the dinner table was $2.50 and the product was offered with a Free Trial Offer (if you lived long enough to return it). Going to really insane measures with this "Radium Craze," men went so far as to wear a bag of Radium tied around their Testicles(!) to make them more virile, and people bought "Radium Inhalers" to breath in the deadly Radioactive element for supposedly invigorating and enriching blood. If the bag of Radium tied around men's testicles did indeed work, and they did become more virile, there was another Radium product designed for them in America: "Radium Condoms!" An original Blue and White Radium Condom package has "The Radium" written with the word "Radium" curving across the entire package, and the name of the company under the word "Radium." Now the name of the company that manufactured and sold Radioactive "Radium Condoms" couldn't have been more of a clear explanation of the eventual results of wearing these Radioactive "Radium Condoms" to the condom's consumers: "NUTEX" (no comment). Not to be left out, these Radium Condoms were sold in other countries besides the states. For Germans they got one of the most memorable of all Radium products manufactured and sold in their country: "Radium Chocolate!" For the Religious, there was "The Magic Radium Luminous Crucifix" which advertised on it's box "Shines in the Dark" - "Size 3.5 x 9.5" - "Entirely Luminous" - Retail Price $1.50, all made possible by "The Pioneer Corporation, Chicago." And - did we leave anybody out of this Radium craze - the Kids! Well up until the late 1940s and early 1950s kids in America could order the "Atomic Bomb" Ring that contained the Radioactive element that the Curies first discovered and named "Polonium," for just 15¢ and one cereal box-top of a very famous children's cereal company that still sells cereal to children today! A photo of this 'killer' ring is in "Something Out of Nothing - Marie Curie and Radium" by McClafferty, and it is sure Ugly! It looks like a little 40's Atomic Bomb on a kid's ring! School children would wear this Radioactive "Polonium" ring, go into the dark, take one end off the ring and put their eye very close to look inside the tiny Aluminum capsule the ring was composed of. With their eye close to the Radioactive source, looking inside the schoolchildren would be fascinated as they saw the splitting of "Genuine Atoms" right before their little eyes! Not only was the ring guaranteed to be "Safe" and "Harmless," but this children's "toy" was in reality an established scientific instrument named a "Spinthariscope" that was used for Radioactive detection. More details about this deadly children's ring along with a very clear full page Color photograph can be found in "The Elements - A Visual Exploration of Every Known Atom in the Universe" by Theodore Gray (2009). Unnaturally, this deadly Radioactive children's ring was sold in the U.S.A., and in 1947 a mere fifteen cents (and most probably a box-top or two) could get you a Gold Colored ring with a cheap adjustable bottom and a Gold Colored band on top of the ring which holds in place a Silver and Red "Atomic Bomb!" Again, this was not something that children had to send away to a scientific research laboratory for, but it was promoted on the box of a Breakfast cereal that they ate every morning named "Kix." It sure had the right name!

In truth, many of the products really did make you feel much better and more energetic for a very short period when initially taking these Radioactive Radium health products, because what happens is that the Radioactivity makes the body create more Red blood cells than is needed and gives the feeling of extra energy for a short initial period, but then as the body continues to produce too many Red blood cells, the body has constant fatigue and eventually may even become cancerous. One of the best of all of these Radium horror products that sold in the early 1900s was the "Revigorator," which consisted of a Radium container, looking like an old fashioned white porcelain water crock, to be filled at night with water and then drunk in the morning and all through the next day! The "Revigorator" was a jar that was made with ore that contained radioactive Radium, and it held gallons of water (eight or more liters) to be taken out of the "Revigorator" through a metal spout at the bottom of the container. The existing example I've seen has the logo on the top part of the vessel and the company name on the bottom part of the vessel next to the metal spout, both in a dark Blue. The top logo has a diagonal "REVIGORATOR" with three bolts of energy around it, and top right is "RADIUM ORE," while bottom right of the logo is "Patd. 7-16-12, (1912) trade mark." At the bottom of the "Revigorator" printed next to the metal water spout is written "The Radium Ore Revigorator Co., 260 California St., San Francisco, Cal." This "Revigorator" was not shaped like an ordinary water container, but looked more like a urinal or something. The bottom was large and round and then about a quarter of the way up from the bottom, it tapers up becoming smaller as it gets towards the top. The White porcelain look of this "Revigorator" is identical to the "Radium Water Jars" and also had a lid made of the same material. On the side of the "Revigorator" came the written instructions that are like a recipe for death: "1. Fill jar every night. 2. Use hydrant or any good water. 3. Drink freely when thirsty and upon arising and retiring, average six[!] or more glasses daily." The advertising pitch for this deadly "Revigorator" was that it was a "perpetual *health* spring in the home." The Radium-containing ore that the "Revigorator" was manufactured with would have made the drinking water that was put into it over night highly Radioactive, and would have created a deadly drinking water, as far from healthy as possible. This 'health spring' didn't come cheap either, in 1926 the "Revigorator" was $29.50 which was alot of money back then, but this didn't stop people from buying them, because there were over half a million "Revigorators" sold. There was another cheaper version of this "Revigorator" called simply a "Radium Water Jar" which was also manufactured during the 1920s and 1930s. This "Radium Water Jar" came in a few models, but all of them were sold on the point of Radium or 'Radon,' which is the Radioactive gas produced by Radium, being put into drinking water as a "Health Cure." These "Radium Water Jars" were not themselves Radioactive like the "Revigorator," so the method of making the drinking water Radioactive was that a small container of Radioactive material derived from Radium was placed into the "Radium Water Jar" and this would irradiate the drinking water over night. One of the most famous of the "Radium Water Jars" was sold as the "Curie Jar!" The famous true nightmare that is often quoted about this insane Radium health cure era is of an American millionaire named Eben Byers who had so much money and was so convinced that the Radium was the "Miracle Cure" that he drank a brand of Radium water named "Radithor" continuously for *Four Years!* Byers drank the "Radithor" Radium water every day, sometimes four bottles a day, with a total of twenty bottles a week, and in the end he died a horrible death of jaw cancer as the Radiation in the Radium caused his facial bones all to slowly disintegrate. Doctors were very much into the Radium health craze, and in the late 1920s and early 1930s there were even "Radium Banks" in several major cities of the world which rented out expensive Radium to doctors for one or two days. In "Radiation: What it is and How it effects you" by Schubert and Lapp, it is stated that one doctor had given more than 7,000 Radium injections to his patients over the course of his practice. The Radium craze continued with even totally obscure products including Radium shirt buttons, Radium plant fertilizes, Radioactive Heating pads, and Radium fishing lures.

  The element that caused this early Twentieth century rage was discovered by Madame Curie and her husband Pierre, and took many years of incredibly hard work to arrive at. On November 8, 1895, Willem Conrad Roentgen discovered a new kind of radiation he named X-rays and this discovery caused a great sensation because it was a ray that could look through solid objects. Next the French scientist Henri Becquerel, the son of Edmond Becquerel who had discovered that tiny impurities which he named "Activators" were the cause of the Fluorescence in minerals, was experimenting with Uranium salts exposed to sunlight and he accidentally placed the Uranium on a metal foil that was covering an unexposed photographic plate, discovering "Radioactivity" after seeing that invisible rays went through the metal foil and actually exposed the photographic plate itself. Henri Becquerel named the invisible radiation after himself initially, "Becquerel Radiation," but, as stated before, Marie Curie thought the radiation behaved like radio waves, so she named it what we still call it today, "Radioactivity." Madame Curie and her husband Pierre would be the two scientists that were to explore the potentials of this new Radioactivity for the rest of both their lives.

  Marie Curie was born Marie Sklodowska in 1867 in Warsaw, Poland, which was part of Russia at that time, with both parents being teachers who believed in the value of education very deeply. Both Marie and her sister wanted to attend the Sorbonne in Paris to get degrees, but neither could afford it, so they made a plan that first Marie's sister Bronya would go to Paris as Marie worked as a governess to support her, and after her graduation she would make money in Paris for Marie to come and study at the Sorbonne next. This resulted in Marie being twenty-four when she finally began to study at the Sorbonne in mathematics and physics, with her end goal being to obtain a teacher's degree and return to Warsaw. All of Marie's plans changed forever when she met Pierre Curie who was head of a laboratory at the School of Industrial Physics and Chemistry. Pierre Curie's father was a physician, who began to teach Pierre at an early age, and together with his brother Jacques, Pierre had discovered "Piezoelectricity" which is the minute amount of electricity that is produced when crystals have physical stress applied to them, such as Quartz crystals, and which has been used for years to create the energy needed for many watches, microphones, and other electrical equipment up until the present day. Pierre Curie married Marie in 1895 and in the same year presented his doctoral thesis, which included a study of the connection between magnetism and temperature, which is now known as "Curie's Law." They had a daughter in 1897, after Marie had received her teaching degree in 1896. After their daughter Irène was born, Pierre arranged for Marie to be able to do research in the school's laboratory, where she initially did research into the magnetic properties of steel. Deciding to continue her research, she began to look for a subject to do her doctoral thesis on. Henri Becquerel's discovery of Radioactivity, then called "Becquerel Radiation," had not made an impact on the scientific community, which was at that time intensely interested in Röntgen's discovery of X-rays. Becquerel made initial investigations into radioactivity, but did not continue to pursue the study of this radioactivity. Marie Curie decided that she would study the "Becquerel Radiation," or as radioactivity was also called at that time, "Uranium Rays." After only a few days of research into "Uranium Rays" Marie Curie discovered that the element "Thorium" gave the same "Uranium Rays" as Uranium, but not one of all the other known elements gave off this energy. At this early point in her career - the actual beginning of her real career - she made one of the most important discoveries of her life, being her insight to realize that the

"Uranium Rays," or radioactivity, was not caused by the arrangement of the atoms in the molecule, but by the actual interior of the atoms themselves.

Marie Curie decided next to study the ores that contain Uranium and Thorium, and with samples from Geological museums, she discovered that the ore Pitchblende contained something which caused up to five times the reaction of just Uranium itself, but was only contained in the Pitchblende in tiny amounts. Marie's research was so ground breaking that Pierre abandoned his research on crystals and joined Marie in her study of Uranium and Thorium radiation. They first isolated the parts of the Pitchblende that had the most reactions and found these parts to contain Bismuth or Barium, which Marie continued to reduce until they arrived at a substance that was three hundred times as active as Uranium itself. In July, 1898 they published a paper in which they announced the discovery of a new element, which they decided to name "Polonium" after Poland where Marie was born, and also they used the name "Radioactivity" for the first time. After several months of additional research the Curies announced to "l' Academie des Sciences" on December 26, 1898 that they had discovered a second new element that has even stronger radiation than "Polonium," and they decided to call it "Radium," which means "rays" in Latin. To be able to obtain the pure element Radium from the Pitchblende, they realized they would need literally tons of this expensive Pitchblende to reduce. The solution was to use the tons of Pitchblende that had been left in slag-heaps at the Joachimsthal Mine in Bohemia, and this was provided to Pierre and Marie Curie through the Austrian Academy of Sciences. This is where the legendary monumental work of the Curies began. To eventually obtain one-tenth of a single gram of Radium - a 'decigram' - they would have to reduce Eight Tons of Pitchblende by hand! Since they needed alot of space to reduce eight tons of Pitchblende into their newly discovered element Radium, the principle of the school where Pierre worked let them use an empty shed to do their research. For this tremendous amount of work needed to reduce the raw Pitchblende ore into Radium, on a daily basis Marie would physically pound and boil in a common acid used in bleaching, while continuously stirring, twenty kilos of Pitchblende at a time while Pierre measured the results of her labour. Marie Curie later wrote that she would be 'broken' at the end of the day after stirring a boiling brew of Pitchblende with a large iron rod that was as tall as her. Marie Curie would have to move around cast-iron pots and empty the mixture of Pitchblende into other pots to separate the precipitates. The residue of the acid boiling process was then boiled in another chemical solution while being flushed with water to cleanse metals from the residue. The further purified residue was then boiled in another chemical bath, flushed with water, and further purified with corrosive chemicals. After many months of this continuous work the Curies were left with a residue of both Radium sulfate and Barium sulfate, which she again boiled to arrive at just Radium salt. The Radium salt was further purified through a long procedure of many processes, most importantly "Fractional Crystallization" which separates impurities from the Radium salt. Marie Curie would then boil the Radium salt in distilled water, and when cooled, the solution would crystallize. It reportedly took *thousands* of steps just of "Fractional Crystallization" to finally arrive at purified Radium salt.

The shed where Pierre and Marie Curie spent years reducing and boiling Pitchblende was described by Marie Curie as a very rudimentary structure with a glass roof that let rain water in and also acted as a steamy glass house when the Sun was out. During the winter months the cold was reportedly just as hard to bear. Six degrees Centigrade (43° F.) was the temperature in the shed which Marie Curie measured on the sixth of February, 1898. There were only rough pine basic tables in the shed, and since there was no storage, the precious residue of Pitchblende that was to become pure Radium was stored openly on tables and boards, and when the Curies would enter the shed at night in the dark, Marie wrote that the residue of Pitchblende around the room would be glowing in the dark. The first time that Marie and Pierre Curie entered their shed at night they were transfixed to see that their Radium glowed in the dark. Both of them sat in the darkened shed and starred at the glowing Radium. Marie said the Radium looked like 'fairy lights' that 'enchanted' them both. One of the first scientists to realize how important was the work on Pitchblende Uranium ore the Curies were doing was Wilhelm Ostwald, and he travelled from Germany to meet them. Upon arriving in Paris and coming out to their shed to meet them, Ostwald found the Curies were not there, but he was allowed into the shed at his request. This famous German chemist wrote that when he entered the Curies' shed he thought that he could have been the victim of a practical joke, because in his description, the Curies' work shed where the new "Wonder element" Radium had recently been discovered looked like the combination of a Horse stable and a Potato shed! "Something Out of Nothing - Marie Curie and Radium" by Carla Killough McClafferty contains many rare photographs, including a photograph of the interior of this shed where the Curies discovered Radium. The shed's interior is essentially four dilapidated wooden tables and two old wooden chairs. The roof beams were exposed and one wall had a complete row of windows. In the middle of the room was one of the wooden tables that had Black fabric hung from the ceiling beams completely to the floor for blocking off light coming from the wall which had waist-high windows lined up from end to end. It looks exactly like a kind of old shed that rain water would leak into, just as the Curies reported. On one of the three tables, by the wall with windows there is the scientific measuring instrument that was invented by Pierre Curie and his brother Jacques called a "Piezoelectric Quartz Electrometer," which provided the incredibly minute measurements need for the Curies' research.

At the same time that Marie and Pierre Curie were laboriously reducing Pitchblende into residue of Pitchblende, both of them also had jobs as well. Marie had a part time job as a teacher in the "Ecole Normale Superieur de Sevres," and Pierre still worked as head of a laboratory in the same school as when he had met Marie, so the life they had together must have left very little time for activities such as sleeping. After an amount of work that is nearly unimaginable, which it took the Curies thousands of repeated procedures of pounding and boiling Pitchblende, at last they had finally reduced literally tons of Pitchblende into a tiny almost pure amount of Radium chloride - a fraction of a single gram called a decigram. To give an idea of how small the amount of Radium is in Pitchblende, Marie Curie initially estimated that Pitchblende contained only one percent of Radium, but after years of work to arrive at this tiny amount of Radium salt, she realized that radium did not constitute a mere one percent of Pitchblende, but only an amount that is hardly possible to imagine: *one-millionth* of one percent of Pitchblende! Mathematically this calculated to the amount of less than one gram of Radium in seven tons of Pitchblende. From this minute amount of Radium chloride Marie could calculate Radium's atomic weight as 225, and finally she could present her doctoral thesis on June 25, 1903. Two of the three members of the committee who would examine Marie's doctoral thesis were eminent scientists who would also go on to receive Nobel prizes, her former teacher Lippmann who would receive the Nobel prize in Physics in 1908, and Moissan who would receive the Nobel prize for Chemistry in 1906. This doctoral committee regarded the doctoral thesis of Marie Curie to be the greatest contribution to science ever to have been contained in a Doctoral thesis. To celebrate the receiving of her doctorate, a small party was given, and was attended by one of the most famous scientists at that time, Ernest Rutherford, who wanted to meet the two scientists that had discovered Radium. The story of the evening is a very good example to illustrate just how very much the phenomenon of Radium's luminescence meant to both Pierre and Marie Curie, and just how personally fascinated and enraptured they were by this glowing miracle. At the end of this warm summer evening of Marie's party, Pierre Curie led everyone, including Rutherford, into the garden to sit in the dark, and then he pulled a tiny tube out of a pocket of his vest that contained a minute amount of Radium salt solution, and in the darkness of the garden the small group of famous scientists starred in rapt amazement as the tiny tube started to glow with it's own light! Rutherford recorded that in the light of the Radium he could see that Pierre Curie's fingers were so scarred and swollen that he was having a hard time just holding onto the tiny tube. The infatuation and divine interest that Pierre and Marie Curie had for Radium it seems was infinite. When Pierre and Marie Curie would return home at night after an evening out, they would mix up a full glass pot of Radium, put it in the open air on the dining room table (!) and they would both sit and stare at the Green glowing radioactive substance emitting it's own brilliant light for hours in the dark. Pierre also was quite wild, and to test the effects of Radium and radioactivity on the human skin he made a truly insane self-experiment, where he tied a small amount of radioactive Radium to his arm one night and then proceeded to go to bed. *Ten Hours later* he removed the Radium from his arm after awaking and was amazed to see that the radioactive Radium had burned all of his skin off of his arm where the Radium had been tied to it. Like a true research scientist, Pierre continued to study the radioactive burn he had inflicted on his own arm for a period of fifty-two days, until in the end he was left with a permanent Grey scar on his arm. This was the first time that either of the Curies had thought of the use of radioactivity and Radium in the medical treatment for Cancer, which would eventually lead to an entire new school of medicine and Cancer treatment that is still being used today in the Twenty-first century. On the subject of cancer, after years of physically working with, and breathing in the dust from radioactive residue of Pitchblende, both Pierre and Marie Curie began to feel sick. After reading about the way that they literally lived with Radium, it's a wonder that they were still alive at all. Pierre was known to almost always have a tube of radioactive Radium in his jacket waistcoat pocket, not to mention that he tied pure Radium to his bare arm for ten hours in his famous self-experiment, and in the end began to have much problems with his health besides his cracked and swollen fingers, such as constant fatigue and legs that shook so badly that he had trouble standing up. Marie also began to suffer from the radiation sickness they had self-induced, including the same swollen and scarred fingers and hands, and also constant fatigue, which is not amazing when reading that she used to keep exposed Radium salts on her night table right next to where she slept, to act like a 'night light' as it glowed all night in the dark! To give an example of the incredible radioactive strength of Radium, there was a spot on the floor of the shed where one day Pierre's scarred fingers had dropped a small amount of their precious Radium solution, and that spot on the shed floor was still found to be intensely radioactive fifty years later. When a visitor wishes to see the three notebooks of Pierre and Marie Curie in which they recorded all their work to arrive at pure Radium over the course of a three year period, that are in the collection of the Paris "Bibliotheque Nationale," the researcher must sign a statement that it is done at their own risk, and which stipulates the Bibliotheque Nationale is not responsible for 'possible risks from radioactivity.' These three notebooks of the Curies' are still highly radioactive and over one hundred years later they will make a Geiger counter go crazy. Pierre, who carried the Radium around in his waistcoat pocket, used to tell people all the time that Radium had a million times stronger radioactivity than even Uranium(!), and the reason that the Curies' notebooks still make a Geiger counter register very strongly is that the half-life of Uranium is 1,620 years.

Another important point to be made here is on the pure intellect and dignity of both Pierre and Marie Curie, who must be considered pure scientists of the highest order, because even after they realized the industrial proportions of Radium and it's projected use in medicine and Cancer treatment, the Curies decided not to patent their discovery, but leave it to the realms of pure science. They even went so far as to regularly provide samples to interested scientists and then even to publishing their laboratory procedure for the production of Radium. Already in May, 1903 the New York Times reported in an article that Radium was valued at an incomprehensible sum of $40 million a pound. Years later, after Pierre's death when Marie Curie was carrying on cancer research in the Curie Institute, the irony of the matter was that Madame Curie - who discovered Radium, did not have enough money to buy Radium anymore after it was industrially produced in the United States in the 1920s and 1930s, so money had to be raised for her in America, and she had to go to America two times to receive two separate gifts of a gram of Radium each so she could continue her research. These two souls were the exact opposite of a new bastardized species that would scourge the face of the Earth many years later, who are called in modern times "Yuppies."

The Nobel prize in Physics was awarded to both Marie and Pierre Curie, and also to professor Henri Becquerel on December 10, 1903. Henri Becquerel won half the Physics award of the Nobel Prize for his discovery of 'spontaneous Radioactivity,' and Marie and Pierre Curie won the other half of the Physics Nobel prize for their 'joint researches' into the 'Radiation phenomenon.' But the Nobel Prize ceremony was not attended by either Marie or Pierre Curie because of their teaching jobs, and as Pierre wrote to the Nobel prize committee, Marie Curie had been sick all summer and had not yet recovered. It took two years for them to get up to Stockholm, and in 1905 Pierre gave a Nobel lecture.

After receiving the Nobel prize the lives of Marie and Pierre Curie changed forever as they became regarded as celebrities and were constantly hounded by the press. Radium had become world famous, and in 1903 it was used for the first time in cancer treatments called "Curie-Therapy" that would later develop into "Chemo Therapy," it was used for the first Fluorescent mineral demonstration in the Natural History Museum in London during June, 1903 and in the fall of 1903 a small amount of Radium was donated to the Museum of Natural History in New York City, where it was put on display for crowds to line up to see this substance that had the appearance of Yellowish table salt. But all the celebration lasted a very short time for Pierre. Soon after, in 1906, Pierre Curie was killed in Paris due to an unfortunate traffic accident, and Marie was appointed to replace Pierre in his teaching position at the school laboratory, becoming the first woman ever to be to be appointed to teach at the Sorbonne. Two years later in 1908 Marie Curie became again the first woman ever to be appointed as a professor in the Paris Sorbonne, during which time she finally managed to isolate Radium in it's pure form as a metal, not Radium chloride as she had only previously been able to produce.

In America Radium production began after the discovery of radioactive ore in Colorado. Mined and shipped to a Canonsburg, Pennsylvania Radium factory, the "Standard Chemical Company" was founded in 1911 and began to sell "Standard" "Radium Solution for Drinking"(!) Each bottle stated on the label to contain two micrograms (millionths of a gram) of the "Element Radium," as well as the deadly user instructions: "Dose: Entire Contents of one Bottle after each Meal." A photograph of an original bottle of this "Standard Radium Solution for Drinking" is in "Something Out of Nothing - Marie Curie and Radium" by McClafferty with a caption informing the reader that the bottle is still radioactive over eighty years later.

In 1911 Marie Curie was awarded a second Nobel prize, this time in Chemistry, for her discovery of both of the elements Polonium and Radium. In 1914 the "Curie Institute" was completed in Paris, but it didn't open until 1916 after the First world war had ended.

One of the greatest achievements in science was achieved with Radium - a dream that had formed Alchemy, which later became known as Chemistry: "Transmutation." In 1919 Ernest Rutherford was world celebrated as he became the first "True Alchemist" when he achieved the age old dream of transmutation - turning one element into another element. Ernest Rutherford would again become world famous in the early 1930s for being the person to finally understand the complete workings of the atom, with it's constituent particles of Protons, Neutrons, and Electrons. In 1919 Ernest Rutherford, in his researching with Radium and radioactivity, quite by accident turned the element Nitrogen into the two different elements Oxygen and Hydrogen, and in this procedure Ernest Rutherford became the world's first true Alchemist, and Radium and it's radioactivity became what was called since antiquity the "Philosopher's Stone."

As Madame Curie got older she developed Cataracts in both eyes and an uneven step to her walk, so together with the sores on her fingers that had never healed, she had to painfully begin to admit that 'her child' - the "Miracle Cure" Radium - was maybe not as healthy as everyone first imagined, later also advertised, and then finally sold in too many products. Many of her laboratory assistants were constantly tired, and Marie Curie began to admit confidentially that the Radium may be the cause of her illnesses, but never warned her lab assistants. As Radium developed into an international industry, with much of it being produced on an industrial scale in the United States, the fears about Radium's effect on health was a real cause for concern. All of Marie Curie's nightmares would be confirmed by a group of extremely unfortunate women who all had the extremely unfortunate job of painting watch dials with Radium paint from the time of the First world war up until the mid-1920s. The "Radium Luminous Materials" company had a very large staff eventually totaling eight hundred women, all of whom painted the numbers on watch dials with Radioactive Radium Paint all the day long! During World war one a number of women and girls, some as young as twelve years old, were hired by the "Radium Luminous Materials Corporation," later known as the "U.S. Radium Corp.," to work in their factory in East Orange, New Jersey to paint the hands and numbers on the dials of wrist watches with Radium paint so they would glow in the dark. This was considered a good job at the time, painting watch dials for twenty dollars a week and working with the world famous Radium as well. Each woman's job was to mix dry Radium paint powder with Zinc sulfide and paint thinner to complete between 250 and 300 wrist watch dials per day. If each "Radium Girl" only sharpened the tip of her Radium brush with her lips one time for each wrist watch dial, which is probably not an accurate number due to the fact that each watch dial has twelve numbers and two watch hands all of which need a sharp brush to paint, but if just say that each woman or girl put the brush in between their lips one time for each dial, it would calculate to a harrowing 62,500 - 75,000 times in just a year. Since most of the 'life expectancies' of these doomed girls was just five years of work with this highly radioactive element, in their careers of five years work each of the "Radium Girls" would have put the Radium brush in between their lips at least 312,000 - 375,000 times. We don't have to be chemists to imagine the profuse *amount* of the deadly Radium that each of these "Radium Girls" must have ingested by putting a brush wet with radioactive Radium (that they had just mixed up from powder without gloves) in between their lips most probably half a million times in their five year careers, especially since the girls said it was tasteless. The super healthy Radium paint that was used in other factories which some of these "Radium Girls," as they became known, used to paint the luminescent watch dials with, was a brand of Radium paint that had the trade name of "UNDARK"(!) It is easy to image that the painting of tiny numbers on watch dials is very precise work with the "Radium Girls" all using very fine camel-hair paint brushes, and keeping the fine tip of the brush very sharp, the "Radium Girls" constantly putting the tip of their brush, containing radioactive Radium paint, again, into their mouths. After a day's work of putting the tasteless gritty Radium paint into their mouths over and over again and mixing up Radium paint by hand, the women were reportedly covered with Radium dust. For laughs (ha ha) some of the women would paint Radium on their clothes, buttons, or belts, and other women went so far as to paint Radium onto their fingernails and *Teeth*, saying that they wanted to look beautiful for their boyfriends. The "Radium Luminous Materials Corporation" assured the women and girls that Radium was Harmless! But every woman and young girl working as a Radium watch dial painter was putting the extremely radioactive element Radium into their mouths each and every time they painted each and every detail of each and every one of the 250-300 watches they painted eight hours a day, five days a week. It wasn't long before problems began to effect the "Radium Girls." By 1919 there had been more than two million wrist watch dials painted by the "Radium Girls." These poor doomed young women, and even girls, mixed up powdered Radium paint with Zinc sulfide, which would react with the Radium to create a very vivid glowing in the dark, brighter than the light of just Radium paint. On the 2010 "BBC" special "Chemistry - A Volatile History - Part 3: The Power of the Elements" the presenter physicist Jim Ai-Khalili explains the discovery of Radium and Polonium in a reconstruction of the original shed that Pierre and Marie Curie used as their laboratory. An original "Radium Wrist watch" was presented and the watch hands and all the numbers are still glowing extremely bright after all these decades. The wrist watch has the manufacturer's company name on the top half of the watch face, which was "Alprosa" and in capital letters the two words on the bottom half of the watch face are "Waterproof" and "Incabloc." This program contains the only movies of the "Radium Girls" painting Radium watch faces that I've ever seen, from between seventy and ninety years ago, for sure in Black and White with constantly changing lighting, etc., like a Charley Chaplain movie. In "Something Out of Nothing - Marie Curie and Radium," there are several very rare photographs of these Radium nightmares, including "Touch-Up Kits" for Radium watch dials that were used by Jewelers to repaint the Radium and Zinc sulfide mixture onto watch dials, because the extremely active Radium even destroys the Zinc in it's mixture, and through this slow destruction of the Zinc sulfide, the watch dials would not glow in the dark as bright as they had when they were new. The photograph of these four "Touch-Up Kits" shows three of the kits opened, displaying similar contents in each of the kits, including two bottles, presumably one of powdered Radium paint and one of Zinc sulfide, and also a glass 'palette' dish to mix the two chemicals together, and some glass stirring sticks. The names of three of these Radium watch dial "Touch-Up Kits" are visible on their respective box tops, including "Hi-Test Radium Outfit - For Retouching Luminous Dials and Hands," the French manufactured "Matiere Lumineuse" ('Luminous Material'), and even the poetic "Sun Ray - Radium Painting Kit."

Not surprisingly the first signs of real health problems for these poor "Radium Girls" were bad toothaches. The teeth of these girls who sharpened their Radium brushes by putting them between their lips, were the first bones in their bodies that absorbed the intensely radioactive Radium paint, followed directly by the jaw bone and all the other bones of the face and skull(!) In "Something Out of Nothing - Marie Curie and Radium" the truly horrible facts of these poor "Radium Girl's" fates are revealed, first in one of five sisters who all painted Radium watch dials in healthy New Jersey ninety years ago: Amelia Maggia's cheek became swollen in 1921 and developed into a painful toothache which she had pulled out. The hole where Amelia's tooth had been extracted never healed, but became terribly infected. In the end, according to "Radium Girls" by Claudia Clark, Amelia Maggia's Dentist pulled the entire rotten *lower jaw bone* out of Amelia's mouth. Not surprisingly Amelia Maggia died within a year. Since this was the first such case, Radium and the girl's job as a Radium watch dial painter were never suspected as the cause of Amelia's horrible death. But then another of the "Radium Girls" developed a painful swollen cheek, a painful toothache, and finally an open hole that would not close or heal after the tooth was pulled. To add to these problems of the bones of the face, the "Radium Girls" began to complain about always being tired, as Pierre and Marie Curie had felt twenty years before after discovering Radium and as many of their laboratory assistants had also complained about. This was a warning sign of serious anaemia that was being caused by the reduced number of Oxygen-transporting Red blood cells in their veins, directly a result of Radioactive Radium absorbed into their bodies. After several similar awful cases of women with swollen cheeks, terrible toothaches, and rotted jaw bones were treated by Dr. Walter Berry, the local New Jersey Dentist, he came to the horrible conclusion that all of these women were Radium watch dial painters. By 1925 the U.S. Department of Labor began an investigation in factories that produced Radium paint to determine if Radium was the cause. In the "New York Times" of May 30, 1925 there was a stunning article about the 'Radium Disease' that had just been discovered that had killed five women, and had 'stricken' ten other women at that point, with what was believed to be 'Radium Necrosis' that the women had been 'infected' with while painting Radium watch dials at the East Orange, New Jersey factory. In the "Times" newspaper of June 25, 1925, less than a month after the previous article, another horrible story of two sisters that were "Radium Girls" was published. The article reported that Sarah Maillefer had already died of suspected "Radium Poisoning," and Marguerite Maillefer, Sarah's sister, was also dying. The very same newspaper article contained a statement from C.B. Lee, the "U.S. Radium Corp." treasurer, in which he not only denies that Radium was the cause of the "Radium Girl's" deaths and incurable sicknesses, but actually restates that Radium was 'helpful' to the health of the "Radium Girls!" Besides the photo of all the "Radium Girls" at work in the Radium Watch Dial Factory in New Jersey, there is an even more severe photo in "Something Out of Nothing," a reproduction of the newspaper article containing five portraits of dying "Radium Girls" that were suing their company "U.S. Radium Corp." for $250,000 each. The title of this nightmarish article announced that 'Five Women' were pleading for justice while 'Facing Death' by Radium poisoning. Portraits of five doomed "Radium Girls" on their way to horrible deaths through cancer of the face bones include Miss Katherine Schaub, Mrs. Albina Larice and Quinta McDonald who were sisters of the first "Radium Girls" to die, Amelia Maggia, as well as Edna Hussman, and Grace Fryer. This newspaper article of the five "Radium Girls" reported on the effects of Radium on the human body after it had been ingested, described by Chief surgeon of the New Jersey Orthopedic hospital of Orange, New Jersey, Dr. Robert Humphries, as the destruction of the bones of the skeleton itself. The Doctor describes the radioactive Radium taken into the body as directly attacking the bones, slowly rotting them for between two and four years, initially indicated through painful toothaches or shortening and pain of the leg bones. The terror of these "Radium Girls" can be imagined through the article's reportage that a "Radium Girl's" breath alone could cause a "Fluorescent Screen" to light up, and perhaps the most unforgettable account of any of the "Radium Girls" comes from Grace Fryer, one of the five girls who's portraits accompany the article, who confessed almost unbelievably that *each time she would blow her nose, her Handkerchief would Glow-in-the Dark!* This Grace Fryer was so weak by the time the court case began that she could not walk any more, and just to sit up she had to be in a back brace. Each of the five "Radium Girls" who's portraits are in the "Radium Poisoning" newspaper article of 1925 were so sick at the trial that not one of them could even raise their arm to take the legal oath. On June 4, 1928 the "U.S. Radium Corp." settled out of court with the five "Radium Girls" giving each of them not $250,000, but a measly $10,000, plus the extremely generous $600 per year for the rest of their lives(!) to five women on their death beds, plus free medical bills. As previously written, this was the highest percentage of workers fatality of any job in history up until the present day, and from the mid-1920s up until the mid-1930s each and every one of the over 800 "Radium Girls" died slow horrible deaths. To give an idea of how total the radiation would spread throughout the body of these "Radium Girls" that were ingesting Radium paint every day, in "Something Out of Nothing" there is another very rare and very disturbing photograph, a photo of an X-ray from one of the "Radium Girls" Sarah Maillefer. After this "Radium Girl," who was in the "Times" newspaper article of 1925, had died of Radium exposure, two metal paper-clips were placed between her leg bone and a piece of unexposed X-ray film. After six weeks the enormous amount of Radium that was absorbed even into her leg bone was sufficient to expose the image of the two paper-clips clearly onto the X-ray film! Facts about these "Radium Girls" are also well documented in a book by David Harvie aptly named "Deadly Sunshine: the history and fatal legacy of Radium." These "Radium Girls" became famous as being the one employment that had the highest percentage of fatality of any job in history: 100%! All of the eight hundred poor "Radium Girls" eventually developed cancer in the bones of their faces and all of them died horrible deaths as their facial bones began to slowly disintegrate, just like the millionaire Eben Byers who drank "Radium Health Tonic" for four full years every day.

Ironically, Radium and radioactivity were both used by Madame Curie in the Curie Institute as the first treatment for Cancer(!) It may sound ridiculous, but it's not quite so ridiculous when considering a full century later "Chemotherapy," the most widely used international treatment of cancer is still based on treatment of cancer with radioactivity, and is not so much different from the original first treatment of cancer that began a century ago called "Curie Therapy." This is still the research going on in the Paris "Curie Institute" today, with advances in the practical technique of radiation treatment for cancer. When Loie Fuller developed breast cancer in the late 1920s at the age of sixty-five, it was well suspected that the Radium dresses she had created and worn for years against her skin in her famous dance performances did not help. For her breast cancer treatment in 1927, Loie Fuller was treated with radioactive needles of Radium because it had been proven to kill cancer cells. Unfortunately, what had not yet been proven at that time yet was that the radioactivity killed virtually all cells - both cancerous and healthy. Through this truly hopeless treatment - something like trying to put out a fire by throwing gasoline onto it - Loie Fuller died of breast cancer on New Year's day, 1928, undeniably the results of her years of direct exposure to radioactive Radium. The major improvement for cancer treatment in the Curie Institute in modern times is the procedure of pinpointing the cancer very precisely, and then treating it with radioactivity in an attempt to destroy only the cancerous cells, without destroying all the other healthy cells in the process.

Marie Curie died of Leukemia in 1934, but it wasn't until she was nearly seventy years old, and it wasn't until thirty-six years after she had discovered radioactive Radium with her late husband Pierre. After Madame Curie died, Albert Einstein, who knew Marie Curie, was quoted as saying of Madame Curie that she was 'of all celebrated beings' the only one who was not 'corrupted by fame.'

What is perhaps as unbelievable as all of these combined facts on Radium, is that today in the year 2016 internet bidders are fighting viciously with each other every day to buy one of these original Radioactive Radium Watches! And not for cheap prices either, but for around $200. The Radium on these 1920s watch dials will still be deadly when all the paper in this book has turned to *dust*! Not to be deterred by idiots of the past, Radium watch dials are not the only radioactive Radium products being fought over on the internet, but even the famed deadly "Revigorator" occasionally still surfaces and is listed, just as viciously fought over, and finally bought by collectors.

In the end this "Radium Craze" nightmare era, which lasted for years, was in my estimation one of the very creators of the eventual Social Stigma of "Fluorophobia." A Dutch visitor to the Museum several years ago, who was a woman about sixty years old, clearly remembered - and mixed up with the Black Light and Fluorescence - the story about when she was a little girl, and in her parent's bedroom, as well as her own bedroom, there were many Glow-in-the-Dark Phosphorescent objects, such a light switch-plates and knobs for lighting. In the Museum collection is a photograph of one of these Radium household light switch items sold in the 1930s and it's got a hilarious trade name: "DARKIZE" = "Dark Eyes"! "A Radium Light" "Shines in the Dark" is at the top of the white board the "Darkize" light switch item was sold attached to. Under the rectangular small odd-looking White Radium devise is written "Finds Lamp Pulls, Door Knobs, Key Holes, Switches, Etc. at Night. Will shine for 10 Years." At the bottom are three drawings illustrating the different suggested uses of this "Darkize" Radium household item, the "Lamp Pull," "Key Holes," and "Electrical Switch." This Dutch woman telling me the story of these household items in her childhood home remembers very clearly that all of a sudden one day her parents removed every single luminescent object in the house and forbid them because they had been found to be very dangerous to the health. These glowing objects that had to be removed from houses were surely remnants of the "Radium Craze," similar or even identical to the "Darkize" item photograph in the Museum collection, and what point I want to make here in this book, is that this woman absolutely put the glowing Fluorescent paint under Black lights before her eyes in the Museum together with - and as being identical to - the luminous phenomenon in her childhood memories of the Radium appliances and the "Radium Scare." Together with the Shortwave Ultraviolet Health Treatment lamps that also eventually were found to cause cancer, this luminous Glow-in-the-Dark Radium revolution which killed countless people, while advertising that it was a "Health Cure" - exactly like the Shortwave Ultraviolet Health Treatment lamps - were the two earliest events of the intrinsically associated Black light and Fluorescence having 'known sin,' and neither of these two nightmare eras have yet to be forgotten over half a century later.

As testament to what a selfless soul Marie Curie was, on April 21, 1995 the French government decided to award the Curies the highest honor, placing them in the Pantheon in Paris, which is the most honored resting place in France, in the company of Voltaire and Victor Hugo. Before this was done, Marie's bones had to be tested for emitting Radioactivity, thought to surely be the cause of her death through he years of work and discovery of Radium with Pierre Curie in 1898, because the Pantheon is a public monument in the center of Paris. Authorities were both shocked and dumbfounded by the lack of what they had been sure to find, high levels of Radioactivity in Marie Curie's bones. In conclusion, and as a testament to her limitless compassion, it was understood that even at almost the age of seventy Marie Curie did not die from her "Miracle Child" Radium, but from X-ray exposure, because during the First world war Marie Curie drove a portable X-ray unit she designed in a truck, and X-rayed countless wounded soldiers in attempt to save their lives. In the end this X-ray exposure from her truly humanitarian efforts is what killed her, not the Radioactivity of her discovery Radium.

On a much lighter side, to offer a bit of 'comic relief' after the miserable ending to the story of Radium, during the same general time period, there began another of the 'Classic" uses of the Black light and Fluorescent paint that everyone today associates with, as well as being advertised as a 'suggested use' by a good deal of the companies selling Black lights and Fluorescent paint presently: Amusement Parks! This afternoon in the Museum one of the visitors was a man named Bob who was born in 1947 and grew up in Cleveland, Ohio. Even before he had put on his foam-rubber slippers to enter the Fluorescent "Participatory" Environment in the Museum, I already began to question him about any memories he might have about growing up in Cleveland, the home of the headquarters of the "Day-Glo" company and of the Switzer Brothers who invented Fluorescent paint, and sure enough he had a wealth of information about a particular childhood memory from when he went to "Euclid Beach Amusement Park" in the suburbs of Cleveland. His precious memories are of the famous Amusement Park attraction named "Laff in the Dark," which was a ride where you sat in a moving cart on tracks and went through a Fluorescent Black Light Fun House in the dark. Bob remembers that you went up an incline as the ride started in the dark Fun house, and then you went through a circular Fluorescent Black light tunnel, with bright Colors all around you (like a 'time-tunnel'), and then you went past a completely Fluorescent Black light mining scene, and onto another Fluorescent Black light scene of Snow White and the Seven Dwarfs. This type of ride is called a "Dark Ride," [this doesn't mean it's like "Dark matter" which would make it an 'invisible ride' (smile)] which is an indoor amusement ride with automatic carts that move the visitors through scenery and specially lit areas - like the "Tunnel-of Love" and the "Spook Houses" in many amusement parks. These "Dark Rides" started in the late 1800s with 'Scenic railways' and boat rides in water for the early "Tunnel of Love." In 1928 Leon Cassidy with the "Pretzel Amusement Ride Company" patented his invention of the first electric rail "Dark Ride," and went on to install over twenty-five of these Dark rides all over America. The most famous of all the Dark rides was the "Futurama" at the 1939 New York World's Fair, but the very first "Dark Ride" to use the Black light and luminous Paint was in 1931 at "Euclid Beach Amusement Park" in both the "Laff in the Dark" ride and another ride called the "Rotating Barrel." The "Laff in the Dark" ride described by Bob in the Museum today had several other Fluorescent Black light attractions to scare the hell out of kids in the dark, including many skeletons, dragons, spiders, gorillas, eyes in the dark, and lightning bolts. The chief engineer at "Euclid Beach Amusement Park" who designed the Black light and Fluorescent Dark rides was Dudley Humphrey Scott. The "Rotating Barrel" that Scott patented in 1931 was copied over the years in Amusement parks all over America and even overseas, having the same fate as the attraction's name itself, "Laff in the Dark," which was copied numerous times, starting only a couple of years after the original Dark ride "Laff in the Dark" in Cleveland, Ohio, and continuing right up until the present moment - there's even a "Laff in the Dark" website! This "Rotating Barrel" Dark ride was about twenty-four feet (almost 8 meters) long and painted inside totally Black, with the addition of Phosphorescent stars painted onto it. Underneath the track that the carts were carrying the visitors on were bright lights that would charge up the Phosphorescent stars inside the "Rotating Barrel," and as the cart approached, the lights would go out and the visitors would enter a completely dark rotating tunnel with Phosphorescent stars flying all around them in every direction. The effect was intended to make the people in the ride feel as if they were turning upside down as they moved through the long turning tunnel in the dark with Phosphorescent stars shinning and revolving all around them.

Already in 1934, just three years after the first "Laff in the Dark" attraction opened in "Euclid Beach Amusement Park" outside of Cleveland, Ohio, there was a second "Laff in the Dark" Dark ride - exactly the same name, even - being used at the "Chicago Century of Progress" exposition, which was going to be sold to "Playland" in Rye, New York upon the exposition in Chicago closing. This "Laff in the Dark" in "Playland," Rye, New York was a large Dark ride with thirty-six different 'tricks' for the riders in the carts to laugh or gasp at in the dark, including a mechanically operated Fluorescent skeleton that would move around in the dark with a Black light bulb right in front of it, and the same exact "Rotating Tunnel" with the Phosphorescent stars on the inside of the Black tunnel, but this tunnel also had a Fluorescent lion waiting in the tall grass right in front of you when your cart exited the dark rotating tunnel. The entrance to the "Playland" "Laff in the Dark" from a 1936 Black and White photograph shows that it had dancing skeletons, and the name made out of wood or some three dimensional material that was White against a dark background. The entrance to the original "Laff in the Dark" of "Euclid Beach Amusement Park" in Ohio, was a complete building with a rectangular arch at it's entrance and "Laff in the Dark" written on the arch in a script typeface. The exhibitions at the "Euclid Beach Amusement Park" all look large and impressive in the few photographs that survive, either in their original Black and White state, or retouched with hand-coloring. The actual entrance to the Amusement park had brick three-story European-styled castle-like side towers with the huge name "Euclid Beach Park" constructed between these two entrance towers.

Another copy of the "Laff in the Dark" Dark ride - again, the exact same spelling - was in 1935 in the famous "Crystal Beach Amusement Park" in Canada on the shore of Lake Erie. Some sources claim that the man who built the Crystal Beach's "Cyclone" and "Tumble Bug" rides, Harry Traver, who built the Amusement Manufacturing Plant in Beaver Falls, Pennsylvania in 1919, also invented the first "Laff in the Dark" Dark ride in 1930. The "Laff in the Dark" Dark ride in the Canadian "Crystal Beach Amusement Park" was most probably the last surviving first generation "Laff in the Dark" when the park closed in 1989.

Another very early pioneer in the field of Black light for entertainment can be found on the "Dark Castle" website, who was a visionary movie director of the 1930s and 1940s named William Castle. This unique movie director used the Black light and Fluorescence in his movies of the 1930s and 40s, and in addition the movie audience had to put on special 'UV glasses' to intensify this early effect. His horror movies must have been terrifying with their production using Black lights, and his most famous films were "13 Ghosts" and the original "House on Haunted Hill." Before William Castle's 1930s and 1940s Black light horror films, in the 1920s a phenomenon began known as "The Spook Show." In high class movie theaters of the 1920s these "Spook Shows" were also called "Midnight Magic Shows," and had magicians, floating phantoms, seances, and spirits which were illuminated. At the end of these "Midnight Magic Shows" all the lights in the theater were turned off, which was termed "Blackout" in the past, and Glow-in-the-Dark ghosts would then appear in the dark movie theater above the heads of the audience and on the stage, which can be easily imagined to have truly horrified the audience over ninety years ago! The sparse documentation of these "Spook Show" performances explains that besides the Phosphorescent ghosts appearing in the "Blackout" movie theater, luminescent spiders would fly from the balcony and other unexpected thrills. This was all just an entertainment for the audience to have the wits scared out of them before the main feature, a horror film, would begin.

After seven years of writing this 'Black light history' a karmic gift was received of truly impossible-to-find issues of "Conti-Glo" "Black Light Beacon" from 1941 and 1942. Now after finding two separate people years ago, during the early stages of writing this book, who had preserved several issues of early 1940s "Conti-Glo" "Black Light Beacon," I never dreamed of finding any of the missing issues of this seventy-three year old series of trade publications from the company formed by the inventors of Fluorescent paint, the "Switzer Brothers," but in January, 2014 a package was put on internet auction which was a dream come true. Not only did this "Black Light Beacon" package purchased for the Museum collection contain six issues of this trade publication in near-mint, unfolded condition from 1941 and 1942, but also some bonus artifacts I had never seen before, such as two pages of an "Index of Subjects," one for just March to July, 1941 "Black Light Beacons," and the other for the entire "Vol. 1, 1941" set of publications. These two pages are filled on both sides with not only "Index of Subjects," but also include complete references by page number of "Index of Fields of Product Use," "Index of Conti-Glo Products," "Index of Black Light Equipment," and an "Index of Installations." Something really precious included in this package perfectly preserved in someone's attic for three-quarters of a century was a two-fold, double-sided brochure containing a "Standard Conti-Glo Products - for Civilian uses" Price list from February 1, 1942, which details every "Civilian" non-military product sold by "Conti-Glo" in 1942 - a literal treasure of a find. As an extra bonus the original printed large envelope from "Conti-Glo" mailed in 1942 and hand-typed to "Mr. Frank Tricker" of "West Philadelphia, Pa." was included in this fantastic find. I wrote to the seller that he sure sold this package to the right person. As can be expected in 1941, the large mailing envelope for "Conti-Glo" "Black Light Beacon" included with this antique set was also very special and recognizable as being from the long past. The hand-typed receiver's name and address is almost unnoticed next to the very large Black "CONTI-GLO DIVISION" return address taking up about a full third of the envelope. The most eye-catching feature of this envelope is the large Black block of advertising for "Conti-Glo" under their return address. With a design representing paint brushed onto a surface, a solid Black area with just as striking large White type exclaims in three different type faces that "Conti-Glo" 'Achieves Glowing and Colorful Magic using Black Light.' "BLACK LIGHT" is also in a funky hand-drawn type face reminiscent of comic book super heroes.

To begin, the issues of "Conti-Glo" Black Light Beacon" that were included in this antique package are "Vol. 1 No. 2" from April, 1941, which was a missing issue in the Museum collection, "Vol. 1 No. 3" from May, 1941 already in the collection, "Vol. 1 No. 4" of June-July, 1941 also missing from the collection, "Vol. 1 No. 6" from September-October, 1941 already in the collection, "Vol. 1 No. 7" of November, 1941 also never seen before, along with "Vol. 2 No. 1" already in the collection. Although half of these "Black Light Beacons" were already in the Museum collection, these issues newly acquired are in near-mint condition and unfolded.

"Conti-Glo" "Black Light Beacon" "Vol. 1 No. 2" from April, 1941 is an eight page issue beginning on page five, which indicates that "Vol. 1 No. 1" was only four pages long since each yearly volume was continuously page numbered. The Black and White photograph on the front cover of this issue No. 2 is of one of the most famous uses of Fluorescent and Phosphorescent paint in history, Instrument Panels. Being during the Second world war these Instrument panels in the photograph are of military aircraft, with the caption under the photo of three clear Fluorescent Instruments dials explaining that a "black light" was used to show the intense light given off from these "Conti-Glo" "Decalcomanias." The text defines this "Decalcomania" as a "transfer process" similar to common "decals," but these luminescent decals were printed using Fluorescent pigment. The vast period of time which has passed since the publication of this "Black Light Beacon" is apparent when reading that whole sheets of decals were only "a penny" in the memory of the article's author, which gave the headline to this article, 'Conti-Glo, Together with a Toy from Old Days, Brings Aviator's Eyes Relief.' The article states that these "Conti-Glo" Fluorescent "Decalcomanias" coating cockpit Instrument panels, control gadgets and dials allow the presence of absolutely no visible lighting in the cockpit, and in this way eliminates pilot eye-strain during night flights. The article clarifies the point that the "ultra-violet" lamp creates no eye-glare or reflections on the glass face of the Instrument panels in the dark, and creates a "Black-out" atmosphere in the cockpit which is not brighter than the darkness outside the cockpit. This cover article ends with the fact that the success of these Fluorescent Instrument panels caused the adaptation of this method using "ultra-violet" and "Decalcomanias" in Great Britain on their new planes. As well as airplanes, this April, 1941 article details applications of these Fluorescent "Decalcomanias" for use on all models of boats and vehicles, dials for clocks, radio transmitter and X-ray machine meters, "gunnery equipment," instruments in laboratories, and Fluorescent markings on "switchboards" of both telephone and stage production. The bottom of page one ends with an invitation to ask advice on these new Fluorescent Instrument markings to "Electronic Laboratories" of Indiana who will send a representative to address the questions. Also added is a note to send a postcard to get a free subscription to this "Black Light Beacon."

The second page of this issue has two photographs of Fluorescence used for American Indian "Smoki" Ceremonials in August, 1940. In Prescott, Arizona this "Smoki" Indian Ceremonial celebrated the Colorful dance ceremonies of the Southwest Zuni and Hopi tribes, and these Indian celebrations were held at night, so "Conti-Glo" Fluorescent Colors were dramatically used under Black lights for both headdresses and costumes, as well as for an Indian Fluorescent Sand Painting. One of the photos is of invisible "Conti-Glo" Fluorescent paints used on Indian "Shalakos" costumes, which had Fluorescent "Invisible Green" used on the masks, feathers, and horns, along with Fluorescent "Pearl White" eyes and "Neon Red" used for the beak. The more spectacular second photo in this article is of an Indian Fluorescent Sand Painting, described as being made with "fluorescent materials" from "Conti-Glo" which glowed like "hidden fires." The very clear photo of this twenty foot wide (6.5 meter) Indian Fluorescent Sand Painting was also taken under Black lights, as the majority of the photographs in all "Black Light Beacons" are. The image created within the Indian Sand painting was a double-eyed stylized bird surrounded with Fluorescent White and Fluorescent Blue, along with Fluorescent Green, Red, and Yellow. The credit is given for the designing of this Black light Indian Ceremonial to "Conti-Glo" West coast distributor Johnny T. Shannon of Hollywood's "Keese Engineering Company," the founder of today's "Shannon Luminous Products, Incorporated." A second small article on the following page also announces that this "Smoki" Indian Fluorescent Ceremonial was so successful that the entire show was invited to the "Palmer House" theater in Chicago to present their Hopi and Zuni rites with Fluorescent Colors under powerful "Conti-Glo" Black lights rented for the occasion. Several other small articles on the second and third pages of this issue document other Fluorescent Black light productions, such as a club of Artists in "Middle America" creating an extravaganza when for their annual party they used Fluorescent lacquer-enamels from "Conti-Glo" to paint paper murals covering the walls of the ballroom which were a hundred feet long (30 meters). Pieces of Fluorescent "Conti-Glo" satin were given with each entrance ticket, and were then by the guests cut into patterns and applied to their costumes, which, along with the huge Fluorescent murals produced what is described as a "flood" of luminosity pouring from all sides into the ballroom. Another small article describes the famous "Switzer Brothers" Fluorescent Movie-Poster display created for the biggest theater in Ohio, the Hippodrome in Cleveland. Reviewed and described already in this book, this early Switzer Brothers Hippodrome theater Black light movie poster lobby display was so expensive that it caused their client to complain about the cost for the rest of his life. Described in this small article, there were apparently several Fluorescent movie poster displays eventually made for the Hippodrome, and included both lobby and foyer Fluorescent poster displays. Details of this Fluorescent lobby display are given, such as being painted with "Conti-Glo" lacquer-enamel Fluorescent paints applied with both an air-brush and by traditional brush on top of non-Fluorescent Colored areas of the display, which gave an effect of "Living Light." This effect must indeed have been dramatic, given the details of a separate 100-watt "Conti-Glo" Black light spot used for each side of the Fluorescent movie poster displays!

On the third page of this "Black Light Beacon" is an important article and two very clear photos of the 'First Theater in Michigan to use "Conti-Glo" Black Light and Fluorescence.' This new "State Theater" of Elk Rapids, Michigan was designed to have Fluorescent murals on the theater's ceiling as well as Fluorescent aisle carpeting, both of which are clearly shown in the accompanying photos. The ceiling Fluorescent murals in this theater are described in this article as being painted with "Conti-Glo" Fluorescent lacquer-enamels in glowing 'Pearl White, Jade Green, Salmon Pink, and Sea Blue,' while being activated with "Conti-Glo" powerful permanent wall fixture Black light units. This Fluorescent mural looks in the photograph to have been enormous, possibly as big as the entire theater ceiling, with a swirling design which could be described as a mixture of Art Deco and American Indian. The Fluorescent Aisle Carpeting used in this 1941 "State Theater" is next described as being a Fluorescent Gold and Tan design on a non-Fluorescent Red carpet base, which was activated using "Conti-Glo" 'Model 67' Black lights mounted on the ceiling. It is further explained that these 'Model 67' Black lights were spotlights, and this allowed the beam of Ultraviolet to be directed at just the Fluorescent carpeting, without causing a "spillage" of Ultraviolet onto the theater audience sitting close to the edge of the aisles and causing their eyes to Fluoresce as well as the carpeting, which was reported as a problem with this carpeting when activated formerly using inferior Black light floodlights. This article closes with a wonderful company motto of the Fluorescent carpeting manufacturers, very reminiscent of this era of "The Miracle of Fluorescence:" "Woven With Light."

The fourth page of this "Black Light Beacon" has a real hard-sell article with a complete commercial sales-pitch on 'Getting Dollars from Light using Fluorescent Sketches.' The rudimentary technique, new in 1941, of highlighting a customer's proposed design with Fluorescent paint to visualize planned electric signs or neon displays is announced in this trade publication, along with a paragraph explaining that since Fluorescent paint literally gives off 'visible light,' then designs touched up with Fluorescent paint and put under a Black light will convince customers of luminous displays on suggested fronts of theaters, marquee lighting, or on roof signs. This article states that almost all of "Conti-Glo's" customers who are involved in this business have tripled sales of both 'electrical displays and lighting equipment.' Below this article is a photograph of what I've described elsewhere in this book as something I dream of finding one day, a set of the first "Conti-Glo" Fluorescent paints in eight little bottles, which are included in the "Sketch and Demonstration" set for "Conti-Glo" Black light. Several small articles are also on this fourth page as well, with an announcement of the police department in Kansas City, Missouri successfully using a "Conti-Glo" Black light 'Model 91' together with Invisible Green Fluorescent Powder to solve cases of document forgery and theft. Another article follows the Kansas City police, in which the definition of the "Angstrom Unit," or "A.U." is clearly explained as having been developed by a scientist named Angstrom to measure extremely short wavelengths below visible light in the Ultraviolet spectrum. Angstrom decided that these wavelengths were too short to measure based on a meter, so he divided a millimeter into ten million Angstrom Units. In effect 366 nanometers, a measurement more commonly used today (which is 366 billionths of a meter), equals 3660 Angstrom Units. A full page article follows on page five, with a headline announcing the use of Fluorescence and Black lights for 'Analysis and Examination.' A long list of industrial-scale production uses for the "ultra-violet rays" in 1941 are presented, beginning with the examination of "Food Products" including additives in butter such as "oleomargarine" or "coconut fat," which are detectable with a Bluish Color under a Black light. Tiny amounts of preservatives not detectable through chemical analysis are also detectable under Black lights, as well as the difference between nearly non-Fluorescent beet sugar compared to Red Fluorescent glucose or sugar cane. Black light examination of Textile is also explained in this article, and used to assess the integrity of fabric and additives. Drug identification is mentioned as pertaining to Black light, along with the use of Ultraviolet in many stages of manufacturing and industry. Two photos accompany this "Analysis" article, displaying a comparison between six "dyestuffs" which look identical in daylight, but under a Black light six different shades of "identical" dyestuffs are clearly identifiable.

Next in this trade journal from 1941 there is a full page article highlighting the sensational 'Black light activated' "Fluorescent Aisle Carpeting," along with a photograph of this very bright theater carpeting. This article begins with the early 'history' of Fluorescent theater carpeting, explaining that a few years before first attempts with extremely weak two and a half watt "Argon bulbs" not surprisingly proved to be ineffective for activating Fluorescent carpeting. It is further explained that the combined efforts of Robert Switzer of "Conti-Glo" and C. M. Cutler from "General Electric Company" finally produced a system and Fluorescent Aisle Carpeting which astounded everyone at a carpeting convention. A demonstration of this Fluorescent Aisle Carpeting manufactured by the Alexander Smith and Sons Carpeting Company displayed under the "Conti-Glo" Black lights 'Model 66' was described as being 'enthusiastically received' at this carpet sales convention. Even an alternative Black light unit for use in theaters with very high ceilings was introduced for 'end seating' installation where many six watt individual Black light units would take the place of powerful ceiling-mounted units. This Fluorescent Aisle Carpeting was such a sensation during the time period of 1941 that there were a total of eight different Black light units available to be used for different situations on this glowing theater carpeting. This article ends with other suggestions for theaters, such as Fluorescent uniforms for usherettes, ushers, ticket takers, and receptionists, all made out of "Conti-Glo" Fluorescent satins and glowing under Black lights as they walk on this Fluorescent Aisle Carpeting in theaters.

This April, 1941 "Black Light Beacon's" seventh page contains three historically valuable small articles containing three very clear Black and White photographs. The first article is accompanied by another one of these photographs from the early 1940s which is nearly unbelievable today because of the image's absolute incongruity to the contemporary concept of Black lights and "Day-Glo" Colors. The title of this article introduces "Miss Fluorescence," who surprisingly enough does not look like a wild girl from the 1960s or even from a rave party of the last decades, but very much like the miserable 1940 Dodge automobile completely painted in Fluorescent Colors rotating in front of massive Black lights described in another issue of this "Black Light Beacon." Again, "Miss Fluorescence" does not look like a wild Hippie girl or party girl in any way, as might be first expected, but she looks about as far as humanly possible from what "Miss Fluorescence" could be imagined today to have looked like - in fact she looks about as cool as what the Fluorescent 1940 Dodge, complete with Fluorescent "White wall" tires, made this author think of - the unimaginable image of Franklin Delano Roosevelt with his pipe in his mouth, painted completely from head to toe with brilliant Fluorescent Colors, rotating on a pedestal in the dark in front of powerful Black lights, sitting in his wheelchair(!) The first glance of 1940's "Miss Fluorescence" is shocking to say the least, and looks more like Martha Washington in the 1700s than who would be first imagined as being "Miss Fluorescence." She was a very traditional serious common woman with a 1940s short hairdo, a frontier-style wide flat formal hat, formal gloves above the elbows, and a gown which looks like it was also tailored for George Washington's wife. In short, as grotesque as the miserable 1940s Fluorescent Dodge automobile. Reading the few paragraphs of text it is learned that "Miss Fluorescence" was introduced during a presentation of a new Fluorescent lamp factory opened by "General Electric Company" in Jackson, Mississippi, and that her costume was purposely made to resemble the gown in "Gone With the Wind." "Miss Fluorescence's" gown was made with Fluorescent "Invisible Blue" "Conti-Glo" satin, and had trimmings on the gown, as well as on her hat and gloves, made of Fluorescent "Saturn Green." What's astounding is to read the description of the amount of Black light used to activate just "Miss Fluorescence" - a tremendous 750 watts (!) being produced by three of the most powerful Black lights "Conti-Glo" manufactured, the 250 watt 'Model 70.' She must have been as bright as burning Magnesium!

There was another Fluorescent bar in Ohio, where the "Switzer Brothers" established their first very successful Fluorescent paint company "Conti-Glo" in association with Carl Moellman's "Continental Lithography" of Ohio. The Hotel Secor in Toledo, Ohio opened the "Peacock Lounge" in their hotel, and living up to the name of their cocktail lounge, this bar was accented by a huge Fluorescent Peacock under a powerful "Conti-Glo" Black light unit. This Fluorescent Peacock was painted on the wall behind the bar facing the customers, and became what the management intended, the focal point of this "Peacock Lounge." The two photos of this article are White light and then Black light versions of this large Fluorescent Peacock painting, and even though not in Color reveal an extremely bright Fluorescent Peacock the full height of the ceiling painted on a dark semi-circular base. The full height of this Fluorescent Peacock in this 1941 Ohio cocktail lounge must have been about fifteen feet tall (5 meters), and the Black light photo proves that this painted Fluorescent focal point of the "Peacock Lounge" was bright enough to illuminate the entire bar. The technical details are given in this article as well, informing the reader that for the full-Color Peacock painting twelve different "Conti-Glo" Fluorescent Colors were used, and that this painting was under a powerful 'Model 81' "Conti-Glo" Black light unit mounted inside the ceiling above the luminescent Peacock.

The last small article in this "Black Light Beacon" gives a very interesting perspective of 'Taking Black Light Photographs' in 1941. The photography of Fluorescent displays or decorations is first mentioned in this article, with good advice to take two different photos of each subject, one in the White light, and another photo with the camera in the same position in the "Black light." Apparently "Conti-Go Division had just published a direction and instruction guide for photographing "fluorescent subjects," and this guide is promoted towards both amateur and professional photographers, as well as businesses of photography supply. Next to this small article on "Black light" photographs promoted towards photographers, on the bottom of the last page there is a notice in a Black box also from the "Conti-Glo Division" which explains that there were so many uses of both "Conti-Glo" Fluorescent products and Black light units that it was not possible to document more than a small amount of them in each issue of "Black Light Beacon," so the invitation is given to contact "Conti-Glo's" department of advisory and engineering if the reader believed that Black light and Fluorescence could be an "advantage" in their work.

The back cover of this 'Vol. 1 No. 2' "Black Light Beacon" from April, 1941 displays a dramatic Black and White photo which looks like a brilliant waterfall of light against an opaque Black background. This is the vivid "Conti-Glo" Fluorescent Satin in a photo which covers three-quarters of this back cover. The short text explains that if the reader thought that this was White satin then they had never been so wrong, because this photo shows satin which is indeed White in daylight, but when put under a "Black light" this material 'brilliantly glows' with the 'characteristic radiant Blue' which all "Invisible Blue" "Conti-Glo" products are known for. It is further stated that these Fluorescent Satins were luxurious, soft material which would not fade even when washed or dry-cleaned. This "Conti-Glo" Fluorescent Satin, originally invented for the U.S. military by the "Switzer Brothers" just a couple of years before the 1941 publication of this "Black Light Beacon," was promoted in this advertisement as having been made in "Invisible Blue," which was described as being 'richly glowing,' or also applicable for this use was "Saturn Green." What is very surprising is the price of this "Conti-Glo" Fluorescent Satin, because for a mere ten yards of this extravagant luminescent satin it would have cost the same amount in 1941 as an ounce of gold!

The second issue of "Black Light Beacon" that I was initially excited by seeing this antique collection of publications for sale on the internet was 'Vol. 1 No. 4' of June-July. 1941. The cover article and photos of this issue presents large Fluorescent murals lighting up the "Ken" Theater in Chicago seventy-three years ago. The title of this article announces this new 1941 "Ken" Theater, with a combination of 'Surrealism and the Magic Black Light.' The text of this article begins with the enthusiasm and fascination signatory of this age of "The Miracle of Fluorescence," beginning with an example of the difference between what is just called "magic," such as "hocus-pocus" acts, and what is "real magic," exemplified in this 1941article as "electricity." The article also goes on to define magic that is "ultra-modern" with the example of using nature's "secret forces" to create the phenomenon of invisible Fluorescence. This introduction on the defining stages of magic being the creation of Fluorescence offers the new 1941 "Ken" Theater of Chicago, with it's Fluorescent theater curtain and Fluorescent murals, as the 'basis' of this magic of the Black light which 'transformed' the theater into a 'brilliant light source through Ultraviolet activation.' These three, nearly poetic, short paragraphs, which would never be seen today, are typical of this era of "The Miracle of Fluorescence, 1930s-1950s," with its awe and innocence. The actual huge Fluorescent murals under Black lights in this 1941 "Ken" Theater are described as representing the skyline of Chicago, with the Artists from Hanns R. Teichert studios using Fluorescent lacquer-enamels from "Conti-Glo" to create these theater murals. The details of this extravagant Fluorescent "Ken" Theater are also given in this article, with four Fluorescent murals on each side of this theater, all painted on "acoustic board." These eight murals were then "activated" by twelve powerful "Conti-Glo" Black lights using "mercury lamps." It is further explained that during the "intermission" when the curtain closed, this stage curtain was also "Fluorescent-treated" by "Conti-Glo" and was activated by Black lights from the stage's footlights. The purpose of this brilliant stage curtain and eight large Fluorescent murals in this theater, which were only turned on during intermission, was to illuminate the theater with the emitted Color's "great spread," and with all the theater's lights off these eight huge Fluorescent murals and entire Fluorescent stage curtain was sufficient to light the entire theater. The article notes that through the combination of all light coming exclusively from Fluorescent Colors activated by Black lights, together with "constant music" being played in the background, there arose an atmosphere described as 'impressive and most unusual.' A comparison is then given between 'early Black light theaters,' which used only 100 watt Black light units on each Fluorescent murals, and the modern new "Ken" Theater, which used powerful 250 watt Black light units on each of their eight Fluorescent murals. The reasoning behind these "early" Black light theaters using only 100 watt Black lights on their Fluorescent murals was to ensure that the Fluorescence of the murals wasn't strong enough to "divert" the audience's attention from the movie being shown on the screen! What resulted from these installations was the bright light of the movie projection nearly obscuring the weak Fluorescence of the theater murals produced by only 100 watt Black lights, so the murals didn't divert the audience's attention away from the movie being shown, but the projected light of the movie did nearly obscure the Fluorescence of the murals. The article closes with the suggested example of this new "Ken" Theater, which only turns on the Black lights and activates the Fluorescent stage curtain with the Fluorescent murals when the movies had been turned off during intermissions.

The two photos with this front page article of this 1941 Fluorescent Chicago theater are what captured my attention when seeing these issues of "Back Light Beacon" on the internet, and display huge Fluorescent murals on either side of the audience on the two side walls of the theater, which are so bright in these antique Black and White photos that even the theater seats can be seen. From the photos it looks like three of the Fluorescent murals on each side of the theater were Chicago skyline paintings, each set making up a triptych, along with a separate stylized Fluorescent collage of theater and music motifs as well. These eight huge Fluorescent murals along with the entire Fluorescent stage curtain being activated by twelve 250 watt Black light units producing a tremendous 3,000 watts of Ultraviolet, would have created a truly astounding ambience in this "Ken" Theater all those years ago.

The second page of this June-July, 1941 "Black Light Beacon" has another article on Fluorescent murals in another movie theater in America. The new 1941 Beechwold Theater in Columbus, Ohio was also built to house Fluorescent murals, decorations, and even Fluorescent statues to be displayed under powerful "Conti-Glo" Black light units. The entrance to this Beechwold Theater had two large Fluorescent circular murals which would have been on either side of the public as they walked into the theater. These two large Fluorescent murals were seven feet in diameter (2.1 meters) had stylized decorations described in the article as a "leaf motif" of "modernized-classic" style. These murals first were created as plaster sculptures and then were painted with "Conti-Glo" Fluorescent lacquer-enamels. Concealed powerful 'Model 96' "Conti-Glo" Black light flood lamps activated these Fluorescent murals in this Ohio 1941 movie theater, as well as many other Fluorescent objects which added to the Fluorescent ambience of the theater, such as three foot tall (1 meter) plaster sculptures of cats, elephants and other figures. The article contains two photos, one of the "leaf motif" Fluorescent circular murals of this theater's entrance, and another of this large Fluorescent cat sculpture, which must have been intensely bright under it's 'Model 99' "Conti-Glo" Black light spotlight in what is described as a "luminescent niche."

Another very interesting article on this second page of this trade publication examines 'Color Science' and 'Color Psychology,' which informs the reader that the "General Electric Company" in Cleveland published a new edition of their "Illumination Design Data" manual which includes for the first time "Conti-Glo" Fluorescent lacquer-enamel paint's reflectance of light and emission of light along with all their listing of paints, wood varnishes, and other prepared decorative surfaces under both incandescent and Fluorescent White light. This is the point of the article, that the inclusion of "Conti-Glo" Fluorescent lacquer-enamels in this "authoritative" laboratory publication 'emphasizes the importance' of "Conti-Flo" Fluorescent paint in the 'decorative field' as well as the field of "display illumination." What was also stressed in this small article was the high reflectance, vivid Colors, and overall beauty of Fluorescent Colors in ordinary White light used for display, decoration, or ornamental use, besides the obvious intensity of these Colors under Black lights. What was very clearly known back in 1941 (and has many times been forgotten today) was that the intensity of the Fluorescence of these Colors was "proportional to" the intensity and amount of Black lights used. This is one of the most important rules of Fluorescence that has been long lost today, with most public displays of Fluorescence using a measly fraction of the original use of Ultraviolet Black lights to create contemporary dim displays, as well as using modern convenient thirty-six watt tubular Black lights, which are a pitiful regression of technology, but are cheap, easy to use, and safer for public displays because of their relatively cool operating temperatures compared to yesteryear's superior state-of-the-Art powerful 250 watt Black light units with immense Longwave Ultraviolet filters on the front of these Black lights from seventy years ago, which created in the end a Black light unit that was vastly superior to any Black light unit made today in the Twenty-first century. Following this technical article, another technical point is clarified in the next tiny article, being that the unhealthy Anthracene was being replaced by less toxic substances in "Conti-Glo" Fluorescent products. Anthracene was explained to have been produced through coal tar distillation, which resulted in this cheap hydrocarbon. It seems that some companies who were manufacturing Invisible Fluorescent criminology powders with Anthracene began to switch to other chemicals because of Anthracene's unhealthy "physiological properties." Specified in this article was "Conti-Glo" 'S-195' "Invisible Green" criminology marking and tracing powder, which had it's formula changed and did not contain Anthracene anymore. Not only was this new changed product brighter under Black lights, but the reader is also informed that no Fluorescent products manufactured by "Conti-Glo" contained Anthracene anymore, and that all "Conti-Glo" Fluorescent products were tested and proven harmless before being sold.

Page three of this June-July, 1941 trade publication has an article with three photos announcing a very early Black light Interactive display. "Gallo Studios" designed an industrial display for an advertising exhibition centered on the hardware field, that was made for a company selling bolts and screws. A photo of the entire display for conventions has elements shown of the various production stages of the company's hardware, and in the center of this industrial display was a circular panel with fourteen Fluorescent nuts, bolts, and screws attached to this panel. At bottom-center of this panel was a large button with 'PRESS HERE' written around it. When visitors pressed this button a "Conti-Glo" Black light unit would light up and create the centerpiece of this display, the fourteen nuts and bolts which had been coated with "Conti-Glo" Fluorescent paint and which would have burst into Colors. This was over seventy years ago during the age of not only far superior Ultraviolet lamp units being used, but also a degree of planning and knowledge of Fluorescent properties which was also vastly superior to what is done, or known about, today in 2016. For concrete proof of this just buy a ticket to a contemporary 'Ice-Capades' performance today, which typifies a present public Black light display, as well as the amount of both planning and knowledge of Fluorescence that has been lost in the decades since the age of "The Miracle of Fluorescence: 1930s-1950s." As an example of this peak of planning, this 1941 public interactive Fluorescent display was built with a "White screen" in front of this Fluorescent display to cut out any auditorium light's glare which would diminish the intensity of this Black light display. Something else that is not even considered (or known) anymore today over seventy years later.

Three additional small articles are also contained on page three of this "Black Light Beacon," the first of which informs that producers of "Motion pictures" had begun to use Ultraviolet lamps instead of White lights to record as well as print movie soundtracks onto film. The use of Ultraviolet to print these soundtracks produced a much sharper recording on the film stock's audio track, which resulted in a better produced soundtrack. As this publication's date was 1941, a presence of warfare was visible throughout these series of "Black Light Beacon," and in this issue the next small writeup was not on the use of Black light for Fluorescent murals and carpeting in movie theaters, or even on Fluorescent puppet shows or ballet costumes, but for the Second world war. The use of Ultraviolet lamps in mining across the entirety of the United States is the subject of this small article, and it explains that these U.V. lamps were essential for prospecting Scheelite's Tungsten throughout the country, and for zinc in the mines of New Jersey. The third of these small articles is a preview of what awaits the reader when turning to the next page of this 1941 "Black Light Beacon," 'Printing With Fluorescent Ink.' Again, as a preview to the following page it is explained that 'recently' a printed example of the new "Conti-Glo" Fluorescent Printing Ink was made by a company in association with the "General Electric Company" to be distributed during "Fluorescent Futuramas." This 1941 card printed with this new "Conti-Glo" Fluorescent printing ink stressed the advance of modernization by contrasting a girl dressed in a bathing suit from 1896 printed in ordinary ink, next to a 1941 bathing beauty in the "ultramodern" bathing suits of the era printed in just as "ultramodern" Fluorescent ink, who would appear on the card only when placed under an Ultraviolet lamp.

Turning the page of this seventy-five year old trade publication an unprecedented surprise awaits the reader - Fluorescent Ink printed in this 1941 issue which vividly Fluoresces under Black lights - with this Fluorescent page being the literal jewel of the entire three series of these "Black Light Beacons" from the 1940s. 'PRINTED WITH LIGHT' is the headline of this full page announcement for printing using the new Fluorescent ink, with the headline printed in "Conti-Glo" "Signal Green" Fluorescent Ink, and even after seventy-five years the half-page photograph, the headline, and the "Conti-Glo Division" footer are still vividly Fluorescent under a Black light, popping off the page in the dark! Being 1941 the half-page Fluorescent photograph is not of Artwork or any other images that may be imagined, but it's a photograph displaying rows of military maps which are surprinted with "Signal Green" Fluorescent ink just on the maps in the Black and White photo, creating a striking contrast with the rest of the Black and White photograph which intensifies the Fluorescence when put under a Black light. The text which follows the highly Fluorescent headline is a testament to the era of enthusiasm for this new Fluorescence technology which existed in 1941. 'You can't imagine holding this page printed with Fluorescent "Conti-Glo" "Signal Green" under an ultraviolet lamp's radiation.' "Conti-Glo" Division associated with "Continental Lithography Company" was introducing the offer of printing with Fluorescent ink for businessmen to make use of the 'ultra-modern attractiveness' in their suggested printing of menus, theater programs, Art reproductions, Advertising displays, and lighting installation designs. Added to these suggested applications of printing with Fluorescent ink are World war two era military charts, maps, and other 'blackout' uses. Ten Colors of "Conti-Glo" Fluorescent printing ink are listed, four of which are stated to be more stable in sunlight and include three different Greens, one of which was "Invisible," and also "Horizon Blue." The more unstable Fluorescent printing inks not suitable for exposure to sunlight include an "Invisible Blue" along with "Arc Yellow," "Fire Orange," "Aurora Pink," "Neon Red," and "Pearl White." There follows instructions to businesses with interest for printing using the new Fluorescent inks, as well as a full paragraph of 'Patent control' by "Conti-Glo" over "all processes" to do with not only the entire printing production of the Fluorescent printing inks, but also with the pigments and formulas that they were made from.

The facing page of this incredible Fluorescent announcement of "Conti-Glo" Fluorescent printing ink has another article on 'Deluxe Fluorescent Carpet Lighting.' In "Upham's Corner Theater" of Massachusetts another use of vivid Fluorescent carpeting lit up four theater aisles through the use of eighteen 'Model 67-A' "Conti-Glo" Black light ceiling units. A total of 340 feet (103 meters) of Fluorescent Aisle Carpeting must have been very vivid under these eighteen Black light spotlights, which were fitted eighteen feet (5.5 meters) above in the ceiling and situated as suggested in the "Conti-Glo" 'lighting layout.' Two photos of this article demonstrate the effect of the carpeting's Fluorescence with a comparison between White light and Black light.

Three small articles follow, one of which unbelievably announces a huge Fluorescent *Cross* under Black lights used for annual sunrise service for Easter by the "Knights of Templar!" In what is described vaguely as a large city in the East, this Easter service used a huge Cross which had been sprayed using several Fluorescent Colors of lacquer-enamel paint, and was mounted in front of a tremendous amount of Ultraviolet coming from four 250 watt "Conti-Glo" 'Model 70' Black light units. The experience must have been incredibly intense with 1,000 watts of Black light on a single huge multi-Colored Fluorescent Cross in a darkened indoor auditorium with 14,000 worshipers in awe. This small article of 1941 adds that use of "Conti-Glo" Fluorescent Colors in "religious services" was 'steadily growing'(!) Adding "mystic beauty" with Fluorescent "Conti-Glo" Paint is unbelievably described as being used on Church Alter backgrounds, religious statues, ceilings of religious centers, and even Fluorescent pigments use on religious windows of stained glass! Another jewel of an article which would be very hard to imagine happening today reports on a recent 1940 high school graduation commencement in which two graduates wore "Conti-Glo" Fluorescent satin graduation gowns along with Fluorescent costume jewelry, and appeared on stage under a normal spotlight while a thesis was being read to the graduating audience on the "Black Light." At a timed point in this "Black Light" graduation speech the spotlights were turned off and a powerful 250 watt "Conti-Glo" Black light was turned on, which caused the two girl's gowns and jewelry to brilliantly Fluoresce under "invisible light."

A full page article follows on page six, with another 'hard-sell' campaign of plainly stated "Selling Light!" A dramatic photo supplements this headline, and displays a very bright Fluorescent picture of a Church with a person in the dark holding a bizarre-looking Black light in front of the picture. The italicized point of the article plainly explains that for "marketing LIGHT" a design created with Fluorescent Color put under a Black light gives the prospective client an 'exact image' in "LIGHT" of what will be bought in "LIGHT." This full page article is directed towards businesses of lamps and fixtures, luminous displays and signs, or lighting and power services. "Conti-Glo" Fluorescent lacquer-enamel paint used to sell designs of building front lighting installations is further explained. Another detail is revealed in this article, which explains that such an expense and planning went into outdoor lighting displays that the Fluorescent designs for the displays were being framed and hung in customer's offices. Proposed Fluorescent designs for store interiors along with plans for Fluorescent night clubs and movie theater murals all intended to be under Black lights are discussed in the article as being proposed with designs using Fluorescent paint as a "selling tool" described as "ultra-modern."

The first of three small articles on the next page is yet another reportage on the highly effective use of Fluorescent "Conti-Glo" Invisible Green powder in crime detection. Two photos and a report of a ventriloquist named Chriss Cross using a Fluorescent doll named Syracuse creating a stage act which is again described as "ultra-modern" closes page seven along with an announcement of the 1941 Ohio Boy Scout Circus making a performance using Fluorescent flags painted "Neon Red," "Pearl White," and "Horizon Blue." Of course this 1941 Boy Scout Circus ended with a fully Fluorescent American flag under Black lights(!) The back cover of this "Black Light Beacon" advertises two "Conti-Glo" Black light floodlights with a headline announcing "Intensely Brilliant." Photos of the portable 'Model 91' and permanent installation 'Model 96' 100 watt Black light unit accompany a list of the lamp's specifications and explained general usage. The first sentence of this full page advertisement's text stresses that the "near-ultraviolet" produced by these Black lights was "harmless," as well as invisible. These 100 watt Black light floodlights are recommended only for small Fluorescent theater murals under fifty square feet. The 100 watt Black light spotlights, the portable 'Model 93' and the permanent 'Model 99' are also described in this ad, and recommended for use when a concentrated beam was necessary. The advertised prices for these Black lights are just as amazing, with prices between $29.75 and $31.75 falling just short of the $35.50 value of an ounce of gold in 1941!

The third nearly-impossible-to-find "Black Light Beacon" that was in the sale that I was fortunate enough to acquire for the Museum collection was the "November, 1941" Christmas Issue. This eight page treasure of antique Black light and Fluorescent practices seventy-five years ago has on each of it's pages a theme of Fluorescent Black Light Christmas! Christmas decorations were always an early application of Black lights and Fluorescent Colors, and this 1941 publication documents just how important an application it was back then. The front cover of this "Black Light Beacon" has a full page article and two photographs of another early famous application of Black lights and Fluorescent paint, the 1942 "Ice-Capades." Still a small part of international Ice spectaculars today, these early 1942 "Ice-Capades" used enormous amounts of Black lights and must have produced breath taking shows in comparison to a contemporary regressed show today. The article's title announces clearly that these "Ice-Capades" had used "Conti-Glo" Black lights together with Fluorescent paints and Fluorescent satins for several years already, with the highlight of these "Ice-Capades" being a Black light "Dutch Treat" performance that can be seen in the two photos of this article. Brilliantly Fluorescent, even in these Black and White photos of 1941, the skaters dressed in traditional Dutch costumes as well as the large windmill and tulip cart stage props, create what is described as an "outstanding feature" in this show 'under the Black light's mysterious rays.' The costumes of the skaters and the stage props were made using "substantial quantities" of "Conti-Glo" Fluorescent satins and Fluorescent lacquer-enamels, with the amount of powerful 250 watt 'Model 70' Black light floodlights all around the skating ring described as "banks." Not only were there thousands of watts of Black light floodlights surrounding the skating ring for this "Ice-Capades" show, but also "carbon-arc" Black light spotlights were used on individual performers as well. Using probably around 5,000 watts of Black lights for this 1942 "Ice-Capades" show, which translates only in wattage, not in superior quality and distance of light-throw, to no less than one-hundred and thirty-eight of today's commonly used tubular Black lights, this show must have been dazzling. Page two of this 1941 Christmas Issue has two photographs and an article on creating a 'Conti-Glo Home Christmas.' The first photo shows what was one of the most popular Christmas uses of the Black light and Fluorescent Colors, the Fluorescent Christmas Tree! The picture shows a fully decorated Fluorescent Christmas tree on the "front lawn" with Black light units in front of it on the lawn which gave the appearance of this Christmas tree being 'lit from within.' In the Museum collection are hundreds of slides that the founder of "Ultra-Violet Products, Inc." Thomas S. Warren sent to me from his personal collection of the Christmas Black light extravaganza he would set up on his whole block every year in Pasadena, California during the 1950s. The second photo in this article is of a woman at home painting all different Christmas decorations with Fluorescent paint under a Black light. On the table in front of her are four medium sized and one large labelled glass bottles of 1941 "Conti-Glo" Fluorescent lacquer-enamel paints, which are explained as being a Fluorescent paint "Christmas kit" consisting of a brush and five jars of Fluorescent "Transparent lacquers" including "Neon Red," "Invisible Blue," "Pearl White," "Arc Yellow," and "Saturn Green." This "Christmas kit" was sold for $10.00 with separate half-pint jars sold for $2.50. It's no wonder the woman painting Fluorescent Christmas decorations is so bright, because the recommended lamp to use for painting Fluorescent Christmas balls was a 100 watt "Conti-Glo" Black light! Beneath this article is another in a series of reports on using Black lights in Movie theaters all across America for Fluorescent Aisle Carpeting, Fluorescent murals, and other decorative objects. The point of this article is very clearly stated as being the increase in customers at movie theaters because of the "beautification" of these theaters with Fluorescent murals and Aisle carpeting under Black lights. The cost of installing Black lights and Fluorescence in a movie theater was described as being "amazingly little" compared to "the impression" that the show made on customers.

Page three of this November, 1941 "Black Light Beacon" has a full page article which today seems nearly as unbelievable and hysterical as "Use Black Light for: Church Groups," the "Conti-Glo" 1941 'Black Light Christmas Dinner Table Setting'(!) No joke, a photograph of a very serious Christmas Dinner Table set for six is displayed in the large photograph, which has a big circular metal Black light fixture in the center of this Christmas Dinner Table that is creating the intense Fluorescence of every single item of all the specifically designed Fluorescent dinner table accessories, including the vivid Fluorescent table cloth! It is explained that since Christmas should be a 'Light Festival,' then 1941's Christmas could be a very special 'Light Feast,' with your own 'Fluorescent Christmas Dinner Table Setting' from "Conti-Glo" creating what is described as a "revelation" for your guests who didn't know about the "marvels" of Ultraviolet and Fluorescence. The 'Fluorescent Dinner Table's' centerpiece was a polished chrome round "silver-like" Black light fixture used for the Annual dinner ball of the United States military and "General Motors" described on another front cover of a "Black Light Beacon." This circular Black light centerpiece lit up the entire 'Fluorescent Christmas Dinner Table Setting,' which included for the expensive $150.00 selling price this 'EH-4' circular chrome Black light, an "Invisible Blue" large Fluorescent satin tablecloth, six wine glasses with different Colored Fluorescent stems, six napkins of three different Fluorescent Colors, a circular wreath of Fluorescent plastic flowers to put around the base of the chrome circular Black light, and also three ashtrays in different Fluorescent Colors. This 1941 'Fluorescent Christmas Dinner Table Setting' under it's circular Black light right in the center of the table must have been spectacular, and should have since it cost the same as more than four ounces of gold(!)

The two page centerfold of this 1941 Christmas special "Black Light Beacon" has one large Christmas article that spreads across both pages, as well as two small Christmas articles underneath. The double-page headline announces that 'Fluorescence and Black Light Add Mystery and Allure to Christmas Displays!' Four photographs of this article show a huge Fluorescent sculpture of a Christmas star outside in a public space both in daylight and under Black light, a very large billboard-sized Fluorescent "Merry Christmas" display also outside next to a building, and the most surprising of all, a huge Fluorescent mural in a public place of the Star of Bethlehem and the Three Wise Men who will announce the birth of Jesus - all under Black lights! The text to this 'Fluorescent Black Light Christmas Display' article explains that Fluorescent Black light Christmas displays were being created through various organizations by 1941, such as big department stores and "religious groups." The large Fluorescent Star of Bethlehem mural under Black lights was displayed by an electrical company in West Virginia for Christmas 1940, with details given of the painting such as dark non-Fluorescent Green used for the olive tree, and the three Wise Men in the foreground of the Fluorescent mural as well painted in non-Fluorescent Green, Purple, and Red. The edge of the olive tree was done with Fluorescent Green to create an effect of penetrating light, along with the painting of the distant rolling hills. The highlights of the robes of the three Wise Men were done with Fluorescent paint, and the entire brilliant sky was done in Fluorescent Blue. The Star of Bethlehem and it's reflected light on the olive trunk were in the brightest Color, Fluorescent Red. Even the small stars were painted Fluorescent Green in the sky and the distant village was done in multiple Fluorescent Colors. That's not all - this huge Fluorescent Star of Bethlehem mural was constantly under powerful Black lights and created to unbelievably change between a daylight effect, then sunset, night, and finally sunrise, by the maneuvering of changing lighting between four 250 watt Black light units and incandescent White lights, which used what is described as a simply archaic lighting dimmer that was "mechanically operated" through the use of a "waterbarrel" type of "rheostat." The large Fluorescent Christmas Star sculpture was made for the 1940 Dover, Ohio Christmas display and was seven feet tall (2.1 meters). This twelve pointed star was made with Yellow, Green, and Red Fluorescent "Conti-Glo" "Permo Sheeting" and revolved outside in front of three 250 watt powerful Black lights. Under 750 watts of Black light this Fluorescent Christmas Star must really have been as bright as a Sun!

Black Light Christmas is still the theme of the two smaller articles of this November, 1941 "Black Light Beacon" centerfold pages, with the first article giving advice on 'Outdoor Lighting for Christmas Displays.' What "Conti-Glo" advises for Fluorescent Christmas decorations is nothing less than the most powerful and expensive Black light unit they ever made, the 250 watt 'Model 70,' that was strong enough to use for "Ice-Capades" and Radio City Music Hall "Skeleton Ballets!" The Fluorescent Christmas displays which this 250 watt Black light was suggested for were entire "house fronts," or decorated Christmas trees and shrubbery. What is surprising about the suggestion of using this powerful 'Model 70' which was also very heavy, has an operating temperature hot enough to fry eggs on, and is not waterproof in any way - or even produced for outdoor use - is the advice to bring these massive, expensive, fragile, very hot, and heavy 250 watt Black light units back in the house every night after the Christmas displays are turned off. A photo of the lamp was included in the article, which was $59.50 in 1941, being the price of more than one and a half ounce of gold. Better advice follows from "Conti-Glo" with the second small article suggesting 'Three Materials from "Conti-Glo" to Create Fluorescent Christmas Decorations," and lists three different Fluorescent products for making these Christmas displays highly Fluorescent. Fluorescent Lacquer-enamel paint is the first suggestion, which "Conti-Glo" manufactured in twelve Colors but were designed only for use on indoor displays because they were not stable under sunlight. This standard Fluorescent paint line sold by "Conti-Glo" is described in this article as being opaque paint which was designed to be used on any surfaces, such as fabrics, metals, glass, plaster, or wood, and could be applied by brush, paint sprayer, or even used for stencils. The typically astronomical "Conti-Glo" price for this Fluorescent Lacquer-enamel paint was $2.50 for a quarter-pint and $8.75 for a pint (half a liter). At these prices a single gallon of this Fluorescent paint would have cost as much as two ounces of gold in 1941. The second Fluorescent product advised for Fluorescent Christmas displays was a newly designed Lacquer-enamel paint for outdoor uses as well. This outdoor Fluorescent paint was sold in "Signal Green," "Invisible Green," and a new deep "Flag Red." The third Fluorescent product suggested in this small article was "Permo Sheeting" from "Conti-Glo," which was explained to be suitable for outdoor Black light displays and designed for long uses. The suggested applications for this "Permo Sheeting" were Fluorescent backgrounds or silhouettes, as well as making cutout letters, designs, or figures. This Fluorescent "Permo Sheeting" was available in "Invisible Green," "Arc Yellow, and "Neon Red" sold by the square foot.

Two articles on the following page are the only reports in this November, 1941 "Black Light Beacon" which do not center on Fluorescent Christmas Displays, with the larger article giving advice on the creation of 'Fluorescent Mineral Displays Using Mercury Spotlights.' The article was reprinted from the September, 1941 "Rocks and Minerals" magazine, and begins with a new Black light unit suitable for the less bright Fluorescence of natural minerals. Early Black light units that were used for Fluorescent mineral displays up until this 1941 publication were discussed in this article, such as "NICO" mercury vapor lamps from "Cooper Hewitt," "Hanovia" Hot quartz mercury Sunlamps, many weak Argon bulbs used together, and even the early "Purple X" Black light bulbs. These examples of Fluorescent mineral display lamps were all "long wave" Ultraviolet lamps, also called "near-Ultraviolet" in this article, and designated in Angstroms (3000-4000), with suggested minerals to be displayed under these lamps being fluorite, hyalite, "wernerite-scapolite," and semi-opal. What is surprising to read in this 1941 article today is that what is called "Shortwave" Ultraviolet now (254 nanometers) was considered "Middle-Ultraviolet" in 1941 (2537 Angstroms, or 253.7 nanometers), and "Longwave" Ultraviolet (366 nanometers) was called "near-ultraviolet" or "long wave" and thought to be 3,000-4,000 Angstrom (300-400 nanometers) which effectively included 300 nanometer "Middlewave" Ultraviolet together with "Longwave" Ultraviolet and didn't even consider that there was "MIddlewave" Ultraviolet between Longwave and Shortwave Ultraviolet. The Fluorescent minerals excited by this "Middle-Ultraviolet" were listed as Red Fluorescing Calcite from Franklin, New Jersey, Blue Fluorescing Hydrozincite and Scheelite, "Sweetwater" Agates Fluorescing Green, and Blue Fluorescing Benitoite. The author of this article from the "Rocks and Minerals"

September, 1941 magazine next admits that he thought the Longwave and Shortwave Ultraviolet lamps he had to display his Fluorescent minerals were as far as could be obtained with a natural Fluorescent display, but he was just astounded when he put a 100 watt "Conti-Glo" spotlight onto his Fluorescent mineral collection. What this "Conti-Glo" 'Model 93' theatrical spotlight did to Mr. Hatcher's Fluorescent minerals he called a "revelation," and he wrote that after he bought the 100 watt Longwave Ultraviolet spotlight he turned it on and pointed it towards his Fluorescent mineral collection that he knew so well, and what he saw he also described as "magnificent." Not only was the "Conti-Glo" 100 watt spotlight brighter than anything that Mr. Hatcher had ever used on his Fluorescent mineral collection, but the superior Ultraviolet filter in his 'Model 93' Back light also excluded most of the visible light which got through the inferior lamps he was used to viewing his collection under, causing him to admit the collection now looked 'extremely spectacular.' The author used his knowledge of geology to make a quantifying test measuring the actual increase in brilliance of the light being emitted from his Fluorescent minerals first under his former U.V. lamp of choice the Nico Black light, and then under his new "Conti-Glo" 100 watt Black light spotlight. The Fluorescent minerals were kept at the same distance from each U.V. lamp, and the brightness of their Fluorescence was measured with a "Weston phototronic" light meter. Cumberland, England Fluorite, "wernerite-scapolite," and "Fluorescent canary" Corning glass ("Depression glass") were methodically measured for brilliance under both U.V. units and the results were also "spectacular," with each specimen emitting ten to twenty times the light under the 100 watt Black light than under the standard Nico Black lights. The author further admits that not only were the Fluorescent minerals ten to twenty times as bright as he had ever seen them before, but that he saw Fluorescence and Phosphorescence in specimens such as Dolomite crystals from Maryland which he had never even seen Colors in before. Italian Gypsum Fluoresced Red, "Ruby Corundum" finally Fluoresced brilliantly in Red, Spodumene Fluoresced and Phosphoresced, "Precious Opal" from Australia also Fluoresced and Phosphoresced, Orange Fluorescence from Agate petrified wood of Arizona and also "Opalized wood" of South Dakota, and varied Calcite specimens of stalactite, septerians, rhombohedral crystals, from Arizona, as well as calcite from Franklin, New Jersey not only brilliantly Fluoresced, but also had some Phosphorescence. Most of these Fluorescent examples listed by Mr. Hatcher using his new powerful 100 watt Black light he had never seen before in his minerals, nor even knew they were capable of luminescence. Underneath the article by this author of the "Rocks and Minerals" magazine, there is a photograph and a short report on a new 'portable' Shortwave Ultraviolet lamp designed for outdoor Fluorescent mineral prospecting. This new 'Model 252' 'short-wave radiation' lamp is correctly termed "Shortwave" by "Conti-Glo," and explained to be 'compact' and designed for prospecting and mining. Directly listed in this short explanation is the prospecting for Scheelite and Zinc, the two most famous Fluorescent minerals which were being searched for in America during the time period of this "Black Light Beacon," the Second world war. Although this lamp may have been considered 'compact' in 1941, the photo and the listed details of this outdoor prospecting lamp look anything but compact or convenient. With a weight of five pounds (over 2 kilos) and looking like a large heavy rectangular iron box, this lamp must have been as 'compact' as it was cheap, costing $54.00, or the price of over an ounce and a half of gold in 1941.

The final two small articles on page seven of this eight page "Black Light Beacon" both are directly related to the Second world war era of this 1941 publication, beginning with a report on the difficulty of manufacturing 'Mercury Lamps' during wartime restrictions of materials. It is directly stated that 'certain elements' used for the manufacturing of Black lights were included on the list of "difficulty attainable" wartime supplies. The small report which closes the page of this 1941 trade publication would convince even the toughest skeptic that this was definitively the Second world war era: Fluorescent "American Flags!" Obvious from the first sentence, the wartime emotions described throughout this super-patriotic article are quite evident. For 'defense rallies' to 'public meetings,' the new Fluorescent satin "Conti-Glo" American Flag was described as 'actually emitting light' and having a 'translucent appearance,' reminding a citizen of religious "stained glass" windows in churches. These new satin Fluorescent American Flags were available from "Conti-Glo" in a four by six foot size (1.2 x 1.8 meter) for $29.00, and a super-sized Fluorescent American Flag of twelve by twenty feet (3.6 x 6 meters) available to rent from "Conti-Glo." This small article also mentions that for $3.50 a yard customers could buy Red, White, and Blue Fluorescent satin and make their own Fluorescent American Flag. As usual the suggested amount of Black light energy to be used on a single Fluorescent American Flag was between 300 and 750 percent more than the single 36 watt tubular Black light which would undoubtably be considered sufficient seventy-five years later, and advises patriotic customers to use a 100 watt Black light spotlight only if lighting up a small-sized Fluorescent American Flag, and only if this small Fluorescent flag was 'totally in the dark' and the Black light spotlight was mounted close by the flag. What was really recommended for these Fluorescent American Flags was the extreme 250 watt Black light floodlight 'Model 70,' which would have made the highly Fluorescent satin American Flag visible from the Moon!

This November, 1941 Christmas Issue of "Black Light Beacon" closes with a back cover article and photos of 'Black Light Christmas Trees!' The Fluorescent Black Light Christmas Tree in the Black and White photo looks extremely bright, and must have been, since the recommended lamp for a single Fluorescent Christmas Tree was the 100 watt Black light spotlight! The intensity of Fluorescence created through the use of a 100 watt Black light spotlight on a single Fluorescent Christmas Tree would be hard to imagine today, when a single 36 watt tubular Black light would surely be considered sufficient for the same installation. The title of this article advertises a 'Black Light Fairyland' being produced with this 100 watt Black light spotlight being used on a Fluorescent Christmas Tree, which either in the house, or on the lawn in front of the house, would be bursting with light without using a single Christmas light. Not only would the modern 1941 Fluorescent Christmas Tree emit it's own light without the use of a single Christmas light on the tree, the new Fluorescent Christmas Tree Ornaments would not be made of old-fashioned breakable glass, but used featherweight unbreakable Fluorescent plastic instead. These Fluorescent plastic Christmas Tree Ornaments are described as being beautiful in daylight, but in the Black light these Fluorescent plastic Christmas Tree Ornaments would become 'visible light sources.' "Conti-Glo" also sold these Fluorescent Christmas Tree Ornaments, which were advertised as modern, plastic and coming in typical Christmas season shapes such as "snow crystals," which were also 'weatherproof, unbreakable, and fire resistant.' These Fluorescent Christmas Tree Ornaments of assorted Christmas shapes were sold for either small or large Christmas trees for $5.00 and $10.00 per 'handsome decorated box.'

Included originally in these 1940s "Black Light Beacon" trade publications was a single page "Index of Subjects" for a portion of each year's issues, such as between 'June-July, 1941,' as well as a page included with the last issue of each year covering the entire year, 'Vol. 1, 1941.' Being an alphabetical index of the full content of a year's "Black Light Beacon" is obviously a source of a wealth of lost knowledge from an era three-quarters of a century ago during the age of "The Miracle of Fluorescence, 1930s - 1950s." The highlights of this double-sided page of 1941 index of "Conti-Glo" subjects will be listed here, such as the 'Fluorescent Black Light Dinner,' 'Ballroom Magic,' 'Black Light Christmas Displays,' 'Black Light Ice Ballets,' 'Black Light Movie Theater Carpeting,' "Black Light Christmas Trees," 'Cleveland Crime Clinic,' 'Safety Features,' 'Kansas City Crooks,' 'Knights-Templar Services,' "General Motors," 'Aviation,' 'Fluorescent Theaters,' 'Fluorescent Instrument Panels,' 'Detectives,' 'Dollars,' "Vodvil Acts," and 'Fluorescent American Flags,' 'Black Light Photography,' 'Industrial Displays,' 'Jugglers,' 'Fluorescent Lighting Installations,' 'Mineral Fluorescence,' 'Miss Fluorescence,' 'Fluorescent Lounges and Ballrooms,' 'Fluorescent Theater Poster Displays,' 'Printing with Fluorescent Ink,' 'Color Psychology,' 'American Indian Celebrations,' 'Spray-Gun used for Fluorescent Paint,' 'Fluorescent Cocktail Lounges' and 'Black Light Dinners,' 'Fluorescent Murals,' 'Velour for Fluorescent Murals,' 'Fluorescent Ventriloquist,' and 'Woven In Light' Fluorescent Textiles. 'Fields of Use' for "Conti-Glo" Fluorescent products follows, including everything the company sold from Fluorescent Black Light Aisle Carpeting for movie theaters to Fluorescent writing ink, as well as an 'Index of Products' sold by "Conti-Glo" and an 'Index of Black Light Units' that the company sold in 1941, including six different powerful 250 watt Black light units from floodlights and spotlights, to units designed specifically for "Carpet Lighting." Four different 100 watt Black light units are also listed, including spotlights and floodlights, as well as several speciality "Conti-Glo" lamps. The final listing in this double-sided "Conti-Glo" Index for 1941 is for 'Fluorescent Black Light Installations,' and includes the "American Theater" in Montana, the "Avalon Theater" of New York, the "Beechwold Theater" and "Boulevard Theater" both of Columbus, Ohio, the "Ken Theater" in Chicago, the "New Mercury" Theater in Detroit, the "Carlos Theater" in California, "Essex Theater" in New York, and "Hotel Secor" of Ohio, the "Princes Theater" of Alabama, the "State Theater" of Michigan, the "Upham's Corner Theater" of Massachusetts, and finally the "Waikiki Theater" of Honolulu, which totals thirteen major Black light installations in major theaters and public places of America covered in the 1941 issues of the "Black Light Beacon."

The final gem of the third "Black Light Beacon" collection acquired for the Museum is a very historically precious document, the February 1, 1942 "Price List" of "Conti-Glo" "Standard Products" made specifically for "civilian uses." The front of this two-fold brochure has two Red stripes at the top and bottom which run completely through the brochure on both sides. The large script logo of "Conti-Glo" is also printed in Red, but this is the only Red text of the brochure. This brochure front has the title 'Standard "Conti-Glo" Products' in large bold type, with "for civilian uses" in smaller type, being an obvious statement of the Price List's front title. Not only is this "for civilian uses" specified in the title, but three lines of small text, printed also as a part of this title make it perfectly clear that this was the era of the Second world war, advising customers who were "officially engaged" in "war operations" or "war planning" to send a request for special prices and details of products manufactured by "Conti-Glo" specifically for "war uses." It couldn't have been more clearly stated. The center of the front of this "Price List A" from February 1, 1942 has a small Black high-contrast illustration of the "Conti-Glo" 100 watt Black light unit. Opening up the two-fold brochure, the three separate 'pages' each have a horribly designed 1940s headline with four different sized types, in two different type faces, announcing again 'Standard "Conti-Glo" Products' "(for civilian uses)." The first two 'pages' of the inside of this brochure are a "price List' of "Fluorescent material," followed by "Black Light Equipment" on the third page. Turning over the brochure the fourth and fifth 'pages' of this six 'page' folded brochure also are all printed with the same - "for civilian uses" - headline and contain the Price List's details, final products, and offered services.

The first and most important of the seven "Fluorescent Materials" on this "Conti-Glo" 1942 Price List is the Fluorescent "Lacquer-enamel" paint, which is described as being "opaque" and "heavily pigmented," for use only indoors, and to be applied by spraying, by brush, or by "dipping." What is also a clear indication that this Fluorescent paint listing was made during the era of "The Miracle of Fluorescence," is that the dozen Colors are listed on a chart with separate "Appearance Under" both in "Daylight" and "Black Light." Another point of this chart is that only about half of the names of the Fluorescent Colors are familiar from using "Day-Glo" paint for the last forty-five years, and the rest are archaic names from the first decade of Robert and Joseph Switzer's Fluorescent paint company "Conti-Glo," years later named "Day-Glo." The twelve Fluorescent "Lacquer-Enamel" paints include the three different "Invisible" Colors Blue, White, and Green, "Pearl White," which has a "Daylight" Color called the retro "Flesh" and Fluoresces White, "Horizon Blue" still called the same seventy-five years later, "Saturn Green" listed as being "Lemon" in Daylight, and "Signal Green" which is still named the same, "Sodium Yellow," which is an antique name, but "Arc Yellow" is still the same as well as "Fire Orange," "Neon Red," and "Aurora Pink" with familiar names. The new Color added at the bottom of this chart was "Flag Red." As always the prices of this Fluorescent paint was inevitably high, with a half-gallon (1,4 liters) being $31.00 and a gallon (3.79 liters) being $54.00 (while an ounce of gold was $35.50). Number two listing of "Fluorescent Material" on this Price List was "Fluorescent Satin," which was available in "Flag Red," "Flag Blue," and "Invisible" White, as well as four other Colors and was $3.95 per yard, with number "2-A" of the Price List being the "Fluorescent American Flag." On this list the price is given for the large eight by twelve foot (2.4 x 3.6 meter) Fluorescent American Flag explained in the "Black Light Beacon" as being available only for rent, and this expensive Fluorescent Flag sold for $77.00, or 2.1 ounces of solid gold! "Transparent Lacquers" are next as the third listing, and are advised to be painted on White bases, Colorless glass, on plastic, or on a shinny metallic surface, and were sold in the same Colors and for the same prices as "Lacquer-Enamels." Number four on this Price List is the obscure 'Liquid for Painting fabrics,' which was advised to be only used on White materials, and sold in the same Fluorescent Colors as "Lacquer-Enamels," but for only two-thirds the price. Fluorescent "Water Colors" were listed next and sold in eight different Colors for the same prices as "Lacquer-Enamels." The last three Fluorescent products were used for security and by the police, including the bizarrely named "Pass Out" Invisible "Check Ink" for entrances to 'dance halls, amusement parks, or rinks,' and sold Fluorescing Blue under a Black light. 'Crime Detection Powder' was sold in "Invisible Green" and the last three items of "Fluorescent Materials" were four different Fluorescent Security Writing Inks including the Invisible "Phanto-Message" Writing Ink, Writing Ink in Fluorescent Blue and a Fluorescent Green, with even Writing Ink in the unique "Fluorescent Black."

'Black Lights and Equipment' is the second major listing of "Standard Products" sold by "Conti-Glo" in 1942, with fifteen lamps and corresponding accessories sold. 'Model 51' was a simple $5.95 Black light, 'Model 91' a portable 100 watt floodlight and 'Model 93' a spotlight, 'Model 94' a 100 watt Black light with it's carrying case, 'Model 96' a permanent-installation 100 watt floodlight and 'Model 94' a spotlight, 'Model 70' the monster 250 watt portable floodlight and the 'Model 72' spotlight, the 'Model 80' 250 watt was a permanent installation floodlight and the 'Model 82' spotlight, the 'Model 86' 250 watt Black light for ceiling "Recessed Mounting" with a 'lightbeam spread' described as '"circular" and then described as "rectangular" in the similar 'Model 87,' the specialty 'Model 67-A' Fluorescent Aisle Carpeting 100 watt Black light, the healthy 'Model 203' Sunlamp, and even healthier 'Model 252' "Hand Lamp" of "Cold Quartz."

The third and final section of "Conti-Glo" Fluorescent products in their 1942 Price List is another product clearly indicating that this brochure is from the pre-stigmatized long past, the 'Fluorescent Black Light Table Setting!' Sold in the 1941 "Black Light Beacon" complete for $150.00, the elements of this "Table Setting" were no longer in 1942 listed for sale as a set, but separately as the circular chrome 'Table Fixture Black Light,' the 'Satin Fluorescent Tablecloth' with six Fluorescent napkins, and the "Accessories" of a Fluorescent flower wreath for the lamp unit, six Fluorescent glasses, four Fluorescent ashtrays, and a candle holder. The complete set would have been $116.00 which is much cheaper than for the original $150.00 price of the prior year.

The final section of this two-fold "Conti-Glo" 1942 Price List has five "Services" available to customers, including Advisory, Engineering, "Theatre," "Fluorescent Lithography" advertised as 'Printing in Light,' and "Equipment Rental" of the 250 watt 'Model 70' Black light unit to be used for 'ice carnivals, stage shows, conventions, or sales meetings.' The last service listed is for Fluorescent printing "Screen Process" of 'posters or displays' in twelve Fluorescent Colors.

"Conti-Glo" "Product Catalogue and Price List" (1941-1942)

From an attic in Cleveland, Ohio, forgotten for many decades, came three extremely rare historic issues of "Conti-Glo BLACK LIGHT BEACON" now in the Museum collection. With these three historic magazines came another precious item: the entire 'Product Catalogue and Price List' of all merchandise sold by "Conti-Glo" at this time period of 1941-1942. This extremely precious Product Catalogue is nine pages long, stapled together, and includes two pages that have been typed by hand, not reproductions. It is evident that the original Cleveland, Ohio owner of the three issues of "Black Light Beacon," together with this complete Product Catalogue of "Conti-Glo" products, may have been a retailer, perhaps operated a store, or had been involved in some other manner with the buying and selling of this "Conti-Glo" Fluorescent paint and Black lights.

This 1941-1942 Price List and Product Catalogue has a front cover with the top third of the page filled with the logo of "Conti-Glo," and what do you know - the logo is in the shape of an Artist's Palette - *Not a Highway Safety Cone!* Inside the Artist's Black Palette is the company name "Conti-Glo" in a type font that is instantaneously recognizable as retro, and in actuality, is the probable grandfather of that ancient miserable type face "Dom Casual." It is so early in the career of the Switzer Brothers (Robert Switzer had only invented Fluorescent paint eight or nine years before as a teenager) that 'Patents Pending' is written under their business name in the logo. 'Paints and Black Lights' is the title of the Product Catalogue and Price List and 'Conti-Glo Sales dept., Continental Lithography Corp., Cleveland, Ohio' is the footer of the cover.

The first page of this "Conti-Glo" Price List and Product Catalogue is the same full page advertisement for "Conti-Glo" Fluorescent Lacquer Enamels with the photograph of the Fluorescent paint production machine that was described in previous pages of this book. The second and third page of this Product catalogue are hand typed, not reproductions, with the impressions of the typewriter letters and symbols clearly visible on the back of both of these pages. The title of page two announces 'Other' "Conti-Glo" Fluorescent Products and begins with a synopsis of the previous printed page advertisement of "Conti-Glo" Fluorescent Lacquer Enamels. The reader is informed that the "Conti-Glo" Fluorescent Lacquer Enamel Paint is designed to use on almost any Color surface and for any use, being opaque and possible to apply by air-brush or spray-gun, by hand with a brush, or applying through stencils. Next the potential customer learns that the "Conti-Glo" Fluorescent Lacquer Enamel Paint could be painted directly onto metal, woods, fabric, and even plastered surfaces, and that these Fluorescent Colors are the best Fluorescent paints made, proven by the large range of Colors, the intensity of the Colors, the permanence, and easy application of these Fluorescent paints. This page consists of a list of all the new products that "Conti-Glo" recently began to produce in 1941-1942, including "Conti-Glo" Transparent Fluorescent Lacquers designed for painting on glass and similar materials, "Conti-Glo" Fluorescent Liquid for fabrics (specifying White as the Color of the fabric to be used upon), "Conti-Glo" Watercolors, which is one of the few products stated as being made specifically for Artists, "Conti-Glo" Fluorescent Satin, 'Phanto Message' Fluorescent Invisible Ink, 'SL-65' Fluorescent Invisible Ink for Pass-out check, and the Invisible Green Powder. The bottom of the page adds a brand new addition to the product line of "Conti-Glo" at the time: Black lights specifically designed to be used for the new innovative Fluorescent Carpeting.

Page three is another completely hand typed information sheet advertising another new "Conti-Glo" product: Fluorescent Satin, which was invented by the Switzer Brothers on commission to the U.S. government as one of the first uses of Fluorescence by the military. The introduction informs potential customers that these beauteous Fluorescent satins are sold in many Colors which will vividly Fluoresce under a Black light, and that this "Conti-Glo" Fluorescent satin is not the same as the inferior stiff Fluorescent materials that have simply been coated with Fluorescent paints, but the first of it's kind ever produced. This extravagant Fluorescent satin came in seven different Colors including the Invisible Blue and Whites, the patriotic 'Flag" Red and "Flag" Blue, another Red, Green and Yellow. This Fluorescent satin was sold thirty-eight inches wide (1 meter) with a price of $3.50 a yard, with reductions for larger quantities. Further details on the Fluorescent satin are given, including the claims of permanence of Color even with exposure to sunlight and after dry-cleaning. Suggested uses for this "Conti-Glo" Fluorescent satin are listed as stage costumes and backdrops, also listing household decoration including window drapery. The suggestion of cutting out designs from Fluorescent satins and sewing them to non-Fluorescent cloth is given for costume or stage use, creating wonderful 'two-way' or 'Invisible' Fluorescent effects when under Black lights. The final suggestion for Fluorescent satin is to sew 'Invisible' Blue or White Fluorescent satin designs onto normal White clothing, creating spectacular invisible effects when the Invisible White or Blue satin designs burst into Colors under Black lights. The suggestion of adding any design of the Fluorescent satins onto non-Fluorescent material of a similar Color also is given for special Invisible effects under Black light, and the page closes with advice of using this Fluorescent satin to producers of Stage shows or Floor shows, for whom this information was primarily directed.

The following page of this "Conti-Glo" Product Catalogue represents to myself one of those things that you dream about for years without really expecting to ever get. Here we have a full page advertisement for a 'Trial Kit' of eight bottles of "Conti-Glo" Fluorescent paints from 1942, offered for sale with just the paint, or as part of the full kit which included a Black light fixture and a screw-in Black light bulb. The entire kit with the Fluorescent Paint Set, the Black light and the large round metal Black light fixture was sold for $10.00. The Trial Kit of eight small bottles of "Conti-Glo" Fluorescent paint was just $5.00, the 'Model 51' Black light fixture was $5.95, or just the screw-in Black light bulb was $2.00. Again, sounds cheap today, but $10.00 in 1942 would have bought you over a quarter of an ounce of Gold. Although in the Museum collection I have several types of Fluorescent paint sets from the 1950s, including a full "Black Light Magic" kit from 1952 also with bottles of Fluorescent paint and including even an older "Argon" bulb, a full set of "Ultra-Violet Products, Inc." "Paint With Living Light" Fluorescent paint from the 1950s, a complete set of "Blak-Ray" Fluorescent Artist Oil Paint in tubes still sealed with still some soft paint inside them from the 1950s, swatches of "Vo-Glo" Fluorescent paints made in San Francisco before 1953, an amazing "Blak-Ray" Invisible Fluorescent Chalk Set in mint condition, and several other Artist's Fluorescent paints and artifacts from the 1950s, this "Conti-Glo" Trial Set of eight small bottles of some of the very first Fluorescent paint sold in the world is something like the "Holy Grail" (without trying to be too overly dramatic). This Trail Set of "Conti-Glo" Fluorescent Lacquer Paint from 1941 to 1942 consisted of eight bottles of paint, each with a paper label bearing the "Conti-Glo" logo and the name of the Fluorescent paint the bottle contained. This Trail Kit contained a selection of Fluorescent paint manufactured by "Conti-Glo" during the early 1940s and included several of the names of Fluorescent paint that "Day-Glo Corporation, Inc." still uses today over seventy years later, and which are instantly recognizable and familiar to me because for over twenty five years I've been mixing Fluorescent paints with "Day-Glo" Fluorescent powdered pigments with the same exact names, including 'Horizon' Blue, 'Neon' Red, 'Arc' Yellow, and 'Aurora' Pink. A few of the names have been upgraded today from their original late 1930s to early 1940s names, but are still similar to the original Color names they had. 'Fire' Orange, 'Signal' Green, 'Pearl' White and 'Invisible' Blue were the other four bottles of Fluorescent paint completing this ultra-rare Trial Set. Here was another rare example of a complete full page advertisement for Fluorescent paint and Black lights that did not mention the Second world war once. Quite the contrary, this advertisement is completely centered on creating Art with this Fluorescent paint and Black light, already suggesting Ice Skating shows and Fluorescent Demonstrations in the headline. The proposed uses for this Introductory Kit included making a Fluorescent sketch or model of a Fluorescent installation for a customer, sketches of 'light-emitting' electrical signs or displays (probably referring to Neon signs), small highlighting uses in advertising, entertainment, or on any other decorations, lecture demonstration, and finally, 'experimentation' and Art. The text of this advertisement goes on to suggest using this Fluorescent paint kit with Black light for demonstrating to a customer what a proposed installation will look like in the dark under only Black lights through a simple drawing made with "Conti-Glo" Fluorescent lacquer enamel paints. I still dream about finding one of these seventy-five year old original Fluorescent paint kits!

The second half of this 1941-1942 "Conti-Glo" Fluorescent product catalogue is devoted to advertisements of the many different models of very powerful Black light units sold by "Conti-Glo" as well. This catalogue was obviously produced for the public sector, without one word or passing comment about the Second world war, the U.S. military, or even sabotage, throughout it's entire eight pages, exactly the opposite of most of the articles and advertisements in the issues of the "Black Light Beacon" during the same time period.

The first page of Black light unit advertisements in this 1941-1942 catalogue has three photographs of two different very powerful 250 watt Black light floodlights intended for use with a Fluorescent Mural or with Fluorescent Carpeting, as the headline states. These two Black light units were very special in their design for their intended usage - unparalleled in today's world - and were meant to be mounted inside the wall or ceiling, so only the round Black Ultraviolet filtered front of the large Black light would be seen by an audience, not the entire obtrusive metal fixture, metal mounting brackets, and all electrical components of the lighting unit, which would be seen and is very typical - actually standard procedure - today in our regressed state. The first sentence of the advertisement's text immediately informs customers that the Longwave Ultraviolet energy emitted by these Ultraviolet lamps is Harmless (most likely stated so clearly because this era was during the Shortwave Ultraviolet medical 'Miracle-Cure' nightmare period), and actually begins with the 'first sentence' of advice that almost all contemporary lighting directors globally have not 'forgotten,' but have *never learned:* the fact that for Fluorescent displays to be fabulous, a fabulous amount of Black light must be used - not one 36 watt Black light tube, only. These two hidden wall or ceiling fixtures, 'Model 86' being designed as a 250 watt floodlight for vertical flat murals, and 'Model 87' was designed as a 250 watt floodlight for horizontal flat murals - are an example of the degree of designing and projection that went into Black light technology over seven decades ago. The text states that 100 watt Black light floodlights were adequate for only small Fluorescent murals(!), but these 250 watt Black light units could be used to cover an area of eight to ten feet (2.5 to 3 meters).

That's 250 watts of Black light, which today would have but a generous two 36 watt Black light tubular lamps in it's place, conveniently and cheaply producing a whopping 72 watts of Black light in the Twenty-first century, compared to 250 watts used in 1942.

The text of this 1941-1942 catalogue goes on to suggest the use of these concealed powerful Black light units for the new Fluorescent Carpeting being installed in Movie theaters and other public venues at that time. The three photographs in this advertisement consist of a cutaway Black and White photo of a ceiling with the square lamp housing concealed for the 'Model 87' Black light unit, another cutaway photo of the ceiling with the round lamp housing concealed for the 'Model 86,' and a center photo of a "Conti-Glo" ceiling or wall adapter for either of these 250 watt units, which had a huge filter surface at about a thirty degree angle that was adjustable to direct the Black light towards wall murals from a ceiling mounting above, for example. Again, the prices were nothing less than astronomical for 1942, the 'Model 87' being $43.80 without a bulb, the 'Model 86' being even more at $55.00 without a bulb, and the missing bulb for these two units was the 250 watt 'AH-5' Mercury lamp sold for an additional $10.75. Once again, either one of these Black light floodlight units would have cost more than an ounce of Gold in 1942. On the following page this angled "Conti-Glo" Adapter for ceiling mounted lighting of flat wall murals is explained through a half page of text, an engineer's drawing plan, and a photograph of the ceiling mounted unit as well. The headline announces that this adapter was designed to be used for Fluorescent wall murals, and the text explains to customers the importance of using powerful Black lights to create spectacular Fluorescent effects, and also the importance of correctly designing and directing that Black light energy efficiently towards the Fluorescent surface to be excited. Restated on this page is the suggested eight foot (2.5 meter) size of the Fluorescent area to be excited requiring a 250 watt Black light, and the suggestions of either ceiling or wall mounting of the Black lights, for either wall or ceiling mounted Fluorescent murals. The engineering mechanical drawing, resembling a blueprint, of the suggested placement of these Black light units in regards to the distance to the Fluorescent murals on the walls beneath them is, like almost all of the Black light technology during the late 1930s early 1940s era of "The Miracle of Fluorescence," nothing less than a revelation to today's 'regressified' lighting designers or almost anyone else working with Black lights. The engineering design in this 1941-1942 "Conti-Glo" Product Catalogue suggests that the Black light's angle should be directed to approximately one-third the height from the bottom of a wall mounted Fluorescent mural, and, crucially, the angled Black light unit itself should be ceiling mounted one-half of the total distance from the bottom of the Fluorescent mural to the ceiling height. Absolutely correct, and absolutely the most efficient design and distances for the greatest amount of evenly emitted Black light. The article closes with the advanced feature of this "Conti-Glo" adjustable adapter for 'Model 86' or 'Model 87' Black lights, being a fixture at the back of the angled adapter to custom adjust the angle and direction of the adapter's front filter surface to correctly suit any installation. Fantastic and also inexistent today.

The next two powerful Black lights to be presented on the next page were intended to be used on small Fluorescent murals or areas that a 250 watt Black light unit was too powerful for. The 'Model 91' and 'Model 96' "Conti-Glo" 100 watt Black light floodlights in this advertisement were intended, like the previous two lamps discussed, to be used in public displays of Fluorescence. 'Model 91' was a portable Black light unit with a small rectangular base containing the electrical components, and a metal bracket attached to the base. The 100 watt Black light floodlight unit was bolted to the inside of this bracket with wing-nuts, making the angle of the lamp easily adjustable. This portable 100 watt Black light was a foot tall (30 cm), weighed ten pounds (4.5 kilo), and had a price of $31.75. This full page ad from these two 100 watt floodlights has a Black and White photograph of each of the lamps, with a cutaway section in the photo of the 'Model 96' Black light designed for being installed permanently, showing the base transformer section of the lamp unit concealed inside the wall while just an adjustable metal bracket holding the Black light was visible to the public. This exposed Black light lamp and bracket was only about half a foot tall (15 cm) and weighed just over two pounds (1 kilo), making it perfect for wall or ceiling mounting, and was sold for $29.75. The 100 watt Black light bulb alone was $12.00, was rated for 1,000 hours of use, and was called an 'EH-4" Mercury 'PAR' bulb. The text block in the ad states clearly in the opening sentence that the Black light Longwave Ultraviolet energy emitted from both these units is harmless and invisible, and was intended to be used for small areas that the 250 watt units would be too powerful for. The customer is advised that these two 100 watt Black lights were designed to be installed only a few yards (meters) from a Fluorescent surface with a maximum size of ten to twelve feet (2.5 to 3 meters), and the suggested area of a Fluorescent theatre mural should not be greater than thirty-five to fifty square feet (10.5 to 15 square meters). There were two other models of the 100 watt Black lights advertised on this page, the 'Model 93' portable unit and the 'Model 99' for permanent installations, both being spotlights designed for intense beams of focused Black light, not floodlights. These two 100 watt Black light spotlight beams of energy were concentrated to an area of sixty degrees from the front of the lamp, while the floodlights had a one hundred degree wide spread of emitted Black light energy, using a different bulb as well, the 'CH-4.'

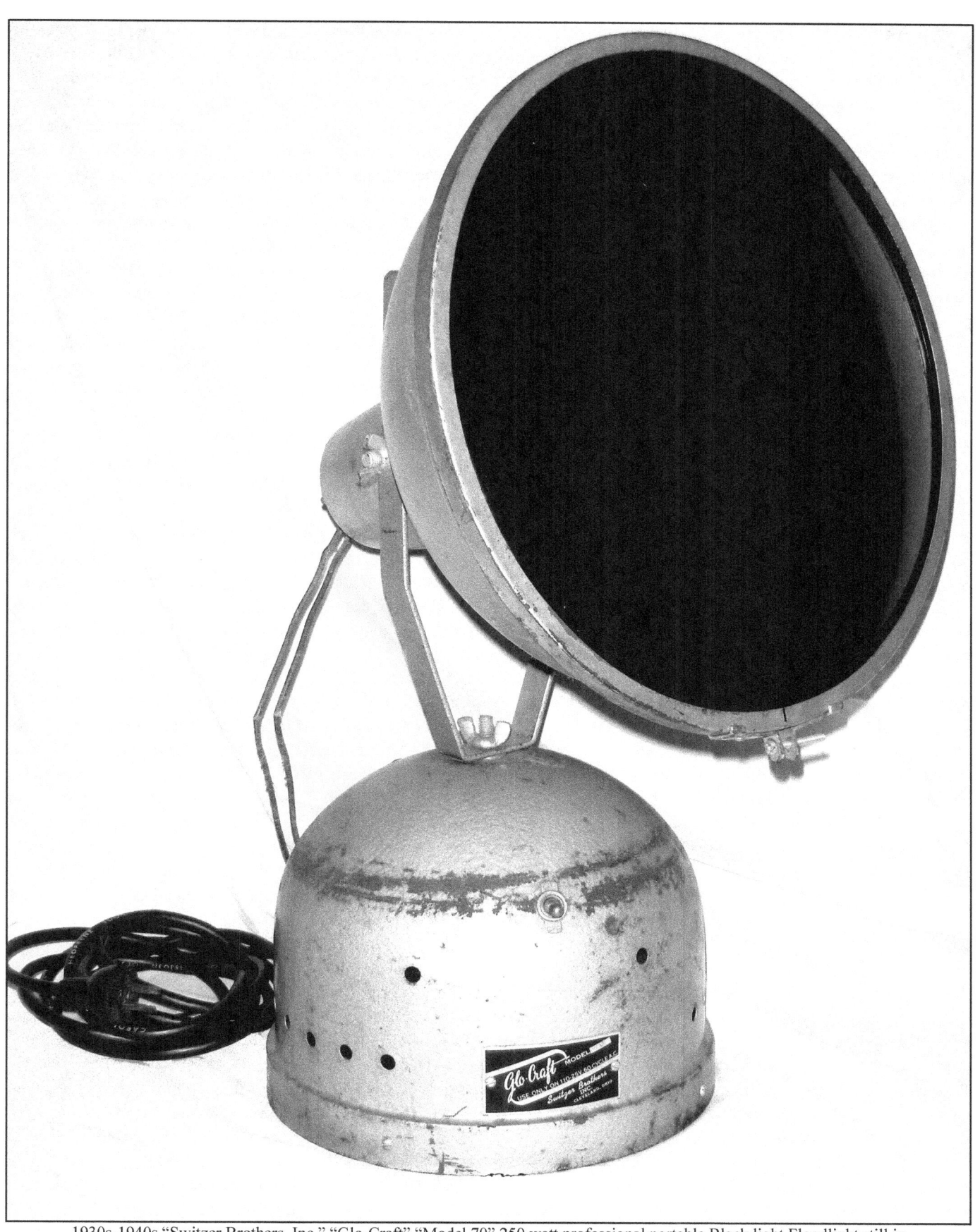

1930s-1940s "Switzer Brothers, Inc." "Glo-Craft" "Model 70" 250 watt professional portable Black light Floodlight still in perfect working condition ("Electric Ladyand - the First Museum of Fluorescent Art" collection)

The final page of this 1941-1942 "Conti-Glo" Product Catalogue and Price List advertises the two most powerful Black light floodlights produced by the company (and probably the most powerful Black lights at that time in the world), the 'Model 70' portable 250 watt Black light unit, and the similarly powerful 250 watt 'Model 80' for permanent installations. The headline at the top of the full page advertisement announces that these two powerful Black light floodlights could be used for stage shows, demonstrations, displays, or just decorations, and that these two lamps of 250 watts would emit three times the amount of Black light than the 100 watt units. These units were also more powerful than the two flush mounted 250 watt Black lights described previously from this catalogue, because of much larger Black light filters used on these two lamps. As with the previous ads of the other "Conti-Glo" Black light units, these two floodlights were available as spotlights also, being the portable 'Model 72' and the permanent mount 'Model 82,' along with a block of text beginning as well with the statement that the Longwave Ultraviolet Black light energy being emitted from these two lamps was harmless. There is a Black and White photograph of the very large and very heavy portable 250 watt 'Model 70' Black Light, which was twenty inches (51 cm) tall, weighed a hefty twenty-five pounds (11 kilos), and cost a fortune in 1942: $59.50 (one and a half ounces of Gold)! A photograph of the 'Model 80' for permanent installations is below on the advertising page, showing a cutaway section of the wall it is mounted on, which contains the transformer base of the lamp unit. The Mercury "AH-5" bulb replacement was $10.75 and the 'Model 80' unit was sold for $52.00. This was such a well known top of the line Black light unit during that time period that there is a full page Black and White photograph of the "Conti-Glo" "Model-80" in "Fluorescent Chemicals and Their Applications" by DeMent and Dake from 1942.

In another attic somewhere in Cleveland, Ohio since my parents were ten years old, in 2008 a "Conti-Glo" 'Model 70' 250 watt Black Light Floodlight unit was discovered in Perfect Working Condition(!) which is now part of the collection of "Electric Ladyland - the First Museum of Fluorescent Art." This director of the First Museum of Fluorescent Art has only ever seen one other 'Model 70' "Conti-Glo" Black light unit in existence, on display in the "Thomas S. Warren Geophysics Museum," which is part of the "Sterling Hill Mining Museum" in Ogdensburg, New Jersey, but this other 'Model 70' unit does not work anymore, and doesn't even have the original connecting electrical wire between the bottom large metal transformer base and the top huge lamp unit attached to it. The 'Model 70' "Conti-Glo" Black light unit in the "Electric Ladyland" collection is in perfect operating condition, and is a monstrous World war two era unit - huge and a very heavy 'Battleship Grey' construction. This tremendous Black light unit consists of a large round metal base containing the 250 watt electrical transformer that is fitted with a toggle-switch, several aeration holes, and a "Conti-Glo" "Switzer Brothers" 'Model 70' metal identification plate including a serial number. The top very large Black light unit itself is like *nothing* made today. The one piece curved glass convex Black light filter for the front of this lamp unit is also a monster. Nowhere in the world today could you get a Black light filter the thickness, size, shape, or weight of this twelve and a half inch (32 cm.) diameter massive early 1940s Longwave Black light filter. Nothing in today's electrical world would prepare the average person for the shock of seeing the foot-long Frankenstein bulb behind the filter though, being a bulb that is hard to describe, and something like I've also never seen before. This Ultraviolet bulb in the unit is a simply tremendous light bulb - almost like something you would expect out of a lighthouse. The construction of this massive bulb is also something - it's like two or three units or bulbs inside of each other with metal plates and connecting wires and enough electrical components to stagger the imagination. In December, 2008, while visiting my sister's house in New Jersey for Christmas (and also to pick up this monstrous 'Model 70' "Conti-Glo" Black light unit), I turned on this unbelievably strong 250 watt Black light unit - it was like nothing I've ever seen! When first tentatively plugging in the seventy year old plug, nothing at all happened for some seconds, then a faint Violet-Red glow of the internal components of the huge transparent light bulb could be seen right through the thick massive convex Black light filter at the front of the lamp (Mary Jean left the room and put away her two dogs on purpose for this). For a few minutes this Violet-Red glow of the bulb became stronger and brighter, until after about five full minutes this massive 250 watt Black light unit was completely lit up and emitting a simply *Copious* amount of Black light Longwave Ultraviolet energy - her entire house was like in a "Purple Haze"! For this experiment I set up six of my recent highly Fluorescent "Thermal Expansion" Paintings about eight feet (2.5 meters), only, in front of the 'Model 70' massive 250 watt Black light, as well as a forty year old Fluorescent painting on canvas I had also recently bought for the Museum collection and had shipped to my sister's house in America. This canvas is the first example I've found of the ancient, forgotten, unknown even, Fluorescent Artist Oil Paint which appeared as normal oil Colors in the White light, but then burst into vivid Fluorescent Colors only when put under a Black light, which creates an 'Autumn' scene in the White light and then changes to 'Summer' in the Black light. When this 250 watt incredibly powerful 'Model 70' "Conti-Glo" Black Light Floodlight was completely warmed up at it's full operating power after about five minutes, my six Fluorescent "Thermal Expansion" Paintings lined up less than ten feet (3.2 meters) in front of this amazing ancient Black light unit were brighter than I've ever seen them. The intensity of the Fluorescent light being emitted by these six paintings was hard to believe - I could see the Colors being *projected* off of the painting surface, like with a slide-projector, where you can see the individual rays of light suspended in the air of the darkened room! The Colors produced by, and the tint of this Black light's emitted energy, is identical to today's Color and tint of normal Black light tubular lamps, not a reddish glow or a warmer Color temperature, like I initially feared. Something that is different in this 'Model 70' 250 watt Black light unit from the Black lights today is the operating temperature. When this 'Model 70' Black light was on for about half an hour you could have easily fried an egg (or your fingers) on the lamp itself - the heat of the unit itself could easily be felt in the room from five or six feet (1.8 meters) away. I have seen over the years several modern (1990s) 400 watt Black light units in operation, in the office of a Black light company in Amsterdam that was something like the 'sponsor' of the Museum when I began construction of the Fluorescent "Participatory" Environment in the early 1990s, and also for the only time I've ever seen a Black light mounted on the ceiling of a Modern Art museum, in the Amsterdam Stedelijk Museum, in the early 1990s for an exhibition entitled "Energieen," in which a Dutch Artist named Rob Scholte mounted several large war maps he had made with Fluorescent paint on the wall of the Museum, a couple of powerful Black light units on the ceiling, and - the best part of all - on the Stedelijk Museum wall opposite the war maps, where the Museum visitors viewed the Fluorescent war maps from, this typically highly informed and knowledgeable Dutch Artist mounted a *Warning* on the wall, once again completely misinforming countless thousands of Museum visitors that 'Black Light is Harmful to Eyes and Skin'(!) For the last seventeen years, before you enter "Electric Ladyland - the First Museum of Fluorescent Art" on the wall there is a framed technical sheet printed by one of the largest lighting companies in the world, "Philips" of Holland, which states in plain English that - for the thousandth time - the "Long Wave" U.V. which is emitted by "Black lights" is "harmless." Anyway, back to the technically-advanced past, the energy of these two different types of contemporary 1990s 400 watt Black light units was only a fraction of the Black light energy produced by this seventy year old 250 watt 'Model 70' "Conti-Glo" Black light. The reason is the simply humongous convex twelve and a half inch (32 cm) very thick and heavy Black light filter on the front of the 'Model 70,' compared to modern compact - much smaller - Black light filters at the front of these modern compact lamps, emits much less modern compact Black light Longwave Ultraviolet energy as well. Yet another example of lost knowledge, the size of the Black light filter at the front of the Black light also determines the amount of Black light energy that is emitted by the Black light - not just the amount of watts that the intense Black light bulb has. So, the enormous one-piece construction of the twelve and a half inch (32 cm) diameter convex Black light filter - incomparable to anything made today in the Twenty-first century - on this 250 watt 'Model 70' lamp from the late 1930s to early 1940s era emits far more Black light energy through this huge Black light filter than the modern 400 watt halogen Black lights fitted with tiny Black light filters, perhaps one-quarter the size of the 'Model 70' massive Black light filter. Talk about "progress" one more time.

The final incredibly difficult step in getting this monstrous twenty inch (51 cm) twenty-five pound (11 kilo) seventy year old lamp, with it's very delicate and impossible-to-replace foot long late 1930s to early 1940s light bulb and huge delicate impossible-to-replace convex twelve and a half inch (32 cm) glass Black light filter, *across the Atlantic Ocean* in my two huge suitcases, and to the Museum in Amsterdam! It literally took me two full days to plan and execute the packing of this lamp. The 'Model 70' lamp had to be taken apart in five separate pieces to transport safely: the heaviest section which is the round metal base containing the electrical transformer, the metal bracket to hold the lamp unit, the metal housing of the large lamp, the impossible-to-replace huge glass 12.5 inch (32 cm) convex Black light filter, and 'last-but-not-least,' the really-impossible-to-replace foot long 1930s-1940s Frankenstein glass Black light bulb. Through careful planning, alot of foam rubber, even more bubble-plastic wrap, plywood, cardboard, and two full rolls of packing tape, I managed to transport this huge ancient 'Model 70' Black light in perfect shape in my two large suitcases across the Atlantic Ocean and back to the Museum in Amsterdam (I forgot to mention praying).

With another stroke of good Karma, the very next year, in 2009, another "Conti-Glo" Black light came up for sale and could be bought for the Museum collection. It is the other major Black light used for public displays in the 1930s and 1940s, the 100 watt "Conti-Glo" 'Model 93' Portable 100 watt Black light Spotlight. Exactly a year later, Christmas of 2009 I made the next experiment with an unbelievably powerful antique Black light in my sister's house again, this time the 100 watt 'Model 93,' which Mary Jean once again put the two dogs away for. I again lined up half a dozen of my Fluorescent "Thermal Expansion" paintings in front of this 'Model 93' and plugged in the seventy-plus year old frayed wire plug (which I had repaired that day by putting electrical tape all over bare, exposed antique copper wiring). The start-up of this 'Model 93' 100 watt lamp was much quicker than the 250 watt 'Model 70' in 2008, about a third of the time, reaching it's peak after less than two minutes. The operating temperature of this 100 watt lamp is also about a third of the 250 watt 'Model 70' as well. But what fascinated me the most with this "Spotlight," compared to the 250 watt "Floodlight" 'Model 70' of the year before's experiment, was the accuracy of the focus for the beam of projected Black light coming out of the lamp. I never expected the lamp to be able to project an actual Black light "Spotlight," but it does so incredibly. I sat on the floor moving the 100 watt 'Model 93' Black light spotlight from painting to painting, and even though my "Thermal Expansion" paintings were lined up very close to each other, the Black light spotlight only lit up the painting directly in front of the lamp, not the two paintings on either side of the painting the lamp was centered on. I am still amazed. Not to mention the intensity of Black light energy that is produced and emitted from this 100 watt 'Model 93,' which is hard to believe, and comparable to the intensity of Colors produced by the 250 watt 'Model 70,' causing rays of Colors to be emitted from the paintings that could be seen suspended in the darkness of the room. What a dramatic difference from the miserable 36 watt Black lights we are left with today! Before installing the two "Conti-Glo" 1936-1946 lamps of 250 and 100 watts each in a permanent display case in the Museum, Michèle and I turned them on separately in front of the Fluorescent "Participatory" Environment in the Museum. We turned all the 1000 watts of standard 36 watt tubular Black lights off, and turned on first the 250 watt 'Model 70' "Conti-Glo" Floodlight - it began to emit copious amounts of pure Longwave U.V. through it's massive antique round filter - and we both then, for the very first time, saw the true Colors of my Fluorescent Environment - after sixteen years of looking at it under today's tubular Black lights. The Colors were *Fantastic* - not off-balanced by visible Blue and Violet light also coming through the cheap built-in filters in today's tubular Black lights, but gorgeous pure Fluorescent Blues, Oranges, Reds, Yellows and all the other Fluorescent Colors as they were intended to Fluoresce when they were invented over eighty years ago.

"Popular Science Monthly - Mechanics and Handicraft" (1939)

Another artifact in the Museum collection is a very dated magazine from December, 1939, "Popular Science Monthly - Mechanics and Handicraft," which has the earliest article about Fluorescent Minerals that I know of. The cover price for this 1939 magazine is enough to amusingly date the publication: 15¢(!), and if the cover price is not enough, then the illustration on the front cover is sufficient to instantly date the era as wartime. The only full Color printing in the entire magazine is on this front cover, with an photograph/illustration of three "U.S. Army" (the U.S. Air Force hadn't even been established yet) fighter airplanes seen from below, which must have been some of the earliest single-wing airplanes constructed. Only six years before this magazine was printed, the U.S. Army fighter airplanes still had the original double-wing design from the first airplanes, as is easily recognizable from the iconic "King Kong" movie's final scene on the Empire State Building from 1933. Opening this crumbling 1939 seventy-six year old magazine, the first difference a person today immediately notices is the absence of Color - the entire magazine, with the sole exception of the front cover, is printed in Black and White with occasional touches of added blocks of the tinted Colors Yellow, Green, or Magenta to highlight the title of articles throughout the magazine. Having degrees in both Fine Art and Graphic Design and with past experience of working in advertising as a package designer on Madison Avenue for years, the graphic design of this entire magazine - from cover to cover - is nearly painful. For example, opening the magazine to the 'Table of Contents' on page two the reader is confronted with a virtual graphic designer's nightmare. At first glance this table of contents looks a little like a "Letraset" type face designer's catalogue with probably every different type font design that existed in 1939 all used on the same page. Including the hand-drawn "Popular Science" logo, there are no less than thirteen different type faces used on this single page of the table of contents. In graphic design school, the golden rule every student learns about page design is that there should never be more than two, or with an exception three at the very most, type faces ever used on a single page, let alone *thirteen*! Instantly recognizable as an antique, this table of contents tutti-frutti type face design is not nearly as retro as the actual contents of some of the articles and advertisements in the magazine.

One of the first full page advertisements in this 1939 "Popular Science" is the announcement of a new invention in the automobile industry: Automatic Transmissions. Again, utilizing about every known type face that existed in 1939, this "Oldsmobile" advertisement looks nearly prehistoric. The type faces, the general design, the logos, photographs, and illustrations all look absolutely ancient. The headline announces the new invention: 'The One Big New Engineering Feature for the 1940 Cars!' - 'No Gears to Shift' ' No Clutch to Press!' "Hydra-Matic Drive" was the name given to this first automatic transmission for the 1940 Oldsmobile, and it was 'more than just a Fluid Flywheel!' There's even a (failed) attempt to explain this "Hydra-Matic Drive" through an illustration of two table fans facing each other. The advertising slogans for Oldsmobile written at the bottom of the ad by the logo are just as antiquated as the ad's photograph, which shows "Rosy-the-Riveter" sitting behind the wheel of a truly primitive car - almost as primitive a design as the car that Fred Flintstone and Barney Rubble used to take to work. These Oldsmobile 1940 slogans border on the ridiculous, like something a moron would think of, and on top of it all they are also written in incorrect English, announcing that the 'Oldsmobile - Is Bigger and Better in Everything' then the logo, which is a hand-drawn front grill of an Oldsmobile resembling a Benjamin Franklin coin, with the profound line from Oldsmobile to end the advertisement, calling the car the 'Biggest Moneys Worth in America.' Another design absurdity not

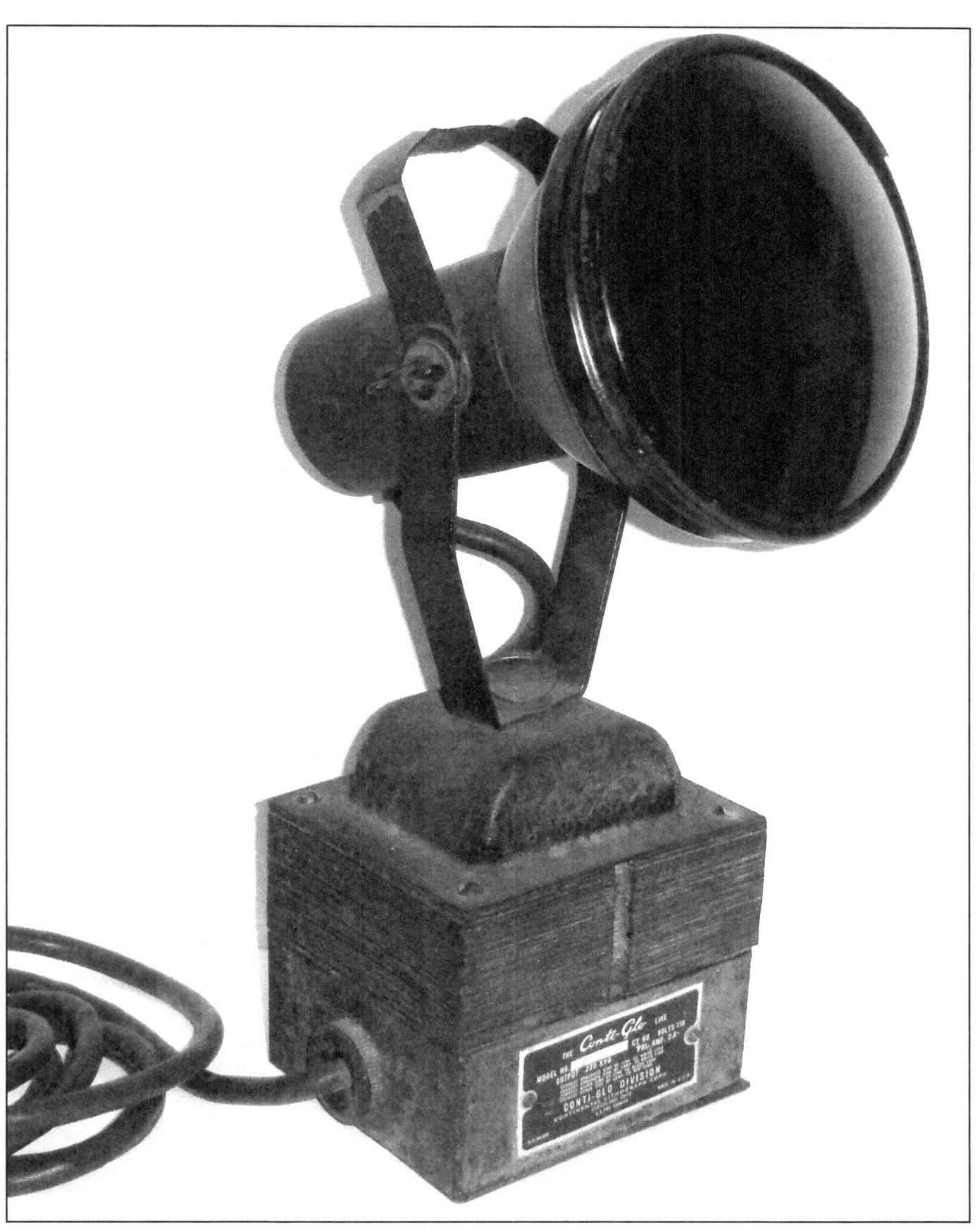
1930s-1940s "Conti-Glo" "Model 93" 100 watt professional portable Black light Spotlight still in perfect working condition
("Electric Ladyand - the First Museum of Fluorescent Art" collection)

mentioned are the no less than eight type faces used on this single page, making it a true masterpiece of graphics in every possible design element.

In this 1939 "Popular Science" there is also an article that dates the time period more precisely than even the miserable design of the Oldsmobile advertisement: 'Forty Years of Automobiles,' with a photograph of a new 1940 typically horrific looking car (designed to resemble a round bread box), next to a comical drawing of a 1900 'car' with a man and woman holding on for dear life as he tries desperately to steer the antique vehicle with a steering-stick. The caption of the compared pictures calls the new 1940 horror car 'streamline'(!) proving that the author of this 1939 article most probably was suffering from cataracts, and then in comparison the 1900 car is called a 'wheezy' 'horseless carriage!' Even older and looking even more like the Flintstone's car, in the article is a photograph of a very early 'speed racer,' the man named R.E. Olds, who sold his first steam-propelled car in 1891 and went on to form "Oldsmobile"(!), driving a contraption that is simply a rectangular frame with four wheels, a steering wheel and chair for Mr. Olds, and two small 'missiles' strapped to the center of this 'vehicle' - it's general appearance is like trying to imagine just the frame of a Conestoga wagon with two huge Roman candles attached to it. The reader is also informed that the first automobile race in America was in 1895 on a muddy track in Chicago, and the fifty-two mile race (85 kilometers) was won in no less than the blistering time of seven hours and thirty minutes! An ad in this magazine that even a small child today would laugh at is a very early "Harley Davidson" 'Motorcycle to Funland' artifact. The two photos in the ad are nearly shocking, with a 1939 smiling whimpy-looking character who looks exactly like an Ice-cream man, riding a "Harley Davidson!" Complete with a total White Ice-cream man's uniform, and a White Ice-cream man's sailor hat and a bow-tie (I'm not exaggerating) the two small photos make Marlon Brando and "The Beetles" in "The Wild Ones" look nearly cool. This was so many years ago, and there were so few motorcycles on the roads, that there wasn't even a law to wear a helmet on a motorcycle yet.

So now that I've typically exponentially overstated the perspective for the time setting of this magazine containing the earliest article about Fluorescent minerals that I know of, the article itself is a real masterpiece and well worth the effort it takes to find the magazine today, written by the person who is regarded as the Father of Fluorescent mineral collecting, Sterling Gleason, who published one of the earliest books about Fluorescent minerals back in 1960 that is considered the 'Bible' of Fluorescent Mineral Collecting. "Ultraviolet Guide to Minerals - With Mineral Identification Charts" was the book published by Sterling Gleason in 1960, and as the author states in the book's introduction, there was no book in existence at that time to act as a field guide for a mineral collector prospecting Fluorescent minerals. This book was written and published on the cusp of a new era, when everything would soon change in regards to 'anything Fluorescent.' The time period that would define the crescendo of experience and research into Fluorescence and Ultraviolet energy that had roughly begun three hundred and fifty-seven years before in 1603 with Vincenzo Casciarola's discovery of the "Bologna Stone," but would change dramatically within only the next six or seven years - less than a decade by any account after the book's publication. This book by Sterling Gleason will be further discussed in it's proper time perspective fittingly at the beginning of the next chapter, which will be very accurately and truthfully representing the change from the era I've called "The Miracle of Fluorescence: 1930s - 1950s," and the beginning of the next era of the 1960s.

Sterling Gleason's 1960 'Bible' for Fluorescent mineral collectors will, again, be examined in the next chapter in it's proper time context, but at this point the article by Sterling Gleason in this 1939 "Popular Science Monthly" is in the proper time period of this book. The article is entitled "Night Prospecting" and announces a "New Hobby" that was for "Amateur Mineralogists," with the three page article containing seven very special Black and White photographs that are about as dated as the photo of R.W. Olds the 'speed racer' in the first pages of this magazine. The dignified style and completely unpretentious, egoless approach to writing in this article is immediately recognizable as the truly professional demeanor that was Sterling Gleason's. In the first sentences of this article already, any person that has read Sterling Gleason's "Ultraviolet Guide to Minerals" will recognize the same friendly 'plain talk' style of Sterling Gleason's writing - as if you are with him in person in the dark both examining the wonders of nature under a U.V. lamp. After reading many books, magazines, professional papers, websites, etc. on the subject of Fluorescence, Ultraviolet, Black light, and Mineralogy, there is no other author I know of that conveyed these not-too-simple subjects of Quantum physics and Geology with such a down-to-Earth demeanor, as if he actually wanted the reader of his writings to *learn something*, not just be impressed by the scope, knowledge, or even ego of the author.

This 1939 article by Sterling Gleason begins, as I've just explained, very humbly talking about a man in the dark prospecting with a primitive Ultraviolet lamp on the side of an unfinished highway in New Jersey. The man picks up a piece of 'rubble' and under his Ultraviolet lamp, it glows with 'blazing internal fires' like an 'Emerald.' The text for this 1939 article on Fluorescent mineral collecting by Sterling Gleason is as dated as the photographs, stating that there were 'nearly 100' different

Fluorescent minerals known in 1939, where today the list is well over a thousand, with over one hundred Fluorescent minerals known to come from only Franklin, New Jersey. All the photographs are precious in this article, and on the first page we see a Fluorescent mineral prospector with his young son in the dark searching for Fluorescent minerals with their 'home made ultra-violet torch' that looks just like it's description. The first photo shows father and son 'night prospecting' for Fluorescent minerals with their home made Ultraviolet lamp that looks very similar to, and most probably is, a converted Miner's lamp. Except for the clothing, the man's hat, and obviously the home made U.V. lamp, this photo is not as dated as the rest and could be a contemporary photo of collecting Fluorescent minerals at night. The second photo is just the opposite, with father and son hooking up their home made U.V. lamp to a car in the field at night for powering their lamp. Now the son in the photo has on a Lord Carnarvon pith helmet (maybe they were night prospecting in Africa), but this is nothing compared to the car they have the U.V. lamp wire attached to, being maybe one model after Ford's first "Model-T." The third Black and White photograph in this 1939 article is one of my personal favorite photos of the entire time period, which I have on display in the Museum for many years, and shows a very serious 'amateur mineralogist' in front of his "blacklight museum" which consisted of a wooden box about a foot wide by ten inches tall (30x25 cm) which had six "Argon Glow Lamp" bulbs with their six porcelain fixtures mounted on the ceiling of this box lined up so close that these bulbs nearly touch each other. These six "Argon Glow Lamps" in fixtures above the small collection of Fluorescent minerals were so close to the minerals that the "Argon Bulbs" also nearly touch the actual minerals themselves. What must be remembered here is that these first commercially available Ultraviolet lamps, the "Argon Glow Lamp" had a vast output of only two and a half watts. There is also a base of Black material underneath the jumble of Fluorescent minerals packed into the tiny space of this "blacklight museum" box, which is noticeably nailed to the two inside walls of the small display box. The caption states that the 'ultra-violet light' was supplied through these 'fifty cent argon bulbs.' Now except for the man in the photo having pants that come up half way to his chest, and also not looking at the tiny design of the "blacklight museum" with it's six Argon bulbs lined up next to each other with porcelain fixtures for each bulb, the photo could be from today(!), but the two other Black and White photos on this page are like something out of the Stone Age. Now in over twenty years of looking for Fluorescent minerals, both in the middle of the night and also in the bright Sun with three feet (1 meter) of snow in the "Buckwheat Dump" of Franklin, not to mention in 1998 at 14,000 feet (4350 meters) reaching the source of the Ganga (Ganges River) in northern India at the border of Tibet on the Gaumukh Glacier collecting the first Fluorescent minerals ever brought from the Himalaya, I have never seen anything as primitive and downright bizarre as the set-up for Fluorescent mineral prospecting with Ultraviolet in the daylight as in the the next Black and White photo in this article. The only photo of the subject that I've seen anywhere that comes close to this third photo from 1939 is the photo of the author Manuel Robbins in the second of his modern day 'Bibles' for Fluorescent Mineral collectors, "Fluorescence - Gems and Minerals under Ultraviolet Light" in which Manuel Robbins is in the midst of prospecting for Fluorescent minerals in the field during the daytime with a big Black terrapin to cover himself and block out the daylight, and with an Ultraviolet lamp to identify the Fluorescence of the minerals he was examining on the floor. But this photo of Manuel Robbins from 1994 is nothing compared to this Stone Age image of Fluorescent mineral prospecting from 1939, in which a man is crouched over a pile of Grey rocks in the daylight with a Black terrapin over him as well, but the first portable battery-powered Shortwave Ultraviolet lamp was just produced by Thomas S. Warren of "Ultra-Violet Products, Inc." only a year before, in 1938, so the common technique still in use at the time of this article in 1939 was illustrated through this bizarre photo revealing the Fluorescent mineral prospecting technique of seventy-six years ago: a huge wooden Black box attached to a large Black terrapin which would be put over almost the full body. The huge wooden box would be worn fully over the head, in which the prospector could place with his hands a sample or two of mineral into this box in which an Ultraviolet filter had been fitted into it's top side, behind the prospector's head facing the Sun, allowing only the Longwave Ultraviolet energy from sunlight to pass through the filter and to cause the prospector's mineral to possibly Fluoresce slightly. This is the identical design used for one of the first Ultraviolet apparatuses known as an "Ultraviolet View-Box" which was constructed by Dr. Robert Wood around 1903, when he invented the first Longwave Ultraviolet filter, and in this way began the modern age of Fluorescence study. I have seen an original ancient "Ultraviolet View Box" in the former "Gerstmann Museum" in Franklin, New Jersey, which was run by the late Ewald Gerstmann for many years, and can bear witness to the minuscule amount of Ultraviolet energy that reaches the Fluorescent mineral inside the box through the filter and causes the mineral to ever so slightly Fluoresce, and I was doing this with a Black light placed right on top of the filter which should have caused the maximum amount of Ultraviolet into the "Ultraviolet View-Box," not just out in the Sun like a hundred years ago.

  Sterling Gleason continues describing the 'new hobby' of 'night prospecting' for Fluorescent minerals and immediately begins to point out that the hobbyist at night with their home made Ultraviolet lamp can discover Scheelite, the Tungsten ore that was being prospected for between 1938 and 1943 in the United States with the help of Thomas Warren's first portable battery-operated Shortwave Ultraviolet lamp, the "M-12," which Warren went before Congress in Washington to produce this "M-12," and which was used specifically with the intention of finding Scheelite in the United States. The reason for the urgency for discovering Scheelite in the U.S. was that in 1938 America was beginning to see the Second world war on the horizon, and at that point the U.S. was importing all of their Scheelite from China, which would be immediately cut off if China allied with the prospective enemy powers, so between 1938 and 1943 America became independent in the production of the Tungsten ore Scheelite, which is necessary to harden steel, an obvious indispensable commodity during the Second world war. There is an original 1938 "M-12" in the Museum collection, and it is a piece of antiquity. This first portable battery-powered Shortwave Ultraviolet lamp was made with the intention of night prospecting for Scheelite and for the war effort in America, so the lamp is very robustly constructed, totally steel and totally flat Black to avoid any distracting light reflections, with the first noticeably ancient feature of this rectangular box-shaped lamp being the real leather handle - like on your Grandmother's suitcases. Even after having this lamp for twenty-five years the ancient large leather handle still fascinates me. This 1930s leather handle isn't the only artifact noticeable, but the actual tubular Shortwave Ultraviolet lamp behind the Black Shortwave filter is something that belongs completely to yesteryear, being a small glass tubular lamp that is bent twice to form a "U" shape. Even if such a seventy year old lamp replacement could ever be found, it is impossible to change the lamp, because - and I've only seen this in one other antique lamp - the "U" shaped tubular glass Ultraviolet lamp has it's electrical connecting wires soldered directly to the wires coming out of the tubular lamp itself.

    Sterling Gleason continues the article by bringing us with him into the field in California at night with our 'high-powered mercury vapor' Ultraviolet lamp on and scanning the desert floor - wait! - an intensely Fluorescent Green Scorpion is walking across our path, and then we see a fossilized tooth or bone in the sand, which Fluoresce like crazy in the still darkness of the desert. Not only is Sterling Gleason's writing approach unique, but the explanation of the phenomenon of Fluorescence that he gives in this article is unlike any of the multitude of explanations for the cause of Fluorescence that can be found. Gleason explains very simply that Fluorescence is caused by the mineral 'slowing down' the 'ultra fast' vibrations of the "black light" to the same speed of the Colors of visible light. A very special unpretentious explanation by a very special unpretentious person. Sterling Gleason advises the reader that they can also do 'night prospecting' for Fluorescent minerals with a very small investment of 'fifty cent argon glow bulbs,' or if they want professional 'factory-built' Mercury vapor Ultraviolet lamps these were the princely sum of $30.00 at that time. The home made Ultraviolet lamp which was the cheapest investment possible during that period is described by Sterling Gleason, and his instructions for building such a contraption entails such antiquated procedures that it would be laughed at today. Gleason tells the reader that for a 'small investment' a flexible tube with Argon gas inside could be bought (!) The next funky instructions are to repeatedly bend the tube with Argon gas inside until a condensed ball of Argon is produced, and then to put a reflector behind this bent Argon tubing, as well as a 'filter glass' in front of the bent Argon tubing to filter out all energy except the "black light." To complete this unimaginable "black light" you are supposed to attach the bent Argon tubing to a 'Ford spark coil' operational through 'dry cells' [batteries] and - viola - you have a "black light!" Jesus. What must be unimaginably imagined in this worse-case scenario Black light, is that the bent flexible tubing with the condensed Argon gas inside of it *is the Light Source!* In rapid succession the very next sentence from Gleason gives directions for the very next unimaginable "black light" contraption. The reader is instructed to 'send High Voltage' (what a difference - today they even warn against watching T.V. shows containing Strobe lights) 'crackling' across a gap between two nails that are attached to a high voltage 'spark coil' or a 'transformer' and then block out all energy except for Ultraviolet through the use of a filter. This is the basic design here (excluding the filter) for the very first mechanical device to produce Ultraviolet energy that was ever made. The simplest instructions of all to create your own home made Ultraviolet lamp Gleason saves for last, telling the reader to just take the glass off of their house flashlight and replace it with a circular piece of 'deep violet' glass filter which the reader is informed will cost only a couple of dollars from an optical supplier. I don't know if anyone reading this book has ever tried any of these types of primitive "black lights," but I can assure you that the name of these lamps should not have been ''Ultra-Violet,' but 'Ultra-Feeble,' because there is such a piteously tiny amount of Ultraviolet energy being created by such contraptions listed in this article that it is difficult to see the Fluorescence of synthetic Fluorescent paint with them, so imagine natural dim Fluorescent minerals. The photo of the first 'bent tubing' design that Gleason described is called a 'black-light torch' in the caption, and looks like a tiny "Camera Obscura" from the 1600s. In the photo a Fluorescent mineral collector is sitting at a plank table with a Frank Sinatra 'Fedora' on examining specimens of Fluorescent minerals. In front of the man, mounted on the plank table by what looks like a Black painted old metal can of tomatoes, is a simply horrid looking 'black light torch' consisting of what looks like three cardboard boxes tilted at an angle towards the minerals; a large cardboard box in the middle and two smaller cardboard boxes, one on each side (I'm surprised this design wasn't also called 'Streamlined!') The article informs the reader that in 1939 Fluorescent minerals were known to

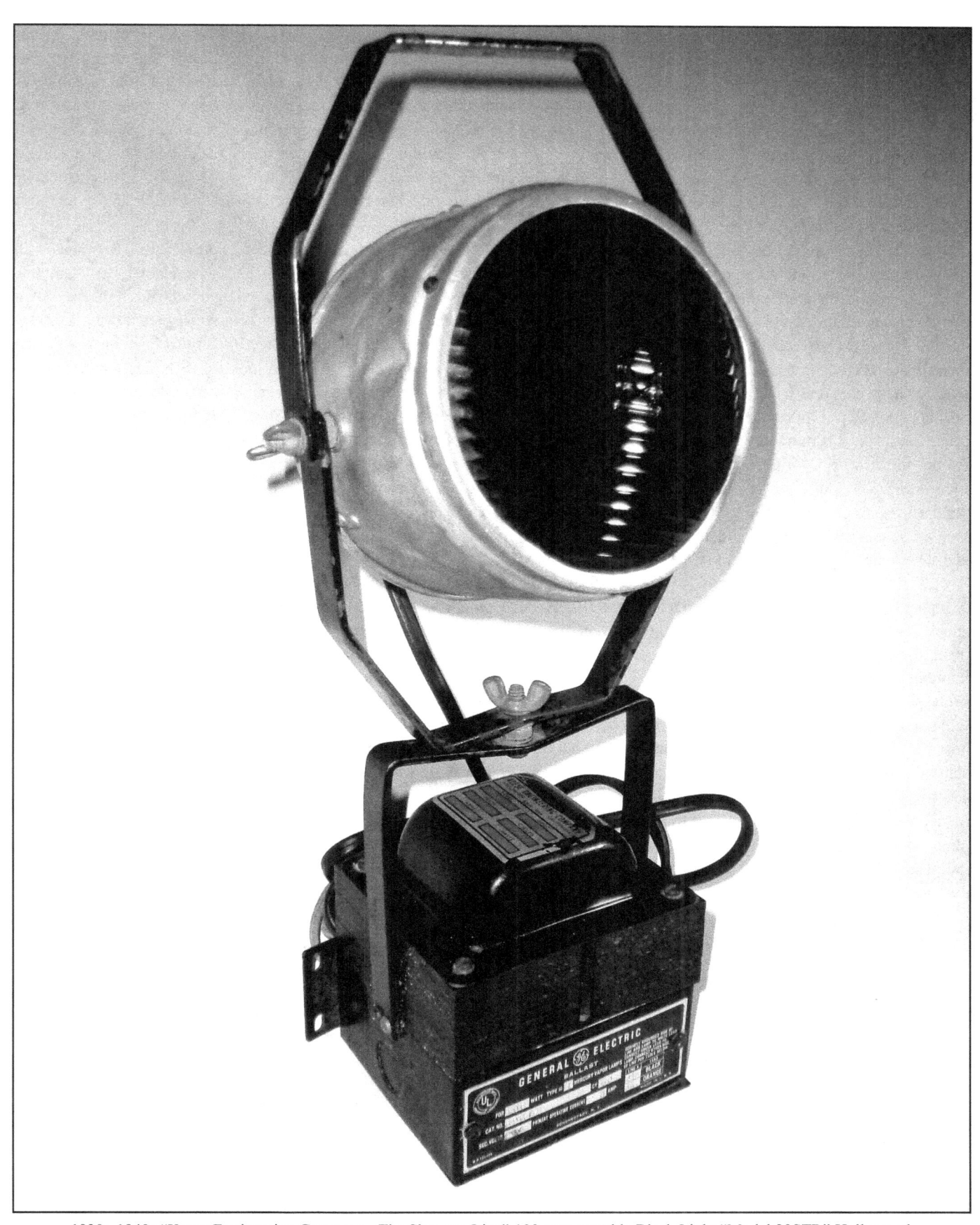

1930s-1940s "Keese Engineering Company - The Shannon Line" 100 watt portable Black Light "Model 90STP," Hollywood, California ("Electric Ladyand - the First Museum of Fluorescent Art" collection)

come from almost every state in America, and typically Sterling Gleason lists half a paragraph of likely 'night prospecting' localities, only to end with his friendly logical advice to look in your own 'back yard' to find 'many things' that are Fluorescent under your portable home made "black light." Gleason also informs the reader of an amateur Fluorescent mineral collector who created his own 'home museum,' and details of the display are given, such as the cabinet that housed the display had Black velvet on the shelves under the minerals and a 'two-way' switch to display the Fluorescent minerals first under White light, and then under the "black light," creating images of 'glowing jewels' and vivid 'moss' from the Grey rocks that were just seen in the White light. Another nut was apparently charging his specimens of Fluorescent minerals with a 'barrage of sparks' cracking across iron electrodes, and Gleason reports that these Fluorescent minerals then looked like they were 'traced' with fire and also Phosphoresced for minutes.

The next subject that Gleason covers is Fluorescence in Gemstones, mentioning the detection of fake Gemstones with the Ultraviolet lamp, and relating the facts that all Rubies are fantastically Fluorescent "Ruby Red" (what else), most Diamonds Fluoresce and with a multitude of different possible Colors, Zircons can be detected from Diamonds through their own particular Red Fluorescence, and the facts that natural Amber's Fluorescent Color is 'bright green' while plastic Amber nearly doesn't Fluoresce. Here either the Black lights, the Black light filters, or the Ultraviolet source itself must have been different than the same contemporary components, because Zircon Fluoresces Yellow and I have been looking at fluorescent Amber for over twenty years and have a collection of four different localities of the most famous Amber in the world, Mexico with it's brilliant Sky-Blue Fluorescence, three different shades and transparencies of Hungarian Amber Fluorescing Yellow, Amber, bright Whitish, the most common Amber from the Baltic regions Fluorescing a Bluish White Color, and finally the rarest Amber in the world, "Blue" Amber - found only washed up on the beaches of the Dominican Republic and having a Bluish Fluorescence both under Black lights and even out in the Sun the Amber is so reactive, which gives this Dominican Republican Amber it's name - but no Amber that's 'bright green.' Sterling Gleason also lists some "Common Items that are Fluorescent" for two sentences, which coincidentally he refers to as 'Common substances,' and informs the reader that kerosene, aspirins, and 'Oleomargerine' were all Fluorescent Blue, while butter Fluoresces Yellow.

The final paragraph of this December, 1939 article in "Popular Science Monthly" with the three "U.S. Army" fighter airplanes overhead on the front cover, gets back to a very large concern in America at that time: Radioactive minerals. Another shock for the lame "Strobe Light Warning" generation is stated by Gleason directly, informing the reader that the 'biggest thrill' for an amateur Fluorescent mineral collector was to find a Radioactive mineral - !! Gleason instructs the reader to make a home made instrument to detect radioactivity. Using two thin pieces of Aluminum foil (alot cheaper than Gold leafing) that are professionally charged with static electricity by rubbing a 'comb with silk.' It is explained that the two leaves of Aluminum foil will stand straight out when charged with the static electricity from the comb rubbing, but if something radioactive is brought near the 'instrument,' the 'bullets' ("Electrons," which were a new discovery in the 1930s) of the radioactivity would stop the static electricity and the two leaves of Aluminum foil would fall back down. The last very healthy advice in this article from 1939 is to make a self-portrait of a radioactive mineral by placing it on top of a photographic plate sealed in Black paper, and then developing the film weeks later, when the visible outline of the radioactive mineral would be easily seen on the photographic print. This is the same procedure that Henri Becquerel used to accidentally discover the phenomenon of radioactivity in the late 1800s, and in the same vein, Sterling Gleason described the photographic image made by the radioactive mineral as being 'Radiumlike!'

"Ultra-Violet Products, Inc." "Mineralight Files" 1943-1950

For nearly seventy years a virtual treasure trove of information about Black lights and Fluorescence was hidden in someone else's attic, very likely the attic of a grandchild of someone deeply involved with Ultraviolet technology during the middle of the Second world war. Actually, this sixty-five year old artifact of the Second world war era was discovered twice, in two separate attics, and I could purchase both of them for the Museum collection. The combination of the two different attic finds completed the largest single artifact of information in the entire Museum collection (besides books), being a total of sixty-one printed pages which form a complete "Ultra-Violet Products, Inc. MINERALIGHT FILE." This is a heavy-stock folder printed in Black and White with Violet headlines and accents, which was meant to eventually store the thirteen different "Mineralight News Bulletin - for your life" publications which were sold one by one from 1944 through 1950 or 1951, and are virtual time warps. Although this "Ultra-Violet Products, Inc. Mineralight File" was published during roughly the same time period as the previously described issues of the "Black Light Beacon," this "Mineralight File" was written more like professional trade publication than the "Black Light Beacon," which was presented much more as a type of public magazine or

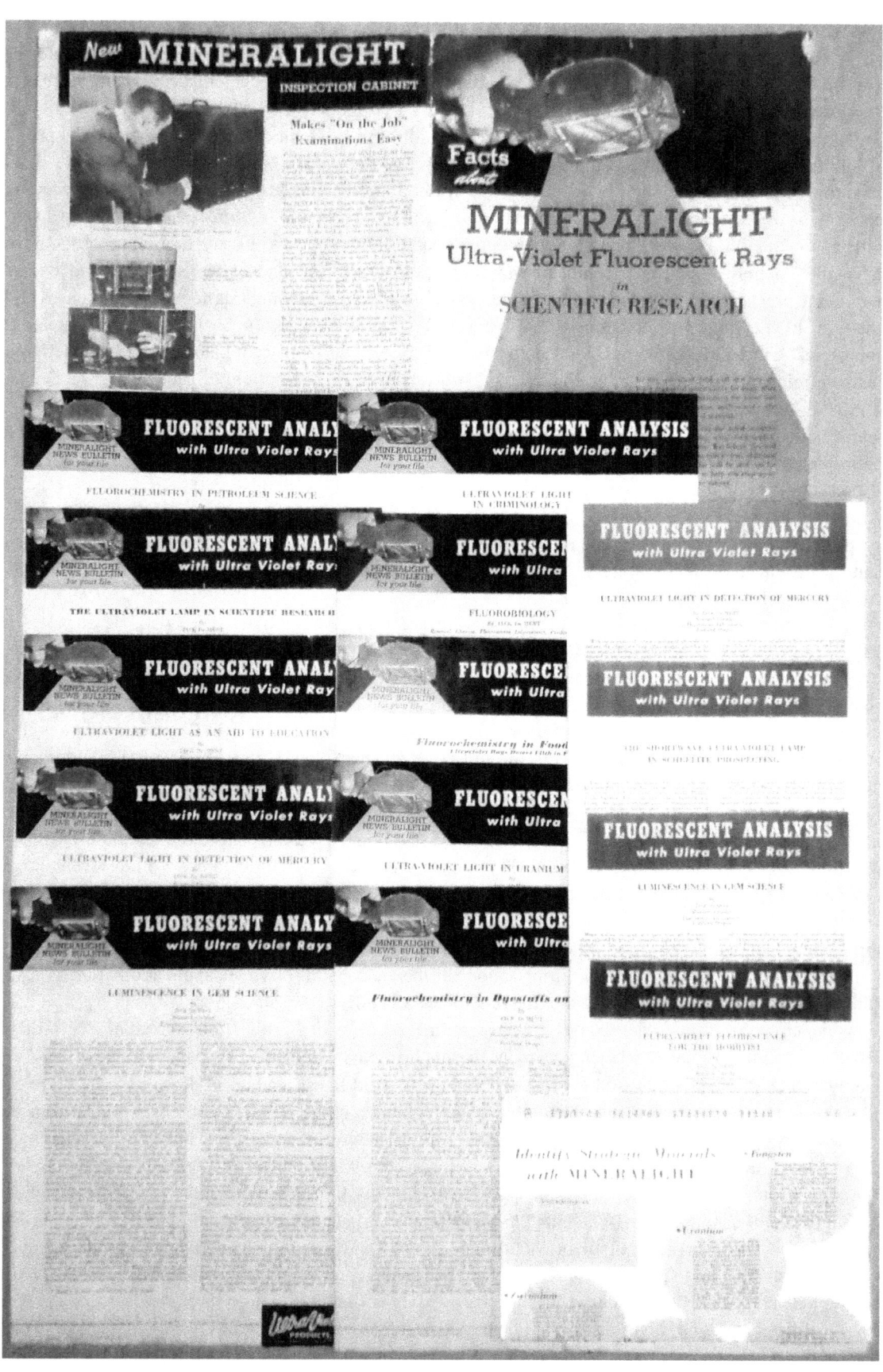

1943-1950 Collection of "MINERALITE News Bulletin - for your life," "Ultra-Violet Products, Inc.," California

newspaper with articles as well as many photographs. What must be explained at this point is that the issues of the "Black Light Beacon" were published by "Conti-Glo," the company of the "Switzer Brothers" that would much later become world famous as "Day-Glo," which was founded by Robert Switzer, the man who invented Fluorescent paint in 1933 as a teenager and his younger brother Joseph Switzer. On the other hand, this "Ultra-Violet Products, Inc. Mineralight File" was published by Thomas S. Warren's company, which he founded in 1932 in California, and which was initially involved primarily with the production of Ultraviolet lamp units, most famously the first portable Shortwave Ultraviolet lamp the "M-12" that was made exclusively for prospecting for the mineral Scheelite in America both before and during the Second world war, and the "V-43" which was made with the same intentions during the middle of the war in 1943. So to establish a proper perspective, the "Switzer Brothers" invented Fluorescent paint and were involved initially in Art, with very first name of their company being "Fluor-S-Art," while Thomas S. Warren's company was founded in the foreground of the Second world war with the clear intentions of mineral prospecting for Scheelite and other valuable Fluorescent minerals to be used exclusively by the U.S. military for the war. In telephone conversations with Thomas S. Warren in the early 1990s, he very clearly stated to me that the initial direction of his "Ultra-Violet Products, Inc." company was not Art or Fluorescent paint, but the production of Ultraviolet lamps to be used in mineral prospecting. The Shortwave lamp was used to find not only Scheelite for the Second world war, but also later in Uranium prospecting for the newly developed atomic fusion. Mr. Warren told me that he did not start to sell Fluorescent paint until after 1953 when he bought the Fluorescent paint company "Vo-Glo" in San Francisco and began to produce an entire line of Fluorescent Art supplies. From this vantage point of historical perspective, it is clear to see why the direction and presentations of the publications of the two separate companies were so different. In short, "Conti-Glo" was founded on Art and Fluorescent paint, while "Ultra-Violet Products, Inc." was founded on mineral prospecting for the war. Not just from my personal contact with Mr. Thomas S. Warren, but even through their respective photographs it is easy to understand that the "Switzer Brothers" were essentially teenage inventors of a new movement, while Thomas S. Warren was essentially a very successful businessman.

Starting with the outside folder of this "Ultra-Violet Products, Inc. MINERALIGHT FILE," it was intended to contain the future publications of thirteen issues of "MINERALIGHT NEWS BULLETIN" starting in 1944 and continuing until 1950 or 1951 after the war's end. Several of the thirteen different "Mineralight News Bulletins" have "10¢" written in pencil on the cover, presumably the selling price for each of these individual publications (the Switzer Brother's "Black Light Beacon" was free), which would be collected and stored in this folder. The front cover of this folder is in Black and White with Violet added, and clearly states the direction of the company with the full cover of this folder being filled with a photograph of an "Ultra-Violet Products, Los Angeles" cast iron ancient looking "Mineralight" in someone's hand, which casts it's Violet beam of energy across the entire cover of this folder. Since Black lights and Fluorescence had developed a whole new school of Criminology, also developed first by the "Switzer Brothers" in 1941 in Cleveland, Ohio, the headline on this "Ultra-Violet Products, Inc." folder is "Facts about MINERALIGHT" with the subtitle of 'Ultra-Violet's' "Fluorescent Rays" for use in Criminology (written in no less than four different type faces). The bottom of this folder's cover has "File and Save" written on it as well as a block of text informing the reader that this 'specialized field' of the 'magic ultra violet light' had many newly discovered applications, including the fields of analyzation and identification. The text informs the reader that their 'business' will be kept up to date on the latest 'scientific information' in the field of 'ultra violet applications.' It is also written that bulletins would be sent to the reader over time, and that this folder was intended to store them.

The inside cover of this folder comes directly to the point with a full Violet headline 'MINERALIGHT For Fluorescent Analysis' and it's use in 'Identifying Many Materials Instantly.' Half this first page is filled with an explanation of Ultraviolet energy, which the reader was told is often referred to as "cold light," and an in-depth description of the company's "Mineralight" technology. There is also an ancient chart that contains many type faces and descriptions from very far in the past. First of all the spelling of "wave-lengths," but even more archaic in this chart's explanation is what's called a 'large crystal Monochromator' utilizing a 'Thermopile-galvanometer system'(?) to measure the peak excitation levels of these "Mineralight" lamps (sounds like a "light-meter"). The text explains the facts that Shortwave Ultraviolet lamps, with a wavelength output of '2540 nanometers,' excite many more materials and natural minerals to Fluoresce than the common Black light, which has a much less energetic output of '3660 nanometers,' and that the "Mineralights" produced by "Ultra-Violet Products, Inc.," were manufactured with the most efficient Ultraviolet producing materials made, especially the Shortwave lamp and it's complementary Shortwave filter. Since Shortwave Ultraviolet does not go through glass, the lamp's tubular bulb and it's Shortwave filter had to be laboriously manufactured out of pure fused Quartz crystals, not glass, which is still the technology used today seventy years later. The reader is informed that this 'genuine pure fused Quartz tube' is the only material that allows the full one hundred percent transmission of Shortwave Ultraviolet, and that a drop of Mercury inside this

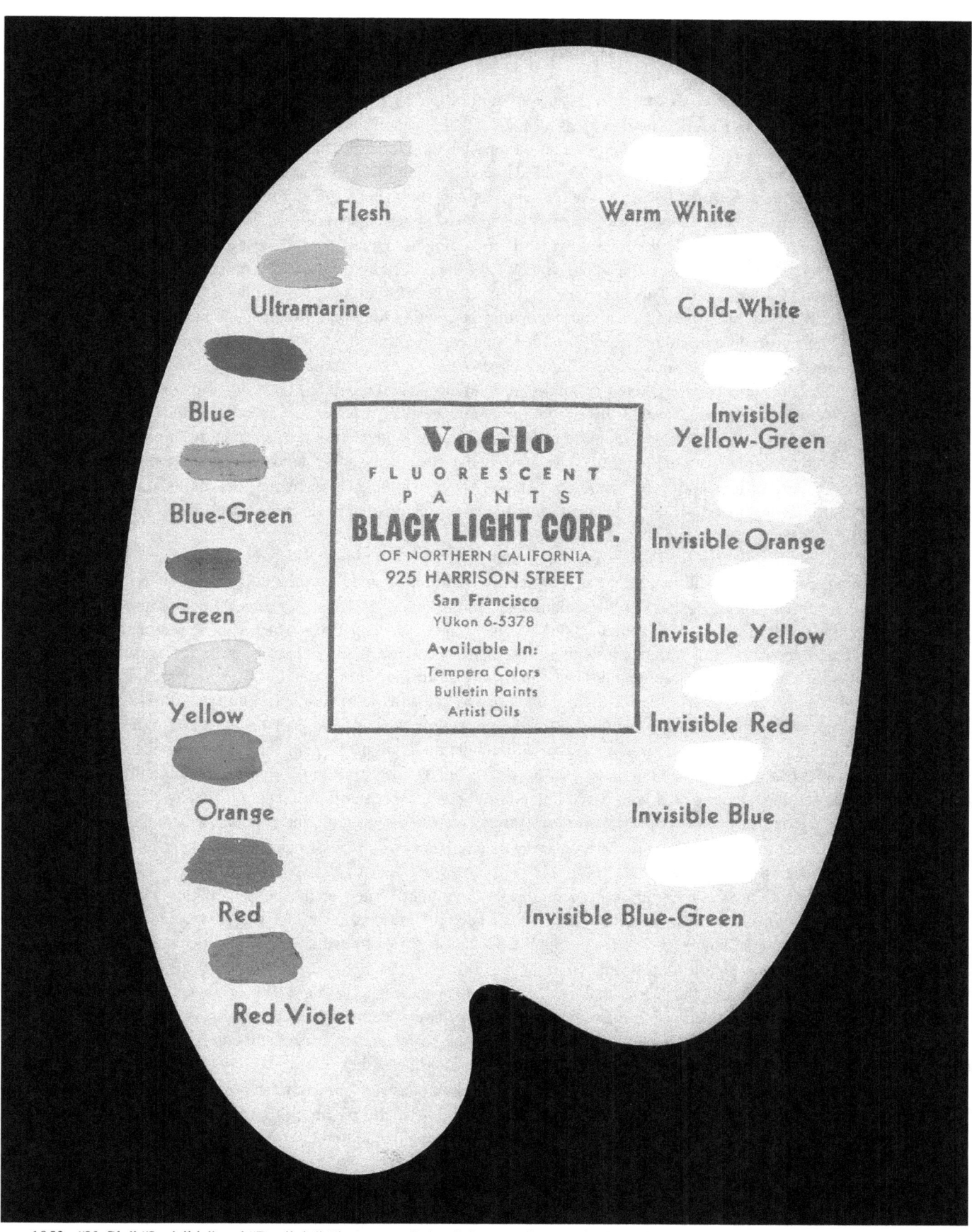

1953: "VoGlo" "Invisible" and "Daylight" Fluorescent Paint Color sample swatch, "BLACK LIGHT CORP. of Northern California," San Francisco (containing the controversial 1950's Beige "FLESH" Color name)

sealed fused Quartz tube was what became vaporized with electrical charge and produced Ultraviolet. What really dates this explanation from 1944, and definitively places it in a nearly archaic context, is the measurement for Ultraviolet energy being in "Calories!"

The bottom of this page holds the general fields of application for these "Mineralights," including a typical headline 'Mineralight Finds the Hidden Values.' The four areas of industrial application for these "Mineralights" that are listed start with the 'Food Industry,' in which the Ultraviolet lamp was used for analyzing food that has been contaminated by rats or bugs, the quality of virgin olive oil compared to the inferior refined olive oil, and also to examine flours for impurities. Next the 'Medical Profession,' with uses of the "Mineralight" entering into an antiquated time slot through an application of the Black light that would shock most people today, including myself. The two suggested applications listed for the 'Medical Profession' are skin analyzation and treatment for skin diseases, which is still being used today for the same exact purposes, but the second suggestion is enough to send shivers down the spine. It looks like the procedure for proving a person was dead in 1944 was by using a Black light and Fluorescence. This gruesome application of Black light is explained through the simple procedure of injecting Fluorescent "Eosin" into the veins and then immediately opening the eyes of the person and examining the eyeballs for Fluorescence. This procedure is another example of developments in Ultraviolet technology that were marketed by Thomas S. Warren's company "Ultra-Violet Products, Inc.," but which also were very similar or even identical to the products that "The Switzer Brothers" had invented and marketed ("Conti-Glo's" Fluorescent Embalming Fluid "Visibalm"). Throughout my contact with Mr. Thomas S. Warren, as well as his friends, ex-employees, and professional associates, there was always present an atmosphere of a "Hard Sell" consciousness quite purged of any notion or intention of spirituality or anything even dimly related to the esoteric world of emitted light. The absolutely most distasteful standard operating procedure for these "professionals" was the outright taking of ideas, concepts, schools of thought - even the idea of making a "Museum of Fluorescence" instead of the already-in-1997-planned same old 'Rock Show' that has repeated itself for as long as this antique "Mineralight File" has been in existence.

The third field highlighted for Fluorescent application was the 'Oil Industry,' with an explanation that Petroleum is a natural compound, making it a substance that is very easily identifiable with a "Mineralight." Not only is Ultraviolet technology used for finding oil fields, but also for making maps of the actual oil fields themselves. In the Museum is an artifact form the 1950s or 1960s that is used as a small "Fluorescent Mineral Viewing Box" which can be seen before starting the Fluorescent mineral demonstrations in the dark, with all the Black lights and White lights still on in the Museum. This small "Fluorescent Mineral Viewing Box" is originally from an offshore oil drilling firm based in Colorado which utilized this small metal instrument for testing oil drill-cores for the presence of the valuable petroleum. The design of this small heavy-duty totally stainless steel Ultraviolet instrument allowed drill-core samples to be examined under Black lights for a trace of petroleum without being in the dark, and in the presence of daylight on an oil drilling rig. The design of this small Ultraviolet instrument included a Black plastic viewing piece that the face is put against, blocking out most daylight and allowing a drill-core sample to be examined under dual 4 watt Black lights in full daylight on an oil drilling ship. The two sides (and front) of this metal Ultraviolet box instrument for petroleum prospecting were fitted with small metal doors, which allowed a long drill-core sample from the sea floor to be slid into the Ultraviolet examination box and tested under Black light for the typical bright Sky Blue Fluorescence of petroleum.

The fourth major professional application for the "Mineralight" listed at the bottom of this page is the 'Mining Industry.' Since the publication of this "Ultra-Violet Products, Inc." information folder was 1944, and the major mineral prospected for with Ultraviolet lamps in America during the Second world war was Scheelite, which contains Tungsten needed for hardening steel, the main application listed for mining in this folder centers around this mineral. Again, Mr. Thomas Warren's capitalized bottom line of the page is that his "Mineralight" can be used to 'Find Hidden Values.'

The third page of this folder, which forms the inside of the folder together with page two, has a listing and photographs of every "Mineralight" sold by "Ultra-Violet Products, Inc." in 1944, which are advertised in the page's headline as being used for field work, laboratory use, and also combination lamps. The entire line of these 1944 Ultraviolet lamps are very antiquated and immediately bring to mind the Second world war era of Battleship construction: completely steel, rubber, and leather, with sometimes a small addition of the newly invented substance "Plastic." Also the general design of these 1940s Ultraviolet lamps was not exactly 'streamlined' or 'space-age' in any way, but more rectangular and brutal. The five different lines of Ultraviolet lamps made by "Ultra-Violet Products, Inc." in 1944 were the original 'Midget' "M" series, the second 'Master' "V" series, and the more recent 'Standard' "Q" series, 'Super' "R" series, and 'Heavy-Duty' "S" series. The "Mineralight Master V Series" is first described, since the series was made in the 1940s exclusively for the war effort ("V" stands for "Victory"). The "V-41" was designed for use only with an electrical cord, the "V-42" was designed for outdoor prospecting utilizing a battery pack, and

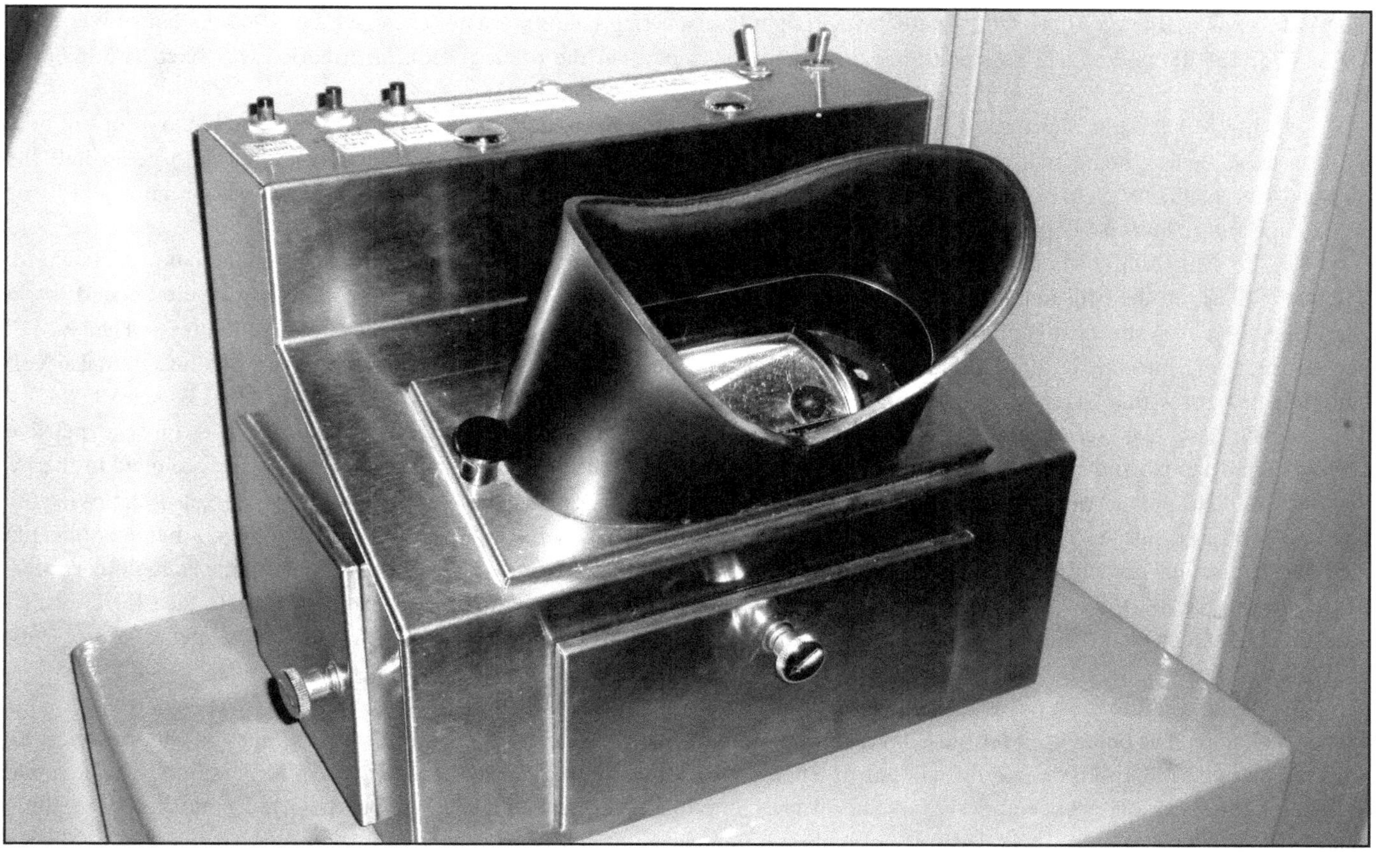

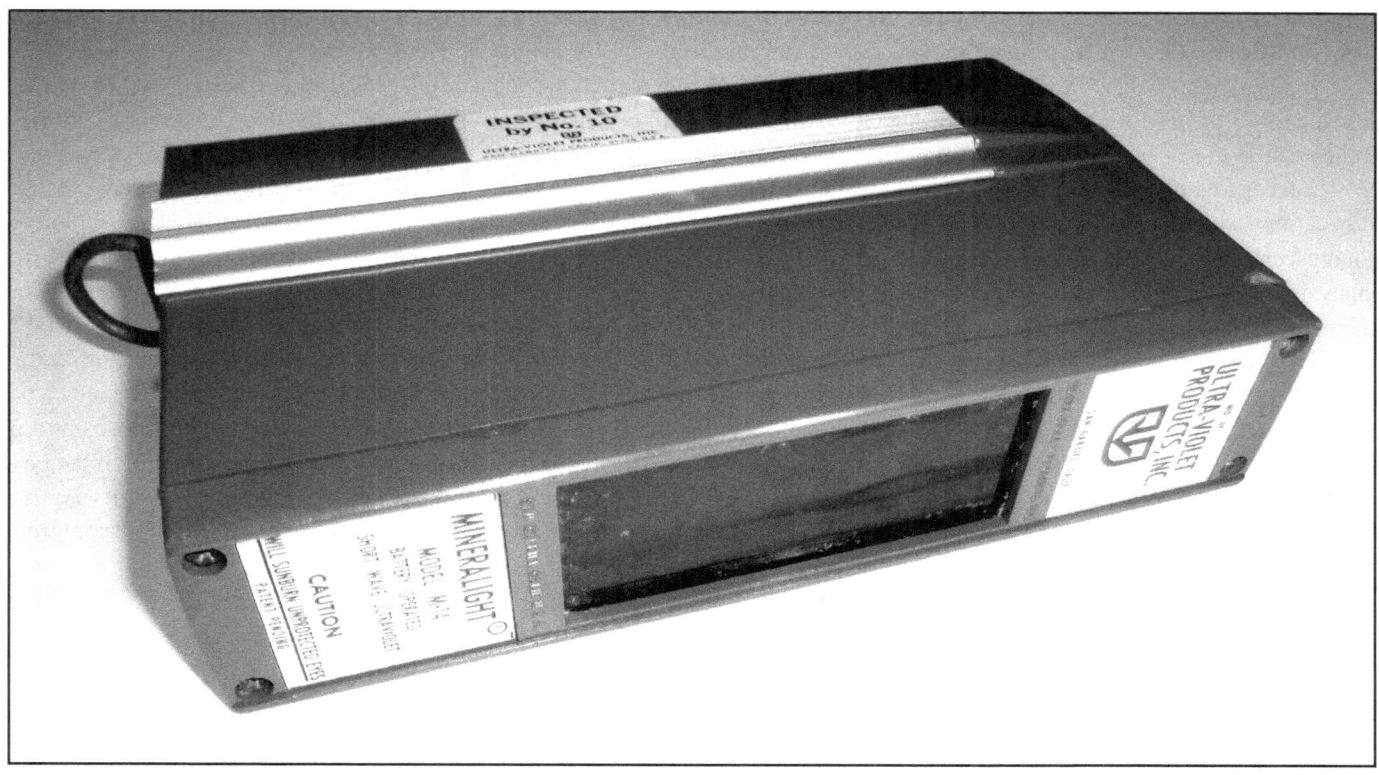

Fluorescent Mineral Viewing Box, "Electric Ladyland - the First Museum of Fluorescent Art," 1940s "Gisco Geophysical Instrument and Supply Company," Denver, Colorado - Originally used for Offshore Oil Drill-Core inspection

1940s-1950s "MINERALITE" "Model M-14 Battery Operated Short Wave Ultraviolet," "Ultra-Violet Products, Inc." This is "The First Pocket-Size Transistor ULTRA-VIOLET LAMP" the "V-44" was usable on AC or DC. These "Mineralight" prospecting lamps were not cheap, and in 1944 the lamps were sold for $48.75, $58.25, and $72.25 respectively. For comparison, in 1944 the price of Gold in America was fixed at $35.00 an ounce.

The 'Mineralight Standard Q Series' also was sold as three separate units, AC, DC, and the combination of the two, and are explained as being half the Ultraviolet energy output as the 'Master V Series,' as well as the lamp being half the physical size of the 'V Series' lamps. This 'Q Series was sold also for cheaper prices than the 'V Series,' the "Q-41" was $39.50, the "Q-42" was $44.50, and the combination "Q-34" was $57.50

The 'Mineralight Midget M Series' is listed third, but it was the first portable Shortwave Ultraviolet lamp in the world, with the "M-12" in the Museum collection being manufactured in 1938 to use in Scheelite prospecting for the Second world war. The "M-12" is shown in a photograph, but the newer models "M-11" and "M-13" are described in the text. The "M-11" was for plugging into an AC outlet, and the "M-13" was designed to use for prospecting, able to run off the internal 6 volt lantern battery, or with a larger external 6 volt 'Hotshot' battery. The "M-12" sold for $24.75, while the "M-13" was $32.75.

The last two series of "Mineralights" described here were the largest, most powerful, and most expensive "Mineralight" lamps sold by "Ultra-Violet Products, Inc." in 1944. The 'Mineralight Super R Series' was similar to the 'V Series' hand held prospecting lamps, but the actual lamp was twice the length of the 'V Series' lamps, and also had twice the Ultraviolet energy output of the 'V Series' lamps. The 'Super R Series' "Mineralight" lamps are described a being applicable for mineral displays and the sorting of ore. The 'R Series' was also sold in three different models, the same as the other series of prospecting lamps, the AC, DC, or AC/DC combination lamps, being the "R-51" which sold for $81.50, the "R-52" which sold for $110.00, and the combination "R-54" which sold for $135.00. The size difference of this 'Super R Series' was equivalent to it's weight difference. The "Q-34" was 8.25 pounds (3.75 kilos), and the "R-54" was 12 pounds (5.5 kilos).

The largest and most powerful "Mineralight" is listed last and was called the 'Mineralight Heavy-Duty S Series.' This was also explained as being used for museum displays, for use on ore sorting tables, or for the photography of Fluorescence, all applications where the most powerful amount of Shortwave Ultraviolet was needed. This "S-61 Mineralight" was a round metal unit that used a very special design of Shortwave Ultraviolet lamp, called a "Coiled Quartz Grid," and was essentially a very long Shortwave tubular lamp that was coiled into a tight space of six by six inches (15x15 cm) like a snake coiled into a circle. This twenty-one pound (9.5 kg) 'S-61 Heavy-Duty Mineralight' was rated as having twice the amount of Shortwave Ultraviolet energy output as the powerful 'R Series,' and ran off AC outlets. The price of this museum or mining Shortwave lamp was a whopping $150.00 in 1944. At the bottom of the text are accessories included with the "Mineralight" lamps, such as a twenty piece Fluorescent mineral sample set and carrying straps for the lamps and batteries.

The back of this "Mineralight File," page four, is fully devoted to the "Mineralight Inspection Cabinet," which was an instrument to be used for analysis together with a "Mineralight" ultraviolet lamp. The headline for this "Inspection Cabinet" indicated the use of this analyzing instrument: 'On the Job Examinations.' Through five photographs and half a page of text the reader learns that Fluorescent Analysis must be performed in conditions as close as possible to being totally dark. Some instructions are given that are not even considered today, such as letting the eyes become adjusted to the dark before beginning Fluorescent analysis. The reader is told that the advantage of using this "Mineralight Inspection Cabinet" was that Fluorescent analysis in the dark with an Ultraviolet lamp can take only some minutes, while the former method of chemical analysis in laboratories could take days. The materials mentioned for Fluorescent analysis in this "Inspection Cabinet" were foods, chemicals, and minerals, as it was explained that the cabinet was intended to be a portable Fluorescent field laboratory with the use of any "Mineralight" Ultraviolet lamp, Longwave or Shortwave. This portable Fluorescent darkroom was designed to be used in conditions of full daylight, such as a laboratory or in the field, complete with two arm holes fitted with rubber to keep light out of the "Inspection Cabinet," as well as a rubber viewing baffle to place the face against for keeping light out of the box which was fitted with a magnifying lens for analysis. Inside the "Inspection Cabinet" there was a 'platform' on an 'elevator' to bring materials to be analyzed into focus for inspection, and in three of the photographs this 'elevator' for the center 'platform' is shown. The three photos of the opened back panel of this "Inspection Cabinet" showing the 'elevator' and 'platform' inside the cabinet immediately bring to mind Dr. Frankenstein's laboratory with the platform he used to bring his creation up to the lightning on the castle's roof, here being an antique contraption equipped with the identical machinery that Dr. Frankenstein himself used: Metal chains, gears, wheels, and springs. The first photograph of this center 'platform' and 'elevator' exemplifies the professional intention of this instrument, with six test tubes in place for Fluorescent analysis.

The size of this large "Mineralight Inspection Cabinet" was about two feet (65 cm) wide and tall, with a depth of about a foot and a half (50 cm) and was designed with the function of the user being able to open the complete front and back panels of the cabinet. The top lid, which was a quarter of the cabinet, completely opened up to place an external hand held

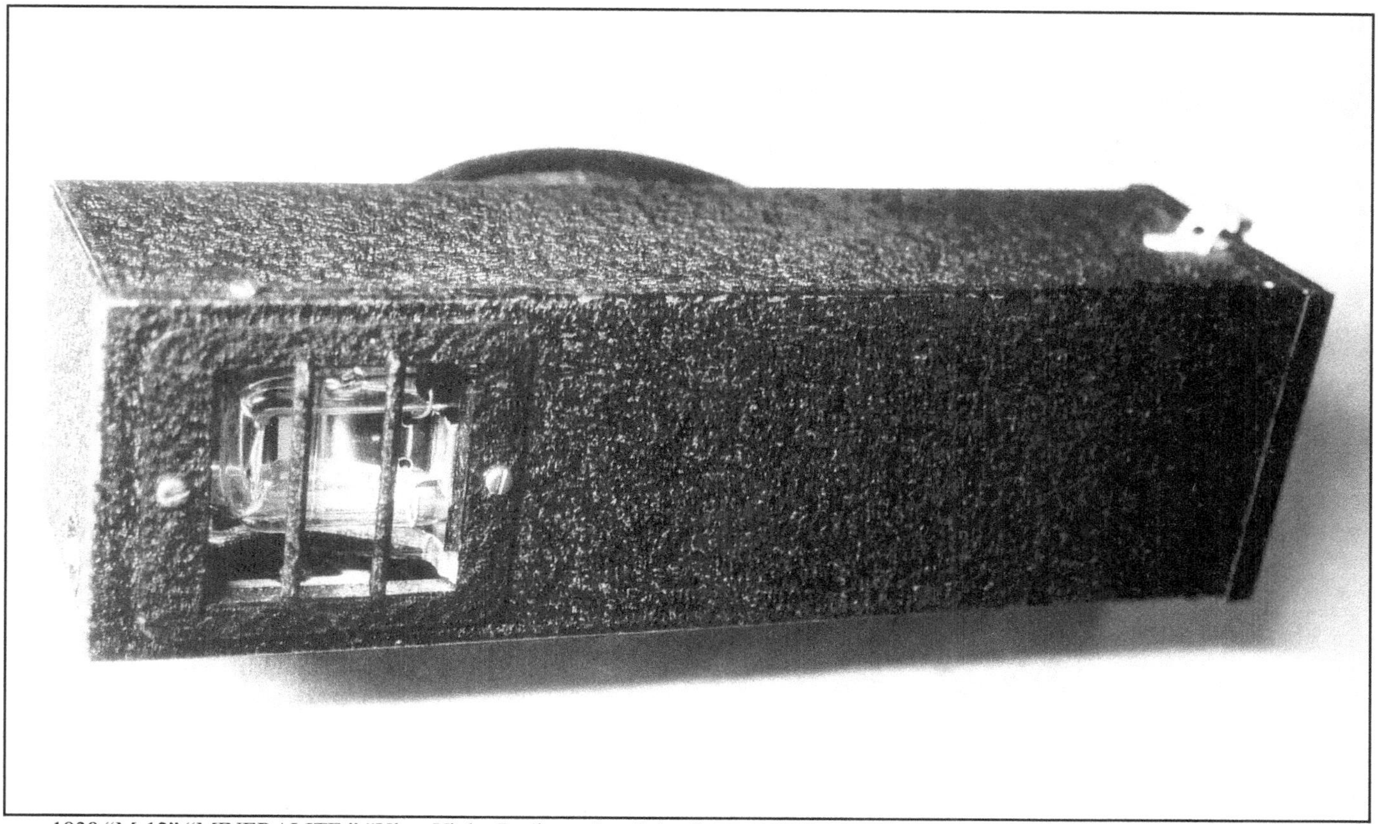

1938 "M-12" "MINERALITE," "Ultra-Violet Products, Inc.," the first portable Shortwave Ultraviolet lamp produced to prospect for Tungsten-containing Scheelite in the United States for the approaching Second World War

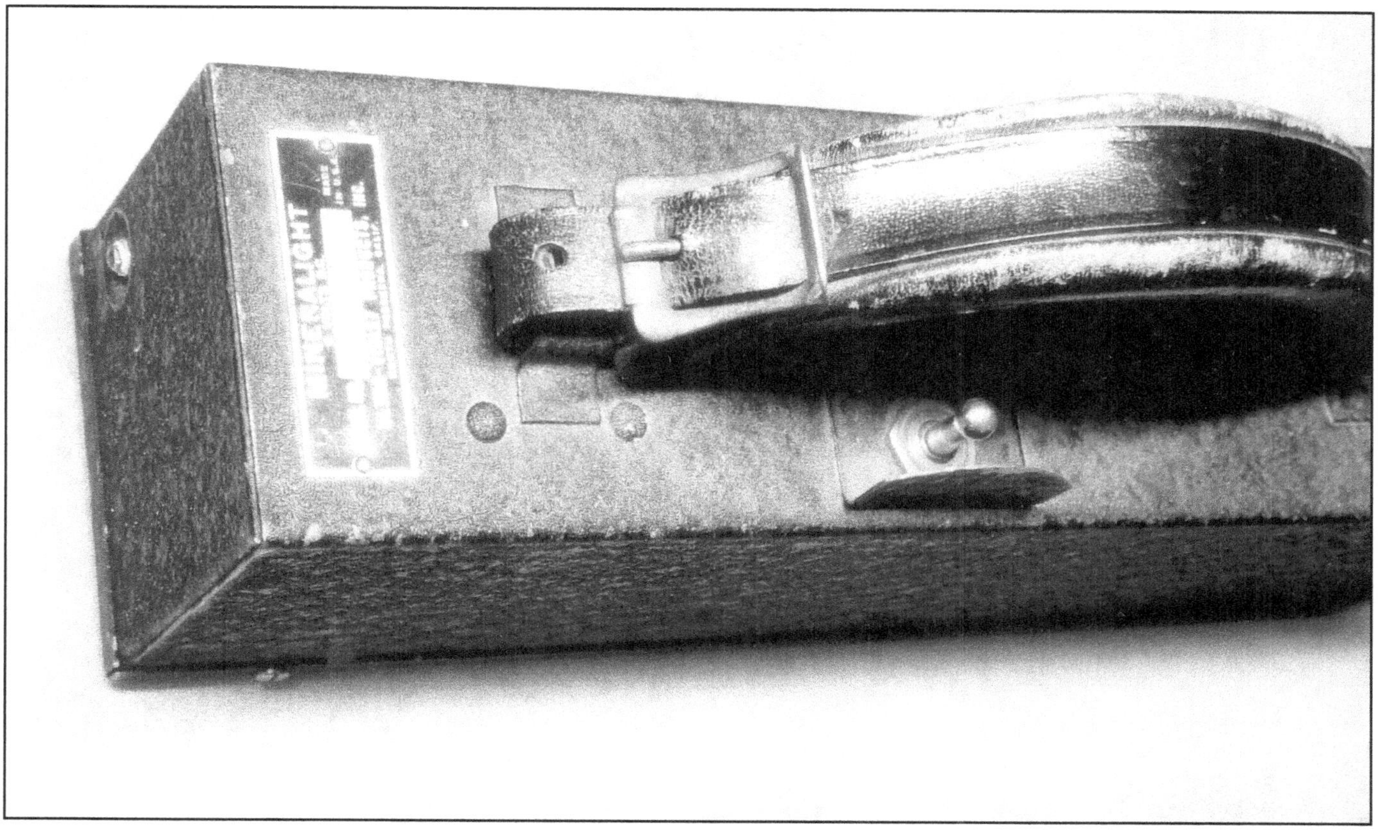

1938 "M-12" "MINERALITE," "Ultra-Violet Products, Inc.," the first portable Shortwave Ultraviolet lamp produced to prospect for Tungsten-containing Scheelite in the United States for the approaching Second World War (top)

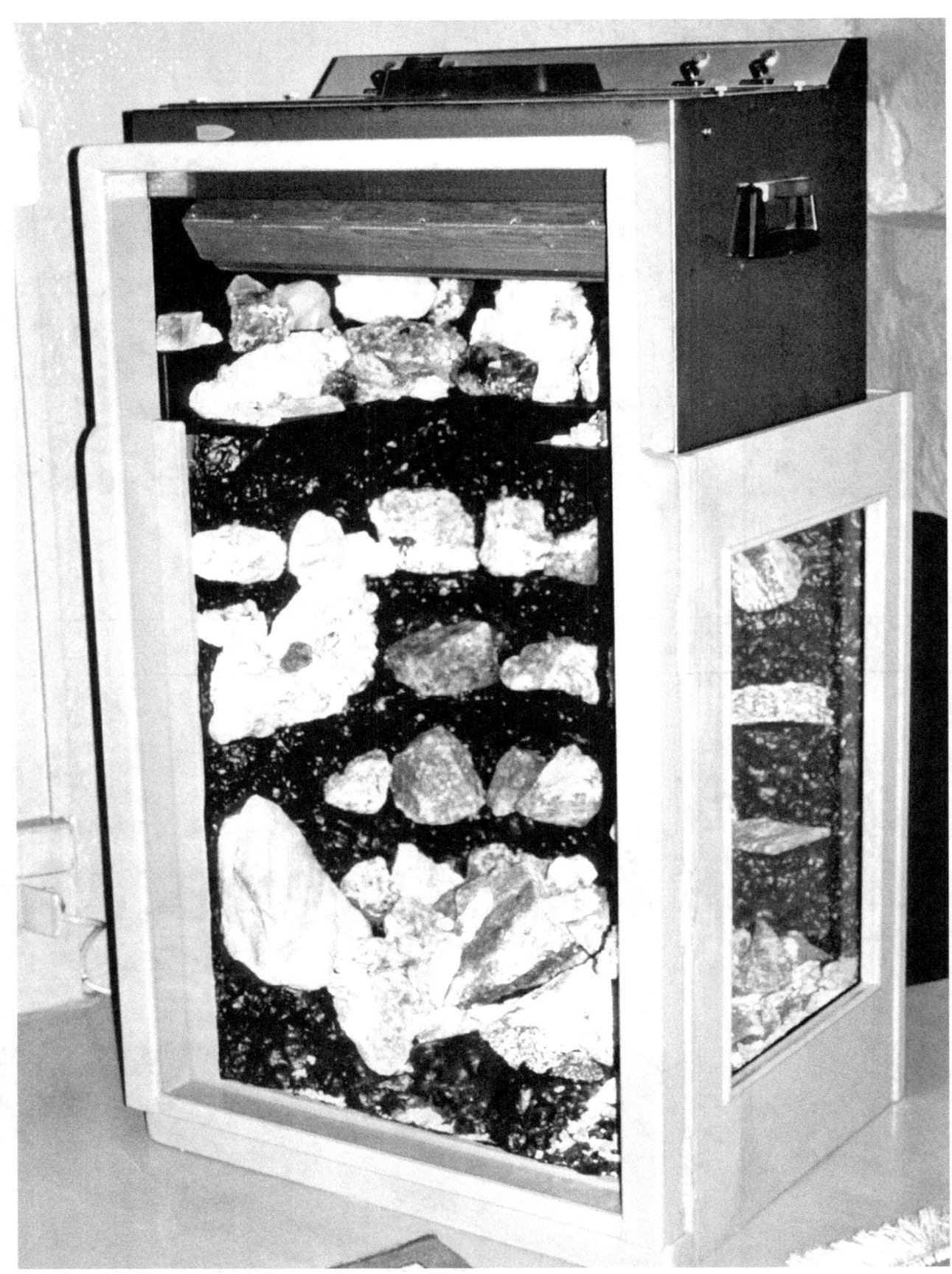

Fluorescent Mineral Viewing Box, "Electric Ladyland - the First Museum of Fluorescent Art" - Originally the top metal section is a 1940s "C-5" "Chromatoviewer" Longwave and Shortwave U.V. Medical Inspection Cabinet

"Mineralight" Ultraviolet lamp into it's fitting, which was the source of the Ultraviolet energy since the cabinet had no Ultraviolet lamps built in, only normal White lights. One of the photos shows the archaic set up, with the large "Inspection Cabinet's" lid opened up and a portable "Mineralight" fitted into place next to a square electrical transformer also inside the top area of the cabinet's lid, which is attached with wires to a huge "Eveready" 6 volt "Hot Shot" battery next to the cabinet, giving the general impression of a complicated science experiment in progress. The reader is told that both solids and liquids were meant to be examined in this "Inspection Cabinet" under White light or "Black Light," with the suggested applications listed being the petroleum Industry, laboratories, police criminology work, and for food and health inspections. This "Mineralight Inspection Cabinet" to be used with an external Ultraviolet "Mineralight," that was bought separately, was sold for $97.50 and is described as being painted a 'crackle Black,' and including a magnifier view piece, a rack of six test tubes made of "Cortex Glass" that was specially manufactured to be transparent to Shortwave Ultraviolet energy (which does not go through regular glass), and an adjustable center Frankenstein 'platform.'

This "Mineralight Inspection Cabinet" is the grandfather of the 1950s "Ultraviolet Products, Inc." later model inspection cabinet, the "C-5" "Chromatoviewer" which is used in the Museum as part of the construction of the "Fluorescent Mineral Viewing Box," and also in "Electric Lady" Art Gallery upstairs from the Museum, with a second original "C-5" being used to introduce visitors to the relatively unknown phenomenon of Fluorescent minerals. The general design of this advanced "C-5" "Chromatoviewer" is basically similar to the original "Mineralight Inspection Cabinet" from 1944, with the major improvement being the inclusion of powerful internal Longwave and Shortwave Ultraviolet lamp units. Inside the "C-5" are separate metal 30 watt Longwave and Shortwave Ultraviolet lamps with tremendous Ultraviolet filters (approximately 42 x 8 cm - 16.5 x 3") creating enough Ultraviolet energy to cause brilliant emission of light by anything that is Fluorescent when placed into the box. The front panel of the modernized "C-5" also was not fitted with arm holes, but with a moveable unit of rubber curtains, since the Ultraviolet energy was so much stronger in the "C-5" with it's internal U.V. lamps that a slight amount of daylight would hardly be noticed. This advanced "C-5" "Chromatoviewer" got it's name from the instrument's intended usage, which was the analysis of blood samples on pieces of paper that were called "Chromatographs," The truly advanced design of this "C-5" "Chromatoviewer" would give the option of a separate Ultraviolet platform being placed into the inspection area, which would allow samples to be supplied with Ultraviolet analyzing energy from above and also from below by use of the extra Ultraviolet platform sold as a "Transilluminator."

So, after receiving this 1944 "Mineralight File" to store future copies of "Mineralight News Bulletin" in for the next six or seven years there would be thirteen issues published and sold for 10¢ each intended to be 'facts about' 'Fluorescent Analysis with Ultraviolet Rays.' The first three "Mineralight News Bulletins" were printed in 1944 and are entitled "Fluorochemistry," 'Fluorochemistry for Petroleum Science,' and 'Ultraviolet light for Criminology.' The third Bulletin uses the word "Ultraviolet" instead of the former spelling of "Ultra Violet" for the first time here in 1944, but will again revert back to the former spelling in future issues of the Bulletin again. In 1945 the bulk of the "Mineralight News Bulletins" were published, from number four to number eleven, and began with 'The Ultraviolet Lamp used for Scientific Research,' then continued on to 'Ultraviolet Light used for aiding Education,'"Fluorobiology," 'Fluorochemistry used for Food Science and it's application of Detecting Filth in Foods,' 'Ultra-Violet Light and it's use for Detecting of Mercury,' 'Ultra-Violet Light used for Uranium Prospecting,' 'Luminescence and Gem Science,' and 'Fluorochemistry and it's use in Dyestuffs as well as Textile Science.' What is interesting and very telling of the Ultraviolet industry towards the end of the Second world war, is it's shift towards non-military applications, with the former military applications virtually falling to zero production after the war's end in 1945. This shift towards the 'civilian' sector of society after the war's end in 1945 is clearly exemplified by the title of the next "Mineralight News Bulletin" printed two years later in 1947: 'Ultra-Violet Fluorescence and it's use for Hobbyists,' number twelve. The final "Mineralight News Bulletin" was number lucky thirteen, and was entitled 'The Ultra-Violet Shortwave Lamp and it's use for Scheelite Prospecting,' perhaps in a final attempt to raise business again when the bottom literally fell out of the Ultraviolet industry after the end of World war two.

The author of all of the first twelve "Mineralight News Bulletins" was one of the leading experts on Fluorescence in the 1930s and 1940s, Jack De Ment, credited on these Bulletins as being a research chemist for the 'Fluorescent Laboratories' in Portland, Oregon. The first two 'Bibles' on Fluorescence I bought years ago and still refer to were both written by world experts on Fluorescence, Jack De Ment and H.C. Dake. Starting in 1934 "The Mineralogist Magazine" was published with H.C. Dake as the Editor and Jack De Ment as the Associate Editor. This magazine was published for over twenty years and specialized in the pioneering study of Fluorescent Gems and Minerals. The magazine was described in 1945 as a publication dealing with 'the field of Ultraviolet light units used in the demonstrations of the Fluorescence of Gems, minerals, and many other luminous substances.'

The book that I've referred to as a 'Bible' of Fluorescence is the first major book published by H.C. Dake and Jack De Ment, entitled "Fluorescent Light and it's Applications - Including Locations and Properties of Fluorescent materials... A Theoretical and Practical Exposition of Fluorescence and Similar Phenomenon." The author's credits are given in the book as 'By H.C. Dake (Editor "The Mineralogist Magazine," Co-Author "Quartz Family Minerals," Honorary President "Northwest Federation of Mineral Societies"), and Jack De Ment (Associate Editor "The Mineralogist Magazine," Research Chemist "The Mineralogist Laboratories"). The publication of the book was "1941 Chemical Publishing Company, Inc., Brooklyn, N.Y." In the Museum Library there are two copies of this 1941 book, one of which is signed by both H.C. Dake and Jack De Ment with fountain pen ink, and dated "5/2/41." This book is a 256 page documentation of the very early days of Black light and Fluorescent technology, ideas, and ideals, with twenty-five illustrations and very rare photographs.

In 1942 H. C. Dake and Jack De Ment published two companion books to "Fluorescent Light and It's Applications" entitled "Ultraviolet Light and It's Applications," with the other book having the full title of "Fluorescent Chemicals and Their Applications - Including a Tabulation of Fluorescent Substances... an exposition of their Utilities in the arts, sciences, and industries." The authors were listed in this book as "by Jack De Ment - Research Chemist "The Mineralogist Laboratories," Associate Editor "The Mineralogist Magazine," Co-Author "Fluorescent Light and It's Applications," and "Uranium and Atomic Power with a Special Chapter on Ultraviolet Radiation Sources," and "by H.C. Dake - Editor "The Mineralogist Magazine," Co-author "Fluorescent Light and It's Applications," "Quartz family Minerals," "Uranium and Atomic Power." This is just as an important book for the study of Fluorescence as the first book "Fluorescent Light and It's Applications," and it has 240 pages and eleven illustrations.

The book referred to in 1941 co-authored by De Ment and Dake was "Uranium and Atomic Power" which was also published in New York. In 1945 Jack De Ment published his own book, without H. C. Dake, and it was entitled with a word that De Ment coined in 1942, "Fluorochemistry." His massive 800 page technical volume 'covers Luminescence's entire field' and in 1945 it was sold for the large sum of $14.50. In this "Fluorochemistry" book, the name of Jack De Ment has been shortened, making it easier to say and less European, to "DeMent." In 1946 another book co-authored by both Jack DeMent and H.C. Dake was published in New York, "Rare Metals." In 1947 the next book to be co-authored by both men has the listing of authors with DeMent before Dake, the opposite of all publications with the exception of the first book of 1941, "Fluorescent Light and It's Applications," which had "Dake" only printed on the spine of the book as the author. This 1947 book was the timely "Handbook of Uranium Minerals" by DeMent and Dake, and is described as 'The only work of it's kind, describes all known Uranium minerals, and their Fluorescent properties, describes the use of the Geiger counter and other equipment used for prospecting Uranium and Thorium minerals.' This book was sold for just $2.00. In 1949 the last book I know of published by DeMent and Dake came out, and is entitled "Handbook of Fluorescent Gems and Minerals - An Exposition and Catalog of the Fluorescent and Phosphorescent Gems and Minerals, Including the Uses of Ultraviolet Light in Earth Sciences." This book was published by their own company, the "Mineralogist Publishing Company."

These "Minealight News Bulletins" with their subtitles "for your life" were all but one written by this author Jack De Ment for the "Ultra-Violet Products, Inc.," "Minealight File" between 1944 and 1947. "Minealight News Bulletin" "Number 1" was published in 1944 and was the first of the technical papers to be written by Jack De Ment in this series of thirteen to be published for this "Minealight File." These papers were compiled out of information from the many books on the phenomenon of Fluorescence that Jack De Ment wrote during the 1940s, with a perfect example being the title of this Number 1 Bulletin, "Fluorochemistry," which is also the exact same title of Jack De Ment's 800 page technical book "Fluorochemistry," which was published in 1945 with the title being a word that De Ment coined in 1942. This "Minealight News Bulletin" "Fluorochemistry" paper is five pages of full text and describes the general principles and definitions of Fluorescence, Phosphorescence, and the new science of "Fluorochemistry." In 1944, during the height of the era of "The Miracle of Fluorescence," new terms were coined that lasted for a very short time in scientific nomenclature, such as this 1940s title coined by Jack De Ment himself, "Fluorochemistry," and the other very dated term used in this paper, "Photochemistry." Jack De Ment was quite an enterprising character, naming scientific "laws" after himself and defining scientific theories with words he had also coined himself. A good example of this practice are the statements in this "Fluorochemistry" paper that there were two different kinds of 'radiations' that could cause Fluorescence, which Jack De Ment lists as "Optical," and "Corpuscular" radiation that is defined by De Ment as energy streams of electrons 'representing the most familiar of all the corpuscular excitants.' Within his paper De Ment informs the reader that over fifty different types of luminescence had been described in the last one hundred years prior to 1944, and notably, De Ment describes the new term coined by E. Newton Harvey, "Bioluminescence." Already in the fifth paragraph the reader is informed by Jack De Ment that 'as early as 1833' Sir David Brewster first described the phenomenon of Fluorescence, and that in 1852 Sir George Stokes 'developed' this new discovery, but 'it was not until 1942, or about 100 years later,' that this new science 'the science of Fluorochemistry was formally named and established by the writer.' Many of the terms that this writer Jack De Ment utilizes are either extremely archaic, or just plain inventions of the author himself, such as "nonthermal luminescence," and the word "phenomenonological" which he uses to completely misinform readers, as he states incorrectly that 'Phosphorescence is physically identical with Fluorescence.' The Quantum mechanics of Phosphorescence is completely different from the Quantum mechanics of Fluorescence, the difference being in the physical movement of the electrons in the atoms. With Fluorescence the cause is termed "Electron Displacement" and it is described as one electron excited with gained energy from a source such as Ultraviolet jumping up to a higher orbit in it's atom, moving through sub-orbits of it's new orbit causing a loss of a fraction of energy through atomic vibrations, and finally jumping back to it's original atomic orbit and releasing the remainder of it's gained energy as Visible Light - Fluorescent Colors. Phosphorescence is not the same Quantum movement, but an altogether different movement of electrons, where the extra energy received from an Ultraviolet source causes the electrons to physically jump out of their atoms completely, and then wander through the crystal lattice of the substance finally falling into the space that was supposed to be occupied by a missing atom, for example, thus 'trapping' the electron for seconds, minutes, hours, or even years, until it is released, and in this process Visible Light is released. This is the reason that the light of Phosphorescence is much dimmer than Fluorescence, and also the reason why the light of Phosphorescence is termed "Glow-in-the-dark," describing the substance giving off a little bit of light for a long time. In his description of 1944 in this "Fluorochemistry" paper that Jack De Ment both wrote and coined the word that is the title itself, the actual explanation of the Quantum mechanics of Fluorescence and Phosphorescence that Jack De Ment describes to readers is wrong, as well as his conclusion that the only difference and 'distinction' between the phenomenon of Fluorescence and Phosphorescence 'is purely phenomenological and historical rather than scientific.' Absolutely wrong, but typically eloquently worded.

After describing the most common Ultraviolet source in 1944 as a "black light," Jack De Ment continues on to humbly name more phenomenon of science after himself, such as "The First Law of Fluorescence" which he renames "De Ment's Absorption Law," and finally "Stoke's Emission Law" comes after his "De Ment's Absorption Law," and is even audaciously called by De Ment the "Second Law of Fluorescence." Mr. De Ment even goes so far as to establish a "Third Law of Luminescence-equivalence" which of course De Ment takes credit for creating in the year 1943, placing himself not only above Sir George Stokes, who named the phenomenon of Fluorescence in 1852, but also within the company of Albert Einstein himself. De Ment continues on using the terms 'Long wavelengths' and 'Short wavelengths' to describe Longwave and Shortwave Ultraviolet, and then three more words that he himself coins, "Macroluminescence," "Microluminescnece," and also "Diluminescence" which is the word De Ment coins for 'Non-Fluorescent.' De Ment continues this 1944 paper "Fluorochemistry" with words of his own invention to describe Quantum physics, such as "ultrachemiluminescence," and then he introduces another new field of science that he personally takes the credit for both establishing and naming: "Fluorobiology." This five page paper on "Fluorochemistry" coined and written by Jack De Ment, concludes with a statement by De Ment that 'Fluorochemistry is a fundamental science,' and then provides a list of 'Suggested Reading' which lists four books by other authors, and then five books by Jack De Ment. Unfortunately, the writing of Jack De Ment, exemplified in this five page "Fluorochemistry" paper, is so heavily weighed with personal achievements and the laying of claim to scientific doctrine, that many times the actual message of the writing is itself obscured.

In 1944 the next 'No. 2' "Mineralight News Bulletin" 'Fluorescent Analysis using Ultra Violet Rays' was published, and it was entitled 'Fluorochemistry in Petroleum Science' by Jack De Ment. The reader learns that the new method of finding petroleum is named the "Fluorochemical Exploration Method," yet another science christened by Jack De Ment. The author informs the reader that all petroleum has a Fluorescence, even when diluted and mixed with mud or water, as is commonly the case with "Drill Core samples" that are tested. De Ment also writes that in industry during the 1940s era, Fluorescence was called "Bloom," and some oils had Fluorescent Green "Polynuclear hydrocarbons" added to them to produce the specified Fluorescent reaction in the marketed oil product. Through this article the reader learns that the 'long-wave lamp' was used primarily in the testing for the presence of petroleum in drill core samples, but also through the use of the 'short-wave lamp' other important minerals could be identified in the same drill core sample, and that the petroleum could be detected with a Black light even when it was greatly diluted to a mere one part in 100,000 parts of Carbon tetrachloride. Since all petroleum has a slightly different Fluorescent reaction under the Black light, other instruments were also employed for petroleum prospecting in 1944, such as 'Color screens or filters, a spectroscope, or a spectrograph.' Jack De Ment lists the different "Technic" that were used in prospecting for oil with 'Ultra-Violet' lamps, the first of which he lists as 'Prospecting,' in which the petroleum drill core sample is quickly placed under a Black light as soon as it is extracted from the ground, and then examined by eye. The other "Technic" written by De Ment is called 'Correlating' and relates to the further examination of the Drill Core sample, where the weight of the sample is 'correlated' to the volume of solvent used to extract the drill core sample.

The last two sections in this "Fluorochemistry in Petroleum Science" paper by Jack De Ment are 'Fluorochemical Exploration By Use of Soil Samples,' and 'Fluoroanalysis of Drill Core,' in which De Ment explains the procedures for analyzing drill core samples, such as the signatory bright Blue Fluorescence of petroleum under Black light in contrast to other Colors of Fluorescence that could be observed in the same drill core sample with the addition of a Shortwave "Mineralight," such as Blue Fluorescing Scheelite with it's Tungsten content, Green Fluorescing Willemite zinc ore, Orange Fluorescing Sphalerite Zinc ore, or even the Yellow, Yellow-Green, or Green Fluorescing Uranium minerals. The conclusion of Jack De Ment is that the petroleum drill core samples should be tested under both Longwave and Shortwave Ultraviolet lamps, and the inspection should be done when the drill core sample is wet and fresh for the detection of oil, or in the dry state for the detection of other minerals.

The 'No. 3' "Mineralight News Bulletin" was also published in 1944 and deals with a common usage of the Black light that is still being employed today, rather than an industrial usage as in the previous two issues, and addresses the rather new science of 'Ultraviolet Light in Criminology' written again by Jack De Ment. In this paper the author introduces the general usage of the Black light in the police field of criminology, which had only been introduced about three years before, in 1941 by, again, the "Switzer Brothers" in Cleveland.

The next section in this Criminology paper is 'Gathering Evidence,' and it deals primarily with the essential step in this gathering of Fluorescent evidence under a Black light at a crime scene: 'Ultraviolet Photography.' The advice that the author gives on the subject of Ultraviolet photography is very well presented, complete, and even contemporary seventy years later. De Ment explains that an ordinary camera with film can be used for Ultraviolet photography, with the simple addition of a 'light filter' put over the lens of the camera, which is today referred to as a "Barrier Filter," and prevents Ultraviolet energy from entering the lens of the camera and fogging the film. De Ment even lists the "Barrier Filters" that were available in 1944, including the 'Noviol A, 3 mm thick, Code 038,' the usage of 'Two Wratten 4-A gelatin filters,' 'one Eastman "Haze" filter,' and a 'Harrison "UV" filter.' De Ment goes on to give the instructions to produce your own "Barrier Filter," which involves saturating a solution of Sodium nitrate in a 2 cm. thick 'glass cell.' The detailed instructions by the author on the subject of 'Ultraviolet Photography' include a discussion on long exposure times to catch the dim light of Fluorescence under Black lights, and even comparisons and advice for the development of the prints made from 'Ultraviolet photography' to be used for 'examination by the jury.'

'Specific Applications to Crime Work' is the title of the next section, in which the individual uses of Black light pertaining to Criminology are examined. Starting with 'Fingerprints,' De Ment discusses the use of Fluorescent dusting and the use of tracers to both record and detect fingerprints. Jack De Ment calls a method of Fluorescent fingerprinting "Fluorographic Fingerprinting" and details the use of different substances that the Fluorescent fingerprint dusting is made of. On display in the Museum is an original 1940s or 1950s "Ultra-Violet Products, Inc." "Blak-Ray" "Invisible Fluor-O-Check System" Fluorescent fingerprint detector unit and the original Fluorescent ink pad used with this apparatus. 'Documentary Studies' is the next area of Fluorescent criminology work to be covered in this paper, and the reader learns that different pencils and pens produce different Fluorescent reactions, as well as any erasures which permanently alter the Fluorescent reaction of the paper that the erasure has been made onto. De Ment also relates the facts that on skin coffee stains, soaps, detergents, lipstick, and even nicotine stains are Fluorescent in their own distinguishable Colors. 'Arson and Explosion' is the next cheerful use of Fluorescent analysis in criminology that is examined, and the facts are revealed that chemicals, corrosives, and inflammables found near crime scenes are all Fluorescent, as well as dynamite wrappings which contain Fluorescent oils, waxes, and resins. Candles and matches are listed as 'Fluorescing intensely,' and the non-Fluorescence of gasoline is compared to the bright Blue Fluorescence of kerosene. The next area of criminal investigation that De Ment uncharacteristically explains is the 'False Psychics and Mediums,' which Robert Switzer also wrote about in the early days of "Day-Glo." Here the author reports on the Mediums 'creating the ectoplasm' in psychic rituals, and how 'mild pandemoniums have resulted' when a Black light and Luminous paint were discovered during seances creating completely false 'spiritual contacts.' Again De Ment delves into the 'dark side' of the use of the "Mineralight" and Fluorescence, and again mentioning the use of a Fluorescent Dye, this time De Ment specifically stating the use of "Fluorescein," to determine if a person is dead or not. Author Jack De Ment now characteristically takes credit for developing 'a technique in this connection' in which De Ment describes his 'invention' of 'injecting a Fluorescent dye (Fluorocein)' into the veins and inspecting the eyes and lips for Fluorescence. As this product was specifically discussed in Liesa Bing's "The Story of Day-Glo," there is good chance that this product was also originally invented by "The Switzer Brothers," who even named the Fluorescent tracer product they developed for injecting into the veins

"Visibalm." In retrospect, Mr. Thomas S. Warren, the founder of "Ultra-Violet Products, Inc." couldn't have picked a better suited author to write for his company, an author who embodied similar techniques and abilities of not only Thomas Warren himself, but his professional associates as well.

The final section covered in this "Ultraviolet Light in Criminology" paper by Jack De Ment is "Tagging and Marking," in which the author discusses examples of dusting objects with Fluorescent powders and then examining suspected thieves' hands with a "Mineralight" to determine if they had touched the stolen object. Added by the author is a small listing of the four major Fluorescent 'Tracers' used in 1944, which consisted of Zinc orthosilicate Fluorescing bright Green, Magnesium tungstate Fluorescing bright Blue, Rhodamine B in water Fluorescing a 'Brilliant red-orange,' and also the most famous of all Fluorescent tracers "Fluorescein" in water (which to this day is still demonstrated on every day in the Museum's "Common Items that are Fluorescent" display) and which De Ment accurately describes as Fluorescing a 'Brilliant Green.'

The fourth "Fluorescent Analysis with Ultra Violet Rays" paper in this series was a detailed eight page discussion on the use of 'The Ultraviolet Lamp in Scientific Research.' Jack De Ment's introduction deals with the limitations of the human eye being able to perceive just a tiny fraction of the Electromagnetic Spectrum as Visible light, and the ability of science to develop devices or instruments that extend the ability of the eye, such as Ultraviolet lamps. The author advises that every person involved in science should own an Ultraviolet lamp, and relates the findings that Fluorescent photography used on the surfaces of objects can reveal unknown facts about the objects themselves, in the course not failing to add two more coined phrases as well: 'selective-Ultraviolet-reflectance' and 'spectrophotometry.' Ultraviolet lamps themselves are next discussed by the author, making a distinction between the 'cold-quartz lamp' producing Shortwave Ultraviolet, and the 'long wave-length' emitting Black light lamp, in which De Ment proceeds to list all the good points of the Shortwave Ultraviolet lamp, without once ever pointing out the major disadvantage of the Shortwave U.V. lamp, which is it's danger to the skin and all biological entities.

The next section in this paper is 'Fluorochemical Analysis,' which is defined by De Ment as the 'method' of causing a substance to Fluoresce through the use of Ultraviolet lamps. De Ment further defines 'Fluorochemical Analysis' as dealing with one of the two forms of luminescence, Fluorescence and Phosphorescence, which the author points out was commonly called "after-glow" in 1944. The example briefly stated by the author is the Fluoroanalysis of vitamins, in which a "Fluorometer" is used to measure the intensity of emitted Fluorescent light in the individual bands of the spectrum of visible light. The section on 'Fluorochemical Analysis' is subdivided into 'Microscopy' and 'Fluorography.' The first 'Microscopy' subdivision begins with the introduction of the 'Fluorescence Microscope,' which is what a microscope designed for studying Fluorescence was termed in 1944. Details of the 'Fluorochemical Analysis' made possible through the use of a 'Fluorescence Microscope' are examined by De Ment, starting with the general division of Longwave Ultraviolet used in the 'Fluorescence Microscope' for analyzing biological and organic substances, while Shortwave Ultraviolet would be generally used for analysis of synthetic and inorganic substances, including minerals. The study of Fluorescence under a microscope is also divided into two fields in this paper, 'Transmission Fluorescence Microscopy' as defined by the method of analysis in which Ultraviolet energy passes through the studied substance with separate Ultraviolet lamps above and beneath the studied substance (the "Ultra-Violet Products, Inc." lamp used beneath the substance was called a "Transilluminator"), and 'Reflection Fluorescence microscopy' in which the Ultraviolet lamp is placed only above the studied substance. This is incorrectly termed 'Reflection Fluorescence' because no light is 'Reflected' from the studied substance under either of the Ultraviolet wavelengths, or in the entire study of Fluorescence itself - the light is "Emitted." A new product is discussed by the author, a specially designed 'cold-quartz' Shortwave "Mineralight" manufactured with a very small opening to fit into the light condenser of a Microscope. To complement the 'Fluorescence Microscope,' the 'Phosphoresce Microscope' was also developed, and is credited to E. Newton Harvey, the famous scientist who would finally discover the cause of the Firefly's Bioluminescent light, and the man who coined the word "Bioluminescent." De Ment also discusses the essential use of non-Fluorescent test-tubes or containing vessels made primarily of Quartz or of 'nonfluorescent pyrex,' and also the general practice at that time to use a "Wratten 2-A" Ultraviolet Barrier filter, or a "EK Haze filter" over the microscope's objective lens to block U.V. from entering the microscope and causing the eye and internal components of the microscope to Fluoresce. The specimens to be 'Fluorochemically' analyzed under this 'Fluorescence microscope' are listed by the author, beginning with the example of 'Auramine-stained Tuberculosis myobacteria,' and then proceeding to the Fluorescent mineral kingdom. De Ment numbers 'over a hundred' Fluorescent minerals known in 1944, while today the number is well over a thousand with over 'a hundred' Fluorescent minerals known to come just from Franklin, New Jersey. First one of the most famous Fluorescent minerals in the world is discussed by De Ment, "Willemite" from Franklin, New Jersey (which was mined for it's Zinc content in Franklin and Ogdensburg, New Jersey from 1852 until the last mine closed in 1986, "The Sterling Hill Mine"). First De Ment makes the common mistake of calling the whole mineral specimen "Willemite" and goes on to explain that the 'Calcite content' of the "Willemite" Fluoresces Reds, the "Willemite" Fluoresces and Phosphoresces a brilliant Green, and then very incorrectly describes the "Franklinite" content of the specimen as Fluorescing a 'deep Violet.' "Franklinite" is Black and well known to be also absolutely non-Fluorescent, so what Jack De Ment is describing in this paper as a 'deep Violet' Fluorescence from the "Franklinite" is the oldest most common mistake in the entire study of Fluorescence, being the incorrect observance of a reflective surface (like shiny Octahedral crystals of "Franklinite") reflecting the Violet glow of the Ultraviolet lamp's filter onto the crystal itself. This is not Fluorescence, and "Franklinite" is never Fluorescent, but this is the most common mistake made by amateurs and Fluorescent novices, like visitors to the Museum every day also thinking that their Silver rings are Fluorescent 'deep Violet' when it is only reflecting the Violet glow of the Ultraviolet lamp's filter. It is extremely surprising to read such a classic novice's reaction from an author who had written several books on the study of Fluorescence already and who obviously considered himself to be a celebrated "expert" on Fluorescence (at least this "expert" on Fluorescence knew that minerals Fluoresce). Fluorescent minerals are listed for Fluorescent study under the 'Fluorescence Microscope,' and include the famous Fluorite, the valuable 1940s mineral Pitchblende, which is the primary Uranium ore, and the Mercury mineral Calomel, as well as Mercury chemicals. 'Fluorography' is next discussed, and simply defined as the photography of Fluorescence or Phosphorescence. Again the author states that any ordinary camera may be used for 'Fluorography' with the simple addition of an Ultraviolet Barrier filter fixed over the lens, which will prevent Ultraviolet energy from entering the camera's lens and fogging the film. The films that are advised to be used by the author are 'Kodak Contrast Process Panchromatic Film,' 'Wratten Process Panchromatic Film,' or 'Kodak Portrait Panchromatic Film' for faster speeds. The exposure times given by De Ment are stated as ranging from thirty-seconds to a full hour, which sound correct, since I often use thirty-two minutes exposure time photographing Fluorescent minerals using modern powerful filtered Ultraviolet lamps.

The second major section of this paper is 'Fluorescent Chemicals,' being divided into three tables of 'Lumi-Tone Phosphors,' 'Sulfides,' and 'Organic Chemicals and Dyes.' The first division 'Lumi-Tone Phosphors' consists of the fifteen different phosphors manufactured by the "General Luminescent Corporation" of Chicago, Illinois, which the reader is informed Fluoresce best under Shortwave U.V., and which include the produced Fluorescent Colors of Green, Yellow, Whites, "Flesh," Reds, Blue, Pink, and "Orchid." The second table is 'Sulfides' and these are listed as the sixteen different phosphors sold by the "New Jersey Zinc Company" which Fluoresced in every Color of the spectrum, as well as several of the phosphors Phosphorescing. There is another small list of seven Fluorescent and Phosphorescent 'Sulfide' phosphors that were manufactured by the "Rhode Island Laboratories" and include all Colors except Red.

The third table is 'Organic Chemicals and Dyes' in which are described thirty-five specific well known Fluorescent 'Organic Chemicals and Dyes.' The most well known of these substances listed is "Fluorescein," which is revealed as being so concentrated that only one part Fluorescein in forty million parts of water will still bear a Fluorescent reaction. In actuality it is known today that only one part of Fluorescein in sixty-four million parts of water will Fluoresce. Other substances in this list include Lanolin, Petroleum, Quinine, and Riboflavin.

The next chapter in this paper 'The Ultraviolet Lamp in Scientific Research' covers the subject 'Fields of Application,' and begins with an example of discovering a tiny amount of an impurity, which is called an "Activator" in a Fluorescent substance that is the actual cause of it's Fluorescent reaction under an Ultraviolet lamp. Edmond Becquerel discovered this fact in 1859 through his studies of Calcite with his father Antoine, concluding that only one part of Manganese per four thousand parts of Calcite was the minuscule amount of impurity needed to cause Calcite to Fluoresce a brilliant Red under an Ultraviolet lamp, and in the end even changed the common reference name of the mineral to 'Mangano Calcite.' De Ment gives the example of the Ruby crystal's brilliant deep Red Fluorescence, and relates the fact that only through 'Fluorochemical Analysis' was it discovered that the "Activator" for Ruby is the "Chromium," and that in 1944 there was still no chemical test sensitive enough to have detected this Chromium impurity without the applications of 'Fluorochemical Analysis.' De Ment also discusses the important research point that a substance may be checked for it's proper impurities with the use of an Ultraviolet lamp in any laboratory in the world, making 'Fluoroanalysis' an important cross-referencing scientific technique.

Under the heading 'Physical Research,' 'Physics' is first covered, and De Ment begins with the physical property of a 'Fluorescent Screen' used in the detection of Mercury. De Ment gives simple instructions for making a 'Fluorescent Screen,' which are to coat a piece of cardboard with glue and then to dust Zinc orthosilicate phosphor onto the glued surface. This 'Fluorescent Screen' will allow for the detection of Mercury in very small invisible amounts through the simple procedure of heating a substance in front of a 'Fluorescent Screen' under a "Mineralight." Since Mercury vapor does not Fluoresce, the presence of Mercury will be immediately detected by opaque Purple shadows on the 'Fluorescent Screen.'

The next physical use of Fluorescence cited by the author is the coating of Instrument Dials, including many parts of the Instrument panels of many vehicles, and is one of the few original uses of Fluorescence from the era of "The Miracle of Fluorescence" that is still in wide use throughout the world. De Ment again gives simple instructions for producing 'Green-Fluorescing' paint to use for coating the various components of the instrument panels of cars, airplanes, etc., by using Zinc orthosilicate or Zinc sulfide phosphor as the paint pigment, and mixing a small portion of this with 'collodion' or 'cellulosic lacquer,' which acts as the paint's "vehicle." De Ment adds instructions for substituting Rhodamine as the paint pigment to produce Red Fluorescent paint, Magnesium tungstate to produce White, Cadmium tungstate to produce Blue, and Uranyl salts to produce Yellow-Green Fluorescent paint.

The instructions for producing Fluorescent Paper that can be read in the dark under a "Mineralight" in a laboratory are next provided by the author, which are to dust paper with a Fluorescent powder like Zinc orthosilicate phosphor or 'Anthracene,' and then to rub it into the paper with the hand. This does not alter the daylight reaction of the paper in any way, but when the paper is written upon with pencil or a pen, under a Black light in the dark the writing is pure Black against the dusted Fluorescent Color of the paper. Obviously, this was long before paper manufactures began to produce almost all of their writing paper with 'Daylight Fluorescent' "Optical Dyes" that cause many substances that are manufactured in White in modern times to vividly Fluoresce under a Black light. Take a look at your T-shirt under a Black light one time, and then compare it's unnatural brilliant Blue-White Fluorescence to the very weak Fluorescence of natural untreated cotton.

Instructions for producing your own Fluorescent Crayons are next given by De Ment, with simple instructions again, telling the reader to mix approximately fifteen percent of a Fluorescent pigment into eighty-five percent of wax or a chalk base, and then to mould them into crayon or chalk shapes. Tracers for detecting cracks or changes in produced materials are mentioned by the author, relating the fact that as little a one part per forty-million of "Uranine" can still give a Fluorescent reaction in analysis. De Ment also instructs the reader that 'Fluorescent Smoke' for detection can be produced by simply 'dispersing' very fine Fluorescent powder into the air, which were valuable tools for industrial production of metals and plastics. Before this 1944 publication, the "Switzer Brothers" had invented Fluorescent Metal Stress Detection with the use of an Ultraviolet lamp and the Fluorescent tracing process they patented as "Zyglo." This was used extensively during the Second world war, for example to test airplane propellers for any imperfections. De Ment reports that it had become such an important aspect of the metal industry that by 1944 several patents had already been issued for this procedure. For a simple unpatented do-it-yourself Fluorescent test for metal-stress, the author offers the simple advice of coating a manufactured piece of metal with highly Fluorescent petroleum, and then examining it under a "Mineralight" to detect highly visible Fluorescent petroleum in stress cracks. For further instructions in the field, De Ment refers the reader to Dr. Wood's book "Physical Optics."

The final chapter in this paper covers the subject of 'Chemical Research' and begins with an explanation of 'Inorganic Chemistry.' Testing Inorganic samples for purity is the example De Ment explains, relating the facts that only the purest Zinc sulfide will Fluoresce Bluish, and if there is a presence of the impurities Iron, Nickel, or Cobalt [known today as "Fluorescence quenchers"] then the Zinc sulfide will not Fluoresce. The limitations and advantages of the advanced testing of Inorganic materials by heating them to a thousand degrees is also discussed by the author. 'Inorganic Chemicals' are examined by the author, with tests for both Fluorescence and Phosphorescence being discussed. De Ment also mentions the fact that if the Ultraviolet filter is taken off a Shortwave lamp for testing Phosphorescence, there is detectable in the air the smell of Ozone [which is produced by the mixture of high energy Ultraviolet energy exciting Oxygen molecules and causing one Oxygen atom to be freed from the Oxygen molecule, in effect producing Ozone and the Ozone layer at the top of the atmosphere which is the Earth's U.V. Filter]. 'Organic Chemistry' is also covered by the author, with similar instructions for testing all new Organic chemicals with an Ultraviolet lamp for the indication of purity through the chemical's Fluorescent or Phosphorescent reaction. The temperature and physical solid or liquid state of the examined chemicals are also discussed by the author, as well as testing with acids and 'alkalis.'

The end of this long technical scientific paper gives a list of thirty-two references, and in these references is something very important to the history of the Black light and Fluorescent Art. In 1944 there was already in business the 'Fluorescent Pigment Corp." in New York City at 445 West Forty-First Street.

The fifth "Mineralight News Bulletin" has a less technical theme, and for the first paper with a 'civilian' audience Jack De Ment writes about 'Ultraviolet Light as an Aid to Education.' The author's introduction begins by informing the reader that ninety percent of all children retain more knowledge through what they are shown than through what they are told, which De Ment calls 'eye-minded.' Further expanding on this theme, Colorful lessons with vivid lighting would logically be the most well retained method of teaching, and this cannot be accomplished with more strength that the results of Black lights with Fluorescent and Phosphorescent Color demonstrations in the classroom. The author writes that a brilliant lesson given with

Black lights and Fluorescent/Phosphorescent crayons on a blackboard will be remembered for longer than the same lesson given with plain White chalk on a blackboard. To give an embolism to both the "Chromophobists" and the "Fluorophobists" alike, De Ment states that a comparison can be made which proves that the effect of an image in the Black light made with Fluorescent Colors is as 'superior' to a normal Color print as the same Color print is to an old fashioned Black and White print of the same subject.

De Ment documents another popular Fluorescent demonstration that had been taking place for 'a number of years' by 1944, and which I wrote about earlier in this chapter: *"Fluorescent Church Sermons!"* The author writes that the "Mineralight" was used together with large pieces of 'Franklin, New Jersey Willemite' in Religious Church Sermons to add incredible drama, and that these 'Fluorescent Sermons' had been and were still in 1944 'widely used.' This is possibly the root of the story of the "Fluorescent Preacher Hofmann" that the Museum visitor from Georgia told me about several years ago, and this is definitively the roots of the "Suggested use" for the set of "Ultra-Violet Products, Inc." "Blak-Ray" Invisible Fluorescent Chalks, with the infamous 1950s 'User Suggestion': "To Be Used With Black Lights For: CHURCH GROUPS!"

Fluorescent and Phosphorescent Plastics are next covered by De Ment, informing the reader that this Luminous Plastic sheeting was produced in many different Colors and sizes, so it could be cut into letters or models to be used for all school lessons, ranging in subjects from geography to home economics, and statistics even. The reader learns that in 1944 the Luminescent Coloring of the plastic was made by dyes or phosphors that were 'organic.'

De Ment relates the success of the use of Black lights together with Fluorescent or Phosphorescent paint in theatre and in the field of advertising to similar success that can be achieved with the very same tools in the classroom. The ultra-lame examples of 'Ultraviolet Created Illusions' to be used as 'Educational Aids' in the classroom exemplify the miserable lack of creativity which I have found in the whole 'clan' of Thomas S. Warren's professional associates. The table of these 'Ultraviolet Created Illusions' presented by De Ment has two columns, one for the intended 'Illusion' and next to it a list of the different Fluorescent paint, dye, or pigment to be used for each 'Illusion.'

Keep in mind while reading the list that this nut intended these 'Fluorescent Illusions' to be literally used in a school classroom in 1944! De Ment's list of ten 'Ultraviolet Fluorescent Illusions' begins with creating the illusion of 'Envy' through the use of a Fluorescent Green dye or Zinc phosphors, the next 'Red-handed' illusion is made with the highly Fluorescent dye Rhodamine, 'Blushing Pink' uses the same dye diluted, 'Fear and Cold' are represented by the Color White and this is made with a Tungsten ore. The fifth 'Illusion' is this list by De Ment is 'Raging Purple' made by the miracle of Calcium sulfide, for science classrooms the 'Illusion' of 'Lava and Hot Metal' is made with the interesting combination of the Fluorescent Red dye Rhodamine used together with the Fluorescent mineral Calcite. This suggestion by De Ment makes me again wonder if the author was just a science writer, or if he had ever physically tested or even tried the suggestions that he fills his writing with. Having experience with Fluorescent Synthetic Phosphors ("paint pigment") for the last forty-seven years, and having experience with Fluorescent minerals for over twenty years, and most importantly, having the experience of endless experiments of the nearly impossible visual balancing act of *combining* the two entities, it makes me question what De Ment is suggesting here: putting natural very dimly Fluorescing minerals together with one of the brightest Fluorescent dyes ever made. The entire design of my Museum "Electric Ladyland - the First Museum of Fluorescent Art" is physically stipulated by this nearly-impossible-to-achieve balancing act. The combination may have sounded very innovative and original even, but that was with his pen writing on paper. Putting the Calcite which Fluoresces typically an Orange-Red with a medium to strong strength in relation to other natural substances, in combination with or even next to one of the strongest Fluorescent dyes ever made, "Rhodamine" which Fluoresces pure Red, sounds very good in theory - 'on paper' let's say - but if you put these two completely different Fluorescent substances next to each other in the dark under an Ultraviolet lamp, the spontaneous response would undoubtedly be: "Where's the Calcite?" Exquisite on paper but nearly impossible to achieve in reality. The Museum design is stipulated by this nearly impossible reality, and has caused me to separate the entire Museum into two different halves, one half being a completely synthetic sculpture coated with hundreds of liters of synthetic phosphors in the forms of handmade Fluorescent and Phosphorescent paints, and the other half of the Museum being a demonstration of about 1,000 pounds (500 kilos) of completely natural Fluorescent minerals, seashells, corals, lichens, gemstones, and many other "Common Items that are Fluorescent." An exception in the Museum to this concept is the use of one of the most intensely Fluorescent minerals known, Fluorite form Weardale in Durham, England, which the name "Fluorescence" comes from, in the middle of one of the most brilliantly Fluorescing areas of the Fluorescent "Participatory" Environment, "The Reactor." In this "Reactor" is a crystal of this Weardale Fluorite, and the reason it is at the center of this area is because it signifies what is taking place inside this "Reactor," which is "Electron Displacement," the Quantum cause of the phenomenon of Fluorescence, thus the crystal of Fluorite from Weardale is the only logical choice, since it was this crystal that Sir George Stokes experimented on with the

Ultraviolet energy contained in sunlight, and in 1852 definitively named the phenomenon "Fluorescence." Having experimented with Calcite inside "The Reactor," which is the Fluorescent mineral suggested by De Ment, and also having tried Scapolite in it's place, the two brilliantly Fluorescing minerals were nearly imperceptible in "The Reactor" - they looked like miserable nearly-Grey rocks next to the Fluorescent paint all around them, in comparison to my first choice of Fluorite. "The Magic Land of Lights, Sounds, and Dimensions," is the area that the Fluorescent "Participatory" Environment was designed around, and the area where the visitor experiences "Participatory Art" through the combined mental actions of their own creative decisions together with the physical action of pressing illuminated buttons they have decided upon, which in turn achieve their "Participation" with the creative process involved in the creation of Art. There is one section in this area called "The Fluorescent Mineral Cave," where about sixty-five Fluorescent minerals are seen under either White light as ordinary common Grey stones, or under five Black lights as brilliantly Fluorescent multi-Colored wonders of nature, depending on which button the Museum visitor decides to press. This "Fluorescent Mineral Cave" is in the middle of the Fluorescent "Participatory" Environment, but it is on purpose of design totally separated from synthetic Fluorescent paint. By experimental comparison, "The Fluorescent Minerals Cave" has five 15 watt Black lights installed in it totaling sixty-five watts of Black light, and the small cave next to it, the "Special Michele Cave" has Fluorescent paint in it, so only a pair of four watt Black lights, or a total of eight watts of Black light produces the same intensity of Fluorescence in paint that sixty-five watts of Black light is needed to produce in Fluorescent minerals. That is almost eight hundred percent the amount of Ultraviolet energy needed for Fluorescent minerals to produce a nearly equal amount of emitted light as Fluorescent paint. Again, I wonder if Jack De Ment had physically experimented with the substances he suggests to use in this paper, or if they were just unfounded ideas of his pen.

Along the same line, the seventh 'Illusion' in De Ment's table is 'Green Plants' with again the suggestion of combining Zinc phosphor with the Green Fluorescing mineral Willemite, and here another suggestion that creates further suspicion that De Ment was either extremely inexperienced with Fluorescent minerals, or completely misinformed by his research materials, because I have seen countless specimens of Calcite, which is one of the most commonly occurring of all Fluorescent minerals, and personally own and give Fluorescent mineral demonstrations on Calcite from over twenty different locations on Earth, as geographically diversified as South Africa and New Jersey, but never once in a collection of books and magazines on Fluorescent minerals ranging in dates from 1939 up into the Twenty-first century have I seen what De Ment next writes about to complete this 'Green Plant' 'Illusion:' '*Green* Fluorescent Calcite'! De Ment is so far off here it is comparable to writing a cooking recipe including instructions to use "Ice-cream flavored Steak," which could only happen if the author knew almost nothing about food. The common name for the Fluorescent mineral Calcite is 'Mangano Calcite' because of it's tiny impurity of Manganese that causes it's Red or Red-Orange Fluorescence. The cause of the Red Fluorescence in Calcite was historically discovered by Edmond Becquerel, the father of Henri Becquerel during the middle of the Nineteenth century - nearly a full century before Jack De Ment wrote this very telling suggestion in this 1944 paper. The last 'Illusions' in De Ment's table are 'Cold,' suggested to be made with Tungsten Scheelite ore that Fluoresces a bright Blue-White, and the 'Illusion' of the abstract 'Time' is accompanied by the suggestion of using all the different Colors.

The second half of this paper 'Ultraviolet Light as an Aid to Education' covers 'Science Education.' The author begins by giving his opinion that all levels of science education should be accompanied by classroom lessons incorporating Ultraviolet lamps and Fluorescent Colors. De Ment also writes the dated 1944 suggestion of using the 'radiation' created by the Shortwave "Mineralight" to demonstrate the rarely seen radiations of 'X-rays' and 'Radium rays' in science classrooms. A series of simple educational experiments is proposed by De Ment in this section and include 'Reflection' in which the fact of the reflectance of Ultraviolet rays is proven through the technique of directing Shortwave U.V. rays into a mirror and then reflecting them onto a Fluorescent screen where Fluorescent Colors are finally produced. The experiment of 'Refraction and Diffraction' is identical to the experiment which was performed by Sir George Stokes in 1852 with sunlight and the crystal Fluorite through which he named the phenomenon "Fluorescence," except that the Sun is substituted by a "Mineralight" and the crystal of Fluorite is substituted by a Fluorescent screen.

The fourteen experiments suggested by De Ment for proof of the existence and the power of invisible Shortwave Ultraviolet energy continues with 'Ionization of Gases,' which is similar to the last experiment with the 'Electroscope' and "Mineralight," but in this experiment a piece of cardboard is used to block some or all of the Shortwave Ultraviolet energy coming out of the lamp and analyze it's effect. The 'Ozone' Experiment' follows and is the most simple experiment of them all, with the short instructions for a student to smell near a "Mineralight" when it is on and generating Shortwave Ultraviolet energy. High energy Ultraviolet collides with molecules of Oxygen, freeing one atom of Oxygen from the molecule, and then the Ultraviolet binds with the Oxygen atom to form 'Ozone (O_3)' and hence the "Ozone Layer," which is the Earth's U.V. filter.

'Bleaching' is the next experiment suggested by the author and is the most frightening for an Artist. Squares of cotton are saturated with Fluorescent dyes like Rhodamine, and then exposed to pure Shortwave Ultraviolet energy and many other wavelengths of Ultraviolet, as the instructions are to remove the Shortwave Ultraviolet filter from the "Mineralight" for this experiment and to expose the unfiltered powerful Ultraviolet energy to the Fluorescent dyed cotton for a period of '2 or 3' hours. This experiment was designed by De Ment to demonstrate the action of sunlight which would fade, or as the author terms the effect, 'Bleach' the Color out of the dyed cotton. This proves how little was known about Ultraviolet energy at the time of this paper's publication in 1944, because Shortwave Ultraviolet energy does not come through the "Ozone Layer" that's what the "Ozone Layer" is for - so the only way that Fluorescent dyed cotton would 'Bleach' as fast and dramatically as the proposed experiment by De Ment is if you were out in space, above the "Ozone Layer."

The last two experiments suggested by De Ment in this paper 'Ultraviolet Light as an Aid to Education' are 'Sterilization and Sanitation' and 'Erythema,' the two effects that are still known to many people these many decades later. 'Sterilization and Sanitation' proves the sterilizing effect of Shortwave Ultraviolet energy, which is still employed today to purify drinking water in many undeveloped parts of the world, and also in most Koi ponds and aquariums to kill the harmful bacteria in the water. The terminology used by the author in 1944 is interesting, with De Ment instructing the reader to place drops of water containing microscopic life, which the author calls 'protozoan' and 'paramecia,' under the Shortwave Ultraviolet of a "Mineralight" for only a short time. After half an hour these microscopic cultures are examined under a microscope to discover that most of the 'protozoan' are dead or deformed. The experiment is repeated with 'Bacillus coli' in two separate plates. One plate is exposed to the "Mineralight" and then both plates are put into an incubator. It was shown in this experiment that the action of the Shortwave Ultraviolet of the "Mineralight" resulted in the plate it was irradiating to contain mostly killed bacteria.

The last experiment is the most fun of all: 'Erythema' ("Sunburn"), and in fact is also the most healthy experiment of them all. Since Shortwave Ultraviolet is famous for causing directly sunburn to the skin, not "suntan" like the less powerful Middlewave Ultraviolet energy causes, the students are directed to remove the Shortwave Ultraviolet filter from their "Mineralight" and to put it directly against the skin on their arm for five minutes(!) Students with different skin Colors are measured next to each other to see the sunburning effect of Shortwave Ultraviolet energy. Another 'healthy' point is that De Ment never once warns of the danger to sunburn the eyes in either of the experiments in which he instructs students to remove the Shortwave Ultraviolet filter from the "Mineralight," and he never even suggests the students wear protective goggles for these experiments. "Photokeratitis" is the sunburning of the Sclerotic Coat (outer layer) of the eye and is caused by the exposure to Shortwave Ultraviolet energy. The effect takes a few hours to happen after the eyes have been exposed to even a second of pure unfiltered Shortwave Ultraviolet energy, and the result is that the dead sunburned outer layer of the eyes 'peels,' like the skin when it is sunburned, and then your eyes run water for about five hours without stopping. De Ment's students must have been used to these symptoms.

The sixth 'Mineralight News Bulletin' is about a science that did not have it's correct name yet: 'Fluorobiology,' which is what "Bioluminescence" is called today, the term coined by E. Newton Harvey thirteen years after this article was published. The first section of this paper is 'Biological Research' and De Ment begins by informing the reader that most biological tissues Fluoresce, but the use of the Ultraviolet lamp in examining biological tissue is greatly expanded and very valuable with the addition of a Fluorescent stain to dye the tissue. It's surprising to see that in a particular example like this, the same technology and general practice that is used today was the same technique used in 1944, Fluorescent staining of cells and biological tissues. The specific example given by the author is the Fluorescent dye (called a "Fluorochrome" in 1944) "Auramine," which was known to bind with 'Myobacterium tuberculosis' and to then cause these Tuberculosis cells to Fluoresce a bright Yellow and be easily identifiable using a 'Fluorescence Microscope.'

By far the most outdated and truly antiquated part of this paper 'Fluorobiology' is the last section 'Medicine,' where the main subject of the entire chapter concentrates on the Shortwave 'Cold-Quartz Ultraviolet lamp,' which is still remembered today as the 'dangerous Black light' to many people. Beginning way back in 1885 as "Actinotherapy," in the 1920s-1940s the Shortwave Ultraviolet lamp was used as a "Miracle cure" in medicine, with advertised miracles attainable through this 'modern' contraption, such a the infamous 'Bald Man Growing His Hair Back(!)' and even the cure for rickets in children's legs was attributed to the Shortwave Ultraviolet treatment of this time period. It was previously written in this book about the nightmare era of "Actinotherapy" being one of the original important factors in the creation in the present Twenty-first century state of the Social Stigma of "Fluorophobia." As his first examples De Ment suggests putting a drop of 'Fluorescein' onto the skin or into the eye, and then examining it under a Shortwave "Mineralight" for diagnostics. De Ment writes about "Murine," which is one of the first Fluorescent natural compounds that Robert and Joe Switzer discovered in their father's pharmacy with a Black light while inventing the first Fluorescent paint in 1933, and informs the reader that the Fluorescent component in "Murine" was 'Berberine,' which caused it to Fluoresce a brilliant Yellow. The author explains that damage to the Sclerotic Coat or the Retina of the Eye can be diagnosed easily with a drop of Fluorescein put into the Eye, and for this prolonged examination, for the first time, De Ment advises the use of a 'long wave length' Ultraviolet lamp to avoid 'Erythema' to the Eye.

The skin is next examined by De Ment, who advises that the Shortwave Ultraviolet "Mineralight" should be used in the following experiments because of it's production of 'Erythema,' or sunburn. De Ment next expands on the subject of sunburn to explain that there are two kinds of Erythema, one kind caused by a 'hot Ultraviolet' source such as a Carbon or Iron-Arc Shortwave Ultraviolet source (like the original "Spark Box") which produced what was called 'heat-erythema.' The other kind of Erythema was caused by the cold action of a "Mineralight" Shortwave Ultraviolet lamp, and the effect on exposure was different depending on if the skin was sunburned from a 'hot' Iron-Arc Ultraviolet spark source or a cool "Mineralight" Shortwave Ultraviolet lamp. The difference being that after exposure to a hot Ultraviolet source the skin becomes Red within half an hour but it would fade very quickly.

De Ment next explains the famous brilliant White Fluorescence of the Teeth, and adds that for Medical diagnostics healthy teeth Fluoresce bright White with a tint of Blue or Green, but some diseased teeth will be easily recognized under an Ultraviolet lamp with a Reddish Fluorescence, due to 'Porphyrins' being present. At this point in the paper the reason for not producing Fluorescent False Teeth anymore, like in the 1940s which I have written about previously in this book, is immediately apparent when reading De Ment's description. The author informs the 1945 reader that the old 'Artificial Dentures' did not Fluoresce, but the modern 1940s 'Artificial Dentures' had been manufactured to Fluoresce like real teeth by design with the simple incorporation of 'Uranium' into these False Teeth! The Uranium additive into the Dentures enabled the False Teeth to Fluoresce Yellow to a Yellow-Greenish and would look natural under a U.V. lamp, before the detrimental radioactive effects of the Uranium gave you cancer in the jaw and all the bones of the face. Better to have non-Fluorescent False Teeth.

The final section of this scientific paper is 'Other Aspects of Fluorobiology' with De Ment writing about the new study of sunburn caused to a welder with the Welding Arc Torch, and discusses the use of the "Mineralight" for research into this new subject. 'Microbiology' cellular life form's Fluorescence is mentioned, in particular the 'Protozoa,' as well as the Fluorescence of the tentacles of the Sea Anemone. The fact that all Organic substances Fluoresce is beginning to be just expanded upon in this paper by the 1940s author, who reports that plants and 'almost any' biological organisms Fluoresce, specifically citing the eyes of Moths and the wings of Butterflies. De Ment ends the paper with the fact that Ultraviolet study had not yet been done on most organic living creatures, and even the known study of Fluorescence of the human eye had not been studied in any detail. In closing, the author writes that the common Fruit Fly has a 'photophily' towards an Ultraviolet lamp in the dark, and informs the reader that studies had not yet been performed on the Ultraviolet 'photophily,' 'photophygy,' 'phototropism,' or the 'phototaxis' of any living creatures including plants, animals, and insects.

The seventh 'Mineralight New Bulletin' is entitled the appetizing 'Fluorochemistry in Food Science - Ultraviolet Rays Detect Filth in Foods.' The author begins this paper by informing the reader that impurities, additives, filth, and spoiled food can be immediately detected through inspection with an Ultraviolet lamp. Since foods and impurities Fluoresce with their own signatory Colors, the Ultraviolet detection of such Fluorescence is very quick.

De Ment examines the differences in Fluorescence of the very important food source Flours, and reports that healthy wheat and rye flours will be determined by a Blue Fluorescence, while potato flour will Fluoresce Grey-Brown and barley flour will Fluoresce White. Bean flour will Fluoresce Blue-Green and pea flour will Fluoresce Reddish according to the author, and it is apparent that through the Ultraviolet lamp purity of the flour was also detectable. Impurities such as rodent hair or dirt would be easily recognizable under Ultraviolet inspection, making the Ultraviolet lamp a very valuable tool for food science. 'Fillers' in flours and other dry foods are also easily detectable under a U.V. lamp, and it is reported by De Ment that the highest quality of wheat flour Fluoresces a Bluish because of it's high gluten level, but inferior wheat flour will Fluoresce only with a Yellowish Color, making the grading of wheat quality a very easy process under a U.V. lamp.

There are three Black and White photographs of very early Ultraviolet lamp food sterilization applications in Dake and DeMent's 1941 "Fluorescent Light and It's Applications," including a photo of a 1930s walk-in refrigerator that is packed with all sorts of meats, and has Ultraviolet 'Bacterial tubes' lined up on the ceiling of the refrigerator. The caption states that these 250 nanometer Shortwave Bacterial lamps consumed very little energy and were cool operating, which is obviously important in a refrigerator. Another photo in the book is a little scarier, showing a cafeteria with Shortwave tubes over the utensil containers, which 'sterilized' the tableware. A sign above the set-up in this photo reads: 'Tableware kept sterile by these

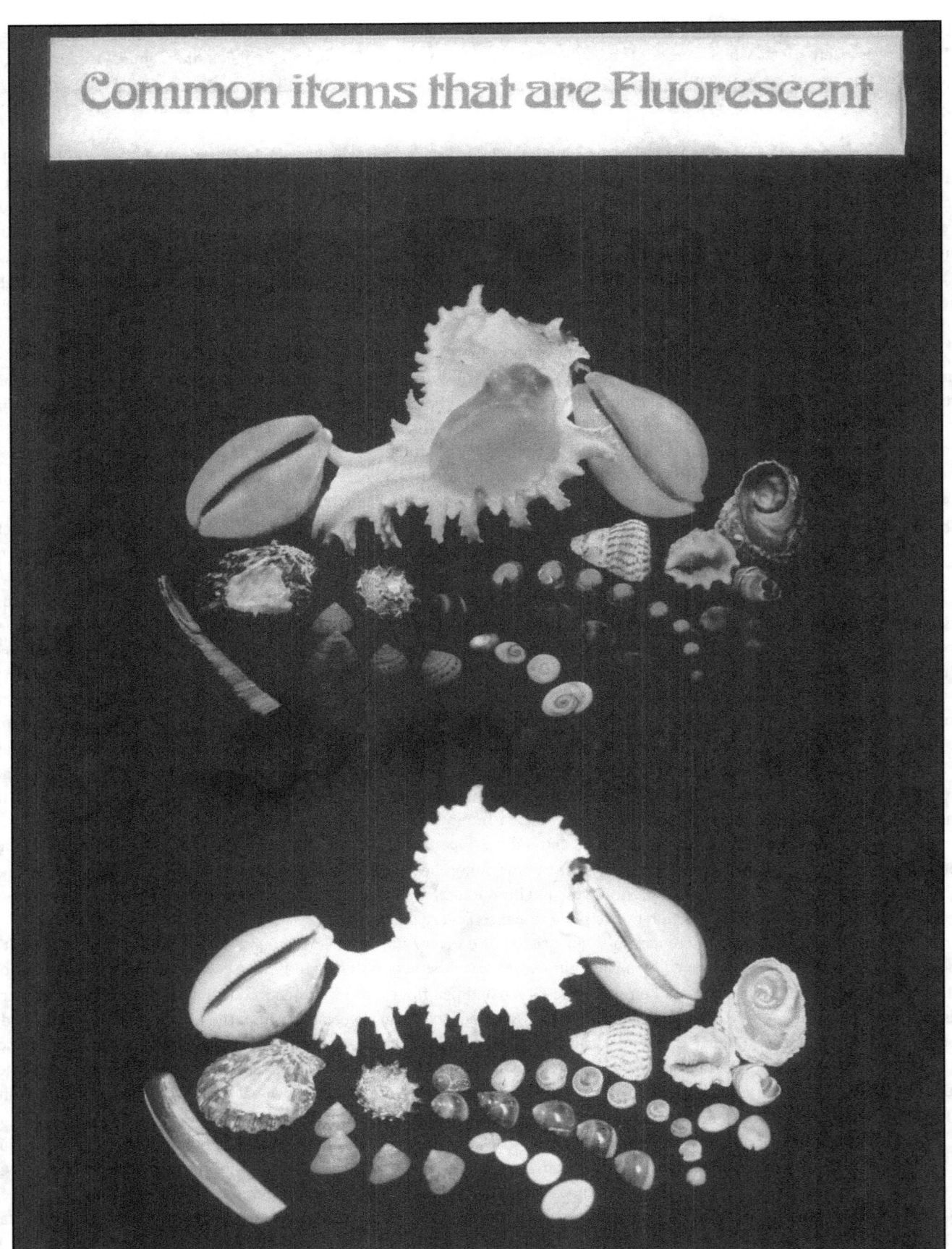

"Common Items that are Fluorescent" Museum book, Nick Padalino, 1997

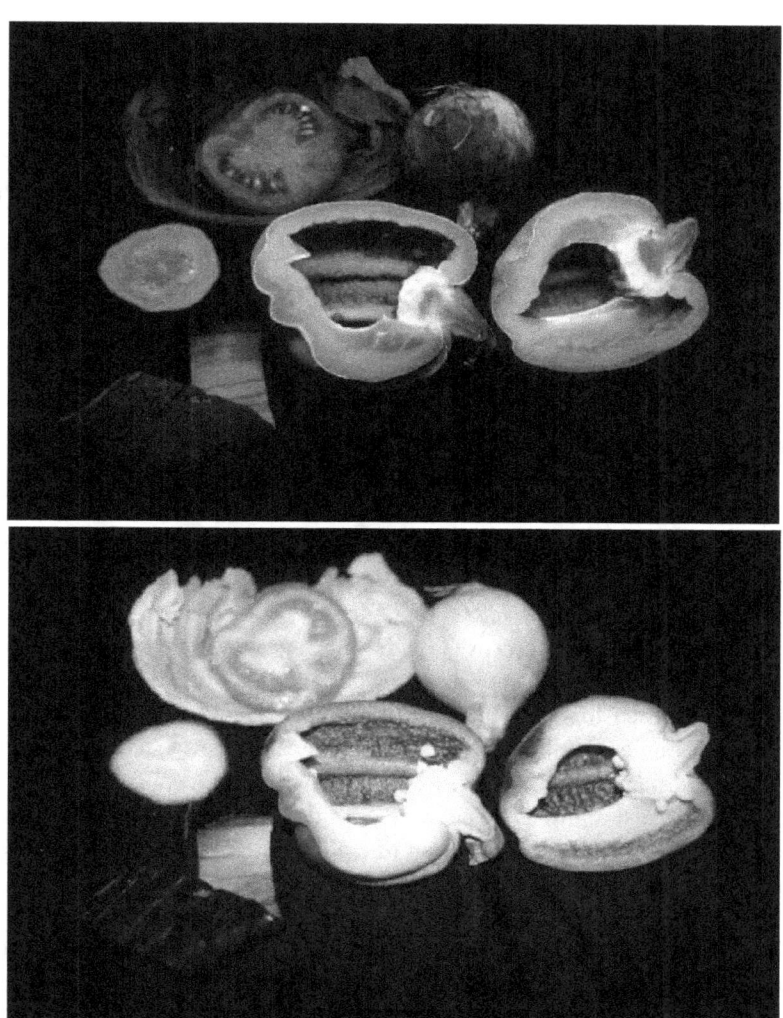

FLUORESCENT FOOD and FLOWERS
Nick Padalino and Michèle Delage

Fluorescent Artichoke, Asparagus, Beans, **Carrot**, **Chives**, Cucumber, Eggplant, Garlic, Lettuces, **Onion**, **Peppers**, Pickle, Tomato, Zucchini, Apricot, Banana, **Kiwi**, **Lemon**, Nectarine, Orange, Peach, Plum, Cheese, **Chewing Gum**, Coconut, Coffee, Corn Flakes, Lentils, **Nuts**, **Pasta**, Popcorn, Rice, Vitamins, Spices, Teas, **Tonic Water**, Flowers, Plants, Trees, Lichens, **Insects**, **Animals**, Sea Shells, and Coral

"FLUORESCENT FOOD and FLOWERS" Museum book, Nick Padalino and Michèle Delage, 2005

Westinghouse STERILAMPS,' and the caption informs the reader that there were pieces of plate glass on both sides of the Shortwave Ultraviolet tubes, so the customers wouldn't get 'sunburned' eyes [only hands and arms]. The third of these Ultraviolet Sterilization photos in Dake and DeMent's book gives credit for all three photos as "Westinghouse Electric Company photo," and this photograph is of a large room in a bakery, where there is a woman with no protection what so ever under at least eight very long Shortwave Ultraviolet Bacterial lamps on the ceiling of this bakery storage room. Next to the woman, who is dressed like a nurse (the same dress as in the photo of the cafeteria workers) there are very large carts with rows of trays containing baked products, and behind her is another unit with eight more Shortwave lamps turned on. This girl's skin tone must have been similar to American Indians(!) There is another photo in Dake and DeMent's book which shows another early application of Shortwave Ultraviolet Sterilization lamps, this time in an Operating room, during an actual operation on a Tuberculosis patient's lung in the 1930s. The caption states the "Westinghouse Sterilamp" was installed over an operating table, and the picture shows this huge circular lamp suspended over the operating table. The operation was in the Duke University hospital, and it is also stated that the operation was a long one, lasting over 'one hour.'

For the remainder of this paper De Ment presents a 'Foodstuffs Listing' of the Fluorescent Color of foods for a full page and a half. This list is the grandfather of the list I published in the early 1990s in my book "Common Items that are Fluorescent," and this list by De Ment includes no less than a hundred and one different Organic substances. Some of his notable inclusions besides the common Foodstuffs are bones, cartilage, cigars and 'cigarettes,' hemp seeds, hair, jute, mold, petroleum, sewerage, shellac, toadstools, urine, and vaseline.

In reality the list by De Ment of one hundred and one Organic Fluorescent Substances is nothing in comparison to other lists he was writing during the same time period. In 1945 Jack De Ment published the book "Fluorochemistry," which is 796 pages long and contains lists that are nearly chapters long. 'Table 30' in De Ment's "Fluorochemistry" book is a list of Colossal proportions, and is entitled 'The Luminescent Organic Substances," stretching over a full sixty-four pages (!) and compiles no less than 2,896 entries of 'Luminescent Organic Substances.' Actually even this list of 2,896 'Luminescent Organic Substances' is nothing compared to the Grandiose list in Jack De Ment's 1945 book "Handbook of Fluorescent Chemicals, Volume 3, Dictionary of Luminescent Substances" which the author also states in the Preface of "Fluorochemistry" that this "Dictionary of Luminous Substances" was an index of 20,000 luminescent substances!

At this point in the writing, as distasteful as it is to me, and after criticizing Jack De Ment many times for his incessant coining of words and phrases along with the generous amount of credit he gives to himself for these achievements, the present writer must admit to having at least a little bit in common with De Ment, if in no other way than in the similarity of a truly obsessive nature. As an example of this obsessive similarity, there are the lists I've published in my book from 1997, "Common Items that are Fluorescent" consisting of over two hundred pages, and the six books I've made for the Museum between 2001 and 2008. In "Common Items that are Fluorescent" from 1997 the natural Fluorescence of Foods, Flowers, Train Tickets, Glass, Pigments, Plastics, Shells, Coral, Petrified Wood, Trees, Lichens, Seaweed, Moss Amber, Diamonds, Rubies, Lapis Lazuli, Sapphires, Turquoise, Emeralds, Ivory, Bones, Fossils and other "Common Items" are photographed and written about in detail. For my book "Fluorescence All Around Us" from 2005, and also "Fluorescent Food and Flowers" from 2005 there are lists included which expand to cover 25 Vegetables, 12 Fruits, 18 Dried or Prepared Foods, 8 Spices, 2 Teas, 5 Psychoactive Organic Substances, 1 Drink ("Schweppes Tonic Water"), and 1 experiment with photographs proving my discovery of "Irreversible Photosensitivity in 'Green Beans.'" For the most recent book I've prepared, the first book of "Fluorescent Flowers," I began listing the minute detail of the Fluorescence of living flowers in our small garden in Amsterdam when we moved into the space in the year 2000, and continued for eight years with a portable filtered Longwave Ultraviolet lamp at night in the garden with Michèle behind our apartment. In the Spring of 2008, and continuing through the summer and into the fall, I photographed over fifty of these Fluorescent flowers with a monstrous "Ultraviolet Dermatology Camera" that was originally made about forty years ago in England and was designed to exclusively take photographs of the human face under filtered Longwave Ultraviolet flash units built into the large, heavy, clumsy, box-like Dermatology camera. The reason I bought this camera and spent half a year in the garden at 1:00 in the morning trying to desperately catch images of natural flower Fluorescence through the combined efforts of calisthenics and cursing is because I wanted photographs of the flowers in their natural setting, unaltered, alive and growing. The first time I photographed the Fluorescence of flowers was in the studio, and I used cut and dead Flowers under Ultraviolet lamps in a complete studio setting during a Summer in the 1990s of photographing hundreds of natural Fluorescent substances, including a large number of the Fluorescent Minerals that were to eventually go into the Museum displays, for the "Common Items that are Fluorescent" book and also for Fluorescent mineral slide demonstrations. This "Fluorescent Flowers" book is the first book ever published on the subject matter of "Fluorescent Flowers," and contains a Fluorescent flower "Lumilogue" of 281 flower's Fluorescence, including Allium, Alstromeria,

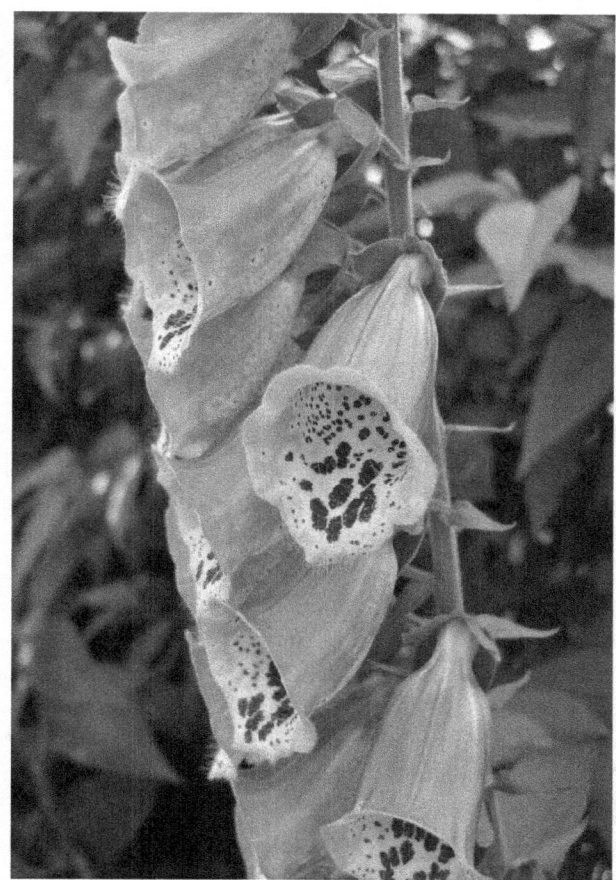
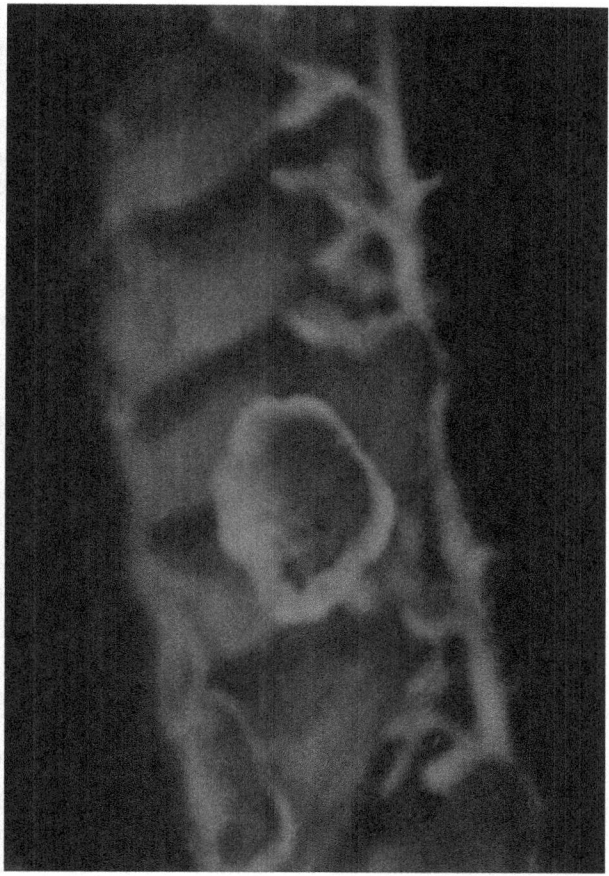

FLUORESCENT FLOWERS

Nick Padalino and Michèle Delage

281 FLUORESCENT FLOWERS including:

Allium, Alstromeria, Anemone, Aster, Azalea, Bougenvillia, Cactus, Canna, Clematis, Cosmos, Crocus, Cyclamen, Daisy, Daffodil, Dahlia, Delphinium, Digitalis, Echinacea, Forsythia, Fuschia, Gladiolus, Hibiscus, Hortensia, Impatience, Iris, Lobelia, Lupinus, Lychnis, Magnolia, Marigold, Margarittas, Monarda, Morning Glory, Muscaria, Nightshade, Orchid, Pansy, Passion Flower, Penstamon, Petunia, Poppy, Primula, Rhododendron, Rose, Salvia, Saxifraga, Snow Pierce, Sunflower, Tulip, Verbena, Veronica, Water Lilly, and Wisteria

"FLUORESCENT FLOWERS" Museum book, Nick Padalino and Michèle Delage, 2005

Anemone, Aster, Azalea, Bougenvillia, Cactus, Canna, Clematis, Cosmos, Crocus, Cyclamen, Daisy, Daffodil, Dahlia, Delphinium, Digitalis, Echinacea, Forsythia, Fuschia, Gladiolus, Hibiscus, Hortensia, Impatience, Iris, Lobelia, Lupinus, Lychnis, Magnolia, Marigold, Margarittas, Monarda, Morning Glory, Muscaria, Nightshade, Orchid, Pansy, Passion Flower, Penstamon, Petunia, Poppy, Primula, Rhododendron, Rose, Salvia, Saxifraga, Snow Pierce, Sunflower, Tulip, Verbena, Veronica, Water Lily, Wisteria and hundreds others. Many of these 281 flowers in the Fluorescent flower "Lumilogue" are listed with the flower's Fluorescence of it's separate components such as the Petals, Anthers, Stamens, Pistols, Septals, Stems, Foliage, and even sometimes, where applicable, are entries including the Fluorescence of a flower's dried seed pods, or it's Fluorescence in the bud before opening, and/or after it has wilted - all completely listed with the Color of each of these flowers and their parts in the "White Light" and in the "Black Light." The list actually began with the first two flowers I photographed under Black lights in the studio in the mid-1990s, while still living in the small apartment behind "Electric Lady" Art Gallery, in the process of preparing "Common Items that are Fluorescent." The two flowers were "Crocusmia" 'Mont Brescia,' which I had bought and were cut fresh flowers, and a dried sample of the Medicinal plant "Monarda" we had found in the Frankendal park in Amsterdam the day I photographed it. The true listing of Fluorescent flowers began when we got our own private small garden behind our ground floor apartment late in the summer of 2000, and maybe the first night we lived there Michèle and I went into the garden with our simple 4 watt battery-powered Black light and had our first great natural Fluorescent Apparition/ Revelation - at midnight watching two intensely Fluorescent Sky-Blue balls jumping around on the floor under our Black light! Turning on a normal flashlight we were both truly astounded to see that the apparition was Fluorescent Frog's Eyes! It eventually took me years to finally capture this apparition of Fluorescent frog's eyes, until the age of digital cameras developed and I could put a tiny digital camera directly in front of a frog's face, while at the same time holding my 4 watt Black light directly above his face in the garden in the dark. The frog was so pissed off that after about three or four minutes he decided he definitely had enough of this, so he bit my finger! As I looked in astonishment at the frog after he bit my finger, he proceeded to bite my finger a second time! I don't know if any of you have ever been bitten by a frog, but I can confess that they have no teeth, and it is a very humbling experience(!) What must be realized here is that this study of Fluorescent natural substances is not something I did with Michèle on purpose, but it started naturally. Understand that we live under Black lights for twenty-nine years. "Electric Lady" Art Gallery with 500 watts of Black lights on the ceiling was our apartment - our living space - for thirteen years, and since then we live in an apartment also with Black light as the normal lighting in the living space. The first time we saw Fluorescent food was not when we made an intentional experiment with food and a Black light, but it was when Michèle brought our dinner out into the middle of the Gallery, where we ate, under 500 watts of Black lights: "What's *THAT*?" So although I've made lists no where near 20,000 items long (I doubt anyone ever has besides De Ment), and I've only coined very few words, such as "Fluorophobia," "Participatory Art," and "Creativatory Art," there still must be admitted a distant similarity in the obsessiveness of natures. Something else that must be admitted to through the use of a very obsessive nature is it's ability to truly inspire others. Some years ago a young couple came to the Museum and were divinely inspired by the "Common Items that are Fluorescent" demonstration, which includes the obscure Fluorescence of Lichens. About a month later I arrive at the Museum door to open for the day, and these two nuts were waiting for me at the front door with a shopping bag filled with - you guessed it - Fluorescent Lichens they had collected with the 4 watt portable Black light they had bought from me, while staying for two weeks in a tent in Lapin Orava, which is no less than 150 kilometers (70 miles) North of the Arctic Circle in Finland!

In the Museum collection is a perfect example of the use of Shortwave Ultraviolet lamps for the medical and sterilization fields, with lamps being named "STERILAMPS" manufactured by "Westinghouse Electric and Manufacturing Co." of Bloomfield, New Jersey. This artifact is an eight page small booklet printed completely in different tones of the old "process Blue," which is a medium-dark Blue, and looks to be printed before the Second world war around 1940. The cover design of this vertical booklet is instantly recognizable as being from a very long time ago - the Color, the illustration, and especially the type-face makes the appearance very obvious. The title is such an old expression that it's meaning is also almost lost to time: "Bugaboo of Bugville" with a medium-dark Blue background and a light Blue ray of Shortwave Ultraviolet energy cutting diagonally across the front cover and in the bottom right hand corner - the place of importance when the scanning eye exits the page - there are seven pitiful cockroach type of bugs begging for mercy. Not something you would see today, for example. Opening up the cover and the inside pages look even older than the ancient cover, with photos and text all printed in this 'Blue-print Blue' and type-faces that are simply archaic. The first page presents a 'Brief History' of "Westinghouse STERILAMP," together with a photo of a very long, very thin ancient looking Shortwave Ultraviolet lamp tube which is oddly much thicker at the two connecting ends of the tubular clear lamp. Surprisingly there is a photo portrait of Dr.

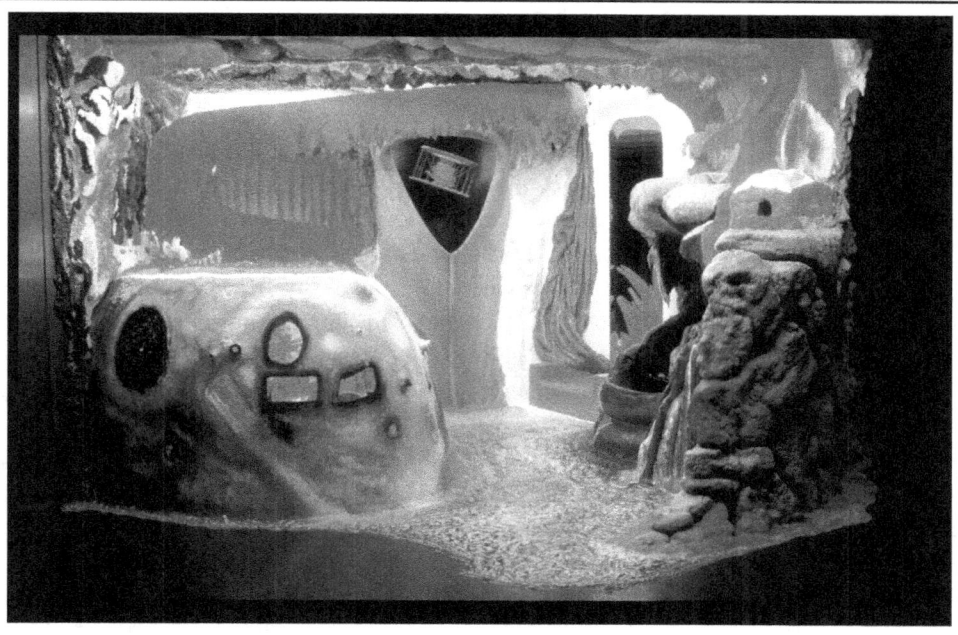

Electric Ladyland
the First Museum of Fluorescent Art

"Electric Ladyland - the First Museum of Fluorescent Art" Museum book, Nick Padalino, 1999

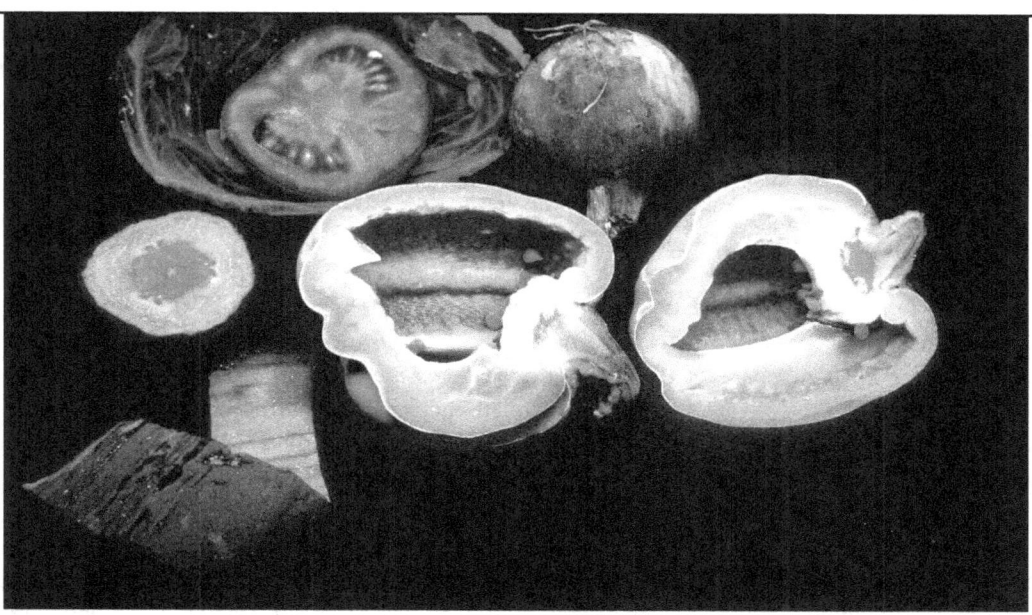

Fluorescence All Around Us

Nick Padalino and Michèle Delage

"Fluorescence All Around Us" Museum book, Nick Padalino and Michèle Delage, 2005

Harvey C. Rentschler, who was the director of research of the "Westinghouse Lamp Division," of whom there is a full page original Black and White photograph in the Museum collection, showing him making a demonstration of the "Sterilamp" during the same general late 1930s to early 1940s time period.

The text of this "Westinghouse Sterilamp" from about 1940 explains that less than three quarters of a century before Louis Pasteur had discovered Bacteria which cause disease and the rotting of food. The text follows with the facts of chemicals and heat used by different developers to kill bacteria since the time of Pasteur, but that the discoveries of the Twentieth century had brought new technology into the field and far advanced the effects of 'Sanitizing.' Typically 1940s style, the text next explains that this new technology is nearly miraculous, and 'as important and far reaching' as Pasteur's discovery of bacteria(!) This new 1940 process was named not surprisingly "Rentschlerizing" obviously from the humble Dr. Harvey C. Rentschler, and the reader is told that this process will fight bacteria, decay, mold, and germs using an "ultra-violet lamp" possessing germ-killing properties. Just ten sentences later the reader is again reminded that this new 'revolutionary' process of sterilization using the "Westinghouse Sterilamp" was called "Rentschlerizing," in case we forgot. For the remaining five pages of the booklet the Applications for the "Sterilamp" are presented as 'Sterilamps at work.'

The first application for the "Sterilamp" was the most common use, for Food Sterilization, and there is a half-page photo of the inside refrigerator of a 'Retail Meat Shop.' This photo has rows of butchered meat in a walk-in refrigerator and two rows of "STERILAMPS" lit up on the ceiling. The caption informs that these lamps 'Protect Purity, Flavour, and the Weight' of the meat, which we are told is composed of eighty percent water. The bacteria and molds that spoils meat is typically combated with very low temperatures, but this effects the butchered meat's Color, texture, and especially it's weight, which is lost by shrinkage in freezers. The cure for all of this is presented, unnaturally, by this booklet of about 1940 informing that the "Sterilamps" make it possible to raise the temperatures of the meat storage rooms to forty-two degrees and humidity to ninety-five percent because the lamps had killed the "bugs." This booklet claims that these lamps not only cause less weight loss to the butcher's meat, but also that the meat is clean and tastes better. Page five has three different applications for these "Sterilamps," starting with "Conquering Mold" in bakeries, with a photo of the back room of a bakery with rows and rows of cakes and breads under two continuous rows of "Sterilamps" on the ceiling and one very large "Sterilamp" unit wall mounted as well. The woman in the photograph must have been perpetually sunburned with such a job. The text explains that with the use of these Shortwave Ultraviolet "Sterilamps" mold and bacteria could be killed and the baked products could be free of bacteria from the "dough-room" to the '"packaged product." Beneath this bakery application there is the restaurant application with a photo of two antique people picking up their forks, knives, and spoons from trays that have a continuous row of Shortwave Ultraviolet "Sterilamps" with a glass top to avoid restaurant customers from getting sunburned eyes, at least. Next to this is the "Drinking Glasses" application with a photo of a large unit, about half the size of a dishwasher, that is filled with Shortwave Ultraviolet "Sterilamps" that are mounted above drinking glasses on a tray. The text explains that this procedure was used after the glasses were washed in the conventional way, providing extra protection against bacteria.

The last two pages of "Sterilamps at Work" present applications that range from idiotically dangerous to downright useful. The applications for these Shortwave Ultraviolet "Sterilamps" are concluded with "Sterile Storage" for dishes, bowls, and other glassware used for eating in restaurants, cafeterias, and an old expression from many years ago, the 'soda fountain.' Same as the 'Drinking Glasses' application of the previous page of this little booklet "Bugaboo of Bugville," this "Sterile Storage" application was applied to restaurant glassware after it had been washed. The photograph, again printed in this 'Blueprint Blue,' shows rows of Shortwave "Sterilamps" mounted under the counter of a restaurant, above the storage of the dishes and other glassware for the customers. "Barber Shops" are also presented in the booklet as applications of "Sterilamps," with a photograph of a 1940 man with the greasiest hair possible, shinning like wet plastic, sitting in a barber's chair waiting to have his very short hair cut even shorter by this greasy-haired barber. There in front of these two WWII characters is a "Sanitizing Cabinet" in which all articles used on the client are stored in a sterilized condition under Shortwave Ultraviolet "Sterilamps." "Bottling Plants" is the next Industrial application for these "Sterilamps," with continuous rows of Shortwave Ultraviolet lamps above long moving conveyer belts of empty glass bottles. It is explained that the photograph is illustrating the continuous sterilization of these bottles from the washing process until they are eventually filled with their products. "Cosmetic Plants" used miles of these Shortwave Ultraviolet "Sterilamps," clearly illustrated by the photo which has a woman packing containers of cosmetics under a continuous row of Shortwave Ultraviolet lamps that stretches for perhaps fifty to one hundred meters (yards). This girl must have had a good dose of sunburn every day of her working life. One of the most obviously dangerous applications for these "Sterilamps" is the next "Hospital" application for these Shortwave Ultraviolet lamps in this booklet, which contains a hair-raising photo of a large square tubular construction directly above an Operating Table, equipped on all four sides with bare Shortwave "Sterilamps." This bank of Shortwave Ultraviolet lamps were above the

Operating table directly over the doctors and nurses heads, to prevent bacteria and germs in the air from infecting patients undergoing surgery. The text states that before 1936 some of the airborne bacteria in the operating theater were the germs responsible for causing infections in post-operation. These "Westinghouse Sterilamps" had already been installed in many hospitals the booklet's text explains, with "hundreds" of operations being performed under these Shortwave Ultraviolet lamps already. Upon close inspection of the photo it is noticed that all the doctors and nurses under these Shortwave Ultraviolet "Sterilamps' are wearing Black 'visors' over their eyes, to at least offer the slightest protection for the eyes against sunburn. These Black accountant-style 'visors' are also worn by laboratory technicians working in similar situations as the doctors under rows of Shortwave Ultraviolet lamps, unfiltered and dangerous, lined up above the 'visored' laboratory workers. It is explained in the text that vaccines and all types of medicines could be manufactured and packaged under virtually sterile conditions. The final fourteenth Industrial application for these Shortwave "Sterilamps" is for public toilets in "Restrooms." "Sterilseats" are the trademark for contraptions which housed a Shortwave "Sterilamp" inside the recessed area of the top section of public toilets where the toilet seat is folded up and into. The text explains that while all toilet seats are lifted up, these would fit snugly into a recessed Shortwave Ultraviolet chamber that would sterilize them after each and every use. The booklet is dated by the explanation which states that all toilets were equipped with "Sterilseats" in the "Westinghouse" pavilion of the 1940 "World's Fair" (known today as the 1939 New York World's Fair).

The back cover of this little booklet from seventy years ago concludes with the predictions of the "Future of Sterilamps" produced by the "Westinghouse Electric and Manufacturing Co." A very dated illustration of a chemist working in a laboratory is printed with these "Future" predictions providing germ-free atmospheres in factories, schools, offices, homes, subways, and theaters - in fact it is suggested that all of life should be filled with Shortwave Ultraviolet lamps, providing all people with a sterile life, free from germs and bacteria (but filled with rampant Vitamin D production in the skin). To close this 1940 era "Sterilamps" booklet, the user is informed that all public buildings, including the fields of medicine and industry, were necessary places to install "Sterilamps" 'Germ-free atmospheres' for schools, homes, factories, subways, and theaters. The reader is also informed of the endless possibilities of these Shortwave Ultraviolet lamps, in which "Sterilamps" are installed and epidemics are avoided, 'surgical operations' could heal miraculously fast, public reservoirs could be irradiated, and cheese could be 'speed-aged.' The customer is assured that with these 'harmless' Shortwave Ultraviolet lamps the whole family could be sterile(!) 'The battle of the Bugs' is what these Shortwave Ultraviolet lamps were created for, properly termed in 1940 "Bactericidal Radiation." The booklet concludes with an entirely capitalized sentence informing the public that a 'New Ray' of 'Light' could now be used to go through the 'veil' into a germ-free and sterile "Future."

The next paper in this series of 'Mineralight News Bulletins' is number seven written by Jack DeMent and published in 1945 announcing a popular pastime in America during the 1930s, 1940s, and 1950s: Fluorescent Mineral Prospecting for valuable ores made into necessary elements of national security, such as Scheelite with it's content of Tungsten which is necessary for hardening Steel, and the present paper's subject, 'Ultra-Violet Light In Detection of Mercury.' De Ment begins the paper by informing the readers that the "Mineralight" Ultraviolet lamp was the most efficient way of discovering contents of Mercury ore in the field. Calomel, called 'Mercurous chloride' in 1945, is discussed by the author through samples found in the very famous Fluorescent mineral locality Terlingua, Texas, where Mercury mining and production went on for decades. Any person who collects Fluorescent minerals knows of one of the most famous Fluorescent mineral that exists, Terlingua, Texas Calcite which possesses the magical ability to change Colors from the Longwave Ultraviolet lamp to the Shortwave lamp, as well as Phosphorescing longer than any other mineral ever discovered: eighteen years measurable on a photographic plate in the dark. In the Museum demonstration of Terlingua, Texas Calcite there is even a large crystal six inches tall (15 cm) that Fluoresces not only the classic Reddish Pink in the Longwave U.V. and then changes to Blueish in the Shortwave U.V., but also Fluoresces a third Yellowish Color when put under the Middlewave Ultraviolet lamp. This area of Terlingua, Texas was the major area for finding Calomel which Fluoresces Orange under Longwave U.V., and also the area for heating the ore to extreme temperatures in house-sized ovens until the flowing natural element Mercury was extracted from the Calomel, and this is the area that De Ment writes about. Besides Calomel the author names another mineral, the obscure 'Terlinguate,' being described as a 'Mecurous oxychloride' from Terlingua that Fluoresces Yellow under a Shortwave "Mineralight." The other major Mercury ore besides Calomel is "Cinnabar" which is also reported by the author to have a dim response under a Shortwave "Mineralight."

The second section of this paper explains the method that was used in 1945 for Mercury prospecting called 'The Fluorescent Screen Method.' De Ment first informs readers that the Shortwave "Mineralight" produces energy concentrated at 254 nanometers (253.7 nanometers to be precise) through it's "Cold Quartz" tube lamp containing the vapor of Mercury. Mercury vapor was already known to both absorb Shortwave Ultraviolet in it's pure state, and also to emit Shortwave

Ultraviolet when the Mercury vapor was excited by an electrical charge, as in both Ultraviolet and daylight Fluorescent lamps. 'The Fluorescent Screen Method' for Mercury prospecting is described by De Ment as a set up using a Fluorescent Screen, made from Willemite powder glued to cardboard or wood, positioned standing in front of the "Mineralight." Between the "Mineralight" and the Fluorescent screen a sample of Mercury ore is heated up to a high temperature, causing Black clouds of smoke to be produced by the ore. The Fluorescent screen emits a bright Green Fluorescence in front of the "Mineralight," but when a Mercury ore is heated between them, producing Black Mercury vapor which is absorbed by the Shortwave Ultraviolet "Mineralight," the Fluorescent screen will appear with Black or dark Purple areas if the smoke contained Mercury vapor, or as De Ment calls it, a 'Mercury Cloud.'

If the reader thought the last paper was dangerous, it was nothing compared to the ninth 'Mineralight News Bulletin' entitled the ominous 'Ultra-Violet Light in Uranium Prospecting,' with the author curiously reverting back to the antiquated spelling of 'Ultra-Violet' after eight papers of using the modern spelling of 'Ultraviolet.' Uranium is introduced by the date of it's discovery in 1786, and by revealing the scientific facts that led to the discovery of radioactivity, but neither the German chemist Martin Heinrich Klaproth who discovered Uranium, nor Antoine Becquerel who discovered radioactivity are credited. The extent that the Ultraviolet lamp (which De Ment again curiously spells correctly in the text of this article) was used as a valuable tool for Uranium prospecting is extended by the author to include prospecting for the ores of Zinc and Tungsten, as well as petroleum.

The first chapter of the paper is 'The Uranium Minerals' and begins by informing the reader that not all the minerals that have Uranium content were important to prospectors because some of these minerals contained very small contents of Uranium. De Ment explains to the reader that the two main Uranium ores prospected for in the United States were "Pitchblende" and "Carnotite." Carnotite was prospected for it's content of "Vanadium" and "Radium," while Pitchblende is the famous mineral used by Pierre and Marie Curie to discover the element Radium half a century before this 'Bulletin' was written, and contained the highest levels of Radium of any mineral known. De Ment writes that "The United States department of Mines" recognized three types of Uranium ores, the first and most important being the 'Uraninites' which bear the most quantity of Uranium known in 1945 and were the minerals "Broeggeite," "Cleveite," and "Nivenite." The author also informs the reader that these three minerals were known as 'Amorphous uraninites,' which is what the name of the mineral Pitchblende is referring to. Pitchblende also refers to the way the actual mineral looks, pure Black or Black-Grey with a shinny appearance like "Pitch." De Ment specifically names Great Bear Lake in Canada as a famous Pitchblende mine in North America.

The second classification of Uranium ore was known as 'Type 2' or 'Secondary Uraninites' and the mineral "Carnotite" is explained by the author to be the most Uranium rich ore in the United States. Carnotite is described as having a consistency like Talc, or waxy, and being much different than Black Pitchblende, with a bright Yellow Color. These 'Secondary Uraninites' were used as additives to the 'Primary Uraninites,' but Carnotite's high content of Uranium meant that this mineral was not used as a mere additive. Other 'Secondary Uraninites' are cited by De Ment and include the well known mineral "Autunite." The third classification of Uranium ores were known as 'Columbium-Titanium-Tantalates' and were found in small quantities, well known to come from the Black sand of river beds. These 'Type 3' Uraninites were first discovered as minerals in Norway and Greenland, but later were found to be also present in Brazil and Madagascar.

The second chapter in this paper is 'Uranium Prospecting' and begins by listing the major Uranium minerals that were prospected for out of over one hundred Uranium ores that had been discovered between 1786 and 1945. The two most important Uranium ores in 1945 were Pitchblende and Carnotite, which De Ment explains provided the largest portion of the supply of Uranium and Radium found on Earth. Pitchblende was the most important of all the Uranium ores and yielded the largest quantity of Radium and Uranium of any mineral discovered, and is still the major Uranium ore seventy years later. "Autunite" is included as a Uranium mineral in the list by the author, and in recent times it is generally recognized that the brightest Fluorescence of any mineral known in the world is the highly radioactive so-called 'Meta-Autunite' coming from Spokane, Washington. 'Meta-Autunite' is so reactive and so unstable that it eventually turns to non-Fluorescent common Lead with exposure to air. The mineral that is referred to as 'Raw Opal' or 'Opalite' today coming from "Virgin Valley," Nevada is also mentioned as containing traces of Uranium, which are properly called 'Uranyls' in modern times. This Opalite from Virgin Valley, Nevada is fossilized volcanic ash which is pure White on the Oxidized surface, giving the name to the locality, "Virgin Valley," but when you break a piece of this White ground with a hammer and pick it up, it has the appearance of opaque dull Brown glass. When a piece of this 'Brown glass' is put under either a Shortwave or Longwave Ultraviolet lamp it Fluoresces a brilliant Green because of it's activator Uranyl. As the majority of Fluorescent minerals known today Fluoresce through the physics of "Impurity Activation," meaning a minuscule amount of a mineral called an "Impurity" is contained inside the host mineral and it is just this tiny amount of Impurity atoms that absorb the invisible U.V. energy, goes through "Electron

Displacement" and then releases most of the gained energy from the U.V. as Visible Light. "Opalite" is one of the few exceptions to this "Impurity Activation," and is known to Fluoresce through the physics of "Intrinsic Activation," meaning that the portion of the molecular make-up of Opalite which absorbs U.V. energy and releases it as Visible Light, is contained in such amounts in Opalite that it cannot be considered a mere Impurity, but it is a necessary component of the mineral itself. I explain it in the Museum by telling that if it was physically possible, the "Impurity" in "Impurity Activated" Fluorescent minerals could be removed from the Fluorescent mineral and it would still be the same mineral, but would not Fluoresce under an Ultraviolet lamp, but for "Intrinsic Activated" Fluorescent Minerals such a Opalite, if the essential Activator could be removed from the mineral it would not be Opalite anymore and would essentially destroy the actual mineral, not just it's Fluorescent ability.

The last section of this paper is a 'Summary' of a 1940 De Ment book on prospecting for Radium and Uranium minerals. The eight major points of reference from the book are listed and include the facts that primary Uranium ores do not Fluoresce, that many secondary Uranium ores are highly Fluorescent, that this Fluorescence is almost always Green to Yellow, that Shortwave Ultraviolet causes the greatest Fluorescence in Uranium ores, and that if Uranium is present in a sample then Radium is present also.

The year was 1945 in which the tenth issue of 'Mineralight News Bulletin' was published, written by Jack De Ment. The subject of this 'Bulletin' is very different for this tenth issue, and since the publication date for the first three 'Bulletins' was 1944, in 1945 the fourth issue was published. By the time this tenth issue of the 'Bulletin' was sold for "10¢" (the pencilled price is still on the cover of this issue) the Second world war had finally ended, and the heavy-duty Mercury, Scheelite, and Uranium prospecting "Rosy the Riveter" days were over. This is most likely the reason that the subject matter of this tenth 'Bulletin' was so 'civilian' and had nothing to do what so ever with the war: 'Luminescence in Gem Science.' There is a small book by Jack De Ment in the Museum collection called "Fluorescent Gems and Minerals" that was published four years after this paper, in 1949, which is a complete study of gem and mineral Fluorescence from the 1940s.

De Ment begins this paper explaining to the reader that many Gemstones are Fluorescent, pointing out the two most famous gemstones, the Ruby with it's spectacular unmatched Red Fluorescence, only comparable to "Eucryptite" in it's saturation of Color, and the most famous gemstone of all, the Diamond, which history records as the first gemstone who's Phosphorescence was recognized. In the medieval times Alchemists thought that Diamonds were magical because when they were brought from outside in the Sun to inside a darkened hut, they glowed-in-the-dark (Phosphoresced). This is the reason that Diamonds became so famous and also the reason that Diamonds became so valuable - not just because of wedding rings. De Ment also informs the reader in the introduction that similar to Fluorescent minerals, Fluorescence was not a definitive test for gemstone identification either, because it varied so much and depended on impurities in the crystal makeup. Also like Fluorescent minerals, De Ment states that the same exact gemstone from the same exact 'species' may react completely different under an Ultraviolet lamp when coming from different localities. What De Ment is complaining about here, in 1945, is the most important reason that Fluorescence has never been embraced by mineralogists or geologists, and remains such an obscure study. In any thick Geology text book, dictionary, or encyclopedia, it is lucky to find one single paragraph written about Fluorescent minerals. Geologists do not like mineral Fluorescence because you can't make a Chart of it. Since many of the Fluorescent minerals vary from specimen to specimen and also from locality to locality, a Chart cannot be made of the Fluorescence of minerals that is standard all over the world, such as the "Chartable" physical characteristics of mineralogy like "Hardness" and "Streak." De Ment words the complaint perfectly, stating that even some gemstones from the very same mine or collecting location will not react with the same Fluorescent Color at all, like identical specimens from the very same mineral locality would be expected to. This is what makes geologists and mineralogists crazy. De Ment next explains the reason for this endless varying response to an Ultraviolet lamp for gemstones, and it is the same exact reason for the variations in Fluorescence throughout the mineral kingdom. As mentioned before in this book, the "Activator" atoms in Fluorescent minerals are what absorb the gained U.V. energy from the U.V. lamp, and these "Activator" atoms must be in precise quantities in the atomic structure of the mineral or gemstone to enable it to Fluoresce. The author again points out 'Opalite,' or 'Raw Opal,' and explains that this 'Hyalite Opal,' as termed by De Ment, was vividly Fluorescent from some localities, but from other localities the same exact Opalite showed no Fluorescence at all. This Fluorescence of Opalite was correctly explained by the author as being due to the presence of small amounts of a 'secondary Uranium mineral' ["Uranyl"]. A second example is given by De Ment on the endless variations of mineral and gemstone Fluorescence, and in this case one of the most 'reliably' Fluorescing gemstones known to exist is explained as a contrast: the most beautifully Fluorescing rock you could ever put under an Ultraviolet lamp, the Ruby. If you ever get the opportunity to put one mineral under a Black light, make sure it's a Ruby, because you will never see a more beautiful saturated Color of Fluorescent Red in any mineral on Earth. The reader learns that the tiny amount of activator atoms in Ruby crystals are "Chromium," and De Ment explains that this Chromium activation in Ruby crystals had been discovered through the use of the Ultraviolet lamp, and even at that point in 1945 there was still no chemical test sensitive enough to have discovered this Chromium content. De Ment also informs the reader that in 1945 this Chromium activation was believed to also cause the activation in Emerald, Alexandrite, and Red Spinel.

After this Gem Fluorescence introduction, the bulk of this paper is a 'Gem Fluorochemistry' alphabetical listing of Fluorescent Gemstones known in 1945:

"Agate" is reported to Fluoresce Yellow-Green in it's state as "Chalcedony,"

"Alexandrite" is weak Red under a Shortwave U.V. lamp,

"Amber" since it is organic fossilized Conifer Tree resin, is invariably Fluorescent in shades from Yellowish to a bright light Blue. The brightest specimen of Fluorescent Amber I have on display in the Museum is from Mexico, Fluorescing a brilliant Sky Blue, and the most famous and rarest Fluorescent Amber is called 'Blue Amber' supposedly coming only from the Dominican Republic, which is also in the Museum collection. This 'Blue Amber' is so highly Fluorescent that it got it's name from the ability to Fluoresce Blue even out in the sunlight, without even being under an Ultraviolet lamp.

"Benitoite" is the extremely rare gemstone coming from only one mine in San Benito County in California, brilliantly Fluorescing a Blue-White Color under the Shortwave U.V. It is so rare that it is the State Gemstone of California.

"Beryl" is reported by De Ment as occasionally Fluorescing a weak Green,

"Chrysoberyl" is listed as being a classic 'Variable' Fluorescent mineral, changing Fluorescent Color and reaction from locality to locality.

"Corundum" 'Gems' are well explained, including Ruby and Sapphire, and the vivid Red Fluorescence of Ruby is, again, attributed to it's "Impurity Activator" Chromium, being excitable to Fluorescence by almost any Ultraviolet source, including either the Longwave or Shortwave Ultraviolet lamp. Ruby is so sensitive, that it will Fluoresce even under visible Violet or Blue light, without any Ultraviolet at all.

"Diamond" is the largest description in the entire paper as it is the undisputed most famous gemstone that exists. Not only is Diamond famous for being the most sought-after gemstone in the world, but it is also famous for having the most variations in Fluorescence of any gemstone, as well. Diamond is famous for Fluorescing a brilliant Sky Blue, but it's Fluorescence can occur in the Colors Yellow, Orange, Green, Purple-Blue, the very rarest Red, or adversely, the Diamond can also be completely non-Fluorescent. The Red Fluorescing Diamonds are the most expensive and rarest Diamonds in the world, and have been known for many years to possess the most beautiful perfect light reflections in daylight - the "sparkle" - of any Diamonds known to exist. The reason for the Diamond's Red Fluorescence and perfect sparkle are interrelated, being due to the presence of Nitrogen in the crystal lattice of the Diamond. This fact was apparently not known in 1945 because it is not mentioned once in this full page description of Diamond Fluorescence by De Ment. The most famous and valuable Diamond in the world is the "Hope Diamond" behind bombproof glass in the Smithsonian Institute in Washington, D.C., which is an incredible 45.52 carats. The "Hope Diamond" is a 'Blue Diamond,' being a beautiful transparent dark Blue in daylight. The completely unique ability of the "Hope Diamond" is displayed when it is put under an Ultraviolet lamp. Due to the presence of both Barium and Nitrogen in it's chemical composition, the Fluorescence of the "Hope Diamond" is not it's unique property, but it's bright Red Phosphorescence. Originally the unique Red Phosphorescence of the "Hope Diamond" was attributed to the wrath of an angry Hindu God after the Diamond had been stolen from it's temple in antiquity, but chemical analysis has revealed that the presence of Barium in it's composition is what enables the "Hope Diamond" to Phosphoresce Red. It has been well known for many years that the Red Fluorescence of a Diamond is incredibly rare, and this is caused by the presence of Nitrogen in the chemical composition. This Nitrogen causes both the most exquisite internal reflections of light and hence the 'sparkle' of the Diamond, and the highest price demanded for any commercial Diamonds in the world, but these Diamonds are clear as air and do not have a Blue Color in the daylight and do not have a Red Phosphorescence as the "Hope Diamond" does with it's added inclusion of Barium in it's composition. This extremely rare demonstration of the Phosphorescence of the "Hope Diamond" was aired on National Geographic Television during 2009 in a show entitled "Super Diamonds." The history of the Fluorescence of Diamonds is presented by De Ment, explaining that the famous Alchemist Robert Boyle ("The Bird was Delicious!") discovered the visible light of Diamond in 1662 through his experiments in heating the Diamond, in which he produced "Thermoluminescence," and also by rubbing the Diamond, which produced the visible light of "Triboluminescence." De Ment wrote that back to 1900 the scientist Crookes was studying the Fluorescent effect of Diamond, and even when he excited Diamond with Radium it was reported to also Fluoresce. De Ment next credits himself, and Oor, as being the first scientists to do a study in the laboratory on the Fluorescence of Diamonds, in 1941. Their conclusions included the fact that the strongest reacting Blue Fluorescing Diamonds were composed of a greater amount of the Activator Chromium than other

Diamond samples. Another study by Chelsey, after De Ment and Oor's, also investigated the Fluorescence of thirty-three different Diamond specimens. The thirty-three Diamonds analyzed were found to be composed of thirteen different elements, and Chromium was found to be present in each of the thirty-three Diamonds. The interesting phenomenon of 'Zone Fluorescence' in Diamonds is described by the author, explaining that different fracture zones in the Diamond crystal could Fluoresce with different Colors. This is caused by the Impurity Activators being different elements or occurring in different quantities in succeeding different growth stages of the physical formation of the Diamond crystal itself. This is clearly seen in the rare specimens of true Fluorescent "Phantom Crystals." In the Museum collection there is a triangular specimen of Calcite crystal from California that is as clear as air in the daylight, but when this crystal is put under a Shortwave lamp it displays it's hidden magical appearance. The interior of this formerly clear crystal becomes a series of six Pale Green translucent triangles on top of each other. These invisible Pale Green triangles of light were formed by the presence of an impurity activator during alternating periods in it's formation, so for instance at one period of the crystal's formation the impurity activator which is responsible for creating Pale Green light under a Shortwave was included inside of the hydrothermal mix creating the crystal, forming a Pale Green band of Fluorescent Calcite, and during other periods in this same Calcite crystal's formation the impurity activator was not included in the hydrothermal mix, the Calcite continued to form minus the impurity activator, and this resulted in another band of the crystal formation which is non-Fluorescent. After perhaps thousands or even millions of years that it took for this Calcite crystal to form, we are privileged to be able to behold a triangular clear piece of crystal which miraculously has six Pale Green pyramids contained inside of it's structure only visible under Shortwave Ultraviolet.

Another scientific investigation into the Fluorescence of Diamonds was done by Nayer, who is explained by De Ment to have found that the Fluorescence of Diamond crystals is excited the most by energy ranging from the top of the Longwave Ultraviolet spectrum right through the visible light of Violet, Purple, Blue, Green, Yellow, and even into visible Orange light, and that Diamonds can vary so much in their Fluorescent intensity that one Diamond specimen can be an incredible ten-thousand times as bright as another comparable Diamond specimen. Concerning the Phosphorescence of Diamonds, Nayer also concluded that the Diamond crystal needs about a full minute of 'charging' from the "Mineralight" before extinguishing the lamp for a Phosphorescence that can be seen for 'several minutes.' In conclusion De Ment restates the fact that in no locality known throughout the world could Diamonds be found that had unvarying identical Fluorescent Color. The final statement by the author was incorrect in 1945, and even more incorrect in the Twenty-first century, stating that the Fluorescent and Phosphorescent capabilities of Diamonds didn't have a 'relationship' to it's high value as a Gemstone. This is absolutely incorrect. If the author would have explored history a little deeper he would have found out that the very reason for both the Diamond's high value and it's social status comes directly from the fact that Alchemists hundreds of years ago considered Diamond to be a magical substance because of the very facts that De Ment disregards: the Diamond was brought into darkened huts from out in the Sun, and it was a *miracle* - the clear Colorless crystals gave off light in the dark - they Phosphoresced! The second reason that makes De Ment's statement double-wrong is that for the last decades, Diamonds sold in the United States for wedding rings were priced more expensively if they had no Blue Fluorescent reaction under a U.V. lamp, because in a new American scam, jewelers had managed to convince the public that common Blue Fluorescent Diamonds will turn Blue in the sunlight and not be as beautiful (or expensive) as Diamonds that did not Fluoresce Blue in the Sunlight. Now the American Jewelers are not lying - you can see a Wedding ring's Diamond Fluoresce Blue out in the sunlight - if you are a Bee.

"Dumortierite" is listed as being from Lyon in France and Fluorescing Blue under a "Mineralight."

"Emerald" is correctly listed as being very seldom Fluorescent, but when Fluorescent the Emerald crystal also Fluoresces Green. Curiously, the fact is given that since the Activator of Emerald was also thought to be the same Activator as Ruby, the element Chromium, then the anticipated Fluorescent Color was logically thought to have been the same as Ruby Red, but in true Fluorescent mineral and gemstone style, the Fluorescent Color of Emerald was just the opposite of Ruby: Green. I can attest to the first of De Ment's statements about the rarity of the Fluorescent Emerald, because the first time I finally found a Fluorescent Emerald crystal was in a fair with my Mother and Aunt Jean during a snow storm in the early 1990s. There were several large tables, about two yards (meters) long each, that were completely covered with tiny crystals of Emerald from Brazil - there were literally hundreds of Emerald specimens, each mounted and for sale, I methodically went through each of these Emerald crystals, one by one with my small 4 watt portable Longwave Ultraviolet lamp (Emeralds barely Fluoresce under Shortwave Ultraviolet, which De Ment is always raving about, and furthermore, Ruby crystals have a very dim Fluorescent response under Shortwave U.V., but they also Fluoresce with the strongest intensity under a normal Longwave Black light). After maybe a full thirty minutes of this methodical searching for a Fluorescent Emerald crystal, my Mother and Aunt definitively had enough, so they went to sit in the car to wait for me in the snow storm with the heater on. I would estimate from the bitter looks on both their faces when I finally returned to the car, that I left both of them waiting close to a full hour to find one single tiny - half of an inch (1 centimeter) - crystal that would immediately be lost forever if it was detached form it's minuscule plastic mineral display box: "WHAT - That's IT!!" In fact, this minuscule Emerald crystal of only one centimeter is the main Emerald crystal on display in the "Common Items that are Fluorescent" demonstration in the Museum for the last seventeen years, and eventually was joined by a much large cluster of Emerald crystals donated to the Museum by my friend Brami who had brought it back from Afghanistan, which is an ancient famous locality for Emerald.

"Garnet" is also correctly stated to be rarely Fluorescent, and it is also reported that since the Garnet crystal is non-Fluorescent, this response identifies it from a Ruby or Spinel, which both Fluoresce a vivid Red. De Ment explains the non Fluorescent response of Garnet due to high levels of Iron, a Fluorescence "quencher," and amounts of Manganese that were so high that they would also inhibit Fluorescence.

"Jadeite" from Burma was listed as having a dull Green Fluorescence, but I have never seen it Fluoresce.

"Lazurite" is also listed as having almost no Fluorescent response, but the locality of Chile is given for Lazurite found with a weak Purple Fluorescence and a weak White Phosphorescence.

"Mother of Pearl" is listed a having the same bright Fluorescence and 'Fluorochemistry' as Pearl.

"Opal" is correctly listed as being Fluorescent Green in a 'raw,' Opalite state of fossilized Volcanic ash, but the beautiful Opal that is used in Jewelry, with all the Opalescent Color effects does not Fluoresce. When an Opal ring is put under a Black light, the bright Blue Fluorescence seen is due to the clear coating that the Opal is permanently set into.

"Pearls" are Organic and their 'Fluorochemistry' is explained by the author as being made of an inner part of Calcium carbonate, and an exterior part made of an Organic substance that was called 'Conchoilin.' De Ment explains that there was no difference in Fluorescent response between the cultured Pearls and the uncultured Pearls [both being Fluorescent with a medium to strong intense White Color tinted with Blue under a Longwave Ultraviolet lamp]. Again, the "Mineralight" that De Ment insists on using throughout his study of gemstones is not the Longwave Ultraviolet, but a Shortwave U.V. lamp. The only two gemstones that I display that have a descent Fluorescent Color under the Shortwave Ultraviolet lamp (like the "Mineralight" that De Ment consistently used) are Spinel and Diamond, both of these examples are more brilliantly Fluorescing under a Shortwave Ultraviolet lamp than under a Longwave Ultraviolet lamp. Almost every other gemstone that is put under an Ultraviolet lamp is multiple times brighter under a Longwave U.V. lamp than under a Shortwave U.V. lamp.

"Quartz," which is stated by the author to be Silicon dioxide, also is correctly stated by the author to be very seldom Fluorescent. Rose Quartz is listed as Fluorescing dull Purple, and clear Quartz crystals from San Diego, California are listed as having a Green 'Zone Fluorescence.' As previously described in the 'Diamond' section, this is absolutely correct, because in the Museum display I have one Quartz crystal from California that is a classic example of a true "Phantom Crystal." The crystal is as clear as air when in the daylight, but when under a Shortwave U.V. lamp, there are six pale Green pyramid shaped Fluorescent zones on top of each other in this formerly crystal clear Quartz. Agate and Amethyst, in the Quartz family, are also listed as being non-Fluorescent.

"Ruby" is erroneously listed as being a 'weak' to bright Fluorescent under a Shortwave "Mineralight." De Ment would have been shocked if he had one time placed what he described as a 'weak' Fluorescing Ruby crystal under a Longwave Ultraviolet Black light! Under Shortwave Ultraviolet, the "Mineralight" which De Ment uses exclusively in this series of 'Mineralight News Bulletins' (I can't imagine why) published by "Ultra-Violet Products, Inc." the company which manufactured the "Mineralight," Ruby Fluoresces only weakly. By contrast I have never seen a 'weak' Fluorescing Ruby crystal under a Longwave Ultraviolet lamp. Every single crystal of Ruby that I have in the Museum collection, from Mysore, India, the Hunza Valley in Pakistan, Tanzania, Madagascar, Brazil, and Burma, although not all exactly the same intensity of Fluorescence, all are *brilliantly* Fluorescent under Longwave Ultraviolet, not 'weak' as these same brilliantly Fluorescing crystals of Ruby appear if I were to mistakenly switch on the Shortwave U.V. lamp instead of the correct lamp to use on Rubies, the Longwave Ultraviolet lamp. The first Laser was made in 1960 with the Fluorescence of the Ruby crystal, because it is so intensely Fluorescing under a Longwave U.V. lamp, and because it's brilliant Red Fluorescent Color is monochromatic: it's Red Fluorescent Color does not vary - it is a very tight wavelength of Red that does not change, hence it was the Fluorescent crystal with the essential qualities that were needed to produce the first Laser (which was Red, of course, not Green like most people have seen for the first time in the 1970s). De Ment lists Ruby from Siam, Burma, North Carolina, Ceylon, and even synthetic Ruby, which De Ment states as Fluorescing very bright. The author explains that Ruby, Spinel, and Alexandrite all Fluoresce with similar reactions that are indicating the Chromium activation for these three crystals. De Ment also states that the Fluorescence of Ruby occurs in the very tight region of 692.7 and 694.2 nanometers, the fact that made it the perfect monochromatic Fluorescent Gemstone to use to create the first Laser. The correct mineralogical name for the 'Ruby' crystal is "Corundum."

"Sapphire" is explained by the author to be more likely to Fluoresce if it is a Colorless Sapphire. Clear Sapphire was listed as Fluorescing Yellow-Orange, while the synthetic version Fluoresced deep Red, and the Yellow Sapphire from Ceylon and Australia is reported by De Ment to Fluoresce in shades of Orange, but in this rare case the synthetic Yellow Sapphire Fluoresces weaker than the natural stone. De Ment informs the reader that the Red Fluorescence of Sapphire has been attributed to Chromium activation, but that both the daylight Blue Color of 'Blue Sapphire' and it's corresponding Orange Fluorescence were believed to be activated through Titanium.

"Spinel" is one of the few gemstones that is Fluorescent only under a Shortwave Ultraviolet lamp, so in this example, De Ment was correct in using the "Mineralight" instead of a Longwave Ultraviolet lamp - but this is one of the only common gemstones which Fluoresces only under a Shortwave lamp, not the naturally occurring Longwave Ultraviolet that reaches the surface of the Earth. Diamond is one of the only gemstones I know of that many times has a similarly stronger Fluorescence under a Shortwave U.V. lamp than under a Longwave U.V. lamp, and also which Fluoresces under either of the U.V. lamps. De Ment explains that if Magnesium is replaced by Chromium in the atomic structure, then Spinel will Fluoresce Red. Artificial Spinel is reported to Fluoresce Green, and ground up heated Spinel was to Fluoresce Yellow-Green.

"Spodumene" is listed by the author as being the Yellow and Green variety called 'Hiddenite,' and also the "Kunzite" variety of light Purple. The 'Hiddenite' variety of Spodumene Fluoresced an Orange Color, while the "Kunzite" variety was described as possibly Fluorescing with a strong reaction.

"Topaz" is next listed, and De Ment states that it rarely Fluoresces, with exceptions being in the clear, Colorless Topaz, which can Fluoresce a dull Red.

"Zircon" from British Columbia is listed by the author as Fluorescing Orange, while the same crystal from Australia is listed as Fluorescing Yellow. Again De Ment states that the Colorless Zircon will Fluoresce the strongest Color, while the darker Colored Blue, Red, and Brown Zircons have less Fluorescence, or none at all.

The eleventh "Mineralight News Bulletin" is the next issue of the publication that, like number ten, is another post-World war two 'civilian' subject matter: 'Fluorochemistry in Dyestuffs and Textile Science.' The introduction by De Ment explains that the definition of a dye is a substance containing a Color that is capable of transferring this Color onto fabric. Fluorescent dyes are, like everything else Fluorescent, in a league of their own because even the simple definition of a dye doesn't necessarily apply to Fluorescent dyes, because the "Invisible" Fluorescent dyes do not contain a Color, and similarly sometimes the Fluorescent dyed fabric does not have a transferred Color either. De Ment proposes that a new definition of a luminescent dye should be established, and this definition should include the corrected facts that a luminescent dye is a Fluorescent substance that is used to transfer the luminescence to a fabric, and in this way, creating a luminescent fabric that does not necessarily contain Color. The "Invisible" Fluorescent dyes did not contain what is traditionally called "Color," but the normal Fluorescent dyes did contain Color, which was similar to the Fluorescent Colors of contemporary times, having brilliant Color in the daylight and even more brilliant Colors under a Black light, which was later called 'Daylight Fluorescence.' De Ment informs the reader that this 'Daylight Fluorescent' visible Fluorescent dye is what the subject of the paper would focus on. The author explains that the traditional science and chemical theories of textile dyes are not applicable to Fluorescent dyes, especially in relation to the 'mordants' used to 'fix' dye on fabric, which are chemical brews that many times contain metal ingredients that are known as 'Fluorescent quenches' because of their ability to destroy the Fluorescent capabilities of a luminescent dye. The example of Fluorescein is explained and the conclusion is that although it is a substance that is brilliantly Fluorescent, it fades in daylight and would not be applicable as a dyestuff.

De Ment defines three classes of Dyestuffs, a visible Color dye, Fluorescent dye, and the "Invisible" Fluorescent dye, and goes so far as to include the effect of the Longwave Ultraviolet contained in sunlight causing 'Daylight Fluorescence' when under the Sun, like the daylight Fluorescent dyes put into all White material in the west for many decades, starting not too many years after this paper by De Ment. This is the reason for the famous 'T-Shirt Fluorescence' under a Black light that everyone is familiar with, caused by the inclusion of "Optical Dyes" in the production of the fabric, enabling the sought after "Whiter-than-White" 1950s dream. The third definition of "Invisible" Fluorescent dyes were used in fabric for Theatre, the example given by the author in which stage effects could be created by the "Invisible" Fluorescent effects under Black lights.

The next subject matter covered by De Ment is perhaps one of the most important uses of Fluorescent dyes in existence today, sixty-five years later: Fluorescent dying of biological samples used in medical and biological research, such as stained cells under a microscope. The author gives the date of 1838 as the first time when Colored dyes were developed for use in staining cells, and then adds that just for the past 'few decades' the advanced procedure of the Fluorescent dying of cells was in use. De Ment would have been pleased with the current Twenty-first century craze of "Green Fluorescent Protein" and the nightmarish "production" of Transgenic Fluorescent Animals. The author discusses the difference of the strength of

Fluorescence in regard to both daylight Fluorescence and Fluorescence under a Black light, and concludes that the Fluorescent dyes which would be the most visible in both of the conditions included the Colors Yellow and Orange, again prophetically predicting the (mis)use of these two Colors on every Highway traffic "Safety Cone" and all Highway repairmen's 'High Visibility' Safety Wear on a virtually world-wide scale. Much of this 'Fluorochemistry in Dyestuffs and Textile Science' paper is similar to De Ment's 1945 colossal book "Fluorochemistry," being filled with scientific explanations, and data, and formulas, making this book and this paper essentially a 'Trade publication,' intended for use in the industry, and hence nearly indecipherable and of very little interest for a non-chemist.

Very politically, De Ment was working as the writer of these 'Mineralight News Bulletins' for Thomas S. Warren of "Ultra-Violet Products, Inc.," the company that manufactured the "Mineralight" and almost every other war time mineral prospecting Ultraviolet lamp made during that era, and was the second company in the Fluorescent industry, after the "Switzer Brothers" "Conti-Glo" (eventual "Day-Glo") corporation. This perspective makes it apparent why the fact that "The Switzer Brothers" Invented Fluorescent fabric as a commission to the United States Military nearly ten full years before this paper by De Ment was published, is never *mentioned* even once. Typical. The 'Pioneer' of Fluorescent dyed fabric is introduced by De Ment as Millson of the 'American Cyanamid Company,' and the date is given by the author of 1942, around half a decade after "The Switzer Brothers" invented Fluorescent fabric for the Second world war, only.

De Ment continues on giving credit to Millson and Royer as the 1942 'pioneers' in the development of Fluorescent fabric, embellishing the credit with too many facts of scientific stature, such as their chemical procedure concerning the different fibers of fabrics and studying cross sections of samples of eight different types of Fluorescent dyed fabrics under the 'Fluoromicroscope.' Very impressive, but it would have been even more impressive if the author would have presented the true historical facts, namely that Fluorescent fabric had been Invented more than five years prior to Millson's 'pioneering' by the "Switzer Brothers" who also were the Inventors of Fluorescent paint in 1933, not bastardized the history of yet another Fluorescent subject to patronize and please his employer Mr. Thomas S. Warren. Again, the 'method of operation' for this Warren clan. Since the "Switzer Brothers" were commissioned by the United States military to invent Fluorescent Fabrics in the 1930s, and since literally millions of yards (meters) of this first Fluorescent Fabric were ordered by the U.S. military during World war two, which had only ended two years before this paper's publication, there is no excuse for De Ment's exclusion of these true facts of history.

The Fluorescent grading of Fabrics is next explored by De Ment, informing readers that Fluorescent analysis can determine different grades of the same fabrics, and different types of fabrics, such as the Yellow Fluorescence of 'Vegetable' fibers, the Blue Fluorescence of 'Animal' fibers, and natural silk and wool Fluorescing with a different intensity of Blue. De Ment states that the hair of animals, and wool were known to Fluoresce with a strong Blue Color through the inclusion of Keratin, while the hair of humans was stated as varying with applications of Hair dye or bleaches. Human hair is not examined that thoroughly by De Ment, and there is no mention about the major difference between light hair, such as blond or the eventual Grey hair which Fluoresces many times brighter than Brown or Black hair. I see this several times a day for seventeen years in the Museum, and the physical reason for this is that the Protein Follicle - the actual hair itself - is what is Fluorescing, and the less pigment that is on top of this Protein Follicle allows more Ultraviolet energy to enter the hair and cause bright Fluorescence. When a person has Brown or Black Hair, or subsequently dyed hair, which is the point about dyed fabrics that De ment is trying to make, the pigment on top of the Protein Follicle does not allow as much Ultraviolet to enter the hair and cause it to vividly Fluoresce, so Brown and Black hair appears much less Fluorescent when compared to Blonde hair, and no natural Fluorescence in human hair can surpass Silver or Grey hair - you should see Michèle under a Black light. As a living example, my mostly Silver beard is about ten times as bright under a Black light as the Reddish Brown Hair on my head.

For Quality Control, the author explains that Oil stained fabric is easily recognized under an Ultraviolet lamp. Techniques for determining the type of oil that stained the fabric, and how to adjust the Fluorescent dying to either light or dark Colored fabric are discussed, including the use of filter paper to absorb oil stains from the material, and the eventual Fluorescent analysis of these stains on the filter paper used to determine the type and possibly even the actual source of the oil that stained the dyed fabric. Again crediting the 'pioneer' Henry E. Millson, this time for the discovery of the Phosphorescence of fabrics, and the year of his "discovery" is stated as 1944, again almost ten years after "The Switzer Brothers" Invented Fluorescent fabric. Imagine this character De Ment crediting someone as the 'pioneer' in Fluorescent fabrics when it had not only been Invented by the "Switzer Brothers" nearly ten years before, but again it is officially documented that Millions of yards had been produced by the "Switzer Brothers" exclusively as commission to the U.S. military forces for use during the Second world war and had been sold to the government over half a decade before this paper was written by De Ment. In reality, by the time this paper was printed announcing the 'pioneer' of Fluorescent fabrics, *Millions* of square yards of Fluorescent fabric had already been very likely used and then destroyed in the war! Millson is also credited with the discovery of the Phosphorescence of human hair, skin, and body tissue(?) - after another healthy self-experiment with Millson putting a Shortwave Ultraviolet 'Cold-Quartz lamp' against his arm for thirty-seconds and then supposedly watching his arm Phosphoresce for some seconds. I have been around U.V. lamps for forty-seven years and I have never seen human flesh Phosphoresce, but then again, I've never been stupid enough to put an unfiltered Shortwave Ultraviolet lamp against my arm for thirty-seconds either. Concerning Fluorescent dyed fabric, the author states that the Phosphorescence of Fluorescent fabrics lasts for only some seconds, and also reports that the Phosphorescence can be seen five times as long if the Fluorescent fabric was moist then if the Fluorescent dyed fabric was dry. For testing the Phosphorescence of Fluorescent dyed fabrics, the author traditionally (and obligatorily) states that the Shortwave Ultraviolet lamp was the U.V. to be used, and then explains that Fluorescent dyed samples would be lined up on a Black background, the eyes would be in the dark for over half an hour to become adapted to the darkness, and that a metal opaque object would be positioned over a part of the fluorescent fabric sample that was to be examined for Phosphorescence, which created a standard of contrast. The 'pioneer' Millson is reported to have studied 'all' the known fabrics and skins used in textiles, both dyed and not dyed, and came to the conclusion that dyed fibers usually have a shorter period of visible Phosphorescence than natural fibers that were not dyed. Again, De Ment uses the Shortwave "Mineralight" from "Ultra-Violet Products, Inc." to make a Phosphorescent dyed fabric test, of course, and the samples are reported to be put under the U.V. lamp for a minute before Phosphorescent analyzation. Chemical tests including the heating of the dyed Fluorescent fabrics were performed, with the result being that the Fluorescent or Phosphorescent ability of the luminescent dyed fabric could be possibly altered, or even completely destroyed, after such heating. The example is given of a skin of 'Vinyon,' which was Phosphorescent for a mere ten-seconds in it's natural state, and after heating for an hour at a high temperature, the Phosphorescence of the fabric was nearly three times as long (although the fabric was also rendered unusable by this procedure). Acetate that was coated with hot Sodium hydroxide Phosphoresced brighter and longer than uncoated Acetate. The effect of light on fabrics causing fading is also considered by De Ment, who explains the revelation that faded Fluorescent fabric will Phosphoresce only one-third or one-quarter the time that Fluorescent fabric that was not faded would.

'Luminescent Fabric' is the last section of the paper and this is described as being either Fluorescent or Phosphorescent, and being included in the division is the fact that all Phosphorescent substances are also Fluorescent, but not the contrary. It is explained how the different kinds of fabrics, such as the proteins wool and silk, and the vegetable fibers of cotton and linen are differently effected by luminescent dyes. The shocking example is given with cotton Fluorescing Yellow after being dyed with 'Flavine S,' but the same Fluorescent dye produced a Blue Fluorescent Color when it was used to dye wool. For the third time in this incorrect, intentionally-misleading paper on Fluorescent dyed fabric, the 'pioneer' of Fluorescent fabric is one more time named as H.E. Millson, and in this third example of changing history, the date of Millson's 'pioneer' work in Fluorescent fabrics is lowered to 1941 from 1942, this time less than five years after the "Switzer Brothers" Invented Fluorescent fabric. In true political incorrectness, De Ment gives credit to Millson as the 'pioneer' of Fluorescent fabrics, and then proceeds to add Meunier and Bonnet, Radley and Grant, and even Seyewetz and Blanc(!) as other 'pioneers' in the Invention and discovery of Fluorescent fabric. Again, not once are the "Switzer Brothers" mentioned. To further buttress the incorrect and intentionally misleading 'fact' that Millson was the first person to 'pioneer' Fluorescent fabric, the date of 1941 is next given as the year that Millson discovered different dyes for creating Fluorescent wool. Next De Ment informs the reader that in 1944 Millson developed Fluorescent wool in Colors such as Yellow, Red, and even different Blues, but alas, these "World-first" discoveries by this Millson were very conveniently 'unpublished' ['Already in 1996 we had the idea to make a Museum of Fluorescence...']. The list of the different Fluorescent Colors of wool 'discovered' by Millson is nearly a full page, and includes the general chemical instructions for producing each of the Fluorescent Colors in wool, including Yellow, Red, three Blues, Orange, Green, and Violet. The 'Vegetable' and 'Animal' dyes are examined in their uses on different fabrics, and the last section of this technical chemist's explanation deals with the same type of material "The Switzer Brothers" utilized to invent Fluorescent fabric: Synthetics - what a surprise! The famous story already in this book of the young newlywed Joseph Switzer in 1935 asking his new wife to "borrow" her White Satin- Synthetic -Wedding Dress because the two young Switzer brothers didn't have the money to buy a piece of Satin to experiment on after their initial investigations into dying silk Fluorescent created Fluorescent fabric that was too stiff for production. The young Switzer brothers experimented on Joseph's young wife's new White Satin Wedding Dress, and in the end, Joseph Switzer's young wife's Wedding Dress is famous for being the first piece of Fluorescent Fabric ever created - I didn't hear the name "Millson" in any of this history of the invention of Fluorescent Fabric! It is very disturbing to see the true facts of history - Discoveries and Inventions - being altered with the intentional result being to actually alter history to the point that the credit for these inventions and discoveries is historically stolen, to be given to someone who actually never did anything near what they are credited with. It was the Method-of-Operation for this Warren clan seven decades ago, and it has not changed since then, just increased exponentially. In 1996 - when it is now claimed on the website of "The Sterling Hill Mining Museum" that the idea of making a 'Museum of Fluorescence' dawned upon them - even the simple idea of making a "Warren Museum of World Class Minerals" wasn't established yet - let alone a "Warren Museum of Fluorescence," and the wall through which the Warren Museum would be established in wasn't even broken through yet, which I photographed for the first time in December, 1997 in "The Sterling Hill Mining Museum." The present director of the Museum, who authored these "facts" on their website, did not even work for the Museum until 1999 when the Museum was dedicated at the end of that year, which was a full year before the Warren Museum officially opened to the public. This is the same director who wrote in 2002 on the "Sterling Hill Museum" website that 'none of us can now remember how the idea for making the Warren Museum came about.' To add to the overwhelming amount of credit awarded by the "Thomas S. Warren Museum of Fluorescence," which opened to the public the year after "Electric Ladyland - the First Museum of Fluorescent Art," about a dozen years ago the director of the Museum (who 'can't remember') came to Amsterdam to buy two of my Fluorescent and Phosphorescent "Thermal Expansion" paintings with the intention of showing something besides just Fluorescent minerals in the "Thomas S. Warren Museum of Fluorescence." About five years ago for what would become my final visit to the "Sterling Hill Mining Museum" and it's annex the "Thomas S. Warren Museum of Fluorescence" (now renamed the "Thomas S. Warren Museum of Geophysics") which opened to the public in the year 2000, I finally could see how they displayed my two Fluorescent "Thermal Expansion" paintings. I wish I would have stayed home! Amongst their many rooms of displays showing everything from the largest Fluorescent geode ever found, labelled and credited to Thomas S. Warren himself, to a rudimentary machine spinning a circular sphere of Mangano Calcite against a Shortwave Ultraviolet lamp to display it's elusive "Flash Phosphorescence," also clearly labelled and credited to Don Newsome who established the "Fluorescent Mineral Society" with Thomas Warren in 1971, I found my two Fluorescent "Thermal Expansion" paintings on display. In a large vertical enclosed display are my two round Fluorescent "Thermal Expansion" paintings mounted in the same display case next to very similar round cut slabs of Fluorescent minerals. As I looked at my two Fluorescent round "Thermal Expansion" paintings mounted right next to round Fluorescent mineral slabs in the "Thomas S. Warren Museum" I casually asked the two Indian visitors next to me looking at my paintings how they liked these "Thermal Expansion" paintings. The couple looked at me very surprised and admitted they had no idea those two round objects were not also Fluorescent minerals, because they were also circular like the cut round Fluorescent mineral specimens mounted along with my Fluorescent paintings in the same display. Not only were my two round Fluorescent "Thermal Expansion" paintings mounted in the same display as other very similar round slabs of Fluorescent minerals, but both of my "Thermal Expansion" paintings were put up in the "Thomas S. Warren Museum of Fluorescence" without a label of any sort, neither crediting myself as the Artist, or even stating that they were not rocks, but pieces of Art, amongst the vast collection in their Museum consisting of almost exclusively just Fluorescent minerals = which was their first intention explained to both Michèle and myself by the original director of the Museum Mr. Richard Hauck in 1997 when they had, again, first broken through the wall of the existing "Sterling Hill Mining Museum" for building the annex of their planned "Thomas S. Warren Museum of World-Class Fluorescent Minerals." The name was changed, as well as the entire concept of the Museum, from the "Thomas S. Warren Museum of World-Class Fluorescent Minerals" to the "Thomas S. Warren Museum of Fluorescence" after both Tom himself and the instigator of the new Warren Museum my friend Dick were generously sent copies by myself in 1998 of one of my first books "Common Items that are Fluorescent," which details the relatively unknown Fluorescence of everything from Green peppers and cucumbers to Fluorescent Frog's eyes = in short, everything that is Fluorescent except well-known "World-Class Fluorescent Minerals."

In the last couple of issues of 'Mineralight News Bulletin' the subject matter has turned from heavy-duty wartime Ultraviolet prospecting for Fluorescent minerals, to much more "civilian" subjects of interest, such as 'Luminescence in Gem Stones,' because for the last issues of this wartime publication, the Second world war had ended. It was now late 1947 for this twelfth issue with the most post-war subject matter yet: 'Ultra-Violet Fluorescence For the Hobbyist.' Pointed out in the last issue of 'Mineralight New Bulletin' that as the Second world war ended in 1945, the subject matter of these 'News Bulletins' also dramatically changed from the wartime subjects such as the prospecting for the Fluorescent mineral Scheelite to be used to harden steel that battleships were constructed out of, and using these Fluorescent Colors and Black lights in warplanes like the "B-17 Flying Fortress" for 'Black-out' night bombing raids over enemy territories. These 'Mineralight News Bulletins' were printed during the height of the Second world war, with issues numbers one through three being published in 1944, issues four through eleven published in 1945, and the last issues numbers ten and eleven were surely being sold at the end of 1945, after the end of the Second world war, with the civilian subject matters of 'Luminescence in Gem Science' and 'Fluorochemistry in

Dyestuffs and Textile Science.' This twelfth issue is a testament to the drop of one hundred percent in the use of Fluorescence and Ultraviolet lamps after the end of World war two, since this is the first issue of 'Mineralight News Bulletin' in the two years since the war had ended, with a publishing date of 1947. So for the first eleven issues in 1944 and 1945 the 'News Bulletin' was printed consistently, and after the war's end in mid-1945, the subject matter suddenly changed to civilian interests, because nobody else was buying Black lights or Fluorescent material. Here we have the proof for this dramatic drop in Fluorescent sales at the end of 1945, because for two solid years this 'Mineralight News Bulletin' was not published by "Ultra-Violet Products, Inc." one of the largest manufacturers of Ultraviolet lights in existence in the 1940s, and when it was finally published again two years later in 1947 with this issue number twelve, the subject matter could not have been any further from the subject matter of the bulk of the first eleven issues, or any closer to the obvious marketing scheme of trying to again interest the public sector in the phenomenon of Fluorescence and Ultraviolet lamps with it's just-as-obvious title 'Ultra-Violet Fluorescence for the Hobbyist.' It always has amazed me how greatly people's attitudes, values, and intent can change just for the acquisition of wealth, or to put it more plainly, 'for the love of money.'

For this ultra-civilian issue of 'Mineralight News Bulletin' author Jack De Ment even begins the paper with a separate quote written by Sir William Osler about the necessity of having a hobby. The paper begins with, predictably, the hobby of collecting Fluorescent and Phosphorescent substances with an Ultraviolet lamp. De Ment characteristically coins a new phrase for this new pastime - the 'Ultraviolet Hobby,' and informs the reader that thousands of Ultraviolet Hobbyists have existed for years. De Ment next adds something to the ancient history of the Black light and Fluorescent paint by including the information that 'numerous' *Preachers* had been giving *Fluorescent Sermons in churches* through the use of Black lights and 'Fluorescent Minerals.' In 1945 this fact was documented by De Ment to have happened in the past, and this Religious use of Black lights and Fluorescent substances from the alter of the church was first known to me through the famous suggestion on the box of antique "Blak-Ray" "Invisible" Fluorescent Chalks with the hard-to-imagine "Use with Black Lights For: CHURCH GROUPS"(!) as well as through the personal memories of Mr. Kenn. of Georgia, a Museum visitor who was in attendance of several "Fluorescent Sermons" of the famous "Fluorescent Preacher Hofmann" when a young boy in Georgia, as I have documented in this book, and other witnesses. Here De Ment adds another fact, stating that '*several*' Preachers were known for Fluorescent Sermons, not just the "Fluorescent Preacher Hofmann," and it was already considered in 1945 as a public Fluorescent phenomenon. De Ment, in fact, uses this phenomenon as a point of possible introduction for the general public into the 'Hobby' of the Black light and Fluorescence. This constitutes evidence from several different independent sources about the phenomenon of Fluorescent Church Sermons being given on the pulpit by Preachers for the very long time period of the 1930s until the last documented Fluorescent Sermon in attendance by Mr. Kennedy of Georgia and given by the famous "Fluorescent Preacher Hofmann" in about 1980. That's nearly half a century of Fluorescent Church Sermons being documented, describing Preachers using Black light with Fluorescent minerals and/or Fluorescent Alter "props" to dramatically accent the Bible passage or similar religious subject that the Preacher was giving the sermon on. Having obviously never heard about such a famous phenomenon after being into the Black light back to 1969, that went on for *half a century* in America, this is a textbook example of social stigmatism and social eradication of documented facts.

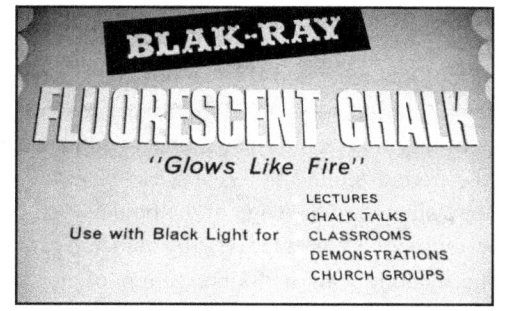

Other possibilities that may have introduced members of the public to Black lights and Fluorescence are suggested by De Ment in the forms of 'Fluorescent Collections' and 'Fluorescent Demonstrations.' The author informs the reader that the 'Ultraviolet Hobby' was very important, and not just a useless hobby, because television, radar, and Fluorescent tubular lights were invented through the study of Ultraviolet and Fluorescence. De Ment also states the fact to hobbyists that many scientists and inventors were initially illuminated by the phenomenon of Fluorescence and the Ultraviolet lamp. De Ment explains that the first of the 'Ultraviolet Hobbyists' were Fluorescent mineral collectors, some of whom were scientists and others were common business men, and that these first Fluorescent mineral collectors were the original people who founded the entire base of Fluorescent research in science and industry. De Ment continues on and reports that it was not unusual in 1945 to go into someone's house and discover a Fluorescent mineral collection that was superior to any of the museum collections of just ten years prior to that period. De Ment adds the fact, still true today, that many amateur Fluorescent mineral collectors can also explain the phenomenon of Fluorescence and the Quantum mechanics involved in causing the miracle of Fluorescent minerals.

The first section in this paper is 'Fluorescent Exhibits,' and it contains extremely valuable information concerning some of the first Fluorescent Mineral Exhibitions ever held in history. De Ment states that already in 1945 there were 'hundreds' of Fluorescent mineral exhibits throughout the United States, which were anything from small private collections viewed under a hand held Ultraviolet lamp, to extravagant exhibitions in people's houses equipped with glass display cases and large professional Ultraviolet lamps. The first private Fluorescent mineral exhibit in the U.S. that De Ment points out is 'The Sutter Fluorescent Show' in the house of Walter Sutter in Tacoma, Washington. De Ment explains that probably no other Fluorescent mineral exhibit had been viewed by more people than 'The Sutter Fluorescent Show' except public museum exhibits. The fact is given that from 1939-1945 'The Sutter Fluorescent Show' was seen by half a million visitors. Walter Sutter divided his show into two separate parts, one part being the extravagant displays of Fluorescent minerals under Ultraviolet lamps in a permanent exhibition in the Sutter home, and the other part of 'The Sutter Fluorescent Show' was a traveling exhibition displaying large Fluorescent mineral specimens under Ultraviolet lamps, reported to total almost five tons. In the early 1941 historically accurate 'Bible' by Dake and De Ment, "Fluorescent Light and it's Applications," there is a full description of 'The Sutter Fluorescent Show' as well as a photograph of one of the most famous Fluorescent mineral display motifs in the U.S. during the period of the 1930s-1950s, the "Fluorescent Fireplace." In Dake and De Ment's 1941 book there is a Black and White photo of the Fluorescent Mineral Fireplace in Walter Sutter's house, which shows a large brick fireplace composed of modules containing slabs of Fluorescent minerals embedded in plaster, that were designed to be interchangeable with similar fireplace Fluorescent mineral modules, allowing the Fluorescent Mineral exhibition of the fireplace to be rearranged at will. These Fluorescent mineral modules simply slid out of their mounting and another Fluorescent mineral module was slid into it's place to change the Fluorescent mineral exhibit. Apparently this was an extravagant private collector's way of showing off his Fluorescent mineral collection in style - and these Fluorescent mineral fireplaces were constructed in a number of collector's houses across America. It was told to me by the director of the Thomas S. Warren Museum that the last surviving Fluorescent mineral fireplace he knew to exist was housed in the inauspicious locality of a pig farm in New Jersey which contained the ruins of an old house(!) I've thought many times that this single fact could exemplify the entire history and present day state of the condition of "Fluorophobia," and if I had not been so disgusted to go onto a pig farm and walk in between the livestock to photograph this last reported surviving Fluorescent mineral fireplace in the late 1990s, I could have used that very photograph on the title page of this chapter: "The Miracle of Fluorescence: 1930s-1950s." Not as famous, but even more extravagant was the style of the period around the 1950s for constructing Fluorescent In-the-ground Swimming Pools, which were made with the casing stone all around the edge of the pool carved from Fluorescent mineral slabs, so at night under Ultraviolet lamps, the entire rim of the pool Fluoresced vividly under Ultraviolet lamps - most likely back then you would have also received a free 'night sunburn' along with the Fluorescent pool display(!)

Another very interesting private Fluorescent mineral collection in the United States during that time of the mid-1940s, was the 'Fluorescent Cave' in Bozeman, Montana put together by Professor H.E. Murdock. De Ment describes this unique exhibition which was in an actual underground cave, where Murdock displayed Fluorescent minerals under Ultraviolet lamps. 'Knott's Berry Farm' in Buena Park, California is next singled out by the author, and described as a combination of a restaurant and a theatre, which housed a public display of Fluorescent minerals under Ultraviolet lamps. Moving from private Fluorescent mineral exhibitions to larger public Fluorescent mineral exhibits in the offices of Ultraviolet lamp manufacturing companies, De Ment describes the 'Smith Collection' put together by Archie Smith of Portland, Oregon as being one of the best Fluorescent mineral exhibitions in the world at that time. The 'Smith Collection' consisted of two rooms filled with 'thousands' of Fluorescent mineral specimens and other Fluorescent substances professionally displayed under Ultraviolet lamps. Next De Ment describes the Fluorescent mineral display of "Ultra-Violet Products, Inc." in Los Angeles. It is a known fact that during that time period the founder of "Ultra-Violet Products, Inc." (who would also go on to found "The Fluorescent Mineral Society" in California many years later in 1971), Thomas S. Warren, had the largest collection of Franklin, New Jersey Fluorescent minerals in the world. This tremendous collection is what is described in this paper by De Ment, who adds that it took Mr. Warren 'years' of collecting to amass this world-class collection. I have several Black and White photographs of the original Thomas S. Warren collection that was housed in the offices of "Ultra-Violet Products, Inc.," which show the incredible scale and completeness of his Fluorescent mineral collection. In one of the known published photographs of this collection, Mr. Warren's secretary is holding an antique U.V. lamp in the middle of this collection, who also was the employee in charge of the Fluorescent mineral collection of Thomas S. Warren. This woman's name was "Sunny" Parker and she was known for collecting only small jewel-like specimens of these Franklin Fluorescent minerals for herself. After she died about a decade ago, her famous collection of small sized 'treasures' of Franklin, New Jersey was sold by the director of the Thomas S. Warren Museum in the Sterling Hill Mining Museum in Ogdensburg, New Jersey. When the director of the Thomas S. Warren

Invisible Ray Transmits Pictures

Ultra-Violet Ray Carries Television Image

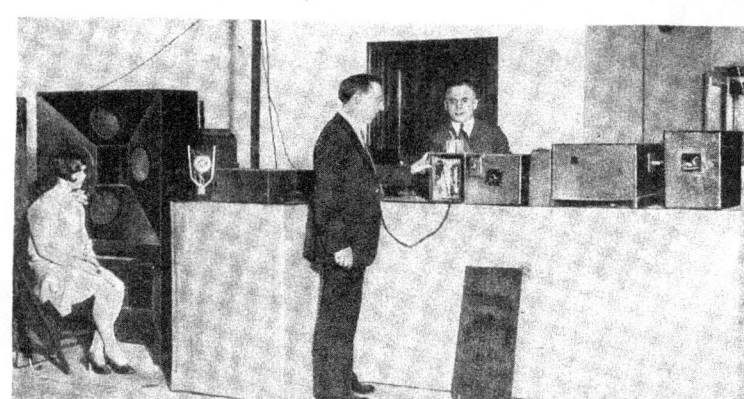

NEW systems of communication are constantly being sought—to relieve the congestion of existing channels and to increase the usefulness of communication apparatus. A demonstration was recently given of such a new system, which used ultra-violet light as a medium over which intelligence could be conveyed.

The ultra-violet ray exhibition made apparent immediate scientific usages and opened a wide experimental field. An example is ship-to-ship communication in time of war, when radio signals and visible light beams would be impractical. The same is true of communication between airplanes. In fact, an invisible ray, for the transmission of

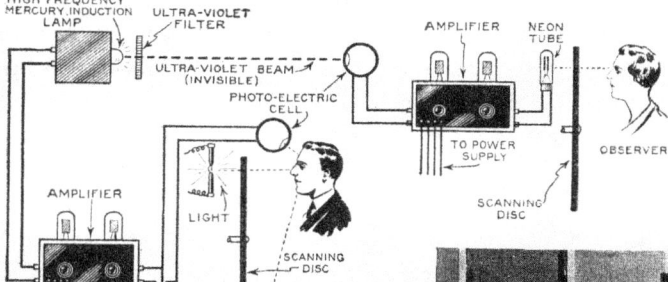

Television transmitter showing person whose image is to be transmitted seated before transmitting screen. Paul A. Kober is at the rear of the apparatus noting its operation.

The complete ultra-violet ray television apparatus as arranged for demonstration at the L. Bamberger & Co. department store in Newark. Dr. Kober is shown examining the mercury induction lamp which makes the phenomena possible.

Diagram of the system used. The picture on the right shows a standard television receiver on which the pictures were received.

sound and pictures, which ray can neither be seen nor heard, has far-reaching potentialities.

The demonstration was held at the L. Bamberger & Co. department store, located in Newark, New Jersey. The casual spectator observed a group of transmitting equipment at one end of the building and a receiving device at the opposite end. A bulb emitted a beam of varying colored light from the transmitting end. The light flickered and changed in intensity in accordance with the words which an official spoke into a near-by microphone connected to an apparatus operating the bulb. The bulb behaved the same way when attached to the television transmitter.

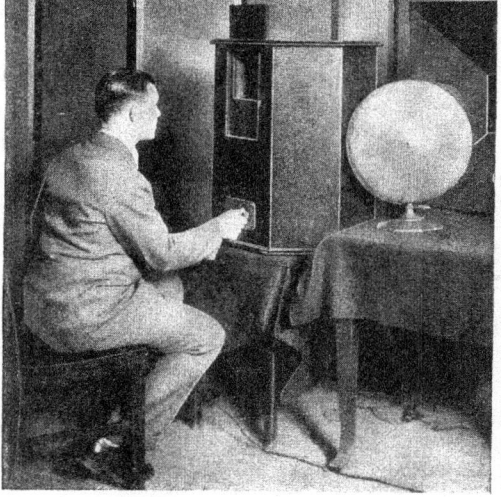

At the opposite end of the floor a loud speaker and head phones delivered the same speech; or when television was being sent, a screen showed the image of the person seated before the television transmitter. Whenever the light or rays were intercepted, reception stopped. Following this, a filter allowing ultra-violet rays to pass through was placed over the bulb. Reception of both sound and television still continued.

The feasibility of the system is due in large measure to the extraordinary qualities of the mercury induction lamp, originally developed for therapeutic work, but recently discovered to have desirable characteristics for light modulation, beyond the highest frequency needed for television. A remarkable feature of this lamp is that the radio frequency which actuates it causes it to darken and glow at least thirty million times in every second.

Museum came to the Museum about five years ago with the intention of buying two of my Fluorescent and Phosphorescent "Thermal Expansion" paintings to exhibit in the Warren Museum as examples of Fluorescent Art, he brought five small absolute jewels from Franklin, New Jersey to trade or sell which had just been acquired from the estate of the late "Sunny" Parker. One of these "Sunny" Parker pieces nearly knocked my eyes out: a four inch (7 cm.) long piece of pure Yellow Esperite encased in a surrounding ridge of Purple Hardystonite, with minuscule veining of Orange Clinohedrite and Red Calcite - a simply gorgeous specimen that is visually much closer to a "painting" than to a 'rock.' Not only is this "Sunny" Parker specimen on display in the "Fluorescent Mineral Viewing Box" in the Museum, but on the back of this specimen is the original hand-written label on very old medical bandage tape by "Sunny" Parker, which is so old that she used the antiquated name for "Esperite," "Calcium Larsenite." In the Black and White photo of "Sunny" Parker just explained, behind her is the largest collection of carved Fluorescent mineral spheres of Franklin, New Jersey minerals ever assembled in one collection. De Ment writes that for some Fluorescent mineral collections the main subject was crystals and minerals under normal lighting, with the addition of a display of Fluorescent minerals under Ultraviolet lamps, but in the more advanced collections the display would be exclusively Fluorescent minerals under Ultraviolet lamps, ranging from just a simple display on a bench or a table under a hand-held Ultraviolet lamp, to displays with a constructed area designed to exhibit Fluorescent Minerals under mounted Ultraviolet lamps. De Ment also passes on the good advice to visit other public or private collections not only to increase your knowledge of the Fluorescent mineral kingdom and techniques of displaying these minerals, but also as a way of increasing your collection of Fluorescent minerals by trading or buying from these other collectors.

'Fluorescent Gems' is the next small section in this paper 'Ultra-Violet Fluorescence for the Hobbyist,' and De Ment explains that some collectors of Fluorescent minerals collect only the pure crystals or 'Gems' of Fluorescent mineral specimens, and these collectors can therefore contain their entire Fluorescent mineral collection in a single suitcase. The obvious size difference is just a part of the advantage of such a 'Fluorescent Gem' collection, but the real advantage of such an exhibition is that all the specimens that are shown are pure examples of the individual Fluorescent minerals, which is a much better teaching aid than large raw stones with crystals just included in the matrix of the specimen. De Ment also includes the possibility of expanding the collector's 'Fluorescent Gem' exhibit by acquiring synthetic gemstones, and even cheap artificial costume jewelry. De Ment gives credit to H.C. Dake, the editor of the "Mineralogist Magazine" that De Ment worked for, and who was co-author of several books with De Ment, for being a 'pioneer' in the field of Fluorescent crystal 'Cabochons,' which are carved and polished crystals.

The third section of this paper describes and lists the essential items that 'Must' be in a Fluorescent display. First De Ment informs the reader that the majority of 'Ultraviolet Hobbyists' prefer Fluorescent minerals to any other Fluorescent substances, and what De Ment lists in this section of the paper is perhaps the first listing of what I call in the Museum "Common Items that are Fluorescent." De Ment refers to these "Common Items that are Fluorescent" as items that 'Must' be in an 'Ultraviolet Hobbyist's' collection:

<u>"Vaseline"</u> or any other Petroleum jelly, or even machine oil, which is stated by the author as Fluorescing brilliant Blue to a Blue-Green because of it's petroleum content.

<u>Fluorescent Plastic</u> such as toys and golf-tees, which De Ment describes a being Red to Red-Orange in the daylight, then Fluorescing vivid Red, and then explains the recognizable "Daylight Fluorescence," in which he describes the '*lifeness*' of the Fluorescent plastic in daylight that makes it recognizable.

<u>"Depression Glass"</u> is next described as 'cheap' glassware made from Bohemia or the commercial glass common in the 1940s. This "Depression Glass" remains today one of the most well known "Common Items that are Fluorescent" in the world, and can easily be found on the internet with full descriptions and photographs of this Green glass from the 1930s era in the White light, and in the Black light vividly Fluorescing. De Ment names 'Bohemia' glass as exhibiting these qualities, but the word 'cheap' does not fit this glass described, because before the 1930s American "Depression Glass" similarly Fluorescent Green glass called "Vaseline Glass" was made in Paris during the second half of the Nineteenth century, but the very first famous Fluorescent Green glass was manufactured in Bohemia around the 1730s, which makes it three-hundred years old, and even in the 1940s anything but 'cheap.' The only examples I've ever seen of this 1700s Bohemian Fluorescent Green glass is on the website "Virtual Glass Museum" from New Zealand. De Ment explains that this Green Fluorescent "Depression Glass" contained a trace of Uranium which caused the bright Green or Yellowish Fluorescence, but as I've stated in this book already, "Depression Glass" does not contain any pure Uranium at all, with the Fluorescent activator in the "Depression Glass" being 'Uranyl,' which is one atom of Uranium combined with one atom of Oxygen creating a new molecule which has similar Fluorescent abilities of Uranium, but just a minuscule trace of radioactivity, similar to old fashioned Color televisions, bananas, and our own bodies!

Glassware is listed separately from "Depression Glass" and is described as being capable of Fluorescing almost any Color, and included in this section are 'spectacles' (eyeglasses) which invariably Fluoresce Blue. What De Ment did not realize yet in 1945 was that *all* glass is Fluorescent, without an exception, but most glass does not Fluoresce with the extravagant intensity of "Depression Glass." First of all, virtually all glassware made before the 1860s is highly Fluorescent under a Black light because of the chemical mixture used by glass manufacturers, which was changed during the period of the 1860s. Aside form vividly Fluorescing 'display' glass, every single piece of glass that is manufactured through the traditional method of melting sand (Silica) is more Fluorescent on one side of the glass than the other. Since the glass is manufactured in horizontal sheets called 'floats,' the heavier microscopic particles of Silica sink to the bottom of this glass 'float' and the lighter particles remain on the top of this float, so when assembling any of the glass display cases in the Museum, as I've stated before, every single sheet of glass must be tested in the dark with an Ultraviolet lamp to determine which side of the glass is more highly Fluorescent, and then when putting together these glass display cases in the Museum, the more Fluorescent side of the glass is put on the outside of the display cases, so when Ultraviolet lamps are turned on inside these Fluorescent mineral display cases the glass has much less of a Fluorescent reaction. To realize the Fluorescence and opacity of glass under Shortwave Ultraviolet, all that has to be done is to turn on a Shortwave Ultraviolet lamp and point it at a window pane. In "Fluorescent Light and It's Applications" by Dake and DeMent of 1941, it is stated that one of the first explorations into the Fluorescence of antique glass was done in 1935 by W.D. Quattlebaum. It is documented that Quattlebaum used a Shortwave Ultraviolet lamp to determine that only glass made before 1864 in America had a Blue Fluorescence, because in 1864 the Glass manufacturers of America changed their formulas to include Soda-lime flint instead of the Lead-flint used up until that date. Quattlebaum also established that old "Continental" glass gives off a Yellow-Green Fluorescence, as well as being most probably the first to document the fact that the very old Bohemian glass and modern Slovakian glass Fluoresces Green from the tiny amounts of Uranium contained in the sand used to make the glass. It is further documented in Dake and DeMent's book that almost all glass made from between 1700 and 1800 in England Fluoresces Blue, as well as the fore-mentioned American glass before 1864, especially the American glass made in New England and Pittsburgh between 1800 and 1864. Before Quattlebaum's experiments, W.B. Lester in 1931 discovered that with Ultraviolet, the difference between glass Colored with Manganese and glass Colored with Selenium could be easily seen, and in 1934 M. Guillott investigated the Fluorescence of iridescent glass.

Material is the next Fluorescent substance included in De Ment's list, and the Fluorescent materials 'Rayon' and 'Calico cloth' are singled out by the author. Antique material is also mentioned as another source of "Common Items that are Fluorescent." This was just at the cusp of the era that did not know of the social phenomenon of "Fluorescent T-shirts," because in 1945 Fluorescent Optical Dyes to make washed clothing "Whiter-Than-White" was not yet used in clothing manufacturing.

Luminous Watch Dials are most probably the 'healthiest' "Common Item that is Fluorescent" in this entire paper by De Ment, because in 1945 "Radium" clocks and wrist watches were still popular and most probably still manufactured in remote areas of the world. As I've mentioned before in this book, the "Radium Girls" were eight hundred extremely unfortunate women who all died of cancer after working in the "Luminous Watch Dial Company" in East Orange, New Jersey, one of the earliest causes of the Social Stigma of "Fluorophobia." De Ment sadistically advises that if these old clocks with luminous dials are thrown away, the collector could save just the healthy luminous dial with numbers that would Fluoresce very vividly in shades from Green to Blue. These deadly "Radium" watch dials are suggested by De Ment to be used in a Fluorescent collection as an example of the original Fluorescent Airplane dials used in the Second world war.

'Old Teeth' are another grizzly "Common Items that are Fluorescent" included as 'musts' in a Fluorescent Mineral display, and the author also includes animal teeth in this category. I have personally seen that a common house cat's teeth are much more Fluorescent than my own teeth under the same Black lights in the same conditions. The author suggests polishing old teeth and exhibiting them along side of old porcelain false teeth to display the big difference in Fluorescence. Now we again experience "Social Regression" as De Ment explains that 'modern' false teeth were manufactured with deliberate Yellowish Fluorescence to have a reaction of a similar luminescence as natural teeth. "What?" For over twenty years I've been amused by visitors to the Gallery with highly polished very expensive modern false teeth, which are absolutely non-Fluorescent, and when these visitors smile under the Black lights it looks like they had a few of their teeth knocked out. In June, 2010 one of my molars fell out and Michèle said to me, "Why don't you put it in the Museum?" After looking at her intensely, she added that it was heart-shaped. My tooth went in the Museum display case "Common Items that are Fluorescent" that day.

Leather is listed by the author as being Fluorescent through the 'Tannins' used to "tan" (stain) the raw leather.

"Quinine" is another of the "Common Items that are Fluorescent" very well known by most members of the public, simply because in many bars there are Black lights, and when someone orders a mixed drink that contains "Schweppes" Tonic water the drink is vivid Fluorescent Blue. Most people that have experienced this think that the gin in 'Gin and Tonic' is the

Fluorescent part of the drink, but similar to all miserable alcohol, gin doesn't Fluoresce, it is the Quinine water that is Fluorescing a brilliant Blue. Some of the very first scientists to experiment with Fluorescence and the Ultraviolet contained in sunlight during the 1700s, Herschel and then Brewster, excited solutions of Quinine water with rays of sunlight and were amazed to see the production of brilliant Fluorescent Colors. De Ment curiously does not mention tonic Water, but suggests melting 'cold tablets' from the medicine box in water and adding a few drops of battery acid to produce a brilliant Blue Fluorescent mixture. Sounds delicious.

<u>Fluorescent Tubular Lamps</u> that are old and don't light up anymore are all filled with Fluorescent powdered phosphors that can be emptied out of the glass tube of the lamp and exhibited under Black light, or as the author also suggests, the Fluorescent lamp can be exhibited with one of it's ends removed, and when a "Mineralight" is placed over the opened end of the Fluorescent lamp, the entire lamp will light up like it was plugged in.

<u>Moth Balls</u> are listed by De Ment as Fluorescing a brilliant Blue or Purple due to the Naphthalene content of the Moth Balls.

<u>Wax</u> is a very common item, and for Fluorescent Waxes, the author lists beeswax, carnauba, paraffin, as well as other greases, cleaning products, polishing products, and floor polish as being highly Fluorescent. In particular paraffin is described as having a vivid Blue Fluorescence.

<u>X-Ray Screens</u> whether old or new, the X-Ray Screens of De Ment's era had a powder coating on them that could be removed and exhibited with a brilliant Fluorescence.

The fourth section of this paper concentrates on the phenomenon of 'Fluorescent Fireplaces' that were popular in the United States during the entire period of "The Miracle of Fluorescence: 1930s-1950s." As I have mentioned before "In-the-ground" Swimming Pools fifty years ago were fitted with Fluorescent mineral slabs as their 'casing stones' around the pool's edge to produce a breath-taking display at night under "Mineralights" (and a free sunburn as well). Here De Ment adds to the Fluorescent fireplace other construction suggestions, such a barbecue pits, aquariums, and fish ponds. De Ment eloquently words the defining point behind these Fluorescent fireplaces stating that Fluorescent Color under Ultraviolet lamps is incomparable to ordinary Colors under normal lighting. De Ment reveals that Fluorescent fireplaces were the most popular household construction using Fluorescent minerals at that time, and adds that although the majority of these Fluorescent fireplaces were built in people's homes, these Fluorescent fireplaces would also be beautiful installations in Movie theaters or nightclubs.

The different methods of constructing Fluorescent Fireplaces are mentioned by De Ment, but the technique of De Ment's college, the editor of "The Mineralogist" magazine H.C. Dake, is considered by the author to be the best design. H.C. Dake's technique for constructing Fluorescent fireplaces began with the sawing of large Fluorescent mineral specimens into tile-like slabs of a suggested quarter inch (half cm) thickness, and into any shape, and although the reader is informed that the common square and rectangular shapes were often used, the shapes of the Fluorescent mineral slabs were up to the builder. The Fluorescent minerals most often used for these slabs are listed, and include the famous New Jersey Willemite and Calcite, 'Wernerite' (called "Scapolite" in modern times), 'Uraniferous silica' (called 'Opalite' or 'raw Opal' today), and Sphalerite. After these Fluorescent mineral slabs have been sawed into quarter inch thickness, a wooden frame is constructed with the suggested size of 13 x 13 x .5" deep (33 x 33 x 1.3 cm deep). This wooden frame is put on a sheet of glass, the flat Fluorescent mineral slabs are positioned in place with the front sides towards the glass, and finally the framework with the Fluorescent mineral slab is filled to the top with Plaster of Paris. When the plaster had dried, the entire unit was taken off the sheet of glass, which is the front side of the slab and the side that would be visible in the finished Fluorescent fireplace construction. Dake recommended that these sawed Fluorescent mineral slabs should not be thicker than three-quarters of an inch. This technique produces a finished Fluorescent fireplace slab that will be one module in it's finished construction, with the flat sawed face of the Fluorescent mineral presented under Ultraviolet lamps in the finished Fluorescent fireplace. De Ment explains that the contrast created by the sawed stone sections of Fluorescent minerals against the base of White plaster could be dramatically increased if Black pigment was added to the plaster, or if 'dead-Black show-card' (flat Black) paint was applied to the dried White plaster surrounding the sawed Fluorescent mineral faces. Alternatively, the author suggests that if the builder did not want to saw the Fluorescent minerals into flat slabs, these raw pieces of Fluorescent minerals could also be used to make Fluorescent Fireplaces by just cementing them into place to create the structure of the Fireplace, in the same manner of construction that ordinary non-Fluorescent stones would be used to build a traditional Fireplace.

'Other Ornamental Mineral Work' follows the fourth section of this paper, and here De Ment suggests using Fluorescent minerals to create household items, such as vivid paperweights, bookends, and penholders. As close as this scientist De Ment comes to "Art" is the advice to create what were effectively Fluorescent Mineral Mosaics out of Plaster of Paris and scraps of Fluorescent Minerals. The author's instructions are to simply fill up a wooden framework with 'Plaster of

Paris' and then with the plaster made into a smooth surface, small scrap pieces of Fluorescent minerals are set into the wet plaster's surface to produce the suggested pictures, portraits, or landscapes that possessed a 'double-effect,' which were seen as different images in the White light, and under the Ultraviolet lamp. Getting slightly and uncharacteristically obscure, De Ment continues on by suggesting to use the scraps of small pieces of Fluorescent minerals in flower pots, as mosaic in vases and other pottery, as mosaic in floor work, or just in the use of what he calls 'Fluorescent boxes,' which were simply boxes filled with scraps of Fluorescent minerals that could be used just as decoration or in demonstration.

'Fluorescent Wood' is the next "Common Item" that is described by De Ment, who suggests using one of several species of Wood known to Fluoresce vividly for constructing into decorative household items. De Ment states that several species of trees produce wood that is vividly Fluorescent and which could be used to create beautiful Fluorescent objects, but doesn't mention the fact that all wood is Fluorescent. The tree made of the most famous Fluorescent wood is the "Black Locust," a fact which has been known since De Ment's time, and which Fluoresces with a very rare vivid Yellowish Color, rare in the tree kingdom as the majority of all wood Fluoresces the same common organic Fluorescent Color as your fingernails: Beige with a tint of Blue.

The Trees that produce the best Fluorescent Wood are listed by De Ment as Black Locust, Oregon Grape root, and Sumac, but in the years of the late 1940s and the 1950s this list would be greatly expanded by Fluorescent Wood collectors. In several other antique books on the phenomenon of Fluorescence I have read in the past that during the 1940s and 1950s there were some Fluorescent collectors in America that exclusively collected Fluorescent trees. The author next makes the brilliant suggestion of using a Fluorescent wood like Black Locust to construct the wooden frameworks for the Fluorescent mineral fireplace modules, or even to turn this wood on a lathe to create such Fluorescent objects as candle holders. The suggestions of cabinets, tables, and other household furniture being constructed from Fluorescent wood like Black Locust are presented by De Ment, who adds the important instruction that the one thing not to forget is that no varnish or clear lacquers could be used to protect the raw wood, because the added layer of varnish would act as a "U.V. Block" and the finished Fluorescent wood furniture would not Fluoresce.

The last section of this civilian 'Mineralight News Bulletin' is 'What you can make with Fluorescein,' which is still today used in medicine, industry, security, and is still today known as one of the most powerful and most concentrated Fluorescent substances in existence. If you get pure Fluorescein on your fingers they will Fluoresce brilliant Yellow-Green for up to three months with no way to get it off. De Ment begins by explaining that for 'Ultraviolet Hobbyists' who are searching for a substance that is greatly concentrated and which will still Fluoresce when highly diluted, Fluorescein is both intensely concentrated and relatively low priced, putting it in reach of 'Ultraviolet Hobbyists.' The author explains that the 'Sodium salt' 'Uranine' in the Fluorescein was the active Fluorescent chemical, which Fluoresces brilliant Yellow or Yellow-Green under a Black light, and which is capable of Fluorescing as a solution with only one part Fluorescein in fifty million parts of water, which sounds amazing, but more contemporary estimates establish the sensitivity of Fluorescein to be one part in sixty-four million parts of water. This means that just one drop of Fluorescein in a literal pond of water would be detectable as producing a visible Yellow-Green Fluorescence under a Black light. De Ment expands on the idea and suggests to the reader that the pond in their backyards or their large aquariums could take on a new highly Fluorescent life by adding only a drop or two of Fluorescein. I often joke with visitors during the "Common Items that are Fluorescent" demonstration in the Museum that one bottle of Fluorescein in a person's swimming pool will cause the bathers to Fluoresce vividly in Yellow-Green whenever entering a club with a Black light for a quarter of a year! If you put a drop in each eye, then they will also Fluoresce for three months! Since the beginning of the Twenty-first century Fluorescein has been used for security in several parts of the world. If a criminal breaks into a store Fluorescein is automatically sprayed onto them, which can be detected by the police with its bright Fluorescence on the skin for up to three months. This is called "DNA Spray" in Amsterdam and "Smart Water" in London. De Ment informs the reader that Fluorescein could be bought from chemical suppliers or from "Ultra-Violet Products, Inc.," and also could alternatively be simply made by the reader. The author instructs the reader to just add a little 'washing soda' or 'lye' to "Mecurichrome" and they would create a substance that was very similar to Fluorescein, having a brilliant Fluorescent reaction under Ultraviolet lamps equal to the intensity of Fluorescein, but differed in the fact that this chemical pseudo-Fluorescein could not be used on living animals or people.

In true 'Ultraviolet Hobbyist' tradition, this paper closes with 'Ultraviolet Tricks' to be performed with Black lights and Fluorescein. The first 'Trick' with Fluorescein is to take one end of a Fluorescent lamp's glass tube off and wash out the powder coating the inside of the glass tube. Next this glass tube is filled with water and a few drops of Fluorescein is added to the top surface of the water, so that the viewers are treated to the sight of vividly Fluorescing Green clouds of Fluorescein gently floating to the bottom of the glass tube. The second 'Ultraviolet Trick' is a technique used by the Dutch here in Holland for many years, but with non-Fluorescent dyes such as Turquoise in White Tulips. The author explains that if a bouquet of cut fresh White Flowers, such as 'Gardenias' are placed into a jar with a Fluorescein solution, the Flowers will absorb this Fluorescein solution into their stems, and when put under a Black light this formerly pure White bouquet will Fluoresce a vivid Green! De Ment also suggests using similar Fluorescent dyes, such a Red Rhodamine to create different Colored 'natural' Fluorescent flower bouquets. The third 'Trick' is very similar, but the flowers are simply floated in a solution of Fluorescein, which would make a great contrast under the U.V. lamp with the vivid Fluorescence of the Fluorescein contrasting with the fact presented by De Ment in 1947 that 'some Flowers' Fluoresce under the "Mineralight." In actuality, *all* Flowers Fluoresce under Longwave Ultraviolet Black lights, which comes through the Ozone Layer and is present in sunlight reaching the surface of the Earth - especially the flower's pollen, which is vividly Fluorescent and attracts Bees, who have the added ability of being able to see Ultraviolet in sunlight as visible light and another visible Color. These points are expanded in the book I completely in 2008, "Fluorescent Flowers," which is the first book created on the subject of Fluorescent flowers, and which contains a list of the individual Fluorescent reactions of two hundred and eighty-one flowers.

The fourth 'Ultraviolet Trick' is the funkiest one of all, as the author instructs to make "Jello" with the addition of Fluorescein in the water! The last 'Trick' has instructions to add some Colorless oil to ground Fluorescein powder, and then to put one drop of this mixture into a large pan of water. Since the oil will not mix with the water, the drop of Fluorescein mixed with oil will spread out into a large area almost covering the surface of the pan of water creating a large Fluorescent Green area under the Black light that seems to expand before the eyes of the viewers.

The conclusion to this paper is a section in which De Ment compares the availability and low prices of Fluorescent substances and Ultraviolet lamps in 1947 to 'years gone by.' This closing section is called 'Other Ultraviolet Experiments' and explains that in 1947 commercially produced Fluorescent and Phosphorescent substances were easily obtainable by the average person, both in availability and price range, giving the example of luminescent substances available at that time for one dollar a pound. De Ment next states some very rarely disclosed secrets concerning the industry of Fluorescent and Phosphorescent pigments [which are called "Synthetic Phosphors"], as he reveals that the Synthetic 'phosphors' are in actuality, only 'artificially made' Fluorescent minerals. Some references state that Robert Switzer's invention of Fluorescent paint in 1933 came about through experiments in which he crushed up Fluorescent minerals and mixed them with wood varnish and "Murine" in the family bathtub. De Ment relates the fact to the readers that these Synthetic Phosphors and other Fluorescent dyes and chemicals were highly concentrated and were therefore an inexpensive way of creating large areas of Fluorescence. Closing the paper De Ment advises all 'Ultraviolet Hobbyists' to have the substances Fluorescein, Sulfide phosphors, Rhodamine, and Eosine, as well as the Organic Fluorescent substance Anthracene in their collections to experiment with.

The last paper in this "Ultra-Violet Products, Inc." series called 'Mineralight News Bulletins' is number thirteen, which is entitled 'The Shortwave Ultra-Violet Lamp in Scheelite Prospecting.' This thirteenth paper is unlike the entire first twelve 'Mineralight Mews Bulletins' by the very fact that the title 'Mineralight News Bulletin' is missing form the header of the paper. The title of this thirteenth paper is simply 'Fluorescent Analysis with Ultra-Violet Rays' which was the subtitle of the first twelve papers. The top header is also printed in Violet, the design is more simplified without the antique illustration of the "Mineralight" lamp as in the first twelve issues, and the copyright date is also missing, but since number twelve was published in 1947 and this entire series of papers was reissued starting in 1952 with a different Color, size, and title design, the booklet being folded to create 4 separate pages, whereas the first series was normal letter size paper stapled together with a title header that was dark Purple and contained a Black and White photograph of the "Mineralight," I date this paper to be from about 1950 or 1951. The reason for my estimate is that in the 'Literature cited' at the end of this thirteenth paper, there is a dated reference from 1950, and furthermore, since the second reissuing of this entire series was begun in 1952, it would have to be from the end of 1950 to the end of 1951. Since I could find and buy this series of 'Mineralight News Bulletins' from two separate people, and neither of the two series went past the undated thirteenth issue, I assume this issue was the last in this publication. Another major difference in this thirteenth issue is that the author of the first twelve issues, Jack De Ment, did not write this paper. This thirteenth paper is such a departure from the style of the first twelve De Ment papers that it can only be considered as part of that series because of it's title, and it's inclusion in this "Ultra-Violet Products, Inc." "Mineralight" folder. The style of writing in this thirteenth paper is typical of the president of this corporation Mr. Thomas S. Warren, as well as the title of this paper going back in time almost a full decade to the first 'Golden Age' of the Ultraviolet lamp, from 1938 to 1943 when Thomas S. Warren went to Washington D.C. to ask permission to use wartime forbidden Mercury to produce the first portable battery-operated Shortwave Ultraviolet lamp, the "M-12," which was designed exclusively for prospecting for Scheelite in the United States which contains Tungsten to harden Steel, and which America was buying from China before the outbreak of the Second world war. Between 1938 and 1943 with Thomas Warren's lamp, the "M-12," America became independent in Scheelite production. So this thirteenth paper is both a testament to the first 'Golden Age' of the Ultraviolet lamp in the 1930s and 1940s wartime era, and also a testament to a final attempt to raise business in desperation during the post-World war two era when the sales of Ultraviolet lamps and Fluorescent products dropped to zero. Very typical of the hard-sell mentality of Thomas S. Warren, this thirteenth paper is also a final attempt to reinspire the public with the possibility of making money by finding Fluorescent Scheelite ore. But it was too late - the Second world war was over and people wanted to forget the past decade of hell forever - including all things that reminded them of that dismal period, which included the new 'magic' technology of the Black light and Fluorescence used extensively by the military during World war two. Many Ultraviolet companies went bankrupt after the end of the Second world war, and only the major companies managed to survive until the present day, including the "Switzer Brothers" which became "Conti-Glo" and then finally "Day-Glo" corporation, "Ultra-Violet Products, Inc." which is still named "Ultraviolet Products, Inc.," and "Shannon Luminous Products, Inc."

This thirteenth paper - the 'last-ditch attempt' to raise business in the post-war late 1940s and early 1950s era - focused specifically on the actual starting point of the Ultraviolet revolution of the Second world war, 'Scheelite Prospecting,' in a failed attempt to create a new beginning. The paper begins with a Thomas Warren hard-sell sentence informing the reader that over one hundred million dollars of Scheelite was found using the 'magic' "Mineralight." The reader is also informed that this "Mineralight" was used to prospect for Scheelite in many countries besides the United States, as this paper includes the North and South Poles, South America, Mexico, Canada, China, Australia, Africa, and even the East Indies - virtually the entire world. This paper also informs the reader that both the valuable ores of Zirconium and 'Zinc Mercury' were also prospected for with this "Mineralight." The Ultraviolet energy from the "Mineralight" is called 'black light rays' in this paper even though it is coming from a Shortwave lamp, making it clear that all wavelengths of Ultraviolet energy were known as 'black light rays' during this era. There is a short description of Ultraviolet energy, and then begins the first section of the paper 'Prospecting for Scheelite' which starts by informing the reader of how essential it was to use a "Mineralight" Shortwave Ultraviolet lamp to prospect for Scheelite. Scheelite doesn't Fluoresce under a Longwave Ultraviolet Black light. It is next explained that Scheelite was often found in contact with 'Limestone granite,' and that in the offices of "Ultra-Violet Products, Inc." there were four hundred specimens of Scheelite that were used to teach about the different minerals that Scheelite could be found in contact with. These minerals that Scheelite is found in contact with are listed as Limestone, then of course Molybendum, and finally Garnet, Quartz, and Granite as the major ores. Other Ores that Scheelite could be found in contact with are also listed, and consist of Epidote, Gold, Copper, Silver, Gneiss, Magnetite, and Iron.

To find Scheelite with a "Mineralight" the reader is instructed to look for a brilliant light Blue Fluorescence that is the signatory Color of pure Scheelite. When impurities such a Molybendum are present in the Scheelite sample, the Fluorescent Color will turn to a Yellow-Beige, and with higher amounts of Molybendum the Fluorescence will become Yellow-Brown. A very rare artifact from the late 1930s and 1940s era is an "Ultra-Violet Products, Inc." Scheelite Prospecting Card to compare the Fluorescent Color of samples found in the field with different standard Fluorescent Colors of Scheelite in a pure state and then with different amounts of impurities present. This artifact, like similar artifacts that are directly connected with the Second world war, is nearly impossible to find anymore, and even the manufacturer of the Scheelite Prospecting Card, Mr. Thomas S. Warren himself did not have one anymore in the 1990s to send to me and donate to the Museum collection. The paper continues and informs the reader that the pure state of 'Calcium tungstate' will Fluoresce a vivid light Blue, with sharp crystals that are Whitish to 'Orange-grey' in daylight. Small crystals of Scheelite often form independently and are many times found scattered inside the matrix of host rocks.

The second section of this paper is dedicated to the most well known and undesirable common impurity in Scheelite, and is entitled 'Fluorescent Light Used in Molybendum Assay.' This part of the paper looks as if it was written a decade before this paper was printed, during the full 'Golden Age' of Scheelite prospecting for the Second world war. The first sentence informs the reader that a 'new' technique had just been developed by the U.S. Geological Survey that would help in the 'war production program' of minerals, when this paper was printed several years after the war ended. The paper informs the reader that Scheelite prospecting was begun by the U.S. Geological Survey in 1938, and throughout the history of this prospecting much Scheelite ore containing the impurity Molybendum had been discovered.

This paper's third part is 'There are Several Tungsten Ores,' which begins with the information that there were fourteen Tungsten ores known in the late 1940s, but only four of those ores were valuable as commercial Tungsten ores. Scheelite, Wolframite, Ferberite, and Hubnerite are listed as the four important commercial ores mined in the 1940s, with Scheelite and Wolframite being the most important of the world's Tungsten ores. In Colorado the Tungsten ore Ferberite was mined, and the ore Hubnerite was the rarest of the four important Tungsten ores to be found in mines.

Scheelite is examined in detail in the fourth section of this paper 'Characteristics of Scheelite.' The information is presented that Scheelite's chemical name is Calcium tungstate (Ca WO_4), and the purest Scheelite contains 80.6 percent of the main Tungsten ore WO_2. In California this was the main source of Tungsten and in it's natural state it appears pure White, or Yellow-White, but can also be light Yellow, Green, Red, and Brown. The Color of Scheelite's "streak" is White, it has a 'greasy' texture and a medium "hardness" of 4.5 - 5.0. All of these are interesting scientific facts, but the main determining characteristic of Scheelite with concerns to the Scheelite prospector reading this paper is Scheelite's brilliant light Blue Fluorescence under a Shortwave Ultraviolet lamp. This is so important a point that the entire sentence is italicized in the paper.

'Uses of Tungsten' is the following section of this paper, directly stating that Tungsten was one of the most important metals needed for the manufacturing of Steel. The reader is informed that the electrical filaments in light bulbs ('incandescent electrical lamps') and inside of 'radio tubes' were also produced from Tungsten. Another major use of Tungsten during the era of this paper was for 'high-speed' steel used to produce cutting tools that would experience very hot temperatures during their use and remain extremely hard. The technical information is given on the actual quantities of metals used as a standard during the era, being '18-4-1,' which was produced with eighteen percent of Tungsten, four percent Chromium, one percent Vanadium, plus less than one percent of Carbon. Being the post-World war two era, the uses for this 'high-speed' steel were listed as 'Armour plating' and 'Armour piercing' steel, along with the less deadly civilian knife blades, razors, and hacksaws. The 'high tech' Tungsten product of the late 1940s was called 'Cemented Tungsten Carbide,' and the reader is told that this constituted the 'hardest' material that was used during that period which was artificial. The very high melting point of Tungsten given as 3,800 degrees centigrade made the use of the metal perfect for the high temperature of light bulb filaments and vacuum tubes in radios (televisions were still a relatively rare and obscure possession during the 1940s), along with the additional uses in production of paints and dyes, X-ray photography, and also as a pigment in the production of porcelain and dyed paper.

The reader is next given facts on the 'Sources of Ultraviolet' that were available, especially in relation to the prospecting of Scheelite, the subject matter of this paper. Again, the Ultraviolet rays that come from the Sun are referred to as invisible 'black light.' Very interestingly, this paper from the late 1940s explains to the reader that outside of the visible light of the spectrum there was invisible 'Infrared' energy longer than visible red, and that on the opposite end of the spectrum, the invisible energy was called 'Ultra-Violet,' which is explained as having no heating action, but possesses the chemical 'actinic effect' of tanning the skin and forming Vitamin D. There is no mention of all the other wavelengths of energy that make up the "Electromagnetic spectrum," such as Gamma rays, Radio waves, etc. As evidence to how little was known even on the source of Ultraviolet during the late 1940s, Ultraviolet energy was separated into only Shortwave Ultraviolet and Longwave Ultraviolet, while today we recognize "Extreme" or "Vacuum" Ultraviolet, Shortwave, Middlewave, and then Longwave Ultraviolet. The two 'classes' of Ultraviolet presented here in this late 1940s professional paper were 'Short Ultraviolet radiations' that were from 13.6 to 300 nanometers, and were 'not found' in sunlight, but was the energy needed to cause Scheelite to brilliantly Fluoresce light Blue. The production of Vitamin D and sunburning by this 'Short' Ultraviolet energy was termed 'bactericidal' in this paper. The other division given in the Ultraviolet spectrum in this paper was the 'Long Ultraviolet radiations,' which were stated as being between 300 and 400 nanometers. Today the information presented in this paper as scientific fact concerning the Ultraviolet spectrum is mostly incorrect and very primitive in both it's scope and projection. First of all, Ultraviolet energy is not recognized today as beginning at 13.6 nanometers, but at 20 nanometers, with X-rays being in the spectrum between .10 and 20 nanometers, and the extremely strong Ultraviolet energy of this region between 20 and 250 nanometers is not called Shortwave Ultraviolet, but "Extreme" or "Vacuum" Ultraviolet. The name "Vacuum" Ultraviolet is precise because this very strong Ultraviolet can only exist in the vacuum of space, and when coming from the Sun and then entering the top of Earth's atmosphere the Vacuum Ultraviolet collides with the Oxygen molecules in the upper atmosphere and frees the Oxygen atoms to recombine into "Ozone," which was not known during the publication of this paper in the late 1940s, along with the fact that the Ozone layer at the top of the Earth's atmosphere is the "U.V. Filter" for the Earth, not allowing dangerous Shortwave Ultraviolet energy to reach the surface of the Earth.

The only Ultraviolet energy that is called Shortwave Ultraviolet today is referring to the invisible energy between 250 and 300 nanometers. This is the harmful Shortwave Ultraviolet that is blocked from coming to the surface of the Earth by the Ozone layer. Here the wonder of Nature in all it's infinite intricacies can be realized: one energy level creating a filter for life against another level of it's own energy. This Shortwave energy is still remembered today for it's use as a notorious "Miracle Health Cure" for decades as a 'craze' in many countries from the 1920s up until the danger was discovered in the same general time era as the publication of this professional paper, an era already discussed in this book as being one of the 'creators' of the Social Stigma of "Fluorophobia." The Shortwave Ultraviolet lamp, such as the "Mineralight," produces energy that is almost exactly 254 nanometers. Between 300 and 350 nanometers is today recognized as "Middlewave Ultraviolet" most commonly used in suntan salons around the world. As the Shortwave Ultraviolet causes sunburn, which occurs when the skin is exposed to under 310 nanometers of Ultraviolet, the Middlewave U.V. is the energy that causes the skin to tan.

The weakest and the only Harmless Ultraviolet energy is between 350 and 400 nanometers and is still today called harmless Longwave Ultraviolet. The most common Ultraviolet source, known as the "Black light," which has been sold for close to the past hundred years, emits only this Longwave Ultraviolet energy. These Black lights emit 366 nanometers, which causes Fluorescent and Phosphorescent paint, inks, dyes, and even organic compounds to produce such intense Color it can make your eyes tear.

The closing section of this paper is an explanation about "Activators," the minuscule amount of Impurity that must be present in Fluorescent minerals at precise quantities to cause the rock to Fluoresce - to cause vivid Colors to be emitted from Grey rocks. In the late 1940s these activators were also called 'Activating agents,' and the paper explains that the pure state of the mineral Calcite will not Fluoresce under an Ultraviolet lamp, but with a tiny amount of an impurity present in the Calcite it will Fluoresce bright Red. It is further explained that the amount of this impurity Manganese will also determine the intensity of the Red Fluorescence of Calcite. It is well stated in the paper, although the amounts were overstated, that the precise amount of impurity in the mineral is crucial in enabling the mineral to give off visible light. The example is also given with Uranium acting as an activator, and it is properly explained that this Uranium-based activation will always cause the emission of Green light. What was obviously not known at the time of this paper's publication is that there are different classifications of Fluorescent activators, not just the activation of Fluorescence caused by impurities in a substance, which is known today as "Impurity Activation" and is the most common cause of mineral Fluorescence, but not the only cause of Fluorescence in minerals. The first example in this paper, Calcite with the impurity Manganese, is a typical Fluorescent mineral and does in fact, like most Fluorescent minerals, Fluoresce through the mechanics of "Impurity Activation," but the second example in this same paper is one of the most well known examples of "Intrinsic Activation," the Green Fluorescence of Uranium-based Fluorescent minerals. This second major classification of Fluorescent mineral activation is termed "Intrinsic Activation" because the activator is not merely an impurity in the mineral, but an essential elementary particle in the physical makeup of the rock itself. I explain it in the Museum by the fact that if it was theoretically possible to remove the impurity from Fluorescent minerals that emit light through "Impurity Activation," then the mineral itself would be physically the same, but when putting it under an Ultraviolet lamp it would be Black. In contrast, if the activator could be removed from a Fluorescent mineral that is "Intrinsically Activated," the mineral itself would be destroyed, because the removed activator is a necessary component in the crystal lattice of the Intrinsically activated mineral. A further complication is the extremely complicated third classification of Fluorescent minerals, "Coactivation" or "Dual Activation," in which a Fluorescent mineral needs two different Impurities to enable the mineral to create and emit light under an Ultraviolet lamp. A classic example of this phenomenon is one of the most famous Fluorescent mineral in the world, Franklin, New Jersey Calcite, which would lack the ability to Fluoresce brilliant Orange-Red if it contained only the impurity Manganese, but with the addition of the other impurity Lead in it's composition, the Grey Calcite becomes vivid Orange-red under a Shortwave lamp. This is explained very precisely in a modern day Fluorescence 'Bible,' "The Collector's Book of Fluorescent Minerals" by Manuel Robbins, in which we learn that the Calcite with only the impurity Manganese lacks the ability to absorb the Ultraviolet energy and to then go through the Quantum movement of "Electron Displacement" causing Fluorescence. With the presence of the other impurity Lead, also called in this case a "Sensitizer," the Lead has the ability to absorb the Ultraviolet energy but not to go through "Electron Displacement", so the Lead then transfers the energy to the Manganese atoms, which do have the ability to go through "Electron Displacement," and the Orange-Red light is then emitted from the Calcite in this way. Manuel Robbins also explains that the activators Manganese, Uranium-based compounds, and Rare Earth elements are responsible for a large percentage of the Fluorescence known in the entire Fluorescent mineral kingdom. An exquisite experiment is cited by Manuel Robbins in which the minuscule proportions of activators can be better realized. The original experiment was performed by H.W. Leverrenz in 1968, and entails simply placing a few crystals of the mineral "Sylvite" on a glass plate, along with another crystal of "Antimony" placed on another nearby glass plate. Under the Ultraviolet lamp neither of these two crystals Fluoresce. Then comes the 'mind-blowing' part: while still under the Ultraviolet lamp, the two non-Fluorescent crystals on separate glass plates are physically slowly moved close to each other - And then as if looking into the source of magic itself, when the two non-Fluorescent crystals get to about half an inch (1 cm) away from each other, the Sylvite crystals closest to the Antimony on the other glass plate will unbelievably start to Fluoresce Yellow! The amount of Impurity needed to cause Fluorescence is so inconceivably microscopic that the Antimony crystal, being a full centimeter apart from the Sylvite is transferring an invisible amount of an Activator element to the Sylvite crystal *through the air before your Eyes*, and as if in a dream, the non-Fluorescent Sylvite crystal begins to emit it's own Yellow light!

In truthful conclusion, this thirteenth and final 'Fluorescent Analysis with Ultra Violet Rays' paper of this "Ultra-Violet Products, Inc." published series dating from 1943 until either 1950 or 1951, closes with the frank admission that very little was yet known about the causes and Quantum movements involved with the 'new' science of Fluorescent minerals.

"DAY-GLO"- 'IT SAVED HIS LIFE' Advertisement, 1959

In the Museum collection is a full page advertisement from the late 1950s, but it could just as easily been made during the mid-1940s, during the Second world war era. This advertisement is a real time capsule, encapsulating the public awe and the high level of respect that "Day-Go" Fluorescent paint had in society during the era of "The Miracle of Fluorescence: 1930s-1950s." In fact this ad is special because we are witnessing the end of an era here at the time the advertisement was published in the late 1950s. Within less than a decade Fluorescent paint and the very name of the company itself - "Day-Glo" - would become intrinsically associated with the 1960s Movement, and we would never again see an advertisement with a serious Mr. America type saying that these "Day-Glo" Colors had saved anyone's life, but possibly just the contrary. This advertisement is a little hard to believe in this current time period of the Twenty-first century, presently immersed in the advanced stages of the Social Stigma of "Fluorophobia," so that upon seeing this advertisement we are left with a feeling of disbelief. This advertisement is for "Day-Glo" Fluorescent Aviation Safety Paint and the huge headline which fills nearly the top half of this full page ad reads like a joke today, quoting a pilot that claimed that "Day-Glo" Fluorescent paint 'Saved His Life!' There is a strange feeling when reading an ad like this today, or closer to a feeling of suspicion like when someone is playing a trick on you and having a laugh at your expense. The photograph of the pilot's face who's quote is presented as this unbelievable headline shows a typical 1940s-1950s man with very short greasy hair, an extremely serious look on his face, and the traditional pipe in his mouth - almost a caricature of a 1940s-1950s man. This was the president of the aviation firm 'C.N. Flagg Company' in Meriden, Connecticut: Pilot Peter Flagg. The introduction of this advertisement informs the reader that the 'C.N. Flagg Company' was at that time the largest pipeline contracting company on the East coast. The text following the small introduction contains the story of how "Day-Glo" Fluorescent paint 'Saved His Life.' While flying in his dual-engined Aero Commander airplane holding seven passengers on board at 8,500 feet (2,590 meters), Mr. Flagg and his passengers were nearly all killed by a jet that was narrowly averted from in-flight collision. Mr. Flagg, the pilot of the airplane and president of his Aviation Company, writes in the advertisement that the jet very quickly turned away from colliding with his airplane just in time to avert a fatal collision, so close that his passengers could see the jet pilot's face at just five hundred feet (150 meters) away. Then Mr. Flagg tells the reader that because his airplane was painted with "Day-Glo" Fluorescent Aviation Safety Paint the jet pilot saw his airplane, turned away a split second before a mid-air collision, and essentially 'Saved His Life'! The facts are next given that "Day-Glo" Aviation Safety paint was four times as bright as ordinary paint, especially in bad weather with decreased visibility, and that only one or two gallons (3.8-7.6 liters) of this Fluorescent paint could save your life, literally. The aviation use of this Fluorescent paint extended to the ground as well, in coating parts of the Air Flight Control Tower for safety visibility, the reader is informed. Facts about the official use of this "Day-Glo" Fluorescent Aviation Safety paint by the U.S. Air Force during the Second world war and during the 1950s are given in the text, relating the fact that 1,600 U.S. Air Force planes were painted with "Day-Glo" Fluorescent paint, and that there were no mid-air collisions of aircraft in a year after which nine mid-air collisions had occurred before the use of "Day-Glo" Fluorescent Aviation Safety paint was applied to the Air Force planes. In the National Air and Space Museum of the Smithsonian Institute in Washington, D. C. is a United States Air-Force jet that has "Day-Glo" Fluorescent paint on it's fuselage in several areas, but in the Museum collection I have photographs of World war two U.S. Air-Force airplanes, not the later jets, that were completely painted with "Day-Glo" Fluorescent Red-Orange paint from nose to tail, not only painted in sections like on the later jets.

This fifty year old advertisement closes with technical facts about the "Day-Glo" Fluorescent Aviation Safety Paint and it is told that a 'Filteray' clear varnish was painted on top of the Fluorescent paint on Mr. Flagg's airplane, and that after nine months flying in the Sun, the Color of the Fluorescent paint had not faded. This paint was sold as "Day-Glo" 'Sunbonded' Fluorescent Aviation Safety Paint for airplanes, by the company name given at the bottom of the ad "Switzer Brothers, Inc.," which had changed since the Second world war from "Conti-Glo" (when they were originally associated with "Continental Lithography" in Cleveland, Ohio). It is stated that the company was the top supplier of daylight Fluorescent paint for aviation, used on both Military and civilian aircraft. At the bottom of the ad is listed the many companies across many of the states in America, and even a firm with five offices in Canada.

A extremely rare acquisition in the Museum collection is a full Color "Day-Glo" printed large brochure from the pioneering "Switzer Brothers, Inc." The 8.5 x 11.5 inch (21 x 29 cm) brochure is for the "Switzer Brothers" "Day-Glo Aviation

Safety Colors." I would date this full Color large folding brochure to a time period not long after the Second world war, because although this brochure and product is strictly marketed towards 'civilian' uses, the military is still mentioned in this "Switzer Brothers, Inc." brochure. The front of this "Switzer Brothers, Inc." Color brochure is a dark Teal, which forms the background Color of almost the entire brochure. In the center of the front cover is a drawing of a stylized paint brush with a Black handle and a dazzling "Day-Glo" Orange Color representing the paint that the brush has been dipped into. There are two small drawings in Black on either side of the "Day-Glo" coated paint brush, one is an airport landscape with a man that has a cowboy hat on standing in front of brilliant "Day-Glo" Orange triangular marking "Wind Tee" on the runway. The other drawing on the cover to the right of the paint brush is a city skyline in Black with a "Day-Glo" Orange water-tower in the foreground. The small block of text on the cover of this "Switzer Brothers, Inc." brochure 'Announces' 'An Improvement in High Visibility Paint for Airport Markings, Observations, and Navigational Aids that are much needed.' This well-designed large full Color brochure opens up to a double page drawing of an airport from the sky that serves as a comparison between normal high-visibility Colored paint, and "Day-Glo" Fluorescent paint. The double-page spread of the airport drawing is printed on the left side with regular high-visibility Orange Colored paint, and on the right side with "Day-Glo" Orange Fluorescent paint. This creates a lucid example of the limited visibility of regular Orange Color compared to "Day-Glo" Fluorescent Orange. This center illustration of the airport is covered with a page on top of it cut diagonally to show half of the airport coated with regular Orange and the other half painted with "Day-Glo" Orange, creating a dramatic, very obvious difference in visibility. This double-page is cut diagonally across the airport illustration to compare the difference between regular Orange and "Day-Glo" Orange coated airport features, and lifts up to reveal a picture of the entire airport illustration coated in only "Day-Glo Aviation Safety Paint." The difference is nothing less than dramatic, and the small block of text at the left of the illustration informs the potential customer that the new "Switzer Brothers Aviation Safety Paint" makes the airport's markings and aerial obstructions "Glow in Daylight" which ensures the safety both up in the air and also on the ground in the airport. The inside double-page illustration is of "Port Durham" airport seen from the sky and completely coated with "Day-Glo" Fluorescent Orange paint on each and every safety point, with the double-page diagonally cut top part of this illustration unfolded, the image is a poster sized at 23 x 33 inches (58 x 84 cm). The top half of this poster-sized total image has a very dramatic total Black background with a large four engine jet printed totally in "Day-Glo" Orange and a block of White type to the left which informs potential customers that "Day-Glo Color's" safety has been proved by the 'U.S. Air Force.' The secondary headline states that 'mid-air collisions' of airplanes have been reduced to 'zero' during a one year test using "Day-Glo Aviation Safety Paint." The paragraph of text that follows the headlines gives the details of this test, informing that for a full year the "Air Training Command" of the "U.S. Air Force" tested about 1,600 planes and although the previous year had nine mid-air collisions, the year that "Day-Glo Aviation Safety Paint" had been applied to the aircraft not a single mid-air crash had occurred. The bottom half of the opened poster-sized four page image is the Fluorescent coated "Port Durham" airport from the air and half a page of text to the left of the airport illustration, with the headline that announces that high-visibility "Day-Glo Aviation Safety Paint" makes ordinary high-visibility paints such as "International Orange" seem dim. Added to the safety of this Color is the statement that this "Day-Glo" paint's 'High-Visibility' will actually increase in visibility at dusk, at dawn, and in overcast weather as well. The fact is revealed that "Day-Glo Aviation Safety Paint" is recognizable 'four times faster' than ordinary high-visibility paint, and that these Fluorescent Colors are visible at great distances. The use of "Day-Glo Aviation Safety Paint" on airport warning markers is also highly advised, including the suggested use of the this paint on 'hangers, runway cones, boundary markings, wind tees, control towers, TV and radio antenna towers, high tension electrical towers, water towers, and smoke stacks' for example. The second paragraph that follows insures the potential customer that the quality of this "Day-Glo Aviation safety paint" is of very high standards and has been specially formulated to provide a long-lasting brilliance that resists to fading in sunlight. The new product from "Day-Glo" was an overcoat of a protective "Filteray." This "Day-Glo Aviation Safety Paint" is explained as being applicable for use with a traditional brush, a roller, or with a spray-gun, with two different types of this paint sold, one for brush application called "Aviation Alkyd Enamel," and the other for spray-gun called "Aviation Acrylic Lacquer." The names of the Fluorescent Colors available in this "Day-Glo Aviation Safety Paint" are listed as 'Rocket Red, Fire Orange, Blaze Orange, Lightning Yellow, and Flash Green.' The final back page of this folded brochure has nine separate "Day-Glo" illustrations of examples of airport features to be coated with Fluorescent Color. The headline above these illustrations advises that "Day-Glo Aviation Safety Paint" should be used where visibility is vital. The ornate brochure closes with a long list of distributors selling this Fluorescent aviation safety paint all across the United States that this "Day-Glo" Fluorescent Aviation Safety Paint could be bought from, including a dozen firms with different offices in Canada as well, and with a footer that also dates the brochure to around World war two, by stating that "Switzer Brothers, Inc." were the 'Major Suppliers of Daylight Fluorescent paint for both the Military and Civilian Aircraft.'

A new acquisition in 2012 to the Museum library is a book that is just as obscure as it is hard to find: "High Viz - US Cold War Aircraft" from the "Osprey Aerospace US Military Aircraft" series of publications. This is the only book the current author knows of with the complete contents centered on Fluorescent "Day-Glo" "High Viz" ('High Visibility') paint on aircraft. The introduction to this book printed on the back cover is quite clear, informing the reader that "today" modern military aircraft built for the armed forces are painted with probably the "drabbest" of all Colors ever used throughout the US Air Force and US Navy history. But, during the 1950s and 1960s "Cold War," what is called a "Riot" of Colors, today labelled "garish," were painted on "all manner" of US military aircraft, ranging from fighter jets to common aircraft used for utility and transport. This obscure book printed in London was published by Michael O'Leary in 1994, however the cover photograph needs no explanation or title, being a Color photo of two "Grumman QF-9G" "Cougar drones" from 1964, which look like they could have been painted by the "Merry Pranksters!" Both of these US military jets were completely painted in eye-watering "Day-Glo" Red Orange from the nose of the aircraft to the back tail wing. The only tiny areas of these two US military jets that are not painted vivid "Day-Glo" Red Orange are the undersides of the front half of each folding wing, and around the US stars and stripes insignias. The very small amount of non-Fluorescent Red Orange surface of these US fighter jets were painted with "Insignia White." The full introduction inside "High Viz - US Cold War Aircraft" is presented to set the stage of the era of the Cold War, starting with the 1950s post-Korean war period icons of the 'new' televisions being bought by families all across America, and the 'star' of this new commodity the T.V. being Joe McCarthy and his "zealotism" for finding "Communists." "Wonder Bread" and "Spam" are both mentioned as 1950's icons, as well as the breasts of Marilyn Monroe and Mr. 1950s Howard Hughes. The author relates the 'idealizing of life' in America during this 50's period to the new threat of the Communist "Red Menace" around the world. This threat in the 1950s lead the Americans to produce tremendous amounts of new military fighter bombers and other aircraft. It is stated by the author Michael O'Leary that the majority of these 1950s and 1960s newly-produced US military aircraft were painted with "Day-Glo" Fluorescent paint, which is interpreted as "somehow symbolic" of that time period. These US military aircraft during the 1950s and 1960s were "splattered," and sometimes virtually covered with "Day-Glo" to improve their visibility, which was officially labelled "Fluorescent Red Orange" and is still listed in the 'US Federal Standard' of paint Colors as number "FS 18913." The author then states that during the 1950s to 1960s era which is now famous for both new huge cars with 'fins,' as well as 'paranoia,' what Color could better symbolize these feelings than "Day-Glo?"

To conclude the book's introduction, the author rightfully points out that these "Day-Glo" "High Viz" US military aircraft of the 1950s-1960s are for the most part "forgotten," and that these Fluorescent Colors, which the author plainly labels "garish," were produced up until the end of the Kennedy administration and the beginning of America's involvement in the Vietnam war. This signifies for O'Leary the crumbling vision of a "bright future" being replaced by a "darker version" of the future.

The contents of this book "High Viz - US Cold War Aircraft" is clear, with the first section of photographs consisting of US Navy, US Marine Corps, and the Coast Guard aircraft, the second section covering the US Air Force as well as the Air National Guard aircraft, and the third section on the US Army Fluorescent military aircraft. The 128 pages of this book contain Color photographs on every page of "Day-Glo" US military aircraft, and from this large number of Fluorescent jets and helicopters a selection of the brightest of all of these aircraft will be singled out. Already mentioned on the front cover of the book, and presented again inside the book, is the totally painted Fluorescent Red Orange "Grumman QF-9G." Photographed in 1964 before it's demolition after being withdrawn from service, the author states that it 'would have been hard' to have made this jet "more visible," because the entire jet is "Day-Glo" Red Orange. Another completely Fluorescent US military aircraft photographed was the "Grumman QF-9J," which was the last of it's type and decommissioned by the early 1970s. This entire jet was painted Fluorescent Red Orange, with the addition of "Insignia Red," "Orange Yellow," and "Insignia White" trim.

A Fluorescent Red Orange military helicopter is another example in this book of a totally painted Fluorescent aircraft. The helicopter was the "Sikorsky HSS-1" and the author rightfully comments that it doesn't get brighter than this. Also documented are the "tech orders" which specified that this helicopter had to be first painted totally "Insignia White" and then Fluorescent Red Orange, which is the standard practice in the creation of Fluorescent Art, and was used in this same manner by the US military on this helicopter to make it "glow." The two photographs of the helicopter are dated 1962 and 1963, with additional information added by the author explaining that the intense Fluorescent glow of the aircraft was difficult to "maintain." A pilotless "drone" photographed in 1970 under the wing of it's 'mother ship' was also completely painted in Fluorescent Red Orange. This military aircraft was the "Ryan Firebee drone," and it looks like it was dipped into a vat of "Day-Glo!" Of the roughly 120 "High Viz US Cold War Aircraft" presented in this full-Color book, each and every one has different amounts of "High Viz" paint coating various parts of it's exterior, and some of these US military aircraft are so complete in their coating of Fluorescent paint that it is nearly hard to believe.

For the majority of this chapter "The Miracle of Fluorescence - 1930s-1950s" the emphasis has been on the social outlook and use of Black lights and Fluorescent Colors in the United States, where Fluorescent paint was invented in 1933, where the first Longwave Ultraviolet Filter was invented by Dr. Robert Wood in 1903, where the Black light was initially used for entertainment in the first "Ziegfeld Follies" in San Francisco in 1907, and where the first Ultraviolet lamp the "Argon Glow Lamp" (which was a Black light that wasn't Black) was sold to the public in 1915.

'The Practical Applications of Luminescence: Fluorescence - Phosphorescence - Black Light'   Maurice Deribere, France, 1938 and 1954

In the following pages I will present an even more obscure history of Black light and Fluorescent Colors being used during the 1930s to the 1950s across the ocean in Europe. The only complete documentation I know of recording the early history of the use of the Black light and Fluorescent Color in Europe during the period of the 1930s to the 1950s is a book that was published twice by the French author Maurice Deribere, entitled "Les Applications Pratiques de la Luminescence: Fluorescence - Phosphorescence - Lumiere Noire" ('The Practical Applications of Luminescence: Fluorescence - Phosphorescence - Black Light'). This book was first published by Deribere in 1938 by "Dunod" of Paris and was a soft cover edition of 263 pages. Later, in 1954, the book was published again as a hardcover edition with 399 pages, incorporating further writings on the Black light and Fluorescence by Deribere. The text of this 1954 edition is nearly as valuable as the many Black and White antique photographs in the book, which are precious and include unique documentation of unbelievable events, such as Fluorescent Black light Store Window displays on the Champs Elysees in Paris in 1936 and 1937! Another very valuable point about this French book from 1954 is that many of the photographs of Ultraviolet lamps and devices are European or French manufactured, which are as unknown in the United States today as they were when the instruments were produced seventy years ago. One of the most notable points about the book's text is the sole use of the term "Wood's Lamps" for the common usage of the term "Black light" or "Longwave Ultraviolet lamp" throughout the entire book. This term is still occasionally used today in the Twenty-first century, and is referring to the American physicist Dr. Robert Wood, who began the modern age of Ultraviolet exploration through his invention of the Longwave Ultraviolet Filter - the Black light filter - which Dr. Wood announced in February, 1903. The book's subject of 'Practical Applications of Luminescence' includes a very detailed introduction presenting Luminescence principles and history, Fluorescent minerals, organics, pharmaceuticals, photographic applications, psychology, biology, chemistry, industry, botany, oils, asphalts, drugs, resins, pigments, plastics, rubber, paper, graphic arts, tanning leather, wood, metals, varnish, paints, signaling, decoration, theatre, and the Arts.

To begin with, this rare book was published both times in Deribere's native French, which my Parisian girlfriend Michèle carefully and painstakingly translated into English for me. As with all writings from over fifty years ago, there are antiquated, forgotten terms and expressions used in the text which must be translated into modern terminology by someone who has knowledge of this past terminology, which Michèle certainly does having been born in Paris and growing up there in the 1950s. The first very curious antiquated term used in Deribere's book is "Biochimiluminescence," which the author defines as the luminous phenomenon that can be produced by the living process of some organic beings, which possess the ability to be permanently regenerated throughout their lives. This is known today as the term that was coined by E. Newton Harvey in 1957, "Bioluminescence."

The first series of Black and White photographs in the Deribere book are ancient machines that were manufactured between fifty and one hundred years ago in France and presumably in other European countries. The first of luminescence instruments I've already mentioned in this book named the "Callophane" was a very early Ultraviolet instrument that utilized no electricity, and had no lamp at all, but was simply used out in the Sun (or with an artificial U.V. source). This "Callophane" was an instrument that utilized the first Longwave Ultraviolet filter invented in 1903 by Dr. Robert Wood to filter out all other light and energy except Longwave Ultraviolet. As already explained, the instrument looked like wooden triangular binoculars, but this construction contained a support that could be unfolded to hold a sample that was observed in the darkened interior of the small hand-held wooden instrument, which was essentially fitted with a Longwave Ultraviolet filter on top of the device and which filtered out all energy but Longwave Ultraviolet - in this way causing a Fluorescent sample to emit visible light - Color.

The next Ultraviolet instrument presented in Deribere's book was called the "Ultrascope Bernheim-Mazo" and this instrument looks more modern, incorporating electrical Ultraviolet lamps into it's advanced design. Deribere explains that this "Ultrascope" contained two lamps of low voltage with special spiral filaments producing it's Ultraviolet energy. These produced Ultraviolet energies go through a heat-absorbing filter ("anti-calor") which absorbs the Infrared energy, then through a second "Wood" Longwave Ultraviolet filter, which absorbs all invisible Ultraviolet energies except Longwave Ultraviolet energy. Through the use of these two separate filters in this "Ultrascope," only Ultraviolet energy between 300 and 400 nanometers could pass. This instrument looks like a real scientific device in the photograph, with two separate angled Black boxes on a platform. The front box is fitted with a large Black baffler that the face is placed against allowing both eyes to examine a sample in darkness. This front viewing box of the "Ultrascope" was also fitted with several small doors to open for putting a sample into the instrument. The back box of this "Ultrascope' was obviously the source of the two low voltage spiral filament lamps which artificially produced Ultraviolet. The angled front section of this back box of this instrument looks to have contained the 'heat-absorbing' Infrared filter, and the back angled section of the front box, separated by just a few inches from the back box, looks to have contained the Ultraviolet "Wood" filter.

Rapidly progressing, the next Ultraviolet instrument in the Deribere book is what most references start with in the history of Ultraviolet devices, the Iron-Arc "Quartz-Burner." This is a complicated small design and was amongst the first instruments able to produce continuous Ultraviolet energy. This French version of the instrument in Deribere's book was originally manufactured by "Le Verrerie scientifique" ('Scientific Glass Factory'). Illustrated in this book as well is another nearly identical instrument with the same manufacturer, also called a 'Quartz-Burner' ("Bruleur de quartz"), but with the production of alternating Ultraviolet energy, not continuous. The only Ultraviolet instrument that is included in Deribere's 1938 edition, but left out of his 1954 edition is called a "Detectolampe" made by the French firm "Mazo." The metal name plate on this antique instrument reads "Marque-Deposee - DETECTOLAMPE - Brevete S.G.D.O.," and the instrument is described as being an interesting example of the use of the 'Electric Arc' as a source of "Ultra-Violets" energy. The instrument itself consisted of two separate tubular sections of metal, the top portion appears to be the section of the instrument where the 'Electric Arc' Ultraviolet-producing device was contained, and the bottom larger section of the "Detectolampe" is shown open in another photo in the Deribere book, making it apparent that this area is where a Fluorescent sample could be placed to observe it's Fluorescence. As with all of these antique Ultraviolet instruments illustrated in Deribere's book, this instrument looks to be quite compact, with a total estimated height of about twelve to eighteen inches (30-45 cm).

Following these small Ultraviolet instruments Deribere presents several large Ultraviolet instruments that were floor-standing with a large base and a large Ultraviolet-producing 'lamp' that had an adjustable height, mounted on a vertical pole extended up from the base to a height of what looks like three to six feet (1-1.8 meter). The first pair of these instruments are the shorter, with an estimated height of about three feet (1 meter) and the same manufacturer of the two previous lamps, 'Scientific Glass factory.' This instrument is described as a 'Quartz Burner' mounted in a reflector on a stand, and a laboratory 'Quartz Burner' lamp with a "Localisator" containing a "Wood" Ultraviolet Filter fitted to the front of the lamp. These both appear as large round lamps mounted on a vertical pole from the base, the first lamp just being an open round metal unit containing a visible 'Electric Arc' Ultraviolet lamp, and the second laboratory 'Quartz-Burner' being identical, except for the front of the lamp, which is covered with a metal unit that is fitted with the "Wood" U.V. filter in a central cylindrical section, and which obviously concentrated the Ultraviolet energy into a much smaller opening at the front of the lamp. The other unit illustrated is similar to these first two 'Quartz-Burners,' but it is twice the height, and it has a base with wheels and a large electrical transformer. The actual 'Quartz-Burner' lamp on this unit appears to be a similar, but advanced version of the previously described laboratory 'Quartz-Burner.' All three of these 'Quartz-Burner' lamps presented here look very similar to the Shortwave Ultraviolet units used in early Ultraviolet "Actinotherapy" "health" treatments.

As a background to just what these lamps were, in "Fluorescent Gems and Minerals" by DeMent from 1949 there is a very clear explanation of the early days of these 'Quartz-Burner' 'Iron-Arc' lamps. DeMent explains that in 1949 the 'Mercury-arc lamp' was the standard lamp, but that the 'Carbon-Arc' lamp and the 'Tungsten Filament lamp' were the predecessors of the modern lamps. The Carbon-Arc was first discovered by Sir Humphry Davy in 1808, when he created a Carbon-Arc three inches long (7.5 cm) through the energy of a 'Voltaic Battery' that contained 2,000 plates. DeMent also states that the modern 1949 Arc lamps were identical in principle to the first Carbon-Arc of Davy in 1808.

Deribere next presents an Ultraviolet instrument that looks like the grandfather of all Ultraviolet Viewing-Cabinets, called an 'Inspection Cabinet' ("Laterne de controle") also manufactured by 'Scientific Glass factory' of France, and this unit contained a 'Quartz-Burner' to produce Ultraviolet energy as well as a "Wood" Ultraviolet filter fitted to it. The photographs of this antique 'Ultraviolet Inspection Cabinet' show a unit about three to four feet tall (1-1.3 m) which consisted of two halves. The top half of this 'Inspection Cabinet' was a closed portion of the unit containing the 'Quart-Burner' that produced the Ultraviolet energy, and the bottom half of the unit was opened and contained an angled platform to mount documents on that were to be examined under Black light. Between the top and the bottom halves of this unit was mounted a "Wood" Ultraviolet filter, which allowed only Ultraviolet between 300 and 400 nanometers to pass, and by which flat documents could be examined under.

After this 'Inspection Cabinet' there is a photograph of an Ultraviolet instrument that looks like another instrument from Frankenstein's laboratory, and is called a "Wood-Hanau" lamp. A short, non-adjustable base which looks to contain the electrical generator has a large round metal Ultraviolet lamp unit attached to it. Similar to the previous round metal 'Quartz-Burner' lamps in design, but this "Wood-Hanau" Ultraviolet lamp has a dark material curtain all around the lamp and a rectangular Ultraviolet "Wood" Filter in the center of the metal front section closing the lamp. I would assume the lamp's material curtain was a new feature of the lamp's design, allowing the Fluorescent subject to be examined under Ultraviolet energy without the necessity of a darkened laboratory, as was needed with the previous units that had no closing curtain.

With the next illustrated Ultraviolet lamp Deribere finally leaves Frankenstein's laboratory and enters the modern times presenting the first actual Ultraviolet lamp that was sold to the public way back in 1915 in the United States, called an "Argon Glow Lamp." The photo in Deribere's book shows a two and a half watt 'Argon Bulb' being used in combination with a circular "Wood" Ultraviolet filter in front of it and a "RA 3" reflector behind the Argon bulb. Deribere explains that the "Wood" filter was used to eliminate the weak Purple visible light also emitted by the Argon bulb. The manufacturer is given as "Compagnie des lampes" ('Lamps Company') and there is an accompanying mechanical drawing of an early version of the Argon bulb's components.

Moving rapidly into advancement, the next photograph looks very similar to a Black light unit that could even be used today. A high pressure Mercury Black light bulb, that looks identical to common pseudo-Black light bulbs most people are familiar with, except that the metal base of this Black light bulb is smooth without the typical screw-in design. An aluminum reflector unit contained this Black light bulb, as well as intensifying it's Ultraviolet emission. Under the photo of this Black light bulb and aluminum reflector manufactured in France by the 'Lamps Company,' there is an extremely antiquated photo of a laboratory from sixty-five years ago containing 'Ultraviolet Rays Apparatus.' The caption of this photo reads 'Apparatus for production of Ultraviolet Rays and Wood Light' and reveals not only just how antiquated a scientific laboratory from sixty-five years ago appeared, but also the most primitive example of photo retouching I have ever seen in my life. The many Ultraviolet instruments photographed in this laboratory are listed by the author as a 'Control Lantern' ('Inspection Box') with a 'Quartz-Burner,' a "Detectolampe' with a 'Quartz-Arc,' and two watt Argon bulbs on the top of an observation chamber fitted with immobile 'Black lamp' filters. The "Detectolampe" in this photo shows that the bottom larger section of this unit opened up, presumably to put in a Fluorescent sample. There is also another sort of Ultraviolet Viewing Box with a small rectangular opening in it's front section, as well as a microscope on the table in the laboratory. Directly in the center of this ancient photograph of an Ultraviolet Scientific Laboratory is a cut-out and pasted-down second photograph of a scientist supposedly sitting in his laboratory. Not only are the cut lines and paste visible all around this second added photo of the scientist, but his back is cut in a perfect vertical line, giving the general appearance of a scientist cut in half.

The next two photographed Ultraviolet lamp units are nearly identical to Ultraviolet units sold today in the Twenty-first century, with the first lamp having the same appearance as most contemporary 100 watt Longwave Ultraviolet industrial inspection lamps. This unit is described by the author as being a portable English lamp manufactured by one of the most famous Ultraviolet "health" lamp companies that ever existed, "Hanovia Ltd.," established in Glough. It is described as a portable powerful Ultraviolet Detection Lamp, specialized in the detection of oil spills in electrical generators, such as car generators. This unit is very similar to Ultraviolet detection lamps manufactured today, with a large metal lamp housing and a pistol-type handle attached to it. The following photo shows a very modern looking White Fluorescent lamp "TL" fixture being fitted with a White tubular Fluorescent lamp that has a tubular Black Longwave Ultraviolet filter slid over it. Deribere describes the unit as a Fluorescent tubular lamp with an inside coating capable of producing a 360 nanometer emission (Black light). The lamp functioned on the fixture of a normal Fluorescent tubular lamp of the same power, and gave an abundant emission of "Wood" light (Black light) that was well diffused. It is explained that it was necessary to put a cylindrical "Wood" Ultraviolet filter around the lamp to be able to select the useful Ultraviolet emission needed.

In the chapter on 'Techniques of the Study of Photoluminescence' Deribere presents very early techniques of Fluorescence Photography. The author gives examples of the applications of Fluorescence Photography, including theatre decor and advertising windows, and explains that two Ultraviolet lamps would be used four meters from the subject along with two Ultraviolet lamps at the distance of two meters from the subject. Deribere details the explanation with camera exposure times of five to ten minutes at an aperture of f18, and includes the information that the exposure times could be greatly reduced with larger camera aperture openings, and also by removing the Ultraviolet filter, which is possible in some cases. The author then assures the reader that with some practice, and by observing the general explanation included in his book, Color

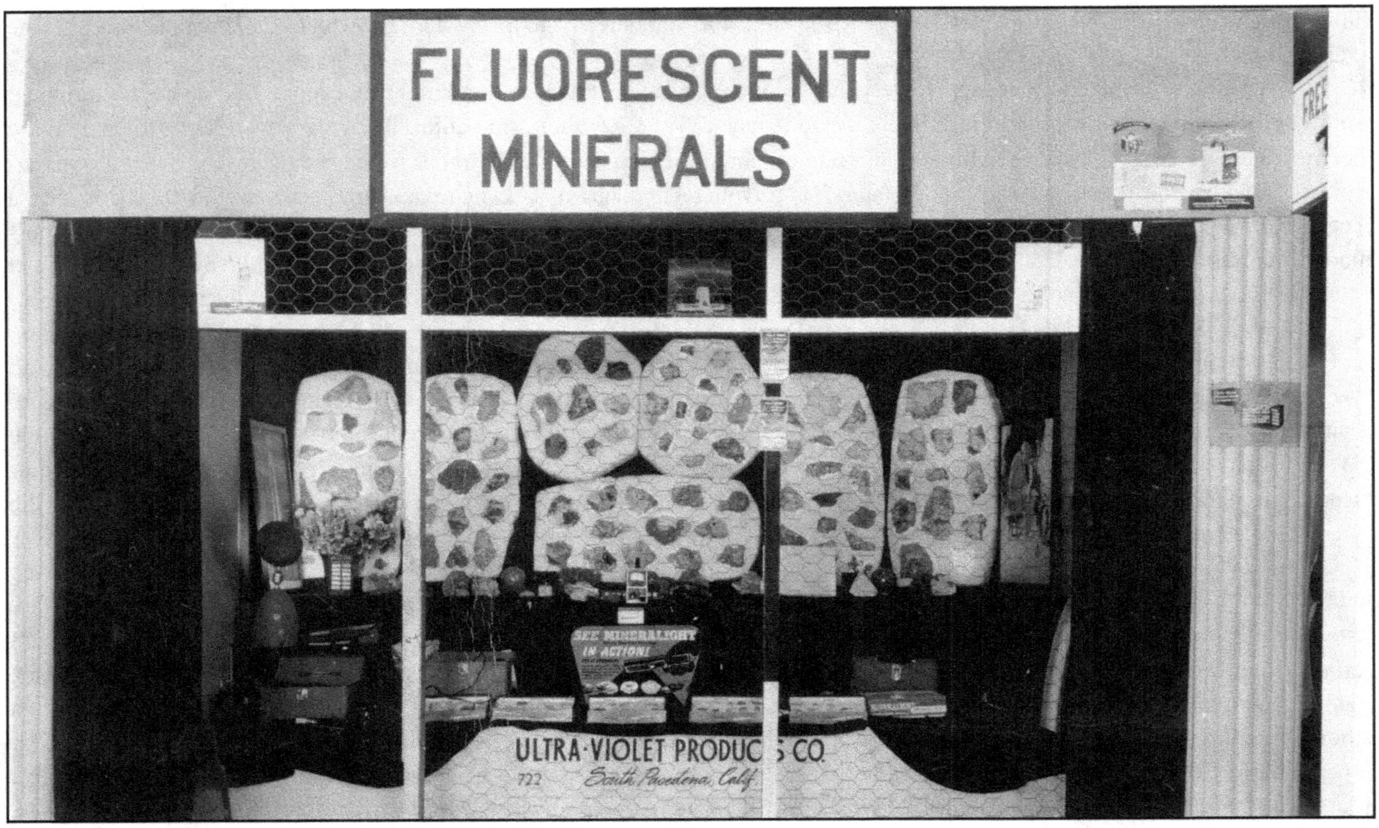

1940s "Ultra-Violet Products Co.," Pasedena, California, Ultraviolet "Mineralite" Lamps convention booth

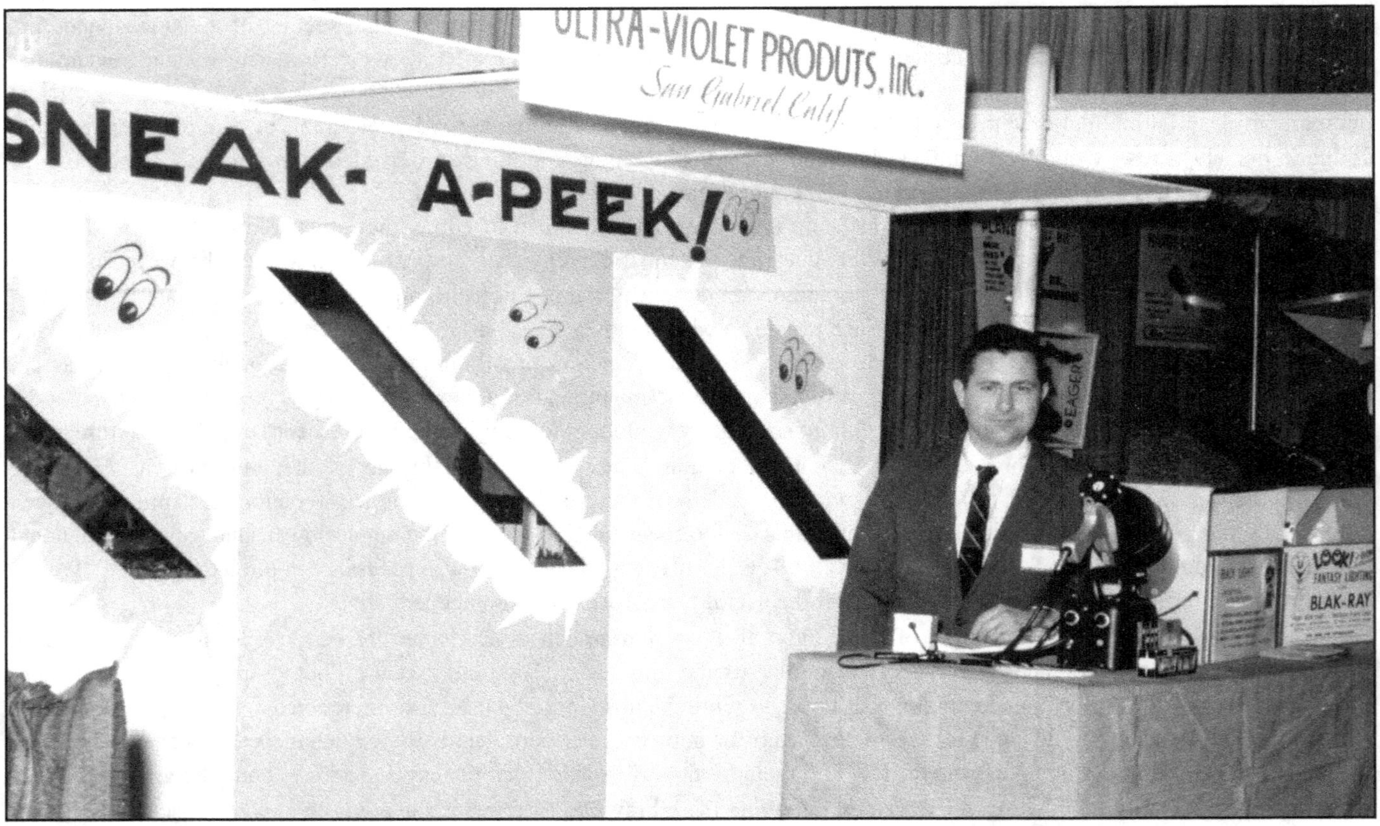

1950s "Ultra-Violet Products, INC.," Pasedena, California, Ultraviolet "BLAK-RAY" Lamps convention booth "SNEAK-A-PEEK!"

photographs of Fluorescent phenomenon could be easily achieved. The author continues on with a detailed explanation of Fluorescence 'Macro Photography,' instructing that two "MAW 75" Black lights were to be used. The examples of very luminescent materials such as Scapolite, Fluorescent paint, varnish, and plastics could be photographed with the extremely varying exposure times of one-second to five minutes are given, followed by medium bright Fluorescent materials such as Fluorite, Willemite, Fluorescent paper, and Ivory, needing exposure times of ten-seconds to twenty minutes. Dimmer Fluorescent materials such a Calcite and Sodalite, are listed as needing between twenty-seconds and thirty minutes. Following is the last category of documents, paintings, stamps, and fossils needing very long thirty minute to two hour exposure times. The credit for this antique Fluorescence Photography information is given as 'C.E. Peterson and H.C. Gibson,' 'The Photography and Colors of Fluorescent Objects,' "Med. Radiogr. Photo.," 1951.

The third section of Deribere's book is entitled 'Natural Mineral Substances - Mineralogy, Paleontology, "Hydrologie" and begins with a description of Fluorescent minerals. The reader is told that although diverse mineral substances are "Photoluminescent," Phosphorescence is rarely observed, but that Fluorescence of these minerals is easily observable. The fact is presented that some of the mineral's luminescence can be considered as characteristic of the mineral, or as the presence in the mineral of a specific element. What Deribere presented here is a simple explanation of what Edmond Becquerel discovered many years before and named Fluorescent "Activators." The credit for this early explanation of Fluorescent "Activators" is given to 'J. Grant, 'Examining Minerals with an Ultraviolet Lamp,' "Sands, Clays, and Min.," 1933,' 'H. Haberlandt, 'Analysing the Fluorescence of Minerals,' 1934,' and 'Deribere, 'The Phenomenon of Luminescence in the Mineral Kingdom,' 1939.'

The author next explains the role of the element Zinc in the phenomenon of Fluorescence, informing the reader that investigations into the phenomenon of "Photoluminescence" discovered that in Fluorescent minerals Zinc is an important indicator. Deribere documents the monumental, historic explorations of Kunz and Baskerville in the collection of the Museum of Natural History in New York, when in 1903 the pair of scientists examined the entire mineralogical collection of the Museum's 13,000 specimens under X-rays, as well as "Radium rays." This monumental examination of 13,000 mineral specimens in 1903 by Kunz and Baskerville was one of the first mass examination for Fluorescent minerals, and probably the most complete investigation of Fluorescent minerals ever performed in history. As so many times, the original enthusiasm and interest in a phenomenon can never be reproduced or recreated as familiarity breeds indifference, but what must be imagined here is the actual physical examination of 13,000 mineral specimens in 1903 using a thundering rolling contraption that must have looked like an entire Monster movie laboratory put on wheels. Kunz and Baskerville rolled this monstrous contraption throughout the entire mineralogical collection of the New York Museum of Natural History in the dark, spewing out X-rays and sparks containing Ultraviolet energy in every direction. In this French book by Deribere it is stated that Kunz and Baskerville used "Radium" to examine the Fluorescence of the 13,000 minerals, but in almost all other English language documentation of this event it is stated that Kunz and Baskerville used the first electrical Ultraviolet-producing instrument called a "Spark Box" on their rolling contraption. Although the first Fluorescent Mineral Demonstration in The Natural History Museum in London in 1903 utilized pure Radium as the Ultraviolet source, most documentation besides this French book by Deribere relates the use of a "Spark Box" by Kunz and Baskerville in 1903. This is clarified in the 1941 "Fluorescent Light and It's Applications" by Dake and DeMent, as well as in Sterling Gleason's 1960 "Ultraviolet Guide to Minerals" which both also document that Kunz and Baskerville used 'Ultra-Violet rays, X-rays, and Radium radiations' on their rolling cart (which defies the imagination) during their 13,000 minerals specimen examination of 1903. The mineral "Kunzite" was named after George Frederick Kunz by Charles Baskerville in 1903, the same year as their monumental examination in the Museum of Natural History. Baskerville was a chemistry professor first at the University of North Carolina and then at the City College of New York. The use of X-rays in examination of the Fluorescence of substances was used for some years before the 1903 Kunz and Baskerville massive study, most famously by Thomas A. Edison. In "Fluorescent Chemicals and Their Applications - Including a comprehensive tabulation of fluorescent substances, an exposition of their utilities in the arts, sciences, and industries." by Jack DeMent and H.C. Dake of 1942 it is stated that probably the greatest examination of Fluorescent substances under the X-ray was done by Edison in 1896. Thomas Edison made an examination of the Fluorescence of 1,800 chemicals, discovering that Calcium tungstate had six times greater brilliance of Fluorescence than Barium platinocyanide, which is the chemical used by Roentgen to discover X-rays only some years before. As all these bizarre early "Age of Innocence" experiments have their human tales, this one is no exception, and DeMent and Dake relate the droll fact that the associate of Thomas Edison's who was operating the X-ray machine for this monumental 1,800 chemical examination died of overexposure to X-rays.

After the examinations of Kunz and Baskerville, other scientists were quick to follow. After the 1903 Natural History Museum of London's first Fluorescent Mineral Demonstration using Radium in a single-person booth, for which people literally waited in line for days to experience, in 1906 W.P Hadden began important examinations on the Fluorescence and Phosphorescence of Calcite from Joplin, Missouri, concluding that the Phosphorescence was attributed to 'Yttrium.' 1912 saw the very important research into Fluorescent minerals by Edward L. Nichols and Ernest Merritt of the Cornell University physics laboratory, which would pave the way for future research into the field of luminescent minerals. In 1912 Liebisch made experiments on the Fluorescent minerals in the Sodalite and Willemite groups. Also in 1912, E. Engelhardt made a large survey of Fluorescent minerals, including 400 specimens of which he measured Fluorescence and Phosphorescence with Longwave Ultraviolet energy. In 1927 the Fluorescence of Willemite and other Zinc minerals was studied by J.L. Spencer of the British Museum, and in 1933 Van Horn made an examination of Tungsten minerals under the 'Iron-Arc.' Dake and DeMent list the earliest public museum collections of Fluorescent minerals, starting with the Philadelphia Public Museum in 1929 creating the first museum collection of Fluorescent minerals ever exhibited. Two-hundred thousand visitors visited this Philadelphia Public Museum Fluorescent mineral exhibition during the first couple of years it was opened, which was composed of eighteen large superb Fluorescent mineral specimens. "Wernerite" [Scapolite], Aragonite, Fluorite, "Common" Opal (Nevada), Willemite, Calcite (New Jersey), Autunite, Hyalite, Sphalerite (Africa), Amber, and Brucite were the eighteen large pieces displayed in Philadelphia's first public museum Fluorescent mineral exhibition. The Ultraviolet lamps used in the Philadelphia Museum consisted of two Carbon-Arc units that had Corning 'heat-resisting' filters on them. This lighting was specially designed to be on for a short period of time and then switch off when White lights were turned on, to surprise the visitors with the Grey, ordinary daylight appearance of these marvelous vividly Colored Fluorescent minerals they just saw under Ultraviolet lamps in the dark. The exhibition in the Philadelphia Public Museum was so successful that a duplicate collection of these Fluorescent minerals were lent by the Philadelphia Public Museum to the "Century of Progress" exposition of 1933 in Chicago. This lent exhibition, upon it's return, was next lent to the biggest department store in Philadelphia, "Wanamakers" which then exhibited the Fluorescent minerals in a large public display window. The display window in "Wanamakers" department store in the early 1930s was painted Black except for a strip that was left bare for the public to look through into the darkened display of astonishing display of Fluorescent minerals, which were under six large "NiCo" Black lights. Between 1933 and 1941 Dake and DeMent give a notion of how many Fluorescent mineral exhibitions were installed in museums all over the United States. The 1933 installation of the Fluorescent mineral display in the Cranbrook Institute of Science in Bloomfield Hills, Michigan is described as housing large specimens of Fluorescent minerals in a darkened room of a Mineral Hall, arranged on Black velvet in a large recessed, glass-covered area of the room. The display is stated as having been ten feet long (3.2 m) and equipped with four large "NiCo" Black lights. The added advantage with this darkened museum exhibition in the Cranbrook Institute was the three phases of lighting, including Black light, White light, and absolute darkness to view the Phosphorescence of the minerals. The largest museum collection of Fluorescent minerals in the 1930s is credited by Dake and DeMent as being in the Paterson Museum in New Jersey. This is perfectly understandable, geographically, because Franklin, New Jersey, "The Fluorescent Mineral Capital of the World" is only a short distance from Paterson, New Jersey. Not surprisingly, the Paterson Museum's Fluorescent mineral collection specialized (and still specializes) in Franklin, New Jersey Fluorescent minerals in it's collection. The Paterson Museum was a very advanced exhibition, with both the Longwave Ultraviolet lamps and the Shortwave lamps as well. As very bad luck would have it, when I went to Paterson years ago the museum had just destroyed the original Fluorescent mineral exhibition and it was under restoration, gone forever. In the early 1990s I met Allen Ginsberg at a book signing show in Amsterdam and after I spoke to him about the Fluorescent Art Museum I was preparing downstairs from the Art Gallery, he told me he remembered growing up in Paterson, New Jersey and being fascinated by the Fluorescent mineral exhibition in the Paterson Museum when he was a boy. The Griffin Observatory in Los Angeles is also listed as a pioneering Museum Fluorescent mineral display, and it is described a being not that large, but comprised of the best of Fluorescent specimens under Shortwave Ultraviolet lamps. The Santa Barbara Museum of Natural History in California is next described as being powered by Cold Quartz tubes and displaying beautiful California and Franklin, New Jersey Fluorescent minerals. As well as adding several East coast museums and Universities to the list of public museum Fluorescent mineral displays in the 1930s, the Field Museum of Chicago and the Houston Museum of Natural History are both described as using automatically controlled "NiCo" tubes as the Black light sources. The Georgia State Museum in Atlanta is described as having perhaps the first "Interactive" Fluorescent mineral display, with a switch that could be operated by the viewer to change between Black light and White light. The Spokane Public Museum in Washington State is also included by Dake and DeMent, describing the exhibition as using a Cold Quartz tube without a filter (must have been alot of free suntans in there), with a six foot "Mineralight" tube. This exhibition would switch between the Ultraviolet lamps, ordinary White lights, and darkness to view the Phosphorescence of the minerals. This long list of extraordinary Fluorescent mineral displays in museums across America in the 1930s closes with two more examples of the displays of Fluorescent minerals eighty years ago.

The Academy of Science Museum in Golden Gate Park, San Francisco, in which an interesting design consisted of viewing Fluorescent minerals lined up in a case under a "NiCo" Black light through an opening in the side of the case. This exhibition was also an "Interactive" display, with the "NiCo" tube operated by the visitor. The Department of Geology in the University of Oregon in Eugene housed a Fluorescent mineral display that is described as utilizing Germicidal Ultraviolet lamps fitted with Filter '986.' This display was in the University's Condon Hall Museum.

On the subject of Paleontology Deribere states that Fossils generally appear more detailed under a "Wood" Ultraviolet lamp than in daylight. Meithe and Wagner created photographs of the Fluorescence of fossils which reveal better detail of the samples than daylight photographs of the same samples. There are also photos of several fossils in Deribere's book, each with a photo in daylight next to a photo in Black light. Deribere briefly mentions the obscure subject of meteorite Fluorescence with a reference to J.D. Buddhue, 'The Luminescence of Meteorites" in the "American Journal of Science" from 1941. Also briefly mentioned is "Hydrology," in which the author relates the point that chemically pure water is transparent to Ultraviolet energy, from a study done in 1925.

As an example of Fluorescent mineral prospecting, Deribere presents a photograph of a prospector using a portable Shortwave Ultraviolet lamp for finding the valuable Tungsten ore Scheelite. Photographed is a mineral prospector utilizing the 'Ultraviolet detector' of John Harvey of Sydney, Australia searching in a mine for Scheelite. A large battery pack is hung from the prospector's shoulder and in his hand is this small Shortwave lamp.

For 'Applications of Fluorescent Minerals' Deribere informs the reader that besides the mining industry, Fluorescent minerals could be used to produce cheap luminescent pigments, which would also be stable in light and water as well as resistant to chemicals. Deribere instructs the reader that after separating all the purest brightest sections of Fluorescent minerals under an Ultraviolet lamp, these sections should be crushed and would produce powders that could be used as cheap pigment to manufacture paint, varnish, paper, plastics, and rubber. The suggestions from the author are Yellow pigment obtained from Scapolite, Orange pigment obtained from mixed Yellow and Red Fluorescent calcite, Red/Pink pigment obtained through crushing Hackmanite, Aragonite, or even some Calcites, and finally Green pigment could be produced by crushing the Fluorescent minerals Uranite, Autunite, or Willemite. This was written by Deribere precisely five years after Robert Switzer did this, and through the knowledge of the Fluorescent minerals along with naturally Fluorescing chemicals, Switzer invented Fluorescent paint in 1933.

The following section in this chapter in Deribere's book examines 'Applications of Black Light in Tourist Caves.' The author explains that in 1938 he indicated the need for good lights in Tourist Caves, and also stated at that time that Black light could be used to display the natural Fluorescence of cave formations (every day I demonstrate this fact in the Museum with the Fluorescence and Phosphorescence of cave formations from the Black Forest in Germany). The author provides an example of the "Nouvelles grottes de Lacave" in Lot, France, which although were already known by tourists, after being fitted with Black lights, these caves became known as the "New" Caves of Lacave. It is explained that the electrical installation and the placement of the Ultraviolet lamps were well designed around the obvious difficulty of water in the caves. Deribere gives a detailed account of this Ultraviolet lamp system in Lacave, including the concealed placement of the Black light units which caused the cave formations to emit light like it was magic. The entrance to the cave had a "Magnetophone" which announced to the visitors that the cave was discovered by Arman Vire, as well as corridor lights that were inside stained glass fixtures. The total electricity used for all the lighting units in the cave system amounted to a staggering twenty-three kilowatts, and included normal incandescent bulbs, Mercury vapor lamps of light Green glass which added a discreet Color to the caves, and Black lights ("Wood" lamps') exciting the natural Fluorescence of the cave formations and adding a 'mysterious and captivating magic.' Details for the Black lights used in the cave are astounding, such as the use of thirty-three "Mazda" Black lights "MAW 80" or "MAW 120" in 'The Lake Room' alone(!), causing the invisible fine edges of the stalactites to be visible. The author goes on to explain that domes of crystals seemed to be emitting their own light under the Black lights. Included is a photograph of the stalactites in the cave's 'Room of Wonders' emitting light through the energy of the large number of Black lights installed. Another photo from the cave shows the bones of a fossilized dog, which were presented to the tourists under Black lights, causing the dog's bones to Fluoresce Bluish White. This information was originally published by Maurice Deribere in 1951. What is to be understood in this French book of Deribere's, originally published in 1938, is that throughout the book the author refers to the use of "Mazda" Black lights in the various installations he describes in France during the 1930s, and that these "Mazda" Black lights were made by "General Electric." In a 1942 advertisement in the Museum collection for "General Electric" Fluorescent lamps, the headline reads "G-E Mazda Lamps - General Electric" and has a photo of a long White tubular Fluorescent light in a person's hand. The text of the ad reveals that in 1942, every year 'nearly 1 million' were sold. Another advertisement in the Museum collection for the same Fluorescent lamps, from the same "General

Electric" company, but exactly ten years later in 1952 reveals that these White tubular Fluorescent lights were not called "Mazda" any more, but "G-E Rapid Start" lamps.

Chapter four of Deribere's book is simply entitled "Luminescence" and in it he explains different luminescent pigments. The reader learns that for pigments containing 'Zinc Sulphur' or 'Cadmium Sulphur,' Phosphorescence can only be produced by manufacturing the pigments in a particular crystal structure, which is obtained through slow and regular heating to a high temperature, followed by a quick cooling. The Sulphur most of the time must also contain an exciting substance, called a "Phosphorogene" by the author, in tiny proportions such as one-thousandth or one-ten-thousandth [an "Activator"]. Deribere informs the reader that the fabrication of these Phosphorescent pigments is simple, but it must be ensured that the products used are pure, and that the homogeneity of the mixture, the heating of the mixture, the fineness of the particles (not ground too fine), and the consistency of the Sulphur must be maintained correctly.

Very healthy Radioactive pigments are next discussed by the author, in which he explains that by activating Zinc sulphates and Phosphorescent Cadmium zinc through small amounts of radioactive substances like the element Radium or 'Meso Thorium salts,' very Phosphorescent and very expensive pigment could be produced.

Discussing pigments based on Alkaline-Earth Sulphurs, the author relates the fact that these were the very first Phosphorescent Colors known. In ancient times these pigments were manufactured with much success starting with Barite (the "Bologna Stone"), Barium 'hyposulfite,' Calcium carbonate, gypse, oyster shells, "sulfure de calcium," and Strontium salts, all added through vast experimentation. In addition to these materials, Magnesium carbonate, "Urane" salt, Bismuth, and Thorium could have been added as well. The results from all the mixtures of these different substances produced what was most of the times a substance that Phosphoresced. After the research of Becquerel, Lenard, and Guntz on the "Sulfures de Zinc" realizing the crystallization state related to Phosphorescence, Earth Sulphurs were used to produce brilliant Phosphorescent pigments. The activator for this Phosphorescence must be well chosen, and the grinding must be just right, not too fine or too coarse, so the desire crystallization state can be obtained. Important also was the intense heating of the pigment, called "Calcination," which was done in a "Creuset" (an oven used to melt metal in a foundry). The heating of the pigment at 900-1,200 C. produces a solid mass that is then grounded. The grinding must be stopped before the Phosphorescent substance is too fine, damaging the crystal structure, and in this way reducing or even destroying the Phosphorescence.

Chapter twelve of Deribere's book covers the subject of 'Products of Pharmacy, Waxes, Resins, Gums, and Pigments.' Solvents are explained as being naturally Fluorescent, such as benzine Fluorescing Purple, and glycerine Fluorescing a Reddish Blue. Siccative oils (additives that promote drying) are also stated by the author as being naturally Fluorescent, and it is explained that with a Black light the cooking of lin oil can be followed, along with it's mixture with wood oil. This information was first published by H. Wolff and W. Toeldte in 1926. The author gives detailed observations of the Fluorescence of lin oil, recording that cooked lin oil has a Purplish Blue Fluorescence if there is the presence of natural pigments in the oil. After boiling Lin Oil for two hours at 150 C., the oil Fluoresced a vivid Blue, and after boiling four hours at 200 C., the same lin oil Fluoresced Purple. After cooking crude oil at 180 C. for four hours the dim Yellow-Brown Fluorescence of the oil became a very luminous Lemon Yellow.

Fluorescent Waxes are briefly discussed by Deribere, referring to a study of waxes under a Quart lamp by Radley in 1932. Deribere lists English or foreign bees wax, Japanese wax, Chinese wax, carnauba wax, and commercial wax made with "Paraffine" all Fluorescing with a Blue or Purple tint, while Colored waxes are reported to have a Fluorescence similar to the daylight Color of the wax.

The next substances described by Deribere are Gums, Rubbers, and natural Resins, which he states give very interesting results when examined under a U.V. lamp. Fluorescence of natural resins and rubbers are reported to have a varying Fluorescent response when the physical states of these two substances is altered. "Colophane" Fluorescence becomes more Green in solution, while the original Fluorescence was Bluish.

A very detailed account of pigment Fluorescence by Deribere follows, beginning with the correct statement that normal Colored pigments, such as Chrome and Zinc based pigments, usually have almost no Fluorescence. As an exception pure White Titanium pigment Fluoresces a Bluish Purple under a U.V. lamp, different from Lead White, which Fluoresces a dim Pink-Brown. Zinc White pigment is also reported to Fluoresce a Yellow or Yellowish Green. Other components of normal White pigments are also discussed, including Magnesium carbonate which Fluoresces Purple, Chalk carbonates which Fluoresce Red-Brown, and finally Talc which is reported to Fluoresce dark Purple. Deribere also writes that the making of White pigments based on Zinc oxide can vary according to the purity, production method, or cooking temperatures. A White Zinc which is very pure Fluoresces Yellow, and this is reported by the author as having been used as a control for making base products for Fluorescent pigments and Fluorescent lamps. There is a list of Colored pigments compiled by Deribere, who states that mostly Red and light tones of Red revealed interesting results under a Black light. "Le Franc" Colored pigments are reported to have only a little Fluorescence under a "Wood" lamp, but the Fluorescence is increased when these Colored pigments are incorporated into lin oil or wood oil from China.

Fluorescent Plastics are next presented by the author, who states that by Colorization with Fluorescent Colorants or by adding Fluorescent or Phosphorescent pigment it is easy to produce Fluorescent Plastics on an industrial scale, which is full of promise for the future [wait until 1959 when "Tide" bottles were initially begun to be manufactured in Fluorescent Red, which is still used today over half a century later]. "Phenolique" resin is reported by the author to be Colorless and almost always non-Fluorescent, but when containing a Fluorescent organic salt this plastic resin reacts with vivid Fluorescence under a "Wood" lamp. Studies of such resins containing Fluorescent Colorants reacted very strong under a U.V. lamp and were reported to become opaque as well as Fluorescent under a Black light, while in daylight the same plastic was transparent or translucent. For Fluorescent plastic applications, Deribere states that it is easy to create very interesting advertising, as well as remarkable decors, including the given examples of lamp shades and other luminescent objects for office and living rooms that would emit ambient light through a small source of Ultraviolet. The author even advises which Fluorescent pigments to be used for such applications, such as Rhodamine's beautiful Red Fluorescence, Eosine's Orange Fluorescence, and the Auramine's or Methylene's Yellow-Green Fluorescence. Also stated is that all of these Fluorescent pigments also have bright and pleasant Colors in the daylight as well, making them suitable for interior design. A photograph of an application is given, displaying plastic Fluorescent flowers for decors, produced with the Fluorescent pigment "Rhodoid" and photographed under "Mazda" Black lights. 'Urine-free' resins are reported to be very transparent under a Black light, allowing the production of many luminescent products. Deribere reports that "The Luminescent Products Society" perfected the pigmentation of synthetic resins in Phosphorescent products. These resins were moulded by "General Electric" to produce electrical components, such as electrical switches, rope switches for lighting, telephone, and "T.S.F." which is a prehistoric term for 'Transmission Without Wires' = "Radio!" It is reported by the author that the best of these early luminescent products have Phosphoresced for over fifty hours, but that the product's emitted light was greatly diminished after about twelve hours. The "Cristallex" produced by the 'Society Cristallex' was reported to be a Phosphorescent plastic made with "benzyl-vinylique" with a Blue-Green emitted Phosphorescent Color.

'Today's [1954] Practical Domain' for Luminescent products is next discussed by the author, in which he lists electrical switches, rope switches for lighting, key holders, hotel doors, luminous letters and numbers, decors, lamp shades, lamps, artificial flowers, and toys as being established Luminescent products, but adds the 'new' products such as ash trays, cups, plates, public signs, bags, spectacles (eyeglasses), signaling, emergency exit signs, advertising, advertising panels, advertising objects, and also included by the author is the past nightmare of watch faces and watch dials. By 1954 every one of the 800 women painting the first luminescent watches, known today as the "Radium Girls," had already died years before.

The author gives a detailed discussion on this section of Fluorescent and Phosphorescent applications, including the hope that products like varnish would be developed further so that the luminosity would not fade so quickly over time. Deribere also mentions a subject that is not even considered any more in regard to the observation of luminescence: 'Light Adaptation' which is termed just the opposite today as "Dark Adaptation." The author states that if the eyes are not adapted to the dark, Phosphorescence cannot be well seen. Continuous displays featuring Phosphorescence can be achieved with a small original "Argon Glow Lamp" or other small source of Ultraviolet energy, and can be very useful when applied to advertising displays or luminescent plastic decors when a large Black light cannot be fitted into the display. Deribere also reports that luminescent plastic products were more common today [1954], and had wide spread use in advertising decors and theater Art, with the given example of Fluorescent stage props under Black lights.

Luminescent Paper is next examined by the author, who begins by stating that old papers and books effected by mold and moisture can be easily identified under a "Wood" lamp, because the mold and moisture Fluoresces with a bright Bluish or Whitish Color, which is usually brighter than the Fluorescence of the paper itself. As in the beginning of all movements, Deribere had wild dreams for Black light applications, such as his idea for 'Luminescent Books' in the future, which could be read under a Black light, which would be very relaxed and void of a distracting White light source. Deribere dreams of these 'Luminescent Books' being produced with Fluorescent or Phosphorescent Paper or even printed with luminescent Text, which would need only a small lamp rich in Ultraviolet to read it. Another invention of the "Switzer Brothers" from two decades earlier, Fluorescent paper is reported by the author as not presenting a problem to produce, with just the use of organic Colorants or Fluorescent salts, who's list was already very large to choose from in 1954. The point is made that what is to consider in the production of luminescent paper is the strength of it's Fluorescence, which was often mediocre, but which also could be increased with the addition of glue, animal fibers, or the addition of Fluorescent mineral powders. This information was originally published by Deribere in 1936 as 'U.V. Rays and Fluorescence in the Paper Industry.'

'Inks, Pencils, and Crayons for Luminescent Writing' is next discussed by Deribere, relating the fact that luminescent writing could be made through the production of luminescent chalk, ink, or crayons. A receipt for making Fluorescent ink is given by the author in which ten grams of "Esculine" and ten grams of 'Silicates of Soda ash' are dissolved in a solution of 1% "Alcali caustique." Twenty-five cubic centimeters of this obtained solution is added to the same amount of regular ink to produce luminous ink.

In 1954 it was reported by Deribere that a process for using Fluorescent Colors for Trichrome photography reproduction had been industrialized by "Eastman Kodak Co." This 'Fluorescence Process' was developed by A, Murray and J.A.C. Yule, in which the pigments used for Trichrome photography absorb a large percentage of 'radiations' that these pigments should reflect or transmit, so there was a necessity of correcting the Colors by reducing Yellow and Pink. This was done manually or by a photographic masking technique, but with the 'Fluorescence Process' of Yule and Murray the document in Color is especially made for Trichrome reproduction, resulting in directly making a Color-correct reproduction. This process was published in 1947 by L.P. Clerc as 'A New Process for Trichrome Reproduction.'

Discussing Security Checking with Ultraviolet lamps [which started in 1941 in Cleveland, Ohio by the "Switzer Brothers"] the author writes about texts, checks, and printed money. Instructions are presented by Deribere as washing a text with an Oxidation (a wash with pomegranate) followed by an acid bath, resulting in revived text when washed in Fluorescent inks, which relieves the original text when again washed in Purplish Black, and which leaves the luminescent background - the letters of the text - visible again. As a historic example of such texts, the "Dead Sea Scrolls" were reproduced onto microfilm in the National Library of Paris using a classic microfilm camera that automatically turns the pages in it's self-contained dark room, fitted with four "Mazda MAW 120" Black lights. The photograph of this Black light microfilm camera shows a huge machine about six feet (2 m) wide and about ten feet (3 m) tall fitted with bellows that must be a full meter (yard) tall. Deribere next presents two photographs of the ancient religious texts, first under a normal White light, which he describes as a text that was washed then put under pressure with wet sand and finally copied by monks. The same ancient religious text is next presented under Black lights, which allowed the discovery of the original writing. A whole volume of these religious texts were restored with this method by the National Library of Paris.

Deribere next presents two photographs of Postage Stamps, the first of which clearly illustrates two identical stamps. The second photo shows the same two stamps put under a "Wood" lamp, and it clear to see even in this Black and White photo that there is a big difference between the two stamps. Under a Black light one of the stamps Fluoresces a bright Pink, while the other identical stamp Fluoresces a dark Red, clearly portraying the different editions of the same stamp. What is next discussed here by Deribere is the use of Black lights in detecting falsified or altered postage stamps, which today has been utilized for over fifty years.

The field of Ultraviolet use in the restoration and examination of old Paintings is a common technique also for many decades in use, but in 1954 this restoration/examination technique was relatively new and was detailed by Deribere. The author reports that in expert Art restoration and examination the "Wood" lamp is playing a very important role. Over-painting, scratches, varnish defects, false dates, hidden indications, and falsified signatures are all easily visible under a Black light. Deribere gives the example of a Goya painting that was examined under a "Wood" lamp, making it instantly visible that a false signature and date was painted over the original Goya signature and date. Another example by Deribere is a painting attributed to Bernado from 1525. Under a "Wood" lamp the Ultraviolet energy proved that this painting was made one full century later than 1525. Ancient Japanese paintings were also proved to be false with the examination under a Black light. While many modern paint Colors have a Fluorescent response, most old paint Colors seldom Fluoresce. Retouched or covered signatures on paintings are also discovered with examination of the Black light, because usually the top layer of paint pigment has a much different Fluorescent reaction from the original oil Colors underneath them. White is easily identifiable, because in ancient times painters used a Silver White, and a Zinc White was used much later on, while in contemporary times Titanium White is used. Cellerier documented examples of these differences of paint pigment Fluorescence from paintings in the "Musee du Louvre" to establish correct pigment information regarding the specific characteristics of each painting master. Since well before the printing of Deribere's book in 1954 the Louvre had used the Fluorescence of paintings extensively for photography and examination. As an example of the Black light in the examination of paintings, two photographs are presented of a late Egyptian Funerary portrait of Fayoum during the Roman period painted on the face plate of a mummy with the ancient "Encaustic" technique (wax and pigment). The daylight photo is printed next to a photo of the same Funerary mask in the Black light. The Black light photograph of the Funerary mask reveals invisible details, such as the brush strokes and texturing

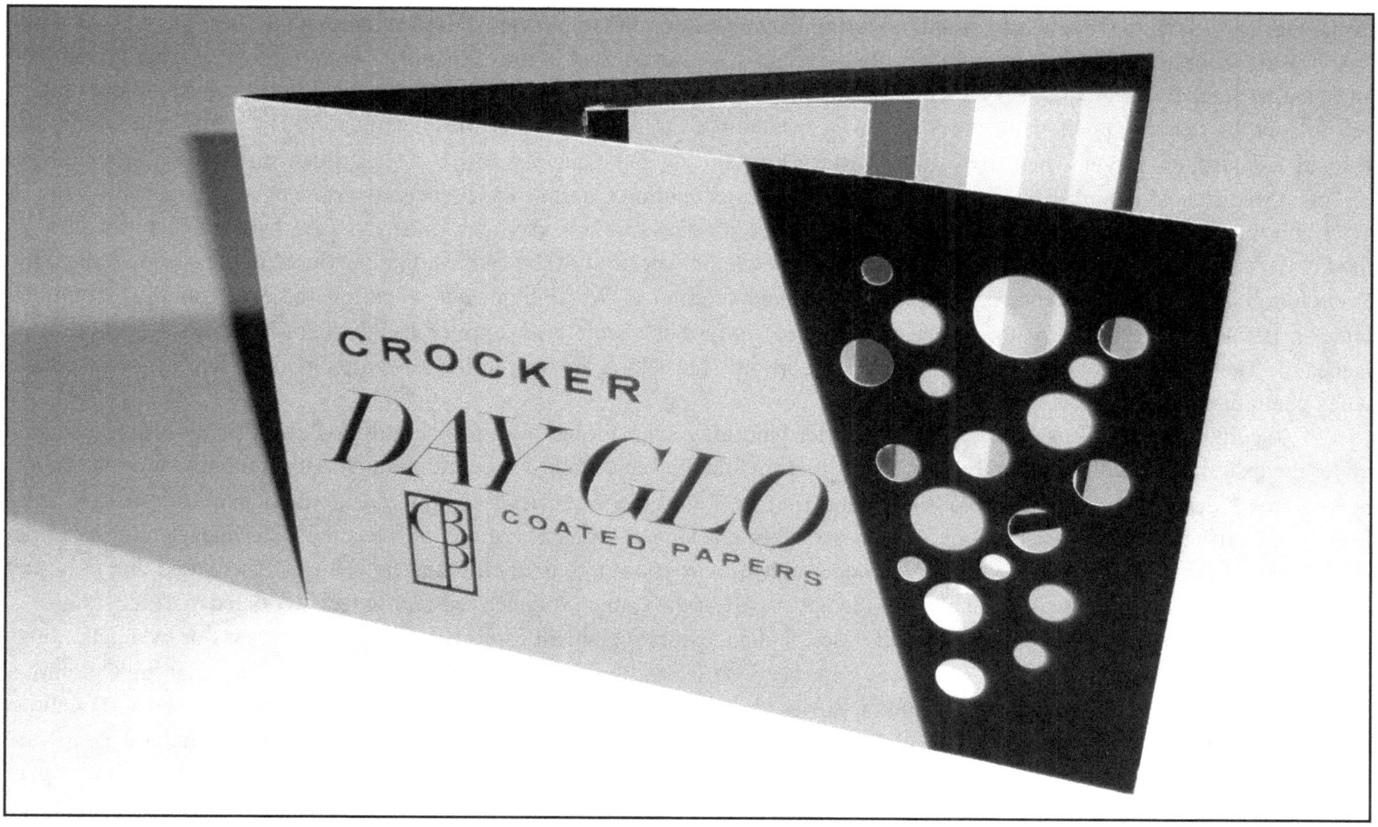

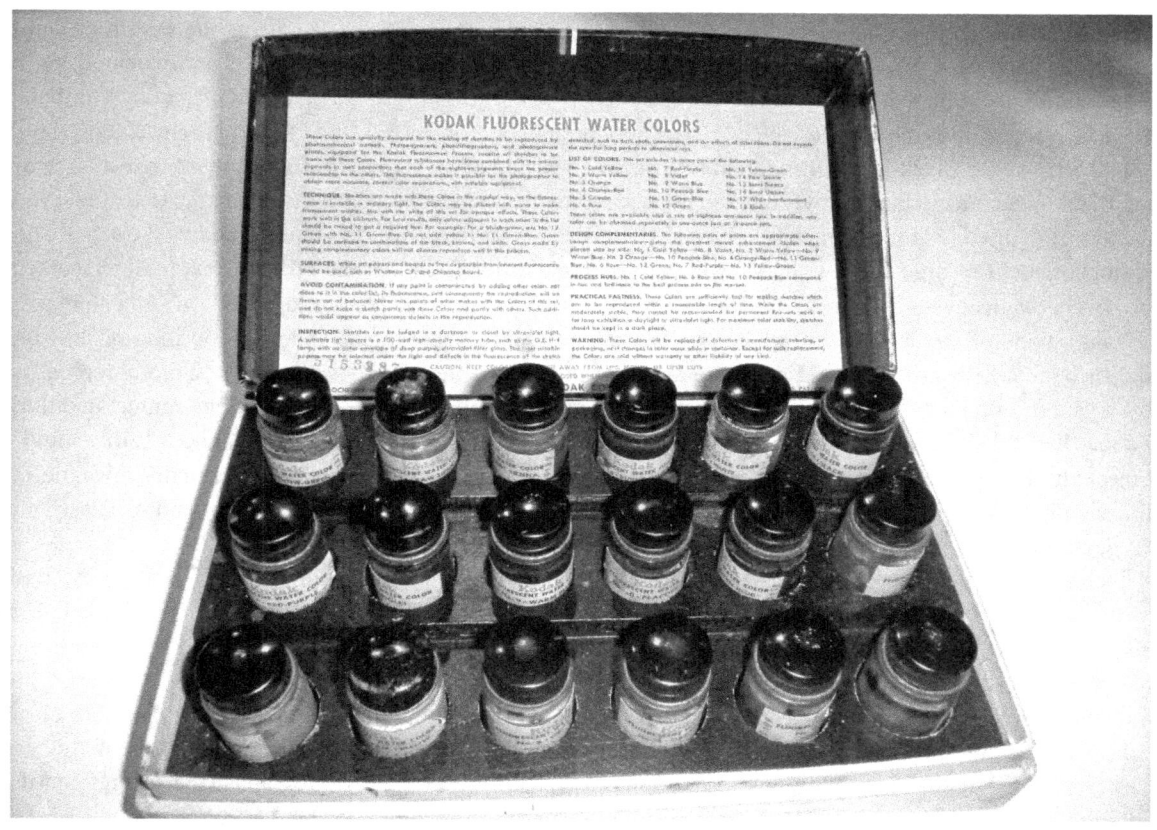

1940s-1950s "Crocker" "DAY-GLO" Fluorescent "Coated Papers," sample booklet

1940s-1950s "Kodak Fluorescent Water Colors" Fluorescent retouch set for photographs

of the hair as well as the brush strokes and texturing of the clothing in the portrait. As illustrated in Deribere's book, the study made in the laboratory of the Louvre on Egyptian Funerary Masks painted in the "Encaustic" technique reveal many unknown and unseen details when examined under a Black light. Through this examination with the Black light it became possible to reconstruct the painting methods of the Artists who painted the Egyptian Funerary Masks around 30 B.C., from the time of the Roman conquest of Egypt when these odd Western portraits on the Funerary Masks of Egyptian mummies prolonged the Egyptian tradition of mummification. A Fresco in the old Accounting Court of the French government was damaged by fire in 1871 and was expertly restored. While this restoration is not discernible in daylight, under a Black light the restored areas of the Fresco are clearly visible. Another given example is a female portrait of the Burges, likely painted in the second half of the Sixteenth century, which appears completely normal and original in White light, but when the same portrait was examined under a Black light, a heavy restoration was revealed. A further example is supplied by Deribere in which the 'Portrait of Isabeaude Baviee' from 1435 had a portion of the portrait's hat which appears to have been painted by two different people when examined under a Black light.

Sculptures are discussed by the author after paintings, with the ability of distinguishing identifiable visual evidence under the examination of the sculpture with a Black light. Old marble statues can be differentiated from modern marble statues, because the Fluorescence of old marble is different from the Fluorescence of newer marble. Alterations in marble statues using heat are identifiable under a Black light, as well as recent cracks and retouches of the marble statue. Ritcher demonstrated on the "Statue of Diogene" in the New York Metropolitan Museum of Art that under a Black light it was discovered that only part of the ancient marble statue was original, with the upper part of the statue produced with more recently dated marble.

Ceramics made with cooked clay, Oil vases, and ancient porcelain all can reveal identifying aspects or even alterations when examined under a Black light, as well as Tapestry. Deribere discusses these substances and explains that the Coloration and the woven support of ancient carpets and tapestries can be easily identified under a Black light as well. Gems and precious stones are mentioned, with the author explaining that important differences and identifying properties of natural gems and precious stones can be easily seen under a Black light. Especially useful, and still being used today, is the examination of gem stones under Black lights to determine if the precious stone is real or a synthetic imitation.

The following chapter in Deribere's book deals with the important subject of Fluorescence Photography, which was known in France as the antiquated "Fluorographie" still in 1954. The author explains that for finding defects in surfaces a procedure was established named 'Fluorography' that could be utilized without fear of damage to the samples. Through the use of a Black light, penetrating cracks could be identified. This was another procedure invented and patented by the "Switzer Brothers" years before used for the detection of what is called "Metal Stress," and was later published by Deribere in 1948 as 'Control of Surface States through Fluorescence.' Two photographs are presented of a 'Fluorography' laboratory, first in the White light, and next in the Black light. The laboratory setup consisted of an angled document stand with a large metal fixture containing a Black light on a stand above the mounted document. There is also a rubber scraper to remove any excess Fluorescent product applied to 'Fluorographed' objects. The Black light photo of the same lab shows the scientist in front of a brilliant document under the large Black light, as well as a brilliant bottle of Fluorescent product next to the document.

For Archeological studies there is presented next a prehistoric Neolithic stick of a commander of "La Marche" (Vienna) made of engraved Reindeer bone. This Fluorescence photograph renders the writing or drawing scratched into the reindeer bone clearly when printed as White marks on a Black bone. The details of this "Fluorographie" are given as being taken by G. Tendron on "Plaque Panchro 32" film stock at f.16, with an exposure time of one minute and thirty-seconds, using an Orange filter "RM" and one "Mazda MAW 75" Black light. The second archeological photo is of a mold for Tibetan butter, and through "Fluorographie" very detailed Tibetan engravings are visible, which were virtually invisible in the White light. Again, the photograph is a negative with the engravings rendered in White and the background as Black, making these symbols very legible.

As incontestable evidence of the advantage of the use of "Fluorographie" in Archeological study, there are four photographs in Deribere's book of a damaged antique marble sculpted head from the Louvre collection. These four pictures are presented first in the White light, and next with a luminous product applied to the entire surface of the marble head. This Fluorescence photograph clearly displays in White only the heavily damaged areas of the marble sculpture. For the third photograph of this marble head the negative of the Fluorescence photograph is printed, displaying even more clear the heavy damage to the marble, this time in Black on the White background of the statue. The fourth image of this same marble sculpture was created by sandwiching both the positive and negative Fluorescence photographs (the second and third photos) revealing a very clear graphic illustration of the surface damage to the sculpture. Deribere states that in the laboratory of the Louvre the process of "Fluorographie" was used for the restoration of damaged prints, marble busts, antique high-reliefs, and also for engravings in metal. For Artistic or industrial reproductions "Fluorographie" was used on drawings, wood, paper, ceramics, and leather to view the 'grains' of the structures. The last five photographs of sculpture are of an Egyptian pot suspended above three supports. The first photo displays the Egyptian sculpture in the White light, which appears uniformly dark Grey with dim indications of engraving. The next "Fluorographie" photo of the same Egyptian sculpture reveals bright White engravings that are lucid against the very dark surface area of the sculpture, and very easy to document. The third photo of this Egyptian sculpture is a negative of the second "Fluorographie" photo accenting the three-dimensionally of the sculpture. The fourth photo is a "Fluorographie" 'drawing' obtained by again the sandwiching of the "Fluorographie" print and the negative of this "Fluorographie" print, and is an absolutely clear rendering of every tiny detail of the engraving on the sculpture's surface. The fifth photo of this Egyptian sculpture is a sandwiching of the first White light photograph of the sculpture and the second "Fluorographie" print, and gives a very precise graphic representation of the engravings of the sculpture, and the naturalistic impression of an actual photographed statue.

Deribere next gives a detailed account of the detection of "Metal Stress" through the use of a Black light, first invented by the "Switzer Brothers." 'Applications in Metal Works and Production' is the title of this section in Deribere's book, and is accompanied by two photographs. The first White light 'Macrography' (close-up photography) of metal stress cracks in a piece of steel reveals what looks like four Black pencil marks on a White background. The second "Fluorographie" print of the metal stress cracks in the Black light reveal the same four cracks, but under the U.V. lamp these cracks are photographed with a greater brilliance, and also illustrates the crack's volume. In this second "Fluorographie" image there are several metal stress cracks clearly visible that were impossible to see in the White light photograph. About eight years after the "Switzer Brothers" invented Fluorescent Metal Stress Detection Maurice Deribere published two papers on the subject in 1949, 'Applications of Fluorescence in the Aeronautic Industry' and 'The Control and Study of Surface Metallurgy with Fluorescence.' For another example of Ultraviolet detection of manufactured stress or defects, Deribere prints a photo of a glass test-tube which is cracked. In the daylight the crack in the glass test-tube is undetectable, but in the photograph under the Black light the crack is very evident, being a White fissure on a Black background. Deribere concludes this very informative section on "Fluorographie" in his book with the statement that he believes the importance and use of "Fluorographie" cannot be denied.

In one of the most important sections of the book Deribere gives an incredibly detailed account of Fluorescent Pigment and Paint production up to 1954, more detailed than the present author has ever seen in any book. This section is entitled 'Coloration in Mass Production' and begins with the historically correct statement that the most important source of information pertaining to the production of "Daylight" Fluorescent Colors is contained in the U.S. patent awarded to J.L. and R.C. Switzer - the "Switzer Brothers" - which is extremely detailed. The Fluorescent pigments consist mostly of a Fluorescent Colorant dissolved in a solvent. Dissolving also a non-polymerizing resin results in the polymerizing state of a transparent glasslike solid substance which can be seen in a very early photograph of Joseph Switzer inspecting this glasslike substance directly from it's production machine in the 1930s. According to the U.S. patent of the Switzer brothers, "Urea" and "Melamine formaldehyde" (a hard thermosetting plastic manufactured from Melamine and Formaldehyde by polymerization and used as a famous kitchen utensil product named "Melmac") resins are very useful for this purpose. If highly concentrated Colorants are used with a higher molecular weight, the wavelength of the emitted light increases as well. This solid glasslike Fluorescent pigment cannot be ground beyond a certain fineness or it will damage the pigment's crystal structure and diminish it's Fluorescent intensity, which is the limiting factor in the production of Fluorescent pigment for commercial sale. Deribere informs the reader that in 1954 there were many companies manufacturing Fluorescent "Daylight" pigments, including the French companies "LUX-Color," "SOFAC," and "Prospa." The process for the production of "Daylight" Fluorescent pigments from the company with the very healthy name "Canadian Radium Uranium Corporation" entails the Coloring of the resin in solution with a Fluorescent Colorant. Through this process fine and vivid Fluorescent pigments are produced which are of a high enough quality to be used for manufacturing Fluorescent inks and translucent or transparent varnish.

For applications of "Daylight" Fluorescent pigments Deribere informs the reader that Fluorescent Colors were introduced to society in a wide variety of uses, such as advertising. The author next gives the origin of public Fluorescent use, stating that in the past years a pedestrian's eyes are attracted by 'shouting' Fluorescent letters and numbers, Deribere writes that this technique began in France from 'Signaling Panels' used on trucks of the Leclerc Army of the French military using Fluorescent Red and Orange panels. It is doubtful that "Signaling Panels" for the military began in France, as Deribere writes, because the U.S. military was using this technique in the late 1930s already, before the Second world war, and it has been documented as the first use of these Fluorescent "Signaling Panels." Deribere next states that these Fluorescent "Signaling Panels" gave an idea to revive the old ideas of the "Tyndall Effect" which scientists presented to their students a very long time before the invention of the first Ultraviolet Filter by Dr. Robert Wood in 1903. John Tyndall was a scientist who lived from

1820-1893 and is remembered for his discovery of the "Tyndall Effect" in 1859, also known as "Tyndall Scattering." This "Tyndall Effect" explained the scattering of light by particles in suspension or by collided particles. As an example, flour suspended in water appears Blue because Blue light is scattered by the flour particles more than Red light. This is also what makes the sky appear Blue, as Sir George Stokes stated in the early 1850s, just a short time before the "Tyndall Effect" was postulated.

Deribere next states that the final application for Advertising, the public display panel ("Billboards") took a long time to be perfected. For rules to create a public display panel with high visibility, Deribere suggests: 1. Creating a strong contrast of brilliance, such as Fluorescent text on a Black background, 2. Choose Complementary Colors to create a strong contrast of Colors such as Yellow on Blue, or Red on Green. The author explains that a pure Red on a bright Green creates one of the strongest Color contrasts there is, causing the eye to correctly adapt to only one of these two Colors at a time, the purest, the brightest, or the most vivid of the Colors. 3. The third suggestion by the author is to use Fluorescent Colors on either a dark or Black background, or even a highly-reflective non-Fluorescent background. Deribere published this information in a 1953 paper 'The Fluorescent Colors.'

The author next explains Fluorescent Inks and states that Fluorescent Lacquers could be adapted to be used to create Fluorescent Inks. Fluorescent textiles are also discussed, explaining that an application of new Fluorescent Colors on textiles had been created. Rayon or Acetate material such a Nylon is treated and Color is dissolved in a resin that will be polymerized, trying to achieve the same structure as "Daylight" Fluorescent lacquers. Solvents can also cause the material fibers to expand, altering the final product. Fluorescent textiles produced in this manner had been used by 1954 for advertising, decoration, airplane signalization, and even lace, umbrellas, and other accessories.

"Optical Bleach" is also explained by Deribere, stating that the technique is only an application of Fluorescence in daylight. The "Optical Bleach" was originally designed to compensate for the Yellowing effect of White textile fabrics. In actuality, this was designed to make T-shirts Fluoresce out in the Sun, creating the dream of an advertising slogan from many years ago: "Whiter than White." Deribere states that this "Optical Bleach" process was used in the textile industry, in the paper industry, and even in manufactured soaps. Deribere concludes this section of his book with a list of many possible difficulties and complexities created by the added use of Fluorescent Colors to the spectrum of ordinary Colors, especially in trying to accurately reproduce consistent Fluorescent Colors.

Deribere dedicates the next entire chapter of his book to 'Varnish and Luminescent Paints.' The author informs the reader that luminescent varnishes for coating an object to make it Fluorescent are created with binders that U.V. energy passes through, such as water, alcohol, nitro-cellulose, or synthetic resins. The manufacturing of these Fluorescent varnishes was relatively simple, even before 1954. A list of luminescent products in use during this era is supplied by the author, including Lacquers or classic Fluorescent pigments, pigments dissolved in varnish, "Daylight" Fluorescent pigments or lacquers, and Phosphorescent pigments.

Formulas to create Fluorescent Paint are given by the author, in which he instructs for the preparation of Luminescent Paint a vehicle and auxiliary agents which must be chosen in proportion to the intended use of the paint. Deribere suggests that vehicles based on oil are to be avoided if they will be in contact with Sulfurs, except Zinc sulfide, and that Dammer gums are widely used as appropriate vehicles for luminescent paints.

Explaining Phosphorescent Paint the author states that Sulphates constitute the normal Phosphorescent Pigments. Suggestions for the production of Phosphorescent paint are given by the author: 1. Lacquer should be used that is Colorless and permeable to Ultraviolet, 2. To avoid any chemical reactions in the Phosphorescent pigment, there should be a weak presence of Acid and a presence of pH to ensure stability of the pigment., 3. Insure enough water is in the pigment to avoid humidity absorption that could cause the destruction of the pigment, 4. And finally, that the Phosphorescent pigment's vehicle should contain no trace of heavy metal, which were already in that era known to be 'Fluorescent Poisoners,' termed today "Fluorescent quenchers." Another bit of advice is added that with use of this Phosphorescent, any "Siccative" (drying agents) based on Lead, Cobalt, or Manganese should be used.

Chapter twenty-five of Deribere's book concentrates on Applications of Luminous Products in 'Signalization, Decoration, and Advertising.' The reader is informed that Fluorescent papers, prints, material, and Inks have made a large impact on applications of luminescence, especially when used in combination with a Black light. The author states that the Black light was used in the development of luminescent advertising, theatre, and decoration between 1935 and 1939, then during the Second world war by the military, so Deribere prophetically concludes that this would become known as *'War Time Lighting.'*

'Normal Lighting During War Time' is next discussed and the author reveals some facts about the Black light's use during the Second world war, and after, in France. Display windows of stores are suggested by Deribere to be created with luminescent displays, and products that would change from White light to Black light could present to the public different aspects of luminescence. The author also states that the use of the Black light in store display windows before the Second world war already was very popular with the public. Then Deribere relates the facts of the importance of the Black light's use during war time, informing the reader that during the Second world war Black light advertising was even more interesting because it could be lit up even during the most severe restrictions of "Black Out," because in the Black light display there are no White lights to be seen in darkness, which made the displays stand out even more to the public during "Black Out," and created no reflection in the dark skies above. The author also suggests the use of a Red light, in combination with the Black light, to give a bit of ambient light to displays. Since this technology produces no disturbing, detectable White light emission it was then possible to create outdoor advertising panels that were Fluorescent and used Black lights even during World war two. This is precisely the reason that only these Fluorescent display panels were allowed for official outdoor displays in France during the Second world war, the reader is informed. The three companies that made these displays in France were "Luminographe" which produced outdoor Fluorescent signs, "Meyer et Chaigne," and "Baezner" which created Fluorescent shop display windows. Photographs accompany this explanation, such as a White light and a Black light photo of a huge generator that had Fluorescent Red paint applied to it as 'Accent lighting.' The actual use of the Fluorescent paint and Black light on the huge generator was termed 'Alert Lighting,' which consisted of Fluorescent and Phosphorescent paint being coated on handles, numbers, and other important parts of the generator.

Other aspects of the Black light's technological use during the war are given as Signalization and Distance Marking Poles, which required the best luminescent paint for permanent use outdoors. Deribere also writes about a 'Luminescent Agent,' who would have a helmet, gloves, and the buttons of the uniform created with Phosphorescent abilities, as well as the placement of this 'Luminous Agent' in a circle under a Black light. There are four photographs presented with this text, a White light and a Black light photo of Fluorescent signs and distance marking poles both with their own "Mazda MAW 75" Black lights installed. The difference between the photos is nothing less than dramatic. The next White and Black light photos are of the entrance to a bomb shelter, with 'Alert Lighting' consisting of a "Mazda" Black light and luminescent directional signals in the bomb shelter, which stand out like beacons in the Black light 'Alert Lighting' photographs. Another use for Phosphorescence during the Second world war, which occurred in Germany, was told to me in the Museum. In Berlin as a tourist you can visit the "Unterwelten" in the underground (which the German word roughly translates to), that consists of one room which had been used by soldiers that is completely painted in Phosphorescent Green for use during bombing raids. This one room "Unterwelten" for German soldiers during the Second world war is so bright that when all the lights are turned off a newspaper can still be read. Michèle has also shown me a famous Phosphorescent building in Montmartre, Paris which was also made for "Black outs" during World war two.

Deribere next explains a design that was invented specifically for the "Black Out" conditions of the Second world war in France, but was never realized because of the slow government administration involved. Since cars could not use their headlights when driving during "Black Out," there was an idea to create U.V. reactive license plates and a Black light installed on the back of each car for identification. The author explains that the technology could have been used on cars, roads, landing strips for airplanes, and harbors, by coating luminous paint on poles, panels, and the even the edge of sidewalks for greater public safety. During war time such a technology could have been invisible to warplanes above and at the same time could have ensured safe auto circulation. Deribere considers using this technology with larger, more luminous license plates after the war. The author also has the idea that maybe the entire car could be coated with Fluorescent or Phosphorescent paint! This was originally published in a paper by Deribere in the middle of the Second world war in 1944, called 'Applications of Luminescence in the Car Industry.' Just two years before Deribere's publication, the 1942 book by DeMent and Dake, "Fluorescent Chemicals and their Applications" contains a section in which the authors explain that the Oregon State Highway Department was experimenting at that time with painting the dividing line in the middle of the highways with Fluorescent Yellow paint. The Fluorescent paint was found to Fluoresce at night and in heavy fog with the bright headlights of the cars. Then DeMent and Dake take a quantum leap into the future by suggesting that not only should the Fluorescent Yellow paint be incorporated in the production of the concrete of the dividing lines, but that perhaps it would be a good idea to incorporate Fluorescent Color into the entire *highway's* concrete! In the Museum collection there is the patent form from Sweden during the 1980s that was issued for a plan involving the whole country of Sweden to do exactly what DeMent and Dake had suggested almost fifty years before: resurface every highway in Sweden with synthetic Fluorescent pigment incorporated into the pavement, and also to fit each and every car front with Ultraviolet lamps to be able to drive at night with the entire highway emitting light. This technological idea will most likely be a standard in the future. After this plan was put into it's testing stage the Swedish Fluorescent highway resurfacing was cancelled because of the hazard to motorists in the event of a broken lens on the Ultraviolet lamps on the front of the car, which doesn't sound like a very good reason, because it is easy to imagine construction of the Ultraviolet lamps that could have prevented this from happening.

This section in Deribere's book contains an antique White light and Black light photograph of 'Dashboard elements' in an airplane, with every dial and number of six different instruments coated with Fluorescent and Phosphorescent paint, and the use of a "Westinghouse" "Wood" lamp (Black light). Another antique set of photographs of an entire U.S. Army Air Corps (before the U.S. Air Force was begun) airplane cockpit instrument panel is presented in the 1942 "Fluorescent Chemicals and their Applications" by DeMent and Dake, in which there is a White photo of the instrument panel in 'glaring ordinary' daylight, and then another photo of the same instrument panel in the dark with each and every instrument dial's details vivid and clearly visible through their coating of 'Fluorescent phosphors' under Ultraviolet lamps. The entire cockpit and the pilots are completely invisible, but the instruments are brilliant. The credit for these two photos is given as: "Official U.S. Army Air Corps photograph."

Deribere concludes this section with the facts that the first Luminescent Green products were created to relate to the maximum sensitivity of the human eye, but by the 1950s there were many different Colors favored, such as Red-Orange in the U.S.A., Yellow in Switzerland, Blue-Green in Italy, Orange-Yellow in Canada, and Red in England. Red was considered the Color that had the least disturbance to night vision, but Red needs more U.V. energy than some of the other Fluorescent Colors to luminesce. In the 1950 "Congress CIE Paris" it was decided upon that the luminescent Color Green should be used to create very legible instrument panels that would be of the least distraction to pilots.

Again, as a conclusion to the book, Deribere discusses in further depth luminescent 'Advertising and Decoration,' explaining that there were many luminescent products available on the market such a luminescent 'Salts' and 'Colorants' in all Colors for fabrics, paints, varnish, and plastics making the creation of Fluorescent and Phosphorescent displays possible. The author also points out that luminescent Art in decoration and advertising was already in public use, but that there was still a 'larger horizon' for these luminescent applications. Store window displays composed of Fluorescent objects or covered with Fluorescent Color under Black lights were already in use, and were very effective opening up an infinite amount of possibilities the author explains, and then continues on with his ideas for Fluorescent decors in 'modern homes,' such as aquariums, paintings, entrance halls, and window boxes. These ideas were already formulated by Deribere in 1938 and presented in his paper 'The Black light at Home.' The four photographs in this section are my favorite images in Deribere's book, and were the reason that this antique book was essential to find. I remember seeing these photos for the first time and being virtually stunned: *Black light Store Window Displays from the 1930s on one of the most expensive and most famous shopping street in the world, the Champs-Elysées in Paris!* The first two photos are separate Black light and White light pictures of an advertising competition in store display windows, and was designed by the 'Lamps Company.' The White light photo at night shows a large store window display with two boxes of different heights covered with Fluorescent patterned fabric. The smaller box had a small bunch of Fluorescent flowers on it, and the taller box had an extravagant large highly Fluorescent flower bouquet in a vase. In front of the two boxes there is another Flower bouquet of Fluorescent roses on the floor. There is a dark curtain behind the entire window display, which appears as a normal store window in the White light photo, but under a powerful "Mazda MAW 3000" Black light, the window display is totally transformed and must have been stunning. These large flower bouquets stand in midair vividly Fluorescent against the Blackness all around them, with the inclusion of the Fluorescent patterned fabric at their bases. The next two photographs are, in my opinion, the most precious images in the Deribere book, a White light and a Black light photo of a Refrigerator Store Window Display on the Champs-Elysées between 1936 and 1937! The store that had this Fluorescent window display on the Champs-Elysées in Paris was "Frigeco" and the display was fantastic! The White light photo shows an antiquated 'new' refrigerator in a large store window display. The refrigerator sits on a piece of 'ice' and there are broken pieces of 'ice' in front of the refrigerator, in the foreground of the display. Amongst these pieces of 'ice' there is the credit sign that is partially legible in the photo and can be read as "Lumiere" and "Mazda," but which completely read 'Lumiere Noire' and "Mazda." The bottom left of the White light photo also includes what looks like a large angled metal lamp unit that was most likely a Black light unit, and behind the antiquated refrigerator is a wall that is White in daylight with odd simple Black sketches on it. This White wall behind the refrigerator becomes tall ice-covered snow-peaks of mountains in the Black light, made with "Invisible" Fluorescent paint, which made it nearly invisible in the White light. The Black light photograph also shows the entire refrigerator itself being intensely Fluorescent and looking like a triangular block of solid ice. I looks to me like highly Fluorescent clear plastic or glass was used to encase the whole refrigerator, the same transparent Fluorescent plastic or glass that the pieces of broken 'ice' in front of the refrigerator and the piece of 'ice' that the refrigerator is sitting on were mostly likely made of. Since there is no given date on this spectacular Fluorescent store window display from Paris's Champs-Elysées, I researched the actual refrigerator for sale in the window. The logo on the refrigerator is from "General Electric," and the design of the refrigerator is something rarely seen even in photographs. It is apparently White with two large door hinges on the right, a large vertical door handle on the left, a raised design element running the entire vertical length of the front of the refrigerator, a horizontal "General Electric" logo near the top of the door, and the best part: two legs that were part of the overall design for the refrigerator to stand on, with an arch between them. After two days of looking at too many pictures of ancient refrigerators on the internet, I came to the conclusion that this "General Electric" refrigerator could have only been the 1936 or 1937 model. Up until 1935 the few refrigerators that were sold were extravagantly expensive - nearly the price of a new automobile - and had a very antique design that most people today have never seen which consisted of a round separate cooling system mounted to the top of the refrigerator. In 1936 and 1937 the first "General Electric" refrigerators were sold with the ugly round cooling system that had been mounted on the top of the refrigerator finally flattened down, condensed, and totally concealed behind the design of the refrigerator, like this refrigerator in the Champs-Elysées store window display. The design of the front of the refrigerators from "General Electric" also then changed noticeably again after 1937.

    Deribere next writes about the 'Project of Rational Irradiation with the Black light' as he explains that in addition to the darkness created in Black light displays, experiments were being made to add a weak Red light to determine if it was possible to add a limited ambient light without disturbing the Black light effect. The following photograph that is presented is also precious: a Fluorescent public billboard under a multitude of Black lights. A very large ten by four and a half yard (meter) "Mazda Lumiere Noire" Billboard is photographed with all it's Black lights displaying the advertisement. Top left is the large company name "MAZDA," bottom left is "Lumiere noire" (Black light) and in the center is a highly Fluorescent masked harlequin holding a candle while dancing amongst two Fluorescent birds, stars and painted curtains. The drawing and the design do not in any way look modern, but instantly bring to mind imagery from the 1930s-1950s. The bottom right of the huge Fluorescent billboard has the Artist's name "Robert Ambroise." There is also included two mechanical drawings of the design of this huge Fluorescent billboard, a front view and side view. The explanation of the billboard states that in the unit which the billboard was installed into, the top section, held ten Black light projectors(!) each being a "PM6" Black light projector equipped with an "MAW 125" Black light. Above this row of powerful Black light projectors emitting a total of 1,250 watts of Black light, there was a small wooden roof constructed to guard from the weather. As if this 1,250 watts of Black light was not enough, the bottom of the billboard held another ten "PM6" Black light projectors, again each holding an "MAW 125" Black light and totaling another 1,250 watts of Black light. The total amount of Black light for this single billboard was a staggering 2,500 watts! These bottom ten Black light projectors were encased in an aluminum mounting covered with glass to protect from the rain. There was most probably several times the amount of Black light on this single French billboard from the Second world war era, then was used on the entire 'Ice Capades' Black light spectacle in Amsterdam in 2008! Although the billboard was only ten by four and a half yards (meters), the actual unit that held the billboard and the twenty Black lights was about eleven meters long and a full seven and a half meters tall. The top row of ten Black light projectors had a sixty centimeter (2 foot) roof over them and a sixty centimeter wide fascia board in front of them. The bottom row of ten more Black light projectors had a similar sixty centimeter wide base as well as a fifty centimeter (20 inch) fascia board in front of them to hide the actual lamps from the view.

    The following important photograph in Deribere's book is an alternative of the preceding Fluorescent billboard, being designed for use inside a store and utilizing tubular Black light units instead of Black light projectors. This photograph of a Fluorescent mattress advertising panel was mounted in the French store "Dunlopilo" and is a good example of a Fluorescent poster mounted in a joined frame and utilizing tubular Black lights, similar to contemporary Black lights. The Fluorescent advertising panel has a man in pajamas waking up and stretching with a smile on his face, and his body is stylized to represent a mattress also, as the advertisement is for "le matelas Dunlopillo" ('The Mattress Dunlopillo'). Bottom left is the company name "Dunlop," as vividly Fluorescent as the entire advertising panel. In front of this Fluorescent advertising panel mounted on the wall in a store are several pieces of furniture that appear to be solely illuminated by the emitted light of this Fluorescent advertising panel. Again, a very useful mechanical drawing of the front and side of this indoor Fluorescent advertising panel accompanies the photograph. The Fluorescent mattress panel was two and a half yards (meters) wide and two yards tall, but the total unit including the Black lights was 3.2 by 2.6 yards. The top section of the unit held two 1.2 meter long tubular Black lights, as well as the bottom section of the unit. The two sides of this unit held a 1.2 meter and a 60 cm tubular Black light each, and around the entire perimeter of the Fluorescent advertisement were fascia boards to hide the tubular Black lights from view. This indoor Fluorescent advertising panel contained a total of six 1.2 meter Black lights and two 60 centimeter Black lights - it must have been Bright!

There follows another special Fluorescent Store Window Display in Paris from the same general time period, and was created by "Establishments C.C.C." of Paris. This surreal Fluorescent window display was the re-creation of a landscape, with a large highly Fluorescent statue of what could be a child angel on an animal, mounted on a four-stepped pedestal with some dimly Fluorescent figures around it in long material cloaks with a Fluorescent tree on the left. The background and tall ceiling of the display are covered with Fluorescent stars as a final touch. The installation of this Fluorescent window display was made by "Establishments Socofray," and it is explained by Deribere that the workers had to determine the types of Black light projectors or reflectors that were needed for this display, as well as the amount of Black light that was necessary for the installation, and also which type of Black light lamp was needed, discharge lamps or Mercury vapor tubular Black lights of either a high or low pressure.

A large Fluorescent Panel is next photographed in the Black light, which was created for a stand in 'The Electricity of France' exhibit of what appears to be the 1940s or 50s by the design and drawings of the imagery. There are two female models made of a simple Fluorescent outline drawing, but both models have highly Fluorescent dresses flying around, which appear to be three-dimensional real dresses collaged onto the large panel. There are also simple Fluorescent outline drawings of houses, a basket in one of the girl's hands, trees, Saturn, the Sun, the Eiffel Tower, stars, and a cityscape. "l'Ete" ('Summer') and "la Nuit" ('the night') are written by each model, and under each of them is the credit "Lumiere Noire Mazda" ('Black light Mazda').

For a real public application of the Black light the next photograph is of a Fluorescent model created by the employees of the "R.A.P.T." in Paris for the fiftieth anniversary of the Metro. The Fluorescent model represents the traffic on the many different lines of the metro in Paris. The model was made with luminescent tubes under a Black light, which contained water in them. When air was circulated through these water-filled Fluorescent tubes, it would give the impression of underground traffic in the metro. The actual Fluorescent model in the photograph looks like it must have been tremendous, about the size of an entire hall in a metro station.

A very popular use for the Black light and Fluorescent paint were Movie theatre interiors, which were somewhat of a rage in the United States in the late 1930s and continuing through the 1950s, but as the photographs in Deribere's book prove, this installation of Black lights and Fluorescence in Movie theaters was also used in France. There are photographs of very large closing Fluorescent stage movie screen doors for the French Movie theatre "Le Francais" in an opened position, and also in their closed position. The first photo of the huge closed Fluorescent stage movie screen doors of this French Movie theatre in the dark gives a general view from the audience seating, and shows the design to be a Fluorescent trellis with about a hundred large and small three-dimensional Fluorescent flowers mounted on the screen doors. The left and right Fluorescent stage screen doors are mirror-images of each other creating a pleasant symmetry. The second much larger and much more detailed photo of these opened Fluorescent stage doors is taken from the stage, looking out into the audience seating, which gives a clear view of the multitude of Black light units lined up nearly touching one another across the entire width of the stage front, but which were also wisely concealed from the audience's view by a sunken position in the stage and a complete row of most likely artificial plants to hide them from them audience. This large photo is in the White light and shows clearly that the three-dimensional Fluorescent flowers and plants were attached to the Fluorescent trellis work on each of the large stage screen doors, which must have been about 12 yards (meters) tall. The stage 'pit' has a row of large Black light units mounted in it so close together that they appear to be on top of each other. I would estimate from this partial view of the photo that there were about twenty huge Black lights with huge circular reflectors, and huge Ultraviolet bulbs in them. In between what I would imagine to be these Black light floodlights, there are an additional twenty smaller units, which I would imagine to be Black light spotlights. The text gives details of these Black lights as the large 'U.V. Projectors' "PM6" each fitted with "MAW 125" Black lights, combined with the smaller "RM3" Black lights in between the larger units, each equipped with an "MAW 80" Black light. It must have been a hell of a Movie theatre.

A very important photograph in Deribere's book is of a dancer of the Fluorescent Ballets of Loie Fuller in the Black light. This photograph was taken at the first of the Fluorescent Ballet shows in 1937, but Loie Fuller had been performing as the "First Luminescent Dancer" complete with her Radium Dress, that she actually invented the Radium paint for in her laboratory of the Latin Quarter in Paris over thirty years before this photo was taken. In fact, by the time Deribere's book had been published Loie Fuller had already died of breast cancer on New Year's Day, 1928, after performing in her Radium dress for years. Loie Fuller was extensively written about in the previous section of this book covering the discoveries of Pierre and

Marie Curie, where it was explained that Loie Fuller's companion continued experimenting with luminescent 'salts' after Fuller's death, and then created these "Black Light Ballets" in the 1930s.

Again discussing Art and the decoration of theaters, Deribere explains that there were already in existence some patents covering luminous effects obtained through luminescent products, and changing or animated decors. In 1921, and then again in 1925 M. Sauvage and the 'Radiana Stores' presented in Parisian exhibitions a Phosphorescent peacock of the highest quality as a promotion for their Phosphorescent paint. During the same period of the 1920s the author states that M. Mercipinetti was using luminous Phosphorescent paint for creating paintings, and then Deribere makes a very prophetic statement, admitting that '*at that time*' already in 1943 - only ten years after the invention of Fluorescent paint, the 'enthusiasm' for Black light and luminous paint had already faded - *Twenty-five full years* before most people ever heard about the Black light! The author also writes about the Painter/Decorator Ch. Blanc-Gatti, who since 1937 was very successful creating "triptychs" of leaded glass that were Fluorescent and Phosphoresced ("Fluorophosphorescents"), which had been revived again by the Artist in the mid-1940s.

Towards the end of the book Deribere presents a section on Fluorescent paintings - Imagine That! The Fluorescent 'changing' paintings that the author details are the same as photographs I have on display in the Museum by Mr. Thomas Goff, an office worker for the Red Cross who was the son-in-law of Thomas S. Warren, the founder of "Ultra-Violet Products, Inc." There is also a painting on canvas by a Russian Artist Tugarinov in the Museum that was made in New York during 1970, which dramatically changes seasons from White light to Black light. Deribere explains that very 'curious' Fluorescent paintings could be created that would change images according to what lamp was turned on. An Autumn landscape in the White light is created with a Whitish sky (made from Fluorescent Salt "NAG"), Yellowish ground (Yellow Methylene), Yellowish trees (Yellow Methylene, Auramine, and Fluorescein), tree branches and bark (with Chrysoidine), all cheerfully painted in front of a Reddish Sunset (Eosine and Rhodamine reflections). When this same Autumn landscape painting detailed by the author is put under a Black light this same Autumn scene will suddenly transform itself into a brilliant Spring landscape! Trees and the meadow will Fluoresce bright Green, and the Sun will shine Yellow with many different tones, in a brilliant Blue sky. Thomas Goff's Fluorescent Landscapes from the 1950s go one step further and have a third transformation into a complete snow-covered Winter landscape when put under a third lamp, a Shortwave Ultraviolet lamp, not a common Longwave Ultraviolet lamp which was used to create the Spring Landscape state of the painting. Deribere explains that fixing a realistic sunset, volcano, or fireplace on canvas was always sought after, going back to antiquity with Chinese paintings, but never really achieved before the invention of Fluorescent paint. These Fluorescent paintings described by Deribere had been made for years already, by the Artist who is credited as being the pioneer in the use of Fluorescent paint in Fine Art in 1945, John Plumer Ludlum. In fact these type of Fluorescent paintings that change scenes from day to night under White light and then Black light are still successful with the public and are still being produced by the Artist that has taken over from John Ludlum's method of "Painting with Living Light," the Oregon Artist Gary Fenske, who's registered trademark for his Art is "Night Visions," and who claims on his website to be recognized internationally as 'the pioneer of Luminous Art.' In 2013 Gary Fenske put out a book on his Art, "The Secret World of Invisible Art," in which he also included a section on the friendship and inspiration he received from John Ludlum.

The author next states that when Pierre and Marie Curie discovered Radium they were naively hoping it would be a beautiful Color. The jars that the Curies had kept their Radium salts in were highly luminescent, but although they emitted much light, it was not a beautiful Color as the Curies has hoped. One night coming back to their modest experiment shed they stopped transfixed in ecstasy: their Radium had more than a nice Color - it very vividly Glowed-in-the-Dark! Since the most distinctive quality of luminescence is the ability to emit light, some painters are reported by the author to have successfully captured this, such as the Artist Durandal with painted reflections in airplanes, and Jeandy who painted the reflective surfaces of fish. Some painters of Deribere's time had managed to created special effects with luminous paints, including the rendering of movement. Deribere closes the section on luminous painting with the common usage of Fluorescent Astral models, such as the incredible walkthrough Fluorescent display of the Universe in the former Hayden Planetarium that was in the Museum of Natural History in New York.

For the more popular and more common usage of Black lights and luminescence, in the Theatre for many years before the date of 1937 that Deribere credits Loie Fuller with the creation of Fluorescent Ballets, people were very excited about this phenomenon in entertainment (again, Loie Fuller died in 1928, but her companion continued experimenting with luminous 'salts' and created the "Black Light Ballets" in the 1930s, after Fuller's death). Other examples of luminescent theatre performances are listed by the author with Jean Saddy's creation of "Dames Blanche" ('The White Lady') and the gnomes in "Griselidis," 'Ghost Dances' were also presented by the big jazz orchestra and the "Comedie Francaise," and the "Satin Shoe" which was finally adapted to the luminescent effect. Deribere also mentions the orchestra and ballet performances that were Fluorescent and that were photographed, such as the original "Skeleton Ballets" [the very first "Skeleton Ballets" using Black lights and Phosphorescent paint were in 1907 for the first "Ziegfeld Follies"]. Moving swiftly along from the sublime to amusement, Deribere next discusses the use of luminescence in the circus, including A. Stasburger who had acrobats wearing Fluorescent stage costumes performing under Black lights to a great success.

In general public Deribere concludes that although Black lights and Fluorescence had been used for years in Movie theaters, such as the huge stage movie screen doors in "Le Francaise" Movie theatre created by Chaigne, experiments had been made to create luminescent movie posters and movie schedules that could be seen in the dark, by companies such as "Arpha." The author concludes that many household objects of Fluorescent Art could be created such as statues, decorative material, religious objects, images, photos, and postcards, which would introduce this luminosity into people's households. Deribere informs the reader that large 'Projector Lamps' of filtered Ultraviolet for huge distance coverage had been manufactured, and these lamps were used in Movie theaters and other large public displays, as well as other applications being possible such as luminescent fountains with water displays featuring Fluorescent fairies and Fluorescent water nymphs. This information is credited to H. Bidou's 1939 paper 'White Fairy, Black Fairy.'

The end of Deribere's book contains recent advances in Luminescent technology (1954), such as the since-lost technique of "Luminographie," which was the process of Luminous reproduction. This technique involved the luminous source of the reproduction, which was a 'plate' covered with luminous Colors. This technique allowed full-size copies to be created from original photography plates by putting the plate into a press under pressure for two to three minutes before developing.

For a photographic headache, the section on 'Photographic Measurements' dealing with Fluorescent Photography is perfect! Deribere restates that the Fluorescent "Screen" covered with Phosphorescent particles created not only many possibilities, but also a photographic standard of control. The author explains that to evaluate exposure time on a photographic enlarger for developing pictures, the method was to experiment on sensitive photography paper with different exposure times and methods. Alternatively, the use of a Fluorescent "Screen" that is immediately removed and examined after it's darkroom exposure, or even simply observing the subject of the photograph through the camera lens with a Fluorescent "Screen" allows 'quick' operation (according to Deribere). Credit for the early information on the lost method of "Luminographie" is given to L. Vanino from all the way back in 1933. For more antique photography lessons, Deribere explains that in the U.S.A. a standard was established for flash units that was named "Check Mate." This "Check Mate" was a simple plastic film that was laminated with very fine Phosphorescent powder. This photographic film is put into a film holder and is designed to accurately determine if the firing of the camera's flash unit was synchronized with the opening of the camera's lens. After the exposure the Phosphorescent film is examined, and if the synchronicity was correct the image on the Phosphorescent film disappeared after about one minute.

A Phosphorescent instrument designed in the U.S. for the Second world war was called an "Icaroscope" and enabled a person to search the sky directly looking into the Sun without effecting the eyes. A diagram of the "Icaroscope" is presented by Deribere, which consisted of an observation eyepiece, a lens which receives the image, and a Phosphorescent screen on which the image forms. This enabled the image to be observed without any damage to the eye. The "Icaroscope" would turn on it's tripod as part of it's function, which allowed the image to be received in direct line with the Sun, and then when the "Icaroscope" was turned away from the Sun, the Phosphorescent image could be safely observed on the Phosphorescent screen in the instrument.

In a curious twist Deribere mentions Jack De Ment ("Mineralight New Bulletins") as the scientist who proposed to use Fluorescent Screens for cinema or fixed projectors. The method was to project an invisible Ultraviolet image onto a Fluorescent screen and then the projector would somehow project an image in Black and White or in Color - sounds like a real Jack De Ment idea.

To finish this book Deribere presents a list of 'Useful Applications' for the Black light with Fluorescent and Phosphorescent paint that were already in use through the industrialization of Fluorescent plastics, varnish, materials, papers:

<u>'At Home'</u> Night tables, door handles, little cups, ashtrays, gas knobs, numbers for hotel rooms, electrical switches, match holders, and of course 'aquarium decors' (too bad they hadn't invented luminescent condoms yet in Deribere's time).

<u>'Outside'</u> Clock faces (!), instrument panels for cars and airplanes, highway milage markers, indicators, fire detectors, railways, bridge fences, ceilings for passenger railroad cars, tunnels, and the body, interior, and diagrams of cars (he forgot Highway Safety Cones).

<u>'Hospitals'</u> Operating rooms, ceilings for sick or nervous patients(!) - imagine putting a nervous patient into a hospital room with a totally Fluorescent ceiling to stare at all the day? Make sure you lock the windows.

'Guns'(!) Handles for guns to shoot in the dark, and targets.
'Boats'   Evacuation indicators, "T.S.F." ('Transmission without wires' = Radio), lifeboats, rescue equipment, stairs, signalization, and handles.
'Electrical Poles' Buttons, indicating panels, handles.
'Defense' Signalization of SOS, maps, shelters, command posts, and bridges.
'Signalization' For security signalization in an Operating room, on boards, and on cars which avoid the terrible danger of driving without any lights at night during war time "Black Out."

    To close the Deribere book there is an exquisite photograph from "General Electric Co." of a woman in front of a pile of Phosphorescent powder with a spoonful of it in her hand. She is perfectly lit for the photograph just through the emitted light coming from the pile of Phosphorescent powder in front of her.

    The book's final antique photograph displays another example of lost knowledge in the form of a Fluorescent Advertising Panel which emits light without any electrical connections - what it claims, but there are wires attached to it in several places. The explanation is that the letters of the "Genolite" company are applied to the base of the sign, which produces a higher frequency field. Since the outer surface of the letters have a Fluorescent coating, the emission of Fluorescent Color is possible. The accompanying diagram slightly explains this method, with a glass plate as a base and an electrical cord that is soldered to the glass base and onto the top layer of metal. In between the glass base is another layer of a Phosphorescent coating ("Phosphore-dielectrique") .25 mm thick. With all this plugged into the electricity, an invisible layer of conducting electricity is created on the glass. This technique was called "Electrophotoluminescence" and was developed by the early 1950s.

    Another rare artifact in the Museum collection gives a clear idea of how difficult and how long it took to professionally document Fluorescence in Photography. The February, 1952 issue of "Photography" magazine has an article "Action in Color - with Black Light" containing what is claimed to be the 'First action color shot taken in the Black Light.' As usual, the front cover of this sixty year old magazine with it's price of thirty-five cents dates the era perfectly, and the cover photo on this magazine looks nearly like a Second world war era image. Three little girls are holding a cat and the fashion (open-toed patent leather double-strap shoes on the three girls) is not nearly as dated as the Color processing of the photo itself. All three girls are printed in the most pastel, dull, flat matt Colors that makes the image look more like a hand-Colored Black and White photograph than an actual Color photo. It even looks closer to an illustration than a real photo. Opening this 1952 "Photography" magazine we are transported back to a long-gone era when "Leica" cameras were being sold for only $99(!) and the very first "Hasselblad" was introduced as the "new Swedish reflex" with a Kodak Ektar lens.

    In this magazine is the article "A Photography First" - the first time an "action color shot" was photographed in the Black light. This 1952 double-page article reproduces a large Color photo on each page - the left page is the dancer Maxine Holman under "Visible White Light" photographed with an "electronic flash," and on the right page is the same dancer in the same pose photographed under "Invisible Ultraviolet rays." With the benefit of nearly sixty years of hindsight, the photograph of the dancer in the Black light is a much more proficient photograph than the White light photo of the same dancer on the facing page. Like the magazine's cover photo, the White light photo of Maxine Holman gives the impression of being a hand-Colored Black and White photo - fake, flat, and looking closer to an illustration than a real photograph. By comparison, the Black light photo of this dancer is an excellent shot vividly recording the brilliance of the Fluorescent parts of the dancer's costume. In fact this 1952 Color Black light photo is a better exposure, reproducing perfect contrast and saturated Fluorescent Colors, than many photographers make today - sixty years later - with Twenty-first century technology.

    Not only does this 1952 article present the first Black light Color action photograph, but the text documents how important the Black light and Fluorescent Colors were during that period sixty years ago - which was a dozen full years before the beginning of the 1960s Movement. The article begins with the contemporarily surprising fact that "almost every" one of the 'large Musical productions' in the early 1950s featured "Black light productions" which are described as "spectacular." This first sentence of the article's text also documents the importance of another 1950s display in the Museum, "Fluorescent Advertisements." It is stated that 'throughout America' there were "Startling" billboards that were changing from "visible tungsten" lights to 'invisible Black lights' to create "fantastic effects."

    After this revealing introduction, the reader is told that photographs using 'invisible Black light' had been taken many times already, but that a 'Color action shot' with Ultraviolet was never achieved before. "Milwaukee Journal" photographer Angus McDougall and John Murray are the two men who realized this first Black light 'Color action shot,' as it is explained that photographing "Fluorescent minerals" and "altered paintings" had been achieved already. The technical difference between still shots taken of Fluorescent minerals and live action shots was that the exposure times were measured in minutes, not seconds, which makes "action shots" out of the question. In truth, the "Color action shot" presented with such pride by this 1952 magazine was, in reality, just another "staged" photo with a dancer still-posing what gives the overall impression of an "action shot," but in actuality was closer to a still-life of Fluorescent minerals than a real "action shot" of a moving dancer. The text goes on to claim that this Black light photo was "instantaneous" and an "action-stopping exposure." Very doubtful. It is further explained that the problem the two photographers had to overcome was to find a source of produced Ultraviolet which was powerful enough to allow exposures in seconds, not minutes. Through a suggestion of an expert on the "electronic flash" and Color, the use of a "speedlight" flash rich in Ultraviolet made the photograph possible. To begin, the two photographers used a "Curtis one-shot Color camera," very fast panchromatic Black and White film along with six high powered flash units. These flash units were filtered with "12 inch Roundel" U.V. filters, as well as a Wratten 2-A Barrier Filter fitted onto the lens of the camera to block Ultraviolet rays from the film.   This technical setup allowed the photography of "only" the visible Fluorescence of the dancer and her costume. To highlight the dancer, who's skin Fluorescence is barely visible against the synthetic Fluorescent pigments used on her costume, a visible Blue light was used in the background.

This article from sixty years ago reveals two things: how difficult it (still) is to get a good exposure under Black lights with any type of camera, and how much knowledge has been lost (or discarded) with high paid professional photographers, such as a Brooklyn-based "National Geographic" photographer who's Twenty-first century Yuppified version of this 1952 exquisite Black light photograph was printed on the last page of a 2011 issue, and which is an incorrect "Ultraviolet" photograph, exposing only the Ultraviolet energy that should have been omitted through the use of a "Wratten 2-A Barrier Filter" if he knew what one was - and not the fascinating "Fluorescence" photograph of the Parrot's feathers (which are specifically Fluorescent for choosing a mate). This contemporary high-paid "expert" not only photographed the "Ultraviolet" of the energy source he used and was supposed to completely omit - and not the Fluorescence of the Parrot's feathers which he was supposed to photograph and which he writes about in the explanation, but as a final statement of his profound ignorance, this schmuck *Covered up his eyes* in this published "National Geographic" photograph because as this prophet again misinformed the public: Black light is *dangerous(!)* I immediately wrote a several page letter to "National Geographic:" magazine in Washington, D.C. and added photographs from "Scientific American" magazine from twenty years ago which correctly document the Fluorescence of Parrot's feathers, not the pure Violet-Colored "Ultraviolet" photograph that this Twenty-first century professional photographer in New York very mistakenly believed was a "Fluorescence" photograph, and went ahead and typically misinformed many millions of "National Geographic" readers. Needless to say, even after being a member of "National Geographic" since 1966 - most likely before this Brooklyn photographer was born - I never received an answer from "National Geographic" magazine, which I formerly had the highest of respect for.

Now that we have travelled through time back to the era that I have called "The Miracle of Fluorescence: 1930s - 1950s" and have concentrated exclusively on the first two decades of that period discovering Black light events and attitudes towards Fluorescence that almost universally seem to be impossible to believe eighty years later after the end of the first decade and a half of the Twenty-first century, we will examine the last period of that era. The 1950s era was a period of the roots of today's modernity with freedom and relief in the air after the misery of the 1940s Second world war era. This was also the decade that could be dubbed 'the calm before the storm.' It was the last period of 'Ignorant Bliss' - the last period when the medieval past seemed to be still connected to the present somehow - the period before the new Age of Enlightenment which began with the movement of the 1960s.   "Bud" and "Sis" were still considered role models of western society, and their miserable show "Father Knows Best" was the most popular show on television in America, promoting the brainless state of mind that is still popular there, in fact it is currently going through something of a revival. As a signpost for inevitable change "Father Knows Best" originally began as a radio show in 1949, then was broadcast on television for six seasons, beginning in 1954 and ending exactly in 1960. Who could forget the 1969 "Dick Cavett Show" with "Father Knows Best" himself Robert "Marcus Welby" Young sitting directly next to none other than Jimi Hendrix! Upon close inspection of this historic "high contrast," it is clear to see that Jimi keeps his back turned to this icon of the miserable existential mindless era of the 1950s for the entire length of his interview with Dick Cavett. He only gives Marcus Welby once a fleeting glance, with a dirty look as well. They looked like two different species next to each other.

In this 1950s postwar Hula-Hoop Elvis Presley decade spirituality and enlightenment wasn't even considered, almost like the point it has regressed to again today. This is recognizable in every facet of the 1950s - just listen to the music created during that period of "Rock Around the Clock." Greasy hair, Black leather jackets, and alcohol were the icons of the 1950s. Veins sticking out of muscled arms and anchor tattoos are what immediately come to mind. "Rosy-the-Riveter's" sons and daughters were born in this era, with the words of FDR ringing in their ears from a few years before: 'Be Good!'

"Black Light - Lamps, Applications, Design Procedures," "General Electric," June, 1956

  Here will be presented a twelve page "General Electric" "Black Light - Lamps, Applications, Design Procedures" catalogue that had it's second printing in June, 1956. Just opening the cover of this sixty year old catalogue is enough to instantly recognize the dated contents and the 1950s design, complete with it's "Dom Casual" and "Futura" antiquated type faces. The first page lists all types of "GE Black Light Lamps" that were sold in 1956, starting with the "Fluorescent Lamps," which came in the standard tubular, "Rapid Start," "Circline," and "Slimline - single pin bases" models. The next category of Black lights listed in this catalogue are the "Mercury Lamps" which were tremendous clear bulbs that would be used in large professional lamps, such as the 250 watt "Conti-Glo" lamp in the Museum collection. These bulbs were sold as 100, 250, and 400 watts, with extravagant prices from $16.50 to $25.00. The simplest, very first, cheapest, and weakest of all 'Black lights' is next listed as the "Argon Lamp." Originally sold in 1915 as the "Argon Glow Lamp," two models were for sale, a measly one-quarter watt "Argon Lamp" for .85¢, and the normal 2 watt bulb for $1.90, which was originally sold for .50¢ decades before. The tiny Argon bulb was designed for instrument panels, which need very little Ultraviolet for small Instrument dials. The last type of Black light listed for sale by "G.E." were the "Filament Lamps" which had 250 watts and cost $2.20.

  An introduction and explanation of "Black Light" and the different types of Black lights follows for two pages, beginning with a 1950s description of the "Black Light" phenomenon. The reader is informed that "Black Light" is a name for 'near-Ultraviolet radiant energy' (today termed "Longwave Ultraviolet"), and that the name "Black Light" is very misleading because the energy doesn't look "Black"(!) "G.E." states in no uncertain terms that the 'weirdly beautiful' Black light effect was very useful for advertising, decoration, and display. Already considered just a common tool in the mid-1950s, "G.E." next considers the Black light's 'work-a-day' applications.

  Under the heading of 'Sources,' "G.E." recommends the use of Black light Fluorescent and Mercury lamps, with "Filament Lamps" considered inefficient and weak, and "Argon Glow Lamps" very weak. Other sources of Black light are given, such as 'Carbon Arcs' and the Sun. "Fluorescent Lamps" (tubular Black lights common today) are explained first, divided into "BL" and "BLB" types. The "BL" Black lights were White, not Black, and appear as ordinary White Fluorescent lamps with the only difference being their emitted energy. Normal Fluorescent lamps emit most of their energy as visible light, while "BL" Fluorescent lamps emit most of their energy as Longwave Ultraviolet energy because of the different phosphors used to manufacture the lamps. These "BL" lamps are used in combination with Longwave Ultraviolet filters to produce laboratory-quality Longwave Ultraviolet lamps which emit 0% visible light. "BLB" tubular Fluorescent lamps differ dramatically in appearance because they are Black, not White. This Black Color is the Longwave Ultraviolet filter, which is made of Nickel and Cobalt contained in the glass itself making it unnecessary to use an external filter. Black light Fluorescent lamps are stated in this catalogue as being the most efficient source of Black light, have 'virtually' no visible light emitted from them (Black light tubular lamps give off about three percent visible light), they are 'Linear' light sources which create even emission throughout the length of the Black light's relatively cool sources, emit their full U.V. energy as soon as they are turned on, and with the 'new' advancement of the 40 watt "Rapid Start" Black light these Black lights had the ability to be attached to a dimmer or a flasher.

  "Mercury Lamps" are next explained along with photos of these Frankenstein laboratory bulbs. There is a photo of a similar Mercury bulb that is in the 250 watt "Conti-Glo" lamp in the Museum, complete with the bulb's interior, which resembles an actual tiny scale-model of the entirety of Frankenstein's laboratory. It is correctly explained that these clear "Mercury Lamp" bulbs emit both visible light and Black light, with a high percentage of their emission being in the 'near-Ultraviolet' (Longwave Ultraviolet), so all of these U.V. bulbs must be used with a Black light filter to remove the visible light from the emission. The examples of 'Black Light Effects' for large productions, such as ice shows and on theatre stages are listed as applications for these intensely powerful "Mercury Lamp" bulbs. Unfortunately, already in 1956 it is written in this catalogue that the more efficient, much cheaper, and much less powerful Black light Fluorescent lamps were already 'largely replacing' the far superior Mercury lamps for such applications. It is also stated that these large powerful "Mercury Lamps" take several minutes to reach their peak after being turned on. I can attest to this with the experience of turning on my 250 watt seventy year old "Conti-Glo" antique lamp in December, 2008 in my sister's house. We waited about five full minutes for this lamp to reach it's peak, and especially the first minute was so slow to turn on that I had to turn off all the lights in the house just to see if it was working or not. For about a full minute all that could be seen in the absolute darkness was a Red-Violet dim glow of the huge bulb's interior behind it's tremendous convex Black light filter. In December, 2009 I got the other major Black light used for large installations, the "Conti-Glo" 100 watt Black Light Spotlight. Again turning on this seventy year old lamp in my sister's house for Christmas, the starting time was amazingly faster. In less than one minute the lamp was at it's peak, and I have to admit to having never seen a true Black light spotlight like this lamp - the beam of very intense Black light was only in a very thin line, so that I could move the lamp along one by one in front of my Fluorescent "Thermal Expansion" paintings I had again lined up in front of the lamp for it's trial, and amazingly only the painting that was directly in front of this Black light spotlight was intensely Fluorescent. Even the paintings right next to the painting with the spotlight on it were dimly Fluorescent, being separated only by a few inches. Amazing intensity of Black light emission that couldn't be compared to any number of today's tubular Black lights, amazing Black light thick curved glass filters, and amazing superior technology gone forever. Comparing today's tubular common Black lights to one of these advanced super Black lights from the 1930s and 1940s, is exactly similar to comparing the doomed superior "S.S.T." to the most common aircraft in the air today, a 747. Another shame. For the advantages of these "Mercury Lamps," "G.E." comments on the fact that these bulbs were the most powerful sources of Black light made, and that they were relatively compact.

"Filament Lamps" is a section that presents just a single "G.E." produced lamp, the 250 watt "Purple X" Black light bulb. This looks like a very large version of those 'Black Light Bulbs' made popular in the 1960s (talk about regression). This bulb is explained to filter 'practically all' of the visible light through it's Black built-in filter. Then comes the fun part: "G.E." recommends that this "Purple X" 250 watt Black light bulb should only be turned on for five minutes at a time(!), with ten minute intervals in between to allow the scalding hot bulbs to cool down. A necessary recommendation is given as well, to use only porcelain fixtures because of the intense temperatures. Even though they already stated that this "Filament Lamp" "Purple X" Black light was weak, it was recommended for close examination of Fluorescent minerals, and for Fluorescent sketches made with Fluorescent inks, chalks, and paints. The advantages listed for this Black light bulb are the same reasons that millions of "pseudo-Black light" Black light bulbs were sold in the 1960s and 1970s, such as the facts that these bulbs were cheap and the easiest to use with their own built-in filters and no requirements of transformers or any other electrical configuration, but most importantly, could screw right into a standard light fixture.

"Argon Glow Lamps" were the first sources of Ultraviolet sold to the public back in 1915. It is plainly stated in this "G.E." catalogue that these Argon bulbs produced visible Blue and Violet light besides the Longwave Ultraviolet energy. The applications of these weak Ultraviolet lamps are given as close examination of Fluorescent minerals, activation of instrument dials and pass-out check marks, ad well as verification of Fluorescent tickets. The biggest advantage of these Argon bulbs was that they were produced with Argon gas, not Mercury gas like all future Black lights, thus they produced mostly Longwave Ultraviolet and had usually presented no need for the Black Nickel and Cobalt Longwave Ultraviolet filter.

"Filters" are presented at the end of this two page presentation of all the types of Black lights that "G.E." made in the 1950s, and it is explained that since most sources of Black light also produce visible light, this must be removed from the lamp's final emission by the Black light filter. It is further explained that several of the Black lights which were produced by "G.E." had their Black light filters built-in to the glass of the lamp itself (like today's Black lights). It is also written that instead of using expensive Ultraviolet filters, deep Blue sheet-glass had been used for a long time, because although it did emit more visible light than true Black light filters, the cost was a fraction of the Black light filters and they could be easily cut into any shape that was needed.

The next four pages - one-third of this entire catalogue - contains a very detailed section of 'Black Light Applications.' The full top third of the page is a large Black and White Black light photograph of an architect's model of a 'Shopping Mall,' that is 'treated' with Fluorescent paint and 'irradiated' with Black light. The full Shopping Mall, including the large parking lot and it's lamp posts, lit up through the Black light is a proposed night scene. Complete with traffic indicators, bright store windows and store names all Fluorescing under a Black light to create a very realistic impression down to tiny details, such as the impression of the light cast onto the parking lot by the eight lights atop each lamp post. A small insert photograph shows the same architect's Shopping Mall model in the White light on a table with a woman standing over it to give it a sense of scale. The introduction to 'Black Light Applications' informs the reader that many existing applications for the Black light will be listed in the following pages, but admits that the list is 'far from complete' and had the insight to admit that there could be even more applications for the Black light than were listed in this 1956 catalogue.

The first 'Black Light Application' given in this publication is a very good example of what society and "G.E." in particular thought of first with their infinite wisdom and their limitless perspective: 'Industry.' The industrial use of Black light begins with the statement that most of the applications for the Black light in Industry centered around the two areas of either Inspection or Identification, in which this miraculous invention and phenomenon of the Black light facilitated the near-surreal results of a 'quicker and more thorough job' completed.

'Foods' are listed first in this 'Industry' section, and the applications are listed as the Black light's use in the inspection of shelled pecans to detect insects, which are a bright White under the Black light while the pecan Fluoresces only a deep Blue.

Contaminated flours and grains are listed next, with applications of the Black light including detecting rat piss, and testing for Riboflavin.

The second 'Industry' application for the Black light is even more celestial than 'Food,' being 'Laundries.' With the first large industrial job of the "Switzer Brothers" being "Invisible Laundry Marking," the idea spread across America in the late 1930s and continued for years with great success until the advent of "Daylight Optical Dyes," which made cotton and other clothing highly Fluorescent White during it's manufacturing.

'Cast and Machined Parts' follows as an important 'Industry' application, which is yet another invention of the "Switzer Brothers" from the early Second world war days, and was properly termed "Metal Stress Detection." This technology was used extensively in World war two, most memorably for inspection of warplane propeller blades. After the "Switzer Brothers" invented Black light "Metal Stress Detection," the former method based on magnetism not applicable to the new aluminum was immediately abandoned in favor of the much more efficient Fluorescent technique.

Another 'Industry' application for the Black light that is still in use today, over half a century later, is "Fluorescent Leak Detection." It is explained that hydraulic systems, pipe lines, and storage containers are all inspected with a Black light for leak detection. This is an old method which consisted of simply adding a Fluorescent Tracer Dye (Fluorescein is commonly used) to the liquid of a refrigerator or to transmission fluid, and then inspecting the exterior of the system with a powerful Black light for easily visible Fluorescent leaks. It is stated in this catalogue that since oil is naturally Fluorescent there is usually no need for adding a Fluorescent tracer to detect Fluorescent leaks, and that this method was also used to inspect airplane fuel tanks for leakage.

'Textiles' is the next 'Industry' application for the Black light presented in this catalogue, explaining that the Black light was being used for many procedures in the textile industry. First the inspection of Grey material for oil stains is listed, the application of Fluorescent patterns for embroidery work is mentioned, as well as the grading inspection of textiles in general.

'Photo reproduction' is explained next, which I have seen evidence of through photographs taken inside of the first photocopier machines that contained about twenty to thirty Argon bulbs. It is basically explained in the text that in the 1950s Black light Fluorescent lamps were being used in 'Photo reproduction' for blueprints, Black and White printing, and for printing on presensitized plates. The Black lights are mounted very close together for these techniques, one and a half to two and a half inches apart (3.8-6.4 cm) as well as being very close to the printing surface, only two and a half to three inches (6.4-7.6 cm).

The final 'Industry' application for the Black light in this 1956 catalogue from "General Electric" is actually one of the very first industrial application of the Black light ever used: 'Mineral Identification.' Before the Black light or Argon glow lamp were ever invented, Ultraviolet "Spark Boxes" were used to identify the Fluorescent Green "Willemite" Zinc ore in northern New Jersey mines starting in 1903. It is accurately explained in this catalogue of 1956 that the Black light had already been used for many years in the field of 'Mineral Identification,' by amateur hobbyists, geologists, and mineral prospectors. Also correctly stated is that a good deal of the Fluorescent minerals need a more powerful Shortwave Ultraviolet lamp to cause their Fluorescence, and that the Longwave Ultraviolet lamp was not powerful enough to make most of the Fluorescent minerals emit light. The Shortwave Ultraviolet lamp is called an 'Ozone lamp' or a 'germicidal lamp' in this catalogue and it is correctly added that these lamps were not classified as "Black lights."

The second major field of Black light application in this catalogue is the very first idea that the "Switzer Brothers" had in 1933-34 after inventing Fluorescent paint: 'Advertising and Display.' The first preserved notes written by the Switzer Brothers after inventing Fluorescent paint in 1933 was the possible use of these unprecedented brilliant Colors under a Black light as a possible source of income that would be acquired through the application of advertising. The first major commission the "Switzer Brothers" could secure and produce was a Fluorescent Billboard for Oranges, which the "Switzer Brothers" themselves were amazed over, and which they together sat in the car and watched for hours, and as the twilight progressed they were transfixed by the absolute brilliance of the Color produced on the billboard as the Sun set and the Ultraviolet in the atmosphere reacted on their Fluorescent paints. This is incidentally the first application of 'Advertising and Display' listed in this booklet's section 'Outdoor Sign Boards.' It is explained that the application of Black light on Fluorescent outdoor sign boards was one of the fastest growing uses in this field. It is stated first that to be the most effective the Black light sign should be in relative darkness, but it is also written that the use of Black light and White light on Fluorescent outdoors signs was becoming more well known. These type of Fluorescent outdoor displays had both White lights and Black lights on different timed flashers, allowing for the Black lights to be constantly lit, but additional White lights would flash on and off in timed intervals automatically. This is explained to have enabled the new type of Fluorescent signs to be created with three distinct different messages, one in the Black light, one in the White light, and a third message created with the combination of the Black light and White light. This technique was achieved through methods including the use of Invisible Fluorescent paint, and Fluorescent paint applied to a non-Fluorescent background of the same Color. Again, the Fluorescent tubular Black light is stated as being the new replacement for the larger, much more powerful Mercury lamps used in the past, because these new lamps were more 'efficient.' The forty watt large Fluorescent Black light was the most popular lamp used for these outdoor sign boards, with a suggested lighting design explained consisting of two rows of Ultraviolet Black lights being mounted above the sign at a distance from the sign's surface equal to one-third to one-half of the sign's vertical dimension. These forty watt Black lights would be mounted in parabolic Aluminum reflectors, and for advertising signs mounted in areas of existing White light it was suggested to use two rows of forty watt Black lights at the top and at the bottom of the sign. It is further suggested that in the design of permanent outdoor signs the use of White inexpensive "BL" Fluorescent tube lamps were used with the additional glass Longwave filters being mounted above them to also protect them from the rain. Indoor signs were usually fitted with regular "BLB" Black light Fluorescent lamps, termed in this 1950s catalogue 'Integral-filter lamps.' A requirement for Black light signs is given as two to five watts of Black light per square foot of sign surface.

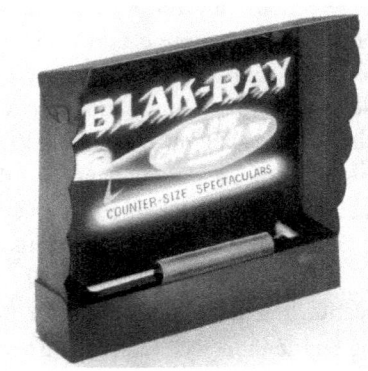

The second major commission of the "Switzer Brothers" twenty years before the publication of this "G.E." Black light catalogue is also presented in the catalogue second: 'Show Windows.' It is stipulated first that Fluorescent Black light Store Window Displays are much more powerful at night than in the daytime with the White ambient daylight detracting from the display of Fluorescence. It is also suggested that these Fluorescent Black light store windows would be separated from other brightly lit windows or displays. Here at last it is conceded that although the new tubular Black lights are more practical and produce an even 'wash' of Black light, the 100 watt and 250 watt Mercury lamp units are the best Ultraviolet spotlights.

The closest this "General Electric" "Black Light - Lamps, Applications, Designs and Procedures" catalogue from 1956 comes to Art is in the next heading of 'Murals.' Don't get the wrong idea here, Art is not properly discussed in relation to this 'work-a-day' Black light of the 1950s, but theater, cocktail lounge, and night club decoration is as close as it gets. As with each and every Black light application listed in this 1956 catalogue it is plainly written that the new tubular Fluorescent Black lights were used in preference of the old fashioned, extremely powerful, and very expensive Mercury lamp units. The only use for these incredible Mercury 100 and 250 watt lamps given in this 1956 explanation is for areas where it was necessary to have a 'long throw' or a round spotlight of Black light. The reader is informed that for these mural displays it was usually designed with the Black lights above the mural, not below it, and a common technique was to mount the Black lights on the ceiling above the murals, with large Mercury lamp units normally recessed and hidden in the ceiling itself. Fluorescent designs on ceilings, popular in Movie theaters, have a suggested design of mounting the Black lights on the walls or on columns hidden from view by decorative structures.

A quarter page photograph illustrates just how effective a Fluorescent Demonstration can be under a Black light, showing a lecturer in a classroom pointing out a specific area of a vivid Fluorescent picture of a house and landscaping on a chalk board. Above the chalk board is a forty watt tubular Black light concealed behind a large wide Aluminum reflector/fascia board, with two large visible metal brackets extending above the chalk board wall unit to hold the Black light. The caption lists Fluorescent pencils, chalk, or crayons as being effective writing tools to use on the chalkboard.

'Medical' is the following Black light application, explaining that for years the Black light had been employed in the medical field (obviously there is no mention at all of the harmful "Miracle Cure" Shortwave Ultraviolet lamp craze that was a rage from the mid 1880s until less that ten years before the printing of this catalogue). It is instead directly stated that the harmless Longwave 'Wood's Light' was the Ultraviolet lamp used for medical purposes, biological studies, and diagnostic analysis.

Another chapter of the "Switzer Brothers" legacy is listed here, uncredited of course, being the Black light application of it's use in the 'Military.' 'Fluorescent Maps and Charts' are listed first with an explanation that wartime maps could be printed with Fluorescent ink, or even could be made Fluorescent by coating the back side of the map with Fluorescent lacquer. This comes directly from the technology used first by the Americans in the Second world war in which bombers and fighter airplanes were equipped with a "Grimes Ultra-Violet Cockpit Light" on their dashboard, and during "Black Out" bombing runs over enemy territory all the lights could be turned off in the airplane so it would not be detectable from the ground below. American bombing charts were printed with Fluorescent ink on Black boards, making them easily readable under this standard

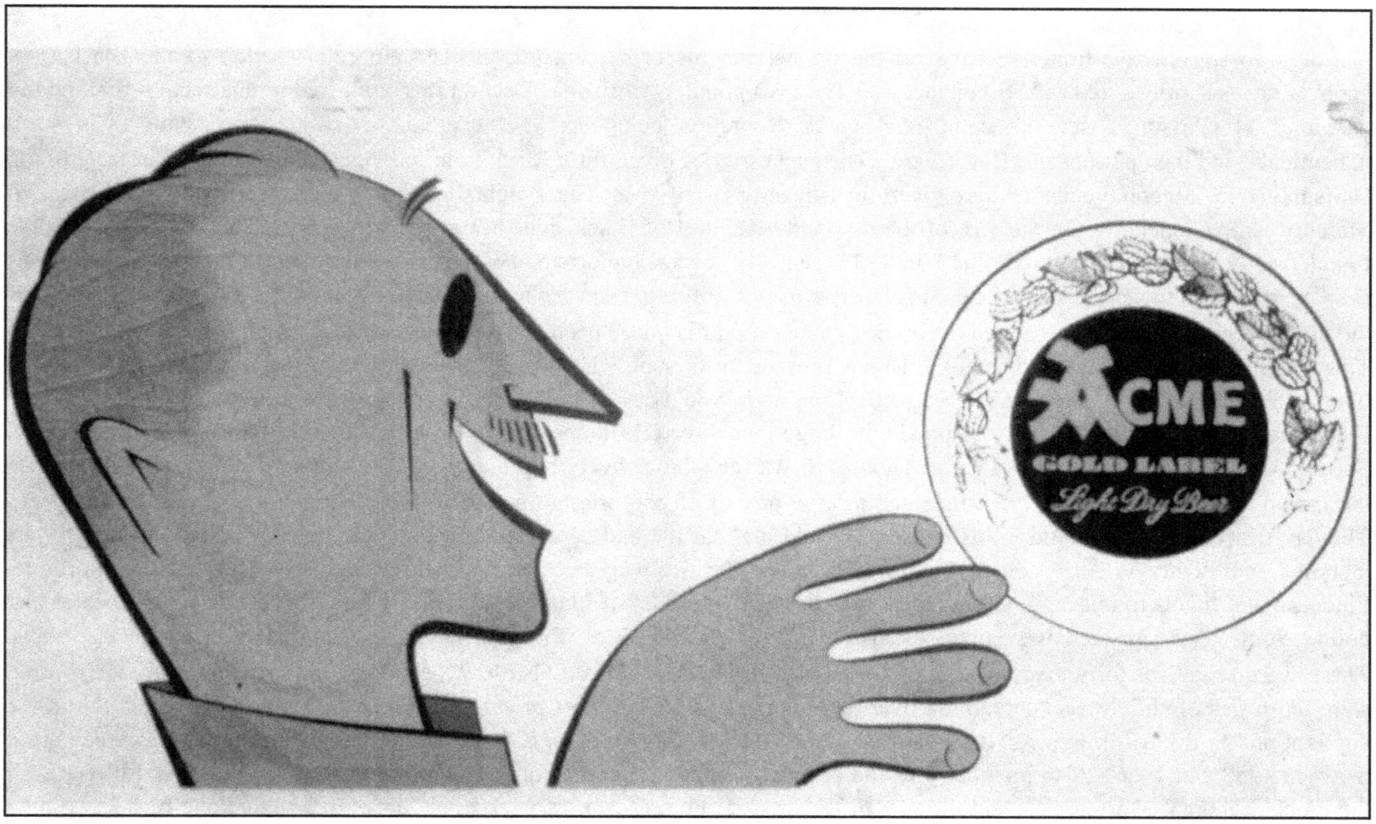

1950s "Invisible" Fluorescent Advertisement for "Acme Gold Label Beer," "Ultra-Violet Products, Inc." - WHITE LIGHT

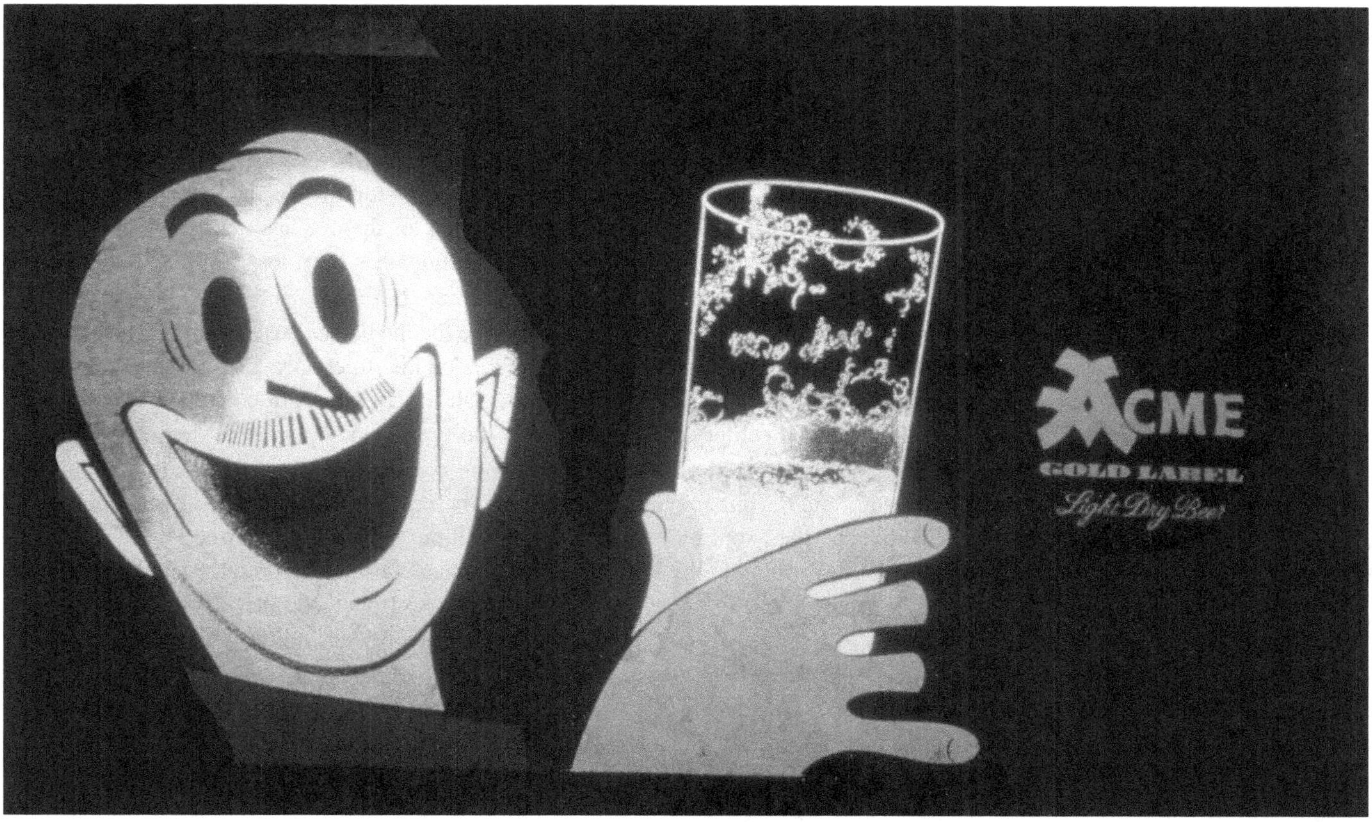

1950s "Invisible" Fluorescent Advertisement for "Acme Gold Label Beer," "Ultra-Violet Products, Inc." - BLACK LIGHT

Black light attached to the plane's instrument panel.

Moving swiftly from the banal to the greater heights of the absurd, the last umbrella section of the Black light applications is simply listed as 'Miscellaneous.' The ever-popular 'Christmas Decorations' are listed in this section first, giving examples of Christmas tree ornaments and other decoration being sprayed, painted, or even dipped with Fluorescent 'Chemicals' and then put under a Black light. The suggestion is given for a Black light to be placed on the floor in front of the Christmas tree. Recommendations are given for fifteen or twenty watt Black lights in Aluminum reflectors, or even 100 watt Mercury lamps depending on the size of the tree and what sort of Black light beam was necessary. Thomas S. Warren, the founder of "Ultra-Violet Products, Inc." in 1932, sent me several hundred slides in the 1990s of the Fluorescent Christmas Display staged on the entire street where his house was in California from the mid-1950s until the mid-1960s, as well as two of the original large Fluorescent painted decorations he used on his house each Christmas under Black lights, one being an angel. This Thomas S. Warren had a special Christmas present for anyone who drove down Marengo Avenue, this street where he lived in South Pasadena, California. Between 1958 and 1966 Warren had all the houses on his street decorated with large Fluorescent Christmas scenes and equipped with large longwave UV lamps (Black lights) on each lawn in front of the house. For two weeks each year cars lined up on Thomas S. Warren's block every night, until 1966 when it was discontinued because the crowds got so large. In 1995 I received a large box of all the original material from "Ultra-Violet Products, Inc." that Thomas Warren still had stored in his house. He told me that if I had contacted him one year before he had a garage full of material from "Ultra-Violet Products, Inc." which he had thrown away because "nobody wanted it." He sent me all original Fluorescent artifacts to put in "Electric Ladyland - the First Museum of Fluorescent Art" which I was preparing to open at that point. Some of the artifacts were precious, like a full set of "Blak Ray" Fluorescent Artist's Paints in tubes from the 1950s. These were saved for forty years in a draw by his son-in-law Mr. Donald Griffiths. Amongst the artifacts from Mr. Warren were ten pages of slide sheets containing over three-hundred slides of the Christmas displays on Marengo Avenue both in the daylight and in the Black light. All the houses on his block were photographed and all the photos are from the whole period between 1958 and 1966. Also included was the original printed invitation from Mr. Warren to anyone who would like to visit the block. Thomas Warren also sent me two of the original Fluorescent displays from Marengo Avenue, one being a painted Fluorescent angel measuring eighteen by thirty-six inches (46 x 92 cm). Two Polaroid photos of Mr. Warren's house at 2045 Marengo Avenue written in his hand and dated 1963 and 1966 completed the collection of material on the Christmas displays on Marengo Avenue and formed a very vivid image of what happened there for eight years. To partially quote from Mr. Warren's letter of March 3, 1995 describing the contents of the box he sent to me in Amsterdam: "A large number of negatives (slides) of fluorescent Christmas scenes. Many of them are of my resident block in South Pasadena, California of scenes showing the only fluorescent Christmas displays that have ever been done anywhere in the U.S. The residents of the block put on this display for eight years and it attracted so much interest that thousands of cars drove by every night for two weeks at Christmas time. We finally discontinued because some residents on the street wanted to stop the display because the crowds were so large that they couldn't get in or out of their driveways during the two weeks of the display. I hope you find these items interesting. I had much more but the displays were nearly forty years ago and much has been lost. If I can help in some way please let me know. I am still interested and would like to do what I can to promote fluorescence." This was written from Thomas S. Warren when he was in his mid 90s. In another letter, Mr. Warren told me that he had an Artist working for him who had painted all of the Christmas displays that were used by himself and his neighbors on his street during Christmas time.

During the last period of preparing this book in late 2015 a new acquisition for the Museum collection was found in another attic where it had been stored for over half a century. This artifact is the type of outdoor Black light unit used by Thomas S. Warren for his yearly Christmas displays on his block, and the same type of unit used for countless outdoor Fluorescent displays from the 1940s to the 1960s and beyond. Although this particular outdoor Black light unit wasn't made by Thomas Warren's company "Ultra-Violet Products, Inc.," but by his biggest competition, the company formed by the "Switzer Brothers" who invented Fluorescent paint in 1933, it is nearly the same unit that Thomas Warren also produced and then sold as his own. On the lawn in front of Thomas Warren's house in the Christmas display photo from 1966 these outdoor Black light units can be seen. They are battleship-Grey iron units which are essentially long rectangular boxes housing a White thirty watt "BL" Longwave Ultraviolet tubular lamp and a full metal curved reflector behind the entire lamp. The front of the thirty-six by five inch (90 x 13 cm) unit is an angled, hinged section which houses a full sheet of Black glass Longwave Ultraviolet filter. This is the original design used back in the 1930s and 1940s when the "Switzer Brothers" developed large Fluorescent Billboards and decided to use the cheaper White "BL" Longwave Ultraviolet tubular

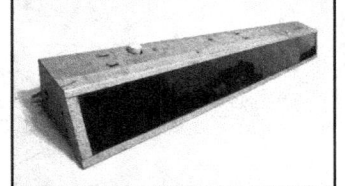

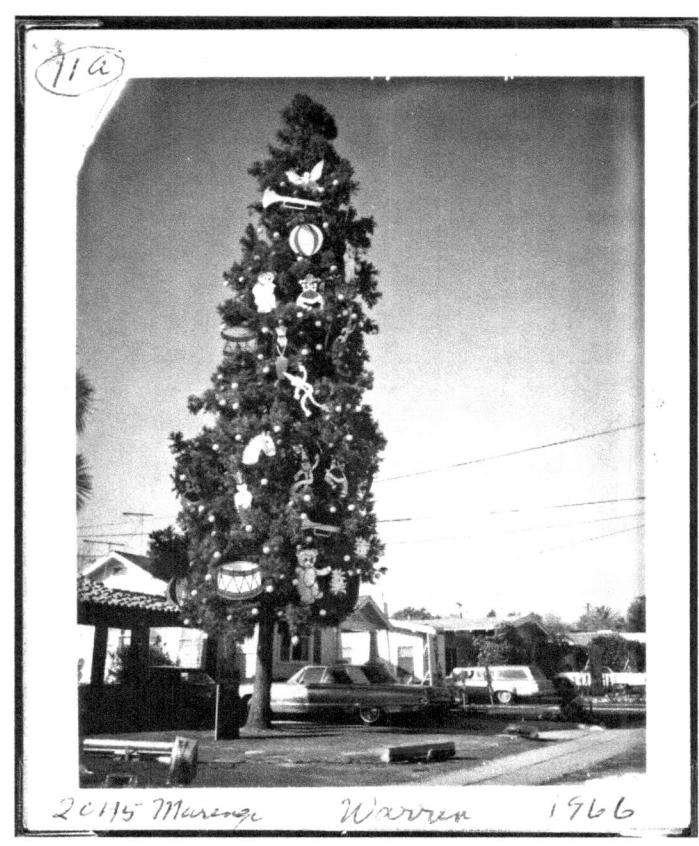

Thomas Warren's Black Light Christmas Show on his entire street Marengo Ave. in California every year from 1958 to 1966

YOU ARE INVITED

To see the most magnificent and dramatic presentation of Black Light Christmas displays, scenes and designs in the world today.

The residents of the 2000 block on Marengo Avenue in South Pasadena (1 block south of Huntington Drive, South Pasadena) cordially invite you to share with them the delight in seeing the unseen in brilliant fluorescent color. To make the entire block one of fantastic beauty, all Christmas decorations are illuminated with black light. Black light causes fluorescent-painted surfaces to fluoresce brilliantly while all other objects disappear into the background.

See Christmas fantasies to delight the children as well as humorous Christmas scenes and inspirational religious scenes. A trip to the 2000 block of Marengo Avenue in South Pasadena is well worth your time and will kindle your Christmas spirit.

ULTRA-VIOLET PRODUCTS, INC.   San Gabriel, California

Invitation to Thomas Warren's Black Light Christmas Show on Marengo Ave. in California every year from 1958 to 1966

lamps, along with long sections of glass Longwave Ultraviolet filters covering the lamps to protect them from the rain. On the bottom of this professional Black light unit is a riveted metal label with "Glo-Craft" and "Switzer Brothers Inc., Cleveland, Ohio" logos etched into it, along with "Model 232." The unit is a heavy-duty industrial design which weighs twelve pounds (6 kilos) and was used for professional Fluorescent displays. With the full thirty-five inch thirty watt "BL" Longwave Ultraviolet tubular lamp behind an entire glass Longwave Ultraviolet filter, the Fluorescent Colors excited by this antique professional Black light unit are pure, and does not include the typical three percent Visible Blue light emitted by today's cheap, simple tubular Black lights which incorporate the inferior Longwave Ultraviolet filter into the glass tube of the Black light lamp itself. Yet another example of the regressed state of Black light technology we are left with over half a century after this 'Golden Age of Fluorescence: 1930s - 1950s.'

'Costumes and Uniforms' are next listed, with credit to this application as being one of the oldest and most familiar use of the Black light [the first Ziegfeld Follies introduced the "Skeleton Ballets" in 1907]. As witness to the onset of "Fluorophobia" the statement given next speaks too many volumes: *'even though they no longer hold the same mystery and novelty that they once did* [this was only 1956] *the Black light still offers the possibility of 'weirdly beautiful' effects of lighting that only Black lights could create.'* Such a nice compliment it could have been written by Goethe! And one more time it is again written that the tubular Black lights were replacing the original Mercury lamps, but that 'Carbon-Arc' lamps with Ultraviolet filters were still employed for 'long-throw' Black light spotlights.

The final section of this 1956 "Black Light - Lamps, Applications, Design Procedures" is perhaps the most important of the catalogue, not because it's knowledge is common and still in use today like many of the 'Lamps' and 'Applications' already listed in the publication, but because of just the opposite: it is in that rarified atmosphere, once again, known as that phenomenon already cited several times in this book and termed not "Lost knowledge," but "Thrown-away knowledge." The technology behind the Black light designers exemplified by the last three pages of this catalogue in 1956 is something that would be nearly unimaginable to today's Twenty-first century extravagantly-paid "Set designers." Showing the advanced state of the Black light technology common in usage in 1956 to the "Set designer" of the 'Ice Capades' extravaganza I saw in Amsterdam would be a little like showing Antonie van Leeuwenhoek an Electron Microscope! Actually it wouldn't be a little like, but it would be exactly like. What is shocking in this chapter "The Miracle of Fluorescence: 1930s - 1950s" is the advanced and damn near perfect designs, scientifically proven as well as proven by concrete experience, that today would be as relevant to a "Set designer" as Aryabhatta's astronomical discoveries thirty centuries ago are to the director of NASA. "Who gives a shit!" would probably be the intellectual opinion of today's Yuppie "Set designer," without a doubt accompanied by the most arrogant grin ever imaginable.

The introduction to this 'Design Procedures' section informs the reader that there are so many variables and different possibilities in designing a Black light installation that it was brought to a point where at least a portion of the design could be figured out by mathematical equation. The Black lights, their reflectors, and their filters all varied in the 1950s (and still do today). Similarly the kind of Fluorescent paint used, as well as the actual Color of the Fluorescent paint used in the installation are all different and were technically measured to correctly incorporate into the overall design. The four Black Light 'Design Procedures' that were covered in this booklet included first converting the common measurement of "Foot candles" of visible light to "Foot lamberts" of Black light emission. Calculating the 'Average Brightness' of an installation followed, as well as a 'Point-by-point' measurement and inspection of displays, finishing with estimating the "Foot lamberts" of the most popular Black light in 1956, the Fluorescent tubular 40 watt "BLB" Black light.

In a detailed list of the Fluorescent products manufactured for sale in 1956 the 'Black Light Equipment and Materials' section of this booklet also has a high historical value: Indoor Fluorescent Lamp equipment, Outdoor Fluorescent Lamp equipment, Portable A-C Fluorescent Lamp, Portable Battery-Powered Fluorescent Lamp, Mercury Lamp, and Shortwave Ultraviolet Lamp equipment. Fluorescent Paints - Lacquers, Watercolors, etc., Fluorescent Ink, Fluorescent Dye, Fluorescent Silk-screen Pastes, Fluorescent Chalks, Pencils, Crayons, etc., Fluorescent Papers, Fabrics, and Cosmetics, Fluorescent Minerals, Fluorescent Phosphors, Powders and Filters.

"The Switzer Brothers" "Day-Glo" Color Promotional Publication, 1959

Another artifact in the Museum collection from the actual dividing point between the 1950s and the 1960s Movement - 1959 - is a definitive example of the manner in which "Day-Glo" Fluorescent paint was promoted by it's inventor's company "The Switzer Brothers, Inc." to the general public, and how total this degree of commercial industrial promotion was. By 1959, the publishing date of this "Switzer Brothers, Inc." four page artifact, the world of Art or the Artist wasn't even vaguely considered anymore by the founders of the "Day-Glo" corporation. The market projection from this 1959 "Day-Glo" artifact is 100% industrial, which is absolutely obvious just by a cursory glance at the publication. Printed in the brilliant "Day-Glo" Colors, this four page printed promotion of the "Switzer Brothers" shows beyond the shadow of a doubt that the philosophy, direct intention, and over-all consciousness of the "Day-Glo" corporation was purged of any even remote connection to Art. Art is not mentioned or even remotely connected with the direction of Day-Glo corporation in 1959 during the era when this publication was presented by the "Switzer Brothers." What must be realized is that this 1959 publication was printed and promoted to the public just twenty-six years after Fluorescent paint had been first invented by Robert Switzer.

This four page "Day-Glo" printed promotion begins with a fully Day-Glo "Fire-Red" cover having a memo 'attached' to it, stating first that the 'Day-light fluorescent colors of Day-Glo' were a "striking concept" with a "visual impact," as well as having 'thousands of uses commercially.' Opening up this total Day-Glo cover page, the inside double-page spread has four separate Black and White photos with added surprinted Day-Glo Colors, as well as a headline, which are all as absolutely void of Artistic feelings as humanly possible. First of all, the philosophical headline announces that "Day-Glo" Colors gives business a "Competitive Edge." But, what is even more representative of this purely commercial advertisement for Day-Glo Colors in this 1959 publication, are the four Black and White photos surprinted with three Colors of vivid Day-Glo inks. The first esoteric use of Day-Glo is presented with the first Black and White photo, which is a box of Day-Glo Orange and Apricot "Tide" washing powder: "Washday Miracle." The title of this first photo is "On" their package. The second Black and White photo surprinted with Orange-Red as well as Magenta Day-Glo inks is entitled "In" their product and has a young boy with a cowboy hat on in a store putting Day-Glo basketballs into a shopping cart, as well as having Day-Glo products on the store shelf behind him. The third photo hows two hunters dressed with Day-Glo Orange-red hunting vests and hunting caps, and includes a title "To See" as well as to "be seen." Fourth on this list of the esoteric, Artistic applications for Fluorescent Day-Glo Color, is the Black and White photo of miserable 1950s cars speeding past a highway billboard printed with - you guessed it - Day-Glo Colors! Magenta Day-Glo is surprinted on this Black and White billboard, and the photo has a headline 'Communicate fast.' After the title informing that Colors from "Day-Glo" will give manufacturers a sought after "Competitive Edge," the subtitle underscores this intention, informing the businessman that not only are Day-Glo Colors 'four times as bright' when compared to "Conventional Colors," but that this 'advantage gives your product a visual difference which will make the sale!' These Day-Glo 'pigments, paints, and printing inks' commercial abilities and advantages are further promoted in the text of this four page promotion, with a paragraph written for each of these four Black and White photos surprinted with pure ungradated Fluorescent printing inks. The first "Package" photo is accompanied by a paragraph explaining that Day-Glo's printing inks were attracting the most attention in "packaging circles" from the first moment "Procter and Gamble" began making their "Tide" soap boxes with Day-Glo Colors [also in 1959]. The text continues with the promotion of beverage, cereal, candy, and soap boxes all 'changing their complexions' by using Day-Glo Colors on their packaging. Furthermore, it is explained that all other innovations of packaging involved expensive redesigns or special new equipment for production, but all that was needed to improve your packaged product was the addition of any of the more than a "dozen" Fluorescent printing inks made by "Day-Glo." The esoteric highlights are listed as being both "trouble-free" for production and the addition of a "sparkle" which was "attention-getting" being added to "your package." The American cowboy child putting Day-Glo basketballs into a shopping cart: "In" their product, is explained as Day-Glo pigment's abilities to add "selling power" for produced plastics. Suggestions include "Eye-Catching" Day-Glo plastic 'inflated play-balls, sponges, tubing, kitchen ware, bottles, fabrics, caps, and toys.' The hard-sell pure businessman is offered a glimpse into Fluorescent Color's magic, as a passing thought, by the added fact that "from within" the product will "glow" when made with Day-Glo Colors, which will then provide the product with "stopping power" that was "extraordinary" for the all-important "point of sale." Finally the businessman is enticed to 'Discover an extra dimension' of appeal for their product which guarantees increased estimated profits.

The 'To be seen and to see' hunting photograph is promoted by the fact that during the previous year, 1958, "Blaze-Orange" Day-Glo Color was tested by experts in vision and safety using Army personnel, and was found to be 'the most visible, distinctive, and safest Color for hunting equipment.' What could be closer to Art than that?

Finally the promotion to the aesthetically-purged and Artistically-void pure businessman concludes with the advantage of being able 'to communicate quickly' and, of course, make more money simply by adding Fluorescent Day-Glo Color to any 'advertising or promotional material.' It is advised that the Day-Glo "glowing colors" will make 'any outdoor advertising, folders, or inserts visible faster and further.'

The back cover of this full-sized 'booklet' is totally dedicated to Day-Glo's use in industry, with a Black and White picture of a jet airliner surprinted in pure Fluorescent "Fire-Red." The entire top half of the jet's fuselage is painted "Fire-Red" as well as half of each wing, the back wings, and the four jet engines. The headline 'When Visibility is Vital' announces in capitals 'Day-Glo Fluorescent Paint SHOUTS SAFETY.' A block of text follows, explaining that in 1958 a twelve month test of the U.S. Air Force Air Training Command was made by painting 1,600 aircraft with Day-Glo "High Visibility" Fluorescent paint. This Fluorescent paint reduced 1957's total of nine midair collisions to 1958's total of zero. The reader is informed of this advantage of using this Day-Glo Fluorescent Aviation paint, being that both the U.S. Air Force and the U.S. Navy had reduced their midair collisions.

The final Black and White illustration surprinted with Fire-Red Day-Glo ink is: "Industrial Accidents." A construction site with Fluorescent safety-helmets, vehicles, beams, fire extinguishers, and other safety equipment completes the illustration, and the 'Reduction of Industrial Accidents' is the headline. Ohio's "Timken Roller Bearing" company is the example given of industries using Day-Glo paint to reduce 'industrial hazards.' This miraculous Fluorescent paint that is hailed as being 'four times as bright as normal colors,' is then reduced to being used for nothing more than 'marking obstructions and for safety equipment.' The list of uses for this Day-Glo Fluorescent paint in this promotional publication concludes with 'Construction, Highways, Signs, Marine, Aviation, and Industrial,' a clear indication of it's manufacturer's intentions and direction, which in the end was as far from Fine Art as possible. In this final example it is once more proved beyond the shadow of a doubt that the intentions and direction of "The Switzer Brothers" was to promote Fluorescent paint in a purely industrial field - the field in which they could make the most money, period. Art or changing the world had nothing what-so-ever to do with the direction of the inventor of this Fluorescent paint - Robert Switzer, or his brother Joseph Switzer, who were both pure American entrepreneurs - businessmen heart and soul, which leaves zero room for aesthetics or non-profitable ventures such as Art.

John Plumer Ludlum - The First Artist Credited with Using Fluorescent Paint in Fine Art, 1945

To close this chapter "The Miracle of Fluorescence: 1930s-1950s," I will 'introduce' an Artist who is credited as being the first Artist who used Fluorescent Paint for Fine Art in 1945. This is not an Artist who is a household name because of his fame in the Twenty-first century, as first might be imagined, but an obscure Artist today who was very famous and successful only thirty years ago. John Plumer Ludlum's Fluorescent masterpiece "Nativity" was sold to the Ohio Tourist Center for two-and-a-half million dollars in 1973, the highest amount ever paid for a living Artist's painting up to that time in history - More money than *Picasso* ever sold a painting for before passing away also in 1973. But, not only has John Ludlum's identity and Artistic career been nearly lost to this Social Stigma of "Fluorophobia," but even his $2.5 million Masterpiece has been lost as well! Nobody even knows where it has been relegated to in storage today after the Ohio Tourist Center was never built. This is by far not the worse thing that has happened to the past-celebrated Artwork of John Ludlum, because through personal correspondence with John Ludlum's former Galley Representative in Oregon, I have learned that the worse nightmare an Artist can imagine is exactly what happened to this Artist: after John Ludlum's death in the early 1990s, and later after the death of his wife, a Trash Compactor was parked in front of his house and was then proceeded to be filled with the canvases of this formerly famous American Artist to be *Thrown Away!* The former fame and present obscurity of John Plumer Ludlum, the first Artist in the world to be credited with using Fluorescent paint in Fine Art in 1945, is a golden example of the entire subject matter of this book: "The Social Stigma of Fluorophobia." What was formerly regarded as 'the new' has now been relegated to 'the past,' but don't get the wrong idea, not just the past, but a past that is Stigmatized. Almost every association with the 1960s Movement has been systematically removed from today's current sociopolitical unacceptance with the measly exceptions of the music and jeans because they both make a fortune.

As a personal example of the subjugated stigmatism that has done a good deal to nearly erase the name of this pivotal Artist, I first got a Black light in 1969 and I have a Fluorescent Art Gallery for thirty years, as well a having given tours to about 50,000 visitors to "Electric Ladyland - the First Museum of Fluorescent Art" in Amsterdam for eighteen years, and the first time I ever heard of the name of this Artist credited as being the first to use Fluorescent paint in Fine Art was not too many years ago by mistake on the internet.

The first time I could find a Fluorescent painting by John Ludlum that I thought was suitable for the Museum, and that I could afford, was in June, 2009, just after the tenth anniversary of the Museum's opening. After searching the internet for a long time the only information in any form that is on the internet consists of a single photo of John Ludlum and a page of text that stands as the only documented biography of this Artist on the entire World Wide Web! After digging deeper on the net I could find on a blog an answer to a question by a man who was the gallery representative of John Ludlum in Oregon years ago, and who very generously sent me a package of impossible-to-find documentation of John Ludlum's career. Thanks solely to

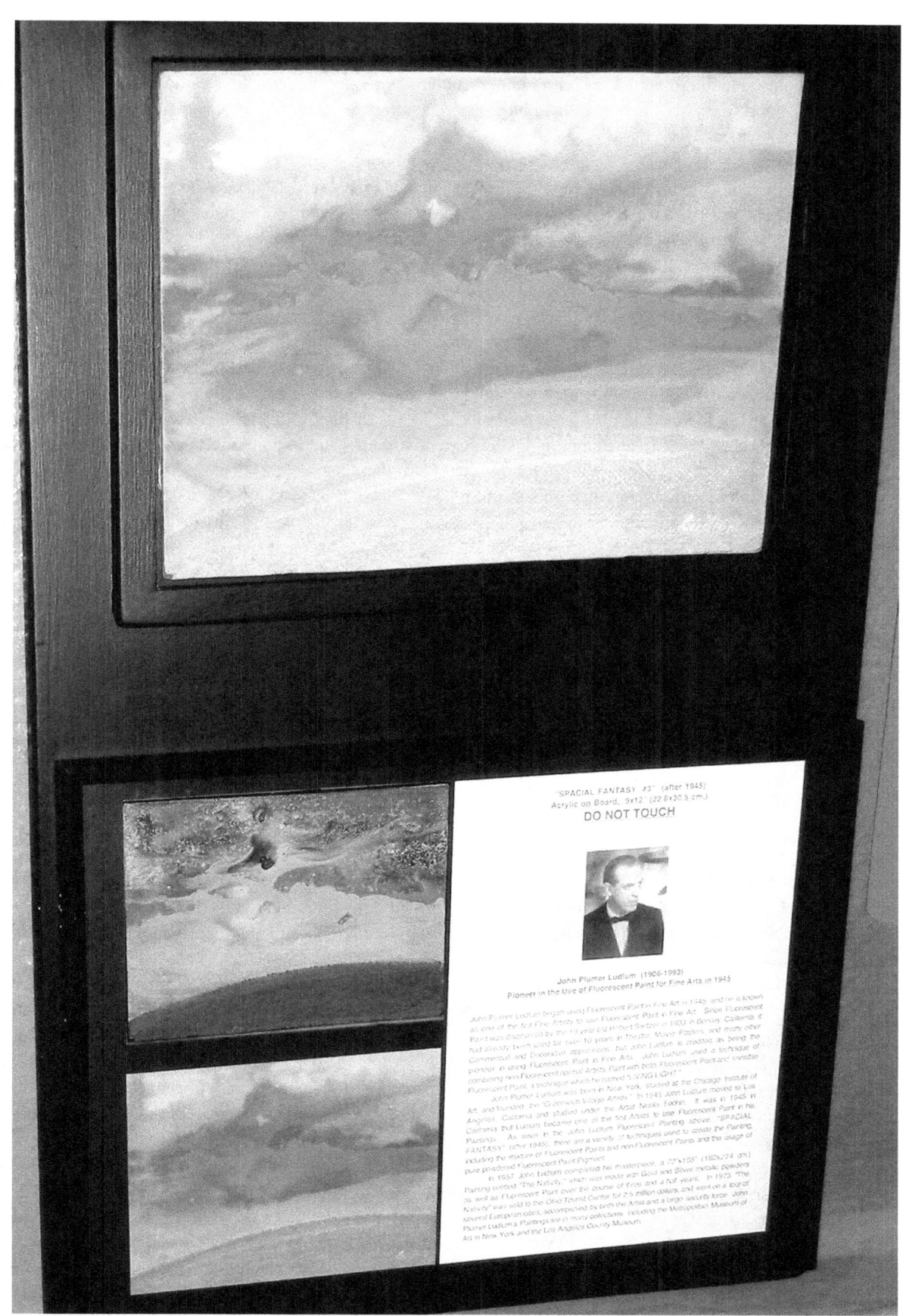

John Plumer Ludlum (1906-1993) - the first Artist to use Fluorescent paint for Fine Art in 1945, "Spacial Fantasy #3"
"Electric Ladyland - the First Museum of Fluorescent Art" collection

this man Marv Taylor this book will contain a good deal more information on the life of John Ludlum than just the single biography that is copied over and over again on the few websites that mention or sell Art by this pioneering Artist John Ludlum.

For a general introduction to the life of John Plumer Ludlum I will start with the text section of this "Electric Ladyland - the First Museum of Fluorescent Art" display of his Fluorescent painting:

<u>"Spacial Fantasy #3" (after 1945), Acrylic on board, 9 x 12" (22.8 x 30.5 cm.)</u>
John Plumer Ludlum began using Fluorescent Paint in Fine Art in 1945, and he is known as the first Artist to use Fluorescent Paint in Fine Art. Since Fluorescent Paint was discovered by the nineteen year old Robert Switzer in 1933 in Berkeley, California, it had already been used for over ten years in Theatre, Movie Posters, and many other Commercial and Decorative applications, but John Ludlum used a technique of combining non-Fluorescent normal Artist's Paint with both Fluorescent Paint and Invisible Fluorescent Paint, a technique which he named "LIVING LIGHT."

John Plumer Ludlum was born in New York, studied at the Chicago Institute of Art, and founded the "Greenwich Village Artists." In 1945 John Ludlum moved to Los Angeles, California and studied under the Artist Nicolai Fechin. It was in 1945 in California that Ludlum became one of the first Artists to use Fluorescent Paint in his Fine Art. As seen in the John Ludlum Fluorescent Painting in this display, "Spacial Fantasy #3" (after 1945) there are a variety of techniques used to create the painting including a mixture of Fluorescent Paints and non-Fluorescent Paints and the usage of what appears to be pure powdered Fluorescent Paint Pigment.

In 1957 John Ludlum completed his masterpiece, a 72" x 108" (182 x 274 cm) Fluorescent Painting entitled "The Nativity" which was made with Gold and Silver Metallic powders as well as Fluorescent Paint over the course of three and a half years. In 1973 "The Nativity" was sold to the Ohio Tourist Center for $2.5 million, and went on a tour of several European cities, accompanied by both the Artist with his wife and a large security force. John Plumer Ludlum's paintings are in many collections, including the Metropolitan Museum of Art in New York and the Los Angeles County Museum."

John Plumer Ludlum was born on September 12, 1906 in Hempstead, Long Island, New York. He was from a family that extended back to the forefathers of the United States, being the descendent of William Ludlum who established the first commercial flour mill in Watermill, Long Island, New York way back in 1630. Ludlum's mother was the daughter of a Presbyterian minister in North Dakota, and his father was the son of a doctor who started his career as a bank director in North Dakota. In 1908 the family moved to Wolcott, Connecticut and bought a farm, and a couple of years later a third child was born only a few years after John's birth. After Ludlum's father got a job as an accountant in the city, the family also eventually migrated back to the city life, leaving their farm behind. In third grade the first signs of Ludlum's Artistic nature began to reveal themselves, such as the drawings in the margins of his third grade school book, and later when sketching pretty girls at age eleven. At this point in his life John Ludlum received a drum for Christmas, then experimented with a trombone, which he returned to the pawn shop that he bought it from after using it for just one weekend. At twelve John was given a violin and organized a five piece Dixieland band, as well as playing violin in the church orchestra and high school symphony. By the third year of High school music had taken over his interests, he lost interest in school, and he discovered painting. It seems to have been John Ludlum's father who suggested that he study the subject that interested him the most, Art, so instead of wasting more time in high school, John began to study the printing industry at the age of sixteen by becoming an Art apprentice at the Lakeside Press in Chicago. Initially an errand boy who learned typesetting, Ludlum discovered Fine Art in this Lakeside Press through Color lithography. Soon Ludlum was studying at Chicago Art Institute and exhibited paintings for the first time when he was just twenty years old in 1926. Pastels became the favorite medium for Ludlum, and his name spread as a fine portrait Artist, but the young student worked so hard that he was confirmed to a T.B. Sanatorium for a year back in Connecticut. After recuperating, Ludlum opened a studio in New Rochell, New York and continued working in pastels, lithography, and in advertising as well, so for four years every day the Artist commuted back and forth to New York City. At this time in Ludlum's career the 1929 stock crash in New York began the era known as "The Depression," and the Artist decided to move directly into New York City and began to study at the National Academy and the Art Student's League.

Soon after Ludlum opened his first New York studio in the fashionable Buckingham Hotel. Becoming friends with Spencer Driggs, who was editor of the "Musical Advance," Ludlum gained customers and publicity, eventually opening up the opportunity to design stage sets for Broadway reviews and other theatre work. John Ludlum also had a show of his pastels at the "Pepper Pot" in the heart of Greenwich Village.

"NATIVITY" EXHIBITED IN GEORGIA, AT FORT GORDON

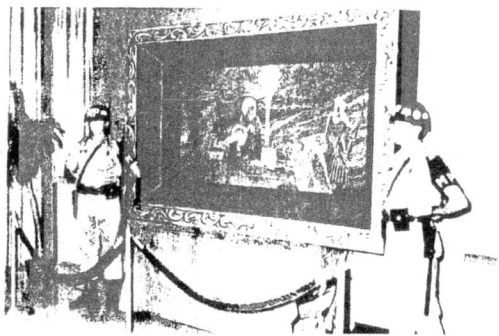

The first major showing of the great, Ludlum "Nativity" since it became associated with Biblelands, took place on Sunday, Ocotber 14, 1973 at a Cultural Fair at Fort Gordon, Georgia before nine hundred people. Featured also at the concert were Mr. Earl Voorhies in behalf of Biblelands, who loaned the painting for this event, Mr. Ludlum, Mr. Frank Roughton who performed his famous dramatic presentation of "The Sermon on the Mount" and the seventy piece Augusta Symphony Orchestra. With an orchestral accompaniment, the beautiful fluorescent painting, depicting the birth of Christ, was unveiled.

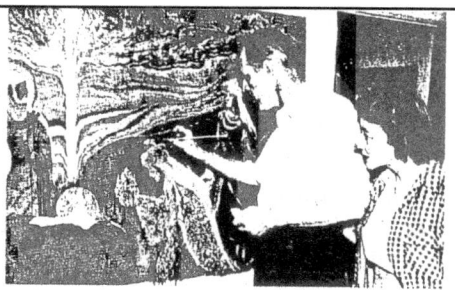

THE ARTIST...

John Plumer Ludlum was born in Hemstead, N.Y., September 12, 1906. He began painting seriously at seventeen and studied at the Chicago Art Institute and the National Academy of Design, N.Y. A master lithographer, his proficiency in the use of oil, watercolor, pastel, acrylic and fluorescent colors has made him internationally known. This is his 50th year of painting.

Mr. Ludlum has garnered ribbons galore. His work is owned by celebrities and heads of industry both here and abroad. For many years he lived and painted in the English manor house in the Hollywood hills. Now they enjoy their studio-gallery overlooking an orange grove and Saddleback Mountain in Tustin, California.

SINCE THE BEGINNING OF HISTORY, the artist has expressed his ideas and feelings through art. Many of his earliest drawings were done with clay and chalk. Later developments provided a variety of pigments mixed in oils, varnishes, lacquers, wax, tempra, etc. In thousands of years there has been little change in basic techniques. There have been variations in styles and materials, but otherwise no radical departure from accepted methods. The artist has

John Plumer Ludlum, "Ludlum Art Center" brochure, Tustin, California 1966-1993 (front)

been working with pigments while thinking in terms of light, doing his best, cleverly to imitate subtle nuances of shadows or the broad blaze of a summer sun. All too often his efforts missed their mark, and at best were a poor imitation of nature, real or imagined.

However, today we have a new, advanced, entirely different medium, as modern as tomorrow's sunrise. Thanks to twentieth century ingenuity we have a new art FLUORESCENT PAINTING! This brilliant and exciting medium is the only basically new achievement in art in thousands of years.

Much experimentation has been done, the most scientific materials and equipment are being produced, and today the artist may at last extend the range of his palette from darkness through the entire spectrum and on into darkness again, using the finest watercolors, pastels and oil paint. He may not only think in terms of light, but can actually dip his brush into the most vivid flame of LIGHT ITSELF, LIVING LIGHT!

JOHN PLUMER LUDLUM discovered the excitement of painting with light and this excitement has remained with him and extends to the viewers of all of his work. Light and form is expressed in his beautiful portraits, sensitive nudes and dramatic landscapes. His space series creates a feeling of movement, depth, and a timelessness of light.

Fluorescent - Ultra Violet - Black Light - has been used in night clubs, skating and theater presentations and for posters for years, but the brilliance of the "raw" color had not been adapted to fine art. Thirty years ago John Plumer Ludlum found fluorescent pigment. It proved a natural medium to an artist so involved with light. Developing his own formula he pioneered fluorescent in fine art. Using this method, Ludlum is able to paint a brilliant sunset, subtly bright clouds and a graduating, lesser degree of light - always expertly done in natural balance - down to the darkest shades. For the first time the sunset is not an imitation.

John Ludlum's fluorescent work has created excitement whenever it has been shown. He is the winner of four first awards in International Competition in this medium. The Nativity, of course, counting for two of those awards!

Society and Religious leaders, heads of Industry and members of news media, from coast to coast and in Europe, are numbered among his collectors.

Among satisfied clients and exhibitors are:

Merrill Lynch, Pierce, Fenner & Smith, Los Angeles
Rutan & Tucker, Attorneys, Orange County
New York Graphic Society
Stokely Foods Products family, Los Angeles
R. C. A. Victor
Max Factor, Hollywood
Ford Motot Co.
Walter Foster Art Books
Los Angeles County Museum
Los Angeles County Airport
Pabst, Schlitz, Blatz
Metropolitan Museum, N. Y. City
Museum of Science and Industry, N. Y. City
Garden Grove Community Church, G. G. Calif.
Mrs. Bonita Granville Wrather
Douglas Aircraft
Paramount Studios
Carnation
Camel
Chesterfield
Canada Dry
Cryson Greeting Cards
Sunkist
Roy Rogers
and
Black light paintings purchased and exhibited by the United States Government Space Program and exhibited at the Armory New York City

Ludlum Art Center
439 El Camino Real
Tustin, Calif. 92680

John Plumer Ludlum, "Ludlum Art Center" brochure, Tustin, California 1966-1993 (back)

About 1936 Ludlum opened up a photography studio on 46th Street near 5th Avenue in Manhattan, began to experiment with lighting effects and costumes in his photography portraits and his studio soon became a place to meet for a weekly Monday evening "Opera House." Ludlum's studio became the meeting place for financial directors, opera singers, dances, and members of the Ziegfeld Follies, and at this pivotal point in Ludlum's Artistic life he had to decide either to continue on with theatre and stage as a designer, or to concentrate on being an Artist, which Ludlum eventually chose. Besides painting, lithography had also deeply interested Ludlum, and at this point in his life the Artist began to work with the very precise "Dot Etching" of Lithography. Basically "Dot Etching" is the microscopic retouching of Color dot-by-dot of an image to be printed. When looking very close at an image in a book or magazine it is made up of thousands of tiny dots, which combined together when viewed at a distance become the image of a person's face or other subject matter. "Dot Etching" is the extremely precise meticulous work of enlarging these "dots" of the printed image, and retouching these individual dots to alter the finished image.

As early proof of the open-minded consciousness that still exists in the world-famous Greenwich Village, Ludlum had a one man show of his Artwork at the "American Saloon" Art Gallery for it's opening in December, 1933. The theme of this 1933 Art Galley in New York was to give exposure to Artwork of both American Indians and Black Americans (called 'Negroes' during that time period) not just White Artists. The "American Saloon" was financed by John Ludlum and was managed by "Chief Letaiyo" (Grey Fox) an American Indian sculptor. In 1938 Ludlum opened up his own Art studio in Greenwich Village, which was a huge loft on the top of a building, where Ludlum concentrated solely on Art and the socialite 'Open Houses' were left behind. During this period of the 1930s John Ludlum founded and was the first president of the "Greenwich Village Artists," and a gallery and museum were established at 144-150 West Fourth Street in New York, right next door to the "Pepper Pot." In 1938 John Ludlum's New York photography studio was reviewed in a magazine in which he was portrayed as an Artist who 'played with light,' a premonition of his signature Artistic legacy which would unfold a few short years later through his introduction to the Black light and Fluorescent paint after moving to California. Ludlum's paintings and photographs all were based on the Artist's deep interest in light; the Color of the light, the direction, and also the intensity of the light. In 1943, as a testament to the success of the Artist in his late 30's, Ludlum's photographs were exhibited with the Rockefeller Center Camera Club and at the prestigious Metropolitan Museum of Art in New York City. Ludlum's serigraphs (silk screens) were also exhibited in the Rockefeller show, which were some of the earliest serigraphs made for Fine Art. Eventually the 'New York life' drained the Artist of his expression, and finding a peaceful place to create Art became the focus of Ludlum's life. On January 7, 1945, John Ludlum left New York City and moved to California. This was the most important move of his life, and just by fate the woman whom he would immediately fall in love with and marry also left her portrait studio in Buffalo, New York, and arrived in California just a month later, in February, 1945. Settling in Hollywood, Ludlum soon became associated with successful photographer Tom Kelly and was working on national advertising campaigns and photographing movie stars. Ludlum met Dr. Isaac Joties during this early period in California, who invited the Artist to stay on the grounds of his luxurious estate in the guest "English Cottage." This was by all accounts a simply gorgeous spot for an Artist, in the Los Feliz Hills which overlook Los Angeles, and was also directly across the street from the huge estate of Cecil B. DeMille, the famous early director in Hollywood. The "English Cottage" had a large one-room studio in it with very high ceilings and a large fireplace which was the size of one full wall of the studio. For nine years John Ludlum created Art in this English Cottage in the Hollywood Hills with few distractions. A special account is the story of Ludlum dealing with a rare distraction in his studio life, in which the ringing of the telephone disturbed him so completely that he decided to stuff the actual bell of the Telephone with cotton to not be disturbed by it's incessant ringing.

The excitement of this Artist, deeply interested with the effects of light in his paintings, on his "discovery" of the new paint that had only recently been invented a dozen years before - Fluorescent Paint - would be virtually impossible to imagine today in the arrogant/banal Twenty-first century. I've only experienced the raw primal discovery of a new emission of light itself through the miracle of the Black light and Fluorescence a few precious times, such as the very first time I saw a Black light - "What the hell is *that*?" - and just as memorable when I showed Fluorescent minerals in India under Ultraviolet lamps to the enlightened Yogi Babaji Santosh Puri and Hindu holy people at the Santosh Puri Ashram in April, 1998: they were *amazed*. The account of Ludlum's "discovery" of Fluorescent paint relates the excitement he felt when finally having the correct pigment to create his paintings of "Living Light." His unbounded fascination with the new Fluorescent paint led Ludlum to think about what many Fluorescent Artists envision: who could imagine the excitement of famous Artists of the past like Gauguin, or Van Gogh, Vlaminck, or Delaunay if it was possible to travel back 100 and some years and give these famous Colorists *a pot of Fluorescent Paint!!* All four of these Artists would have been so enthralled by this Fluorescent Color - without a Black light at all - just out in the Sun, that they would have probably smeared some of the Fluorescent paint onto their faces(!) With his "discovery" of the new Fluorescent paint - the first and only paint in the world that could create and emit it's own light - John Ludlum began to experiment with light again. As many Artists for many years had done, Ludlum had experimented with the effects of two different lights on his paintings, the electric light and natural daylight. Now Ludlum began to experiment with three different 'lights' on his paintings: electric light, natural daylight, and the new Twentieth century invention the "Black Light." Ludlum quickly learned through experimentation that the Black light Longwave Ultraviolet was the most effective and caused the Fluorescent paint to emit the most vivid light when the room was dark, without the distraction of too much ambient White light. Ludlum found the perfect combination of lighting for his paintings was when the room had just enough ambient light to see the Colors of his Artist oil paints, but not too much ambient light to disturb the effect of the Black light on his Fluorescent pigments. Further experimentation led Ludlum to his signatory technique of mixing the use of classic Artist oil Colors and the use of new Fluorescent paint on the same canvas. These new paintings took the Artist three or four times the amount of time to paint them, but offered an extension to his palette that was formerly both unimaginable and impossible. John Ludlum quickly developed his fascination with the new Fluorescent paint into the creation of canvases in which there would be a normal landscape in the White light, but as the White lights were turned down and the Black light effect became visible, this same common landscape would change before the eyes into a blazing sunset or a snow-covered winter scene. Ludlum's excitement could hardly be contained as we imagine him discovering the fact that Fluorescent paint is the actual source of the painting's light itself, and in this way he actually held "Living Light" in his paint jars.

  At just this pivotal point in his life John Ludlum met a Hindu dancer named Bhupesh Guha, whom he helped to establish an Indian dance class, and whom Ludlum asked to model for a very early "Living Light" painting, "Lord Krishna." In 1933 at a party of the Hindu dance troupe during this period, John Ludlum met and proposed to Shirley Grote, a portrait painter whom he would remain with for the rest of his life. For years John and Shirley Ludlum lived in the beautiful Hollywood Hills "English Cottage," with a large studio to freely create. This wealth of information on the early years of John Ludlum's career comes form the first public records of the lives of John and Shirley Ludlum created in 1978 upon request of the National Archives at the Smithsonian Institute in Washington, D.C. to be permanently added as a biography of these two Artists.

  The best explanation of the unimaginable "newness" of Fluorescent paint to the history of Art itself is contained in a simple brochure of the "Ludlum Art Center," 439 El Camino Real, Tustin, California printed in the mid-1970s. On the cover of this one-fold small brochure there is a photograph of John Plumer Ludlum painting his masterpiece, the "Nativity" while his wife watches intently. The text begins with a simple two paragraph introduction to John Plumer Ludlum, presenting the facts that his Artwork was owned by both leaders of industry and by celebrities in both America and abroad. The lifestyle of Ludlum is also described in this text, explaining that after living for years in the Hollywood Hills English manor house, he and his wife were now relocated to Saddleback Mountain, with a studio-gallery in Tustin, California which overlooked an Orange grove. The most valuable section is the bulk of the text, which explains what the invention of Fluorescent Paint meant to the History of Art. This is a very rare documented detailed discussion of the confrontation in Art which began with this formerly unimaginable and unprecedented Fluorescent paint. This brochure gives a feeling of the time era that the brochure was printed in, and also gives a taste of the passion and perspective of the Artist John Ludlum. In his brochure text John Ludlum explains that Artists have expressed their feelings and their ideas through their Art since before history began, primarily with clay and chalk during the earliest times. Developments later produced a variety of different pigments which could be mixed with a variety of 'vehicles,' such as oils, lacquers, varnishes, tempera, or wax, but after the production of new pigments, these techniques and mixtures of pigments with a variety of vehicles has changed very little. Ludlum observed that although the styles and materials of Artists changed dramatically throughout the long history of Art, the techniques and pigments used by Artists to produce their paint has not changed that much. Since Art began, the Artist has been creating with classic pigments, while trying to imitate pure light. Ludlum plainly states in truth that most of the time these attempts resulted in 'poor imitations' of both light and nature. Ludlum continues, announcing to the reader that "today" the Artist has the opportunity to use a new painting medium which is as modern and new as *"tomorrow's sunrise"* - the Art of "FLUORESCENT PAINTING!" Ludlum describes clearly this new Art of "FLUORESCENT PAINTING" as being the first new innovation for "thousands of years" in Art. It is also clearly explained by Ludlum that after years of experimentation in science, Fluorescent Colors were available as oil paint, pastels, and watercolors, and through the use of these different choice of Fluorescent mediums, the Artist was not limited to only imitating light, but by using Fluorescent mediums the Artist could now paint with "LIGHT ITSELF," with the 'LIVING LIGHT" of Fluorescent pigments. The text of Ludlum's small brochure goes on to inform readers that John Plumer Ludlum had discovered painting with Fluorescent mediums in Fine Art, and that the excitement of this light-emitting pigment has remained with him through his years of creating portraits, landscapes, and classic nudes. Ludlum's "Space series" is also mentioned in this brochure, as creating feelings of both movement and depth, as well as light's "timelessness." The John

Ludlum painting displayed in "Electric Ladyland - the First Museum of Fluorescent Art" is part of this "Space series," being named "Spatial Fantasy #3."

This text of Ludlum's brochure concludes with the facts that Fluorescent Colors and the Black light had been already used for years in night clubs, and for public performances, such as skating clubs and theater, but also with his opinion that these "raw" Fluorescent Colors had been too bright and not "adapted" for use in Fine Art. However, John Ludlum is credited with being the first Artist able to adapt these Fluorescent Colors for Fine Art through the use of his own pioneering "formula." This brochure text closes with the statement that for the first time in Art history, through the use of the new Fluorescent pigments, an Artist can paint a sunset which is not a mere "imitation."

The third page of this "Ludlum Art Center" brochure lists famous clients who bought Ludlum's paintings, including Merrill Lynch, R.C.A., Max Factor, Ford Motor Co., Los Angeles County Museum, Los Angeles County Airport, Metropolitan Museum of Art, Douglas Aircraft, Paramount Studios, Camel, Chesterfield Cigarettes, Canada Dry, Sunkist, Roy Rogers, and the United States Space Program.

The back of this John Ludlum brochure centers on his masterpiece the "Nativity" which he worked on for three and a half years and which was first officially exhibited on Sunday, October 14, 1973 at a Cultural Fair at Fort Gordon, Georgia to a crowd of 900 people. The photograph on the back of this brochure shows Ludlum's masterpiece, the Fluorescent painting "Nativity" with a free standing hand-carved large frame around it containing the painting's Black lights, as well as a two person military police guard team flanking the masterpiece. But this is getting ahead of the story of John Ludlum's Artistic legacy.

In the eighteen room English manor house where John and Shirley Ludlum lived for about ten years there was a huge thirty-four foot (10.3 meter) studio. During this period in the mid-1950s John Ludlum began the three years work on his Fluorescent masterpiece "Nativity." The mantle above the fireplace in the Ludlum's studio was eleven feet long (3.2 meter) and no painting that was hung there filled the large space properly, so John told his wife he would paint a very special painting to hang over the fireplace mantle that would be nine feet (2.74 meter) long and would fill the mantle piece space. Work on the "Nativity" progressed over the course of three and a half years, and when it was completed in 1957, Ludlum entered it into the Los Angeles "Madonna Festival" where it won first prize and the prize for most popular painting. Visitors to this week long "Madonna Festival" travelled from around the world and would vote on the 300 paintings exhibited, and in 1957 the "Nativity" received more votes than any other painting had in the entire twelve year history of the festival. In 1954 Ludlum had entered his first major work in "Ultra-Violet Oils," the "Madonna Del Vetro," which won the highest award in that ninth "Madonna Festival" in Los Angeles, and which caused "Who's Who" to announce John Ludlum 'Foremost of Artists of Fluorescent Painting and Portraiture.'

John Ludlum's Fluorescent masterpiece the "Nativity" is a six by nine foot (102 x 274 cm) painting on panel which the Artist worked on for three and a half years. It is complete with a large free standing hand-carved frame which was designed to incorporate the painting's Black lights. Ludlum painted the "Nativity" scene of the birth of Christ in a Byzantine style combining Gold and Silver metallic pigments, Fluorescent pigments, and Artist oil paints to create the sparkling religious image. After the first exhibition of this "Nativity" painting at the 1957 "Madonna Festival" in L.A., it went on to sell for the highest price ever paid for a work of Art made by a living Artist in history up to that point in 1973, when it was purchased by the Ohio Tourist Center for $2.5 million. The masterpiece was unveiled at Fort Gordon, Georgia in front of 900 people under heavy armed guard, while the seventy-two piece Augusta Symphony Orchestra played. Included in the Opening ceremony was a presentation of "Sermon on the Mount" by Mr. Frank Roughton, and a presentation by Mr. Earl Voorhies on behalf of the "Biblelands" of the Ohio Tourist Center who lent the painting for the event. The Fluorescent masterpiece also travelled to Europe for a one man painting tour in Mantz, Germany and in Madrid hosted by the United States Air Force complete with heavy security and armed guards.

The details of the ownership of the "Nativity" were printed in the "Ohio Tourist center News Letter" and "The Rambler, Fort Gordon, Ga." The "Ohio Tourist Center, Inc." bought "The Nativity of Living Light, Inc." through a stock exchange for $2.5 million at $20 per share of Class A common stock. The painting is described as being comprised of 'jewel-like' dots that create a kaleidoscope of Color through the 'fluorescent salts' with the addition of Gold and Silver metallic pigments. The few photos of the painting from old articles displays a painting that immediately brings to mind the Pointillist Neo-Impressionist Artist Georges Seurat. Not only the composition of the painting, made totally from tiny dots of paint, but also the statue-like figures portrayed in the painting are very much the two defining points of Seurat's oeuvre. The "Ohio Tourist Office Newsletter" gives a background to the Artist's career, stating that Ludlum was a pioneer in Fluorescent Fine Art, and that he had been working with the combination of Artist oil paint and Fluorescent paint for over thirty years. The value of the "Nativity" is reported to have been appraised by one of the country's top appraisers, Harry Muir Kurtzworth, the former director of the Los Angeles County Museum. The "Ohio Tourist Office Newsletter" closes with the announcement that the "Nativity" had just returned from an exhibition tour of Europe, and that it will eventually be on display at the "Biblelands Theme Park" in the "Ohio Tourist Center." A book was published for the occasion, both on the "Nativity" and the Artwork of John Ludlum.

"The Rambler, Fort Gordon, Ga." published by the Richmond County Times of Georgia gave a detailed account of the unveiling ceremony of the "Nativity," beginning with the statement that the unveiling ceremony of the "Nativity" would be the first religious-cultural fair ever to be held on a military base, and that this 'musical-drama' would be held on Sunday, October 14, 1973 at 3:00 PM in Alexander Hall. While the "Nativity" was being unveiled in Fort Gordon, Georgia, the United States presidential car was brought to Georgia to be John and Shirley Ludlum's limousine for the event. This newspaper article also adds France and Austria to the German and Spanish cities that the "Nativity" had just returned from on it's European tour. The prophetic statement that follows in this "Rambler Fort Gordon" newspaper is a statement that was instantly apparent and just a matter of plain old logic, but, apparently this plain and logical conclusion never was realized, and stands as one of the prime reasons why I wrote this book: Fluorescent oils, Artist's oils, Gold and Silver metallic pigments on a tempered masonite panel of forty-eight by eighty-four inches (122 x 213 cm) in a frame fitted with Ultraviolet lamps, characterizes the masterpiece, *'which marks a new era of visual Arts.'* It is further explained that every one of the paintings of the "Old Masters" who's works are worth 'fabulous prices' was a work by a 'Master of Beauty,' and that John Plumer Ludlum 'today reigns in these ranks.' The closing statement is another blatant proof of the Social Stigma of "Fluorophobia," proving how something that was so obvious and such a logical extension that it was written about by even newspaper reporters, stating that John Ludlum was a pioneer of Fluorescent painting in Fine Art, and this had made him a 'leading Artist' of the new movement of the Art world. These prophetic statements that were nipped in the bud by the stigmatization of "Fluorophobia" are all the more logical when examining the decades of events that led up to the unveiling of the "Nativity" in 1973. The "Nativity" was considered such a national treasure that when the painting returned to the United States after it's European tour, military armed guards were in position at the airport before the plane transporting the "Nativity" even landed! A mere "Yuppie's" lifetime later - thirty-nine years - this same national treasure that had a military squadron guarding the airport the painting was being transported to, this same $2.5 million painting that sold for more than any painting by a living Artist up to that time in history - including *Picasso* - now a mere thirty-nine years later nobody knows *where* it has been put into storage in some dark shitty corner of Ohio. From a 'National Treasure of America' to a 'Better-Forgotten Mistake,' hidden away for good to free Ohio and America from it's association with the sordid past - the "Hippie Era" when people unimaginably spoke against the government and did things that were illegal - "Quelle Horreur!" Almost unimaginable today in an era when the vast majority of American citizens would be happy to simply 'bend over' in an instant, with a smile, at the slightest request from the government. The "Support Our Troops" society of America today is downright *embarrassed* that the 1960s movement ever happened, and will fight until the end of their lives denying that they were ever involved in any way with that forbidden past. In December, 2008 I went to Rockefeller Center to see the world famous grandiose Christmas tree, and across the street at the New York City landmark the "Lord and Taylor's" Christmas windows, there was an odd display, complete with animated puppets, etc., showing a man and woman portrayed as typical "Hippies," complete with "Headbands," "Long Hair," "Tie-Dyes," "Beads," and "Peace signs" (man), and on the wall behind these "Hippie" puppets was written the message 'Remember when your Mom and Dad were Hippies *Six Million Years Ago*(!)' Was it really that long ago? Besides the point that very few, if any, of the rich gentrified Yuppie bastards with a child in their arms in front of that million dollar "Lord and Taylor's" Christmas window were even *born* during the Hippie Movement of the 1960s!

The first Fluorescent Art Class was given by John Ludlum in 1952 at the "Kit Kat Art Club," which was the name with a long history of Art clubs behind it, given to the club Ludlum formed with his friend the Hindu dancer Bhupesh Guha. In 1952 Ludlum also had an exhibition in the "Nik-Rick" Restaurant on Sunset Boulevard in Hollywood. This was the same year that Ludlum unveiled one of his first Fluorescent Paintings, "Lord Krishna" modeled from Bhupesh Guha. In 1953 Fluorescent "Madonna and Child" was accepted by the eighth annual "Madonna Festival." In 1954 the Fluorescent "Madonna del Vetro" won the ninth annual Madonna Festival in Los Angeles, and there was the unveiling of the new painting "Mystery of Life." In 1955 John Ludlum married Shirley Louise Grote, gave a Fluorescent Art Class, and was involved in the "Black Light Center and Bank of America." In 1956 one of the few traceable documented events that took place in Ludlum's life can be found in the March 11, 1956 copy of the "Los Angeles Times:" 'Artist Discussing Fluorescent Colors during Friday Club Meeting.' This three sentence article announces that the Artist John Ludlum will lecture on using Fluorescent paint in Fine Art, and that this lecture would be held in Mrs. Jack Chertok's home in Beverly Hills, who was a member of the "Art Patroness Group" of the Friday Morning Club. It is also announced that Ludlum would display some of his Fluorescent 'prize-winning' paintings.

In 1960 the first full exhibition of Ludlum's Fluorescent paintings, Fluorescent drawings, and Fluorescent Art was held at the "American Art Academy" of the city of Los Angeles.

In 1963 the infamous 'smog of L.A.' began to be a health problem for it's residents. At this time the smog would roll over the city of Los Angeles and stop just at the incline of the Hollywood Hills. Reportedly one day John Ludlum got stuck in a traffic jam and was trapped in this smog for quite a while, so long that he became sick for several weeks. This event seriously made the Ludlums think about moving out of their eighteen room dream house in the Beverly Hills, and at the same time they were becoming associated with a printing company "Walter Foster Artbooks" which was settling in Orange County, Tustin, California because of the beautiful weather. From the period of June, 1965 to the end of 1966 the Ludlums first rented an apartment in Tustin, then decided to buy a townhouse, so for the next two and a half years the Ludlums spent three days a week in the 'Grand Central Station' of their Hollywood Hills home at 2836 N. Beachwood Drive, and four days a week in their peaceful Tustin townhouse. Eventually the Ludlums decided to leave the English Manor house in the Hollywood Hills and live permanently in Orange County weather. This is documented by the October 30, 1966 "Preview Opening" of the "Ludlum Art Center" in Tustin, California, the November 2, 1966 Invitational Unveiling of the "Ludlum Art Center" for the Chamber of Commerce, and the official opening also in November, 1966. 1967, remembered as "The Summer of Love" would bring an advertisement in January of Ludlum's work, which was entitled "Psychedelic Painting," which is the only time I've ever seen that word used in association with John Ludlum's Fluorescent paintings. 1967 also saw the beginning of Fluorescent Art classes given at the "Ludlum Art Center." Throughout the late 60s and into the 1970s the Ludlums received letters from Mrs. Richard Nixon each year, and in 1973 after the unveiling of the "Nativity" had been news for months, December saw the publication of newspaper articles in the "Register" and the "Herald American" acknowledging Ludlum as the pioneer in Fluorescent Fine Art and announcing the record-breaking sale of the "Nativity" in 1973. In October, 1975, John Ludlum was interviewed on a television show along with a showing of his Fluorescent paintings on KBSA TV, entitled "John Plumer Ludlum - Special." In 1976 John and Shirley Ludlum design and write an Art course on "Possibility thinking" for Dr. Robert Schuller of the "Garden Grove Community Church" and the "Hour of Power" television program. June, 1976 the "Columbus Dispatch" newspaper has an article and a photo of the "Nativity" 'done with Fluorescent Paints,' and the "Nativity" was also featured in the "Freedom Train" Central Ohio Bicentennial Exhibition that year. In 1977 John and Shirley Ludlum appear on two television programs and speak about their attitude of "Possibility Thinking" during the infancy of the "New Age" movement, and a large ten page Color article was published in the new magazine "Virtue" for it's special edition which featured a three-page foldout of the "Nativity."

The details of John Ludlum's exhibits and commissions are impressive with a major United States government commission to paint a number of eight foot (2.43 meter) Fluorescent murals for the first Space and Rockets Exhibition building, which was subsequently exhibited at the Armory Show in New York in 1955. In 1964 Ludlum's Fluorescent Artwork was exhibited at the dedication of the "Tower of Light' in Garden Grove, California along with the "Dead Sea Scrolls."

1984 was an important year for John Ludlum, because early in 1984 John and Shirley Ludlum met Julie and Marv Taylor who had recently opened the "Oceanside Studio Gallery" in Lincoln City, Oregon. In personal correspondence with Marv Taylor in late 2009, Mr. Taylor wrote the details to me:

"We met John and Shirley Ludlum early in 1984. We were in the process of opening a rental Art gallery in the tourist city of Lincoln City, Oregon. We spent some time at their home and studio in Tustin, Ca., and during that visit we became their agent and established the only public display of his works for sale. I created a special display area in our gallery ("Oceanside Studio Gallery") where we displayed several paintings under controlled lighting conditions. That section of the galley was called "The Hall of Living Light." John and Shirley spent approximately a month every year onsite at our gallery and painted many pieces while there and while the patrons watched and interacted with them. We sold the gallery in 1994, and the new owners continued to carry his works."

The "Hall of Living Light - Masterpiece Collection" in Marv Taylor's "Oceanside Studio Gallery" was opened on May 30, 1985, and it is estimated that more than half a million people viewed the exhibition "Hall of Living Light," and that more than 650 of John Ludlum's Fluorescent Paintings were purchased by collectors from around the world. On May 1, 1989 the gallery was sold by Marv Taylor and a new location in Depoe Bay, Oregon in a three story building was established. The opening of this new gallery "The Harbor Gallery" at 211 SW Highway 101, Depoe Bay, Oregon was on October 1, 1990.

A sheet of "Appraisals of Paintings by John Plumer Ludlum" was sent to me by Marv Taylor along with the collection of very rare articles and documentation on the life of John Ludlum, and this "Appraisal" is a good indication of the great values that Ludlum's Fluorescent paintings were assigned approximately thirty-five years ago in the late 1970s. Fifteen Fluorescent paintings dated 1979 are valued at a combined total of a staggering $11,205,000! Almost all of these appraisal prices were given again by Harry Muir Kurtzworth, the former director of the Los Angeles County Museum, who was recognized as one of the most important Art appraisers in the United States at that time.

The most recent newspaper interview with John Ludlum that I was sent by Marv Taylor, is the June 7, 1983 issue of "The Register Community Weekly" newspaper of Orange County, Tustin, California. Ludlum, then in his 70's, speaks candidly about Fluorescent Art in general, and more importantly about the public's opinion of Fluorescent Art in 1983. The title of the article states that an early Greenwich Village Artist of Tustin is still creating Art with 'individuality.' For historical purposes, the fact must be emphasized that that this article was published just ten years after John Ludlum's masterpiece "Nativity" was sold for the highest amount of money ever paid for a painting by a living Artist - including Picasso who was still alive in 1973 - two-and-a-half million dollars, and was exhibited with armed guards on a tour of American and European cities hosted by the United States Air Force. These facts must be kept in perspective when reviewing the following interview with John Ludlum in 1983. The opening paragraph speaks too many volumes about the way society's viewpoint had changed towards the Black light and Fluorescent paint from the early 1970s to the early 1980s, a decade that saw the collapse of any dream of Fluorescent paint and the Black light being accepted by, used by, or even acknowledged by Artists and the Art community in general. This is the decade - the 1970s - that saw the ultimate demise of the entire dream and movement of the 1960s and everything that had to do with the 1960s Movement, including the Hippies themselves, and any paraphernalia they carried on them, such a their ideas and ideals, their references and preferences, and even their Black lights and their Fluorescent Colors.

The 1983 interview begins with an introduction of the Artist, explaining that John Plumer Ludlum is a Artist that creates paintings with Fluorescent paint and are to be viewed under a Black light. Ludlum states that he knew that his 'approach' was not 'artistically respected.' Ludlum then paraphrases society's outlook of Fluorescent Art saying that to most of the people Fluorescent painting is thought of as 'tacky' and only acceptable in 'offbeat locations.' John Ludlum then sums up all of society's profound judgement on the phenomenon of Fluorescent Art in two simple ugly words, labeling it a 'tourist attraction.' This statement is documented proof in a published newspaper interview of the *depths* that Fluorescent Art had sunk to in ten short years since the "Nativity" masterpiece by Ludlum had sold for $2,500,000 to the Ohio State Tourist Office. Then comes similar proof by the newspaper reporter who's opinion is that *even though* Ludlum's more conventional early paintings hung and sold next to Pablo Picasso's paintings, Ludlum himself says that he is 'committed' to continue painting with Fluorescent Color. The intention of the reporter is more than obvious in this statement, comparing a formerly famous Artist who was in the same league as Picasso, now brought down to the level of near-obscurity because of his own insistence on using those damn unacceptable Socially Stigmatized Fluorescent Colors. This short statement by the newspaper article's author epitomizes the dramatic swing of society's acceptance of Fluorescent Colors and Black light from before the era of the 1960s, to the complete unacceptance, disapproval, and stigmatization of Fluorescent Colors and their Black lights after the 1960s. Almost as an excuse to justify his stubborn use of these Artistically and socially unacceptable Fluorescent Colors and Black lights is the short statement that followed by Ludlum, in which he admits to being 'crazy' about all Color as well as being 'fascinated' by both light and Color with the addition of their combined 'reflections.' The point is that using these Fluorescent Colors and Black lights in Fine Art was socially unacceptable by the early 1980s, and could compare to the same long lasting, defining career move as a physicist writing their Doctoral thesis on "UFOs."

The description by the newspaper reporter of Ludlum's oeuvre is typical of those times, and continues unchanged until the present day, calling the Artist's paintings 'unusual' and demoting his status to just showing in a store in a small shopping mall. The article explains that this "Ludlum Art Center" had been in existence for seventeen years by 1983, where the Artwork of both John and Shirley Ludlum was exhibited and sold, and that the gallery attracted both local customers and customers that had heard about the gallery across the ocean in Europe and the Far east. This newspaper article also gives some facts on Ludlum's masterpiece the "Nativity," which had been sold ten years before. The article explains that the Ohio Tourist Center in Cambridge, Ohio bought the six by nine foot masterpiece by John Ludlum for it's planned "Biblelands Center," but that this "Biblelands Center" was never built, and in 1983, ten years after the record-breaking famous sale, Ludlum's masterpiece was already relegated to being hung in somebody's private home in Ohio. If you think that is bad, it's nothing compared to the eventual fate of Ludlum's celebrated masterpiece, because today on the internet the true facts about the present Twenty-first century location of Ludlum's masterpiece is almost hard to believe, but the truth is that nobody even knows *where* this celebrated masterpiece that toured America and Europe in 1973 has been put into storage! This Fluorescent masterpiece by the famous pioneer of Fluorescent paint in Fine Art has been a defining example of the infinite respect and general high regard that Fluorescent Artwork and the entire phenomenon of Fluorescence itself has come to only forty-three years after it was sold for $2.5 million in 1973. A textbook, classic example of the Social Stigma of "Fluorophobia."

Concerning their personal life, John Ludlum explains in the interview that although the "Ludlum Art Center" was only a small store that was hidden away in a shopping canter, they had managed to remain financially independent and to have earned enough money over the last forty years to live a comfortable life. The article explains that both John and Shirley Ludlum owned the "Ludlum Art Center," as well as giving Art classes through the Tustin Recreation Services Department, and also paint in both their home and the gallery. The reporter describes the Art of John Ludlum's classic portraiture in oil or watercolors, but explains that the Art Ludlum was famous for are his Fluorescent paintings that are changing images depending on the lighting they are put under. The writer reports that Ludlum's Fluorescent paintings are viewed with different amounts of Black light, and before the eyes a summer landscape will transform into a blazing sunset with brilliant Colors in the sky as the Black light is turned on and the White light is gradually reduced. These are the classic Fluorescent paintings that John Ludlum built his Artistic career on, and this Ludlum style has been copied countless times by countless painters, until it has been reduced to it's present day depth.

Along with the many artifacts that Marv Taylor sent me, who was the former owner of the gallery that John Ludlum exhibited in, there is a page announcing Ludlum's Art with four Color reproductions of his paintings on it. This Color page comes from "Artists of Southern California" and the addresses are given for Ludlum's "Studio" at 14741 Devonshire Avenue in Tustin, California, and the "Harbor Gallery" in Depoe Bay, Oregon on the back of the page along with a biography of John Ludlum and three B/W photographs. In the bio John Ludlum is described as always having been a pioneer, first by showing the first Fine Art serigraphs (silk screens) in New York City in the Museum of Science and Industry in Rockefeller Center in 1953 for six months. Ludlum is credited in this biography as being the pioneer Artist in his use of Fluorescent paint in Fine Art in 1945, and for the ten page Color article in the magazine "Virtue" about his Fluorescent paintings. The biography closes crediting John Ludlum as a "Master of Light" and explains the details of Ludlum's Fluorescent masterpiece the "Nativity" touring American and European cities. The reproductions on the front of this Color sheet are classic John Ludlum Fluorescent paintings, including a classic nude "The Slave Girl" and three paintings that change scenes from White light to Black light. "The City at Night" is a Ludlum Fluorescent painting that is done in shades of Blue depicting a cityscape of tall skyscrapers in the White light that would 'light up' as the White light was reduced on the painting and the Black light caused the street lights, cars, windows, and peaks of the skyscrapers to emit light and change the daylight cityscape into a "City at Night." "Hansel and Gretel Cottage" is the second Ludlum Fluorescent painting reproduced on this Color sheet of Ludlum's paintings, and is another daylight/night time Fluorescent painting that transforms with different degrees of Black light and White light present on the painting. The daytime painting of "Hansel and Gretel's Cottage," complete with a fenced garden in the foreground becomes another painting when White lights are turned off and the Black light causes the lights in the cottage windows to become lit, as well as the moonlit garden with it's fence and rocky path taking on a nocturnal light. The third Fluorescent painting by John Ludlum on this Color sheet of his paintings is the "English Cottage" that John and Shirley Ludlum lived in for many years in the Hollywood Hills. The painting represents the "English Cottage" and it's very detailed garden, complete with the two empty chairs of the couple in the garden. From the Color photograph it is obvious that this day time scene became a beautiful sunset when the light was turned down and the Black light caused steaks of the Orange sunset sky to emit light. Many of the paintings for sale on the internet today by John Ludlum are on the website of the same gallery that represented John Ludlum decades ago during his lifetime, "The Harbor Galley" in Depoe Bay, Oregon. The paintings of Ludlum on this website are displayed with separate photos in the White light and in the Black light. These paintings are typically landscapes during the day, but when the White lights are turned off and the Black light is turned on, these landscapes are transformed into blazing sunset scenes, for example a medieval walled city becomes a moonlit citadel in the Black light, complete with lights in every window of the castle shining like candles in this painting "Provincial Winter Scene." "The Lost Cove" is also on "The Harbor Gallery's" website photographed in both it's daylight state and it's Black light state, in which the bay of water disappears and the brilliant sunset sky appears. Another theme of Ludlum's Fluorescent Artwork is represented by the reproduction of the religious painting "Adoremus" on "The Harbor Gallery" website, showing a brilliant Fluorescent scene of the nativity. The Fluorescent painting by John Ludlum that I could purchase for the Museum collection in 2009 is also a classic John Ludlum Fluorescent painting in which an abstract "Spacial Landscape" with a daylight cloudy Orange sky in the White light becomes transformed into a brilliant nighttime star-filled sky revealing mystery and depth that did not exist in only the painting's White light state. Through the mixed media of Artist's Acrylic paint and Fluorescent paint, along with what appears to be pure Fluorescent powdered pigment, Ludlum creates a cosmic, timeless landscape on a tiny 9 x 12" (23 x 30.5 cm) piece of masonite wood panelling (with the addition of a Black light).

Along with the information that John Ludlum's former gallery representative Marv Taylor sent me, he referred to me of the contemporary Fluorescent Artwork of Gary Fenske, who has a website of his paintings, and has taken over from the late John Plumer Ludlum in the painting of landscapes which are transformed before the eyes when the White light is reduced and the Black light is increased. Marv Taylor told me that Gary Fenske is also in the process of writing a book on the subject of the Black light, and on his website it is clearly stated that the Artist is taking over the role of painting with "Living Light," which is exactly the phrase used by John Ludlum during his lifetime ("Hall of Living Light"). The book that Marv Taylor told me about was recently published in 2013 as "Gary Fenske - The Secret World of Invisible Art & A Collection from the Pioneer of Luminism" by the Artist, and in this book Fenske writes about his inspiration and association with the first painter to use Fluorescent paint for Fine Art in 1945, John Plumer Ludlum. This book is for the most part a catalogue of Gary Fenske's invisible Fluorescent paintings, which are similar to John Ludlum's paintings, displaying a daylight scene under White lights, that then turns into a night scene gradually when the lighting slowly changes between White and Black light. Fenske's book also includes a small section introducing the history of what the Artist terms "Luminism." Fenske was from Montana, and has listed an inspiration that was also a fascinating memory for the Artist writing this book, but I didn't have to travel across America for the inspiration because I was born just across the river in Brooklyn, New York. The gigantic Black light Astronomy murals of the former Hayden Planetarium in the American Museum of Natural History in Manhattan is the inspiration Gary Fenske lists in his book, along with details of their creator Helmut Karl Wimmer, who lived from 1926 until 2006. Wimmer was a German immigrant in New York who painted the fourteen Fluorescent Astronomy murals in the former Hayden Planetarium, that were massive and totaled 4,000 square feet of painting, and which were seen in the darkened circular hall surrounding the actual Planetarium theater, vividly Fluorescing under Black lights. Fenske documents the facts that Wimmer was considered the best Planetarium Artist in the world, and that his Artwork was published both by the American Museum of Natural History and the Smithsonian Institute in Washington, D.C. Unfortunately these fourteen Fluorescent Astronomy murals, as well as the Hayden Planetarium itself, were both demolished in the early 1990s to make way for the ultra-modern "Rose Center for Earth and Space," which is spectacular, but contains not a single Fluorescent Astronomy mural.

    A very interesting section of Gary Fenske's book is the detailed biography of his mentor John Ludlum, who was not only the first Artist to use Fluorescent paint for Fine Art in 1945, but also knew secret information. In April, 2011 the United States government released top-secret declassified military information about the usage of "Invisible ink" during the First world war approximately one-hundred years ago. Somehow John Ludlum knew of this top-secret classified military information and told Gary Fenske about the use of this "Invisible Ink" during World war one. Ludlum told Fenske that trenches were dug to protect soldiers all the way between Belgium and Switzerland, which were imaginably treacherous places to be at night. Flashlights were suicidal to use, because they would immediately illuminate your hidden position to the enemy, so John Ludlum told Fenske that Fluorescing paint was used along with Ultraviolet lamps, and then in the dark, soldiers were able to see the Fluorescent trail without the enemy seeing them. Ludlum went on to explain that not only were the bottom of the trenches painted with Fluorescent paint to mark the way, but also that the Artists stationed in these trenches would paint Fluorescing pictures on the walls of the trenches for the benefit of their fellow warrior's spirits. The top-secret military classified documents pertaining to this Fluorescent World war one pigment was finally made public by being declassified after lawsuits and public demand just five years ago in 2011, which followed with a media flood of information on this Fluorescent and Ultraviolet history from a century ago. Headlines from the top news agencies in the world were very similar at the time of this declassification of military secrets, when the "washingtonpost.com" announced a "CIA recipe" to make "invisible ink" from World war one documents declassified on April 19, 2011, with "cbsnews.com," "bbc.co.uk," and the "telegraph.co.uk" all reporting similar stories as their headlines on or about the same day. The articles of these and more listed media sources are as similar as their headlines, detailing these amazing secrets of invisible military ink used in warfare two decades before Robert Switzer invented Fluorescent paint. "The Washington Post" announces in their first sentence that the released "Invisible Ink" government secret was one out of the six classified documents which were the oldest Classified documents of the CIA. Almost a full century after it's creation the secret formula for military "Invisible Ink" was published in this 2011 article, instructing to use five grams of copper acetol arsenate with three ounces of acetone, all mixed into one pint of amyl alcohol and then heated in a bath of water - toxic fumes rising not to be inhaled, but to be used to make top-secret "Invisible Ink." Six of these World war one documents were released by the CIA in April, 2011, almost all of which have to do with the declassification of this "Invisible Ink," and all were classified between 1917 and 1918 before the CIA was even a government agency. One of the declassified government documents gives formulas for making "secret writing" invisible ink, while another June, 1918 declassified government document is written in French and reveals another secret formula that was used by the Germans to produce invisible ink during the First world war. These six declassified government documents were initially held during World war one by the office of Naval Intelligence, with one coming directly from France, according to this 2011 "Washington Post" article, as well as one of the documents containing seven formulas for invisible ink being from the U.S. Department of Commerce. Another of these documents released by the CIA teaches U.S. Postal workers how to detect secret invisible ink, with a list of fifty possible uses on letters for this secret ink. Other methods used by spies or smugglers are detailed in these declassified government documents, such as putting the invisible messages under postage stamps, or in medicine capsules, or even writing secret messages with invisible ink on their toe-nails(!) The "dailymail.co.uk" article from July 13, 2011 explains that one of these six declassified CIA documents had been put on public display after ninety-five years of being top-secret. This declassified document is in the fore-mentioned French language, and explains how the French discovered and revealed the German's secret formula for "Invisible Ink." This declassified June, 1918 CIA document "L'Aspirine et l'eau" explains that the Germans made their secret "Invisible Ink" with the simple procedure of mixing water with just powdered or capsuled Aspirin (also discovered by "Bayer" in Germany during this era), and that this war secret of the Germans was cracked by the French during World war one.

    The last years of John Ludlum's life portray him as a very spiritual person, detached from the material wealth of the common person. The end of the June 7, 1983 article contains a few statements from Ludlum that are proof of his transcendence, such as his admission that he 'intentionally' has remained out of the public eye and lets his 'Artwork speak for him.' The article closes explaining that every morning John Ludlum does Meditation, and that according to Ludlum his Artistic inspiration comes only 'from God.'

    As I've already written, John Plumer Ludlum, who was celebrated as the pioneer Artist in his use of Fluorescent paint in Fine Art, and who's masterpiece was sold for more money than any painting of a living Artist up to that time in history, including Pablo Picasso, this Artist who was chauffeured around in the U.S. presidential limousine suffered a fate that is so incongruous to the celebrated life he lived that it is nearly inconceivable. This pioneering Artist's life stands as the epitomizing *definition* of the Social Stigma of "Fluorophobia." Some things we learn or hear in our lives are so distasteful and so downright painful that we go on living wishing that we would have never even learned or heard them: they haunt us! The following statement written to me by Marv Taylor, the former Gallery representative, agent, and personal friend of John Ludlum, is one of those things that I wish I had never read or found out about, because it literally gives me nightmares. I will quote directly form Marv Taylor's email:

    "We attended John's funeral in Tustin [1993], but soon Shirley became ill and was in a nursing home and we lost contact with her. We understood that the state of CA. took over her home and most of the paintings were lost or destroyed. Their next door neighbor stated that a large dumpster was brought in by the State and paintings were piled in and hauled away. We have no first hand knowledge of what happened, however. I do know that in their house were several spectacular paintings that had been appraised by Harry Muir Kurtzworth of the LA County Museum of Fine Arts with values of over $50,000 each. I would estimate that there were over 300 pieces of Fluorescent Art in their home the last time I visited them." There is no greater horror to an Artist, in this life or even in the next one.

    To end this section on John Plumer Ludlum on a less catastrophic note, and to give an example of how far John Ludlum went with his lifelong fascination and creation of Fluorescent Art, we will examine a United States Patent that was filed by John P. Ludlum and Shirley G. Ludlum on Aug. 5, 1985 for "Printing Fine Art with Fluorescent and Non-fluorescent Colorants" (U.S. Patent 4652464). The "Description" of the patent issued to the Ludlums begins with the '1. Background of the Invention' and explains that the Ludlum's invention was for a new method of printing Fine Art with use of both Fluorescent and non-Fluorescent Colorants. '2. "Description" of the Prior Art' follows, explaining that previously Fluorescent Colors had been used with visible light Colorants, daylight Fluorescent Colorants had been mixed with visible light Colorants to brighten the Color, and that Invisible or 'black light Fluorescent Colorants' had also previously been used for special effects and in theatre. It is further explained that the difference with prior uses of Fluorescent Colorants and with the invention of the Ludlum's, is in the use of visible and invisible Fluorescent Colorants used in combination with visible light Colorants to produce Fine Art paintings that are capable of creating different day and night scenes when displayed under either White light or Black light. The U.S. patent also states that only a few Artists had ever attempted combining Fluorescent and non-Fluorescent paints in the past, with 'questionable' results.

    The U.S. patent that was finally awarded to the Ludlums on March 24, 1987 indicates the sociological outlook at the time: 'the Art community has largely avoided such style of painting because it is so difficult to create natural results, or aesthetically pleasing results.' Furthermore the U.S. patent office writes that also printing with Fluorescent and non-Fluorescent was never achieved successfully in Fine Art because of the printing technology limits.

    The 'Summary of the Invention' is explained in the patent awarded to John and Shirley Ludlum, as an Invention of a method for printing fine or commercial Art prints with applications of many preselected Colors or Colorants. The method specified the use of visible and/or invisible Fluorescent Colors or Colorants that would create different pictures whether viewed in daylight conditions, where the Fluorescent Colors would be seen together with the non-Fluorescent Colors also used in the prints, or whether viewed in just the Black light, when only the Fluorescent Colors would react and create a different image than the image seen with the addition of daylight. The patent 'Summary' specifies that the relative proportions, Colors, and shades of Colors of the non-Fluorescent Colors, the daylight Fluorescent Colors, and the invisible Fluorescent Colors are selected to enable a gradual gentle change in the piece of Art, where the finished Artwork would have a subtle transition between the daylight image of a summer landscape, for example, to the Black light image of a snowy winter landscape in the same piece of Artwork.

This extremely detailed and descriptive U.S. patent of John and Shirley Ludlum goes on to explain for several pages the different printing techniques that the patent would be applicable to, including virtually any printing process that was known in the mid-1980s, including stencil printing, silkscreen printing, hand or machine lithography, block printing, or the most common rotogravure rotary or Flat bed printing presses. It is further explained that the Colors are applied several times to produce saturated Color in the prints, and that between three and twenty-five applications of Colors or blends of Colors were used. It is specified in the patent that this printing process could be used on any surface, including paper, canvas, silk, wool, hair, straw, acetate, mylar, tracing paper, metal, and leather. Details are given about the process of printing non-Fluorescent Colors in addition to the Invisible Fluorescent Colors (which react with vivid Colors only under a Black light and are only White or off-White in normal lighting), which must be printed without disturbing the effect of the non-Fluorescent Colors. It is stated in the patent that this process was achieved by printing gradations of both the non-Fluorescent Colors and the invisible Fluorescent Colors. It is stipulated in the patent that the invention was for achieving a subtle transition between the two different pictures that the Artwork would contain: a White light image that would subtly change into a completely different image in the Black light. The example cited in the patent is of a 'Street Lantern.' This street lantern would appear unlit in the White light state of the Artwork, but as the White light is gently decreased and the Black light is gently increased, a dim glow of light would appear in the previously unlit street lantern. As the White light is gradually brought down, the same street lantern would begin to shine brighter in the Black light, resembling a realistic transition between day and night. The final state of this piece of Art would be in only the Black light, and in this final state the street lantern would be brightly lit and would also illuminate it's surroundings in a naturalistic manner.

The patent continues on to great detail in it's explanation of the different patented applications of non-Fluorescent Colors. Daylight Fluorescent Colors and Invisible Fluorescent Colors that would achieve the desired result of a changing Artwork, which would portray not just two different images of a White light and Black light scene, but also the gentle transition that would occur between these two dramatically different scenes. The details of both the pigments to be used and the solvents that the pigments would be used in are also specified in several paragraphs of this patent, beginning with the Colorants which would be either paints or inks. Fluorescent ink Colorants were not as permanent as Fluorescent paints, so Fluorescent paint Colorants were preferred by the Ludlums over the water-based Inks. It is also explained that non-Fluorescent pigments are usually made up of inorganic salts and metal oxides, but that the Fluorescent pigments were powdered from their original brittle plastic, glass-like "Melamine-formaldehyde" or "Triazine-formaldehyde" resin state. It is further explained that both the Daylight and invisible Fluorescent pigments were really just Fluorescent salts or Fluorescent dyes that are initially produced in a brittle plastic glass-like composition that must then be ground to particles between one and ten microns. This detailed account of the materials to be used, and how they are to be used, in this Invention Patent of John and Shirley Ludlum ends with the statement that at any time in the printing process, hand application of pigments whether Fluorescent or non-Fluorescent, could be additionally used.

The final third of this patent clarifies the technical specifications with a seven paragraph "Example" of this patented invention of the Ludlum's. An example of a typical Ludlum subject, a "Landscape," is presented to conclude the Ludlum's U.S. patent. The landscape will be printed so that in the daylight the sky is Blue with White and Grey clouds, and beneath is a Green landscape containing trees on rolling hills. In it's second state, under a Black light, this same landscape is dramatically transformed into a sunset scene with a dark Blue sky containing Yellow and Orange Colors of the sunset, and a Purple cloud that also has these Yellow and Orange tints of sunset. The technical details of making this silkscreened sunset example are given in five paragraphs, including the printing techniques, the paper choices, pigment choices, pigment preparations, and actual printed pigment applications for this highly technical technique of White light/Black light Art printing patented by John and Shirley Ludlum, as issued on March 24, 1987 when John Ludlum was eighty-one years old.

The eventual fate of John Ludlum's lifetime of Fluorescent Artwork is nearly unbearable to even contemplate, because just six years after the issuing of this U.S. patent of John and Shirley Ludlum, he died at nearly ninety years old in 1993. Ten years later Shirley Ludlum would be dead, and nobody quite knows how it happened, but most of John Ludlum's Fluorescent paintings were piled into a trash dumpster and hauled away by the state of California, undoubtedly not to hang in museums, where these Ludlum Fluorescent paintings were destined to go, but into the garbage to be destroyed. How could this have happened? Unfortunately very easily, and even legally. Heartbroken and despondent, Shirley was left with her house full of a fortune worth of her late husband's Fluorescent paintings. No one knows why she didn't disperse Ludlum's canvases to other, more secure, younger owners, but it could be highly suspected that she just couldn't part with the only things she had left of her late husband, whom she had spent a lifetime with, and was deeply grieved after his passing. To give an idea of the kind of relationship that John and Shirley Ludlum had, not only did they fall in love when they first met each other and even decided to marry at this first meeting together, but in the Tustin 1983 newspaper interview, John Ludlum admits that in the entire fifty years of their relationship and marriage, they never once had a fight. Unfortunately, 'like humans do,' Shirley Ludlum's health deteriorated to the point where she had to be put into a nursing home, where she passed away in the year 2003. No children or family survived these two old Artists, so there was no one left to claim the ownership of the Ludlum's house after Shirley died. It could be imagined that Shirley Ludlum could have realized the eventual fate of the 'hundreds of paintings' that filled her lonely house after John's passing in 1993, and could have simply given the Fluorescent paintings away, to Marv Taylor their gallery representative for example, instead of the most awful fate of being destroyed as trash after being confiscated from an abandoned home who's owners had both died. But she didn't, and John Ludlum's Fluorescent paintings went into the garbage, lost forever. How many years of his life spent creating this new body of Art, and how much of his life's energy did he dedicate to the infinite number of tiny measured brushstrokes of paint which filled the hundreds of canvases that went into the State of California's trash dumpster that fate-less day in 2003? "Too Many" is the answer for both these obvious questions.

Now in the Twenty-first century John Ludlum's pioneering Fluorescent paintings are again gaining respect and being placed in museum collections. In "The National Museum of Catholic Art and Library" in Washington, D.C., John Ludlum's large Fluorescent painting "Adoremus" is in their permanent collection. On NMCAL's website it is written that for their second Annual International Holidays Traditions Exhibition, which ran from December, 2009 until January, 2010, from their "old master collection" would be on display John Plumer Ludlum's Fluorescent painting "Adoremus." Although the museum spells Ludlum's middle name wrong and confuses their painting with "The Nativity," stating that their painting "The Adoremus" is the famous Ludlum painting that sold for "three million dollars," the description of the "Adoremus" Fluorescent painting is more correct. "Adoremus" is described as a "special Nativity" that can be seen only with the black light. The museum states that this Fluorescent six by four foot (1.8 x 1.2 m) painting by John Ludlum "Adoremus," of a sparkling "Nativity" scene with a taste of Pointillism, "drew thousands" of visitors the previous year, and that visitors had never seen something like Ludlum's Fluorescent painting under black light.

Concerning John Ludlum's six by nine foot (1.8 x 2.75 m) masterpiece "The Nativity" which he spent three and a half years working on, and which was the Fluorescent painting that sold for over two million dollars in 1973, making his painting the largest amount ever paid for a pice of Art by a living Artist up until that time, more information on the painting's cryptic provenance, and current location, has been published on the internet. On the website of the late Minister Frank Harvey it is written that a lawyer in Columbus, Ohio owned "The Nativity" by Ludlum after "Biblelands" in Ohio closed through bankruptcy. On the Artist's blog "Ask Art" there is more information by several different people over the course of 2009. Steward Douglas wrote that the painting "Nativity" "is now owned" by himself through an arrangement he made with the Ohio State Tourist Center (which "Biblelands" was associated with) after the Center went bankrupt. Stephane Y. on the blog states that "the couple" who owned "The Nativity" (apparently Steward Douglas and his partner) had been given the painting by the bankrupt Ohio State Tourist Center in return for money the couple had initially invested in the Center. This blogger also writes that the couple later "donated" "The Nativity" to a Christian group "The Living Word Outdoor Drama," which exists in Ohio, giving religious public stage shows that are posted on their website. Another blogger on "Ask Art" Ann H. answers with confirmation that Ludlum's masterpiece "The Nativity" is in the "care of" this "Living Word Outdoor Drama" religious group in Ohio. Next she gives very disturbing details, stating that this religious drama group doesn't even 'have a place to store the painting,' which has been crated up for more than "fifteen years," and that this Catholic group complains that the crated up Ludlum masterpiece is always "in the way"(!)

A new 2014 acquisition to the Museum collection is a poster which epitomizes this era of "The Miracle of Fluorescence: 1930s-1950s." Way back on February 18, 1944 there was a one-night 'Black Light Spectacle' in a High School Auditorium of Ogden, Utah, and the original fragile paper poster from that night seventy-two years ago is now in the Museum. This poster is not just a historical piece, but it is very appropriate in "Electric Ladyland - the First Museum of Fluorescent Art" because the presenter of this 1944 one-night "Black Light Spectacle' was both a Scientist, as well as being an Artist and Musician. This nine by eighteen inch (23 x 46 cm) vertical poster is printed in Black on very thin Orange paper in four different typefaces, and this long poster introduces at the top: "Chas. M. Dawson - Musician - Artist - Scientist." The headline of the poster follows: "Presents the Scientific Wonder" "BLACK LIGHT" which is printed in huge Black letters filling the entire center of the poster. Under this headline "A Brilliant Spectacle IN THE DARK." "BEAUTIFUL -- DRAMATIC" is the next headline introducing the text:

"BLACK LIGHT is the phenomenon of fluorescence with the Invisible Ultra Violet Rays.

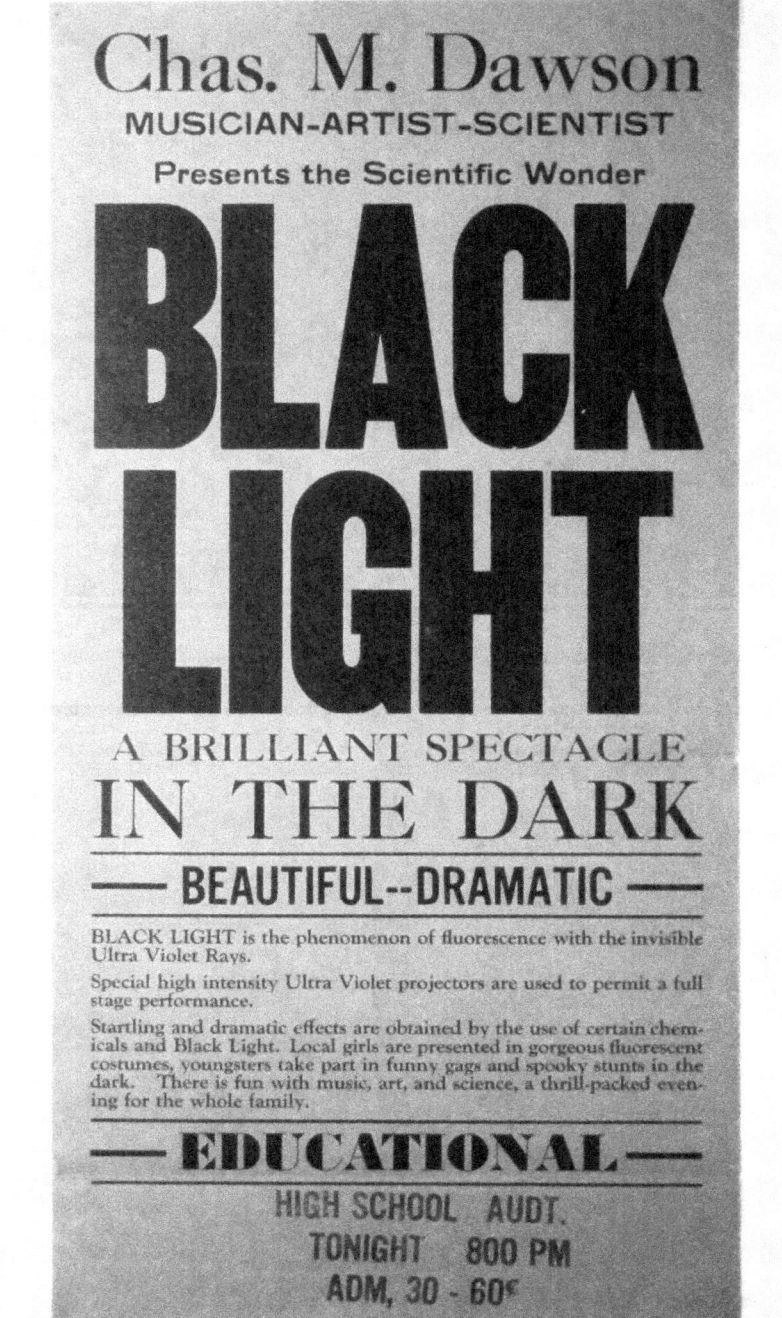

Special high intensity are used to permit a performance. Startling and dramatic the use of certain Light. Local girls are fluorescent costumes, funny gags and dark. There is fun science, a thrill- whole family." The February 18, 1944 headline and the event details, night event were rubber-stamp:
"HIGH SCHOOL TONIGHT 800 PM Imagine an between thirty and

To totally this long-lost era of that was dubbed 'the an era in which remembered as us not forget today bomb and the Second extremely rare copy weekly from 1949 exemplify this Fluorescence.' From seventeenth of 1949, 190 of "Goodliffe's The Only Magical was published by This small four by cm) booklet bound printed "each "GOODLIFFE THE Birmingham, England.

Ultra Violet projectors full stage effects are obtained by chemicals and Black presented in gorgeous youngsters take part in spooky stunts in the with music, art, and packed evening for the bottom of this poster ends with the "EDUCATIONAL," which for this one- applied with a simple

AUDT.
ADM, 30 - 60 ¢"
"Admission Price" of sixty *cents*(!)

close the chapter on the pre-1960s, an era age of innocence,' and everything is "good," an era that let included the atomic world war, there is an of a Magician's which can serve to 'Golden Age of Saturday, September Volume eight, number ABRACADABRA - Weekly in the World" "Hamleys" of London. eight inch (10 x 20 with two staples was Saturday" by MAGICIAN" of A year subscription of fifty-two weekly issues of this publication was priced at just one English pound. The hand-drawn illustration of the cover is printed in Black with tones of a Red/Orange, and is instantaneously recognizable as being antique with it's five different archaic typefaces all used together in a single illustration. These hand-drawn typefaces range from the 100 year old "Futura," to the attempted curved Black "ABRACADABRA" which has a Red shadow cast onto the background Earth floating in space. The inside cover of this small extremely rare publication has two boxed advertisements, one for "The British Rings (International

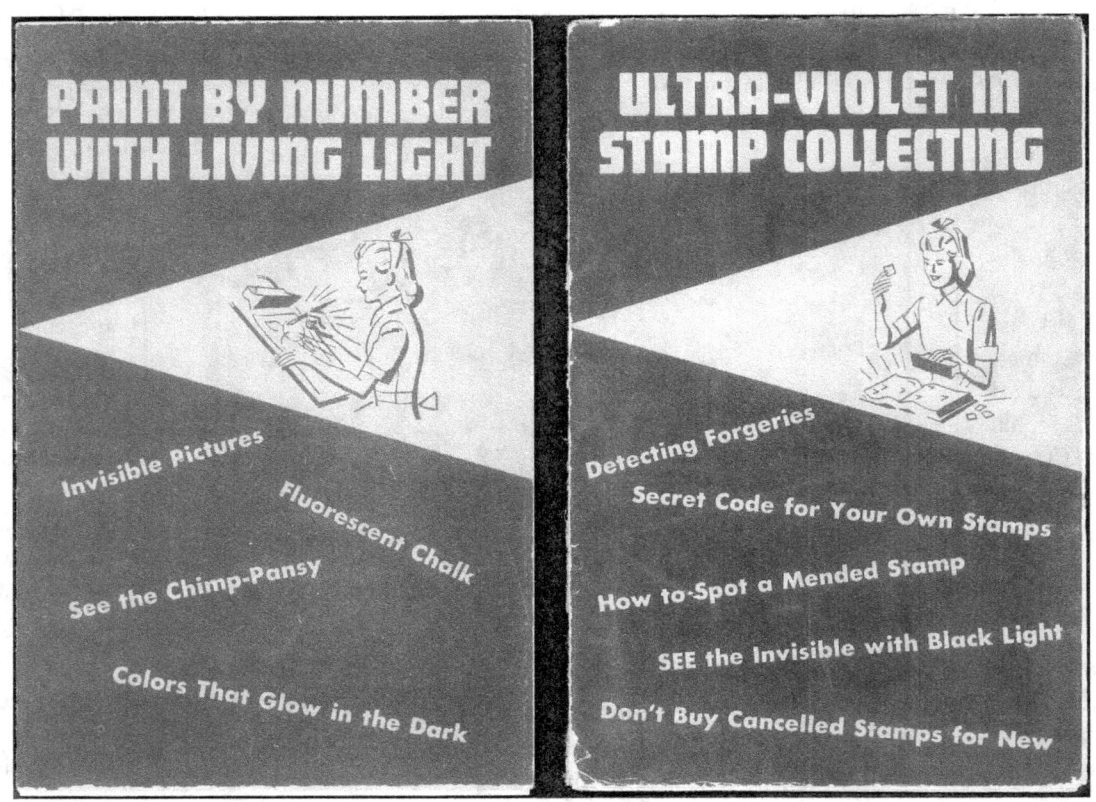

1959: Booklets from the "Ultra-Violet MASTER SCIENCE LAB," "Ultra-Violet Products, Inc.," California

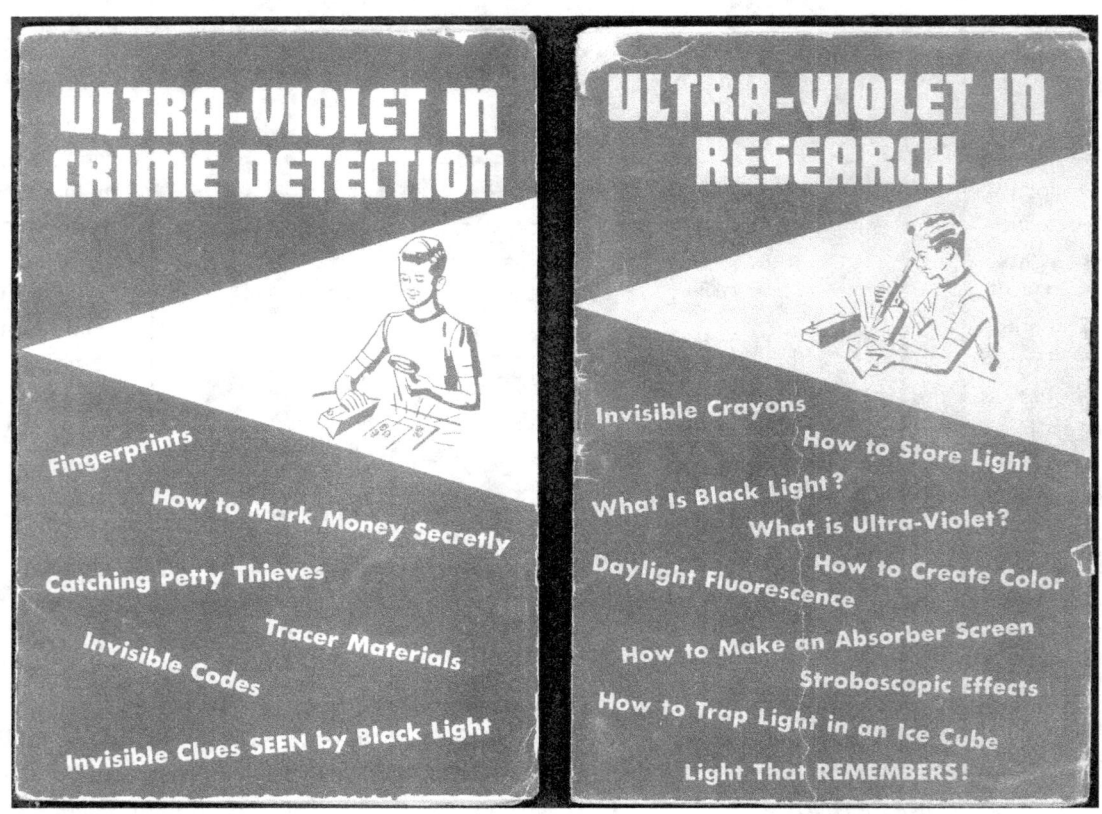

1959: Booklets from the "Ultra-Violet MASTER SCIENCE LAB," "Ultra-Violet Products, Inc.," California

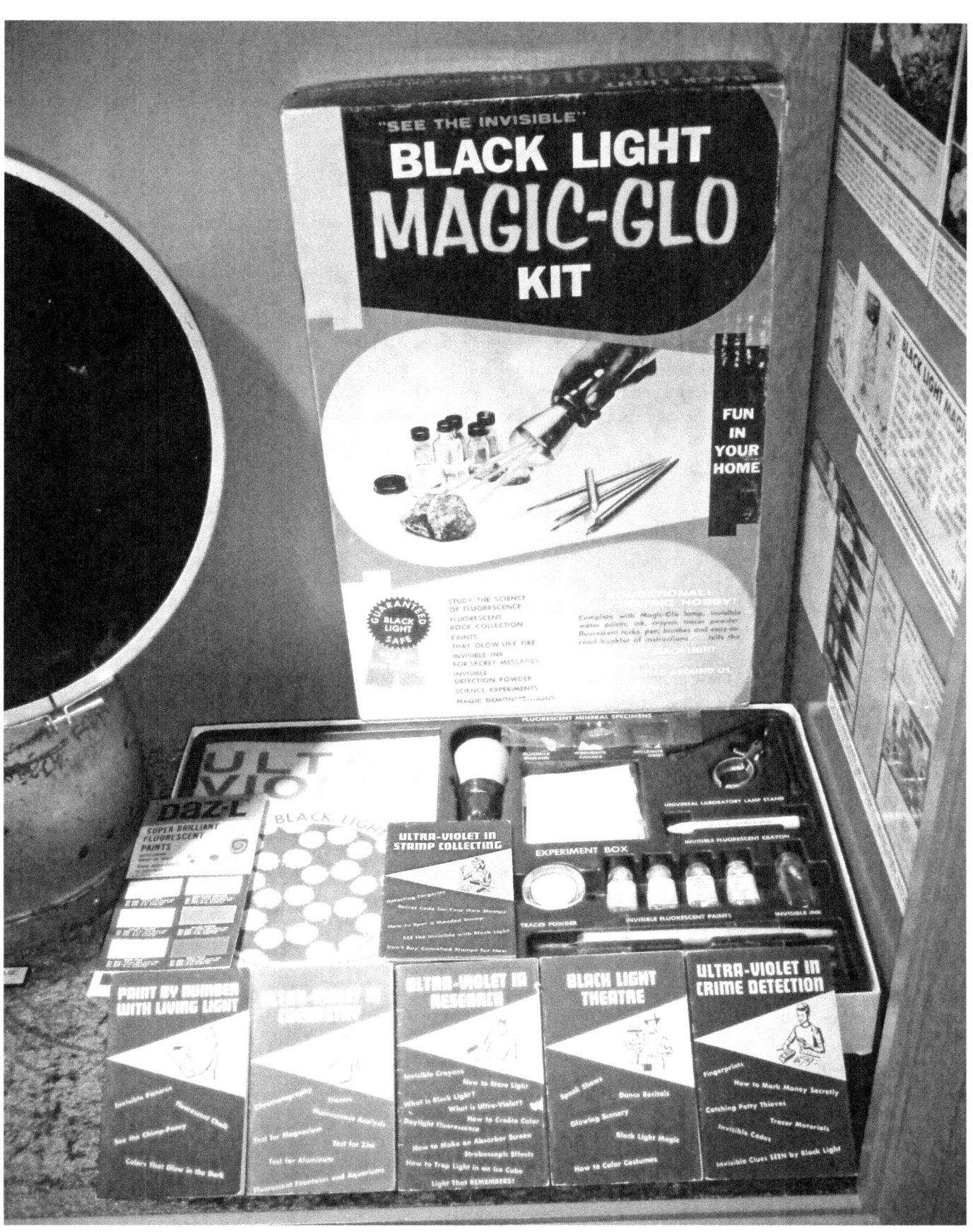

1959 "Black Light MAGIC-GLO Kit" - "See The Invisible," "Black Light Eastern Corp.," Bayside, New York

Brotherhood of Magicians)" and another for "Burtini's Magic Shop" in Birmingham. The bottom of the inside cover has an offer for back issues of "ABRACADABRA," advertising fifteen back-issues for just "a one-dollar bill." The back cover and it's inside back cover page also contain nearly twenty small ads for Schools of Magic, Magic Clubs, and various magic tricks for sale, including such 1940s magic tricks as "Run Rabbit Run," the "Scarlet Pimpernel," and the popular "Lemon Egg." Talk about retro.

"BLACK LIGHT - Ultra-Violet Rays in the Service of THE MAGICIAN" by Jack Potter is the first article in this magazine and begins after a two page introduction "Edited by Goodliffe, Literary and Technical Editor - FABIAN." The small title of this Black light article itself consists of five different mis-matched typefaces, only. This three page article "BLACK LIGHT" in this 1949 Magician's weekly contains the technical instructions for building an extremely complicated fixture to house a single Black light bulb. This article is complete with two full pages of written instructions, as well as a half-page technical drawing including an Operating panel and several wiring schematics - all to house a single Black light bulb! The article begins with technical instructions stipulating that if more than one Black light bulb was to be used with this design, then each Black light bulb would require it's own "individual choke coil." A reflector for the Black light bulb is also recommended, with "chrome-plated steel" advised, as well as advice for obtaining the best results with magic tricks under a Black light, which are achieved by working very close to the lamp. Black lights are also termed "Black glass lamps" in this ancient 1949 article, which in the end is a much more precise definition than "Black light." The technical instructions for mounting this single Black light bulb are so complicated that they are hard to believe today. A single Black light bulb was mounted on an iron rod with a metal reflector around two-thirds of the bulb. This was attached to a wooden box at it's base which contained a wooden "Control panel." To operate this single Black light bulb in 1949 required a "small mains switch" used for radios, "2 removable fuses," a non-essential "luxury" of a "voltmeter," a "Bulgin Type" "three pins mains connector," a "four- or five-pin valve plug," and finally a "choke coil and the condenser" mounted in the back of the "Control panel," (and an electrical engineer's degree). Next, this 1949 Black light bulb didn't even screw into it's fixture, but had a "three-slot bayonet holder." And that's not all. The actual "Control Panel" wooden base of this single Black light bulb would weigh an astounding *"14 pounds"* (6.5 kilos)!

The second half of this Magician's article details the actual method of this magic "Ultra-violet" bulb's application, with suggestions of mounting it about three feet (one meter) off the stage floor, which would be about the same level of the audience, and would importantly not obscure the audience's view of the Magician's hands. The author Jack Potter gives essential technical advice for the use of a Black light with an audience present, suggesting to position the circular metal reflector so that the "U.V. rays" emitted from the bulb are directed towards the Magician and his Fluorescent Magic tricks, not towards the audience. Once again, sixty-seven years ago in 1949, the distant past had more knowledge about the effects of a Black light, and also designed their applications of a Black light with their gained knowledge to such a high standard which is rarely attained since this 'Golden Age of Fluorescence.' This obscure Magician's journal, with it's even more obscure "BLACK LIGHT Ultra-Violet rays - in the service of THE MAGICIAN" three page article from 1949 gives advice that most of today's Twenty-first century exuberantly-paid Stage designers have never heard of - or considered - which is that the audience's "eyeballs themselves fluoresce" which, as Jack Potter explains sixty-seven years ago, would create what looked like a "glare" if the Black light was directed towards the audience. Potter further correctly explains that this "glare" was created by the "U.V. rays" entering the eyeballs of the audience and causing the eyeballs themselves to Fluoresce, and this literally creates visible light "within the eyes." This tiny, totally obscure twenty-page Magician's weekly from 1949 would be nothing less than a revelation to most of today's gentrified Stage designers. The last part of this article details the complicated "Control Box" at the base of this single Black light bulb, which shows how much work went into creating the effect of this single Black light. The "Control box" was approximately five by nine inches (13 x 23 cm) and contained an array of electrical components including the fore-mentioned "choke coil" and a "condenser" which was used to indicate if the bulb was to be operated on "A.C." or "D.C." If the interested party was not an electrical engineer, and incapable of building the complicated Black light fixture and it's "Control box," then it is suggested at the end of the article that complete "U.V. Lanterns" could be purchased by a firm in London, which included a "black lamp" with it's "choke coil" and it's stand. The article's final advice clearly indicates just how long ago it was published, by it's suggestion of an alternate source of U.V. production to this Black light bulb, being an antique "Carbon arc lamp." The author explains that an old Carbon arc lamp could alternatively have it's "U.V. rays" "focussed" onto the Magician's stage using a "stage-type" spot light that had a "special dark filter" attached to it. This is suggested by the author as a secondary alternative, and admittedly inferior to the use of a 'modern' Black light bulb. The last sentence of this article is a true teaser from the past, advising the reader to buy the next issue of "Goodliffe's ABRACADABRA" because the coming issue would contain an entire article on "Fluorescent Paints," their applicable

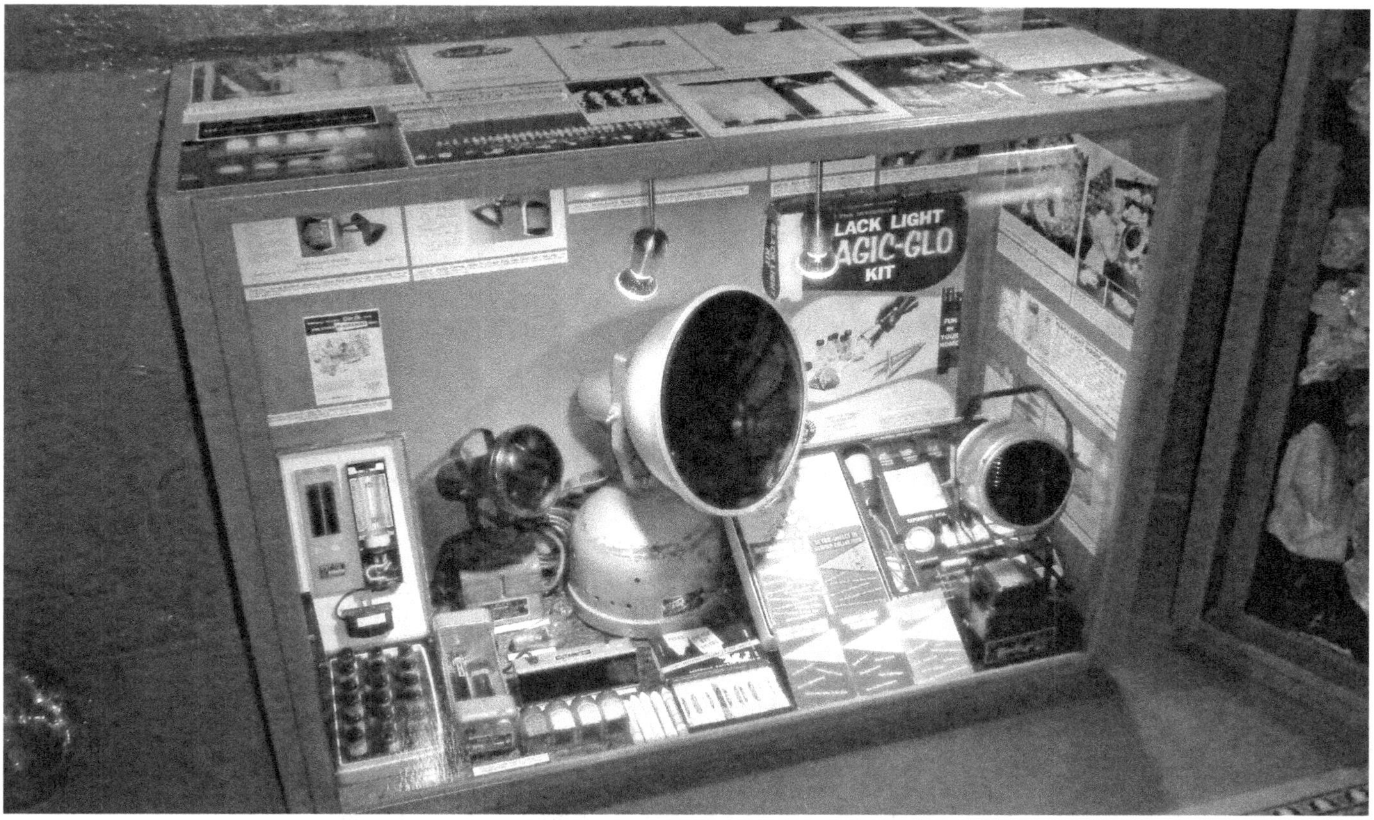

Antique Black Light Display Case, "Electric Ladyland - the First Museum of Fluorescent Art"

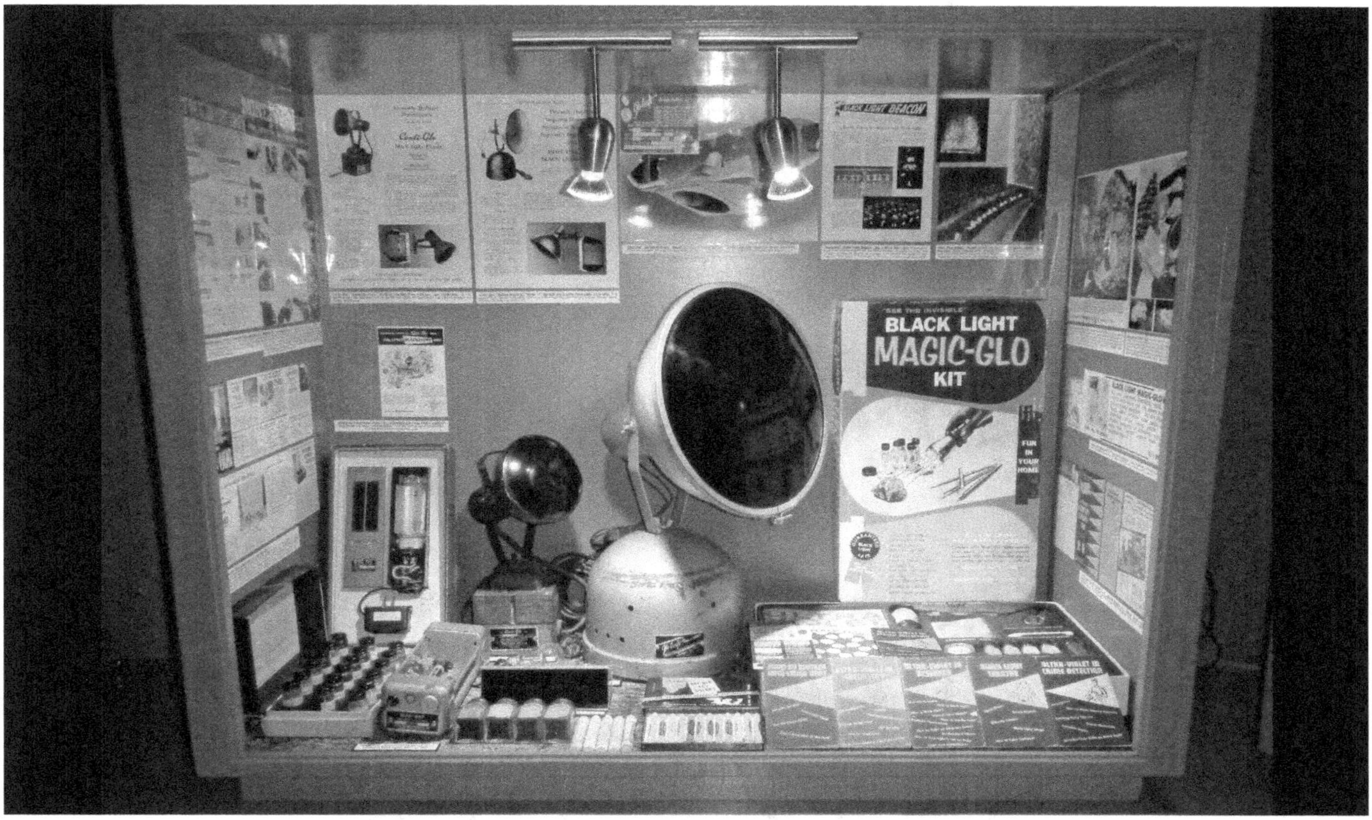

Antique Black Light Display Case, "Electric Ladyland - the First Museum of Fluorescent Art"

varnishes and solutions, and instructions for the reader on how to use these Fluorescent paints and the Fluorescent Magician's objects produced with them. This would have been the "no. 111" "Goodliffe's ABRACADABRA" that came out way back on Saturday, twenty-fourth of September, 1949, which I have no great confidence of finding in the future. Could it be - as the Computer/Digital age of the early Twenty-first century has proven - that as things became *"Easier"* - such as finding virtually any information in the world with just the click of a computer button - or by simply going to the store and buying a tubular cheap Black light - that much of the knowledge gained in the past when things were not *"easier"* - knowledge gained through insight and experimentation - has been lost simply because it was not needed anymore? The loss of the tremendous effort and knowledge that went into creating objects, as well as research, in the past has, for the common person, been lost forever. More profoundly, not only has the knowledge of the past been lost forever, but it has also been replaced by a grandiose arrogance that absolutely personifies the contemporary gentrified "Yuppie:" empty and self-contained - precisely the way Ayn Rand instructed them in "Atlas Shrugged."

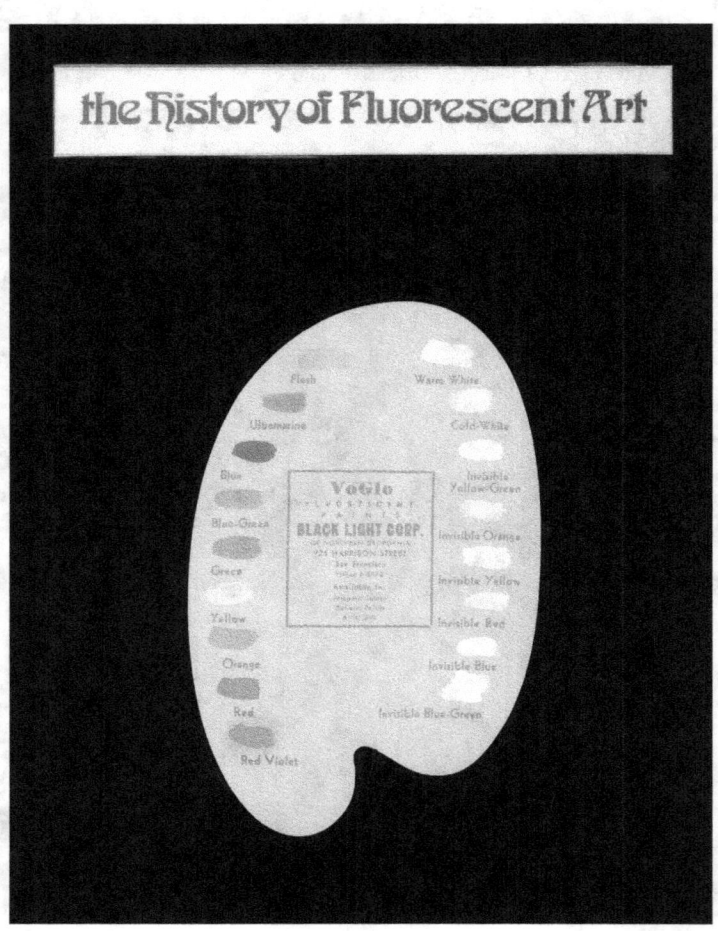

"the History of Fluorescent Art," Museum book, Nick Padalino, 1995

4. The Social Phenomenon of Fluorescence: "The 1960s Movement"

So here we arrive at the great 'Turning Point' - that pivotal time in history when the Black light and Fluorescent Paint fell 'far out' of grace with all established society, and sunk from it's high pedestal of "the New" and "the Future" to just the extreme opposite, a low point where the Black light and Fluorescent Paint were not acceptable to be even talked about any more, let alone used. So what, you may quite rightfully ask, could have caused such a dramatic 180 degree complete change and reversal in established public opinion regarding Black lights and Fluorescent paint formerly used by the square miles in such respected sectors of society as the United States military? In short, a very descriptive and contemporarily unacceptable era: the 1960s. Johnny Weissmuller, Judy Garland, and Benny Goodman *Did Not* want to be associated with the 1960s Movement. Neither did the United States military, or "Radio City Music Hall" in New York City, or the Church (!) obviously, or even General Motors Corporation, for that matter. But how, might you ask, could public mass opinion change so dramatically, so immediately, and so permanently? That is what the word "Stigma" means. It's less of a kind of public "prejudice," and more of a kind of public "call to arms," if the truth be told. The 1940s generation of Americans - my parents - did not like Hippies in any way, form, or notion. To my parent's generation of Americans that heralded in the coming of a new age with Black lights and Fluorescent Colors, the era that adopted and, in actuality, gave 'birth' to these "Day-Glo" Colors and Black lights around the world through the 1960s Movement represented just about every single thing the Second world war generation detested, despised, and fought against all their lives. Everything that this Second world war Harry Truman, John Wayne, and 'Rosy-the-Riveter' generation thought was indecent and undesirable was *signatory* for the Hippies. All that the Second world war generation loved the Hippies hated, and all that the Hippies hated the Second world war generation loved. Simple as that. There was never even a chance. Even just the God damn *Hair* drove them crazy! Black lights and Fluorescent Colors - "Day-Glo" Colors - as they became known in the 1960s (the "Switzer Brothers" even officially changed the name of their company to "Day-Glo" in the 1960s) had intrinsically become associated with the entire movement of the 1960s as well as with the choice of illegal drugs over established legal alcohol. Through this constitutional association with all that established society stood against and detested, Black lights and Fluorescent Colors had "known sin." For established society throughout the world, the Black light and it's complementary Fluorescent Colors had fallen from grace, period.

Another example in history to compare to the immediate, dramatic, and apparently irreversible Social Stigma of "Fluorophobia" forged by society, is an example that is so utterly distasteful to me personally, but undeniably a close comparison of Social Stigmatization for historical analysis. In the 1930s and early 1940s the newly developed Atomic Fusion research was heralded in as the new miracle future for the world. A new "trouble-free" energy source that would literally usher in a new age for humanity. Atomic researchers like Ernest Rutherford and Nils Boer were world celebrities - the new pioneers in the wonderful new world of Nuclear Physics! Nils Boer and his team of pioneer Atomic physicists were so enthralled by the new Atomic discoveries that they literally wrote a *Musical* about the event. In 1932 the Neutron particle was discovered, finally completing the entire physical make up of all Atoms with their Protons, Neutrons, and Electrons. For Christmas, 1932, famous physicists at the Nils Boer Institute in Copenhagen celebrated the Neutron's discovery and the completion of the Atom by writing and performing an "Atomic Musical!" This Neutron, the final piece of the elementary Atomic structure, was the Future - what everybody wanted a piece of and what everybody wanted to be a part of. Then they dropped the Atomic Bomb. From one day to the next, the party was over. Nils Boer never wrote another musical about the Atom, needless to say. The "Future" - what everybody had wanted to have a part of and be a part of - had now "known sin." By studying the Neutron atomic particle, Nuclear Fusion had been discovered, and eventually developed into instruments of mass destruction for the Second world war by physicists under the direction of Robert Oppenheimer. Robert Oppenheimer, "The Father of the Atomic Bomb" himself left the historic quote at the time, stating that physicists including himself had "known sin." Sociological Dreams changed into sociological Nightmares.

'Fantasy Lighting for After Dark using Blak-Ray,' "Ultra-Violet Products, Inc." (1960)

An exquisite example which perfectly announces the birth of the "1960s Movement" and typifies society's outlook, as well as their physical applications for the miraculous Black light and it's light-emitting Fluorescent paint, is a four page booklet published in the first year of that era, 1960, by "Ultra-Violet Products, Inc." The design of this booklet is immediately recognizable as being from the distant past, and on close inspection it looks as though it could have even been from the 1940s or 1950s, not 1960. The cover of this 1960 booklet has such a miserable illustration as an introduction that it's hard to believe it was printed like that. The top third of the cover has a rectangular box containing the lamest drawing of a "stage" possible, looking as though it was drawn by a young school child. Stage curtains and footlights frame the dark flat Blue title/ introduction of this "Ultra-Violet Products, Inc." 1960 booklet, which announces "FANTASY LIGHTING" for "AFTER DARK" using "BLAK-RAY." Underneath this headline (in two different type faces and Colors) the 'starred' applications for this miraculous technology are listed, which in the end are almost as lame as the stage drawing surrounding them. The extremely common amusements which are listed as the applications for this miraculous Black light and Fluorescent Paint in the first year of "The 1960s Movement" are pitiful. "Waterfalls," "Enclosed Porches," "Rock gardens," "Garden Settings," and "Patios" are the major celestial applications suggested in this 1960 booklet from one of the biggest Black light companies in the world, back in the 1940s as well as today. "Also" included with the "Blak-Ray" introduction are equally esoteric applications for the Black light and Fluorescent Paint such as "Christmas Decorations," and "Halloween Decorations" along with "Parties" and "Festive occasions." Out of the ten applications for the Black light's "Fantasy Lighting" for varying levels of amusement in 1960 by this major Black light company, at least "Murals" was included. The lamest part of this miserable illustration on the cover of this booklet is standing next to the stage curtains, where pointing at the headline is a childlike drawing of a "stick-figure" person wearing a bow-tie and having a round ballon head and a face made up of a "U" for the nose and a "V" for the mouth = U.V.(!) This illustration is so terribly drawn it must have been made by Thomas Warren himself.

    The text of this booklet's front cover is again introduced by another headline, which begins 'Blak-Ray's Function and Fun.' In the dull Blue box the first paragraph's heading explains that 'Black Light is Blak-Ray' and begins with a feeling reminiscent of an age of innocence, very similar in fact to the feeling of Sterling Gleason's book "Ultraviolet Guide to Minerals" also published the same year in 1960. The reader is explained that in the same way that some sounds can't be heard, there is also light that cannot be seen. These 'invisible rays' called "ultra-violet" are described to "radiate energy" that can cause a 'glow in certain substances' or to 'brightly Fluoresce' in what is described as a beautiful Color "fantasy." A reminder that this was 1960, just a decade or so after the nightmare of the "Actinotherapy" Shortwave Ultraviolet "Miracle Cure" era, so assuring customers that this "Blak-Ray" Black light was "completely safe" and that the lamp was emitting "rays" of "ultra-violet" known as "long wave" during that time period "was essential." This "ultra-violet" "Blak-Ray" Black light was advertised as being able to produce "lighting effects" described as "unusual," good for use inside or outdoors, and reacting with Fluorescent paint which was vivid both under the Black light or out in the daylight. The second dull Blue heading is typical of the 1950s and typical of the founder of "Ultra-Violet Products, Inc.," Mr. Thomas S. Warren: "Lightscaping." It is advertised here that any backyard can have normal landscaping for the daytime, but can also be "Lightscaped" with "Colorful beauty" using "Blak-Ray" for night. A 'plain stone wall' can be transformed into 'festive colorful gaiety' at night under "Blak-Ray" when painted with either "Invisible" or "Visible" Fluorescent paint. A "supernatural glow" can also be achieved in your garden's waterfall simply by adding some "specially developed" Fluorescent dye tablets to the pond water. The 'festive colorful gaiety' continues onto the rocks and the waterfall which are advised to be 'streaked or dappled' using waterproof Invisible Fluorescent paint, and then position rocks halfway into the water so the Fluorescence would also be visible under the water, which goes on to include Fluorescent painted artificial flowers and plants around the waterfall and pond.

    The last artifact of Fluorescence acquired for the Museum collection during the writing of this book was an ancient Fluorescent paint set specifically made to use in the 1950s for the "Garden and Patio." This is the "Blak-Ray" six bottle paint set number "A-192" of "Invisible Magic Colors" made for "Garden and Patio." This entire sixty-five year old Fluorescent "Garden and Patio" paint set is complete, with it's cardboard box and top, as well as the six original small glass bottles of Fluorescent paint, all looking like truly ancient artifacts. The cardboard box-top has a paper label on it which is so old it is almost indecipherable, but begins with the company name "BLAK-RAY," the "A-192"number of the set, and "Invisible Magic Colors" specifically for "Garden and Patio." A list of the six bottles making up the Fluorescent paint set is next listed, including "Invisible" Orange, Invisible Blue, Invisible Green, Invisible Pink, and Invisible Yellow, along with the sixth bottle containing six of the Blue "Water Glow Tablets." Four lines of type conclude the label on the cardboard box-top, which explain that by using these five "Invisible" Fluorescent paints, the "objects" painted "should retain" what is called their "natural appearance" when in daylight. 'Suggested applications' of this "Invisible Magic Colors" set for "Garden and Patio" are listed as 'rock gardens, waterfalls, cascades, statuary, and any exterior or interior decorative painting.' This early Fluorescent paint set even lists the "Life expectancy outdoors" for the Invisible Fluorescent Colors, and states that it depends on both the paint "concentration" as well as "exposure," going so far as to differentiate between the "Life expectancy" of this Invisible Fluorescent paint when situated under "Northern exposure." As stated before, this cardboard box-top is instantly recognizable as an ancient artifact, with the typed label in such decrepit condition parts of it are unreadable. The six small glass bottles of Fluorescent paint look just as ancient as their cardboard container, with Black iron caps which are so rusted and corroded they have physically bonded with their respective glass bottles. The labels on these small bottles are not only in just as ancient condition as the rest of this antique set, but they are also instantly recognizable as antiques by their design. These tiny labels on the six small glass bottles contain just eight lines of words, and the eight lines of words are printed in four different type faces! The five bottles of paint all have Pink labels reading "BLAK-RAY" "BLACK LIGHT" (in two different type faces), "fluorescent" "BULLETIN PAINT" (in two different type faces), and end with the number and name of the Color, such as "A-171" Invisible Orange. The sixth bottle has an Orange label reading "BLAK-RAY" Black light "WATER GLOW TABLETS," with 'for Waterfalls, Cascades, etc' before the number and name of these six Blue tablets of "Water Glow." Through slides sent to me over twenty years ago from Mr. Thomas Warren, founder of "BLAK-RAY" and "Ultra-Violet Products, Inc.," I have Color images of both indoor and outdoor Fluorescent "Garden and Patio" rocks, waterfalls, and ponds from the 1950s, but I never knew there was a Fluorescent paint set specifically made for these Fluorescent 'Gardens and Patios' back then.

The third block of dull Blue contains the closing text of this 1960 booklet's cover, advising that 'Getting the Best Gets You the Most,' accompanied by the second failed attempt at a simple drawing of a stick-figure person, who also has the "U.V." face(!) The text which follows clearly states that these "Blak-Ray" Black lights were made by the largest manufacturer in the world of "Ultra-Violet" products, "Ultra-Violet Products, Inc.," which had been the result of 'over 30 years' of research. As an example of the "superior quality" of "Blak-Ray's" lamps, the polished "specular reflectors" used to increase the lamp's intensity are claimed to be 250% more reflective than normal similar reflectors.

This four page 1960 "Ultra-Violet Products, Inc." booklet encapsulated the end of the Black light and Fluorescent paint's age of innocence, being printed during the first year of the 1960s. This 1960s decade and it's world-changing "1960s Movement" would come to finally announce this miraculous Black light and Fluorescent Colors to the world.

Another historical comparison of Social Stigmatization, that is a little 'closer to home' in regards to contemporary society's concept of the subjects of Black lights and Fluorescent Colors, is the history of the use of psychoactive substances. In fact there is such an intense social stigma presently concerning the subject of these substances, that I initially decided to not even include it in this book, but in the end it must be included as part of the history of "Fluorophobia," and in actual truth, it is a closer and more accurate comparison, in regards to social stigmatization, than the subject of Nuclear energy, so in spite of my trepidation I have included a limited comparison here - after the comparison of a contemporarily less volatile subject than psychoactive substances: the Atomic Bomb(!)

The inclusion of the history of the 1960s Movement in this book on the history of the Black light and Fluorescent Art has two purposes. First of all, to demonstrate how wrong the accepted "common knowledge" of society is, and how far from both the truth and historical facts common knowledge actually is. The history of Fluorescent Colors and the Black light, as well as the history of Psychoactive substances *both* did not begin in the 1960s when society in general found out about Fluorescent Colors, Black lights, and Psychoactive substances, but decades, centuries, or even millennia before the 1960s began - and before any one of the Hippies were ever born. These are two extremely accurate examples of both the ignorance and the lack of any historical perspective that contemporary society has laid as it's foundation. The second reason for the inclusion of the 1960s Movement in this book is because the 1960s Movement was the only example of total acceptance, infinite fascination, and a literal permanent adoption of the unseen magic realm of these Fluorescent Colors and the Black light. The 1960s Movement represents an absolute break with the past and all of it's miserable baggage consisting of ignorance, hatred, and prejudice. A new era of human existence was the dream of the 1960s Movement, including new concepts, technologies, and social acceptance, which manifested itself in the ikons society remembers today from the 1960s Movement, such as the new styles of dress and hair, the use of psychoactive substances, freedom of expression, and of course the Music - with the Black light and it's Fluorescent Colors as the 1960s Movement's palette of choice.

Exactly as with the Black light and Fluorescent Colors, the controversial and highly illegal substance L.S.D., or acid as it is more commonly known in the last half of a century, was used extensively by the United States Military and Government organizations, as well as by the Militaries and the Governments of several other countries around the globe, including England, in the 1940s and 1950s for research. Acid was discovered by Dr. Albert Hofmann, the director of the Organic Chemistry department for Sandoz Chemical company in Switzerland during 1938, but the psychoactive effect of the substance wasn't discovered by Dr. Hofmann until 1943 during the middle of the darkest time in modern human history. In 1947 the first paper on the mental effects of the substance was published by Dr. Werner Stoll, a colleague of Dr. Albert Hofmann, in the "Swiss Archives of Neurology." This psychoactive substance first entered the United States in 1949 when Dr. Max Rinkel brought the substance from "Sandoz Pharmaceuticals" in Switzerland to Boston, and Nick Becel also commenced study on the substance in 1949 in Los Angeles. In 1949 Charles Savage was working on Mescaline research in Bethesda Naval Hospital in Maryland, as well, which is where research on this psychoactive substance supposedly first began in the USA, according to some references.

This substance was used in many countries during the 1940s and up until it became illegal in the United States in 1966, including extensive psychological studies and medical therapy, as well as positive treatments documented for alcoholism and drug addiction. During this period the substance was not only socially acceptable, but it was also taken by many important people under the guidance of their psychoanalysts, including the owner of the Time-Life Magazine corporation at the time, Henry Luce. As with Nuclear energy, the substance was something newly discovered and generally viewed with great positive potential for social benefit (who could today believe the book "LSD - the Problem-Solving Psychedelic" by Peter Stafford). There are many thousands of books and documented medical and psychological studies and papers on the substance from the 1940s up until 1966. Creating a law that made this substance an illegal substance is obviously what changed everything. Immediately all research, studies, medical/psychological treatments were shut down. Society making the substance something illegal created the criminal social stigma immediately, and public opinion in regards to this whole subject changed literally over night, including public opinion in regards to everything which was intrinsically associated with the 1960s Movement.

This social stigmatization of acid was eloquently worded, professionally and conclusively defined, and examined in a scholarly fashion in "The Road to Eleusis - Unveiling the Secrets of the Mysteries" by Robert G. Wasson, Dr. Albert Hofmann, and Carl A.P. Ruck, which was originally published in 1978. Reprinted recently in 2008 for the "Thirtieth Anniversary Edition," this new edition begins with a preface by Robert Forte written in 2008. This 2008 edition also reprints the preface to the Second Edition by Huston Smith from 1998, followed by a hindsight written by Carl A.P. Ruck for the 1998 Second Edition as well. Today, a full fifty years after the 1960s Psychedelic Movement, at a point in time when any surviving member of the original Hippie Movement has reached their "retirement age" of sixty-five years old, and at a point in time when any of their signatory long hair and beards are now quite Grey (if still there at all), it would be thought that after all the metaphysical 'dust' had settled over five decades, the sociopolitical stigmatism could also be retired, but in fact quite the opposite is true. In the current state of the conservative mentality that governs effectively every nation, there exists a more severe, prejudicial social stigmatization of the substance and anything that is even remotely associated with this substance today in the Twenty-first century, than had existed when the book was first published in 1978. The hindsight in the Second Edition of "The Road to Eleusis" was written in 1998 by one of the original authors, a scholar on ancient Greek Ethnobotany, Carl A. P. Ruck, and lucidly lists the causes and effects of the social stigmatization of this substance. The reader is informed by Carl A.P. Ruck, already in the second paragraph, that for the first twenty years the book was relatively ignored by the professional community, and only after twenty years, in 1998, had a new generation of younger non-stigmatized scholars begun to examine "The Road to Eleusis." Carl A.P. Ruck clearly states in 1998 that other people of his age and generation that were part of the 1960s Movement don't want to remember that pivotal time in history not only for the negative ramifications it would cause on their own lives decades later in today's, or even 1998's political climate, but also so that their children won't be so fool-hearty as to repeat their 'mistakes.' In this 1998 edition Carl A.P. Ruck informs the reader that the encouraged social stigmatism and exponential prejudice had reached such a degree any student who chose to work with this professor would be "blacklisted" as a result. In such a stigmatized state at the dawn of the Twenty-first century even Carl A.P. Ruck's Grammar textbooks were viewed with classic suspicion of containing subversive messages.

"The Road to Eleusis - Unveiling the Secrets of the Mysteries" is a history of the Eleusian Mysteries of ancient Greece which were held every year for over two thousand years, with it's participants including the men who created the schools of Philosophy, Science, the Arts, Mathematics, and Democracy in civilization. What is as unimaginable today as the suggestion of "Church Groups" using Black Lights and Fluorescent paint in America, is that the world famous ancient Greek civilization held yearly the passage of the "Eleusian Mysteries," during which Socrates, Aristotle, Plato the "Father of Philosophy," and most of the Greek thinkers and politicians still known by name in history today, most likely participated in a ceremony which was created for and centered around the expansion of the human consciousness through the ingestion of substances very similar to today's very stigmatized and highly illegal psychoactive substances. Another textbook example of this stigmatization and social eradication is revealed in R. Gordon Wasson's equally controversial book of 1968 "Soma - Divine Mushroom of Immortality." This scholarly examination by the Ethnobotanist R. Gordon Wasson reveals that in the oldest religious text in existence, the Hinduist "Rig Vedas," the word "Soma" is contained in over ten percent of all the thousands of passages it is composed of. R. Gordon Wasson come to the conclusion that "Soma," the mystical substance written over and over again in the founding Rig Vedas of Indian Hinduism thousands of years ago, was in fact the psychoactive "Amanita muscaria" Mushroom ('Fly Agaric'). Not only did R. Gordon Wasson conclude that one of the biggest religions in the world today, Hinduism, which one-sixth of the entire population of the Earth belongs to, was founded on human experience with a psychoactive substance, but R. Gordon Wasson continues on in his book "Soma - Divine Mushroom of Immortality" to conclude that when the world climate changed thousands of years ago, which caused the loss of the "Amanita Muscaria" psychoactive Mushroom in northern India, a practice was developed by Hinduists to bring back and try to relive the ecstatic divine enlightened states they had formerly reached with the "Amanita Muscaria" Mushroom - it was called "Yoga." It is not suggested, in any way, that you repeat these conclusions to your contemporary Indian Yoga instructor.

The Rig Veda itself is specific and quite clear about Soma being a very auspicious potion, and the mention of "drugs" in the translated text is a historical fact. Aside from the controversy created by R. Gordon Wasson's 1968 book "Soma - Divine Mushroom of Immortality," in which Wasson clearly explains that Soma was a psychoactive drink made from the "Amanita muscaria" 'Fly Agaric' Mushroom, an exploration of the original Rig Veda makes it clear that Wasson was not exaggerating. Many documentaries on Hinduism, or specifically on the Rig Veda over the last twenty-five years have touched on the controversial subject itself. A majority of these modern documentaries, from books, to magazines, and television include a discussion of the controversial Soma directly from the Rig Veda, and the majority of these documentaries have found through scholarly exploration, that Soma in fact was a mind-altering inebriant ranging in effect and description from Marijuana (which ancient "Bhang" is still made with today in modern India), to Opium, to a mild stimulant with a name nearly identical to Soma. All that a person need do to prove these theories is to open up a translation of the actual Rig Vedas, in fact. My classic copy of the Rig Veda was published by "Penguin Classics" in 1981 and was translated by Wendy Doniger O'Flaherty. This Rig Veda translation is one hundred and eight hymns, but the full Rig Veda is 1,028 hymns with about ten verses in each hymn, and is studied by scholars in it's original Sanskrit. The Rig Veda is generally accepted by history to be the oldest religious text in existence, predating the Islamic religion by centuries, and predating the Christian religion by millennia, extending it's origin back to about 5,000 years ago.

This "Penguin Classics" translation from 1981 included the part of the Rig Veda entitled "Soma," which is divided into the separate sections of 'Restless Soma,' 'Soma Pressed,' 'Pressing-Stones,' 'Butter,' 'Soma, Indra, the Eagle,' 'Soma-Drinker Praised,' 'Soma Ecstasy,' 'Have Drunk Soma,' and 'Long Hair Ascetic.' The introduction to the "Soma" hymns states that Soma is visualized as being a God contained in a liquid that is pressed through stones into a wooden bowl filtered by a sieve made of wool. It is clearly stated in this introduction that in the Rig Veda drinking Soma was considered dangerous, but with it's effect also being admired, including great personal power, knowledge and assurance of being immortal, as well as a trance of "hallucinations." It is just as clearly stated in the "Butter" hymns (4.58) of the "Soma" section of the Rig Veda that the 'stalk of Soma' is mixed together with water to make an 'immortality elixir,' as well as in the section 'Soma, Indra, the Eagle' (4.26-7) where it is written several times that the drinker of Soma becomes "ecstatic," and a "wise one."

In the crystal clear section of the Rig Veda entitled plainly 'Soma Ecstasy' (9.113) a poet invites the God Indra to a drink of Soma, and then when Indra is inebriated, he asks the God for immortality. The introduction to this section of the Rig Veda clearly states that the inebriation of the Soma "drug" was "hallucinogenic." Nothing in the Soma section of the Rig Veda clearly indicated that this Soma was a psychoactive drink more than the hymns entitled 'Long Hair Ascetic' (10.136). In the introduction to this section, Kesin, the 'Long Hair Ascetic' who represents the first Yogi is plainly documented as drinking a 'hallucinogenic drug,' which is also clearly documented as being a hallucinogenic drug similar, but different than the 'hallucinogenic drug' Soma. This substance and it's produced hallucinations are described as being 'related' to the Soma drink and it's effect, but not exactly the same.

What is the most surprising after rereading these original hymns of the Rig Veda translated in a respectable book published by "Penguin Classics" in 1981, not written in a book by R. Gordon Wasson or any sort of 1960s-era publication, is how it is clearly stated in plain English by a scholar of the Rig Veda that 'Hallucinogenic Drugs' were used in the Rig Veda. For decades there has been vicious opposition to this very same conclusion reached by R. Gordon Wasson in his 1968 book "Soma - Divine Mushroom of Immortality." What was all the opposition about? Any idiot with a "Penguin Classics" translation of the Rig Veda can easily come to precisely the same conclusion that Wasson came to almost half a century ago, without fear of the professional and public ridicule Wasson had to withstand.

For the point of view of an Indian scholar on the subject of the origin of "Soma," there is an article that was published two years before the death of this very famous teacher and politician in India named Dr. Sampurnanand. Dr. Sampurnanand lived from 1891 until 1969 and was known as not only a teacher and politician, but also as a political activist and a member of India's "Freedom Fighters." Dr. Sampurnanand was elected to the Uttar Pradesh legislative assembly and held the office of Chief Minister of Uttar Pradesh, India from 1954 until 1960, the longest the position was held by anyone. This Hindu and Sanskrit scholar was then elected as the Governor of Rajasthan until the year this article "Notes on Soma" was published, in 1967. Dr. Sampurnanand was originally from the oldest populated city on Earth, "Kashi," later named "Banares," but more familiar by it's modern name Varanasi. To just give an idea of the vast period of time considered here, Varanasi was called "The Ancient City" when Buddha visited during his lifetime over 2,500 years ago. Dr. Sampurnanand was not only a classic Indian scholar and politician, but had very controversial ideas, such as the "No Bars Prison." This was put into use on an experimental basis in Rajasthan in 1963, and was known as the 'Open Prison.' Being a scholar of ancient Hindu culture and it's ancient language Sanskrit as well as the astrology of ancient India called "Phalit Jyotish," he would teach astronomy to his jail mates while incarcerated as a "Freedom Fighter." Also, after India's independence finally from England, Dr. Sampurnanand was elected as Educational Minister of the first independent government of Uttar Pradesh. With the power of this office, Dr. Sampurnanand could finally fulfill his dream of constructing an Astronomical Observatory in the Government Sanskrit College of Banares, now renamed in his honor as "Sampurnanand Sanskrit University."

When Dr. Sampurnanand wrote this article "Notes on Soma" he had already achieved all that has been outlined here, and was seventy-six years old, which was only two years before he passed away in 1969. Obviously, Dr. Sampurnanand was in no way considered a "Hippie" or a member of the western "Psychedelic Movement," justifying his opinions in this scholarly article that was published in 1967.

"Notes on Soma," Dr. Sampurnanand (1967)

The short introduction to this article of 1967 by Dr. Sampurnanand informs the reader that 'mystery' was still surrounding the subject of "Soma" from the ancient Indian religious text the "Rig Veda." The reader is introduced to Dr. Sampurnanand as a known scholar of the Hindu culture and is informed that this scholar would examine the origins of Soma with regards to Twentieth century discoveries.

Dr. Sampurnanand begins the article by loosely comparing "Soma" to "Bhang," a drink still consumed by the population of India, especially on the religious festival of "Holi," which is a psychoactive drink made with Cannabis and holy Mantras. Dr. Sampurnanand concludes that this Soma was made from a particular plant and that it did have an 'intoxicating' effect, which is what was considered the opinion of many Indian scholars at that time. The author concedes that Soma was an intoxicating drink, but that it was not used as a daily intoxicating substance, like wine for instance, only as an elixir that was reserved for specific purposes. Dr. Sampurnanand states that the early Aryans did have the knowledge for preparing wine and fermented intoxicants, but that this Soma was completely different from these common substances and reserved for a special purpose. In the ancient Aryan culture there were strict laws which stipulated the sale and even the transportation of the holy Soma, as well as a religious law that stated that even in the event of a war between two states of India, there could not be interference of the delivery of Soma to either fighting states. For further proof of it's special significance in ancient Aryan culture, Soma was not allowed to be sold in shops (like wine), and it could not be made by anyone, or at any time that was chosen. The only time that Soma could be prepared was during a Vedic sacrifice, called a "Yajna." The highest caste of priests, the "Brahmanas," prepared the sacred intoxicating drink, documented by the ancient saying of "Samosmakam Brahmananam Raja" ('Soma is the king of the Brahmananam') still used today. Obviously just the religious doctrine of this Soma puts it in a class far removed from ordinary intoxicants, such as wine. Dr. Sampurnanand continues with his historical description of Soma, stating that Soma was 'praised' in the literature of the Vedic times. The word Soma is used in Hindi both as a general description of all plant life on Earth, and also as a definition of the nutrition and strength given to all life on Earth which eat plants. Soma also symbolizes "Prana," which is defined as the all important force omnipresent in the Universe that encompasses spiritual as well as physical energy, and which represents God, consciousness, and physical action that is known by Hindus as "Shiva" and "Shakti." Obviously, again, this Soma was not wine, or any other common intoxicant.

Dr. Sampurnanand quotes the Rig Veda in his explanation of Soma, specifically the third Mantra of the eighty-fifth hymn in the tenth book, which informs the reader that although Soma was a plant 'pressed' to prepare, Soma could not be experienced by an 'ordinary' person in the same way as the Brahmanas. Here, Dr. Sampurnanand explains, is the actual 'mystery' of this historic Soma, being that a mere drink could create a psychoactive experience comparable to the highest level of Yoga, "Samadhi." Also incomparable to mere wine, the author states that Soma could give the ability to live a detached life free of the outside distractions of existentialism. Of the greatest significance, Dr. Sampurnanand next explains why such a definition and great understanding of Soma was possible in 1967, by crediting the Psychedelic Movement in the United States as the reason. 'Recent experimentation with the juices of particular plants' is how Dr. Sampurnanand tactfully words it, explaining that these experiments have rediscovered the amazing psychoactive powers of particular plant species. In particular, Dr. Sampurnanand discusses the cactus extract Mescaline and certain Mushrooms. The author recounts the tale of a general psychoactive experience manifested by the ingestion of this Mescaline Peyote Cactus or Mushrooms, which causes the expansion of the consciousness and the transcendence of time as well as space. Sampurnanand then states very significantly that in light of the information and personal experiences documented by the 1960s Movement, he had not a 'doubt' that the historical Soma of the Rig Veda possessed similar properties to the psychoactive substances used in the 1960s. In Hindi, the "Psychedelic Experience" is translated as "Baja," and is known as the experience produced by Soma, which is not normally accessible to mortal beings in their daily lives.

The bulk of Dr. Sampurnanand's article "Notes on Soma" is contained in the second half, where he discusses his opinions on the 'Interpretation of the Veda' dealing with the subject of Soma. In this respected Indian scholar's opinion, the culture of the Aryans and the era of the Rig Veda and the Atharva Veda was not a primitive time period, but highly refined, with people evolved and living during a time of new spiritual and intellectual horizons. The elite Aryan priests of this era were expanding the horizons of consciousness and questioning existence itself, such as the questions of reality, the afterlife, and about the gods they worshipped. Dr. Sampurnanand gives examples of these profound questions being raised during this Aryan period of ancient India in the form of a quote which asks about the Earth's end, the Sun's cause, and the highest reaches of the human intellect. Dr. Sampurnanand discusses the changes in the Hindu culture brought about by the enlightenment achieved through this age of profound questioning, and parallels it with a quote from the Rig Veda which states that this message of enlightenment must be experienced by 'all,' not just the elite. The author concludes this thought with the fact that although a new spiritual attainment had been achieved during this era of enlightenment, and that the mystery had been passed down from generation to generation, today unfortunately modern people have lost this 'key.' As a lucid example of this point, Dr. Sampurnanand quotes fantastical scenes directly out of the Rig Veda, which indicate the degree of knowledge and meaning from the Rig Veda that has been lost. The author quotes Yaska, who stated that no one could truly understand the Rig Veda until they had become a Saint ("Rishi"), and in the author's opinion only the experience of living a life of an enlightened Yogi would bring the necessary understanding needed to comprehend the Rig Veda.

Dr. Sampurnanand concludes that the actual psychoactive substance Soma in itself did not hold the key to the profound knowledge of life and the universe, but that this psychoactive substance could act as a catalyst in the mind of a person that had already raised the level of their consciousness. This author of "Notes on Soma" also wisely concludes that Soma was not essential for everyone, and that it was not necessary for the already enlightened.

To finish this article, Dr. Sampurnanand definitively states that this famous Soma of the Rig Veda had intoxicating effects, and that there were many restrictions imposed on it's production and use, which eventually led to Soma's use by a certain class of society and only for specific ceremonies. The author further states that Soma grew in the region of Afghanistan or central Asia, and as the Aryans moved deeper into India's interior, the availability of Soma became more rare. With the rise of Buddhism in ancient times in India, the Vedic ceremonies became obsolete, and with this obsolescence came the loss of the knowledge of Soma from the Hinduist Rig Veda.

In conclusion, the origin of the Iranian form of "Soma," known a "Haoma," is an open question that has never been proved, but the Hindu origin of Soma that has been the main point of two-hundred years of scholarly pursuit is much clearer, and has been documented in the last half of a century as possibly being the hallucinogenic "Amanita muscaria" 'Fly Agaric' Mushroom. Many researchers have offered over a hundred suggested psychoactive plants as being the origin of the famous Soma deity of the ancient Hindu Rig Veda, including "The Encyclopedia of Psychoactive Substances" with their suggestion of 'Syrian Rue' "Peganum harmala." The concluding documentation by R. Gordon Wasson in his historical "Soma: Divine Mushroom of Immortality" lends evidence to the theory that Soma was the "Amanita muscaria" Psychoactive Mushroom in the Hindu Rig Veda from thousands of years ago. It is known that R. Gordon Wasson was never in India, and it is also doubtful that most of the western 'experts' writing with expertise about the Rig Veda and the culture of India have never been in India either. Quite the contrary, this current author has lived in India three times during the last twenty-nine years, amongst Siddhis and Hindu priests and Holy people, in Ashrams and even caves. This is a culture that is so different from the western society that it is virtually impossible to truly imagine or to learn about in books. This is a country where hundreds of gallons of precious clean drinking water will be thrown away into the street in an instant of rage, only if an impure Western person merely *touches* the huge stainless-steel container that the drinking water was contained in. This is a country where the subject of sex is absolutely taboo - no talking about physical body movements, asking about physical body movements, or even thinking about physical body movements. The point that I am trying to make is that India is the last place on the Earth in which a ceremony of "Urine-Drinking" would be imagined unless it was for an extremely good reason(!) Michèle has been in and out of India since 1978 - thirty-eight years - and when I spoke to her about imagining ceremonial "Urine-drinking" in India she gave me an incredibly incredulous look, as if I was asking her something truly absurd. This ceremonial "Urine-Drinking" is clearly documented in the Hindu Rig Veda, as pointed out by Wasson in "Soma: Divine Mushroom of Immortality." This fact must be contemplated in combination with the other fact that the "Amanita muscaria" 'Fly Agaric' hallucinogenic Mushroom is the only psychoactive plant known on Earth to possess the ability to pass unchanged through a person's body, and when another person drinks an inebriant's Urine, the psychoactive ingredient in this hallucinogenic Mushroom causes the Urine-drinker to have the same psychoactive experience as the original inebriant. This ceremonial "Urine-Drinking" has been documented for millennia, not only in the Hindu Rig Veda, but also in other cultures of the world including the Siberian Shamans who carved ceremonial wooden Urine-collecting bowls specifically for this purpose, as well as ceremonial Reindeer Urine-collecting wooden vessels to also get access to the psychoactive substance of the "Amanita muscaria" Mushroom which is well known to make up a portion of the Reindeer's diet.

In collaboration with Dr. Albert Hofmann, the chemist who discovered acid in 1938, Richard Schultes published the definitive book on the subject of Hallucinogenic plants with regards to their history and their relationship with human development: "Plants of the Gods - Their Sacred, Healing and Hallucinogenic Powers." In the preface of this historic book, the authors explain the role of plant life on Earth, going back to the earliest fossil records of 3.2 billion years ago. Plants led to the development of all life we know on Earth today, including ourselves. The plant kingdom was used by early humans basically as a food source, but also with some special plants used as a healing source, or medicine. Amongst the plant kingdom there were a small number also discovered to have incredible effects on the mind - causing the prehistoric explorer hallucinations and a refined, expanded view of their world and the universe around them. Hofmann and Schultes state clearly that out of the more than 1,000 holy hymns of the oldest religious text known, the "Rig Veda," again, there are one hundred and twenty hymns written about "Soma."

In 1730 a Swedish Military Officer was held as a prisoner of war for twelve years in Siberia, and during his incarceration, he witnessed native tribesmen ingesting "Amanita muscaria" in rituals of Shamans. These Finno-Ugrian tribes of Siberia included the "Koryak," have documented the use of the native "Amanita muscaria" Mushroom. According to this Koryak account, the "Amanita muscaria" first had water poured on them and were boiled. The boiled liquid was then drunk, and it was this liquid which brought on the Hallucinogenic experience. It is also clearly written in this ancient Koryak Siberian account that the poor people who could not afford the sacred psychoactive Mushroom would patiently wait outside the huts of others experiencing Mushrooms, and during their hallucinogenic experiences these well-off people would come out of their huts to urinate, and the poorer inhabitants of the tribe would hold wooden "Urine-Collecting" bowls for them to urinate into. Again, some of the strongest evidence for the identity of "Soma" from the Hindu Rig Veda being the "Amanita muscaria," is the inclusion of hymns describing very accurately urine drinking of Soma.

For a new Twenty-first century version of the history of "Soma" in the Rig Veda, we are treated to a truly unique interpretation. After millennia of debate about the origin of Soma, the mystical substance which opened the eyes and minds of sages and countless others back thousands of years ago and inspired the written testament which is now known to be the oldest religious text in existence, the full circle has now been turned by modern society, with a retelling of history in which Soma is not a substance that participants took thousands of years ago to open their minds and lay the foundations of Hinduism - not something external they ingested to change them, and certainly not a hallucinogenic substance like the "Amanita muscaria" mushroom, or even marijuana or any member of a long list of possible substances that Soma might have been, and which have been written about by scholars over the last several millennia as well. The new version of the origin of "Soma" from the Rig Veda has been published in the July/August/September 2012 issue of the American magazine "Hinduism Today," based in Hawaii. On page fourteen of this issue of "Hinduism Today," a revealing half-page article is entitled "Soma" 'the Potion of the Rishis.' The small article begins by explaining that Soma was a potion with "ritual importance" that had the capability of 'transforming a mortal into a God,' and was drunk by the Hindu Gods Agni and Indra. The fact is documented that "Soma" was written about in many lines of the Rig Veda where the "Soma Mandala" of 144 hymns praise it's "energizing qualities." Clearly the 2012 "Hinduism Today" article states that "Soma" was described in the Rig Veda as being a "plant" which had the juice from it's stalks extracted, as well as the fact that the identity of this transforming energizing plant was a secret and has been lost to the passage of time. The article continues with more accepted historic facts, such as the fact that the drinking of Soma was "restricted" and also "documented" during the formation of Hinduism at the time the Rig Veda was being written. It is also stated clearly in this 2012 article that the effects of drinking Soma was the 'stimulation of the inner faculties of the Sage,' who were able to soar into the god's realms through their consciousness and through yogic powers. The article next explains that the formula for making the divine potion Soma has been lost to time, which makes the substance unavailable today. This 2012 article continues, explaining that the origin of the plant used to create Soma has raised "much speculation," and that this original plant was described in the Rig Veda as being 'bright and shining' and having a tint of "Green." There is even a recipe instructing Soma juice to be filtered using lamb's wool and then mixed with cow's milk amongst other ingredients. The drinker was described to "roar" in this article. The "Spiritual practices" of Yoga, mantra, pranayama, and also meditation are listed in this 2012 reinterpreted version of history, with these self-created divine alterations of the self, which 'releases' what is described in "Hinduism Today" as a self-created "bliss" through the whole body. The literal 'bottom line' of this short article states in existential clarity that what is described as this self-created brain secretion's "inner soma," is in the end the actual "main subject" of the Rig Veda, but the true "Soma" - the substance which induced visions described for thousands of years, and which helped to form Hinduism, is now relegated to being labelled the "outer somas," and reduced to having once upon a time been "also important." In 2013 I could ask a true Indian Yogi who was born in a holy Ashram and had lived his whole life there up until the present, about "Soma." His answer was precisely the same as the new version written in 2013's "Hindu Times," being that through a lifetime of Yoga the body itself creates a secretion between the brain and the top of the throat which spiritually enlightens, and this is what the mystical substance "Soma" is. This is not to state that only the opinion that psychoactive substances were the origin of Soma is correct. The point is that no one knows, and in all cases of the unknown at least an open mind must be kept.

The paper "The Hallucinogenic Fungi of Mexico: An Inquiry into The Origins of The Religious Idea Among Primitive Peoples" was first presented at the "Annual Lecture" of the "Mycological Society of America" in Stillwater, Oklahoma in 1960 by R. Gordon Wasson. In 1961 it was printed in the "Botanical Museum Leaflets," Harvard University. R. Gordon Wasson's paper begins with his introduction as a banker, and the introduction of his Russian wife Valentina Pavlovna, who was a pediatrician and originally got her husband fascinated with Mushrooms. Growing up in Russia, Wasson's wife was knowledgeable about Mushrooms, which were very much a part of Russian childhood. Wasson and his wife gathered as much information as they could on Mushrooms, including studying the names of these Mushrooms in as many languages as they could find, and traveling to the Basque country, to Japan, Friesland, Provence, and even Lapland in search of Mushrooms. Wasson and his wife's work began to be published in 1956, and in 1957 one of the rarest books on the study of Mushrooms was published by Wasson and his wife, "Mushrooms Russia and History." Wasson also gives thanks for the greatest help he and his wife received along their Mushroom studies from Professor Roger Heim, director of the Paris "Laboratoire de Mycologie."

This lecture and paper by R. Gordon Wasson from 1960 begins in earnest with Wasson stating that way back in the 1940s either he or his wife first formulated the question of whether these Mushrooms thousands of years ago were worshipped. Wasson could not remember whether this was before or after they had learned of "Amanita muscaria's" role in the formation of the religion of several Siberian tribes as well. In the Fall of 1952, Wasson and his wife learned of a Sixteenth century writer's descriptions of Mushrooms being worshipped in Indian cultures of Mexico, and they also learned of pre-Columbian stone Mushroom statues being found in the highlands of Guatemala, which they labelled "Mushroom stones." This began to form the realization that the Mushroom cult of central America was formed into a religion by the Indians of pre-Columbian times around 1,500 BC.

After finding out to their great surprise that the Magic Mushroom was still worshipped in Mexico, Wasson and his wife set out to find the Mushroom cult in Sierra Mazateca of Oaxaca, Mexico in 1953. Wasson also states that the exact day that he participated in the first Magic Mushroom ceremony in Mexico that included White people, was the night of June 29-30, 1955. Wasson tries to describe the state of the Magic Mushroom experience, beginning with the fact that the psychoactive experience is about as different from the known inebriation of alcohol as 'Night from Day.' Wasson puts forth the example that the futility of trying to explain a psychoactive experience in our languages is like trying to explain "seeing" to a person born blind.

R. Gordon Wasson begins to explain the actual area in Mexico where he travelled to in the mid-1950s to find Magic Mushroom cults still in existence, beginning with villages in southern Mexico. In these "monolingual villages," where Spanish is barely even spoken, the men are typically prone to alcohol abuse, which they speak about like everywhere else, but with regards to Magic Mushrooms the same people prefer not to speak about them, especially when "White strangers" are present. The Magic Mushrooms are highly revered in the southern area of Mexico, and even the collection of Magic Mushrooms was done before sunrise, during a new Moon, and in some regions also only collected by a virgin. The Magic Mushrooms are collected before sunrise and wrapped in a leaf so as to not even be seen by "irreverent eyes," and in some of the villages the Magic Mushrooms are taken to the church and placed on the alter in a gourd bowl. Wasson begins to explain the divine respect for the Magic Mushrooms by the Mexicans, starting with the fact that the original Aztec's name for these Mushrooms was "Teo-nanacatl," meaning "God's flesh."

For anthropological comparisons, Wasson next presents similarities between the secret Magic Mushroom ceremonies in Mexico, which were performed during the rainy season as the Mushrooms were growing between June and August, and the famous secrecy of the ancient "Eleusian Mystery." The "Eleusian Mystery" was also performed during the growing season of the Mushrooms, being September or early October in Greece, and the secrecy was so intense that a death penalty was the punishment for revealing the secret. Wasson explains that countless thousands of ancient Greeks were initiated into the secrets of the "Eleusian Mysteries" every year for nearly 2,000 years, with evidence in writing from Greeks, and in fresco from Pompeii, that the initiates drank a secret potion. These initiates saw great visions after drinking the potion, and it has been recorded that many of these initiates felt they would never be the same person again after drinking the secret potion. In the 1955 edition of "The Mysteries," the paper "The Meaning of the Eleusian Mysteries" was published by Walter F. Otto and also in this scholarly work are quotes that support the point that a psychoactive potion was drunk by all initiates of these ancient Greek rites. One initiate is quoted as calling the "Eleusian Mysteries" "new," "astonishing," and even inaccessible to "rational cognition." Wasson expands on the similarities between the ancient Greek "Eleusian Mysteries" and the Magic Mushroom cults of Mexico on the other side of the world, and sites the similar name that the ancient Greeks also called Mushrooms "broma theon" 'the Food of the Gods.' Wasson explains that the early Greek word for Mushroom was "sponge," but was replaced by a word that means "mystery," which came from a word that meant to close the ears and eyes, signifying a 'secret' or a religious taboo. Wasson next lectures about the Mazatec country in Mexico, where no Magic Mushrooms are growing, and reveals that Dr. Albert Hofmann had isolated psychoactive agents in the 'Morning Glory' seed ("Ololiuqui" to the Mexicans, and "Rivea corymbosa" in Latin). This was first documented by Richard Evans Schultes in 1941 with his paper for the Botanical Museum of Harvard University, "A Contribution to Our Knowledge of "Rivea corymbosa," the Narcotic Ololiuqui of the Aztecs." 'Morning Glory' seeds used as a psychoactive substance were also documented by Dr. Humphrey Osmond fourteen years later in 1955 in the "Journal of Mental Science" with his paper describing the effects of 'Morning Glory' seeds upon himself, "Ololiuqui: The Ancient Aztec Narcotic." Another 'Morning Glory' seed is used for it's psychoactive abilities in Mexico, and is very commonly grown in Europe as well, "Ipomoea violacea." These two different types of 'Morning Glory' seeds have different shapes and Color, but as Dr. Hofmann first discovered both of these seeds contain "Lysergic acid amide," a weaker psychoactive substance than "Lysergic acid diethylamide" (L.S.D.), also discovered by Dr. Hofmann in 1938 which is though to be contained only in Ergot. Wasson concludes that the modern chemist discovering that the same Lysergic acid derivatives are found in Ergot on grasses, and also on the lower plant form of Mushroom ("fungi"), finally completes our knowledge and brings our understanding of these psychoactive substances to the same level as it was thousands of years ago in ancient Greece.

Wasson finishes his lecture in 1960 with a conclusion of timeless similarities between the modern age and the prehistoric age with regards to the psychoactive experience, agreeing with ancient Greeks for keeping the "Eleusian Mysteries" an absolute secret, which in turn preserved the 'miracle' of this experience, and not reduced it to the contemporary view of the experience as merely "drug-induced." Wasson further concludes that perhaps with our advanced knowledge of today we don't need the Magic Mushroom experience as we did in the past, or perhaps the contemporary person is in need of this experience more than ever.

After traveling to many countries and amassing a huge amount of information Wasson decided to coin a term for the study he had done with his wife, and called it "Ethnomycology." Back in September, 1952 the Wassons had received two letters that changed their lives forever. The first letter had a drawing from Guatemala of a pre-conquest Mushroom statue. The other letter was from the poet Robert Graves who had read an article by the famed Ethnobotanist Richard Evans Schultes who not only had claimed that Magic Mushroom cults were still in existence in Mexico, but even more incredibly, that he had brought actual samples back from Mexico of Magic Mushrooms to the Harvard Botanical Museum. In the article by Schultes he claimed to have witnessed a Shamanistic ritual of Magic Mushrooms, but admitted that he hadn't taken them himself during the ritual. In 1953 the Wassons left for Mexico in search of the town that Schultes had written about where the Magic Mushroom cults were still in existence, and which was named "Huautla de Jiminez." The Wassons brought with them the anthropologist who had made the first claims that Magic Mushroom cults had still existed and who inspired Richard Evans Schultes to search in quest of them, Roberto Weitlaner. In another article of October, 1987, written by John W. Allen and entitled "Wasson's First Voyage," it is also stated that the Wassons had received two letters about the existence of Magic Mushroom cults in the early 1950s. Besides the letter from poet Robert Graves, another letter had informed the Wassons about shamans using Magic Mushrooms for healing and religious ceremonies amongst the Mazatec Indians of Oaxaca, Mexico. This letter was sent by a protestant missionary living amongst these Indians who was named Eunice Pike, and who informed the Wassons that these Magic Mushroom ceremonies had mixed christian ideals with the original Aztec rituals inherited by their ancestors.

The first Magic Mushroom ceremony that was witnessed by Wasson, which is called a "Velada" by the Mazatec Shamans who are called "Curanderas," was performed by a Mazatec Shaman named Don Aurelio. Wasson was allowed to take notes on the procedure and to be in attendance of this "Curandera," but not allowed to be an actual participant by eating the Magic Mushrooms. Over the next two years the Wassons travelled to Mexico two more times exploring the Magic Mushroom cults, and on this third trip to Oaxaca, being their second trip into Huautla, Wasson and his friend Allen Richardson arrived in the very small village of Huautla de Jiminez in the Sierra Mazatec Mountains, south Mexico on the morning of June 29, 1955. After finding a place to stay in Huautla de Jiminez, Wasson and Richardson separated and began to question people in this tiny town about the Magic Mushroom cults. After hours of getting nowhere because of the secrecy surrounding the Mushrooms, Wasson had the idea to talk to a government official about the Magic Mushroom secrets, so he went to the local town hall ("municipio"). Wasson could meet with the 'vice-president' ("sindico") of Huautla de Jiminez, named Cayetano Garcia Mendoza, and was diplomatic enough to first discuss with this vice-president simple matters, such as the weather, the price of corn crops and coffee, as well as problems with drinking water, before Wasson leaned towards Cayetano and whispered the name for the Magic Mushroom in Mazatec. Cayetano was shocked that this White "Gringo" knew the secret of the Magic Mushrooms as well as the Mazatec name for this secret. After recovering from his shock, the vice-president Cayetano replied to Wasson that it would be very easy for him to get information about the Magic Mushrooms, and that he should meet him at 4:00 that afternoon after his work was finished. Wasson and Richardson were very excited about the proposal of the town "Sindico" Cayetano, and went to his house at 4:00 as instructed. Cayetano led them to living Magic Mushrooms growing out of a sugar cane patch that was only about one hundred feet (30 meters) from his house. Richardson began photographing the first living Magic Mushrooms that either of them had ever seen, and Wasson picked several of the Mushrooms out of the patch and gently stored the specimens in a 'pasteboard box' he had brought with him to collect samples. While Richardson was fascinated photographing the first Magic Mushrooms he had ever seen, and Wasson was fascinated by picking the first Magic Mushrooms he had ever seen, the vice-president Cayetano went to the house of Dona Maria Sabrina, his friend. Cayetano asked Dona Maria Sabrina if she would be willing to teach the two White strangers the "true knowledge" of the Magic Mushrooms, and although she stated fifteen years later that she should have refused the request of giving the secret of the Magic Mushrooms to the two White strangers, she felt obligated because of Cayetano's elected position in the village and agreed to meet with Wasson and Richardson. After Wasson and Richardson had finished photographing and picking Magic Mushrooms they returned to Cayetano's house. To accompany them as an interpreter, Cayetano sent his son Emilio along with Wasson and Richardson to Maria Sabrina's house. After meeting Dona Maria Sabrina, Wasson took the Magic Mushrooms he had just picked out of his pasteboard box and Maria Sabrina cried out joyously as she talked in Mazatec to the Mushrooms while holding them in her hands. Dona Maria Sabrina then agreed to let these two White strangers join a Magic Mushroom ceremony "Velada" that very evening. That night, June 29, 1955, a Magic Mushroom Velada was performed by Curandera Dona Maria Sabrina in the house of her friend Cayetano, making the historic event the first documentation describing White people eating the Magic Mushrooms of the Aztecs. Wasson's notes from that night of June 29, 1955 state that all of them ate their Magic Mushrooms sitting and facing the wall where there was a small alter table. They all ate the Magic Mushrooms silently, except for Cayetano's father don Emilio, who was talking to the Magic Mushrooms about an infection in his left arm. Wasson was sitting in the corner of the room, to the left of the alter table, and Dona Maria Sabrina asked him to move to another spot because the "word" would be coming down in that spot. Wasson moved behind Maria Sabrina, joining Allen Richardson, as everyone continued eating their Magic Mushrooms, of which each person ate six pairs. By eleven o'clock that evening all of them had finished eating their dozen Magic Mushrooms, and Dona Maria Sabrina made the sign of the cross as she ate her last piece. Twenty minutes after eleven Allen Richardson leaned to Wasson from his chair and whispered that he was chilly, so they wrapped him in a blanket. A short time after this Richardson again leaned to Wasson and admitted to him that he was 'seeing things,' to which Wasson replied that he was also 'seeing things.' Wasson's account of this first Magic Mushroom ceremony with White people reveal notes scribbled with the wondering of the universe, which in turn reveal just what a life-altering incredible experience it truly was to Wasson. 'Architectural patterns of brilliant Colors grew to dimensions that went beyond sight,' and which seemed 'Oriental' to Wasson. A bouquet of flowers on the table transmuted itself before Wasson's amazed eyes into an 'imperial car' being pulled by 'mythological zoological creatures' and carrying a 'royal woman.' The walls of the house seemed to have completely vanished to Wasson, and only when he consciously made an effort to touch the three-dimensional wall of Cayetano's house did he feel the nausea of reality. After the intensity of the Magic Mushroom hallucinations subsided, Wasson decided that he would never eat Magic Mushrooms again, but then after just a few days he asked Maria Sabrina to perform another Mushroom Velada so he could properly document the ceremony. This second Magic Mushroom Velada a few days later was photographed by Allen Richardson who had not taken the Hallucinogenic Mushrooms on this second occasion so that he could properly photograph the event. Less than two years after these life-changing Magic Mushroom Veladas, the world would find out about the secret of Mexican Magic Mushrooms.

In 1957 the Wassons published their first book, "Mushrooms, Russia, and History" which is an extremely rare two-volume set of which only five hundred copies were printed. This, however, is not the publication of 1957 that literally changed the world by ushering in the Psychedelic Movement, since only five hundred were printed and these copies were astronomically priced. The 1957 publication that changed the world and literally ushered in the 1960s Movement was the May 13, 1957 "Life" magazine, which was probably the most well-known magazine in America at that time, and which printed a fifteen page article documenting and announcing to the general public through the millions who read "Life" magazine that there was a substance "unlike wine" that could cause hallucinations and change both your consciousness and your life. The way that R. Gordon Wasson explained and documented this first Magic Mushroom ceremony with White people - such as the sacred conditions and the proper setting of the experience, would inspire a young generation of Americans to seek out such an experience themselves, and thus began what is known as the "Psychedelic Movement."

After Wasson's return from Asia and his "Soma: Divine Mushroom of Immortality" was published, Wasson began to explore with Dr. Albert Hofmann and Carl A.P. Ruck, the "Eleusian Mysteries" of ancient Greece. In the 1978 publication "The Road to Eleusis - Unveiling the Secret of the Mysteries" the authors would go on to also conclude that the ancient Greek "Eleusian Mysteries" held every year for almost 2,000 years was centered around the ingestion of a 'magic potion' which was made from Ergot, and which contained a Lysergic acid very similar to contemporary psychoactive substances, which the founders of modern society including Aristotle, Socrates, and Plato all drank and were deeply effected by millennia ago. In later years Wasson continued publishing, and just before he died on December 23, 1986 he had finished "Persiphone's Quest," which further explores the role of psychoactive substances and the formation of early religion.

"GREAT ADVENTURES III: The Discovery of Mushrooms that Cause Strange Visions," "Life" Magazine, May 13, 1957

"GREAT ADVENTURES III: The Discovery of Mushrooms that Cause Strange Visions"(!) was the main headline on the cover of "Life" magazine on May 13, 1957. The second major story in this issue of "Life" magazine from fifty-nine years ago is the equally esoteric "Teen-Age Allowances," but what always brings a smile is the portrait on the cover of this historic issue of "Life:" "The Cowardly Lion" from "The Wizard of Oz," Bert Lahr. Perfectly suited for the underlying theme of what this one issue of a "20 cents" "Life" magazine did, which was introduce most of the 1950s world to a substance that was "Unlike Wine" and had the potential to change a person's life - *What?* This was 1957 - the "Space Age" hadn't even started just yet, but in half a year Sputnik would be launched by the Russians. This 1957 magazine was the beginning of the story for most of the members of the western society, nine years before psychoactive substances would become illegal. Imagine the time period when this magazine was published, the third of a "Great Adventure" series in "Life" magazine, following "Great Adventures l: Romantic Voyage of the Varua" in the South Pacific in the February 25, 1957 "Life" Magazine, and "Great Adventures ll: Over the Andes by Light Plane" in the April 8, 1957 magazine, and now for "Great Adventures lll: Taking Mushrooms That Cause Strange Visions" - *What?!*

This was the very first issue of a major magazine which literally introduced the concept of a substance unlike alcohol that caused the alteration of a person's consciousness, and this is the issue of the magazine that initially introduced the concept of a psychoactive substance to millions of people across America. This May 13, 1957 "Life" magazine could be compared to the play millennia ago by Plato, loosely entitled "Touchstone for Courage" in which he hinted at the 'Magic potion' of the ancient Greek "Eleusian Mysteries" which was as much "unlike wine" as possible. This is the one magazine that in many people's opinions, literally started the 1960s Movement.

"Third in a Life Series: Great Adventures" "SEEKING THE MAGIC MUSHROOM." The bold type at the beginning of the text informs the reader that the author R. Gordon Wasson was a New York Banker and went to "Mexico's Mountains" to be a participant in an age-old ritual of Indians who chewed "strange growths" that would "produce visions." What? The page before we were looking at the first "Ford Automobile" with a "disappearing steel top" and when turning the page from the portrait of normality, we are greeted with a full page Color portrait of the Mexican "Curandera" "Eva Mendez" (Maria Sabrina) putting large "Hallucinogenic Mushrooms" into the smoke of smoldering "aromatic leaves" to prepare them for the ceremonies of June, 1955 in which the article's author R. Gordon Wasson participated as the first White person in a Mexican Magic Mushroom ceremony. The smaller Black and White photo of Wasson on the facing page shows him in his New York apartment dressed in a suit and tie, with a reel-to-reel tape recorder and a "Mushroom Stone" sculpture from Central America. The reel-to-reel tape recorder was the piece of equipment Wasson used to record his fourth Magic Mushroom ceremony performed by Dona Maria Sabrina, which the Wassons also published in 1957 as a long-playing record ("LP"). The record was also limited to just five hundred pressings and is as rare today as "Mushrooms Russia and History," and just as impossible to find, so realizing the cultural value of such a unique recording as this "Mushroom Ceremony of the Mazatec Indians of Mexico" it was released by "Folkway Records" as a CD from the "Smithsonian Folkways Recordings" in 2006.

The introductory text of the 1957 "Life" magazine article explains that the Wassons had spent the four summers before 1957 in "remote mountains" of Mexico, having been searching for the "cultural role" that wild Mushrooms play in the world's culture. It is also written that the new book "Mushrooms, Russia, and History" limited to an edition of just five hundred copies had just been published and was sold for one hundred and twenty-five dollars. Wasson explains in his article that Allan Richardson and himself were initiated into the world of Magic Mushrooms in an Indian village so remote in Mexico that almost no one even spoke Spanish. In the first sentence of the article Wasson uses a quoted "holy communion" to describe the Magic Mushroom Ceremony in which he and his friend had eaten "divine" Mushrooms. Wasson states for the record that Richardson and himself were the only White people in "recorded history" to have participated in a Mexican Magic Mushroom Ceremony, and furthermore, no anthropologist had ever witnessed what they had been a part of. The fact that R. Gordon Wasson's wife Valentina, and his daughter, were joining them the next day explains the reason that she was not a participant in this first Magic Mushroom Ceremony. After nearly thirty years of searching the world for the secret of the Mushroom, in one night the entire timeless story was finally revealed to Wasson. In the "Life" article Wasson recounts the story of talking to the town "Sindico" and using the correct Mazatec word for the Magic Mushroom "'nti sheeto" in his request for learning it's "secret." There is a Black and White photo in the "Life" article of the house that Wasson and Richardson had their Magic Mushroom initiation in, being a simple adobe structure with a hay-thatched roof. Wasson's describes the Shaman or "Curandera" Dona Maria Sabrina as a middle-aged, short woman.

R. Gordon Wasson goes on to describe his first Magic Mushroom ceremony in detail, beginning with the fact that about twenty people were involved in the ceremony, all Mazatec Indians except for Wasson and Richardson. At eight o'clock in the evening the ceremony began, with members of the group translating into Spanish for Wasson. It is explained that the two White strangers were treated very friendly, accepted completely by the Mazatec members of this ceremony who had dressed in their "best clothes" for the auspicious occasion. To begin the actual Magic Mushroom ceremony everyone was given chocolate to drink which Wasson remembered was a very old tradition before eating the Magic Mushrooms in ceremony. Wasson also explains that during the ceremony the actual Magic Mushrooms were respected as sacred, and never vulgarly joked about, like "White men" do with their alcohol. At about half past ten that night Curandera Maria Sabrina cleaned the dirt off the large amount of Magic Mushrooms and then while praying she passed the Mushrooms through incensed smoke while sitting on a mat. Maria Sabrina took thirteen pair of Magic Mushrooms for herself (which are only served in pairs) and then gave thirteen pair to her daughter. Wasson admits that at this point he was on "tip-toe," waiting after decades of searching for this experience, and to his great happiness Maria Sabrina handed six pair of Magic Mushrooms in a cup to him. Then she handed the same amount to Allen Richardson, who had promised his wife Mary he would not eat the Magic Mushrooms, but he did the right thing and forgot about his lame promise. There are two Color half-page photos together at this point in the "Life" article, at the top a superb image of "Curandera Eva Mendez" handing the Magic Mushrooms to R. Gordon Wasson, with the caption including the French anthropologist Guy Stresser-Pean kneeling behind Wasson who had already began to eat his Magic Mushrooms. The bottom photo shows R. Gordon Wasson seated on a chair eating his Magic Mushrooms from a glass cup, with Maria Sabrina next to him on the floor in front of the table alter of two christian pictures, one of John the Baptist baptizing Jesus, along with a crucifix in a small bouquet of flowers in front of the pictures. Wasson had a camera and an old-fashioned flash unit attached to it on his lap, complete with the coiled flash wire and battery pack in a case over his shoulder. The caption explains that it took half an hour to chew the six pairs of Magic Mushrooms. Wasson documents the event by explaining that before midnight "Senora" Maria Sabrina broke off a flower of the bouquet and extinguished the only burning candle in the room. After half an hour in silence Wasson and Richardson told each other that they were "seeing things," and then the Magic Mushroom visions came in all their intensity and lasted until about four o'clock in the morning. Wasson states that they laid down on mats on the floor as the hallucinations began, and that they had never been more "wide awake," with the visions continuing whether the eyes were opened or closed. Wasson details his visions as coming from the center of his "field of vision," being "harmonious" and of "vivid color," with "art" patterns such as "carpets," "wall-paper," or "textiles" becoming palaces with inlaid jewels. The next two pages of the "Life" article contain four Color photographs of Maria Sabrina before and during the Magic Mushroom ceremony. One of the most unforgettable photos of the article is printed here, with Maria Sabrina helping her seventeen year old son at half past three in the morning on Magic Mushrooms, who is laying on the matted floor and holding on tight with both fists to his hair, cosmically smiling, and apparently blind in one eye. The caption of the photo of Maria Sabrina praying states that she was giving her "qualifications," such a being a "creator woman," and a "star," "moon," and "cross" woman. She calls herself a "cloud person," and finally a "dew" of the grass person. There is also a quote from R. Gordon Wasson, in which he admits that for the first time in his life he truly experienced "Ecstasy."

There is next presented in this 1957 article a Botanical catalogue of Mexico's Magic Mushrooms as a double-page spread, represented by seven different species, each illustrated in Color. The headline announces that "Vision-giving" Mushrooms were presented for the "first time." The illustrations consist of four to eight specimens of each separate species of Magic Mushroom, including "Psilocybe Aztecorum" Heim, also known to the ancient Aztecs as "Children of the Waters," "Conocybe siligineoides" Heim originally collected by Wasson in 1955, "Stropharia cubensis" Earle that was discovered in June, 1904 in Cuba, a variety called "Mushroom of Superior Reason," another called "Crown of Thorns" first found in 1955, the variety that looks like the species collected, photographed, and eaten by Wasson and Richardson, named the "Landslide Mushroom" or "Psilocybe caerulescens" Murrill variety "Mazetecorum" Heim which grows in sugar cane patches, and finally the 'most prized' by the Mexican Indians and the most common of these varieties called "Psilocybe Mexicana" Heim. The "Heim" part of these Mushroom species' names indicates the name of Professor Roger Heim of France's "Musee National d'Histoire Naturelle," who is shown in a Color photograph with Wasson on a mountain side near the village where the Magic Mushroom ceremony had been held. The text explains that the seven Magic Mushroom watercolor illustrations are "life-size" painted by Professor Heim. It is also explained that Wasson had sent Heim specimens from the last three trips to Mexico, but during his latest expedition Heim accompanied Wasson to Mexico to study the Mushrooms in their natural setting. Professor Roger Heim also ate the Magic Mushrooms with the Mazatec Indians, and developed techniques to grow these Magic Mushrooms in the laboratory. The text also states that four of the seven species of hallucinogenic Mushrooms presented are "new to science." The early date of this publication is evident as the text admits that the actual "drug" that the Magic Mushrooms contain was as yet undiscovered. The text also wisely advises precautions, clearly indicating that the Mexican Indians treated these Magic Mushrooms with the highest respect, which included never selling them, or eating them for recreation, and that the Indians consider the experience as "muy delicado" or 'perilous.'

The large "Life" article continues for seven more half-page sections, the first of which has a Black and White photo of New York photographer Allen Richardson eating Magic Mushrooms, and to just give some perspective into how early this "Life" article on Magic Mushrooms was, next to Allen Richardson eating Magic Mushrooms on the page of this "Life" magazine there are heavily airbrushed antique-looking portraits of two of the most famous people of the 1950s, Lucille Ball and Desi Arnaz of "I Love Lucy." The text continues with a description by Wasson of his second Magic Mushroom experience three days after his initiation with Allan Richardson. Wasson explains that for the second ceremony he was in the same room with the same Curandera Maria Sabrina, but the visions that he experienced during his second ceremony were not mountains like the first ceremony, but flowing rivers that included a statue-like woman breathing "woven colored garments." Wasson admits that it occurred to him that he was being allowed to glimpse a world of which he was not a part, nor which he could ever "establish contact" with. The quality of his hallucinations was described by Wasson as being not hazy or "blurred," but were composed of "lines and colors" that were "more real" than anything that he had ever seen before. Wasson immediately understood that he was seeing the "archetypes" of the "imperfect images" we usually see throughout our lives. At that moment during his vision on his second Magic Mushroom experience, the thought occurred to Wasson that this hallucinatory Mushroom experience could be the actual source of "ancient mysteries," such as the tales from northern Europe of "flying witches" from folklore. Wasson contemplated, at that moment during his experience, the workings of the mind in regards to the Magic Mushroom experience, and came to the conclusion that the Mushrooms create a "fissure" of the consciousness, in which one side of the brain continues to be "rational" and reasonable, while the other side of the brain is soaring through the universe with a freedom previously untapped.

Wasson describes the parts of the recording he made of the Magic Mushroom Ceremony, stating that from the beginning of the experience when the visions began Maria Sabrina was waving her arms and began humming, which developed into an ancient "canticle." During the Mushroom experience Maria Sabrina's daughter also sang these ancient Magic Mushroom incantations. Wasson admits that the singing was sensitive as well as having a poetic beauty, which led the author to wonder whether the Magic Mushroom experience also effected the hearing as well as having visual hallucinations, which it certainly does, effecting the gathering of all sensory information and effecting especially the processing of this sensory information in the brain. Wasson contemplates the origin of the chanting, wondering if it is indigenous or European, or a mixture of both. Wasson continues his description of Maria Sabrina's songs, and explains that her daughter was singing at one point when Maria Sabrina stood up in the absolute darkness of the room and began a dance with clapping and sometimes slapping. Richardson and Wasson wondered in the darkness if Maria Sabrina was chanting to the four directions of the compass, and the two of them were amazed remembering that the clapping and singing were coming from different directions, disorienting and giving the effect of a "ventriloquist." Wasson remembered that during these Mushroom songs of Maria Sabrina or her daughter, the other Indians in the room would 'answer' the singer with exclamations, as Richardson and Wasson desperately scribbled notes in absolute darkness laying on their mats, with their new consciousness floating free while their physical bodies felt like "lead." The first Magic Mushroom ceremony ended for Wasson and Richardson by falling asleep at about four in the morning and awaking only two hours later. Their hallucinations were over and upon awaking they had clear heads, being served coffee and bread before walking back to the house they were staying at about a mile away. There is a Black and White photo accompanying this half-page section of text showing R. Gordon Wasson siting very seriously at a table the "morning after" this first Magic Mushroom experience reviewing his scribbled notes with his wife Valentina, who had just arrived with their daughter, standing behind Wasson and in deep concentration as well. The caption states that the jars on the table were full of Magic Mushroom specimens collected for Professor Roger Heim.

At this point in the text, Wasson explains that by the "Life" article's writing in 1957, he had taken Magic Mushrooms nine times. It was clear to Wasson that amongst the Mazatec Indians the "congregation" was a necessary part of the experience, but also that the experience is just as strong if eaten not in a congregation. Wasson's wife Valentina and his eighteen year old daughter Masha arrived a day after the first Magic Mushroom ceremony, and he explains that a week later on July 5, 1955 his wife and daughter ate the Magic Mushrooms in their sleeping bags alone with Wasson and Richardson. Valentina and Masha also experience the same intensity of visions in their private Magic Mushroom ceremony without the Indian congregation, with Wasson's wife seeing the "Palace of Versailles" complete with a costume ball and people dancing to a minuet of Mozart (in her sleeping bag). Six weeks after Wasson had gathered the Magic Mushrooms in Mexico, he had his first experience with them after returning to New York. On August 12, 1955 Wasson ate the Magic Mushrooms in his New York bedroom and reported that it felt as if the Mushroom's "hallucinogenic potency" had increased.

The different journeys to Mexico to study Magic Mushrooms are discussed by Wasson, and by 1957 he had discovered that there were at least five "distinct" areas of southern Mexico in which the Magic Mushroom ceremonies were still performed, and although it was known that each area's usage of the Mushroom differed from area to area, Wasson suggests the need of a trained anthropologist who had knowledge of Magic Mushrooms. Professor Roger Heim of Paris is singled out by Wasson as uniquely qualified by both his academic degrees as well as his personal experience with ingesting Magic Mushrooms. It is explained that in 1956 Professor Roger Heim accompanied Wasson to Mexico to study the Magic Mushrooms, along with a chemist from the University of Delaware Professor James A. Moore, Guy Stresser-Pean an anthropologist from the Paris Sorbonne, and the New York photographer Allan Richardson. The quest of this 1956 expedition to southern Mexico was to identify the Magic Mushroom and to somehow learn how to create a constant supply of these Mushrooms for "laboratory use" outside of their native Mexico. Through their combined personal experiences, Wasson and his guests to Mexico over the last years had confirmed by 1957 that four Mushroom species were hallucinogenic, as well as two other species that they were reasonably sure were also hallucinogenic, and a seventh that they had heard claims of. The seven different Magic Mushrooms of Mexico known in 1957 were belonging to three different "genera," and six of these Mushrooms were totally unknown to science.

At the end of this fifteen page "Life" magazine article Wasson admits that the "chemical" which causes the hallucinations that is contained in the Mushrooms was unknown to science in 1957, but that it was reasonably sure that this activating chemical was different from the known chemicals in hashish, opium, coca, and mescaline. The isolation and synthesizing of this chemical remained for science, as well as the study of this chemical and it's potential use in psychology. This article and initial study of Magic Mushrooms in 1957 is concluded by Wasson with the fact that he and his wife had studied the Mushroom for thirty years, and were on the way to leave for their fifth expedition to Mexico to increase their knowledge of the Magic Mushroom ceremonies of the Mexican Indians, but that their study in Mexico was just the "beginning." The study of the European cultures' use of the Magic Mushrooms in the distant past, which perhaps shaped the present day, is also contemplated by Wasson at the end of this article. The final page of the article presents, as evidence of their success, a Black and White photograph of 'Psilocybe mexicana" Heim Magic Mushrooms growing in a Parisian laboratory, which were brought back as "cultures" from Mexico by Professor Roger Heim.

Before the end of his eighty-eight years, R. Gordon Wasson came to the very lucid conclusion that the modern Human being had evolved from the 'wise, understanding, and compassionate' "Homo sapien" species, into another 'ruthless, cunning, pleasure-greedy, foolhardy' "Toolmaker" species he referred to as "Homo faber" - "the fabricator" - Wasson stated that 'psychactive substances' provide perhaps a slim chance to revert back to "Homo sapiens," and back to an understanding that Art, religion, politics, and science are one.

Here I have tried to comprehensively define a historic state of "Social Stigmatization," and to illustrate just how far a stigma can *change* or even *remove completely* not only details, but the actual facts and events that occurred in our history. The point is immediately proven just by today's absolute disbelief and inability to even comprehend real facts and actual events that are documented to have occurred. Nowhere is this more evident and plain to see than in the pure human reactions today when confronted with facts of a prestigmatized past. The degree that society has eradicated sections of history that do not, in any way, conform to today's extremely conservative Human acceptance can bring back memories of Winston Smith at his desk in Orwell's "1984."

Today, eighty-three years after the invention of Fluorescent paint - the first paint to emit it's own light through the invisible Ultraviolet energy of the Black light, this wondrous, unprecedented invention has been relegated by society, with all it's truly divine wisdom, to Safety Cones for highway repair, 'High-Visibility' Safety Wear for maintenance men, Golf balls, Tennis balls, and Skis! But, unfortunately, this squandering of the miracles of the Black light did not start in the 1960s. In 1941, one of the early books on the subject of the Fluorescent phenomenon was "Fluorescent Light and It's Applications" by Dake and DeMent. This 225 page book covers almost every conceivable use for the Black light and Fluorescence in eleven chapters, and on the very last page - page 225 - in the very last paragraph of this book, in one sentence, there is mention of the obscure possible application of painting Fluorescent "Murals," and this is in the last section of the book, in the last chapter, entitled 'Theatrical Application.' Again, the newly discovered miracles of Ultraviolet Black lights and Fluorescent paint - the first paint in the world to emit it's own light through the energy of an Ultraviolet lamp - are not commonly used by Artists, and Fluorescent paintings are not hung in museums all over the world, nor did Fluorescent paint usher in a new era of Fine Arts.

Before getting too far ahead, the 1960s did not start with the Hippies and the things that most people think of immediately in reference to the 1960s, but with an age of innocence that was it's inheritance from the late 1950s. 1960 was the year of the Kennedy-Nixon television debates in which the U.S. chose John F. Kennedy as President, the year that the U.S. launched the first Communications Satellite, as well as the first weather, navigational, and Spy Satellites, the year who's favorite T.V. shows were "Bonanza," "My Three Sons," and the "Andy Griffith's Show," and who's hit records were "Are You Lonesome Tonight," "Let's Do the Twist," and "Itsy Bitsy Teeny Weenie Yellow Polka Dot Bikini." This is not to say that the seeds of the 1960 Movement had not already been sown by this early 1960 year of relative innocence. In October, 1957 the "Space Race" began with Russia's launch of "Sputnik," which was less than half a year after the "Magic Mushroom" R. Gordon Wasson article had appeared in "Life" Magazine, and in 1959 L.S.D. first became available to Artists and students in California during which Ken Kesey was paid twenty-five dollars a session to take part in experimental drug testing and was given, amongst a cocktail of other drugs, acid for the first time in 1959 while a graduate student. After discovering the mystical side of the substance in a sterile hospital testing environment, Kesey became a volunteer at the testing center, got the keys to the medicine cabinet, and soon enough the very first acid parties were being held on "Perry Lane," the small Stanford University neighborhood that Ken Kesey and other graduate students were housed in.

These were the first prototypes of what would become a movement in a mere five or six years time, not the 'norm' for 1960. The 'norm' for 1960 was the first "Teflon" pans ever sold, and Pittsburgh beating the New York Yankees in the World Series. The cosmic highlights of 1961 were the invention of the Electric Toothbrush, and the introduction of "Barbie's" lifelong soul-less mate "Ken." The 1960s did not *really* begin until 1963 with the first hit record of "The Beatles." "The Beatles" embodied, and also introduced the signatory icon of the 1960s Movement: Long Hair. The Greaser "Rosie-the-Riveter" 1940s/1950s generation was *over* the day the first "Beatles" single crackled across the airwaves around the Earth, and on that very same day, the 1960s Movement began. "The Beatles" incontestably began the 1960s Movement - they embodied it, they created it, and they broadcast it all over the world. The "Fab Four" with their long 'grease-less' hair were the epitome of revolutionary - they *changed* the world - and they were not exactly loved for it by the older generations of the 1940s/1950s War mongers, greasers, World war two veterans, Korean war veterans, and in general a very heavy, macho, extremely prejudiced mentality that pervaded the planet's societies in 1963. "The Beatles" and the Long Hair they preached were not exactly loved by my parent's generation who grew up during the Second world war - they thought it was outrageous even for a man to grow his hair, so how could they possibly feel about people - their *children* for Christ's sake - altering their consciousness with illegal psychoactive drugs? The "Be Good" 1940s/1950s World war two generation who had fought for their country and beat the Nazis did not exactly embrace men growing their hair like girls, smoking pot, taking acid, or even playing unearthly music at auditory-impairing volumes: *"Turn it DOWN!!"* Like I wrote before, there was never even a *chance*. So, until the world was changed by "The Beatles" and the 1960's Revolution they began in 1963, the first few years of the 1960s were relatively boring and very similar to the last few years of the 1950s.

In excruciating irony 1963 is also the year that the proponents of the self-deitzed "Yuppies" were born. The Creation and the Destruction going on simultaneously and continuously, as the Cosmic dance of the Shiva Nataraja teaches. To exemplify these 1960-1962 early years of the 1960s Movement which would also in turn create the 1960's Black light and "Day-Glo" Movement, there is a book that was published in 1960 by a person who is referred to as the "Father of Fluorescent Minerals," Sterling Gleason, who wrote the very early 1939 "Popular Science Magazine" article previously covered in this book, "Night Prospecting for Fluorescent Minerals." This book "Ultraviolet Guide to Minerals: a Complete Working Manual for Use of Ultraviolet Light in Locating and Recognizing Minerals, Including Field Identification Charts" of 1960 by Sterling Gleason, with it's very innocent title, is the perfect example of the innocence of this time period, just at the edge of the coming cultural revolution.

As a preface to this 1960 book by Sterling Gleason, the stage was set many years before in an age of true purity in regards to the public opinion to Fluorescence and Black light - an era when this phenomenon was seen as having limitless positive potential and arose in it's viewers pure awe and fascination. Eleven years before Gleason's book, the "Handbook of Fluorescent Gems and Minerals - A Practical Guide for the Gem and Mineral Collector" was published by Jack DeMent, again with a title from an age of innocence. In the Preface to his book, DeMent writes that at the time of the book's publication in 1949, it was almost a century since the study of Fluorescent minerals had been actively begun, and the author ponders what the second century of the study of Fluorescent minerals might bring for the betterment of the race. DeMent states that in his opinion the study of Fluorescence would bring forth an era in which 'matter' would be understood, and through this understanding the 'energy' that is 'inextricably bound' in Fluorescence could be utilized for a 'better life.' I wonder what these true dreamers would have thought about "Green Fluorescent Rabbits" fifty years later?

"Ultraviolet Guide to Minerals: a Complete Working Manual for Use of Ultraviolet Light in Locating and Recognizing Minerals, Including Field Identification Charts" Sterling Gleason, 1960

From the 1960 hardcover first edition of Sterling Gleason's book (which is so old that the identification number on the copyright page is written by hand) this cusp of the 1960s era will be examined through the analogy of the innocence of this book. On the inside flap of the book's slipcover there is a short biography of Sterling Gleason, which includes a Black and White photo of the author that gives the impression of it coming from the late 1800s. Sterling Gleason's appearance matched his personality: pure, egoless, and reminding the viewer of a scientist, with his gaze fixed off into the distance. Old fashioned round spectacles are worn by Gleason, complete with the scientist's signatory bent eyeglass frames. The four paragraph biography of Gleason introduces the author as having been a contributing writer of "Popular Science Monthly," "Outdoor Life," and "Reader's Digest to American Weekly" amongst other published articles. Directly the reader is informed of the author's involvement with the Fluorescent mineral phenomenon by the fact that Gleason had already organized the largest night prospecting expedition with Ultraviolet lamps ever done in the Mojave Desert. Mr. Gleason's credentials with the "U.S. Department of Commerce" are given, along with his membership in the "Los Angeles Mineralogical Society," "Compass Club," and the "Institute of Radio Engineers." This small bio closes with the personal information of Gleason, including that he lived in Venice, California and had received his masters from the University of Southern California in 1944.

The back cover of Sterling Gleason's 1960 "Ultraviolet Guide to Minerals" has six "Van Nostrand" published books listed on the subject of "Gems and Minerals," and gives the price of Gleason's hardcover edition as $6.95. The listing before Gleason's book describes an "Identification of Qualitative Chemical Analysis of Minerals" by Orsino C. Smith that contained every recorded mineral at the time of it's publication, given as 'more than 2,000,' which amounts to only a fraction of the minerals known today. The slipcover of Gleason's book also contains a small description of the contents, beginning with the capitalized word "FLUORESCENCE." It's not only the overall demeanor of the style of this book that brings to mind an age of innocence long gone, but also some of the words in this book, exemplified by the use of the very old fashioned expression appearing several times in the short six paragraph description, "rockhound." The reader is first informed of the fact that nothing in a "rockhound's" collection can produce exclamations of such wonderment and awe as the 'gorgeous glow' produced in a 'drab' mineral when it is placed under an Ultraviolet lamp. The reader is also informed that just finding a Fluorescent mineral was not enough and that the understanding of this miraculous phenomenon was also of interest to the "rockhound," being the very reason that Gleason published his book. If there is still any doubt as to what the definition of a "rockhound" is, a quick glance at the Color picture on the cover of Gleason's book will show you. There is a "rockhound" in typically filthy clothes walking into the desert at sunset time with nothing but nature and rocks around him.

The inclusion of extremely detailed "Field Charts" by Gleason, which are divided into seven identifying Colors of Mineral Fluorescence, stretch to a considerable fifty-eight pages across four chapters! The Preface of Sterling Gleason's book contains a special acknowledgement to 'an ultra-violet pioneer' Thomas S. Warren of San Gabriel, California, who was president of both "Ultra-Violet Products, Inc." and "Black Light Corporation of America," as well as having been the past president of "American Gem and Mineral Supplies Association." Gleason informs the reader that no other person was as closely related to the "Ultra-violet" development of mineral prospecting as Thomas S. Warren, who is described as having been a manufacturer of U.V. medical lamps in the 1930s when he first saw the life-changing revelation of Fluorescent minerals under a Black light.

In complete keeping with the retro feel of this 1960 book, Gleason chooses to use a typeface that is immediately identifiable as being from the 1920s and 1930s era: "Futura," and with this typeface presents what is normally called the "Table of Contents," but in this unique book by Gleason it is demurely entitled 'What This Book Contains,' and stretches for four pages. The book's thirteen chapters are divided into four sections, which begin with the 'Beginner's' section, and then continues on to 'Mineral Identification,' a section for 'Collectors,' and finally a section for the 'Advanced.' Out of all the thirteen chapter titles in Gleason's book, the title of the second chapter describes the intimate feelings that are still an identifying part of his book: 'Your First Night Out With The Ultraviolet Lamp.'

The first chapter on the history of 'Ultraviolet and Minerals' begins with the amateur interest of these minerals during the late 1930s and relates how important the timing was to the bombing of Pearl Harbor in December, 1941, when America overnight had also lost it's supply from China of Tungsten needed for hardening steel. Gleason explains that at the Bradley Mining Company in Idaho the largest deposit of Tungsten-containing Scheelite had been found with the use of Ultraviolet lamps, and retells the famous story of how mining went on day and night throughout the Second world war at this "Yellow Pine Mine." The fact that the Scheelite ore was so close to the surface enabled the excavation of the mineral through just the use of 'Steam shovels' that were equipped in front with massive Shortwave Ultraviolet lamps. After the most important of the Ultraviolet lamp's prospecting legacy concerning Scheelite, the prospecting of the 1940s and 1950s for Uranium is next explained, and finally the famous prospecting for the Fluorescent mineral that is still the most important Zinc ore in the world "Willemite," most famously coming from the "Fluorescent Mineral Capital of the World" Franklin, New Jersey, where the primitive "Spark Box" had been used as the identifying Ultraviolet source dating back to 1903.

Gleason's historic 1960 book actually begins with the second chapter 'Your First Night Out With The Ultraviolet Lamp,' because in this chapter the reader is introduced to the intimate writing style of Sterling Gleason, which gives the reader the lasting impression of having been brought by your friend Mr. Gleason out into the dark of night, armed only with your portable Ultraviolet lamp, to discover together one-by-one the formerly invisible 'Wonders of Nature.' Mr. Gleason tells us that tonight we will become 'acquainted' with our new Ultraviolet lamp by going outside in the dark. We are instructed to switch on our Ultraviolet lamp before stepping outside into the darkness and - look - your fingernails are Fluorescing 'off-White' and not only that, but your hands reveal a Purple Fluorescing scar, small freckles and even the reddish-orange Fluorescence of nicotine stains! The world-famous Fluorescence of your T-shirt is next pointed out by Mr. Gleason, as well as the historic remnants of days gone by: the 'Fluorescent Laundry markings.' Walking through a room in the house with Mr. Gleason he shows you that Fluorescent ink is also used in ordinary poster printing and then points out the bright Fluorescence of a plastic dish and some plastic costume jewelry. We follow Mr. Gleason on his Black light night of discoveries next outside in the dark as he points out Fluorescent Blue oil drippings on the driveway. Driving to an area to look at rocks with our Ultraviolet lamp we are informed by Mr. Gleason even of the different Fluorescent Colors our car's motor oil could contain. We reach a city park and go through the dark discovering first Fluorescent Lichens and then pebbles Fluorescing in a small stream. Mr. Gleason scoops up a handful of sand and shows us that the tiny specks of Fluorescent Yellow are Zircon and the Blue could be grains of Scheelite. As we walk through the woods, he shows us that even blades of dried grass are Fluorescent and twigs of wood, next informing us further as we walk that some species of wood are used especially for creating Fluorescent 'decorative objects' such a Locust, Sumac, and Cypress. Amongst the rubble we find another wonder - a broken glass bottle that is bright Green from the traces of Uranium that Sterling Gleason tells us are often found in this former era's glass.

The Black light night of discoveries along with our expert guide begins seriously with our next drive to an abandoned rock quarry. Immediately upon entering the quarry our Ultraviolet lamp causes a thick vein in a Grey rock to Fluoresce bright Green! Sterling Gleason shows us with a few rudimentary mineralogical tests such as the smoothness of the rock, and the fact that his fingernail or knife will not scratch the rock to determine what the mineral could be. He explains to us that these tests are for hardness, texture, and Color of the mineral, and that these simple three facts could reveal the specimens as being Silicas in the huge Quartz family. Gleason tells us that Silica minerals are found everywhere on Earth and that Agate, Opal, Jasper, and Chalcedony are members of this family. Opal and Chalcedony we learn from our guide are famous Fluorescent minerals, but Jasper rarely Fluoresces and Agate only sometimes Fluoresces. Mr. Gleason explains deeper that these Silica minerals are known to replace dead wood cell-by-cell transforming it very slowly into "Petrified Wood." Our guide has brought us to common Silica minerals in the Quartz family, but the most famous Fluorescent Silica mineral is pointed out as being 'raw' Opal called 'hyalite Opal.' A few molecules per million of Uranium are all that is needed of this Fluorescence activator to cause the raw Opal to typically Fluoresce bright Green. Today this mineral is commonly known as 'Opalite.' Yet another mineralogical test by our guide proves that the specimen in hand is a Silica of the Quartz family: the lack of Phosphorescence. As we slowly walk through the abandoned rock quarry with Mr. Gleason and our Ultraviolet lamp at night, all of a sudden there is a beautiful Orange Fluorescence in a whole area of rock. This mineral crumbles as our guide picks up a piece and examines it's physical consistency, pointing out that the tight crystals it is composed of look like 'matches' all packed together. The next geological test for this Orange Fluorescing rock sample is to quickly run the Ultraviolet lamp over it and then turn it off, revealing a noticeable White Phosphorescence. A further geological test in a lab is explained by our guide, and we are told that if a drop of acid was put onto our sample it would cause the rock to 'fizz,' and this would prove that it was a Carbonate which is a family of some of the most common rocks in the world, which Calcite is a member of. More detailed geological tests are performed by our experienced guide, instructing us as he goes along that the Fluorescent Colors of our sample varies slightly from a Pinkish to a deep Reddish in gradated bands which may vary towards Orange-yellow, and also that our sample has a visible Phosphorescence comparable in Color but less bright than it's Fluorescence, usually a Pinkish, so Mr. Gleason concludes in the end that the glowing Orangish mineral we have discovered is "Aragonite." Further stumbling through the quarry in the dark with Mr. Gleason we trip over a round rock sticking out of the ground. Picking up this next specimen we see that it is as round as a ball, and as our guide takes it he strikes it with a hammer and it magically cracks in half like an egg! This is called a 'geode' and it is a miniature crystal pocket in our hand with it's interior filled with beautiful tiny pin-like crystals. The surprise of our guide as he turns on the Ultraviolet lamp is caused by the extremely rare Red Color of these tiny crystal's Fluorescence. Mr. Gleason tells us that on our first night of Ultraviolet mineral prospecting we have been blessed with finding this Red Fluorescing geode, which we will eventually treasure for the rest of our lives and will most likely never find another like it. Since we have been exploring for quite a while our guide decides that it is getting late and that we have found enough wonders of nature to satisfy us on our first Ultraviolet prospecting night. As we drive back home Mr. Gleason tells us about the famous American quarries of Fluorescent minerals that we could have visited tonight in our imagination, such as the famous "Virgin Valley" of Nevada composed of fossilized volcanic ash giving it's signatory White surface veneer, with it's interior being an entire valley of Green Fluorescing 'Opalite.' The next dream destination that Sterling Gleason tells about on our drive home are the mines of Arizona where tri-Colored Fluorescent samples are commonly found, as well as the world-famous Clay-Center, Ohio where creamy Fluorescent Yellow samples of 'Butter' Fluorite are easy to prospect with our Ultraviolet lamp. Oregon, Montana, and Wyoming's volcanic plains, as well as the pegmatites of Grafton, New Hampshire are also dream quarries that we hear about, along with which Fluorescent minerals we would collect at each of the quarries, of course.

We are instructed by Sterling Gleason that even if we live in a city, like too many people, we could still go out prospecting for Fluorescent minerals in places such as gravel pits, along railroad tracks, in stores where they sell garden rocks, and also in construction projects such as the building of a tunnel. An amusing story is told to us by Sterling Gleason to prove just how easy it is to prospect for mineral samples in such unthought of places as New York City, in which a former director of the Museum of Natural History Dr. Pough brought a box full of freshly cut Amethyst crystals to a mineralogical meeting and explained to his amazed audience that the Amethyst crystals had been 'quarried' from below the streets of the Bronx!

In conclusion to our first night prospecting trip with our Ultraviolet lamp our guide wisely points out to us that there may be many more famous Fluorescent mineral localities discovered in the future because, as an example, new Fluorescent minerals had recently been discovered in Texas and California, and that the incredible Red Fluorescence of Eucryptite, thought to be found only in South Africa had also been recently discovered in Wyoming as well. Our first night of discovering Fluorescent minerals with our new Ultraviolet lamp ends with our guide suggesting us to join a Mineralogical club where other people also interested in the phenomenon may be met, and more importantly Sterling Gleason tells us to take the whole family out in the dark with our Ultraviolet lamp to share this wonderment and the discoveries of the natural world with our loved ones which will increase our knowledge and enrich our lives at the same time.

This five page chapter two of Sterling Gleason's book contains the essence of his legacy as he reaches out with his knowledge to the common person in his attempt to attract universal interest to the miracle he has been witness to. This is what Sterling Gleason is still remembered for over half a century later, and this is why he is known as one of the founding fathers of the entire movement of the Fluorescent phenomenon.

Another feature of Sterling Gleason's book that reflects the innocence of the period of 1960 are both the Black and White as well as primitive Color photographs printed in it. The first photo in Gleason's book is in chapter four 'Ultraviolet Field Techniques' and is a precious historic image of a U.S. Geological fieldman out in the field putting samples of minerals under an Ultraviolet lamp to test for Fluorescence. The fieldman has a metal helmet on and his entire well-equipped Geological Fluorescence laboratory unfolds from the whole side of his truck, which has "Geochemical Exploration Section Mobile Laboratory" written across the side of the vehicle. There is a platform which is formed by the unfolded side of the truck, and three sections of equipment in front of the fieldman, who is bent over looking into a concealed box-like Ultraviolet inspection cabinet. In front of the fieldman are test-tubes and different small containers in a picture that describes exactly how America became independent in Scheelite production in the few short years between 1938 and 1943. On the book's next page is another photograph of 'Ultraviolet Field Techniques' with Mr. Gleason himself "lamping" sand, gravel, or crushed mineral samples with a portable Shortwave Ultraviolet lamp attached to a battery unit. The caption informs the reader that this was the best technique to find Fluorescent heavy metals, and for further identification if the filter is removed from the U.V. lamp then "Monazite" and members of the Cerium family of minerals could be found. Next comes the first section of Color photos of Fluorescent minerals, which for a photographer who has been photographing Fluorescent minerals for over twenty years, is just as dated, if not more so, than the older Black and White photos in Gleason's book. In short, many of the primitive Color photographs of Fluorescent minerals from this 1960 book are nearly miserable. Almost all the Color photos in this book are recognizable to this author as being the commissioned work of Thomas Warren because they have been reproduced numerous times in numerous books on Fluorescent minerals, in almost every book that Thomas Warren was author, publisher, or just plain instigator of since 1960, including the small and early "Rainbow Minerals of Franklin/Sterling Hill New Jersey - a Color Portfolio of Minerals from the Fluorescent Mineral Capitol of the World" by Bob Jones, with copyright by Thomas Warren and including the name of the mineral photographer David Grigsby. Compared with modern Twenty-first century books with photographs of Fluorescent minerals, exemplified by "Collecting Fluorescent Minerals" and "The World of Fluorescent Minerals" both by Stuart Schneider, the Color photos in Gleason's book look nearly prehistoric. The Colors which were printed in this 1960 book are faded and lean towards Brown tones, as well as the obvious misalignment of Color plates that reproduces a slightly out of focus image. The four Color photos on the first page are of Fluorescent Mercury deposit's Hydrocarbons, weathered Lime, and an Orange-Brown image of a 'major Zinc ore' Sphalerite along with an indication that this photo was taken under Longwave Ultraviolet. The fourth photo is of Green Fluorescing Adamite which the reader learns is indicative of Zinc ore bodies in the field. The second page of Color photos are slightly better quality and nearly Color correct, with Halite salt crystals Fluorescing Red-Orange from Amboy, California, Tremolite from Balmat, New York Fluorescing Pink and Reddish Colors, and bright Blue Fluorite that 'gave it's name to Fluorescence' as the caption reads. All three of these Fluorescent minerals are correctly captioned to have been photographed under Longwave Ultraviolet lamps. The fourth photo in this first small two page Color section in Gleason's book is one of the most beautiful of Fluorescent minerals, Eucryptite from Bikita, Rhodesia, which is one of the only minerals to possess the intense Red Fluorescence unsurpassed by Ruby crystals, and is one of the only photos in the book that correctly reproduces the mineral's Fluorescent Color.

Chapter five of Sterling Gleason's book begins the Color Identification Charts which cover more than fifty pages of his book. The title of the chapter is 'Recognizing the Minerals' and the Color Chart begins very wisely with Red. Each Fluorescent mineral in Gleason's chart stretches across two pages and lists the Name of the Fluorescent mineral, it's Formula, Color of Fluorescence, Daylight Color, Physical characteristics, Hardness, Luster, Streak, "G," and finally 'Distinguishing Tests' for each and every mineral.

This monumental listing of Fluorescent minerals for over fifty pages has never been surpassed in the last half century of published books on Fluorescent minerals, and can only be compared to one modern printed listing of Fluorescent minerals which is in Manuel Robbins "The Collector's Book of Fluorescent Minerals" of 1983, in which Fluorescent mineral Identification Charts spread for thirty-five pages.

The second Color photograph section (page) of Gleason's book has three very familiar images of one of the most famous of all Fluorescent minerals, Terlingua, Texas Calcite first reproduced in the White light, then as 'Blue-White' Fluorescing under the Shortwave U.V., and finally as 'bright Pink' under the Longwave U.V. The next page of Color photos has three more images of Fluorescent minerals that would be reproduced in many books after Gleason's book of 1960, including a Color-incorrect photo of Franklin, New Jersey Calcite and Willemite reproducing the Color of the Calcite not as it's natural Orange-Red, but Magenta-Violet. A dark photo of one of the most beautiful and famous Fluorescent minerals Scapolite is understandable because the caption informs the reader that the incorrect Shortwave U.V. lamp was used for the photo, not the correct Longwave lamp. The last of the three photos is of Calcite which the reader is told 'glows fiery Red,' but must use their imagination because the Color of the reproduction is only pastel Pink. The third Color section (page) of the book is entitled 'Fluorescent Treasures for the Lapidary,' and presents a familiar Color photograph of Diamond Fluorescence. The Colors of the Fluorescence of the Diamonds on this photo range from shades of bright Turquoise-Blue through to Greens, Yellows, and even two Orange-Red Fluorescing Diamonds. Six individual photos are beneath the Diamonds, which are of reasonably good quality, and are of the faceted gemstones Kunzite in LW, Scheelite in SW, Zircon in SW, synthetic Ruby in LW, synthetic Green Sapphire in LW, and Spinel under LW Ultraviolet. Following is a Color page with photos of Franklin, N.J. '"Cabochons" which are Fluorescent minerals carved into 'heart' and 'egg' shapes. As a visual guide to Mineralogists, there are two photos reproduced next to test for synthetic Emerald crystals. Credited to the "Gemological Institute" the first photo shows three Green Emerald crystals in the White light, including one synthetic and two natural Emeralds. The second photo of the same three Emerald crystals reveals immediately the synthetic crystal, which Fluoresces in a shade towards Red, while natural Emerald Fluoresces rarely (as my late Mother and Aunt Jean would swear to) and when the crystals do Fluoresce, the Color is from a Greenish to a Yellowish, without a trace of Red or Orange.

The fourth Color section in Gleason's book contains more 'Fluorescent Treasures' for the Lapidary. The first page has a photo in the White light and another one in the Ultraviolet of the largest collection of carved spheres of Fluorescent minerals in the world at that time, owned by Thomas S. Warren, which is a display of forty-six spheres consisting of every Color imaginable arranged on a six-stepped presentation covered with Black material.

The next page of Color photos is the most surprising of all, with three rare photos of "Fluorescent Mineral Artwork" from the 1950s that were owned by Thomas S. Warren. These Artworks are made with crushed Fluorescent minerals put down on boards with glue in the dark under Longwave and Shortwave Ultraviolet lamps using tweezers. I have written in this book several times about the ten pieces of "Fluorescent Mineral Artwork" in the "Electric Ladyland - the First Museum of Fluorescent Art" collection made by Mrs. Eva Phillips of New Jersey, "Miera," a Japanese Fluorescent Mineral collector that lived in New Jersey, and one of the miners of Franklin, New Jersey. In 1994 I could photograph all three of the actual Fluorescent Mineral Artworks that are in Sterling Gleason's book, in the White light, Longwave U.V., Shortwave U.V., and with the intended combination of the LW and SW Ultraviolet, through Richard Bostwick in New York City. Richard Bostwick had worked for Thomas S. Warren in his famous company "Ultraviolet Products, Inc." in California in the 1970s and remained a close friend of Mr. Warren's until 2001 when Mr. Warren passed away at the age of 98. The collection of Terlingua, Texas Calcite I have in the Museum I bought at that time from Richard Bostwick who had the crystals from the vast collection of Mr. Warren's. This was the way I could have contact with Thomas Warren on the telephone in the early 1990s and then eventually through letters and parcels. Richard Bostwick was also kind enough to let me photograph his large collection of Thomas Goff's Fluorescent Paintings from the 1950s, which I have also previously explained as changing scenes between the White light, Longwave U.V., and Shortwave U.V. and would become a Summer, Winter, and Fall scene all in one painting, for example.

One of the three "Fluorescent Mineral Artworks" in Gleason's book I clearly remember being signed by a woman named "Colet" from the West coast in the states that was a friend of Mr. Warren's, as I was told by Richard Bostwick when I photographed this "Poinsettias" in his New York City apartment. This "Poinsettias" by Colet is created in a different manner than the "Fluorescent Mineral Artwork" by the three people from New Jersey that are in the Museum collection, as far as the actual method in which the pieces of Art were made. In Colet's work the fragments of Fluorescent minerals are large and they form almost a mosaic of an image, but the work from the three people from New Jersey in the Museum collection is much finer in it's application because the Fluorescent minerals have been pulverized into a sand and thus when applied, create an image closer to a painting than a mosaic. Gleason explains that one of the "Fluorescent Mineral Artworks" in his book was done by a doctor in New York, but by the time I had photographed these pieces thirty-four years later that information had been lost. Gleason details these "Fluorescent Mineral Artworks" and explains that Fluorite was used for the Blue Color that make up large flowers in one of the works, and that the Green leaves were made with Willemite that had veins of Sphalerite. Yellow flowers are explained by Gleason as having been made with 'Wernerite' from Canada, which is the old name for Scapolite, and that small Red flower buds were made with Calcite from Franklin, N.J. Gleason also correctly observed and documented the fact that all these "Fluorescent Mineral Artworks" were originally made and intended to be viewed under both Longwave and Shortwave Ultraviolet lamps simultaneously. In the late 1990s Richard Bostwick helped form the new "Thomas S. Warren Museum of Fluorescence" in the "Sterling Hill Mining Museum" in Ogdensburg, N.J. after also having worked as a miner there before the mine closed in 1986.

Chapter nine of Gleason's book covers the Ultraviolet lamp's use in mining, in the mill, and in the laboratory, with this chapter containing very dated Black and White photographs that are historical documents, such as an image of two 'operators' at the "Nevada Massachusetts Mill" in Tungsten, Nevada examining Scheelite on a mine separating table where the valuable Tungsten-containing ore was being separated from the Garnet and Iron sulfides. One of the simply ancient looking 'operators' has a just as ancient looking Ultraviolet lamp in his hand, and a 'Lionel' trainman hat on his head. In front of him there is the other just-as-ancient-looking 'operator' peering into extremely retouched White lines of Fluorescing Scheelite. The next Black and White photo is of another miner, who looks like Roy Rogers after he fell into a mud pit with his horse. The photo in Gleason's book was reproduced from "Mining World" and I don't think I've ever seen a photo of a person or of a place that was filthier. The character in the photo not surprisingly has a Shortwave Ultraviolet lamp mounted which points directly into his face(!) and is examining a sample of the waste material (called 'tailings') of the "Linka Mine" in Austin, Nevada to make sure no Tungsten was lost in the milling process.

One of the valuable photos in Gleason's book clearly illustrates a procedure for testing if ore contains Mercury, a process which is written about in this book. This field test was used for Mercury prospecting and involved heating a mineral sample in front of a "Fluorescent Screen" and a Shortwave Ultraviolet lamp. If Mercury was contained in the heated sample then a dense Black shadow would be created on the Fluorescent screen, which would not be created by samples that contain no Mercury.

The next Black and White photograph in Gleason's book is of probably the most important Ultraviolet artifact from the Second world war era, the "Scheelite Fluorescent Analyzer" card made 'under license' by the 'Department of Interior of the United States Government.' This was the field testing card that was constantly used in the search for Tungsten-containing Scheelite in the U.S.A. for the Second world war. The "Scheelite Fluorescent Analyzer" contains twelve Fluorescent samples of the Color that Scheelite Fluoresces with different amounts of the weakening impurity Molybendum included in it's composition. The label on this "Scheelite Fluorescent Analyzer" states that the card was made by "Ralph S. Cannon Jr., Geologist and Kiguna J. Murata, Chemist, Geological Survey" and manufactured by "Ultra-Violet Products, Inc."

The final Color photos in Gleason's book are also familiar photos, including the largest piece of Franklin, N.J. Wollastonite ever found, originally in the collection of the late Ewald Gerstmann, who sold it to the "Franklin Mineral Museum," where it still remains today as the centerpiece of it's enormous collection. Four photos of Uranium minerals are next presented on the page facing the beginning of chapter eleven 'Radioactive Minerals.' There follows Color photos demonstrating the most important use for Ultraviolet in 1960 when Gleason's book was published, prospecting for radioactive Uranium, illustrated by a "beading" test for Uranium and the simple 'Bottle-Cap' "Halo" Uranium tests. The last page of Color photos in Gleason's book appropriately illustrates one of the most fascinating Fluorescent phenomenon in the entire mineral kingdom: "Tenebrescence." Three photos of 'Amazing Hackmanite' are presented by Gleason, the first in the White light showing a Grey rock, the second in the Longwave Ultraviolet shows an Orange Fluorescence in the Hackmanite, but in the third photo is seen the 'Amazing' quality of Hackmanite's Tenebrescence, it's magical ability to turn 'Reddish-Purple' in daylight after being exposed to the energy of a Shortwave Ultraviolet lamp. The Color in the White light changes from Grey to Purple after just an exposure to a Shortwave Ultraviolet lamp, and then back to Grey again when put under a White light - it is something that is amazing to behold (even after doing it several thousand times in the Museum).

The last chapter in Gleason's book "Ultraviolet Guide to Minerals" leaves us with the final chapter of dreams and miracles of the Black light's miraculous future. Thankfully for them, true visionaries like Sterling Gleason died a long time ago, before their dreams and visions for the magical future of the Black light were stigmatized by society. This final chapter in Gleason's 1960 book has a visionary title about the search for 'New Keys' to Fluorescence in the future. This search for 'New Keys' to Fluorescence begins with Sterling Gleason explaining that so many minerals and substances that had very little or no response to Ultraviolet in the past have been reported to have some Fluorescence after they are re-examined with newer Ultraviolet technology, which usually translated to more powerful Ultraviolet lamps in combination with better Ultraviolet filters. Gleason logically concludes this thought that in the future when the correct 'key' is found to 'unlock' every mineral's hidden secrets, then there will be more Fluorescent minerals discovered. This 1960 visionary Sterling Gleason closes the thought with the possibility of combining Ultraviolet energy with 'Electrical' or even 'Nuclear' energy in the future.

Before returning to these visions of the future with Ultraviolet energy used in combination with other sources of energy to unveil further the magic of nature, Gleason puts the search into perspective by starting with what many people consider the 'beginning' - Vincenzo Casciarola's discovery of the "Bologna Stone" in 1603 (written as 1602 in Gleason's book). Gleason explains Casciarola's discovery, in which he calcined the mineral Barite, it then glowed Red in the dark, caused a mild sociological pandemonium, and includes the belief that this magical substance could cure diseases or maybe even cause miracles to happen. Gleason writes that it took two hundred years before Casciarola's discovery of the "Bologna Stone" was finally expanded upon by the next Fluorescence visionary Sir David Brewster, who in 1833 to the Royal Society in Edinburgh described his experiments into Fluorescence that had led him to call the phenomenon "Internal Dispersion." Brewster had created a 'Chlorophyll solution' by extracting the Green Colored portion of plant leaves, then he concentrated Sunlight on a bottle of his solution of 'Chlorophyll' using a lens, and must have been duly *shocked* when the single ray of concentrated Sunlight turned brilliant Red in the pure Green solution! Brewster named the phenomenon of Fluorescence "Internal

Dispersion" because of his idea that the Colored particles of Red he saw were held in suspension. Gleason explains that Brewster got the same results when experimenting with the English variety of the mineral Fluorite, and that it was precisely this mineral that led Sir George Gabriel Stokes to coin the term "Fluorescence" in 1852 after his experiments with Sunlight's effect upon the mineral. The reader is informed of the "Stoke's Law of Fluorescence" which states that certain energies can excite a mineral to emit light, but that Fluorescence occurs when the emitted light is of a longer wavelength then the energy which excited it. This law of Stokes finally and truly described the mechanics of Fluorescence and for the first time also separated it as being an independent energy form from the already known magical energies of Thermoluminescence, Chemiluminescence, Bioluminescence, and Triboluminescence. Gleason further explains that it took fifty years before "Stoke's Law of Fluorescence" was finally proved by Albert Einstein, and that in between this period of time Antoine Becquerel invented the "Phosphoroscope," Roentgen discovered "X-Rays" and the Curies discovered "Radium."

Gleason's book follows with a superbly detailed description of the monumental Kunz and Baskerville 1903 American Museum of Natural History historic expedition. It is explained first that Dr. George F. Kunz was a Tiffany's mineralogist and that Charles Baskerville was a professor at Amherst College, and that their experiment was the largest such experiment ever performed in history. Gleason describes what must have been a monstrous apparition: Kunz and Baskerville pushing a huge wheeled contraption sparking, flashing, and flaming in the darkness of the American Museum of Natural History in Manhattan. Gleason himself also envisions the contraption of Kunz and Baskerville to most probably have looked like something out of an old horror movie, with it's giant "Spark Box" that is described in Gleason's book as a huge spark coil that was connected to two 'Leyden jars' which were covered in tin foil and that dramatically sent White sheets of 'flame' that were directed between the four iron terminals of a gigantic "Spark Box," and then finally through an opening fitted with Quartz. Another apparatus that Kunz and Baskerville's contraption was fitted with was a primitive X-Ray tube, which consisted of a vivid Green glowing bulb that emitted potent X-Rays onto the mineral samples. Here in Gleason's description of this monumental historic mineralogical expedition into the vast collections of the American Museum of Natural History in New York City, it is once again confirmed that Radium was indeed used on the rolling contraption. Gleason describes that the two experimenters used a 'well shielded' bottle of Radium 'salts' to excite specimen by specimen with the intense energy of it's Gamma rays. To complete their sparking, flashing, flaming barrage on the 13,000 mineral samples and 15,000 Diamonds of the American Museum of Natural History collection, Kunz and Baskerville ignited blinding strips of Magnesium that must have lit up the pitch Black display cases in the museum like spotlights! Through the raw unharnessed energy these experimenters were armed with, along with the obvious infinite curiosity and wonderment that these two men were possessed with, the wonders which they discovered are astounding, and leave this writer of one hundred and thirteen years later envious. As an astonishing example, after Kunz and Baskerville exposed a specimen of Green Fluorescing Willemite from Franklin, New Jersey to X-Rays, they next exposed the same specimen to the Gamma rays of the vial of Radium salts that they placed one hundred feet away (30 meters) from the Willemite specimen, and amazingly it Fluoresced brilliant Green, and then what was even more amazing, continued to Phosphoresce Green for more than twenty-four hours! Not only that, but after the experimenters suspended this specimen of Willemite in a glass vessel the Willemite would emit a flash of Green light just by hitting the outside of the glass vessel it was suspended in, thus displaying truly unbelievable Triboluminescence. This 1903 historic expedition by these two pioneers remains the most comprehensive examination of minerals for Fluorescence in history up until the present day.

In this final chapter of Gleason's book, which deals with the search for 'New keys' to the Fluorescence phenomenon, the final two photos are presented in Black and White. First a photo of Sterling Gleason looking through what he calls an 'inexpensive' pocket Spectroscope at a Fluorescing mineral under a World war two era "V-43" Shortwave Ultraviolet lamp. This closing advise of Gleason's is to buy this portable Spectroscope to analyze the Fluorescent Colors emitted by your Fluorescent minerals, which could also give a hint to the Activators causing the mineral's Fluorescence. The last photo faces the picture of Gleason with his Spectroscope, and this image has a full page explanation of how to read the Spectroscope's "Spectrogram." The image has the numbered scale of the nanometers of the visible spectrum at the top, going from 400 to 800 (Violet to Red). Underneath this scale there are ten lines that are the Spectroscope reading of the Color of light emitted by eight different Fluorescent minerals, and also the reading of the U.V. lamp itself, with it's U.V. filter off the lamp, and then on the lamp for a double reading. The antique "V-43" "Ultra-Violet Products, Inc." Shortwave lamp without it's filter gives a Spectrogram reading of Violet, Green, and Yellow visible light. With it's antique Shortwave filter in place the lamp still reads some Violet visible light (the Shortwave Ultraviolet filter wasn't 'perfected' until two decades later in 1980). Typical of Sterling Gleason, the explanation of such an intricate machine measuring the emitted Spectrogram of Colors of individual Fluorescent minerals and even the minuscule amount of their activators, is made simple, understandable to everyone, and nearly impossibly made to sound like fun! In conclusion to the Spectroscope discussion, Gleason presents a table of known Activators for Fluorescent minerals in 1960, including twenty-five specimens of Fluorescent minerals ranging from Ruby to Halite, with respective Activators listed from Chromium to Manganese. Gleason writes about the research that went on all over the world to find the Activators of Fluorescent minerals, including the University of Jena, the "Institut fur Radium forschung" in Vienna, and Cornell University.

The incredible reaction to Ultraviolet in a small group of Fluorescent Minerals, which is termed "Tenebrescence" or "Reversible Photosensitivity" is briefly discussed by Gleason in the last pages of his book, rightfully being described as 'exotic' by the author. The actual discovery of Tenebrescence is revealed by Gleason, as he writes about a mineralogist named Giesecke who was prospecting in Greenland in 1806. Giesecke broke open some mineral specimens and found them to have a beautiful Magenta-Pink Color, but to his shock the same broken specimens had completely lost their beautiful Magenta-Pink Color and had faded to dull Grey after only a few hours. This is a phenomenon that even in the Twenty-first century is absolutely astounding. Giesecke had discovered the Tenebrescence or Reversible Photosensitivity of Sodalite, or more properly Hackmanite, which is a member of the Sodalite group. This Sodalite was also described by another geologist working later in Rajputana, India, and also a geologist working with Sodalite in Bancroft, Ontario. What is also striking about Tenebrescence is that over two centuries after it's discovery, the physical cause of the magical phenomenon is still not completely known, but it is thought to be caused by the movement of electrons to higher orbits through the energy of Ultraviolet. In some references the electrons trapped are in new orbits of higher energy that are defined as the "F-Center" (derived from the German word for Color, 'Farbe'), and these trapped electrons in higher orbits are explained as the actual cause of the Color of Tenebrescence. It is further thought that when the Tenebrescent mineral, which has changed Color to bright Raspberry-Violet from it's exposure to a Shortwave Ultraviolet lamp, is next put under a White light, the fading of this bright Raspberry-Violet Tenebrescent Color back to Grey again is caused by the less energetic White light. It seems that the lower energy given to atoms through White light may dislodge the trapped electrons in their new higher energy "F-Center" orbits, causing the electrons to return to their usual lower energy orbits, and back to Grey again.

The end of Gleason's 1960 book is a perfect example of the dreams of that time period, a rare era in human history when everything seemed possible and the world was to be discovered. The 1960 era was a time when the future of Nuclear energy seemed absolutely positive, and was thought of as a "Miracle!" Gleason discussed Fluorescent Colors being read from natural Radioactive elements, which he 1960-terms 'Atomic Reactors' of nature. Gleason also quotes Dr. Robert Wood, the inventor of the Black light filter in 1903, who wrote he believed that almost all physical substances have a degree of Fluorescence, but that in many cases it's faintness was almost impossible to record. Gleason next discusses Triboluminescence as a possible clue to very faint, nearly invisible Fluorescence, and in his final page writes about 'King-Size' Ultraviolet lamps that could be created in the 'future.' Sterling Gleason dreams about 'new Fluorescent effects' that could be discovered through the use of gigantic, extremely powerful Ultraviolet lamps of the future, or even through the utilization of strong 'Ionizing beams.' It's most likely Sterling Gleason's good Karma that caused him to die relatively young, and not live to see the era of Green Fluorescent Protein and it's production of man-made Fluorescent Transgenic Animals. Imagining what this true visionary of yesteryear would have thought about Fluorescent Transgenic man-made animals, is like trying to imagine what Jimi Hendrix would have thought about Rap.

To put things into painful perspective, flashing across the "BBC" News last night: "Ringo turns 70!" Jesus. "The Beatles" started the story for me and countless others in 1964 when they arrived in New York when I was a kid. My Aunt Jean bought me "Songs, Pictures, and Stories of the Fabulous Beatles" on the obscure "Vee-Jay Records" because I asked for it, and which I still display in my apartment in Amsterdam over fifty years later. "The Beatles" *started* the 1960s Renaissance, period. The signatory traits of the 1960s movement were the signatory traits of "The Beatles" - the Long hair, Youthful rebellion, changing the world to suit their standards, and last-but-not-least - the Music! John Lennon formed "The Beatles" after he met the younger Paul on June 15, 1956 at a small show of John's band "The Quarrymen," and from these humble beginnings, in the end, John will be remembered forever as a Peace maker and an Artist who changed the world. Of course the "Rolling Stones" and countless other early 1960s groups also contributed to the birth of the "Sixties," but none of these groups (regardless of their present day elevated and semi-deitized statuses almost half a century later) had a fraction of the energy, genius, or capability to transform the world as "The Beatles" did so famously in less than a decade.

Today's fat-assed, lazy, sponge of a human cannot begin to even *image* the energy and impetus of the world changing 1960s movement. This movement was complete - not just in the famous centers like San Francisco, but it happened right across the western world.

The credit that is due to these four "Beatles" is truly incalculable. They changed the world in a positive way. Some rare avatars make not just Art, but also Magic, and the combination of the simultaneously created two energies is what changes the world. This is the basic forgotten difference between an "Artist" and an "Entertainer." Originally, before the days of celebrity millionaire statuses, an Artist's main occupation in life was to change the world, not just make themselves rich and famous. The energy and excitement of the 1960s is nearly impossible to relate to today in this sea of malaise. An obese bespectacled *pig* of a human stands in $500 worth of tailored material with a Smart phone and a Bluetooth in each pocket. Thankfully for this monster his pockets are not as empty as his head or spirit is.

Embodying a miserable conclusion, the end of the first decades of the Twenty-first century was an era when the caveman meet the computer head on and created a crash of monumental proportions. An era when technology made our lives "better" we are told. An era of instant information access and retrieval. An age when books are going not only 'out of fashion' but becoming something even further removed from our daily lives, further to the point of antiquity nearly. The common idiot can buttress themselves with a profuse number of technological appendages - enough to actually make them feel like a human being(!) The imbecile with an "Smart phone" is instantly transmuted into a new-age instigator - all for $400! A precise contemporary version of Edgar Allen Poe's "Brevet Brigadier-General John A.B.C. Smith," in actual fact. The outright pretentiousness of this transmutation is what is called "society" today - a superiority complex *en masse*. It's more than a movement, more vicious and self-centered, more exclusively individual to be called a "movement." So now that you have your electrical appendages we must ask a question that I assumed would be obvious, but is truthfully seldom heard: have these technological advances of the modern age improved our daily lives (as we are constantly reassured that they will not only "improve" our lives but will actually change our lives)? And further more, is this "change" for better or for worse, he asks and is greeted with looks of obvious aggression. Have these technological advances and endless personal electronic gadgets we are avalanched with on a daily basis truly added something positive to our lives, or - the unthinkable (and unsaleable) - has this endless stream of technological devices created *Idiots*, in plain English! This question is raised on a regular basis as part of a short presentation on "CNN," in which presenter Anderson Cooper compiles the "RidicuList." Obviously from the presentation's name the list of what is shown is truthfully 'ridiculous.' In January, 2014 Anderson Cooper presented a new "App" that can be downloaded and which works in combination with moisture-sensitive detectors to send you an *Email* when your baby Wets it's diaper(!) Pitiful.

As a lucid answer to this more-than-important contemporary dilemma, I have a personal experience that occurred only recently. I grew up in the 1960s and was in college during the 1970s, so I have seen the beginning of the modern age developing since I was a boy. I was born before the "Space Age" began in October, 1957 with the launching of the Russian "Sputnik," so I have lived through the generation that changed from the caveman into the egotistical new-age leaders of the world. Something happened in December, 2009 that is a prototypical example of a suggested answer to the great question "have technological advances improved our lives?" For our planned dream journey to India in April and May for the 2010 Kumbh Mela in Hardwar, North India, I bought a very inconspicuous "Sony" digital camera which looks only like a shinny Black credit card in your hand. Now I was very impressed with this minuscule "Sony" camera, especially with it's "Touchscreen," which can even be considered a marvel of the modern age, let's say. So on Christmas day at my Uncle Viggie's house for dinner in America on my yearly journey to visit my family, I typically took too many pictures with my brand new camera. The photo that I will never forget, and which I have been thinking about since then is a perfect example of an answer to the pondered question about the improvement of our lives through today's technological advances. My nephew Nicholas was about four years old and is a perfectly normal, average American boy. I took a portrait of him with my new "Touchscreen" "Sony" camera I was so proud of, and then made the mistake of calling little Nicholas over to me and his father to show him his picture on the camera. What must be explained is an advanced function of this "Sony Touchscreen:" you just touch the screen with your finger on a photo you took, and the photo is instantly enlarged by just the action of touching the screen(!) And not only that, but every time you touch the screen the photograph is again enlarged! Now I must admit that this was nearly mind-blowing to me, and I don't consider myself backwards or uneducated in any way, but I admittedly did make the mistake of calling little four year old Nicholas over to the camera to also take part in the witnessing of what I consider nearly a miracle. Little Nicholas came sauntering over to the camera, looking about as bored and uninterested as humanly possible and starred at me like I was an antique. I show him the "Touchscreen" on the back of my new "Sony" digital camera and then display the photo I just took of him so he can see it. Now as he is blankly starring uninterestedly at my "Sony Touchscreen" and his portrait, I touch the camera screen and instantly blow up his portrait so that just his face fills the camera screen, and I look at him truly expecting to see him amazed - but to my ultimate and eternal surprise, little four year old Nicholas was down there with his little face looking back up at me like I was *retarded!* The look little Nicholas had on his face towards me after being shown this 'wonder of technology' was nothing less than philistine! His little face looked back up at me without so much as a vestige of a smile - a measuring and condescending look from this little four year old prick, as he informs me with his all-encompassing critique of not only my shitty little camera, but myself as well, and tries to desperately educate me to my obvious mistake by telling me *"You didn't take the Red out of my eyes!"* What!! Without so much as a nanogram of appreciation or of the feeling of wonderment present in his reaction to me, just the ultimate feeling of 'what an idiot, he doesn't even know how to remove Red-eye!' Nothing about "Wow" being elicited from this four year old after showing his portrait on the "Touchscreen" of a camera, and then even enlarging his face by just touching the screen with the finger. He just focused on the one mistake that was made that did not create an image that measured up to his four year old standards of perfection! Jesus. I don't think this lucid example needs any more commentary, explaining the point of what degree personal wonderment and exploration has been obviously lost by the contemporary technological advancement in the world. I am almost sixty years old and have lived through and experienced things that most people could never imagine, yet wonderment and personal exploration are at the very top of the conditions of my life, and have not been relegated to the level of "parlor jokes," nor even to the level of little Nicholas' feelings of absolute disinterest and disregard.

While examining the evolution of the species in basic regard to the overwhelming inundation of the technological and computer era, as here exemplified by the total lack of interest and fascination elicited by little Nicholas the four year old camera enthusiast, we ask ourselves in basic regard to the subject of the Black light and Fluorescence, once again, "Qu'est-il arrive au miracle?" - "What Happened to the Goddamn Miracle?" In this era of absolute regression and zero spirituality, there can obviously be no space or even need for personal awe. The current "evolved" technological soulless marvel is what today's world citizen is proud to be. Technological advances in a person's everyday life have produced an entity that not only doesn't "Question authority" like the 1960s impassioned movement, but this bunch has demystified all of birth, life, death, and even the afterlife to such a degree that not only does the contemporary young member of the human race not "Question authority," but they don't question *anything at all*. The technological advances in your pockets at all times of your modern lives (except when your sleeping) have changed more than your 'schedules,' and they have also caused an exponential expansion of the individual's ego. Godless visionless technological slaves are what the average common person has thus evolved to - and proud as can be of it. It took me two years to find out that "LOL" means "Laughing Out Loud"(!) The wonderment and awe of life is now something of a human trait that is not only discouraged, but can be treated with suspicion or even met with physical aggression. This is the present state that the modern person has regressed to, with all of the profound questioning of our existence now replaced by zeros and ones. Profound questioning, wonderment, and fascination replaced by empirical arrogance and a baseless ego formed out of the very elixir of today's technologically advanced society: *Nothing*. Imagine for a second Sir Isaac Newton without wonderment or questioning - what would he have been, we ask? Just a common "asshole," like almost every other person today has become, we are immediately answered.

A perfect example of today's technological advancement can be clearly seen in the example of NASA's achievements since the early 1960s of it's infancy. Fired with enthusiasm, fascination, and cosmic wonderment, NASA put two humans on the Moon in less than a decade by July, 1969, utilizing less computing memory than an infant's toy has today. In the nearly forty years that have slipped through their fingers like sand, not one human has been "put" anywhere in the universe since the enlightened era that culminated Moon walks with the ending of the Apollo program in 1972. What NASA has done in a time period that has quadrupled the time it took an enlightened fascinated generation to send men to the Moon and get them back to Earth safely, is what the entire world has become masters at: spending money! Today in 2016, more computer memory is needed to go to the *Toilet* than Neil Armstrong used in 1969 to go to the fucking Moon! This is the Buddha-like look of profound enlightenment that little Nicholas gave me for Christmas. If his look could be translated into words, they would have to have been a combination of fifty percent of one of my all time favorites - "So What" - mixed with another fifty percent of outright "Go to hell." I did not elicit these reactions from a college student, but from a four year old. It is extremely easy to imagine what will happen to a race that has lost it's most valuable trait of evolution - in a single word: stagnation. Everything that has brought the contemporary person their non-innocent bliss is now what is directly threatened by their measured and intentional demystification of life and the universe they live in. It's like comparing the philosophy of wonderment imbued in one of the Artists that led the way into today's future, Paul Gauguin and his 1897 masterpiece "D'ou Venons Nous? Que Sommes Nous? Ou Allons Nous?" ('Where do we come from? What are we? Where are we going?') - to the Transgenic Artist Eduardo Kac's "GFP Bunny" of the year 2000. Gauguin questioned the infinite mystery of the universe, while Kac typically created a new technological false life and existence. What a difference.

Just the uses of the simple subjects of this book, the Black light and Fluorescence can be a comprehensive analogy of what the evolution of the species has produced thus far. From it's primitive discoveries by a chapter full of humans fired with the fundamental questioning of life and the universe, epitomized by Colorful characters such as Vincenzo Casciarola, John Ritter, and Eugene Chevreul, the fire has absolutely gone out for the cast of today's Colorless characters. Unless of course the fire that is being referred to is this contemporary bunch's financial reports. The personal quest for the wonderment of life and existence itself was the subject matter and the impetus for Art created for thousands of years by our predecessors. Actually in the Museum where I've introduced thousands of visitors for the very first time to the spiritually questionable "GFP Bunny" - Eduardo Kac's Green Fluorescent Protein Rabbit which he commissioned a laboratory in Jouy-en-Josas outside of Paris to create for him in the year 2000 - the most common praise that is showered onto Transgenic Artist Eduardo Kac's Genetically altered Green Fluorescent Rabbit is: "That's Sick!!" I have to admit that after not eating meat or drinking alcohol for the last half of my life since 1986, as well as after living in India amongst Sadhus and Indian Holy people and being a Hinduist, I agree with my Museum visitors. To be precise, I think it is even more 'dangerous' than it is sick.

The technological advances of Black lights and Fluorescent pigments created the era of "The Miracle of Fluorescence" from the 1930s to the 1950s, then during the 1960s era the Black light and Fluorescent Colors became the palette of the Psychedelic movement, and through this explosion the world became aware of these Black lights and Fluorescent Colors. Admittedly the interest for the Black light and Fluorescent Colors gradually faded as the 1970s turned into the 80s an 90s, absolutely coinciding with the infancy and rise of the technological and digital age we are presently immersed in - but fading is not the same as stigmatization.

The present Fluorescent Transgenic movement started with Osamu Shimomura's discovery of "Green Fluorescent Protein" in 1962, which was contained in a small Bioluminescent Jellyfish "Aequorea aequorea" found in Victoria Bay, Vancouver Island in British Columbia, and was initially facilitated by Martin Chalfie of Columbia University in New York City who created the first two Fluorescent Transgenic life forms in 1993 and 1994, the intestinal bacteria "E. coli" and Flatworms. After the first series of Green Fluorescent Mice, Rabbits, dead Monkeys, Pigs, Fish, Silkworms, and Chickens horrified the world for the first four consecutive 'bumper crop' years of "GFP" animals, in 2007 a Russian scientist discovered Red Fluorescent Protein in a Sea Anemone and a new generation of Red Fluorescing Transgenic living animals shocked the world, including the infamous Red Fluorescent Frogs created in Hiroshima University in 2007, and everybody's favorite - the Red Fluorescent Cat! Since 2007, in a few short years, the living Green Fluorescent Monkey has been achieved in Japan, as well as a Green Fluorescent Beagle and an Orange Fluorescent Beagle. It has gone so far now that to the average visitor to my Museum of Fluorescent Art, "Glo-Fish" are old fashioned 'things' that they remember from when they were kids. Starring in awe at the world with wide opened dilated pupils witnessing the miracle of life cannot, in any dimension, be compared with the dull bored peering into personal fame and fortune. What has been lost is *unimaginable*. What has been gained consists of a huge mountain of filthy paper, and a truly incalculable increase of ego and social position.

So here he sits, an obscure Artist in Amsterdam criticizing the rich and world-famous Transgenic Artist Eduardo Kac of Chicago, who has been compared to Leonardo da Vinci on the internet. I have never had a computer chip implanted in my ankle, or any other part of my body in fact. I have never commissioned a laboratory in France to create a new species of life for my Art. And finally, I am not the "Chair" of any department of any University anywhere, and undoubtedly will never be one. Hari Ram Ram.

A very sobering thought to keep in mind while exploring this chapter on the 60s Movement, is that January 1, 2010 marked the anniversary of half a century since the 1960s began. The 1960s movement will be examined here for perspective into a period that caused the present social stigmatized state of "Fluorophobia," but was not the focus or prime interest in writing this book on the history of the Black light. The 1960s movement's bonding with the Black light and Fluorescent Colors is what everybody already knows too much about in contrast to the pre-1960s era that I have documented in detail, and which era's deep involvement with the Black light and Fluorescent Colors is not only unknown, but after the early stigmatization can be interpreted as being anywhere from truly unbelievable to downright hysterical.

Exactly forty years ago this time this morning I was standing at my locker between 'Homeroom' and 'First class' between eight and nine o'clock in the morning when I heard news from other frantic Junior High students that I will never forget. I first I thought it was just a fashion of the times to report that famous musicians had died ("Paul is dead" was the famous scarer of the day). Sadly as I kept hearing the same news over and over for the next few hours of September 18, 1970 I slowly had to admit to myself that it might actually be true that Jimi Hendrix had died that morning in London. Talk about painful perspective. The absolute essence of the 1960s Movement - all it contained and to what unreachable heights it had soared to - all could be represented by the unsurpassed contribution of Jimi Hendrix. A total Artist who's life was dedicated to his music and to living a lifestyle which was also representative of the music which he composed. Jimi Hendrix used to bring his guitar to bed with him - even way back when he was a teenager in the Army. He would sit in the tiled bathroom playing his guitar for ages because he loved the sound of the tiled toilet's echo! When he was shortly an Army Paratrooper, he said that the sounds he heard as the wind rushed passed his ears after jumping out of an airplane in 1960 were exactly the sounds he was trying to reproduce on his guitar. The unprecedented and never-again reproduced absolute control over "feedback" was the consciousness-altering musical energy that Jimi was the master of. The unwanted overload of electrical impulse combined with the volume of all his immense "Marshall" amplifies turned up to '10' produced a wall of abstract sound and energy that had never been used in such a masterly way before Jimi Hendrix, or in the last forty years since he passed. In interviews of the late 1960s Jimi talked about his approach to altering the consciousness of his audiences "en masse," which was directly related to the practice of Sorcery, and which he achieved through the seemingly endless repetition of guitar cords that would put the brain waves of his audience into a nearly meditative state; into a state of profound openness, into which he could insert what he wanted precisely at that point of infinite absorption. This is what the Artist Jimi Hendrix, who's memory today is also a good example of social stigmatization since his passing in 1970, being remembered as only a "Sex, Drugs, and Rock and Roll" God, was deeply involved with during the last part of his extremely short four year career. This can both be easily heard and experienced by anyone today who plays the "Jimi Hendrix at Woodstock" DVD of 2004 and pays attention to this enlightened formula of Jimi's, especially on the track "Jam Back at the House." For the 2010 fortieth anniversary marking the passing of Jimi Hendrix, "Are You Experienced, Ltd." the Official Jimi Hendrix company set up in the 1990s by Al and Janie Hendrix (Jimi's father and young stepsister) after they won back the rights to Jimi's music through a hugh court battle, has released a new collection of interviews by Jimi Hendrix in which he tells his life story. This new compilation of four DVDs is also entitled "West Coast Seattle Boy," which is what Jimi referred to himself in an offhand sarcastic way, and which is also the title of an autobiographical song of his. Through Jimi's recorded interviews is where I first realized the Artistic sensitivity of Jimi Hendrix when I was a young teenager. On an old double record that was released just after he died, and which is the soundtrack to the 1971 movie "Jimi Hendrix," there is a clear interview with Jimi in which he is talking about his memory of some dreams he had that he said he could never forget. One particular dream was about his mother, a dream he said that he had right before her early death when he was just a teenager, and he retells the dream as seeing his mother being carried away on a stretcher through some trees in the Sun, and his lucid memory of the Green patterns of the shadows crossing her face formed by the leaves of the trees overhead being dappled by sunlight. He stressed that he still remembered this Green pattern of leaf shadow and sunlight crossing her face and the Colors it created. The intricate way he explained the details of his memory of this teenage dream, and how important it was to him, instantly made me realize the deep sensitivity and spirituality that were intrinsic compositions of his nature. In the last twenty years this sensitive Artistic makeup of his personality has been stressed by the Official Jimi Hendrix company in an attempt to counter-balance the stigmatized "Drugs, Sex, and Rock and Roll" persona that Jimi Hendrix is most often remembered by. This started with the "discovery" of many Colored drawings by Jimi Hendrix in the 1990s by one of his old countless business managers, who put them all up for sale in a large auction house in England which also published a small Color catalogue of the show containing the first Color images of the Artwork of Jimi Hendrix. Needless to say, I sent to England for this catalogue and was not disappointed with it's contents. A series of abstract and semi-abstract full Color "Magic Marker" drawings on paper make up this first show which introduced the visual Art of Jimi Hendrix. Following this example, which is a 'method-of-operation' for the Official Jimi Hendrix company, their website began containing a separate page with Artwork made by Jimi Hendrix. Very expensive "Limited edition" prints of a collection of 155 Jimi Hendrix Artworks saved by the late Al Hendrix and now belonging to the Official Jimi Hendrix company, are slowly being offered to the public. As an example of these Artworks by Jimi Hendrix, in 2010, the year of the fortieth passing of Jimi Hendrix saw the release of a new Hendrix album, which is entitled with one of the most prophetic of all his compositions, and one of my personal favorites, "Valleys of Neptune." The CD's Artwork is a very special collage of Blue-Green imagery surprinted with Jimi's image. The original Artwork for this CD was chosen by his step-sister Janie when she saw a watercolor that Jimi had made in 1957 when he was fifteen years old. This watercolor by Jimi was recolored and was used as the base of the album's cover, but displaying a formerly unprecedented degree of Artistic taste, his step-sister's Official business also released a vinyl record (45 rpm) in which this 1957 watercolor by Jimi Hendrix is reproduced on the cover in it's original unaltered state. For sure in the very near future a very large 'coffee table' Art book will be published by the Official company on the Artwork of Jimi Hendrix.

  The not-so-underlying theme of these projects is an all-too-obvious strategy to intentionally attempt to alter society's opinion about Jimi Hendrix, away from a God of "Drugs, Sex, and Rock and Roll" and towards the respect automatically granted classically to visual Artists. This is similar to Leonardo Da Vinci's campaign in the 1500s to intentionally raise the social opinion of Artists to the level of respect that is awarded to Artists universally today, just by changing society's opinion towards them. Society's cliché of a "Peynter-Steyner," who was a sociological misfit who spent all his life in a dark Alchemist's laboratory grinding Colored chemicals into pigments, had to be changed into a new ideal of the Artist as a refined educated member of high society, and this was done simply by the alteration of society's opinion from a Alchemist grinding

Colors in the dark to a socialite drawing with Black chalk out in the Sun dressed in fine socially-acceptable clothing, all the while creating his Colorless drawing to the accompaniment of live chamber music (only!) History has proven that this tested technique works nearly miraculously.

The 1960s Movement and all it's iconography took many years to gain momentum, through the 'dark ages' of the1950s which cried out for a touch of anything beyond it's existential self-imposed perimeters. One person who is rightfully credited for jump-starting the 1960s Movement and all that it stood for, began the adventure in 1958-1959 while on a creative-writing fellowship at Stanford University in California. Like the true leaders of the 1960s Movement, who were enlightened people that were trying to change the world, his name is not instantly recognized by everyone because he was not a common socialite more interested in fame and fortune and all the old-fashioned ideals of life than in changing anything, like Timothy Leary for example, who's name and questionable reputation instantly come to everybody's mind. Ken Kesey is the person I am referring to as a person responsible for initiating the true 1960s Movement - the consciousness of the 1960s Movement - more than any other single individual. After being paid $25.00 per session at the "Veteran's Hospital" in Menlo Park, California to be a guinea pig given experimental "Psychomimetic" drugs such as acid in 1959, Ken Kesey became a "volunteer" in the testing center, got access to the keys for the medicine cabinet, and soon enough the first acid parties were being held in "Perry Lane," which was the student neighborhood of Stanford University where Ken Kesey and his wife Faye lived. These life-changing parties were attended by such luminaries as the young Jerry Garcia, the iconic Neal Cassady, and even the famous Richard Alpert. On July 21, 1963 a land developing company bought Perry Lane and decided to tear it down and build modern houses, and this led to the establishment of Kesey's infamous ranch in La Honda, California. But, for the last 'going away' party for the historic Perry Lane, it was imagined that a solemn ceremony would be held with tears and long-winded speeches given in constant succession, as had happened since time began, but when the Newspapers arrived to document the solemn event they were plum *Shocked!* Laying on mattresses in the trees were the jovial, laughing students of the doomed Perry Lane stoned as hell and carrying on like it was the best day of their lives - and also offering the shocked reporters to taste the "Electric" Venison chili they were all enjoying so much. When the time came for the tears over the loss of historic Perry Lane to Land developers, etc., etc., which the newspaper reporters had come to the event for and were all hyped up and eager to sentimentally document, this crazy Perry Lane resident Ken Kesey who had not shed a single tear, in front of the crowd and to the utter amazement of every witness to this historic 'solemn' event, dragged the oldest antique on all of Perry Lane - a piano - out of his bohemian Perry Lane accommodations and then he and all the other supposed-to-be-solemn Perry Lane crazies began to chop up the antique piano with axes and then finally set it on fire - What?! And in true future-Prankster emotions, these residents of Perry Lane demolishing the piano did not shed a single tear, but to the shock of everyone - especially the newspaper reporters - all these nuts were actually laughing and carrying on like it was the most enjoyable deed of their lives - What the hell is going on here?? Those reporters and highly perplexed spectators who were present at this Perry Lane happening never did figure out just what in the world was going on with those madmen on Perry Lane, and like almost every other defining moment of the 1960s Movement, they *still* have just no idea about what had happened, or even what the cause was for this completely unexpected illogical behavior, obviously completely unaware of the fact, again, the defining fact of the moment, that the venison chili that all those Perry Lane gigglers were carrying on about and constantly offering to every stunned, open-mouth reporter who starred at them, had been seasoned, or to use the vernacular of that moment "Electrified" with some of the exotic "Psychomimetic" experimental drugs that had somehow managed to escape from the Menlo Park Veteran's Hospital where Ken Kesey was working as a "volunteer." Kesey had already bought a ranch in the Redwood forest of La Honda, California and had already also invited a dozen of the Perry Lane nuts to join himself and Faye for relocating to his new place with the conscious intentions of changing the world as the eventual "Merry Pranksters."

This acid experimentation on civilians, in which Kesey had been given his first experience, happened at two different locations in 1959: in Stanford, California, where Allen Ginsberg had his first experience, and in Menlo Park right next to Stanford. These experiments were part of the historic brutal C.I.A. "MK-ULTRA" Program which translates in government code to "Mind-Control Ultra" and needs not too much commentary with such an obvious name. The ultimate "Karma" of this historic event is an exquisite example of how the American CIA tried to "Mind-Control" the people by paying them to take acid. In "Sweet Chaos: The Grateful Dead's American Adventure" by Carol Brightman, Ken Kesey admits that he never knew that the CIA "MK-ULTRA" Program was behind his initial experiences in the Menlo Park hospital in 1959. He said that Allen Ginsberg used to tell everybody that the CIA had been behind these experiments, but that nobody ever believed him. After the Freedom of Information Act was passed Kesey and everyone found out that Ginsberg had been right, and that they had both been CIA guinea pigs. When Kesey found out this truth, he was delighted and realized that this constituted a 'proof of Angels:' the fact that the American C.I.A. actually created the "Acid Tests!" The original audio recording of Ken Kesey's first experience with "Hallucinogenic drugs" administered at the Menlo Park Veteran's Hospital in 1959 was released in 2011 on the DVD "Magic Trip" documenting the famous Merry Prankster's 1964 bus ride across America. On this first psychedelic experience, into his tape recorder Kesey speaks specifically about the "Day-Glo Colors" he knew from advertising "billboards" by 1959, and as he explains, the very particular intensity of these "Day-Glo Colors" was precisely what the altering patterned Colored visions on his first experience were composed of.

In the wide open natural setting in La Honda, Artists, Musicians and other Vision-seekers began to move in and eventually would become a group very similar to the "explorers" of Hermann Hesse's "Journey to the East," a book loved by this group of characters who came to be known as "Ken Kesey and the Merry Pranksters." Another novel that the Pranksters were very involved in was "Stranger in a Strange Land" by Robert Heinlein, in which a man from Mars comes to Earth and is recognized for his infinitely superior intellect and perspective, which causes a separate society to form around him, complete with their own separate ceremonies, just like the Pranksters and Ken Kesey in the La Honda ranch, and they loved the obvious cosmic parallels.

After half a century the facts and credit for such a world-changing movement become blurred, and of course socially stigmatized, but the true fact remains that "Ken Kesey and the Merry Pranksters" invented many of the icons of the 1960s Movement. They began the "Acid Tests" which were the very first mass acid parties long before the drug became illegal on October 6, 1966. The first iconic "Day-Glo School bus" of the 1960's Movement was also bought by Ken Kesey for the group of Merry Pranksters to drive all the way across America in and visit the 1964 New York "World's Fair." The other person who was very pivotal in the Merry Pranksters was one of Kesey's old friends from Stanford University a few years before, Ken Babbs, who had been to Vietnam in between and is the Prankster who is credited as being the one who discovered what would instantly become yet another icon of the 1960s Movement: "Day-Glo" Paint! The story goes that the 1939 "International Harvester" School bus was bought by Ken Kesey to go to the New York "World's Fair" with the Pranksters, but it was the normal miserable Yellow and Black of all school buses in America, so they typically decided to "personalize" the bus with their own paint job. Pots of "Day-Glo" paint were poured out in preparation of the painting of the bus and apparently a neighbor walked into a tray of Fluorescent Paint and then began to walk across the roof of the school bus in her bare paint covered feet - this is how the paint job began! This was the first iconic "Day-Glo School bus" of the 1960's Movement, which would be copied hundreds if not thousands of times all across America on freak's school buses, and exemplifies once again the creative and establishing force that "Ken Kesey and the Merry Pranksters" represented during the infancy of the 1960s Movement. Actually, Kesey's first idea was to buy a station wagon to drive across America to see the New York World's Fair, shoot some film on the way, and eventually be in New York for the publication of his second novel "Sometimes a Great Notion." Yes, Kesey was already a celebrated new writer in America since the 1961 publication of his first novel "One Flew Over the Cookoo's Nest," which would be made

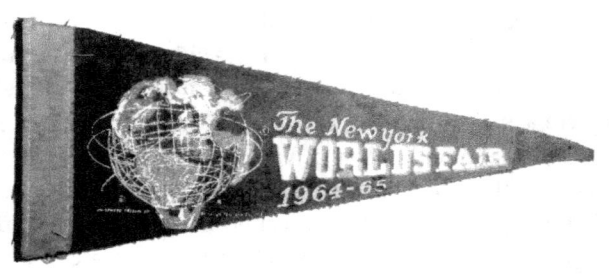

into a classic film starring Jack Nicholson in 1975, and which would win five Academy Awards. Kesey was one of the most promising new young writers in America at the time of planning the ride to the New York "World's Fair" in 1963. Then someone saw an ad for a school bus for sale, most people agree that it was Ken Babbs, and this bus was also from an owner in Menlo Park, California who was a real family man with eleven children. In recent years on the internet, the identity of this man has arisen, and is Andre Hobson, who lived in Atheron, California. The special part is that this family man Mr. Hobson had already stripped out the school bus seats, and had installed living quarters for his huge family, including bunk-beds, benches, a refrigerator, and even a sink and small kitchen area in the bus: it was perfect for the dream and Kesey bought it for fifteen-hundred dollars. This bus was destined for history, in fact the "Smithsonian Institute" in Washington, D.C. begged Kesey for years before he passed away in 2001 for this very first Psychedelic Bus for the Museum! The bus remained as a permanent feature of the forest behind Kesey's house in Oregon, because Kesey never agreed to the Smithsonian's plan of completely restoring the bus to it's original condition before putting it on display in the museum in Washington. Kesey agreed to put the bus "Furthur" on display in the Smithsonian Institute only in it's unaltered, unrestored, moss-encrusted condition. He even - Kesey-style - insisted that the Smithsonian preserve the dead leaves inside the bus that had fallen from the forest trees over the course of decades. As can be expected, the Smithsonian never did agree to Kesey's stipulations, and "Furthur" remained in the woods of Oregon rapidly returning to it's elemental composition as it should naturally. One of the original Prankster commandments was that "Nothing Lasts." On the nineteenth of April/twelfth anniversary of the Museum in 2011 I was honored with the visit of one of Ken Kesey's Merry Pranksters, Phil Dietz who joined with Kesey in the late 60's. Phil Dietz told me that Kesey's son Zane finally has pulled "Furthur" out of the swamp behind Kesey's house and the mortal remains of this world-famous bus are now sheltered from the Oregon elements in what has been christened the "Furthur Barn." Anyway, after Kesey bought this 1939 "International Harvester" school bus the Merry Pranksters took to customizing the bus with their exuberant energy and creativity that others would be in awe of. They cut a huge hole in the bus' roof and installed a transparent dome, built a whole area on the roof of the school bus for the Pranksters to ride upon and where they would be able to play instruments and make music while driving down the highway. They installed an incredible sound system that this band of Merry Pranksters could broadcast from the inside of the bus, and it would be blasted out of speakers on the roof of the bus. There were microphones mounted even outside the bus that would broadcast the sounds of the road on speakers inside the bus, and high-tech sound systems that would delay recorded sound's broadcasting for a second, creating a very trippy "variable lag." The painting job of the bus was, in the end, the defining personalization on this 1960s icon, and turned out alot like Tom Wolfe described it in his book, 'Hieromeus Bosch on acid!' "Day-Glo" and the most primary of Colors covered the entire bus front-to-back, top-to-bottom, inside and out - it was complete and more wild than most people can even imagine. Amongst the Merry Pranksters there was a practicing painter named Roy Sebern who had created beautiful parts of the bus-mural, but overall it could only be described when finished as 'shocking.' Roy Sebern had been one of the first to begin the painting of the bus, and he is the Prankster who named the it. The sign on the front of the School bus announcing it's 'planned destination' to the stream of constantly-shocked spectators starring, read the infamous *"FURTHUR!"* Again, the legend goes that the "Day-Glo" painting of "Furthur" was not started by one of the Merry Pranksters, but by one of Kesey's neighbors named Janet, who accidentally stepped into the "Day-Glo" Green paint and then walked barefooted across the roof. The very beginning of the painting of "Furthur" can be witnessed in all it's Glorious "Day-Glo" in 'Part one' of the DVD that Ken Kesey and the Pranksters finally completed and put on their website in 1999, "Ken Kesey and his Band of Merry Pranksters Search For the Kool Place." So in this Day-Glo very first Hippie Psychedelic Bus, this bunch of crazies leave from La Honda and begin to drive 3,000 miles across America to the "World's Fair," and in the course of their legendary ride, they would shock countless thousands of citizens, take an amazing amount of acid, and shoot miles of film that they would create into a Movie out of the entire trip. This famous movie originally entitled "The Merry Pranksters Look for a Kool Place" would wind up taking literally decades to edit and put together and wouldn't really be even partially completed until most of the original Pranksters were middle-aged or even not far from 'old,' in the 1990s. At the wheel of this "Furthur" Psychedelic bus full of extra-dimensional passengers, there was the most famous driver in America - Neal Cassady - the middle-aged 1950s Beat generation iconic figure that had been the actual "Dean Moriority" in Jack Kerouac's classic "On the Road," driving endlessly across America in search of meaning in life. Neal Cassady is probably the most memorable of all the Pranksters after Kesey, and he is still remembered for his endless chemically-enhanced monologue that was called 'Cassady's rap.' Neal Cassady is still remembered driving back and forth across America in 1942 Dodges, and a long list of unknown similar vehicles, and listing every single part of the car in his endless rap on the journey, along with their metaphysical counterparts in parallel universes(!) Meanwhile, back to the 'beginning,' the Redwood forest behind Kesey's ranch in 1964 La Honda, California began to be inhabited by characters that were just as Colorful as the vivid "Day-Glo" paint they were coating the Redwood trees themselves with. Ken Babbs discovered this "Day-Glo" Fluorescent paint for sale, and then he started painting even the trunks of the Redwood trees with "Day-Glo" paint, and not only the trunks, but Babbs would even paint the leaves of the tree! I've seen "Day-Glo" paint on the trunks of coconut trees in Goa which was left from unimaginably wild parties ages before - this was in the 1980s, still happening twenty years after the Pranksters started it. One of the wildest of these 'Kesey forest dwellers' was a eighteen year old unearthly kid that the Pranksters called "the Hermit," who would wear an old war helmet painted with "Day-Glo" paint to match his face which was also entirely painted with "Day-Glo" paint as well! He lived in a cave he built in this Redwood forest that is described in Tom Wolfe's book to sound something like Aladdin's lamp, and this Redwood forest behind Kesey's ranch was itself wired with microphones and speakers way up in the trees (!) so sounds of the forest were echoing from speakers hidden from sight way above your head mounted in the Redwoods, as well as the wailing music of Bob Dylan, etc. Walking through this Redwood forest in the dark must have been a life-changing experience in itself. This is all lucidly transcribed in what could be called the best book to unbiasedly document the 1960's Movement, "The Electric Kool-Aid Acid Test" by Tom Wolfe published in 1968. Forty full years after the 1960s have ended, there exists a long list of books that have attempted to document that nearly-undocumentable unique period of evolution, but most attempts have too many fingerprints on them, usually consisting of the author's clearly stated and obvious prejudicial attitude towards the 1960s Movement. The epitome of this extremely biased attitude can be found in a 1984 hardcover publication of "The Haight-Ashbury - A History" by a

Berkeley, California ex-Hippie named Charles Perry. All that is really necessary to realize the obvious distaste this Charles Perry has towards the world-changing 1960s Movement that he was also obviously regrettably a member of, is to just look at the enlightened, truly compassionate look on his bald-faced portrait on the dust-jacket of his book - Wow! This is the most condescending look I have ever seen on a human's face. Unfortunately Mr. Perry did not leave his condescending state of mind on his face, but it bled into every sentence of the 306 pages of his book. His "interpretation" of the era he lived through in the 1960s is already presented in the words of the preface of his book, and his obvious detachment was the source of the author's whole 'historic' interpretation. And by the way Mr. Perry, Eric the original "MC" of Chet Helm's "Family Dog" was not an Australian as you wrote in your Haight-Ashbury 'History,' and his "Liverpoolian" accent was not "fashionable" but real, because, as a good example of the accuracy your "History," Eric was *English*, you idiot! Although the author Charles Perry was living in Berkley in the late 1960s as a Hippie and even published a photo of himself in 1968 in his book, in the photograph on the 1984 slipcover of the book he looks about as far from a "Hippie" or from a person that had any involvement what-so-ever in the 1960s Psychedelic era as he could possibly have managed to become in the intervening decades. In contrast to most books written on the "History" of the 1960s Movement, Tom Wolfe wrote the unbiased, crystal clear "Electric Kool-Aid Acid Test" in 1968, during the actual movement itself, not with twenty years plus of "hindsight," dramatic personal change of lifestyle and values, or just plain prejudice. Tom Wolfe lived with Ken Kesey and the Merry Pranksters for a short time while writing his documentary of this small group of Artists, Writers, Poets, Musicians, and Vision seekers who literally changed the world by being the very catalysts of the 1960s Movement. Tom Wolfe is an extremely gifted social critic of our time, from "The Painted Word" that caused bonfires in the Art world, to "The Right Stuff" about the Space Race that changed the world, and to list just a few of his masterpieces, "The Bonfires of Vanity" revealing the hidden sordid lives of New Yorkers. Tom Wolfe's style of describing the Colorful characters in his works with multiple descriptive adjectives is unique, and he was the perfect author to document the complex nearly-indescribable 1960s Movement.

Once the Merry Pranksters with their Day-Glo psychedelic bus "Furthur" finally reached New York City in July, 1964, they even managed to startle New Yorkers. The 1964 hip scene's "cool" was tested by these wildest of all humans "the Pranksters," and they met Jack Kerouac himself, the 1950s icon, who came drunk to the party in Manhattan the Pranksters held for him, then continued to become drunker and drunker as Ken Kesey and the Pranksters were high on acid and made him definitively look like an artifact. New York with all it's ego, power, and endless money was, according to Kesey himself, way behind the Psychedelic revolution that was happening that moment in 1964 in California, and this was proved in rapid succession by the movie the Pranksters made on their historical journey. First of all in 'Part two' of the Pranksters bus movie "The Merry Pranksters search for the Kool Place," which is accurately entitled "North to Madhatten," there is a section of film that documents the new world Merry Pranksters and Ken Kesey at the party in New York for the meeting between the old Beatnik 1950s Jack Kerouac, and the new Hippie 1960s Ken Kesey. It is as clear as crystal. Ken Kesey and the entire entourage of Merry Pranksters are running around the New York apartment with whistles, bells, fringes, Day-Glo, tape recorders, movie cameras, head-dresses, sunglasses, American flag turbans, and every type of musical instrument ever invented - all laughing and giggling and carrying on and filming and tripping, while Jack Kerouac is sitting on the couch in the middle of this celestial event drinking "Budweiser" beer out of a can, like the 1950s iconic figure of the past that he was. Kesey with sunglasses, a flute, an American flag turban, and laughing cosmically on acid, next to Kerouac guzzling cans of "Budweiser" beer one after the other on a couch looking about as enlightened as a dusty redneck at a Cowboy Rodeo. This meeting and the world of difference between Jack Kerouac and Ken Kesey of the Merry Pranksters was also documented with still photographs in Black and White's harsh reality by one of the New York Beatnik/Hippie that had one foot in New York's Timothy Leary's world and the other foot in Ken Kesey's free La Honda California acid parties: Allen Ginsberg. I met Allen Ginsberg many years later in 1990 in Amsterdam when he performed "Howl" in Amsterdam's "Paradisio" along with one of the most important Amsterdam factors of the Psychedelic Movement, Simon Vinkenoog. Allen Ginsberg was holding an 'Open House' at the "Canon" Photography center in Amsterdam where he was signing his newly published large book of his Black and White photographs documenting the 1940s to the 1980s. After talking to Allen Ginsberg about India and Fluorescent minerals, with Ginsberg clearly remembering the early Fluorescent mineral display in the Paterson, New Jersey museum where he grew up, I went downstairs in this "Canon" Photography center to the exhibition of Allen Ginsberg's photographs, which included the haunting image from 1964 of 'Jack Kerouac yawning on DMT.' The very next day after the disappointing meeting between Kerouac and Kesey in New York City, Allen Ginsberg had another brilliant idea and suggested that Kesey and the Merry Pranksters drive up to Millbrook, New York to the Timothy Leary headquarters in the Hitchcock mansion, which was known by the Leary group as the "Castalia Foundation." "Castalia" is from Hermann Hesse's final novel which he was awarded the Nobel Prize for, "Magister Ludi - The Glass Bead Game," and it exists as a place in Hesse's novel where only advanced research into all fields of learning takes place continuously. That is the sole reason for the existence of Castalia in Hesse's work, the increase of knowledge, hence the reason for Leary's adoption of the same name for his foundation exploring acid. This experience the Pranksters had with the cold, East coast's "I.F.I.F." "International Federation for Internal Freedom" was even more of disappointment than the meeting between Jack Kerouac and the Pranksters the night before.

A further comparison to the altered, enlightened experience is made by Tom Wolfe to the 1932 book that was light years ahead of it's time, "The Journey to the East." The Pranksters all knew that Hesse had been somehow attuned to the alteration of consciousness caused by psychoactive substances decades before these substances became widely available to the masses, and the Pranksters were, of course, correct. Before the writing of "Steppenwolf," which preceded "Journey to the East," a German scientist who has been cited numerous times to have known Hermann Hesse named Karl Beringer, wrote the second book ever published on the Mescaline experience entitled "Der Mescalinrausch" ('The Mescaline Inebriation') in 1927. It is no great surprise that one of the members of Hesse's 'Prankster' society in "The Journey to the East" was a very famous Swiss Artist that people *still* are trying to figure out three-quarters of a century after he painted: Paul Klee. This is precisely documented in Hesse's "Journey to the East," a new society that was so advanced and which had attained such a divine state of awareness that 'moving Time and Space around like props in a theatre set' became a routine event.

The evolution and the advanced thinking, planning, and lives of Ken Kesey and the Merry Pranksters began to manifest itself into a grand plan that foreshadowed the movement that would eventually happen in entertainment and in Art. The concept of the audience being a part of the Art - the mental process and the physical creation of the Art itself - is known today since "Interactive Art" became a concept in the 1980s. This concept was also created by Ken Kesey and the Merry Pranksters in the mid-1960s, and grew out of an idea Kesey had of an environment that people would climb in and immerse themselves into a place that was like a superconductor of the psychedelic experience. There would be Light Projection shows by Gerd Stern and Roy Sebern, which would be another eventual icon of the 1960s introduced to the world by the Pranksters, movies, lights, and video projectors projecting simultaneously, microphones and speakers, all recording, playing back, variable lagging, etc. etc. etc. This is what was envisioned by Ken Kesey in 1965, and which would also become eventually known to the public in a typical watered-down, demystified version commonly known as a "Multi-Media Event." What the Pranksters actually did with this concept some consider their crowning achievement: "The Acid Tests." All that they had experienced and learned in the last years at Perry Lane and then at La Honda would be manifested into a multi-media Artform that was foreseen in another favorite book of the Pranksters, "Childhood's End." Sir Arthur C. Clarke's "Childhood's End" of 1953 brings the reader to the concept of what I have called "Participatory Art," in which the reader is guided through the evolution of a common movie experience, which began with "Silent Movies," then had sound added, and eventually Color. Next came "3-D" movies and other technical advances to bring forth an experience that became more and more 'life like.' "Childhood's End" asks the obvious question that would be formulated about such a series of advancements: what would be the final result? Obviously this series of advances would lead the primitive "Moving Pictures" into a dream-like creation which then became a virtual reality in itself = the breaking of the boundaries between the "movie" and the "audience;" the "entertainer" and the "entertained;" the "Artist" and the "viewer." This extremely advanced state of consciousness is still - sixty years later - barely understood by the average person, and is in no way a part of their collective consciousness. In other words, this concept the Pranksters had sixty years ago is still barely understood by most people today in the Twenty-first century.

"Day-Glo" paint, Black light parties, Psychedelic posters and Psychedelic Art, "Multi-Media Events," "Acid Rock" music and the "Grateful Dead" all came out of these "Acid Tests" by Ken Kesey and the Merry Pranksters. Tom Wolfe lucidly explains that almost every single icon of the 1960s Movement was started by Ken Kesey and the Merry Pranksters. The Light shows, the Music, the complete break with all pasts up until the Acid Movement were all brought out by the Pranksters. Wolfe also puts this into proper perspective by stating that all of these ideas and ideals of the Pranksters that became in the end the "1960s," would be copied and reproduced an infinite amount of times in the future with an infinite amount of "improvements" and money, but without the essential world-changing fascination and state of mind that the original Pranksters had.

When asked about Kesey's famous first psychedelic school bus "Furthur," Mountain Girl remembers the sections of the bus that were constructed by the Pranksters themselves, using an old dryer drum out of a 'laundromat' that had first been welded to the back of the bus, and then cut open to make space for a ladder on the inside of the bus which brought the Pranksters up onto the roof of "Furthur," where a platform with a small railing around it had also been built by the Pranksters. This platform was for riding on the roof of the bus while it was driving down the highways of America, complete with a car windshield mounted at the front of the platform to cut the wind. Mountain Girl fondly recalls that with two mattresses on the platform, it was a perfect place to lie down and smoke joints while rolling down the road. There was also a sound-system with Pranksters to talk to each other over headphones while on the roof of this moving bus that was barreling down the highways.

The "Day-Glo" paint job on the outside of the Prankster bus "Furthur" is described by Mountain Girl as being 'bizarre' swirls and patterns which was in a constant state of flux - a 'work in progress' being added to on a daily basic. She said that every morning she would continue the painting of "Furthur" with another Prankster George Walker. At the early stage of the Merry Pranksters, the entire group of these world-changing absolutely unique "Merry Pranksters" that threw the first "Acid Tests" only amounted to a core group of eleven people, by Mountain Girl's memory. What follows in this 1991 Mountain Girl interview is the best and most complete memory of the Black light and Fluorescent Paint in Ken Kesey and the Merry Prankster's "Acid Tests" that this author has ever seen published. She also remembers the nearly instant revolution inside of people that came to the "Acid Tests," first coming dressed in a sport shirt and a neat jacket, and then coming back to the next "Acid Test" with jewels glued to their painted faces. Mountain Girl remembers that a specific 'Black Light Corner' was set up at "Acid Tests" with 'lots' of Black lights and a large case of "Day-Glo" paints! The "Day-Glo" paint was prepared in separate cups complete with a brush in each, but Mountain Girl remembers that the prepared brushes were rarely used, because people at the "Acid Tests," would love to stick their fingers directly into the "Day-Glo" paint, and get the Fluorescent paint onto themselves under the Black lights, which makes you look like your skin disappeared and all that is left is Fluorescent Colors! A plastic woman's bust is remembered as well by Mountain Girl, which was also a constantly evolving "Day-Glo" sculpture at the "Acid Tests." The heights that people reached at these "Acid Tests" of the Merry Pranksters are also nearly impossible to be imagined today. Wolfe describes a woman named Clair who went on an "Acid Test" of the Pranksters while Kesey was in Mexico, with the Pranksters going down to Los Angeles and "Wavy Gravy" (Hugh Romney from New York - "What we have in mind is Breakfast in Bed for 300,000!") joining the Pranksters and proceeding to initiate the free "Electric Kool-Aid Acid" story at the "Acid Tests." This girl Clair walks into the "Acid Test," having never even smoked Marijuana before, and is unaware that the little paper cup of free "Kool-Aid" drink she just drank had acid in it. She describes this very first experience amongst the Merry Pranksters at this "Acid Test" in Wolfe's book, and was very definitive about the Black light and Fluorescent paint being an integral part of these public mass-acid parties. Clair Brush remembers getting off the first time in her life with the accompaniment of the "World's Fair" Bus Movie playing on the walls, and also a room in the "Acid Tests" that had only a Black light in it. This girl Clair remembers that about ten people on acid were sitting directly under this Black light, which she described as turning the people into beautiful Colors and textures. Clair remembers going under the Black light with the other tripping people and that there was a Fluorescent painting draped around the Black light that was dripping Fluorescent paint onto all the mesmerized people under it, as well as onto herself. This woman on her psychedelic initiation remembers clearly returning to this Black light over and over again throughout this first experience, saying that it was both 'peaceful' and that it's 'beauty' couldn't be described. She remembers that her skin had a texture and a depth under the Black light of Purple velvet, and how much that she loved it, concluding her description with the statement that she still wished her skin would have remained the Color and texture it had under the Black light at the "Acid Test." The Sunday morning after-party cleanup of the different venues that the weekly Saturday night "Acid Tests" were held in is also fondly remembered by "MG," as Mountain Girl is known by her friends, with the cleaning of "Day-Glo" paint off the walls and floors of the hall, which contained Fluorescent images made by people in extremely altered states of consciousness, such as footprints of "Day-Glo" paint leaving disoriented trails of wonderment, or Fluorescent dots on the wall made by transfixed initiates with their "Day-Glo" coated fingers creating unforgettable 'miracles' under mind-arising Black lights.

Just stop for a moment and examine what has happened in the past half of a century. I've been writing about the social stigmatization of the Black light and Fluorescent Colors for the last three-hundred pages. As is typical with all social stigmas, which are in the end just plain old prejudice multiplied exponentially, the truth becomes so altered and distorted that it disappears completely, and if society had it's way, forever. As I've documented in this book, the Black light and Fluorescent Colors were not an invention of the 1960s Movement, and the use of the Black light and Fluorescent Colors did not start in the 1960s either, but many years - decades - before they became infamous during the Psychedelic Revolution of the 1960s. This is identical to the case of acid and all other mind-altering drugs that became famous during the 1960s Psychedelic Movement. Psychedelic drugs had also been around for many years - decades as well - before the 1960s Movement began. In actual fact acid was discovered by Dr. Albert Hofmann in 1938 in Switzerland before almost all of the "Hippies" were even born. But, like the Black light and Fluorescent Colors, nobody talks anymore today about Black lights being used by Preachers in America decades ago to conduct Holy masses combined with Fluorescent and Phosphorescent Alter props. The very same is true about psychoactive drugs, nobody talks anymore today about the thousands of alcoholics that were cured with acid, or the positive ways that it altered the world forever - just the nightmare scenarios. If the reader is wondering just what the Hippies and the 1960s devilish "Psychedelic Movement" help bring to the world - in a very offhand way the dreams of the 1960s did come true

- watered down and palatable to the average person, but even in it's diluted form, the 1960s dream of Freedom and "Power to the People" did come true - did anybody out there ever hear of the *"Internet"*?

So to put "things" in proper perspective once more, we will begin at the real beginning, not in the 1960s which people consider the "beginning." The fact is that this beginning of the mind-altering drug history was, again, not in the 1960s, or even in the Twentieth century, but in reality centuries ago. One of the only books put out in the late 1970s on the stigmatized subject was "Psychedelic Drugs Reconsidered" in 1979.

The third chapter of "Psychedelic Drugs Reconsidered" is entitled "Psychedelic Drugs in the Twentieth Century" and within this chapter the authors document the centuries of use and acceptance that psychedelic mind-altering drugs had. Again, the 1960s were not the first time that people used drugs, and these drugs were not an invention of the 1960s. Authors Grinspoon and Bakalar correctly decide not to start with the discovery of distilled alcohol in the Thirteen century, and just as correctly also not to start with Tobacco or Coffee of the Seventeenth century. The authors do not even start with the more contemporary Hashish and Opium, favorite elixirs of the Nineteenth century. And definitively Cocaine is barely even mentioned because it has nothing to do with psychedelics or mind-alteration, just it's user-preferred 'mood alteration.' The documented history of drug use goes back so many centuries that it is nearly amusing when considering the last fifty years of public outcry over these "new" drugs. The documented history of drug use goes back many centuries, making it quite clear that drugs have been a part of the lives of people even before the act of documentation began. In ancient times the Sumarians called Opium the "Joy Plant," and even harder to believe in today's society of unacceptance, way back in 1898 the famous drug company "Bayer," known worldwide for it's ever-popular "Bayer Aspirin," literally and legally marketed Heroin for the first time. During the last decades of the 1800s two chemists of the "Bayer" company in Germany created two new drugs - one drug was Aspirin, and the other was Heroin. The truly unbelievable part of this well-documented historical fact is that these two newly developed drugs went before the drug testing board of the "Bayer" company and Aspirin was rejected because it was believed to be bad for your heart, but Heroin was found by the drug testing board of one of the biggest pharmaceutical companies in the world to be an excellent drug for marketing to the public. Grinspoon and Bakalar correctly start their history with the first "new" mind-altering substance - psychoactive drug - "Nitrous Oxide," known commonly today as 'Laughing gas.' Now the people to introduce "Nitrous Oxide" to the public were not "Hippies" as is most probably first imagined by the reader, but as with all the psychedelics that are known today these substances were invented or discovered and then introduced to the public by scientists and chemists, many which of whom are surprisingly very familiar names in history. "Nitrous Oxide" was the first 'new' drug that Europeans and Americans began using, again, not in the 1960s, but nearly two-hundred years before the 1960s in 1772! To put events in the proper historical perspective here, the first new mind-altering drug in modern times was discovered four years before the United States became a country. The names that are involved with this discovery of this first new psychoactive drug are instantly recognizable as some of the actual "fathers" of modern science, and may cause more than just a few eyebrows to raise. Joseph Priestly, who is the scientist that discovered the element Oxygen in 1774 (with the 'borrowing' of Swedish scientist Carl Scheele's work), first discovered Nitrous Oxide in 1772. By 1798 the first book on this new psychedelic substance was published after it was experimented on extensively by another very famous scientist Humphrey Davy, the English scientist who invented the first Electric Light in 1809, and had also been part of the team that discovered the element Boron in 1808, as well as having been the teacher of another famous scientist Michael Faraday. In 1798 Humphrey Davy used Nitrous Oxide extensively and discovered the effects of the drug, as well as giving it to Artists and scientists that were his friends. Humphrey Davy then published what could be considered the first book on a psychoactive substance in 1798 as well, which was a six-hundred page book he named "Researches Chemical and Philosophical, Chiefly Concerning Nitrous Oxide and It's Respiration." Again, this was one-hundred and sixty-two years before the 1960s even began, and about one-hundred and forty years before the "Hippies" were born. Humphrey Davy describes the philosophical effect that this new psychedelic substance Nitrous Oxide had on himself and on his Artist and scientist friends in his book of 1798. Grinspoon and Bakalar list poets and writers that were deeply involved in Nitrous Oxide in the late 1700s and early 1800s, including Robert Southey, an English poet best remembered for his 1834 children's classic "The Story of the Three Bears" starring "Goldilocks"(!) Also mentioned is a friend of Southey's named Samuel Taylor, an English poet as well, who founded the "Romantic Movement" in England with his friend William Wordsworth, and was also an Opium addict before using Nitrous Oxide. Josiah Wedgewood, the grandfather of Charles Darwin and the person who industrialized the manufacturing of pottery, is included in the list of famous Nitrous Oxide users, well over a hundred years ago, as well as the person who wrote "Roget's Thesaurus," Roget himself. In the 1840s William Morton and Horace Wells began the use for Nitrous Oxide that it is known today for, as a dental and medical anesthetic, but before and after that period, it was used by the social elite as an elixir. In 1874 the philosophical state induced by the inhalation of Nitrous Oxide was documented by Benjamin Paul Blood of America who wrote "The Anesthetic Revelation and the Gist of Philosophy," which inspired William James, the famous American psychologist and philosopher who's godfather was Ralph Waldo Emerson, to also try the substance and experience it for the purpose of describing it in his publications.

Mescaline is a naturally-occurring psychoactive substance contained in the Peyote cactus "Lophophora williamsii," the San Pedro cactus "Echinopsis pachanoi," the Peruvian Torch cactus "Echinopsis peruviana," and in other members of the Cactaceae family of plants as well as in members of the bean family "Fabaceae," such as "Acacia berlandieri." Peyote has been used for well over three-thousand years by native American Indians in Mexico and the United States, most famously by the "Huichols" of Mexico. The San Pedro cactus has also been used for centuries in South America, from Peru to Ecuador. Then the White people arrived. Putting the time period in it's proper social perspective, from the Fourteenth to the Seventeenth century in Europe, the association of Witchcraft with mind-altering states of consciousness, or as they were called back then "Healing," was strictly taboo and could easily cause a person to be literally burned alive at the stake. According to Dr. Charles Grob's publication of 1995 "Psychiatric Research with Hallucinogens: What have we learned?" in those three-hundred years leading up to the Seventeenth century several million women were executed after being accused of witchcraft in Europe. So, in the late 1500s and the early 1600s when European Spanish conquistadors arrived in the Americas they were plum horrified at the Shamanistic practices using these psychoactive substances ingrained into the fabric of the society itself. Peyote Cactus, Psilocybin Mushrooms, and Morning Glory seeds were the main psychoactive plants in common use by Shamans and healers of the "New World" at that time, as well as the usage of Datura, Mandrake, Henbane, and Belladonna. In 1616 "The Holy Inquisition of Mexico" ordered the excommunication with the Catholic church and the combined legal persecution of anyone using any of these substances formerly considered "Entheogens." These threatened punishments were as severe as they get, and included being burned alive at the stake and public flogging, only. This had it's desired effect, namely causing the Shamans and the healers of the New World to be considered as witches and associates of the devil himself by the invading Europeans. As anyone who has read the body of Shamanistic work by Carlos Casteneda, for example, already knows this European stigmatizing did not eradicate these mystical psychoactive substances, just brought them underground where they still remain in their original power until this day. It seems that the only indigenous Indians not to conquered by the Spanish Invaders were the "Wayuu," who managed to hide in the Columbian mountains from these Spanish Conquistadors.

1880 was the year a woman in Lorado, Texas mailed Peyote samples to different medical researches and especially to "Parke-Davis Pharmaceutical Company." The American Plains Indians had already formed a religion around the experience of Peyote's Mescaline after the Civil war in the United States, so it was the perfect time to attract the attention of further scientific study. Way back in the Seventeenth century Spanish Jesuit priests had documented the use of Peyote in ceremonial practices of the Aztecs, who called it "Teonanacatl." Between 1886 and 1888 the German pharmacologist Louis Lewin tested the Peyote extract on animals, and in 1888 he published the first scientific report on Mescaline after he received the Peyote samples that had been sent to the "Parke-Davis Pharmaceutical Company." The name that was first given to the Peyote cactus was named in honor of Louis Lewin, the 1880s German toxicologist that is considered today as the "Father of Psychopharmacology," and that name given to the Peyote Louis Lewin first experimented on is "Anhalonium lewinii." The historical perspective of this should be examined right here. We are considering the discovery of the psychedelic effects of Mescaline by German scientists in 1880 - which was exactly eighty years, eight full decades, before the 1960s even began - which was forty-seven years before Hermann Hesse published the book that started this discussion "Steppenwolf" - and which was actually when Hermann Hesse was just three years old. Like the Black light and Fluorescent colors, mind-altering drugs were not a product of the 1960s, but this is when society became aware of them.

After this woman of Lorado, Texas sent these first Peyote to the "Parke-Davis Pharmaceutical Company" and several medical researchers in this year of 1880, German toxicologist Louis Lewin received them through "Parke-Davis." After succeeding to isolate different alkaloids from the Peyote cactus, Lewin tried to identify the psychoactive alkaloids amongst these isolated alkaloids, but was unable to determine this simply through the standard animal testing. It seems that this Louis Lewin's scientific curiosity was greater than his personal courage, because he did not want to experiment with these potentially mind-altering alkaloids on himself, so a more courageous scientific college of Lewin's named Arthur Heffter was the first person to eat these Peyote derived alkaloids. Arthur Carl Wilhelm Heffter became the first person to ingest these alkaloids that Louis Lewin had separated from the Peyote cactus, and after experimenting with them one at a time he discovered the alkaloid that was truly psychoactive and Lewin named it "Mescal." Arthur Heffter (1859-1925) was a German pharmacologist and a chemist, and after his courage to be the first person to take the pure psychoactive alkaloid in Peyote, he also became the first scientist to isolate pure Mescaline from this Peyote cactus in either 1896 or 1897 (both dates are given for the event in many different sources). Heffter's achievement with isolating the pure Mescaline from Peyote was the very first time that a

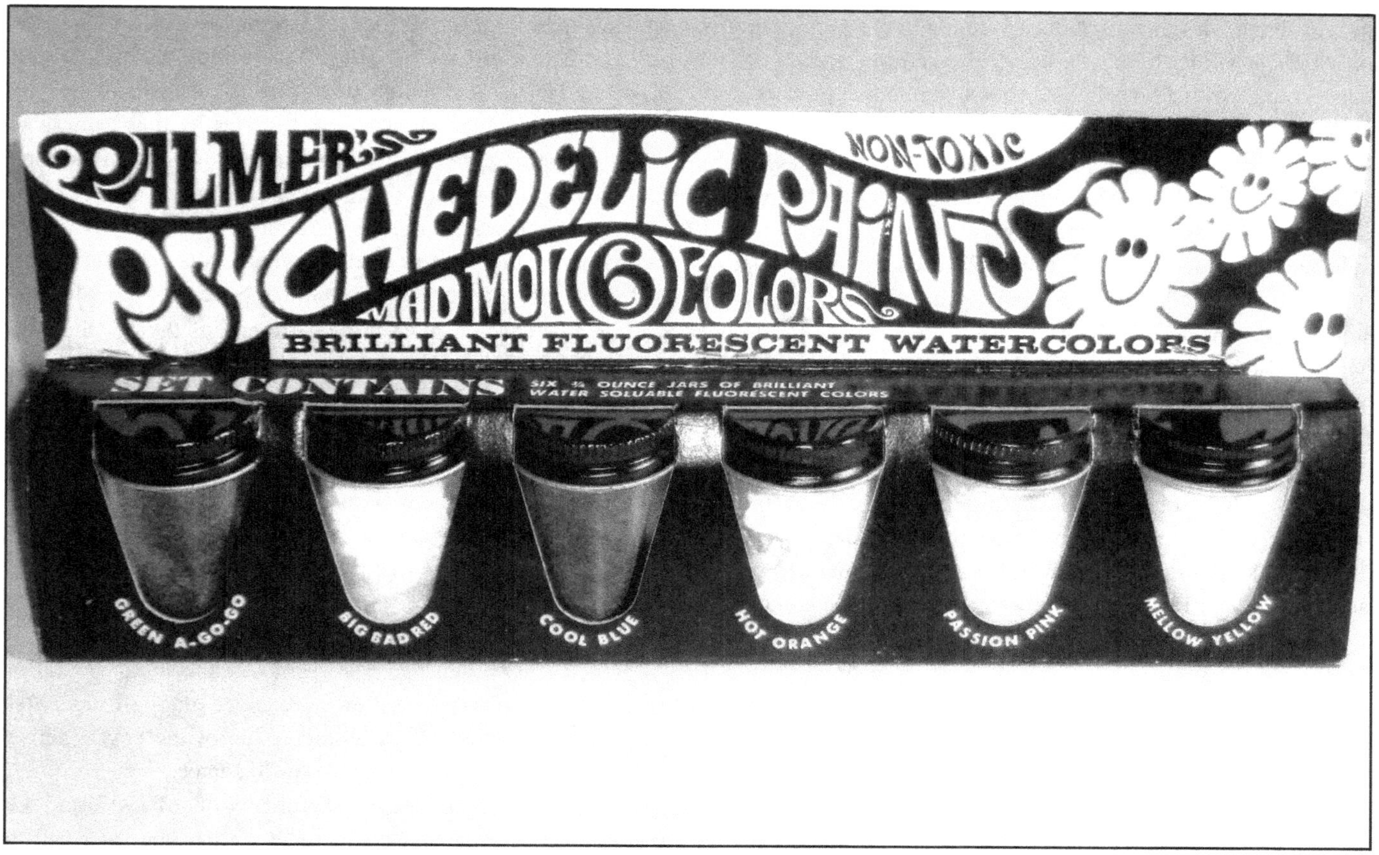

1960s "PSYCHEDELIC PAINTS" Set - "Poster Paint," "Palmer's Paint Products Incorporated," Michigan

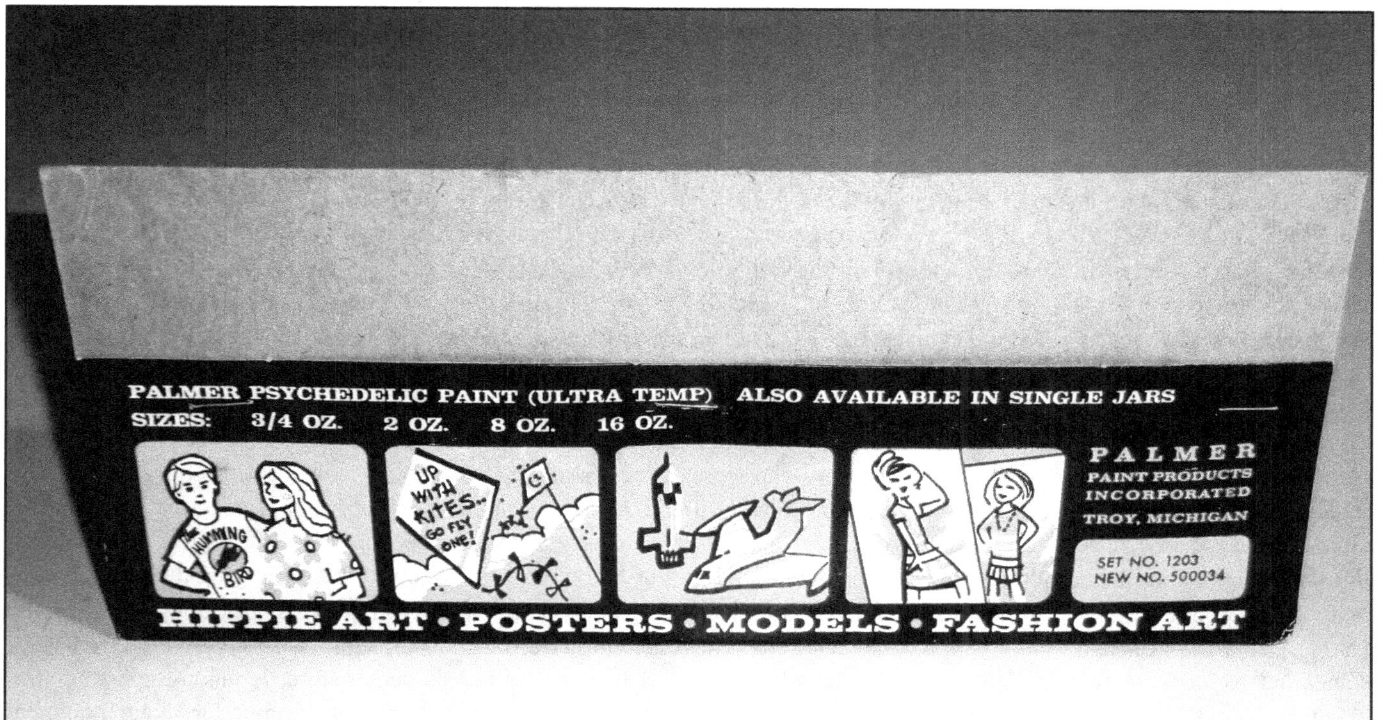

1960s "PSYCHEDELIC PAINTS" Set - "Poster Paint" (back) "HIPPIE ART - POSTERS - MODELS - FASHION ART"

psychoactive substance had been isolated in it's pure naturally-occurring state. Arthur Heffter is also famous for, and was the only person of that time who was truly qualified to publish, the first "Handbook of Experimental Pharmacology" after his self-experiments with Mescaline. Almost immediately after news of Arthur Heffter's isolation of pure Mescaline from Peyote, researchers around the world began to experiment with it. In America a doctor who was the founder of the "American Neurological Association," Weir Mitchell, obtained Peyote from a south-western native American Plains Indian, and then took it himself. After his Mescaline trip in 1896 he wrote an account of this early experience that has a modern and contemporary content. Wier Mitchell wrote what could be seen as the very first "Hippie" description of an experience with a psychoactive substance, and while reading it in the present day the reader may be convinced that they're reading a manifesto from the 1960s, not 1896. Mitchell describes precisely the movement of the Psychedelic Revolution of the 1960s in his paper of 1896 after his self-experiment with Mescaline, giving his personal opinion that after most people have the experience of the 'Enchanting Magic' of the psychedelic trip it may be impossible to resist returning to this enchanted magical place of 'Fairy Colors.' After Wier Mitchell published this first account of his psychedelic experience it attracted the attention of other scientific researchers, namely Havelock Ellis, the English sex psychologist who in 1897 also made a self-experiment with Mescaline. Similar to Arthur Heffter, Havelock Ellis' Mescaline experience was, in modern terminology, a "Mind-blowing" experience on every account. Ellis wrote that after taking Mescaline twice, the 'unforgettable delight' of the experience, in his opinion, could only be compared in intensity to the 'Education' a person received from the Mescaline experience itself. This was written by Ellis in 1897, but in 1898 he was not surprisingly reprimanded in his native England by the "British Medical Journal" for publicizing and even promoting the auto-experimentation with hallucinogenic 'magical' plants.

At that point, in the 1920s it was exactly forty years after Louis Lewin began the history of the established use of Mescaline in the west when he received the very first sample of Peyote in 1886 that had been sent in 1880 by a woman in Lorado, Texas to researchers including "Parke-Davis Pharmaceutical Company" where Lewin received them from. After Spath's synthesizing of Mescaline in 1919 the interest, experimentation, availability, and documentation of the psychoactive substance and experience took off in both the medical and science sector, and also in the private sector of society.

Finally, back to the point that began this exploration pages ago with Hermann Hesse's "Steppenwolf" of 1927, and the "Journey to the East" of 1932, in which Hesse's knowledge of the psychoactive experience is clear. Like the Pranksters in La Honda in the mid-1960s knew for sure, Hesse was so aware of, and had documented the psychoactive experience so masterly, that his personal knowledge of the experience is very apparent. It seems that Ken Kesey and the Merry Pranksters, and Tom Wolfe as well, had no idea about the friendship between Hermann Hess, Carl Jung, and Karl Beringer (who was also German), but Beringer is the key to the understanding of how knowledge of the Mescaline experience spread to both Hermann Hesse and Carl Jung already way back in the 1920s. After Mescaline was synthesized in 1919 several books were published including the early 1927 "Peyotl: La plant qui les fait yeux emerveilles" ('Peyote: The plant that gives eyes of wonderment') by Alexander Rouhier, and the famous 1927 book by Karl Beringer "Der Mescalinrausch" ('The Mescaline Inebriation') who was the friend of both Hermann Hesse and Carl Jung. In 1928 followed the first book to try to analyze and classify Mescaline visions, "Mescal: The Divine Plant and It's Psychological Effects," by Heinrich Kluver. The friendship between Hermann Hesse and Carl Jung is the subject of published books over the last half of a century, and the friendship that existed between Hermann Hesse, Carl Jung, and the author of the first book in German describing the Mescaline experience, Karl Beringer, has also been documented many times in different languages. 1927 was the year that Hermann Hesse published "Steppenwolf," arguably the first major novel to discuss the psychoactive experience to the mass public, and 1927 was also the year that Karl Beringer published "Der Mescalinrausch" in German. The passage in "Steppenwolf" where Hesse documents the psychoactive experience of Henry Haller is not that hard to find in the book. Standing in the "Magic Theater" with Hermine (who represents Herman Hesse's female counterpoint), Harry Haller (who represents Herman Hesse himself) is asked by his companion if he is 'ready.' Harry nods yes, then as if on cue Hermine's bizarre friend Pablo appears, and to Harry it appears at that moment that Hermine and Pablo were something close to witches. Pablo then tells Harry that he has been invited to be 'entertained' and that this entertainment is (the actual subtitle of Hesse's book) 'Only For Madmen,' with Pablo further informing that there is only one admission price, Haller's mind. Pablo appears completely uncharacteristic this particular evening, leading Hermine and Harry up to a charged round room with a Blue unearthly light containing three chairs, and begins what appears to Harry to be something like a 'ceremony.' This bizarre Pablo, who Harry had barely ever heard speak before, is talking non-stop with eloquence, and then announces at the round table in the Blue room that he has invited Harry and Hermine for an entertainment that Harry has been dreaming about for a long time. Out of the wall from a hidden compartment Pablo takes three glasses and a small bottle, as well as a small special box decorated with oriental Colored inlaid woods. He fills the three glasses from the small bottle and opens the special small box, removing three long Yellow thin cigarettes. The three of them drink from the

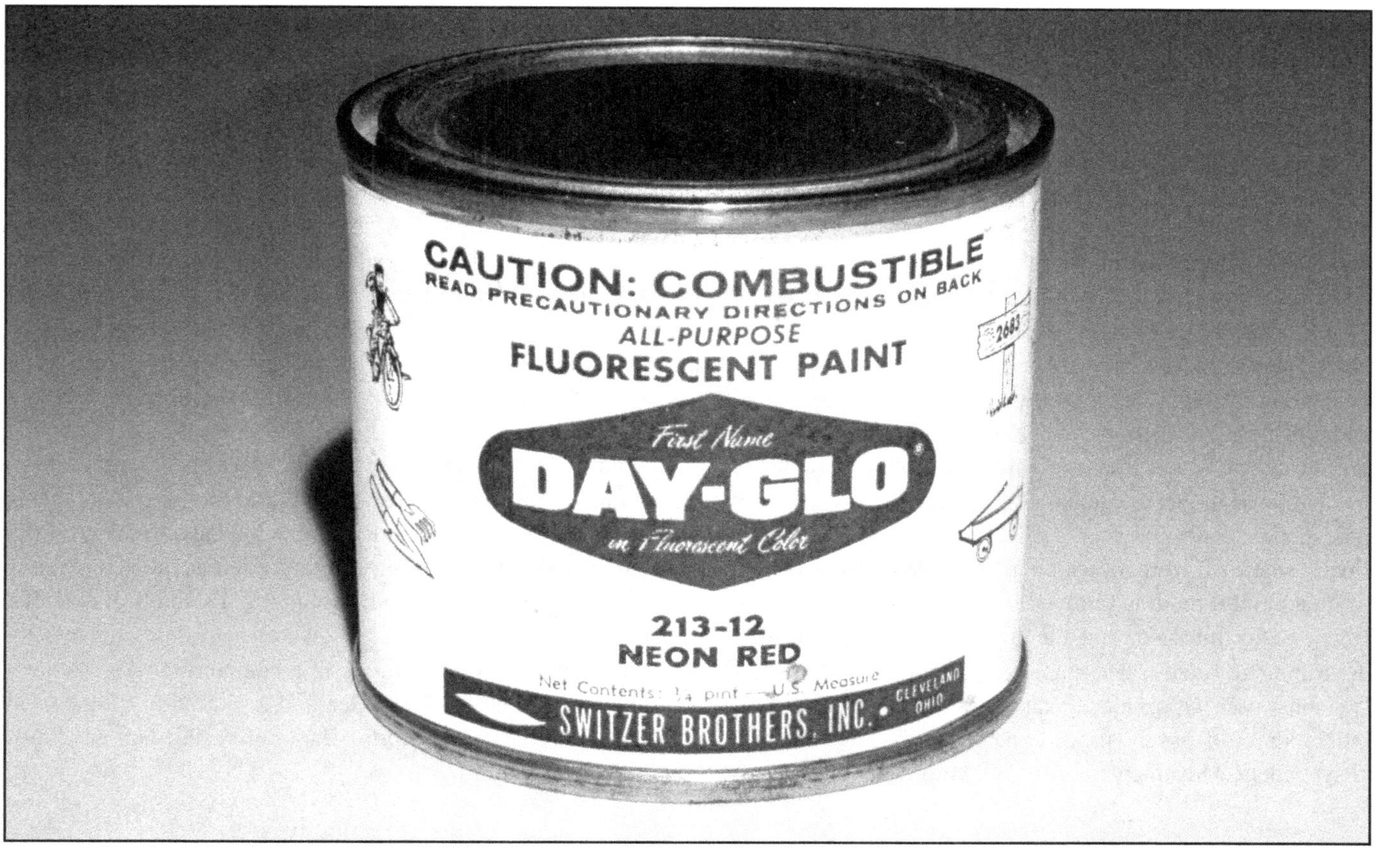

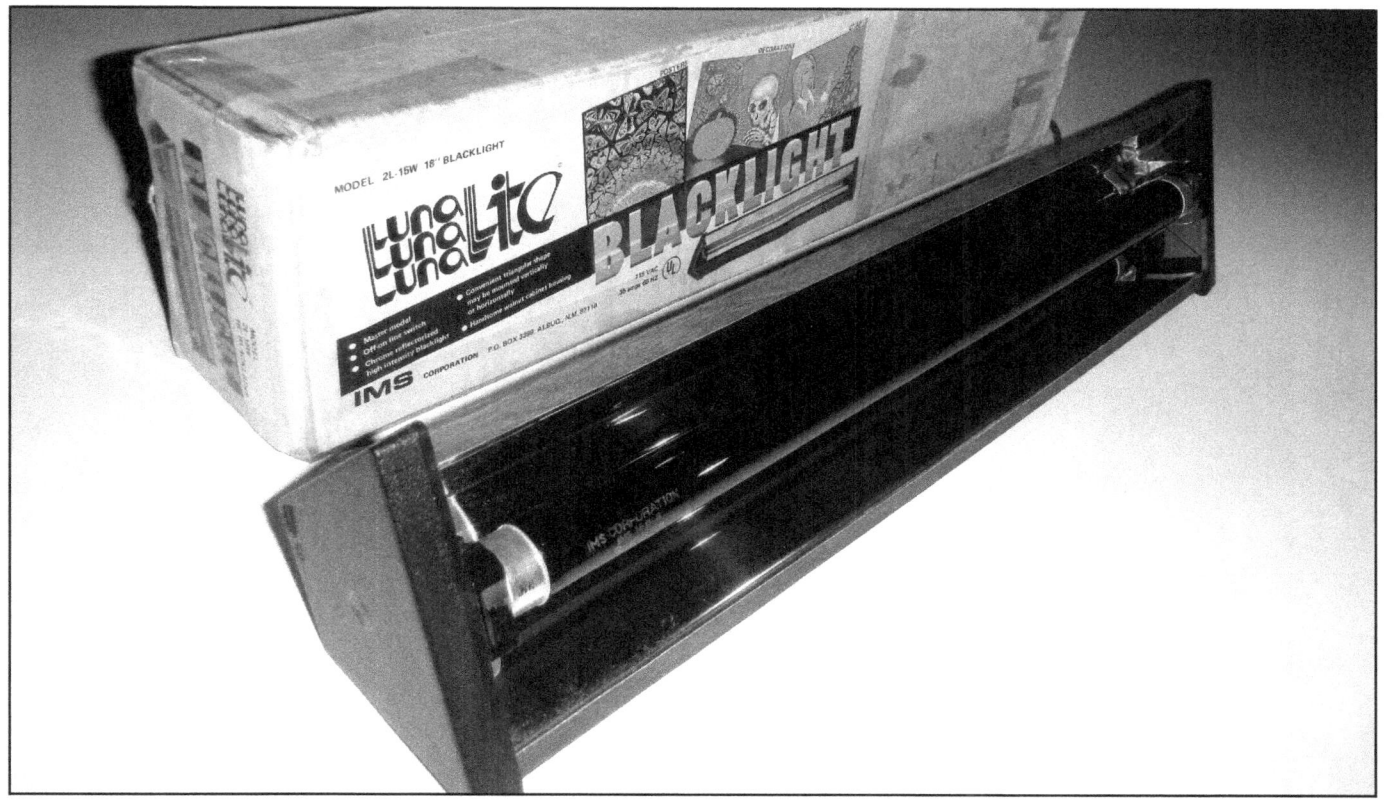

1960s "DAY-GLO - First Name in Fluorescent Color" "Neon Red" Fluorescent oil paint, "Switzer Brothers, Inc.," Cleveland, Ohio

1960s "Luna Lite" "BLACKLIGHT" Poster lamp, with Fluorescent box - "Posters - Decorations - Crafts," New Mexico

small bottle's contents, which Harry considers having a special aroma as well as a taste that is not familiar to him in any way. Then they smoke their three long Yellow thin cigarettes, which also have a strange thick incensed smoke to them. Immediately after this Harry feels the effect of the drink, which is also not like the effect of alcohol that he is 'familiar' with, and makes him feel weightless, as if he was a gas balloon floating free of gravity. As they sit sipping their strange drinks, which Harry considers having a taste that he also never experienced before, and smoking their strange cigarettes, which have thick incensed smoke to them, Harry, not surprisingly, feels that the three of them are becoming progressively more light, and that they are at the same time filled with serenity. Finally Pablo announces to Harry, who he is sitting right next to, in a voice which strangely seemed as if somewhere off in the distance, that he was privileged to be Harry's 'host' on the occasion of that evening, to give Harry an escape from his world's reality into an altered reality which he has always dreamed about, and which transcends time. This timeless altered reality, Pablo explains to Harry, is in actuality his very own soul, and that in fact, all that he can give him is the 'key' to make visible all that he has inside of his own soul. Pablo then leads them into his "Magic Theater" all the while explaining to Harry Haller that to conquer time and reality, it was imperative that the prison of a person's ego must be removed and left in the 'coat-room,' where he will be able to pick it back up after the theater show. Pablo further reveals to Harry that this event, in which they have just partaken a "stimulant" which Pablo clearly announces to them was the 'Steppenwolf's treatise,' was in fact the actual preparation for leaving his ego behind him. Pablo leads Harry into a world of visions by first, as he explains, causing a small 'suicide' inside of him. Pablo holds up a small mirror and shows Harry his face, causing him to finally shake off his ego, which makes Harry feel lighter and finally free, commenting to himself that it felt as much a relief as when a painful tooth is finally pulled out. What is very clear in the passage in which Pablo is discussing the small suicide that Harry Haller must commit for this experience is that this is the death of the ego, referred to since ancient times universally describing spiritual transcendence, which Hesse, in his gracious, unique style, gently disguises in a common term as Haller's "personality." Upon close examination it is obvious that Herman Hesse, Carl Jung, Paul Klee and a multitude of unnamed others knew of psychoactive experiences by the late 1920s and early 1930s, thirty to forty years before the famous 1960s "Psychedelic Movement" began, and before any one of the "Hippies" were even born.

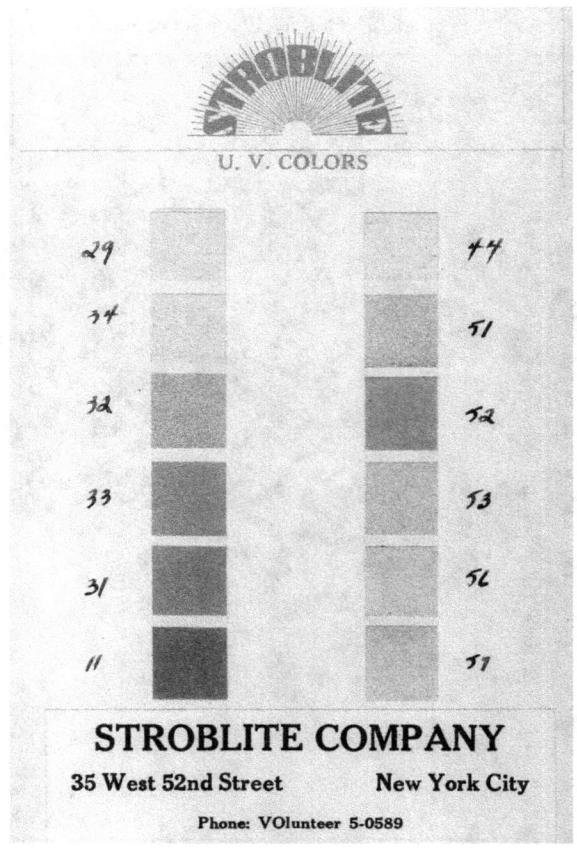

1930s-1940s "STROBLITE COMPANY-First in Fluorescence ... Since 1924," Fluorescent Paint Color sample swatch

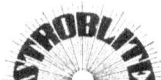

MAGICAL DISPLAY EFFECTS with Fluorescent STROBLITE ULTRA VIOLET COLORS and ULTRA-VIOLET BLACKLIGHT

for all types of ADVERTISING EXHIBITS, DISPLAYS, POSTERS, MURALS, BILLBOARDS, DECORATIONS, SHOP WINDOWS.

INVISIBLE DESIGNS
Your display can change radically with a switch of light. Over an ordinary white background, paint your copy or design with Stroblite "Invisible" UV Paint. This "white-on-white" design will not be noticeable under incandescent white light. By illuminating with Blacklight, the hidden fluorescent message will glowingly appear. Stroblite UV Temperas or Oils can also be tinted with ordinary artist's colors to match a colored background.

SILHOUETTES
Paint the background solidly with one of the "Invisible" UV Colors. Then overpaint your design with an ordinary white paint which, under Blacklight, will appear darkly silhouetted against the glowing background. Trade Marks or slogans can be "brought to light" with this technique.

SHOW WINDOWS
Select windows where surrounding light will not shine directly on to the fluorescent surface. Multiply attention value with mysterious and beautiful glowing settings, transformation of "2-in-1 posters (see illustration).

Our Display Dept. will be glad to make recommendations for your Blacklight ideas.

MERCHANDISE MAGIC
Treat products such as a refrigerator, auto, or machinery with Stroblite UV Colors, featuring its improvements and advantages. When white light is off, Blacklight makes these treated areas glow.

DECORATIONS with Depth and Dimension.
Stroblite is popular for dim interiors of Night Clubs, Lounges, Theatres, Cafes. Artists can create amazing murals, or enhance the simplest existing decorations under Blacklight illumination.

DISCOTHEQUE SCENES
Blacklight is an integral part of the multi-media Psychedelic Light Works, a sure eye-catcher for the interested public. Use Blacklight lamps to accent Mod Fashions, and for fluorescent UV copy in windows and interior displays. Other lighting techniques can be used in conjunction with a Stroblited display, such as projections, reflecting mirror balls, and flashing colored lights.

HOME DECOR
The Fantasy of Fluorescence has come of age in private homes, too, featuring glowing murals, starry UV ceilings, brilliant posters. UV ART works in this exciting fluorescent medium are offered by leading galleries, and can be illuminated with our attractive tubular fixtures. Party themes and table settings can create festive, dramatic moods for a discoteque atmosphere with a flick of a Blacklight switch.

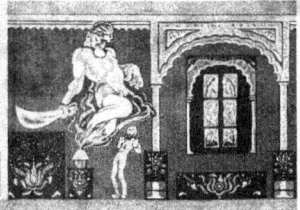

White-light scene . . .   changes under UV Blacklight.

STROBLITE COMPANY, INC.
"First in Fluorescence" . . . Since 1924
75 West 45th Street, New York, N. Y. 10036
Phone: (212) Circle 5-7911

© 1968, Stroblite Co., Inc.

1968 "Stroblite Company, Inc. - First In Fluorescence ... Since 1924" brochure, "Magical Display Effects," New York (inside)

BLACKLIGHT ILLUMINATION
Best Blacklight effects are obtained in relatively dark surroundings and where interfering outside lights can be eliminated or reduced. Use shadow boxes or canopies to create darkness. In displays using both Blacklight and white light, the Blacklight is left on continuously. The incandescent white light is flashed on and off to "wash out" the glowing Blacklight effect.
STROBLITE UV Blacklight Lamps are available in several scientifically designed models to meet individuals requirements.
For shadow boxes and other close range illumination, the STROBLITE Tubular Type UV Lamps are recommended. On bulletins and murals, the lamps are placed along the top or bottom, if over 10 ft. long.
If the Blacklight has to be located at some distance, the STROBLITE High-Intensity UV Lamps should be used. For good UV illumination, place the 100 Watt UV Projector Lamps at 6 to 8 ft. intervals. The wide-angle 250 Watt UV Reflector Lamps can be placed at 10 to 12 ft. intervals.

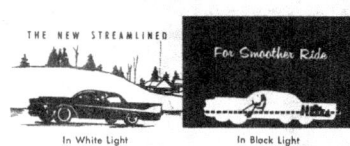

SPECTACULAR DISPLAYS
STARTLING SCENIC CHANGES can be produced by combining Blacklight with white light illumination. In a scenic diorama, for instance, street lamps and windows painted with Stroblite "Invisible" UV Colors would appear as a normal daylight scene under white light. Under Blacklight, these areas will glow as though lighted from within, for a unique change to a night scene. For such effects, the Blacklights are left on continuously, and only the white light is flashed on (to wash out the Blacklight effect) and flashed off (for the glowing night effect). This basic effect has been adapted in many ways by creative displaymen since its introduction by Stroblite Co.

CHRISTMAS & SNOW Scenes are especially effective with "Invisible" Stroblite Fluorescent UV Paints, superimposed over backgrounds of regular white paint. The UV designs and copy will become visible only when the Blacklight activates the fluorescent areas.

STROBLITE UV COLORS
STROBLITE CO. has pioneered in luminescent color effects for over 42 years, and is still the leading innovator and manufacturer of brilliant Blacklight Fluorescent UV Colors and Ultra-Violet Blacklight Lamps.

FLUORESCENT UV COLORS come in many hues that can be mixed for almost any desired shade. They glow brilliantly under the invisible rays of Blacklight Lamps.

INVISIBLE UV COLORS (Vinyl Latex, Oils, Chalks) are white or off-white colors under regular light, and so are not visible when applied to white surfaces. Blacklight transforms them into mysteriously glowing colors. Blank walls or ceilings treated with these "Invisible" UV Colors can reveal exotic designs when Blacklight is switched on.

To match pastel backgrounds of non-fluorescent colors, our "Invisible" UV Oils or Vinyl Latex Paints can be tinted with ordinary artist's colors.

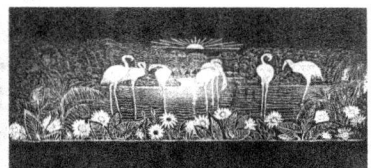

STROBLITE FOR DECOR
"Painting with Light" by means of STROBLITE UV COLORS is a unique medium for creating unusually beautiful color and light effects that successfully arouse curiosity and interest. STROBLITE is an important contribution to the art of display. Spectacular scenic backgrounds in brilliantly glowing colors — Advertising posters that change with light — Merchandise with important features emphasized in glowing "neon" hues — these are just a few of the dramatic effects possible. These glowing effects are being tastefully presented in Night Clubs, Theatres, Hotels, Stores, Exhibitions, Museums, World Fairs, and in the Home.

STROBLITE-"First in Fluorescent UV Color Effects"

How to Put Stroblite UV Colors and Blacklight to Work for You

UNUSUAL

Glow in the dark

DISPLAY EFFECTS

- AROUSES CURIOSITY AND ATTENTION!
- CREATES STARTLING VISUAL IMPACT!
- SPARKS YOUR SALES STORY!
- REGISTERS A LASTING IMPRESSION!
- INCREASES VALUE OF DISPLAY!

STROBLITE CO., Inc.
75 West 45th Street
New York, N. Y. 10036

1968 "Stroblite Company, Inc. - First In Fluorescent UV Color effects ... Since 1924" brochure, New York (outside)

Not even a short discussion of the 1960s Movement, as is presented here for the perspective it provides, is complete without mentioning the person who is considered the father of the Psychedelic Movement, Aldous Huxley. Huxley was a famous visionary who had already published "Brave New World" many years before, and he came across an article about acid by Dr. Humphrey Osmond in the early 1950s. On May 4, 1953 Dr. Humphrey Osmond gave this visionary Aldous Huxley four-tenths of a gram of Mescaline, and solely from this life-changing initial psychoactive experience Aldous Huxley wrote "The Doors of Perception." "Heaven and Hell" was written by Huxley in 1956 after he was given acid by Captain Al Hubbard. "The Doors of Perception" was the first major book ever published discussing, or more correctly "introducing" psychoactive drugs, and it was in 1954, many years before most people ever heard of these substances (and a dozen years before Jim Morrison would be so inspired by this book that he would name his band after it). The last book Aldous Huxley wrote was his masterpiece and which was awarded the Nobel Prize for Literature, "Island," a novel about a remote island society that lives in a higher consciousness due to the use of 'Moksha medicine' from their initiation at puberty, and continuing for the rest of their lives. 'Moksha medicine' in Huxley's "Island" are psychoactive Mushrooms. The difference is portrayed by Huxley between the peace, wisdom, and respect for the world that the "Island" enlightened society certainly had, in direct comparison to the vulgar, brutal, backwards outside world that destroys their Island society for oil in the end.

Aldous Huxley, and countless unnamed others who were spiritually awakened through their experimentations with mind-altering substances, did not just talk about a new life, but literally *Lived* a new life. "This Timeless Moment" is a book by Laura Huxley about November 22, 1963, the day that Aldous Huxley died, which was also the same day that President John F. Kennedy was assassinated. Laura Huxley explains that on that day when Aldous Huxley died he was sick in bed at the end of his battle with cancer and knew that he was at the end of his life. Even though he was so close to death that he couldn't even speak anymore, he communicated to his wife several times during that day he died that he wanted her to give him acid. Again, on his deathbed Aldous Huxley asked several different times at intervals between each other for acid, and through this experience the medical research into easing the pain of dying with the use of psychoactive substances was born. In the 1950s through correspondence between Aldous Huxley and the Canadian Dr. Humphrey Osmond, the very word "Psychedelic" was coined. In a letter Huxley had suggested a name for this new altered experience, "Phanerothyme" (Greek for 'spiritedness'), but Osmond being a scientist thought that Huxley's suggestion sounded too poetic, so in a return letter to Huxley, Osmond suggested the combination of two Greek words: "psycho" meaning "mind," and "delos" meaning "Manifesting" or "Arising." Osmond had changed the spelling from "Psychodelic" to "Psychedelic" to avoid the obvious connotation, and first presented the term in June, 1957 to the New York Society of Sciences.

Hubbard was forty-nine years old at the time of this first acid trip, which in 1951 was a few years before even Aldous Huxley had taken psychedelics. In Canada as well was Dr. Humphrey Osmond, the famous British psychiatrist working with acid and Mescaline in Saskatchewan at the Weyburn Hospital. In 1952 Osmond was the first person to publish his findings on the fact that the Mescaline structure was very similar to the adrenaline molecule, and that schizophrenia could very well be created through the act of the body producing it's own psychoactive compounds. This led to the proposal of Osmond's that all medical personnel working with schizophrenics should be trained with Mescaline to have an innate understanding of the mental condition personally before trying to cure it. Dr. Humphrey Osmond is famous for coining the word "Psychedelic" and giving Aldous Huxley his first psychedelic, Mescaline, in May, 1953, which was historically less than a month after the CIA began Operation "MK-ULTRA." After Huxley's second Mescaline trip in 1955, Captain Al Hubbard became the first person to give Aldous Huxley acid, which inspired Huxley's writing of "Heaven and Hell" after "The Doors of Perception." These two mentally and physically opposite people, Aldous Huxley a famous author from England and Al Hubbard a loud American former spy became close friends and had great respect for each other in the end. Al "Cappy" Hubbard is the first person to see the potential of acid as a medical therapeutic tool, and he gave massive doses of the substance to severe alcoholics for the first time. Hubbard guided these alcoholics with religious symbols and achieved extremely positive results. Many of the former severe alcoholics that Hubbard had treated described the breaking of their addiction to alcohol "miraculous."

Once again, as documented in the book "Acid Dreams," acid was a highly respected substance with unlimited resources in the fields of medicine and psychiatry after it's arrival in America in 1949. Dr. Max Rinkel was the first person in America to work with acid in 1949 in Boston. By 1959 over a 1,000 professional papers had been written on the substance, with over 40,000 patients having been administered the new drug. Positive results were recorded all those decades ago even on the treatment of Autistic children, sexual frigidity, the treatment for easing the fear of dying to patients terminally ill with cancer, as well as treatment with acid to alcoholics. One of the most famous of these 1950s therapists was Dr. Sidney Cohen, author of the book "The Beyond Within: The LSD Story" (1964), who was the psychiatrist who gave acid to Henry and Claire Boothe Luce, owners of "Time-Life Magazine." In a published questionnaire of the late 1950s by Dr. Sidney Cohen, forty-four

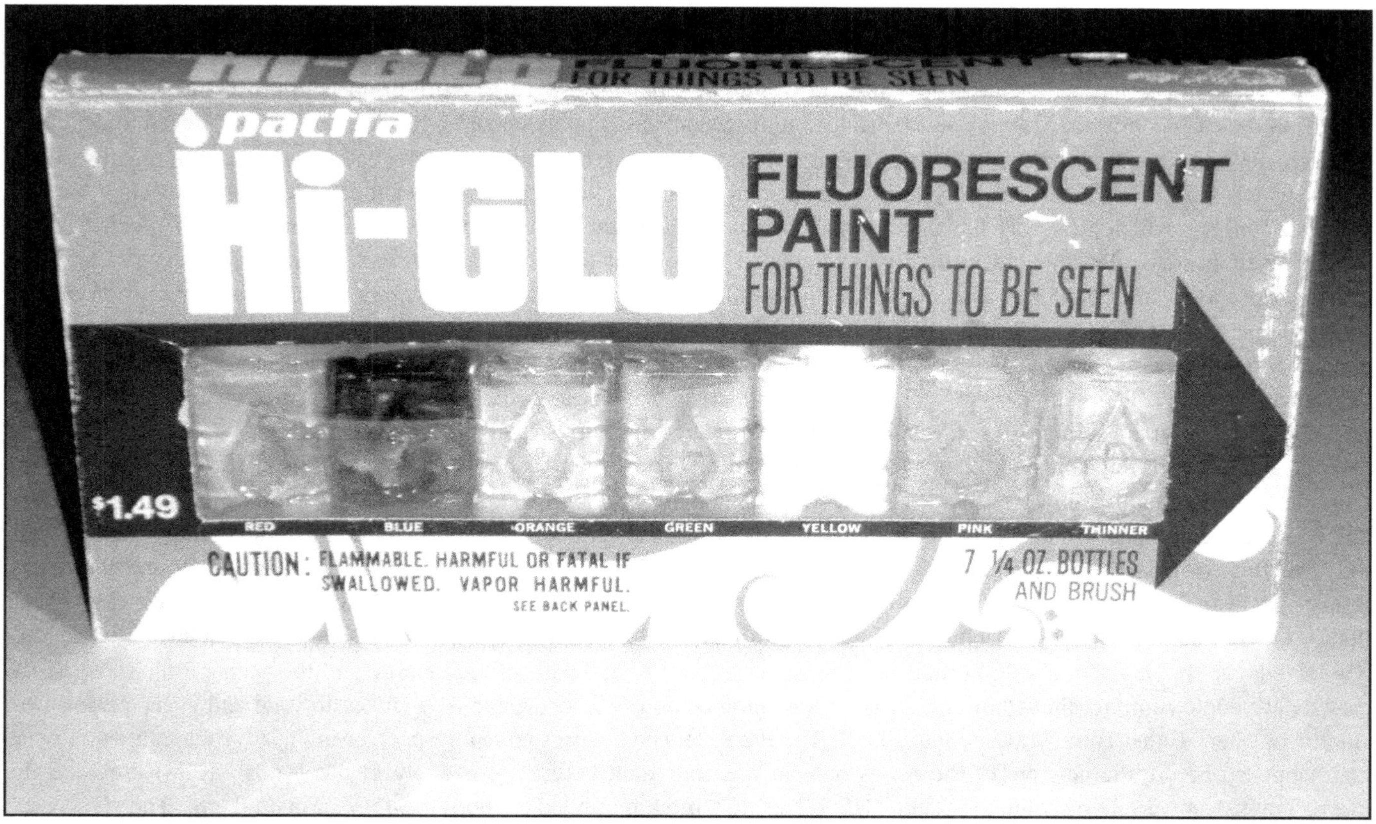

1960s "HI-GLO Fluorescent Paint - For Things To Be Seen," "Pactra Industries, Inc.," Los Angeles

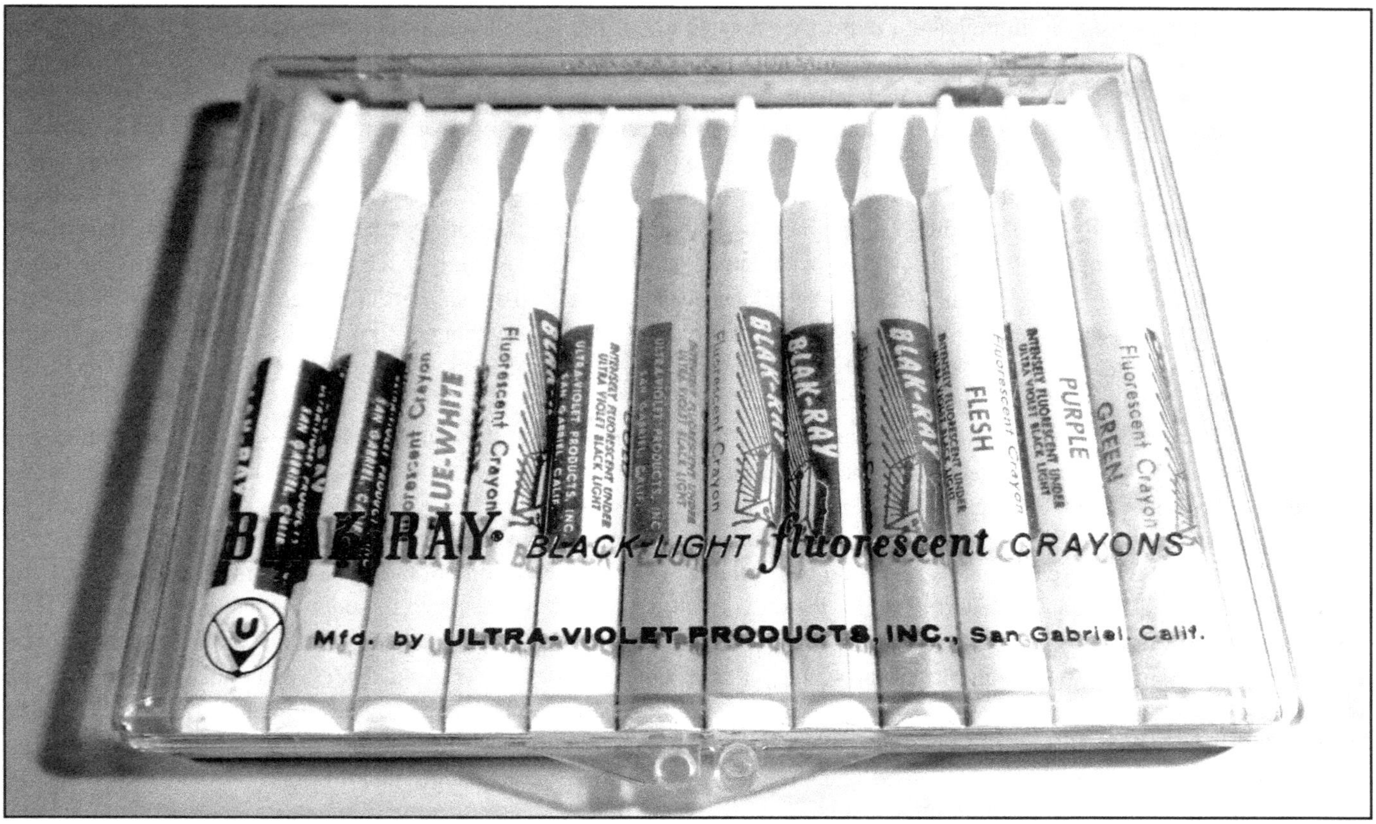

1960s "BLAK-RAY Black Light Fluorescent Crayons," "Ultra-Violet Products, Inc.," San Gabriel, California

doctors replied with data stretching over 5,000 patients who had been given more than 25,000 doses of acid or Mescaline. Why did this miracle drug with so much promise to the world of psychiatry fall from grace? After ten years of positive results on many thousands of tested patients, the drug itself was not the problem, but it had more to do with professional jealousy and greed. In the early 1960s the "American Medical Administration" and the "Food and Drug Administration" began to denounce acid. In 1962 the power of these two American organizations help bring into law in Congress new regulations in regards to new drugs, which left the substance as only an "Experimental drug," not an FDA approved medicine. This new law had it's calculated effect, which first was the that the psychoactive substance that had been used for ten years in medicine with thousands of positive documented results, was stipulated to be used only for research as an "Experimental drug" not for treatment purposes in psychiatry. This all had the effect that the government was instigating, namely the termination of acid research totally. Not only did this effect the United States, but it had universal repercussions, such as the chemical firm that Dr. Albert Hofmann was working for in Switzerland, "Sandoz," also terminating it's manufacturing of acid in April, 1966. Not everybody was as thrilled with these results as the government agencies who initiated them, and a Congressional probe into this question was held in the spring of 1966 with Senator Robert Kennedy as it's leader.

A reason for the inclusion of all these examples of the lifestyles and aspirations of the 1960s Movement was to set the perspective into a totally unique era that was open enough mentally, spiritually, and in actuality, to embrace the strongest Colors that had ever been made - Fluorescent Colors - along with the Black light, which could alter conventional reality literally with only the flick of a switch. The unbelievable characters of the 1960s Movement epitomized by Ken Kesey and the Merry Pranksters, wanted absolutely no part of the established, tested and failed, old-fashioned ways of doing things, looking at things, acting, talking, thinking, alcohol-drinking, conforming, contorting, distorting Past. As an example that will make any one of today's Yuppies split a vein in their neck, at some of the "Acid Tests" of Ken Kesey and the Merry Pranksters, which crowds of people came to, the Admission Price at the entrance door was presented as a choice to each and every person who wanted to enter: Either Burn $1.00, or Pay $5.00! The Pranksters had almost no real respect, or interest for that matter, in what had happened before the new era of the 1960s or who was important before the new era of the 1960s. Ken Kesey and the Merry Pranksters were living in the absolute "NOW," as they often reminded anybody who was around them. The "Day-Glo" Fluorescent Colors and the Black light were the setting of their "Now" stage, which would become known to the world through the Merry Pranksters spreading it to the entire "Psychedelic Movement."

The lines that we pass through and eventually over step in this life bring about the combination of lucidity, perspective, and the boundless unknown. Although the first two properties are essential, the most attractive and important is the infinity of the unknown - the abstract in life - the untested, unquestioned, and unanswered areas of existence - the "Grey area" so to speak. Ken Kesey put it typically in very accessible terms, telling an interviewer that "Answers" are not what we should be looking for, but exactly the opposite: "Questions." Like the 'destination' on the journey of life, the 'answers' are also what we should not cherish as important or significant, but the actual impetus that began the action; such as the "Journey" being much more significant and life-altering then the dubious destination that many times will not be reached - and the formation of the "Question" being more important than the eventual calculated "Answer." We have only taken a few baby steps from the water, still with mud on our feet. The arrogance that can be gained by "Knowing" - the "Answers" - can create obstacles on the path to the attainment of knowledge. In justified company, Kesey was not the only Visionary to place the highest of all values on "Questioning." Another very great thinker left a similar message, stating that the "important thing" was to never "stop questioning." His name was Albert Einstein.

As a lucid example of how important and ingrained in society psychoactive substances were in long past history, the "Eleusian Mysteries" of ancient Greece are one of the most well-documented events of this kind and will here be further examined. The most well researched book on the subject was published in 1978, and again in 2008 for the thirtieth anniversary: "The Road to Eleusis - Unveiling the Secrets of the Mysteries" by R. Gordon Wasson, Dr. Albert Hofmann, and Carl A.P. Ruck. The 2008 Preface of this revealing book from 1978 is for the printing of the thirtieth anniversary edition of this historic volume. The Preface by Robert Forte is already very clear and comes directly to the point, which is that if the United States (and the rest of the world as well) ever changed their attitude and became 'reasonable' about psychoactive substances, than it would be realized that the majority of the scholars that actually founded the Western schools of Philosophy, Democracy, Science, Mathematics, and Theater in ancient Greece were active participants in the well documented historic "Eleusian Mysteries" which have been known to be the first organized mass gatherings of society in which a substance was used as an Entheogen. It is also very well documented that the men who founded these schools of Philosophy, Democracy, Science, Mathematics, and Theater in the world of ancient Greece considered these Eleusian Mysteries the most important event of their lives.

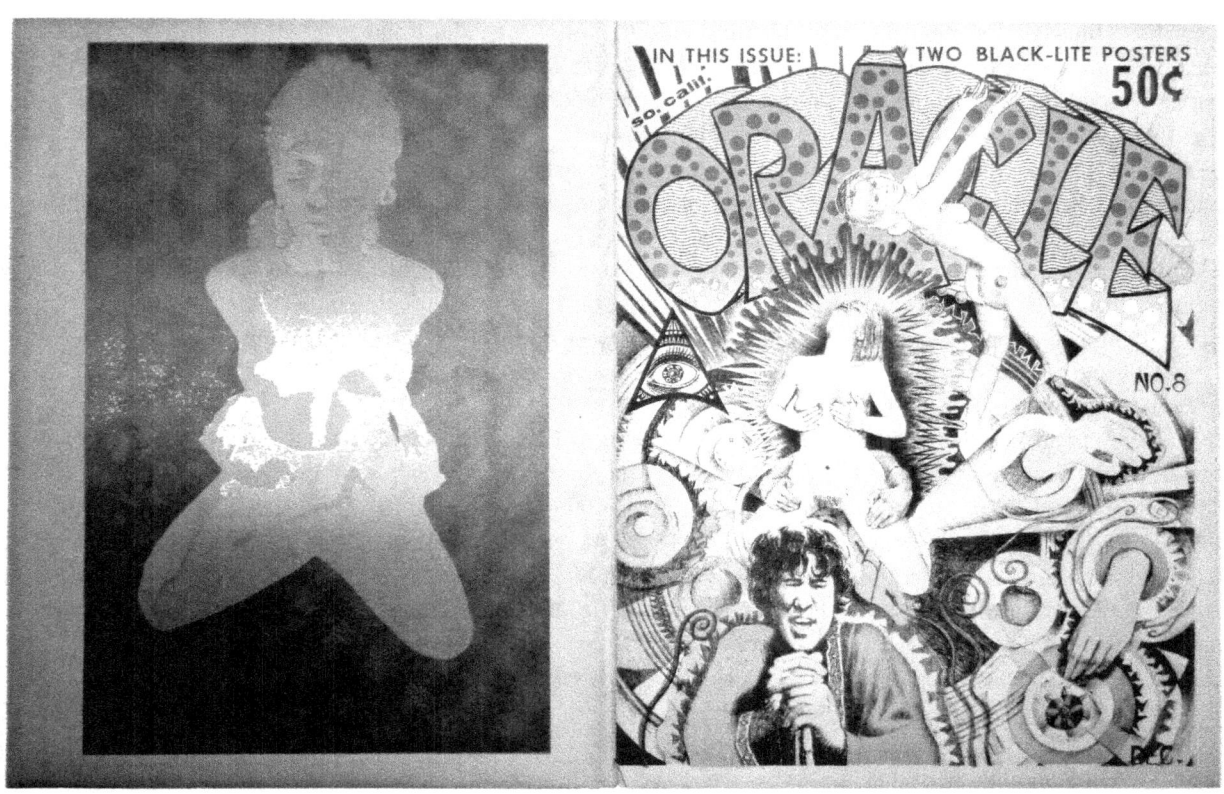

"The Oracle of the City of San Francisco," Fluorescent cover of Black Light Poster Issue, Dec. 6, 1967, vol. 1, nr. 8

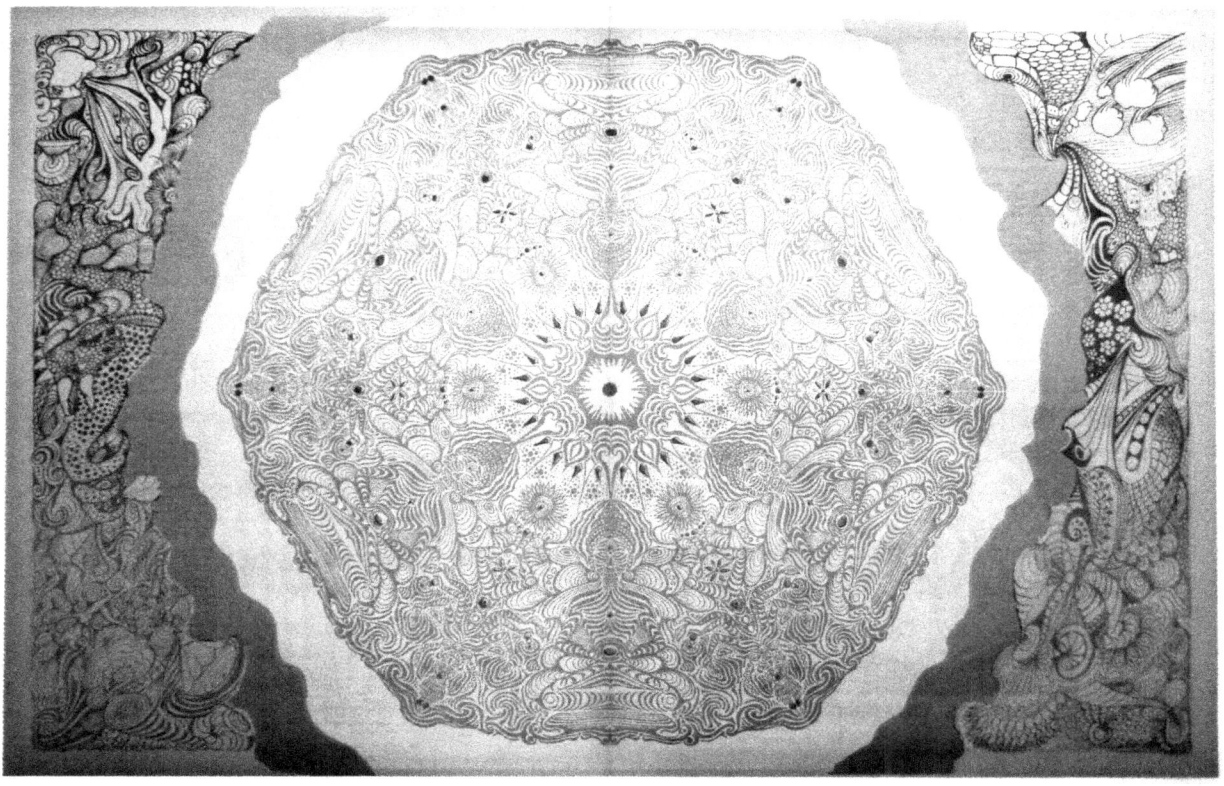

"The Oracle of the City of San Francisco," Fluorescent poster in Black Light Poster Issue, Dec. 6, 1967, vol. 1, nr. 8

In the "Hindsight" section also introducing the 2008 edition of "The Road to Eleusis" Carl A.P. Puck states very clearly that the punishment for revealing the secrets of the Eleusian Mysteries in ancient Greece held every year in September for centuries was death, and nobody was above this supreme law, not even the famous philosopher of the ancient world Socrates. It was well known in ancient Greece that if the secret of the Eleusian Mysteries was told to anyone the punishment would be nothing less than the death penalty, but Socrates went one step further than this and committed the unthinkable crime of using the sacred substance of the Eleusian Mysteries to give 'private parties,' thus condemning himself to the penalty. This is the subject of one of the paintings that Art historians in the 1970s considered the beginning of Modern Art, "The Death of Socrates" by Jacques Louis David, which clearly depicts Socrates on his death bed about to drink the poison that was the punishment for disclosing the secret of the Eleusian Mysteries. This has been presented in the paper 'Plato, the Greeks, and Ethics of the Symposium' in 1998 at the meeting of the "Midwest Political Science Association, Society for Greek Political Thought" in Chicago, and also in the New York State Political Science Association 1998 "Profaning the Mysteries: Recovering the Deep Context Behind the Execution of Socrates."

In the "Forward" to this thirtieth edition of "The Road to Eleusis" R. Gordon Wasson writes that the present day is nearly two thousand years after the last Eleusian Mysteries and four thousand years after the first Eleusian Mysteries. It is a historical fact that the Eleusian Mysteries went on for nearly two thousand years, every year except one, held during the month of September. Every person who spoke Greek could apply for admission to these Eleusian Mysteries, with the sole exception of condemned murderers. Amongst the individuals granted permission were also the most important factors of the Arts and Sciences - the thinkers of ancient Greece. These Eleusian Mysteries were shrouded in nearly total secrecy, except for fragments of documented references to this life-changing yearly event. The most significant of these fragments of 'proof' is contained in part of a play written by Plato, which will be examined after the facts are first presented regarding these Eleusian Mysteries. Many of the carefully screened and selected applicants who were participants of the Eleusian Mysteries, including Sophocles, stated that after they came back from this night of wonderment they were changed forever and would never be the same again.

The two famous authors of this book "The Road to Eleusis" who were scholars of psychoactive substances, Dr. Albert Hofmann, who discovered acid in 1938 in Switzerland, and R. Gordon Wasson, who wrote "Soma: Divine Mushroom of Immortality" in 1968, needed a scholar of ancient Greece to collaborate with, and Carl A.P. Ruck of Boston was chosen because of his work in the 1970s on the obscure subject of Greek Ethnobotany. The first chapter of "The Road to Eleusis" written by R. Gordon Wasson puts the contemporary era into context by stating that the substance which the ancient Greeks changed and developed the world with, in today's jaded world is considered just an illegal drug, but this same substance that is disregarded and actually criminalized in today's society, the ancient Greek Philosophers, Politicians, and Scientists thought was nothing less than a miracle.

Chapter two of "The Road to Eleusis" is written by the man who discovered acid in 1938, Dr. Albert Hofmann, and is an account of a 'Challenging Question producing his Answer.' Dr. Hofmann begins by the beginning: the fungal growth that changed the world many times, most famously by being the key ingredient in the discovery of L.S.D. in 1938: "Ergot." Dr. Hofmann explains that Ergot is the name of the "sclerotium" of a parasitic tiny mushroom "Claviceps purpurea" which grows on Rye, Barley, and Wheat. This tiny mushroom has been the root of "Saint Anthony's Fire" in the Middle Ages, which was "Ergotism" caused by eating bread made with grain that was contaminated with Ergot mushroom parasites. In German folklore, "St. Anthony's Fire" was known as "Mad Grain" or "Drunken Rye," leading to gangrene and death. In 1582 Adam Lonitzer, a German doctor, first used Ergot as a medicine, prescribing it for accelerating childbirth. In 1808 the first scientific paper on Ergot was written by the American doctor John Stearns, and in 1824 one of the most famous doctors in New York, Dr. David Hosack, initiated the accepted use of Ergot only for childbirth hemorrhaging. Since 1918 more than thirty alkaloids have been found in Ergot, the first to find it's way into medicine was isolated by A. Stoll in 1918 as "Ergotamine," and was used for migraine headaches and to treat nervousness. Dr. Albert Hofmann and A. Stoll of the "Sandoz Pharmaceutical Laboratories" in Switzerland developed medicines with Ergot alkaloids that would treat geriatric and circulatory disorders. Then in 1937 Dr. Hofmann began working with another of Ergot's alkaloids "Ergonovine," and in combination with naturally occurring Lysergic acid, he unknowingly discovered the most powerful psychoactive substance ever known, Lysergic acid diethylamide. Dr. Albert Hofmann's discovery and self-experiments with "L.S.D.: My Problem Child" led him to a life-long interest in psychoactive substances, lasting until his passing at 102 years old in 2008. Dr. Hofmann met R. Gordon Wasson, the pioneer Ethnomycologist who began the study of magic mushrooms in the early 1950s during his initiation in Mexico with Maria Sabrina well documented in "Life" magazine in 1957, as well as Roger Heim, head of the "Laboratoire de Cryptogamie" and director of the "Museum National d'Histoire Naturelle" in Paris, who was an associate of Wasson in the field of Mushroom studies. What is a relatively unknown achievement of Dr. Albert Hofmann is the fact that he eventually travelled with R.

Gordon Wasson to Mexico to research the psychoactive mushrooms in the field after isolating, identifying, and naming the hallucinogenic substance in sacred Mexican Mushrooms: "Psilocybin" and "Psilocin." With his colleges at "Sandoz Research Laboratories" in Switzerland, Dr. Albert Hofmann synthesized Psilocybin and Psilocin, an accomplishment that the American government had failed to achieve for years.

The first samples of sacred Mexican Mushrooms that Dr. Hofmann used to identify and synthesize Psilocybin, the hallucinogenic substance of the psychoactive Mushroom, were sent by R. Gordon Wasson, and after his success at isolating the substance that eluded the American government, Wasson helped Dr. Hofmann get a huge amount of another historically famous psychoactive plant of Mexico, "Morning Glory" seeds, known to indigenous people as "Ololiuhqui." The Indians of Mexico and the American southwest had been using these "Morning Glory" seeds, which they revered as "divine," for centuries by the time that Dr. Hofmann isolated and identified the psychoactive substance of the two types of "Morning Glory" seeds that had been used, named "Turbina corymbosa" and the more common "Ipomoea violacea." Dr. Albert Hofmann was very surprised to discover that the psychoactive substance in the two different divine "Morning Glory" seeds was a very similar substance to what he had already isolated and identified many years before in acid, "Lysergic acid amide" and "Lysergic acid hydroxyethylamide," both water-soluble Ergot alkaloids, and both in the same family as acid ("Lysergic acid diethylamide"). These two psychoactive substances of the "Morning Glory" seeds from Mexico are also the two important alkaloids of the acid derivative Ergot that grows on the wild grass "Paspalum distichum." This wild grass species is growing throughout the Mediterranean basin and it is common for this wild grass to be infested with "Claviceps paspali" Ergot.

Examining the Eleusian Mysteries that went on for well over a millennia in ancient Greece, during which a substance was drunk and what followed has been described as nearly indescribable and nothing less than a life-changing event, Dr. Albert Hofmann concludes that with only ancient techniques, as well as with only the equipment available in ancient times, it would have been very easy to produce a psychoactive drink from different kinds of Ergot that were easily found in the ancient Greek world. Although no Rye grew in ancient Greece, Barley and Wheat did grow and the Ergot "Claviceps purpurea" is a parasitic psychoactive Mushroom that grows on both of these cereals. Dr. Hofmann explains in "The Road to Eleusis" that although it is not possible to visit the fields of grain growing in ancient Greece 4,000 years ago, it is not a stretch of the imagination to believe that the Ergot parasite of the Wheat and Barley grains growing on the famous Rarian plain of the ancient Greek city of Eleusis outside of Athens in ancient times is the same parasite growing on these cereals there today. Dr. Hofmann deduced that it would have been a simple process for ancient Greeks to just add water to the Ergot alkaloids and produce a psychoactive drink, or even simpler, to just create a powdered form of dried Ergot growing on the "Paspalum distichum" wild grass of ancient Greece. Dr. Hofmann states more than one time in "The Road to Eleusis" that the Ergot "Paspalum distichum" grows everywhere around the Mediterranean basin.

In the ancient Greek world the mythological gods Demeter, Kore, and Triptolemus were responsible for the growth of Wheat and Barley. Dr. Hofmann also describes another form of Ergot that grows on a wild grass named "Lolium temulentum." This wild grass appears even in the Bible, where it was called "Tares" and this grass is incorrectly often called 'Wild Rye Grass.' The name for this wild grass in French is "Ivraie," and in German is "Taumellolch," which Dr. Hofmann states indicates in both languages an indication of it's folkloric history of Europeans using it for the psychoactive properties the Ergot on this wild grass contained. In French "Ivraie" has been found in documents dating back to 1236 A.D. Dr. Hofmann's laboratory work on this wild grass that grows amongst the grains of ancient Greece proved that "Lolium temulentum" and "Lolium perenne" contain no psychoactive alkaloids, but these wild grasses are famous for being infested with the parasitic Ergot. Dr. Hofmann concludes that the Ergot that grows on both "L. temulentum" and "L. perenne" collected in Switzerland, Germany, and also France contained high amounts of the alkaloids "Ergonovine," "Ergotamine," and "Ergotoxine" which must be unchanged since the times of the Eleusian Mysteries and in Dr. Hofmann's professional opinion, his answer to the question that formed the title of the chapter he wrote on his 'Challenging Question and his Answer' is "*Yes*," it would have been possible to consider the ancient Greeks producing a hallucinogenic drink, famously used in the "Eleusian Mysteries," out of the Ergot growing on one of several choices of grains in ancient Greece: Wheat, Barley, and at least three types of wild grasses.

To supply the details of the actual "Eleusian Mysteries," Carl A.P. Ruck, a scholar on ancient Greek Ethnobotany, explains the process that was involved in taking part in this yearly historic event. A citizen of ancient Greece could pay what was roughly equal to a month's salary to take part in these Eleusian Mysteries and be a part of the secret religious ceremony that took place in the village of Eleusis, a suburb of Athens just fourteen miles (22.5 kilometers) by foot. Even though it was a death penalty to reveal the secrets of the Eleusian Mysteries, to reveal that this ceremony was considered by all to be an experience of a lifetime, and to reveal the details leading up to the ceremony was not a crime. To be an initiate in the Eleusian Mysteries a person would have to live in Athens for half a year to prepare themselves for this ceremony. Thousands of pilgrims who were allowed just a single participation in the Eleusian Mysteries in their lives, would walk from Athens to the village of Eleusis at it's outskirts, on a path known as the "Sacred Road" crossing a bridge still existing today which separated the city of Athens from the suburb of Eleusis. Carl A.P. Ruck writes that every year this "Sacred Road" was a pilgrimage for initiates of the Eleusian Mysteries, which consisted of a large group as varied as scholars, philosophers, mathematicians, prostitutes, and slaves. The only requirement to be an initiate in the Eleusian Mysteries was to be fluent in the Greek language, the costs of a sacrificial pig, a guide, and priests, which would amount to about a month's average wage, as well as the expense for living in Athens for half a year in preparation for the ceremony. When the initiates arrived at the village of Eleusis they danced throughout the night in honor of Greek gods including Dionysus, the god of inebriants. At last the initiates would pass through the gates of the fortified walls of Eleusis and into the Initiation Hall inside the sanctuary called the "Telesterion," which held about 3,000 initiates. All writers on ancient Greece agree that something extraordinary was seen by the initiates in the Initiation Hall "Telesterion" inside the Eleusian sanctuary. It is known throughout history that what the initiates did see was a vision, and that after the initiate had this sacred vision they were known as a different person - as an "Epoptes," which means 'a person who saw.' It is also agreed upon by scholars of ancient Greece that this great Initiation Hall in Eleusis, the "Telesterion," was not built with either the intention or with the physical accommodations to house performances or any kind of theater, and further more there are no records from Eleusis of stage props or actors being used, being paid, or being present in any way. The recorded evidence from 1,500 years of "Eleusian Mysteries" makes it historically clear that there were no theatrical performances, actors, or plays involved in the Eleusian Mysteries, but only pure "Phasmata" which means 'Spiritual apparitions' in Greek. It is believed that the Greek Goddess Persephone would appear in their "Phasmata" of the Eleusian Mysteries, along with her infant son, and it is also firmly believed that these ancient Greeks who were well versed in Drama and had invented theater, could never have been fooled by a simple sober play being performed. The poet of ancient Greece Pindar together with the famous playwright Sophocles would have both never personally testified that the ceremony they were initiates of was overwhelming, if the Eleusian Mysteries had been a mere theatrical performance. Further more, there are historically documented facts also about the physical effects on the initiates of the Eleusian Mysteries which do not come from simply watching a play, such as cold sweats, nausea, fear of heights, terror, and a trembling in the arms and legs. The visions that have been documented through the millennia and a half of Eleusian Mysteries are even stronger evidence that a psychoactive substance was taken by initiates. What was described in the Initiation Hall was a brilliant light, and has been documented by many initiates as a 'vision.' A poet of ancient Greece described this indescribable 'vision' he had at the Eleusian Mysteries as seeing the actual beginning of life and the end of life, and coming to the realization that they are both the same divine occurrence. The poet's short description included his account of the Earth and the sky not being separated anymore, but melting together and becoming a column of light, keeping in mind that these ceremonies were held in an enclosed Initiation Hall. These documented reactions and memories of initiates to the Eleusian Mysteries are very similar if not the same as well documented visions of initiates of psychoactive substances universally since time began and up until the present day. Logic would suggest that these visions could not have been produced or induced by simple stage trickery or a common play, and also the fact that thousands of initiates into the Eleusian Mysteries received this same visionary experience together, on schedule, each year for over 1,500 years in a row, logic would also suggest that a psychoactive substance was involved.

There are two more historical documentations that suggest that the Eleusian Mysteries involved the ingestion by the initiates of a psychoactive substance. First it is well known that a special "potion" was drunk as a ceremony by every initiate described in all historical references as the intended beginning of the Eleusian Mysteries, before their indescribable visions of Heaven and Earth began. Further proof that this extraordinary "potion" that the initiates of the Eleusian Mysteries drank contained a psychoactive substance is given by the arrests of several Athenian high-ranking aristocrats of the classical age of Greece, including a famous General, and none other than Socrates himself, on the grounds that these influential members of the Greek elite had hosted their own private "Eleusian Mysteries" at home with their aristocratic guests. Carl A. P. Ruck continues his scholarly investigation into the source of the "Eleusian Mysteries" in "The Road to Eleusis," and provides examples in ancient Greek history that indicate a psychoactive hallucinogenic "potion" was drunk by initiates, including his rendition of the Homeric hymn to Demeter written in the Seventh century B.C., which is a time period seven hundred years after the Eleusian Mysteries began, as well as in the famous "Odyssey" by Homer in which Helen adds a substance known as a "euphoric," which was called "Nepenthes," to the wine of her husband and the guests he was entertaining. It was a fairly common practice for the Greeks of the ancient world to customize their wine with a variety of "additives," including herbal chemicals, spices, and unguents, all with known psychoactive abilities. These psychoactive additives would clearly have been added to the wine during the documented ceremony of the diluting of the wine with water. This was a custom of the Greek culture that was born from the advice given to mortals by Dionysus, in which the God advises mortals to dilute their wine with water to make it 'calmer.' This ancient Greek tradition of adding water to wine to dilute it must be seen with knowledge of the process of the Greek's wine production, which was not distillation, for this technique was unknown to the ancient Greeks. Carl A.P. Ruck informs the reader that in fact there wasn't even a word in the ancient Greek language for alcohol, and that the simple process the Greeks used to produce wine could have never have made a strong wine that needed to be diluted with water, just a weak wine having a maximum content of about fourteen percent alcohol. So since this common wine of ancient Greece was weak with a maximum of fourteen percent alcohol, why was the custom to add water to wine that was already weak to begin with? Historic records of ancient Greek wine state that it was always produced by diluting it with up to twenty parts water because it was so powerful, and after it's production, this wine was again further diluted with eight parts water to finally be able to drink the wine. It is also documented in ancient Greece that drinking the wine undiluted was very dangerous, because the powerful effect of the wine could cause not only permanent damage to the brain, but even in it's worse case could cause the wine drinker's death. It was well known in ancient Greece that just three small glasses of this wine could make the drinker come close to loosing their minds. Obviously weak wine which started with only fourteen percent alcohol - that was then diluted with twenty parts water - could never have got a person inebriated, let alone drive them to madness by drinking only three small glasses of this heavily diluted weak wine. If you take fourteen percent alcohol wine and then add twenty parts water to it, you get a wine that has just seven-tenths of one percent alcohol content. Then if you would further dilute this wine containing less than one percent alcohol by another eight parts of water, the resulting "wine" would contain not but the fractional eight-hundredths of one percent total alcohol, and would have not been able to get a baby drunk, let alone cause permanent brain damage or even death to an adult. What is relatively interesting here is the fact that "Lysergic acid amide," the psychoactive substance in Ergot growing in the Greek plains of Eleusis, is so powerful that an infinitesimally small amount of seven-hundred and fifty millionths of a gram can cause a psychoactive experience in a person. This means that only a single gram of the psychoactive substance in the Ergot growing on the plains of ancient Greece could have given 133 people a experience. Now it could be reasonably considered to dilute with twenty parts of water to arrive at a "potion" that would still make a person have a very strong experience. It is also a documented fact of ancient Greece that there were different produced wines with different known effects, including a wine with an effect that would cause the drinker to stay awake all night and not be able to fall asleep, another wine that would cause the drinker to easily fall asleep, and a third type of wine that was known to cause it's drinker to have hallucinations. This points to the obvious conclusion that the wines of ancient Greece were similar to most of the produced wines of many cultures of antiquity, which had been commonly produced with alcohol and the addition of different herbal infusions with known mild psychoactive abilities.

In a papyrus fragment a portion of an ancient Greek comedy was discovered that was written by Eupolis in the Fifth century B.C. and was named "Demes." The comedy's time coincides with the well documented Fifth century B.C. arrests and prosecutions for disclosing the secret of the "Eleusian Mysteries" by high ranking members of the Greek aristocracy who held private "Eleusian Mysteries" in their homes with their guests by drinking the sacred "potion" of the "Eleusian Mysteries" called the "Kykeon." This "Kykeon" potion is further revealed as a 'drug' in this Eupolis Greek comedy of the Fifth century B.C., and a sacred drink that specifically contained Barley.

In the examination of the sacred "potion," called the "Kykeon" of the initiates of the Eleusian Mysteries, it is known through the Eleusian traditions that Triptolemus was a different form of the god Dionysus, who taught man to cultivate vines, and that Demeter's son Ploutos was conceived with her mate Lasion, who's name translates as the man 'of drug.' It is further documented that it was the Sacred Barley of Triptolemus that only grew on the Rarian plain outside of Athens next to Eleusis, which was the most important ingredient in the initiate's "potion" at the Eleusian Mysteries, having been known throughout history to have induced indescribable visions. The formula for this "potion" drunk by the initiates of the Eleusian Mysteries is also documented, and it appears in a hymn of Homer. The ingredients were simply Barley, water, and a variety of mint known as "Bleachon." Clearly the "Bleachon" variety of mint was not the psychoactive ingredient in the initiate's potion, "Bleachon" being neither known for psychoactive properties nor respected as a sacred plant. Barley is the only other ingredient in the potion besides water, making Barley infected with Ergot containing well known alkaloids with psychoactive properties, similar to acid discovered by Dr. Albert Hofmann millennia later in 1938, the substance that could have easily been in the initiate's potion that they drank to begin the ceremony of their initiation into the Eleusian Mysteries of ancient Greece.

Carl A.P. Ruck explains the Barley grain that was grown in ancient Greece had come from the primitive wild grass "Lolium tenulentum" called "aira" in Greek, and in English known by the many names 'wild rye,' ivray, darnel, and cockle. This same wild grass was called 'Tares' when referred to in the Bible, and this wild grass, or 'weed' as it was properly known to farmers, is commonly infested with Ergot "Claviceps purpurea" called simply "rust" because of it Reddish Color. Ergot's "sclerotia" fell to the Earth and sprouted minuscule Purple mushrooms, which are the 'fruit' of the fungus Ergot, and which contain the most powerful psychoactive substances ever discovered, including the alkaloids "Ergonovine," Ergotamine," and "Ergotoxine" that were likely the cause of the life-changing visions of the "Eleusian Mysteries," as well as being the same alkaloids in which Dr. Albert Hofmann discovered "Lysergic acid diethylamide", which changed the world once again 2,000 years after the Eleusian Mysteries were over.

In the ceremonial preparation of the sacred "potion" used in the Eleusian Mysteries for over 1,500 years, the priest, called the "Hierophant," who could trace his lineage back to the very first priest of the Eleusian Mysteries, took the "sclerotia" from the Ergot out of a room in the Telesterion that had been constructed in the most auspicious spot, which was directly above the original temple's remains from the Mycenaean era. The Ergot-containing Barley was put into chalices and then onto the heads of priestesses who would dance in the Telesterion. The Barley grain was then mixed together with water and mint into special urns, and finally into special cups for the initiates. The Hierophants would then chant to the Gods telling them that they had drunk the "potion" and that they had used the secret ingredient that had been brought with them on the Sacred Road pilgrimage, and which had been contained in baskets that were sealed. The Hierophants - priests - then sat on bleacher-type stone seats, that were all around the walls of the huge Initiation Hall the "Telesterion" in darkness and waited for their visions to start. With a true psychoactive substance Carl A.P. Ruck points out that not just the sense of sight would be affected, but that typically all the senses are profoundly effected, including hearing, so in his opinion there would have been the accompaniment of both vocal and instrumental music in the hall. For other sensory excitation the Hierophants would have used several different types of perfumes that they would have brought out at different intervals. All of this spiritual preparation performed during the Eleusian Mysteries ceremony would have been brought to a climax when the huge doors to the Telesterion were suddenly opened and light beamed into the Initiation Hall. This would have been the apparition for the initiates of the Goddess Persephone with her infant son returning from hell. The Hierophant would chant and thunderclaps of musical instruments would accompany this climax of the Eleusian Mysteries.

In conclusion the authors of "The Road to Eleusis" compare the "Eleusian Mysteries" to the sacred Magic Mushroom use going on for millennia on the other side of the world from Greece. Magic Mushrooms, Morning Glory seeds, and the Peyote Cactus have been used in religious ceremonies in the Americas for thousands of years before the Eleusian Mysteries began, and for 2,000 years since the Eleusian Mysteries ended. If these "Eleusian Mysteries" went on for more than 1,500 years and were life-changing events to countless thousands of our ancient Greek forefathers, including the founders of Philosophy, Democracy, Science, Mathematics, Medicine, and Theater, who literally changed the world, the obvious question begs for an answer: why doesn't anybody know about such a world-changing substance and a founded 'Movement?' The answers to that question are many, and the answers originate from just as many arenas. The comparison in "The Road to Eleusis" between the Magic Mushroom's ceremonial use in Mexico and the Americas, that began at least a millennia before the compared Eleusian Mysteries in Greece, gives a clue to one answer to the question of why nobody ever heard of the Eleusian Mysteries: Fear. Not only was the well documented persecution for disclosing the secrets of the Eleusian Mysteries the death penalty, but throughout history it is also well documented how outside uninitiated people in general reacted to substances that are psychoactive and "world-changing."

Carl A.P. Ruck concludes that previously only a few scraps of information on the "Eleusian Mysteries" were left to history by a small number of initiates who figured out a way to document the ceremony without breaking the law and being sentenced to death. The bits of information, none the less, left centuries of their discoverers and readers 'enthralled,' enlightened and wishing for further explanations of this world-changing ceremony of ancient Greece. Ruck closes his chapter in "The Road to Eleusis" with praise of the research done by his two co-authors Dr. Albert Hofmann and R. Gordon Wasson, and stating his deep gratitude to both of these pioneers for allowing contemporary explorers of inner-space through psychoactive mind-expanding substances to feel finally again part of a 'brotherhood' or part of an unbroken ancient lineage of free explorers.

One of the few times that the "Eleusian Mysteries" were well documented was in play written by an Ancient Greek writer, who has survived through time as one of he most respected philosophers of all time, Plato. Although it is well known that the death penalty was the severe punishment for revealing the secrets of the "Eleusian Mysteries," Plato wrote a play that did not break his vow of secrecy, by the use of the subjunctive. The play that Plato wrote hinting at the secrets of the "Eleusian Mysteries" is from "The Laws," which were written by Plato just a few years before he died. "Book I" of "The Laws" contains this play by Plato, and it is especially valuable, because this is documented proof of the knowledge of a psychoactive substance in ancient Greece during the time of Plato's life. Just as important, this play was written during the ancient Greek era, not 2,000 years later by an author on the other side of the world that maybe had never even been to Greece in their life.

Plato's writing on a 'substance that is unlike wine' and which could create a psychological effect, instead of just an inebriation, is in the form of a conversation between three men, a Cretan, a Spartan, and an Athenian stranger. The June, 1963 publication with the title "A Touchstone for Courage" of this revealing play written over 2,000 years ago by Plato, states in it's introduction that it has been suggested through history that Plato himself had 'firsthand experience with psychoactives' after his initiation into the "Eleusian Mysteries," which scholars through history have also believed involved the ingestion of a 'psychoactive potion used as the central rite.' This suggestion was also published back in 1959 by Friedlander in "Plato: An Introduction."

Why didn't anybody ever hear about the Magic Mushrooms of Mexico that were taken as sacred "Food of the Gods" since 3,000 B.C. until R. Gordon Wasson went to Mexico in the early 1950s and took part in the first Magic Mushroom ceremony with White people? The reason is all too clear when you know that the Mexican Sorcerer Maria Sabrina, who indulged the secret of the sacred Mexican Mushrooms to R. Gordon Wasson and the White people, had her house burned to the ground by the locals after this event appeared in the May, 1957 issue of "Life" magazine. Why didn't anybody ever hear about the psychoactive Ayahuasca ceremonies that had been going on for countless centuries in Brazil and South America until William Burroughs went to South America and wrote "The Yage Letters" in 1953 with Allen Ginsberg? Why was it also unknown to history that for thousands of years in Mexico and South America the "Morning Glory" seed was used as a sacred religious substance as well because of it's psychoactive properties, until Richard Evans Schutes wrote about the subject in the 1950s? The answer to all of these questions is relatively the same. Fear of the death penalty. Fear of persecution. Fear of releasing sacred knowledge to the vulgar herd. Fear of ridicule and ostracization from this same vulgar herd. Fear of what other people may think or do is the general simple answer, and remains unchanged on the subject up until the present day.

To discuss the 'secrecy' that surrounded the Eleusian Mysteries, we only have to look at the parallel sacred Magic Mushroom cults of Mexico which have existed for thousands of years. The early christian friars wrote of 'secret' Magic Mushrooms taken by Mexicans in the south of the country during the Sixteenth and Seventeenth centuries. But as R. Gordon Wasson and Dr. Albert Hofmann discovered by going to Mexico themselves, the Magic Mushroom was never a 'secret' between the Mexicans, just a 'secret' to outsiders. This stemmed from the Mexican's first encounters with outside foreign christian invaders. The church's "Holy Office of the Inquisition" in the Sixteenth and Seventeen centuries naturally was against the Mexican's Magic Mushroom ingestion and naturally tried to typically eradicate it's use in Mexico through vicious persecution. What did happen was the wise decision of the Mexicans, a decision in many ways similar to the Greeks, to have no further communication with the outside, unknowing, unenlightened vulgar catholics, christian missionaries, Spanish, English, German, or French that were steadily invading their country, on the private subject of psychoactive substances. As Carl A.P. Ruck clearly explains, the secrecy of the Mexican Magic Mushroom cults was not chosen by the native Mexicans, but 'imposed' on the Mexicans by the ignorance and blindness of the invading European christians. This wall of secrecy was finally broken on June 29-30, 1955 when R. Gordon Wasson and Allan Richardson became the first White people to take part in a Mexican Magic Mushroom ceremony with Sorcerer Maria Sabrina, and is the subject of Ruck's conclusion to the 'mystery' that has surrounded the "Eleusian Mysteries" for millennia. The author admits that the laws and persecution of ancient Greece were nothing at all like in Mexico only several hundred years ago, but that the 'secrecy' surrounding the "Eleusian Mysteries" was identical to the 'secrecy' surrounding the Mexican Mushroom cults, being essentially self-imposed, with the intention of preserving the actual ceremonies and also protecting one's self from the public.

The "Eleusian Mysteries" were stopped and the movement was destroyed by the invading early christians finally in the Fourth century A.D., who are famous throughout history since the actual birth of the organized religion christianity itself, for their intentional destruction of natural native cultures around the globe, again, for their own personal gain. Unfortunately, this is something else that is still unchanged in the present day, as well. In the end, the "God-on-thier-Side" christians have destroyed more cultures throughout history than any other unnameable troops did.

The experience that the ancient Greeks had during these celebrated "Mysteries" they held every year is documented by Cicero, one of the most important philosophers and statesmen of the later era of the Roman Empire who lived for a part of his life in Athens. Cicero is quoted on the life-changing event of the "Eleusian Mysteries," writing that although Athens was filled with things that were 'divine,' in his opinion nothing more 'noble' than the "Eleusian Mysteries" had ever been created in Athens. Cicero continues, informing the reader of the changes in the lives of initiates, who, after their experience were transformed into 'gentler' and more 'advanced' people than they were in the 'barbaric' lives they had formerly lived in the woods. The end of Cicero's prophetic statement foreshadows the Twentieth century's "discovery" that psychoactive substances can be used to bring peace to the dying. Cicreo documents that not only did the initiate who experienced the "Eleusian

Mysteries" afterwards live a more 'joyful' life, but they also went on to finish their lives and to eventually die with 'better hope.'

Finally, to sum up what the "Eleusian Mysteries" meant to the ancient Greeks themselves involving the life-altering "Kykeon" initiate's ceremonial drink, Aelius Aristides stated his feeling on the experience, writing that the "Eleusian Mysteries" were both the most 'awesome' and the most 'Luminous' of all the divine experiences that were available to a person in this life. Before he died, Dr. Albert Hofmann confided in Carl A. P. Ruck, clearly claiming that the only event which could possibly "help mankind" survive the 'threatening Sociological and natural catastrophes' as well as bring about 'a new era of happiness' was a "new Eleusis."

What would be both inconceivable and unacceptable to the average egocentric Twenty-first century member of the human race, is that they are in reality only an empty shell - a reduced fraction of their wise, spiritual, humble forefathers who lived for countless centuries. Any one of the citizens of ancient Greece 2,500 years ago who took part in the Eleusian Mysteries - even the prostitutes and slaves - would make the average rich, obese, bespectacled pig of a Twenty-first century human fittingly look pitifully reduced. The arrogance of this "New Society" of this Twenty-first century, along with their egos, has invented a fictitious image of themselves as superior members of their species, so superior in fact that they embody and represent a literal culmination of all the knowledge and advancement of the Human race. It is universally accepted in the modern world that almost all of humanity before the 1990's "Computer Age" began were nothing more than ignorant ape-like unevolved idiots who would be in awe of the highly evolved advanced intelligence of human beings today. If only this was even fractionally true.

In addition to the world-changing abilities of the parasitic Ergot which are famous from the Eleusian Mysteries of ancient Greece to the discovery of acid by Dr. Albert Hofmann in 1938, a new mushroom which looks like Ergot, being an organic string-like structure, is also similar to Ergot through it's life cycle. "Cordyceps" is this recently 'discovered' Mushroom, which is also a parasite living in insects, infecting them, and finally destroying the insect from the inside out. Cordyceps only grows at about 5,000 meters (over 15,000 feet) in the Nepalese Himalaya and these tiny mushrooms are sold for as much as twenty dollars each. This newly 'discovered' Cordyceps is used as a health elixir for the rich and famous, as well as being a rare strong aphrodisiac and energizer. Since the turn of the Twenty-first century this tiny rare Mushroom has been hailed as something like a "miracle drug" and is included in vitamins taken by every Olympic athlete. Currently the opinion of this new "miracle drug" is to such a high level that Cordyceps has been compared to Penicillin, and also dubbed 'the most important drug of the Twenty-first century.' Researchers believe that the cures for cancer and AIDS may be contained in this Cordyceps Mushroom.

Perhaps the most important conclusion documented in the final book by Wasson, "Persephone's Quest - Entheogens and the Origins of Religion" is the correspondence between himself and Dr. Albert Hofmann. While staying at Wasson's house in July, 1975, Dr. Albert Hofmann was asked by Wasson if he thought that "early man" in ancient Greece could have created an Entheogen from Ergot that would have been "comparable" to Magic Mushrooms or acid. Dr. Hofmann took two years to reply to this question, and in 1977 Dr. Albert Hofmann wrote back to Wasson that "Yes" early man in ancient Greece could have easily produced an Entheogenic potion from the water-soluble Ergot, or "rust," of Barley or Wheat grown on the "Rarian plain" next to Eleusis, or even from the common grass "Paspalum distichum" growing wildly throughout the Mediterranean.

In "Plants of the Gods - Their sacred, Healing and Hallucinogenic Powers" Dr. Albert Hofmann and Richard Schultes discuss the beginning of the modern era of psychoactive plant use, beginning with the first psychoactive to be produced from a plant into a pure substance being Morphine, in 1806, by the pharmacist Friedrich Serturner. This was the first discovery of an "Alkaloid," which Serturner named after the Greek god of sleep, "Morpheus." The authors inform the reader that out of approximately half a million species of plant life on Earth, we have only discovered a small amount of these plants to be hallucinogenic, a mere one-hundred and fifty. The world map is presented by Hofmann and Schultes, with indications of the use of psychoactive plants throughout history, and the parts of the globe with the highest concentration of psychoactive use are India and the Americas. Once again, in this book as well, it is clearly stated by the authors that the ancient God-drug of the Rig Vedas of India, "Soma" has 'been identified' as the psychoactive "Amanita muscaria" Mushroom, which is also most likely the first hallucinogen ever discovered by humans. As with "Soma" the use of these psychoactive substances in ancient cultures of the world died out as hunter-gatherer societies settled down and began farming and agriculture, leaving the hallucinogenic plants only to the use of 'witches' and Shamans throughout more recent history. The importance of psychoactive substances in India has been documented throughout history, most well known being the "Soma" god of the ancient Rig Veda, but to describe the deep history of psychoactive plants in the Indian Hinduist religion, a statue is explained at the beginning of this book "Plants of the Gods" which is the very same statue that Aldous Huxley intricately described in his masterpiece "Island:" the

"Shiva Nataraja" or 'Dancing Shiva' which represents the "Cosmic Dance" of Shiva. In Hinduism this "Shiva Nataraja" is called the "Tandava" and is seen as two separate Cosmic Dances in itself, the "Rudra Tandava" is the aspect of Shiva which signifies the Destruction, and the "Ananda Tandava" is the Creation aspect of Shiva. This is a representation of the continuous and simultaneous Creation and Destruction of the Universe that, as Huxley wisely states in "Island," is a symbol which is unmatched in our western culture. "Shiva Nataraja" represents the entire "Dance of Life" - and death - the creation and the destruction of life, the universe, and nature itself. Each gesture of the "Shiva Nataraja" specifically represents the different aspects of life and death that we can experience as human beings. Shiva dances within a ring of fire, which represents all of nature, and is standing on a subhuman malignant little monster named "Muyalaka," who is the embodiment of "Ignorance," and who is having his back broken by Shiva's left foot. Shiva's right foot is raised into the air and one of his four hands is pointing directly to this raised foot, thus showing us that we are cosmic creatures not at all tied to the Earth, but flying freely through the universe. Hinduists refer to this gesture as "Gajahasta." In one of Shiva's right hands he also holds the "Damroe," a little drum in which Shiva calls all of nature into existence: the "Creation." In one of Shiva's

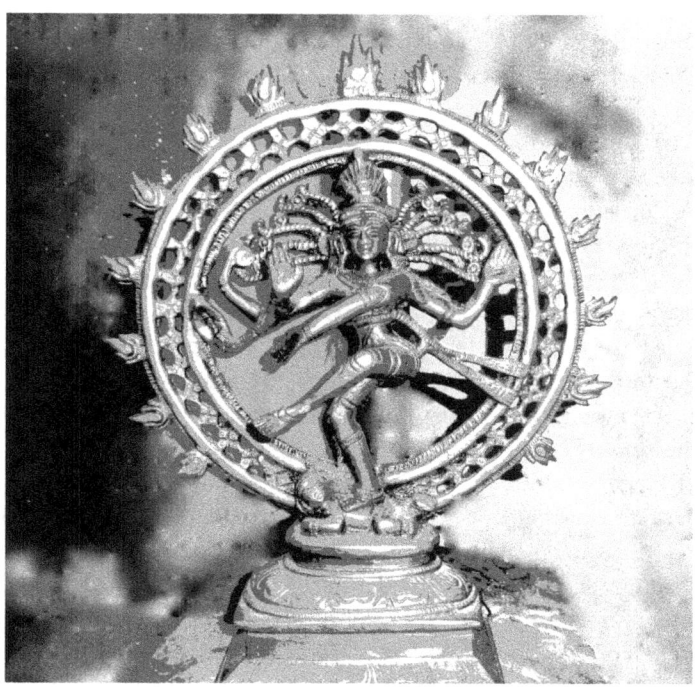

left hands is the opposite symbol, a flame, which symbolizes "Illusion" and represents the "Destruction." The forth hand of Shiva is raised towards us in a gesture that indicates to us mortals that even though the destruction and creation of the universe, life, and all matter is a constant, simultaneous, eternal event, it is "All right." It is all right: life, death, creation, and destruction, because they are all interrelated necessary stages of existence. This is referred to in Hinduism as the "Abhayamudra." Recently physicists are questioning the "Big Bang" theory in favor of a theory which describes the endless cycle of creation and destruction that brought the universe into being, and will in turn destroy it and bring another universe into being, not just one event that 'started' everything, which is what the "Big Bang" theory states. Shiva's hair is bound by Cobras holding a skull, which represents the destruction of life naturally, and finally, interwoven into all of his flying jettas of hair, there are many Datura flowers. The opened mind and expanded consciousness brought about by the psychoactive experience induced through the Datura plant, is here plainly and simply rendered in the "Shiva Nataraja" - the "Cosmic Dance of Shiva."

Today is forty-seven years that Aldous Huxley left his body on acid, which he had asked his wife to give him two times that last day of his life, which was also the same day that President John F. Kennedy was assassinated. In "This Timeless Moment - A Personal View of Aldous Huxley" written by Laura Huxley in 1968, the author states very clearly that along with many other scientists of the era, Aldous Huxley believed that the discovery of psychoactive substances was one of the most important discoveries of the Twentieth century, along with atomic fusion and the study of genetics. To Aldous Huxley acid, Mescaline, and Psilocybin, from Ergot, the Cactus, and the Mushroom respectively, brought to the species the chance to peek into the infinity of the universe - a chance to personally experience mysticism and magic itself - a chance for a person to experience what Aldous Huxley often referred to as "Gratuitous Grace."

Laura Huxley wrote that Aldous Huxley died on November 23, 1963 on acid 'as he lived,' in total awareness. She wrote in her book that Huxley died on acid the way he lived, in an expanded consciousness, and that the doctrines and life he wrote about in his masterpiece "Island," along with it's introduction to society of the concept of dying with the comfort of a psychoactive experience, was the actual way that Huxley himself chose to die, in total conscious awareness. In her book Laura Huxley admits that a few days after Aldous died she realized what a trauma it had been to Aldous that 1963's society had not taken the advice to live a completely new life as in "Island," but regarded this masterpiece and 'Guide book' of Huxley's to be nothing more than "science fiction." The very reason for Laura Huxley to write her book is stated by the author as the communication with the public of the actual way that Aldous chose to die - exactly as he wrote and exactly as he communicated to others - in full conscious awareness, exactly as he described in his 'Manual' for a new life: "Island."

Aldous Huxley was a Visionary in every sense of the word. He tried to give people a new manual for living a new life, but he was so far ahead of his time that it is doubtful who he was talking to will ever catch up with his mental capacity, or ever understand what he was talking about. To give an idea of the reaches of Aldous Huxley's inspiration, there is a little book in the form of an essay that Huxley published the last year of his life named "Literature and Science" (1963). In a unique writing style that is comprehensive, abstract, and totally riveting, Huxley puts forth his philosophy in a paragraph-long sentence, informing the reader that a true Artist seeks to make the incomprehensible comprehensible, and to further conceptualize the unconceptual. The life of an Artist is written about during the last part of Huxley's life and he specifies that the true Artist creates pieces of Art that manifest meaning out of the random chaos of existence. The true literary Artist has the task of communicating through language the thoughts and subtle workings of the mind and emotions that are all but impossible to express in words, according to Huxley's "Literature and Science." Aldous Huxley continues with the task of a literary Artist, stating that they should not center themselves on the physical realities of life, giving the example of the "Stamens" and botanical parts of a flower, but he advises that after the literary Artist 'cleans' the "Doors of Perception," that the enlightened being then sees not "Stamens" in a flower, but it's true divine identity, "Heaven." Huxley comments on the astounding bipolar abilities of human beings, with their capacity for creating and existing in an enlightened life - or - in a life of 'squalor' - for possessing the ability to refine the senses and our lives to a higher plane - or to live a truly 'vulgar' life. This thoroughly bipolar human life form is actually capable, in Huxley's clear view, to an almost infinite intellect - or to an almost fathomless idiocy. Albert Einstein shared the same viewpoint, and believed that 'Two things were Infinite,' listing "the Universe" and also "Human Stupidity." The subject of this late essay by Huxley is the seemingly unbridgeable worlds of 'Poetry' and 'Science' - the mystic unexplainable subtle shadow dances of our consciousness, and the literal, dissected, catalogued and existential world of scientific research. Huxley calls for not only a new way of approaching our thoughts of the world around us, but also for a completely new way of expressing this new approach to the world through the writing of a completely new style which combine both "Nature" and "Literature." To make mystic again the demystified. Huxley concedes that, in the end, it is literally 'impossible' for the language of literature, the language of science, or even the imagined language of an advanced convergence of literature and science, to be able to not explain, but merely express the truly infinite depth of nature or of our infinite experience of living. Huxley tried more than once during his visionary life to wake people up. He gave numerous new 'manuals' to live new lives - literally 'Brave New Worlds' - he warned of our detrimental treatment of nature and the world we live in over half a century ago, and he even went so far to do his best to prepare people for what will come in the future - what can be realized and considered literally as "today." As an example this essay in the last year of his life was desperately trying to console a meeting ground between the infinite subtle world of Art and Mysticism, with the finite demystification of dissecting science.

In 1937 Aldous Huxley moved from his native England to the United States and settled in Los Angeles. In Hollywood Huxley began to study Vedantic Hinduism at a newly developed Ashram supervised by Swami Prabhavananda, who had been sent to the west to introduce Eastern philosophy and religion. The Indian Swami Prabhavananda would speak for many hours to Huxley as a council, and just a short time later this Swami would also council the famous Alan Watts, who wrote another of the early 'Psychedelic guides' "The Joyous Cosmology." Living in this Hollywood Ashram of Swami Prabhavananda that was built to represent the Taj Mahal, Huxley invited a friend to stay in the Ashram, Dr. Humphrey Osmond who would become the most influential person in Canada during the Psychedelic Movement. Later during the 1950s through correspondence with Aldous Huxley, Dr. Humphrey Osmond would coin the term "Psychedelic." In 1952 Dr. Humphrey Osmond and John Smythies published a six page article on Mescaline that was seen by Aldous Huxley in the "Journal of Mind Science." It was during this visit to the Ashram in Hollywood the next year, in 1953 that Osmond had talked to Huxley about Mescaline, which was done only two days before his visit with Huxley was to end. This was the main interest of Huxley's, and probably a portion of the reason he invited Dr. Humphrey Osmond to the Ashram in the first place. Huxley had prepared for his first psychedelic experience by borrowing a tape recorder to document the trip. The next day - the day before Dr. Osmond was supposed to leave - he dissolved a large dose of Mescaline - four-tenths of a gram - into a glass of water. It was May 4, 1953 and has been documented as a beautiful sunny Los Angeles morning, but Osmond was much more nervous and filled with anticipation over what he had just done: given one of the most famous authors of his day a psychoactive uncontrollable substance that had the potential for either an extraordinary or disastrous experience. Osmond had been quoted many times as being in fear at that moment of becoming infamous as the person who drove Aldous Huxley to madness. But he worried for no reason, because taking Mescaline is what Aldous Huxley had been dreaming about for some time already. A portion of the letter that Huxley sent to Osmond inviting him to stay with himself and Maria at the Hollywood Ashram was partially published in an article by Jay Stevens in January, 1988, which proves that Huxley was very eager to experience the magic of a psychedelic substance and had envisioned this experience to allow him to glimpse the "heroic perception" of William Blake. Huxley's letter to Osmond inviting him to stay at the Ashram clearly depicts Huxley's state of mind in 1953 America, of which he openly criticizes the entire system of education that he believes causes the destruction of the awareness and openness of the student, reducing their inventory of mentality to what Huxley refers to as the "Sears-Roebuck" Catalogue. He was dreaming about changing the world dramatically, as well as people's lives on this world, during the early 1950s - only a mere eight years after the Second world war had ended- during a period when alot of the world-changing "Hippies" were either little children, or even just being born. Some visionaries are so far ahead of their own personal time on this planet that even half a century or more after their visionary proposals, their ideas seem hard to imagine - or even closer to the truth - virtually impossible to imagine. In the early 1950s Huxley was already imagining giving Mescaline to students of higher education to crystallize their newly acquired knowledge, and exactly ten years later, preceding his death in 1963, Huxley had published his "manual" for living a completely new and different life, which would allow all members of society to develop with awareness, compassion, and divine wonderment - all in his last book for which he was awarded the Nobel prize for in literature, "Island."

All was very clearly revealed to Aldous Huxley on that morning of his psychedelic initiation when he was given almost half a gram of Mescaline. He had proof in this initial Mescaline experience of what he had always personally believed - the fact that we have a huge source of sensory information input into the brain constantly, but that the individual learns to reduce this immense flow of information down to a minuscule drip-drip-drip of information only, for reasons mostly of survival - Huxley finally had incontestable proof of this fact. This first experience on Mescaline was understandingly life-changing for Aldous Huxley, who wrote to his editor in New York that he was preparing a manuscript of this experience, which he called the 'most significant and extraordinary' experience a person could possibly have. This manuscript would be named after a quote from William Blake, which states that 'if we cleanse the doors of perception, then everything would appear as infinite to us - the way it really is.' "The Doors of Perception" was written by Aldous Huxley as a personal account of his first psychedelic experience on that May 4, 1953, and would become a literary classic, recognized universally as a piece of work that planted the literal seeds of a world-changing revolution. This slim volume that took Huxley but four weeks to complete is this visionary's statement proving the proposals of other wise scholars, such as the English philosopher named Broad and his associate Bergson who had been absolutely correct when they wrote that the brain's modern function was to be an actual "Reduction Valve," reducing all of the infinite sensory input down to a very small palatable amount which has been proven through monkey evolution to be "practical," and just what is necessary to survive.

Then Aldous Huxley - the already famous English author who had written the very popular "Brave New World" years before - published "The Doors of Perception" in the spring of 1954. The social climate for such a book is almost impossible to imagine today, for the average post-World war two veteran who fought the Nazis against world domination less than ten years before - to the 'other world' of Aldous Huxley's drug-induced "Doors of Perception." Jay Steven's Aldous Huxley article of January, 1988 gives a typical example of a horrified early 1950s book reviewer who had just read Huxley's account of his Mescaline trip, being a Marvin Barrett who wrote for "The Reporter." Barrett's typical review of Huxley's book, which was the first popular book on the subject of a psychoactive experience, was that if anyone besides the eminent English author Aldous Huxley would have suggested to all people, especially intellectuals, to take the hallucinatory drug Mescaline the author would have been called a "crackpot." This reporter Barrett searched for early experimenters with Mescaline to compare with Huxley's unprecedented proposals and of course found some technicians who had easily managed to provide the dramatically different result of schizophrenia compared to this author Aldous Huxley's initial wonderful Mescaline experience. What also must be put into perspective here is that only about twenty-five years before Huxley's "The Doors of Perception" were the very first books on the Mescaline experience ever published. Jay Stevens makes the correct vivid analogy between the negative critical response to Huxley's "The Doors of Perception" and the way that the "British Medical Journal" condemned Havelock Ellis' unbounded enthusiasm to also 'spread the news' about this newly discovered 'miracle' named Peyote. Huxley rightfully defended himself, stating that it was sociologically acceptable for writers like Chesterton and Belloc to document accepted alcohol, which Huxley correctly pointed out as killing thousands of people each year in drunk car crashes and other acts of social violence, but when another substance is suggested that will allow a person to make available the possibility of transcending existentialism, Huxley just as rightfully complained that this person is treated as a mere drug addict.

In 1960 Aldous Huxley was diagnosed with throat cancer and he told no one except his closest friend Humphrey Osmond. Realizing he wasn't going to live many more years and that he had one last chance to help the human race, he worked even faster to complete his "manual" for a new life which he entitled "Island." The reader of "Island" sees this Utopian society as the reader should, as a foreigner. The 'narrator' of "Island" is a common westerner who gets shipwrecked and floats onto Pala's shore. This last novel of Aldous Huxley concludes and includes all the wondering and philosophy of this Twentieth century visionary's life. Huxley's views on Art and Music, Religion and death are all weaved into a society in which psychoactive Mushrooms are taken by all children as they are initiated into adulthood. Huxley spoke to his own son about the challenge he faced of writing a 'manual' to give as advice on changing people's lives without his book loosing it's captivating force as a novel. "Moksha" medicine was what these psychoactive Mushrooms in "Island" were named by Huxley, the Hindi word which means the 'liberation' from the repeated cycle of death and reincarnation in this existence. This "Moksha medicine" was the most important underlying theme of Huxley's message to his readers - to cleanse "The Doors of Perception" by clearing the mind and reducing it's ego through the ingestion of psychoactive substances. Huxley's "Island" has a similarity to one of the most important movies of the beginning of the Twenty-first century, "Avatar" by James Cameron. By the final cut of the movie there is a loose similarity to "Island" that is not as apparent as the extended DVD of the movie, including scenes that were edited out of the final release of December, 2009. November, 2010 saw this "Collector's Edition" of "Avatar" released and sure enough in this extended version there is a totally removed scene of the movie in which a psychoactive 'worm' is given to Jake Scully's Avatar body as part of an initiation ceremony which he is a member of, and will then enter into manhood and become a member of the society. The scene is done with the same clearness and intensity as the rest of Cameron's movie, so it is no great wonder why it was edited out of the final release to movie theaters around the world. On "Pandora" the humans try to destroy the indigenous being's lives for the substance under their feet: "Unobtanium," and in "Island" the humans destroy the lives of Pala's inhabitants for miserable Oil - both substances not only useless to the indigenous peoples, but even unknown to them.

As an example of Aldous Huxley's message in "Island," the subject of the "Moksha medicine" is being discussed in the book, and the fact is realized that the "timeless bliss" of the experience will pass, and the question is raised asking what a person will "do" with this experience and all similar experiences that they will receive on "Moksha medicine?" Will the divine experience that the "Moksha medicine" has brought be enjoyed only as mere entertainment, like a "puppet show" and then will you return to a normal unchanged life acting like these "silly delinquents" that people imagine themselves as? Or after having "glimpsed" infinity will a person change and become what they were really meant to be? The conclusion is that the only thing that the "Moksha medicine" can do is to show you a series of "Glimpses" of enlightening and liberating "Grace." The decision is up to the individual whether or not to change their lives after becoming aware of the opportunity.

The importance of Aldous Huxley's "Island" can be measured in the achievement of winning the Nobel prize for Literature. No other critical acclaim is necessary, but the book and it's author received this as well. It is known that Huxley himself was very disappointed that most of the public read "Island" as a typical novel and typically translated it's infinite knowledge into something like a science-fiction book, not a "manual" to give directions on how to live a complete life which fuses physical action with deep meditative contemplation seamlessly. Similar to all profound messages of visionaries throughout time, Huxley's message is no closer to being understood than it was half a century ago when it was first published. One of the few literary reviews that came close to grasping Huxley's final message was the "New York Times Book Review," which wrote that the 'reaction' of the reader of "Island" would depend on their own values and their individual life experiences, and also would depend on the reader's opinion of the possibility of the human race saving itself through an expanded awareness and spiritual development. Like Sterling Gleason, the author of the first real manual of Fluorescence and the magic world of the Black light who also did not live to see the 1960s Psychedelic Movement which he in a small way predicted, the two most important authors to summons the 1960s Psychedelic Revolution into existence would both die on the very pivotal point between the 'old world' and the 'new world:' 1962-1963. Hermann Hesse, author of "Steppenwolf," "Journey to the East," and "Magister Ludi - The Glass Bead Game," which would be 'manuals' of the 1960s Movement, with his "Journey to the East" also being a literal premonition of the movement itself and present on Ken Kesey's La Honda ranch "Merry Prankster's" book shelf, would leave his body the year before Aldous Huxley, in 1962. These great two Visionaries of the Twentieth century who both wrote about psychoactive experiences, who would both become the guiding authors of the 1960s Movement, both died during the very first years of that Movement in 1962 and 1963. Many people believe that 1964 was the beginning of the 1960s Movement, and there is even a book published on the subject "The Last Innocent Year - America in 1964 [The Beginning of the "Sixties"]" by Jon Margolis from 1999, but by the current author's estimation it was the preceding year of 1963, when the rise to fame of the 'spokesmen' of the 1960s generation, "The Beatles" began to become known. The four English boys did more to actually begin the 1960s than any other four people on Earth, and this is what I base my decision on of 1963 being the 'first' year of the 1960s Movement. In 1964 "The Beatles" and "The Rolling Stones" were both already on tour in America. It may be thought of as cruel and unfair that Hesse and Huxley both died on the literal cusp of the 1960s Psychedelic Movement which they themselves helped to create into existence, but to see the eventual bastardization and eradication of the precious initial dreams of these two Visionaries would have most probably been crueler than death itself. We can only imagine that it was the divine Karma of these two great Visionaries to leave their bodies before the disastrous confrontation of the enlightened world of the 1960s Movement running head-on into the world of the common person composed only of mud.

To understand how important and controversial acid was in America during it's 'turning point' of 1966 when the U.S. government made it illegal on October 6, 1966, half a year before that, on March 25, 1966 "Life" magazine published it's only issue with acid as the cover story. The front cover of this March 25,1966 "Life" has a photo of a Black and White hand with a pill in it's palm, overprinted with a dull illustration of six squares of Violet, Orange, Blue, Yellow, and Green which are meant to represent the headline at the top of the "Life" cover, announcing the substance as an "Exploding Threat." Next to the photo of the hand and the Colored squares is the secondary headline, which describes Acid as a capsule of "Turmoil," and informs it's reader that a single dose of the substance was enough to start a "mental riot" with insights and vivid Colors, or "terror."

As another example of how dramatically society's attitude and acceptance have changed in less than fifty years, another issue of "Life" magazine will be presented here, this time published less than a month before the final illegalization of acid. This September 9, 1966 issue of the American 'family' magazine "Life," presents it's cover story in full psychedelic Colors: "LSD ART." The cover photograph is of an Artist sitting in a chair naked from the waist up and with iron bug-eye glasses. Very vivid Red, Orange, Yellow, and Blue light in flowing psychedelic triangular sections cover this Artist's face and body, as well as completely filling the area around him. Again, this was a mere three and a half weeks before the final illegalization of the substance, so this issue of "Life" magazine could literally represent the end of an era in which society accepted the substance as a new miraculous substance of the Twentieth century, since it's political leaders, Artists, musicians, and members of it's elite had taken it in the 1950s or early 1960s had been changed positively and permanently by their experiences, and then proceeded to announce their startling revelations to the rest of the members of society. In actual fact, after the substance was made illegal, society was so effective at their total reversal of public, private, and professional opinion, that after a full fifty years it is still nothing less than shocking to hold an issue of "Life" magazine in your hands with a full Color psychedelic cover story announcing "LSD ART!" In this is revealed the impetus for writing this book: Social Stigmatization.

To give an idea of this magazine's era, printed was the first ever fuzzy (and pretty miserable) photograph of the Earth from "deep space" (which in 1966 meant just behind the Moon) as the "Lunar Orbiter" was mapping sites for the 1969 Moon landing. Dating the era precisely, the page after a long article on the Vietnam war this article entitled "Psychedelic Art" begins. With a dramatic introduction the article begins with a double-page spread printed vertically, so the "Life" magazine had to be turned sideways to begin this altering article. This article on "Psychedelic Art" gives a background on the modern influences of the movement, such as the slide projection and kaleidoscope, as well as it's incorporation of ancient knowledge and imagery of "Oriental philosophies" and American Indian "lore." The article centers on the exhibition of Psychedelic Art in the former "Riverside Museum" in New York City, and was presented by the pioneering group "USCO."

This fifty year old "Life" magazine printed just weeks before this psychoactive substance became illegal, ends with a positive and very optimistic conclusion, being both surprising and at the same time nearly impossible to believe after half a century of pure stigmatism. The final two pages of this nine page article form this surprising conclusion and a headline is spread over both pages announcing that 'The Logical Outcome of half a century of Art is Psychedelic Art'(!) This conclusion that Psychedelic Art was the logical conclusion of Art since the beginning of the Twentieth century, begins with the very precise example of "DaDa" during the beginning of the Twentieth century, with it's similar breaks with established society and Art itself, and is just one of many similar documented examples of this very logical conclusion.

The conclusion of this article begins with the example of "DaDa," which during the early part of the Twentieth century with it's anti-Art break with society and established customs, drove audiences wild, but the 'prime sources' this "Life" article cites as the foundations of "Psychedelic Art," were Robert Rauschenberg's "Combines," which are still famous for mixing elements of Fine Art with discarded items found literally on the street. Another prime source of Psychedelic Art cited by this "Life" article were the "Happenings" of Allen Kaprow which introduced "environments" in Art to the general public and used 'lights, textures, and sounds' to create an Art form based on an "event," not a finished piece of Art hung on the wall. The "DaDa" movement with it's most outrageous spokesman Marcel Duchamp, is credited first as the "prime source" of "Psychedelic Art," then Robert Rauschenburg's "Combines, Allen Kaprow's "Happenings," "Op Art" which began to explore the limitations of human perception, and finally "Kinetic Art" which also altered the perception with rapid motion.

Just to give an example of the depth involved in the "DaDa" Art movement nearly one-hundred years ago, the final masterpiece of the Artist who was instrumental in the formation of the movement, Marcel Duchamp, shall serve this purpose.

This is a piece of Art that is still as raw, shocking, and modern as it was the day it was completed (also in 1966): "Given: 1. The Waterfall 2. The Illuminating Gas" (1946-1966). This is an "environment" that is permanently installed in the largest public collection of Duchamp's Art in the world at the Philadelphia Museum of Art, and involves one of the most shocking experiences a person ever had in a museum in their lives. The museum viewer enters a small inconspicuous room in the left corner of the Duchamp room in Philadelphia and sees to their right a small museum label on the wall with the already obscure name of Duchamp's piece of Art, and to their left in the semi-darkness is a very old worn wooden door. This is as far as the majority of visitors to the Philadelphia Museum of Art get. Some of the more adventurous may walk the vast distance of about five steps to this worn-out door to inspect it in the low light, and a precious few may even notice the two worn "peep-holes" at eye level in the ancient door. But, alas, only the smallest amount of the visitors who enter the semi-dark small room in Philadelphia will actually put their eyes to these small worn "peep-holes" in this door. When they do they will be confronted with a vision they could never have been sufficiently prepared for - and will never forget. A vision that is at once as simple as life itself and as complicated as the very limits of human consciousness - like Marcel Duchamp himself. This image was stipulated by Duchamp not to be photographed for fifteen years after it's installation. This piece of Art is explained by Duchamp with the viewer's "Participation" as the act of a "voyeur" being the most important "integral element" of the experience itself. Duchamp further explained that the *reaction* of the viewer was the most important element in the piece of Art. Duchamp also explained that although the viewer's 'vision and understanding are restricted' (with reference to the design and construction of this piece of Art), without the viewer's "reaction" this piece of Art "is incomplete." This pioneering theme of Duchamp's Art fifty years ago is still being discovered by Artists today.

The conclusion of this "Life" magazine cover story on 'Acid Art' in September, 1966 continues, explaining that the "Psychedelic Art" movement included both ancient Hindu philosophies and contemporary writers such as the influential ideas of the 'Global village' through mass-media from Marshall McLuhan. This "Life" article gives credit to the "USCO" psychedelic Art group in New York for supplying "the World" discotheque in New York City with 2,000 slides, two and a half hours of 16-mm films, and a control console for operating this psychedelic light show which mixed flashing slides, strobe lights, and movie projections simultaneously. This article goes on to credit three "Psychedelic Artists" in New York who had made these installations, in clubs such as "The Cheetah" discotheque in the city, and gives the overall impression that this new form of Art and expression was invented by these New York Artists, but what it does not inform it's readers is that this new Art form was not invented by these New York psychedelic Artists in 1966, but had been done for two years before this "Life" article was even written on the opposite side of America in California. In 1964 Ken Kesey and the Merry Pranksters in California had begun working with these concepts, which culminated in their "Acid Tests" of 1965 and 1966. This was a well established and unique movement created by the Pranksters to bombard the human senses with every element they could - to intentionally overwhelm the viewer externally with light and sound. Gerd Stern of the USCO group was the member of these East coast Artists that had been with Ken Kesey and the Merry Pranksters for the start of the "Acid Tests," and it was his light projections that were an integral ingredient in the multi-media assemblage that would overload the senses, as well as the Prankster painter Roy Sebern who had also done alot with these light projections and would continue using them throughout the Acid Tests.

"The Symbolism of Color," Faber Birren (1988)

To understand the physical and spiritual energy contained in Color itself, and how this energy is channeled, the late work of one of the most respected Color Theorists of the Twentieth century, Faber Birren, must be examined. Faber Birren published more than twenty-four books on Color Theory, and in turn he is regarded as the most widely read Color Theory authority of the Twentieth century. Applying his published Color Theory to the real world, Faber Birren has also worked as a Color consultant for corporations as well as government agencies. Birren explains in the introduction of "The Symbolism of Color" that as a professional Color consultant his expertise was centered on the psychological effects of Color, and that he had been employed by public institutions such as Neuropsychiatric hospitals. Amongst his published books are "Color: A Survey in Words and Pictures," and "Color Psychology and Color Therapy." Birren also confesses with pleasure in the introduction of "The Symbolism of Color" that over the course of his long career he had witnessed the change of society's acceptance towards the "mystic," which he lists as the "esoteric realms" of Color Therapy, ESP, the human aura, precognition, and faith healing. Birren also correctly interprets a portion of the reason for society's change of attitude towards the mystic subject matters as being the involvement in meditation, "Biofeedback," and the perfection of measurements analyzing brain waves and physical body response. As proof that the "occult" or "mystic" knowledge had begun to be regarded as accepted scientific studies, and to what extent these added viewpoints contributed to the scientific quest, Birren informs the reader of a relatively unknown fact, being that one of the most famous "Fathers of Science," Sir Isaac Newton, wrote extensively on the subject of religion leading to a higher understanding of God, in fact Newton wrote over one million words specifically on this subject. Faber Birren quotes Stanley R. Dean who wrote that the "New Age" has dawned, an age after the "Atomic Age," and the "Space Age," which Dean names the "Psychic Age."

Faber Birren's book "The Symbolism of Color" has a statement on the front cover that can be seen as a sub-title, and which informs the reader that the 'Magic and Beauty' of Color has been vital for 'Life, Mysticism, and Religion.' Mr. Birren closes his introduction with a hope that Color's magic and beauty will once again not just "enthrall" people, like in past ages, but also that Color will become "vital" and an "essential" part of people's lives once more.

Faber Birren begins "The Symbolism of Color" with a background he researched for a book published decades before, "The Story of Color," in which he uncovered the fact that Color was guided by "Mysticism" and not by aesthetics in ancient times, and quotes Darwin's "Decent of Man" in relation to the three main skin Colors of humanity, White, Yellow, and Black, symbolizing "racial purity" being representative of "Color purity." Birren expands this concept to include the people of ancient Egypt who divided humanity into four races, being the Red race of Egypt, where applying Red dye to the face was a common practice, the Yellow Asiatics, the Whites of the north across the Mediterranean, and Black Africans. The Aryan's culture also divided humanity into the same four races, and in India as well the four castes were established with the same distinctions. The "Arabs" typically did not conform with the Western frame of mind, and saw humanity as being only "two races," the Red race and the Black race, exactly as in Africa, where the Red race was believed to be descendants of the hunters who killed the first Ox and ate it's blood and lungs, while the Black race had descended form the eaters of the first Ox's liver. The American Indians were not as existential as the Africans or "Arabs," and believed their Red Color to have come from the "Morning Star," who is painted Red and which they considered the "Color of life." Amongst the American Indians, "Dawn people" wore Red painted clothing, the Color Gold represented Sunlight, and the Rainbow was a "Magic bridge" leading to heaven from Earth.

The point that Faber Birren brings to light is that Color was part of the "Mysteries" of humanity from the earliest formation of civilization. In ancient China the four "heavenly kings" were the Black-faced Northern guardian, the Red-faced Southern guardian, the Green-faced Eastern guardian, and the White-faced Western guardian. In comparison to the importance of Color representation, Mr. Birren explains that the American Indian tribes universally elevated Color to mythical proportions, giving the example of the "Navahoe" creation story in which their distant relatives lived surrounded by mountains, that in turn rose and set causing the day and night. The Eastern White mountains created the day, the Western Yellow mountains created the sunset, the Black mountains brought the night, and finally the Blue mountains brought the dawn. The "Hopi" Indians create Art by first using the Yellow Color representing the North, then in a specific order, the Hopi Artist uses either the Color Blue or Green representing the West, Red representing the South, and finally the Color White is used which represents the East. The Cherokee Indian considered Red to represent triumph or success, Blue to represent defeat, White to represent peace, and Black stood for death.

Expanding the boundaries of Color representation to cultures of the past, Faber Birren explains that in Tibet the belief was that Color actually had an effect and a "mystical relationship" with a person's state of mind. Tibetans believe that a "mild nature" was represented by a Yellow or White skin Color, while Blue, Red, and Black represented a nature that was "fierce," and light Blue represented only natures of the "celestial." In turn Tibetans symbolized gods as being White, devils as being Black, and "Goblins" as being Red. The religious text of the Hindu "Upanishads," which Birren states was written between nine and ten-thousand years ago, also teach the age old concept of the world being made up of "simple elements," specifying the three Colors of Red representing burning fire, the White Color of fire representing water, and the Black Color of fire representing the Earth being "what is true."

In more recent history Birren further explains that the Jewish religion associated the Earth with the Color White, water with the Color Purple, fire with the Color Red, and air was represented by the Color Yellow. In the mind of the great Leonardo da Vinci, the Color Blue represented air, Red represented fire, Green represented water, and the Color Yellow signified the Earth. The civilization that our modern society has it's roots in, ancient Greece, also considered Color as indicative of mysticism. The ancient Greek poet Hesiod wrote in "The Mythology of All Races" that the beginning of humanity was created by first the enlightened god-like "Men of Gold." The Greeks believed that the inferior "Men of Silver" were created by the gods second, and were child-like dim comparisons to the superior "Men of Gold," and would also lower themselves to kill one another. Then came the modern person, whom the ancient Greeks considered the "Men of Bronze" in possession of hard hearts, lust, strife, and jealousy. It is also correctly foretold by Hesiod that the "Men of Bronze" fell from their former realm of light into the darkness of "King Hades" by the workings of 'their inventions.'

Expanding on the subject of Color and mysticism creating the concepts of religion, Faber Birren points out that the Sun was always revered as the ruler of "heaven and earth" and the creator of life itself. Through it's various representations by ancient cultures, the Sun was seen as Red, White, and Yellow respectively by the ancient Egyptians, the Assyrians, and the Babylonians. In India the Sun was seen to be the totally different Color of Blue in it's purity, but when the Sun shone on the Earth, the ancient Indians believed that the Orange Color was created by a "diffusion" of substances which make up the "illusionary world." Faber Birren also relates the fact that much of our contemporary viewpoints or "chromophobic" unacceptance of Color directly caused by not the consciousness of mankind, but to weathering in the end. Birren recalls how all the sculpture as well as all the architecture of the great ancient Greece were long ago painted in "brilliant hues" that were used to symbolize the universe's "mystic principles," but what the brilliant sunlight of Greece, along with millennia of rain and changing temperatures have faded and reduced all the temples of ancient Greece to their present state of sterile White, which has once again been passionately embraced and standardized by the spiritually-purged Western society. In ancient Rome Vermillion was used to Color the faces of the gods, and through Greece Purple was adapted by Rome to be it's imperial Color as well. Thousands of kilometers away, the ancient British Druids also saw the Colors as representative of magic, and used astral light for healing. Closing the section of Color's influence on the creation of culture and religion throughout humanity's history, the ancient culture of India and the main trinity of the Hindu religion was also represented according to Color, with Brahma the creator represented by being Red or Gold, Vishnu the preserver represented by Yellow, and Shiva the destroyer and creator represented by Black. For a clue on how Black and somber dull Colors became the accepted tone of refined contemporary society, it all began about a thousand years ago with the educated class of China (not surprisingly) wearing only dark Purple, and the respectable Chinese wearing only Browns, Grays, and light Blue. The Chinese a thousand years ago also set the standard for men wearing Black, or deep Blue which is still the preferred Color in China all these centuries later (as well as most other places in the world). On a closing note, Faber Birren also writes that the Islamic prophet Mohammed entered Mecca wearing totally Black cloth and a Black turban. In modern history Alchemy and Mysticism are expanded upon by Birren, with Alchemy begun by Hermes of ancient Egypt, developed by Babylonians and in Asia Minor, further refined by the ancient Greeks who in turn transferred the early knowledge of Alchemy to the Romans, and then to the early Christians, and finally to Islam after China. As an example of a contemporary Alchemist, Faber Birren quotes Carl Jung and his book "The Integration of the Personality," in which Jung specifies four distinct Colors as well. In old alchemy Jung explains that the Colors used were the four Colors of the "old painters," Red, Black, White, and Yellow which were also the four Colors used for the four points of the compass. Jung explains that in modern times the basic Colors chosen by the "unconscious" are Red, Yellow (or Gold), Blue (representing Black), and Green (replacing White). Jung also states that the appearance of the Peacock's tail, called the "cauda pavonis" by Alchemists, auspiciously signaled the ending of a period. The principle Colors of alchemy were specified, and also represented in a specific order, being Black, White, Gold, and the Color Red, after Yellow was lost to time. To the Alchemists Black signified fire's action, and was identified by the symbol of a cross. White represented perfection and was represented by the swan. Orange or Gold was the third Color, which they considered the passage between White and Red, symbolized by sunrise. The final Color for the Alchemists was Red, which was representative of the phoenix and "extracted from White." Alchemists believed that the Red of the Sun perfected Sulphur, which they considered the male sperm.

Faber Birren next discussed the symbolism in another important ancient study, Astrology, which he states had it's beginning four-thousand years ago in Chaldea. Astrology identifies the planets with Colors and believes that these planets, along with the Sun and Moon, are the ruling powers of humanity. Astrology believes that the Sun's Color is Yellow or Gold, represented by Amber, and that the Moon's Color is White or Silver, represented by Diamond. For the planets, Astrology states that Mars is symbolized by Red and the Ruby, Mercury is symbolized by a neutral Color and represented by the neutral Colored Agate. Jupiter was represented by Blue and symbolized by Amethyst, Venus was symbolized by Green and the Emerald, while Saturn was represented by Black and the Onyx. The facts are that hundreds of years ago Astrology was an "occult science" involved even with christianity, and that Astrologers were respected by the leaders of the day, including the Egyptian pharaohs and the kings and queens of nations.

The beginning of Color Healing, or what is known as Color Therapy in modern times, is considered by Birren, who states that the symbolism of Color used in early healing was formed by direct association. It was believed that Colors were representative of disease because Colors were produced by disease. Minerals, flowers, and plants were used for healing by association of their Colors to visual signs of disease, such as Red representing fever, Yellow representing plague, and Black representing death. The Color Red used in healing stayed with society through the ages, being used up until the Eleventh century to stop bleeding. The combination of a substance's Color and it's composition, made specific through use of crystals in medieval healing and treatment for centuries, citing the example of Amber which was used to prevent miscarriages. Amethyst cured gout, Asphalt (Buitemen) treated broken bones, Green Beryl for eye disease and Yellow Beryl for jaundice, Carnelian ("Blood stone") treated hemorrhages, Chalcedony treated fevers, Crystal of Quartz treated swelling, Coral treated sterility, Diamond was used to cure almost anything, and Emerald was used with eye disease. To complete the ancient Color healing list, Garnet was used for the skin, Hematite was used for blood-shot eyes, Jade for childbirth, Jasper for pregnancy, Jet for epilepsy, Lapis Lazuli also for miscarriage, Opal also for eye diseases, Peridot for liver ailments, Ruby for stomach or blood, Sapphire was used to prevent diseases, and Turquoise protected it's wearer from poisons. The clear fact is that the power of a mineral was "endowed" by ancient healers many times strictly based on their individual Color. The "Medicine man" of the American Indians used Color for healing and treatment even in their dress, while the Shaman of Siberia were respected as priests and healers who were involved in medicine and used for medicinal purposes quinine and psychoactive substances. Along with dressing as birds or animals the American Indian Medicine man thus extended the healing power to the Color of their clothing, especially the western and southwestern American Indian tribes of the Navajo, Pueblo, and the Creek, with an example of the Navajo making paints in the Colors White, Red, Yellow, Blue and Black. William Z. Park documented the fact that the two "native paints" of White and Red were made from pigments of natural Earth substances and were also used by American Indian Medicine men for curing. During some healing practices of American Indians the Colors are painted onto both the Medicine man and the spectators, while the patient has dried powdered pigment dusted onto them with feathers used for the healing which have also been painted. The Navajo Medicine men "Sand Painters" create healing mandalas of natural Color sand that must be completed and destroyed in one day, before the sunset. The Blackfoot Medicine men would paint a young man Yellow to endow him with the Sun's power, while the Creek Medicine man would paint Black circles around his eyes to identify himself. As a conclusion to his discussion of Shamans, Medicine men, and "Witch doctors," Faber Birren expands on the "Peyote cult" of the Rio Grande Valley Indians, and states with clear vision that the effect of the Peyote taken by Medicine men of the American Indians was "similar" to the effects of the contemporary substance L.S.D., which both bring "religious ecstasy" and which both are hallucinogenic. Birren states that both Peyote and Acid heighten a user's Color "sensitivity," as well as creating respect for Colors because of their "spiritual meaning."

After chapters discussing the esoteric subjects of Color therapy, Astral light, the Aura, brain and body emanations, meditation, and sensory deprivation, the final sixteenth chapter in Faber Birren's "The Symbolism of Color" explores the "Eyeless Sight" and "Eidetic Imagery" of L.S.D. To find the final chapter of the most respected Color theorist of the Twentieth century's book from 1988 exploring the effects of Color with regards to the expanded consciousness and higher sensitivity to Color brought about by acid is nothing less than astounding, but in the end also absolutely accurate. Faber Birren begins with the fact that our vision, including dreams, hallucinations, and afterimages, is only collected by our light receptors (the eyes), but in actuality all that we perceive is processed by the brain, not the eyes. This has been known by the "Mystic" all along, but science always centered our perception only in the realm of the light receptor - the eye. On the first page of chapter sixteen Birren already makes the bridge between society's higher understanding and acknowledgment that the brain is the center of perception not the simple light receptor the eye. Explaining that the "celestial trips" that thousands of people were going on after taking psychedelics had a very "notable feature," being an explosion of Colors, which Birren also accurately describes as "flashing," "flowing," and "brilliant." Birren goes on to explain that the psychedelic experience is what brought about an "amazing discovery," which is that our vision comes from our brain, where it is processed into consciousness, not from our eyes, where it is merely collected, or as Birren poetically put it, from the "inside out," not from the "outside in." Faber Birren also clearly states the applications of acid during it's earliest accepted days, such as the 'wonder drug's' treatment of mental patients, treatment of patients who were terminally ill, as well as a treatment for the transition and fear of dying, all came about because the substance is "mind expanding." Birren informs the reader that these "mind-expanding" substances had been well known throughout history in the forms of Hashish, Peyote, and Opium, but Birren is quite correct in pointing out the similarity in the religious use of Peyote by the American Indians and the ritualized use of acid in America during the 1960s and 1970s, which sought to 'achieve harmony with the infinite.' Birren gives the example of Aldous Huxley, who is quoted on his first Mescaline experience describing Colors being raised to a "higher power" and perceived in "fine shades" which were "innumerable." Heinrich Kluver is also quoted by the author as stating that it was "impossible" to describe in mere words "Mescal Colors." "Psychiatry and Mysticism" by Dr. Stanislav Grof is also highlighted by Birren, in which fifteen years of Acid research and experiments were published, with a total of over two-thousand psychoactive sessions documented by Dr. Grof. The death of the ego and the experience of radiant divine light are culminations of positive experiences recorded for over fifteen years by Dr. Grof. Birren also relates Carl Jung's "collective unconscious" theories to experiences on psychoactives, with which a person's literal conception and prenatal life in the womb may be clearly relived, as well as episodes including the meeting of deities or mythological gods. Birren explains that Dr. Grof was most interested in medical treatment with acid for cases of alcoholism, drug addiction, mental disorders including schizophrenia, and sexual frigidity, and that he ended up administering the substance to a wide spectrum of society, which included teachers, philosophers, scientists, and Artists.

Faber Birren next clearly states that acid had led directly to forms of "new art." The visions and altered ways of perceiving the world and life itself led the Artist to try and document these "mosaics" and "geometric patterns" of their experiences onto "canvas." The late 1960s "discotheque" is also documented by Birren as being a direct result of the 1960s, and a conscious attempt to recreate a psychedelic experience without drugs, using "Stroboscopic" and ""flashing lights," "fluid designs" and "flowing colors."

"Subjective color," or Colors that are registered by the brain without being before the eyes, is discussed in "The Symbolism of Color," particularly with Aristotle who wrote that he saw a "flight of colors" after looking into the Sun. Birren also documents the fact that Goethe made the same experiment as Aristotle, and that his dangerous "Sun-gazing" can be harmlessly recreated using a light bulb. The area of this visual research was explored by E.R. Jaensch, who categorized human images being created by the three experiences of the memory, afterimages, and "eidetic images." "Eidetic imagery" is explained by Jaensch as being the "intermediate experiences" between physical reality and mentally created images - a 'gift from childhood,' insanity, and the "mystically inspired." The projected images created inside a child's head while they are playing with their toys, as well as drug-induced hallucinations, are both defined as "Eidetic imagery" by Jaensch, including the visions of mystics. "Eyeless Sight" is presented at the end of this last chapter by Birren, in which he states that it was in 1924 the French author Jules Romains published the book "Eyeless Sight." Romains documented the proposal that the skin of humans is light sensitive, just as the skin of lower life forms, which he termed "Paroptic perception." Experimenting with screens that could project light onto parts of the body without reaching the eyes, Romains claimed the hands to be the most receptive to "Eyeless Sight," and further claimed that a "paroptic function" existed in humans which allows "visual perception" of objects, including form and Color, without using the eyes in any way. This led Jules Romains to state that a person could read while blindfolded, as well a being in possession of the ability to "smell" Color. These mystical abilities of "Eyeless Sight" were later explored in "Psychic Discoveries Behind the Iron Curtain" by Ostrander and Schroeder, with Rosa Kuleshova, a girl from Russia who was experimented on in Moscow during 1964. This story was published by "Life" magazine on June 12, 1964, which showed Rosa reading, typing, and naming Colors with her fingertips alone. This Russian girl proved to the Russian Biophysics Institute in Moscow that she could "see" Red, Blue, and Green Colors with her fingertips alone, which the researchers termed "dermo-optics." This led to a huge amount of research, and eventually developed in the first years of the Twenty-first century into the present day cutting-edge field called "Neuroplasticity." Exactly as documented by Faber Birren twenty-five years ago, "Seeing" with the tongue - not the eyes - has been scientifically proved, documented, and even broadcast on public television.

In this 'Black Light History' there have been many subtopics included, which have served the purpose of creating the 'set and setting' of either the time period or state of mind representative of this long history of both Fluorescent Colors and the Black light. The margins of both society and Art are important to this history and are included because they are the only groups which have truly embraced Fluorescent Colors and Black lights. How many people or even Artists in today's world even consider the Spirituality of Colors? And these are 'normal' Colors that humanity has seen for millennia - what could be expected for 'new' Twentieth century Fluorescent Colors that emit light through the energy of a Black light, which was also invented less than one century ago? The answer is quite obvious, and it is the answer that gave this book it's theme and title: "Fluorophobia." The Visionaries who spoke in the 1950s about Fluorescent Colors and Black lights heralding in a "New Age of Art" were truly inspired and did not consider the malaise of their species, who in the end are nothing more than partially-evolved monkeys. These visionaries could today be compared to the just-as-enthusiastic and clear sighted few who believed that after the 1969 and early 1970s Moon landings, that humanity would step on Mars by 1980(!) These visionaries believed in what they experienced and saw, and then clearly projected a future that was quite possible and entirely logical - without considering that the majority of the people are extremely close-minded and virtually lame. All the "i" appendages in the universe will not change this. A tiny sector of humanity has finally evolved advanced mentally and spiritually to the level of inventing such wonders of technology, but as it has always been, the majority of the users of these wonderous new inventions are only just a few steps from the caveman. Around the first decade of the Twenty-first century a series of conclusions crystalized which brought about a new school of thought as well as a new field in the study of human consciousness. This new field proves nothing less than the fact this author has known for the last three-quarters of his life - that the human brain *can change* because of, and adapt to, different situations and experiences. Specifically, this is not referring to a simple, common change of personality, moods, attitude, or choice, but to the fact that the brain can literally rewire itself to adapt to our experiences. This new field of Neurology is termed "Neuroplasticity," and has broken down the rigid walls of academic knowledge in place for centuries - literally in place since the brain began to have been pondered upon millennia ago. Classically the opinion has been that all areas of the brain have extremely specific 'jobs' or 'functions,' such as sight, balance, hearing, etc., but in just the last decades what has been finally realized is that our brain does not resemble what it's owner until recently referred to as a simple, reduced 'filing cabinet' or an unchanging computer hard drive, but that the brain is 'plastic' and does not stay the same as was formerly taught and believed. This is now referred to as "Cross-Modal Plasticity," which has proven definitively that the experiences we have in this life can in actuality permanently change our brain. Similar to the old-fashioned concept of our brain being an unchanging filing cabinet, the belief until very recently was also that each of our senses was a rigid area or 'department' of our brain that could never be altered or cross-referenced by ourselves. This has also been proven in recent times to be absolutely wrong, and what is now known is that all of our senses work together (logically). This Twenty-first century epiphany of Neuroscience is a clear new understanding of life, sweeping away the antiquated cob-webs of millennia from our eyes, and is comparable to the concept of Evolution brought about by Darwin 150 years ago was.

This unprecedented concept of our brain changing it's wiring to adapt to new experiences and situations - nearly instantly - and that these experiences or situations of our lives can permanently change our brain - seems in hindsight so utterly obvious that it, again, is compared to the 'discovery' of the concept of Darwinian Evolution. As with many new schools of thought or new concepts, when it is broadcast to the public arena through the mass media of magazines, newspapers, and especially the television, it is already well established. This is the level that the new fields of "Neuroplasticity" and "Cross-Modal Plasticity" have reached, with several science shows being broadcast in the last decade. Proof of these newly accepted concepts of Neurology are present on these public media presentations, including an undeniable experiment performed on several of these shows which is termed the 'Rubber Hand Trick.' A person sits down at a table with a vertical partition on it. Their left arm and hand is concealed behind the partition from their sight, and a surrogate fake rubber hand and arm are positioned on the table in front of the person with a small Black cloth used to complete the illusion of this rubber hand and arm being their own flesh and blood. In just one single minute of talking to this test subject with their new rubber hand in front of them on the table, as well as gently touching this obviously rubber fake hand with a soft paintbrush, the subject has adapted to this new experience and transfers their feelings to this fake rubber hand - their brain has nearly instantaneously rewired itself to it's changing experience.   This is proved well beyond the proverbial shadow of a doubt by the scientist conducting this experiment, through the simple but extremely effective act of taking a hammer that was completely hidden from the test subject's view under the table, and *slamming* it without warning onto their newly adapted (or adopted) fake rubber hand! Not only does this scare the hell out of each and every test subject the experiment is conducted on, but the undeniable proof of the brain rewiring itself very quickly to adapt to this new experience is clearly illustrated by the fact that every one of these test subjects actually <u>feel pain</u> in their real flesh and blood left hand when they see the hammer smashing their obviously fake rubber hand(!) Again, this does not take years to develop, and the reaction is not subtle in any way, with test subjects nearly jumping out of their chair at the experiment's partitioned table - as well as truly feeling pain in their real left hand when the hammer suddenly hits their 'new' fake rubber hand after about a mere sixty-seconds of 'reconditioning.' Just the simple words of the experimenter along with their gentle touching of this fake rubber hand with a soft paintbrush for only a single minute was more than enough for the test subject's brain to change it's wiring and adapt the sight of this fake rubber hand on the table in front of them as their own. Not only that, but when this fake rubber hand was hit with a hammer after only one minute of this 'reconditioning' or 'transference,' every test subject felt real pain in their real left hand and continued rubbing their real left hand like it had been hurt! What scientists think is responsible for this amazing 'transference' in the brain is what they explain as "Mirror Neurons," through which the brain alters the senses.

Another undeniable proof of these concepts of "Neuroplasticity" and "Cross-Modal Plasticity" is embodied in a man that was blind from birth and has such amazing capabilities that he was not only on the "BBC," but was also presented on "Discovery Channel." This man Daniel Kish comes riding down the street on his mountain bike to meet the show's presenter, who is staring incredulously at this man riding the bicycle, because this man is blind! Amazingly, Daniel Kish who was born blind has rewired his brain completely by being able to see using "Echo-location" like a bat. This amazing man clicks his tongue and creates "echo-location" with which he literally assembles an image of the world around him through the creation of his sound and with the formation of a visual image in his brain created by this sound of his clicking tongue bouncing back to his ears through space. Do not get the wrong idea and think that this is a simple parlor-trick performed by this blind man, because this echo-locating person has rewired his brain extensively, being able to ride a mountain bike through a series of obstacle courses that even a person with normal sight would have to approach slowly. This same man is brought into a underground cave and with his tongue clicking and echo location he is shown to be able to not only judge the size and shape of

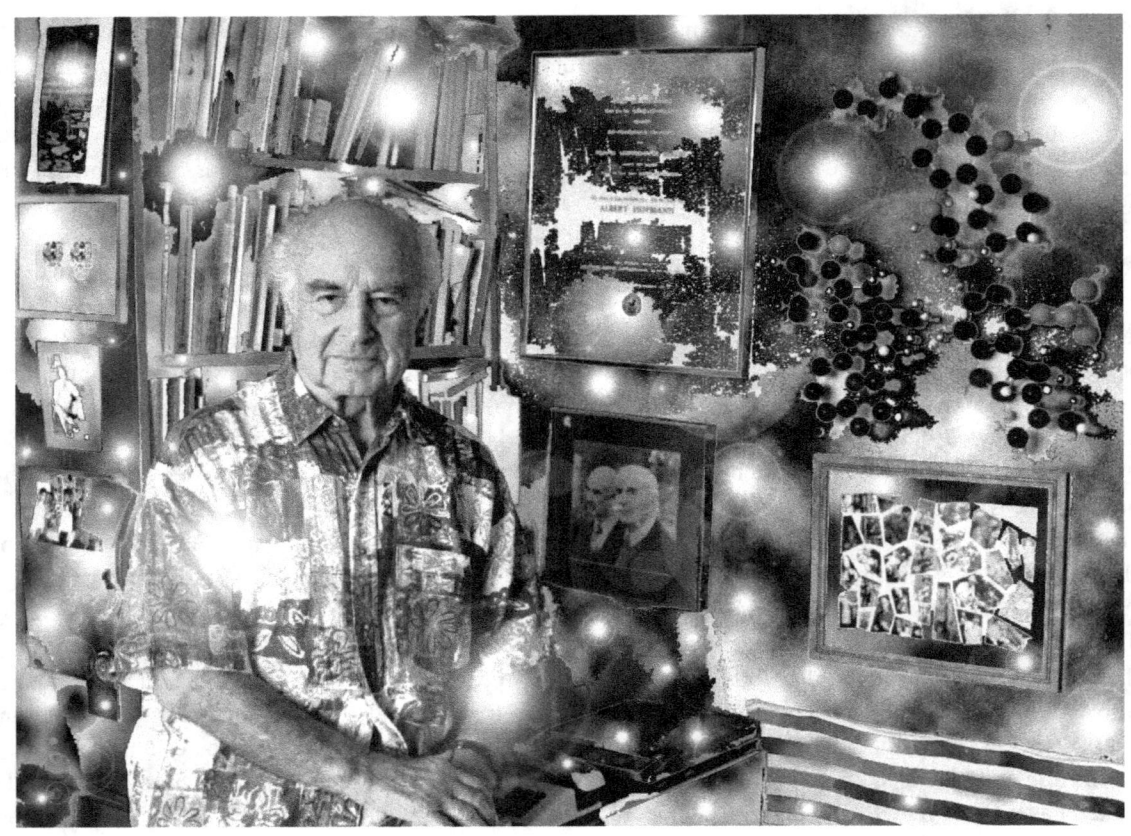

"Dr. Albert Hofmann in his study, July 21, 1998," Fluorescent bubble-jet computer print, ©Nick Padalino

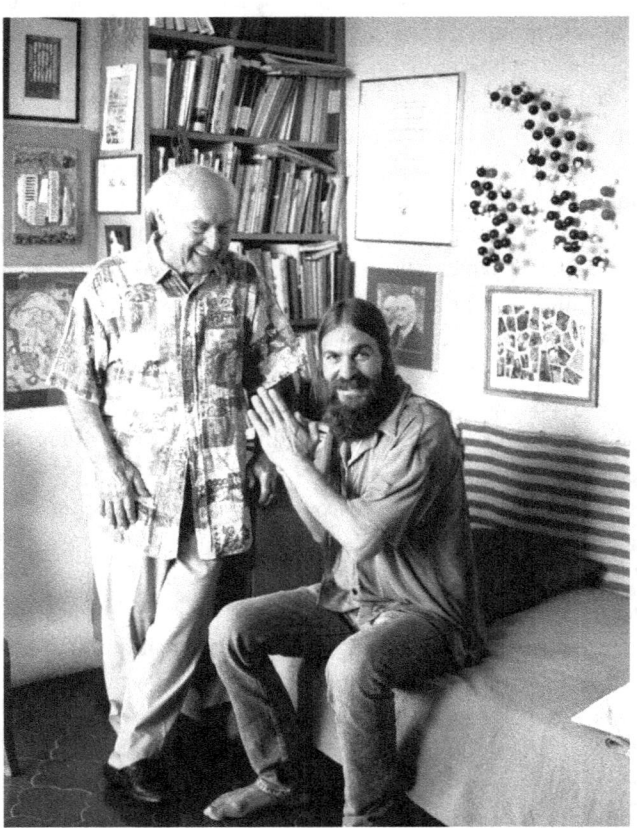

Dr. Albert Hofmann in his study with the author, July 21, 1998

this cave, but can even "see" that on one wall of the cave there was a big bump, which was not as smooth as all the other walls of the cave surrounding him. This proves that through clicking his tongue like a bat sending out sonar, the returning sound is used by Daniel Kish as "echo-location," and that furthermore the visual part of his brain is activated and that this creates an actual image of the invisible world around him.

This raises another question, which is if only people already effected in an uncommon way, such as blindness, are capable of this seemingly impossible rewiring their brains and creating sight from sound. This question is also raised with an experiment conducted on subjects who have no disabilities. A college student working on his bicycle for a delivery service was fitted with a special belt which is sensitive to magnetism, and then went about his daily life. This belt the subject wore would vibrate and constantly alert him to the presence of the Earth's magnetic lines. After, again, a very short time period the test subject had become so accustomed and tuned into the invisible magnetic lines of the Earth all around us, that he personally felt and also physically exhibited that he had developed another - or 'sixth' - sense through this simple adaption of wearing a vibrating magnetism belt. Further proof of this has been shown with Rajesh Malek born in India in 1959 and blind since birth, who has his tongue stimulated with computer-generated "images" through pin-pricks of what is in front of him, and with astounding similarity to the the "echo-location" of Daniel Kish who clicks his tongue and creates a visual image, this blind man's tongue is stimulated and an image is sent to his brain through this physical stimulation of his tongue, not his eyes. Rajesh Malik has switched sensations from his eyes to his tongue through the working optic nerves and it is believed that these sensations have stimulated his optic nerve to create an image in his brain.

What all these facts should awaken in a person's mind is the idea of not only the insufficient, limited amount of knowledge we have of the vast plains of the brain, which is now believed to consist of the nearly unimaginable one-hundred billion Neurons and the truly unimaginable two-hundred trillion connections between Neurons, but also the insufficiently limited amount of knowledge we have on the infinite universe around us.

Another lucid example of "Neuroplasticity" is embodied in a girl named Dominique, also broadcast on public television. This girl was born with access to just half of her brain's abilities, and she uses the primitive part of the brain to replace the inaccessible visual circuit to half of her brain. In this way Dominique has rewired her own brain to gain the ability to see for the missing half of her brain. The list of what we do not know gets longer and longer, such as the 'new' field of "Optogenetics." This new field of "Neuroplasticity" has advanced to the point of getting specific parts of the brain to react when simply stimulated with light. There is such a strong stimulation to the brain from light it was proved that through simply this light-stimulated brain activity, researchers could trigger a female fly to have male sex reactions. This new field of "Optogenetics" has now promised to turn off neurons in the human brain related to specific emotions such as Fear, Love, and Hate, while having no effect on other neurons or emotions. To turn on just specific neurons in the brain these neurons are made sensitive to light. To achieve this genes are extracted from light-sensitive cells already occurring in nature, such as cells creating photosynthesis in plants, and then these cells are put into neurons in the human brain. Sounds very 'natural' already, but this is nothing. With these light-sensitive plant photosynthesis genes in neurons of the human brain, it becomes a "switch" to turn brain neurons on and off, which thus enables the ability to turn on and off targeted emotions such as Fear and Hatred(!) Another wonderful part about this targeted emotional switch for Human beings is a network of fiber optics being next implanted into the brain as well. It is calmly explained by the lisping developer of this madness that the same optical fiber which connects us to the Internet would be implanted directly into the brain. Can't wait. This network of fiber optics implanted into the human brain would be further divided into many individual optical fibers which would distribute light into all areas of the brain. Just as calmly and emotionlessly it is also explained by it's developer that simply by changing the "geometry" of the cluster of optical fibers implanted into the brain delivering light, it would be possible to then turn on and off "Emotions," "Feelings," and even "Cognition" in the human brain.

Added to this list of new fields of Twenty-first century research must be "Synthetic Biology" that grows flesh back by starting with stem cells and "blanks," "Transhumanism" which is the merging into an entity of both Human being and robot, and "Epigenetics" which studies a newly discovered 'second' layer of genetic information on top of DNA.

An afternoon with Dr. Albert Hofmann, July 21, 1998

On November 27, 1992 Michèle and I opened "Electric Ladyland - the First Museum of Fluorescent Art" as an initial two week "50th Birthday Celebration" for Jimi Hendrix. We had a large collection of extremely rare Jimi Hendrix posters fromthe archive of the "The Jimi Hendrix Information Center," organized by Dan Foster. This 1992 Museum opening also displayed a section on the Artwork of Monika Dannemann, who was with Jimi, as well as a ninety page Movie script that Jimi

Hendrix wrote in 1970 which the current author spent two full days at Sotheby's Manhattan in 1990 transcribing into a recording Walkman. One of the most auspicious meetings of this initial two week opening in 1992 was the visit of an American named Dave. He stayed in the Museum for hours, and he was the first person I met that knew Dr. Albert Hofmann personally. Dave gave me the telephone number of Dr. Hofmann and his address. Five months later for the April 19, 1993 "50th Anniversary celebration" commemorating Dr. Hofmann's famous bicycle ride on the first acid experience in the world, this author wrote to Dr. Hofmann for the first time. Naturally expecting nothing in return from this world famous chemist, I was overjoyed to receive two months later a small inconspicuous White envelope with an even more demure return address printed on it: "Dr. A.H." from Switzerland. This first letter I received from Dr. Hofmann was written in two different Colors and was dated from June 13, 1993 with a letterhead introducing "ALBERT HOFMANN Dr. PHIL.II, Dr. H.C. MULT."

Five years later during the Kumbh Mela in Hardwar, India, I met a character from Switzerland who told me that he had called Dr. Hofmann on the telephone and had been invited to his home to talk. After seeing the way this questionable Swiss guy acted in India, I came to the conclusion that if this person could be invited to Dr. Hofmann's house then so could I. After returning from India, a month later while in Switzerland I telephoned Dr. Albert Hofmann's house. I introduced myself to the gentle voice of Dr. Hofmann, and explained a little about my Art gallery and Museum of Fluorescent Art in Amsterdam, and then I asked Dr. Hofmann a question that nobody had ever asked him before - or after, for that matter - a question I had been thinking about for years - a question that nobody else besides Dr. Hofmann was qualified to answer - and a question that got me invited to Dr. Albert Hofmann's house. This question that I asked Dr. Hofmann on the phone in July, 1998 was admittedly a very unique question, for which I needed to first explain that the "Cause of Fluorescence" was "Electron Displacement" in which invisible Ultraviolet energy was absorbed by the atoms of a Fluorescent substance, such as paint or minerals, and that this extra energy received from this invisible U.V. would cause electrons to move and produce visible light - Color. So, my question to Dr. Hofmann was in two parts - number one: did he think that there could be a physiological effect on a human being immersed in a Fluorescent environment, like in the Museum, painted with hundreds of liters of Fluorescent paint and under one-thousand watts of Black light, and number two: did he think that this physiological effect of the Electron Displacement of Fluorescence would be altered or increased in any way if the person immersed in a Fluorescent environment under a thousand watts of Black light was on a psychoactive substance? After asking this unheard of question to Dr. Hofmann there was absolute silence on the telephone - I thought he had hung up on me - but after a very memorable silence came the unforgettable answer of Dr. Hofmann: "I...don't...know, but what day would you like to come to my house?"(!) Two days later we arrived on a secluded hilltop with a very beautiful contemporary home that looked like it had been built within the last twenty years, which was the house of Dr. Hofmann. This was about noon on July 21, 1998, in Europe, where the time is six hours ahead of the East coast of America, and where July 21 is often cited as the anniversary of the 1969 first Moon landing, only, making it a truly auspicious day.

The front door to Dr. Albert Hofmann's house was opened by a woman about ninety years old who was smiling and as polite as could be, telling that she was Dr. Hofmann's wife Anita, and that her husband would be with me in a second. She was about five feet tall, thin, looked about thirty years younger than she was, but the most noticeable feature about her were her knowledgeable eyes. A minute later inside the front door of the house, and in walks a man also about just five feet tall, ninety-two years old, and beaming with a welcoming smile! He rushed to shake hands as I stood transfixed at my first sight of the man who had discovered L.S.D. in 1938. My first words to Dr. Hofmann were that I had just returned from the Kumbh Mela in India, to which he was smiling broadly. He lead us to an open porch of his house where we could talk. I began by giving Dr. Hofmann a portrait I had made of him in which he is holding the Hindu instruments of Creation and Destruction - the Trishule and the Damroe. I also had prepared a prototype of the "Electric Ladyland" Museum booklet we would be giving to Museum visitors when we eventually opened the coming April, which I had also signed and dedicated to Dr. Hofmann. I did not immediately begin to speak to Dr. Hofmann about the obvious subject of his world-changing discovery exactly sixty years before, acid, but began to speak about a subject that was 'neutral' and which I knew he was deeply interested in: Science. Sitting at an outdoor picnic table with Dr. Hofmann at the head of the table I slightly introduced the Gallery and Museum and began immediately to speak about "Electron Displacement" and the cause of the phenomenon of Fluorescence. I then began to describe the hundreds of pounds of Fluorescent minerals which I had been collecting for the Museum displays - and Dr. Hofmann looked directly at me with simply fathomless eyes and asked in shock: *"Minerals Fluoresce??"* He had earned his PhD. as an Organic chemist such a long time ago that it wasn't even taught about the newly discovered invisible world of mineral Fluorescence. I began as rapidly as I could to explain "Impurity Activation" and other essential details causing the phenomenon of Fluorescence, and to my great surprise Dr. Albert Hofmann stood up from his chair and walked away from the picnic table. I stopped explaining the quantum mechanics of Fluorescence, looked at Dr. Hofmann standing at the table, and wondered what was going on. Dr. Hofmann then excused himself for getting up right in the middle of my explanation of "Electron Displacement" - because he had to go and get paper and a pen to take notes(!) We sat for quite a while on this outdoor covered porch of Dr. Hofmann's, eating cherries from his trees while it on-and-off poured like mad. He showed something which was truly a representation of this gentle, enlightened creature, being a small Yellow and Green car battery with a very low electrical charge that he had wired around his beloved roses, so that the neighborhood rabbits would receive a gentle harmless charge when touching the wire attached to the car battery, and then not eat his roses. I also photographed this car battery and wiring. After Dr. Hofmann had excused himself for getting paper and a pen to take notes on what I was telling him about the Fluorescence of natural minerals and it's cause of "Electron Displacement," and I definitively knew for sure that there was no more fear of getting thrown out of his house, the conversation turned towards his "Wonder Child" acid and the 1960s Movement. He spoke with a partial smile about the early 1990s last European tour of "The Grateful Dead" when his secretary had received a multitude of calls and requests from a man who would not take no for an answer and insisted that he meet Dr. Hofmann - he was traveling with "The Grateful Dead" tour, and his name was Owsley, who had been the most famous underground chemist of the 1960s Movement. That had been the last European tour of "The Grateful Dead" for which Michèle and I had travelled to Paris for their Saturday night concert in the "Zenith Theatre," which Owsley had also been at. We spoke for quite a while with Dr. Hofmann on the outdoor porch of his beautiful contemporary mountain-top home, about Baba Ram Das, our experience just a few short months before in the Hardwar Kumbh Mela of 1998, as well as our second pilgrimage up to 14,000 feet (4,350 meters) in the Himalaya to Gaumukh, the holy source of the Ganga (Ganges River) at the Indian border of Tibet, from where I had brought back the first Fluorescent Minerals collected in the Himalaya. This is a two day journey of thirty-eight kilometers by foot, which Michèle and I have made in 1987, 1998, and 2010. We spoke about R. Gordon Wasson, and Dr. Hofmann's trip to Mexico with Wasson decades before, after Wasson's discovery and during his study on the Mexican Magic Mushroom culture and it's history. We also discussed the "Eleusian Mysteries" and the book "The Road to Eleusis" that Dr. Hofmann had published with R. Gordon Wasson in 1978. If only one thing could be changed of the meeting we had with Dr. Hofmann at his home, I wish I could have had a tape-recorder rolling or some instrument to record all that Dr. Hofmann spoke, but alas, this was 1998, at just the cusp of the digital age and I did not own a digital camera yet, quite unfortunately. But, I did not leave my Nikon film camera home, and continued to take photos of Dr. Hofmann for our entire afternoon together at his house.

After quite a while of talking about everything from "Electron Displacement" to acid, I told Dr. Hofmann that I had brought him something, and he invited us to his private study on the opposite end of his house. Upon entering this small coveted private study of Dr. Hofmann I was charged with energy - immediately I see on the wall the original, very first model made by Dr. Hofmann of the L.S.D. atomic structure. Models of the two other Psychoactive substances first isolated by Dr. Hofmann, Psilocybin in Magic Mushrooms, and L.S.A. in Morning Glory seeds, are also mounted on the wall next to the acid molecule. Then I opened up my small handbag and take something out that I had brought to Switzerland dreaming that I could actually meet this famous avatar. Before I left Amsterdam, I packed the only possession I had that I though Dr. Hofmann would be interested in having in his collection, knowing that Dr. Hofmann had travelled to Mexico during R. Gordon Wasson's quest of the 1950s (and early 1960s) for the Magic Mushroom, and that Dr. Hofmann had been the first person to isolate Psilocybin from these same Magic Mushrooms of Mexico collected by the Wasson expeditions, I thought there was a slim possibility that Dr. Hofmann might not own a copy of the world-changing May 14, 1957 R. Gordon Wasson "Mexican Magic Mushroom" issue of "Life" magazine, since it was published on the other side of the Atlantic in the states. As I told him this, while taking the forty-one year old "Life" magazine out of my handbag - his eyes widened with anticipation. When I got the "Life" magazine out I asked him 'do you have a copy of this Wasson "Life" magazine?' to which he replied in excitement that he had only heard for many decades about this very special 1957 "Life" magazine, but that he had never even *seen* it before! I was ecstatic - having brought something that many people claim helped start the "Psychedelic Movement" of the 1960s to Dr. Albert Hofmann, that he not only didn't own, but had never even seen before - Hari Om! I quickly flipped through the pages and held open before him the double-page Color photographs from the first Magic Mushroom ceremony with White people in Mexico attended by his friend R. Gordon Wasson, and Dr. Hofmann's eyes were as wide as stars. The only picture that Dr.Hofmann has of himself on the wall of his private study is a faded photograph in which he is walking with R. Gordon Wasson in 1976. He immediately took a small stone carving of a Mushroom God from Mexico off his shelf and we both were astounded to touch an original Mushroom God, but Dr. Hofmann quickly replied very surprised 'No, no, this is just a copy - the original is in the museum in Mexico!' I still remember that as we talked in a charged atmosphere about the Wasson "Life" magazine and Mexican Magic Mushrooms, Dr. Hofmann took the forty-one year old precious "Life" magazine I had kept stored completely flat in protective plastic for decades, and rolled it up like an old newspaper and put it under his arm. A very subtle, but true lesson in detachment(!)

After surprising Dr. Hofmann while discussing personal experiences, I asked him if he had ever been close to another "Father of the Psychedelic Movement" Aldous Huxley, and he led us directly from the inner doorway of his private study into the main room of his house, which contained a literal wall of bookshelves stretching about a quarter of his house's total length. From this large collection of books Dr. Albert Hofmann directly pulls out a hardcover, first edition of "Island" by Aldous Huxley, and opens the front cover to show me the hand-written dedication "To Dr. Albert Hoffman, the original discoverer of the Moksha Medicine, from Aldous Huxley 1963." This time my eyes were as wide as stars! It was the first (and only) time I've ever had something hand-written by Aldous Huxley in my hands, and I immediately asked Dr. Hofmann if I could take a picture of the book(!) He laughed like I was absolutely crazy and looked at me with big eyes: "You want to photograph the BOOK??" Just behind us was a large glass contemporary dining table, which I laid the hardcover first edition of "Island" on, and photographed Aldous Huxley's dedication to "Dr. Albert Hoffman, the original discoverer of the Moksha Medicine" (who's misspelled name did not go unnoticed by the doctor himself). The biggest laughter of Dr. Hofmann during our afternoon together at his house came when I asked for a picture of Dr. Hofmann and myself in his private study specifically in front of his original model of acid's atomic structure on his wall. First of all, I sat down in front of Dr. Hofmann, because the height difference looked ridiculous with myself being a full head taller than (and half the age of) Dr. Hofmann. Then what made him burst out with laughter, which can be seen in the photographs of us together, is that I had just bent down from my sitting position in front of Dr. Hofmann a second before the photograph was taken and touched his feet! I very much doubt that Dr. Hofmann had ever had his feet touched in reverence before, and he laughed out loud! He was even still laughing in the second photo of us a minute later. It was a wonderful, unforgettable experience with a truly enlightened human being.

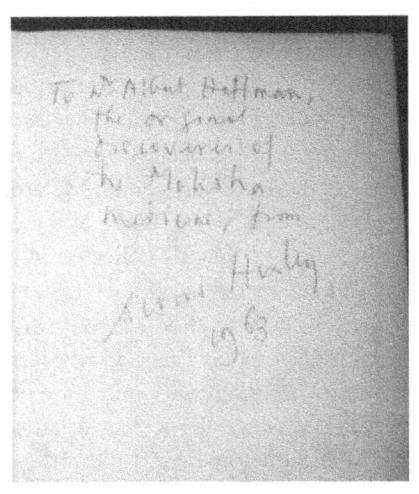

A fact about Dr. Albert Hofmann that is relatively unknown is that he was also a ceramic Artist. In his private study there were several pieces of his ceramic Art, including a work on the wall of a cityscape of skyscrapers. As we walked from the wall of books to the dining area of his house, Dr. Hofmann stopped to explain the large glazed cat he had sculpted and fired, informing me that the several pieces of ceramic Art in his house and study were all made by himself. He described the creation of this ceramic cat in detail, including the basic sculpting and the Colors used in the final glazing of the Artwork, proving that Dr. Hofmann did indeed possess the traits of an enlightened Renaissance person, excelling in Science, Literature, and even Art. To the left of where we stood around Dr. Hofmann's ceramic cat there was a light-filled glass room containing a shinny baby-grand piano, and to our right was the entrance of the house where we had met a few hours before, with a large painted family portrait of Dr. Hofmann, his wife Anita, and their children.

Several hours had passed talking to Dr. Hofmann, and after seeing the house and his private study the rain had stopped and the Sun was out again on this late July afternoon, so we went to take a walk on his property. This contemporary mansion was built specifically on a small mountain top to have peace and a contact with nature. We exit again onto the enclosed porch where we had sat talking next to the rain, and Dr. Hofmann - at ninety-two years old - shows us his pair of "Nikes" next to his wife's pair of "Nikes!" One of the reasons they both looked so much younger than their actual ninety plus years was that every day they walked some kilometers together on their vast property. We began to walk down a mountain path in a landscape of rolling hills and pure Greenery. After a distance we arrive at an ancient stone marker on his property from the Napoleonic reign, with a date of 1863 carved into it ("18" on one side and "63" on the other side). Dr. Hofmann explains to us that this is the stone marker put up during the reign of Napoleon to divide Switzerland from France. Dr. Hofmann was such a pivotal person that on his property was the dividing line between two countries. After laughing and walking in the woods like kids, Albert Hofmann leads to a special spot for him, being his "Meditation bench" that was built for him by his son. This was a simple construction using fallen trees from the property left in their natural state with the bark at the edges giving the impression of a 'log cabin' construction. I sat on this "Meditation bench" with Dr. Hofmann, and the view was superb as you scanned the rolling hills of Switzerland juxtaposed by the Greenery of France. It was obvious that this person was deeply in touch with the energy of nature, being not only an Organic chemist, but a person who saw the "White Light" of enlightenment when he was still just a boy walking in the forest of Switzerland. This initial revelation that Dr. Hofmann had experienced as a small boy is detailed in a wonderful late publication of his entitled "Insight/Outlook" which is one of the two books Dr. Hofmann gave to me after signing a dedication inside the front covers. This slim volume is perhaps the most reflective writing ever published by Dr. Hofmann, without a word written about his "Problem/Wonder Child" acid, but filled with a tale of an enlightened person's philosophical journey through this physical world. Dr. Hofmann details the account of his first life-changing experience, when walking through the woods as a young boy he saw this energy and force of nature as a "White Light" - which fills not only your vision, but your mind and being as well. This is an experience that is never forgotten - a true turning point in life.

This same "Meditation Bench" hewn out of fallen trees from the property of Albert Hofmann and constructed by one of his sons, where I sat with Dr. Hofmann on that late July afternoon was so important to him that on the card informing the passing of Dr. Hofmann in 2008 sent by his son there is a photograph of his "Meditation Bench" with no one sitting on it anymore, empty except for Dr. Hofmann's cap and the cane he used the last couple of years of his life.

Unfortunately at about 6:00, this afternoon with Dr. Hofmann was coming to an end as he had other invited guests arriving shortly for dinner that evening. I promised Dr. Hofmann to send him a collection of Fluorescent minerals and a portable Black light to examine these wonders of nature with, and after just a few all-too-short hours together a bond was established with Dr. Hofmann that would exist through correspondence for the next ten years until his passing. After hours of talking about electrons, Fluorescence, Alchemy, acid, and life itself, we were disappointed to end the conversation, and Dr. Hofmann said he wished we could continue talking through the evening, but the guests to arrive that evening had already been invited some time ago.

What must be recorded here is the overall impression that was formed by meeting Dr. Hofmann and his wife Anita, both around ninety years old. Neither of them wore eyeglasses at ninety, both of them walked kilometers in "Nikes" every day on their mountain property at ninety, and both of them were about five feet tall. Honestly, both of them gave the impression of gliding effortlessly across the floor as they walked - like hovering. These physical attributes, absolutely incongruous to a couple both around ninety years old, were nothing compared to looking into the eyes of these two enlightened human beings. That is my lasting memory: of meeting a truly enlightened human being - a spiritual being - not just a mortal being or a Swiss chemist.

In truth, one of the most precious memories of meeting Dr. Hofmann was the astonishment he showed as he exclaimed in question: "Minerals *FLUORESCE??*" To bring that concept to such an enlightened human being was just as astounding for this author, who was just less than half his age, as it was for Dr. Hofmann himself. A month later, back in Amsterdam I prepared a large parcel to send to Dr. Hofmann containing a full selection of different major Fluorescent mineral specimens from around the globe, along with a detailed explanation of each Fluorescent mineral specimen and a written explanation of "Electron Displacement - the cause of Fluorescence." Also included in this first large parcel I sent Dr. Hofmann was the essential portable Black light with batteries for him to examine this miracle of Fluorescence for himself. I remember that the parcel I sent to Dr. Hofmann in August, 1998 was so large that I photographed it(!) A month later I received a letter from Dr. Hofmann:

"Coming home from a vacation in France I was surprised to find a magic box on my desk. I thank you very much for your nice and instructive letter and for your generous gift, the selected collection of fluorescent minerals, the ultra violet detector, the phantastic colored picture from Electric Lady, the set of wonderful photographs from your expedition to the Himalayas, and for the excellent pictures of your visit at Rittematte [Dr. Hofmann's house].

Anita and I were deeply impressed by your personalities so full of life and love. It seems to me that you enjoy the best of both, the Western and eastern wisdoms.

I have already had a short look at the fascinating colors that appear under the light of the ultra violet detector. I shall study with much interest the single minerals, following the comment you gave to each species.

May be that I shall attend the conference PSYCHOACTIVITY that will take place 1-4 October in Amsterdam. If this will be the case I shall not miss the opportunity to report about my experiences with your fascinating minerals.

My wife joins me in sending you best wishes and kind regards,

Albert Hofmann"

In 2001 I made a portrait of Dr. Albert Hofmann with Fluorescent bubble-jet inks I printed in the gallery from a photo I took in his private study with the first model of the molecular structure of acid on his wall behind him. I added stars, energies, clouds, and many Colors to the original photo on my Apple and sent Dr. Hofmann the Fluorescent mounted portrait, an eighteen watt Black light, and instructions for viewing his Fluorescent portrait: "I've printed the portrait with Fluorescent bubble-jet inks, so if you turn off the lights and switch on your "Ultraviolet Detector" the portrait is completely <u>Fluorescent</u>." Along with this Fluorescent portrait I also wrote to Dr. Hofmann and asked him again my question about the possible physiological effects on a person immersed in an environment of Fluorescence with the energy of Electron Displacement taking place all around them, and furthermore, the effects on a person in the same environment with an added psychoactive substance in their minds. Dr. Hofmann finally wrote me the answer that I had been asking him since my first letter to him in 1992. In my second letter of 1993, and in my first telephone call to him in 1998 I had also repeated the same question - the question that ultimately got me invited to his house, which no one had ever asked him before. In my May 15, 1994 letter to Dr. Hofmann I addressed the question in this manner:

"Congratulations on the 51st Anniversary of your "Wonder Child." I wrote to you last year and sent you photographs of my "Mind-Arising Boxes" and "Electric Lady." We are in the process of preparing "Electric Ladyland - the First Museum of Fluorescent Art" downstairs from the gallery. It is an environment we've planned for many years - a Fluorescent environment you can enter physically as well as spiritually. All the parts of the environment were designed to have the viewer become a <u>Participant</u> in the piece of Art. The person visiting the museum must interact with the piece of Art. All the interaction is not fruitless - the gentle changes of perspective and even body-motions that the "participant" goes through exploring the areas of the environment are carefully designed to capture the Attention and center the Awareness. Nothing is 'taught' to a viewer in this Art - but many things can be learned by a participant on their own by just entering and exploring the environment I've been building for years downstairs. It is an attempt to communicate in a gentle, non-imposing way to others what your "Wonder Child" and living and Art have taught. In lesser or greater degrees, all true Art is gentle sorcery - the altering of awareness and perspective. The museum won't be opened for many more months, but you will certainly receive an invitation to the opening.

My question to you is something I've wondered about for years:

A.) Could this "process of Energy Exchange" taking place on a massive scale - with 1000s of watts of ultraviolet lighting exchanging energy with an immense amount of fluorescent color (like in the museum we are opening) effect a human being on a Physiological level?

B.) And further more, would being on a psychoactive substance like acid compound or alter the physiological effect of the "energy exchange" in a person?

This may seem a little like "out in left field," but after seeing the effect of the "Energy Exchange" in people that come into our gallery for the last years and experience Fluorescent Colors on a large scale, and learning about the Electron Displacement and the energy given off on an atomic level, I think that it must effect a person physiologically.

Your professional opinions on this matter would be extremely important and are greatly anticipated."

That original question which I had asked Dr. Hofmann in both of my first two letters to him of 1992 and 1993, and which I repeated to Dr. Hofmann on my first telephone call to him in July, 1998, was finally answered nine years later in this hand-written letter back from Dr. Hofmann dated December, 2001. The spelling is quoted from the original letter. In this December, 2001 letter, Dr. Hofmann not only answers the question I had been asking him for nine years, but also writes me one of the highest compliments of my life:

"You made me a wonderful surprising Christmas gift to me and Anita by your lovely letters and extra-ordinary pictures and photos. We send you our heart-felt thanks.

I remember with great pleasure my visit in your museum of fluorescent art in Amsterdam, and Anita and I are happy to have you even both as guests at Rittematte.

I must express my highest astonishment and respect about your talent as artist and your faculty as master of the new techniques in computer art, which find the expression in the great marvellous picture of myself - <u>a really psichedelic artwork</u>. I send you my heartfelt thanks for this gift.

And now your question: I do not believe that fluorescent light has any physiological effect on human beings, even under Acid. Effects on the psyche are probable.

Pictures produced by UV-light are as real as those produced by normal light. They become consceous, real, only on the inner screen, of an individual.

Anita and I wish you both enduring good health and good luck and happiness in the new year."

Also sent by Dr. Hofmann in his letter was a page of "The Entheogen Review" from the "Summer Solstice 2001" in which he is quoted as stating the fact that he was both a "chemist" and a "natural scientist," and explains that from the beginning of his "philosophical thinking" he was interested in the "relationship" between spiritual and material worlds. Dr. Hofmann next states that although the material and spiritual worlds are "often regarded" as being two separate worlds, in his opinion just the "opposite is true," with the material world and the spiritual world being complementary.

One of the precious books given by Dr. Albert Hofmann on the day we visited his house in 1998 will be presented as a conclusion to this open question of the origins of religion being rough-sculpted by prehistoric experiments with psychoactive substances. This book is "Entheogens and the Future of Religion" from 1997, and is a collection of essays from Dr. Albert Hofmann, R. Gordon Wasson, and others. In the introduction by Robert Forte, the author clearly states in plain English that one of the biggest "problems" that the past fifty years of the "Psychedelic Movement" had encountered was the world-encompassing ego of 'the Prince of Acid' Timothy Leary, who Forte very tactfully labels as the past "cheerleader" of psychedelics. Forte clearly documents the facts that his contemporaries, who were much more wise and had only a fraction of Leary's ego, such as the visionary Aldous Huxley, understood these psychedelic substances were sacred and should be treated with something that Leary hardly understood, respect.

In Dr. Hofmann's essay on 'The Eleusian Mystery's Message for the World Today,' in "Entheogens and the Future of Religion," the facts and preparation of the "Kykeon" potion drunk by every initiate of the Eleusian Mysteries are very clearly examined by Dr. Hofmann. First of all Dr. Hofmann examines the parallels between the Eleusian Mysteries of ancient Greece and to the "magic cults" of Indians in southern Mexico. In the research laboratories of "Sandoz" in Basel, Switzerland, Dr. Hofmann explains discovering that seeds of some of the "Morning Glory" species used for millennia by Mexican Indians contain active psychoactive substances such as lysergic acid amide that are "near relatives" of lysergic acid diethylamide, both products of the parasite Ergot. Further experimentation by Dr. Hofmann concluded that the "very same" psychoactive hallucinogenic substances found in both acid and Morning Glory seeds were also contained in the Ergot on the wild grass "Paspalum districhum" found around Athens and in the entire Mediterranean area. In fact Dr. Hofmann writes that this wild grass was so common in the area of Eleusis that it must have grown in "the vicinity" of the temple of Eleusis itself. Dr. Hofmann definitively answers a very old question by further explaining that it was just plain simple for the Eleusian priests 2,500 years ago to have continuously for millennia prepared a hallucinogenic potion - the "Kykeon" - for the initiates of the Eleusian Mysteries on schedule. Just by collecting the Ergot off of this wild grass by hand, which was again found commonly in the areas of Athens and Eleusis itself, the Eleusian priests then had to simply crush the Ergot and pour it into water.

To close this historical inquiry into the deep past of ancient Greece and the Eleusian Mysteries, Dr. Hofmann bridges the lessons of antiquity to the present day and addresses the question of how the Eleusian Mysteries can be used as a "model" for psychoactive use in today's society. Dr. Hofmann recognizes the fundamental differences between the ancient Greek consciousness and the "Dualistic" European world view equipped with an inflated ego, which is sufficiently capable of objectively regarding all nature and the universe around them as outside of themselves - being completely dislocated from nature, thus able to efficiently rape and plunder everything around themselves as well. This global environmental crisis that contemporary humans have single-handedly created as their modern "masterpiece" in such an astonishing and alarming short span of time, is the real "Problem Child" of the world today, in actuality. In typical clarity Dr. Hofmann also states that the most serious consequence of our modern christian-based dualistic view of the world is not the well-publicized raping of nature, but an even deeper wound: the "spiritual damage" that such an egotistical consciousness creates. The completely "materialistic" individual has totally lost their "connection" to the divine and the spiritual. Dr. Hofmann continues with the consequences, which are the natural extensions of existing in this reduced spiritually-void manner, and concludes correctly that the "human individual" becomes a "soulless," "unprotected" being, and in the end is reduced to being alone "with oneself."

Dr. Hofmann offers society's attempts in the modern day to return to a spiritual existence, such as the "Eastern religions" which provide the opportunity for adherents to such timeless philosophies an experience into the mystical side of existence. The world of "psychology and psychiatry" and "ecclesiastical circles" are included by Dr. Hofmann as paths towards global and individual healing, as well as the reattainment of a civilization and culture with a spiritual foundation. Just as lucidly Dr. Hofmann counters with the facts that the "official" christian churches are in control of today's sociological pulse, and that their "dogmas" not only perpetuated, but literally helped initiate the modern "dualistic" materialistic view of the world around us. Dr. Hofmann clearly also states that this christian-dominated state of modern mind offers "little room" for the evolution of society to return to a spiritual life. The alternatives are offered by Dr. Hofmann, as a path to healing and spirituality, including 'yoga and meditation' and private groups of people seeking "self-encounter," all with a common goal of the expansion or alteration of the consciousness.

Dr. Hofmann concludes his discussion with the fact that throughout human history groups of people, or individuals, on the journey of the expansion of their consciousness have used substances to induce altered states. The ancient Greeks named these consciousness-altering substances "Pharmacotheon" which translates as "divine drug." Dr. Hofmann also clearly points out the dramatic difference between the preparation for taking a "divine drug" in the ancient world, and the lack of any preparation for taking these "divine drugs" in modern society, as well as the differences between the Mexican Indian's ceremonies for "divine drugs" such as Morning Glory seeds, which involved fasting and praying in preparation for their life-changing psychoactive experience and even the guiding light of a shaman present during their experience, compared to the relatively opposite way it was taken during the 1960s and in contemporary times. The Mexican Indian's long history of psychoactive use, and the Eleusian Mysteries of ancient Greece are two examples that Dr. Hofmann offers as "models" for today's society on the journey of spirituality and expanded consciousness.

The journey on the path to higher understanding and a better life is lucidly pointed out by Dr. Hofmann to be obtainable only by the "individual person" themselves - and not by the brutal vulgar herd of society in mass.

After personally having met many Sadhus and holy people in India since first traveling there in 1987, the truth is that very few of these holy people came close to the state of enlightenment that I witnessed in the ninety-two year old Dr. Albert Hofmann; the memory of Dr. Hofmann sitting right next to me on his outdoor porch while we spoke that July 1998 afternoon when he looked directly into my eyes and asked with utter surprise and excited anticipation: "Minerals FLUORESCE?!?" My letter describing the contents of the small selection of Fluorescent minerals I sent to Dr. Hofmann in August, 1998, after returning from his house, will be presented in conclusion:

"Dr. Albert Hofmann,

In deep appreciation of your hospitality on the occasion of our visit to your house on July 21, 1998, I send you a small selection of very fascinating FLUORESCENT MINERALS. We spoke for a long time about the phenomenon of Fluorescence on the quantum level, involving Electron Displacement, and how it is related to the Museum of Fluorescent Art we are opening in Amsterdam, such as the question of a physiological effect on a person immersed in a massive amount of energy being emitted by the 32 cubic meter Fluorescent Environment lit by 1000 watts of Ultraviolet lamps in the Museum. While speaking of the phenomenon, we talked of Fluorescent Minerals. We have been collecting Fluorescent Minerals for displays in the Museum for years, and have been to "The Fluorescent Mineral Capital of the World" = Franklin, New Jersey many times to find large and special pieces. The pieces we send to you are the most well known and brightest of the Fluorescent Minerals excited by Longwave Ultraviolet (365 nanometers). There are also Fluorescent Minerals that are excited by Shortwave (254 nm) and some excited by Middlewave (300 nm). There are even some very special Fluorescent Minerals that react to Longwave <u>and</u> Shortwave UV, changing Colors dramatically from the Longwave to the Shortwave lamps. A good example is the little piece of Calcite crystal from Terlingua, Texas, which is Salmon-Pink under the Longwave U.V., and then turns Sky Blue under the Shortwave U.V. - when the Shortwave is turned off, it has a bright and long-lasting Phosphorescence of <u>Sky Blue</u>. We hope that you're fascinated by these Fluorescent Minerals as well - look at them on the Black cloth I've sent, and do it in the <u>DARK</u>, so as to see the Colors the best. After holding the U.V. lamp over the mineral selection for some time, switch off the lamp and you'll see the Phosphorescence of at least 1 of your minerals.

<u>After</u> viewing the Fluorescent Minerals, look at the small pieces of Fluorescent Art we've sent you, to see the difference between natural Fluorescence, and the intensity of the Fluorescence of Synthetic Phosphors in Fluorescent Paint (as well as the Fluorescent and Phosphorescent Holy Mala from India for Mrs. Hofmann).

After returning to Amsterdam, I read your book that you gave to me, "Insight/Outlook" two times, as well as "Entheogens and the Future of Religion." "Insight/Outlook" is a book written from the soul itself. Even though much of the writing is about facts of Life and Science, it has an incredible organic quality - like the famous "Owner's Manual" we were never given at birth with the most complicated of physical/spiritual entities known in the universe - namely, ourselves. Thank you for the opportunity to have met you and to have spent an afternoon in true "psychedelic communico" at your house. It was a day that we will never forget. After years of hearing many people <u>speak</u> about true enlightenment in many places around the world, it was a rewarding experience to meet a truly Enlightened Human Being who also changed the world for Better and Forever.

If you have some moments we are very much interested in your reaction to the Fluorescence of the minerals with the U.V. lamp, so please write us.

I can't thank you enough for all you've done, and for the afternoon we spent together.

Gratefully yours,"

[The second half of this letter to Dr. Hofmann consisted of seven pages, which contained the name, locality, and description of each of the Fluorescent Minerals I sent to Dr. Hofmann, along with the details of their individual Colors under the "White Light" and then under the "Black Light." Next to each Fluorescent Mineral's descriptive paragraph was a drawing of the individual specimens I sent, made to it's exact size and shape, so Dr. Hofmann could match them up if the labels were lost on the specimens themselves:]

"1. FLUORITE
   - crystals of Fluorite
   - Weardale, Durham, England
   - This is the mineral that FLUORESCENCE got it's name from in 1852 from Sir George Stokes
   - <u>White Light</u> = clear to Pinkish/Purplish crystals
   - <u>Black Light</u> (U.V.) = Bright <u>BLUE</u>
2. "RUBY" = CORUNDUM
   - most of the famous Gemstones are Fluorescent, including Diamonds, Sapphires, Rubies, Emeralds, Coral, and Amber explaining why people have always had a fascination for tiny chunks of translucent minerals.
   - The Ruby has the most intense and unvarying Red Fluorescence, and it is the basis of the Laser.
   - <u>White Light</u> = Red
   - <u>Black Light</u> = Deep Red
3. SCAPOLITE
   - Bancroft, Ontario, Canada
   - one of the brightest and most famous Longwave Fluorescent Minerals along with Fluorite.
   - <u>White Light</u> = Grey/Grey-Greenish
   - <u>Black Light</u> = Bright <u>Yellow/Apricot</u>
4. OPALITE (Raw Opal)
   - Nevada, U.S.A.
   - Formed from Volcanic Dust compacting on the flat lands of Nevada for millennia
   - <u>White Light</u> = translucent Beige
   - <u>Black Light</u> = Bright <u>GREEN</u>
5. AUTUNITE
   - Queensland, Australia
   - This is one of the "Uranium" minerals
   - It's Fluorescent "activator" atoms are of the "Uranyl" group, composed of one atom of Uranium and two atoms of Oxygen. They are very <u>slightly</u> radioactive, so slight as to have no harm
   - <u>White Light</u> = Brown
   - <u>Black Light</u> = bright <u>Green</u>
6. MANGANO CALCITE
   - Peru
   - Calcite is the most common Fluorescent Mineral coming in every color of the Spectrum, but the most famous of the Fluorescent Calcites is MANGANO CALCITE which is activated by a trace amount (impurity) of MANGANESE in the Calcite, and always has shades of Red Fluorescence
   - <u>White Light</u> = White with a tint of Pinkish
   - <u>Black Light</u> = <u>Red</u>
7. STRONTIANITE
   - Massa Marittima, Italy
   - One of the Brightest Red Fluorescent Minerals in the world.
   - <u>White Light</u> = Grey/Greenish
   - <u>Black Light</u> = Bright <u>Red</u>
8. CALCITE crystal
   - Terlingua, Texas
   - This is a natural, perfect crystal of Calcite. It's crystal structure is "Rhombohedral."
   - <u>White Light</u> = White/Grey
   - <u>Longwave U.V.</u> = Salmon Pink
   - <u>Shortwave U.V.</u> = Blue
   - <u>SW Phosphorescence</u> = Blue
9. HYDRO ULEXITE
   - Faras, Turkey
   - A very odd mixture of crystals and Fluorescent Color response.

  -<u>White Light</u> = White-Grey-Beige
  -<u>Black Light</u> = Orangish/Yellow
10. ADVERDISSEN/ARAGONITE
  -Saurerland, Germany
  -Much of the Stalagmites, Stalactites, "Draperies," and other Cave structures formed by groundwater leaving trace minerals while seeping through cracks in the Earth's crust are composed of this mineral and/or Calcite.
  -<u>White Light</u> = White; "Marble" like sparkle
  -<u>Black Light</u> = White/Beige - Bright
  -<u>Phosphorescence</u> = Green
11. CALCITE, FLUORITE, WILLEMITE
  -Purple Passion Mine, Arizona, U.S.A.
  -This tiny piece is composed of <u>three</u> Fluorescent Minerals, but only <u>2</u> can be seen with the Longwave U.V. lamp.
  -<u>White Light</u> = Grey/Beige
  -<u>Longwave</u> = <u>Fluorite</u>=Blue / <u>Calcite</u>=Red
  -<u>Shortwave</u> = <u>Fluorite</u>=Blue / <u>Calcite</u>=Red / <u>Willemite</u>=Beige/Whitish Green
12. "<u>Xanthoria Parientina</u>"" LICHEN
  -organic and Living
  -<u>White Light</u> = Yellow Orangish
  -<u>Black Light</u> = Red/Orange

- When you brought us on a walk into the field of your property, at the beginning of the walk near the top of your drive-way, before you come to the path that leads to the field with the stone marker, there was a tree over-grown with several kinds of <u>Lichens</u> = I mentioned it as we walked by, but now you can see the response with your portable U.V. lamp. This Lichen can be clearly seen on the bark of that tree, as well as a White Fluorescing Lichen called "Pleopsidium Oxytonum" ('Lizard Semen' from the Red Indians).
- Last Summer I made a 2 volume Book and Slide Show called "Common Items that are Fluorescent." It was a fascinating project for both of us, seeing Fluorescence in many places we never expected it. The 10 sections of the Book and Slide Show were:
1. <u>Money, Stamps, and Train Tickets</u>
  -(all <u>Swiss</u> paper money, Stamps, and local train tickets are <u>Highly</u> Fluorescent)
2. <u>Depression Glass</u>
  -Green Glass made in the USA in the 1920s and 1930s (originally called "Uranium Glass" before the 1950s scare, and is activated by URANYL, like the mineral "Autunite")
3. <u>Fluorescent and Phosphorescent PLASTICS</u>
4. <u>Fluorescent and Phosphorescent PAINT PIGMENTS</u>
5. <u>Household Items = FOODS, SPICES, and TEAS</u>
  -By far the most fascinating section:
  20 fresh vegetables
  19 dried or prepared foods
  10 fruits
  8 spices
  Teas
  and Psychoactive Substances, such as Magic Mushrooms, Peyote cactus, Marijuana, and Hashish
6. <u>Shells, Sand, and Coral</u>
7. <u>Trees, flowers, and Lichens</u>
8. <u>Amber</u>
9. <u>Gemstones</u>
10. <u>Bones, Fossils, and Ivory</u>

-More than 15% of the known mineral kingdom is Fluorescent, totaling more than 550 different minerals, but <u>ALL</u> ORGANIC Substances - living, dead, or petrified, are FLUORESCENT (to a greater or lesser degree). One of the most precious natural resources of the earth is Fluorescent: CRUDE OIL! And all the photographs of Galaxies and Nebulas from Deep Space are, in fact, the largest display of Fluorescence known to exist. Young, hot Stars give off tremendous amounts of Ultraviolet, illuminating gases and particles of galaxies. This phenomenon of FLUORESCENCE is truly amazing to me after years of working with it."

    A year before he passed away, Dr. Albert Hofmann wrote a letter to Steve Jobs of "Apple" Computers on Valentine's Day 2007. Dr. Hofmann had learned from "media accounts" that Steve Jobs had stated that he had been 'helped creatively in his development with Apple Computers by LSD,' and in his handwritten letter to Steve Jobs, Dr. Hofmann points this out in his first sentence. Dr. Hofmann then asks Steve Jobs how acid was "useful" to him in developing Apple Computers as well as in his personal spiritual quest. Dr. Hofmann explains to Steve Jobs that he had just passed his 101st birthday and that he was requesting his support for the Swiss psychiatrist Dr. Peter Gosser, who is doing the first acid-assisted psychotherapy study in over thirty-five years, which is on people suffering with 'anxiety from life-threatening illnesses.' Dr. Hofmann closes his letter hoping that Steve Jobs will help make the "transformation" of his "problem child" into his "wonder child."

    On the back cover of the most comprehensive book on the one-hundred and two year life of Dr. Albert Hofmann, "Mystic Chemist" from 2013, there is a quote from Steve Jobs, billionaire founder of "Apple" Computers, one of the most successful corporations in the world. After being an Art student, traveling to India, and taking acid in the early 1970s, the lasting impression of his experience was that 'taking acid' for Steve Jobs was what he defined as a "profound experience," as well as being what he considered one of the experiences which were the 'most important of his life.' This opinion of the extremely successful billionaire who changed the world, Steve jobs, as shocking as it will be to the average person, is contrary to popular belief, and is the identical opinion of the majority of the millions of people who have experienced acid in the last seventy-plus years. One of the most precious photos in the three-hundred and eighty-four pages of this book by Dieter Hagenbach and Lucius Werthmuller, is an image of Dr. Hofmann sitting absorbed in deep contemplation in the year 2000, at the age of ninety-four, on his only journey to the Temple of Eleusis in Greece, used for over fifteen-hundred years during the "Eleusian Mysteries." Hari Om. At the age of one-hundred and one, in 2007 Dr. Albert Hofmann was voted the "Greatest Living Genius" by the "Daily Telegraph" in London.

    The weakest of all the true "Psychoactive" substances is still used throughout the world as it has been for thousands of years: Cannabis. Richard Evans Schultes lists hemp fabric from ten centuries ago having been discovered in Turkey, as well as hemp fabric from ancient Egypt from four thousand years ago. 3,000 years ago Marijuana was made into an intoxicating drink in ancient Thebes, and the Scythians burned leaves and seeds of 'Pot.' 4,800 years ago Cannabis was already used in Chinese traditional medicine, with names indicating it's usage, including "Liberator.' For over 3,000 years Cannabis has been used in India for medicine with similar names indicating the usage of this Cannabis, such as "Heavenly." This Marijuana, the weakest and therefore the most palatable psychedelic substance commonly used, has literally changed the world again in the last half of a century. The famous astronomer Edmund Halley, who is still known today for his discovery of "Halley's Comet" was one of the founding fathers of the first scientific formation, "The British Royal Academy." What is both unknown, as well as being shocking in today's very sober atmosphere, is that Edmund Halley as a founding father of "The British Royal Academy" wrote a paper on Marijuana!

    In the end all Cannabis came originally from central Asia, including "Cannabis Stavita," most commonly used in the west today, "Cannabis Indica," most common still in it's native locality of central Asia, and the obscure "Cannabis Ruderalis." Cannabis was transported from the "Old World" to the Americas by the actual "Pilgrims" who brought hemp to New England to produce fiber, and by the Spanish and Portuguese to central and South America. Richard Schultes in "Hallucinogenic Plants" states that Cannabis entered the United States in the 1920s through the vicinity of New Orleans, with most references citing Jamaica as the island where it was brought from to New Orleans.

    In a very recent reportage on the subject of Cannabis, "National Geographic" Television broadcast a show in the Fall of 2010 named "Drugs, Inc. - Cannabis." In the respected style of "National Geographic Society," this contemporary show on Cannabis was non-bias, and stated clearly and fairly both the psychological and medical effects of smoking Marijuana. This "National Geographic" 2010 documentary states quite clearly that seventy years of prohibition has conclusively not worked, and for the broken system of prohibition, in the United States alone two Trillion dollars have been wasted since the 1970s on the so-called "War on Drugs." This was enough money to feed the population of the planet. And the best part is that after spending over two thousand Billion dollars on this "War," today more people smoke Marijuana than ever before in history -

even more people than in the psychedelic 1960s! In 2010 forty-seven percent of all citizens in the USA admit to having smoked Cannabis, including the current President of the United States, and at least one other President who has also admitted to having tried Marijuana, President Bill Clinton. But it doesn't stop the 'small town' and empty-headed religious fanatics of America from spending $142 Billion dollars *a year* on their "Pipe dream" of eradicating "Pot." Let us not forget that in 2005 of this Twenty-first century there was a Supreme Court case centered on Dover, Pennsylvania ruling that it was illegal to teach "Creationism" in high school(!)

What are the current results of seventy years of failed Cannabis prohibition in the mighty United States? The result of spending two trillion dollars on stamping out the "Evil Weed" - or as it was originally stigmatized almost one hundred years ago - "Reefer Madness(!)" - is that in the state of California in 2010, the biggest cash crop was not Grapes for the famous California wine industry, or Vegetables for eating, or even Corn for human and livestock consumption, but - wait for it - *Marijuana!* Not only is Marijuana the biggest cash crop of California - outselling even Grapes - but in 2010 there were over 2,100 legal stores selling 'Medical Marijuana" for legal use! The statistics are enough to make Richard Millhouse Nixon stand up straight in his well-deserved grave: In 2010 there are more legal Marijuana stores in California - selling up to one hundred different strands of Marijuana in each store - than there are "McDonalds," "Starbucks," and "7-11" Convenience Stores *all combined!* Another good example of how good prohibition of Cannabis has worked during the last century, and also a good justification for wasting two trillion dollars when a good portion of the world's population is still starving. The author assumes most readers are aware of the new Marijuana laws established in Colorado and other states in America between 2013 and 2016 as well.

As a conclusion to this discussion on the 1960s and the doors it opened both socially and psychologically, during the beginning of this Twenty-first century many old prejudices and stigmatized subjects, as well as substances, have begun to be reexamined. There have been recent studies in both America and Switzerland using legally sanctioned psychoactive substances such as acid and psilocybin, and public opinion has become slightly more open minded in regards to these stigmatized, formerly legal and medicinal, illegal substances. "National Geographic" television released the first publicly broadcast show that was not prejudice in either direction entitled "Inside LSD" in 2009, and this professional presentation began with naming major life-altering events in a person's life, such as 'You graduate from college, you fall in love, you take acid.' Another movie which won documentary film awards in 2011 on the life and work of Dr. Albert Hofmann was made by a Swiss director and was entitled "The Substance: Albert Hofmann's LSD." It seems society has come to a point where the questioning of everything is currently ongoing. People are starting to see that old ideas and attitudes were sometimes formed too swiftly, or without the proper depth of study. This is a common occurrence on the path to understanding. When DNA study was in it's infancy, this "Genetic code of life" was initially referred to as the "stupid" compound of the body, and one of the first widespread applications that society so wisely formulated for this world-changing discovery of DNA was "Eugenics!"

This is a very late addition to this book, which I have accumulated over the past eight years, and this addition is written on July 5, 2015, the day of a historic occasion: the Fiftieth Anniversary of the band and the final performance of the "Grateful Dead" playing in the same stadium that they played in for their last show together before Jerry Garcia passed away twenty years ago. This final addition to this book would have never happened in any possible way if it wasn't for the "Grateful Dead" and the entire "1960s Movement" which they fronted. It is in a very real way nothing less than a "crowning achievement" of the entire 1960s Movement and everything it not only stood for, but was quite literally founded on. Going to the Schiphol Airport with Michèle on route for my birthday to Basel's exquisite Gauguin exhibition, in which would be Gauguin's masterpiece "Where Do We Come From? Why are We Here? Where are We Going?" on only it's third excursion out of the Boston Museum of Fine Arts in history (that Michèle and I had travelled to Paris in 2003 to see on it's second excursion from Boston) there was amazingly a magazine plastered ten feet high all over every magazine shop in the airport with a full "Pot" leaf on it's front cover! Now I know that this is the Amsterdam Schiphol Airport, but upon closer inspection I was amazed to find that these multitude of Marijuana leaf-covered magazines were not "High Times" or something like I immediately thought of, but the magazines were - wait for it - *"National Geographic!"* Even more amazingly, when getting close and reading the article's title on the front cover right next to the life-sized "Pot" leaf it was not something negative or a warning of some sort which might easily be imagined, but: "WEED: the New Science of Marijuana"(!) Imagine *That!!*

From February fifteenth to May nineteenth, 2013 an exhibition was held in Paris at "Le Maison Rouge - Foundation Antoine de Galbert" entitled "Sous influences, arts plastiques et psychotropes" - "Under the Influence, Plastic Arts and Psychotropics." Directly from the website of "Le Maison Rouge," translated from French, the introductory text for this enlightening exhibition in Paris last year is very clear:

'Le Maison Rouge presents from February 15, 2013 'Under the Influence, Plastic Arts and Psychotropics,' that includes Artworks, documents, and films, the theme of this exhibition being the relationship that exists between 'Visual Arts' and 'Psychotropic substances.' Since the beginning of time, actually since the beginning of humanity, our ancestors have discovered Psychoactive substances contained in plants, fungi, and other life forms, which resulted in self experimentation and led to amazement, mystical access, relief, dependence, intoxication, death, or even illumination. Many Artists, who are always mentally curious could not avoid trying the effects of these Psychoactive substances.'

This 2013 exhibition in Paris, the center of the Art world a century ago, was curated by Antoine Perpère, and on the webpage of "Le Maison Rouge" announcing this exhibition, not only is the title and description of this exhibition clearly stated, but it is accompanied by a Color photograph of the oldest known Psychoactive Mushroom, "Amanita muscaria," the spotted Red-capped 'Fly agaric,' making the theme of this exhibition also very clearly stated, being the use of these Psychoactive substances throughout history by Artists as access to creation of the 'imaginary.' As with so many subjects that were never supposed to be talked about or explored, the subject of psychoactive drug use by Artists throughout history is also now being reexamined in a clear, new light, which is not only free from millennia of social stigmatization, but amazingly even helping to alter some of the traditional prejudice. It is still possible to find, over a hundred years after one of the initial Color-masters of Art died, authors who base their entire prejudicial biography on their stigmatized viewpoint that Paul Gauguin was an Artist as well as a drug addict, and created his Artistic oeuvre on his addiction to Morphine. Documented facts about Artists throughout history, especially in the last century, have been met with not only unacceptance, but also downright disbelief. Not only were the shocking, world-changing Colors used by Gauguin credited to his altered consciousness achieved through drug use, but there is a long list of not only famous Artists who were inspired by these consciousness-altering 'Psychotropic substances,' but entire Art movements which were inspired by these experiments with these substances. This is documented history, not public or personal opinion. A simple search on the internet will bring a wealth of references citing the association of the psychoactive experience with one of the movements in France that founded Modern Art, Cubism, members of which included Pablo Picasso and Robert Delaunay. Two early Surrealist movies that suggest an inspiration of 'Psychotropic substances' are "Un Chien Andalou" by Bunuel and Salvador Dali from 1928, and "Le Sang d'un Poète" by Cocteau in 1930, which has a loose similarity to Hesse's famous "Steppenwolf" of 1927. The list of movements of Art and Artists effected by 'Psychotropics' is quite substantial, even beyond Cubism, Dada, and Surrealism, exemplified by this 2013 exhibition "Under the Influence, Plastic Arts and Psychotropics" of "Le Maison Rouge" in Paris, the city of one of the most well documented inspired Artists, Henri Michaux, who wrote the book "Misérable miracle" about the Mescaline experience in 1956. Nobel Prize winner and world-famous author Rudyard Kipling wrote "The Jungle Book" many years after he was very involved with Opium, Morphine, and Indian Marijuana while living in India for seven years when he was young. Scholars have also written about the Dutch Renaissance Artist Hieronymus Bosch being inspired to create his incomparable creatures and worlds such as "The Garden of Earthly Delights" in the late 1400s and early 1500s from his experience with Hallucinogenic substances (psychoactive Mushrooms have been around for millions of years before humans evolved).

The main point of this investigation into the 1960s - the generation that brought the Black light and Fluorescent Colors to the world - and in particular, the main point about this investigation into the true history of the 1960s Movement, was to illustrate the parallel stigmatisms which have obscured history, including the true history of the 1960s Movement, and the true history of the Black light and Fluorescent Colors. This examination of the 1960s Movement and the use of psychoactive substances throughout recorded history was presented with the intentions of serving several purposes, including showing how wrong the viewpoint that both the Black light and Fluorescent Colors, as well as psychoactive substances were inventions of the 1960s, when the historic fact is that all of these were either invented or discovered decades, or even centuries before the "Hippie Movement" of the 1960s began, and in fact, a long time before the "Hippies" were even born.

To understand the physical and spiritual energy contained in Color itself, and how this energy is channeled, the late work of one of the most respected Color Theorists of the Twentieth century, Faber Birren was examined earlier in this chapter. Faber Birren published more than twenty-four books on Color Theory, and in turn he is regarded as the most widely read Color Theory authority of the Twentieth century. Applying his published Color Theory to the real world, Faber Birren has also worked as a Color consultant for corporations as well as government agencies. Birren explains in the introduction of "The Symbolism of Color" (1988) that as a professional Color consultant his expertise was centered on the psychological effects of Color, and that he had been employed by public institutions such as Neuropsychiatric hospitals. Amongst his published books are "Color: A Survey in Words and Pictures," and "Color Psychology and Color Therapy." Birren also confesses with pleasure in the introduction of "The Symbolism of Color" that over the course of his long career he had witnessed the change of society's acceptance towards the "mystic," which he lists as the "esoteric realms" of Color Therapy, ESP, the human aura, precognition, and faith healing.

"The Day-Glo Designer's Guide," "Day-Glo" Corporation (1969)

In reference to the 1960s Movement, which in reality made "Day-Glo" Fluorescent Colors world-famous, Robert Switzer, the inventor of Fluorescent Paint was no less derogatory or prejudice than any other middle-aged American at that time. In Liesa Bing's "The History of Day-Glo - The Switzer Brothers" the inventor of "Day-Glo" Fluorescent paint first lists the 1960s Movement as the "biggest market" for these Colors, after recementing the social fact that "designers consider" these "Day-Glo" Colors to be "garish." Robert Switzer's list of applications for these "garish" Fluorescent Colors, again bordering on the surreal, also recements society's decision to relegate this palette - the first in the world to emit it's own light through the energy of an Ultraviolet lamp - to the totally non-artistic uses of "Traffic cones," and also the equally banal "Traffic vests." "School guards" are added from Switzer's grandiose perspective, as well as "crossing flags," and finally "fire hydrants."

Robert Switzer, after unveiling his futuristic, esoteric applications of this unprecedented light-emitting paint, next goes on to unveil his equally common, typical outlook of the 1960s Movement in Liesa Bing's book, beginning with the statement that he couldn't "leave out" the 1960s "psychedelic period." His deep philosophic viewpoint is covered in one short sentence, stating that during this "psychedelic period" "Day-Glo" Fluorescent Colors were used "for whatever"(!) Just as deep is Robert Switzer's conclusion of the 1960s "psychedelic period," being that "we benefited" because of the "literally millions" of Black light posters "painted" with "Day-Glo" "psychedelic designs." This extensive investigation into the 1960s "psychedelic period" by Robert Switzer goes on for a vast seven whole sentences, where in the middle of this intensive codex Switzer mentions Ken Kesey, and in just a single sentence manages to not only mislead history, but also to change the name of Tom Wolfe's book, credit the misnamed book to Ken Kesey, and finally also manages to accuse Ken Kesey of plagiarism of the misnamed book that Kesey (or anybody else) never wrote. Again, this is the historic "Father of Day-Glo Paint!" Robert Switzer, in this third sentence of his all-encompassing seven sentence history of the "psychedelic period" is quoted in Bing's book as believing that Ken Kesey who wrote "One Flew Over the Cuckoo's Nest" also wrote - wait for it - *Electric Color Aid*"(!) In one swift blow Robert Switzer transmutes the name of the book "The Electric Kool-Aid Acid Test" into "Electric Color Aid," transmutes the author of that book Tom Wolfe into the book's main character Ken Kesey, and then - in the same sentence - accuses Ken Kesey of *Plagiarism* because "Color Aid" is a "Day-Glo" Corporation trademark! Robert Switzer concludes his expert, opulent seven sentence history of the "psychedelic period" with the unknown revelation that "sometimes" the 1960s psychedelic posters were used under "blacklight" (also managing to even spell "Black light" wrong). The cosmic conclusion reached by Robert Switzer, again: "business" for "Day-Glo" had gone "straight up." A tremendous amount of two whole other applications of "Day-Glo" Fluorescent Colors during the "psychedelic period" are listed by Robert Switzer as "textiles," which he adds the example of clothing with "bright Colors," as well as the application of "Day-Glo" Fluorescent 'packaging' for commercial use. The totally predictable conclusion from the inventor of Fluorescent Paint is that "the negative" part of the "psychedelic period" was "of course" the connection with "drugs."

As literal proof of "Karma" - or if the reader prefers, "poetic justice" - when the inventor of Fluorescent paint Robert Switzer, who spoke in such derogatory terms about the 1960s Movement and the Hippies, died in 1997 at the age of eighty-three his obituary was in the "New York Times" Sunday edition newspaper. After his published obvious distaste and negative feelings towards everything that the Psychedelic Movement of the 1960s represented, including its famous "Black light Posters" which sold with his "Day-Glo" ink by the millions, the full-Color photograph accompanying and announcing Robert Switzer's death in the "New York Times" was not a Fluorescent traffic cone, a Fluorescent police car, or even a Fluorescent World war two airplane, but - wait for it - one of the most famous 1960s Psychedelic Movement's "Black light Posters" (man)! This "Day-Glo" Black light poster accompanying Robert Switzer's obituary read by millions of people in the "New York Times" was not an abstract geometric design or even a rock star, but as "Furthur" proof of Switzer's Karma, the Back light poster was an illustration of one of the most famous stories ever written about the 'unfortunate illegal drugs,' "Alice in Wonderland!"

Typical of almost every middle-aged American business man who detested the 1960s "Hippie Movement," when there was money to be made they magically and dramatically changed their attitude towards this generation. Proof of this magical and dramatic transformation is contained in the countless thousands - or even millions - of gallons of "Day-Glo" Fluorescent Color used during the 1960s for Black light posters, Artwork, and again quoting Robert Switzer, "for whatever." Concrete proof of this dramatic, and not so 'magical' transformation of attitude towards the 1960s "psychedelic period" where a fortune was ripe to be made, exists in 1969 during the height and final climax of the 1960s "psychedelic period" when Robert Switzer published the lavish, extremely rare "Day-Glo Designer's Guide." This large book is in the Museum collection, and is a real "Designer's Guide" printed on very thick stock for practical use by a graphic designer, and also printed totally in Fluorescent ink. The very first impression when seeing this book printed by Robert Switzer in 1969 is that it is a "Hippie" book (!) which was absolutely intentionally designed this way to appeal to the 1960s consumer market, obviously. The front cover has a full illustration printed in brilliant "Day-Glo" Fluorescent Color which is an extremely proficient outright copy of 1960s famous Artist Peter Max's style, being a typical 1960s Peter Max landscape; the style which will fill a large part of this 1969 "Day-Glo Designer's Guide." Underneath this pseudo-Hippie landscape is the title "The Day-Glo Designer's Guide" and "price ten dollars" both also printed with round "Mod" letters. Opening the cover, the very first page is a large 1960s style collage printed with "Day-Glo" Colors in which Robert Switzer manages to plagiarize not only the world famous 1960s style of Peter Max, but also the world famous "Campbell's Tomato Soup" Artwork of Andy Warhol, also made famous in the 1960s.

The introduction of this 1969 "Day-Glo Designer's Guide" sets the stage, immediately beginning with the selling point to graphic designers that Fluorescent paint from "Day-Glo" was 'frequently used' to make a product 'shout,' giving the impression that all Fluorescence could do was "scream." The intention of this "Designer's Guide" was for 'shattering that illusion.' The "other dimension" of "Day-Glo" Colors is the intention of this book, illustrating that Fluorescent Colors were also capable of 'whispering, warming, and laughing.' The introduction of the 1969 "Day-Glo Designer's Guide" closes with the point that this book could make the user "experience" nothing less than "deja-vu" (man). The first chapter of this "Designer's Guide" recounts - and changes - 'The Day-Glo Story,' with historical facts leading to the invention of "Day-Glo" paint being changed in this 1969 publication, beginning with the altered fact that the younger brother Joe (at eighteen) is stated as being alone, not with his older brother Robert in the back room of his father's drug store, when he found some 'drugs which glowed' under his "improvised" black light, and then proceeded to be the first person who mixed these 'drugs together with shellac,' produced the first primitive Fluorescent paint, proceeded to paint "props" with this mixture, and then also made a black light show for a "magician's convention." Only at this point in the 'Day-Glo Story' is the actual inventor of Fluorescent paint, his nineteen year old brother Robert Switzer first introduced. After brother Bob had been impressed by Joe's black light Fluorescent Magic show, he is in this book first credited with a suggestion to his brother 'the inventor' to 'sell this stuff.' With $1.75 the Switzer brothers established "The Switzer Brothers' Ultra Violet Laboratories Company, Inc." in Berkley, California in their mother's kitchen. This "Day-Glo Story" continues, informing the reader that 'Night clubs, Theaters, Chorus girls, and the police' began to order vast amounts of the Switzer brother's newly invented Fluorescent paint. Credit is again given only to younger brother Joe in this revised history, explaining that prior to 1940 Joe invented a "revolutionary step" in allowing Fluorescent paint to glow in the daylight, without the assistance of a black light and still managing to produce four times the amount of light as "conventional colors." At least both brothers are credited as 'coining' "Daylight Fluorescence." The 'Day-Glo Story' next states that their invention "Fluorescent Fabric" was used to create Fluorescent "signaling" and "visual communication" devices by the military who used millions of meters (yards). After the war, this "Guide" explains that "Day-Glo" Fluorescent Colors began to be used industrially in Graphic Arts for silk screening, and states that the first use was in Canada during 1947. The text continues, listing the registration of "Day-Glo" as the trademark of the Switzer brother's Fluorescent Color first in Canada in 1944, next in the U.S. in 1947, and later worldwide. The "Guide" also lists 1956 as the date that mid-air collisions began to be avoided by use of "Day-Glo" paint at Hondo, Texas' Air Training Command. In 1959 the Division of Fish and Game in Massachusetts, the Strategic Army Command in the U.S., as well as the "American Optical Co." all proved that Fluorescent Orange was the only Color that could be seen by both normal visioned people and people with Color deficiency, which resulted in the mandatory laws of hunters wearing Fluorescent Orange clothing. Not to be excluded from the surreal applications of Fluorescent Colors, 1959 is also listed in the "Guide" as the date when Proctor and Gamble changed the Color of their "Tide" detergent package to "Day-Glo" gravure ink. 1962 is the year listed as when 'one-impression Litho-letter-press' Fluorescent ink was invented, and 1963 is the date "ROP News Ink" was first made Fluorescent. "Flexographic ink" is listed as being made Fluorescent first in 1967 with "chips" of "Day-Glo," and then in 1969 industrial strength "Day-Glo" "Letter-press Litho" Fluorescent ink was first made. The story of the history of "Day-Glo" ends in 1969 in this "Guide" with the realization by graphic designers that, again, "Day-Glo" Fluorescent Colors could be used not only to "shout" for Hard Sell packaging and promotion, but also to 'whisper in good taste' with their new medium.

After referring typically in a very derogatory manor about the 1960s "psychedelic period" and in just as derogatory manor about one of it's main instigators Ken Kesey, famous for the Merry Pranksters and the famous first "Day-Glo" psychedelic 1960s Hippie school bus "Furthur," the first page of the first chapter in this 1969 "Day-Glo Designers' Guide" presents one of the biggest, most Fluorescent full-page Peter Max plagiarized illustration in the entire book: a "Day-Glo"

1960s Hippie School Bus(!) *Not only that,* but the chapter title of the first chapter in this "Day-Glo Designers' Guide" - printed in far-out Hippie lettering as well - unbelievably plagiarizes the most famous quote of Ken Kesey that exists: *"You're either On the Bus, or Off the Bus"(!)* Again, just as typically, Robert Switzer and the "Day-Glo Corporation" not only do not credit Ken Kesey as the author of the title of the first chapter in their book, but use this plagiarized quote for their own purposes, stating in the opening lines of the chapter that "few designers" were "neutral" in opinion of "Day-Glo" Colors, but that - again plagiarizing Kesey's quote - "you're either on the bus or off the bus(!)"

Further cementing in history the 'frivolity' of these first full palette of Colors in the world to emit light through the energy of an Ultraviolet lamp, the "Day-Glo Designers' Guide" states that in the "early days" Fluorescent Colors were viewed as nothing more than a "novelty." Momentarily becoming philosophical, this "Designers' Guide" reflects on the point that perhaps the reason that "Day-Glo" paint was only used in 'black lit bars' and for 'signs which shouted,' was because these listed early formed associations have effectively labelled "Day-Glo" Fluorescent Colors "too crass" to use for "delicate sensibilities." Worded so poetically it could have been written by Goethe or Charles Blanc. This all-too-obvious sales pitch ends with a predictable line that only the "adventurous" graphic designers interested in designing for "tomorrow" are using "Day-Glo" Fluorescent Colors. The following two pages reproduce graphic Art in full "Day-Glo" as examples of work of graphic designers who were "on the bus." The "Day-Glo" record album covers of the 1960s group "Cream," "Wheels of Fire" and "Desraeli Gears" are presented first, along with a black light 'Cat' poster, and then finally a real Peter Max "Captain Midnight" poster from 1967. These four are printed together with the facing page giving a full page illustration in "Day-Glo" of Toulouse Lautrec also by Peter Max, from 1966. So after three whole pages the next chapter is aptly titled "Sales Promotion." The full page "Day-Glo" collage that starts this chapter "Sales Promotion" is a collection of the most lame examples of the graphic use of "Day-Glo" Fluorescent Colors - of course with the "psychedelic period" in mind - including "Jesus" and "Soul Food." For example, turning the page - after three pages of 'hippie' - the reader is presented with just the opposite: 'Madison Avenue.' Two Fluorescent illustrations of football players are followed by many more obvious examples of 'respectable' uses of these Colors, such as "Lord and Taylor," "Universal Studios," "Conductron Corporation," and "Color Engineering." These are followed by still more 'respectable' uses for "Day-Glo" Colors, exemplified by "Lenmore Press, Inc.," the "Diamond-Shamrock Chemical Co.," and "Westinghouse." After five full pages of 'respectable' uses for "Day-Glo," page sixteen presents the 'respectable' corporation "Bell and Howell's" "Protest" with a "Day-Glo" print of two "Peace" signs during a demonstration which they use as an example of the theme entitled "today's filmmakers," along with four other psychedelic illustrations. The next page in this 1969 "Designers' Guide" is a full die-cut "Day-Glo" package which was intended to be removed from this "Guide" and used as a three dimensional example of a Fluorescent package. The flat package is in the shape of a christian cross, and this folds into a six-sided box. This "Sales Promotion" chapter ends with a final effective stab at respectability with the classic old fashioned American technique of justification through European acceptance. A "Day-Glo" design printed by a Dutch company "A.W. Bruna & Zoon's Uitgeverij Maatschappij," as well as a "Day-Glo" design by a German company "J. Walter Thompson GMBH" are presented in conclusion, after the just-as-respectable "Unicard" credit card company advertisement. Page twenty of this "Day-Glo Designers' Guide" begins the "Magazines" chapter of the book, and misleadingly reproduces a "Day-Glo" Fluorescent magazine cover for "Collier's" magazine from April 18, 1931 - What? - Fluorescent paint was not invented until 1933 by the owners of the corporation printing this "Designers' Guide!" Swiftly turning to the "Production Notes" in the back of this exuberantly priced antique book, it is written that the 1931 "Collier's" magazine cover in the "Guide" originally printed two years before Fluorescent paint was invented, as well as the "AT&T" full page advertisement in the "Guide" were both originally printed with non-Fluorescent 'conventional four Colors,' but were reprinted in this book with "Day-Glo" "Aurora Pink" and "Saturn Yellow" substituted for the conventional Magenta and Yellow used in the original printed magazines. Next are presented magazine advertisements that were actually printed with "Day-Glo" Colors originally, and again representing very reputable corporations who chose to use "Day-Glo" Colors, including "CBS Television Network," "Continental Airlines," "Owens Illinois" cosmetics corporation, and "Plymouth Division, Chrysler Corporation."

On page twenty-four of this "Day-Glo Designers' Guide" the association of Fluorescent Color with Fine Art was presented obviously as a well-calculated attempt to further elevate the social standing of "Day-Glo" paint. First there is a Marilyn Monroe "Trip" which is the title of this chapter of the "Guide," and consists of "Day-Glo" prints from the last photographs of Marilyn Monroe taken in Hollywood at the Bel Air Hotel on June 21, 1962 by Bert Stern. The text begins with the statement (in 1960s hip terminology) that Artists by the "hundreds" had been "hung on" the icon Marilyn Monroe since 1963 when she died, including Dali, De Kooning, and Robert Rauschenberg, all of whom had participated in the "Homage to Marilyn" 1968 show in New York's Janis Gallery. It is further explained that Bert Stern was never "entirely satisfied" with these last images of Monroe that he took, and spent five years experimenting with different "new techniques" to capture the "dazzling image" he saw of Marilyn Monroe as he was photographing her. Finally Bert Stern found the answer to reproducing the 'dazzle' of Marilyn Monroe's photographs through silkscreening ("serigraphy") and "Day-Glo" Fluorescent Colors. The "phantasmagoric" images of Marilyn printed in "Day-Glo" by Bert Stern are presented for the next twelve pages of this "Designers' Guide." The brilliant dazzling "Day-Glo" prints of Marilyn Monroe are very psychedelic images of a very non-psychedelic era and it's non-psychedelic queen, creating in the end a very incongruous bank of photographs, giving the same overall impression to this author as the 1941 old-fashioned automobile painted in full "Day-Glo" Fluorescent Colors in "Conti-Glo's" "Black Light Beacon" from the Second world war era. The text explaining the images at the end of this chapter explains that the twelve pages of Bert Stern's "Day-Glo" Marilyn Monroe prints were first printed in the second issue of "Avant Garde" magazine a few years before and made the issue a collector's item. It is also explained that to reproduce the "heavy" Colors of silkscreens the magazine pages were printed by the technique of "gravure." Bert Stern's technique is also detailed, starting with Black and White prints and then layering of transparent "Day-Glo" Colors on opaque Colors to achieve the desired results. The conclusion is that this photographer was able to go beyond the "mechanical restraints" of photography and create an "individualistic" set of images using "Day-Glo" Fluorescent Colors applied originally by serigraphy, and next in print by the "gravure" process.

The next chapter in this "Day-Glo Guide" is what many people remember from "Day-Glo" Colors, and remains as one of the original applications of Fluorescence still in existence today: Fluorescent "Packaging." The accompanying Fluorescent collage contains a multitude of "Day-Glo" package examples, but strangely omits the most famous package of them all: "Tide" detergent packages, begun in 1959 and still produced with brilliant "Day-Glo" Red-Orange over half a century later. The actual first package printed with "Day-Glo" Fluorescent Colors is on display in the Museum: the 1956 "Chesterfield" cigarettes "Christmas carton(!)" The first package printed in this 1969 "Designers' Guide" is Fluorescent, as well as being a psychedelic design, and is for "Le Canned Dress" from "Wippette Sportswear, Inc." Next presented is one of the most famous perfume corporations in the world, "Faberge, Inc." with a full line of perfumeries printed with abstract Fluorescent designs. Shopping bags printed in Fluorescent "Day-Glo" follow with six pages of packages made by "Famous-Barr," "Andy Warhol," "The Higbee Co.," and "Arnold Constable 5th Avenue," all with "psychedelic period" designs. Placemats, napkins, and bridge sets all printed in floral "Day-Glo" Colors are the next "Packaging" examples, all from "Hallmark." Following these very respectable uses for "Day-Glo" Colors comes a page of four record covers printed in Fluorescent ink, not rock music, but respectable classical music including a Leonard Bernstein record with a Fluorescent portrait of Berstein painted by a famous psychedelic Artist Mati Klarwein, known for creating the "Abraxas" record cover from Santana. "Pictures at an Exhibition" record cover is next, followed by "Aaron Copland" and finally "Stockhausen." The next page of "Day-Glo" "Packaging" presents fully Fluorescent psychedelic designs for "Touch Boxes" designed by Peter Gee. Five examples of 1960s "Day-Glo" "Packaging" closes the chapter, with designs for "Rayette, Inc.," "Westinghouse Electrical Company," "Farrar Straus & Giroux," and an "Aspen magazine" cover by Andy Warhol designed to look like a Fluorescent Soap box.

"Newspaper" is the next chapter in the "Day-Glo Designers' Guide," with many examples from "Newspaper" that were originally printed in non-Fluorescent Colors, but are reproduced in this "Designers' Guide" as an example of how they would have looked in Fluorescent Colors. "Little Orphan Annie" is the first example, followed by "Sunkist" Oranges, "Continental Airlines," and "The East Ohio Gas Company." Four examples of newspaper ads originally printed in "Day-Glo" Colors follow, including "Stop and Save Food Stores," "Eaton's," and "Famous-Barr Department Stores," all printed with Fluorescent "psychedelic period" designs. The next example of Fluorescent "Day-Glo" Colors used in graphic design is the winner of a "Day-Glo" firm contest from 1966 in which Japanese "Haikus" were designed using Fluorescent Colors. "Haiku" is traditional Japanese dating to the Seventeenth century, and consists of a three line poem accompanied by seventeen symbols.

The last chapter of the "Designers' Guide" is for 'Outdoor - Posters - Displays' and consists, again, mostly of designs originally printed with non-Fluorescent Color and reproduced as examples of how they would have looked if they had been printed with "Day-Glo" Colors.

This "Day-Glo Designers' Guide" from 1969 closes with the most valuable section of the book for graphic designers, two pages of "Production notes" listing each and every design in the book, page-by-page, detailing which ink and paper stock originally was used to print the presented designs. These "Production Notes" are clear technical directions for designers to follow and achieve the brilliant results printed in this "Designers' Guide."

The most valuable part of this "Designers Guide" for this Artist are the three Charts/Color wheels which are included in a flap at the back of the book, and are the "Day-Glo" "Tone Chart," the "Day-Glo" "Bonus Color Chart," and the "Day-Glo" "Four-Color Chart." These two removable Color Charts and one "Day-Glo" Color Wheel are included after the closing two page graphic designers' technical section, which is called 'Getting the Most from Day-Glo Fluorescent Colors' and is introduced as the explanation of Fluorescence, the "advantages" as well as the "limitations" of printing with "Day-Glo" Colors, and also which mediums can be used as a base to print the Fluorescent Colors onto. "What is Fluorescence?" offers a two paragraph simple explanation of "light conversion" [more accurately known as "energy conversion"] which is the cause of Fluorescence. 'Black Absence' is next explained as being the essence of Fluorescent Colors, and Fluorescent Colors are defined in this "Guide" as 'conventional Colors minus the Black' [which is quite misleading and completely false]. The designer's application for this 'Black Absence' is that if a "Black halftone" of twenty percent is printed on top of any Fluorescent Color, the result will be a match for a non-Fluorescent Color. "Design Tips" divides the way Fluorescent Colors can be used into two distinct categories: "Hard sell" to add impact, and "Soft Sell" in which "Day-Glo" Colors can be used to 'enhance the design.' Techniques for "Hard Sell" follow with five clear instructions, beginning with the use of Fluorescent lettering surrounded by Black or a saturated complementary Color to achieve the "Neon Light" effect. The second instruction for "Hard Sell" is the use of Fluorescent lettering on a White background, which requires special adjustments such as 'Black outlines' or 'drop shadows.' Third is the advice to use Black letters or lettering with "Contrasting Color" to the "solid" Fluorescent Color of the background. Fluorescent Colors applied to a "middle tone" or for "shadow reverse" is the next tip given, followed by the fifth technique for "Hard Sell," producing a "3-D effect" using Fluorescent Colored lettering containing an "outline," or overprinting two separate Colors to create a third Color, which is explained will create a "3-D effect."

"Bonus Colors" is the next section covered, explaining that Fluorescent Colors are very transparent, allowing overprinting, which creates a nearly infinite amount of new Colors, in which can be designed to add an extra "third color" without extra printing cost. Effects creating "Multi-Color" is explained as being almost the same technique of "overprinting" Fluorescent Colors on top of non-Fluorescent Colors, or on top of Fluorescent Colors, to create a "broad spectrum" of Colors for printing. The technique of substituting Fluorescent Colors for one or two of the conventional Colors of a print, and thus producing an 'enhanced Artwork' is detailed for designers as well. "Tonal Scales" are next discussed, explaining that "Soft Sell" layouts do not use the pure, vivid Colors of "Day-Glo" inks, but that these Colors are used 'toned down,' with Black added up to fifty percent. Sounds wonderful.

"Applications" is the next interesting designer's tip, first explaining that the Fluorescent Colors are "extremely practical" for use in the printing process to produce coated Fluorescent paper, vinyl film, paint, fabric, or even plastics. A very simple chart is offered, with Packaging, Magazines, Newspapers, POP displays, and Outdoor posters all plotted against the printing applications Letterpress, Lithography, Gravure, Screen process, Flexography, Coated paper, Paint, Fabric, Vinyl, Film, and Plastics. "POP" is usable for every Fluorescent application, packaging is second, followed by Magazines, Outdoor posters, and finally Newspaper.

"Printing Tips" is on the second page of "Designers Tips" and proceeds to explain that different type of "printing processes" give different results with Fluorescent Colors. Advice is given for attaching a "Color chip" to the mechanical layout sent to the printer, as well as using Fluorescent markers on the rough layout to indicate Fluorescent Colors to be used in the final printing. "Contamination" follows, and is so easy to achieve. Fluorescent Colors are pure and, normally, void of Black, so to avoid contamination of these transparent vivd Colors, it is advised to clean the printer as thoroughly as if the Color Yellow was to be used next.

"Stock" lists and explains the various different types and Colors of paper to print Fluorescent "Day-Glo" ink onto, and the final tip "Sunfastness" clearly states that Fluorescent Colors should not be used where direct sunlight occurs. Whereas "Day-Glo" Colors are applicable for all interior printing, such as packaging and magazines, even one month of exposure to the Sun on outdoor posters or billboards could dramatically fade "Day-Glo" Colors, so it is advised to use silk-screening, Fluorescent paint, coated material, or vinyl film outdoors.

As stated previously, the removable "Day-Glo" Color Wheel and removable large Color Charts are the most valuable part of this "Designers' Guide" to this Artist. The 'Daylight Fluorescent for Selling Combinations of Colors' is a valuable Color Wheel tool for designing with both non-Fluorescent and Fluorescent Colors combined in a design. The text at the bottom of the "Color Selecting Tool" instructs to start with either the non-Fluorescent Colors (printed on the Color Wheel itself) or with the "daylight" Fluorescent Color (which is printed underneath the spinning Color Wheel). A cut-out window in the top 'wheel' allows any of the Fluorescent Colors to be juxtaposed to any non-Fluorescent Color by simply lining up the windows on the non-Fluorescent Color Wheel with the Fluorescent Colors underneath the Color Wheel. The logo of "Day-Glo" Color Corporation" is followed by the company policy in 1969 stating that their "main interest" was communications which were more Colorful. The largest of the removable 'Day-Glo designer's tools' is a folded 'Day-Glo Four-Color Process Chart for Lithography' in which a vast array of Color samples are printed by substituting "Saturn Yellow" and "Aurora Pink" for non-

Fluorescent standard Process Yellow and Magenta. This large chart about two feet across (65 cm) reproduces a huge amount of variations in Color by substituting these Fluorescent Colors in printing, and each subtle change is presented on the chart in steps of just eighths. The fourth "designer's tool" is a removable "Tone Chart." "Blaze Orange," "Arc Yellow," "Rocket Red," "Signal Green," "Saturn Yellow," "Neon Red," "Fire Orange," "Aurora Pink," and "Corona Magenta" are each printed as Solid blocks of Color, and then each "Day-Glo" Color is printed as ten, twenty, thirty, forty, and fifty percent tones. This entire chart is printed with a White background, and then with a Black background to illustrate the differences obtained with opposite surroundings.

This fourth and final "Color Chart" for "Day-Glo" Fluorescent Colors printed with the "screen process" is the most valuable of all the removable charts in this "Designers' Guide" to this painter. I have my own identical chart of Fluorescent paint which I spent many hours making over twenty years ago because it was so important to use as a Color painting guide. Along the left side of this valuable "Color Chart" are printed horizontal strips of each of the nine "Day-Glo" Colors. Then across the top of the chart is printed the same entire palette of nine "Day-Glo" Colors vertically, overprinting on each of the nine "Day-Glo" Colors printed first horizontally. What this precious chart clearly shows is the third Fluorescent Color which was created by each of the nine Fluorescent Colors that were painted on top of the same nine Fluorescent Colors underneath. To complete this 'Fluorescent Color Overprinting Chart' there are two removable sections at the bottom of the chart, one in White and one in Black, each with a window cut out of the centers, allowing the entire combination of overlaid "Day-Glo" Colors to be seen in reference to being used on a White or a Black background. If only this single valuable chart was the entire contents of this 1969 "Day-Glo Designers' Guide" it would have still been worth the "ten dollars" cover price.

This 1969 "Day-Glo Designers' Guide" is a unique and very important documentation of the historical and sociological perspective of the 1960s Movement towards the phenomenon of Fluorescence and the Black light. This "Designers' Guide" was published in 1969, during the height of the 1960s Movement and is included in this book as an example of some of the rarely published personal viewpoints of the inventor of Fluorescent paint, Robert Switzer.

Again, there are two reasons for the inclusion of this extended history of the 1960s Movement in this book on the Black light, Fluorescent Art, and the "Social Stigma of Fluorophobia," First of all the history of psychoactive substances, as well as the history of Fluorescent Colors and the Black light *both* did not begin in the 1960s when society in general finally found out about both psychoactive substances and Fluorescent Colors under Black lights, but decades, centuries, or even millennia before the 1960s began or any one of the Hippies were ever born. These are accurate examples of the ignorance and misinformation which contemporary society has laid as it's foundation. The second reason for this extended inclusion of the 1960s Movement in this book is because this 1960s Movement was the sole example of total acceptance and infinite fascination for not just a different technology or an advance in lighting, but for an unseen magic realm that had been completely unknown, undiscovered, and was totally Twentieth century new - the Black light and Fluorescent Colors. The 1960s Movement represents an absolute break with the past and all that it created and represented, such as the millennia-old-fashioned concepts of human race inequality, male domination of the species, and eternal sexual repression. The past and all of it's miserable baggage consisting of ignorance, hatred, and jealousy was thrown out of the window in hope of a new era of human existence being created with new concepts, technologies, and social acceptance, including the dress, the hair, the substances, freedom of expression, the music - and naturally Fluorescent Color under the Black light was the 1960s Movement's palette.

5. The Greying of the Miraculous Fluorescent Rainbow: "Post 1960s - Social Stigma and Fluorophobia / "Alba" the Green Fluorescent Rabbit and Transgenic Fluorescent Animals" ("Qu'est-il arrive au miracle?")

Catering to "Little Nicholas the four year old camera enthusiast," and his generation of children that were born into such a jaded era of human developmental technology, a new type of book has been presented for children. In 2010 this new style of book was published by Herve Tullet, which caters to children for whom "Touchscreen technology" is a given - something common even - and is presented as a design technique that has seamlessly been integrated into the classic format of a paper book which a person physically holds in their hands. This children's book is cleverly entitled "PRESS HERE," which is displayed as the cover illustration of the book with a Yellow circular spot between the two words "PRESS" and "HERE," and which would be instantly recognizable to a child born with Touchscreen technology as a normal everyday fact of their lives. Even a mere decade ago if a young child was presented with such a conceptual book they would have been completely unable to understand the actual concept of this "PRESS HERE" book, but today the little child of four or five grabs the paper three-dimensional classic millennia-old design of this book and *instantaneously* bridges the conceptual gap between the "real world" of a paper book in their hands - and the "virtual reality" of this paper three-dimensional book in their hands, which possesses the invisible fictitious functions of an electronic computer, telephone, and a computer game "Touchscreen." If this same new "PRESS HERE" children's book was given to an eighty year old today, they would be unable to make the same instantaneous bridge between the "real" and the "virtual" - because to everybody on the planet with the exception of this new generation of little computer children that are like four or five years old, "real" and "virtual" "Touchscreens" remain just that: "real" and "virtual" with a distinct concrete non-conceptualized unblurred division between the two, thankfully. A four year old today would be more spontaneously prepared and educated to the concept of the "Touchscreen" and this "PRESS HERE" book than Albert Einstein or Leonardo da Vinci. These two wise old men would have picked up this "PRESS HERE" book, pressed the Yellow circular form printed on the paper cover of the book between "PRESS" and "HERE," and when nothing obviously would have happened, they would have put the book back down dismissing it as a child's game of some sort. But, today the little child picks up this book, instantly presses the printed Yellow "button" on the cover - and although obviously nothing visual "happens," it is virtually enough to satisfy the child *just by the act of touching the Touchscreen.* The child touches the printed circular Yellow spot on the cover of this book, between "PRESS" and "HERE," then opens the book and begins to press all the printed different Colored spots on every page of the book - again with absolutely nothing visually "happening" (obviously) when each of these different-Colored spots printed on paper pages is "pressed" by the child today, but this is *more than enough!* Just the basic act of physically pressing the fictitious "button" on the paper page's fictitious "Touchscreen" is enough to satisfy today's child. Nothing has to "happen," nothing has to be "learned," "experienced," "gained," or even the very basic of all - "seen" - for today's four or five year old to be absolutely satisfied - *happy* even - with this "PRESS HERE" book. Personally, if I would have received a "PRESS HERE" 2010 book when I was four years old half a century ago, I would have pressed the Yellow spot printed on a nearly translucent piece of paper between the instructions "PRESS" and "HERE," nothing obviously would have happened, and I would have thrown the book on the floor in full lucid awareness that nothing was ever going to happen when I pressed that printed Colored spot on a paper book - no matter how many times I pressed it - there would be obviously no visual "reaction" caused by the "action" of my finger pressing the Yellow printed spot, but for a four year old child of today who has literally been born with a "Touchscreen" device in their little hands - *This is Enough!* Just the physical act of pressing all these different Colored printed spots on every page of this child's book "PRESS HERE" is enough to totally satisfy a child today - the mere act of touching the "buttons" without anything at all gained or lost even considered in the action.

What has been gained here by the innate reaction of a child today inherently interacting with "Touchscreen" technology is a mere recognition of a rudimentary technique - <u>Only</u> - similar (and about as life-changing) to a child learning to eat with a fork - but what has been lost here is hard to begin to even categorize. Imagine loosing human fascination and the pursuit of knowledge just to learn to eat with a fork?! Little Nicholas the four year old camera enthusiast in America proved this point to me a few years ago when he looked at me like I was an idiot when I excitedly showed him his photo on my new "Sony Touchscreen" camera. No "WOW!!," or any word at all in fact, was exclaimed by this three-foot-tall American four-year-old when presented with technology that would have made Leonardo da Vinci's eyeballs literally fall out of his head. Little Nicholas, again, merely looked up at me like I was an idiot and tried to desperately educate me to the obvious fact that I had not taken the "Red-Eye" out of his photo - WHAT!! Personally I can't imagine what my limitless fascination would have been if someone would have shown me my photo on the back of a camera when I was a kid a second after taking the photograph, then merely by touching with their finger they would have instantly enlarged the image of my face on their magic screen on the back of a camera - I probably would have been screaming, but for sure I would not have been unimpressed and bored, or looked at the person holding this magical camera like he was an idiot.

The mere comprehension of a technical technique is all that has been gained in the end - a four year old today would inherently know to press the fictitious "buttons" of the new "PRESS HERE" book (and be totally satisfied with absolutely no reaction from their action of pressing said "buttons"), but any one specimen from the millions of years of evolution of the human species - out of the estimated one-hundred and eight billion people who have lived on Earth so far - would not have been satisfied or even interested in this "PRESS HERE" virtual book before these computer children. So what has been gained here in reality? A comprehension of a technical technique - a completely new "intuitive" way for the child to "interact" with their book - has been gained, but along with gained comprehension of one rudimentary technical technique, the individual has forfeited their natural expectations and natural experiences. Only the physical act to "PRESS HERE" is more than enough to completely *overjoy* the little four year old child today. What a pity.

On the business front, the "International Business Times" report of August 3, 2011 announced a lucrative new "upcoming" business venture: the world's first brand-new market of "Glow-in-the-Dark Pets!" The "Ruppy" is introduced here: the Beagle that was spliced together with genes from a Sea Anemone, and passes this genetic "defect" onto it's offspring, allowing mother Beagle and puppies to Fluoresce Orange under a Black light. The "Ruppy" is a word created between "Ruby" and "Puppy." The "I. B. Times" article continues with Green Fluorescent Pigs, which were created in 2006 in Taiwan to coincide with the Chinese "Year of the Pig," when a research team for the "National Taiwan University" successfully bred three Fluorescent Green male pigs by injecting "GFP" into the pigs during their embryonic stage. This was originally done with Taiwan's Stem cell research in mind. In January, 2008 a Chinese Fluorescent Green Transgenic pig was mated with an ordinary pig, and her piglets Fluoresced Green - which the researchers were extremely proud of! This article goes on to highlight prospective Transgenic Fluorescent Animals for the "upcoming" market, starting with the 'Angelfish' ("Herophyllum scalare") which was displayed at the 2010 Taiwan International Aqua Expo Fluorescing a vivid Blue and Green under a Black light. At the same Aqua Expo of 2010 in Taipei on October 29, the 'Convict cichlids' ("Amatitlania nigrofasciata") fish Fluoresces both bright Blue outside as well as having bright Green Fluorescent internal organs. Taipei saw the first "Glo-Fish" in 1997, then the "Medaka" fish on September 6, 2001, and recently has included yet another Green Fluorescent fish "Archocentrus nigrofasciatus" in this 2010 Aqua Expo in Taipei as well.

The "Glo-Fish" are currently the only genetically-altered Fluorescent animals for sale on a mass scale so far, and only in China, Taiwan, and the continental U.S. (except California). Photos in this "I.B. Times" article also reveal the Colors of the "Glo-Fish," which are still sold Fluorescing in the original three different Colors, and were originally highlighted at the 2007 Bio Taiwan exhibit. This book took much longer to write than I ever imagined it would, and during these years along with the enormous amount of changes and advances that have taken place, "Glo-Fish" have also had new members, or better stated "Colors," added to their commodified Transgenic species. In December, 2013 I went into a large pet store named "Petsmart" in Toms River, New Jersey. To my surprise I found three fishtanks full of many different Colors of "Glo-Fish," when there originally had been only one fish tank of these "Glo-Fish" in just three different Colors a few years before that time. These three Colors, sold since the late 1990s in China and Taiwan and then since 2003 in the United States, are still sold as the "Glo-Fish" "Starfire Red Danio," "Glo-Fish" "Sunburst Orange Danio," and "Glo-Fish" "Electric Green Danio," all for $5.99 each. To my surprise, at the end of 2013 these three original "Glo-Fish" have had seven new members of new Fluorescent Transgenic Colors added to their incorporated Transgenic species. "Glo-Fish" "Sunburst Orange Tetra" is a different small Transgenic fish than the original "Sunburst Orange Danio" and is sold for $7.99, along with the "Glo-Fish" "Moonrise Pink Tetra" also for $7.99 each. The new "Glo-Fish" "Cosmic Blue

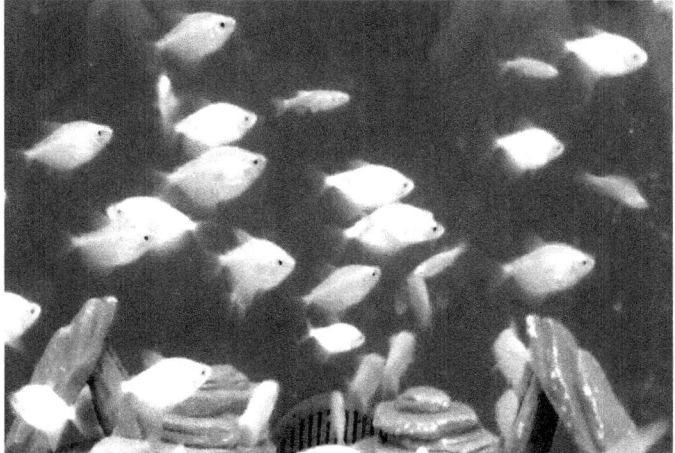

Transgenic Fluorescent "GLO-FISH" for sale in New Jersey(!)

Danio" and the "Glo-Fish" "Galctic Purple Danio" are both sold for the original $5.99 each, with the "Glo-Fish" "Elecric Green Tetra" being sold for $7.99. The two highest priced "Glo-Fish" are the "Electric Green Barb" for $9.99 each, and the "Glo-Fish" labelled "NEW" on it's tank, the "Galactic Purple Tetra" sold for more than twice the price of the original "Glo-Fish," at $12.99 each. Still up until the present day these three fishtanks loaded with 'pets' for sale to the public which are genetically crossed with Jellyfish DNA and are highly Fluorescent, are astoundingly sold without a Black light advertising their full palette of Transgenic Fluorescent Colors, as well as without mention in any way that they are Transgenic or Fluorescent. This is a primary example of the far reaching effects of "Fluorophobia," proving that even in America where an addition of a Black light over the "Glo-Fish" tanks, or at least even an indication that they are Fluorescent, would have multiplied sales of these Transgenic Fluorescent fish, but, again, there is absolutely no indication that these fish are Transgenic and Fluorescent in the several huge American pet stores I've seen these "Glo-Fish" in during the past years. The only single solitary difference between the presentation and labeling of these ten different "Glo-Fish" compared to all the other species of non-Fluorescent natural fish in these major American pet stores are the multi-Colored Fluorescent aquarium stones covering the bottom of all three "Glo-Fish" tanks. Typically over-enthused, I took out my 3D camera and took pictures of these three "Glo-Fish" tanks, the ten individual different types of "Glo-Fish," as well as the ten different sales labels for these "Glo-Fish," and then also began to take 3D video of these three fishtanks, which attracted the attention of the "Petsmart" staff. In the middle of taking video of these ten "Glo-Fish" a young employee of the store came up to me and asked what I was doing. I answered her with a question, asking her if she knew these ten "Glo-Fish" she was selling were Genetically Manipulated - Transgenic - mixed with Jellyfish DNA - and that they were Fluorescent under a Black light. Unbelievably, this young girl working in the aquarium department of this "Petsmart" looked at me as if I had lost my mind, and then reacted by stepping away from me about twice the distance she had been, looking at me with true suspicion(!)

    The newest life form which began to be marketed to the public during the final writing of this book in January, 2014 is the world's first Transgenic Bioluminescent Plant, or as the company "Bioglow" terms it, the world's first "Autoluminescent" plant "Starlight Avatar." On Bioglowtech.com potential customers are introduced to the facts that this "Starlight Avatar" "Autoluminescent" plant, announced first in December, 2013, is their first glowing plant, and in fact the first commercially available Bioluminescent plant in the world. The website states that "Starlight Avatar" is not only the first, but the "only" glowing plant existing that is "genuine." This is explained as the reason, along with the "limited production" of these Transgenic Bioluminescent plants, that "Bioglow" decided to hold an "online auction" selling twenty of the first "Starlight Avatars." Auctions for these plants, which have an estimated life-span on just one to three months, began at $1.00 each and according to the company's website went up to almost $800.00 per plant, with the bidding averaging over $300.00 per plant. The bidding so impressed the company that they promise the next "Autoluminescent" plant they produce will be sent free to all winning bidders. This "Bioglow" company is based in Saint Louis, Missouri, with this biotechnology company's "Autoluminescent" world-first commercial plant having been developed through the work of Dr. Alexander Krichevsky, the molecular biologist who founded "Bioglow." The company's co-founder is Tal Eidelberg, head of the board of directors for "Bioglow." This world's first Bioluminescent commercially available plant "Starlight Avatar" is explained to be a Transgenic variety of the original "Nicotiana alata" plant. Also explained on the company's website is the point that these plants do not need Ultraviolet lamps or chemicals for them to give off light, and that these "Starlight Avatar" plants are "genetically modified" through the mixing of "marine bacteria" into the DNA of the plant's "chloroplast." This is followed directly by the statement that these "Bioglow" plants have been approved by the U.S. "Department of Agriculture." Potential customers are also advised to raise their "Autoluminescent" plants indoors only, and then they are assured that the "Starlight Avatar" "genes" cannot through pollen be transferred to any other plants.

  The selling point for these world's first commercially available Transgenic "Autoluminescent" plants from "Bioglow" is not just that it is a unique glow-in-the-dark plant, but for a proposed purpose that is so contemporary that it has almost become a cliché: "Green Energy." The claim made by "Bioglow" is that through development and production of Transgenic "Autoluminescent" plants we will use less electricity for lighting with this 'cleaner, greener energy alternative.' "Bioglow" admits that this will be for the future, going on to explain that their first Transgenic "Autoluminescent" plant developed in 2010 emitted a dimmer light than the improved "Starlight Avatar" begun to be marketed in January, 2014. The company states that their goal is to increase the light output of their "Autoluminescent" plants with the dream of the creation of a replacement to electrical lights, with these plants also being more affordable, sustainable, and cleaner. In the center of the "Research" page of "Bioglow's" website is a serene image of a young couple with their upper bodies and faces illuminated by the Blue-Green Transgenic Bioluminescence of the plant they are both holding and looking into (which is a hauntingly reminiscent image of 'Radium skin-creme' advertisements from a century ago). Again, the headline announces 'energy which is clean and sustainable,' followed by a paragraph of the company's projections, such as future "Bioglow" plants being brighter than the first Blue-Green emitting "Starlight Avatar," and the addition of Bioluminescent Yellow and Red plants being introduced. The goal is again restated for a future clean, affordable and sustainable lighting source, with recommended applications from the company of 'backyard lighting,' marking the edge of highways and driveways, and for what the prospective customer is told yet again, reducing the use of both fossil fuels and electricity. The distant projections by "Bioglow" include the marketing of Transgenic Bioluminescent plants which will glow different Colors, such as "Autoluminescent" plants with leaves that will glow a different Color than it's flowers, as well as plants that will be engineered to glow only when responding to pollution or environmental stress, protecting both the environment and food crops. Also explained on the "Bioglow" website is the name "Starlight Avatar," which represents actually how dim the "Autoluminescence" of the company's plant is, comparable to the weakness of "starlight." Several full sentences of directions for adapting your eyes in a dark room just to be able to *see* this "Autoluminescent" plant's glow follow.

The final reviewed Transgenic Bioluminescent plant which is intended for sale is so new that at the time of this writing it is several months before the projected release date to donors of the company. In September, 2014 - Transgenic Bioluminescent "Glowing Plants" will be shipped to donors of "glowingplant.com," a "Kickstarter" company started by three men in San Francisco. Not only will seeds for the Bioluminescent Transgenic "Glowing plants" be marketed to the public, but living Transgenic plants will be available as well, for $100.00 each. Packets of 50-100 seeds for these "Glowing plants" will be sold for $50.00 starting possibly also in September, 2014. This Bioluminescent "Glow-in-the-Dark" product is a Transgenic creation of the "Arabidopsis" plant in the mustard seed family. There is even a "Maker kit" being sold for $300.00 which is a 'do-it-yourself kit' enabling consumers to genetically transform their own plants at home! This mini-lab that is intended to be available to ship to customers in August, 2014 includes everything needed to create a Genetic transformation lab right in your own house - all for $300.00! This "Glowing Plant" "Maker kit" consists of an instruction manual, a coffee table book "How to Make a Glowing Plant" (which will also be available to buy separately for $70.00 in Autumn, 2014), a container of the DNA from the "Glowing plant," Arabidopsis seeds, and several other simple laboratory instruments to complete a "DIY" Transgenic plant laboratory right at home. Can't wait.

Of corse the underlying theme of this new "Glowing plant" company is not to make money, but to bring to the Human race and the whole world a solution and salvation, by providing a new 'product' which creates "Natural Lighting" with no use of Electricity. Wonderful, electricity will be saved by the distribution of a new Transgenic Bioluminescent plant species into nature. Anyone who wants these Transgenic plant seeds, grown living Transgenic plants, or even "Maker kits" for producing your own Transgenic Bioluminescent plants in your kitchen, can order them today - in fact thousands of these Transgenic seeds are already to be sent to a huge amount of the company's donors. This is all plainly written on "glowingplant.com," with the additional information of these Transgenic plants being an "Open Source," meaning that consumers of these "Glowing plant" seeds are free to "edit" the DNA and seeds, free to "grow" these seeds, or even to sell these seeds or give them away for free. Next the consumer is informed that these Bioluminescent Transgenic "Glowing plants" are nothing less than a "Symbol" of a sustainable future. Consumers are enticed to 'show their friends' that they care about synthetic biology's potential to improve the world through sustainability. The first page of the "glowingplant.com" website also informs the public that already 8,433 backers of this "Glowing plant project" have their seed packs reserved through their donations of $484,013.00.

The "Objectives" of "Glowing plant" are clearly presented on the homepage of the project's website, with text and illustrations of our "unsustainable" life on Earth compared to the sustainable contrast of "Biology," which is exemplified by the crossing of Firefly DNA with plant DNA to create "Glowing plants." This "Glowing plant project" is not a plan or projection of the future, but is ready to ship to thousands of donors across the United States in 2014. The reader should not get the idea that this is a one-off project which will soon be forgotten, because Transgenic Bioluminescent "Glowing Roses" are also available to order for shipping in June, 2015. In fact these "Glowing Roses" are so new that the "Glowing plant" company doesn't even yet know what Color these Roses will glow, but for $150.00 you can already reserve your own for shipping in mid-2015.

So here we have in the winter of 2014 two Transgenic Bioluminescent plant companies already not only established, but either distributing these Transgenic life forms to the public, or on the verge of distributing not only seeds, but living Transgenic plant specimens, and even a "Maker kit" to produce your very own self-made Transgenic plants in the kitchen! "Bioglow's" twenty auctioned living Transgenic "Autoluminescent" tobacco plants have already been sent out and distributed to twenty of the highest bidders on an online auction for these plants in January, 2014, and within six months "Glowing Plant" will be sending literally thousands of Transgenic seeds, as well as living specimens of their Transgenic Bioluminescent plants to thousands of donors across the United States in September, 2014. Anthony Evans, head of "Glowing Plants" has no fear about distributing many thousands of these Transgenic seeds and living Transgenic plants into the environment, of course, and only dreams about creating a sustainable future consisting of "natural lighting." Evans and his colleges of "glowingplant.com" dream not of disturbing life on Earth or disturbing the food chain, but of a utopian future which will be entirely illuminated through light bulbs that are filled with Firefly and Jellyfish DNA as well as future streetlights being cheerfully replaced by Transgenic Bioluminescent Trees.

The very simple, nearly automated procedure for creating these new Transgenic Bioluminescent life forms is explained on the company's website as merely taking genes of natural Bioluminescent "bacterium" from the sea, and inserting this bacterium DNA into seedlings of the plant "Arabidopsis." This procedure is further explained as simply putting into a computer this marine bacterium's DNA sequence, and then a computer program alters the Bioluminescent bacterium's DNA sequence to allow it to "work" for plants. Next the "Glowing Plant" researchers simply Email the altered bacterium's DNA to a Chinese company along with $8,000.00, and a couple of weeks later in the mail (!) they receive usable DNA back from the company in China. The final step is to insert into the plant this newly created DNA sequence programmed in China, through the use of a "Gene gun." This procedure from the beginning to the end sounds simple enough, but according to Anthony Evans the real challenge is to create a Transgenic Bioluminescent plant which is bright enough to use for lighting, not only dimly glowing in a pitch Black room where you have to adapt your eyes to the dark just to be able to see the plant's light. Evans admits that the best his company hopes for at first is not the current impossibility of a plant as bright as a light bulb, but merely as bright as the plastic stars which glow-in-the-dark on ceilings. The final goal that is dreamed about by Evans and the Transgenic plant companies is the attainment of Bioluminescent plants as bright as - and replacements for - electric light bulbs.

In April, 2013, the "Glowing Plant Project" initiated a "Kickstarter" campaign of fundraising in hopes for raising $65,000.00, but in just forty-four days this fundraising campaign collected $484,013.00! This is not to say that everyone was overjoyed by the prospect of having Transgenic plants and Transgenic plant seeds distributed throughout the United States, because an environmental protection agency called the "ETC Group" started an online petition to stop what they refer to as a Silicon Valley "biotech threat," which was signed by almost 14,000 people. Then in August, 2013 it was announced that "Glowing Plant" would ban further genetically modified gifts to it's company's donors, but would still honor their promise and send many thousands of the Transgenic seeds to the multitude of it's donors across the United States. Not surprisingly this "Glowing Plant Project" initiated a scientific and public debate about releasing genetically modified life forms to a widespread public. The debate centers around a new field known today as "Synthetic Biology," that the "Glowing Plant Project" is at the forefront of, and which involves the genetic manipulation of life forms which can be used to replace electric light bulbs, or make new medicine, biofuels, or even food flavorings - What! It doesn't *grow your hair back?"* The results scientists and the general public fear is not only the simplistic procedure of creating "GMOs" (Genetically Modified Organisms) with natural DNA which is then reinvented into a "GMO" by a computer program, but the mother of all fears: releasing Transgenic plant seeds by the thousands to the general public in America. Nobody knows what will result with these Transgenic Bioluminescent plants once they are introduced onto the natural environment, and yet these very seeds are already waiting to be sent all over America in 2014. Again, this is not a one-off amusement, because these thousands of Transgenic plant seeds will grow untold thousands of living Transgenic plants all across America, which does not in any way end when the individual plants die, because the DNA modified to create the "GMO's" plant's glow will be passed on to all future generations of all plants from each of the thousands of original seeds. In an article from the end of 2013, "The Washington Post" includes "Bioethicist" Arthur Caplan's opinion, who asks the hypothetical question, what if somebody wants to plant Transgenic Bioluminescent plants to light up one of America's national forests? This September, 2013 "Washington Post" article explains that the amount of these Transgenic Bioluminescent "Glowing Plants" seeds to be sent across America in September, 2014 exceeds 600,000 (!) to 8,000 donors who funded the project through the internet site "Kickstarter." The spokesman, and one of the project's founders Anthony Evans counters all fears of the release of over 600,000 Transgenic seeds across America with words, quoted by "The Washington Post," offering assurance that the "Glowing Plant Project" has taken "precautions," including the selection of which plants are to be created as Transgenic, and also controlling how the Transgenic plants will be transported around America to donors and then customers. Evans, again merely with words, assured all concerned that everything is safe, that everyone's concerns are what he calls "over blown,"and that he and his "Glowing Plant" company are being "prudent." This all was reported during the end of 2013, with "The Washington Post" article on the "Glowing Plant Project" of the "Kickstarter" website sparking debates over 'DNA Modification Regulations.' What this article reveals is disturbing to say the least, and a classic example of "passing the buck." The United States Department of Interior creates legislation safeguarding the land and ecology, but the Bureau of Land Management and Fish and Wildlife Services says that the DNA modification issue is outside of their jurisdiction. Next the Food and Drug Administration says the exact same thing, that the DNA modification is also outside of their jurisdiction because it is not meant to be eaten. Finally, completing this vicious circle, The Environmental Protection Agency says it's a matter for The Department of Agriculture. Bottom line is contained in an Email sent to the founders of the "Glowing Plant Project" from the "U.S. Drug Administration," in which they inform the company that regulating this type of DNA modification is also outside of their powers because of the method that the "Glowing Plants" are being created with. Since "Glowing Plant" is shooting DNA into tissue of the plants through the use of a "Gene gun," the government agency cannot regulate their DNA modification because regulations have laws only pertaining to older methods of DNA modifications, not the current standard use of the "Gene gun." Government regulations covering DNA modification were established in 1986, while the standard method also used by the "Glowing Plant Project," the "Gene gun," wasn't created until 1987. The absurdity of these statements by several U.S. government agencies is a very conclusive example of the world today, and the direction the world of tomorrow is headed in. This "Washington Post" article also quotes Dana Perls, of "Friends of the Earth," who clearly concludes that these findings of several government agencies which exclude them from being able to regulate DNA modification could prove to allow "dozens" more projects of "synthetic biology" to literally do what they want without fear of regulations, because there are no government regulations existing to stop them. Perls continues, explaining that what these government agencies are doing is believing the "Glowing Plant" developers when they are assuring the public that what they are creating is "safe" without being aware of the very obvious 'risks involved.' The number of which 600,000 "Glowing Plant" seeds that will develop into living plants of the future is incalculable. As usual, one of the three partners of "Glowing Plant," Kyle Taylor has an answer to this. He claims that before the eruption of the controversy over environmental concerns even started he was already thinking about this, experimenting with "biocontainment methods." He says he "could try" making these Transgenic plants deficient in a kind of vitamin, which would ensure that the plant's "caretakers" would always have to give this vitamin to the plant or it would die. This would almost ensure that if a Transgenic plant escaped into nature it would almost surely die. Taylor, 30, who is originally form a Kansas farming community, says that he is a believer in "stewardship," which takes care of the land you grow, and which he believes "applies" to this situation. This is all highly commendable, but Taylor only says he "could try" this method, not that it is already in place in the 600,000 Transgenic plant seeds to be sent across America in 2014, or in any of the living Transgenic plants they planned to sell. In conclusion, the "Glowing Plant" company spokesman and founder Anthony Evans not surprisingly claims just the opposite of most of the public, that regulations for genetically modified life forms should be "scaled back," and not increased, because if they were increased than entrepreneurs such as himself might have been prevented from beginning their companies in the first place. Evans claims that what is needed is finding ways which are "cost-effective" for many more "start-up" companies to form and bring many more of these products to the market, and that only this will bring the "economic" as well as the "social" promise for this new technology to realization.

    The last in a long list of scientific "advances" which will be presented in this book is perhaps the most serious, the most dangerous, and the most difficult to believe of them all. This last scientific "advance," comparatively speaking, makes the creation of new species of Transgenic Fluorescent animals seem nearly old-fashioned, because in short this relatively new scientific advance is the ultimate in scientific creation: the creation of nothing less than *Life* itself. In 2010 Dr. Craig Venter and his team were the first in the world to actually create synthetic life! This not the simple cloning of Sheep, the basic crossing of species such as the created "Geep," or even the Transgenic creation of Fluorescent Rabbits which are mixed with Bioluminescent Jellyfish DNA, but the actual creation of a new species of Life through the writing of it's genetic code, and the synthesis of the life form with chemicals in 2010. This new synthetic life created by Venter and his team is hailed as the first new species capable of self-replicating on Earth - with a computer as it's 'parent.' Already in the introduction of articles, papers, and broadcast programs on Dr. Craig Venter's creation of the first synthetic life, the dreamed about miracle-cure claims of applications for this unprecedented breakthrough in technology are announced, such as the invention of new medicines to alleviate Human suffering, as well as the contemporary dream of inventing new clean, "Green" alternative energy sources.

    In 2010 Dr. Craig Venter and his team created single-cell man-made, self-replicating living Bacteria. Proponents call it the beginning of a new branch on the Evolutionary Tree, as well as claiming that this advance will define the third major revolution of the Human race after the discovery of Agriculture 10,000 years ago, and the Industrial revolution beginning a few hundred years ago. Opponents consider this advance of the creation of the first created synthetic life to be something like 'the Final Solution' - something so powerful and something which we know so little about that the results both intentional and unintentional are unimaginable. All of life on Earth started with, and can be traced all the way back to, the very first cell capable of self-replicating approximately three billion years ago, and now at the beginning of the Twenty-first century for the first time we have the first cell which is not an offspring of this first natural biological cell, but is the offspring of computers and a scientific laboratory in America. As for Dr. Craig Venter, he believes he has led a team which is on the way to nothing less than 'saving the world' through the projected inventions of new clean Biofuels, new foods, new vaccines for medicine, and also new technologies for cleaning up the polluted Earth. Dr. Venter dreams of new "Designer bacteria" created through synthetic DNA providing new benefit to humanity, as well as creating new industries born out of, and centered on these advances.

DNA is composed of genes that determine basic traits of all living things, such as Color, size, digestion, and reproduction, all achieved in pairs of just four chemicals, Adenine with Thymine, and Guanine with Cytosine. All of our DNA put together is the "Human genome," or 'software/operating system.' The human genome is composed of three billion chemical "base pairs," and during the 1980s and 1990s the U.S. government stated it would take fifteen years and three billion dollars to write the entire Human genome. This is when Dr. Craig Venter first made news, claiming that he and his team would write the entire Human genome in three years, and at a cost of only three-hundred million dollars. To complete this unprecedented job in only one-fifth the time and one-ninth the amount of money, Venter's team discovered a new technique known a "shotgun sequencing," which breaks up DNA into small pieces and then with a laser the chemical sequence of this DNA is read and coded into four different Colors.

On July 26, 2000 Dr. Craig Venter was honored by President Clinton for completing the entire human genome (in the three years he said he would do it in). After the professional as well as the financial success of writing the Human genome in 2000, Dr. Venter decided it was the perfect time to try and fulfill a dream he had many years: to literally manufacture the very "software" for creating Life. After their success at reading the entire Human genetic code, Dr. Venter and his team now attempted just the opposite, to write the four DNA letters on a computer, and then to put these chemicals together in the right order and in the correct places to create a living, self-replicating new life form. Dr. Venter clearly states that it was this writing of Life's genetic code on computers which advanced genetic engineering up to the current Digital age. Venter explains that it is now possible to just design on a computer a new species, build this new species, and then see if it 'works,' lives, and self-replicates. It is also clearly the goal of Dr. Venter to not merely genetically modify existing species, but to physically *Create* new species. Venter recruited two old collaborators, one a Nobel prize winner, and they began on their quest of creating synthetic life by first creating a copy of the DNA molecule of a virus for their initial step. By the summer of 2003 Venter and his team had announced the creation of a living synthetic virus microorganism in their lab. This announcement and direction caused not just Dr. Venter and his team, but countless others including the United States government to be concerned over just what could be created through these unprecedented technological breakthroughs. Inventing new clean energy sources, new food, or even new medicine is admirable, but what happens if the ability to create any virus on earth - or any virus not on Earth - is realized also by the dark side of humanity? What did happen was a very large review by the U.S. government including sessions in the White House for deciding just how to regulate the new technology of creating life. It was questioned whether the work Venter and his team accomplished should be kept as military secrets, or could the team publish their work to the public? The administration under Bush allowed publication of Venter's work, but a review process having safety protocols was established.

In 2005 Dr. Craig Venter puts together a team with twenty of the top scientists from around the world who have the common passion to create life. This new life they create will not be a virus, because they are not true life forms, but they will create a self-replicating, self-sustaining Bacteria, which is by all definitions a true life form. The team of scientists are broken into two separate teams, one of which will work on the Synthesis of the created new DNA, and one team would work on the Transplant procedure that gets the created synthetic DNA into an existing cell, replaces the existing cell's natural DNA, and then begins producing it's own proteins inside the cell, which defines the creation of a new living life form. To make this immense task as easy as possible, the smallest Bacteria known was chosen to use, "M. Genitalium." The procedure was designed to make an "assembly" of small sections of DNA into finally the complete circular form. By 2006 the team was still not able to "assemble" a full DNA form, until a member of Venter's team decided to try an old method used for the last thirty years in DNA research, Yeast, which is one of the only substances known that can link particles of DNA together into a complete chromosome. In 2007 Venter's team finally achieved the creation of a man-made DNA genome of a living Bacteria after two years of work. The next step towards the creation of a living organism was to develop a method of inserting this synthetic DNA into an already existing cell, so that it would be able to work, self-replicate, and live. In comparison to the human brain and the body, the DNA chromosome is something like the brain, or 'operating system/software,' and the biological cell is something like the body, or functioning 'hardware.' This step, the "transplanting" of synthetic DNA into an existing cell was much more difficult to achieve than the team thought it would be, and decided to use "M. Mycoides," another Bacteria which is larger, to achieve the transplantation of DNA. One benefit of this Bacteria is that it forms Blue colonies which can be seen with the naked eye. After a year's work, the idea to take "M. Mycoides" DNA and transplant it into another species worked, and for the first time, through gene transplantation, one species was transformed into a different species. After the success, Dr. Venter decided the team would try to transplant their synthetic DNA into an existing "M. Mycoides" cell to create for the first time, new life. The two years work copying the DNA of "M. Genitaliym," the smallest Bacteria known which the team could not transplant into a biological cell was put aside, and work began on copying the biggest DNA genome that had ever been attempted, the Bacteria "M. Mycoides," twice the size of "M. Genitalium." Already at that point in time, before Dr. Venter had even created one living synthetic cell, he formed a new company "Synthetic Genomics" getting ready for the future industry which would spring from his accomplishments. Dr. Arthur Kaplan, the "Bioethicist" who also commented on the Bioluminescent Transgenic plants, describes future "Miracle Cure" applications for this new technology which creates life, and lists the environment, with utilization in oil-spill cleanups, medicine utilizing microbes acting something like vaccines that will enter the body, and even space exploration through the alteration of the human body until it is resilient to high levels of radiation during space missions. Kaplan believes that there is no limit to what can be done using microbial life. Again, it doesn't "Grow Your Hair Back?" Huge facilities are dreamed of by Dr. Venter that would be the size of a full city and which would contain microbial synthetic life first removing carbon dioxide from the atmosphere, and then creating usable fuel with it. Against the threat of leakage of any kind out of the labs, facilities, or another containments, Venter's team plans on adding "suicide genes" into the synthetic life forms they create, so when removed from essential environments, the synthetic life is supposed to die. Members of Venter's team firmly believe that they are going to save our world and create a better life for future generations.

Finally in March, 2010 everything falls together, Venter's team is able to transplant DNA using yeast, and everyone prepares to literally create Life. On March 29, 2010, after transplanting man-made "M. Mycoides" DNA into host cells this synthetic DNA takes over the host cell's natural DNA, and a new species of Life has been created for the first time in history by Dr. Craig Venter and his team. That was the first time in the world that a synthetic cell had been made. This discovery has been said to have changed Human being's viewpoint of life itself, as well as having been proclaimed as being the beginning of the third major Revolution of the Human race after the Agricultural and Industrial Revolutions. In comparison, this first creation of synthetic man-made Life makes "Glo-fish" and "Alba" the "GFP Bunny" seem nearly safe(!)

This is the concluding chapter in a very long history of trials, errors, dreams, prayers, and accomplishments. Countless thousands of generations of biological entities evolved into an all-consuming, self-destructive, self-deitized animal. The ultimate parasite. Look around: Artists - formerly who's role it was as a *"Teacher"* going back to the birth of Art itself - today making "Art" in the totally new medium of Genetically-altered Monsters who Fluoresce under Black lights(!?) Technically advanced, but Spiritually malignant. What "lessons!"

Let us imagine ourselves in a world such as the one we actually live in. Mass - Global even - societies that have completely lost their link to nature around themselves in every way. A "creature" - and this word is used in all it's meanings - that is the working physical manifestation of it's ego and it's ego-produced and buttressing machinery. The inside has been relegated to nothing more than a "hardrive" memory machine. The outside veneer has been elevated to the ultimate - a God-like state. This is how society stands and operates for the majority of people walking on Earth today.

One of the subjects that will be examined closely in this final chapter "What Happened to the Miracle?" was just outlined in the previous paragraphs, which is one of the most controversial subjects ever breeched by humanity, and truly contains the elements to make it a greater potential threat than any other of the pleasant treats to all life on Earth, such as nuclear annihilation. If historical perspective is developed enough in a person, it doesn't take a huge leap of imagination to picture the "Green Fluorescent Protein Revolution" being eerily similar with it's seemingly "Miracle-Cure" contemporary status, to the "Actinotherapy" revolution which went on from approximately 1885 until about 1949, raising public enthusiasm with claims of being a tool on the way to creating a "Brave New World." The other "Miracle-Cure Movement" that immediately comes to mind is the "Radium Craze" of the first few decades of the Twentieth century - again extremely similar to the "Actinotherapy" misguided and deadly movement. The vast potential immediately realized in the weak little minds of greedy entrepreneurs - throughout history - has almost inevitably produced monstrous results, which "Actinotherapy" and the "Radium Miracle-Cure" movements are without question at the very top of the list of naming such atrocities. Extremely similar in it's nearly fetish-like state, the Green Fluorescent Protein revolution is also another deadly invisible energy "discovered" by human beings which - again - everybody wants a piece of - like Radium and Shortwave Ultraviolet Medical Treatments exactly one-hundred years ago, and - again - also possesses the potential for catastrophic results. At least "Actinotherapy" and the "Radium Craze" a century ago only killed the individuals who were naive enough to expose themselves to these Miracle-Cures, but the "Fluorescent Protein Revolution" of today has advanced exponentially over these old fashioned Miracle-cure threats, and currently holds the potential to threaten all life on Earth - talk about progress!

Discovered in a small inconspicuous Jellyfish living in the "Friday Harbor" in Washington State by a young Japanese scientist named Osamu Shimomura over half a century ago in 1962, the "Green Fluorescent Protein" Revolution took off after the first life was created which artificially glowed under a Black light in 1993 in the 'holy land' of Manhattan, and then just a year later Martin Chalfie went beyond the "GFP" intestinal bacteria 'E. coli" he was first to "create," and produced the second "GFP" life-form, a flatworm, and then just as important to this revolution the cloning of Green Fluorescent Protein was achieved. Altering the genes of many living creatures on this Earth for two full decades now will be seen in the future in the same light - and with just as much respect and admiration for - as the most important medical procedure used by people for centuries: "Bleeding" a patient to make them healthy. This current "Transgenic" revolution will perhaps even surpass the mundane status of "Actinotherapy" and the just-as-deadly "Radium Craze" a mere century ago.

"Glowing Genes - A Revolution in Biotechnology" Marc Zimmer, Ph.D. (2005)

For proof of the "Miracle-Cure" mentality in this Twenty-first century, merely read the dust-jacket of one of the few books written on the subject for the general public, "Glowing Genes - A Revolution in Biotechnology" by Marc Zimmer, Ph.D. from 2005. The very first sentence of the dust-jacket of the book informs the reader that altering life through "Biotechnology" will give us the power to "understand cancer," to develop "New products," improve our "agriculture" - and last but not least: to also "Combat Terrorism" as well. If the reader just runs over that last sentence in their heads once more, only, it is an undeniable repetition of "Miracle-Cure" history from exactly one century ago. Something that everyone wanted a piece of, and through their extremely limited knowledge which was greatly supplemented by enthusiasm, ego, and dreams of wealth, humanity looks back in absolute horror a mere century later. From 'Understanding Cancer' to 'Combating Terrorism' sounds like a clear, unchanged echo of the "Grow Your Hair Back," "Improve Personality Disorders," and "Curing Rickets in Children's Legs" outrageous claims of the deadly "Actinotherapy" that went on until less than ten years before this current author's birth in the 1950s. In fact, the creation of new species of Genetically Manipulated life-forms seems as insane to this current author as a popular technique 'to improve virility' a hundred years ago: tying a bag of Radium around the Testicles(!) By only the fourth sentence of just the dust-jacket introduction, Dr. Marc Zimmer restates the miraculous potentials of the Green Fluorescent Protein genes discovered in just a single Jellyfish species which has been around for one-hundred and sixty million years, and again informs the reader of the 'brand new exciting discoveries' this "GFP Revolution" will create for us, such as - again - tracing "bacterial infection" as well as 'detecting biological and chemical threats' of Terrorism (yet again - it doesn't Grow Your Hair Back?). The fifth sentence of this dust-jacket of "Glowing Genes" adds the imaging of cancer cells and the detection of pollution to the list of 'miraculous' attributes of the Transgenic manipulation of life-forms on Earth. By only the third paragraph of just the dust-jacket of this book - the book hasn't even been opened yet - we are enticed by more 'miracles' of "Glowing Genes," such as crops which glow to signal their need for watering, and Red Fluorescent Protein contained in coral which is envisioned to be used to engineer Sheep born with Red wool, so the wool doesn't have to be dyed. Along the similar lines as the Green Fluorescent Protein Silkworms created around the turn of the century over a dozen years ago, scientists are producing Transgenic monsters that have never populated the Earth before in it's four-billion plus year history - just so we don't have to dye wool or silk. Similar to going under Middlewave Ultraviolet lamps all over the world today to get a quick, artificial suntan, logic would suggest very, very strongly that it is better to go out into the Sun to get a suntan - and to *Dye wool!* Dr. Zimmer cheerfully reminds the prospective reader of his book, in it's dust-cover introduction, not to forget that this Transgenic Coloration of Sheep's wool, etc. will also help the 'Environment' because harmful chemical Dyes won't be washed down the sink into the water system - avoiding 'Pollution.' Wonderful. This proposal and logic sound like an echo of the past, when it was believed that sitting under Shortwave Ultraviolet Miracle-Cure "Actinotherapy" lamps - which we clearly know today would eventually kill the patient through it's greatest gift, skin cancer - was considered and taught - and also written in countless books as well - to be much *better* for you than going out into the Sun.

The mother of all horrors is the possibility of our extinction as a result of radical change to the Earth's food chain and endless other unseen possibilities. The reason Homo-sapiens are here, as well as each and every species on the planet, is because of the Darwinian concept of "Evolution," and evolution is often created by a genetic anomaly - a mistake in the DNA of an individual member of any species who may be born with a different size or shape beak, for example. This individual bird has an advantage over other members of it's species, because of it's genetic "mistake," and through reproduction this advantage multiplies very rapidly, until this chance genetical natural mistake which gave one bird in one species a longer beak than all other members of it's species eventually will reproduce in greater and greater numbers resulting, in the end, to only the offspring and generations created originally by the bird with a chance natural DNA alteration finding more food, raising healthier offspring, and finally becoming the more successful reproducer. This species, naturally, will then change until all that is left is the offspring of the bird with the longer beak - the advantage over the original members of it's species will be a new species of the same genus - "Evolution" - the reason we are here and not Neanderthals. Now if this can happen literally a countless number of times in nature, it would be more than absurd to think it couldn't happen with Transgenic animals. Let us imagine just one of the one billion or so "Glo-Fish" sold since 1997 on both sides of the world with direct access to both the Pacific and Atlantic Oceans through the seashores of China, Taiwan, and the United States - just one of these unnatural "Glo-Fish" has a naturally occurring DNA "mistake" which allows it to become not "sterile" like they all were programed genetically to be born, but had a chance evolutionary change to it's DNA, naturally as any other species on this planet, which allowed it to now reproduce. Let us now imagine a common practice for owners of unwanted aquarium fish - this "Glo-Fish" bought for $5.99 that is unwanted by it's owner in the United States flushes this genetic "mistake" with the ability to reproduce down their toilet. This "Glo-Fish" enters the waters off the coast of the United States and begins to mate - and reproduce - with other non-Transgenic, natural members of it's species in either the Atlantic or Pacific coasts of the U.S. For some unthought-of, unstudied, and unforeseen reason, the Transgenic man-made advantage in this new species of combined "Glo-Fish" and natural "Zebra fish" thrive and have, again, an unforeseen hunting advantage through their genetically manipulated ability to emit light through Longwave Ultraviolet energy passing through the Earth's atmosphere at all times. This new species with the man-made hunting advantage eventually reproduces more and also has healthier offspring because of their unnaturally genetically engineered hunting advantage, which quite naturally leads to evolution - the stronger and greater numbers of the advantaged "Glo-Fish"/"Zebra fish" species have become an evolved new creature on the Earth - not arriving after millions of years of "Natural selection," but through not even millions of *hours* - this man-made monster can easily be imagined as becoming the dominant, more successful member of it's species, which again naturally leads to "natural selection" and this new "Glo-Fish"/"Zebra fish" creature replaces all previously completely natural "Zebra fish" - again, this is also how we got here. So What? Nobody for sure has stopped to research - or even consider - the outcome of these Transgenic monsters made in a Taiwanese laboratory over twenty years ago and for sale to the public in China and Taiwan since 1997, and to the public in the United States since 2003, entering the food chain and being eaten by other fish and creatures in the sea, and maybe even by Human beings. What if the genetically-altered genes of this "Glo-Fish" creates something capable of causing a mutation like cancer in the other fish it eats in both the Atlantic and Pacific Oceans - and what if people eating fish that ate these now wild "Glo-Fish"/"Zebra fish" can get cancer from eating these fish that ate the wild "Glo-Fish"/"Zebra fish." What happens - again naturally - could lead to nothing less that a change in the complete food chain of the Earth, and to many species alive for countless millions of years on our planet - including Homo sapiens going extinct. If you run this seemingly farfetched concept presented here to a person of science, they would probably not even raise their eyebrows it is so common an occurrence in nature. You would be telling them something they already know - something that is also a natural fact. Now with the addition of the other "Transgenic Pets" on the horizon this possibility presented here obviously also multiplies correspondingly. There are about fifteen different Transgenic aquarium fish either being sold or on the way to being sold in China, Taiwan, and the United States. Also the "Ruppy" - a mammal - a Transgenic Red Fluorescent dog is on the near horizon to being sold to the public as well, along with other fish, animals and even plants.

    Back to "Glowing Genes," if avoiding pollution through genetical manipulation producing "Transgenic" new species on Earth, curing cancer, monitoring bacterial infections, and also genetically modifying our crops to Fluoresce Red so we know when to water them, are not enough "Miracles," the last two paragraphs of just the "Glowing Genes" dust-jacket introduction already informs the reader that 'Anthrax, land-mines, and chemical agents used in wars' could be combated by the creation of genetically-modified Transgenic Fluorescent "organisms," again, in the fight against the threat of "Terrorism." The very next sentence also introduces the "emergence" of a brand new Art form: "Transgenic Art." This dust-jacket introduction to "Glowing Genes" closes with one sentence presenting a very lucid premonition for the future - that this new Transgenic manipulation and production of new man-made species of Fluorescent animals on Earth 'Promises to soon *Revolutionize* the world.' In the era before the Second world war, Nils Boer and other scientists pioneering the new field of Nuclear fusion went on to 'promise' that Nuclear fusion would also 'Revolutionize' the world - and they were not exaggerating in any way - who has forgotten about the Atomic bombs dropped on both Nagasaki and Hiroshima? Ask any ex-citizen of the formerly inhabited city of Chernobyl their opinion on this as well.

    On the back cover of this dust-jacket of "Glowing Genes" the quoted praises for the "Fluorescent Protein Revolution" are listed from the top to the bottom, starting with the President of "AntiCancer, Inc." who states once again that Transgenic manipulation of life-forms on Earth is one of the two most important of history's "revolutions" in medicine and biology, and furthermore - to cement the "Miracle-Cure" mentality of this movement - the President of "AntiCancer, Inc." is quoted as predicting nothing less than a coming "wonderful future" which 'we cannot even imagine,' of course being miraculously invented for us by "Fluorescent Proteins." Next in this list of quotes on the back cover of the dust-jacket of "Glowing Genes" is a "Research Fellow" of "Promega Corporation" who also praises the Transgenic "Miracle-Cure" for advancing the revolution in "molecular biology," and restates for all to know that this will lead to 'improving the quality' of nothing less than 'our life' in "surprising ways"(!) The praise continues to be poured onto the back of "Glowing Genes" dust-jacket, with 'Science Advisor and Manager' of the "US Department of Homeland Security" excited about another "miracle" of Transgenic manipulation of life on Earth: 'counter measures against biological and chemical international Terrorism threats.' This manager of "Homeland Security" also claims that the "Miracles" of Transgenic manipulation have gone beyond the 'initial findings' "wildest expectations." Along very similar lines, a "Distinguished Professor" in the field of "Reproductive Biotechnology" is also quoted on this back cover with the confirmation that this Transgenic movement has led to 'revolutionizing biomedical science' and has 'begun to revolutionize our daily life.'

These "Miracle-Cure" claims, praises, and quotes - dreams of beating Terrorism, Cancer, bacterial infections, and even of watering plants - are all printed on just the "Glowing Genes" dust-cover, again, before you even open up the book.

The Introduction inside the "Glowing Genes - A Revolution in Biotechnology" book immediately states that Genetically-altered "Glowing proteins" are going to be used as a tool in many diverse fields, such as medicine, national defense, agriculture, and even Art. Dr. Marc Zimmer explains that these Fluorescent proteins are such important tools to research and analysis that they are referred to as the "microscopes" of this new millennia. Dr. Zimmer also goes on to explain the basic procedure of nothing less than creating a new species of life on Earth. An example is used of finding out how well an "antibody" works by simply injecting bacteria that has been manipulated genetically through the mixture of genes from a firefly into a lab rat. It is then very easy to follow the infection spreading throughout the lab rat's body by simply putting the living rat under a Black light. If the tested "antibody" is working as planned, the amount of the laboratory rat that Fluoresces under a Black light will shrink as the infection is cured. In this "Introduction" Dr. Zimmer informs that there are an abundance of Bioluminescent creatures on Earth, but out of this zoo of Bioluminescent life only five lifeforms have altered life through this "glowing gene technology," including first the Jellyfish, and then the most well known Bioluminescent creature the Firefly, as well as bacteria, coral, and 'Sea Pansies.' The Bioluminescence DNA from just these five creatures have created a new contemporary "Miracle-Cure" era which we are right in the middle of today in the Twenty-first century, and which will allow us the incredible abilities of being able to image as well as monitor "biological processes" of genetics, gene therapy, molecular biology, transplantation biology, cellular biology, and to also be used for analyzation in areas of defense, the environment, our food, and of course in medicine.

Dr. Zimmer clearly explains that our most well known Bioluminescent creature the Firefly is not the host of our Transgenic Revolution, but an unseen sea creature the Jellyfish. In fact only one "GFP" Jellyfish species known is the creature that in 1962 Osamu Shimomura discovered containing Green Fluorescent Protein: "Aequorea aequorea" coming from "Friday Harbor" in Washington State. Even back in 2005 when he wrote the book, Dr. Zimmer calls the movement a 'GFP Revolution.' After Columbia University professor Martin Chalfie created the first Green Fluorescent Protein life form, "E. coli" bacteria in 1993, he went on to create the first complex Fluorescent life form the Flatworm the following year in 1994, through which he proved that the GFP gene could be extracted from this "Aqueorea aqueorea" Jellyfish and be inserted into a cell of another species to make it Fluorescent. By the turn of the Twenty-first century, just five or six years later, throughout the world in most of the laboratories of molecular biology Green Fluorescent Protein - "GFP" - was being used as a tool already. By 1999 the eclectic mix of Rabbits, Zebra fish ("Glo-Fish"), Grape vines, and Cancer cells all would Fluoresce under a Black light. Dr. Zimmer expands on the workings of the GFP explaining that it can be "fused" together on the ends of a protein, which creates the new ability to Fluoresce under a Black light without effecting the protein's natural abilities and functions, such as moving through cells. This has been used in science to give the ability to see when living organisms make proteins, as well as how these proteins move.

To prove how little is known about what these scientists are using to both manipulate and to even create new life forms on Earth, Dr. Zimmer states clearly that nobody even knows why Jellyfish are naturally Bioluminescent after over 9,000 papers had been written on the specific subject. One more "Miracle" of the GFP revolution is added to the long list in Zimmer's book, the reduction of laboratory animal's deaths through former radioisotope analysis. Still in the Introduction of his book, Dr. Zimmer adds yet another "miracle" use of Fluorescent proteins: to avoid the food and water shortages on the future's horizon when the Earth's population reaches a critical point. Dr. Zimmer explains that the "World Health Organization" predicts nine billion population by 2050, which calculates to the impossible - being a doubling of food production with just the same amount of land and water we now use. A genetically altered potato which has the new ability to glow when watering is needed presents a prospective partial "solution" to future famine, according to "Glowing Genes." It is further explained that even the quality of drinking water can be analyzed with the Firefly's and Jellyfish's "Glowing genes." The example is given of Bangladesh, where half of the drinking water supply contains toxic arsenic, and where "cheap" accurate sensors detecting arsenic in water are being created through the use of bacteria which has been genetically manipulated.

A very fascinating fact is contained in the first paragraph of "Glowing Genes'" first chapter, which is that scientists believe that the most common communication on Earth are the light signals given off by both light-emitting plants and animals: "Bioluminescence." It has been documented in numerous studies outside of the book "Glowing Genes" that not only is Bioluminescence the "most common" communication on Earth, but most likely Bioluminescence was the absolute first form of communication on this planet. Marc Zimmer explains that Bioluminescent life probably began during the "Cambrian explosion" which the first life form's fossils come from that have the addition of eyes. The enormous number of different Bioluminescent creatures on Earth is estimated at between sixty and eighty percent in the sea by Dr. Zimmer, where incredible abilities of this Bioluminescent light are used by fish, including "Flashlight fish" with patches of Bioluminescence under each eye as well as false 'eyelids' to open and close their Bioluminescence. The "Bristlemouth" fish has Bioluminescence on the underside of their stomach, so predators from beneath do not see a dark outline of the "Bristlemouth," which creates a life saving "camouflage," and which is a common use of Bioluminescence in the deeps sea. The "Lanternfish" also uses their Bioluminescence for two different purposes, first as a camouflage against predators, and second for attracting a mate with it's light. The prehistoric-looking "Anglerfish" is another of the first examples given by Dr. Zimmer, explained to use their light emission as a fish bait, hung strategically by a body protrusion directly in front of this "Anglerfish's" mouth. The "Tubeshoulder" fish lives to 3,000 feet deep (1,000 meters) and survives thanks to it's Bioluminescence, which is contained in some "slime" it releases from it's shoulder area when it is threatened by a predator.

The Color of sea creature's Bioluminescence is Blue, not Yellow as in most land Bioluminescent creatures, because Blue light can travel the greatest distance of any Color in seawater. This is the reason that the majority of Bioluminescent light given off by sea creatures is either Blue, Green, Violet, or Indigo. The estimates for the number of Bioluminescent creatures is stated by Dr. Zimmer at being minimum 'seven hundred individual genera' containing Bioluminescent species.

One of the smallest of these lifeforms with the ability to luminesce is Bioluminescent Bacteria, which Dr. Zimmer notes are "fairly common," and known to people before the days of refrigerators, freezers, and medical antiseptics. From open infected wounds on a person, to the killed animals they stored before eating, Bioluminescence was a far more common occurrence for the average person before the modern era of refrigerators and antiseptics than today. Dr. Robert "The Bird was Delicious" Boyle will attest to this, and Aristotle recorded dead fish 'shining' on the beach in the dark thousands of years ago. But outside of the ocean and the insect world, Bioluminescence is rare. There are only a small amount of Bioluminescent freshwater fish, and no Bioluminescence has ever been discovered in the entire Plant kingdom, or in higher invertebrates besides the fish family. The mammal, bird, amphibian, and reptile families contain not one known species which is Bioluminescent. The two main creatures that the Green Fluorescent Protein Revolution is based on are Jellyfish and Fireflies, so Dr. Zimmer explains the Bioluminescent mechanics of Fireflies and Glowworms very thoroughly, along with the important point that just four elements are needed for the magical Bioluminescence of all species of Fireflies, which are oxygen, "ATP," Luciferase, and Luciferin. Oxygen enters the Firefly's body through minuscule openings on it's abdomen and the energy needed for producing the light in the Firefly's body is the molecule "ATP." "ATP," oxygen, and Luciferin are kept in close contact to each other by the fourth necessary enzyme Luciferase, and this causes the reaction of produced visible light. These Firefly mechanisms and chemical reactions were explained in depth previously in this book, along with what Dr. Zimmer rightfully describes as "spectacular:" the synchronized flashing of Fireflies found in Thailand, the Philippines, Malaysia, and India. This spectacular natural phenomenon occurs when multitudes of Fireflies collect in individual trees and flash their rhythmic luminescence mating signal together by the thousands, which can be seen by female Fireflies in a dark landscape for many miles.

The Jellyfish is next thoroughly described in "Glowing Genes," starting with the point that there are over a thousand species of Jellyfish in the ocean, who can live down to thousands of feet of depth, and which have been alive in our oceans at least back to, and some even before, the Dinosaurs. In the boneless, shellless body of the Jellyfish there are three distinct layers known as the outer "exumbrella," then the middle layer of it's body called the "mesoglea," and finally the inner section of it's body the "subumbrella." These extremely basic evolutionary champions have none of the components which make up the majority of almost all other animal species on the planet, such as blood, brain, bone, eyes, and ears. Also missing from the Jellyfish species are lungs, heart, a head, and any kind of central nervous system. What the Jellyfish does consist of is water, containing up to ninety-six percent, one percent mineral, and the remaining three percent consists of protein, the subject of this entire "GFP Revolution." Dr. Zimmer explains that Jellyfish stay upright in the ocean without the need of a brain, by a clever self-contained "balancing" system all around the edge of their bodies, which consists of tiny particles which touch sensitive cilia hairs and signal to the Jellyfish that it's body is off the horizontal axis and tilted, or upside down in the water. The only single Jellyfish that is important to this "GFP Revolution" is the Jellyfish that Osamu Shimomura discovered containing "Green Fluorescent Protein," "Aequorea aequorea" also known as "Aequorea victoria" or the 'Crystal Jelly.' This is a small Jellyfish growing only up to a maximum ten inches (25 cm), but commonly found up to just 4 inches (10 cm) living off the West coast of the United States from California to British Columbia, with the highest concentration between Washington State and Vancouver. Dr. Zimmer closes his Jellyfish description with the not-so-surprising fact that people have never discovered why the Jellyfish "Aequorea aequorea" is Bioluminescent in the first place, because there seems to be no apparent need of this "living light" for their gathering of food, in their reproduction, or even for defense.

In "Glowing Genes" the history of Jellyfish research is covered, after Pliny the Elder described his glowing walking stick and documented for the first time the Jellyfish Bioluminescence way back about two-thousand years ago during the First century, it took one and a half millennia for the next documented experiments with Jellyfish luminescence. In 1646 a famous early experimenter with Luminescence, Athanasius Kircher, wrote "Ars Magna Lucis et Umbrae" and described the "Sea Lung's" Bioluminescence. A century later another German explorer and scientist Alexander von Humboldt made the first experiments on Jellyfish Bioluminescence. An important early experimenter of Jellyfish Bioluminescence was Abbe Lazzaro Spallanzani who in the 1700s discovered that the substance causing Jellyfish Bioluminescence was "mucus" at the edge of the Jellyfish's body. After experimenting with sea water, and then fresh water which brought out Bioluminescence, Spallanzani wrote that when a dead Jellyfish was placed in milk, the Bioluminescence became so intense that he could read a letter at three feet (1 meter).

So, after a rather short history of Jellyfish Bioluminescence experimentation, the history of the scientist who made the most profound discovery in the field of Jellyfish Bioluminescence will be examined: Osamu Shimomura. Osamu Shimomura discovered "Green Fluorescent Protein" in 1962 contained in the Bioluminescent Jellyfish "Aequorea aequorea" that populated the Friday Harbor of Washington State, which has led to a true "revolution" in the medical analysis field and, as mentioned before, a multitude of other applications ranging from Fluorescent Red Sheep to Green Fluorescent Monkeys. In 2011 a Green Fluorescent Beagle and an Orange Fluorescent Beagle were "created."

In Osamu Shimomura's lecture from when he was awarded the Nobel Prize in 2008 for his discovery of Green Fluorescent Protein, this wise scientist in his eighties spoke of his extraordinary life. At sixteen Shimomura was working 15 kilometers outside of Nagasaki - in 1945 - and watched as a B-29 flew overhead towards Nagasaki and then actually witnessed the *Atomic Bomb* explode less than seven miles in front of him. Desperate for education in post-war Japan, Shimomura studied Pharmacy which he admits to having no interest in. After working as a teaching assistant Shimomura was sent to Nagoya University, where he was a research assistant in the laboratory of Professor Hirata. This Professor Hirata assigned Shimomura the nearly impossible job of isolating the Bioluminescent substance in a mollusk "Cypridina" commonly known as "Ostracod," which the most famous scientist in the field of Bioluminescence, E. Newton Harvey, who coined the word "Bioluminescent," had been unable to achieve for thirty-nine years since 1916. Professor Hirata didn't tell his young ambitious research assistant about Harvey's decades of work at Princeton, or even about how seemingly impossible the task he assigned him was going to be. Osamu Shimomura worked on isolating the Bioluminescent substance in this mollusk "Cypridina" from the mid-1940s until 1956 - more than ten years - before he both isolated and then crystallized the Bioluminescent substance that makes this mollusk glow. Shimomura explains in his Nobel Prize Lecture that this "Cypridina hilgendorfii" crustacean 'Ostracod' emits a Blue light when it's Luciferin is present with Luciferase and also molecular oxygen, causing the Luciferin to oxidize. After over ten years Shimomura finally accomplished isolating and crystallizing the substance which makes this "Ostracod" Bioluminescent, and after his results were published in 1959 they were read by Professor Frank Johnson, a former student of Professor Harvey in Princeton, and Shimomura was invited to Princeton University as a research assistant. In September, 1960, a short time after arriving in Princeton University, Shimomura was asked by Professor Frank Johnson if he was interested in researching the Bioluminescence of a Jellyfish "Aequorea." Johnson told Shimomura about the brilliance of "Aequorea's" Bioluminescence and about the place where it could be easily found, Friday Harbor in Washington State's Puget Sound. During the beginning of the 1961 summer Professor Frank Johnson, Yo Saiga his assistant, as well as Osamu Shimomura and his wife all packed Johnson's station wagon with a huge "photometer," laboratory equipment, their baggage, and then proceeded to drive across the whole United States from Princeton, New Jersey to Friday Harbor in Washington State - three-thousand miles - over 5,000 kilometers. Immediately upon arrival in Friday Harbor, these scientists began to collect and experiment on "Aequorea" Jellyfish, which were scooped up with a shallow "dip net" one-by-one. The outer ring of the "Aequorea's" body contains about two-hundred Bioluminescent organs which the scientists had travelled to study, so using a scissor, this Bioluminescent outer ring of this Jellyfish was cut off also one-by-one. The outer rings of twenty to thirty "Aequorea" were collected and removed, then "squeezed" into a filter of rayon gauze, finally producing a luminescent liquid which they called "Squeezate." Shimomura and Johnson tried for days to isolate the Bioluminescent substance in "Aequorea," but failed because they based their methods on the false assumption that the Jellyfish's Bioluminescence would be similar to the Bioluminescence of the most well known luminescent creature the Firefly.

Shimomura clearly states that the assumption in 1961 was that all Bioluminescent creatures produced their Bioluminescence from the reaction of Luciferase and Luciferin, like the Firefly. Shimomura was first to realize that that they were heading in the wrong direction trying to find Luciferin in the Jellyfish, so in disagreement with Dr. Johnson he started to work at finding another chemical causing the Jellyfish's Bioluminescence. This pursuit led to "soul-searching" and Shimomura even taking his row boat out into the bay to be absolutely alone and distraction free to think. On one of these solitary boat excursions Shimomura saw the answer in a flash, which was that 'protein was probably involved' in the production of the Bioluminescence of the Jellyfish, and if so, a "certain pH" could inhibit this Bioluminescence. With this gained insight Shimomura could extract the luminescent substance of the Jellyfish, and when he threw the extract into the sink which also had seawater in it, the mixture gave off a "bright blue flash." The composition of the seawater was the breakthrough, and for the rest of the 1961 summer Shimomura and his team in Friday Harbor extracted the Bioluminescent substance from around 10,000 "Aequorea aequorea" Jellyfish. This yielded only a few grams of pure protein after purification back in Princeton, and this protein in the presence of a trace of calcium (which acted as an "activator") emitted Blue light. The team named the protein "Aequorin," which was the first "photoprotein" ever discovered. In "Glowing Genes" Shimomura's world-changing experiment is expanded upon, with this famous experiment in perspective rightfully called a "kitchen experiment" because it was so rudimentary, using just the extracted Bioluminescent substance from the organs on the Jellyfish, baking soda, vinegar, and seawater. Through this experiment Shimomura had proved that protein was involved in the Bioluminescence of this Jellyfish, and that it could also be isolated from "Aequorea aequorea." He had also proved in this simple experiment that it was the presence of "calcium ions" contained in seawater which caused the brilliance of the emitted light. Through this "kitchen experiment" Shimomura was able to eventually isolate the protein causing the Bioluminescence in "Aequorea aequorea." While the scientists had been purifying Aequorin, they discovered another protein which Fluoresced brilliant Green, and after purifying this second protein, they named it "Green Protein." This same protein would four decades later literally change the world, known to us today by it's title after being renamed by Morin and Hastings in 1971: "Green Fluorescent Protein."

Shimomura explained in his Nobel Prize lecture that he and Dr. Johnson wanted to understand the "Aequorin" Bioluminescent "mechanism" because by 1967 it was already realized that it would become in the field of biological study an important "calcium probe." These two scientists found a procedure to discover these "mechanisms" of "Aequorin's" luminosity, but this procedure would need at least one milligram of "AF-350," which could only be obtained from about 150 mg of purified Aequorin, and which in the end could only be obtained by extracting it from approximately 50,000 Jellyfish. Cutting the Bioluminescent ring off of 50,000 Jellyfish would take an enormous amount of time, so Dr. Johnson designed in 1969 an electric "Jellyfish Ring Cutting Machine" which used a circular meat cutting blade ten inches across (25 cm), and which allowed one person working on this machine to cut ten times the amount of Jellyfish Bioluminescent rings they could by hand, or about six-hundred Jellyfish rings per hour. A precious Color photo from the summer of 1974 with Osamu Shimomura, his wife, his two young children, Dr. Chang and his wife, Dr. Johnson and his wife, along with a helper, all with small Jellyfish-catching nets in their hands is printed in Shimomura's Nobel Prize Lecture, where it is explained that this team together collected between thirty and forty bucketfuls of Jellyfish every day. Shimomura further explains that Jellyfish collecting started bright and early at 6:00 AM, then at 8:00 AM part of the team began to cut off the Jellyfish rings. The entire afternoon was then spent extracting the "Aequorin" from these collected and dissected Jellyfish rings. Then again between 7:00 and 9:00 PM the team went back out and collected more Jellyfish for the next day. Shimomura admits that their laboratory looked and smelled similar to a "Jellyfish factory." Marc Zimmer adds details to this massive operation, such as the fact that so many Jellyfish were needed it was impossible to collect and dissect them all, even with their brutal schedule and "Jellyfish Ring Cutting Machine." High school girls were paid two cents a Jellyfish ring after being trained to cut, as well as any children of scientists, who were paid one cent a Jellyfish ring. Even with this monumental work force, the "Aequorea aequorea" only live for half a year and die off by mid-autumn, so the Jellyfish eventually ran out in Friday Harbor. Ten-thousand Jellyfish was all that they could collect, and this load was preserved using dry ice, and then driven by the team back all the way across the United States returning to Princeton University. After another half a year of incredible work back in Princeton, just .005 gram - 5 milligrams - of the pure protein was collected. The team named this pure protein from the "Aequorea aequorea" Jellyfish

"Aequorin" in honor of it's host. This went on for five full years until the team determined that the chemical structure that they had been working half a decade in search of was related chemically to the 'luminescence system' of the "Ostracod" mollusk. This revelation led to the team finally being able to discover the structure of "Aequorin's" chromophore to be "coelenterazine." In more understandable terms, Shimomura further explains that in the living Jellyfish "Aequorea aequorea," "GFP" and "Aequorin" are both contained in it's "light organs," and when the Jellyfish produces it's Bioluminescent Blue light the energy of this Blue light produced by the Jellyfish is next transferred to "GFP," and then finally this GFP produces Green light. The Shimomura team continued to collect and extract the Bioluminescence from the "Aequorea" to study because there was such a minuscule amount of GFP in each Jellyfish. It eventually took up until 1979 for the team to collect enough GFP to study. What Shimomura did eventually discover is that the chromophore of GFP is part of a "peptide chain," which gave the possibility of the cloning of GFP. Shimomura closes his 2008 Nobel Prize lecture by admitting that after he had found "GFP's" chromophore in 1979 he thought that he had concluded his research with GFP, but then something "mysterious" happened. The "Aequorea aequorea" Jellyfish population dropped dramatically, making the collection and extraction of "GFP" and "aequorin" nearly impossible anymore. In 1985 "Aequorin" was cloned by Inouye and Prasher, and then in 1992 "Green Fluorescent Protein" was cloned by Prasher, which made the collection and extraction of these two chemicals from their natural host the "Aequorea aequorea" Jellyfish unnecessary.

In 1992 Martin Chalfie, who shared the Nobel Prize for Chemistry with Osamu Shimomura and Roger Tsein, created the first "GFP" life-form, the intestinal bacteria "E. coli," and then in 1994 Martin Chalfie also created the first "GFP" living higher organism, the flatworm. After Roger Tsein succeeded in creating the Fluorescent proteins in the full spectrum of Colors in 2007, he shared the Nobel Prize for Chemistry in 2008 with Osamu Shimomura and Martin Chalfie. This will be expanded upon in the coming pages of this book.

Before venturing further into the truly 'unknown,' some deep thought should be given to the direction and possible seemingly endless ramifications of the permanent genetic altering of life on Earth, along with it's "creation" of brand new life forms that were never designed by the infinite wisdom of nature to have been born. Transgenic Fluorescent animals are only part of it, adding to this the amount of experimentation involved in this field which must be impossible to calculate. Where will this lead us as a species, and what could happen if an unforeseen anomaly in the literal zoo of Transgenic animals causes, again, 'unforeseen' consequences to not only Human beings, but the entire food chain of the planet? A mere hundred years ago there were just the first cars running around on dirt tracks - and "areoplanes" were a new invention(!) There was no T.V. - it wasn't invented yet. The unfathomable detail involved in the DNA code of life, which people are so arrogantly proud of having "mastered" and "cracked" today, will not be truly understood until these egotistical researchers are all long dead and turned to dust, and the Twenty-first century is a dim historical footnote, comparable to our present memory of the "Dark Ages" many centuries ago.

In 1962 Osamu Shimomura discovered Green Fluorescent Protein in the "Aequorea aequorea" Jellyfish and is today called the "reluctant Grandfather" of this GFP Revolution, but he is not the person who is called the "Father of the GFP Revolution." The scientist who "created" the first two Transgenic Green Fluorescent life-forms on Earth, Martin Chalfie of Columbia University in New York City, is the person who started this "GFP Revolution." Late in his scientific career Martin Chalfie first heard about Green Fluorescent Protein in 1988 while working at Columbia University. In 1988 the entire genetic code had been sequenced for a tiny worm "C. elegans" which Chalfie had been studying for years, and after hearing for the first time about GFP Chalfie began to immediately picture useful applications for this Fluorescent protein in his "C. elegans" study. Chalfie contacted Douglas Prasher who was working on sequencing and cloning GFP in 1988, and asked him if he would consider working together. Chalfie suggested his research worm "C. elegans" to test GFP because it only has 959 cells and a transparent body, so it would be vey easy to detect GFP in any cell. Chalfie thought of using GFP as a "marker" which could then be attached onto a "promoter." A "promoter" is an area of DNA that is in front of genes, and if a cell needs to produce a protein, it binds with the promoter, which in turn activates the gene. Chalfie then dreamed of attaching this GFP gene to "promoter" genes in the cells of "C. elegans," which would transmute his 'roundworm into a flashlight.' By 1992 Douglas Prasher succeeded in sequencing and cloning GFP, was contacted by Chalfie, and then sent him his GFP clone. In Columbia Martin Chalfie and his graduate student Ghia Euskirchen set to work on trying to incorporate the Green Fluorescent Protein into the simple intestinal bacteria "E. coli." After just one month Chalfie's graduate student succeeded in creating Transgenic Green Fluorescent "E. coli" bacteria by simply inserting the GFP gene originally from "Aequorea aequorea" Jellyfish into the intestinal bacteria "E. coli," which 'magically and easily' allowed the bacteria to produce Green Fluorescent Protein visible under a Black light. Martin Chalfie, his technician, Prasher, and Ward then set to "transform" the flatworm Chalfie had been researching for years "C. elegans" into a Transgenic life-form using Green Fluorescent Protein. In the February 11, 1994 issue of "Science" magazine Martin Chalfie and his team announced to the world that they had created the first Transgenic Green Fluorescent life-forms, the intestinal bacteria "E. coli," and then next the flatworm "C. elegans."

Something a little more unknown is that Martin Chalfie's wife Tulle Hazelrigg was also instrumental in the GFP movement, having been the first at succeeding in "tagging" a protein with this Green Fluorescent Protein, and she is called 'perhaps the mother of this GFP Revolution.' Hazelrigg didn't use the flatworm for her GFP Transgenic work, but the more interesting fruit fly "Drosophila."

"Bioluminescence - Chemical Principles and Methods" Osamu Shimomura (2006)

In 2006 Osamu Shimomura's 'masterpiece' was published: "Bioluminescence - Chemical Principles and Methods" credited to Osamu Shimomura "Formerly Senior Scientist at the Marine Biological Laboratory, Woods Hole, Massachusetts." This book is the next generation to E. Newton Harvey's 1957 Bioluminescence 'Bible' "A history of Luminescence - From Earliest Times Until 1900" (of which there is a first edition signed by Harvey in the Museum collection), with Shimomura publishing every known Bioluminescent creature on Earth in his typical concise, scholarly method. Even the front cover of Shimomura's book has an elegant design, with a Black background and the "Aequorea aequorea" Jellyfish with it's famous Bioluminescent "ring" photographed from below printed twice, incorporating this circular Bioluminescent "ring" of the Jellyfish to create the "O" in the book's title: "Bioluminescence." In the "Preface' of this 470 page book Shimomura basically explains that the 'chemistry of over thirty different systems of Bioluminescence will be described,' along with over 1,000 references specific to each system of Bioluminescence as well. Shimomura further explains that 'practical reviews' of Bioluminescence's "chemical aspects" were few and hard to find before his book's publication, except on the subject of Bioluminescent bacteria. Also included in his book are details of the original experiments he performed decades ago during his discovery of Green Fluorescent Protein during the first years of the 1960s, as well as contemporary "experimental methods" and "new data." For proof of the humble nature of this true scientist, on the brink of winning the Nobel Prize for Chemistry in 2008 and already one of the most famous scientists in the world, Osamu Shimomura dedicates his book to the memory of his three greatest mentors from many decades ago, Yasunaga who advised Shimomura to switch his research from pharmacy to chemistry in 1955 at Nagasaki University, Hirata of Nagoya University who set Shimomura on his life's path by giving him his first major challenge of finding the origin of the "Ostracod's" Bioluminescence, and finally Frank Johnson who gave Shimomura the "Aequorea aequorea" Jellyfish to research after having him invited to Princeton University in 1961.

After Shimomura's "Introduction" going from the study of Bioluminescence during the 'Last Hundred Years" to "the Future," his book's first three chapters begin with "Fireflies," then "Luminous Insects" followed by "Luminous Bacteria," continuing onto "Ostracod Cypridina" and also other "Luminous Crustaceans." Chapter four is sixty-nine pages of details on the world famous Bioluminescence of the "Jellyfish Aequorea" with also other "Luminous Coelenterates," and chapter five is dedicated totally to "The Coelenterazines." Chapter six covers "Luminous Mollusca," followed in the next chapter by "Annelida," and then "Dinoflagellates" including "Other Protozoa" in chapter eight. The last two chapters are "Luminous Fungi" followed by "Other Luminous Organisms" and then an Appendix. To give a hint at Shimomura's detail, the "References" of his book stretch for a full seventy-six pages, and the actual book begins with two full pages of "Definitions" to scientific and chemical 'Abbreviations and Symbols.'

In this contemporary Twenty-first century new Bioluminescent 'Bible,' Shimomura begins by naming the most important scientists of the past centuries of Bioluminescence study, starting way back with Aristotle and Pliny. Robert Boyle is the first scientist of the modern era and credited with proving that Bioluminescence needs oxygen, then Benjamin Franklin is next credited, followed by Paolo Panceri (1833-1877) who published early documentation on "luminous organisms." Raphael Dubois (1849-1929) is rightfully credited with the discovery of Luciferase and Luciferin, and the two "modern" scientists of the Twentieth century, when 'the secrets of Bioluminescence's chemistry began to become uncovered,' who are credited by Shimomura are Eilhardt Wiedemann (1888) who coined the word "Luminous" for the phenomenon of "the emission" of specifically "cold light," and the scientist who coined the word "Bioluminescence," E. Newton Harvey.

Shimomura restates in his "Introduction" that most of the Bioluminescent creatures on Earth live in the ocean, and that there are very few "non-marine animals" which are Bioluminescent. This small list is given by Shimomura as Fireflies, beetles, the earthworm, the limpet "Latia," the millipede "Luminodesmus," the "Quantula" snail, the "Orfelia" and "Arachnocampa" glow worms, and Bioluminescent mushrooms. The scientific fact is also stated that all Bioluminescence is literally a "Chemiluminescence reaction," and that the term "photoprotein," coined by Shimomura and Johnson, specifically covered the "unusual" Bioluminescent proteins first found in the "Aequorea" Jellyfish, which differentiates itself from the known "Luciferase" Bioluminescent system of the Firefly.

Some interesting facts about Harvey are disclosed by Shimomura in his section on "Ostracods" ("Cypridina"), such as the first time that Harvey saw Bioluminescence was in 1916 on his honeymoon during his first trip to Japan. Harvey quickly found that even when the Ostracod was dried, it could quickly light up again just by adding moisture. Harvey then collected, dried, and sent to Princeton dried "Ostracods." As Shimomura proudly points out, this meant that Harvey began his lifelong study of Ostracod's Bioluminescence with a "large quantity" of Ostracods dried and sent from Japan. Shimomura points out that the Japanese army had also been collecting "hundreds of gallons" of Bioluminescent Ostracods during World war two in a plan to mark soldiers at night, but it was never carried out. After more than half a century there exists still the original bottles containing dried Ostracods of Harvey from decades ago, which were given to Shimomura in Princeton after Harvey died in 1959, and for which Shimomura attests to their ability to still luminesce when moistened so many years later.

The method of collecting large amounts of Ostracods developed by Harvey many decades ago was to use a bowl with fish bait in it which was covered with a cloth secured to the edge of the bowl. This cloth covering the fish bait had a small two centimeter (±1 inch) hole cut into into it's center. The cloth-covered bowl containing fish bait was then simply sunk to the sandy bottom of the bay attached to a line to be left for one hour, and eventually pulled up with a bowl full of living, undamaged Ostracods. So many decades later Shimomura would collect his Ostracod specimens in the exact same locality in Japan where Harvey had originally collected, Tateyama, an hour's drive south of Tokyo.

Osamu Shimomura's section on the Hydrozoan Medusa "Aequorea aequorea" includes many interesting details about the famous Jellyfish, starting with it's name. In 1927 "Aequorea aequorea" was named following two former names going back to 1775, and Shimomura explains the difference of the alternate name used for this Jellyfish which is "Aequorea victoria," and which originally came from the Puget Sound British Columbia area's population of "Aequorea aequorea." The specific "Aequorea" population found in Friday Harbor, Washington State is described by Shimomura as having a diameter of seven to ten centimeters and a weight around fifty grams. The Bioluminescent light organs found all around the edge of the Jellyfish's "ring" are "distributed evenly" and number about two-hundred. Shimomura remembers that at Friday Harbor Laboratories of the University of Washington he and his team collected about fifty to eighty-thousand "Aequorea aequorea" from 1966 until 1980, and also states that the Jellyfish disappeared around 1990 in Friday Harbor for unknown reasons.

Even the "Collection of Aequorea" is detailed in Shimomura's book, explaining that the net used to collect the individual Jellyfish one-by-one was "specially designed" so that the most important Bioluminescent organs around the jellyfish's "ring" or "umbrella," would not be damaged. Interestingly Shimomura states that Harvey was probably the first scientist to study the Bioluminescence of "Aequorea" in 1921, and that up until the 1950s he was still researching this Bioluminescence of the Jellyfish from Friday Harbor.

The details are also revealed in Shimomura's book on the 'Extraction and Purification' of "Aequorin" from the "Aequorea aequorea's" "tiny granular" Bioluminescent light organs. The 2-3 mm wide strip of the light organs cut off of every Jellyfish was the only part used, totaling merely an approximate one percent of the "Aequorea's" body weight. In the end Shimomura and his team purified between two and five tons of the "Aequorea aequorea" Jellyfish and obtained only 125 mg of pure "Aequorin." Shimomura also explains the answer to a question which puzzled him during his early research on "Aequorea," being that the live specimens of "Aequorea" emit a Green light, but the isolated "Aequorin" photoprotein emits a Blue light. The difference he discovered was due to the Green Fluorescent Protein present in "Aequorea's" "photogenic cells." This Green Fluorescence had first been found in "Aequorea" in 1955 by Davenport and Nicol, but Shimomura and Johnson were the first to isolate the substance and then identify it as a protein in 1961. Shimomura explains that Green Fluorescent Protein is found in many Bioluminescent "Coelenterates," which emit Green light through this Green Fluorescent Protein in their "photogenic cells." The "photogenic cells" photoprotein, or "coelenterazine-luciferase system," produces light energy, then this light energy is transferred to GFP molecules, and then these GFP molecules emit Green light. Shimomura lists the "Hydrozoans" Aequorea, Mitrocoma (Halistaura), Phialidium, and Obelia, the "Anthozoans" the 'Sea pansy' (Renilla), the 'Sea cactus' (Cavernularia) and the 'Sea pen' (Ptilosarcus) all as containing a Green Fluorescent Protein.

Another full chapter in Shimomura's book is dedicated to a different very important Bioluminescent creature, the "Dinoflagellate," which is one of the well known Bioluminescent life forms on Earth, and which are tiny Protozoa responsible for the 'phosphorescence of the ocean' documented throughout history. "Bioluminescent Bay" in Puerto Rico is the most famous place in the world to see the Bioluminescence of Dinoflagellates, which are plankton that prefer warm waters, and are subsequently seen the most in regions close to the equator. Dinoflagellates are microscopic, so individual plankton can't be seen with the naked eye, only the brilliant Blue Bioluminescent light they produce. Microscopic Dinoflagellates are simple to differentiate from Ostracods, because Ostracods are about the size of a sesame seed, and the Blue light of the microscopic Dinoflagellates appears to be like paint or ink - an unbroken mass of Color - not individually seen points of light like Ostracods. This single cell organism Dinoflagellate is explained by Shimomura to be "distributed worldwide" in the ocean's surface water. Another detail presented by Shimomura is that there are three different species of Dinoflagellates, which are "Noctiluca," "Gonyaulazx," and "Pyrocystis," clarifying that although Bioluminescent Dinoflagellates have been studied since the mid-1800s, their "chemical aspects" were not discovered until about 1957 when J. Wodland Hastings and Sweeny published the facts that the Bioluminescent light emitted from the Dinoflagellate "Gonyaulax polyedra" must have three conditions to occur, being an enzyme which is "heat-labile," a great concentration of salt, and oxygen, leading scientists to believe that the Bioluminescence of Dinoflagellates is based on the same chemicals as Firefly luminescence, Luciferin and Luciferase.

The last two chapters of "Bioluminescence - Chemical Principles and Methods" by Shimomura covers obscure Bioluminescence, such as "Luminous Fungi," which include mushrooms and also decaying wood which has been known since ancient times through Aristotle and Pliny the Elder, when it was then called "Shining wood" or "Fox-fire." Robert Boyle used an air pump to prove that oxygen was needed for decaying wood to produce light in 1667, and during the beginning of the 1800s Derschau discovered that the Bioluminescence of rotting wood came from the fungal mycelium. Today about forty species of Bioluminescent Fungi are known to science, spread over nine genera. Other "Luminous Organisms," the final chapter in Shimomura's book includes the obscure of the Bioluminescent world, such as 'Star fish' and 'Brittle stars,' 'Sea cucumbers,' 'Sea lilies,' and 'Feather stars.' Another extremely obscure Bioluminescent creature described in "Bioluminescence" is one single "Millipede" living at 1,500 meters only in California's Sequoia National Forest, an it's 'relative' a "Centipede" found in Micronesia, the East Indies, Okinawa, Formosa, Indochina, and the Malay Peninsula. This six centimeter (2.5 inch) "Centipede" secretes a luminous Green slime when disturbed. Shimomura's very concise book closes with the Bioluminescence of several types of worms, and then "Luminous Fishes" divided into fishes of "Costal" regions as well as "Shallow-water" fishes, and 'Deep Sea Oceanic Fishes.'

Shimomura's "Bioluminescence - Chemical Principles and Methods" concludes with a full seven page list of "Luminous Organisms" including a large amount of individual species documented as being Bioluminescent in the following Phylums of life: Bacteria, Fungi, Protozoa, Cnidaria, Ctenophora, Mollusca, Annelida, Arthropoda, Echinodermata, Hemichordata, Chordata, and Vertebrata (Fishes). Osamu Shimomura's "Bioluminescence - Chemical Principles and Methods" is what it sounds like: a textbook for students and scholars studying or researching Bioluminescence, and was not meant for the general reading public like Marc Zimmer's "Glowing Genes." This means two things, first the knowledge contained in Shimomura's textbook of 2006 is contemporary and very likely the most complete knowledge of Bioluminescence that has been published, and second that over half the contents of his new Bioluminescence 'Bible' is nearly incomprehensible to the average person without degrees in science. The very last section at the end of the Appendix in Shimomura's "Bioluminescence - Chemical Principles and Methods" is clearly named 'Advice to Students that have an Interest in the Study of the Chemistry of Bioluminescence.' Osamu Shimomura's 'Advice for Students' begins with the fact that in the field of Bioluminescence, very valuable knowledge has been discovered through the research on Fireflies, "Cypridina" Ostracods, and more recently the "Aequorea aequorea" Jellyfish which contains two important proteins that were discovered, the "photoprotein" "Aequorin" used today as a "Calcium probe" in biology, and the world-changing Green Fluorescent Protein - "GFP" - which Shimomura clearly labels a "Genetic Marker" which in today's world has become "indispensable." Shimomura points out that one of the most essential qualities of a student exploring Bioluminescence is to possess an 'innovative and creative mind' because the "chemical mechanisms" of Bioluminescence are known to be "very diverse," making an 'established methodology or protocol' for studying or isolating new systems of Bioluminescence non-existent. Shimomura concludes that "amateurism" in the study of Bioluminescence can prove to be the student's "valuable asset," just as long as the investigator is not just 'creative and innovative,' but also in possession of 'adequate and basic knowledge.'

In "Glowing Genes" by Marc Zimmer the facts are documented with Osamu Shimomura given the title of the GFP revolution's "reluctant grandfather," and Matin Chalfie the 'proud and enthusiastic father' of the GFP Revolution. An interesting story is told in Zimmer's book about Martin Chalfie going to a pet store after his creation of the first two Transgenic Green Fluorescent life-forms, the bacteria "E. coli" and then the flatworm, and seeing "Painted Glassfish" (which were literally 'painted'), after which Chalfie asked the pet store owner if he thought he could sell real Fluorescent fish which had been genetically modified. The answer was 'you could sell millions of them,' which was nearly a decade before Transgenic "Night Pearls" and then "GloFish" began to be sold by the hundreds of millions in Taiwan, China, and the United States.

Marc Zimmer clearly and correctly concludes in "Glowing Genes" that Green Fluorescent Protein has indeed become the Twenty-first century's "Microscope," because it makes visible to scientists both the inner and outer workings of a protein, which led to the reality of Transgenic Fluorescent aquarium fish for sale first in Taiwan. Before being sold in the continental United States (besides California) beginning in 2003, these "GloFish" were first sold in Taiwan in the late 1990s as "Night Pearls" for about fifteen dollars each. These Transgenic aquarium fish were altered from natural "Zebra fish" by H.J. Tsai of the National University of Taiwan, who was trying to make just the organs of the Zebra fish Fluoresce to study their development. Instead of just organ Fluorescence, the GFP caused the entire Zebra fish to Fluoresce, which Tsai photographed and then showed these photos in a conference, which were then seen by a worldwide aquarium company "Taikong." As can easily be imagined the financial potential of these newly "invented" Fluorescent fish was nearly infinite, so "Taikong" company funded Tsai's research of nearly three million dollars to develop the first Transgenic Fluorescent animals for sale on Earth, these "Night Pearls" which were from the beginning sold "sterile," and included a Black light, Fluorescent plastic coral, as well as Fluorescent food for the fish. Red, Yellow, Green, and then Orange separate Transgenic Fluorescent "Night Pearls" were "invented" using the Green Fluorescent Protein of the Jellyfish and protein of Coral, which Fluoresces Red. By May, 2003, 2.3 million dollars of orders for these Transgenic Fluorescent fish came from all over the world outside of Taiwan, but all foreign countries did not embrace these Transgenic monsters and instead intelligently immediately illegalized them. Singapore illegalized Transgenic animals for sale and Japan quickly passed laws in 2004 regulating these Transgenic fish in their country. Besides Taiwan and China, the only other country on Earth which not only allows the sale of the Transgenic Fluorescent aquarium fish, but enthusiastically embraces the sale of these lab monsters is - of course - America! In every continental state except California these Transgenic Fluorescent fish began to be sold in the United States in January, 2004 through the Texas company fittingly named "GloFish." In the end Red, Yellow, Green, and also Orange Fluorescent "GloFish" were invented and have sold over 1,000,000,000 pieces in the past fifteen years, in 2014 selling ten different types and Colors with the "GloFish" corporation owner Alan Blake who was in his mid-twenties, along with his partner, obviously both becoming immensely rich. In "Glowing Genes" some typically American reactions to this new century's "GloFish" are documented, including an article published in the "Star Phoenix," which immediately relates these newly invented "Transgenic Pets" to the glow in the black light of 'your old Jimi Hendrix poster' rolled up in your closet, and announces that this 1960s technology of "glow-in-the-dark" is not just for 'your basement wall' anymore, but through genetic engineering's "miracle," you can now have pet fish which also react like your old Jimi Hendrix Black light posters(!) These "GloFish" were, again, voted "The Coolest Invention of the Year" in "Time" magazine in 2004. The "consensus" amongst scientists when "Glowing Genes" was published in 2005 was that "GloFish" were not dangerous if released into the wild, stated by both Frank Greco of the New York Aquarium and William Muir of Perdue University. However, in the very next paragraph Zimmer quickly presents the first Green Fluorescent Protein Flower, the humble "Daisy" created in San Remo, Italy, with the very terrestrial, as well as existential intention of the American government being able to genetically create marijuana plants which are modified with GFP, so legal hemp can easily be tested under a Black light to Fluoresce Green, while marijuana that Fluoresces only in it's natural Beige Color will be easy to distinguish as being illegal. This quickly led to Edinburgh University scientists creating Transgenic Potatoes which Fluoresce Green when they need water. The list of Transgenic applications to life on Earth continues in "Glowing Genes," with "Transgenic tadpoles" Fluorescing Green in the presence of pollutants Zinc and Cadmium, which were very intelligently invented by injecting Mouse "metallothionein" into unfertilized eggs of Frogs. That's not all, because Potatoes have been mixed genetically with Chicken genes to prevent fungal growth as well as increase the potatoes' "shelf life," and Flounder genes have been put into Tomatoes to protect the tomatoes from the cold(!) These new "inventions" begin to frighten scientists of the new possibilities of not only Transgenic fish and other animals cross-breeding and getting into the food chain, but the new horror of Transgenic crops spreading their Pollen worldwide, possibly also *pollenating crops* that were not genetically modified. This, in the end, could easily through airborne pollen effect not only the crops of the entire world, but even the crop's pollinators, such as the valuable and already disappearing bees. This has the disastrous potential of nothing less than a worldwide alteration of wheat, rice, and corn, just to mention a few unimportant and unused food sources.

Another shocking fact revealed in "Glowing Genes" about the "GloFish," which can easily be imagined happening in Transgenic plants as well, is that the GFP injected into the zebra fish's embryo which created the "GloFish" remains and is passed on to future generations, of course. What was not at all expected, of course, was to find that the children and the grandchildren of the first original Transgenic Fluorescent Zebra fish evolved into creatures with *Green Fluorescent Blood* flowing through their little bodies(!) Marc Zimmer closes his chapter on the subjects of "Thirsty Potatoes" as well as "Green Blood" with the clear insight to levitate Green Fluorescent Protein's importance and indispensability in science today right up to the level of the "Microscope" or to even the "Test Tube."

For some 'comic relief' from these Transgenic monsters altering the food chain and creating the downfall of life as we know it, Bioluminescent Glow-in-the-Dark Toys for children have been developed and sold by the millions in the last decade!

A company "Prolume" in the biotechnology field working with Bioluminescent genes from deep water sea creatures, has launched a new company which is selling only Bioluminescent Toys for children: *"BioToy."* The best selling product of "BioToy" is a children's "squirtgun" sold for $4.99 which squirts powdered "Aequorin" mixed with water onto other children, amongst other things. The powdered 'Sea pansy's' "Aequorin" is used, and when distilled water is added to the gun, children squirt out a Bioluminescent mixture which looks like just ordinary water, but when this "water" hits something containing Calcium, like other children's skin, it bursts into light! That's not all - another Bioluminescent Toy from "BioToy" that can be bought for $9.99 is a children's Chemistry Kit of Bioluminescence. This kid's Bioluminescent "BioToy" is called "H2OGlow," and with this "Bioluminescent Chemistry Kit" your little kid can now work with the chemicals Luciferin and Luciferase in your kitchen sink to create their own brilliantly Bioluminescent water - all for ten bucks.

Three years after Martin Chalfie created the first GFP Transgenic life-forms, Biotech companies were realizing the nearly unlimited potential of GFP and had already begun to create "mutant" GFP of different Colors. Blue Fluorescent Protein was developed, along with the "mutants" Yellow, Citrine, Gold, and Cyan, but Red Fluorescing protein was the most elusive. The search for true GFP in other species besides "Aequorea aequorea" proved fruitless because researchers were looking for the wrong indications in the wrong species. The "Crystal Jellyfish" "Aequorea" is not Fluorescent or even Colored - it is clear and Colorless in daylight, so researchers began to change their hunting tactics and realized that the Color of the specimen was not important, and could even be misleading.

In the Russian Academy of Sciences Mikhail Matz and Sergey Lukyanov began to explore species that had not been thought of before to have the ability to produce GFP, through the advice of fellow Russian scientist Yulii Labas in the Russian Academy of Sciences' "Institute of Ecology and Evolution." Lukyanov and Matz originally wanted to test all the species that were already being researched by scientists, but Labas showed them that other species which only Fluoresce under a Black light, making them only Fluorescent (today termed "Biofluorescent") but not Bioluminescent, could also contain "GFP analogs." Labas told Matz and Lukyanov about a friend who had a 'Reef aquarium' which contained many specimens of the Anthozoa family which Fluoresced bright Green under a black light, but had no Bioluminescent capability, so Matz and Lukyanov began to search species beyond the Jellyfish and other known Bioluminescent creatures, such as creatures which were the "evolutionary ancestors" of GFP and are naturally Fluorescent, brightly Colored in the daylight, but which are not Bioluminescent. Labas had made Matz and Lukyanov realize that Bioluminescence may be a "recent" biological evolution, but before this ability evolved there were proteins in this pre-Bioluminescent era which still exist today, proteins that are similar to GFP. This changed Matz and Lukyanov's approach completely, and led the two Russian scientists to search for proteins which were similar to GFP in Coral Reefs, particularly reefs of the "Indo-Pacific Ocean." The brilliant Colors as well as the Fluorescence of the Corals were what made the two scientists choose these specimens to research. It wasn't even known what pigments caused the Coral's Fluorescence, which was mostly found in the Coral to be Green or Blue emitted light but also occurred in many Colors. The two Russian scientists decided that using the same isolation and purification techniques which Shimomura used to discover GFP in the "Aequorea" Jellyfish was not the right direction to find Red Fluorescing protein, so Lukyanov decided to try contemporary biochemical techniques combined with inspiration from Prasher who found the gene of GFP in the Jellyfish "Aequorea aequorea." Lukyanov decided on five different Indo-Pacific Corals which all had bright Colors, and searched through the DNA of these brightly Colored 'body' sections of the Corals. Six proteins were found and then cloned, all of which were Fluorescent and were similar to GFP. The most important point was that one of the proteins that was found in the Corals Fluoresced the elusive Color *Red*. Matrz and Lukyanov then proved that this Red Fluorescent Protein which was similar to Green Fluorescent Protein and could be used to cause the cells of frogs and mammalians to Fluoresce Red, could be used similarly to GFP. That was the beginning of "RFP."

The Russian team also discovered that the Fluorescent proteins of the Coral have only about one-third of the same sequence of amino acids as the GFP discovered originally in the "Aequorea" Jellyfish, hence the structure, in addition to other similarities, suggest that Fluorescent proteins evolved into the ability of an organism to chemically produce and emit light, which we term "Bioluminescence." This Red Fluorescing protein discovered in Moscow from Coral is described as "GFP-like," has been very helpful in science as a tool used in conjunction with, or independent of GFP for analysis, and which also has become a commercial product called "DsRed" named after the Coral it was originally discovered in, "Discosoma striata." The working differences between GFP and DsRed is that GFP was discovered in the Jellyfish "Aequorea aequorea" who lives in the cold water of the Pacific Northwest in the United States, and in great contrast the DsRed protein was found in Coral living in warm tropical ocean, so these natural situations created a "GFP" which forms in extremely cold temperatures, while the "DsRed" forms at room temperature. By the publication date of "Glowing Genes" in 2005 there had been already twenty-seven different proteins cloned that are "GFP-like," and which Fluoresce the Colors Green, Yellow, Purple-Blue, and Orange-

Red. Closing this section on Red Fluorescent Protein - "DsRed" - discovered in a Coral by Matz and Lukyanov at the dawn of the Twenty-first century in Moscow, Lukyanov originally dreamed of industrial applications for "DsRed" which would not only make a fortune, but would also join the ranks of other "industrial applications" for these assorted Fluorescent proteins that could alter life on Earth. The 'brain-storm' idea of Lukyanov's gives a good example of a genius-like intelligence inherent in great scientists, which is coupled too many times with a social ignorance as well as a total lack of personal spirituality - this 'brian-storm' of Lukyanov's was to create Transgenic Red Fluorescent Sheep! Lukyanov's great idea was to create a man-made new life-form on Earth - a genetical monster invented by pairing genes of *Coral* with a *Sheep* in a laboratory in Moscow - and raising such animals on Earth, for the huge advantage their invention would provide the Human race: we wouldn't have to dye clothes Red anymore(!) Again for the thousandth time, Logic would intensely suggest that rather than inventing and raising a new Transgenic livestock animal on Earth, like Sheep mixed with Coral, which obviously has never before walked the Earth (or was ever intended to walk the Earth by nature) - it is better to *Dye Wool!* The nearly absurd advantage claimed by these spiritually-void scientific inventions is something truly mind-blowing: eliminating the use of toxic chemical dyes for simply making Red clothing(!) Again, it makes about as much logical sense as tying a bag of "Radium" around the testicles to improve virility.   Dr. Zimmer asks if it can be imagined that our grandchildren and even our great-grandchildren will see Transgenic Red Fluorescent Sheep grazing on Transgenic meadows of Purple grass. Can't wait. This was at least only a 'brain-storm' of Professor Lukyanov's, but in reality just as absurdly in 2000 the first GFP Silkworm "Bombyx mori L." was created for uses in the Pharmaceutical and Veterinary uses, as well as in the Textile industry - for the explicit purpose of not having to *Dye Silk!* Dr. Zimmer cheerfully explores the nightmares which could easily be invented in the very near future, or even at the present time during the writing of this book. The question in 2005 was presented: could a "GFP Human" be invented with the technology we now hold? The answer was even back then in 2005 a definite "Yes." In fact is was confirmed in "Glowing Genes" that it would be easier to create a GFP Human than to clone a Human being. Even though it is illegal to even try in countries around the world, it is nearly absurd to think that it has not been done already. The first GFP primate was created during the very first year of the Twenty-first century, a Green Fluorescent Monkey! In Oregon on October 2, 2000 the first primate carrying a gene from another life-form was born: a Transgenic Rhesus Monkey which is also mixed with DNA originally from the Jellyfish. Since Humans and Rhesus Monkeys share ninety-three percent of the same DNA, you don't have to be a geneticist to conclude that it would also be possible to create GFP Humans. As if the act of the creation of a Green Fluorescent Monkey wasn't irresponsible enough, this Transgenic GFP live Monkey received a name befitting it's creators as well: "ANDi," which was coined by it's method of invention - "inserted DNA" spelled backwards. Gerald Schatten in Oregon is named 'the father of ANDi,' and typically this scientist began to wonder about the ramifications of his new invention of a Transgenic primate - the birth of the first Green Fluorescent Protein Monkey on Earth - *after* he had invented it. Schatten and his team wondered if "technological discoveries," such as their creation of a Transgenic GFP Monkey, could be "unethically extended" and inclusive of the creation of Transgenic Fluorescent Human beings, typically, again, after he had already created the first GFP Monkey. Schatten was a professor at the Oregon Health and Science University involved with cellular and developmental biology in the field of gynecology and obstetrics at the time of the creation of "ANDi," as well as being associated with the Oregon Regional Primate Research Center. The reason for Schatten's thirteen million dollar research into Transgenic primate Fluorescence was to find out if healthy Monkeys could be born from Monkey eggs which had the genes of other animals "inserted" into them. Transgenic mice are commercially available for years which were, and are, created and "produced" exclusively for research in medicine. In the end the entire experiment by Gerald Schatten and Anthony Chan to create a Transgenic Green Fluorescent Monkey was only a partial success, because just the umbilical cord, blood, hair, and urine of "ANDi" Fluoresced Green under a Black light, but none of his body. A true Fluorescent Monkey was only achieved years after the "Glowing Genes" book was printed, in Japan, with a "Marmoset" Monkey during May, 2009 which Fluoresces brilliant Green under a Black light - inside and out. It seems that Schatter and his team in Oregon still had reason to celebrate in 2000, and the "celebration" was caused by two dead Monkeys, stillborn "sisters" of "ANDi" who's fingernails, only, Fluoresced in Green under a Black light. What a celebration. The applications dreamed of by Schatter and his team creating this first GFP primate are to make available Transgenic Monkeys as the new "human model" for researches, because when Transgenic Mice have human diseases "introduced" into them they don't get the disease, but Transgenic Monkeys will contract AIDS, Alzheimer's disease, and Cancer when they are given these human diseases. It is clearly stated in "Glowing Genes" that "ANDi" was the first living example of that "direction." The public outcry that resulted in the announcement of the birth of the first Monkey born with Jellyfish DNA, included a TV reportage on "Saturday Night Live" the very next day after the paper introducing "ANDi" was published in "Science" magazine on January 12, 2001. More seriously, the "BBC" quickly ran a show about this first Transgenic Monkey "ANDi," and the 'British Union for the Abolition of Vivisections' spokeswoman was quoted as believing that the "end result" in genetic manipulation of primates will be "terrible suffering," and furthermore, that 'playing god' with primates to her was "morally abhorrent."

2006 was "The Year of the Pig" in China, and marking the occasion was the creation of - obviously - the Green Fluorescent Pig! A whole family of Transgenic Green Fluorescent Pigs were created, Fluoresced vividly under Black lights, and were even mated and reproduced quite a few generations of Piglets which carried Green Fluorescent feet and tails! This proved that the DNA of another animal which has been added to the host animal could be passed onto the offspring of the host animal, at least in Pigs. The first "YFP" Pig was created half a decade before made by Randy Prather of the University of Missouri, Columbia, for research in medicine, which was a Transgenic "EGFP" Pig cloned by Professor Prather with the addition of another protein, "Yellow Fluorescent Protein" used as a marker. This famous Pig has it's picture on the front cover of Zimmer's book "Glowing Genes," with it's signatory Yellow snout looking about as alien as you could get, compared to the normal Pink-snouted Pig next to him. The bottom line in the creation of this first "YFP" Yellow-snouted Pig was to prove it is possible to create a "transgenic clone."

The largest, most important application for the entire "GFP Revolution" has been and is today Medicine, and indicative of it's importance two of the final chapters of "Glowing Genes" are dedicated to "Cancer" and the Medical uses of "Glowing Genes." One of the most striking photos in Dr. Zimmer's book displays the use of GFP and RFP for breast cancer detection in a mouse, on which clearly is shown vivid Green and Red Fluorescence of it's breast cancer cells. This was done through the research of AntiCancer Inc. way back in 1997 when it was announced that "GFP-expressing" cancer tumor cells were implanted in mice and could be traced, and then a few years later visible Fluorescence of breast cancer cells in a living mouse was achieved. Using GFP to "label" cancer cells, which can be easily seen under a Black light, was an early objective in medicine centering on "monitoring" the spread and growth of cancer cells.

A little of that "Miracle-Cure" echo is heard, as the "future applications" of "Glowing Genes" used in Medicine are both documented and predicted, with "Stem cells," "Organ regeneration," Repairing Human eyes with "EGFP" Pig eye parts, "Lou Gehrig's disease," "Parkinson's disease," Strokes, "GFP-labelled" skin cells, "Diabetes," boosting the immune system, "Salmonella," "Herpes," "AIDS," and last but not least: "Obesity" all being covered as being analyzed, treated, or even cured with this new "Miracle-Cure." What - for the thousandth time - it doesn't *Grow Your Hair Back*?

After the terrible attack and destruction of the World Trade Center towers in New York City in 2001 the most important thing on the minds of Americans is "Terrorism," which is on television, in magazines, an on the lips so often that it has become an expression and movement in itself. This is the final application documented in Dr. Zimmer's book, using "Glowing Genes" for 'Defense and Security' in the possible use of "Bioterrorism" in warfare today. Besides the planned use of Ostracod's Bioluminescence spread on the backs of Japanese foot soldiers to see each other while marching through the dark at night during the Second world war, Bioluminescence of Dinoflagellates was caused by the movement underwater of a German submarine, which gave away it's position, and was used to sink the German U-34. The story has also been told in books about Dinoflagellates changing the course of history: while Christopher Columbus was going to land on the mainland of America for the first time and he saw bright lights of Dinoflagellates, he assumed them to be the fires on shores of native inhabitants and then decided to divert his course and land first in the East Indies. Dr. Zimmer explains a similar story of the early British explorers of 1634 sailing past the island of Cuba and believing that the Spanish had beaten their navy on Cuba because they saw "flickering lights." The British sailing past Cuba who thought they were looking at victorious Spanish warships, most likely only saw the Bioluminescent "flickering lights" of much more beautiful creatures than the Spanish soldiers - what they saw were Fireflies! Again, in the 1967 war in Israel soldiers shot into the water at night when they saw lights, thinking that they were killing underwater espionage troops of the enemy, but when daylight arrived all they found were floating dead Bioluminescent "Lantern Fish."

Quickly moving into the present, the use of Bioluminescent light emission in the detection of landmines is a modern use in Twenty-first century warfare. The shocking figure is an estimate of twenty million landmines worldwide produced and buried by the countries of China, Russia, Italy, and the United States just since 1980. A method developed to detect buried landmines employs Transgenic Fluorescent Bacteria that is sprayed over the dirt that landmines are buried in, and this bacteria has been genetically manipulated to have the ability not only to detect landmines but also to "digest" TNT that has leaked out of buried landmines. An Ultraviolet lamp is suspended above the ground to detect the Fluorescence from the "digestion" of this bacteria, which has been tagged with GFP. Another even more bizarre "technique" being developed for finding landmines uses plants which have been genetically modified to Fluoresce Green in the presence of TNT, so these plants are grown on a landmine field and if they are above a landmine the roots of an individual plant will absorb TNT from the landmine and have a Green Fluorescence of it's leaves under a black light. The landmine is then deactivated, and the plants are then "uprooted" to prevent these Transgenic plants 'spreading.' Great idea to alter plant life on Earth and possibly disrupt the world's food chain to find buried landmines.

Moving swiftly from extremely dangerous buried landmines to "warfare agents" using chemicals, the fact is that an enzyme labelled with GFP has already been created with the ability to 'degrade nerve agents' as well as pesticides. In 2003 at MIT a sensor was created which emits light through Aequorin in the presence of Anthrax, smallpox, the plague, SARs, and even "Legionnaire's disease," to detect the use of these chemical pathogens. This Fluorescent Transgenic enzyme marker is named "CANARY," which also uses White blood cells which are from the immune system that can clearly detect pathogens, and when the blood cell is attacked by a pathogen like Anthrax, the cell gives off a Calcium signal and begins to glow in Blue due to it's Aequorin content. Mention of other techniques for the detection of chemical warfare pathogens such as Anthrax involve the U.S. Army Medical Research Institute of Infectious Diseases and other researchers developing Transgenic enzymes to detect Anthrax through cell Fluorescence.

Typically with a "Miracle-Cure," the boundaries of ability are spread very far, in fact as far back as the Vietnam war during the 1960s and early 1970s. A very pleasant chemical used by the Americans to kill all vegetation Vietnam soldiers were hiding in was called "Agent Orange," which was "Dioxin." Typically after too much of this Dioxin had been spread over the whole country of Vietnam by American soldiers spraying it from the air, it was discovered that Dioxin caused severe health problems in people as well(!) In this genius technique, the American government sprayed no less than the unbelievable amount of 42,000,000 liters - or over 1,000,000 Gallons - on the country of Vietnam, Vietnamese soldiers, and of course, also on American soldiers as well. In 1969, with half a decade of the Vietnam war behind them and the second half still to come, American scientists suddenly discovered that these 42,000,000 liters of Dioxin they just sprayed over an entire country, as well as on themselves, causes birth defects. Research began during the war of the negative health problems caused in soldiers who were sprayed with this Dioxin - after 1,000,000 gallons had already been sprayed from helicopters all over Vietnam. What the research found was nothing less than alarming, being that Dioxin was, of all man-made chemicals that they ever had tested, "the most toxic." The best part is that over forty years after American soldiers sprayed 1,000,000 gallons of Dioxin onto the country of Vietnam, science still doesn't know how susceptible humans are to Dioxin, but it has been definitely proven by science that Dioxin causes Cancer in not only Human beings, but also in other animals as well. While most methods used for detecting Dioxin are expensive and slow, a faster and cheaper method named "CALUX" based on luciferase from the firefly has been developed at the University of California, Davis. Dr. Zimmer closes his chapter in "Glowing Genes" on 'Defense and Security' as well as "Bioterrorism" with the suggestion that most likely there exists many more "Glowing Gene" technological applications for the fields of Bioterrorism, Security, and also Defense, but that they are unknown government secrets.

In the conclusion of "Glowing Genes" the Transgenic Green Fluorescent Protein Movement is clearly summed up with the fact that already in 2005, over a decade ago, "Glowing Genes" were used in every one of the research universities on Earth, along with the fact that every student studying biological sciences has already at least learned about the Transgenic Fluorescent Protein Movement, if not having already used it in their research. The current author can verify this fact today, because in the Museum one of the final displays presented to visitors five or six times a day is a flip-chart on the GFP Movement and Transgenic Fluorescent life-forms, of which many visitors are not only familiar with but have personally been involved with through their own university laboratory work, or the research of a professor they learn from, or a colleague. Dr. Zimmer clearly announces that Biotechnology has been "revolutionized" by "Glowing genes," and goes on to question what the future will bring now that we are inundated with Transgenic animals, plants, food, and medicine - but only examined are the *positive* changes that genetic manipulation on a mass scale could bring, not the possibilities of disrupting the food chain and effecting all life on Earth, or of Transgenic life-forms getting into nature. The cheerful possibility that is only considered in the final pages of "Glowing Genes," is of GFP and Luciferase being capable of "revolutionizing" all life on Earth as well as all science. To justify this question and point, Antonie van Leeuwenhoek's invention of the microscope two and a half centuries ago in Holland is presented. It is clearly explained that when Leeuwenhoek invented the microscope he could magnify the specimen he was studying 270 times, and that today's microscopes are capable of routinely magnifying a specimen 100,000,000 times and studying individual atoms. Also examined is the social fact that the spread of new information two and a half centuries ago was unimaginably slower than today's internet, so the "GFP Revolution" took off with unprecedented speed. The question is presented that with this Bioluminescent "Glowing genes" technology what will be discovered in the next fifty years, and if our grandchildren will possess the ability to use "kits" to inject new species of their pets with Bioluminescent proteins? In wonderment about the future of this Transgenic Revolution the name Roger Tsien comes up, who's opinion is stated as being that the Twenty-first century's quest will be to discover how the proteins in DNA can create living cells, and how to use that newly gained knowledge to improve our health and lives.

Roger Tsien is the third scientist of this "GFP Revolution" who shared the Nobel Prize for Chemistry in 2008 with Osamu Shimomura and Martin Chalfie. Osamu Shimomura discovered GFP in 1961 in the "Aequorea aequorea" Jellyfish, Martin Chalfie created the first two GFP life-forms in 1993 and 1994, and Roger Tsien extended just the two existing Colors of Green Fluorescent Protein and Red Fluorescent Protein into a virtual painter's palette of Fluorescent Proteins in every Color of the rainbow. Having at least a partial sense of humor, Roger Tsien illustrated his monumental achievement in 2007 with his creation of the "Beach Tsien," which is a 'Beach Scene' in every Color, and immediately reminds one of a Gauguin Tahitian masterpiece, but upon closer inspection it is clearly revealed that this "Beach Tsien" is not a Gauguin, in fact it's not even a painting at all but the full palette of Colors of Fluorescent Proteins developed by Roger Tsien "painted" into a petri dish in a lab, then placed under a Black light! The achievement of Roger Tsien has since also been compared to the invention of the microscope in the Seventeenth century by Antoine van Leeuwenhoek, just as the whole "GFP Revolution" has been compared to Leeuwenhoek's invention. GFP is compared to the microscope in the way that Leeuwenhoek's invention opened up an entire new world not only to scientist's eyes, but by seeing single-celled organisms for the very first time it opened the minds of scientists to finally understand that the human body and all living things are made up of individual microscopic cells. What Roger Tsien's achievement of extending the palette of just Green and Red to the entire spectrum of Colors for Fluorescent proteins has done is to give scientists the tools of analysis that enable them to look into the cells with detail that was never possible before. Officially what Roger Tsien was recognized for to receive the Nobel Prize in 2008 was his work on the "GFP Marker" discovered by Shimomura from the Jellyfish, in which Tsien manipulated this Green Fluorescent Protein genetic marker and created an extension of just the two Colors of Green and Red Fluorescent proteins to the entire spectrum of Colors. These Fluorescent proteins can be made in any Colors of the painter's palette thanks to Roger Tsien, which allows scientists to attach these Colored genetic markers to any of the multitudes of proteins that make up the cells of living organisms and their DNA. This spectrum of Fluorescent proteins developed by Tsien can be used as genetic markers on any species of life, as well as in a nearly infinite field of research.

Roger Tsien began his important work with GFP twenty-five years before he received the 2008 Nobel Prize, in the mid-1980s at the University of Cambridge with his graduate studies, during which time he created new Fluorescent dyes that would label the three very significant "Messenger molecules" calcium, nitric acid, and "cyclic AMP." These three extremely important "Messenger molecules" transmit information between cells and are thus known as "intercellular messengers," which are of the utmost importance in the brain's Neurotransmitter activity, the contraction movement of muscles, hormone response, fertilization, and the intricate workings of both "glucose release" and "hormone response." The Color palette of Fluorescent proteins developed through Tsien's work enables the study of these vital processes in the cells of living organisms. The early work of Roger Tsien involving Fluorescent dye and the labeling of messenger molecules was very difficult to accomplish because Fluorescent dye had to be injected into every individual cell. The contribution to infinite applications of the Fluorescent Protein Revolution by Tsien was to create not infinite Colors of Fluorescent dyes, but a "genetic marker" that could be used to create Fluorescent markers on any individual protein of a Transgenic organism. The initial work began in 1985 when Douglas Prasher of the Woods Hole Oceanographic Institute first identified and then isolated the individual gene responsible for the creation of Green Fluorescent Protein. Roger Tsien then received a copy of this GFP gene from Douglas Prasher and began research, which led to his understanding that only a small part of this GFP gene produces protein which Fluoresces Green. Roger Tsien then worked on making a new version of the GFP gene, which Fluoresced a much more vivid Green, and then worked on modifying versions of this GFP gene which were not just Green anymore, but also Yellow and Cyan. This development by Tsien enabled scientists to finally observe protein interactions through their new ability of labeling multiple proteins at the same time with different Colors.

In 2007 Roger Tsien created the full spectrum of Colors of Fluorescent proteins after another major achievement in the GFP Revolution, the creation of Red Fluorescent Protein found in Coral by the two Russian scientists Matz and Lukynov. Roger Tsien modified RFP to create a genetic marker that was not only a quarter of RFP's size, but also most importantly Fluoresced additional Colors which he named "mPlum," "mCherry," and others. This is the achievement for which Roger Tsien shared the Nobel Prize in Chemistry with Osamu Shimomura and Martin Chalfie. The Royal Swedish Academy of Sciences in awarding Roger Tsien this Nobel Prize praised Tsien's achievement of the development of a full palette of Colors of Fluorescent markers, which they called a "Tool box" for studying living system's "dynamic processes." Roger Tsien's work has advanced since the 2008 Nobel Prize into developing "Infrared Fluorescent Proteins" which can be used to study the internal organs of an animal from the outside, without the obstruction of blood and body tissue encountered during surgery which obscures the observation of Fluorescent proteins. In addition to the development of "Infrared Fluorescent Proteins," Roger Tsien is also developing techniques of making cancerous cells Fluoresce, which allows much easier and efficient monitoring of these cells. The photograph of the mouse with Fluorescent breast cancer visible under a black light which was mentioned from the "Glowing Genes" book, is a photo of Roger Tsien's work. The mouse infested with breast cancer led the way to surgery assisted by GFP and RFP, which causes the cancerous cells to Fluoresce vividly, resulting in a three-hundred percent increase for "tumor-free" surgery recovery. Roger Tsien also developed "tools" for brain research, specifically in regards to observation and understanding of "memory formation." New techniques have been created by Tsien that measure when individual proteins form, thus indicating to researchers that memories are in the process of being formed in the brain.

Recently there have been more independent discoveries made concerning Bioluminescence, and in the February, 2013 "National Geographic" magazine an announcement was made in a small section on another discovered use for Firefly Bioluminescence. In the United Kingdom scientists are using the fundamental chemistry of Firefly Bioluminescence to find bacteria, such as the harmful E. coli, salmonella, and listeria in contaminated foods. The "Fluorescent molecule" and the "catalyzing enzyme" which together create the light of a Firefly's Bioluminescence are being used in a test tube along with a small amount of DNA with the ability to identify these harmful bacterias in foods. A sample of contaminated food is put into this test tube for examination, and when the DNA positively identifies that the food is in fact contaminated with E. coli, salmonella, or listeria bacteria, the test tube lights up. It is also reported in this small announcement of "National Geographic" magazine that Laurence Tisi, a molecular scientist, believes that this test tube containing Firefly Bioluminescence will someday be used also to identify infections in hospital environments, such as "MRSA," and perhaps even used to monitor the "HIV/AIDS" virus in patients who have no access to hospitals.

The previous pages tell a story of the development of new "tools" for science and medicine, as well as almost every application possible just short of 'growing your hair back.' Whether or not Transgenic life-forms should be created by Human beings even if they bring forth the alleviation of disease and cancer is still an open debate. Genetic manipulation of crops such as important Soya beans has not exactly been proven one-hundred percent successful, and is still a hotly debated, controversial, and in some places even an illegal issue. Should individuals with cancer and other life-threatening diseases be cured with technology that could bring about the downfall and possible eradication of the species - or perhaps even the eradication of numerous species? Too much research and development has already been done towards the creation of Transgenic life-forms, with not enough research done towards the long term effect of life on Earth after a virtual "zoo" of Transgenic life-forms have already been created. The extremely fragile relationships that exist and which have evolved for uncountable millennia are just that: extremely fragile. Not only are these interrelationships of nature very simple to disturb, but very easy to completely decimate without even knowing they existed. It took science thousands of years just to begin to understand that there exist little known symbiotic relationships which are essential to the workings of all nature, and that the disturbance or destruction of these for the most part undiscovered symbiotic relationships has ramifications for other, or possibly all, life-forms on Earth. Imagine that a simple, brutal act of killing Hippopotamuses who stir up water in streams and rivers results in an alarming increase of local deaths of humans because of Malaria. The Hippos stir up the water, which doesn't allow mosquitos to peacefully land and lay their eggs, which doesn't allow an infestation of mosquito births, which doesn't allow the numbers of mosquitos infested with Malaria to rise dramatically, which doesn't result in a dramatic increase in the number of humans infected by Malaria-carrying mosquitos, and finally which doesn't increase the number of Human beings dying from Malaria. So the simple, mindless act of killing a Hippopotamus is the *direct cause* of an increase in deaths of Human beings through Malaria. Now let us imagine this rudimentary example of human death resulting from our manipulation of just Hippopotamuses can be also imagined to be exponentially multiplied with the advent of the manipulation of DNA. The obvious results that could be brought about from the human manipulation of the very building blocks of all life-forms should be just that: Obvious. Humans are just beginning to understand the very basics of natural interrelationships which form the trellis of all life as we know it on Earth, so logic would very strongly suggest that if simple very visible acts such as killing Hippopotamuses can result in an 'invisible' reaction of many Human beings dying from Malaria, imagine what interrelationships of nature are being disturbed or destroyed when Transgenic living Monsters are being invented in a laboratory in Manhattan? It doesn't take much perspective, or even much simple imagination, to realize that what has already been done could easily result in not just alteration of life as we know it, but the actual demise of life as we know it. These incredibly tender and incredibly important interrelationships of nature were the subject of an examination by Chris Packman of the "BBC." An intricate interaction between three totally separate species was clearly illustrated, and proven to be the underlying skeleton that all of life and nature is constructed upon. Indeed it is clearly stated that Acacia trees need Ants to protect their leaves and keep healthy, but the Giraffes eat the leaves of the Acacia trees, so the Acacia tree forms very sharp thorns which serve as pockets for Ants to live inside of, which protect the tree's leaves from hungry Giraffes, and which also keep Monkeys alive, because Monkeys eat these Ants of the Acacia tree to survive. If any one of this chain of natural interdependence is disturbed or broken the entire chain is destroyed. This is admittedly a very basic example, which should serve it's purpose of imagining just how many more unimaginably intricate and complex interrelationships exist at the molecular and cellular level. This Chris Packman wisely states that the interrelationships that exist in the natural world are so intricate that it is impossible to predict what the end result of removing or indeed - as the "GFP Revolution" has done for the last two decades - "adding" new species will be, until it is unfortunately "*too late*."

As another example of the incredible interconnected interrelated extremely fragile world of nature, Chris Packman expands the story of the 'Secrets of Our Planet' to clearly show how the Brazilian Nut Tree could not survive without the Orchid. The seemingly unconnected rodent "Agouti" is the only animal adopted to be able to break open the large thick pod of Brazil nuts from the tree, which contain about eight nuts inside. The Agouti cannot eat all eight nuts of the pod it breaks open, so it buries most of them under carefully placed leaves on the floor of the forest up to several hundred yards away from the tree they fell from, with the efficiency of what the show's presenter calls a "gardener." Orchids living at the top of these huge Brazil Nut Trees need male "Orchid Bees" that use the Orchid's perfume to attract female Orchid Bees, so the male rubs himself against this Brazil Nut Tree's flowers to collect this perfume that is essential for their breeding, which in turn also pollenates the Orchid. This clearly shows that the Brazil Nut Tree needs the Agouti rodent to dispense it seeds. The Agouti rodent needs the male Orchid Bee to pollenate the Brazil Nut Tree's flowers so Brazil Nuts are produced for it to eat. Female Orchid Bees need the male Orchid Bees, obviously for reproduction, and the male Orchid Bees both need and pollenate the flowers of the Orchid plant through his action of collecting perfume to attract the female Orchid Bees. Once again, if this intricate mind-boggling example of the interrelationships essential for life at a visible scale exists, as with Brazil Nut Trees, Orchids, rodents and Bees, the complexity that exists in the essential interrelationships between life at a microscopic or submicroscopic scale is nearly unimaginable, and obviously should not be manipulated.

During the final phase of the writing of this book, on the twenty-third of June, 2015 the mother of all "Fluorophobia" newsflashes occurred in the French newspaper "Le Parisien," which announced to a horrified French population that a "Genetically Modified" Sheep that had been born as a "Transgenic" "Mutant" containing genes of "Green Fluorescent Protein" from a bioluminescent Jellyfish had not only been sold as meat in France, but had unbelievably also been bought and eaten by members of the French population(!!) As can easily be imagined, the fact that a "Transgenic" Sheep containing Jellyfish "GFP" DNA was sold and eaten by the French public horrified the citizens of France, and was announced by every manner of media immediately upon being discovered on June 23, 2015. In the major French newspaper "Le Parisien" last week the story broke to the French population, which revealed the hard to imagine facts being that a Genetically Modified Transgenic Sheep engineered to contain Green Fluorescent Protein Jellyfish DNA, which had been raised by the "French National Institute for Agricultural Research" (INRA) with the purpose of monitoring stem cell transplants visually for 'restoring heart functions' had actually been sold as food to the French people! Even the individual "Mutant Lamb" is identified and named, as well as it's mother! "Emeraude" is a Transgenic Green Fluorescent Protein Sheep who gave birth to "Rubis," who although carried the Jellyfish GFP from it's mother, did not express this Green Fluorescent Protein and subsequently also did not glow under an Ultraviolet lamp. What this stipulated as "Lab policies" in France was that "Rubis" had to be separated from non-Transgenic Sheep, and being classified as a "class 1 GMO" was not allowed in any way to be sold as food for people(!) But sold as Food for human consumption this GFP "Mutant Lamb" was - and in of all countries France(!) What must be appreciated here is the irony of the matter - the French people's love for food as well as the French Culinary Arts are famous throughout the world, so for this to have happened in the Gastronomic center of the world is especially poignant. The grizzly facts are now also known world-wide, with "Le Parisien" reporting last week that a statement was released by the "INRA" disclosing that what had actually happened was that this GFP Transgenic Sheep had been initially intentionally released for sale to be eaten by people during last August, 2014 by who is now referred to as an unnamed "unhappy employee." Months later this Green Fluorescent Protein Transgenic Sheep was sold to an "unidentified individual" as food. In December, 2014 these horrifying facts were discovered and then duly investigated by the "INRA." Sales of all livestock in France were halted, all experiments on livestock were also immediately stopped, and all "materials" that were genetically modified were destroyed. "Le Parisien" also reported that the penalty for such a crime is a year in prison and a €75,000 fine, so the laboratory responsible for this "Mutant Lamb" being sold as food to the French public was quick to respond with the statement that there was "no risk" to either the environment or to humans presented by this GFP Lamb. As can easily be imagined these released statements caused sparks to fly from environmental groups and European officials. Not a single country on Earth has approved Genetically Modified animals to be sold as food for humans, and in France the restrictions are reported to be "much stricter" then, for example, in the United States. What is also a major concern is the fact that since this "GFP "Mutant Lamb" made it out onto a French citizen's dinner plate this time, it could obviously happen again. Of course scientists across the world were quick to answer that 'eating DNA is safe,' and that according to their research there is no (discovered) way for the DNA from the food eaten to be "incorporated" into our own DNA. What is pointed out by these reports is that if Rubis' mother, the Transgenic Lamb who expresses "GFP" and did glow under a Black light, had been eaten instead, there might have been more danger to the individuals who consumed this true "Mutant Lamb." In "The Guardian" of England it was also reported on the same day last week that the French police had been called in to investigate this 'Lamb containing Jellyfish Genes' ending up on a French dinner plate. Apparently both this "Rubis" and "Emeraude," the mother of "Rubis," were Transgenic Sheep part of the "Green Sheep" program begun in 2009, which was striving to make Genetically Modified Sheep who would be born with "transparent skin" making it easier to 'visualize heart transplants.' "The Guardian" report of June 23, 2015 ends with accusations of employees responsible in France for the release of this "Mutant Lamb" as food for the French public, and states that for this "unacceptable" act there will be 'disciplinary hearings' quickly following in July.

Like the majority of people, the first Green Fluorescent living animal this author heard about was the infamous "ALBA" of Eduardo Kac. "The Rabbit Fluoresces bright Green under a Black light and hops around alive!" Michèle and I were told by Swiss visitors when first opening "Electric Ladyland - the First Museum of Fluorescent Art." Either in 1999 or the year 2000 three Swiss science students visited the Museum and told us about this Green Fluorescent Rabbit "You mean it's not paint or dye but was born that way?" Admittedly there was a mixture of fascination and disgust personally felt, which most likely is a universal reaction. "No, it wasn't painted or dyed, but born Fluorescent Green!" - as our fascination turned to disgust and our smiles faded rapidly. The reason that "Alba" the Transgenic "GFP" Rabbit was heard about first by the majority of people is because the Brazilian "Transgenic Artist" who "created" (actually "commissioned") this Fluorescent Green living Rabbit has a fetish for the mass communication of the world media. Bearing a certain similarity to another Artist who's piece of Art was, in actuality, the hysteria the piece of Art created in the media, Jeff Koons, Eduardo Kac's fame rose from his press announcements and the shocked reactions they elicited nearly universally in the public arena. But that's where the similarity ends, because all that Jeff Koons did was shock the public with blatant sexual photographs blown up about twenty feet wide of himself with his Italian partner. The current author remembers going to his opening when the Leo Castelli Art Galley was still in Soho more than twenty years ago, and it was so packed with people that you could hardly walk. Clear, sharp billboard-sized Color photographs of Jeff Koons squirting semen into his Italian lover's hair was admittedly surprising, but the only part personally shocking was the setting for these blatant huge sexually explicit photographs, which was at the time one of the most important Art Galleries in the world. But, to repeat, this is where the similarity ends, because Jeff Koon's "media manipulation" controversial Art of two decades ago was shocking and possibly even offensive to almost everyone, but coming in your partner's hair cannot be compared to mixing Jellyfish DNA with Albino Rabbit DNA to create a living, breathing Transgenic Fluorescent Monster. Eduardo Kac "created" not just a Transgenic Fluorescent Green living animal as a piece of Art, but also "created" both the name and the movement itself: "Transgenic Art." Now while semen in your lover's hair blown up twenty feet wide and hung in the Leo Castelli Art gallery may not be to everyone's taste, or even acceptance, the printed and presented photographs, as well as the original physical sexual act in itself, did not include Genetic alteration, or even the most "unnatural act" of all - the intentional act of physically combining DNA of a Jellyfish with the DNA of a Rabbit. In retrospect Jeff Koons' blatant sexual images twenty feet wide in an intensely crowded Art Galley seem nearly 'quaint' - or even 'old fashioned' - compared to the monstrosity that Eduardo Kac created. I have been an Artist for over half a century - all of my conscious life - and I have always been fascinated by and involved with Art that stretches the imagination as well as the social and physical limitations - Jackson Pollock, Paul Gauguin, Marcel Duchamp - I opened the "First Museum of Fluorescent Art" seventeen years ago with the first Fluorescent physical environment that is entered into by visitors who then experience "Participatory Art" - but the entire Artistic oeuvre of the "Transgenic Artist" Eduardo Kac, as well as the school of like-minded followers who call themselves "Transgenic Artists" or "Bio Artists" to me is not only disgusting, but closer to *insane*. Much more than just the 'club-tie and the firm hand shake,' these "Animals" are not just content with altering or destroying sociological outlooks or perception anymore, but have progressed to the new, contemporary level of embracing and possessing the personal potential of physically altering life itself, only. The obvious fetish for the amassment of both wealth and ego has not only led to the current miserable state that the world is currently dying from, but has bled into the species' imagination, wonderment, and even Art itself.

In Marc Zimmer's opinion "ALBA" the Transgenic Green Fluorescent Rabbit that Eduardo Kac commissioned a Parisian laboratory to create for him is just one of the "miracles" of the "GFP Revolution" - in between Transgenic Tadpoles and Transgenic Sheep. In fact this creation of "Alba" is hailed by Dr. Zimmer as an 'indication' of the beginning of the "GFP Revolution," because the "transition" between science and Art has been bridged by "Transgenic Artist" Eduardo Kac. "Alba" the Green Fluorescent Transgenic Rabbit created by Eduardo Kac and other Genetically Manipulated life-forms have been elevated to the status of being considered this new Art form's "Paintbrush," in fact. Eduardo Kac himself states that what

Transgenic Art has been created for was to both 'raise public awareness' allowing the inclusion of this new world of Transgenic Fluorescent animals, and also very humbly Kac suggests that by Transgenic Artists "inventing" new Transgenic Fluorescent species of life on Earth they will 'increase the biodiversity' of our planet. Just what the Earth was waiting for, and just what it needed the most: Transgenic monsters invented by "Transgenic Artists." So not only is the "invention" of new Genetically manipulated life-forms on Earth for the acquisition of fortune and fame acceptable to Eduardo Kac, but - unimaginably - these Transgenic life-forms are 'helpful to the increase of Earth's biodiversity'(!) The current author has used the term 'self-deitized' many times previously in this book, and is here indebted to Eduardo Kac for providing the epitome of the perfect definition. Now it is wrong to assume that fame and fortune were the dreamed of spiritual goals of this first "Transgenic Artist" Eduardo Kac, but after studying at the Art Institute of Chicago, where he had relocated to after being born in Rio de Janeiro in 1962, he created and became "chair" of the newly-created department of this "School of the Art Institute of Chicago:" "Art and Technology." That's a little of the 'fortune' part of it, and in regards to the 'fame' part of the spiritual quest, Eduardo Kac is probably multiple times as famous as the three "GFP"" Nobel Prize winners Osamu Shimomura, Martin Chalfie, and Roger Tsien all combined.

The grand plan of Eduardo Kac - the first "Transgenic Artist" - was a series of three public demonstrations and media hysterias which he would call his "Creation Trilogy." Now this "Creation Trilogy" of Kac's would be logically divided into three parts, or exhibitions, and these three exhibitions would be named "Genesis," the "GFP Bunny," and as a witness to his lack of ego, "The Eighth Day." For a Brazilian performance Artist who rose to public recognition by first wearing a Pink miniskirt while reciting poems of pornography on Rio's Ipanema beach, and then by being the first Human being to have a microchip implanted in his body which he surgically implanted himself as the media recorded the event as his "Art performance," Kac added to the "six days" and the day of rest, during which christians worldwide believe God created the world in, to create his "Eighth Day."

Eduardo Kac's first exhibition of what he called his "Creation Trilogy" was the 1999 show entitled "Genesis" held in galleries around the world including San Paulo and Linz, Chicago, New York, and Pittsburgh, as well as Athens, Madrid, and Yokohama. First of all for this "Genesis" piece of Art Eduardo Kac invented an interface for translating the Bible's "Old Testament" into "Morse Code!" Now the reader may be excused for wondering how on Earth the "Old Testament" could be translated into "Morse code," but Kac very typically had a quick explanation for that, being that since DNA and "Morse code" are both composed of just four characters, it was just a matter of converting dots, dashes, and spaces into the words of God(!) These dots, dashes, and spaces of "Morse code" were easily "translated" by Kac from the four "C,T,G,A" nucleic bases of DNA. What the DNA/Morse code interface was used for was to project a quote from the Bible's "Old Testament" Genesis 1:26 about 'man having dominion over the fish of the sea and the birds in the air and all living things on earth' onto the walls of the Art galleries that "Genesis" was exhibited in. Basically Eduardo Kac placed DNA in a central chamber of the exhibition, the visitor would turn on a Shortwave Ultraviolet lamp above the contained DNA, which would mutate the DNA, and which would have the dramatic result of - wait for it - altering the Bible's quote of "Genesis 1:26" being projected onto the walls of the Art gallery the visitor was standing in the middle of. The DNA used for Kac's "Genesis" exhibition was the "Genesis Gene" that Kac had commissioned a Biotech firm to synthesize and inject into Fluorescent bacteria. This "Genesis Gene" was newly created for each of the exhibitions, and to complete the media fetish circuit, where it was possible there was a connection established so that the "Genesis Gene" could be both seen and mutated by turning on the Shortwave Ultraviolet lamp above the gene via the internet. These "Genesis" exhibitions are not surprisingly praised in the book "Glowing Genes," where the conclusion reached is that Eduardo Kac was attempting to bridge the division between life and Art.

In the second stage of the "Creation Trilogy" Eduardo Kac managed to not only shock, but also to effect people at a very deep level, because almost everyone who heard about "ALBA" the "GFP Bunny" were learning about the existence of Transgenic Fluorescent life-forms for the very first time. Eduardo Kac states that he commissioned a laboratory outside of Paris in Jouy-en-Josas, the "French National Institute for Argonomic Research" to create his Green Fluorescent Rabbit "Alba." According to Eduardo Kac it was totally his concept to create a Green Fluorescent Rabbit, but that is in great contrast to what Louis-Marie Houdebine of this laboratory outside of Paris remembers. Kac claims that the production of "Alba" the Transgenic "GFP Bunny" was totally his own idea, but Houdebine discloses just how much discrepancy exists in the oeuvre of this first "Transgenic Artist," which is not at all surprising. Eduardo Kac insists that the concept of the creation of the "GFP Bunny" was exclusively his idea, and furthermore that he independently formed the concept and then found a laboratory to create his concept of a Green Fluorescent Rabbit, but Houdebine states clearly that the idea for creating a Green Fluorescent Rabbit was not Kac's at all, but was the idea of this French scientist Louis-Marie Houdebine, who has stated that not only was the idea of creating a Green Fluorescent Rabbit his own, but in fact that numerous Green Fluorescent Rabbits had already been created by

Houdebine in the French laboratory before he was even initially contacted by Kac. Houdebine states with scientific lucidity that already in 1998 he and his research team were the first to inject "commercial GFP" into an unfertilized White albino Rabbit egg, chemically fertilize the egg containing the unbelievable mixture of Jellyfish DNA and Rabbit DNA, and to then raise living adult "GFP" Rabbits - the year before he ever heard of Eduardo Kac. These living Green Fluorescent Rabbits were raised to maturity by Houdebine and his team, and then even mated, and generations were bred of newborn Green Fluorescent Transgenic Rabbits. In fact Houdebine documents the fact that over one-hundred and fifty Green Fluorescent Transgenic Rabbits were raised at the "French National Institute for Argonomic Research" until one day he was contacted by Eduardo Kac, who simply came to this French research institute and proceeded to just 'pick one out!' How typical and completely believable. These facts are all documented in "I Love My Glowing Bunny: Genetically Modified Objet D'art? Crime against Nature? Transgenic Protein Machine? The Inside Story of How a Reengineerd Rabbit Named Alba Became the Center of an International Tug-of War" by Christopher Dickey from the April 2001 "Wired," as well as in "Glowing Genes."

    For a bit of 'comic relief' (but surely not 'Karmic relief') during the middle of the writing about "Alba" the "GFP Bunny" and the new Twenty-first century "Miracle-Cure" Transgenic "GFP Revolution" which hails the Genetic Manipulation of life-forms on Earth as being not only our new "microscope" and "test tubes" of science, and nothing less than leading to our salvation from disease, old age, and even of late, "Terrorism" - but apparently not everybody is in agreement with this new "Revolution," and not everyone believes this misguided egotistical "Glowing Genes Revolution" to be anything close to a "Glowing Genes Miracle" either. Outside the arena of individuals and professional groups who stand to profit immensely financially by this "GFP Revolution," the general public is not only unenthusiastic about this genetic manipulation of life-forms on Earth, but on a whole the general public understandably believes logically that the manipulation of DNA for the creation of completely man-made "evolution" and again, immense profit, is nothing less than *insanely dangerous.* But as concrete proof of this, for a perfect example of what the general public thinks of Genetic Manipulation of life on Earth, who could be a better spokesman for the general public than the television? During the writing of this section on the most offensive of all Transgenic Manipulation - the creation of "Transgenic Art" first begun by Eduardo Kac's "GFP Bunny" during the dawn of the Twenty-first century, there was a truly revealing television program on "Discovery Science" station which had the cheery title of '10 Ways that the World Will End'(!) As the program's title suggests, this show listed what Discovery Channel believes to be the ten most dangerous events that could bring about the annihilation of not just Human beings, but the absolute eradication of all life on Earth. The '10 ways that the World Will End' "Discovery Science" channel program aired July, 2012, and begins listing the disasters that 'Will End the World' from number ten all the way up to the number one threat to all life on Earth. At the bottom of this list the program began with the tenth greatest threat to all life on Earth which is listed as an 'Astroid Hitting the Earth.' Number nine threat to life on Earth continues with 'Robots taking over the Earth,' and then a 'Super Volcano' is the eighth threat. The seventh greatest threat to life is described as an 'Alien attack,' the sixth threat is the Earth going into a 'Freeze,' or new Ice-age, and the fifth greatest threat is believed by "Discovery Science" to be a 'Mathematically-created substance' that runs wild and annihilates life on Earth. For the final countdown of these 'Top 4 Threats to Life on Earth,' number four is nothing less than 'Global Warfare,' and number three is listed as an unknown 'Plague' from space arriving via a meteorite. Now for the 'Top 2 Ways to End the World' after a list of annihilating disasters - the public opinion is that far more dangerous than an 'Astroid Impact,' 'Robot' or 'Alien' take over of Earth, a 'Super Volcano,' a new 'Ice Age,' 'Global Warfare' or even a 'Plague' coming to Earth by meteorite, the general public opinion is that the Second Greatest Threat to All Life on Earth is - wait for it - nothing less than this insane "Miracle-Cure" of "Genetic Manipulation!" Only beat by the number one threat to all life listed as the 'Earth spinning off it's Axis,' again, "Discovery Science" television station lists "Genetic Manipulation" as the Second Greatest Threat to All Life on Earth, only. The ten minutes devoted to this 'Second Greatest Threat to All Life on Earth,' - "Genetic Manipulation' - of course showed a "GFP Mouse" Fluorescing in bright Green under a Black light, and which was clearly labelled as being 'genetically spliced with Jellyfish DNA,' then right next to this "GFP Mouse" the camera pans to a model of a brilliantly Fluorescing Green Human baby (!) clearly explaining that although it's illegal, it would be very possible to create a "GFP Human being." What the "Genetic Manipulation" concentrates on in this program is the Enhancement of Human beings through this Genetic manipulation, with a professor of Princeton University very nearly drooling over the new possibilities within our grasp of eradicating sickness, disease, and human suffering - which Discovery Science channel soberly retranslates into the creation of nothing less than what the program literally defines as a "Brave New World," in which Genetically Modified Human beings will resemble us as much as we resemble an Earthworm - can't wait! So after the scientists profit and drool over what they consider the greatest accomplishment of Humanity since the dawn of creation, the general public, here fairly represented by the television station "Discovery Science," believe Genetical Manipulation of Life to be nothing less than the 'Second Greatest Threat to All Life on Earth' - not a "Miracle-Cure" - and more dangerous than an 'Astroid Hitting the Earth,' or even a new 'Plague!' Like the subtitle of this final chapter in this book asks: 'What Happened to the Miracle?' It seems, aside from drooling and profiting scientists, that the general public is not exactly overly enthusiastic about creating a "Brave New World" through the new "Miracle-Cure" of Genetic Manipulation. In fact even some clear minded scientists have retained enough professional perspective to realize how very dangerous the creation of Transgenic life-forms on Earth is.

As another example of society's fear and reaction towards Genetically Manipulated Transgenic life-forms being created on Earth, these planned "GFP Bunny" exhibitions of Eduardo Kac's never happened at all. The entire media outcry about "Alba" the "GFP Bunny" was all that happened - there was no public exhibition in any Art gallery anywhere - period. The concept and words were typically all that this "piece of Art" came to be. What actually happened is that Eduardo Kac planned three stages of his super-controversial "GFP Bunny" piece. The first part of the piece of Art was the birth of the "GFP Bunny" "Alba" which Kac insists was exclusively his idea. The second planned part of this piece was the 'hysteria' that was produced when the birth of "Alba" the Transgenic Rabbit mixed with Jellyfish DNA was announced to the world media. On the website "Glowing Genes" also created by Marc Zimmer, the political story of "Alba" and Eduardo Kac is expanded upon, claiming that Kac first read about GFP Fluorescent technology and then formed the concept of the creation of a "GFP" Rabbit. Zimmer's website goes on to explain that Kac then searched for a laboratory that was capable of creating a living Green Fluorescent Transgenic Rabbit and found one in France outside of Paris. According to Kac, when the laboratory completed his request of creating a Transgenic GFP Rabbit they contacted him, and then Kac announced to newspapers and television both the birth of the "GFP Bunny," and the plans for the new Transgenic Art exhibition he was to stage. The grand plan that never happened - only in Eduardo Kac's head and in books - was the public exhibition of this "GFP Bunny," in which Eduardo Kac was to be sitting in a room behind a large piece of glass on a public street in front of the public who would be walking by the room that Kac was sitting on a couch in, and who would look through the large glass window to see Kac living an apparently normal life style with a White albino Rabbit hopping around this room as well. There was going to be a big button by the window of Kac's room for the public to push, which would have caused the lights in the room to turn off and a Black light to turn on, so all that would have been left visible would have been a Transgenic Green Fluorescent living Rabbit hopping around the room/exhibition. In addition there was also planned the playing of an audio tape that would come on when this button was pressed by the public, with a recording about the story of Genetically Modified Fluorescent organisms and how you can't see any difference between a normal animal and a Transgenic GFP animal. The audio tape was supposed to have then continued on to explain that in the case of "Alba" there was an advantage in that you can instantly see that the Rabbit was Genetically Modified just by turning on a Black light.

As for the public reaction of the French after the announcement of "Alba's" birth, they loved it and ran stories in newspapers and on television - that is until they found out that this Transgenic Green Fluorescent Rabbit was created in France. Realizing that this "GFP" monster was created in their own country turned the decision as well as the stomachs of the French citizens, who went against Kac's plan of exhibiting this "GFP Bunny" as a piece of "Transgenic Art." This was greatly compounded by the publication from Eduardo Kac of his master plan to first create public hysteria by announcing his creation to the media, second to exhibit publicly the "GFP Bunny," and finally completing the "GFP Bunny" piece, the insane plan of bringing this Transgenic "GFP Bunny" "Alba" back to Chicago to live with his family. Logic would suggest that this could have easily led to then letting "Alba" out into Chicago to mate with other Rabbits and start a new species of Rabbits in America. This "GFP Bunny" could be considered the first 'positive outcome' of the "GFP Revolution," because "Alba" was, in the end, most likely killed by either the French laboratory, or the French government, or both, which no one knows.

As faith would have it, the very night before the first public exhibition of "Alba" the "GFP Bunny" in France, the director of the "French National Institute for Argonomic Research" would not allow the Transgenic Rabbit to be released to Eduardo Kac. This was the night before "Alba's" 'public debut' in the first of a planned series of public installations with the living room behind glass and Kac with "Alba," the first of which was to have been in Avignon, France at a Digital Art exhibition. Kac's living room was supposed to signify how the Biotechnologies of our age are entering our lives, even to the point of being part of our private lives in our living rooms. This living room setup was ready for "Alba" and Kac's first public exhibition with the large button for the public to press turning off the White light and turning on the Black light, but his exhibition in Avignon was cancelled, because "Alba"was not going to be released to Eduardo Kac. Of course a huge fight started between Kac and the French Institute he was supposed to get his Transgenic Rabbit from. Marc Zimmer states that the worldwide headlines of the "Alba" fight included the ABC news, as well as the "BBC," the "Boston Globe," France's "Le Monde," and literally was such a huge story that it competed with the 2000 Olympic Games on the news. The political details of this "Alba" fight are expanded upon on the "Glowing Genes" website, explaining that initially the French public was in total agreement with Kac's plans and exhibitions, but the big change in attitude came when it was discovered by the French media that this actual Transgenic life-form, which as unnaturally as possible Fluoresces Green under a Black light because it was mixed with Jellyfish DNA, was created in their own country - France. These "GFP Bunny" exhibitions planned around the world were intended by the "Transgenic Artist" to be a "political project," and he sure got his wish. The exhibitions were supposed to bridge the barriers that exist between politics, science, and also Art, but in this author's opinion all Kac did with his 'shock therapy' was fortify and construct an even greater impenetrable barrier between the public and science than existed before. What Eduardo Kac did first was create a media scandal worldwide - which was a planned part of the "GFP Bunny" 'Artwork' - and second, he created public detestation, resentment, and political opposition to his planned intentions. The living, Transgenic Green Fluorescent Rabbit confirmed the public's fears and nightmares about Genetically Manipulated life-forms entering our own lives. "Alba" first represented the public's fears of Transgenic animals when his birth was announced to the worldwide media by Kac, but the actual living Rabbit mixed with Jellyfish DNA also made the public realize that these Transgenic animals were being "created" right under their noses in their own countries without regard in the least to the opinions or approval of society. In the end, as a good example of society's opinion towards Transgenic life-forms on Earth, "Alba" was never given to Kac to either exhibit behind glass in exhibitions worldwide, or to bring back to his family in Chicago and possibly reproduce with other native Rabbits beginning a new Transgenic Rabbit species in America. What did happen in reality is that the "French National Institute for Argonomic Research" reported that "Alba," who they claim was born in 1998, died at the age of four years old in July, 2002. "Alba's" true creator, the French scientist Houdebine, reported that "Alba" who's real name was "GFP.014" lived a normal lifespan of Institute Rabbits of four years, but naturally Eduardo Kac does not believe this French scientist and insists that "Alba" did not die, but that he was lied to by the French Institute which desperately wanted to end the worldwide negative 'publicity stunt' initiated by this Transgenic Artist. Kac declared, typically, that he knew more about Transgenic Rabbits than "Alba's" French creator and the French director of the "French National Institute for Argonomic Research," and that "Alba" should have lived to be twelve years old, and furthermore, that "Alba" was only two years old, not four (according to Kac's insistence that he first created the concept of a "GFP Bunny" and commissioned the French laboratory to produce the Transgenic Rabbit in January, 2000). These facts are denied by Houdebine and the "French National Institute for Argonomic Research," where it is still upheld that "Alba" was not in any way Eduardo Kac's idea, was not at all commissioned for Kac, and was born out of a long list of one-hundred and fifty Transgenic Green Fluorescent Rabbits in 1998 before Houdebine ever heard of Eduardo Kac. As of 2005 when the book "Glowing Genes" was published, Marc Zimmer, who is not surprisingly in complete agreement with Eduardo Kac and the "Transgenic Art" movement, states that Kac still hadn't given up on his dream of returning home with "Alba" the "GFP Bunny" and that he still published a website 'Free Alba.'

    Eduardo Kac's masterpiece was the third part of his planned "Trilogy," and was humbly named by the Artist "The Eighth Day." This was an Art exhibition of Transgenic life-forms under a four foot (1.3 meter) wide acrylic plastic dome, which was called by the Artist a "Transgenic Biosphere." The Transgenic life-forms mixed with Jellyfish DNA under Kac's clear plastic dome in "The Eighth Day" included some fish, amoebas, and mice, as well as plants, all Fluorescing brilliant Green in the dark under a "Blue light." This "Transgenic Artist" Eduardo Kac's intentions for creating "The Eighth Day" was to "symbolize" nothing less than a "new ecology" that is currently in formation in the United States between Transgenic "GM" crops. This "Eighth Day" of the creation of the world now falls into the hands of a Brazilian "Transgenic Artist." "Glowing Genes" also clearly reveals the concept of "The Eighth Day," being that this piece of Transgenic Art represents the "eighth day" of the creation of Earth and the creation of life on Earth. In the center of this four foot clear lucite dome populated by several Transgenic Fluorescent life-forms, there is a robot that is controlled by the physical activity of Green Fluorescent Amoebae "Dyctioslelium discoideum." The movement of this robot was activated by the activity of these Transgenic Amoebas, so that when they were inactive the robot was also static. The visitors of "The Eighth Day" exhibition's website also were in control of this Transgenically-driven robot's camera.

    Dr. Zimmer presents the questions that are the pivotal point of the entire "Transgenic Art" movement: first, 'is it Art?' - and second 'is the creation of Transgenic life-forms for Art ethical?' To justify Transgenic Art, "Traits of Life" exhibition in 2002 at "The Exploratorium" museum in San Francisco is offered. The exhibition showed the GFP Transgenic flatworm of Martin Chalfie as part of this show centering on the newest in scientific research, and apparently there was no controversy or scandal. This begs the question: why was the GFP flatworm accepted by the public and not Eduardo Kac's "GFP Bunny" "Alba?" Dr. Zimmer asks whether it was because the flatworm was considered not a piece of Art, but science, or possibly even because the "emotional response" in the public is much more subdued when considering a mere flatworm compared to a mammal. What is not considered (or written about in his book) by Dr. Zimmer is that perhaps people were petrified when they understood Kac's intentions of bringing the Transgenic Fluorescent Green Rabbit back to Chicago to live with his family. Another Art exhibition of the same theme and in the same year, 2002, also held in California was entitled "Transgenic Light" in the "Cantor Center for the Visual Arts" of Stanford University. This exhibition meant to 'connect the aesthetic and scientific,' and consisted of three separate parts. Viewers could look into a Fluorescent microscopic world through live video of fruit flies' Fluorescent Green Transgencially-produced eyes, and also at the newest produced "GFP" life-forms of science, which was the second part of the show and which were shown on a separate large monitor. For the third part of this "Transgenic Light" Stanford University exhibition of 2002 a movie was presented to visitors that ran five-and-a-half minutes, and sounds a little like a propaganda film. Apparently this movie concluding the "Transgenic Light" exhibition attempted the impossible, which was the "reinterpretation" of Transgenic Green Fluorescent Protein life-form images into - of course - "natural landscapes"(!)

With enthusiasm the chapter on "Alba" in "Glowing Genes" is closed with examples of other Artists working in what are considered explorations comparable to Transgenic animals used by Eduardo Kac in his GFP installations. The short film "Le Mouvement des plantes" shown in 2000 at New York's "MOMA" was created by two French pioneers in the field of "microcinematography" who led the direction to Transgenic Art and the controversial Genetically-Manipulated life-forms used by Eduardo Kac. The second example presented was a competition of the "European Life Science Organization" in 2002 and 2003 for multimedia Art entitled "Cinema of the Cell." Remi Dumollard is singled out as an example of an Artist working in a similar field as Kac, and the film made by this doctoral student of the University College of London used Fluorescent proteins added to rhythmic music for an interpretation of the waves of "calcium oscillations." The literal 'bottom line' is clearly stated that the "GFP Revolution" has arrived, and does not just include science, but also Art.

Three years ago in 2010, the director of the museum in which the 2002 exhibition "Traits of Life" was presented, where Matin Chalfie's GFP Transgenic flatworm "C. elegans" was viewed by the public, visited "Electric Ladyland - the First Museum of Fluorescent Art." Neuroscientist Richard O. Brown, Ph.D., the director of "Exploratorium - the museum of science, art and human perception" in San Francisco, spoke with the current author in "Electric Ladyland" for about an hour during his Museum tour, and said that Eduardo Kac had done his internship at "Exploratorium," during which Kac had planted clones of trees all over San Francisco. We discussed Eduardo Kac and the "Genetically Manipulated" Revolution after Dr. Brown went through the small "GFP" presentation in "Electric Ladyland," and we also talked briefly about the role that Fluorescent proteins have come to play in Art. The one highlight of what I discussed with Dr. Brown which stands out is about a permanent installation in "Exploratorium" in which there is an entire ceiling of one room that is made of an enormous glass Longwave Ultraviolet Filter(!), and when museum visitors enter this room under Longwave Ultraviolet that has come from sunlight through the filtered ceiling, parts of their clothing, fingernails, teeth, eyes, and other natural and unnaturally Fluorescent components of their clothing and bodies light up brightly as if the visitor went into a room with Black lights. Dr. Brown gently explained to me that this was specifically made to teach museum visitors that the Ultraviolet they all know about from Black lights is precisely the same harmless Longwave Ultraviolet energy that is constantly reaching the surface of the Earth after passing directly through our Ozone layer. An exquisite interactive exhibition which directly teaches a museum visitor through their own actions and direct revelations, which results in the visitor experiencing something profound, learning from this profound experience, and most likely remembering this knowledge gained through their own interactive experience. The reason the current author still clearly remembers this learning experience that Dr. Brown explained is because this is the precise 'experience' - combined with - 'learning experience' that I built the "Participatory Fluorescent Environment" in "Electric Ladyland" for in the 1990s. The initial intention was always clear in my mind, long before beginning the years of construction and Color application. As a footnote, the business card of "Exploratorium" given to me by Dr. Brown is very fitting to their theme of "science, art and human perception," with a large circular hole die-cut into the Black card which creates something that reminds one of a magnifying glass or microscope. My lasting memory of Richard O. Brown, Ph.D. is of meeting an intelligent, gentle scientist.

"Signs of Life, Bio Art and Beyond," Edited by Eduardo Kac (2007)

In "Signs of Life - Bio Art and Beyond" edited by Eduardo Kac and published by MIT in 2007, the 'Series Foreword' by Sean Cubitt, Editor in Chief of the Leonardo Book series, concisely explains in just one paragraph what the creation of Genetically Manipulated life-forms on Earth presents to all of us. This 'Foreword' begins by explaining that profound changes are occurring in the fields of science, technology, and the Arts, and that these profound changes bring with them also the "urgent" need of questioning the "ethics" and the "care" for both the Earth and all it's life. Both unforeseen knowledge and "beauty" is presented as being possible, but the warning is given of also "unforeseen" threats.

The Introduction to "Signs of Life" written by Eduardo Kac has a title including 'Hybrids, Mutants, Synthetics, Clones, and Transgenics' which consists for Kac of 'Art which looks at you straight into the Eye.' Not surprisingly with such a title, Kac begins a list of the 'new Art mediums' with the common radio, and in the first sentence directly explains that Biotechnology has currently brought about possibilities in Art which were "unprecedented." In just the first paragraph by Eduardo Kac the reader is introduced to concepts that are mind-boggling, as well as horrifying, visions of the very near future. Kac initially mentions the biotech industry's Genetically Modified food products, and directly states clearly that the benefits of "GM" food are unknown, and also what is unknown are the "consequences" to the environment brought about by Genetically Manipulated foods. In the very next sentence Kac also clearly admits that the research done in "genomics," including the "Human Genome Project" and advances in "proteomics" studying the functions and physical structures of proteins, bring together to society both the hope of "social benefits," and what he calls the horror of "genocracy," which Kac explains as the nightmarish possible future government policy of determining social legislature, health, labor, and law solely on the basis of genes. In just the first sentence of the second paragraph of Kac's Introduction, this first "Transgenic Artist" introduces another term, "bioinformatics," which he explains as a threat to society arising through a 'reduced analogy' occurring, effecting "binary data" and it's relationship to both the environment and genetics. Kac goes on to explain that the consequences of such social changes brought about by genetics could also bring about both the "objectification" of our lives, and the general disregard for the individual, as well as their rights. The subject of the "erosion" of the dividing lines between artificial and natural, as well as between technology and biology is expanded upon by Kac, listing achievements such as the production of new, unnatural DNA forms, and unnatural newly invented proteins which could create a future that has the capability to invent living creatures who are "entirely synthetic." The present realm we are immersed in is also reflected upon by Kac, reveling in the facts that the new age of society includes transferring genetic features from one individual to another of the same species, as with the example of the cloned sheep "Dolly" - and also the transference of genetic information between very different species, of which "Alba" the "GFP Bunny" is offered as an example.

Kac explains that "gene therapy" techniques are improving rapidly and lead the path towards developments which include "oocyte fusion" (allowing two eggs from different females to conceive a child), "haploidization," and ultimately to the cloning of Human beings. A point that Kac makes in his Introduction is that Artists are now working in the present day with what he calls "biomedia" - media that is alive - and through this new 'medium,' Artists are today "inventing" both concepts and actual Artforms that were impossible to create until the present era. Then Kac takes this to the next level, explaining that to create Artforms with "biomedia" involves directly the manipulation of life itself, and expanding on this concept, to manipulate life directly results in "evolution." The simple conclusion that Kac's logic comes to is obviously that Transgenic Artists who work with "biomedia" and who manipulate life to create their Artforms are creating nothing less than "evolution." Included in the strongest forces influencing evolution of species on Earth, Kac lists not only "Wall Street," but also adds "FedEx" to these questionable 'forces of nature.' On top of this the accelerated pace at which evolution now occurs is also unprecedented, with examples given by Kac of plant species becoming extinct and other new species being produced all within the short span of a single human life.

As a foundation for the contemporary era of Genetic Manipulation, Kac discusses a nearly amusing list of personalities, including Aristotle, Horace of Rome, Julien Offray de La Mettrie, Descartes, Darwin, Koko the communicating Gorilla, Thomas Aquinas, Theophrastos the ancient botanist, Ulisse Aldrovandi the naturalist, Hieronymus Bosch, H. G. Wells' "The Island of Doctor Moreau," and - of course - Mary Shelly and her famous monstrous creation "Frankenstein." For examples of true contemporary "Frankensteins," Kac adds the equally monstrous "Geep" who appeared on the front cover of "Nature"(!) magazine in 1984, which logically is the animal born from both a 'goat' and a 'sheep,' and for which Kac also supplies the definition of an animal born with cells that originate from two different species, termed a "chimera." Interestingly, the origin of that word has several definitions, including a mythological fire-breathing monster that is made up of a lion's head, a goat's body, and a snake's tail. The next example is even further from nature, and was created in 1997 when a *Human Ear* was grafted onto a *Mouse's Back!* This creature Kac refers to as the *"ear-mouse,"* and was in fact a sort of tiny mutant grandchild of Mary Shelly's "Frankenstein."

The "Transgenic Art" movement and the "GFP Revolution" seem to have relatives deep in the past, in fact both of these grotesque caricatures of natural life have roots going back hundreds, if not thousands of years. Not only does Mary Shelly's monstrous literary creation immediately come to mind, but even some of her inspiration for writing her novel "Frankenstein - A Modern Prometheus" in 1818. A certain parallel, and even comparison could be realized between this Italian scientist Luigi Galvani of the Eighteenth century who helped inspire Mary Shelly's "Frankenstein," and the first "Transgenic Artist" Eduardo Kac of the Twenty-first century. Luigi Galvani, like Eduardo Kac, took the technical advances of his day and created a spectacle that simultaneously horrified and fascinated the general public. Today Kac is working with Genetic Manipulation, the Twenty-first century "Miracle-Cure," but the miraculous power discovered and harnessed back in the Eighteenth century was Electricity. Similar to Kac, Galvani was a "showman" who went out of his way to create 'public spectacles' that simultaneously enthralled and disgusted the general public of the era. Luigi Galvani wanted to demonstrate to the public the invisible magic power of electricity, and is remembered for his grotesque experiments - his famous public spectacles - designed to shock not only dead animals, but also his audience as well. The first famous experiment/public spectacle Galvani performed was to demonstrate this invisible life-giving miraculous force of electricity on a dead frog. Now it may not seem so spectacular today, but attaching electrical wires to a dead frog - and then making that dead frog move when miraculous invisible electricity was supplied to the wires - this was astounding in the Eighteenth century. But, this was nothing for Galvani, he was just getting started. The culmination of his macabre experiments on the dead frog and other animals came to it's climax when Galvani formed the concept of the ultimate public spectacle: making a dead man move! Again, with similarities, Galvani was not a scientist and did not advance science in any way, but was a showman who became famous from his reinterpretation of the scientific advances and discoveries of his day into unforgettable, unbelievable, historic public spectacles. Luigi Galvani convinced a relative to find him a human corpse, and a dead prisoner's body was found for him. In his most grotesque public spectacle, extremely strong electrical currents were run through the dead body of this prisoner in front of an assembled crowd of spectators, and to the combined fascination and horror of his audience, the dead man twitched and then opened his eyes! To make this public spectacle as unforgettable and unforgivable as a living Green Fluorescent Transgenic Bunny, Galvani turned up the electricity attached to his dead prisoner's body, and in front of a simply mortified audience Luigi Galvani produced his most famous public spectacle: making a dead man sit up! The similarities are nothing less than obvious. Galvani was one of the first scientists to explore "bioelectricity," which is still studied today in the field of medical research on the electrical signals of the nervous system. Galvani's paper on "electrical reanimation," which he referred to as "animal electricity," was on Mary Shelly's reading list for the summer in Geneva during the competition between her and her literary friends to write the scariest novel. That was part of Mary Shelly's inspiration, but for her creation "Frankenstein," the similarities are just as obvious. Mary Shelly wrote "Frankenstein" as a teenager during that summer bet with her literary friends over who could write the scariest story, and was fascinated by Luigi Galvani's experiments including the public spectacles of her era, but the source of her inspiration were most likely first sparked by the events of her own young troubled life. For a start, her mother had died giving birth to her, and this effected Mary Shelly for the rest of her life. She used to go to the cemetery as a teenager and read to her mother's grave. This was not the only mixing with death that Mary Shelly was unfortunate enough to have throughout her life, because five of her childbirths ended in death, and then came the early death of even her husband. It is easily understandable that Mary Shelly began to think she was cursed, and that in her mind, proven by the many unfortunate events of her life, creation could very easily be seen as destructive. In her masterpiece "Frankenstein - A Modern Prometheus," which is considered the first science-fiction novel ever written, Dr. Victor Frankenstein constructs his monster out of a combination of different species, such as the use of both human and also animal bones as well, because it was easier to work with larger bones. There is a certain thread of similarity in this logic that also still extends it's shadow into the present era's Fluorescent Protein revolution. Today, almost two centuries after Mary Shelly's literary creation, scientists now possess the ability to make life-forms, and already have succeeded at producing such examples of their abilities, including "Dolly" the 1980s first cloned Sheep, the "Geep" of 1997, the "ear-mouse" of the same year, and in the past decade plus, Green Fluorescent Rabbits, Red Fluorescent Cats and a virtual zoo of Fluorescent Transgenic life-forms. Now that scientists possess the knowledge to create life, it is only a matter of time (and law) before scientists manufacture synthetic Human beings. In the same vein as the Fluorescent Protein revolution, Transgenic life-forms produced through Genetic Manipulation were created with precisely the same goals in mind that Doctor Victor Frankenstein had: to alleviate human suffering. In reality, Dr. Frankenstein and the Fluorescent Protein Genetic Manipulation movement of today have both achieved the same final result: the dream of merely alleviating human suffering - which both also resulted in the creation of living *monsters!* Mary Shelly in her pioneering science-fiction novel "Frankenstein - A Modern Prometheus" asks the question if it is really wrong for Human beings to play god and create life, and then also answers this question by stating that it is alright to create life and new species on the Earth, as long as the scientists act responsibly in both their creation of new life and it's nurturing.

Eduardo Kac explains the details of the ongoing "Alba" the "GFP Bunny" saga on his website "GFP Bunny." Clearly Kac states on www.ekac.org/gfpbunny the three stages of his Transgenic Art work, which began with the birth of the Green Fluorescent Rabbit, followed by the second stage of what Kac terms the "public dialogue" brought about by this birth of the Transgenic Fluorescent Green Rabbit. The third and final stage was envisioned by Kac as the Transgenic Rabbit's "social integration" when "Alba" would have been brought back to Chicago to live with Kac and his wife and daughter. An "Art journal" article has the opinion from the chief curator of the Centre Georges Pompidou Musee in Paris, who is quoted as comparing the shocking impact of Eduardo Kac's "GFP Bunny" to Marcel Duchamp's urinal/drinking "Fountain," and claiming that no one has 'redefined' aesthetics to such a degree since Marcel Duchamp as well. An article in the "Chicago tribune" of May 10, 2002 on the "New Kac show" that was an opening of his prints and "Alba" posters, also clearly reports that the public debut of "Alba" the "GFP Bunny" was planned for the June, 2000 "Digital Art" exhibition in Avignon where Kac would be publicly displayed in a reconstruction of his own living room in Oak Park, Chicago to live with "Alba" for the exhibition. The article also reports that the director of the French research center NIAR outside of Paris refused to release the Transgenic Rabbit to Kac the day before the exhibition was to have opened in Avignon. Kac defines "Transgenic Art" as a new form of Art which is founded on "genetic engineering" used for transferring genes and creating a final result of "unique" new life-forms, and states next that this must be carried out with the greatest "care," the "acknowledgment" of the complexity of the act, and finally that the created "unique" life-form must be 'respected, nurtured, and also loved.' The famous photograph of Eduardo Kac holding the albino "Alba" in his arms accompanies the second small paragraph of text on his website, where Kac explains that he would always remember the first time he held the living Transgenic Rabbit "Alba" in his arms on April 29, 2000 in Jouy-en-Josas outside of Paris. Kac writes that the name "Alba" was given to the Rabbit by himself, his wife, and daughter. The nine reasons for "Alba's" creation are next listed by Eduardo Kac after explaining that the Genetic Manipulation of the Rabbit and it's Transgenic ability to Fluoresce Green under a Black light is just a 'single component' of the Transgenic Artwork. Kac directly states that the actual animal was only a fraction of the Artwork, with the intentionally created "social event" brought about by the birth of a "chimerical animal" being the defining point behind this "GFP Bunny" piece. These nine listed reasons for the creation of the Transgenic "GFP Bunny" in 2000 are given by Kac, starting with the ongoing public debate initiated by "Alba's" birth across the board between Art, philosophy, science, literature, communications, law, and the general society. DNA supremacy, extending the definitions of both "biodiversity" as well as "evolution," communication at an "interspecies" level beginning a dialogue between Transgenic mammals and Human beings, the "integration" of this Transgenic Rabbit into society, the reexamination of "normality's" definition and meaning, the extension of the meaning of "communication" to include sharing DNA from one species to another, the "respect" from society towards these Transgenic life-forms, and finally the "expansion" of Art's boundaries to also accept the "invention" of Transgenic life-forms as a new Art 'medium,' are all numbered and listed by Eduardo Kac on his "GFP Bunny" website as projected goals of the "Transgenic Art" movement.

"Alba's" 'technical specifications' are next given by Kac, beginning with the fact that the Rabbit was albino, and including the facts that the Transgenic mixture of Jellyfish DNA with the Rabbit allowed the Fluorescence in bright Green (509 nm) when placed under a "blue light." Kac goes on to explain that under "blue light" of 488 nanometers "Alba" the Transgenic Rabbit also Fluoresces bright Green. Ruby crystals and Fluorescent synthetic paint pigments are also so reactive that light of the visual Blue spectrum will cause their Fluorescence (similar to fake screw-in 'Black light' bulbs from decades ago - but in no comparison to the intensity of an actual Longwave Ultraviolet "Black light").

Another fact that is given by Kac is that the Fluorescent brightness of "Alba" under a "blue light" was doubled when comparing these mammal cells of the Transgenic Rabbit to the cells of the original "Aequorea aequorea" Bioluminescent Jellyfish. The Rabbit was created not using the original "GFP" Green Fluorescent Protein found in "Aequorea aequorea," but with "EGFP," which is an "Enhanced" GFP produced synthetically. Kac also gives May 14, 2000 as the date that the second stage of the "GFP Bunny" Artwork began, with the first announcement to the media of "Alba's" birth at the conference "Planet Work" in San Francisco. Kac closes the section with the plans of the third and final stage of the "GFP Bunny," when he had hoped to return to Chicago with "Alba" who was to become part of his family and live with his wife Ruth and daughter Miriam, which in any way did not happen.

On his "GFP Bunny" website Edouard Kac next begins to justify the Genetic Manipulation of "Alba" this Transgenic "GFP Bunny" by retelling the history from "Domestication" of Rabbits to their "Selective Breeding." It takes a signatory unimaginable leap of the imagination to believe that the 'domestication and selective breeding' of Rabbits going back thousands of years could possibly be compared to the mixing of Jellyfish DNA with Rabbit DNA! With this signatory stretch-of-the-imagination, Kac begins to try and justify what was done to create this Transgenic Rabbit "Alba" in the year 2000, by retelling the gentle tale of people mating Rabbits intentionally to change their features subtly over generations. Once again Kac relates to the Bible, with the first documentation of the interactions between Rabbits and people, which started with the 'discovery' of the Rabbit by Phoenicians about 1100 B.C., according to the "GFP Bunny" website. Kac directly states that the evolution of the Rabbit was already altered by human intervention way back in the Sixth century with monks domesticating and breeding the animal in South France, and writes that this selective breeding and the Rabbit's adoption into the houses of it's keepers lead to the evolution of the Rabbit, which turned it into the animal that is known to us in the present day. Although documentation of the Color of a Rabbit's fur and their range of sizes is found way back to the Sixth century, the Eighteenth century is singled out by Kac as the era when a new species of "Angora" Rabbit was created. The combination of human domestication of the Rabbit added to the selective breeding of the animal, which then led to new Rabbits being developed over centuries - not the minuscule time scale of minutes or seconds, as comparable to the laboratory insertion of synthetic Green Fluorescent Protein in the form of Jellyfish DNA into the DNA of a Rabbit. "Evolution" not only 'speeded up,' but in plain English, also 'fucked up!' Not to mention that this Transgenic "Evolution" was not a product of millennia of "natural selection," but an invention of 'ego selection' by a Brazilian Artist living in the 'nature reserve' of Chicago.

To buttress his point Eduardo Kac states that the domestication of Rabbits going back 1,500 years, combined with the trade of Rabbits worldwide, has resulted in more than 1,000 "breeds" of Rabbits known in the world today. Not stopping at historical text, Kac also reproduces the image of a Roman coin from the year 134 AD which has the emperor Hadrian on it's face, and Hispania on it's back along with a Rabbit. As further proof of this human intervention causing the creation of new Rabbit breeds throughout history, the "genetic variations" that happen in nature are explained through the example of the genetic condition which "Alba" had as a White "albino" Rabbit. The point made by Kac about albino Rabbits is that humans have also intervened in nature by both breeding and raising these White albino Rabbits, causing their population to increase unnaturally worldwide, because in nature the albino Rabbits would have never thrived due to both it's lack of pigment in it's fur allowing it no camouflage, and it's albino poor vision for hunting.

The following section of the "GFP Bunny" website embodies the great leap effortlessly transversed by Eduardo Kac, from human "breeding" of Rabbits - to Twenty-first century "Transgenic Art." Kac explains that Rabbit breeding by humans was driven by first the improved physical condition achieved by breeding, and as time went on, also the physical appearance of the Rabbit. In complete contrast, Transgenic Art and specifically the example of "Alba" the "GFP Bunny" is explained by Kac to have "aesthetics" that were based on the Rabbit's impact on society, not it's outward physical appearance. Clearly declared by this first Transgenic Artist is the fact that the creation of Transgenic creatures is not what interests him, but the 'social impact' created by the creation of Transgenic animals. With his signatory self-contained logic, Eduardo Kac explains that for him the point behind the Transgenic Art is the 'social integration' of the invented Transgenic creature, which fuses biotechnology, domesticated family life, and social opinion. In a typical convoluted, impressive style the point is reached by Kac that Transgenic Art 'promotes' social "respect" for the invented Transgenic animals' spirituality(!) If the Artist looked beyond the sphere of his eyeglasses, into the real world, it would be realized how astronomically distant from reality, and the plain truth, this distorted perspective has travelled. Using words such as "hermeneutical" only serves to impress society, not to permanently alter society's opinion on life. Kac continues to the climaxing point of his statement, which is (not surprisingly) that Transgenic Art and pieces such as "GFP Bunny" will alter permanently the future of Art, and furthermore, that the future's "interactive art" will bear no resemblance to the Art of the distant past (being understood as the Twentieth century). The Artist is definitive in documenting that his "GFP Bunny" not only altered society worldwide, but also altered both Art and human aesthetics as well. "GFP Bunny" is claimed by it's creator to have brought about a new "interface" between humans, plants, mammals, birds, insects, robots, and bacteria (only). The conclusion to the objective of his "GFP Bunny" include for Kac the potpourri of: the interrelationships of a family, differences in society, procedures of science, communication between species, public debate, social ethics, the interpretation by media, and finally the context of Art itself.

To justify Transgenic Art Kac also lays it's foundation with the claim that during the Twentieth century Art began to distance itself from the traditional image reproduction of visual Art, and away from the actual creation of objects of Art, towards - of course - sociological aspects of life and conceptual Art. This was all remedied and evolved by the emergence of his new media of Transgenic Art (according to Kac) by offering a "radical departure" from Art itself in the creation of Genetically Manipulated life-forms, replacing old fashioned paintings and sculptures. Of course, next Kac charts Transgenic Art's development on the basis of other fields, such as the discovery of new planets in astronomy, the discovering of "extremophiles" in biology, and the invention of the cloning of life itself. Eduardo Kac closes his argument with his, again, self-contained knowledge which leads to his own unique conclusion that Genetically Modified Transgenic animals, which are created by scientists in laboratories by mixing for example Jellyfish DNA with Rabbit DNA, or even Coral DNA with Cat DNA, are - get ready for it - *'Regular creatures'!* If the genetic cross between a Jellyfish and a Rabbit is "regular" it is unimaginable what "irregular" could mean to this character.

The very predictable general conclusion for Eduardo Kac is twofold, first being that "Green Fluorescent Protein" from a Jellyfish inserted into a Rabbit is - of course - "harmless" for the Rabbit, and second that his "GFP Bunny" broke no rules of society, because humans have been altering the Rabbit's evolution for already 1,400 years. Surprisingly the only point Kac stops short of is to claim that mixing Jellyfish DNA with it's own DNA was *beneficial* for the Rabbit.

The Artist goes so far as to defend the Rabbit species in general, with facts of it's vision having a blind spot right in front of it's face that causes people to think that Rabbits are not as intelligent as the dog, which is the example given by Kac. Another important point explained in detail by Kac is that the Transgenic Green Fluorescent Rabbits such as "Alba" are not 'monstrous' Genetically Manipulated creatures as society imagines, but that quite the contrary, "Alba" is just the same as every other albino Rabbit in outward appearance, Coloration, and behavior. Somehow extending this logic, Kac concludes that by Genetically Modifying Human beings at the beginning of the Twenty-first century we can also change our way of 'communicating' with animals. This change as well as the knowledge that has been gained by this Genetic Modification movement of the last two decades reveals for Kac that our "human genome" does not differ in any way from other species, and that it is not special or even important. In other words, Human beings can be Genetically Modified with precisely the same disregard for spirituality as the Genetic Manipulation of Bacteria, Monkeys, and Rabbits. This approach to the spirituality of animals is examined by Kac through the eyes of Aristotle, Descartes, Kant, and Nietzsche (to mention just a few). Humanity's parameters are also examined by Kac, with the predictable conclusion reached that we have extended the limits of humanity by creating life through 'genetic engineering.' In Kac's opinion science has not 'eliminated' life's mystery by it's intervention of Genetic Manipulation, but again quite the contrary, science has 'reawakened' humanity's awe at the wonder of life. To believe that humanity's opinion towards the beauty and mystery of life itself is unchanged and undiminished through the combined actions of Genetic Manipulation and the intervention of new life-forms in laboratories, is about as far from reality as believing that the "Industrial Revolution" also did not change humanity's respect towards nature and the environment.

Eduardo Kac may not have gone so far as to claim that the Genetic Manipulation of "Alba" was actually beneficial for the Rabbit, but he does go extremely far with his claim that Human beings should not only "*welcome*" the manipulation of our genes, but that we should see the Genetic Manipulation of our genes as "*desirable!*" This logic is based upon the record of genetic therapy in humans which is considered successful by the Artist, and through this "success," the projection of imagined health and living benefits for all of us. In the very next sentence, after the assurance of the undreamed-of benefits to Human beings that Genetic Manipulation is sure to bring all of us, and after the claim of Human beings both 'welcoming' their own Genetic Manipulation and even 'desiring' it - the nightmare is next revealed of nothing less than "biological warfare"(!) Kac continues on, listing additional events that the human race will also surely 'desire' and even 'welcome,' such as the Genetic Manipulation threats of "eugenics" (which history remembers through it's past success with "racial hygiene" during the Nazi reign), and the cheerful "biopiracy" which will be the state of the 'theft and patenting' of individual's DNA without any regards to it's owner. Both sound like something truly 'desirable' and something we all would 'welcome' without a doubt. Eduardo Kac uses the same blueprinted argument that has been used throughout history to convince society of the benefit of virtually anything that begs their acceptance and approval: the promise of "curing diseases" and relieving humanity of it's eternal animalistic condition of existential suffering. The two most infamous of medieval-minded "Miracle-cures" in history also were both based on precisely the same mentality - curing diseases - and alleviating human suffering - through the miracles of "Actinotherapy" and "Radium Treatments," and these two deadly "Miracle-Cures" also were highly 'desired' and truly 'welcomed' by all of society - exactly as Eduardo Kac talks of this new Twenty-first century "Miracle-Cure" Genetic Manipulation. Trying to convince his subjects even further, Kac lists what must be done by society worldwide to not only embrace this new "Miracle-Cure" of Genetic Manipulation, but to both 'welcome' and 'desire' the altering of their own DNA. In a truly detached utopian state of dream-like consciousness this first Transgenic Artist lists instructions for society's projected acceptance, 'welcome,' and 'desire' for their own - and their children's - Genetic Manipulation: society's studying all the different viewpoints of Genetic Manipulation, learning the historical basis behind this new "Miracle-Cure," understanding the new terminology and research that is taking place during the present era, developing "alternative" viewpoints by expanding their own concepts of Genetic Manipulation, debating this new "Miracle-Cure," and finally arriving at new conclusions on the subject. Even the sentence is too long just listing these 'instructions' for society to carry out proposed by Kac.

The historical basis of Transgenic Art is detailed by Eduardo Kac in "Signs of Life - Bio Art and Beyond." After his role call of history's elite, including Aristotle, Art is examined from the Twentieth century with the first 'signs of life' used, such as the first use of animals in the creation of Art, which was 1910 when not an Artist - but a journalist - named Roland Dorgeles had three paintings accepted by the "Salon des Independents" which were created by a Donkey who had a paintbrush attached to his tail. This was no ordinary Donkey though, as explained by Kac, because "Lolo" the painting Donkey was owned by Frede, who ran Montmartre's "Lapin Agile" where Picasso and other artists used to meet. 1938's "International Exposition of Surrealism" in Paris' Gallerie Beaux Arts had a piece of Art, which consisted of living fish swimming in a fishbowl that represented the stomach of Leo Malet's "Mannequin," removed from the show because it was too much for the public at that time. The same Surrealism exhibition had an installation by Dali, "Rainy Taxi," which included two mannequins in a car, one of which represented the driver with a shark's head and the other represented a female passenger who was sitting in the back seat immersed in a large amount of lettuce that was being eaten by living Burgundian snails. Marcel Duchamp's 1946 "Paisage fautif" drawing he made with semen is mentioned by Kac, as well as the use of urine and blood being employed to make Art in the 1960s by the "Vienna Actionism" group. Andy Warhol's 1970 "Piss Paintings" are naturally examined as well by Kac, in which the chemical reaction between urine and metallic paint containing copper was used to create paintings. Less acidic Art containing life is also mentioned by Kac in his Introduction to "Signs of Life," such as "Ecological Art" during the 1960s and 70s employing microorganisms that were used for the specific purpose of cleaning up pollution or deforested landscapes. The 1978 "Time Capsule: Greenwich Village, New York" of Alan Sonfist is singled out as an example of this movement of "Ecological Art," in which the Artist attempted to restore the entire area of lower Manhattan known as Greenwich Village back to its former "natural habitat." These examples given by Kac from "Semen Drawings" to "Ecological Art" are all assembled with the common denominator being the utilization of body fluids or living organisms to produce Art. The final example in Kac's section on 'Art made with Plants or Animals' is a true forecast of "Transgenic Art" made decades ago in 1968 by a Swedish composer Sten Hanson, who is also credited as being an Artist of "Text-Sound." Hanson wrote a piece of music that was performed for the first time in 1969 in Stockholm which is based on the DNA code, and which is translated into a composition of 195 arbitrary condons. This DNA code is "mutated" in the musical composition, which represented the mutation of DNA nucleotides due to an individual's 'Destruction of the Genetic Code through Drugs, Toxins, or even Irradiation' which doubles as the title of this 1968 composition translated from it's original Swedish.

Eduardo Kac concludes the section with the point that "Bio Art" and "Transgenic Art" are separated from these past Art movements employing body fluids and living animals, because although blood, semen, urine, living snails, trees and other organisms were included in a concept or actual piece of Art, the life-forms or life-form fluids were unaltered, unmutated, and were in no way Genetically Manipulated like the life-forms which make up Twenty-first century "Transgenic Art."

The role of the "Transgenic Artist" or "Bio Artist" is perfectly clarified by the first Transgenic Artist Eduardo Kac, and is clearly defined in "Signs of Life" as not a mere "commentator" or 'observer' that is just documenting the Genetic Manipulation movement, but as activists that are creating the debates and decisions on policies that shape society. The "Bio Artist" and "Transgenic Artist" is not a creature of the past that merely 'documented' or 'illustrated' history, but like Kac's title for this section of his Introduction, "Art" that goes "Beyond Biology," the role of the "Transgenic Artist" is clear: to both make and change history. Kac next states that the Artists and writers who are "Transgenic Artists" also have "acute awareness" of the ethics involved in the manipulation of DNA and the resulting creation of new species and life-forms, which is extremely easy to write in words, but virtually impossible to believe. The quest is very clearly documented by Kac, who writes that "Biotechnology" isn't the mere subject of Transgenic Artist's interest, or of their Art, but that "Biotechnology" is nothing less than the Transgenic Artist's "medium." Kac goes so far as to compare the 'new technology' of "Genetic Manipulation" to the "Impressionists" (!) who's movement arose because of the 'new technology' which brought about the collapsable tin paint tube and the new flat brushes of the Nineteenth century. "Furthermore" Kac explains that Transgenic Artists which work in this new Art medium of invented new life-forms must now understand that their Artwork is no longer "objective," as an observer or only a commentator's work would be, but that their creation of life-forms make them absolutely "subjective." The "True Art" of what Kac directly states as nothing less than "nature," now uses the medium of invented or manipulated life-forms which are specified as "living organisms" and which were either merely bred, or were completely invented to be "unique." These new "Art mediums" that are listed by Eduardo Kac are bunnies, bacteria, flowers, and frogs, which include a member from almost all the phylums of life on Earth excluding the insects, and are claimed by Kac that in their modified or even invented uniqueness these Transgenic life-forms constitute the components of a new "true art" of nothing less than "evolution."

Clearly the subject is examined in a publication of 2010 named "Green Light: Toward an Art of Evolution" printed by the MIT Press as part of the "Leonardo Books" series, and written by George Gessert. The first chapter of this publication is entitled "Divine Plants" as well as "Magical Animals" and begins with the joke that Eduardo Kac gives as an example of the first use of 'Animals in Art:' 'The Painting Donkey of 1910,' which Kac had already written about three years earlier in "Signs of Life - Bio Art and Beyond" of 2007. This joke began when the Parisian journalist Ronald Dorgeles decided to tie a paint brush to a Donkey's tail, dip it in paint and create "masterpieces!" Exhibited at Paris' "Salon des Independents" of 1910, the three pieces of 'Art' were made by placing these canvases in the path of "Lolo" the Painting Donkey's tail, which had a paint brush attached to it that had been coated with the bright Colors of the contemporary "Fauvist" movement. Since the "Painting Donkey" was also a 'friend' of Picasso and the group of Artists surrounding him gathering at the bar in Montmartre where they met, a new Art group arose inspired directly by "Lolo's" work - and by the "prank" on the Art world. This new Art group was formed by "cubo-futurists" from Russia including Marc Chagall and Kazimir Malevich, who named the movement after

"Lolo's" inspiration: "Donkey's Tail." This Artists group "Donkey's Tail" was nearly as short-lived as the "prank," lasting just a single year, but according to George Gessert, this 'idea' which included "non-humans" involved in the creation of Art was never "forgotten." Gessert next discusses the first important exhibition of modified life in Art. "Edward Steichen's Delphiniums" ran for just one week in the MOMA in New York, from June 26 to July 1, 1936. Edward Steichen bred the Delphiniums himself on his West Redding, Connecticut farm, and the actual cut hybridized Delphinium flowers were on display in this MOMA exhibition. Steichen bred other flowers as well, including hybridized sunflowers, poppies, and cleomes. It is reported that this Delphinium installation in the Museum of Modern Art was not well received by the museum curators, but that the press (naturally) was very 'enthusiastic' about this new "Artform." Precisely as Eduardo Kac believes that Genetically Manipulated living animals and plants will confirm this Twenty-first century "Miracle-Cure" technique and it's monstrous results as "Fine Art," Edward Steichen also firmly believed that the one week installation of hybridized flowers (which are as common today as grass itself and found in every flower shop on the planet) would confirm the breeding of plants also as "Fine Art." Eduardo Kac's hysteria-creating "GFP Bunny" in eighty years will most likely be a similar 'footnote' of Art that Steichen's "Delphinium" are today.

In "Green Light: Toward an Art of Evolution" the differences between "Bio Art" and "Transgenic Art" are clarified, with "Bio Art" being Art which is either made up of living organisms, or Art that contains also living organisms. Around the world, from the United States to China, living organisms have been used in Art throughout much of the Twentieth century, with a list of over thirty-five living plants, animals, and bacteria given by Gorge Gessert. The author also explains that not all "Bio Art" consists of living organisms, but also can contain pollen, cuttings from plants, or just cells, with examples of sheep, rat, pig, goldfish, and lillie cells having been used in "Bio Art." The "Bio Art" installation singled out by the author had a "hybridoma" made up of the very desirable mixture of one White blood cell of a Human being "fused" together with a Mouse's Cancer cell. The next form of 'expression' listed is a hybridized version of "Bio Art" named "Biotech Art," which contains what the author compassionately describes as the "living components" of the piece of "Biotech Art" which have been altered "Biotechnologically." The term is defined by the person who introduced it to Artists, Jens Hauser, who includes both the modification of life-forms in traditional terms such as breeding, as well as the Genetic Modification of life-forms, for the creation of "Biotech Art." "Transgenic Art" is considered a "subset" of this "Biotech Art," and consists of exclusively Genetically Manipulated life-forms as it's Art form. The large amount of publications on "Bio Art," "Biotech Art," and "Transgenic Art" which have come out in the past decade-plus since these forms of expression were invented, are reviewed by George Gessert as dealing mostly with not surprisingly the ethics of these movements consisting of Transgenic life-forms, as well as the political and social impact of this movement. "Tactical Biopolitics" was published in 2008 and is exemplary of these publications, announcing the treats of "eugenics," as well as the important issue raised of how movements such as "Bio Art," "Biotech Art," and "Transgenic Art" can not only 'alter' the DNA of it's Transgenic victims contained in it's installations, but also can alter human understanding of such things including 'race and gender,' as well as the concept of our 'man-made environment.' Jens Hauser clearly admits that Art which uses Biotechnology for it's medium in expression is today considered closer to "public debates" which are void of aesthetics, than Art. George Gessert's conclusion is that "Bio Art" consists of the meeting between "cultural histories" which are contained in the 'histories of living organisms,' and that in these meetings (or collisions) the meanings of "Bio Art" are to be found. Again very compassionately explained, the author describes living organisms as just "art materials," and divides these "art materials" into just two categories. "Sentient" organisms are described as living things with the ability to feel or have consciousness, exclusive to animals who have nervous systems, and "Nonsentient" is all other living organisms. The 1930 writing of Olaf Stapledon could be considered nearly prophetic, as he described a form of Art consisting of bred animals eventually evolving into a movement where "monsters" were created "deliberately" by Artists in their quest of expressing both 'hatred for life' and "cruelty." Pleasant past pieces of Art are included by Gessert such as Hermann Nitsch's "Orgien Myterien Theater" in which the Artist commissioned animals to be slaughtered, "Portable Fish Farm" by Newton Harrison which consisted of the electrocution of these fish, Mark Pauline 'tossing' into a shredder live pigeons, Ana Mendieta cutting off the heads of living chickens, and finally Kim Jones setting fire to live rats.

Coincidentally, as well as conveniently, it is next directly presented by the Gessert that "animal sacrifice" very likely is contained in Art's "roots." George Gessert considers it "easy" to be able to imagine the evolution of Art into an expression consisting of "appalling forms" of animals intentionally altered by Human beings, but to the current author there is no need to imagine this - it is already contemporary "Art History."

For an assumed comparison to "Transgenic Art" which is made up of Genetically Modified life-forms, the installation of Joseph Beuys' "Coyote: I Like America and America Likes Me" in 1974 at the Rene Block Art Gallery in Manhattan is presented by Gessert. The author has the audacity to use the Coyote's "experience" and it's "considerable distress" caused by being in a New York gallery for one week out of it's natural preferred environment - for the assumed comparison to the invention of a new species of Transgenic life-form on Earth making up "Transgenic Art." The poor Coyote had to "endure" the agony of "close proximity" to the Artist and not only that, but the Artist must have scarred the Coyote by "sudden movements" and the 'loud sounds' both intentionally created by Joseph Beuys' installation. The conclusion by Gessert is that neither Joseph Beuys nor anyone else involved with this "cruel" treatment of this Coyote in the Art installation considered that the Coyote may have "suffered" by being a part of Beuys' installation. If the reader can imagine shouting at an animal and keeping that same animal in an Art gallery for the unimaginable span of seven days - used as an assumed comparison to mixing a Rabbit's DNA with a Jellyfish's DNA and inventing a new species of Rabbit that Fluoresces under a "Blue light" - if this can be seriously imagined by the reader, than you are perfectly suited and prepared both emotionally and spiritually to become a "Transgenic Artist." As an example of a trait which is signatory for this Twenty-first century "Bio Art," "Biotech Art," and "Transgenic Art" movement, the author goes on for, unbelievably, *several pages* about how cruelly Joseph Beuys treated the living Coyote in his 1974 installation. For photographic evidence, the author also includes a picture of the wild Coyote biting and pulling cloth off of the Artist during this Art installation. The author goes so far as to call Joseph Beuys the Coyote's "jailor," and lists the incomparable cruelty to this Coyote as 'probably being Bored,' as well as the horrible cruelty of being in a state of "considerable" stress. The author goes on buttressing his point by stating that "today" Artists and viewers are more *aware* and *considerate* of the "sensitivity" and the "needs" of the animals used in Art. The photographic evidence of the Beuys installation is described by the author as a portrait of an animal in 'distress,' made obvious to the author by the Coyote's "panting," "pacing," and even holding it's ears back. During the final writing of this book the current author attended a viewing of the long video made by Joseph Beuys of this 1974 performance "Coyote: I Like America and America Likes Me," and during this Joseph Bouys retrospective in the "Kunstmuseum Basel - Museum fur gegenwartskunst" came to the same exact conclusion reached by simply reading about the Bouys performance, being that obviously this claim of compared animal cruelty between a Coyote living in an Art Gallery - and the mixing of Jellyfish DNA with Rabbit DNA to create a new Transgenic life-form on Earth is exponentially *ABSURD* - to the tenth power - that's "ABSURD" with ten zeros after it.

    The author Gessert next states that Joseph Beuys' quoted justification for the Coyote Art installation was at the same time "noble," but also an "arrogant" form of "wishful thinking." The social and spiritual crime that Joseph Beuys committed is clearly declared by the author as 'forcing this Coyote to endure' human contact for a full week and being placed in an 'alien environment.' In "defense" of Beuys the author admits that he acted like any Artist beginning with a "new medium," being only aware of their experiences with other mediums. Further inspired by Kac's "GFP Bunny," the author also states that Beuys' "photographic documentation" of the pieces of Art was more faithful to the Artist's intentions than the actual original piece of Art was. To the present author the assumed comparison between the treatment of the Coyote in Joseph Beuys' "Coyote: I Like America and America Likes Me," to the Genetic Manipulation of "Alba" the Transgenic Green Fluorescent "GFP Bunny" of Eduardo Kac is as absurd as comparing Edward Streichen's "Delphiniums" to Mary Shelly's "Frankenstein!" The present author also believes that the audacity of comparing Joseph Beuys or even Marcel Duchamp to this first Transgenic Artist Eduardo Kac, is also as absurd as comparing Vincent Van Gogh to Roland Dorgeles the 1910 "Donkey-Tail Artist!" What surprises this current author is that contemporary protagonist writers supporting this "Transgenic Art" movement have gone so far as to compare this glorified "social commentator" Kac even to the enlightened visionary Leonardo da Vinci: that's the biggest "Art Prank" of them all. Finally, the current author who has been an Artist all his life and was infatuated with drawing and Color over fifty-five years ago, before he ever wrote his first words, considers this "Transgenic Artist" to be nothing more than a fantastically pretentious Twenty-first century social commentator, who's greatest aspirations are the acquisition of his own personal fame and fortune. As far as this "new medium" for Art consisting of Genetically Altered Fluorescent life-forms, Gessert relieves the horror created by these life-form's creations in a single sentence, reassuring the reader that 'all new Art mediums' also contain a chance of "slippages" or "misunderstanding." What is not clear in the author's statement is whether he meant "misunderstanding" on the part of the viewing public, or on the part of the Transgenic Artists themselves. George Gessert continues to compare the "Coyote" installation to contemporary "Bio Art," "Biotech Art," and "Transgenic Art," writing that it could only be imagined what the Coyote "experienced," and that the "trick" was on Joseph Beuys because the Artist "forced" his own actions onto the Coyote and "reenacted" the old story of humans exploiting nature. If keeping a Coyote in an Art Gallery for a week can be called "exploiting" nature, it is unstated by the author what mixing Jellyfish DNA together with Rabbit DNA could then be called, perhaps 'exponential exploitation.' Proving beyond the shadow of a doubt the boundless compassion of the author, a statement is presented in "Green Light: Toward an Art of Evolution" that plants, bacteria, fungi, and components of living organisms such as tissue or cells, "permit" the Artist to also "make mistakes" - even mistakes that lead to the death of the living organism in their piece of Art. Delving deep into philosophical areas of ethics,

Gessert begins to elaborate on the question of what life-forms are acceptable to genetically alter and even kill in a pice of Art, and what life-forms are not. Killing Plants is stated as "permissible," but killing living organisms that humanity recognizes as "kin," and therefore also recognizes 'itself' in, is obviously not "permissible." Becoming just as "cosmic" as Jack De Ment in 1942, or even Charles Blanc, Gessert continues with the supposition that vertebrates are considered "kin" to humanity because of their 'body organization' and their recognizable reactions to pain and pleasure, but this raises the question 'how did humanity recognize itself in the plant kingdom?' The facts are presented that plants neither have a nervous system nor a recognizable consciousness, which explains that humanity does indeed share kinship with the plant kingdom through a common existential similarity Gessert describes as the "nonexperience" of our lives. An example is given of an accident of Gessert, who was unconscious for resulting surgery due to anesthesia and which brought about the understanding that his life was not at all "synonymous" with his consciousness. Connecting with the cosmic consciousness Gessert questions the 'experiences' of internal organs and components of cells. The conclusion is reached that all of our life is spent adrift in "eternal unconsciousness," akin to plants which Gessert states remind people of their "forgotten selves." The point of aesthetics is brought back with the introductory fact that humans have altered life on Earth intentionally for over 10,000 years. The span of time when our species began to alter other species is extended back to a truly absurd span when the author questions our alteration of other species Colors, for example, by choosing or avoiding them when we were perhaps "lemur-like." Back to the relative present, Irises are given as an example of "Domestication" of life-forms by humans in the crossing of flowers to produce "hybrids." The point is next made that "cross-pollination" caused by human intervention is exactly the same as cross-pollination brought about naturally by bees or other insects in the wild. The conclusion is that this natural "cross-pollination" isn't deliberate or done consciously. Not stopping at bees, the example of "Leafcutter ants" is next given, with the point, again, that humans are not the only species guilty of domesticating life-forms. These "Leafcutter ants" collectively form many different species, and these individual species "cultivate" different species of fungi, which is most of the time a type of fungi they "created" and exists nowhere else except in their individual species' colonies. It is explained that this Leafcutter ant "domestication" of fungi most likely has been taking place for many millions of years, so the point that the author is trying so desperately to convince the reader of is that ants have been guilty of domesticating life-forms for an almost inconceivably longer time than humans have(!)

The beginning of human domestication of life-forms is proved to have begun about 10,000 years ago with plants, but the examples are given of early forms of domestication with both animals and plants for purposes of aesthetics, or even magic, perhaps much further back in our history. The author states that domestication was most likely undertaken by "well-fed" humans who had both the time and the means to develop crossbreeding for generations, and furthermore, most of the domestication done for the past five-hundred years has also been carried out by "well-fed" people who created new species for sheer curiosity, luxury, or just aesthetics. The example is given with the majority of domestication done by humans on "ornamental plants," and with the number of domesticated ornamental plants being greater than the combination of all other domesticated life-forms. The life-forms that humans have domesticated in the recent past centuries are expanded upon by Gessert, beginning with domestication for "displaying wealth" which includes furs of the animals mink, fox, and chinchillas. Next the life-forms domesticated for pure aesthetics are listed as guppies, swordtails, angelfish, tetras, and canary. The last list contains life-forms who were domesticated by humans in recent centuries which were made mostly to create "pets" for people, similar to several members of the 'aesthetic' list, and are gerbils, parakeets, parrots, cockatiels, mice, and even skunk.

Next, to further justify animal alteration throughout history, the example is given by Gessert of life-forms domesticated by science to experiment upon in labs. The example is meant to represent one of the only examples in the field of human domestication that was 'essential,' and not done just for pleasure or aesthetics. The point the author is, again, so desperately trying to convince the reader of is that humans both began and continued to alter life-forms on Earth since the early times of our species - sheerly for amusement - with absolutely no 'essential' uses or reasons for altering these life-forms through domestication - which obviously begs the conclusion that if humans have been altering life since history began, or earlier, for their own amusement and for totally "nonessential" alterations in these life-forms, then obviously this makes it also sociologically acceptable to mix Jellyfish DNA with Rabbit DNA and Coral DNA with Cat DNA. The author even manages to twist the sole example of scientists in laboratories domesticating life-forms into of course the direction of his point, claiming that science is very often done only for the sake of "curiosity" leading the author to conclude that 'scientific curiosity' is "nonessential." The example given of "nonessential" 'scientific curiosity' altering life for sheer amusement is the fruit fly "Drosophila melanogaster" bred by science initially in 1901 and used for research into the 'nonessential scientific curiosity' called "genetics." The first fruit fly which was discovered mutated was in 1910 by Thomas Hunt Morgan, and then during the 1920s H. J. Muller, a student of Morgan's, discovered that he could mutate fruit flies himself simply by exposing the insect to

X-rays. This led to the standard practice by scientists of the 1930s intentionally inducing mutations in fruit flies by this procedure of exposing them to X-rays. Furthermore, after World war two scientists began to change methods with new technology and used chemicals instead of X-rays to mutate fruit flies - all of course for the "nonessential" reason of 'scientific curiosity.' These "nonessential" 'scientific curiosities' that drove the scientists to mutate fruit flies are listed as the unimportant amusements of genetics, agriculture, animal breeding, horticulture, and medicine, only. To steer these facts into the direction of the author's point, it is next claimed that since the scientists mutating fruit flies for decades did not know what was going to happen with their experiments, they were essentially amusing themselves with their own 'scientific curiosity.' Since these scientific experiments initially benefitted no one except the involved scientists, this indicates for Gessert that these researchers on the fruit fly going back to 1910 have merely followed the same "ancient pattern" of life-forms domesticated to benefit the very few people who's 'survival,' essentially, does not depend on 'eating' the domesticated life-form. So if the ultimate 'survival' of the species - food - is the not the goal, then according to the author it enters the classification of mere 'scientific curiosity.' To conclude this chapter on "Divine Plants" as well as "Magical Animals" in "Green Light: Toward an Art of Evolution" the author restates the point that almost all of the human domestication of animals over the past five-hundred years was for "nonessential" reasons, such as the example of "Parakeets," and adds to his statement that the human domestication of plants over the past five-hundred years has also been for the same "nonessential" reasons. Gessert states that "several dozen" food plant species have been domesticated by humans in the past five centuries, including strawberries, blueberries, pecans, cranberries, and grapefruits. The point, again, that the author is trying to make this time with food plant domestication and alteration by humans, is that even though strawberries, pecans, blueberries, etc. are nutritional foods, they are "nonessential." This is supported for the author by the decision of society in the United States, where Gessert explains the acceptance of a new "food" derived from a new crossbred plant is through the new food being used as a "novelty item," meaning a flavoring, a dessert, or additive, but nothing more than a "nonessential" food. Besides "nonessential" food plants, the author expands crossbreeding by Human beings over the past five-hundred years done for a purpose close to "nonessential," and to the really "nonessential" association with the production of cosmetics through recent domestication of "oil crop" plants. Further examples of "nonessential" crossbreeding which results in useless "nonessential" animals and food plants are added by the author, including the domestication of deer as well as elk for the "nonessential" reason of providing a new choice in available meat to buy, not for 'solving hunger.' The grand conclusion by Gessert is that out of all the hundreds of animals and food plants that Human beings have domesticated over the past few centuries, only a mere dozen have been "useful," and he provides the sole example of "Penicillium chrysogenum," which was developed into "Penicillin" by Alexander Fleming after domestication in the late 1920s. For the author, this proves that aside from "Penicillin" and merely about eleven other species, most other human domestication of life-forms for the past five-hundred years has been done with "nonessential" intentions, and as a result have had almost no effect on Human being's "basic needs."

Gessert in "Green Light: Toward an Art of Evolution" states in conclusion that human domestication of life-forms throughout our history has been done with the "nonessential" intentions of nothing more than compassion, curiosity, aesthetics, luxury, or even because of "magic," and that eventually these "nonessential" intentions may have become important or even necessary - but that the initial intentions of human domestication of life-forms was essentially "nonessential." The increase in the population is the determining factor stated by the author which caused the domestication of life-forms to increase, and this is considered to indicate the determining point when humans began to disregard the origins of these food sources, as well as disregarding thoughts of the food source's "social" impact or even "environmental" impact. Once more, the assumed point by the author is that if the domestication of both Animals and Food Plants over the last five-hundred years has been done for "nonessential" purposes, combined with the points that this "nonessential" domestication by humans was done without regard for either social or environmental impact, then the Genetic Manipulation of life-forms to produce "nonessential" pieces of Art, such as "Transgenic Art," is totally justified and virtually the same as domesticating Food Plants, which makes it just another chapter in our long history of amusing ourselves.

To stop for just a moment and take toll of this Transgenic epidemic, a quick search on the internet will deliver an enormous amount of books published on the subject of the "GFP Revolution." Just a small representative selection of these books will be listed here, with the purpose of both revealing the depth of subject matter that is covered with self-explanatory book titles and publishing dates, and also as an example of the sheer number of published books existing on the subject of Genetic Manipulation and the creation of Transgenic life-forms. "What's wrong with my Mouse?" 2000, "Virus-Resistant Transgenic Plants: Potential Ecological Impact" 1997, "Transgenic Wheat, Barley, and Oats" 2008, "Transgenic Plants, Methods and Protocols" 2004, "Transgenic Plants: A Production System for Industrial and Pharmaceutical Proteins" 1996, "Transgenic Plants in Agriculture, Ten years experience of the French Biomolecular Engineering Commission" 1999,

"Transgenic Plants and Crops," 2002, "Transgenic Plants, New Research" 2008, "Transgenic Organisms: Biological and Social Implications" 2002, "Transgenic Organisms and Biosafety" 1996, "Transgenic Mouse Methods and Protocols" 2010, "Transgenic Microalgae as Green Cell factories" 2008, "Transgenic Mammals" 1999, "Transgenic Maize, Methods and Protocols" 2009, "Transgenic Horticultural Crops" 2011, "Biotechnology in Agriculture and Forestry" 2007, "Transgenic Crops of the World" 2005, "Transgenic Crop Plants" Volume one and two, 2010, "Transgenic Animals in Agriculture" 1999, "Transgenic Animal Technology" 2002, "Transgenic and Mutant Tools to Model Brain Disorders" 2010, "Tau Pathophysiology in Transgenic Mice" 2009, "Safety Assessment of Transgenic Organisms" 2006, "Models of Risk Assessment of Transgenic Plants" 1997, "Environmental Risk Assessment of Genetically Modified Organisms - Vol. 3 - "Methodologies for Transgenic Fish" 2007, "Environmental Effects of Transgenic Plants" 2002, "Environmental Costs and Benefits of Transgenic Crops" 2005, and "Transgenic Cereals and Forage Grasses" 2009. A book on the long list of literature published covering the subject matter of Transgenic life-forms that deserves a special mention was published in 2010 by an original character of "Ken Kesey and the Merry Pranksters" from the mid 1960s, who went on to publish the famous "Whole Earth Catalog" for years (as well as many other books), and was in the 1990s a pivotal person in the social development of the internet: Stewart Brand. The book needs no explanation and is entitled "Whole Earth Discipline - Why Dense Cities, Nuclear Power, Transgenic Crops, Restored Wildlands, and Geoengineering ARE NECESSARY." The publications on the subject of "Genetic Engineering" that Steward Brand lists in his book as recommended reading include "Tomorrow's Table: Organic Farming, Genetics, and the Future of Food," 2008, and "The Doubly Green Revolution: Food for All in the Twenty-first Century," 1999.

After the 'Introduction' written by Eduardo Kac to the book "Signs of Life, Bio Art and Beyond," the first chapter deals directly with both "Life Transformation" and "Art Mutation," and in the first sentence Kac states that in his Art he had been 'exploring the boundaries' between the human, the animal, and the robot. Second sentence already concludes that "Transgenic Art" should then be considered the "natural development" from all of the Artwork that he's done up until the development of "Transgenic Art." Kac lists and defines his previous forms of Art as "Teleprescence Art" beginning in 1986, in which humans are 'coexisting' with both other humans and with "telerobotic" bodied animals the Artist describes as 'non-human." In 1994 Kac developed "Biotelematic Art," in which the Artist sought to create a "hybrid" of the mixture between what he describes as the "living" with the "telematic." Kac states 1998 as the beginning of the development of "Transgenic Art," and explains simply that in this work "animate" cannot be distinguished from "technological" any longer. Kac concludes his first paragraph with the admission that the "implications" of this "Transgenic Art" have "social ramifications" and also 'cross several disciplines.'

Not only is the future in which "Biotechnology" will be as common as today's personal computer next quickly and clearly envisioned by Kac, but he also predicts the future in which "Biotechnology" is seen as something personally desirable, with the comparison by Kac again of the computer, formerly seen as a tool of the military and presently which almost every single person has or wants. In other words "Biotechnology" will become 'cool'(!) Further supporting this point is the example of language, in which technical computer terms such as 'Megabyte' have entered popular culture. Kac immediately presents his vision of the future in which new "Biotechnological" words enter pop culture such as "protein." What Kac terms today's Biotechnological "presence" is further supported by routine Transgenic Bacteria kits used by U.S. high school students, according to the Artist. Kac states that Art should bring about 'alternative world views' and compares his Artwork to the the Artists Tinguely and Moholy-Nagy through the similarity of his 'subverting' technology of his day - not merely for the old-fashioned purpose of social commentary, but for the explicit purpose to "*enact*" (and Kac italicizes this word) "critical views." The additional purpose of his Art follows, explained as the opening of a new experience for both the emotions and the intellect through the invention of newly created "entities" and "transgenic organisms." The Artist closes his Introduction to this first chapter by explaining that he has been using the term "Bio Art" to define his Art since 1997, and that in 1998 the term "Transgenic Art" was introduced by Kac in a paper that he "proposed" to not only create a living Green Fluorescent Genetically Manipulated Dog, but also (as planned with "Alba" the "GFP Bunny") to 'socially integrate' the Transgenic Fluorescent Dog which was envisioned as being called the "GFP K-9." The purpose behind the Green Fluorescence of the Transgenic animals planned for use in his Artwork is admitted by Kac as being the creation of a "social marker." Kac abandoned the plans of the "GFP K-9" because technology wasn't advanced enough in 1998 to create a GFP Dog, and this led to the creation of Kac's first "Transgenic Art" piece called "Genesis" in 1999.

"Genesis" is described by the Artist as being an 'exploration' between 'relationships' including biology, ethics, "belief systems," technology, and the new miracle of the 1990s the Internet. Directly stated by Kac is the defining point of this "Genesis" installation being the "artist's gene" at the center of the piece. The Artist explains that this synthetically-made "artist's gene" was created to transmute a sentence of the Book of Genesis from the Bible's Old Testament, which was first 'translated' into "Morse code," and then this translated Morse code from the Bible was 'converted' through Kac's own "conversion principle" developed specifically for the "Genesis" piece. The quote especially chosen by Kac is, again, the quote proclaiming "man's" power over the sea's fish as well as birds and all other living things. The Artist states that this particular quote was selected because of this divine "dubious notion" announcing man's ruling of nature itself, and further explains that Morse code was used because it represents the first "dawn" or "genesis" of the present global "information age." The Artist explains that this "Genesis" gene created for the show was inserted into bacteria, and that this bacteria would be mutated by "Genesis" "participants" who would turn on a [Shortwave] "Ultraviolet light" via the Internet. Kac goes on to also explain that after the "artist's gene" was mutated by [Shortwave] Ultraviolet energy, the effect was the 'changing' of the 'Biblical quote.' This DNA mutation altered the quote used in "Genesis," that was then put on the website which was created as part of this Artwork. The changed Biblical quote was also projected onto the walls of the Art installation's space, which again was in several Art galleries across the world simultaneously, and is the pivotal point of the piece, defined by Kac as a "Symbolic gesture" of our ability to change not only the quote, but of our ability to change the meaning of the Biblical quote itself.

Kac writes that during the "Genesis" show he also gave a lecture concerning the "GFP K-9" plans, which were to create a Green Fluorescent Protein Dog as his piece of Transgenic Art. To justify this invention of the mixture of Jellyfish DNA with Dog DNA, Kac typically begins a dialog about man's domestication and crossbreeding of the Dog, which he states goes back 14,000 years. What the objective of the show intended, again, was the creation of not only a "Jellyfish/Dog," but also of the creation of "shock." Kac adds that this "shock" led an Art critic of the era to claim that "Transgenic Art" was "the end" of Art itself.

The "GFP K-9" couldn't be realized in 1998, but by the turn of the Twenty-first century in the year 2000 Eduardo Kac announced his second Transgenic Artwork, the super-controversial "GFP Bunny" "Alba," which would make the Artist world famous. Directly stated by the Artist is, again, the point of the three stages of the "GFP Bunny" piece, being first the Green Fluorescent Protein Rabbit's "creation," second the "public dialog" created by the "GFP Bunny's" creation, and third the Fluorescent Rabbit's "social integration." Kac explains the actual creation of "Alba" through the mixture of Jellyfish DNA and Rabbit DNA in a few short sentences, beginning with his meeting of Louis Bec at the September 1999 "Ars Electronica" show in which "Genesis" had it's premiere. Kac quickly explains that Louis Bec contacted Louis-Marie Houdebine to propose the "GFP Bunny." Kac also states that "Alba" was born months later during the year 2000, and naturally does take credit for the concept of creating a Green Fluorescent Rabbit which is mixed with Jellyfish DNA. Again, in "Glowing Genes" it is plainly stated by Dr. Marc Zimmer that over a hundred and fifty Green Fluorescent Rabbits had already been conceptualized, then technologically developed, and finally had also been born in the French center outside of Paris where Louis-Marie Houdebine was employed, before Houdebine had ever heard from Kac. Kac also restates the objective of "Transgenic Art," which he introduced in his 1998 paper, and which he first defined in this paper as being a "new" form of Art based on the creation of "unique" life-forms through "Genetic engineering." Kac proceeds to follow this definition of "Transgenic Art" with his warnings or guidelines of this newly created "art form," being that "Transgenic Art" must be made using "great care," and with knowledge of what the Artist calls "complex issues" that will be created by the Fluorescent Transgenic life-form's creation. Finally the Artist must be "committed" to 'love, respect, and also nurture' this newly invented Genetically Manipulated life-form. This was all not to be with "Alba," as Kac goes on to explain that the director of the French institute which created and gave birth to the "GFP Bunny" refused to release "Alba" to him for the premier installation of this Transgenic Rabbit in Avignon, or for this Transgenic Rabbit's newly planned home: Kac's house in Chicago. Kac next has the audacity to claim that the reasons for the French director's refusal to release the Transgenic Rabbit to himself are "unknown," but what did occur was a media explosion on the story and a debate over a virtual zoo of newly-created topics. Claiming headlines and all forms of media worldwide, the debate over the "GFP Bunny" intensified and then went on literally for years. The account of Kac's "custody battle" for "Alba" the "GFP Bunny" is listed by the Artist, from the public staged campaign of December, 2000 in Paris, to the creation of "The Alba Flag" in 2001 for Kac to fly in front of his house in Chicago.

In "Signs of Life" of 2007 Kac details the 'evolution' of "Transgenic Art," with a new direction formed known as "Proteic Art," which is also called "Protein Art." "Proteic Art" involves the creation of 'sculptures' that are on the scale of "Nanometers," or billionths of a meter, which is the scale of atoms, with these 'sculptures' composed entirely of amino acids, and created within strict assemblage according to natural principles of biology. At this nanometer scale, these described "Proteic" 'sculptures' are so far from visible that they nearly enter the realm of "Conceptual Art." Another direction that "Transgenic Art" has "evolved" in is explained by Kac as a creation of an environment containing different Transgenic organisms interacting on a complex level with "biobots," or robots that are "biological" and run in part by the 'regulation' of "microorganisms" which are Transgenic and an integral, essential part of the "biobot's" composition. Eduardo Kac expands on the concepts involved in his first piece of "Transgenic Art" entitled "Genesis," explaining that a "first phase" of the piece centered on the "creation" and then the "mutation" of the synthetic gene in "Genesis" caused by participants on the Internet who logged onto the website of the galleries "Genesis" was installed in, and then switched on a Shortwave Ultraviolet lamp through this website to mutate the gene. The "second phase" of "Genesis" was completed in 2000-2001, and this time centered on the resulting protein formed by the synthetic gene, which Kac calls the "Genesis protein." The Artist explains that this "Genesis protein" stands as "another step" involved in the Biblical text's translation for this "Genesis" piece. The actual translation that utilized Morse code and DNA to mutate the Old Testament Bible quote, and then was downloaded to the Internet as well as being projected onto the walls of the Art galleries the "Genesis" project was installed in, is an exquisite definition of "self-contained logic," and Kac attempts an explanation. This "Genesis gene" is explained by Kac as the actual translator which 'encodes' English, and is then translated into "amino acids." This 'translation' from written language into three-dimensional amino acids is termed "transmogrification" by Kac, who manages to also use the word "intersemiotic" in the same sentence. The Artist defines the study of "Proteomics" as researching proteins and protein functions, and states that the "logic," "methods," and "symbolism" of this field was investigated in "Genesis," along with the potential of "Proteomics" being used for "artmaking."

In "Signs of Life" Kac goes on to detail the concepts and structure of his next major installation "The Eighth Day" of 2001. The Artist brings the reader into the show by describing the entrance into the space where "The Eighth Day" was installed in the "Institute for Studies in the Arts" of Arizona State University. As you walked in you saw a round transparent dome glowing Blue in a dark exhibition space. Kac explains that the dome is four feet wide (1.3 meters) and that it is lit from within and 'evoking' the sight of Earth floating in space. In the background could also be heard water flowing, which served as a "metaphor" for Earth's life and is reinforced with video projection of flowing water onto the floor of the installation space. Kac states that to see this installation "The Eighth Day" the viewer experiences what it is like to be 'walking on water.' In the exhibition the circular transparent Plexiglas dome was mounted about chest level on a dark circular base, making visible Transgenic Green Fluorescent living fish, mice, plants, and even amoebae emitting Color through the "blue light."

The purpose of "The Eighth Day" is given by the Artist, being the formation of a new Bioluminescent 'synthetic ecosystem' of different Transgenic "GFP" species and a "Biobot" biological robot. This 'artwork' - or 'experiment' - was created to see this 'biological synthetic system' as the first example of what it will be like when these Transgenic creatures coexist with natural life-forms on Earth. This living 'biological synthetic ecosystem' populated by four species of newly created life-forms was visible to viewers during the installation from the outside of the Plexiglas dome looking in, and also through the 'eyes' of the "biobot" by both viewers in the gallery and visitors to the website, who could see the Transgenic ecosystem from inside this 'new world.' This is not surprisingly expanded upon by Kac, who describes the fact that viewers could also experience the Transgenic ecosystem in the dome through another camera mounted inside, at the top of this dome, giving a bird's-eye view of the 'new world.' Being able to maneuver this camera, viewers could also see the faces as well as the upper bodies of gallery visitors looking into "The Eighth Day," which Kac naturally describes as the Human beings in the gallery becoming a "part" of this Transgenic Green Fluorescent synthetic bioluminescent ecosystem. Directly stated as well by Kac is that "The Eighth Day" 'presented biodiversity's expansion' outside the limits imposed by nature, of what the Artist labels "wildtype" forms of life. Humbly stated next by Kac is that this "self-contained" synthetic ecosystem intentionally entitled "The Eighth Day" adds one more day to the Biblical scriptures in which the world was created in seven days. What "The Eighth Day" was designed by Kac to create was the sociological and scientific question of nothing less than "transgenic evolution." As part of this experiment in "transgenic evolution" and unnatural expansion of biodiversity, in addition to four species of Transgenic Fluorescent life-forms, the "Biobot" in this synthetic ecosystem was created to integrate a "biological element" into it's "body" that would control a portion of the Biobot's "behavior." Kac explains that this "Biobot" was created with a "brain," which consists of a living colony of "GFP" amoebas. These Transgenic amoebae "brain cells" of the "Biobot" naturally divide, and when that occurs physically, it causes the "Biobot" to move physically as well. Added to all of this is the fact that the viewer could see this synthetic Transgenic ecosystem through cameras mounted as the "Biobot's" 'eyes,' enabling a "first-person" point of view in which the viewer could experience this synthetic Transgenic ecosystem as if they were a part of it. Eduardo Kac's "Conclusion" states clearly in the first sentence that as far as the worlds of Art, society, politics, economics, and medicine go, "genetic engineering" has and will continue to create not only Transgenic life-forms, but also "profound consequences." What Kac states clearly as his goal is nothing less than to change "genetics" into a new form of "art medium." Kac goes on to just as humbly claim that what was "developed" in his Transgenic Artworks, which was both the "symbolic" as well as the "tangible" state of "coexistence" between the Human being and Transgenic forms of life, demonstrates that Human beings as well as "other species" presently are "evolving" in ways which are new. This, according to the Artist, warns of the need for developing "new models" to understand all the changes which will come about through the development and creation of Transgenic life-forms, clones, and Genetically altered "chimeras."

The grand concluding statement by Eduardo Kac is that Human beings are partially made up of DNA sequences that "come from" forms of viruses, which is in itself incorrect, as Human beings merely "share" the same sequences of DNA as viruses and all other forms of life on Earth. Kac continues, coming to the very predictable conclusion based on his own self-contained logic that since Human beings possess DNA within our bodies from other outside organisms, then it means that - a drum roll can be distinctly heard - *we are all Transgenic!* The entire logic which Kac bases his grand conclusion on would be feasible if it were correct that Human beings are made up of DNA sequences that "come from" viruses, horses, kangaroos, and chimpanzees - but this is currently believed by scientists to be incorrect. Human beings, viruses, horses, kangaroos, etc. all "share" the same basic sequences of DNA - in fact all of life on Earth is currently believed by science to "share" exactly the same DNA sequences. It is now believed that Human beings share ninety-five percent of their DNA with Chimpanzees. Humans also share eighty-five percent of their DNA with mice, and forty percent of our DNA is believed to be shared with the cabbage. This is not the same as what Kac mistakenly states as our DNA "coming from" Chimpanzees, mice, or cabbage, because we do not get our DNA from any other species, but all species "share" the same DNA. This does not equate to the grand conclusion reached by Eduardo Kac that we are all Transgenic, because we haven't received our DNA from other species, but all species on Earth share the same sequences of DNA. This also proves that some of the identical Genetic Instructions are shared not just between animal species, but also between Plant and Animal species as well. It is now believed by science that all of life on Earth has a source from which all life-forms still today share DNA from, and this ancient relative of us all is named the "Last Universal Common Ancestor" or "L.U.C.A." which was alive 3.8 billion years ago. It has also been discovered that chicken eggs contain the evidence to prove that chickens today still possess DNA shared with the Dinosaurs, and that this Dinosaur DNA is no longer used, or 'active,' in today's chicken. It is also believed that just five percent of our own DNA is actually 'active' and still used by ourselves. As proof of the fact that all life-forms on Earth including ourselves are interrelated genetically, a large portion of the DNA we possess has become 'silent,' or inactive, simply left over from our distant past and presently unused. Evolution has created an immense amount of life-forms on Earth, estimated at about 8.7 million species today (excluding microscopic life-forms), of which we have managed to catalogue approximately 1.7 million species. Natural extinction has been just as astounding, eliminating an estimated ninety-nine percent of all the species of life that have ever lived upon the Earth as well. Unnatural extinction, meaning extinction compounded by the intervention of we Human beings, has increased this rate astronomically, to a figure of a thousand times the rate of Natural extinction. But, not to worry about Human beings increasing the rate of natural extinction one-thousand times, because across the news - again - flashes the answer to all our prayers - another stupendous dream achieved by the Twenty-first century "Miracle-Cure" Genetic Manipulation: the resurrection of the *Woolly Mammoth!* No joke - in 2011 Japanese and Russian scientists announced to the world that they would resurrect a living Woolly Mammoth from the Ice Age. The technique that the international team will use is a plan to inject the preserved DNA from a frozen dead Woolly Mammoth's thigh bone into the egg of the Mammoth's closest living relative: the Elephant. The egg, containing DNA from an extinct Woolly Mammoth mixed with the DNA of a Twenty-first century Elephant, will then be inserted into the womb of a living Elephant. This should develop into a living Woolly Mammoth. This team of Japanese and Russian scientists forecast 2016 as the year that the living Woolly Mammoth will return to walk the Earth. The December 11, 2011 edition of "Scrape TV" on the internet ran a story with the headline: 'Woolly Mammoth Back on your Dinner Plates In Five Years.'

So the grand conclusion by Eduardo Kac that 'we are all Transgenic' because we all "come from" other forms of life is incorrect because our DNA does not "come from" other life-forms, but is universally shared by all life-forms on Earth, meaning we are not all "Transgenic" but in actuality (and not surprisingly) absolutely the opposite is true, being that all life-forms on earth are the "Same." Trying to find similarities in the beauty and perfection of nature within the brutality of man-made Genetically Modified monsters is clever, and is also not surprisingly next attempted by Kac. The Artist develops another of his own logical conclusions, being that all Human beings, as well as all other species alive, are "Transgenic" because we all have contained in our bodies the DNA from other organisms, so that before Human beings 'decide' that Transgenic life-forms are "monstrous" we must all "look inside" for seeing that we are all "monstrous" because of our own individual "Transgenic condition"(!) What a character. What Kac next tries to convince the reader of is that their common belief today of Transgenic life-forms being "Unnatural" *is incorrect!* This Transgenic Artist explains that the movement of genes from one species to another is not just a product of Human intervention, but just another natural process of "wild life." The well known household animal that Kac cites as an example to prove this 'common' natural "Transgenic" process is the "agrobaterium" bacteria, which the Artist explains as entering the roots of a plant and then 'communicating' it's DNA to the plant. This bacteria can transfer it's DNA to the cells of plants and then "integrate" it's DNA into the chromosomes of the plant.

Kac ends his conclusion with the multiple points which "Transgenic Art" calls into question, including the 'romantic notion' of what is considered "natural" and what is not, as well as 'acknowledging' that Human beings have now played a role in 'evolution.' While questioning what is "natural" and what is not, and acknowledging both that Transgenic life-forms are "natural" and that humans altering life-forms have in effect also altered evolution, Kac explains that we must also be 'respectful' and 'humble' before the "amazing phenomenon" known as "life"(!) Reminds one of the old famous advice of doctors worldwide who instruct their patients: "Do what I say, not what I Do."

"The Eighth Day, The Transgenic Art of Eduardo Kac" edited by Sheilah Britton and Dan Collins of 2003 gives a good insight into not only the Artwork of the first Transgenic Artist, but also independent viewpoints through essays contained in the book. The introduction to the book on the back cover was written by the director of the School of Visual Arts in Penn State University, Charles R. Garioan, Ph.D., and informs the reader that "Transgenic Art," the "controversial topic," will be examined to document opinions on an Artform which manipulates genetic as well as biological matter, and to give an idea about Eduardo Kac, this first "Transgenic Artist" who insists that his "palette" contains "life itself."

The actual introduction to "The Eighth Day, the Transgenic Art of Eduardo Kac" begins with a quote from a 1988 "Artforum" article "Curie's Children" which predated Kac's "GFP Bunny" "Alba" by a dozen years, and asked the questions why Blue and Red spotted dogs and Phosphorescent horses don't yet exist. After Edward Stiechten's crossbred "Delphiniums" are obligatorily mentioned, other Artists of the Twentieth century who dealt with life-forms or manipulated life-forms are mentioned as well, including Peter Gerwin Hoffman who in 1983 cultivated bacteria he had collected off a Kandinsky painting's surface and called the 'Artwork' "Mikrobenbei Kandinsky." The short history of Genetic Manipulation follows, with the early example given of 1986's splicing of Firefly DNA into Tobacco plants, which was the invention of the first Tobacco plant that was luminescent. Moving swiftly to "The Eighth Day" by Eduardo Kac, it is plainly stated that the intention by the Artist was to create a vision of the future in which new invented Transgenic life-forms coexist with Human beings and all other life-forms that have managed to escape extinction. In his first Transgenic work "Genesis" of 1999, Kac worked on the parallels he saw between DNA's discovery in 1953 and the Rosetta Stone's discovery in 1719. According to Kac the Rosetta Stone was a "key" for unlocking the secrets of the past, and the "Genesis project" by himself with it's three 'systems' of language, DNA, and binary logic, stands as the "key" for understanding nothing less than the "future." Not everybody (obviously) enthusiastically agrees with the absolute self-contained logic of Eduardo Kac, and in "The Eighth Day," Katherine Hayles clearly states that there is nothing in nature or culture that exists as an interface between DNA and Morse code, with the exception of the "associations" invented by Eduardo Kac, only.

The book "The Eighth Day, The Transgenic Art of Eduardo Kac" begins with a list of Kac's collaborators on "The Eighth Day" project, which number over thirty, and then directly launches into a campaign to legitimize "Transgenic Art" by the age-old tested recipe of placing this new Twenty-first century Artform, as well as the first Transgenic Artist Eduardo Kac, in the context of the "Old Masters." Edward Lucie-Smith is the author of this first chapter, and in the very first sentence "links" that occur between science and Art going back to the Renaissance are presented. The second sentence presents none other than Leonardo da Vinci and his anatomical drawings from half a millennium ago, followed by Titian in the third sentence who provided the basic Artwork for the first major anatomical treatise. After dropping several other Artist's names, including Caravaggio, the conclusion is reached that the common "element" in the presented early Artwork of anatomy is the presence of 'magic and also the forbidden.' The example of science's "newest discoveries" directly producing a new Art described as "radical" is next presented, with Vassily Kandinsky's "Concerning the Spiritual in Art" published in 1911 discussed. By the third paragraph the author has intimately bound together Eduardo Kac, as well as other Artists working in this new field, with Leonardo da Vinci, Titian, Caravaggio, and Kandinsky, stating clearly that Kac's Artwork constitutes a "continuation" of these luminous Artist's legacy, as well as a reversal of their "attitude."

Edward Lucie-Smith then concludes that Kac's first Transgenic installation "Genesis" containing the "Artist's gene" mutated by [Shortwave] Ultraviolet and then changing the Bible's Old Testament quote on both the internet and the walls of the Art galleries it was exhibited in, brought back science as both an important driving force and 'moral force of human existence.' An early work "Time Capsule" of Kac's is included in Edward Lucie-Smith's chapter, beginning with the fact that the Brazilian Artist is from a Polish lineage who were persecuted by the Nazis because they were Jewish. "Time Capsule" was a performance by Kac in 1997 where he surgically implanted a microchip into his ankle, becoming the first person to have a microchip implanted in their body. The author makes the connection between the microchip in Kac's ankle (where Brazilian slaves were tattooed) that also registered a number on the U.S. 'lost dog' database, and the tattooed arms of concentration camp victims of the Second world war containing their identification numbers.

"Transgenic Art" and it's expansion beyond the work of Eduardo Kac is discussed by the author of the first chapter of "The Eighth Day," and includes "davidkremers" who began in 1992 to create 'Artwork' - "paintings" as they are called by Kremers - by applying bacteria to sheets of clear acrylic. The bacteria Kremers applied to the clear acrylic was genetically engineered to grow enzymes that would be different Colors after the 'piece of Art' spent eight hours inside one "incubation chamber" - effectively 'growing' the 'piece of Art' - and then these acrylic sheets with different Colored bacteria incubated on them would be first dried and next sealed with synthetic resin. This is not the end of these pieces of Transgenic Art, as Kremers envisions Art conservators a millennium from today removing the sealing resin of his work, feeding this Colored bacteria of his Artwork, and in effect bringing them back to life, as well as continuing these pieces of 'Art' by "davidkremers." The author also explains that a website was created around the "Transgenic Art" of Eduardo Kac, David Kremers, and other Artists working in the field of genetics who held a group exhibition entitled "Paradise Now."

Surprisingly the reader is warned to beware of 'imitations' of "Transgenic Art," such as Artists who look not "forward" like Eduardo Kac, but "backwards" like Thomas Grunfeld the German Artist who produces "hybrid creatures" which Edward Lucie-Smith labels as "old fashioned" and similar to "natural history" museums as well as 'sideshows of fairgrounds.' Grunfeld's images are described as "Hybrid creatures" that are reminiscent of "mermaids" created by the mixtures of fish and monkeys by showmen of days gone by. Lucie-Smith labels Grunfeld's images "nostalgic" because he claims they are reminiscent of a time when "wonders" such as mermaids could be appreciated without today's signatory "irony." Grunfeld's work is used as an example of what the opposite of Kac's work represents, which for Lucie-Smith is the excitation of the imagination through examples of what is currently possible with "contemporary science." It is understandable why Grunfeld's biting work is criticized by Edward Lucie-Smith after seeing the taxidermy creatures the Artist created, such as a monster consisting of a Pig's head and a Flemish Blue-Jay's body or a Moose with antlers fused onto the body of a Giraffe, as an obvious social commentary directly criticizing this Genetical Manipulation movement.

Kac's large installation "The Eighth Day" of 2001 is next discussed by Edward Lucie-Smith, who clearly again documents the fact that this 'Eighth Day' represents the day that the creation of the universe was complete, and the day that the "creator" left the creation "to develop." Eduardo Kac tells us through his "Eighth Day" that the creator's creation has now developed so far it has attained it's own God-like state and is currently capable of creating new forms of life "independently" of divine intervention. This is another exquisite definition provided by Eduardo Kac of a phrase the current author has used throughout this chapter: "Self-Deitized."

Edward Lucie-Smith presents the question of whether these Transgenic creatures are viable as 'pieces of Art.' The scientific side of involving Genetic Manipulation in the Transgenic invented life-forms presented as pieces of Transgenic Art is not surprisingly barely examined in relation to the individual's reaction, and reduced to only 'worrying' society because these Genetically engineered species are somehow "inappropriate." What is centered on by the author is the three-dimensionality and "interactivity" that a living Transgenic organism possesses, in great contrast to static 'Renaissance sculptures' and "Impressionist paintings." All that the disturbance "some people" have with their confrontation of these invented Transgenic Green Fluorescent life-forms used for a piece of "Transgenic Art" is brought down to the author's conclusion of merely an 'unexpected physicality.' Nothing about inventing new Transgenic life-forms by mixing Jellyfish DNA with a rabbit or mouse or even a tobacco plant's genes. Lucie-Smith's first chapter is concluded by the assertion that "The Eighth Day" is in fact a "turning point" similar to cited works by Kandinsky, Jacques-Louis Davis, Eugene Delacroix, and Picasso, and furthermore, that what "The Eighth Day" calls to question is society's contemporary "attitudes" towards creativity, pointing out that the word "Creativity" was used in this context defined by it's "fundamental sense."

In "Telepresence and Bio Art, Networking Humans, Rabbits, and Robots" of 2005 Eduardo Kac 'proposes' that "Transgenic Art" is an "artform" that is founded on the creation of unique Transgenic life-forms through "genetic engineering." The methods listed by Kac to create Genetically Manipulated life-forms for "Transgenic Art" are through the transference of "synthetic genes" into another life-form, through the genetic mutation of a life-form's DNA, or through the transference of non-manipulated "genetic material" between different species. With zeal Eduardo Kac excitedly continues, beginning with the fact that through the modern wonder of "Molecular Genetics," Artists can now engineer plant as well as animal "genomes" to create new life! Kac exclaims that this new Art's "nature" can be defined beyond the mere birth of a Genetically Modified invented new life-form, as well as being defined more profoundly by the "relationship" that will exist between the Transgenic life-form invented for a piece of "Transgenic Art" and it's inventor - the "Artist" - as well as added to the "relationship" the Transgenic life-form will develop with the "public." Eduardo Kac next cheerily advertises that these Genetically Modified "Organisms" created for "Transgenic Art" can - wait for it - now be made available for the public to 'take home' (!) and grow these Transgenic plants in their "backyard" or even to be "raised" by people as their Pets. This character Kac goes so outrageously far as to suggest that since every day one species of endangered animal is going extinct on Earth, Artists could actively "contribute" to the cause of increasing "global biodiversity" through their 'inventions' of new forms of Transgenic life!

In "Telepresence and Bio Art, Networking Humans, Rabbits, and Robots" Eduardo Kac defines the movement itself and his Art in particular, inclusive of "telepresence" and "biotelematics" as well as "biorobotics" and finally "transgenic art," as the 'commitment and investigation' into what is simply stated as just "communication."

A contemporary masterpiece of Eduardo Kac has been reverted back to a less hysteria-producing Transgenic life-form than the "GFP Bunny" "Alba," in fact back to the first cited Genetically Manipulated life-form exhibited as Art in 1936 by Edward Steichen: flowers. The 2009 opening of Eduardo Kac's "Natural History of the Enigma" at the Minneapolis "Weiman Art Museum" featured a new invented Transgenic Petunia mixed with the Artist's own DNA. The new species of Transgenic "Petunia" is humbly named the "Edunia" by Eduardo Kac, who does not call the Transgenic flower a 'plant,' but a "plantimal." Between 2003 and 2008 this Transgenic Petunia "Edunia" was created, and Kac states on his website "ekac.org" that he "invented" as well as "produced" this new "Edunia" through the techniques of "molecular biology." The "Edunia" Petunia that Eduardo Kac invented is light Pink with blood-Red veins running all through the flower's petals. The point is that the blood-Red veins of this invented "Edunia" contain Eduardo Kac's "gene" which was first "isolated" and then "sequenced" from, of course, the Artist's own blood. Kac continues his description with his observation that the light Pink Color of the "Edunia's" petals 'evoke' the Color of his own skin, as well as the climax being that the Red veins of the "Edunia" produced with the Artist's own DNA derived from his blood 'creates a living image' obviously representing "human blood" pumping through "Edunia's" little Genetically Manipulated 'veins.'

Kac explains that the gene he sequenced from his own blood was specifically chosen because of it's responsibility of identifying "foreign bodies." In this way Kac has 'integrated' into this "plantimal" "Edunia" precisely what is rejected and identified by what it was 'integrated' into - thus he claims to have created a "new kind" of what he calls "self," which is part flower and part Human being.

Photographs on this "ekac.org" website include a 'portrait' of the "plantimal" "Edunia" created by Eduardo Kac, as well as an image of the Artist in 2009 watering his "Edunia" Petunia which contains his blood's DNA. The 2009 exhibition "Natural History of the Enigma" contained the actual living "Edunia" Petunia in the show on a pedestal, as well as six lithographs of studies for "Edunia" Seed Packs, and actual seeds of this "Edunia" in six limited edition "Seed Packs."

For Eduardo Kac the creation of the "Enigma" exhibition and the "plantimal" "Edunia" was to reflect on what he terms a "contiguity" of all life that exists or will exist, between completely different species. "Edunia" expresses for Kac a "marker" representing our "shared heritage" of life thorough his use of the Red Color of his blood and the Red Color of "Edunia's" veins. Again, Kac states he creates a "realization" of this "contiguity" of all life that exists or will exist between completely different species, by his combination of Plant and Human DNA producing a "Plantimal" that literally appears to have human blood flowing through it's blood-Red veins.

"Edunia" the "Plantimal" invented by mixing Petunia DNA with Eduardo Kac's blood DNA, is claimed by the Artist to "instill" the public with nothing less than a feeling of "wonder" over what is the 'amazing phenomenon' called "life." Kac next states that although the "general public" understands that Human beings are genetically close to apes, dogs, and cats, most people don't realize that they are closely related genetically to many other forms of life, including "flora."

To support "Edunia" the "Plantimal," Kac again cites Art history as well as philosophy and "contemporary science." Inspired by the writing of Descartes, in 1748 Julien Offray de La Mettrie already documented the fact that the basic "principle parts" are quite the "same" between plants and humans. The completion of the sequencing of the genome of a mustard family plant in 2000 adds to the human genome already sequenced, and equates for Eduardo Kac to a grandiose 'extension' of the similarity between ourselves and plants, or to use the scientific terminology, "homologies" have been discovered between the human and the plant DNA sequences. This proves for Kac that the most important aspect of the "Enigma" occurs down at the level of molecules. The "Edunia" is both a newly created life-form by Eduardo Kac, which he labels as "physical realization," and simultaneously an idea and an emotion evoked by an actual flower, which Kac labels the "symbolic gesture." The Artist details what was done to make this "key gesture" of the "Enigma" work, which involved a selection of part of his blood to sequence the section of his genetics making up his immune system. The key point behind using the genetic sequencing of his immune system was that this system is responsible for protecting the body against anything that is not part of the individual, such as 'disease, invaders, or foreign molecules.' This is more precisely known as the "Immunoglobulin," from which Kac had a sequence of his DNA isolated. The Artist details the procedure used for the creation of this "Edunia" Petunia that has his blood DNA expressed in it's Red veins, which involved creating a "chimeric gene" made up of his blood's DNA along with a "promoter" that would "guide" his blood's DNA to be expressed only in the Petunia's Red veins. This was achieved by using a promoter developed by a professor at the University of Minnesota specifically produced to target "gene expression" just in the veins of plants. Kac stresses the fact that since his blood's DNA is mixed into the chromosomes of this invented "Edunia," every new plant grown through seeds will also carry with it Eduardo Kac's genes in it's flower's veins.

As part of "The Natural History of the Enigma" installation, a large sculpture made from metal and fiberglass was created. The twenty foot long (6.5 meters) "Singularis" sculpture was "derived" from the particular "molecular procedure" used to create the "Edunia" flower, and this translates for Kac as the revelation unveiling mankind's close relatives contained in the Plant kingdom. To complete the similarity visually, this "Singularis" sculpture representing Kac's blood DNA as well as the Red Coloration of the "Edunia" veins, was created also Colored "blood Red."

Of course Eduardo Kac envisions the future where "Edunias" will be "distributed" throughout society and will also be "planted everywhere," and to create this vision he has produced also the "Edunia Seed Packs" manufactured as a "limited edition" and containing seeds for this "Edunia" Petunia. Completing "The Natural History of the Enigma" exhibition, Kac added the six lithographs he created as "studies" of the Seed Packs for "Edunia."

Eduardo Kac concludes this "Enigma" section of his website "ekac.org" with details of the design of these "Seed Packs," which he calls "hybrid objects." The seed packets open like very expensive Art books through a design utilizing an 'embedded magnet' and also, like a book, the seed packet opens up to text including instructions on "Growing Notes" and "Bloom Period." The final works in the "Enigma" exhibition are described by the Artist as photographs and watercolors. Eight diptychs make up a series of watercolors entitled "Mysterium Magnum" which explore what Kac admits has always been interesting to him, the "relationship" he calls "inextricable" that exists between communication and life. This series of "Mysterium Magnum" watercolors are explained by the Artist to "oscillate" between "sign systems" and "biomorphic patterns." Another series included in the exhibition was "Plantimal" photographs which were images of the first germinated "Edunias" from 2009 in Minneapolis. Kac points out in conclusion that although the photographs were taken of genetically engineered "identical clones" of this "Edunia" Petunia, all of the individual flowers that bloom are different from each other. Thus, this "Plantimal" "Edunia" invented by Eduardo Kac allows the Artist to proclaim that regardless of "how similar" life is, life remains "fundamentally different" as well as "singular." What a revelation.

Documenting the "Revolution" or history of "Transgenic Art," "Biotech Art," and "Bio Art" was not the intention of this book, and to do so would not only distort the physical size of this book, but also the consciousness of it's author. In precisely half a century of first being conscious of Art, then fascinated by Art, and finally dedicating my life to Art, the present author has never before encountered an Artform that he not only considers distasteful, but which has also been elevated to the position of both being offensive to ethics, religion, and spirituality, as well as being an obvious irreverent physical threat to life on Earth. These multiple points combine to create a lack of respect by the current author for these Artforms, which was crystallized by the Artists of these Artworks obvious intrinsic association with a typical and signatory self-deitized, incompassionate, self-absorbed and self-created 'hybridized' subspecies of contemporary Human beings. Contrary to popular belief, this sociological 'hybrid' did not just begin to rule the Earth in the 1980s and 1990s, but have been around since the formation of the species. Countless examples both throughout and beyond history exist of selfish mindless acts which were done by individuals without the least regard for the opinion of anyone but themselves, and even less regard for the consequences of their actions upon anyone else, or the Earth and it's countless species of inhabitants. The current reader will know beyond the shadow of a doubt that they are eligible members of that 'hybridization' if they arrogantly smiled as they read the last words of the previous sentence.

Now currently into the eighth year of writing this voluminous 'Black light history,' another "Artist" has achieved what the current author thought was the impossible: going beyond the Artistic Abominations of Eduardo Kac(!) In March, 2015 towards the end of a Museum demonstration to about fifteen visitors during which Green Fluorescent Protein's discovery and it's uses both in medicine and society are explained along with the Transgenic Artists who have used Transgenic Fluorescent animals as their "Art" such as Eduardo Kac's "GFP Bunny," one of the Museum visitors told me that he teaches a college corse in California on Transgenic and Bio Art. This teacher then asks me if I knew about "Stelarc" = the Performance Artist who has had a Human Ear permanently grafted onto his Arm?(!) As I looked in shock at this teacher he continued unbelievably with this: 'You can go onto his website and listen to what the Ear on his arm is hearing(!)' 'A Human Ear on his Arm - and he did it as his Art?' 'Yes.' Then I went on the internet and found that there is more information published about this "Stelarc" than about most entire nations.

This "Performance Artist" was born in Cyprus in 1946 as Stelios Arcadiou and changed his name in 1972 to "Stelarc." His website's biography describes him as a "Performance Artist" who has both "acoustically amplified" as well as "visually probed" his body. The inside of "Stelarc's" body has been the subject of three of his films, and "Stelarc" has created performances of his body being suspended by hooks piercing his skin for twenty-five exhibitions between 1976 and 1988. To 'explore interfaces' relating to the body, "Stelarc" has utilized the internet, biotechnology, virtual reality, robotics, prosthetics, and even medical instruments, as his biography goes on to boast. "Stelarc's" performances have also involved a walking robot with six legs, his "Stomach Sculpture," what he describes as a "Virtual Hand," and a performance with a "Third Hand." Choreography between the muscles being directly stimulated, and the body, have also been explored in performances by "Stelarc," as well as what he calls his "Prosthetic Head," which is described on his website as a "conversational agent" that of course speaks.

'Naturally,' on his website is also what "Stelarc" calls his "Extra Ear," and it is explained that this "Third Ear" of the Performance Artist was 'surgically constructed' onto his Forearm, and that his Third Ear will have the ability to Hear(!) Not only that, but this Third Ear will be an "acoustical organ" that is "publicly accessible" for anyone who wants to hear what the grafted Third Ear on "Stelarc's" forearm is listening to - all on the internet. There are a multitude of photos of "Stelarc" promoting this Third Ear on his forearm to be found on the internet, as well as a mountain of articles and publications about his "Extra Ear" as well.

On October 11, 2007 the "BBC News" published an article on "Stelarc" which was called 'Performer who gets a Third Ear for his Art.' The first sentence of the article already announced that this "Australian Performer" has "sparked controversy" by getting an Ear grafted onto his forearm as his Art. "Stelarc" responded by stating that his "Third Ear," which has been made of human cartilage, is what he calls an "augmentation" of his body's form. The sixty-one year old "Stelarc" also aded that it took years for him to find a willing surgeon to graft a human Ear onto his arm, as well as the fact that his future plans were to have a microphone implanted into his "Arm Ear," so that anybody will be able to listen to what his "Arm Ear" is hearing(!) What is amazing/amusing to the current author is the extremely close resemblance of "Stelarc" to Peter Boyle in 1974's "Young Frankenstein." "Stelarc" could perhaps then also represent valid proof that David Byrne was absolutely correct about a person's 'physical appearance' actually changing directly because of their consciousness and conscious desires(!)

As a stark contrast to the Twenty-first century's Bioluminescent monsters and "spectacles," in "Cold Light - Creatures, Discoveries, and Inventions That Glow" it is stated that during the 1900 International Exhibition in Paris, jars were filled with Bioluminescent glowing bacteria by a scientist and positioned around a room. These jars of Bioluminescent bacteria emitted so much light during this 1900 International Exhibition that people attending could read by the light of this naturally glowing bacteria, and could even recognize the faces of people almost seven meters (20 feet) away!

Is this the beginning of the era which will end life on Earth? During the last century plus Human beings have damaged Mother Earth so continuously that it seems beyond the point of no return. Can the brutality and the blind ignorance of the Human race extinguish all life on Earth? This Artist believes that the infinite wisdom of Nature, which has been alive on Earth for nearly four billion years, is no comparison to the blatant obvious ignorance of the human race. For years it has been running around in my head the quote that would predict the uprise of Nature and the reclamation of it's Grandmother Earth, which was presented at the end of H. G. Wells' "War of the Worlds" when the superior alien invaders who nearly take over the Earth are totally decimated and absolutely conquered by 'the tiniest creatures that the infinite wisdom of God had placed upon the Earth.' In the past several decades a worldwide crisis has been created by the still mysterious disappearance of food-pollinating Bees. A shocking amount of the food which feeds the human race is produced solely through the service of Bees pollinating flowering plants. "Coincidentally," during the exact same span of time - the last several decades - Jellyfish numbers have begun to explode, resulting in a staggering overpopulation of these Jellyfish worldwide, which is currently leading to the seas across the Earth being taken over by Jellyfish, which are not exactly a staple diet of Human beings, and which are also adding to the drastic and increasing reduction of eatable Fish in the world's oceans.

So it may be asked what can these 'tiniest and insignificant of all creatures' do to effect the world? The answer is nothing less than the alteration of all life on Earth. Is this a coincidence that just in the last decades - when the Earth has been polluted and perturbed well beyond the proverbial "point of no return" - that the Jellyfish by their billions began to take over the world's oceans and the Bees began to mysteriously disappear by their billions? Coincidence is for fools. Are these two natural explosions and disappearances caused by Human being's stupidity, greed, superiority, and selfishness - or are these two simultaneous natural disasters happening in *Self-defense?* After countless millions of years, to consider the mass-disappearance of food-pollinating Bees and the extensive explosion of the numbers of Jellyfish which are taking over the oceans - happening simultaneously all in the course of a few mere decades - decades during which the intensity of humanity's inconsideration towards, and raping of, nature came to it's climax - to consider these two natural explosions and disappearances simultaneously happening as a "coincidence" is nothing less than absurd. What will be left to eat after the Bees disappear - along with three-quarters of our land-grown eatable plants, such as flowering fruits, vegetables, and grains? What will be left to eat after the crops are not pollinated by Bees and our grains, vegetables, and fruits do not produce food anymore on land, combined with the fish of the seas diminishing rapidly because of their oceans being suffocated and taken over by Jellyfish? These billions of Jellyfish eat the fish, by the way. Besides the limited number of birds which will never sustain over seven billion people, one of the only living sources of food that will left for people to eat in large quantities will be Insects! Bon appetite.

Now suppose that these 'tiniest and insignificant of all creatures,' such as Bees and Jellyfish, began to 'fight back' against humanity's brutal raping of nature by using other means than just their disappearances and explosions in numbers? On July 1, 2011 an article appeared on the internet by "Reuters" announcing to the world for the first time that the "Jellyfish Invasion" kept Power Plants in the UK "Shut Down"(!) In Scotland the two Torness Nuclear Power Plants of "EDF Energy" were shut down for a few days solely because of this "Jellyfish Invasion." To avoid the damage, destruction, or possible total meltdown of these two Scottish nuclear reactors, which would be caused by this invasion of Jellyfish clogging up and stopping the cooling water pumped into the reactors, the decision was made to keep these two Scottish Torness Nuclear Power Plants "Offline" for a few days during July, 2011. Not only did this "Jellyfish Invasion" stop these two Nuclear Power Plants in Scotland from producing energy for a few days, but the Reuters' article goes on to explain that this alteration of human events by the "Jellyfish Invasion" will become increasingly a common occurrence since the world's oceans now absorb more carbon dioxide, resulting in the water's pH balance being changed. These are perfect conditions ensuring an over population and literal explosion of Jellyfish numbers in the seas. Combine this change of pH balance in the world's oceans caused by carbon dioxide absorption, with the rise in temperature of the actual ocean water worldwide, and what is created is a perfect situation for an explosion of the numbers of Jellyfish across the globe. The article closes with the information that officials hoped "Reactor 1" would return to operation on July 5, 2011, and that the following day on July sixth "Reactor 2" was hoped to resume operation. This was a year before the writing of this section in this book.

During the year 2012 the "Japan Times" reported that in Ise Bay Jellyfish have endangered the operation of *nine* Thermal Power Plants. "Chubu Electric Power Co." of Japan reported on "worldnews.com" that there were approximately 24,000 tons of Jellyfish living in the Ise Bay where these nine Thermal Power Plants are located, which amounts to double the normal population of these Jellyfish as well as the second highest number of Jellyfish recorded in that area in the last ten years. The same reason that the two Scottish Nuclear Power Plants were stopped for a few days in 2011 also caused these nine Thermal Power Plants in Japan to be very worried, which was the possible clogging of the "intakes" for the Power Plant's cooling water by countless Jellyfish.

At the beginning of 2008 "National Geographic" aired a show on this phenomenon, which was clearly entitled "Jellyfish Invasion." The show was a reportage on the discovery of giant Jellyfish in the seas around Japan in unprecedented exploding numbers. This "National Geographic" show "Jellyfish Invasion" over five years ago reported that on the night of August 25, 2005, Japanese fishermen of the Tsushima Strait pulled in fishing nets filled with tons of not salmon or anchovies, which was usual, but tons of deadly stinging giant Nomura's Jellyfish. On that August night these Japanese fishermen caught over three tons of Jellyfish, which was just the very beginning. The fishermen in Japan didn't know what to do, so a practice began of slaughtering the tons and tons of Jellyfish caught every night by cutting them up into pieces and then just throwing them back into the sea. This was most probably the very worse thing that the Japanese fishermen could have done, because in their brutal attempt to reduce the numbers of the Jellyfish by slicing them up and throwing them overboard, they were actually increasing the number of invading Jellyfish *exponentially!* When Jellyfish are cut up and thrown back into the water, which is what the fishermen of Japan were doing for a long time, each and every cut-up section of the Jellyfish responds to this brutal attempt at their destruction with a clever literal explosion of Jellyfish eggs. So in all their infinite wisdom, the human brutality of these fishermen cutting up countless numbers of giant Jellyfish and then throwing them back overboard into the seas, actually caused countless millions or billions more of these Jellyfish to be born. And this is just what we have discovered so far. This 2008 "National Geographic" "Jellyfish Invasion" reportage went on to explain clearly that these Jellyfish are not content to remain out at sea, but have a real intent on heading towards the ocean's shores. Dr. Jamie Seymour clearly demonstrates on this show that in Australia, where the Jellyfish Invasion first began to be noticed, Jellyfish are moving in definitive directions that they choose, and that they are also very quick to reach these chosen destinations. In Australia "Box Jellyfish" and "Irukandji" Jellyfish are responsible for more swimmer's deaths than both Crocodiles and Great White Sharks combined. On the "Daily Telegraph's" website from England, this "Jellyfish Invasion" show was also reviewed in February, 2008, and begins with the opinion that the Jellyfish Invasion could have easily been what the article calls the "role model" for the monster in the movie "Alien!" The fact is revealed that in just three minutes the "Box Jellyfish" can kill a person who merely brushes up against it in the water. Not only that, but as witnessed in Japan if the Jellyfish has it's life threatened, or if it is attacked, it can reproduce at a shocked emergency exponential rate. This "Jellyfish Invasion" "National Geographic" documentary clearly determined the source of the problem, being that the world's seas are being fished dry by humans. This "Telegraph" 2008 article goes on to elaborate on the "Jellyfish Explosion," which at that time was focused around Japan and Australia, who were under 'attack' by countless Jellyfish who were attracted to the Pacific waters because of the depleted food supply caused by overfishing. A 2008 "Popular Science" article documented an unbelievable event which occurred in November, 2007 on the coast of Ireland. North Ireland's salmon farms were stocked with 120,000 salmon worth approximately two million dollars. In just one night in November, 2007 a simply huge "swarm" of Jellyfish that were measured at forty-two feet thick (13 meters) and an astounding ten miles wide (16 kilometers), reduced this salmon farm worth two million dollars to 120,000 floating dead fish. The salmon couldn't survive with the combination of oxygen deprivation and stings from an unimaginable number of "Baby mauve stinger" Jellyfish in this "swarm," which was reported as being in the billions. This "Popular Science" article stated in 2008 that it was believed the 500 million year old species of Jellyfish and their related similar "cousins" such as "comb jellies" together account for up to a full third of the combined life of the seas. Other estimates of Jellyfish population are higher, with percentages reaching a full fifty percent of the combined mass of all living creatures on Earth. The largest Jellyfish has been reported at over 40 yards (meters) long.

  The way that Jellyfish have been helped to overpopulate the world's oceans is also directly related to human intervention. The 'Warty comb jelly' or 'American comb jelly' was originally like it's name suggests, only found around America, but for over thirty years it's habitat has spread as far as the Black Sea, where it was already found in 1982. This spreading of the 'American comb jelly' as far as the Black Sea was, again, thanks to humans. 'American comb jellies' had "stowed away" contained in the ballast water of a ship, and when the same ship emptied it's ballast water in the Dead Sea at the end of it's journey, the Jellyfish had 'migrated' to the other side of the Earth with a truly unnatural speed. That's not all. A short seven years later in the Black Sea the population of this 'American comb jelly' invaders had exploded in such large numbers that they literally caused the "total collapse" of Dead Sea fisheries which raised millions of sardines and anchovies. These sardines and anchovies were unfortunate enough to share the same basic diet of the Jellyfish: plankton. What caused the "total collapse" of these Dead Sea fisheries was the fact that the countless Jellyfish invaders didn't stop at just eating the sardine and anchovies' food supply of plankton, but they also ate the fish's eggs and their living young as well. This 'American comb jelly' which had "stowed away" in a ship's ballast water had caused the "total collapse" of the Dead Sea's fishery industry, and then moved on to spread to the Caspian Sea and the eastern Mediterranean Sea, where they continue their path of death and destruction. Seventeen years later in 2006, these 'American comb jellies' had managed to spread even further, being found in the waters of Holland, Denmark, and Sweden. In 2007 it was found that Danish costal waters were infested with an astounding twenty-five Jellyfish per cubic foot (30.5 cm) of water, and these waters of the area contain the largest population of valuable cod. It has also been found that an 'Australian spotted jellyfish" as well as other foreign species had been introduced to North America before the turn of the century as similar "stow aways" in other ship's ballast water. By the year 2000 these 'Australian spotted jellies' had reproduced to an astounding number of 5,500,000 and were documented in a fifty-seven square mile (91 square kilometer) "bloom" across the Gulf of Mexico. The "Popular Science" article adds another tactic of the Jellyfish to travel worldwide effortlessly at a very quick pace. Even simpler than getting sucked in and dumped out as ballast water of globe traveling ships, the Jellyfish have found a truly effortless way to travel the globe, simply by sticking themselves to the bottom of a boat and taking a free ride, which is called "hull-fouling." The article reports that sixty-nine percent of Jellyfish 'migration' to other parts of the world are directly caused by ballast water "stow aways" and ship's "hull-fouling." The example of the European native 'Moon Jelly' is given, with it's population now found in every single ocean of the Earth. Besides humans fishing the seas dry causing the Jellyfish explosion, we transport them globally to relocate and populate other oceans without even knowing about it. That surely is not all, because the process called "Eutrophication" grows huge amounts of algae through the incredible amount of waste from our sewerage plants and agriculture runoff. These "blooms" of huge amounts of algae deplete the water of oxygen, which quickly kills all fish and creates great conditions for Jellyfish to live in. The last very large factor attributed as a cause of the "Jellyfish Invasion" is the warming global temperature, which in recent years has been hotly and constantly debated, but is nevertheless still believed to be caused by humans and their fetish for industrialization going on the past two centuries. The top 1,000 feet (300 meters) of the world's oceans has risen in temperature half a degree in Fahrenheit over the past half a century, creating ideal conditions for Jellyfish to thrive. Humans have contributed to yet another factor responsible for the "Jellyfish Invasion," because Jellyfish polyps must attach themselves to a surface during their growth, and one of these 'surfaces' they find in ever-growing numbers with ease, are the tremendous amount of new waterfront construction sites worldwide. This increased waterfront construction builds surfaces on shorelines that countless Jellyfish polyps can attach themselves to and develop. As witness to this, across from the huge boom of waterfront construction going on in China, the Sea of Japan has been invaded by countless Jellyfish native to China. Already in 2003 Japanese fishermen had lost twenty million dollars due to this "Jellyfish Invasion." The Jellyfish can be well over 400 pounds (200 kilos) and six feet wide (1.8 meters) each, easily crushing all the fish in the fishing nets, destroying the nets, and even in 2009 capsized a fishing boat. In November, 2009 off the eastern coast of Japan the ten ton fishing boast "Diasan Shinsho-maru" was capsized trying to haul in it's nets which contained dozens of these giant two-hundred kilo Nomura Jellyfish.

In conclusion Human beings have not only created the conditions that are ideal for an explosion of the population of the world's Jellyfish through their combined wizardry of raising the global temperature, fishing the world's seas dry, and pouring an unimaginable amount of waste and pollution into the oceans of the world - but have also been wise and considerate enough to transport these Jellyfish freely and quickly anywhere in any of the seven seas of the Earth, as well as providing housing for their young to safely develop by the incalculable billions. Then as their masterpiece, Human beings in all their deep, studied, measured, and seemingly infinite wisdom began to brutally attack and slaughter these billions of Jellyfish - which they themselves had 'created.' The enlightened wisdom of the Japanese government made a decision which was engineered to be just the opposite of what actually happened: the "fatal blow" to the Jellyfish, but as usual turned out in reality to be the "fatal blow" to any effort designed to decrease or wipeout the Jellyfish. In a true poetic example of "Karma," the Japanese government attempted to eradicate the "Jellyfish Invasion" by dragging wires which were razor sharp through countless numbers of these Jellyfish making up massive "Jellyfish swarms." Fishermen also began cutting up the countless Jellyfish hauled in their fishing nets, and threw the butchered pieces of Jellyfish back into the sea. After that it was discovered that huge female 'Box Jellyfish' being caught after these brutal killing practices were put into action, contained an unnaturally tremendous amount of eggs - millions of eggs each - and that each male being caught also contained an unnaturally large count of sperm, numbering in the billions. The brutal slaughtering efforts designed to decimate the Jellyfish had backfired *exponentially*, in actuality causing an exponential explosion of Jellyfish births! These 500 million year old creatures have survived half a billion years because of their natural defenses. When Jellyfish are attacked or have their lives threatened, such as running razor sharp wires through their colonies or slicing them up into little pieces and throwing them back overboard, they are programmed genetically to unleash a "Breeding Explosion" which ensures their survival. So, simply, by trying to eliminate the Jellyfish, Human beings have increased their numbers exponentially. It is not at all surprising.

On the website of New York's "NBC" a story ran on August 10, 2011 announcing that 'New Jersey's Barnegat Bay was Invaded by Jellyfish numbering Tens of Millions.' New Jersey's shore is a famous seaside resort area with beaches running for miles at a stretch. It was estimated in August, 2011 that Jellyfish numbering in the "tens of millions" had taken up residence in Barnegat Bay, the largest estuary in New Jersey. The article reports that at times swimming was not possible, and for this and other reasons rentals of beachfront accommodations had also been effected. These Jellyfish in Barnegat Bay are commonly called 'sea nettles,' and their invasion was begun to be noticed around the year 2005 or 2006, but over the last five or six years it has been described 'like a tsunamis' with millions of Jellyfish invading swimming areas and also disrupting boating. What Monclair State University biologist Jack Gaynor calls a first-class "pest" is this 'sea nettle,' which can produce 40,000 eggs each day. This biologist also explains one of the strengths of this seemingly unstoppable "Jellyfish Invasion" is that the polyps of the Jellyfish can themselves become "asexual" and go on to reproduce "dozens" of offspring. As the New York "NBC" article then clearly states, this "gets worse." As was discovered on the shorefront construction sites of China, in New Jersey Jellyfish polyps also need a solid surface to attach themselves to for their developmental stage. So, in New Jersey the fore-mentioned "Jersey Shore" beachfront resorts and homes have also contributed to the "Jellyfish Invasion," because the Jellyfish polyps have a perfect surface to attach themselves to and develop in the multi-millions. This article goes on to reveal that besides the thousands of existing shorefront buildings for Jellyfish polyps to attach themselves to, there is an additional development along Jersey shores currently with the construction of additional "thousands" of new homes. The other major contributor documented in this 2011 "NBC" article is the increasing nitrogen in the New Jersey waters caused by runoff from people all over "The Garden State" fertilizing their lawns. Along with the enormous amount of cars burning fossil fuels in New Jersey giving off nitrogen, added to the New Jersey's power plants which are coal-powered and also give off huge amounts of nitrogen, and you end up with what the "NBC" article calls an 'upended ecosystem.' Increased nitrogen causes huge blooms of algae which deplete the water of oxygen when dying, and then are consumed by bacteria. The fish that are naturally the Jellyfish's predators and would in normal circumstances eat the Jellyfish and stabilize the population, are killed by the oxygen-depleted water, and the same worldwide story is repeated in New Jersey: the water is left just for the Jellyfish, because oxygen-depleted water is just fine for Jellyfish. First humans have polluted the oceans of the world with excess nitrogen coming from their cars, fertilizers, and industries, which was efficient at wiping out the Jellyfish's predators, and which also created the right environment for Jellyfish to take over the oceans of the world. A perfect recipe for global disaster.

After reading the previous horror stories of the "Jellyfish Invasion" the reader may think to themselves 'So what - who gives a damn - I'm not a fisherman.' Besides the essential food supply that is being decimated by massive explosions of Jellyfish numbers throughout the globe's oceans, and can lead to a disruption in the food chain of life on Earth including Human beings, even the 'nonessential' is being dramatically effected. Over the past not-too-many years there has been a new "Forecast" added around the world to the existing forecasts, such as 'weather forecasting,' for major global areas of seaside resorts and areas even for swimming: "Jellyfish Forecasts!" At first impression these may seem like the rantings of a madman - or someone in a doomsday cult - until you realize that this news report came from one of the biggest television stations in New York City: "NBC." And that is only the very beginning. As an example of just how serious this worldwide "Jellyfish Invasion" is, on June 28, 2012 the Washington D.C. radio station "WTOP" gave a news report about not only "Jellyfish Forecasting," but a new smartphone "App." that allows anyone to check their "Jellyfish Forecast" before thinking about going to the beach(!) The "NBC" news report explains that in the Washington D.C. area swimming waters there lives the same Jellyfish which caused the New Jersey Barnegat Bay "Jellyfish Explosion" during the summer of 2011: 'Sea Nettles.' An oceanographer Christopher Brown of the National Oceanic and Atmospheric Administration reported that although these 'Sea Nettles' begin appearing every summer around Washington D.C. in July or August, for 2012 they were forecast to appear earlier, and were also forecast by Brown to be present in the D.C. waters longer than in previous years as well. Not only that, but the oceanographer also reported to the "Delaware Coast Press" that the right conditions exist in 2012 to expect the Jellyfish to appear in Washington D.C. swimming waters in "large numbers." The majority of this "WTOP" news report is centered on this new mobile telephone App. available for Washington D.C. and surrounding area residents who swim in the nearby Chesapeake Bay. This App. for smartphones forecasts both the weather conditions in the Chesapeake Bay, as well as giving swimmers a "Jellyfish Forecast." Over the past several years buoys have been strategically placed throughout the Chesapeake Bay which constantly monitor the salinity of the ocean, the temperature of the water, and the height of the waves. This "WTOP" news story proudly announces that now anyone in the Washington D.C. vicinity can simply connect with their mobile smartphone to the nearest floating forecasting buoy in the Chesapeake Bay and receive their forecast, called a "Sea Nettle Probability." The buoys' forecasts are based on the temperature and salinity of sea water, because 'Sea Nettles' prefer warm waters between seventy-nine and eighty-six degrees (26-30 C.), as well as a specific range of sea water salinity. So, not in the movies, but in Washington D.C., anyone on the way to go swimming in the Chesapeake Bay can now pick up their smartphone and receive a real-time Jellyfish forecast from the "Chesapeake Bay Interpretive Buoy System." Once again, this is not something used only by 'doomsday prophets,' but perhaps even by the President of the United States(!)

Almost at the same time, in April 2012 a large report about the 'Soaring Global Jellyfish Population' appeared in the "National Post" written by Brian Hutchinson. The news report began with the very first sentence warning of exploding Jellyfish populations worldwide. The report was based on the findings of five scientists of the University of British Columbia, who published their work in the scientific journal "Hydrobiologia." Details are given of the "Jellyfish Invasion" such as sometimes lethal stings obviously ruining seaside holidays, as well as huge numbers of Jellyfish clogging drainpipes and seawater intakes (which effected Nuclear Reactors already both in Great Britain and Japan), clogging the nets of fishermen, and even capsizing their fishing boats. Lucas Brotz, who is a doctoral student at the University of British Columbia has been studying changes in the sea over the past sixty years which universally point to the same thing: Jellyfish populations are greatly increasing worldwide. It has been found in these studies that the largest increase in Jellyfish population worldwide is concentrated around areas most densely populated by Human beings as well. The hardest hit areas with literal "Jellyfish Invasions" are reported by Brotz to be the coasts of Europe, Asia, and the former sardine and anchovies fishery area of the Black Sea. Another disturbing fact revealed by the UBC report by Brotz and his team is that the "Jellyfish Invasion" is not exclusively centered around areas of human activity, but that swarms of Jellyfish have also infested the waters surrounding Antarctica. The causes for this worldwide "Jellyfish Invasion" are reported over and over again in each newspaper, magazine, or scientific paper, and again in this Brian Hutchinson "National Post" report: the deadly combination created solely by Human beings, who overfish the seas dry, as well as throw more pollution into the world's oceans than is conceivable. The less fish that are left in the oceans through human overfishing directly means more food for the Jellyfish in the form of plankton. As well as giving the Jellyfish more food to eat, humans overfishing the seas have also greatly reduced the natural predators of Jellyfish such as salmon. This "National Post" article also published a map of the world with Color-coded "Jellyfish population" indications. This "University of British Columbia Public Affairs" Jellyfish map clearly shows that the highest level of increased Jellyfish population is in the vicinity off of Alaska, the northeast coast of the United States, Hawaii, the entire coast of China, southwest Africa, and completely surrounding Antarctica.

This "National Post" report from April, 2012 concludes with the facts that Human beings, who are directly responsible for the worldwide "Jellyfish Invasion," have no use or love of the half billion year old Jellyfish inhabiting the oceans of the world, and even refer to them as the sea's "cockroaches." Besides the large number of Jellyfish used in pet foods worldwide, the Russians have discovered another use for these Jellyfish, which are mashed up and added to cement to construct stronger buildings out of. One of the most disturbing parts of this "National Post" April 2012 news report are the public comments posted at the end of the article. One genius suggests nothing less than the creation of a genetically altered "Peanut Butter and Jelly Fish." On a website reporting on the "Jellyfish Invasion" a typical reaction was published by someone who states that she knew the Jellyfish have been on Earth many millions of years longer than humans, but despite this she also claims that the Jellyfish are spoiling her favorite seaside resort areas, so they "must go."

A news report on the internet announces that France has also released a similar "jelly-fish forecast." The famous seaside region of the French Riviera began on July 1, 2012 to publish what this internet report labels as an "unusual" jelly-fish "forecast" designed to be an early-warning system warning visitors to French seasides of a jelly-fish "raid." The French ocean laboratory by Villefranche-sur-Mer now publishes on-line early-warning Jellyfish Warning Forecasts every forty-eight hours. This news report also lists two other websites which are subsidized by the EU, and which will regularly release "jelly-fish alerts" for the seaside resort areas from Saint Tropez to Marseilles. These websites are named "Medazurs" and "jellywatch."

On the "Practical Fishkeeping" website from July, 2012 as well, another report appeared announcing the new 'Jellyfish Forecasts in the French Riviera.' Also explained in this report is the new French Riviera Jellyfish "early-warning system" started on July 1, 2012. This "Practical Fishkeeping" article states that up to five-hundred swimmers a day are stung by the 'Mauve stinger' or "Pelagia noctiluca" in these French Riviera waters. Besides the new on-line "Jellyfish Forecast" reports being published every forty-eight hours by the oceanological institute in Villefranche-sur-Mer, there are already "anti-jellyfish nets" used in the area. The report closes with little hope in view, because to reverse the 'Jellyfish explosion' there must be environmental changes, as well as the natural predators of the Jellyfish such as the turtle and tuna's return to the seas. Dream on.

In August, 2012 a news report was published by the "Telegraph" announcing that 'Deadly Jellyfish Close Spanish Beaches.' The grim report begins with what is called an "unprecedented plague" of "deadly jellyfish" for the beaches all across the northwest coast of Spain. This "unprecedented plague" of jellyfish has caused the authorities to warn swimmers to stay out of the ocean. The areas most severely effected were the seaside resorts between Galicia and Asturias of the northwest coast of Spain. Hundreds of thousands of Jellyfish wash ashore and 'Portuguese man o' war' were also seen in the region's coastal areas, as well as "enormous blooms" of the 'Mauve stinger jellyfish.' Details are given of these 'man o' war' Jellyfish stings, with thirty yard (meter) long tentacles and a stinger at each tentacle end that can cause painful welts for three days, or even heart failure. This "Telegraph" article also reports that these 'Mauve stinger jellyfish' are Bioluminescent, emitting a "yellowish glow" in the dark. Luis Lara, in charge of the marine species protection organization "Cepesma" was quoted as calling the "Jellyfish Invasion" a plague with proportions that have never been seen before.

The tourist website 'Getting by in Malta' posted a warning as well in July, 2012, which informed swimmers in the Malta waters of Jellyfish. The 'Jellyfish Warning' was posted in Malta because of an anticipated increase in the numbers of Jellyfish populating the swimming waters for the summer of 2012. The article publishes a 'Spot the Jellyfish' public awareness chart with photographs of a dozen different Jellyfish which swimmers might see in the waters, with the title "Painful Sting" at the top of the chart. The author of this Jellyfish warning article suggests that to avoid getting stung by a Jellyfish while swimming in Malta it is best to swim only inside restricted areas containing 'Protection nets" in the sea which keep the invading Jellyfish out.

To clarify the warnings for swimmers in the Malta area, the "SD Weather Service" publishes on the internet a "Year Round" Sea and Jellyfish Forecast which is posted every sixteen days. This extensive charting system is divided into sections on Malta, Comino, and Gozo, with two separate charts for each of the three localities that are published as "Sea Forecast" and "Jellyfish Forecast." The "Sea Forecast" and "Jellyfish Forecast" charts are divided into sixteen different swimming locations in Malta, such as Anchor Bay, Blue Grotto, and Paradise Bay, four different localities in Comino, and ten in Gozo, with the "Sea Forecasts" advising either "Suitable," "Not Suitable," or 'Suitable only for good swimmers.' The same extensive charts are next published every sixteen days for these three localities as a "Jellyfish Forecast," with each day for each locality showing either a Green check or a picture of a Jellyfish, indicating that Jellyfish are predicted in the swimming waters of that particular area charted, and to avoid swimming in that area on that day. Sounds wonderful. To give an idea of the seriousness of the

"Jellyfish Invasion," almost all of the thirty individual swimming bays or areas charted in Malta, Comino, and Gozo are infested with Jellyfish and unadvisable to swim in for more than half of the sixteen days presented on the internet. In the "Blue Lagoon" in Comino it is advised to stay out of the ocean for all sixteen days. Nice vacation.

As imagined with these examples presented, "Jellyfish Forecasts" have become a common essential system in place throughout many swimming areas of the world already - this is not 'proposed,' or 'in the planning,' but reality in 2012. The 'Israel Oceanographic Research' website also published a "weekly report" and a "Watch poster" for Jellyfish in 2012. Also easily found on the internet is the "Arrival Calendar" published as a "Jellyfish Forecast" for the beaches of Hawaii. The 2012 calendar is broken into twelve months on this Hawaii "Jellyfish Forecast," with indications on the individual days of the year for both "Jellyfish invasion" and the full moon. At the bottom of this "Arrival Calendar" for Jellyfish on Hawaiian beaches, it is advised to observe Jellyfish "warning signs" on beaches, swim only on "guarded beaches," and to ask lifeguards about Jellyfish in the water. This website also states that the 'box jellyfish' is the most common type found in the swimming waters of Hawaii, usually on the west and south shores, and that these Jellyfish almost always arrive between nine and twelve days after the full moon. The 'Portuguese man o' war' is also found on the eastern shores of Hawaii, and it is warned in general not to swim at unguarded remote beaches.

So Saint Tropez and the French Riviera, Malta, Israel, Spain, France, and Hawaii, all found nearly instantly on the internet with their individual published warnings or entire "Jellyfish Forecasts" on a regular basis today. These are not the rantings of a madman or even science fiction - this is the world in 2012. If "Jellyfish Invasions" shutting down Nuclear Reactors, killing the fish, taking over the oceans for themselves, destroying fishery areas of the world, destroying fishing industries, capsizing fishing boats, and even invading in such unprecedented numbers which necessitate countries around the world publishing "Jellyfish Forecasts" to warn swimmers to stay out of the sea - if all of this doesn't sound extremely serious, it's questionable what could. The "International Business Times" website of July 15, 2011 published a news report with photographs of the "Jellyfish Invasion" shutting down four Nuclear Reactors in Israel, Japan, and Scotland. This 2011 news report documents four Nuclear Reactors being forced to "shutdown" because of enormous Jellyfish swarms which clogged the cooling systems of these Nuclear Reactors. In July 2011 the Orot Rabin Nuclear Reactor in Hadera, Israel had to shutdown when the reactor's coolant water was blocked by swarms of Jellyfish. Towards the end of June 2011 a Nuclear Reactor of Shimane, Japan also was forced to shutdown, as well as the two Nuclear Reactors of the Torness power station in Scotland. The four Nuclear Reactors from Scotland to Israel and Japan were shutdown exclusively by the "Jellyfish Invasion" clogging the "cooling waters screens" of all four of these Reactors.

Again, these were not insignificant public facilities such as Sewerage plants or Water recycling - but crucial Nuclear Reactors. Also not considered in the news reports covering these Jellyfish shutdowns of four Nuclear Reactors from Great Britain to Japan are the consequences of these Jellyfish attacks on these four Reactors. If the "Jellyfish Invasion" had not been detected as the source of the clogging of the cooling waters for these four Nuclear Reactors, and the Jellyfish had completely clogged the cooling water intakes, the final result would have been nothing less than catastrophic, because all four of these Nuclear Reactors spread from Great Britain to the Middle east and Japan would have been cut off from their essential cooling waters for the nuclear reactions taking place in the four reactors - and finally would have caused a complete "Meltdown" of all four reactors, which would have spread Radioactivity in massive amounts from all four of these Nuclear Reactors. Chernobyl times four - and not in a remote area of Russia - but in Scotland, Israel, and Japan - densely populated areas of human inhabitation spread around three-quarters of the globe. Another nearly unbelievable report was in 2006, when close to Brisbane, Australia the huge aircraft carrier "Ronald Reagen" during it's maiden voyage was crippled and defeated not by a military maneuver, but also by Jellyfish. Think of it - the Jellyfish have begun taking over the oceans of the world, which has two direct effects on humans: one effect is the loss of a huge amount of human's food supply in the form of fish, crabs, lobsters, etc., while the other effect is to keep people out of the water or get stung by Jellyfish. Not only does this "Jellyfish Invasion" have the potential to eradicate a portion of the food supply of the Human race, but with the recent attacks on the cooling water intakes of four reported shutdown Nuclear Reactors in densely populated regions of the globe, this "Jellyfish Invasion" has obviously increased in potential.

As stated at the beginning of this section, the quote from the end of H.G. Well's "War of the Worlds" in which it is clearly explained that of all of God's creatures on Earth to stop the 'Alien Invasion' by Martians, the most insignificant of these creatures accomplished this seemingly impossible feat. The quote also explains that these 'Invaders' of Earth had not earned the right to live here, which only comes about from countless millennia of generations living and dying on this Earth and very gradually becoming immune through countless deaths to this same bacteria which quickly killed the 'Alien Invaders.' Not in a book or a movie - but in the real world - the extremely disturbing fact is that we must think of *ourselves* as the Earth's 'Alien

Invaders' - *not* the Jellyfish. The Jellyfish have been living on Earth for half a billion years - five-hundred million years - millions of years before the first Dinosaurs were born, and nearly infinitely longer than Human beings. We must realize that to assume a similar situation as the end of H.G. Well's "War of the Worlds," the *Jellyfish* are the creatures who have earned the right through countless millions of generations to inhabit the Earth - and the Human beings who have done nothing but pollute and shit upon the Earth for the past centuries are nothing less than the 'Alien Invaders.' As written at the beginning of this section, what the "Jellyfish Invasion" can be seen as is the "Self-Defense" of the Earth, the last-chance effort of our planet - our "Grandmother Earth" - to rebalance itself and to heal itself from the relentless onslaught of the 'Alien Invaders' called Human beings. And the "Jellyfish Invasion," as serious as it has become today, is only a mere fraction of the Earth's "Self-Defense," because just by "coincidence," another pivotal 'insignificant' creature has begun to greatly effect the human race, most significantly in our food supply as well: Bees.

If it is not believed that Human beings have altered the Earth beyond the point of no return, then it is probably not known that science has named a new Geological epoch to include the present era we live in: "The Anthroplescien" - "The Human Epoch"(!) Every year twenty-six million tons of Plastic ends up thrown into the oceans, in fact so much of it that there is a name for a huge deposit, "The Eastern Pacific Garbage Patch." The plastic eventually gets broken down into smaller particles by sunlight, and these smaller particles of plastic sink to the floor of the oceans where they get buried, which is the first stage of the plastic's transformation into the Sedimentary rock of the Earth. This plastic which is buried on the bottom of the oceans will eventually form into the new strata of the planet and will forever be identified as our "Plastic Legacy." In just a year's time human machinery transforms more Earth than all of nature's processes put together. Humans have altered over three-quarters of the ice-free landscape of the Earth. In just a year's time humans burn into the atmosphere thirty-one billion barrels of oil, which calculates to an unbelievable *one-thousand barrels of oil a second!* In just a year's time the human race burns the amount of oil that the Earth took three million years to create. In 2006 the Human race achieved another commendable accomplishment: for the first time a volcano was caused to erupt through human intervention. In 2006 developers were probing for gas in Indonesia and drilled 3,000 meters (yards) deep. When the drill was withdrawn from the 3,000 meter deep hole it caused first the pressure to drop in the drilled hole, and then the fracturing of the underground rock. The underground water under pressure burst through the drilled hole and combined with ground mud to form a boiling mixture called a "Mud Volcano." Every day after this "Mud Volcano" was created by drilling for gas, forty Olympic size swimming pools worth of boiling mud erupted out of it. On "National Geographic's" website a report was published in March 2011 in which the amount of boiling mud that will erupt from this "Mud Volcano" caused by human intervention was quoted at 56,000 Olympic size swimming pools over the course of twenty-six years after 2011. On the "Voice of America" news website it was reported in May 2011 that some scientists estimate more like eighty years until the "Mud Volcano" stops erupting boiling mud. A Durham University geologist is quoted as saying that this Mud Volcano 'behaves entirely unnaturally,' and that it has now erupted 'continuously for the last five years.' This geologist Davies states that the human drilling for gas caused the unnatural development of a Mud Volcano in just five years, instead of nature's 5,000 or 10,000 year timespan, and that this has never happened before in history. Not only does the company drilling for gas in 2006 'deny responsibility' for the brand new Mud Volcano, but this same company was planning to begin a brand new project drilling for gas again - only a little over a mile away from the still-erupting Mud Volcano they created! Many methods of stopping the continuous flow of boiling mud from the volcano have been attempted, such as building huge levies around the volcano opening, and even just throwing concrete blocks into the hole, but nothing has stopped the power of nature that was unleashed by drilling 3,000 meters deep into the Earth in their financially-driven search for gas. Let's not even begin to discuss the new swiftly-spreading genius idea of "Fracking."

Human intervention in the natural condition and mechanics of the Earth began about 11,000 years ago when the development of farming spread from just the Fertile Crescent, and then again 7,000 years ago when farming spread around the world. Early farmers used fire to clear forest for creating farm lands, which caused the carbon dioxide level in the atmosphere to rise, and their farm animals produced additional methane. Scientists believe that these increased levels of carbon dioxide and methane directly caused by human farming was the reason that a new Ice-age did not begin 10,000 years ago. This increase globally of human farming alone is believed to have stopped the beginning of this new Ice-age. That began our role as a force of nothing less than planetary change. 5,000 years ago humans made the discovery of metal ores inside of rocks, such as copper inside of malachite, which could be used for making tools. Huge civilizations could form by 2,000 years ago when humans discovered ways to tap and exploit natural water supplies. Sailors learned to develop major trade routes by exploiting the power of the wind 500 years ago. Perhaps the most environmentally damaging discovery of humans happened relatively recently within the last few centuries, with the discoveries of coal and oil's potentials of enormous energy trapped inside these fossil fuels of the Earth's interior.

The distance the contemporary 'modern' Human beings - "Homo sapiens sapiens" - have strayed from their natural path is infinitely further than the point of no return - so much further that it could be unfathomable. Trying to imagine the absolutely natural roots of our very long-lost ancestors would be as impossible as trying to identify the source of the individual atoms of our bodies one by one. The distance that the modern person has travelled from their birthright as completely natural beings living in a symbiotic harmony with the world around them - the plants, the water, and the air - the distance that the modern person has strayed from these absolute natural beings that they began as millennia ago, was achieved by the advent of modernism, then industrialization, and presently gentrification, to arrive after thousands of generations of evolution into the present state of self-consuming egotists. What a fruitful journey! All that remains today is the husk of this formerly enlightened creature - only the crumbs of aware, completely natural beings who lived in perfect harmony and with deep respect for their world. Just the skeleton of this enlightened creature remains, who has evolved after countless generations into nothing more than Bipedal Bacteria - or clearer to the truth, Bipedal Virus.

Two years ago when returning to the west from a spiritual journey in India for the Kumbh Mela in Hardwar, you wonder what the world's people could possibly be thinking about living their lives the way they appear to. The shallowness, the life void of spiritual values, or even rituals, which are imbued in the lives of people in India. You wonder "Is this ALL?" Can life be so empty and purged of it's most essential elements? Can people live all their lives like this? Apparently so, and they also multiply like rats. Only the thinest veneer is acceptable anymore - and even that must be "transparent." The most profound primitive composition of ourselves is being chipped away person-by person, one-by-one. Compassion, non-violence, love - in this western society these are only words spoken in church - or on talk shows. The loss of wonderment and personal exploration, which are signatory of more contemplative times, deserves the greatest mourning of all. The mad Lemming-like rush for commodities and commerce has numbed the senses, and through this loss of feeling, the ability to acquire more commodities and commerce for the individual multiplies exponentially. A hopelessly vicious cycle. But, besides this majority numbering in the billions on this world, there is none the less a minority of the population who have chosen to not go along for the entire miserable roller-coaster ride. A precious few have even managed to amazingly get off the roller-coaster ride all together with, if this can be imagined anymore. The third question in the great trio asked by Gauguin in his masterpiece is perhaps the most important question to contemplate in this era of the human race: "Ou Allons Nous?" 'Where are we going?' Can the spiral towards the individual person being inspected microscopically by society be rapidly gaining momentum? The loss of the individual is such an old concept that it has become a cliché, but these words should ring in people's ears every day, because if not, then the eventual loss of individuality will be the inevitable result of the equation that is now in the process of being calculated. Greed and Lust have become the universally acknowledged calling cards of society; the most base and primitive parts, which society has managed to manifest into the most desired for assets that life can offer anymore. In the end, and this is surely what it is, most folks today can't even imagine that there exists anything better than money and sex.

Luckily for most 'folks,' after the Jellyfish take over the oceans of the world, and the pollinating Bees disappear from the face of the Earth, there will be nothing left except 'money and sex.' This other reciprocal catastrophe that is simultaneously upon the planet is the "Bee Catastrophe." Besides the disappearance of the fish from the sea caused by both overfishing and the "Jellyfish Invasion," a full *one-third* of all the food eaten by the human race will not exist anymore after the Bees disappear. The "Washington Times" reported in March, 2012 that the amount of food pollinated by Bees and then eaten by humans is in the order of nineteen billion dollars per year in the United States alone, and for the worldwide estimate the figure of two-hundred and seventeen billion dollars worth of food will disappear each year. The Bees are disappearing and the world's agriculture will be on the verge of collapse because of this loss. March 27, 2012 saw a government action in the United States in which the beekeepers were asked for advice on saving the remaining Bee populations to avoid a literal "collapse" of the agriculture in the U.S. Jeffrey Pettis of the U.S. Department of Agriculture reported that the situation in America with the Bee collapse is on the borderline of becoming a "crisis," and that the "pollinating demands" are barely being met. Millions of dollars are being spent by the U.S. government on a "Bee Catastrophe" data base to try and find just the cause of the Bee disappearance. Pettis reported that the "Bee Catastrophe" began to be felt in national production of food about 2007, when the population of the Bees began to disappear by up to one-third in numbers. U.S. Congress along with the "National Institute of Food and Agriculture" granted 5.6 million dollars for the establishment of a massive national Bee database "Bee Informed Partnership." The plan is to employ the same methods used by cancer epidemiologists for human populations, which will then be applied to the Bee populations in an effort to discover what causes the Bee disappearance. The "BIP" also began a website on which beekeepers across the U.S. will report and compare notes and procedures in an attempt to arrest this massive disappearance of pollinating Bees. The severity of the "Bee Catastrophe" is summed up in the bottom line of this "Washington Times" 2012 news report, where it is plainly stated that 'If the U.S. looses it's Bees, then the United States as it is known today is also lost.' According to the Bumble Bee Conservatory website, the loss will be approximately eighty-four percent of all of Europe's crops, which are exclusively Bee pollinated.

A very clear scholarly report in 2010 was made by Maneka Gandhi of "People For Animals," the largest Animal Welfare Organization in India. The very first sentence of Gandhi's report is a clear warning to the future, in which it is plainly stated again that a full one-third of all the food we eat is the direct result of pollination by Honey Bees. The essential pollination of plants through their fertilized flowers is what makes fruits and vegetable grow. Without pollinating Bees these pollinated fruits and vegetables will simply disappear like the Bees themselves, causing worldwide starvation as well as financial disaster.

Gandhi reminds the reader that the partnership which has existed for millennia between plants and Bees is nothing less than "essential" for life. Almost all of humanity's main crops are absolutely dependent on pollinating Bees, as well as all of the fruits. Not just humans, but human's food source, such as the cattle raised for meat, also depend on alfalfa to eat, which is again pollinated by Bees.

The massive Bee disappearance has been named "Colony Collapse Disorder" - "CCD" - by scientists, which precisely describes what is happening around the world as Bees fly away from the colonies in vast numbers to search for pollen, and then they simply disappear. Not only hasn't a cure for this catastrophe been found, but even the *cause* hasn't been discovered yet. The odd part is that researchers have found that the Bees die in the field from disorientation and exhaustion, but that they have never found the dead Bees. The shocking fact is that since 2006 over one-quarter of the 2.4 million Bee colonies in America have disappeared. This estimates at tens of billions of Bees. All across Great Britain, Greece, Germany, Italy, Portugal, Poland, Spain, and Switzerland as well as in other countries using pesticides, the Bee colonies have been devastated. Even far from Europe, in India and in Brazil the "Bee Catastrophe" begins to be reported.

One of the most intelligent Human beings ever to have lived, Albert Einstein himself knew this (of course) and is quoted, some say falsely, as believing that 'If Bees disappear from the Earth, then humanity would have only four years left to live. No Bees, no pollination, no plants, no animals, no man.'

Maneka Gandhi writes about society barely noticing the disappearances of other recently endangered animals, such as the cheetah, but rightfully concludes that if the Bees are lost, then "everything" is lost. The three main culprits of this "Bee Catastrophe" are still far from positive, but are now believed by scientists to be pesticides, mercury, and Genetically-Modified crops. It has been discovered that Bees crawling into flowers come into contact with pollutants such as pesticides and heavy-metals, which sticks to their bodies and are then carried back to the colonies. These pesticides and heavy-metals such as mercury are then mixed into the produced honey, pollen, and beeswax by being rubbed off the body of the Bee. Research into the DNA of Bees has discovered that these ancient insects have no genes to remove poisons from their bodies, and very few genes to fight disease.

Forty-eight tons of Mercury is released into the atmosphere each year by power plants across the world, while the estimate for the annual use of pesticides worldwide is in the millions of tons. Mercury is a very well known cause of brain damage as well as damage to the nervous system, even in higher animals such as Human beings. Pesticide use on crops and seeds has been studied in respect to the "Bee Catastrophe" in the countries of the United States, Italy, France, the Czech Republic, and Romania. The President of the American Beekeeping Federation believes that the "Bee Catastrophe" is being caused solely by pesticides. This opinion is also supported by reports of "organic" beekeepers who use no pesticides or chemicals on their Bees, and have suffered no "Bee Catastrophe" or "CCD" at all, even in cases where they are situated close to nonorganic Bee colonies which have been effected by this "CCD."

Also closely being examined as a cause of the "Bee Catastrophe," are the ever-popular "Genetically-Modified" crops, such as corn and wheat. These Genetically-Modified crops have been positively discovered to cause butterflies to die, so these "GM" crops are also being studied as possible killers of the Bees. Gandhi discusses the book "Beware of the Coming Food Apocalypse" in which a German study found that Genetically-Modified corn contains bacterial toxin, which may have caused the alteration of the intestines of the Bee, and which weakens the Bee and makes them susceptible to parasites. Gandhi concludes her article with the wise observation that 'When the Bees start dying, it's just a short time before humans do too.'

An alarming article was published in "The Observer" by Alison Benjamin in May 2010 where the facts are presented of the United States loosing one-third of their Bee colonies for a forth year in a row. Also again documented is the possible cause of this "Bee Catastrophe" being pesticides. In the U.S. scientists have discovered one-hundred and twenty-one different pesticides in both the Bee's bodies as well as in the beeswax and the pollen. Beekeeper Dave Hackenberg of "Hackenberg

Apiaries" was the first to notice the "CCD" only some years ago, and reported to "The Observer" that between May 2009 and April 2010 a full sixty-two percent of Bees living in his 2,600 Beehives died. Another researcher compared the inability to find a definitive cause for the "Bee Catastrophe" after so much time and money has been spent on the cause, to the inability of finding a cure for AIDS after decades and billions of dollars in research has been spent on the cause.

This May, 2010 article in "The Observer" concludes with a section 'Why Do Bees Matter,' in which the facts are given on Bee population, and in which it is revealed that ninety different food crops which are sold commercially worldwide are absolutely dependent on Bee pollination. No Bees, no ninety different food crops worldwide-period. Such well known foods like fruits and vegetables, including apples, oranges, carrots, strawberries, onions, nuts, and products such a coffee, alfalfa, and cotton would disappear if the Bees disappear. Not to mention the obvious honey. The results of a Bee-less environment would be what "The Observer" calls a 'meatless colorless diet consisting of rice and cereals, cotton-less clothing, a landscape barren of flowers, and a collapsed food chain for animals and birds.' Sounds wonderful.

A general review of endless articles on the "Bee Catastrophe" all point to identical findings, which report on over three million Honey Bee colonies being completely lost around the world since 1996, and the cause of this "Bee Catastrophe" being suspected as pesticides. "Bee Blessed" honey of North Carolina reports that business is great and that there has been no "Bee Catastrophe" on this Beehive farm. What's the difference between the "Bee Blessed" Bee farm and most other Bee farms with massive Bee death counts? The "Bee Blessed" Bee farm is an "Organic" Bee farm that does not use pesticides or any other unnatural chemicals on their Bees, and does not feed their Bees with corn syrup containing pesticides. There are many examples of this same story easily found in magazines, newspapers, and on the internet, all which retell the same details of their Bee population being healthy, and completely unaffected by the drastic "Bee Catastrophe" - and every single one of these examples are written about Beekeepers who run "Organic" Bee farms without using pesticides and who feed their Bees with "Organic" corn syrup which is pesticide free. In 2010 the World Organization for Animal Health made a global review covering the Bee deaths worldwide, and concluded that although there seems to be no single cause for the "Bee Catastrophe," the organization singled out what they believe to be the most likely cause: pesticides 'irresponsibly used.'

In May, 2010 even a children's book was published on the contemporary subject, "The Hive Detectives: Chronicle of a Honey Bee Catastrophe" by Loree Griffin Burns. It seems to be a universal finding that the Bees are disappearing and that the rest of life will be effected in lesser or greater degrees because of it. Even articles written with a conservative view by people of science also agree without hysteria that there is a worldwide "Bee Catastrophe." One such long article is entitled "Disappearing Bees," with very clear facts given. First of all the article begins by stating that the Einstein quote about 'Bee disappearance' might not be written by Albert Einstein himself, but by a group of French Beekeepers in 1992. Also stated in this article is the opinion that if the Bees did indeed disappear, humans would not also disappear, but just have a much more unpleasant life. "Disappearing Bees" quotes Dr. Roberts of the Centre of Agri-Environmental Research in Reading University speaking before the Federation of Middlesex Beekeepers, who clarified the fact that there are around the world nine Honey Bee species, two-hundred and forty Bumble Bee species, and 19,300 other varied Bee species. Having said this, Dr. Roberts went on to explain that keeping statistics on Bee disappearances worldwide would be nearly an impossible task, so his team has concentrated on just the UK and the Netherlands. The results were very disturbing, just in this small examined area, with Bee colonies having decreased in numbers by twenty-three percent and Beekeepers disappearing by thirty-six percent across central Europe since 1985. The research also clearly proved declines in both insect pollinators and the pollinated plants across both the UK and the Netherlands. This proves that the Bees are disappearing, that the "Bee Catastrophe" effects all Bees, and that this catastrophe is widespread. Besides the pesticide pollution, this article also points to the effect of "Habitat loss" for Bees worldwide as another cause of "CCD." A further very graphic point made by this "Disappearing Bees" article is that there is simply no alternative to insect pollination of fruit and vegetable plants globally. Dr. Roberts has experimented with a team of students in Reading University, who were given the task of pollinating plants by hand with paint brushes. Even the Oman government experimented with human pollination by hand of Date palms, and both teams in Reading University and Oman came to the same conclusion, simply that it is impossible. The findings of Dr. Roberts and his team were published in the paper 'Parallel Declines in Pollinators and Insect-Pollinated Plants in Britain and the Netherlands.'

In 2011 a film opened named "Queen of the Sun," in which the Bee situation and all the mystery surrounding the Bee disappearance is carefully examined. The film goes back to the first person who foresaw the present "Bee Catastrophe," Rudolf Steiner in 1923. This scholar gave lectures in 1923 named "The Bee," in which he clearly predicted that within eighty to one-hundred years the consequences of human mechanization of Beekeeping and Bee farms, which for all of time had been natural without human intervention, would become very apparent. Rudolf Steiner saw into the future with scientific accuracy, warning humanity that if they continued to disturb natural Bee hive production, disturb Queen Bees, and create a mechanized human profit-driven approach to a natural organic balance achieved through countless millennia by Bees, this human intervention would in eighty to one-hundred years cause a 'mass disappearance of bees.' Eighty years after his prediction was indeed 2003. As a testament to his vision and intelligence, Rudolf Steiner, who died just two years after his 1923 lecture series on "The Bee," also stated clearly that the greedy side of human intervention in Bee production is to blame. Steiner warned to not apply the same 'regressive and materialistic' human conditions to the Bee hives, or they would die, period. Obviously, failing to heed the warnings of Rudolf Steiner in 1923, Human beings have materialistically decimated Bee populations worldwide in the name of greed through such unnatural techniques including artificially inseminating Queen Bees, clipping the Queen Bee's wings, and by using tons of pesticides along with a huge amount of other chemical pollutants.

On March 11, 2011 the United Nations Environmental Programme (UNEP) presented their report named "Global Honey Bee Colony Disorder and Other Treats to Insects." This United Nations report also concluded that increased chemical use in agriculture, especially insecticides and chemicals used for coating seeds, are either toxic or damaging to Bees. This UNEP report concludes with the fact that this Bee decline points to "serious consequences" for the world's "food security."

This "Disappearing Bees" article gives the same advice as a multitude of other contemporary articles on the "Bee Catastrophe" subject, advising individual gardeners to plant flowers which are "Bee-friendly," create habitats for Bees in your private garden, educate yourself about the "Bee Catastrophe," don't kill wild flowers or flowering 'weeds' in your garden, Do Not use pesticides or chemicals in your garden or on your lawn, and support and eat "Organic" food grown without any pesticides or unnatural chemicals.

In "The New Yorker" magazine an article was published on April 20, 2012 entitled "Silent Hives." This clear scholarly study on the "Bee Catastrophe" was published on the fifty year anniversary of a three-part series in "The New Yorker" magazine from June, 1962 similarly entitled "Silent Spring." In this "Silent Spring" series from half a century ago it's author Rachel Carson warned deaf ears about the effect on wildlife from the use of pesticides. The author of this article "Silent Hives" fifty years later in "The New Yorker," Elizabeth Kolbert, begins with the early warnings given in 2006 when the Bee disappearances began to be seen worldwide. As mentioned in many other articles, the Beekeeper from Pennsylvania Dave Hackenberg was the first person to try alerting others about the Bee collapse "CCD." Elizabeth Kolbert states that in her 2007 interview with Hackenberg he was sure that a virus, or stress, or a fungus was not causing the worldwide "Bee Catastrophe," but a new class of pesticides called "Neonicotinoids." In 2012 the journal "Science" published three new studies on the "Bee Catastrophe" in which Neonicotinoid pesticides are examined. The first study published in "Science" centered on British scientists who raised Bumble Bees on pollen treated with a Neonicotinoid pesticide called "Imidacloprid." The Bumble Bees fed this pollen containing this Neonicotinoid pesticide clearly showed poor, reduced rates of growth as well as producing 'dramatically less new Queen Bees.' The second study published in 2012 by "Science" was based on French scientist's research, who had attached tiny tags on individual Bees so that they could trace them with radio-frequency. After feeding Bees with sucrose dosed with another common Neonicotinoid pesticide "Thiamethoxan," the Bees were free to leave the hive. The French experiment results were that Bees who are fed with sucrose including this Neonicotinoid pesticide were very unlikely to again return to the hive, and simply disappear. The third study, also reported on in the "Silent Hives" article of April, 2012, is to be published in 2012 by the "Bulletin of Insectology," and is nearly undeniable evidence of the Neonicotinoid pesticides killing billions of Bees worldwide. This third study was based on a series of very healthy Honey Bee colonies, which had their diets changed by scientists. The new diet exclusively fed to these healthy Honey Bee colonies was a high-fructose corn syrup which had the Neonicotinoid pesticide "Imidacloprid" added to it. The undeniable result was that no less than fifteen out of the sixteen healthy Bee hives fed with the Imidacloprid pesticide *died*. The study also revealed the fact that on commercial Bee farms, all of the Bees are "routinely fed" this same corn syrup - and that best of all - the corn grown to produce the Bee's corn syrup has all been just as "routinely" treated with Neonicotinoid pesticide. This third study produced undeniable evidence that this corn syrup containing the pesticide from the Neonicotinoid family killed *93.7* percent of the sixteen healthy Bee colonies experimented upon. The leader of the team making this third undeniable experiment is a professor from Harvard University, Chensheng Lu, who's paper was not surprisingly "disputed" by the world's producer of the most Neonicotinoid pesticides "Bayer CropScience." This huge multinational chemical company "Bayer CropScience" also denied the findings of the first two experiments in Britain and France which also clearly found that Neonicotinoids in corn pesticide are killing the Bees. The author of this article in "The New Yorker" telephoned Hackenberg in Pennsylvania to ask his opinion on the three definitive scientific studies. Hackenberg's Bees were pollinating an apple orchard in Pennsylvania, and then were on the way to Maine for blueberry pollinating after the apple tress. Not only does Hackenberg agree with these three studies, but claims that the findings of the three studies simply proved what he knew for six years already. Hackenberg, the first Beekeeper to recognize "CCD" in 2006, also explained that several organizations of Beekeepers filed a lawsuit against the Environmental Protection

Agency in March, 2012 because the "EPA" violated the rules it created itself. The EPA never performed "field studies" on the Neonicotinoid pesticide "Clothianidin," and then went ahead and deemed it safe for use on crops anyway.

It seems that in the end "Neonicotinoid" pesticides are Neurotoxins, which resemble nicotine chemically and were the first new class of pesticides to be introduced to agriculture in fifty years. These Neonicotinoid pesticides began to be used in the 1990s as "Systemic pesticides," which are pesticides used to treat the seeds of crops such as corn, which then get absorbed by the growing crop's "vascular systems." The findings that are very shocking came from the "Pesticide Action Network," which reported that an area of crops larger than the total combined large states of Florida and California - one-hundred and forty-million acres - were already planted with seeds treated by Neonicotinoids - and that was just in the year 2012. Precisely fifty years ago in "The New Yorker" Rachel Carson wrote in the "Silent Spring" article a premonition of this Twenty-first century "Bee Catastrophe," in which she very clearly and precisely claimed the "Systemic pesticides" used on crop seeds 'surpass the Brothers Grimm imagination.' Carson wrote in 1962 of a world in which former fairy tale 'enchanted forests' have turned into 'poisonous forests,' and where a flea dies after biting a dog, and where a Bee carries a "poisonous nectar" to it's hive to ultimately produce 'poison honey.' With the mad dash to desperately find a cause and possible solution for the present worldwide "Bee Catastrophe," what has been overlooked is the end result of this neurotoxin Neonicotinoid's effect on the millions of Human beings both buying and eating the Bee honey that has been made by Bee's nectar that contains Neonicotinoids. The Harvard University leader of the definitive experiment on "CCD," Chensheng Lu, reported that the Bee hives treated with corn syrup containing the Neonicotinoid "Imidacloprid" became unfortunately "dead silent." Lu also wonders if this will be a repeat from "Silent Springs," as well as the good question of 'what *else* is needed to prove that pesticides cause C.C.D.?'

A conclusive article also appeared on the "Time" magazine's website section "Science and Space" in April, 2012, and was clearly entitled 'Study Links Pesticide With the Honeybee Collapse.' This "Time" article began with the facts that since the middle of the 1990s Colony Collapse Disorder - CCD - has produced deaths of Bees on the magnitude of thirty to ninety percent. The Bees don't only disappear, but just as uncharacteristically the Bees abandon both their Queen and their hive to go out by themselves to disappear. Again, "Time" restates the facts that one-hundred and thirty food crops in the United States alone are dependent on Bee pollination, which "Time" estimates at annually fifteen billion dollars, and defines this as a pending "agricultural disaster" in the making.

This "Time" article of April, 2012 clearly reports that several possible culprits of the "CCD" have been studied over the past years, including mites, viruses, fungi, bacteria, and new techniques in Beekeeping, but that the new study by Harvard University's biologist Chemsheng Lu published in "Bulletin of Insectology" has actually for the first time "isolated" what is labelled a "single risk factor" of the cause of "C.C.D." This "Time" article candidly points out to the reader that since the corn syrup that is used to feed the Bee colonies has been made from corn that was treated with a pesticide containing the neurotoxin Neonicotinoid "Imidacloprid" which has been proven to kill these Bee colonies, then the both uncomfortable and undeniable truth is that Human beings could, not surprisingly, be the ones killing the Bees. "Time" explains that this neurotoxin pesticide containing Neonicotinoids is transferred in trace amounts directly to Bees regularly fed with standard "high-fructose" level corn syrup made from corn plants that have been grown through corn seeds treated with the Neonicotinoid "Imidacloprid." The obvious solution offered by "Time" magazine is that Beekeepers must feed their Bees with something other that the standardly used and commercially produced corn syrup. It is clear that the "CCD" disaster began about 2005 - the very same year that corn crops first began to be treated with the Neonicotinoid "Imidacloprid." What more conclusive evidence is needed?

Harvard University's Chensheng Lu and his team began their conclusive experiment with Neonicotinoids and Bees during the spring of 2010, when they set up commercial Bee colonies in four groups, each containing five Bee hives. The trace amounts of Imidacloprid given in corn syrup to these sixteen colonies of test Bees was incredibly small, ranging from twenty parts per billion to four-hundred parts per billion, but proved even at this minuscule amount to cause all of the Bees in fifteen out of sixteen Bee hives to disappear. The actual offered statement released by "Bayer CropScience" corporation about their pesticide Imidacloprid not surprisingly denounced Lu's findings with five presented opposing points, being first that the tested concentration of Imidacloprid were not based on 'residues' of the neurotoxin normally measured in the "High-Fructose Corn Syrup" normally fed to commercial Bees. "Bayer" goes on to claim that the Bees in Lu's experiment were fed High-Fructose Corn Syrup containing different levels of Imidacloprid than used in commercial Bee feed, and also that in different research no residues of Imidacloprid were found in samples of High-fructose Corn Syrup that had been grown with corn treated with the neurotoxin. "Bayer" went on to criticize the experimental technique of Harvard University's Lu, claiming that this study also did not replicate the experiment to prove it, and that Lu's team used too few Bees to arrive at a correct "statistical analysis" of the "Bee Catastrophe" cause. Finally "Bayer" claimed that Lu and his team "ignored" the consensus of science, believing that the health of Bees could be effected by "multiple factors" besides pesticides, such as the "varroa mite," poor diet, disease, poorly managed colonies, or even genetic diversity loss. Of course "Bayer CropScience" does not include their neurotoxin pesticide "Imidacloprid" in their list. This is the very same famous drug company, "Bayer" from Germany known worldwide for selling "Bayer Aspirin," which was the company that initially also decided in the late 1800s that a good, very healthy product to sell to the general public instead of "Aspirin" was "*Heroin!*"

What is absolutely true of the criticism from "Bayer" on the Harvard University report by Lu's team is that the team did use "different" levels of Imidacloprid to feed the Bees in their experiment than is used in commercial Bee hives - but typically what this powerful multinational corporation "Bayer" does not reveal is that the levels of Imidacloprid used on the Bees in the experiment were actually "less than" what typically is used on crops or in Bee foraging areas. This well publicized study by the "Harvard School of Public Health" was published on their website on April 5, 2012. The study was led by Chensheng Lu, who is an associate professor of environmental exposure biology for the Department of Environmental Health. The study which was published in the June, 2012 publication "Bulletin of Insectology," is concluded by Lu to have found dramatically decimated experimental Bee populations while using amounts of pesticides that were 'below the amount normally found in the environment.' This study found that Bees could be in contact with "imidacloprid" either through the pollen they collect from plants that had been treated with the neurotoxin pesticide, and/or through the "High-Fructose Corn Syrup" they are commonly fed on Bee farms, which had been made from corn that has also been treated with "Imidacloprid."

Details of the Bee study done by the Harvard School of Public Health during the summer of 2010 are published on their website, explaining that this experiment was carried out in Worcester County, Massachusetts. Four different Bee farms were monitored over a period of twenty-three weeks, and each of the four Bee farms housed five Bee hives treated with different levels of the pesticide "Imidacloprid," as well as one untreated 'control' Bee hive on each farm. The experiment resulted in no Bee deaths after a period of twelve weeks, but after twenty-three weeks the catastrophic results were recorded of fifteen out of the sixteen Bee hives - 94% of the multitude of healthy Bees tested - were Dead. The Bees that had been exposed to the highest levels of "Imidacloprid" were also the Bees that died first. What really surprised the leader of this Harvard study was the small amount of the neurotoxin pesticide "Imidacloprid" that it took to kill all of the Bees and caused "Colony Collapse Disorder" - 'less than typically used for crops and in Bee foraging areas.' This study by the Harvard School of Public Health was accurately entitled "In Situ Replication of Honey Bee Colony Collapse Disorder."

It seems that the "Bee Catastrophe" was created by not only by the pesticides that the Bees are ingesting in the High-fructose corn syrup they are fed, but also in the corn plants that they are pollinating as well. One of the biggest American seed companies is "Monsatno," and in 2006 this company Genetically manipulated corn plants so that the corn would switch on an insect toxin contained in the plant itself. This Genetic manipulation produced plants which release much more poison than is naturally made by the plant, so when Bees pollinate the corn they also ingest the poison and die. The hives of these poisoned Bees are so infested with poison from the Genetically manipulated corn they pollinated, that other Bees won't go near these hives.

So here we have gathered information on two 'insignificant creatures put upon the Earth' who have lived here for millions of years before Homo sapiens sapiens, and have lived on Earth for all those millions of years in perfect symbiotic harmony with the world around them and all of interrelated nature. Then Human beings came along and literally fucked up the world around them. The air, water, and land polluted beyond the point of no return in only one century. A literal blink-of-the-eye, only, for these ancient guardians of Grandmother Earth. Did people really think that the infinite wisdom and ancient spirituality of nature would allow them to do anything they wanted for the rest of their delinquent carcinogenic little lives? To compare the wisdom of nature to the wisdom of an average Twenty-first century Human being, would be like comparing the wisdom of Albert Einstein to the wisdom of dirt. Can people really delude themselves into believing that the "Jellyfish Invasion" and the "Bee Catastrophe" endangering the very Food cycle of life on Earth is happening simultaneously now by *coincidence?* An exquisite documentary entitled "l'Invasion des Meduses" ('The Jellyfish Invasion') was aired in 2010 on French TV5's "Thalassa," and ended with a very clear bottom line which translates as 'If the Jellyfish could speak they would tell us that they have been here for so long on the Earth. They have seen the man coming, and in the worse case scenario, they will see the man disappear.'

If two of these 'insignificant creatures put upon the Earth' are not enough to turn against the new invaders (Human beings) and combine their forces as a form of nature's "Self-Defense," there is a third unsensationalized and unpublicized 'insignificant creature' that is even tinier and more 'insignificant' than Jellyfish and Bees, which has also begun to create a worldwide effect that could have a devastating effect for Human beings as well: Phytoplankton. Just by 'coincidence,' again, in just the same amount of time and in just the same period of history as the "Jellyfish Invasion" and the "Bee Catastrophe," the plant-like organism Phytoplankton in the world's seas, being one of the most important creatures on Earth making up the basis for the Food web on this planet, are now beginning to also react to Human intervention on the Earth. Phytoplankton's main contribution to life on Earth, besides making up the basis of the food chain for life, is absorbing billions of tons of Carbon dioxide from the atmosphere, and then producing more than half of the oxygen making up the Earth's atmosphere, which almost all other life-forms on Earth, including Human beings, breath.

Human beings have intervened in every possible way with nature, from the rampant and unending pollution of the seas, air, and land, to the manipulation of DNA to create their own obviously "man-made" life-forms upon the Earth - all with a rapidity and unwavering intent driven by 'man,' who will settle for nothing less than absolute world domination. Just as obviously, this human intervention has rarely ever led to a positive outcome for nature or the Earth, which is just as rarely even considered anymore in any way. Human intervention during the last one-hundred years has resulted in the 'positive outcome' for the Earth of a full 1.1 degree global temperature rise since 1940. That doesn't sound like such a big deal, but it's enough to cause polar ice caps as well as glaciers to melt and recede, which not only causes the sea level to rise across the globe, but also changes the temperature of the oceans and the temperature as well as the dynamics of the crucial ocean currents. In plain English, Human intervention has literally changed the physics of the atmosphere. The unending burning of fossil fuel in cars, factories, and power plants across the globe has raised the temperature of the Earth's atmosphere and the Earth's oceans. "Global warming" and the "Greenhouse effect" are current phrases that are so often repeated in society today that even little school children know what they are. This human intervention has also resulted in the creation of vast areas of the oceans of the world which are uninhabitable for most forms of life and are aptly named "Dead Zones."

"Dead Zones" are areas of the world's oceans which have become nearly devoid of oxygen, and in these "Dead zones" all living species either are driven out by the lack of oxygen in the water, or die. These "Dead zones" are created by dying Phytoplankton and are so vast that they can be seen from space. The superior life-form on Earth, Human beings, are visibly unavoidable on the face of the Earth, like ants running on a cake, but their actual numbers or total weight as a life-form on this Earth is as 'inconspicuous and tiny' as what their superiority considers most other life-forms they coexist with. Human beings, with all their disruptive, destructive intervention on Earth, not to mention a hell of a superiority complex, ego, and a big mouth to match, only consist in total to an 'insignificant' two-tenths of one percent of the total weight of life on Earth. Plant life on Earth, as a comparison, makes up an incredible 3,800 times the total weight of Human life, but this is just nothing when considering the total weight of microbial life-forms. The largest amount of life-forms on this Earth are not the superior loud-mouthed Human beings, or even the quiet Plant life such as the mighty trees, but 'the tiniest and most insignificant creatures placed upon the Earth:' silent microbial life-forms such as Phytoplankton and bacteria. A full eighty percent of the weight of all life upon the Earth is not animal or plant, and certainly not Human beings, but amazingly microscopic life-forms. As so often happens, the ones with the biggest mouths are also the ones with the smallest 'contents.'

"Dead Zones" are created by blooms of Phytoplankton which die and fall to the bottom of the sea to decompose. When the immense number of Phytoplankton are consumed by bacteria at the bottom of the sea the bacteria deplete the water of most of it's oxygen. Previously there were "dozens" of "Dead Zones" in the world's oceans, but by 2011 there were an estimated four-hundred "Dead Zones" around the Earth. Off the coast of Oregon there is a "Dead Zone" which has the enormous size of over 16,000 square kilometers. This increase in areas of oxygen depleted ocean are not only growing in numbers, but currently also found throughout the world including Asia, China, Australia, the Americas, and even Antarctica's seas. What should be obvious is that the increase in the numbers of global "Dead Zones," from dozens in former times to over four-hundred in 2011, is caused directly by a change in the Ecosystem. "Global warming" is the change in the Ecosystem that is believed to be causing "Dead Zones" to increase in numbers so greatly. As everyone knows, including little school children, "Global warming" is a direct result of Human beings burning fossil fuels in their cars, factories, and power plants at the almost inconceivable rate of one-thousand barrels *per second* around the Earth. The change in the Ecosystem has effected the ocean temperatures, which changes the dynamics of the ocean's currents, which normally drive the dead Phytoplankton up from the bottom of the ocean's floor. As is well known, a slight nearly inconspicuous alteration of nature has a ripple effect which reverberates throughout nature's inner workings. For example, winds effect the upwellings of water and the movement of dead Plankton from the bottom of the ocean to the top. Global warming has also changed the winds, which has in turn effected the way that upwellings of dead Phytoplankton and nutrients are transported from the ocean's bottom to it's surface, and which has the dramatic increased effect of the creation of the "Dead Zones" in the seas. As a small reminder of Human being's intervention in nature and their self-made masterpiece "Global warming," today in 2012 it is estimated that over a full eighty percent of the world's forests, consisting of an incalculable number of carbon dioxide absorbing and oxygen producing trees, have been cut down by humans. It's not only the loss of the world's forests, but as nature's fractal principle has shown, every negative effect, such as a dramatic increase in "Dead Zones" in the world's oceans, has a definitive negative cause, such as the destruction of the Ozone layer by human intervention, of course. Way back in 1989 "The New York Times" published an article warning of the "Threat to Plankton." The article clearly explains that the hole created by human intervention in the Ozone layer above Antarctica allows solar radiation in, and is believed to be the cause of Phytoplankton dying in massive numbers, which effects the food chain and all wildlife. Researchers at the Texas A and M University found in the late 1980s that certain Ultraviolet wavelengths don't allow the growth of Phytoplankton in the oceans. Phytoplankton is a member of the plant kingdom, and as such uses photosynthesis like other plants to create it's own food out of carbon dioxide. "The New York Times" article goes on to explain the importance of Phytoplankton, which is the very base of the world's food chain. Plankton are eaten by krill, which are then eaten by fish, squid, and whales worldwide. Besides these animals, seals, penguins, and birds also survive by eating animals which also live by eating plankton. The research group of A and M University carried out experiments at Antarctica's Palmer Station, where varying degrees of Ultraviolet radiation were experimented upon, in regard to the growth and reproduction of Phytoplankton. The healthiest Phytoplankton which also reproduced the most were found in waters which had all of the Ultraviolet filtered out of their sunlight, and just as clearly the increased level of Ultraviolet radiation that the Phytoplankton were exposed to appeared to be destroying plant chlorophyll, which is the 'catalyst' of the Phytoplankton's food source through photosynthesis.

    The "National Science Foundation" also published a long article recently which asks the question if "Climate Change" is "Suffocating" the seas? This report begins with the facts that the "Dead Zones" of the oceans have increased to include over four-hundred worldwide, with the number of "Dead Zones" doubling every decade, and increasing to the sizes of these "Dead Zones" that have been measured in recent years exceeding 10,000 square miles. This "National Science Foundation" article clearly explains that "Dead Zones" are created when Phytoplankton are over fed by nutrients coming directly from Human being's sewerage and fertilizers, which are dumped into rivers and oceans unendingly. This human intervention through their sewerage and fertilizers being dumped into the world's seas has dramatically increased the number of "Dead Zones" globally. What is also explained by the "National Science Foundation" is that naturally occurring "Dead Zones" are a process of the oceans and have been known for many years. What human intervention has created, in the form of pollution directly producing changes in the Ecosystem, results in a huge increase of both the size and numbers of the ocean's "Dead Zones." The mechanics that create the ocean's "Dead Zones" work through a combination of northerly summer winds and the rotation of the Earth, which together move oxygenated surface ocean water offshore. This oxygenated coastal water is then replaced by nutrient-rich waters with low level of oxygen pushed up from the ocean's depths by upwelling. When this high nutrient low oxygen water from the depths of the sea is driven up and reaches surface waters and sunlight, it "fertilizes" huge blooms of Phytoplankton. This has both positive as well as negative results. The Phytoplankton blooms, which reach vast sizes, create one of America's most productive fisheries in the Pacific Northwest, but also create the formation of "low-oxygen water" in the depths of the sea where the dead Phytoplankton are decomposing in unimaginable numbers. Studies funded by the "National Science Foundation" have been led by two scientists, one of whom is Jack Barth from Oregon State University. These studies have discovered that low-oxygen water has increased in area, stretching from the continental shelf up all the way to the coast of Oregon and Washington State, expanding each summer since 2002. Also found was that these created "Dead Zones" have moved closer to the shorelines than was ever recorded before 2002, and that these "Costal dead zones" are more "hypoxic" than the "Dead Zones" of the continental shelf. What has also occurred recently and could lead to very dramatic consequences, is that the individual numerous "Dead Zones" scattered along the Pacific Northwest coast have become "connected" to each other, resulting in the formation of an entire area of oxygen depleted water, or "Dead Zone," running along the sea floor of the coast. The largest "Dead Zone" recorded in the Pacific Northwest happened in 2006 off of Newport, Oregon, where it was measured at nearly 1,200 square miles (1,930 square kilometers). Researcher Jack Barth believes not surprisingly that "Climate change" is the reason for this recent phenomenon in which the formation of "Dead Zones" in the world's oceans has dramatically multiplied. The details are explained by Barth, including the climate change lowering the oxygen content in the "subsurface offshore" water, as well as changing coastal winds. Climate change can result in deep waters having depleted oxygen because the surface water is warmer. Climate change, brought about by human intervention, warms the surface waters of the world's oceans, which 'insulates' the deeper water underneath it, and which in turn doesn't let this deeper water come into contact with oxygen in the atmosphere. This is the crucial point behind the vicious cycle begun by the burning of fossil fuels around the globe for the last century plus.

    A beautiful photograph was published with one news report on the 'Ocean System's Peril' by "Al Jazeera" in June, 2012. In the article a swirl of Blue Bioluminescent lights stream across a photograph of "Dinoflagellates," which are members of the Phytoplankton family. The "Al Jazeera" article explains that Phytoplankton is also called 'marine algae,' and that it is the "most important" life-form on the planet because it produces half of our oxygen - an amount equal to all the oxygen that is produced worldwide by the trees and all plant life - and also is vital for the food chain. What is reported by this 2012 article is that the total population of Phytoplankton is forty percent lower than in 1950. The measured drop of the ocean's Phytoplankton is one percent per year since 1999, with the blame going to the rise in the surface temperature of the seas, caused by Global warming. Dr. Michael Latz of the Scripps Institute of Oceanography studies Bioluminescent Dinoflagellates and believes that by monitoring their Bioluminescent light produced through photosynthesis, the condition of the seas can be analyzed. Latz explains that global warming has increased the ocean's "temperature stratification" and resulted in less nutrients in the surface waters, which is the food source of the Phytoplankton, and which has caused a decrease in Phytoplankton populations. Latz has studied Bioluminescence for thirty years and gives a warning for the famous "Bioluminescent Bay" in Puerto Rico and other such bays of Bioluminescent Phytoplankton in the Caribbean, because in 2010 a storm in Puerto Rico caused a "large decrease" of Bioluminescent Phytoplankton which was replaced by a bloom of non-luminescent Phytoplankton. Latz is concerned with the possibility of greater stress on the world's ocean systems eventually resulting in a "Non-Bioluminescent Bay" in Puerto Rico. This exemplifies what Latz considers an Ecological monitor, which might indicate an "ecological degradation" through a reduced amount of Bioluminescence.

   The "Dead Zone" of the Gulf of Mexico is the subject of yet another report, which explains that in 2003 this "Dead Zone" was larger than the entire state of Massachusetts. The report details the process of oxygen depletion of the sea floor, which is caused by colonies of bacteria who are feeding on the vast amounts of dead Phytoplankton. What is causing this Gulf of Mexico "Dead Zone?" Again, fertilizers, sewerage, pesticides, and industrial waste is singled out as increasing the nitrogen level of the world's seas. The level of nitrogen measured from the Mississippi River and dumped into the Gulf of Mexico has almost tripled during the last fifty years with 1.6 million metric tons of nitrogen being dumped into the river each year. The Phytoplankton are dying because of many reasons, including the increased levels of Ultraviolet radiation caused by the partial destruction of the Ozone layer, which was caused by human intervention through their use of fluorocarbons in spray-cans around the world for many decades. These areas of dead Phytoplankton on the bottom of the world's seas are becoming larger, and because of human intervention in the form of Global warming, the upwellings that transport water from the sea's floor to it's surface levels have also been disturbed. To add to these man-made disturbances, the change of winds and the increased temperature of surface waters in the oceans has the combined effect of the creation of massive areas of the world's oceans that are oxygen depleted and which either totally drive out fish and all other life-forms from these "Dead Zones," or kills them.

   The conclusion is that a dangerous pattern is forming, and increasing, where human intervention is directly causing the death of one of the most important life-forms on Earth, which produces a full fifty percent of the oxygen in the planet's atmosphere, and the death of these Phytoplankton combined with other changes in the climate and Ecosystem of the Earth, also caused by human intervention, is causing the creation of vast areas of the world's oceans which kill all life-forms inside of these "Dead Zones." Not only has human intervention caused the loss of Phytoplankton, which creates half our oxygen, but has also caused the creation of "Dead Zones" in the world's oceans which kill all fish or other life-forms which cannot escape these areas of oxygen depleted water. A killer combination of less oxygen as well as less food is the grand result of, once again, human intervention.

   These 'doomsday prophecies' coming from a Fluorescent Artist are not just the beliefs of an individual person. For a good example of similar beliefs aired by public media, on "Discovery Science" a question was proposed asking if the 'Ocean Thinks.' Some scientists today believe that the entirety of all the Oceans on Earth may be the biggest living, and possibly thinking, creature known. The Ocean is believed to have an Immune system to protect itself, which could react to our mass pollution and create a mass extinction that could wipe out ninety-nine percent of life on Earth. This is thought to have happened several times already throughout Earth's history, and although scientists until recently believed that mass extinctions had only been caused by astroids or massive geological events, some scientists have found lethal Hydrogen Sulfide in high amounts present during mass extinction events. When the temperature of the Ocean water rises only a few degrees, which is happening at the present moment due famously to our "global warming," there is no cool water to sink to the Ocean's bottom and circulate Oxygen to the deep sea. When the deep sea has no circulation of Oxygen, Hydrogen Sulfide producing Bacteria becomes abundant and fills the Ocean bottom with a poisonous sludge, which then releases toxic Hydrogen Sulfide that rises out of the seas and poisons all plant and animal life, causing a mass extinction. Some scientists believe that a vast bacterial electrical network is present throughout the mass of the Ocean, possibly giving it a form of consciousness. The conclusions to this public broadcast stated clearly that if the Ocean is a conscious living thinking being which rightfully views Human beings as "a threat" to it's existence, the Ocean may defend itself with a mass extinction. Instead of us killing the Ocean, which we have very nearly accomplished, the Ocean may defend itself and kill us.

Here are basic examples of the way that nature has been dramatically effected by Human being's cars, factories, and power plants burning billions of tons of fossil fuels, and throwing billions of tons of pollution into the oceans, which has the extremely detrimental effect of changing the physics of the Earth's atmosphere and the temperature of the ocean's waters, which in turn effects ocean currents and winds. Between the "Jellyfish Invasion," the "Bee Catastrophe," and the death of Phytoplankton causing the creation of vast areas of "Dead Zones" in the oceans of the world - all happening simultaneously - the notion of these 'tiny and insignificant creatures placed upon the Earth' becoming the "Natural Defense" of the planet can now be considered. The "Jellyfish Invasion" could kill all the fish in the seas, the "Bee Catastrophe" could wipe out most of the fruits, grains, and vegetables on the land, the death of Phytoplankton could take away half of all the oxygen we breath in the air, and/or the Ocean could react to our pollution and emit poisonous Hydrogen Sulfide - like I wrote before most folks will be ecstatic, because all that will be left will be money and sex!

Back to the main subject of this book, in this first decade and a half of the Twenty-first century Fluorescent Colors and the Black light have most often still been used as the same 'entertainment prop' as they have for the last three decades, clearly indicating that this miraculous technology is no closer to being taken seriously than it was forty years ago. There has been no change in the attitude of Museums and Art galleries worldwide, still steeped in tradition, towards Fluorescent Colors and the Black light with these institutions continuing to stigmatize Fluorescent Colors as being unacceptable for serious 'Fine Art.' One reason for this is the closed minded attitude of the majority of Art Museum and Art gallery directors worldwide, who operate in a manner that is stipulated by tradition. Society in general seems to be less stigmatized by the Black light and Fluorescent Colors, and is as always very open to any technique or gimmick to increase their profits, especially in the entertainment industry. In the last years, between 2008 and 2015, several notable "MTV" music videos have been broadcast, all using the 'entertainment prop' of the Black light and Fluorescent Colors as the video's theme, and all of these videos are of varying degrees of reinforcement of the typical sociological cliché of the Black light and Fluorescent Colors. Obviously reinforcing the seemingly intrinsic 1960s roots of the Black light and Fluorescent Color's stigma to the greatest degree, was an "MTV" video from about 2010 by "Ke$ha." Every single possible cliché about the 1960s, 'Hippies,' and drugs (even in the name of the song), is embedded in this music video made by an American girl who wasn't even born until 1987. Of course since the name of the song, as well as it's theme, was founded on "drug," the Black light and Fluorescent Color's stigmatized association with the 1960s Movement and drugs was the obvious choice for this typical video. For sure there's a young character with a beard and long hair in this video to 'authenticate' this prototypically stigmatized Twenty-first century viewpoint of the Black light, Fluorescent Colors, and the 1960s Movement all at once. Three other popular "MTV" music videos between 2008 and 2012 also used the 'entertainment prop' of the Black light and Fluorescent Colors, but without the stigmatized association of the 1960s Movement. The German group "Laserkraft 3D" made a video containing dance scenes under Black lights with Fluorescent dance costumes, the "Black Eyed Peas" made a music video with the simple use of just a single bucket of Green Fluorescent paint and a Black light, and "Ludacris" used even less props, producing a video using just a typical Fluorescent T-shirt and Fluorescent sunglasses under a Black light(!) 2014 saw the release of a Rita Ora music video in which the girl shows how to party and "bullshit" under full Black lights and Fluorescent paint. In 2011 a music video using the Black light and Fluorescent paint with descent feelings was released, by "Coldplay." This video features a large Fluorescent backdrop painted under Black lights, and is a rare example of the Black light and Fluorescent Colors used in a slightly creative way. Two more miserable Black light clichè music videos that deserve to be added to this list were broadcast globally in 2015. The music video by "Kygo and Kyla La Grange" embodies what could be termed "clichè-plus" imagery - as well as imagination - with it's contents centered on a group of teenage girls dressing up in Fluorescent skeleton costumes while wearing Day-glo makeup under Black lights in the dark. How unique! Comparable in terms of it's "clichè-plus" use of Black light and Fluorescence, a 2015 music video by "Dr. Lektroluv" deserves similar distinctions on an equal level to "Kygo and Kyla La Grange."

What must be pointed out here in high contrast to "MTV" is the use of Black lights and Fluorescent Colors in Rave parties all across the world for decades, which is still very much going on. This wild sub-culture of the current era has truly embraced and taken as their signatory Colors "Day-Glo." Goa parties, Rave parties, Ibiza parties, and countless others in constant procession make full use of Black lights and Fluorescent Colors. The wild, altered brilliance of the Colors and the rebellious social unacceptance of these Fluorescent Colors under Black lights made this "Day-Glo" the obvious choice for the current movement.

In this "Black Light and Fluorescent Art - The Social Stigma of Fluorophobia," the thinnest part of the book will be on "Fluorescent Art." Obviously if there was a universal acceptance by society and Artists towards Fluorescent Color and Black lights there would have been no "Social Stigma" or creation of "Fluorophobia," and also no reason to write this book in the first place. The one point that has kept the strength of Fluorescent Colors is precisely this "Social Stigma of Fluorophobia," which by unnatural selection has kept Fluorescent Colors off of "Cola" cans and your mother's Chocolate box, and through this unacceptance the dissipation of Fluorescent Colors brought about by familiarity thankfully hasn't occurred. Over the past half century of visiting Museums, beginning with the "Brooklyn Public Museum" when I started grade school, there has been only one single unforgettable experience with Fluorescent Colors. When I began working as a graphic designer on Madison Avenue during the end of 1980, the Museum of Modern Art was preparing for it's first major renovation. After filling the Museum only with Picasso for the final exhibition in the original museum space, the Museum of Modern Art closed to build it's 'Museum Tower' and virtually a new museum. Throughout this renovation/construction period the Museum of Modern Art had small temporary exhibitions of Artists such as Anselm Adams and Giorgio de Chirico. During this time of approximately 1981 when the new Museum of Modern Art was being rebuilt above, in the basement of the original building a show was held of a radical new Artist Jonathan Borofsky that I myself will never forget. I must admit that this Jonathan Borofsky opening in the basement of the original Museum of Modern Art in about 1981 was the absolute first time in all my lifelong visits to museums that I've seen Fluorescent Color used as the theme in a major museum. Now if the work of Jonathan Borofsky is known, he is still a radical Artist who still at over seventy years old has thankfully shown no sign of decadence, and remains a cutting edge Artist creating sculptures of working humans as huge public installations all across Europe. In 1981 he was becoming internationally known, and for his opening in the basement of the Museum of Modern Art's temporary exhibition space Jonathan Borofsky painted in pure "Day-Glo" Magenta directly onto the pristine White walls and then continued up onto the just-as-pristine White Museum of Modern Art ceiling! It was brilliantly vivid, completely unexpected, unprecedented, and shocking. This "Day-Glo" installation painted directly onto the walls and ceiling of the Museum of Modern Art gave me the immediate very rare impression of having my own acceptance tested - 'Have I walked into the wrong building - is this the Museum of Modern Art?' That's how strong the experience was, and that's how strong Social Stigmatization is. The Jonathan Borofsky Fluorescent exhibition entrance was painted directly onto the wall and ceiling of the Museum of Modern Art in pure "Day-Glo" Magenta obviously in a wild state, and was strong enough to take your breath away - without even a black light. Don't get the wrong idea here, the Museum of Modern Art did not get carried away by installing a Black light for the Fluorescent paint of Jonathan Borofsky, but this unique appearance of pure "Day-Glo" Magenta onto the pristine White wall and ceiling of the Museum of Modern Art was more than enough. In contrast, the actual pieces of Art by Borofsky in the exhibition were small studied graphic pieces with pencil-drawn mandalas which were captivating, but not at all Fluorescent.

As a very clear indication of the amount of Fluorescent Art in major museum collections today, the Museum of Modern Art in New York City will serve as a perfect example. On the MOMA website today in 2012 there are 7,729 Artists represented, with a tremendous total of 45,046 works of Art viewable online from their collection. Out of these almost 8,000 Artists from all across the world, and out of these over 45,000 Artworks, there is a grand total of *Four* pieces of Art specifically listed on the MOMA website as being made with Fluorescent Color, by Two different Artists which are included in the Museum of Modern Art's collection represented on their website. To add to this, these four pieces of Art using Fluorescent Colors out of the 45,046 Artworks listed on the MOMA website are only displayed online, and are plainly stated as being "not on view" to the public in the actual museum. One of these two Artists is John Armleder from Switzerland, who is represented by a collection of thirteen screen prints "not on view" in the museum, and there isn't even a photo of these Artworks on the MOMA website. There is however a quote from this Swiss Artist who rather clearly is both uniformed about the history of Fluorescent Colors, and is plainly in agreement with the common person about these "modern colors." Armleder states that he uses Colors in his Art that are 'one way or another about Art history.' The Artist then gives the comparison between using the Color Gold to 'go back to the paintings of the middle ages' inclusive of Gold's "specific significance," and using the Fluorescent Colors which Armleder labels as "modern colors" which will 'reflect the context' of the period of time that Fluorescent Colors 'were introduced' - which is doubtful that this Swiss Artist meant the 1930s, but almost undoubtably meant the common conception of the "period" of the 1960s. Armleder on the MOMA website adds surprisingly a common person's observation, stating that Fluorescent Colors have a "very edgy" optical effect.

Growing up and going to the Museum of Modern Art in the 1960s and 1970s, there was one piece of Art in the lobby of the Museum behind the rows of visitors paying their entrance fees (which was about one-sixth of the entrance fee today) that had a few square centimeters - about a square inch - of Fluorescent Pink: Marilyn Monroe's lips on Andy Warhol's huge Gold silkscreen. The one other piece of Art in the building that was made using Fluorescent Color was an actual full painting made with "Fluorescent Alkyds" in the 1960s by one of the only world famous Artist who has been associated with Fluorescent paint for the last half a century: Frank Stella. Although there was never a Black light installed above this single Fluorescent Frank Stella painting which hung in the Museum of Modern Art for over thirty years, and although the Fluorescent paintings by Frank

Stella are typically made with pastel, toned down gentle shades of Fluorescent Colors, the mere presence of one painting made with "Fluorescent Alkyd" hung in the Museum of Modern Art made a life-long impression on me - I still clearly see the rectangular room and space the Stella painting hung in the MOMA, in the company of Yves Klein's Ultramarine paints and Swiss Artist Tinguely. Again, this Frank Stella Fluorescent painting was not made with the pure vivid Colors of Fluorescence, and were toned down to pastels which gave no immediate impression that the painting was made with Fluorescent Colors, but was bright enough to make a viewer aware that a different kind of paint was used. This painting has been taken off the wall of the MOMA, and the three works of Art by Frank Stella which are made with Fluorescent Colors in the MOMA collection are only available to be seen online today via their website, and are all, again, "not on view" to the public in the museum. The earliest Stella painting on the MOMA website made with Fluorescent Alkyd is "Fez (2)" from 1964 on canvas, followed by "Abra Variation 1" also on canvas from 1969. These are both large paintings made traditionally on canvas. The third work of Art including Fluorescent Colors by Stella on the MOMA website is a large aluminum sculpture hung on the wall, a style Stella developed and is known around the world for. These three-dimensional sculptures replaced canvas and are coated with a long list of mediums, such as sparkles, Fluorescent Alkyd, acrylic paint, oil paint, and other materials, with the piece on the MOMA website being entitled "Giufa la luna, i adri, e el guardic," and was created by Stella in 1984.

Another Frank Stella painting on canvas made with "Fluorescent polymer" is in the collection of another very important museum in New York City, the Solomon R. Guggenheim Museum. "Harran II" is the large ten by twenty foot (three by six meter) canvas by Stella in the Guggenheim collection made with Fluorescent Color, and is similar in it's geometric design to the two 1960s Stella Fluorescent paintings in the MOMA collection, and signatory for this period of Stella's oeuvre. On the Guggenheim website Frank Stella's "Harran II" made with both Polymer and Fluorescent Polymer in 1967, is described as being made through the combination of the "protractor" and with Colors that are "almost psychedelic." Stella is next credited with bringing the painting of "decorative pattern" and "Abstraction" "into congruence," by using 'a manner which challenges both tradition's conventions.'

On the occasion of a new opening in 2009 of Frank Stella's 1960s and 1970s Art, which was called "Geometric Variations," the magazine "Time Out - New York" interviewed Stella and asked the Artist about 'taking risks' and 'using Fluorescence.' The "Time Out" interview asked Frank Stella in September, 2009 about the first time when he used Fluorescent Colors. Stella answered that he began to 'deliberately' use Fluorescent Colors in his paintings either in 1962 or 1963. The idea Stella had was to make a series of paintings on the theme of Morocco, and to include the feelings of the desert and the heat there. Stella explains that the series was basically painted in just two Colors, with one of the Colors being Fluorescent Yellow, and these paintings were composed of stripes, each painting being one Colored stripe, such as Red, Blue, or Green - in combination with Fluorescent Yellow stripes. It is stated by the Artist in this interview that this Moroccan series was "All fluorescent." The decision to use Fluorescent Colors for the first time in 1962 or 1963 in his paintings is explained by the Artist, beginning with the fact that Fluorescent paint had already "been around," but the intention of Stella was to make paintings which didn't have any "other reference" except for the fact that they were painted with Fluorescent Colors. Frank Stella then admits in the interview that this first series of his Fluorescent paintings in the early 1960s didn't really look that Fluorescent, and goes on to state that Fluorescent Colors usually look more Fluorescent 'in relief surrounded by a color such as Black.' Stella closes his interview with the surprisingly common observation, being that the technique of putting Fluorescent Colors against Black is what nightclubs do to create the Fluorescent effect. If Fluorescent Colors are left pure, and not mixed with other non-Fluorescent Colors - especially White to tone the Fluorescent Colors down - the brilliance of these Fluorescent Colors is more than enough to stand by themselves without the need of being used in combination with the old technique of a Black relief. Several other Fluorescent paintings by Frank Stella can be referenced from major museums worldwide, including a work from the Geometric design period of Stella's paintings "Flin Flon" from 1970. This Frank Stella Fluorescent canvas is in the collection of the National Gallery of Australia and is described as being made with 'Fluorescent paint and Synthetic polymer.' A very good description of this Geometric period of Frank Stella's paintings, known collectively as his "Protractor Series" comes from the Guggenheim Museum, which describes the break with Abstract Expressionism of the 1940s and 1950s through Stella's "Black Paintings" of the late 1950s and early 1960s, which consisted of measured areas of Black stripes and bare canvas. In 1966 Stella's work evolved into large canvases of Color fields divided into geometric forms which became known as his "Irregular Polygons." This work developed into huge canvases which are described by the Guggenheim Museum as being 'more Color-oriented and open' while being based on curved forms, which became the "Protractor Series" of Stella's. This describes the Fluorescent "polymer paint" and polymer ten by twenty foot (three by six meter) "Harran II" painting by Stella from 1967 in their collection. The painting's titles from Stella's "Protractor Series" come from Asia Minor's cities of the long past, with a Roman numeral at the end of the name indicating one of three designs Stella was working with during this

"Protractor series," such as "fans," "rainbows," or "interlaces." The Stella painting "Harran II" in the Guggenheim collection was created using the "rainbow" design, being composed of large complete vertical circles interlocked with a horizontal circular protractor shape. These protractor shapes, both horizontal and vertical, in "Harran II" are composed of eight circular bands and constitute the "Rainbow" design of Stella's "Protractor series." This combination of what is described as a "decorative pattern" and "abstraction" in Frank Stella's "Protractor Series," which incorporated the 'protractor shapes' and Stella's use of what is described as Colors which are "almost psychedelic," is what the Guggenheim Museum states "challenged" both abstraction and decorative pattern painting's "conventions."

For this thin 'history' of Fluorescent Art, the Artist John Plumer Ludlum has been documented as the first Artist to use Fluorescent paint in Fine Arts way back in 1945, just a dozen years after Robert Switzer invented the first Fluorescent paint, and has been written about extensively in this book. Only six years after John Ludlum began to "Paint with Living Light," another Artist held an exhibition of his Fluorescent mobiles under Black lights in 1951, which he referred to as "Luminous Mobiles." This Artist's name was Robert Mallary, who was called a "Junk Artist," or a "Neo-Dadaist" because of his use of found materials, but he was also one of the first Artists to use plastics and computers in Art. Robert Mallary is today considered one of the Artists who 'contributed to American sculpture's blossoming during the late 1950s and early 60s,' as was written in his 1993 obituary in "The New York Times." Mallary is counted along with Claes Oldenburg, John Chamberlain, Antonio Tapies, and Alberto Burri as one of the Artists who brought to Art 'a new fierce physical reality' through their use of both 'unusual materials' and 'found objects.' Known for his large sculptures made from cardboard, cloth, and wood found on the streets, Mallary also created lucid social commentary through his tuxedo sculptures with the help of polyester resin. The most prominent of this series was a large sculpture made of tuxedos impregnated with polyester resin held together with welded steel and wood which measured twenty by twenty feet (six meters by six meters). This was Mallary's "Cliffhangers" of 1963-1964, which was on display at the New York World's Fair in 1964-1965. "The New York Times" considers these cutting sculptures of Mallary's tuxedos as an intermediate Art between the schools of Abstract Expressionism of the 1940s and 1950s, which preceded his tuxedo sculptures, and Pop Art of the 1960s.

Robert Mallary, born in Toledo, Ohio, began studying Art at the early age of eight, and grew up in Berkeley, California. As a teenager Mallary was fascinated with Mexican muralists, and by his early twenties the Artist went to Mexico City to study with Siqueiros and Jose Orozco. David Alfaro Siqueiros had already been an early experimenter in the world between Art and technology since roughly 1932, and through his inspiration Mallary began to experiment with the new invention of "plastic" in his Art of 1938. While visiting New York during 1936 Mallary met a disciple of Siqueiros named Roberto Berdecio, who introduced the Artist to new cutting-edge Art tools such as the airbrush and "Duco" paint. Following this, Mallary in the 1940s developed interest in three-dimensional projection and stereoscopy, which developed into the Artist's idea of "sequential contour projection." Mallary's interest in 3D projection led to his creation and exhibiting of a "Stroboplane" in 1951. On the Robert Mallary website it is also documented that during this period of the late 1940s the Artist began to experiment with the newly developed liquid plastics called polyester and acrylic which were known as "monomeric plastics," as well as the newly developed "Fluorescent Colors." In the same exhibition of 1951 that Mallary showed his "Stroboplane" in Los Angeles, the Artist also exhibited his "Luminous Mobiles" made with Fluorescent paint on clear acetate sheets and exhibited under Black lights.

Before exhibiting his huge sculptures "The Cliffhangers" made with 'impregnated tuxedos' at the New York World's Fair of 1964-1965, and before Mallary was one of the pioneers of "Computer Art" in 1967 with his creation of the 'sculpture computer program' "TRANS2," Mallary was teaching in New Mexico. In 1958 Elaine de Kooning also was teaching at the University of New Mexico for one semester and during this period inspired Mallary to relocate to the center of the Art world, New York. Mallary moved to New York City during the summer of 1959, and the city itself made a huge impact on both the Artist and his Art. In the catalogue for the exhibition "Contemporary Urban Visions" of 1966 held in the New School Art Center, Mallary wrote of this impact of New York City, which included the Artist 'assimilating' the actual city of New York into his Artwork. Mallary wrote about the old walls full of peeling paint together with the eroded broken streets and sidewalks, which he collected fragments of and brought back to his studio. Mallary's sculpture "Broome Street," named after a street in Greenwich Village, is made of torn billboards, sand, gravel, broken wood and other pieces of detritus held together as a sculpture with "synthetic plastic." After 1961 Mallary used his found detritus from the streets of New York to create "leaning" wall sculptures with very apparent anthropomorphic references. This reassociation with figurative forms led to Mallary's well-known 'Tuxedo Series,' which utilized three, five, or up to ten tuxedos made into hollow skin-like structures evoking a "human figure." In 1963 Mallary asked for a Guggenheim grant to be able to combine his new "Junk Art" with the 'classic Art of Cubism,' and to link this new Art with even older Artistic traditions by casting his "Junk Art" assemblages in bronze. While teaching at the Pratt Institute of Brooklyn since moving to New York in 1959, Robert Mallary showed his new "Junk Art" at the University of New York, Potsdam.

One of the major reasons which caused Mallary to stop using polyester resin for creating his Art was because of health problems caused by this toxic medium, and this decision led to his brief association with bronze casting. What is more recognized today is Mallary's use of the computer as an Artistic tool, and in 1968 Mallary exhibited in London one of the very first sculptures which was "computer designed." In "The New York Times" it was clearly stated that although the Artist continued to create assemblages, the majority of Mallary's Artistic output towards the end of his life was involved with both sculptures which were "computer-designed," as well as actual computer programs. In 1993, the year Mallary died (by fate being the same year that the first pioneer of Fluorescent Art John Ludlum also passed away) an exhibition of the Artist's new assemblages and works of his computer graphics was shown in SoHo at the Mitchell Algus Gallery.

Although there is no record of Robert Mallary creating Fluorescent Art under Black lights after his early "Luminous Mobiles" exhibition in 1951, these mobiles attracted such attention that they were reported on in "Time" magazine. In the March 10, 1952 issue of "Time" magazine there is a two page article appropriately entitled 'Colors in the Dark' presenting Mallary's "Luminous Mobiles." This "Time" article from over sixty years ago begins with a comparison between the Artist of 'yesteryear' who only needed 'a stick, a stain, and space' to create their Art, and the modern 1952 Artist who had at their disposal "modern technology" which offers a 'thousand innovations' for the creation of new Art. The "Time" article goes on to announce that amongst the innovations offered by modern technology the "newest mediums" include an "invention" by Robert Mallary in California at the age of thirty-four, which was then on exhibition in Sacramento. "Time" magazine gives credit to Robert Mallary and the creation of his Fluorescent mobiles under Black lights, as being 'most likely the only Artist' who chooses to make his Art not in the light, but in 'darkness.' Mallary's "Luminous Mobiles" presented in Color photos are stated as being twenty-four by thirty inches (61 x 76 cm) in size, and are described as being created on "transparent acetate." "Time" explains that Robert Mallary uses the new "luminous pigments" to paint his mobiles, which then "glow" when under "Ultraviolet," commonly known even back in 1952 as a "black light." These "Luminous Mobiles" of Mallary were described in "Time" as having been exhibited hanging from the ceiling of the Sacramento, California gallery by wires, and when they were in this darkened Art gallery "gently twirling," the Fluorescent mobiles were described as looking like 'unfading fireworks under black light.' The article ends with this description of these "Luminous Mobiles" exhibited under Black lights being similar to fireworks, with their 'resemblance' of a form which is three-dimensional, brilliantly Colored, and also in motion, all combined into one display which glows "eerily" under the ultraviolet light's "invisible beams."

This 1952 "Time" magazine article on Robert Mallary's "Luminous Mobiles" contains a very clear Color photograph of three of these Fluorescent mobiles under Black lights along with two more Black and White photos showing details of these suspended acetate works of Fluorescent Art. The impression that the photographed Fluorescent mobiles gives is one of convoluted transparent planes turning in on themselves creating something resembling a vortex of energy or a vision of the nano-scale. The Color photograph in "Time" magazine includes three separate and different "Luminous Mobiles" exhibited by Mallary in 1951, the most striking of which has precise straight lines of the Fluorescent Colors Yellow, Orange-Red, and Blue applied to the curved planes of acetate turning in on each other. This multi-Colored "Luminous Mobile" has very precise crosshatched lines of Fluorescent Colors overlaying each other, which create multiple moire patterns where the transparent acetate planes overlap and convolute. The crosshatched Fluorescent lines are so closely patterned that they give the first impression of being something like a screen of Fluorescent Color on this mobile. The second "Luminous Mobile" in the "Time" photograph has almost all it's Fluorescent Colors applied also in precise lines, with the pattern being not so precise and screen-like, but much more painterly and random. Also used on this second "Luminous Mobile" are the Fluorescent Colors Yellow, Orange-Red, and Blue, along with the addition of three circular Fluorescent linear forms, which create a feeling of an almost organic quality amongst the straight random lines. The third Fluorescent mobile in the Color photograph of 1952 is similar in it's screen-like pattern of tightly spaced lines of Color applied to the first of Mallary's "Luminous Mobiles" described in this photo, with the major difference being that this third Fluorescent mobile is monochromatic, having painted lines of pure Fluorescent Blue only. These three "Luminous Mobiles" of Robert Mallary may sound similar to one another but they are visually very different from each other, with the first full-Color Fluorescent mobile discussed being the most dynamic and the brightest of the three. The first and the third of the Fluorescent mobiles with their paint patterns applied tightly together in a nearly screen-like manner create more movement and give a stronger impression of fields of energy interacting than the second mobile patterned in a looser painterly method.

In the traveling exhibition's catalogue for the show "Forty California Painters" in 1956, which was organized by the University Gallery of the University of New Mexico where Mallary was teaching, the Artist described in detail what is quoted as "Unorthodox Methods" of painting on the Robert Mallary website. Mallary himself stated that he used "unorthodox methods" to apply paint, which he lists as 'oil cans, basters, and hypodermic needles.' The Artist explains that by utilizing these unorthodox tools, "lines" of paint can be created which cannot be made using a brush or even the 'drip' techniques.

Robert Mallary is included in this short account of Fine Artists using Fluorescent paint to create their Art, which includes Luciano Fontana experimenting with Fluorescent and Phosphorescent Art, and one of the few Artists with a painting still today hanging on the walls of the Museum of Modern Art in New York that was made partially with Fluorescent paint: James Rosenquist. This Artist, famous for his Pop-Art was interviewed at MOMA on April 17, 2012, and during this interview spoke about his use of Fluorescent paint on his monumental "F-111" mural. The interviewer referred to Rosenquist's use of Color on his mural "F-111" as being "shocking," but the Artist's response was exquisitely clear, stating that he didn't consider his use of Color as shocking as the use of Color by the "Fauve painters." Rosenquist then refers to his distant past as a billboard sign-painter when he used 'every paint imaginable,' including Fluorescent paint. Detailing his use of Fluorescent paint on the iconic "F-111," Rosenquist explained that he decided to use some Fluorescent paint on top of the already painted surface of the mural for "an experiment," and that even if the Fluorescent paint "wears out," the surface Color under the Fluorescent paint will still be there. Rosenquist then states in his 2012 interview that this Fluorescent paint on "F-111" is still intact and has "held up" amazingly. Although the Artist admits that a small section of the painting doesn't look as good as when he painted it in the 1960s, the "F-111" as well as other paintings Rosenquist has made with Fluorescent paint "forty years" ago are still considered by the Artist to be in good condition.

During the seventh year of work on this 'History of the Black Light and Fluorescent Art' a paper was sent to me by an Art conservator of Belgium. This conservator has focused her attention and recently written papers for her master's degree on the subjects of the restoration of Fluorescent paintings, as well as the history of Fluorescent Art, after working on problems with restoration of the work made by the Artist whom she states was the first painter in Belgium to use Fluorescent pigments, Felix De Boeck. After internships in America researching the beginning of Fluorescent Art and for restoration work on the Fluorescent paintings of Frank Stella, this conservator has written papers on whom she presents as the first Artist to have used Fluorescent paint, Richard Bowman, and the first Artist to have used Fluorescent paint "successfully," Herb Aach. In her initial correspondence with the author this Art conservator explained that although the "appreciation" for Fluorescent Art remains "still problematic," she wishes to present a different viewpoint, and her viewpoint is included in this book as an example of a contemporary perspective of the history of Fluorescent Art, independent of the viewpoint of the Artist writing this book. After an internship working on the restoration of Frank Stella Fluorescent paintings in New York, it led to this conservator's thesis on the conservation of Fluorescent Art, which was published by "CeROArt." Another paper written by this Belgian Art conservator focuses on the history of the beginning of Fluorescent Art, and is centered around whom this conservator concludes was the most important Artist who 'developed' Fluorescent Art, the German-American Artist Herbert Aach. What introduced and inspired this conservator to a paper on Herb Aach was a 1970 article written by Aach in "Leonardo" on both the phenomenon of Fluorescence, and the use of these Fluorescent pigments for Art. Very curiously, in the introduction of her paper on Herb Aach this conservator informs the reader that Fluorescence can not be photographed or even printed - What?? The first photograph of Fluorescence was taken one-hundred and thirteen years ago in 1903 by the scientist who invented the Black light Longwave Ultraviolet filter, and whom the Black light is still named after in professional circles, Dr. Robert Williams Wood, of the "Wood's Lamp." In addition, Joseph Switzer (the younger brother of the teenager who invented Fluorescent paint, Robert Switzer) invented a completely new printing process exclusively for Fluorescent printing, as well as filing a patent for this invention of Fluorescent printing, both in 1935, which revolutionized industrial Fluorescent printing. What really caught my eye in both this conservator's paper on Herb Aach and his original 1970 article in "Leonardo," was the astounding arrogance of Aach, who states plainly that after painting with Fluorescent pigments in his Art for the vast time period of more than "five years," this humble Artist claimed that although 'Fluorescent paint had not been developed recently' and 'although he was not the first Artist to use these Fluorescent Colors,' Aach states that he 'may have been' the first Artist to have used these Fluorescent pigments "relatively successfully"(!) As this Herb Aach paper on the history of Fluorescent Art is read it becomes quite apparent that neither Herb Aach or the Art conservator writing this paper ever heard of John Plumer Ludlum, the first Artist to have used Fluorescent pigments in Fine Art ("relatively successfully") in 1945, nearly twenty years before Aach. Furthermore this paper on Herb Aach and Fluorescent Art history claims that Richard Bowman of California was probably the first Artist who used Fluorescent paint in Fine Art during the 1950s. Only partially through this paper three questionable points have already been made, first being that Fluorescence can not be photographed or printed, when Fluorescence has been photographed since 1903 (the current author has taken many tens of thousands of photographs of Fluorescence during the past decades, with 35mm film, 6x6 medium format film with a Hasselblad 503, a multitude of digital cameras and digital video cameras, including 3D digital photos as well as digital 3D HD video, only, in addition to perhaps twenty-five thousand digital photographs of visitors to the Museum in the Fluorescent "Participatory" Environment, the first book in the world on "Fluorescent Flowers," and the first published photograph of Fluorescent Frog's eyes). The second questionable point made by this Belgian Art conservator was that Richard Bowman was probably the first Artist to have used Fluorescent pigments in Fine Art in the 1950s, the decade after John Ludlum began to use Fluorescent pigments in Fine Art in 1945 (also in California), and the third point in question was that although Herb Aach was not the first Artist to have used Fluorescent pigments in Fine Art, he was humble enough to claim, after using Fluorescent pigments for only "five years," that he was probably the first Artist to use Fluorescent paint "relatively successfully." What does become very apparent throughout the reading of this paper on Herb Aach is the common attitude of both the Artist himself, and this conservator writing about him, through the statement that Aach used Fluorescent Colors in his painting also 'correctly,' which is apparently considered by the author of the paper to be 'frugally, well-considered,' and not, as Aach explains, the "kitschy" way many other Artists use Fluorescent Colors. Aach goes so far as to criticize Andy Warhol's Fluorescent silkscreens, which in his opinion 'miss the effect' because about Color and it's use in Fluorescence, Andy Warhol didn't "know much." Furthermore this Aach states that Andy Warhol's use of Fluorescence in his Art was "merely intuitive," as well as the results of Warhol's Fluorescent Art being just plain "accidental." In conclusion of his criticism of Andy Warhol, Aach writes that Warhol wasn't aware that Fluorescent Colors are not "tuned" to an "equal value," which is defined by Aach as a "medium value." Apparently Aach mixed up his own Fluorescent paint without the 'U.V. absorbers' added to Fluorescent paint commercially sold, according to the Artist. It is clearly stated that the intention of Aach was to use Fluorescent paint as an 'extension' of the known, 'visible world,' and not for something such as a 'psychedelic experience.' Comparing the effect of the stained glass windows of Chartres, which are appreciated throughout the changing natural light of the day, Aach states that viewing a Fluorescent painting in the gradual shifting effects between daylight and Black light is what he terms "multi-leveled." However, when Aach actually begins to paint with Fluorescent pigments, he uses also Black and White paint for 'creating depth' on his canvas, and in the end does exactly what he criticized Andy Warhol for: not using only Colors of "medium value."

Herbert Aach was born in 1923 in Germany and began to study Art at an early age until his family left Germany for New York in 1938. After studying at The Brooklyn Museum Art School, Aach studied Art in Mexico City for two years. During this period of study Aach developed his fascination for Color, and between 1954 and 1963 he developed through experimentation what he called "Color Expressionism." This is what Herb Aach is remembered for during the period of the 1960s through the 1980s, his 'unique and individual use of Color.' While living in remote Hazletown, Pennsylvania as the director of a children's Art-supply company, he experimented with a multitude of pigments which led him to begin mixing up his own paints, and upon his return in 1963 to New York he began teaching Art and Color Theory at Queens College in 1965. It was during this period of the mid-1960s that Aach began to use Fluorescent pigments because of their intense Colors and 'inner light.' In his 1970 "Leonardo" article on the "Use and Phenomenon" of Fluorescent pigments, Aach wrote that it took him more than "three years" for relearning "Color behavior" using Fluorescent paint. Aach also discovers and admits that Vasarely or any Color theory based on non-Fluorescent pigments was "inadequate" to use in any way with these light-emitting Fluorescent Colors. Aach also concludes correctly that Fluorescent Colors are "the frontier" of both research and usage of Color. Philosophically, Aach explains that up until the use of Fluorescent pigments the Twentieth century technology had 'fit in' with the texture of the "natural environment," but with the advancements and discoveries of the Twentieth century a "synthetic environment" has begun to be produced. Logically, Aach explains, the invention and use of these synthetic Fluorescent Colors was a product of the Twentieth century when the move towards a synthetic environment began to develop. In conclusion Aach states that during the period from the mid-1960s to 1970, when he began to use Fluorescent pigments, it felt as if he had begun to learn to see with his eyes "over again." After Herb Aach's Introduction to his article in 1970's "Leonardo," the second section "Fluorescent Pigments" begins with Aach proclaiming that 'although Fluorescent pigments weren't developed recently' and 'although he wasn't the first Artist to use Fluorescent Colors,' Aach states, again, that he may have been the first Artist to use Fluorescent pigments "relatively successfully" in regards to his 'technical and aesthetic' use of these Fluorescent pigments. Aach next explains that what Fluorescent Colors have been used for, and have come to represent are "bright, brash" Colors used as "attention getters." This usage and representation is what Herb Aach concludes caused society and Artists to deem the "brazen" Fluorescent paint "not suitable" for the creation of 'Fine' Art. To his eternal credit, Herb Aach next writes clearly that he believes this viewpoint of society and Artists about Fluorescent pigments is what he terms nothing more than "erroneous myth." In this 1970 article Aach explains the differences between the luminescent phenomenon of Fluorescence, Phosphorescence, Bioluminescence, Chemiluminescence, and Photoluminescence, concluding that under any possible lighting condition or wavelength of the spectrum - in daylight or under Black light Ultraviolet energy - more light is always emitted by Fluorescent pigments than "ordinary" pigments.

The third section of Aach's 1970 article pertains to his "Experience" using Fluorescent pigments, and the Artist explains that during the 1960s "Day-Glo Corp." of Cleveland, Ohio sent him some samples of Fluorescent paint and reassured the Artist that the quality of the pigment had been improved over the earlier pigments that quickly faded, and which Aach explains he had tried before without success. Since Aach had been used to the common Artistic practice of mixing dry powdered pigments into acrylic mediums (a practice unchanged until the present day, and the exact way the current author has always made his Fluorescent paint) the powdered Fluorescent pigments he began to incorporate into his palette were mixed precisely the same way. In amazement Aach explains that by juxtaposing the brilliant "Cadmium Orange" with Fluorescent Green, this formerly brilliant non-Fluorescent Orange magically changes it's appearance to "dirty ochre"(!) Aach next states correctly that there is an actual 'increase' with this intensity of Fluorescent Colors in a person's "Color perception," as well as a change in the viewer's response 'psychologically and physiologically' in regards especially to "spatial illusions." The Artist further explains the response of Fluorescent pigments under Ultraviolet Black lights, as well as the response of his Fluorescent Art in sunlight which has a component of Longwave Ultraviolet that also makes Fluorescent Art "glow."

The turning point in Aach's opinion of Fluorescent pigments in his painting occurred after his neighbor, who painted human bodies as "Living Sculpture," asked him about using Fluorescent paint in her "Living" Art. Aach referred his neighbor to the "Day-Glo Corp." who had sent him his pigments, and a representative of the company then brought a thirty watt Black light to test the response of their Fluorescent paint with. Herb Aach admits that it was his practice to paint under a mixture of both incandescent and Fluorescent White lights, and not under Black lights with Fluorescent paint. The effect of seeing his Fluorescent paintings under the black light emitting brilliant Colors of light for the Artist who's Art was based on Color - the effect on himself was described by Aach as being "enthralled"(!) *Nothing* surpasses the intensity of Fluorescent Colors under a black light in the dark! The Artist wrote that his entire studio became "lit up" and was "glowing" under a single thirty watt Black light, as well as being what Aach calculated as ten times the illumination of an ordinary thirty watt incandescent White light. The 'enthralling' effect of seeing his Fluorescent Art under a Black light for the first time was caused in part by what Aach explains as the technique by which he made his own Fluorescent paint. This handmade Fluorescent paint was mixed by Aach using a very high concentration of Fluorescent pigment, and without what the Artist calls "ultraviolet absorbers" added to his paint, like used in commercially produced Fluorescent paint. It is further explained that a high concentration of Fluorescent pigment in an emulsion creates a paint less prone to fading, and by comparison paint manufacturers do not use high concentrations of Fluorescent pigments in their manufactured Fluorescent paint because when using less pigment in the mixture of paint it produces paint which has a longer "shelf-life" and will not dry out. Aach explains that he counterbalances the shorter "shelf-life" and drying out of the Fluorescent paint made with a high concentration of Fluorescent pigment by simply mixing up his Fluorescent paint when he needs it, not in advance. The current author has found that, unfortunately, the amount of Fluorescent pigment in Fluorescent paint is not the only problem with commercially produced, or even with handmade Fluorescent paint, because the quality of the Fluorescent pigment itself is crucial. If the size of the particles of the Fluorescent pigment are ground below a certain micron size during the manufacturing of the Fluorescent pigment, the resulting Fluorescent paint will not Fluoresce as brightly as Fluorescent paint made with pigment ground to the correct micron size. The Fluorescent Artist writing this book has mixed up thousands of liters of Fluorescent and also Phosphorescent paint by hand with powdered pigments in the last thirty years, and began before that in the late 1960s and 1970s by experimentally adding first glue, then advancing to adding acrylic mediums and acrylic binders to manufactured Fluorescent paints in an attempt to raise their quality for painting.

Personally speaking, Herb Aach next explains in his "Leonardo" 1970 article that his use of Fluorescent paint began roughly two years ahead of "Psychedelica," and while the Artist claims that he was not actually "opposed to" what he calls the "mind-blowing" use of Fluorescence, his "intentions" for this Fluorescent phenomenon in his Art were "far removed" from this mind-blowing use of Fluorescence with "Psychedelica," which is described by the Artist as being composed of "high-pressure" drama and "light jabs" which are "eye-piercing." The Artist continues on this theme, describing his use of Black light as being nothing more than "an extension" for "traditional" viewing of paintings. Furthermore, Aach explains that what he finds fascinating is the technique he uses of a slow transition for his Fluorescent Artwork between the ordinary White light and the Black light, which he writes "contributes" visually to the 'overall experience.' Concluding on the social standing of Fluorescent Colors, forty-six years ago in this 1970 article Aach wrote that Fluorescence has accumulated over the ages a "bad name" because of it's original association with rotten food glowing and other fears, such as "oil slicks." This, according to Aach, caused society's association of Fluorescence with "spoilage" and other undesirable states of "deterioration." In addition to these associations of unhealthy rotten foods and deterioration with the glow of Chemiluminescence and Bioluminescence since the dawn of civilization, Fluorescent paint itself had a "bad name" since the beginning of it's commercialization due to it's original inferior quality regarding stability and fading. The Artist concedes that although there exists "some truth" in these negative associations with Fluorescence, "erroneous conclusions" can also easily be obtained by them [and usually are]. The current author would have to add also the insane "Miracle Cures" Shortwave Ultraviolet "Actinotherapy" as well as the luminescent "Radium Craze," both a century ago, as well as the Second world war's immense usage of Fluorescence, added to the association with the Psychedelic Movement of the 1960s, and the "Green Fluorescent Protein's" "Transgenic Fluorescent animals" created by Genetic manipulation of the present day - all to the associations which together have caused society to give Fluorescence a "bad name" in the end.

Herb Aach closes his article with the subject which opened the article, his large Fluorescent mural "Sonic Boom" which he painted for over a year. The Artist states that with his painting "Sonic Boom" he developed a technique he would explore the rest of his life. Coating this painting with up to thirty coats of paint, Aach used the flat hard-edge technique of the 1970s, achieved with masking tape and endless coats of paint on canvas. This was the most common "Color field" painting technique of the 1970s, which the current author can fondly remember, having painted about one-hundred canvases during the 1970s with this hard-edge technique, using miles of masking tape and endless coats of paint to achieve an almost industrial surface of Color. To achieve this minimalist appearance Aach began to even use an industrial tool, applying his many layers of flat fields of Color with paint rollers, which further erased any evidence of an expressive human touch. In this way Aach explained that he had reduced Color to being just a "component" of the painting, "impersonal," and nearly "clinical." In mixing the paint for "Sonic Boom" Aach used 'flattening agents' with this Fluorescent paint, as well as developing his own Fluorescent Colors. Aach developed his own Fluorescent Colors because he felt that there weren't enough Fluorescent Colors produced at that time, and the quality of the pigments could be improved. In relation to this large Fluorescent painting "Sonic Boom" of 1969, Aach again very humbly states clearly that in all the fields of Color, he considered himself to be the first authority of not only the present, but in all the past history of Art itself. To close his discussion of this "Sonic Boom" Fluorescent painting, Aach explains the Color photographs of the mural which were included in this 1970 "Leonardo" article, and again makes a claim that reveals the true limit of his knowledge regarding the history of Fluorescence (while again displaying his truly humble nature) explaining to the 1970 reader that as far as he knew, the Color photographs taken of his "Sonic Boom" painting were the very "first photographs" made of paintings using only the "black lights"(!) *In 1969?!* Here, in this statement, Herbert Aach is about as incorrect as he was stating that he was the first Artist to use Fluorescent pigments "relatively successfully." First of all, in the very first magazine article written about the "Switzer Brothers," one of which whom invented Fluorescent paint in 1933, in "Scientific American" magazine of October, 1934 this first article included a photograph in 'only the Black light' of a very early example of their Fluorescent paintings made with "Invisible" Fluorescent paint. This photograph of a Fluorescent painting under Black light was taken and published when Herb Aach was eleven years old and still living in Germany, which was thirty-six years before Aach claimed that the photographs of "Sonic Boom" were the first photographs of a Fluorescent painting under only Black lights. Now if Aach meant to say the first 'Color' photograph taken of a Fluorescent painting with only Black lights, it's not what he wrote, but even then he would have been incorrect by only by a couple of decades, not thirty-six years. These absolutely incorrect sweeping statements made by Herb Aach, such as the photographs of "Sonic Boom" being the first photographs of a Fluorescent painting taken under only Black lights in 1969, which is more than thirty years after Fluorescent paintings were already photographed, are mirrored in the writing of this Belgian Art conservator presenting the 'history' of Fluorescent Art. Unbelievably, once again on page thirty-one of this Art conservator's thesis written in 2012, it is plainly stated that 'even today printing Fluorescent Colors is *impossible*' because of the Fluorescent pigment's "vulnerability." Again, Joseph Switzer invented a printing process exclusively for Fluorescent inks which was the actual first patent filed by the "Switzer Brothers" in 1935, seventy-seven years before this Belgian thesis was written. In "Electric Lady" Art Gallery there are hundreds of Fluorescent prints for sale for over a decade, which the current author even prints using Fluorescent inks with a "bubble-jet" computer printer!

With this hard-edge Color field technique he had used to create "Sonic Boom" in his hopes of achieving 'Color's optimal experience,' Aach began to create canvases in series, inspired by Claude Monet's experiments in changing sunlight achieved with his famous series 'Haystacks' as well as the series experimenting with shifting sunlight on the facade of the 'Rouen Cathedral.' The first series of Fluorescent paintings by Aach were exhibited in 1969, and it becomes understandable that the technical planning, variables, value ranges, numbers of Colors, and other extremely complex rules which come to govern his Art are artifacts of his deep and prolonged study of the scientist who wrote the most prejudiced, 'Chromophobic' "Theory of Colours" every published (as well as being the scientist who stole the discovery of Ultraviolet itself from the unknown German scientist John Ritter two-hundred years ago and claimed it as his own for history): Johann Wolfgang von Goethe himself. Three "rules" are what Aach explained create his Fluorescent paintings, first of which (like Andy Warhol) all of his Colors have to be of a "medium value," second, the limit of Colors used is stipulated by the twelve Colors of the Color-wheel, and third (which stinks of Goethe) numbers are assigned to each Color and sequenced to regulate Color transitions. This results in a total of three-hundred and eight-four possible Color combinations, of which Aach chooses sixteen. These mathematical exercises to create Art, according to Aach, also create forces of "axial tension," as well as the "expansion" of all the Colors themselves. From 1973 to 1974 a series of twenty-six acrylic paintings on canvas were created by the Artist, done in the hard-edge 1970s technique, and are composed of Fluorescent circles sequentially arranged inside each other. This series was inspired by the spring and fall equinoxes, of which the comparison between day and night's balance is analogous to the balance between White light and Black light. The dynamics of this "Equinox" series is created by the 'movement' of circles in the series of paintings which are arranged in different positions on each canvas and then seen through sequence. It is also mentioned by Aach that a three-dimensional illusion is created on these flat two-dimensional paintings through the juxtaposition of monochromatic pure areas of Color.

The last two Fluorescent series of paintings created by Aach were during the latter part of the 1970s, which consist of the twenty-five acrylic paintings of the "Equinox" series just described, and another series of thirty gouache paintings. Similar circular forms are used in these two last series of paintings, and is clear that Aach was once again strongly inspired by Goethe. This flavor of an almost self-contained logic which Goethe was so proficient at not only creating, but also of convincing others of, is very similar to the reasoning written by Aach in his quest to create a stronger vibration between Colors. The last Fluorescent series by Aach is know as the "Split Infinity," which is split into the "A" and "B" series and dealt with the dynamics set in motion through sequencing of the large number of individual images in the series, as well as the creation of the illusion of three-dimensionality achieved on the flat canvases through the use of form and the vibration of juxtaposed pure areas of Fluorescent Colors. The title Aach assigned to this series of Fluorescent paintings "Split Infinity" refers to the Colors as well as the shapes used on this series of canvases, specifically referring to a beam of light split into it's infinite number of component Colors when refracted by a prism, and to the circular forms broken into just partial views and juxtaposed on his canvases which add to the illusion of infinity. What apparently fascinated Aach was the three-dimensional perspective which viewers would experience, and this effect was varied by the Artist, who in the "Equinox" series created the illusion of entering into the canvases, and for the "Split Infinity" series created just the opposite illusion, with the circular forms on the canvases seeming to be projected off of the surface and towards the viewer. Aach himself attributed the use of Fluorescent Colors to this illusion of three-dimensionality, but also went to great lengths carefully designing the sequencing of circular forms on his series of paintings, making it clear that it was a combination of both form and Fluorescent Colors which created these illusions of different states of three-dimensionality. In addition to these illusionary techniques creating three-dimensionality and dynamics, Aach used Color sequencing in his series of paintings which was coordinated to the inherently known progression of the Colors of the spectrum. At the end of his life during the mid-1980s Aach still used Fluorescent Colors, but changed his technique by adding dark and light Colors to his compositions, and in the end not creating paintings of "equal value," which is what, again, he criticized Andy Warhol for over a decade before, saying that about Fluorescent Colors and their use in painting, Warhol didn't "know much."

The Belgian paper on Herb Aach closes with, again, the incorrect, misleading point that the Artist's "oeuvre" changed dramatically with the introduction of the "first" paint marketed and sold which was Fluorescent - in the 1960s?! The time period when the first Fluorescent paint was marketed and sold was when Herbert Aach was a boy, actually. The 'introduction' of Fluorescent paint did not change the "oeuvre" of Herbert Aach, because Fluorescent paint had been introduced, marketed, and sold since Aach was twelve years old and still living in Germany in 1935. The historical fact is that Fluorescent paint had been used by Artists since Aach was an adolescent, and Aach himself did not begin to use Fluorescent Colors until they were over thirty years old, and after he had been an Artist and painting for years already. It is further stated that this "new" Fluorescent paint of the 1960s is what Aach had been searching for his entire Artistic career. Through his questionable technical calisthenics inspired by his study of convoluted Goethe and his work on the publication of Goethe's "Theory of Colours," as well as his astounding arrogance proclaiming after just five years of working with Fluorescent Colors that he was the first Artist to use Fluorescent pigments "relatively successfully," a clear picture is formed of this Artist.

However, the Fluorescent Artist writing this book must give credit to Herb Aach who did in fact believe that due to his Artistic contribution and his work with Fluorescent pigments, Art would gradually accept Fluorescent Colors and that these modern Colors would be added to the palettes of Artists worldwide. The "Conclusions" written by Aach in his 1970 article consist of just two sentences, but they are very hopeful. The Artist writes that his experience over the several years before 1970 'convinced' him that as Fluorescent pigment's quality is improved many more Artists would begin to use these Fluorescent Colors. Aach last point is that there is still "much exploration" to be done with "glowing paintings," especially in the field of 'aesthetics.'

Another well known Artist who used Fluorescent Colors extensively was Richard Bowman. Bowman was one of the first Artists to use Fluorescent pigments, and began his use of these Colors through his initial experiments with Fluorescent lacquers in 1950. This was however half a decade after the first Artist to use Fluorescent paint in fine Art began to use these Colors in 1945, John Plumer Ludlum. Richard Bowman is remembered for his abstract dynamic canvases which he created primarily in the San Francisco Bay area. The Artist was born in Illinois in 1918 and graduated in 1942 from the Art Institute of Chicago School, going on to earn his Fine Arts Masters degree in 1949 from the University of Iowa. During the 1940s Bowman also taught Art in the Art Institute of Chicago School, where he painted a portrait of one of his students he became involved with, the abstract expressionist Joan Mitchell during the mid-1940s. In 1950 Bowman began teaching in Canada at the University of Manitoba, Winnipeg, and it was during that year in 1950 when Bowman found the captivating magic of Fluorescent Colors.

There was only one book published on Richard Bowman, the 1986 "Richard Bowman: Forty Years of Abstract Painting," but there were several catalogues from his exhibitions published throughout his life, including "Richard Bowman: Paintings and Reflections, 1943-1961," from his November third to December third 1961 exhibition in the San Francisco Museum of Art. This 1961 San Francisco Museum of Art Richard Bowman catalogue was a historical event in itself, because the front cover has a painting by the Artist printed in Red and Yellow Fluorescent ink, and it has been documented that this cover of Bowman's painting was the first time a piece of Art had been printed and published in Fluorescent Colors, which was fifty-five years ago. Since the first commercial package was printed in 1956, the timeline of 1961 for the first Artwork to have been printed in Fluorescent ink is feasible (the first package printed with Fluorescent ink documented in the November, 1956 "Chain Store Age" trade magazine advertisement announcing the event for "Chesterfield Cigarettes" - which had printed on it "The Christmas Carton" with a label also printed on the carton of "Christmas" cigarettes to write who you were giving the cigarettes to for Christmas - is displayed in "Electric Ladyland - the First Museum of Fluorescent Art"). This 1961 "Richard Bowman - Paintings and Reflections, 1943-1961" catalogue of the San Francisco Museum of Art is not that easy to find since only 1,000 copies were printed fifty-five years ago, but the author could find one copy in good condition for the Museum collection. This is a medium sized format six by nine inch (15 x 23 cm) softcover publication with a thick cover stock of what appears to be Artist's paper, which has on it a piece of Art printed in Fluorescent Colors for the first time. Even after half a century the Fluorescent Colors that this historic cover of the Bowman catalogue were printed on are so vivid it looks like it could have been printed today. This White Artist's paper cover of the catalogue has the signature "R Bowman" printed in Black at the bottom, as well as energetic lines of Black making up the structure of the Bowman Fluorescent Artwork. Over these Black energetic lines bursting out from a central point are areas of Fluorescent Magenta and Fluorescent Yellow brushstrokes. The transparency of Fluorescent Colors is used to it's full extent by Bowman on this catalogue cover, because when Fluorescent Magenta is printed on top of Fluorescent Yellow a third Color of Fluorescent Orange is immediately produced, exactly as if you would take a sheet of transparent Magenta glass and place it on top of a sheet of Yellow glass. What is the most striking point of this Bowman exhibition catalogue cover is the incredible strength and freshness of the Fluorescent Colors, even after half a century. This is nothing compared to Bowman's cover placed under a Black light in the dark - the cover stock has correctly been chosen to be non-Fluorescent White Artist's paper, so the Fluorescent Colors of Magenta, Yellow, and the third created Orange are stunning. The catalogue begins with a small dedication by Bowman in 1961 to "creative people" from all nations and all races. Although the interior of the catalogue is printed with nineteen Black and White reproductions of Bowman's Fluorescent paintings, there is one painting "Kinetogenics 36" from 1960 made with oil paint and "Fluorescent oil" paint printed on a full page in Fluorescent Colors. This large 73 x 84 inch (185 x 213 cm) canvas is ablaze with Fluorescent Color and bursting with energy, giving the immediate impression of what Bowman was most interested in, the invisible and "magical" forces of the universe revealed. A pale Pinkish Mauve background of this canvas is barely visible behind the Fluorescent Reds, Magentas, Oranges, Yellows, and touches of Fluorescent Green and Blue which make up the majority of this Bowman painting. The catalogue of nineteen Bowman paintings reproduced from the San Francisco Museum of Art 1961 exhibition are listed, with three being painted in the 1940s, six painted in the 1950s, and the remaining ten paintings from 1960 and 1961. The Forward to the catalogue is written by the director of the San Francisco Museum of Art at the time, George D. Culler, who clearly describes Bowman's very early pioneering work with Fluorescent paint, as well as his inspiration being the invisible worlds described by science. Culler describes Bowman as an Artist 'exploring new realities in an age which is ruled and created by science.' Culler goes on to explain that Bowman was an Artist painting 'intuitions of energies' both subatomic and

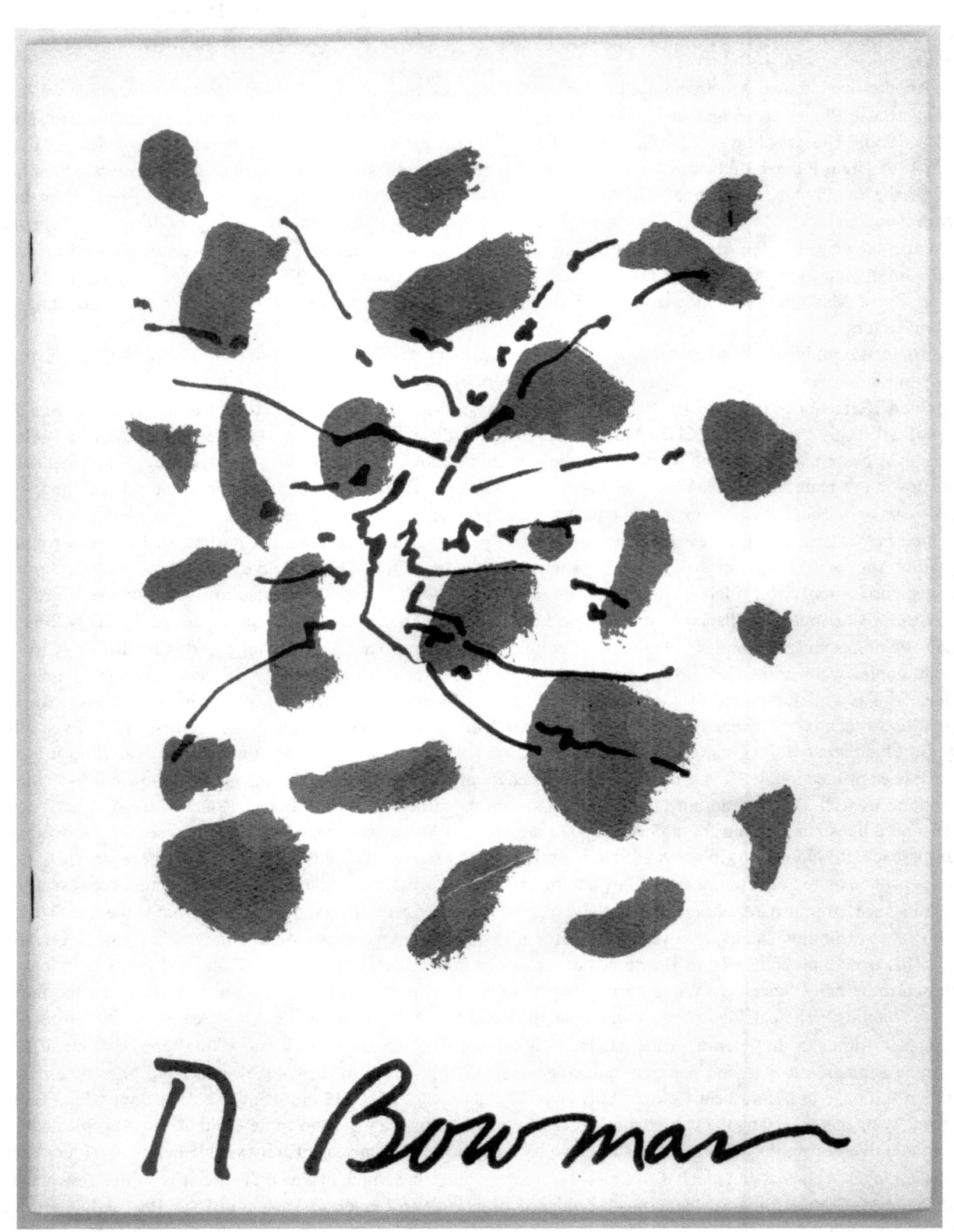

"Richard Bowman: Paintings and Reflections, 1943-1961," 1961 San Francisco Museum of Art catalogue containing the historical front cover, which was the first piece of Art that had been printed and published in Fluorescent Colors

on a scale of the known universe, who captures a 'reality which cannot be known through direct experience.' Culler also places Bowman's inspiration from the Color master Pierre Bonnard at the beginning, right before his description of Bowman's discovery of early Fluorescent lacquer in 1950 and Fluorescent oil paint in 1956. With very clear perspective, and with great respect from the Fluorescent Artist writing this book, in 1961 this San Francisco Museum of Art director wrote what I have personally dreamed about for many years, going back in time to give a few pots of Fluorescent paint to the original great Color painters of the past, such as Gauguin! Culler wrote that he was "quite sure" if Pierre Bonnard 'would have lived to see Fluorescent Colors, he would surely have been delighted to find supercharged Colors.' Culler goes on to describe these new Fluorescent Colors as being comparable to light itself, and being 'beyond any paint previously available for an Artist.' What George D. Culler closes his Forward with in Bowman's 1961 catalogue is nothing less than crystal clear and prophetic, stating very plainly that what this museum director was really interested in, more than the "technical properties" of Fluorescent Colors, was the human "reactions" to these new unprecedented Colors. Culler cannot figure out why 'in an age which allows almost anything, from the new synthetics to the trash of industrialized society' to be used by Artists through both experimentation and creation of their Art, it's "strange" to this 1961 museum director that a "strong exception" would be made, and that these newly invented Fluorescent Colors which create the possibility of 'extending the range of Color's intensity' would be rejected by almost all Artists. In this rare questioning of the validity of Fluorescent Color's use in Fine Art, and it's almost immediate rejection by Artists universally, Culler goes on to very correctly further describe the main culprit behind this universal rejection: *Tradition.* Culler writes that 'Judgements of what materials can be proper for making Art' are still based on tradition and by 1961 were becoming difficult to categorize. The example of Fluorescent Colors 'arousing irrational antagonisms' and of being unfair, or "unsporting" - like using dynamite instead of a fishing pole to catch fish - are all given by Culler, who clearly reacts with the fact of the matter, being that Art is neither a "sport" or a damn game having rules - but that Art is essentially a "search," 'a way to see the invisible magic universe around us.' This very clear museum director closes his statement of 1961 with the fact that Artists do not learn what they should paint by 'consulting definitions,' but that they create by themselves through their vision of 'the laws which relate to their Art.'

The text of this Bowman 1961 exhibition catalogue closes with a statement by the Artist in 1959 in which Bowman explains in the first sentence that since 1943 his Art was based on 'the energies of nature (or reality).' The Artist describes his "Rock and Sun" 1943-1950 series of paintings being centered on "atomic concept" and his interpretation of this energy, his 1950-1953 "Kinetograph" series being similarly based on both the atomic and subatomic worlds, and his "Micromacrocosmos" 1953-1955 series inspired by the visual "structural similarities" of the universe seen through either an electron microscope or a telescope. Bowman describes the inspiration for his most recent painting series of 1956 to 1961 being from forms which were "energy-generating." Bowman concludes his 1959 statement in his exhibition catalogue with his 'discovery and his use of Fluorescent lacquer in 1950 and then in 1956 Fluorescent oil paint,' which were in Bowman's words "natural mediums" for him to both 'integrate and express his concepts of the universe's great forces, known but unseen, more fully.'

One last point to make about this Bowman catalogue is the page listing the Artist's major exhibitions, in which it is written that Richard Bowman showed in Peggy Guggenheim's "Art of this Century" in 1945, which was an extremely influential Art gallery in which the painting of Jackson Pollock was first 'discovered' by Piet Mondrian and then announced by Peggy Guggenheim herself to the media.

An article of 1973 written by Bowman in "Leonardo" documents the Artist discussing his career, his first use of Fluorescent Colors in 1950, and his paintings going back to 1943. Bowman explains the forces which deeply inspired his paintings, particularly atomic physics as the underlying "energy phenomenon" in nature. It has been documented that the forces of science which inspired Bowman's "Kinetographs" series were atomic structure, subatomic structure, nuclear particles, cloud-chamber atomic tracking, and also force fields. It was while working on this series "Kinetographs" in 1950 that the Artist decided to highlight energy areas of his paintings with Fluorescent lacquer paint for the first time. Bowman's "Leonardo" article of 1973 reveals his inspiration immediately through it's title, with his deepest interests of making 'Painting of both the Microcosm and the Macrocosm created with Fluorescent Pigments.' In this article Bowman gives a background to the beginning of his use of Fluorescent lacquer in 1950, and to the beginning of his Artistic career, which started with his study at the Art Institute of Chicago where he graduated in 1942. Bowman next went to paint in Mexico where he began his first important series of paintings, the 'Rock and Sun' paintings. This 'Rock and Sun' series began with Bowman making a simple watercolor of a sunset over Lake Patzcuaro in which he saw the Sun's energy, and formulated the idea of expressing the energy of both radioactive minerals and the Sun itself. This led to his first paintings in oil of this series, which he completed in July, 1943, 'Rock Formation in Sunlight.' Bowman describes this first canvas of simple forms, explaining that this painting beginning the 'Rock and Sun' series is of the Sun prominently painted as a "flat disc" in the sky, and the mountain-like rocks painted as 'curved surfaces overlapping.' Initially, after finishing this first oil of the 'Rock and Sun' series, the Artist defined the concept of this series with his written statement questioning the 'stability of rock' as we come to see it with our eyes and brain. Bowman then delves deeply into the "atomic state" of this "Rock" and perceives it as it truly exists, as an atomic structure which is not only as stable as we perceive it with our eyes, but also an infinitely dynamic world of atoms, which are anything but "stable," and which Bowman describes as "kinetic." What the actual painted image of 'Rock Formation in Sunlight' from 1943 reminds one of is nearly a Cubist view of the surface of a large iron meteorite. Bowman describes this surface in his 1943 canvas as 'curved surfaces overlapping,' as well as the inspiration for the painting being his dramatic climate change when he moved after four years from the windy city of Chicago to the 'brilliant sunshine' of Mexico. The Artist wrote in his 1973 "Leonardo" article that the intensity of the sunlight in Mexico was stronger than he had ever experienced before in his life. Back to the 'curved surfaces overlapping' in his 1943 canvas, Bowman states that the Mexican landscape was also the first place he had ever seen "rugged mountains." This timeless ancient culture of Mexico further inspired Bowman to delve deeper into the subatomic world, and the Artist began to be 'enchanted' by the rapidly developing 1940s field of "atomic physics." The Artist began to follow common 'newspaper and popular magazine accounts of atomic physics,' and then advanced to attempt learning deeper science through the "Bulletin of the Atomic Scientists." It has also been noted that Richard Bowman's friendship with Bern Porter, who was a scientist, Artist, and publisher, as well as a true character known for his development of the Cathode Ray tube, added to the Artist's collection of influential scientific knowledge. In discussing his first important series 'Rock and Sun,' which begins with his initial 'Rock Formation in Sunlight' canvas of 1943, these paintings are described in general as "contrasting colors" which are "very bright" and used to evoke a visual effect that is strong, such as painting a sky bright Red with a Sun in this sky painted brilliant Green. The imagery from his 1943 'Rock Formation in Sunlight' is reconfigured and reduced in his 1945 'Rock and fragment' canvas, transformed and fragmented onto an upright almost organic form, with the flat disc of the Sun remaining in the upper area of the painting. By 1946, in his 'Rock' canvas the organic form of 'Rock' has become even more representational of a figurative form, slightly similar to the paintings of Picasso and Miro. This representational figurative form of 'Rock' in Bowman's 'Rock and Sun' series gets elevated to a pedestal (or a statue base) in 1944's "Abstract (Blue)" canvas. In August, 1947 Bowman documented his experience with this 'Rock and Sun' series, and states clearly in his first sentence that "the factor" in his painting since the beginning of the 'Rock and Sun' series which had preoccupied him, has been "kinetics," and expanding on the subject Bowman next states that he also 'stresses' the importance in 1947's contemporary Art, of "Kinetogenic forms." As witness to the Artist's immersion into the deep abstract particle world of atomic physics, Bowman next explains that "kinetics" are not only a "dominant factor" of reality in the objective world such as physical contact with external stimuli, but that the state of "kinetics" can also be used 'psychologically' in Art, expressing feelings of "subjective nature" as well. The discussion by Bowman of his 1943-1950 series 'Rock and Sun' ends with his last canvas of that series, 'Atomic Rock and Sun' of 1950, which is described by the Artist in "Leonardo" as "fragmented forms" from which he had formulated through his perception of the world based on the study of atomic physics. Bowman admits that by 1950 he had finally described in his painting what he had learned, being that the energy of the universe is composed of 'tiny bits of quanta.' Bowman further states that this concept of the 'transmission of energy' being either matter or light had been "a factor" of his Art the last thirty years. Bowman closes his August, 1947 statement with the humble fact that he was aware of other Artists who were 'similarly influenced by modern physics' as well. The last canvas in this series 'Rock and Sun,' 'Atomic Rock and Sun' of 1950, is a dramatic departure from the first canvas of the series 'Rock Formation in Sunlight' of 1943, and depicts the world around us as quanta, or particles.

    The discovery of small jars of 'daylight' Fluorescent lacquer paint which were being sold in 1950 was nothing less than a major turning point in Richard Bowman's life, and this is of such importance that the event is separated and begins section three of his 1973 "Leonardo" article. In 1950 the Artist first found 'daylight' Fluorescent paint sold in these small jars, described by the Artist as paints which were intended primarily to be used for "advertising" as well as "decoration," and goes on to claim that he 'might have been' the Artist first using these Fluorescent lacquer paints for paintings. This, however, is not so, because it is well documented that John Ludlum had been using Fluorescent paint in fine Art since 1945 in Los Angeles, and Lucio Fontana had also used Fluorescent paint by 1948. Bowman explained that his attraction to Fluorescent lacquer paint was caused by the paint's "added brilliance" over ordinary Colors which 'assisted him in expressing' how he personally conceived and then interpreted "energy." The Artist goes on to state that since he found the first Fluorescent lacquer paint in 1950 he had been interested in, and had used this brilliant pigment ever since. By 1956 Bowman had found a Fluorescent paint of better quality, the relatively new Fluorescent Oil paint, which the Artist described as being easier to work with and to "spread," as well as being an improvement in quality over the Fluorescent lacquer paint which in the end 'cracked.' Finally Richard Bowman found Fluorescent paint that was a far superior quality than old-fashioned lacquers and oil paints, the 'new' water-based Acrylic Fluorescent paint of 1965. The Artist explains that he found "Politec, Inc." Fluorescent acrylic paint made in San Francisco in 1965, and like most Artists enjoyed the fraction of the drying time modern acrylic paint has over traditional oil and lacquer paints. Unfortunately, something that has not really changed amongst most acrylic Fluorescent paints is also what Bowman cited as a disadvantage, the limited range of Fluorescent Colors available with premixed store-bought paint in jars. The five Fluorescent Colors Bowman was limited to he lists as Cerise, Red, Orange-Rose, Yellow-Orange, and Lemon-Yellow, with his Blue Fluorescent paint being just as nearly non-Fluorescent as it still is in common Fluorescent acrylic paint up until the present day. Bowman also mixed non-Fluorescent Ultramarine and White acrylics together first, and then glazed over this non-Fluorescent Blue with Fluorescent Cerise to create Violet (this is still the most elusive of all the Fluorescent paint Colors, and for the large central Purple area of the Fluorescent "Participatory" Environment in the Museum, the current author sprayed alternating coats of Fluorescent Red and Fluorescent Blue for two weeks over a base of custom-made "Purple" Fluorescent acrylic paint from "Shannon Luminous Pigments, Inc.," which is still run by the grandchildren of Johnny Shannon, who was the first distributor of Fluorescent paint for the "Switzer Brothers" during the 1930s). Bowman also described the intensity of his Fluorescent acrylic paint, with the Yellow-Green available to him being less Fluorescent than his Yellows, Oranges, and Reds. In the last section of Richard Bowman's "Leonardo" article of 1973 the Artist described his inspiration for painting going back to 1950, when he was introduced to Fluorescent Colors and his Art and life were changed forever. The Artist begins with his love of Pierre Bonnard's rendering of "light effects," and explains that from 1950 when he found Fluorescent Colors all of his paintings emphasize this abstractly. Bowman also details the inspirations for his 1950-1953 "Kinetograph" series, which were photographs of a "cloud-chamber" used in physics to show the trails of nuclear particles and cosmic rays, as well as his personal study of 'subatomic particles and atomic structure.' The Artist further explains that his paintings inspired by this atomic physics were only his Artistic "interpretation," made with Colors and shapes on canvas, of such energies and phenomenon of science, and he makes it clear that these canvases were never meant to be representational or "illustrations" of these phenomenon. "Kinetograph #5" of 1950 is in the permanent collection of the Utah State University Museum of Art, and is created with oil paint and Fluorescent lacquer. The imagery is a far departure from Bowman's "Rock and Sun" series, and it is quite apparent that the Artist's painting had transformed itself dramatically with the Fluorescent lacquer he had found for the first time the year he painted this canvas. For a start, this is a horizontal image on a horizontal canvas, not the traditional vertical picture which Bowman had used throughout his 1943-1950 "Rock and Sun" series before he found Fluorescent lacquer paint. The actual painted imagery of this "Kinetograph" series is just as dramatically altered from the former series "Rock and Sun," as the format change from vertical to horizontal, with images of what could be the Sun painted three times in "Kinetograph #5," along with particles of matter on a nearly pattern-like base of subtle lines. The overall feeling of this "Kinetograph #5" from 1950, with it's highlights of Orange-Red, Orange, and Yellow Fluorescent lacquer paint, is very reminiscent of the atmospheric and basic imagery of Paul Klee. In "Abstract (Brown)" of 1953, Bowman's inspiration through photographs taken from trails of nuclear particles and cosmic rays captured inside of cloud-chambers, and his study of subatomic particles and atomic structure, seems to be transferred onto this monochromatic horizontal painting. Bowman's inspiration went deeper into atomic physics, as he states that between 1953 and 1955 he began to incorporate images into his paintings of both the 'microcosm' seen through "electron microscopes," and of the 'macrocosm' through cameras on "sounding rockets" miles above the Earth's surface. This series of Bowman's naturally became known as the "Micromacrocosmos" series. "Micromacrocosmos ll" of this series is a vertical canvas by Bowman which also marks a departure for the Artist into a more overall field of imagery in his painting, using atmospheric and interconnected areas of Colors applied in a loose painterly style which nearly fill the entire surface of his canvases. This feeling of the cosmos at it's subatomic level, and also at it's infinite physical dimension, is translated by Bowman into fields of interconnected energy, some rendered sharply in focus and others vague and atmospheric. Another canvas by Bowman that seems to be a part of this "Micromacrocosmos" series is "Aerospace" of 1952, which is the year before Bowman wrote that he started the series, but the title of the painting and the atmospheric quality of the imagery both in sharp focus and soft focus juxtaposed, is very similar to the overall field of imagery and painterly application of pigment in "Micromacrocosmos ll." During the next period of Bowman's life, from 1956 to 1965, he created "about 100" Fluorescent oil paintings, which he called the "Kinetogenics" series. The Artist clearly wrote that with Fluorescent Colors he could not only 'present his ides more freely,' but also could capture his conception of energy. Richard Bowman's use of Fluorescent paint in his Art was expanded upon in a November, 1975 flyer in which the Artist definitively explains that with his first use of Fluorescent lacquer back in 1950, Fluorescent oil paint in 1956, and finally Fluorescent acrylic paint in 1965, he knew that this pigment was a natural choice which allowed him to more fully "Integrate" as well as "express" his concept of the universe's "great forces," which are known but remain unseen. Bowman's painting of this "Kinetogenics" series are some of the brightest canvases he made, with his use of pure Fluorescent oil Colors thickly applied, or 'smeared' onto the canvas, as the

Artist found the higher quality of Fluorescent oil paints allowed him to do, and which was not possible with Fluorescent lacquer paints he had first used since 1950. "Kinetogenics 2" of 1956 is an overall field of Orange-Red and Orange Fluorescent oil paint thickly applied in a manner close to Abstract Expressionism, but with an overall rendering of what Bowman referred to as an 'integrated' concept of the 'universe's unseen great forces.' "Kinetogenics 39" from 1960 is a large canvas by Bowman from the series and is visually greatly altered from the overall field of Color in "Kinetogenics 2" four years earlier. Two distinct fields of energy on opposite sides of the horizontal canvas interact with each other, but retain their individual integrity on a base that is nearly Colorless, and similar to the feeling of Georges Mathieu. The image of the painting has a distant feeling of the 1950s Abstract Expressionism inspiration, but with it's liberal use of Fluorescent oil paint it becomes part of the early 1960s era.

Quite unfortunately the San Francisco Museum of Art today has taken a contemporary stance on Fluorescent Art similar to most of the majority of Artists and society (with just as obviously a director now possessing only a fraction of the vision of it's former director George D. Culler), and has decided to sell it's large collection of Richard Bowman's paintings to "benefit" (or 'pay for') new Artwork "acquisitions" for the museum, resulting recently with this "Kinetogenics 39" Fluorescent painting being auctioned off for the surprisingly low price of just a little over forty-five hundred dollars. The painting that is printed in Bowman's 1973 "Leonardo" article and which is part of this series was the next canvas, "Kinetogenics 40" also of 1960. Painted in Fluorescent oil, this canvas is a field of Color punctuated in the center of the painting with an area of paint very similar to the Artist's later "Dynamorph" series. On top of this in the 'foreground' are very graphic dark lines. The canvas that followed these two paintings, "Kinetogenics 41" of 1960, is painted in a vertical format with a flow of naturalistic Colors giving the initial feeling of an Artist Bowman was deeply inspired by, Pierre Bonnard and his impressionistic rendering of natural light. This canvas is a good example of what Monet could possibly have painted in his paradise of Giverny if he could have been sent a few tubes of Fluorescent oil paint back in time! It's a shame (and something I've thought about for years), because just *seven* years after Claude Monet died at eighty-six years old in 1926, Fluorescent paint was invented by Robert Switzer in California in 1933. The later series of "Kinetogenics" paintings by Richard Bowman become an overall field of Fluorescent Color similar to the first canvas in 1956 of this series painted after the Artist found better quality Fluorescent oil paint. "Kinetogenics 72" of 1963 is a good example of these later paintings of the "Kinetogenics" series, with a long vertical canvas covered with an atmospheric mist of mostly Yellow and Yellow-Orange Fluorescent paint highlighted with touches of Fluorescent Red and Blue. Other "Kinetogenics" canvases from 1963 are similar in their execution and Fluorescent Colors, with an undulating field of Color pulsing with inner dynamics. 1964's "Kinetogenics 83" moves into another visual dimension, with an atmospheric base of soft-focus Fluorescent Yellows, Oranges, and Reds overlaid with a translucent plane of White thin curving lines, which gives the impression of organic neuron-like structures seen in front of a field of energy. Richard Bowman's inspiration for his Fluorescent paintings came not just from images of the microcosm at the atomic scale through electron microscopes, or of the macrocosm through images of the Earth from space, but also from images of nature around him. Another 'natural' inspiration of Bowman's was the jazz improvisation coffeehouses in the San Francisco Bay area, having a close friend Kenneth Patchen who was a jazz poet of the era. From natural inspiration, the Artist retells the story for what he named his 'Environs' series, which began in 1960 while he was starting a large painting. While working on this large canvas Bowman "suddenly realized" that what he had painted was a cluster of California poppies, which had inspired him through their natural bright "Fluorescent Colors" which he had seen 'in his neighborhood.' Bowman explains that this canvas began his "Environs" series, which he would return to for the next eight years while working on his "Kinetogenics" series and other Art. Bowman directly states that it was the Colors of the flowers being 'naturally Fluorescent' which created his fascination for this "Environs" series of the 1960s, but this 'natural Fluorescence' of flowers, such as "nasturtium" or the "geranium" specifically named by the Artist, is for the most part an optical illusion. For the last twenty-five years Michèle and I have explored and examined "Common Items that are Fluorescent" in most forms of life - from Basmati rice to Frog's eyes - but what has always surprised us, and continues to fool us, is the apparent 'natural Fluorescence' of brightly Colored flowers. In 2008 I completed the first book on "Fluorescent Flowers," which has the Fluorescence of petals, stems, leaves, and pollen of two-hundred and eighty-one individual kinds of flowers listed, many of which were photographed in the daylight and at night in our small garden in Amsterdam with a Longwave Ultraviolet Dermatology camera, and what has always surprised us is just what Bowman was inspired by - the apparent Fluorescence of the Colors of Flower petals. The fact is that if Bowman had put one of these California poppies, or even nasturtiums or geraniums under a black light he would have been very disappointed, because the apparently Fluorescent Colors of most flower petals is partially an illusion - the flower petals are only dimly Fluorescent. What does Fluoresce with the intensity expected of the brilliantly Colored flower's petals, is the flower's pollen. The pollen of flowers universally is about the same intensity as synthetic Fluorescent paint pigment, which is naturally expected of the flower petal's Fluorescence after seeing them in the daylight with such a brilliant 'Fluorescent' Color, but the actual Fluorescence of the flower's petals is just a fraction of the intensity of it's pollen. This is an evolved natural attraction for the flower's main pollinators the bees, who are fortunate enough to be able to also see what is invisible to us - Ultraviolet. The apparently "Day-Glo" petals of flowers universally have surprisingly a dim Fluorescence compared to what is expected when seeing some flowers looking as bright as Fluorescent paint in the sunlight. A few exceptions to this dim flower petal Fluorescence out of the 281 flowers in my "Fluorescent Flowers" book are "Anchusa" with small brightly Fluorescent Sky-Blue petals under a filtered Longwave Ultraviolet Black light, "Crocusmia" 'Mont Brescia' with also bright Orange-Apricot flowers, the famous "Dahlia" 'Bishop of Llandaff' having some of the brightest Red Fluorescing petals you can see, the "Oenothera biennis" better known as the wild 'Evening Primrose' also Fluoresces a very bright Yellow that is much brighter than most flower's Fluorescence, "Monarda" which Fluoresces bright Red, and "Cheiranthus cheiri," known as 'Wall Flowers,' which have flower petals that Fluoresce very bright Red and are as bright as the Fluorescence of their seed pods (which is very rare). Again, this is not the easiest "Common Item" to examine under a Black light in the dark, and is best seen when under filtered laboratory Longwave Ultraviolet lamps, not simple tubular Black lights which give off also three percent visible Blue light in addition to Longwave U.V., which distractingly add this visible reflected light to the natural emission of Fluorescent Color. What you get is a 'Blue haze' over photographs taken with normal Black lights and long exposures, such as thirty-two minute exposures needed with film or slides. Use of a "Kodak" "Wratten Barrier Filter" in a plastic carrier mounted on the front of the analogue camera's lens compensates for this, blocking U.V. from entering the camera's lens and 'fogging' the film, but laboratory filtered Longwave Ultraviolet lamps which emit zero percent visible light should be directly used, along with this "Wratten Barrier Filter" in place on the camera's lens as well. With this apparatus I photographed hundreds of Fluorescent gemstones and minerals, flowers, seashells, lichens, fossils, Green Peppers and a multitude of other vegetables, fruits, spices, and psychoactive substances, glass, plastics, petrified wood, trees, ivory, and coral (to mention just a few "Common Items that are Fluorescent").

    Bowman specifies 1965 to 1967 as the years he concentrated on his "Environs" series inspired by Fluorescent flowers, but also during the same years worked on his "Synthesis" series, which he compares to his earlier 'Rock and Sun' series, except for his use of Fluorescent Colors instead of ordinary oil Colors he had used in the original 'Rock and Sun' series before the Artist found Fluorescent paint. Another departure from his earlier 'Rock and Sun' series is this simplification and abstraction of forms in the 'Synthesis' series, which the Artist expands on, giving an example of his rendering the Earth as just a horizontal bar signifying "rock."

    From 1966 until the writing of his 1973 "Leonardo" article Bowman worked on his newest series of Fluorescent paintings, the 'Dynamorph' series, which is explained by the Artist to be an 'extension' of his 'Kinetogenics' series. This 'Dynamorph' series was composed of "symbolic forms" the Artist had previously used, combined with energy's "different concepts" he imagined through what he called his 'fierce eye' perceiving nature. What immediately sets this "Dynamorph" series of Bowman's apart and in advance of his previous work, both in Color and technique, is the Artist's use beginning in 1965 of Fluorescent Acrylic paint, not the traditional dense paste of oil paint. The difference between water-based Twentieth century acrylic paint and oil paint credited to have been invented by Jan Van Eyck many centuries ago, could fill a book in itself. You can create paintings with acrylic paint that are not possible to create with oil paint, with an example being several of Bowman's later "Dynamorph" paintings in which the treatment of the surface Color caused it to fragment and reveal the underlying surfaces of contrasting Colors. Acrylic Fluorescent paint is amazing to mix by hand and use to create effects not possible to achieve with traditional oil paint. Working with up to twenty-five different Colors of Fluorescent acrylic paint, and surfaces of paintings consisting of up to fifteen liters (quarts) of wet Fluorescent paint, the current author has created close to five-hundred "Thermal Expansion" Fluorescent and Phosphorescent paintings. Even if the impossible could have been achieved and these "Thermal Expansion" paintings containing up to fifteen liters of paint could have been created with oil paint, they would never dry in this Artist's lifetime. "Dynamorph 3" from 1966 is a perfect example of the difference between the vibrancy of Color, freshness of execution, and technical ability that Fluorescent acrylic paint gave to the painting of Bowman. There is a fraction of the drying time between acrylic paint and oil paint, so the Artist can work fresh acrylic vibrant Colors on top of under-layers without smearing together the still-wet Colors if oil paint had been used instead. Bowman's "Dynamorph 3" has a vibrant dynamism created by the use of pure Fluorescent acrylic Colors. Fresh vivid pure Colors are easily recognizable as acrylic Fluorescent paintings of Bowman's when seen in direct comparison placed along side of Fluorescent paintings made by the Artist during the previous decade with Fluorescent lacquer and then oil paints. No Browns or muted smeared Colors of the oil paint years are seen in the majority of Bowman's later acrylic painting series. "Dynamorph 55" of 1971 is nearly monochromatic, and consists of pure vibrant Yellow and what appears to be an area of bare White canvas, creating the feeling of a portal. In Bowman's "Leonardo" article the seventh painting reproduced was "Dynamorph 58" from

1971, which has a strong visual feeling of Bowman's previous "Synthesis" series, but also contains a treatment of paint that sets it apart from the former series and creates a new layer of dynamics. This new treatment of paint is fully realized in Bowman's "Dynamorph 83" of 1973, in which Blue Fluorescent paint has been physically fragmented on the surface layer of the painting, revealing a surface of contrasting Colors. Richard Bowman closes his 1973 "Leonardo" article on Fluorescent painting with a quote from the San Francisco Museum of Art's former director Gerald Nordland, who describes Bowman's Fluorescent paintings of his 'Dynamorph' series as 'the inside of matter's structure' seen in "electron micrographs." Nordland writes of the "energies" and "elements" that Bowman formerly used subtly in his work now being recognizable in all of this 'Dynamorph' series. In the opinion of this former director of the San Francisco Museum of Art, Bowman "simplified" the elements of his painting's "structure" by the large scale of his paintings, as well as the use of "energy-charged" Fluorescent paint. Towards the end of Bowman's life his Fluorescent paintings retained their energy and search. "Nuclear Move" of 1995 is a vibrant painting created with pure Orange and Orange-Red Fluorescent acrylic Colors, and is a testament to the Artist's quest throughout his lifetime and of what he finally achieved by creating paintings which are not only Artworks of energy, but which are energy itself.

  To conclude this thin section on a selection of Artists who have used Fluorescent Color, there are a few Artists that the author has had personal contact with. Anders Knutsson is an Artist who created large abstract canvases which were seen in the White light, and which then transformed themselves into completely different paintings when the lights were turned off, achieved through his use of a wide palette of Phosphorescent pigments incorporated into his paintings. The author was at one of Anders Knutsson's exhibitions during the 1990s in Manhattan and still remembers it very clearly. As an example of how far the magic of the Black light has reached, in January, 2015 the author received emails from an Artist Leon Coetzee who works with two Black lights in a single fixture and creates Fluorescent paintings in South Africa. In Prague there are ten Black Light Theaters today in 2016 going all the way back to it's invention in 1959 by Jiri Srnec. These are world famous full Fluorescent/Black light theater performances in both small private venues as well as the "WOW" Black Light Theater in the National Theater of Prague. There is even a "Zauber Licht Theater" based in Germany which performs Black Light Puppet Theater for years by friends of ours, Thumpah and Angie.

  In the end at the risk of seeming narcissistic, the last Fluorescent Artist described in this book will be the Fluorescent Artist writing this book. He bought his first Black light and Fluorescent "Poster paint" in 1969, opened the Fluorescent Art gallery "Electric Lady" in Amsterdam twenty-nine years ago with Michèle in 1987, opened "Electric Ladyland - the First Museum of Fluorescent Art" seventeen years ago in 1999, and contrary to most of the Artists reviewed in this book, he is obviously still alive. I've been an Artist all my life, inspired by my Aunt Toni who is an Artist, and showed me that I was an Artist at about the age of five. I was also very inspired as a kid by the 'modern mythology' of comic book illustrations, particularly Steve Ditko and John Romita who drew the first two series of "Spider-man" comics in the 1960s, and I already had created and drew my own first comics when I was ten. Having been born and raised in Brooklyn, New York, my family moved across the water to the 'farmlands' of New Jersey in the mid-1960s, and this is where I saw my first real Black light display in the late 1960s. The actual first time I saw a Black light was in 1964 at the "Futurama" "GM" pavilion of the New York "World's Fair" with my parents, sitting in the 'driving seat' of what clearly was a 'futuristic' view of the world, complete with monorails and moon bases. This was one of the only displays in which Black lights were used in the 1964-1965 New York "World's Fair" in great contrast to the 1939 New York World's Fair, and especially in great contrast to the 1939 San Francisco World's Fair, which was probably one of the greatest uses of Fluorescent paint and Black lights in history. There was an unearthly glow coming out of one or two of the large dioramas you 'drove' past in this 1964 "Futurama" pavilion, but it was subtle and similar to a display made with neon or other lighting effects, not a display that was instantly recognizable as something that had never been seen before. The little six inch (15 cm) "World's Fair 1964-1965" souvenir I still have displayed in my apartment in Amsterdam is also printed in "Day-Glo" Orange on Blue felt. Then, in New Jersey there was a funky place to shop called the "Englishtown Auction" opened on weekends where this kid from Brooklyn had his eyes opened wide seeing for the first time how these New Jerseyites lived their lives(!) This was the totally inauspicious setting that I saw my first real Black light display, in a brand new small "Mod" clothing stand next to the giant food stall and handmade French-fry stand of this Englishtown Auction between 1967 and 1969. I still clearly remember the event like I'm standing there now, with this unearthly glow of the most indescribably beautiful and brilliant Colors I ever saw in my life. This "Mod" clothing stand was set up like a tiny discotheque with 1960s rock music blaring and an entrance on the right side of the stand where you got in line to walk into and through this enclosed glowing effervescent small rectangular clothing stand, and then exited on the left. With it's specific 'entrance' and 'exit,' this "Mod" Black light clothing stand was set up to loosely create something like a 'discotheque experience,' not just a clothing stand. What first absolutely captivated me was what almost everyone who has ever been under a Black light also has been surprised at: the heavenly Blue glow of T-shirts and other White clothing under a Black light - I could see that this was something different than anything else I'd ever seen in my life, with this indescribably beautiful Blue Color seeming to be projected out of these plain White T-shirts and all other White clothes displayed up in the air over your head close to the Black lights. I clearly remember the rare feeling of seeing something completely different from anything I'd ever seen before, staring at this "Mod" 1960s clothing stand/discotheque with Black lights and the strongest, most beautiful glowing Colors I'd ever seen. This place was nothing tremendous in size, with the whole "Mod" clothing stand being perhaps a mere ten feet wide and twenty feet deep (±3x6 meters), but the way it was set up, with a central dividing wall which cut the U-shaped interior in half, effectively made it seem like two rooms. You walked into the entrance on the right side of the stand and entered into a space with Fluorescing material up to the high ceiling on both sides of you, and you were surrounded by brilliant Colors of Fluorescing clothes. Again, there was blaring 1960s rock music bombarding your senses as you walked through what appeared to be a Black light 'environment,' and when you got to the back of the right side in this clothing stand, you turned left with the constant crowd walking in amazement through this clothing stand/discotheque, and then came back down the left side of this Black light display to the exit. I still am there - looking up with unblinking eyes and a wide-opened mouth (along with all the other people walking through this 1960s "Mod" Black light clothing stand) wondering what I was looking at for the first time - light and Color seemed to be coming out everywhere - like it was coming out of the air itself. Of course like everyone else in the late 1960s I bought my own small eighteen watt Black light, Black light posters, and also some of the worse quality Fluorescent "Poster paint" that was commonly available in 1969. I clearly remember painting with this Fluorescent "Poster paint" very thick, and the next day most of this terrible quality dusty paint cracked dramatically - and unbelievably fell off the paper and onto the floor! This is when I first started to mix simple water-based transparent household "Elmer's" glue with the powdery Fluorescent "Poster paint" trying to improve the paint's quality by binding it together. At college in Art school during the 1970s Fluorescent Colors were not even considered or mentioned, and obviously during that post-1960s period society was desperately trying to not only forget their nightmare of the 1960s Movement, but to downright eradicate any memories or links to the "Psychedelic Movement," including Fluorescent Colors and Black lights. Naturally this did not stop the culture which had started in the 1960s, obviously, and I clearly remember the Black light posters everywhere into the mid and late 1970s (especially in my friend Marc's cosmic room). Special mention here for "Autobahn" in Sam's "Mansion" as well. Needless to say I painted with non-Fluorescent acrylic paint in Art school in the 1970s, creating nine foot long triptychs of hard-edge vibrating Colors. From 1977 until 1981 I made a large series of nine foot (3 meter) triptych canvases with this 1970s hard-edge masking tape technique and endless coats of paint to create a plastic-like pure coating of vibrating complementary Colors. This is when I was introduced to the master of "Vibrating Colors:" Eugene Chevreul of the 1800s, by my "Color-Theory" professor Bruce Rigby, who exhibited at the West Broadway Gallery in Soho which was the same gallery in which my painting professor for three years Howard Goldstein also exhibited, who painted in this hard-edge 1970s style along with air-brushing tints of brilliant Colors onto his "Prismatic" canvases, and hailed my work. After Art school, about 1981, I began to move on from the hard-edge vibrating canvases and started introducing some freely painted expressionistic areas into my paintings, and during this time again bought Fluorescent "Poster paints" in the landmark "Pearl Paint" on Canal Street in New York City. Never forgetting the miserable experiences of these Fluorescent "Poster paints" falling off of the piece of Art you painted the day before, I began to again experiment with improving the quality of this "Poster paint," but instead of simply adding clear glue which I had tried for my early experiments, I tried adding clear acrylic matt medium to these premixed water-based Fluorescent "Poster paints" and it amazingly worked easily, with the paint remaining on the painting and not winding up on the floor(!) While working on Madison Avenue as a graphic Artist and package designer from 1980, I incorporated these self-improved Fluorescent Colors into my large three meter canvases which became free of the 1970s hard-edge vibrating Colors influence and had moved into thick sculptural surfaces and free expressionistic brush work.

In 1984 I finally left America for the first time and travelled for half a year in Europe on a museum and Art tour of most of the countries in Europe to see the Artwork I never saw growing up in the United States, like Michelangelo and Leonardo da Vinci as very good examples. This is when I first arrived in my "home" - Amsterdam - thirty-two years ago only planning to see the Van Gogh Museum(!) Returning to America after six months traveling freely in Europe, life would never be the same again. All that I could think of was returning to Amsterdam, with my dream from the very first morning in Amsterdam walking on the Prinsengracht and seeing the Artist "Dig Space" painting in his studio through the window: imagine *painting* here! After meeting a special German friend Dieter in John's "Fancy Free Coffeeshop" when coming back to Amsterdam in 1985 for seeing how I liked living in the city, I made my first series of Art in Amsterdam. Fully utilizing Dieter and Rosie's house, this was a series of two large silkscreened collages of my photos of Amsterdam, and I remember going crazy trying to find Orange Fluorescent silkscreen ink to include with the normal silkscreen Colors used for this series. This was from September to November 1985, and before returning to America I had made plans with Dieter and his friend Jorgens for opening a coffeeshop in Amsterdam all together in May, 1986. The name of the coffeeshop was to be "Electric Lady," which I had chosen because it was the name of Jimi Hendrix's recording studio on Eighth Street in Greenwich Village, which was not only still in existence in 1986, but is still an important recording mecca today in 2016. I could finally get a tour of "Electric Lady Studios" after a recording engineer named 'Frenchy' from "Electric Lady" came to "Electric Ladyland - the First Museum of Fluorescent Art" that end of 2001. On January 21, 2002, which was auspiciously Martin Luther King Day, I finally got to enter "Electric Lady Studios," and it was like a *dream*. From the original curved facade of the brick building, to the round reception window (which was Jimi's design request), the feeling of Jimi Hendrix is everywhere. In "Studio A," which is last studio Jimi recorded in, there is an Artist's lounge next to the Recording Room that has hanging the Isaac Abrams psychedelic oil painting that originally was in Jimi Hendrix's apartment some blocks away. There is a huge eighty-track mixing board and a multitude of recording machines including the original large analogue Mastering machine from Jimi's time. In this Recording Room there is also something I personally waited years to see: the Color Control Panel that Jimi wanted so that he could change the Colors of all the lighting throughout the Recording Room, the Studio, and "Electric Lady Studios!" It's like an equalizer with eighteen vertical sliders to bring up the Colored spot lights in all different areas, depending on his feelings and moods. These sliders are all labelled in Jimi's hand from left to right: "CEILING, SIDES, MACHINE, CONTROL BACK, CONSOLE, RED, GREEN, BLUE, LEFT WALL, CENTER, RIGHT REAR, DOOR, MURAL." Jimi Hendrix's presence could be felt in every corner of "Electric Lady Studios." What is an extremely amazing parallel, and something I've been thinking about a long time, is that two Artists who definitively changed not only their respective fields of Art, but also the world itself, both changes the world in the same incredibly short period of three and a half years. Vincent Van Gogh journeyed to Paris in 1886 and began to seriously create the body of paintings which would change the world. Three and a half years later in 1890 he was dead. Jimi Hendrix journeyed to London in 1966 and formed "The Jimi Hendrix Experience." After changing the world, three and a half years later in 1970 he was dead. Both of them gave us the same message, but at different volumes.

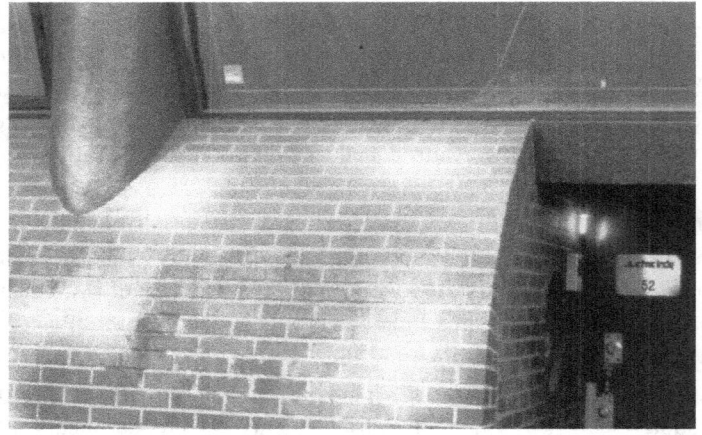

"Electric Lady Studios" built for Jimi Hendrix in 1970

The last weekend before leaving America forever I took my Red 1977 "Trans-Am" on a five hour drive to find Jackson Pollock's barn/atelier on the Hamptons of Long Island, which wasn't even a museum yet but had been recently abandoned since the death of Lee Krasner, Pollock's widow. As fate would have it, I came back to Amsterdam in May, 1986 with my two friends thankfully not wanting to open a coffeeshop anymore, and miraculously within one month met the most magical person I had ever seen or been around, Michèle, who had just returned from the Kumbh Mela Hindu festival in India. It was something like magnets in the way that there was an instant attraction between opposite polarities, we fell in love with each other instantaneously, opened "Electric Lady" Fluorescent Art Gallery together on April 19, 1987, "Electric Ladyland - the First Museum of Fluorescent Art" downstairs from the gallery on April 19, 1999, and have lived together for exactly thirty years. In our first apartment in 1986 I remember mixing up Fluorescent paint from scratch in the kitchen sink with Fluorescent powdered pigments and clear acrylic matt medium - without a blender - by hand with a spoon in left-over glass jars from the only food that I ate when I met Michèle a month before: peanut butter. Since I decided before even leaving America that I wanted to live for good in Amsterdam, the only way to live here permanently was either to get a job or open a business, so within six months

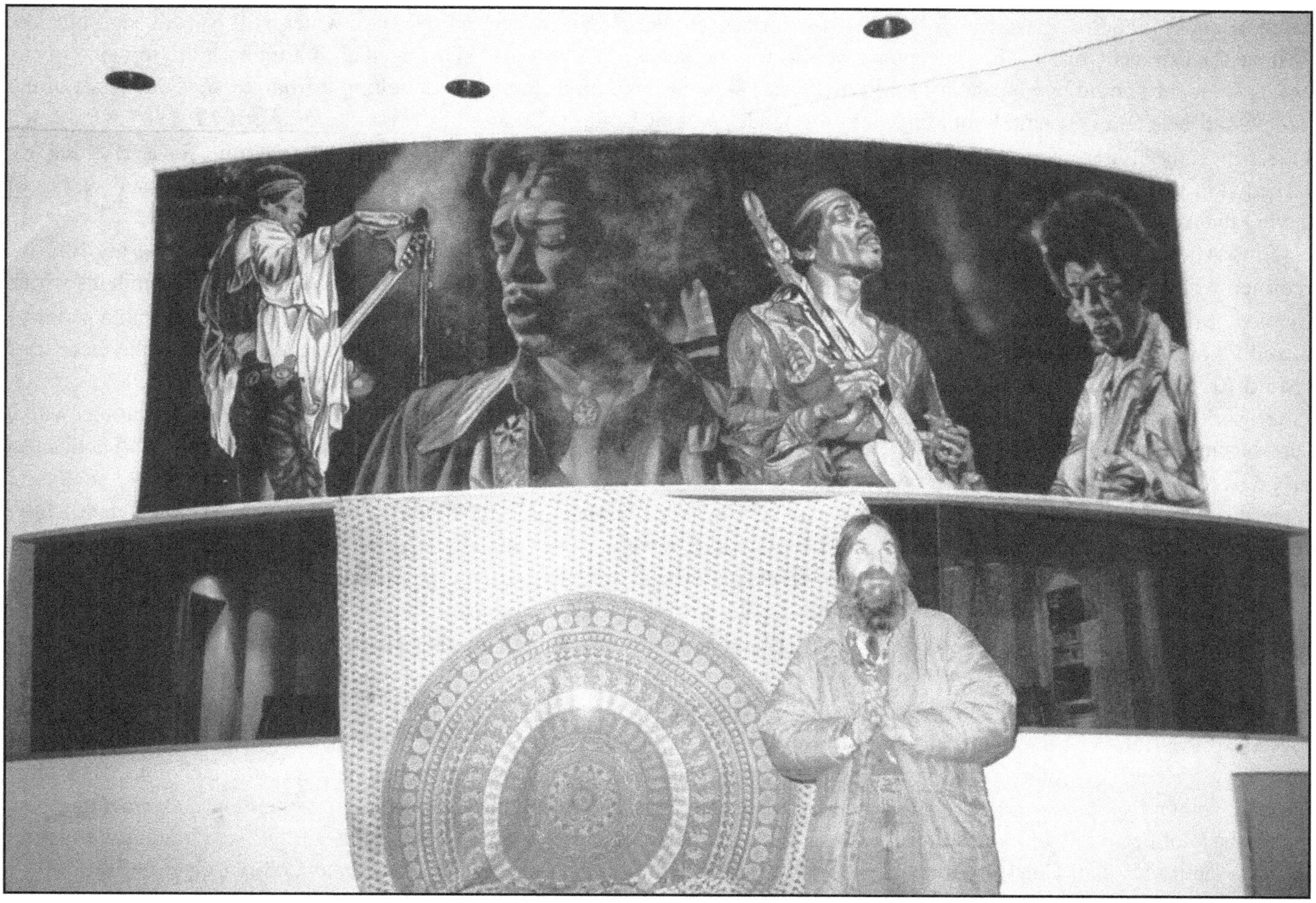

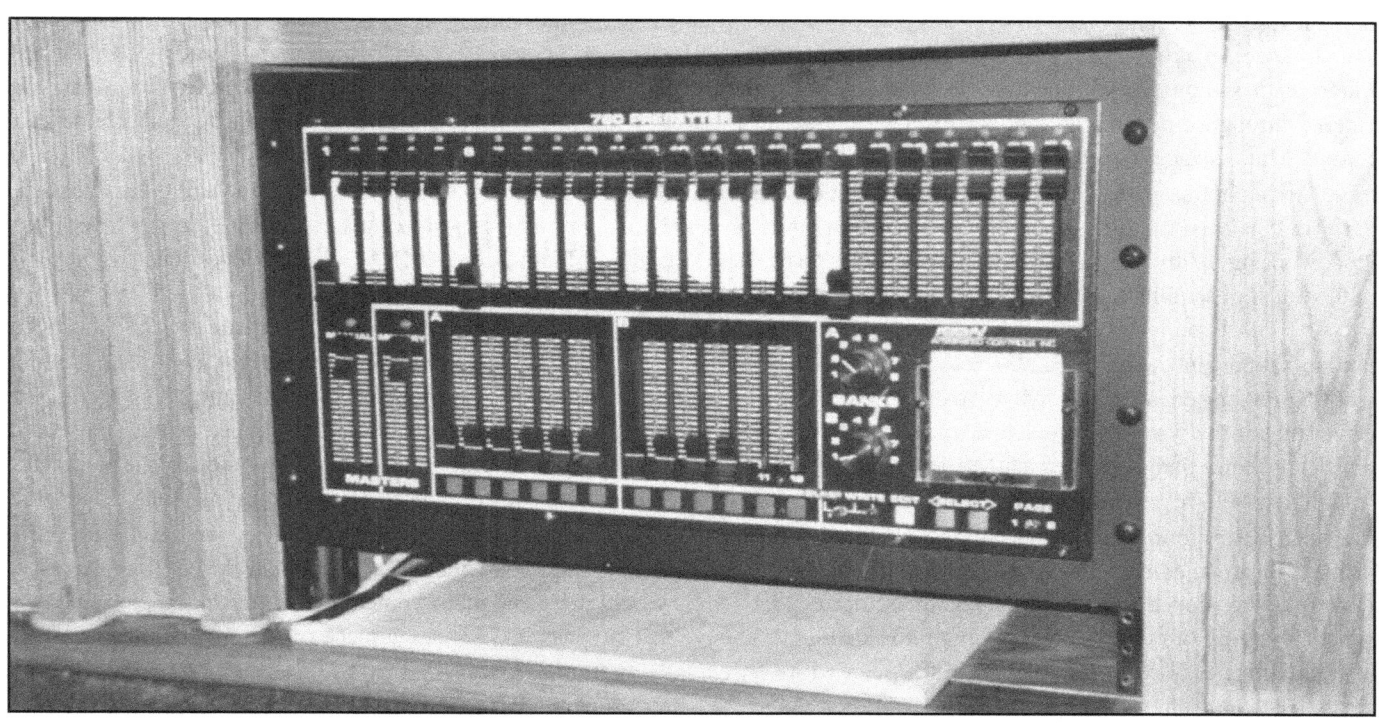

The author in Jimi Hendrix's "Electric Lady Studios," "Studio A," January 21, 2002

"Electric Lady Studios," Color Control Panel with original Light Color-indicating labels written by Jimi Hendrix

Michèle and I found the beautiful area called the Jordaan in Amsterdam to rent an old shop which still had it's sign outside: "Coma"(!) Anyway, one of the first things we did was take down this "Coma" sign together, with me on the top step of the cheapest ladder I could buy balancing the iron "Coma" sign on top of my head while unbolting it from the outside facade of the galley, and Michèle desperately holding onto the ladder so that I didn't fall and kill myself. On April 19, 1987 we opened "Electric Lady" Fluorescent Art Gallery with almost no money, but with enough inspiration to make up for everything we lacked, and lived an enchanted life in the tiny room behind the gallery for thirteen years, being in a nearly magical setting of having the Art Gallery and Atelier just ten steps from your bed.

After traveling to India for half a year between 1987 and 1988 with Michèle and definitively changing my life, we returned with full new inspiration, and by the spring of 1990 I had begun to make large boxed Fluorescent environments which I called "Mind-Arising Boxes." These "Mind-Arising Boxes" came after three years of exploration, beginning with a series of boxed Fluorescent environments that were not enclosed, and didn't have a Black light mounted in each sculpture like these later "Mind-Arising Boxes," but were a series of thirteen open Fluorescent sculpture 'Acid Boxes' made between 1987 an 1988. After working on three-dimensional Fluorescent sculpture boxes for two years I went back to 'flat' Fluorescent paintings with a series using discarded wooden doors. In 1990 I began a new series of Fluorescent paintings on wood, but for this series I began mixing up a large amount of Fluorescent White with thicker acrylic mediums and gels with which I could apply sculptural three-dimensional levels of this Fluorescent White acrylic as a complete base for Fluorescent paintings. This is when I fully realized the increased strength of Fluorescent Colors which have not been manipulated themselves (as in physically mixing with other Fluorescent Colors) but have been manipulated through the effect caused by layering of the Fluorescent Colors. Not only is Fluorescent paint under Black lights "emitting" light which is just the opposite of all other paint in the world that merely "reflects" light, but through this process of emitting light gives results from combining Fluorescent paint Colors that would be expected from combining Colors of light, not pigment. Simply put, when mixing all of the Colors of normal non-Fluorescent paint together you get something close to Black (the "Subtractive System" of Color), but just the opposite happens when you mix all of the Colors of light-emitting Fluorescent Colors together, because you end up with a Color that is an off-White (the "Additive System" of Color). This in itself can take years not only getting used to as another, opposite technique than when using all other Colors and other paints together, but it goes much further than that, with experimenting and inventing new techniques not necessary or even applicable to all other non-Fluorescent pigments. For me it is a little like painting with layers of glass - pure brilliant Color emitting from the Fluorescent paint, which is also very similar to Colored glass because of it's incredible transparency. Layering of Fluorescent paint Colors on top of each other is how I've 'mixed' most of my Fluorescent Colors for the past twenty-five years, with an added set of variables and creative results involved whether the Fluorescent paint being layered is wet paint layered over wet paint, or wet paint layered over dry paint.

After making a series of these "Mind-Arising Boxes" between 1990 and 1992 with Black lights contained inside the Fluorescent sculptures, we decided we would open up the abandoned miserable basement below our Art gallery (that you entered through a decrepit trap-door) so that I could have a work-shop to construct the fine woodwork dowelled boxes for future "Mind-Arising Boxes." Work on the basement windows began on fourth of July, 1992, and by that fall, with Michèle traveling in another part of the world to escape the construction downstairs, at about 3:00 in the morning sanding the Canadian hardwood beams on the ceiling of the basement I had an epiphany: what I was making here was not a workspace for woodworking on my "Mind-Arising Boxes," but ... "The First Museum of Fluorescent Art!!" I laughed uproariously by myself in the midst of sanding the ceiling above my head in the middle of the night!

The basement beneath "Electric Lady" Fluorescent Art Gallery was the perfect space to create what I had been thinking about since working on the series of Fluorescent sculpture boxes in the late 1980s, and especially thinking about while working on the series of later "Mind-Arising Boxes" for two years just prior to beginning work on the basement: a Fluorescent Environment that you would not just traditionally look at on the wall like a painting on canvas, but a piece of Art you would physically enter and become a part of the piece of Art. For a year I had sent proposals to museums around the world for installing a Fluorescent environment, but never received answers back from my proposals. The defining point behind the Fluorescent environment I would build, sculpt, and paint for the next seven years beneath the Art gallery would come from a brilliant idea that Michèle had for a large Fluorescent sculpture she made in 1990 called "The Hanuman Space Ship Trip" - in which she envisioned a set of buttons on the sculpture that people would press and make something happen in the piece of Art - What!! - having thoroughly 'blown my mind,' I couldn't believe that she wanted to create a piece of Art in which the 'viewer' has something to do with the creation of the piece of Art by actually altering it themselves! At roughly the same period of time that Michèle made this sculpture, about 1990, I returned to the States for Christmas and went with my brother Tony to the

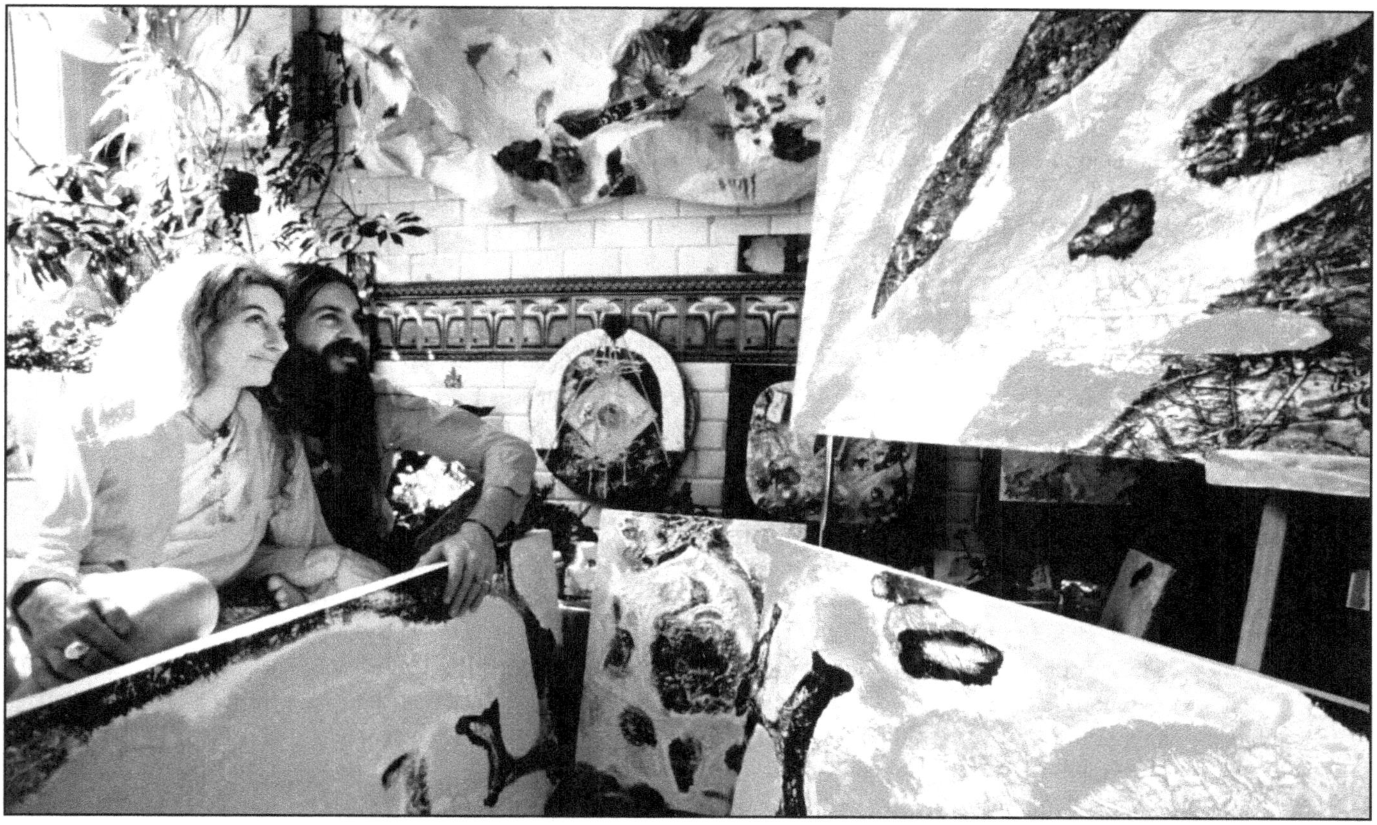

Nick Padalino and Michèle Delage in "Electric Lady" Art Gallery, Amsterdam, 1990

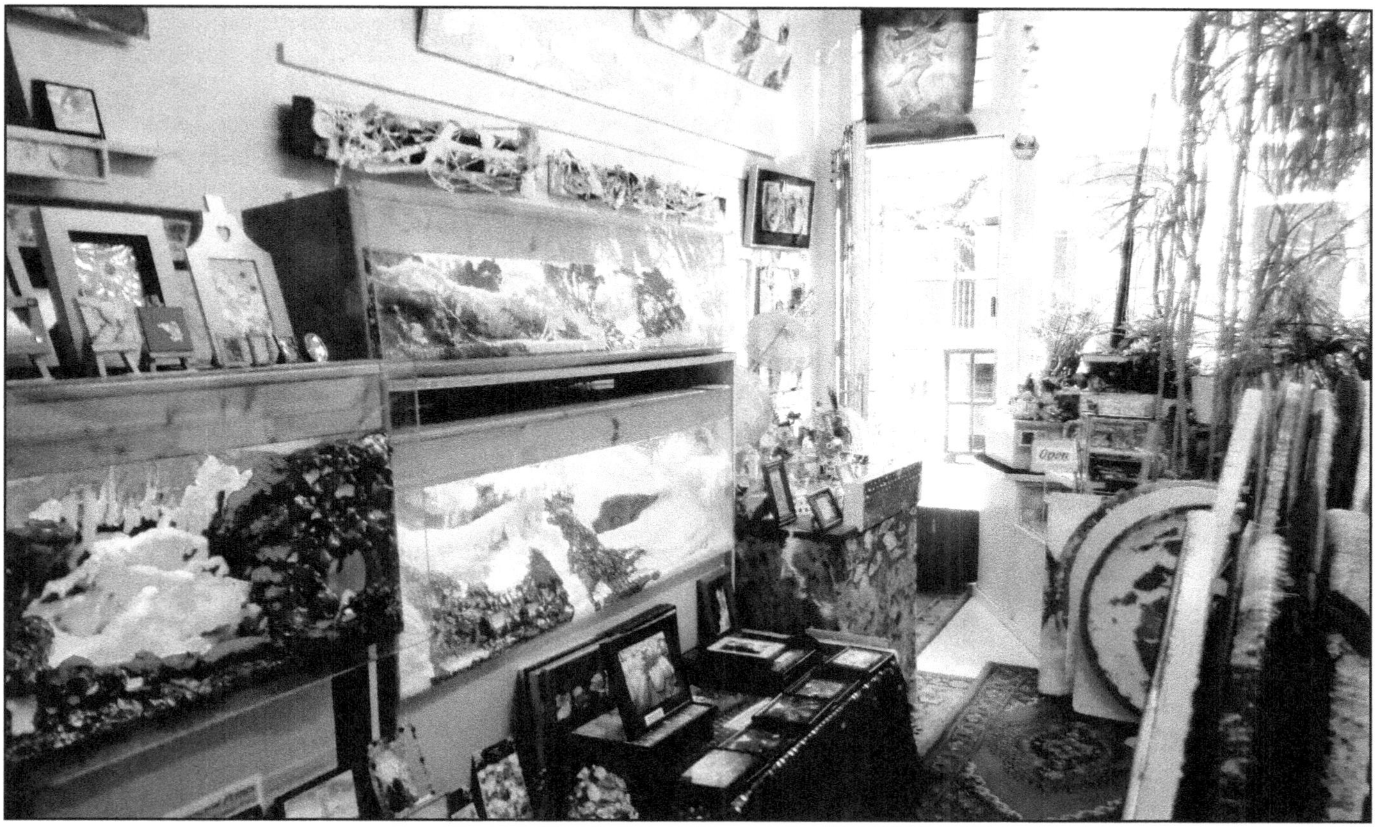

"Electric Lady" Art Gallery, 2015

Metropolitan Museum of Art in New York, where they had installed a huge "Interactive" sculpture/environment by one of the Artists who inspired me since I was a teenager, Robert Rauschenberg. This huge hall-sized environment was entered, and as you walked through the space music began to play, and as you continued walking through the large Rauschenberg environment the music changed through the effect of your own body motion. Incredible - and brought back unforgettable memories from 1984 in the Centre Pompidou of Paris entering into and sitting in rapture for half a day in Jean Dubufette's 1969-70 cave-like environment "Jardin d'Hiver." A few other pieces of Art I saw in the early 1990s also were activated with body motion, and a name for a new movement of Art arose at that time: "Interactive Art." As unique and absolutely new as it was, "Interactive Art" had some shortcomings for me, mostly because the "Interaction" in these pieces of "Interactive Art" was merely triggered by "motion detection" and could have also easily been caused by simply rolling a bowling ball into these Artworks, without any need for mental participation. Michèle's idea incorporated into my own ideas advanced the concept of "Interactive Art" because there is a mental process involved - the viewer first enters the piece of Art physically and then by choosing which buttons to press does not just "Interact" with the piece of Art, but "Participates" with the ongoing creation of the piece of Art. This became what I call the Fluorescent "Participatory" Environment in the Museum, in which visitors experience "Participatory Art." Like explained before in this book, it is a little like there is a painting three-quarters finished, and when you enter the piece of Art in the Museum, the visitors complete the 'painting' by pressing the buttons in the "Fluorescent Participatory Environment." A mental process is involved with the viewers choice of which of the eleven buttons to press, and then is further effected by the reaction they cause by pressing these buttons in the environment. In this "Magic Land of Lights, Sounds, and Dimensions" there is a small button pad containing ten Red switches and one Green switch which have lights inside them that light up when turned on, and which cause sixty-five Fluorescent minerals to change from their normal daylight Grey Color into all the brilliant Colors of the spectrum in "The Fluorescent Mineral Cave;" there are switches causing tiny series of lights to begin flashing along with two-centimeter tall traffic lights and street lights as well as a one-centimeter telephone booth with a light inside of it in the "Special Michele Cave;" halogen lights causing crystals from all over the world to display their optical qualities in "The Crystal Cave;" seven Colors of Phosphorescent paint in "The Crack Between the Worlds" first Fluoresce, and then when the button is turned off, brilliant Phosphoresce is emitted from Red to Orange, Yellow, and a Blue that will glow-in-the-dark for twelve hours. There is one switch on this button pad that causes music to begin from a tape I made of nineteen different pieces of music broken up into five second clips one after another, in order, for ninety-one minutes. I made this in 1998 manually with nineteen labelled music cassettes being put into a cassette deck one after another, in order, for recording five seconds of music from each, which went on constantly for about twelve solid hours one very memorable night and morning. The crystals in "The Crystal Cave" also reflect in three mirrors up to a "Hanuman Mandir" modeled after the Hanuman temple in Hampi, India where Michèle and I climbed a few hours in 1987 to get up to. In this "Hanuman Mandir" in the Museum there is a marble Hanuman statue three and a half centimeters tall which was custom made in India for this cave by Dr. Shilipi, a sculptor and a doctor in Bheraghat, India, the "Marble rock area" in the center of the country. In 1995, during the middle of the seven years of creating the Fluorescent "Participatory" Environment Michèle went back to India with two sized drawings I made, one of this Hanuman statue I wanted at three and a half centimeters tall, and another of an even tinier one centimeter tall (half an inch) marble Shiva statue for the top of "The Shiva Linga" in the Museum environment, which has the Himalaya with the Ganga (Ganges River) flowing down the left side of the six foot tall Shiva Linga into "The Fire of Creation" inside of the Linga. The source of the Ganga, which is called "Gaumukh" (the cow's mouth) and where Michèle and I have been three times at fourteen-thousand feet (4,350 meters), is represented in the Museum by a tiny cave at the top of this "Shiva Linga" in the Himalaya, and inside this cave is the one centimeter White marble Shiva statue also custom made by Dr. Shilipi in India. To give an idea of what life was like in India, this one centimeter hand-carved marble statue - complete with a cobra lifting off Shiva's neck - made to fit inside the cave in the Museum environment cost less than two dollars to have custom made (!) (which was actually alot of money in India in 1995, being one-hundred rupees). Three of the switches which cause reactions in "The Magic Land of Lights, Sounds, and Dimensions" directly in front of the viewer at the button pad also cause the lights in "The Crystal Cave" to be reflected in three mirrors behind the Hanuman statue in "The Hanuman Mandir." These three switches also have another use, which is lighting for the five "Hidden Caves" down on the right outer edge of the Environment, behind the Participatory Art button pad, that house a five centimeter tall marble Taj Mahal Michèle bought in Agra, where the Taj Mahal was built, and an Amethyst pyramid: "The Two Wonders From the World Cave:" 'Who needs seven, when two are plenty, sir!' There is also "The Smokey Quartz Cave" with other crystal wonders of nature, all included as part of the same area of "The Hidden Caves." The Fluorescent "Participatory" Environment in the Museum also has a central area called "The Land Between Tick-and-Tock," inspired by a phenomenon Ken Kesey named, and represents visually what Einstein wrote about "Time" being an artifact of human intelligence. The "Jumping Through Time Wall" in the

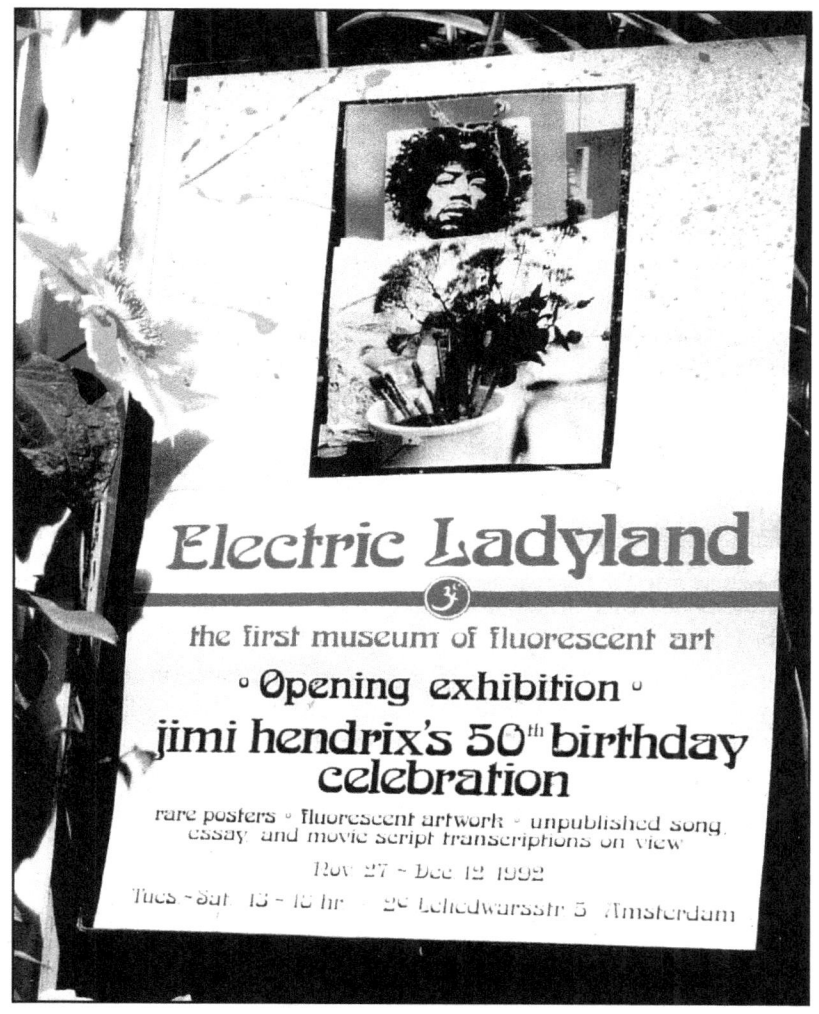

"Electric Ladyland - the First Museum of Fluorescent Art"
Temporary Opening Exhibition, November 27 - December 12, 1992

Museum was inspired by the incredible "String Theory" in physics, and "The Skyline Caverns Pool" is an area of Fluorescent stalactites hanging over a pool of glass containing Fluorescent stalagmites, which was inspired by my first trip to a cave back in 1977 in Virginia with Janis, someone who deeply inspired me, and someone I am thankful for having been inspired by. The left side of the Fluorescent "Participatory" Environment has "The Reactor," which is a semi-circular construction housing a Fluorescent environment inside of itself, and which contains nineteen lenses and windows to look through that have magnifying glasses, kaleidoscopes, enlarging and reducing lenses, a backwards glass lemon squeezer, a microscope, binoculars form my Aunt Jean, two rectangular translucent 'doctor' windows from my Mother, and a sawed-off telescope which was originally three feet long (one meter) before I sawed it down to five inches (thirteen centimeters) and turned it backwards, which is to make people get down on their hands and knees about sixty-five centimeters (two feet) away from this sawed-off telescope to see a tiny Blue crystal of Fluorite upside-down in perfect focus(!) As the reader has probably understood by now, this was the underlying theme of the Fluorescent "Participatory" Environment: getting people to create Art, or even just their vision of a piece of Art, by their own movement and participation. It's the way that everything is learned much more efficiently, through self-discovery, and by having a good time while doing it. The reason that there is a natural crystal of Blue Fluorescing "Fluorite" from Weardale, Durham in northern England at the heart of "The Reactor" is because the reaction that is taking place inside "The Reactor" is the cause of Fluorescence - "Electron Displacement" - and this Fluorite crystal from northern England is what Sir George Stokes named the phenomenon "Fluorescence" after in 1852. After three years of construction, which began with metal brackets, wooden beams, industrial heavy-duty plastic plumbing pipe, countless bolts and screws, and many thousands of pins, I formed a sculptural base with plastic that I heated to five-hundred and fifty degrees, carved with serrated-edge large bread knives, and then coated with combinations of glues, epoxies, and hardeners that came close to the feeling (and smell) of 'Plastic Alchemy.' This all happened after the initial opening of the Museum for two weeks on November 27, 1992 for the "50th Birthday Celebration of Jimi Hendrix." After making new walls, a new ceiling, and a new floor for months in 1992, artifacts were loaned to the Museum by Dan Foster, who was one of the members of the "Hendrix Information Centre" that was originally formed in 1967 in Amsterdam. For this opening the loaned artifacts included reproductions of drawings and paintings by a girlfriend of Jimi Hendrix, Monika Danemann, some of which she made with direct input from Jimi. The back wall of the Museum space for this two week Jimi Hendrix Celebration in 1992 contained black lights, and mounted on the wall Fluorescing were two original Jimi Hendrix posters printed with Fluorescent ink in 1967, a pair of Fluorescent Jimi Hendrix collages, one made by Michèle and the other by myself, and a large Fluorescent sculpture on the left side, "South Saturn Delta" which we both made in-place for this exhibition. The ceiling beams of the Museum were lined up with an entire movie script that Jimi Hendrix had written in 1970, and which I had transcribed page-by-page into a recording "Walkman" in Sotheby's Manhattan during my Christmas trip to New York in 1991.

The complete Fluorescent "Participatory" Environment in the Museum took seven years to finish, with approximately three years taken for the building, carving, and forming of the environment itself, and an additional four years to mix hundreds of liters of Fluorescent paint and Phosphorescent paint by hand, and finally to apply it under one-thousand watts of Black light to the environment. This application of the Fluorescent paint to the Museum environment began with the techniques I already knew and had used for all my life up until the point I began to paint the environment. After initially painting only the specific areas of the environment that were to be closed inside of structures that would be physically built around and covered up in the final environment with glass or other materials, I began to paint the surface of the thirty-two cubic meter structure. On the actual first day of painting the surface of the Fluorescent "Participatory" Environment, again, I began with techniques I had developed and used for many years, which included brilliant areas of hot Fluorescent Colors juxtaposed with cool Colors such as Phthalocyanine Blue. To begin the surface of the Museum environment I started at the source of energy, above "The Shiva Linga," which would lead the viewer into this area through the use of pure Fluorescent Yellow vibrating with Fluorescent Magentas and Reds. On this first 'ceiling' section that I began painting the surface of the environment, I was searching for new techniques of painting to create this environment.

To give a slight example of both the amount of preliminary planning, and the Fluorescent paint that I mixed and applied to the Fluorescent "Participatory" Environment in the Museum, "The Spectrum Pole" which runs through the entire environment, and the Fluorescent Colors that were used to create this six meter gradation from Fluorescent Yellow to Fluorescent Magenta will be explained. For this huge six yard gradation running from Fluorescent Yellow to Fluorescent Magenta I used a total of *sixty-six* Fluorescent Colors, which were created from twenty-two jars of different acrylic Fluorescent Colors that were each 'broken' into 'light' and 'dark' shades by first mixing fifty percent of the preceding Fluorescent Color with the Fluorescent Color used, using the pure Fluorescent Color unmixed, and then using a mixture of fifty percent of the next Fluorescent Color with the Fluorescent Color used. What I prepared "The Spectrum Pole" with before the final sixty-six Fluorescent Colors was many coats of Fluorescent White paint, and then coated the entire "Pole" structure with several more coats of Fluorescent Yellow. I next poured and painted sixty-six Fluorescent Colors going from Magenta to Yellow onto the six meter structure for about twelve hours. The entire mass of many liters of Fluorescent paint was left to dry for a full twenty-four hours on and off under heat guns, and when it was completely dry and finished, I started all over again and poured and painted the same sixty-six Fluorescent Colors all over again on top of the finished first painted surface of "The Spectrum Pole" for another twelve hours. This ensured that even in my lifetime if the many liters of the second coat of sixty-six Colors of Fluorescent paint on "The Spectrum Pole" ever faded slightly from being so close to the ceiling of the environment full of Black lights, then the pristine vivid first coat of many liters of the same sixty-six Fluorescent Colors would be underneath to maintain the brilliance of all the Colors. Today in 2016, almost a full twenty years later and after something like 50,000 visitors have entered the Fluorescent "Participatory" Environment in the Museum and have experienced as well as touched the Fluorescent paint surfaces, the Colors of this "Spectrum Pole" and the rest of the Environment are still brilliant and fresh.

The Fluorescent "Participatory" Environment in the Museum took me seven years to build and paint, begun in 1992 and finished in 1999, during which "Electric Lady" Fluorescent Art Gallery had been opened since 1987 upstairs from the Museum. During this vast period of time life went on and many things changed - I was thirty-five when I started to make the Museum and forty-two when I finished it; my father died in between and many other things happened in seven years of living. During this entire period I was always working on the Museum in one form or another, but between 1992 and 1999 there were twenty major "Sessions" of extensive and extended work during which the bulk of the Museum was built, painted, and completed. Everything had to be made - the floor, the walls, and the ceiling to start, before the Museum construction could

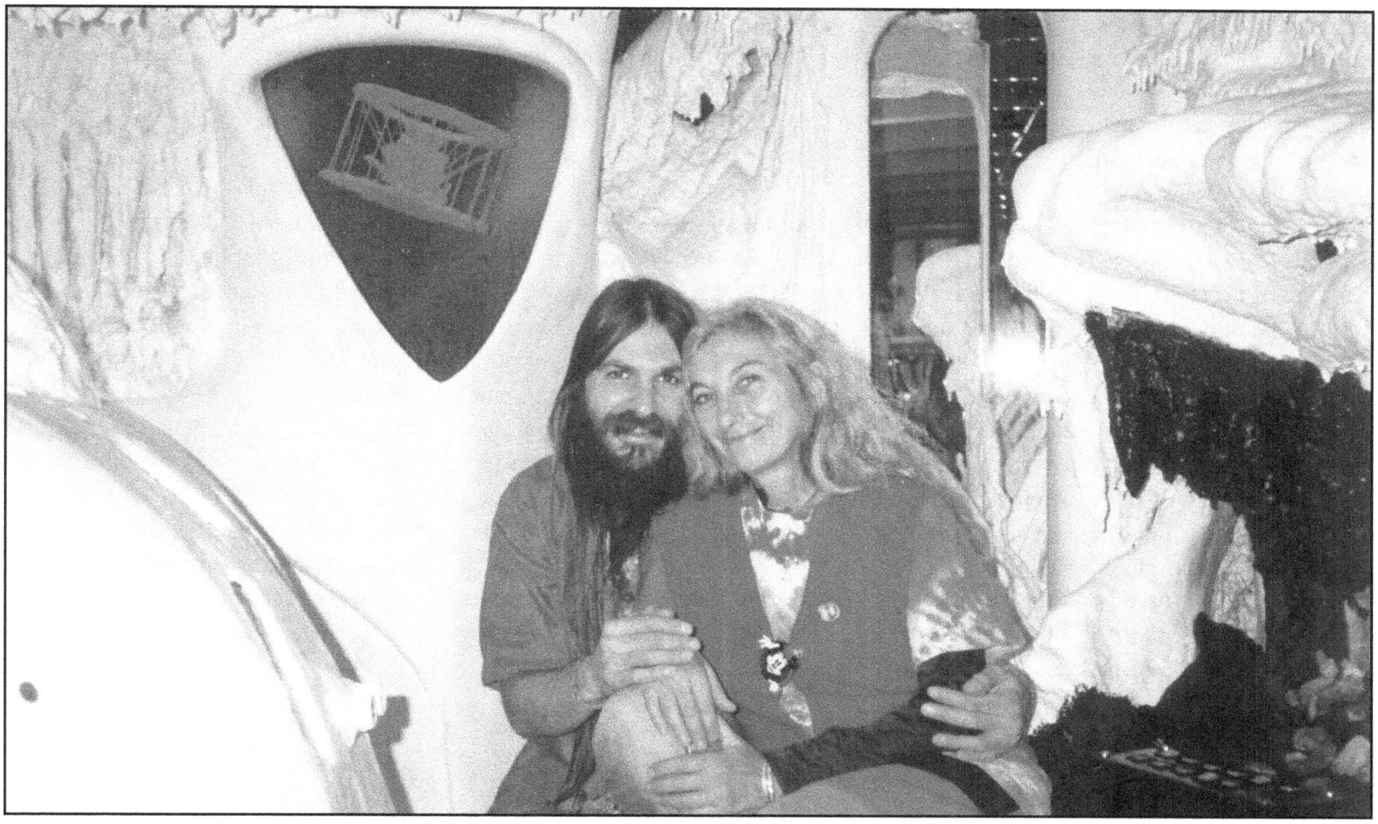

Nick Padalino and Michèle Delage in "Electric Ladyland - the First Museum of Fluorescent Art" under construction, 1995

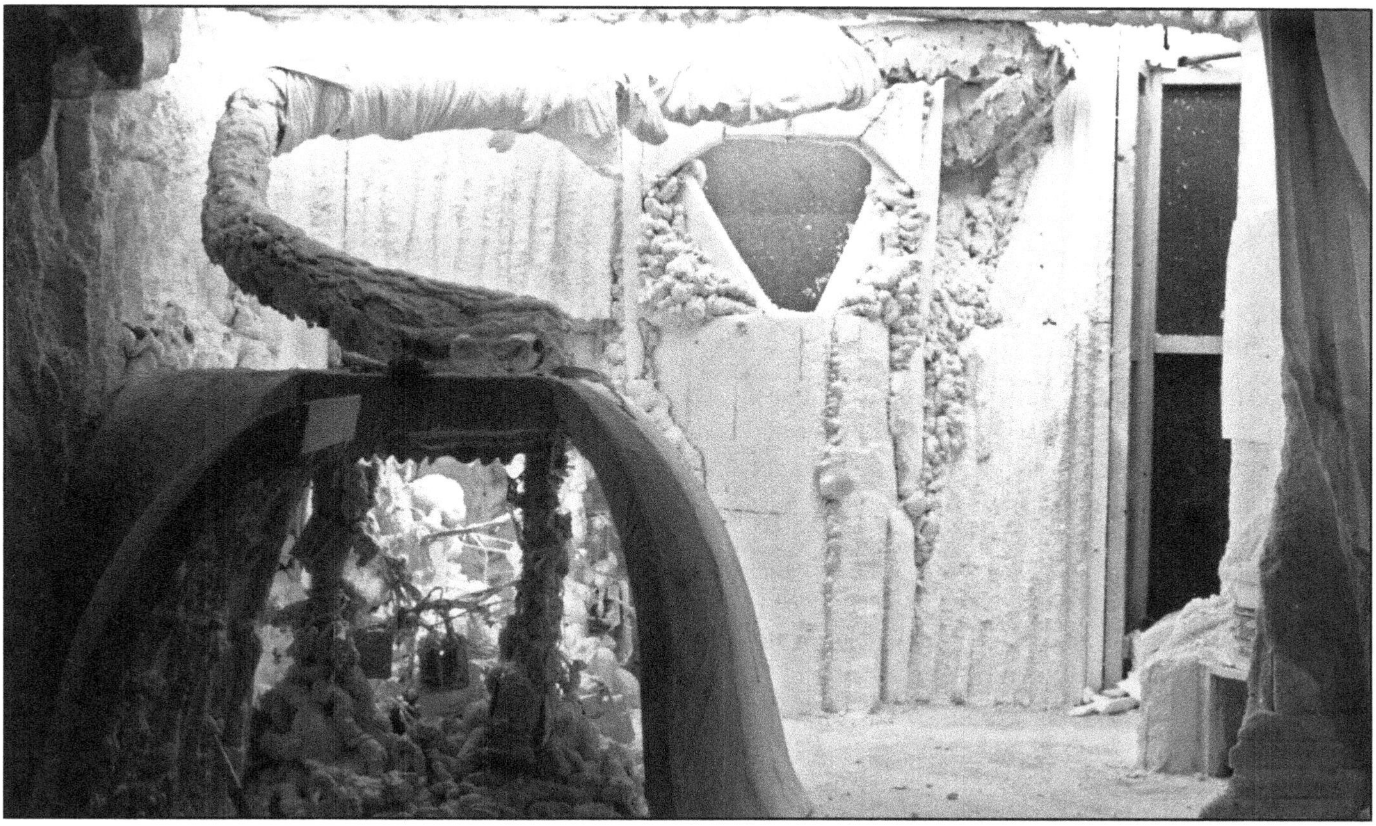

"Electric Ladyland - the First Museum of Fluorescent Art" Fluorescent "Participatory" Environment under construction, 1993

even begin. During these extended Sessions Michèle would escape to India, Bali, Switzerland, or France for weeks or months, and work in the Museum went on ceaselessly, sometimes for three or four days without stop or sleep. It was an experience filled with infinite wonder, work, creating, inventing, and learning - that I wish would have never ended. The twenty major Sessions of creation between 1992 and 1999 on the Museum will be listed along with a short description of what was completed during each Session.

Session #1 - September 20 to November 20, 1992: "Initial Space Construction."
This first Session centered around the construction, painting, and completion of the initial Museum space, literally meaning the building of the floor, walls, ceiling, and steps into the Museum, the painting of all in one light and one dark shade of Purple, as well as the mounting of the first November 27 - December 13, 1992 'Opening' of the Museum in honor of what would have been Jimi Hendrix's fiftieth birthday on November 27, 1992.

Session #2 - Mid-February to end April, 1993: "Initial Electric Ladyland Environment Construction."
After the two week Jimi Hendrix Celebration was over the new Museum space was emptied again, and I began to build the Fluorescent "Participatory" Environment in the Museum. I still remember twenty years later that first day of real construction, with the building of the wooden skeleton of the Environment as well as the large shelving unit that would be in the storage space around the Environment driving me crazy. The major work that took place during these intense Sessions of initial construction of the Fluorescent "Participatory" Environment involved the raw construction of the industrial plastic heavy-duty large pipe which I used to create the base of "The Spectrum Pole." After two months of solid work I had completed only such a basic rudimentary skeleton of the planned Fluorescent "Participatory" Environment that I was nearly ashamed to show it to Michèle when she returned.

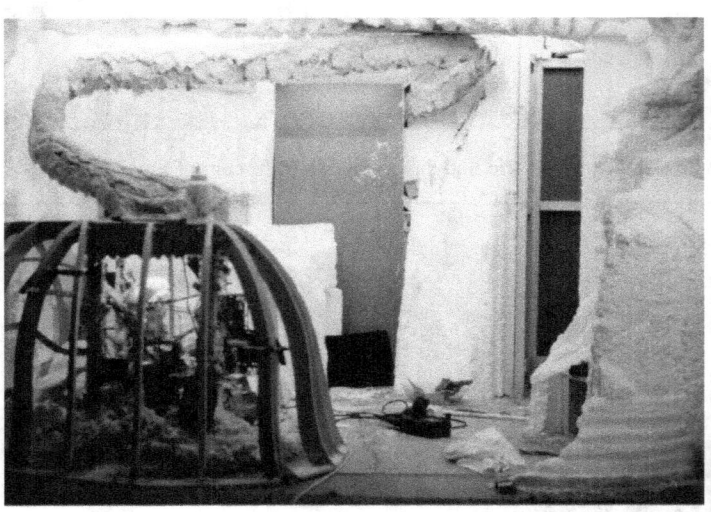

Session #3 - June, 1993: "The Plastic Sessions."
A good portion of the 'skin,' or 'sculpture,' on top of the wooden skeleton of the Environment is plastic that I heated and carved. I would glue, screw and/or bolt the plastic sheets together and then to the wooden skeleton of the sculpture, next heating them to 550 degrees with industrial heat guns, then carving forms with large knives, and finally many layers as well as many different kinds of plasters, glues, and industrial epoxies would be applied just to create the hardened structure of the Environment before paint or Color was considered.

Session #4 - August to September, 1993: "The Cutting Sessions. This was almost two months of cutting (or 'sculpting') plastic by the square meter in the Museum Environment. One time I bought out the entire supply of professional wood glue from the construction store near the Museum in Amsterdam for the endless coating of the Environment. After using layers of epoxies to stabilize the surface of the plastic sculpture, I coat it with
many thick layers of a special finishing plaster before again coating it with many more layers of glues to make the surface hard and strong. Again, this is all done before paint or Colors were even considered.

Session #5 - February 22 to April 26, 1994: "The Unbelievable Session."
Endless sculpting, forming, and coating of the Museum Environment as well as the building of individual areas within the Environment, such as the 'Stalagmite Pool,' "The Reactor," "The Land Between Tick and Tock," "The Shiva Linga," and the

"Participatory" cave area. The stalagmites making up the 'Stalagmite Pool' were not sculpted individually and then assembled in place, but were all carved out - or 'relieved' - from a solid block of plastic. This also included each of the large foot-long Stalactites above the Stalagmite Pool which were carved out and 'relieved' from a solid block of plastic, and then immediately were heavily coated with glue before having a foot-long screw driven up into the stalactite from the bottom, prior to starting to carve the stalactite next to it. The sculpture inside "The Land Between Tick and Tock" was made up of many layers of very thin plywood glued together, and then strings were threaded and individually knotted through tiny drilled holes from the top to the bottom of this sculpture in a very delicate balance of tensions. "The Shiva Linga" was an experience in itself, with four custom-made mirrors carried by hand across Amsterdam. These four tall mirrors were then mounted inside of "The Shiva Linga" in the sculpture, allowing the viewing of nineteen repeated mirrored reflections visible in three different directions as you gaze into "The Shiva Linga's" 'Passage of Infinity.'

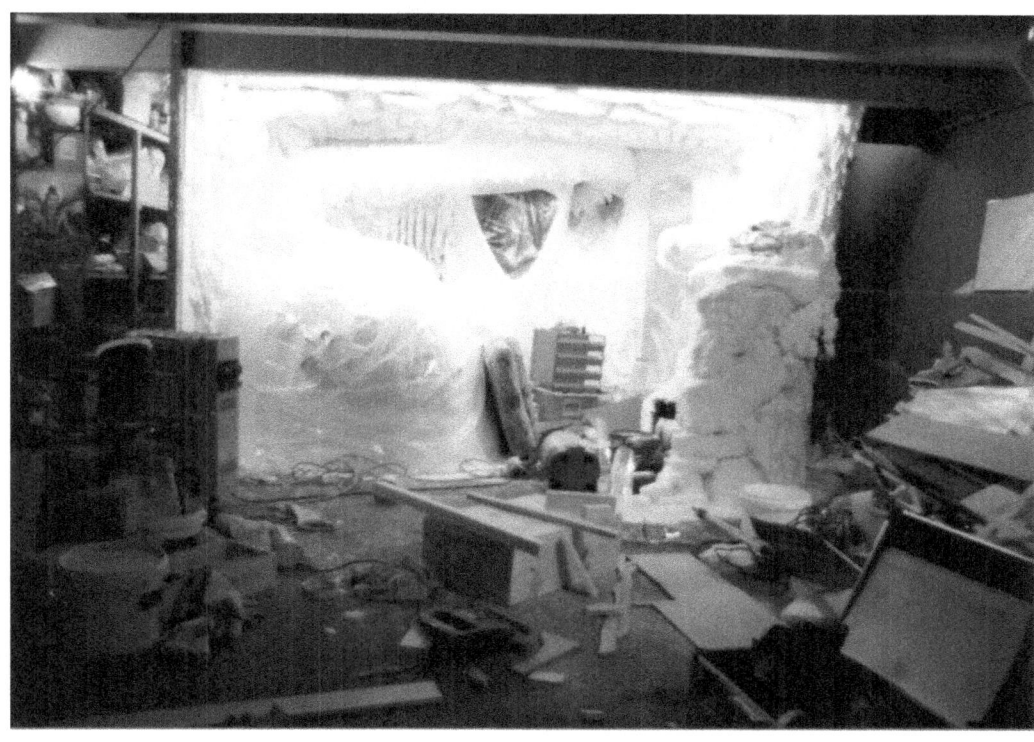

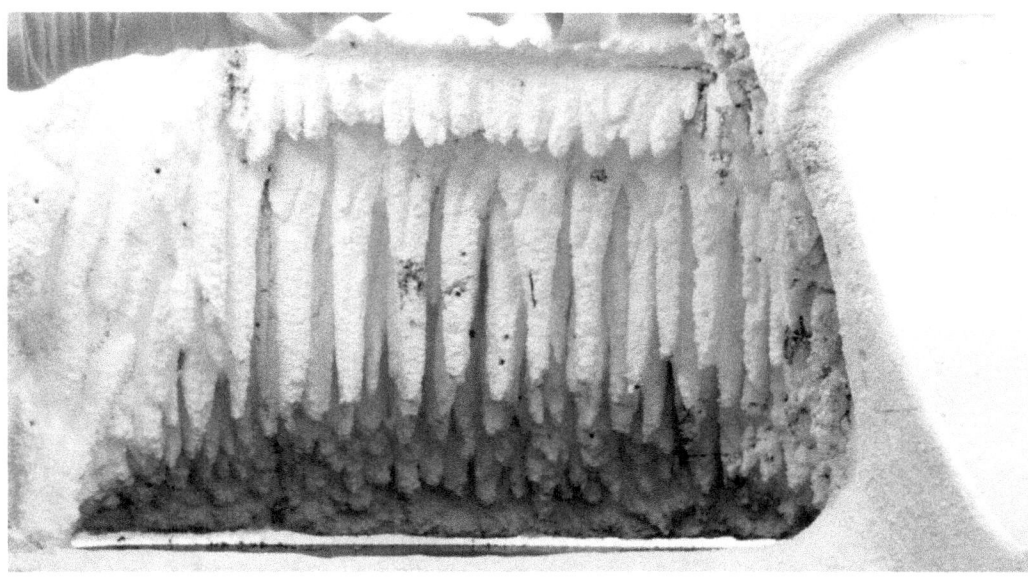

Session #6 - July, 1994: "The Jupiter Collision."
This was the Session during which the unforgettable "Comet Shoemaker-Levy 9" collided with Jupiter as the world watched amazed. It was one of the premier astronomical events in recent history which was witnessed by people across the world. On the actual main day of the collisions of the many fragments of this scattered comet that was witnessed to bombard Jupiter between July 16 and July 22, 1994, I sawed off the entire 'Hampi Mountain' containing the "Hanuman Mandir" and the "Ganesh Mandir" at it's top, which makes up the front/right side of the Museum Environment, and extended it about two feet (65 centimeters), allowing a new space in which to carve "The Crystal Cave" within "The Magic Land of Lights, Sounds, and Dimensions." This "Crystal Cave" is filled with over a hundred crystals, meteorites, tektites, impactites, geodes, an "Optical Effects Cave" with examples of Asterism, Labradorescence, Iridescence, Adventurism, Opalescence, Chatoyancy, and 'Double Refraction,' mirrors, fossils, fossilized Dinosaur excrement, plastic, feathers, and even a tiny Phosphorescent Red 'Tête de mort' of Jerry Garcia.

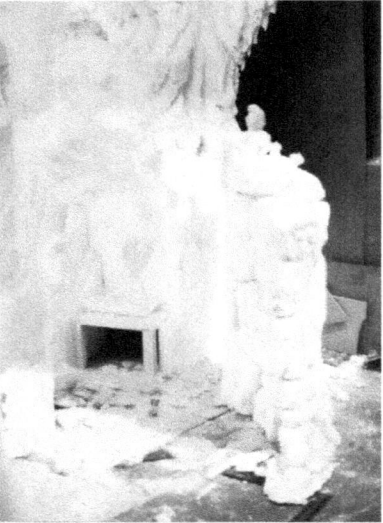

Session #7 - September to November, 1994: "The Spaghetti-wire Lighting Session."
Along with much other construction, the main event which took place during this several month Session was the wiring of the switches of the "Participatory" Button Pad in "The Magic Land of Lights, Sounds, and Dimensions," which contains eleven switches with lights in them, each which must be soldered to two different wires before being mounted on the plastified plywood mounting board I had made. Sounds straight forward enough, except for the fact that I have two degrees in Art and never held a soldering iron in my hands before(!) So, I went to an electronics store in Amsterdam and told the guy that I would buy the soldering gun if he would first show me how to use it. Then I proceeded to solder, in a tiny working space, for the first time - on eleven tiny switches - twenty-two wires leading to seemingly the very four corners of the Earth through a network of tangled wires that truly resembled what became the 'title' of this Session: "Spaghetti-wire."

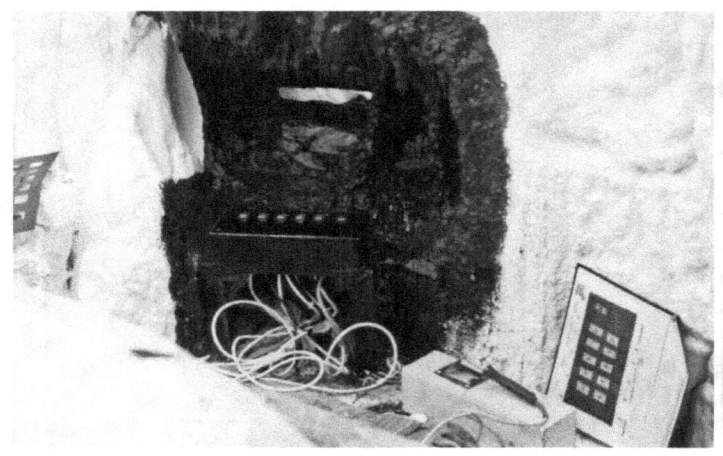

Session #8 - February 19 to April 26, 1995: "Le Bouttons Rouge!! The Caves Session."
This was another two month Session during which all the cave areas of the Fluorescent "Participatory" Environment's "Magic Land of Lights, Sounds, and Dimensions" were finished, including a full line of "H.O." scale model train set electrical transformers soldered to switches of the "Participatory" button pad, three Halogen lamps and two more "H.O." train transformers as well as another tiny light fixture for "The Crystal Cave." Besides three "H.O." train transformers there would be also two small four-watt Black lights wired up and mounted in "The Special Michele Cave," a hidden trap-door eighteen-watt Black light activated by yet another Red lit switch on the "Participatory" button pad, and finally six individual fifteen-watt Black lights turned on by one of the Red switches, as well as a White spot light for comparison of the Fluorescent minerals which is activated by the only Green lit switch - both for "The Fluorescent Mineral Cave's" sixty-five Fluorescent minerals mounted under these two different types of lamps which produce absolutely opposite shocking effects on the same plain rocks.

Session #9 - July, 1995, "The Floor Session."
This was the Session during which the entire formed floor of the Fluorescent "Participatory" Environment was made. One of the key ingredients which made the construction possible of this thirty-two cubic meter piece of Art which has been entered by 50,000 visitors as of this writing period sixteen years after it's opening, is an industrial product which is used as an epoxy for construction in Holland. It is as expensive as it is dangerous to use and unnatural. I used a virtual pool full of this epoxy to construct the Museum Environment. The defining point of this epoxy which is so toxic that it's not sold commercially in America, is that after it is poured or painted onto a surface it slightly expands and then hardens to such an unbelievable degree that it's difficult to drive a screw into it. A huge amount of this industrial epoxy was used to create the entire seamless floor of the Fluorescent "Participatory" Environment in the Museum. It expands and slightly creates it's own formations during it's slow drying process, which hardened into an industrial surface on the Museum floor giving the overall impression of a natural flowing river of water.

"Session # 10" - November 2 to November 19, 1995: "The Final Construction Session."
The entire Fluorescent "Participatory" Environment was structurally finished during this Session, all in preparation after three years of construction for the final four years of mixing up Fluorescent paint by hand and applying a huge amount of Fluorescent and Phosphorescent Colors to this large Museum surface.

Session #11 - March 3 to April 27, 1996: "The First Painting Sessions."
Finally after three years of construction and sculpting I could begin to only paint. First, areas which had to be sealed off permanently in the Environment had already been painted during the last couple of years, such as the inside structure of "The Reactor," which was sealed with the three modules of the front, left, and right 'walls' containing nineteen lenses to look through, and then the Stalagmite pool in "The Skyline Caverns Pool" had to be painted, using more than ten Colors of gradation before being covered with a large piece of oval glass. During this two month "First Painting Session" I began with "The Jumping Through Time Wall" on the left in the Environment, which was loosely inspired by the new theories of the universe, such as "Quantum Foam" and "Super String." This first area of the Environment was painted in relatively the same techniques I had used for years in the "Mind-Arising Boxes" series as well as most of the other series of Fluorescent paintings back to 1987. Continuing from the end of "The Jumping through Time Wall," I next painted the Stalactites above the Stalagmite pool in "The Skyline caverns Pool" with another gradation of very hot Oranges becoming brilliant Orange-Reds. This painting of the Stalactites above "The Skyline Caverns Pool" continued, extending up above the "Pool" to "The Plains of Heaven," which was inspired by John Martin's masterpiece in the Tate Gallery.

"Session #12" - September to November, 1996: "The Second Painting Sessions."
I remembered the first day of painting when I accidentally discovered the "Thermal Expansion" technique as being the first day of painting the Environment, but it was the first day of painting the Environment during these "Second Painting Sessions." To begin I was slightly overwhelmed with the massive unpainted surface of the Environment, and began the only way I could - above "The Shiva Linga" and Gaumukh in the Himalaya, coating brilliant contrasts of Fluorescent Magentas vibrating with Fluorescent Yellows on "The Energy flow." This 'Starbirth Ceiling' of the "Energy Flow" represents the continuous, ceaseless flow of cosmic energy between the physical realm of "The Jumping Through Time Wall" and the physiological/spiritual realm of "The Shiva Linga." After completing "The Energy Flow" of the 'Starbirth Ceiling,' I began the front-top ceiling portion of the Environment, with "Grandmother Earth and Grandfather Sky." While painting this portion of the Environment a combination of events manipulating physical energies resulted in the chance discovery of a new incredible painting technique above my head on the ceiling! Being enthralled with this new "Thermal Expansion" technique I continued it onto "Grandmother Earth and Grandfather Sky," after beginning with the Blues of the sky and water of Earth. On the left of

"Grandmother Earth and Grandfather Sky" there are upside-down tiny peaks of the White snow covered peaks of the Himalaya, the source of the Ganga, and then the Ganga continues across the width of "Grandmother Earth and Grandfather Sky" until it reaches it's delta in Kolkata above "The Magic Land of Lights, Sounds, and Dimensions" on the right side of the Environment. I could have a Monet trip on the ceiling section of this area, by running endless loaded brushes of Fluorescent Orange-Reds over a surface of Orange, where just the 'highlights' of paint would be laid thicker and thicker, similar to the technique which Monet used on his late "Waterlily" masterpieces. The actual ceiling of 'clouds' suspended upside-down above the surface of the Earth was painted completely in this new technique I found and came to call "Thermal Expansion." The end of this three month 1996 Session was spent painting the outside of "The Reactor." First the top boiling hot section of "The Reactor" was painted, representing the intensity of atomic reactions such as "Electron Displacement," the cause of Fluorescence, and this was achieved with every hot Fluorescent Color beginning in vivid Yellow and continuing up to brilliant Magentas. Constantly looking for new painting techniques, I used a painting 'tool' from the Artist who inspired me more than any other, Jackson Pollock, who was very fond of cooking 'basters,' which are like huge syringes with a rubber ball at the end that can be filled with paint and exploded out onto a surface. I also used straws and other primitive instruments to 'blow' into the wet Fluorescent paint areas, as well as incorporating mixed Fluorescent glue areas into the surface of Fluorescent paint on "The Reactor's" top. In the end I achieved what I envisioned with the outside of "The Reactor," creating an area of the Environment in a style of painting I had never before attempted, including on the outside of "The Reactor" "The Atom/The Universe," and "The Electron Trails" which still inspired my painting seventeen years later in 2013, but the ultimate measure of my success after making an area of painting I had never created before happened when Michèle returned, and after showing her what I had painted for the last three months she asked me in a very sensitive way if "The Reactor" was "finished" the way I had painted it...or not?

"Session #13" - February to March, 1997: "The Airbrush Purple Session."
During this Session I continued from where I had finished painting with the back wall of "The Reactor" and it's "Electron Trails," and began painting the area in front of "The Skyline Caverns Pool." This area was sculpted, as the entirety of the Fluorescent "Participatory" Environment, and the creation of what became "The Shiva Pectorals" was an extremely humbling, as well as unforgettable experience. In symbiotic relation, this "Shiva Pectorals" sculpted area of the Environment was also representational at the same time of the "Trans-Am/Batmobile nose," identically shaped into the form of the front nose of my 1977 Red "Trans-Am" I owned decades ago, and from what this 1977 "Trans-Am" was copied from, the original front of the "Batmobile" from the 1965-1966 Adam West series. This whole area I created with flowing, thin coats of Blue, evoking the feelings of underwater. This area was, however, the minor part of this "Session #13," because for several weeks after painting the "Shiva Pectorals/Trans-Am/Batmobile nose," I began a long, strange journey of painting the central focus-point of the Fluorescent "Participatory" Environment in the most elusive of all Fluorescent Colors: Purple! The preparation for this central Purple area of the Environment was formidable, beginning with the ordering the year before of a custom-made Fluorescent Purple pot of very expensive paint from California after talking to the company on the telephone about the problems with this most elusive of all Fluorescent Colors, Purple. Unfortunately, all of this story was not worth the finally-delivered custom-made Fluorescent Purple paint, because although it had been prepared just for me with the written promise of being a "Real Fluorescent Purple," it was only marginally better than all the previous nearly non-Fluorescent Purple paints I had used going back to the late 1960s - a dull, Brownish Purple which only barely Fluoresced, and looked in plain English pitiful next to all my other brilliant, sparkling Colors of Fluorescent paints I make by hand. Even before drying and becoming flat, this custom coat of Fluorescent Purple paint on the outside of "The Land Between Tick and Tock" looked miserable! In a state of mortal despair I next wondered what the hell I was going to do now - I had ordered a custom-made Fluorescent Purple paint that had travelled literally a quarter of the way around the Earth from California to Amsterdam - 6,000 miles - but after using it next to my brilliant palette of Fluorescent Colors, this expensive custom-made "Real Purple" Fluorescent paint was totally disappointing and unusable. What I decided to do, after realizing that even the best Fluorescent paint companies in the world could not make the impossible - brilliant Fluorescent Purple paint - was to make my own multi-layered painting of Purple, which would create an optical mixture of an incredible Fluorescent Purple in this central focal-point of the Environment. In "Pearl Paint" on Canal Street in Manhattan some weeks before, during my yearly Christmas visit, I had already prepared thoroughly for this Purple Session, and besides ordering and picking up my "Real Fluorescent" Purple bottle of custom made paint, I bought a professional "Pasche" airbrush with all needed accessories, as well as an air-compressor for this airbrush. So I taped off the Environment with plastic around the area to be airbrushed, then sealed off the entire Environment from the other half of the Museum space with a complete clear plastic wall. For two solid weeks, from the morning to about ten o'clock at night I constantly airbrushed. After the first full day of painting with a simple mask, goggles and about eight to ten hours of

airbrushing, the entire central focal-point of "The Land Between tick and Tock" looked only very slightly better than miserable. I was exhausted, half deaf, and in desperation wondering if this endless airbrushing was ever going to look good. Day after day I sprayed with my "Pasche" airbrush, which admittedly was designed for tiny areas of photo retouching, not an area six feet wide by six feet tall. After several days a glimmer of sparkling Fluorescent Purple began to appear almost like iridescence (which is impossible to achieve in the Black light because it is an effect of White light) with a shimmer of Reddish Purple and then a shimmer of Bluish Purple (like on the neck of a pigeon) as you moved your head back and forth . Very gradually an incredible vivid Purple arose from countless coats, which is a living, nearly iridescent dynamic Fluorescent Purple that slightly changes as you look from different angles, and is a dimension beyond what I had ever hoped for.

"Session #14" - March 31 to April 29, 1997: "Thermal Expansion."

This was a one month Session during which in thirty days I painted thirty 'rocks.' These thirty 'rocks' making up the front/right of the Environment, represent the mountain that is climbed in Hampi, India to reach "The Hanuman Temple," and then continued onto the 'rocks' above, around, and in front of "The Magic and of Lights, Sounds, and Dimensions." These were exquisite Sessions, with the peak not surprisingly coming on April nineteenth, when for twelve hours I painted the top, front 'rock' of the Environment, which is still one of my favorite areas of the Environment even nineteen years later.

"Session #15" - September to November, 1997: "The Darkest Ages Session."

The 'dark' name of this Session which went on for three months had not to do with what was done in the Museum, but was named because of extremely negative external forces which nearly caused the closing of the Museum before it was even completed. During these Sessions the most Phosphorescent area of the entire Fluorescent "Participatory" Environment was painted, using the most amount of extremely expensive Phosphorescent paints I had ever used at one time in my life for this "Crack Between the Worlds" area. Very expensive Phosphorescent light Orange and Orange-Red pigments from Amsterdam, Phosphorescent Yellow and "Phat" Phosphorescent Yellow-Green pigments from New York, Extremely expensive Phosphorescent Blue pigment form "Sennelier Paints" in Paris, "Crayola" Yellow-Green Phosphorescent paint, and even Yellow, Orange, and the extremely rare true Red Phosphorescent paints which were sent to me in small plastic tubes from my mother in America (!) were all used to create "The Crack Between the Worlds." Seven distinct Phosphorescent Colors can be seen immediately as the one-thousand watts of Black lights are turned off all together in the Environment, and these Phosphorescent Colors are visible for several hours after turning off all the lights. The next Sessions of painting were already described in this section of the book, with the sixty-six Colors of gradations used to paint "The Spectrum Pole" not just once, but twice. This is the most visually striking form in the Fluorescent "Participatory" Environment, being over six meters (yards) long and imperceptibly changing from Fluorescent Magenta-Purple to Fluorescent Yellow.

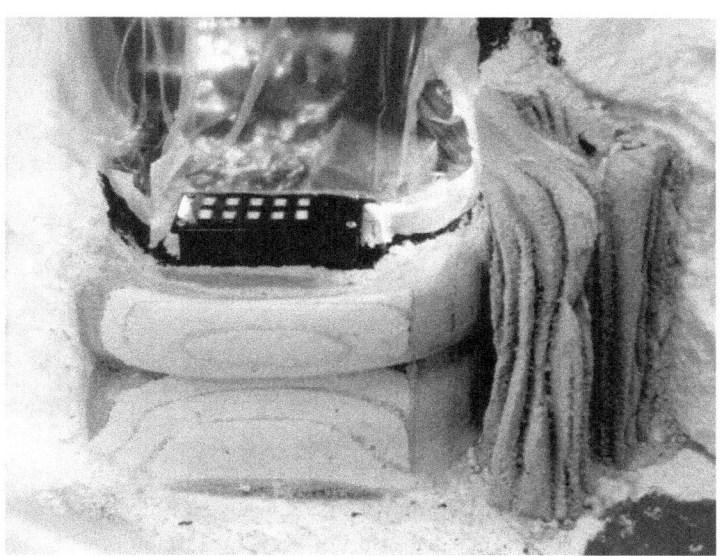

"Session #15a" - June 15, 1997: "Painting of 'The Draperies' with Michèle on my Fortieth Birthday."

This was by far one of the most memorable nights of the entire seven years of making the Museum, on my fortieth birthday pouring and painting Fluorescent Colors onto 'The Draperies' formation, the structure of which was inspired by our trips to

Belgium a couple of years earlier when we went into four different cave systems. Of course being my birthday and being a night we painted from midnight until dawn in the Museum together, it was a very special event indeed. Not only were we altered, but the entire city of Amsterdam was itself altered at that moment. Thankfully, even the constant bizarre noise and vibrations of helicopters over the roof for the coming "United Europe 2000" throughout the all-night Session could not distract Michèle and I from having a wonderful adventure with a substance we never used in such a large quantity before, Fluorescent glue. Fluorescent Colors had once again come back slightly into fashion during the mid to late 1990s and as always major companies had 'jumped on the bandwagon,' such as famous classic "Elmer's Glue" in America who began to make a full line of high quality Fluorescent glue. The December before in New York's "Pearl Paint" I had bought a tremendous amount of these tubes of Fluorescent "Elmer's Glue" - about $100.00 worth - I bought so much that we still have some unopened tubes nineteen years later. With these seven Colors of Fluorescent "Elmer's Glue," which are translucent and shinny when dry, we layered Colors like sheets of Colored glass filters on top of each other the entire night until sunrise, and created some mixtures of Colors which are unique to these Fluorescent glue 'Draperies.'

"Session #16" - February 23 to March 23, 1998: "Pre-India Kumbh Mela Session."

Before leaving to go to India for the first Kumbh Mela of my life in Hardwar during the Spring of 1998, I made two smaller environments that are separate from the large Fluorescent "Participatory" Environment in the Museum. First I painted the environment at the entrance of the Museum, at the top of the stairs, which is seen as visitors descend these entrance steps, and which I played upon by creating an environment which changes Colors as you descend these entrance steps in front of it. The scalding Fluorescence of Yellows, Oranges, and Reds gradate into Magenta-Red on the top surface of a series of sculpted levels, which then turn to a Fluorescent Turquoise as you descend the entrance steps into the Museum. You control the speed and the directions of decent or ascension, of course. In front of you is a large curved acrylic protection for this "Jurassic Environment," which contains parts of an environment that Michèle had begun to create in the Gallery itself on the floor in front of my "Mind-Arising Boxes" for the previous couple of years, being models of dinosaurs that she painted with full Fluorescent skins. These Brontosaurus, Pterodactyls, and other species of the dinosaur family became the inhabitants of this "Jurassic Environment" at the top of the entrance steps into "Electric Ladyland - the First Museum of Fluorescent Art." The last thing I did before leaving to join Michèle in India for the Hardwar Kumbh Mela - the biggest religious gathering on Earth - in March, 1998 was to build the second separate environment, which Michèle would create in the Museum, the "Bernadette Grotto." This Bernadette environment is on the other side of the Museum, the "Demonstration side" with 1,000 pounds of Fluorescent minerals and display cases containing "Common Items that are Fluorescent," and Fluorescent Mineral Artwork from the 1950s. This second separate Museum environment of Michèle's also had a long evolution, beginning with me finding an antique statue made years ago in Lourdes, and Michèle repainting this antique plaster grotto containing Bernadette Soubirous kneeling in front of the apparition of Mary. I added details to Michèle's Fluorescent painting of the antique Bernadette Grotto statue, such as Fluorescent plastic 'stars' around the head of Mary, tiny Fluorescent minerals added to the garden in front of the Grotto, and on each of the roses at Mary's feet I tried to represent the original vision of Bernadette and applied twenty-four carat Gold leafing. Finally, the night before my flight to join Michèle in India for the Hardwar Kumbh Mela, I filled the 'pool' in front of the "Bernadette Grotto" with five liters of plastic which had Fluorescent Blue pigment added to it, and after two and a half months in India, upon returning to Amsterdam this "Bernadette" 'pool' had nearly finished drying(!)

The First Fluorescent Minerals Collected in the Himalaya

From March to June, 1998 I was in northern India with Michèle for the Kumbh Mela in Hardwar, just south of Rishikesh. During this trip we also went on a pilgrimage deep into the Himalaya where I collected more than thirty pounds (14 kilos) of Fluorescent Minerals.

On March 27, 1998 I gave what was possibly the first Fluorescent Mineral Demonstration in the Himalaya. At the Santosh Puri Ashram in Saptor Rishi, between Hardwar and Rishikesh, I gave a Fluorescent Mineral Demonstration to a group of about fifteen holy people, including the Yogi Babaji Santosh Puri, Sadhus (Hindu priests), and Indian Babas. This was the first time that any of them had heard about Fluorescent minerals, or even "Black Lights!" Everyone in the Ashram reacted with astonishment and much excitement. What amazed them the most was that these seemingly common, Colorless rocks burst into brilliant Colors. After the demonstration when I turned the White lights back on, Babaji Santosh Puri picked up a Grey piece of the Calcite and Willemite from Franklin, New Jersey that he had just seen as bright Red-Orange and Green under my U.V. lamps, and he then turned it over in his hands, looking to see where the amazing Colors had gone(!) I brought both the

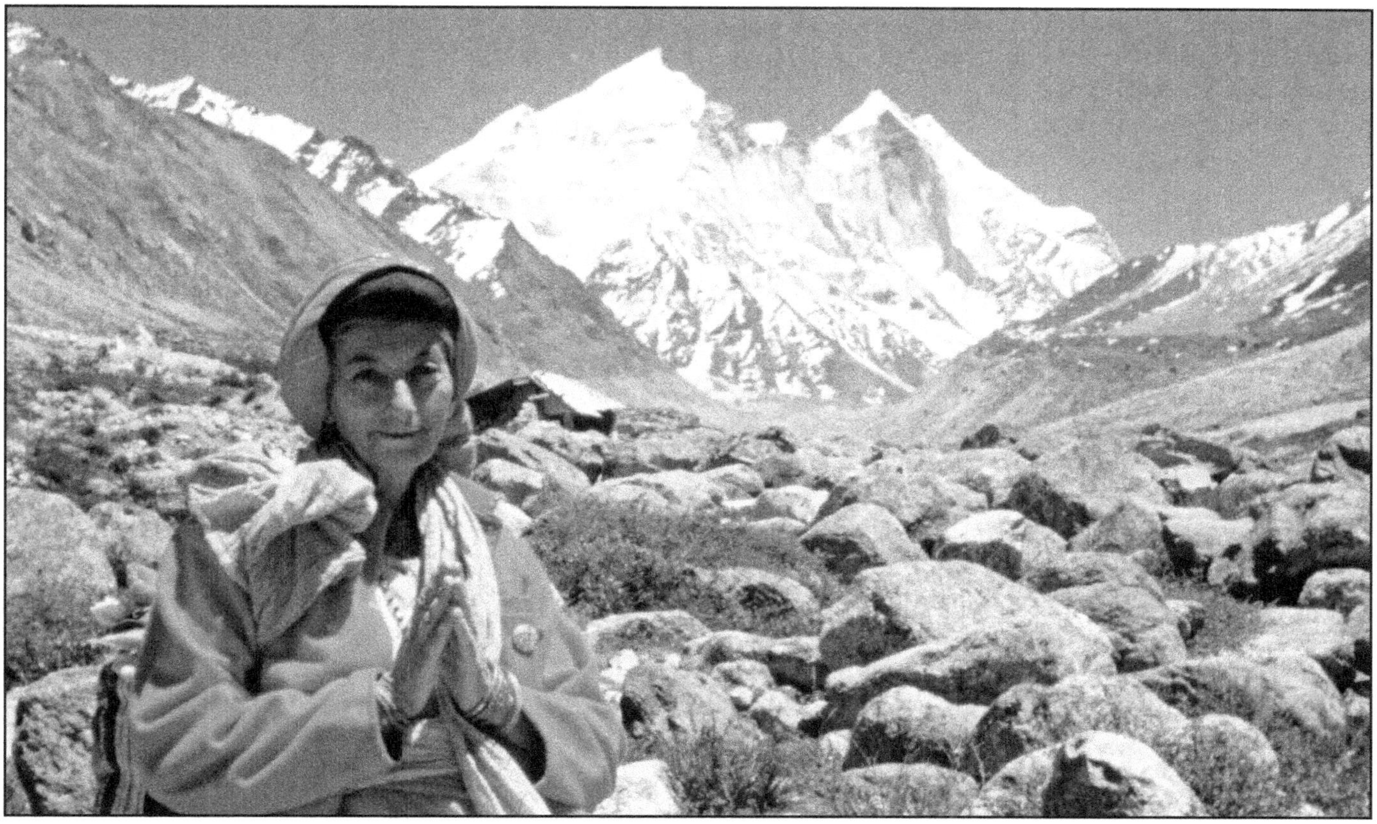

Michèle Delage at 14,000 feet elevation (4,350 mtrs.) in Gaumukh, India - the Source of the Ganga, May, 1998

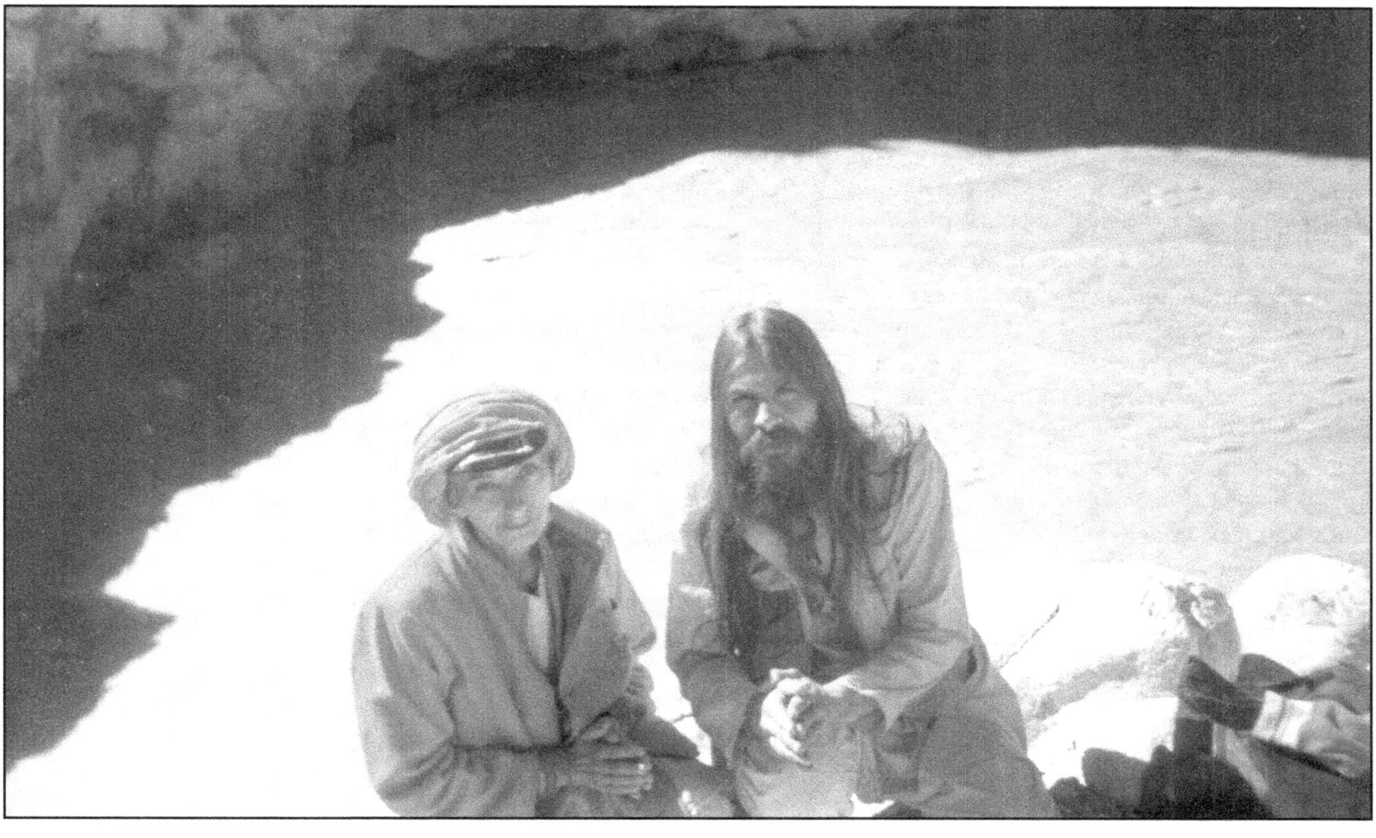

Nick Padalino and Michèle Delage at 14,000 feet (4,350 mtrs.) in Gaumukh, India - the Source of the Ganga, May, 1998

Longwave and Shortwave Ultraviolet lamps with me to India for the Fluorescent Mineral Demonstrations, and for the show I brought a selection of seven different kind of Fluorescent minerals to the Ashram. Fluorite from England with Blue Fluorescence, Scapolite from Canada with Yellow-Apricot Fluorescence, and Red Fluorescing Mangano Calcite from Peru were shown for the Longwave Ultraviolet Demonstration. I next showed a rare phenomenon of Fluorescent minerals changing Colors with Terlingua, Texas Calcite, which is Pink-Red in the Longwave U.V., and then turns Blue in the Shortwave U.V., and when the Shortwave lamp is turned off they also all saw the crystals Phosphorescing Blue - Glowing-in-the-Dark! I then showed Aragonite from Sicily which turns Colors from Red-Pink in the Longwave U.V., to White in the Shortwave, and Phosphoresces a Greenish. The strongest reaction came last from the Shortwave Fluorescent mineral demonstration, where I showed a six inch (15 cm) slab and about a pound of pieces of brilliant Red Fluorescing Mangano Calcite and just as brilliant Green Fluorescing Willemite from Franklin, New Jersey, as well as a three-Colored Fluorescent mineral from the Purple Passion Mine in Arizona, amazingly made up of Blue Fluorite, Red Calcite, and White-Greenish Willemite. At the end of the Fluorescent Mineral Demonstrations, I also showed a small selection of "Common Items that are Fluorescent," like Basmati Rice, Dal (Orange lentils), and Coconut, which are very common in India. When I left India, I gave all the labeled Fluorescent minerals and the portable U.V. lamp to Mandakini in the Ashram, where she gave Fluorescent Mineral Demonstrations with her amazing "coloring stones" for years.

The highlight of this trip to India was a pilgrimage to the source of the Ganga (the Ganges River), deep in the Himalaya during the end of May, 1998. Traveling to Gangotri, which is in the very north of India at an altitude of 10,500 feet (3,350 meters), myself, Michèle, and an Indian friend went on the thirty-eight kilometer (20 mile) pilgrimage - nineteen kilometers to Gaumukh, and nineteen kilometers back. If you walk eight more miles beyond these two mountains Shivalink Topovan, then you reach the border of Tibet. Gaumukh is at an altitude of 14,000 feet (4,350 meters) and this is the source of the Ganga (Ganges River). The Ganga comes from within the Gaumukh Glacier, that measures at almost twenty miles long and two to four miles wide. When standing in front of this advancing face of the Glacier, where Gaumukh is, it is nearly hard to believe it is ice - the face of the Glacier stretches twenty or thirty stories over your head, and is about a mile wide. At this holy pilgrimage, Gaumukh, I climbed up onto this enormous Glacier and collected three very special Fluorescent mineral specimens that are Red, Blue, and Yellow under the Shortwave U.V. lamp. On this often hair-raising thirty-eight kilometer round trip pilgrimage walking back and forth to Gaumukh, I collected and carried back more than thirty pounds of Fluorescent minerals. In the finest of the thirty-five best specimens from Gaumukh, the strongest Fluorescence is under the Shortwave U.V. lamp. Many of the specimens contain a very particular Yellow-Apricot Fluorescent mineral that is most likely Apatite, which is famous for coming from Gilgit, Pakistan, geographically very close. Some of the most interesting Fluorescent minerals I collected on the Gaumukh pilgrimage consists of a group of nine sparkling crystallized pieces which are possibly Microcline, because the specimens Fluoresce deep Red under the Shortwave U.V., and then turn to cold Blue under the Longwave Ultraviolet. These Fluorescent minerals I collected in Gaumukh at 14,000 feet are probably the first Fluorescent minerals collected in the Himalaya. When I returned from India I spoke to founding members of the "Fluorescent Mineral Society" (established in 1971) and asked if they had ever heard of anyone collecting Fluorescent minerals in the Himalaya, then I wrote a detailed article about the journey to Gaumukh and the Fluorescent minerals I collected, which was published in the "Fluorescent Mineral Society's" "U.V. Waves" in 1998, and in this article I also specifically asked if any one of the hundreds of expert members had ever collected Fluorescent minerals in the Himalaya, or had even heard about Fluorescent minerals ever having been collected in the Himalaya, which I've never received a reply to after eighteen years.

"Session #17" - June 15 to July, 1998: "Opening the Museum Session."

Returning to the west after the Kumbh Mela in Hardwar, India was even ruder than the rude awakening it always is, especially from that 1998 Kumbh before finishing the Museum. Michèle and I had just come from the biggest religious celebration of Earth with fifty or sixty-million pilgrims on a spiritual journey, and for the last two weeks of our journey we had gone for the second time to Gaumukh, the source of the Ganga (Ganges River) at 14,000 feet (4,350 meters). This Ganga source on the Gaumukh Glacier had receded about one-hundred meters from the spot where the source of the Ganga had been in 1987, the first time that we made the thirty-eight kilometer pilgrimage bare-footed to Gaumukh. On returning to Amsterdam work continued, and I began construction which does not need infinite contemplation or even a clear state of mind. I ran the wiring and began to mount the lighting units on the "Demonstration Side" of the Museum, which consists of a series of halogen lights as well as several smaller Black lights, all used for Fluorescent antiques and artifacts on display in the Museum. After running these lighting units in the Museum, I cut and mounted the large curved piece of clear acrylic on the front of "The Jurassic Environment" in the entrance to the Museum. Before leaving the 1998 Hardwar Kumbh Mela, I had bought a large brass "Trishule" and a brass "Damroe" in Hardwar, as well as a solid marble "Shiva Linga," all Hindu religious items to be mounted

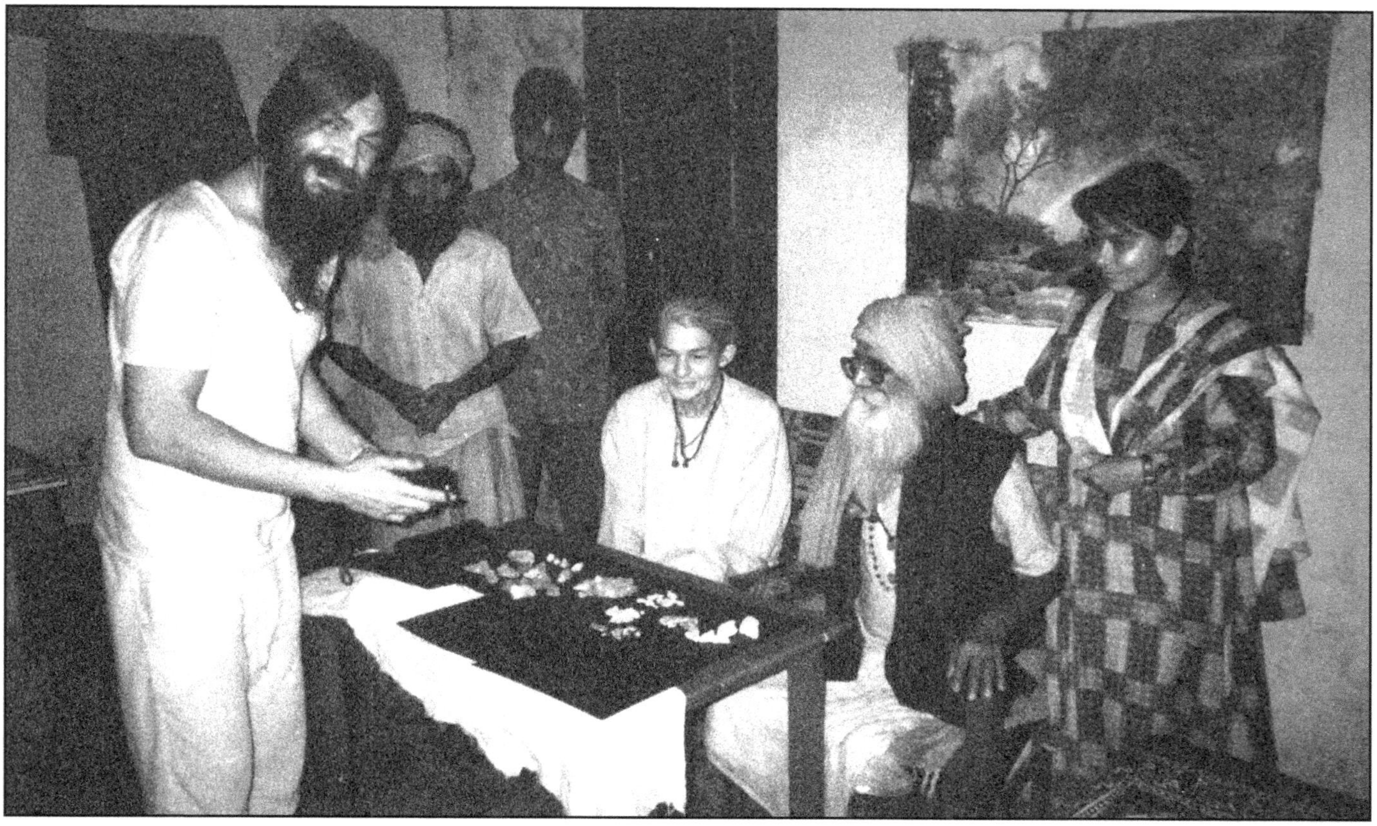

The author giving possibly the First Fluorescent Mineral Demonstration in India at "The Santosh Puri Ashram," May, 1998

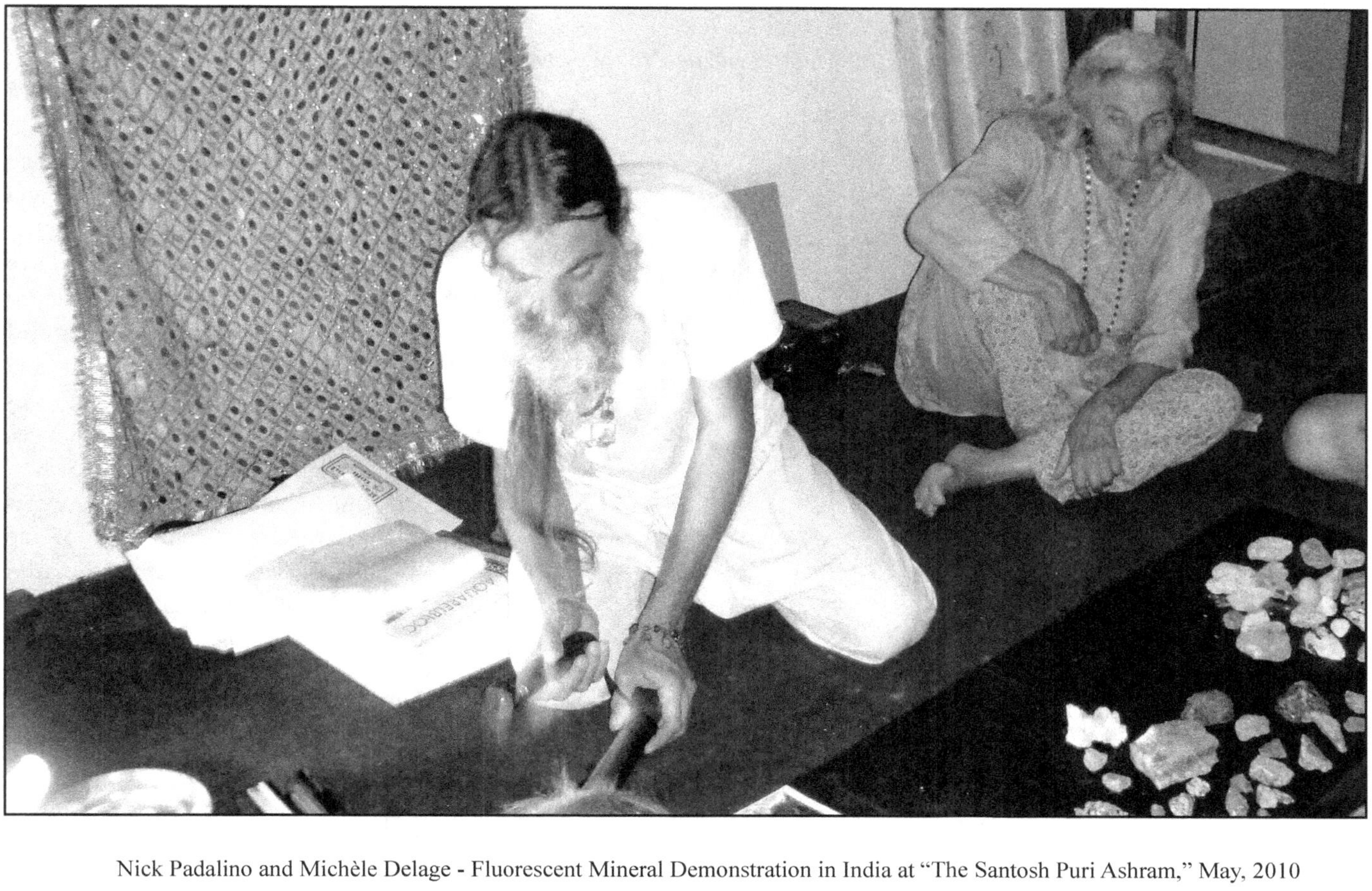

Nick Padalino and Michèle Delage - Fluorescent Mineral Demonstration in India at "The Santosh Puri Ashram," May, 2010

in the Museum after being blessed by our spring guru Babaji Santosh Puri the day before we left the Ashram. I wanted to build a base for the Trishule and Damroe in the Museum that would be similar to the base of the Trishule and Damroe in the Santosh Puri Ashram, so I photographed Babaji's base of his Trishule and reconstructed it in Amsterdam out of bricks and cement, as it had been originally made in the Ashram, complete with Hindu symbols formed into the top of this cement Trishule base. I used these same materials of brick and cement for the base of the marble Shiva Linga that would be mounted right next to the Trishule and Damroe in the Museum. This was done at the same time that a new floor was made for the Museum. During this period Michèle had escaped to Switzerland, and after the last night of making this floor on the entire "Demonstration Side" of the Museum, I decided to also escape from the negative forces acting upon the Gallery and planned Museum, and joined her in Switzerland by train. Before leaving India and the Hardwar Kumbh Mela just the previous month in June, 1998, a questionable Swiss person also staying in the Santosh Puri Ashram where we live in India told me that he had called up Dr. Albert Hofmann in Switzerland and that he had been invited to Dr. Hofmann's house to talk. In Switzerland together, Michèle and I decided to make a large Fluorescent and Phosphorescent mural of Gaumukh, the source of the Ganga where we had just been for the second time in May. This large four by four meter (twelve by twelve foot) Fluorescent and Phosphorescent painting would be done on thick Fluorescent White fine cotton directly on the floor of an apartment we had been loaned for a week by vacationing friends of Michèle. The morning of finishing this Fluorescent mural of Gaumukh, still in a very special state of mind, I telephoned Dr. Albert Hofmann for the first time. As I previously detailed in this book, I asked Dr. Hofmann a question that he had never been asked before, and through this question got invited to his house outside of Basel in the mountains. The lasting impression of spending an afternoon with Dr. Albert Hofmann eighteen years ago on his mountain retreat outside of Basel, is that we were in the presence of a truly enlightened human being.

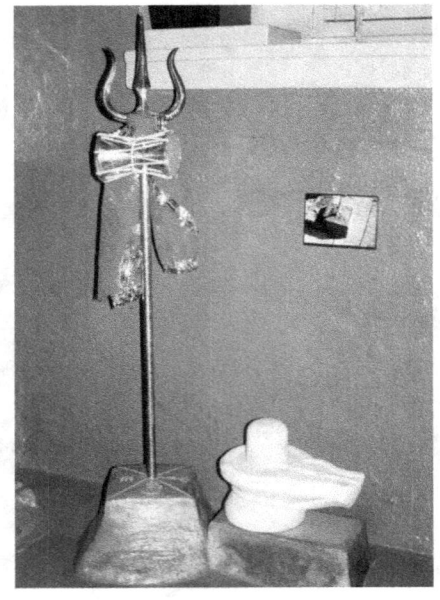

"Session #18a" - September, 1998: "Painting of 'The Bernadette Grotto' by Michèle."

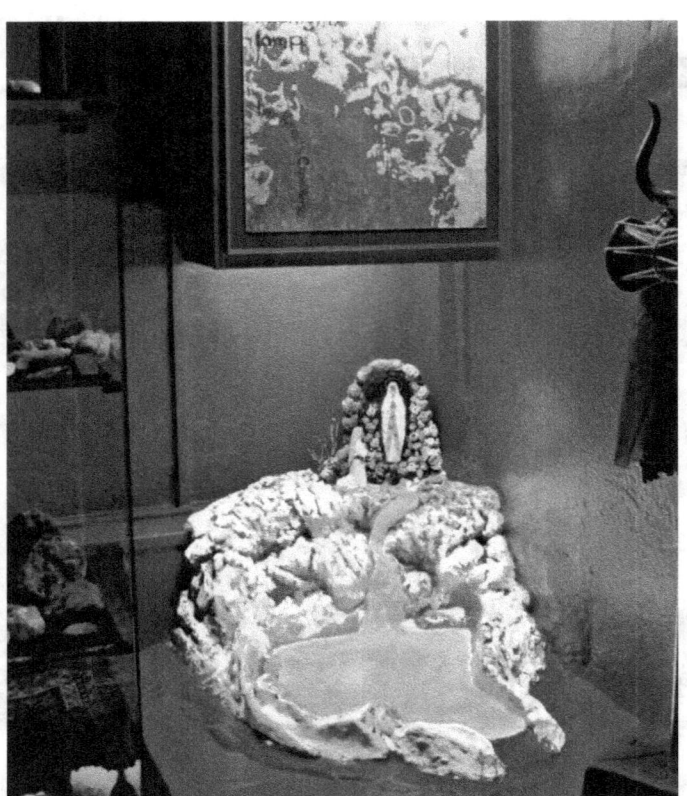

Another unforgettable night of the seven years of creating the Museum was the full evening-morning I could enjoy completely, by only photographing and taking video of Michèle painting "The Bernadette Grotto" using vivid combinations of Fluorescent Colors with her hands. The organic Colors as well as the mixtures of Colors that Michèle uses were especially suited for this piece, being a representation of a natural grotto and pool, since she lived many years in India and has experienced many varied terrains, from the ice-covered peaks of the Himalaya to the tropical jungles of south India, as well as being drawn since she was a young girl to nature and the natural aspects of life. After constructing "The Bernadette Grotto" out of the original antique Bernadette statue from Lourdes Michèle had repainted in Fluorescence, and with the broken plastic pool form I found, I filled in the 'pool' with five liters of Fluorescent plastic and left for India the next morning. Again, this 'pool' was just about finished drying when we returned from India together over two months later.

"Session #18" - September to October 4, 1998: "Waiting Session."

I assembled the first tall glass display case on the "Demonstration Side" of the Museum, next to the "Common Items that are Fluorescent" and Fluorescent Artifacts displays, and proceeded to fill it with five shelves of the wonders of nature. The top shelf has one of the highlights of the entire Museum collection on it: the Fluorescent Mineral Artwork masterpiece of Miera, the Japanese Fluorescent mineral collector in New Jersey during the 1950s. This sculpture of a Japanese house and landscape is made completely out of a multitude of different natural Fluorescent minerals which have been first pulverized with a hammer by hand, then separated into twenty shades of Green and twelve shades of Red under Ultraviolet lamps, and finally for six months applied with wet cement and tweezers to the surface of the sculpture in the dark under two different types of Ultraviolet lamps. Beneath this top shelf of this display case there are shelves of magical changing and glowing Terlingua, Texas Calcite, rare Fluorescent minerals and crystals, Fluorescent minerals which change Color from Longwave to Shortwave Ultraviolet, and in the dark on the bottom shelf, 'Glow-in-the-Dark' or Phosphorescent minerals.

"Session #19" - October 4 to December 1, 1998: "The Traveling Session"

During this next-to-last Session a few months before the completion and opening of the Museum, displays on the "Demonstration Side" were finished, including what for many visitors is the most memorable display of the Museum, the "Fluorescent Mineral Viewing Box." This is a large display with over five-hundred pounds (250 kilos) of Fluorescent minerals from all over the world shown to be nearly Colorless first in the White light, then burst into Colors in the common Longwave Ultraviolet Black light, next in the very powerful Shortwave Ultraviolet (which most Fluorescent minerals react under), and then together both the Longwave and Shortwave Ultraviolet separate thirty watt lighting units are turned on displaying the full brilliantly Colored collection of hundreds of kilos of Fluorescent minerals. After this, both these Ultraviolet lighting units are turned off together, and in the darkness of the Museum visitors next see natural mineral Phosphorescence (almost always for the first time), then finally the White lights are turned back on, and to the universal shock of all viewers these incredible marvels of nature emitting brilliant, pure, saturated Colors - right before the eyes - turn back into plain, ordinary, common Grey rocks(!) The top third of this display in the Museum consists of an Ultraviolet laboratory examination box for medicine from many decades ago named the "C-5" by it's famous manufacturer "Ultra-Violet Products, Inc." The bottom two-thirds of this "Fluorescent Mineral Viewing Box" I built out of wood, combining the structure with the antique metal "C-5" to create a large display about four and a half feet tall (1.5 meters) which fifteen to twenty visitors can easily see during a demonstration in the dark. The entire front of the display, from the top of the "C-5" to the bottom of the wooden display case it's incorporated into, is a complete window and glass door which the display is mostly viewed through, by visitors sitting on the floor in a semi-circle in the dark in front of this "Fluorescent Mineral Viewing Box." To make the display more naturalistic, I sculpted forms out of plastic which also are used as supports and platforms for the many specimens of Fluorescent minerals in the display. This entire interior of the bottom two-thirds of the display built out of wood and plastics was then painted completely Black as a background for the vividly Fluorescing rocks in the dark. The 'right' side of this display also has a large window built into it, the entire height and width of the bottom wooden section. So, combined with the full sheet of glass totally covering the front of the display, and the top sliding small laboratory window, these three windows form three different viewing angles allowing a very close, intimate examination of almost a quarter of a ton of natural Fluorescent minerals just inches away from your eyes behind glass. After completing and preparing the "Fluorescent Mineral Viewing Box" I framed and mounted an antique 'invisible' commercial advertisement looking like it was made in the 1950s, also manufactured by Thomas Warren's "Ultra-Violet Products, Incorporated." Richard Bostwick in New York had worked for "UVP, Inc." and Thomas Warren in the 1960s and he gave me this "invisible" Fluorescent advertisement during the early 1990s.

The last part of this two month Session was occupied by filling in another five-hundred pounds (250 kilos) of Fluorescent mineral crystals and Fluorescent Mineral Artwork into the new tall glass display case on the "Demonstration Side" of the Museum, in front of the "Fluorescent Mineral Viewing Box," and next to the "Common Items that are Fluorescent" display, and then finally the completion of the Fluorescent Artifacts display.

"Session #20" - March 3 to April 1-2, 1999: "The Final Sessions."

As the title declares, these were "The Final Sessions" to complete everything before we opened the Museum on April 19, 1999. In one month an incredible amount of painting and work had to be accomplished, such as one of the most important areas of the Fluorescent "Participatory" Environment, the entire "Shiva Linga" section. This whole area had been built with four huge mirrors juxtaposed into a "Chamber of Infinity" inside the six foot tall "Shiva Linga," as well as "The Fire of Creation" built into the inside base of "The Chamber of Infinity." Finishing the area a massive solid wood Yoni was built and secured into place in front of "The Shiva Linga." The inside top area of "The Linga" had been painted long before with flat Black and

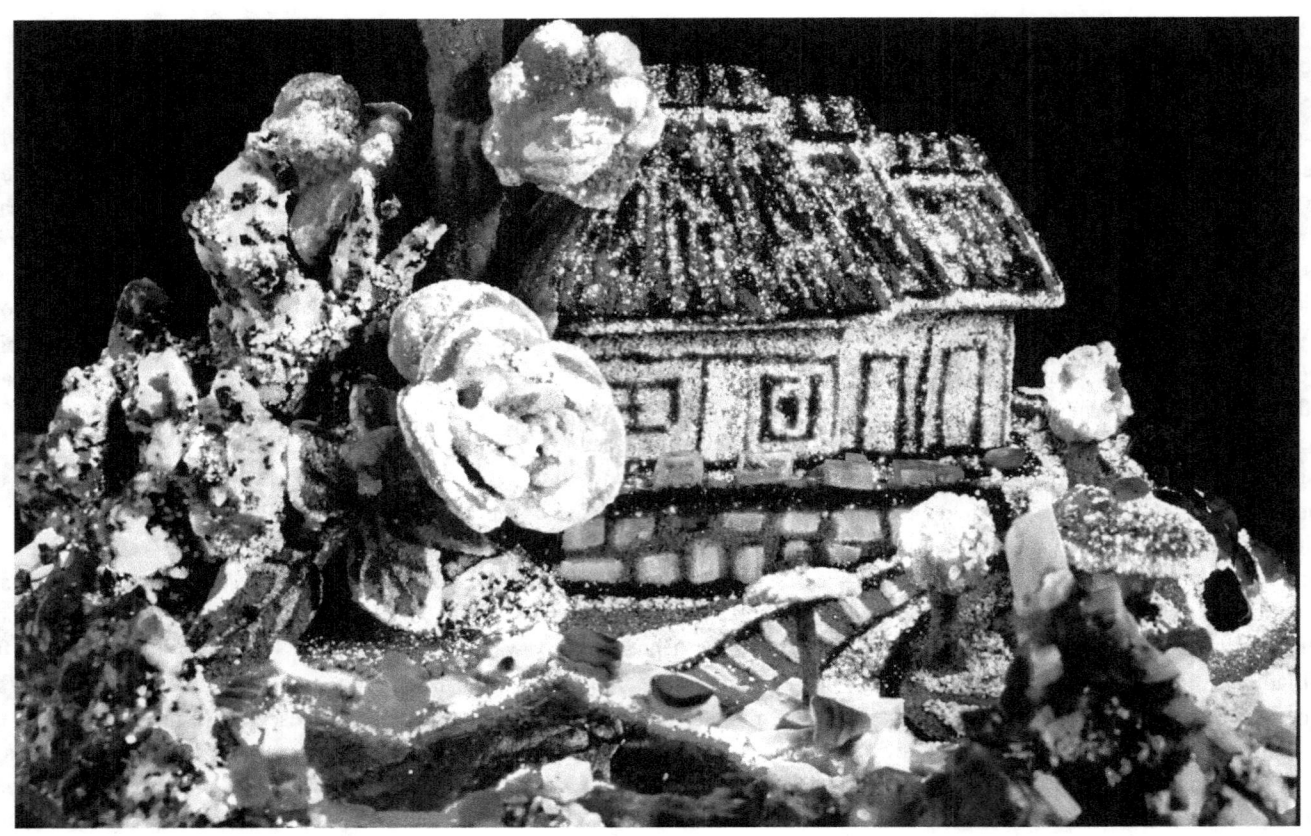

Fluorescscent Mineral Artwork from the 1950s in New Jersey - Miera's masterpiece which took six months to create

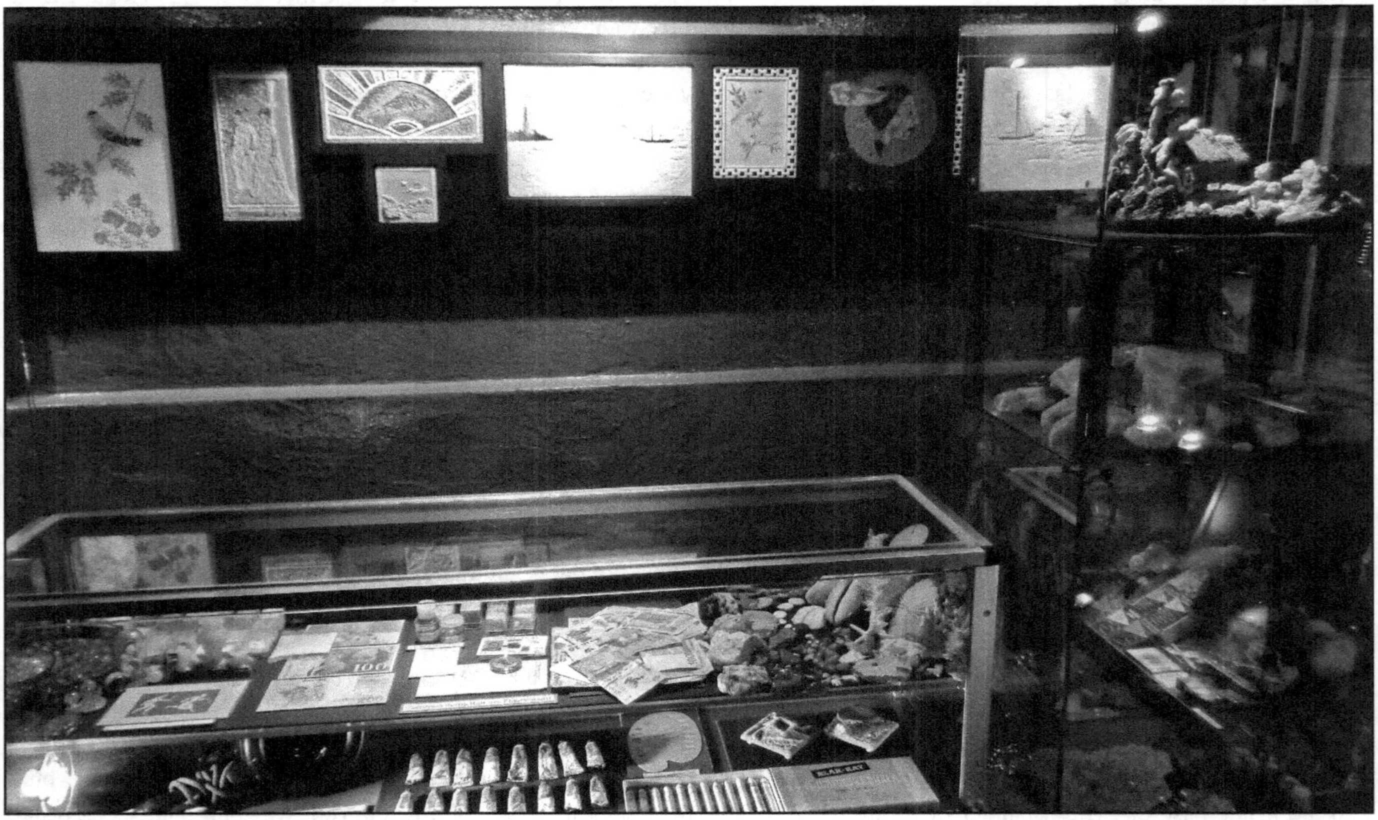

Fluorescscent Mineral Artwork from the 1950s - "Electric Ladyland - the First Museum of Fluorescent Art" collection

sprayed by hand above the head in this tight spot, to create a representation of the universe. It took weeks to finally get all the tiny White Fluorescent 'stars' out of my beard(!) First I painted the interior of "The Shiva Linga," which is "The Fire of Creation," using the Colors I love the most, every hot Fluorescent Color from Acid Yellow to brilliant Red. The only difficult areas of the Environment to create for me were the only areas in which I tried to represent something natural, such as the 'rocks' making up the 'Hanuman mountain' of Hampi, India, and the hardest of all, the eternally flowing water of "Mata Ganga," or the 'Ganges River'

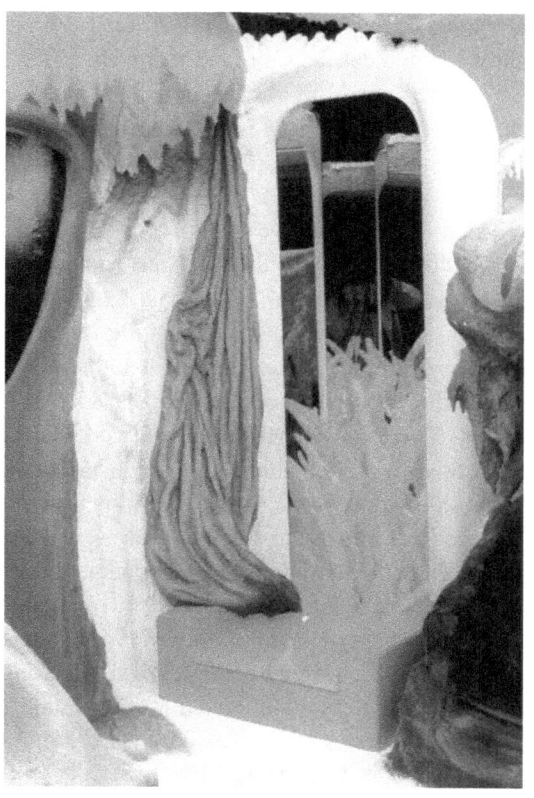

"The Shiva Linga" starting in the Gaumukh, and then flowing down extremely difficult construction of linen that was thick and heavy, of liquid acrylics, epoxies, and glues Attaching the heavy dripping form began a full day of bending and attempts to create a form of natural between breaks on "Mata Ganga" at my late friend Harry of the near-attempting to create. It was so remember the day, using almost the used in my life, second only to the Spectrum Pole" created a few years had soaked into the heavy suit linen of desperately folding, bending, and resemblance of flowing water began the end, after about twelve hours of form of the holy "Mata Ganga" pinned-together, very unlikely difficult of all forms - naturally and in the Fluorescent "Participatory" "Mata Ganga" I used a large variety shiny Fluorescent glues, transparent coming down from the left side of heights of the Himalaya and into "The Shiva Linga." For this "Mata Ganga" I used expensive suit which I then soaked in a toxic stew that resembled a witch's brew. to the top of "The Shiva Linga" I pinning this soaked linen in many flowing water. I remember in the front door of the Gallery telling impossibility of what I was difficult that I still very clearly largest amount of sewing pins I ever meters of stalactites on "The before. As the toxic emulsion that I began to slowly dry over the hours endlessly pinning, a dim to slowly and thankfully emerge. In pinning, bending, and cursing, the arose from these toxic-smelling, substances. This was the most unnaturally inspired - that I created Environment. Finally, to 'paint' this of substances, such as translucent Colorless acrylic mediums, iridescent translucent sparkles, and even Fluorescent paint. I layered these translucent and then transparent acrylics and glues, interspersed with iridescent Blue-Green sparkles that are also translucent, on top of layers of more opaque Fluorescent paints to create a variable Bluish-Greenish Color which changes as you move around in front of it, much like the surface of water. The translucent Blue Fluorescent "Elmer's Glue" was also a good part of the changing surface of "Mata Ganga." I remember running endless loaded brushes of Colors and clear or translucent acrylics over each other coating the "Ganga." The peaks of the Himalaya and the tiny cave representing Gaumukh, the source of the Ganga were then carved at the top of "The Shiva Linga." The tiny cave with the one centimeter marble statue of Shiva in it, on the left side of the Himalaya above the "Linga"

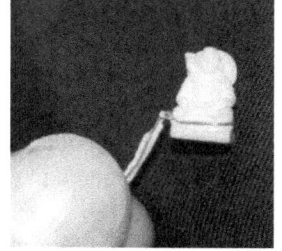

is where the Ganga begins. The area to the left Between Tick and Tock," is where I next formed twenty kilometer long "Gaumukh Glacier" the Glacier" in the Museum there is also a tiny cave in India by the same sculptor who made the tiny S. Shilipi. "The Himalaya" and "The Gaumukh Fluorescent White, and then even more coats of both look like ice. The actual "Shiva Linga" I White," which means that it is a 'true' White White of most other Fluorescent White of "The Shiva Linga," in between "The Land the "Gaumukh Glacier." From underneath this Ganga's spring flows.   In this "Gaumukh with a one centimeter Shiva Linga custom-made Hanuman statue in the "Hanuman Mandir," Dr. Glacier" were both coated with many coats of high-gloss clear acrylic medium to make them painted with a Swiss Fluorescent "Optical under the Black light, not the typical Blue-pigments. As an added surprise (we discovered while painting the "Gaumukh" mural in Switzerland during July, 1998) this Swiss "Optical White" Fluorescent paint also Phosphoresces in Green. So, along with all the other eight to ten Phosphorescent Colors glowing in the Fluorescent "Participatory" Environment when the lights are all turned off before the natural "Demonstration Side" of the Museum is shown, this pure "Optical White" Fluorescing "Shiva Linga" then Phosphoresces Green. To finish the entire "Shiva Linga" area of the Environment I made a cushion for kneeling on in front of "The Mirrors of Infinity" and "The Fire of Creation" inside the "Shiva Linga," for which I had bought industrial heavy-duty Fluorescent Fuchsia vinyl on Canal Street in New York the December before in preparation. A thin wood base and many layers of rubber exercise mats were contained inside this Fluorescent Fuchsia vinyl covering. For the solid wood "Yoni" in front of "The Shiva Linga" I wanted a unique Color, not used on any other part of the Environment in a pure state, so I used a highly Fluorescent Fuchsia-Pink which is nearly the exact same Color as the Fluorescent Fuchsia vinyl I used for the cushion of the "Yoni," and I painted it with a tremendous amount of coats. Gluing in the Fuchsia "Yoni" cushion completed this entire "Shiva Linga" area. With less than a month left before opening the Museum I still had two major area of the Environment to begin and to finish. First I assembled about one-hundred crystal clusters, fossils, geodes, meteorites, opals, tiny statues from around the world, and many other obscure objects, and began to create "The Crystal Cave" in "The Magic Land of Lights, Sounds, and Dimensions." The list of natural and unnatural objects in this "Crystal Cave" is large, but is divided into three main areas of "The Optical Effects Cave," the center "Crystal Cave," and "The Gods Cave."

As can be imagined, the final Session of this seven year journey was an unforgettable experience in itself. The last night of work which completed this last Session began with the final job I kept for the end: the Floor of the Fluorescent "Participatory" Environment. First the floor was prepared and then about $250.00 of Dutch professional construction epoxy was poured carefully, starting from the bottom of each vertical form making up the Environment, so as to create a seamless bond and a floor that is a continuous part of the sculpture. After pooling about two 750 ml. pots of this pro epoxy all along the bottom of the Environment forms, I poured three to four more 750 ml. pots of this industrial epoxy onto the entire large horizontal surface of the Environment's floor. The overall smell of these six pots of industrial construction epoxy was enough to curl your hair(!) About twelve hours later this wonderful industrial epoxy had first expanded slightly, in this process creating small forms by itself, and then had become harder than wood. Since I had poured the liters of epoxy in relatively the same time, the entire floor of the Environment dried seamlessly, and in the process created by itself the form of a body of water naturally flowing from the interior of the Fluorescent "Participatory" Environment and out onto the shinny Purple floor of the Museum in the foreground. Next, I painted many coats of Fluorescent White paint onto the floor in preparation of painting it with Colors. For this entire floor of the Fluorescent "Participatory" Environment I used just one Color - the exact same Color I used to paint the entire outside of "The Reactor" - the Color I discovered in "Painting 1" in Art school in 1977 which I still love: "Liquitex" Phthalocyanine Blue. Besides areas of diluted Phthalocyanine Blue which allowed the brilliant base Fluorescent White of the floor to show through, there was alot of undiluted Phthalocyanine Blue used as well, creating a dramatic floor which together with the natural flow of the epoxy, creates what looks like flowing water - like a river flowing from inside the Environment out into the Museum space. To complete this Environment floor I painted maybe ten full coats of high-gloss clear acrylic medium onto it, which gives a very convincing image of a bed of water flowing before your eyes. After the final coat of high-gloss clear acrylic medium it took a few seconds to realize that after seven years of constant planning and work - I was *Finished*(!) In near disbelief I went upstairs to the Gallery and got my Nikon and one of the last rolls I had saved of a particular cool-balanced 1990s pro Fiji film, and came down and took a full roll with different light exposures of my finally finished Fluorescent "Participatory" Environment. I had started this piece of Art when I was thirty-five, and now I was forty-two. In the middle of the night after finishing the Fluorescent "Participatory" Environment and the roll of film with photos of the finished Environment, I planed to finish completely with a celebratory session right in front of the finished Environment. I finished the session and into the Fluorescent "Participatory" Environment I went. In a very excited state of mind I experienced for the first time the finished Environment - it was like a dream - and at this moment I looked down to the floor I had just finished last, particularly down to the area where the bottom of "The Reactor" meets the Environment floor, and I saw a 'hair' in the Phthalo Blue paint. As I knelt down to look closer and pick up the 'hair,' it didn't move - in fact I could feel it with my fingernail - it was a small crack! In fact there was a series of tiny hairline cracks barely visible running all along the bottom/front area of "The Reactor" in the new floor I had just made over the past several days. It was a desperate situation and desperate measures were required, so in the middle of the night I poured pure industrial construction epoxy onto the whole front area at the base of "The Reactor," and then - the only time I had used such a technique in the whole seven years of creating the Fluorescent "Participatory" Environment - I began to spray by hand Fluorescent Red-Magenta paint directly into and onto the wet Industrial construction epoxy. I added some layers more of construction epoxy on top of this, and then sprayed more Fluorescent Red-Magenta paint onto the whole wet area. After several repeated layers of construction epoxy and Fluorescent Red-Magenta paint, I began to spray only Red-Magenta Fluorescent paint onto the surface. Gradually after much Fluorescent paint had been sprayed by hand onto the wet epoxy surface, it began to create an image of it's own, and began to look like a brilliant Red form coming from an unseen area behind, and then advancing around, the base of "The Reactor." Not only was this an essential visual element in the overall reading of the three-dimensionality of the Fluorescent "Participatory" Environment, but it is also one of my favorite parts of the entire Museum environment because it was not only completely unplanned, but was absolutely spontaneous. Not at all surprisingly, this extra unplanned spontaneous final job and painting of the Museum Environment meant that I actually completed the Fluorescent "Participatory" Environment on April first to April second, 1999, which were "April Fool's Day" and "Good Friday!" I was not surprised. "A suitable ending."

For the first ten years the Museum was opened every one of the 25,000 visitors received a fifteen page illustrated Museum booklet to keep as part of their entrance. This was sadly reduced after the rent for the Museum space was raised in January, 2010, but the bulk of the information contained in the Museum booklet which was printed and then assembled by hand into English and French booklets, is on the sixteen page website I designed and built for the Museum. This Museum booklet began with "What is a Black Light?" explained, accompanied by one chart of the "Electromagnetic Spectrum" and another chart of "Invisible Ultraviolet Light and Visible Light." The second page explains the "Four Kinds of Ultraviolet," including the harmless Longwave Ultraviolet (Black lights), Middlewave Ultraviolet (Suntan salons), Shortwave Ultraviolet used in science, and "Extreme" or "Vacuum Ultraviolet" which creates the Ozone layer at the top of our atmosphere and keeps Shortwave Ultraviolet and the harmful region of Middlewave Ultraviolet from reaching the surface of the Earth. Page three of the Museum booklet is "The History of Fluorescence" with Sir George Stokes, the scientist who named Fluorescence in 1852, and the beginning of the section "The First Sources of Ultraviolet Light and the First U.V. Lamps" starting with the "Light Box" and "Spark Box" of 1900 and 1903, and continuing onto the contemporary Black lights on the next page. Page five is "The Cause of Fluorescence: Electron Displacement," with a clear basic explanation of the energy exchange at an atomic scale which causes Fluorescence, as well as a three picture chart showing a simple diagram of electron movement causing the creation of visible light. The next page of the booklet details closely the quantum mechanics involved in the cause of Fluorescence, particularly involving the movement of electrons through "sub-orbits" of their orbits, with "A Closer Look at Electron Displacement." There is also a small explanation of the "Different Sources of Light," including Fluorescence, Phosphorescence, Thermoluminescence, Triboluminescence, Cathodluminescence, Radioluminescence, and Bioluminescence. The seventh page is "The First Fluorescent Paint," describing the circumstances and eventualities of the teenager Robert Switzer, who in 1933 invented Fluorescent Paint in the family bathtub in Berkley, California. There is also included a photo of an early "Blak-Ray" tube of Fluorescent paint for Artists from the 1950s, which is part of the full set donated to the Museum by Thomas S. Warren in 1995. "The First Fluorescent Art" follows on page eight with photographs and a page of text describing Mrs. Eva Phillips' "Fluorescent Mineral Artwork" from decades ago, as well as John Plumer Ludlum's painting "Spacial Fantasy #3" in the Museum collection, who was the first Artist to have used Fluorescent paint in Fine Art in 1945. The actual 'Museum guide' begins on the tenth page of the booklet, with a photograph of the Fluorescent "Participatory" Environment in the Museum labeling nineteen major sections. The text begins with an introduction to the Museum, and then continues on for two pages explaining all nineteen sections of the environment, ending with a short description of the "Demonstration Side" of the Museum containing over one-thousand pounds of Fluorescent minerals and other natural as well as unnatural Fluorescent items displayed in glass cases.

The last four pages of this Museum booklet create a guide to the Fluorescent Mineral displays in the Museum as well as a description of the many antique instruments and kits in the display case "Ultraviolet Artifacts." Page twelve of the booklet describes these "Ultraviolet Artifacts" in the Museum, and has a numbered drawing of this display along with the "Ultraviolet Artifacts" in the main display case which houses the "Common Items That are Fluorescent" display. Two blocks of text describe each item in these "Ultraviolet Artifacts" displays. The items listed are: 1. "Experimental U.V. Color" Kit (1950s), 2. "Ultraviolet Science and Hobby Set" with "Mineralight" (1950s), 3. "Black Light Magic" Kit (1952), 4. Fluorescent Fingerprint Checking Lamp (1940s-1950s), 5. Ultraviolet Lamp for Checking Metal Stress (1940s), 6. Ultraviolet Criminology Lamp (1940s-1950s), 7. NASA "Extreme Ultraviolet Explorer" patch, 8. Fluorescent Leak Detector - Tracer (1940s-present), 9. Ultraviolet Criminology Kit (1940s-1950s), 10. Ultraviolet Lamp for Medicine (1920s-1940s), 11. "Ultra-Violet Ray Treatment" Folding Goggles (1932), "Alpine Sunlamp" Advertisement (March, 1928), 12. Argon Bulb (1915), 13. Very early "Black Lights," 14. Very early "Black Light" with original fixture (1930s-1940s), 15. "M-12 Mineralight" Shortwave Ultraviolet Lamp (1938), 16. "Blak-Ray" Fluorescent Artist's Oil Paint Set (1950s), 17. "Blak-Ray" Fluorescent Invisible Chalk Set (1950s), 18. Original "Visible" and "Invisible" Fluorescent Paint Color Sample Card (pre-1953), 19. Fluorescent Mineral Artworks (1950s).

Page thirteen of the Museum booklet has two numbered drawings of all the specimens from across the globe in the "Fluorescent Mineral Viewing Box" display on the "Demonstration Side" of the Museum. The top section of this display is a grey metal lighting unit called the "C-5" "Chromato-Viewer," that is an artifact from the 1950s made by "Ultraviolet Products, Inc." in California. From 1994 to 1998, before the Museum was opened, the "C-5" alone was used to give Fluorescent Mineral demonstrations upstairs in "Electric Lady" Art Gallery. On top of the "C-5," there is a control panel with switches to turn on the different lights. Furthest left is the "Longwave U.V." switch, next to this is the "Shortwave U.V." switch, and to the right is the "White Light" switch. Another block of numbered text follows below the two numbered drawings of the collection of Fluorescent Minerals, with each specimen described by mineral name, origin, and Fluorescent Color.

The next page of the Museum booklet is similar, with half of the page displaying a numbered drawing of the specimens in the separate "Fluorescent Mineral Display Case" in the Museum. This "Fluorescent Mineral Display Case" has five shelves, with the top shelf containing the magnificent Fluorescent Mineral Artwork masterpiece of Miera, the Japanese Fluorescent mineral collector who lived decades ago in New Jersey. Shelf two of this display contains a large collection of world-famous Calcite crystals from Terlingua, Texas which magnificently change from a Pinkish-Red Color to just the opposite Sky Blue when put first under a Longwave U.V. lamp, and then under a Shortwave U.V. lamp. Terlingua, Texas Calcite is also known to be the crystals which Phosphoresce the longest time of any crystals on Earth. This collection in the Museum is the private collection of the Ultraviolet pioneer who started "Ultra-Violet Products, Inc." in 1932, Thomas S. Warren. Shelf three of the display case has "Fluorescent Crystals and special pieces" including two specimens of the first Fluorescent Minerals collected in the Himalaya, which I brought back with Michèle from 14,000 feet (4,350 meters) at the source of the Ganga, in

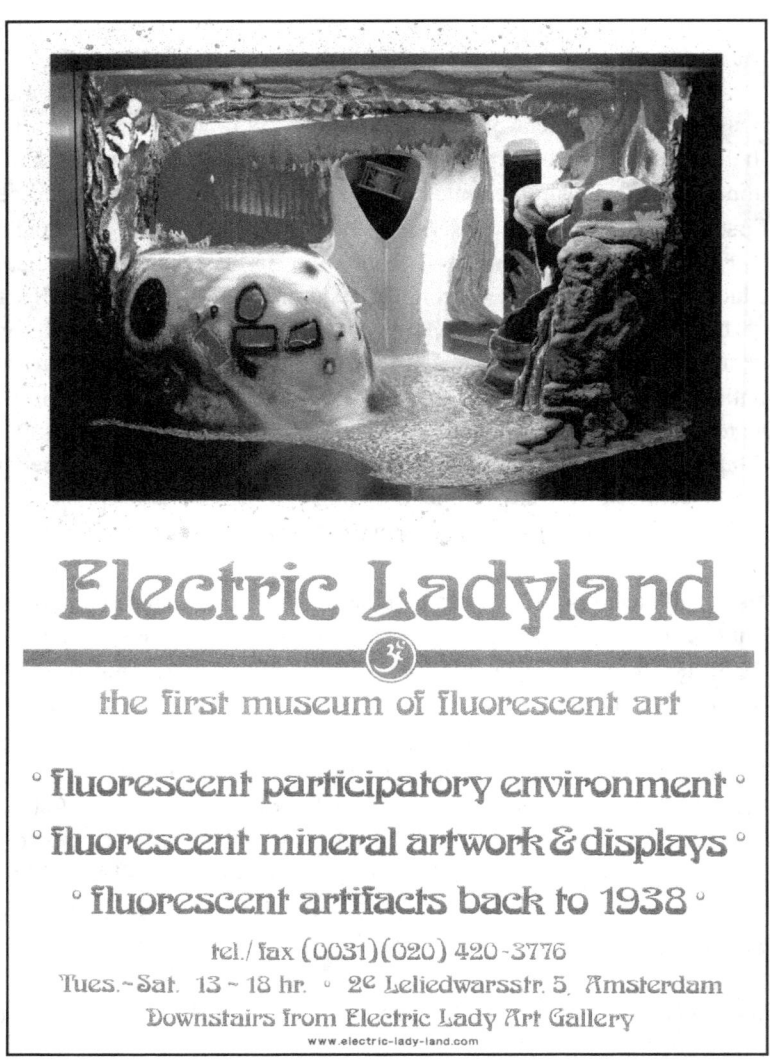

"Electric Ladyland - the First Museum of Fluorescent Art"
Opening Poster, April 19, 1999

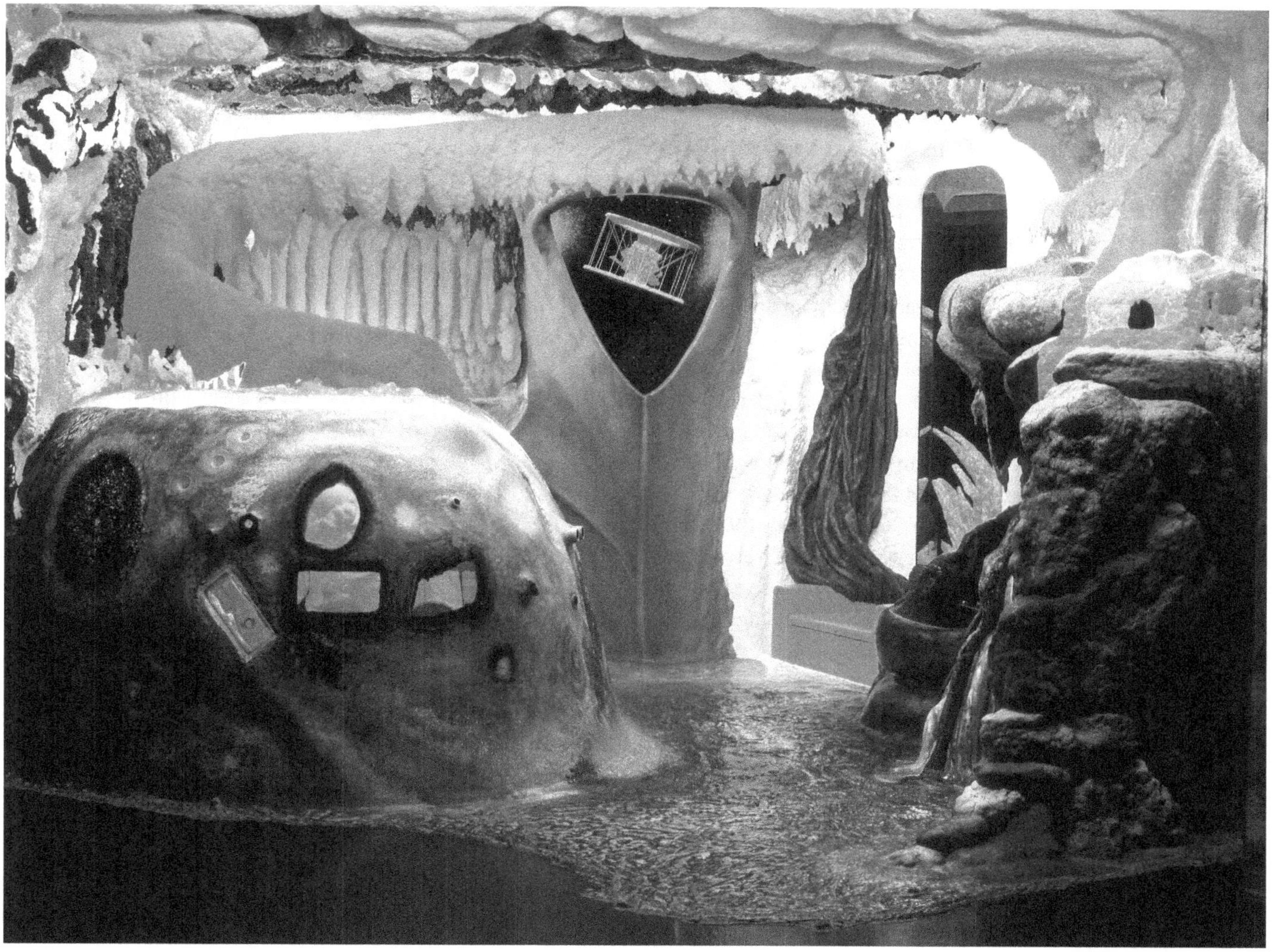

Fluorescent "Participatory" Environment, "Electric Ladyand - the First Museum of Fluorescent Art"

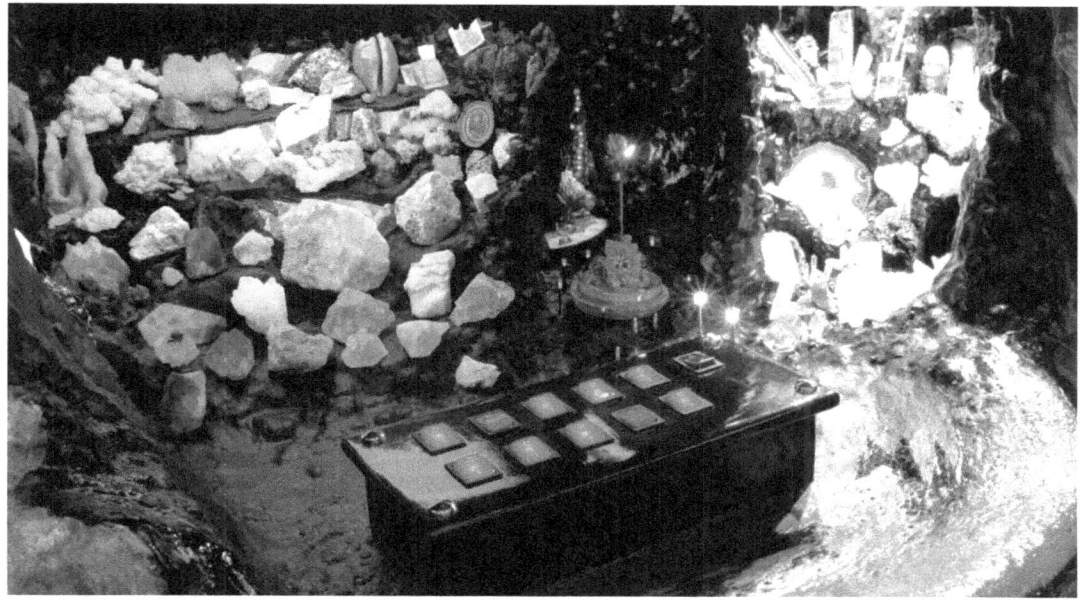

"Participatory Art" in the Fluorescent "Participatory" Environment,
"Electric Ladyland - the First Museum of Fluorescent Art"

1998. Shelf four has a collection of rare Fluorescent Minerals which change Color from Longwave to Shortwave U.V., including rare specimens of Tugtupite found only on Greenland which changes from a dramatic Red to a brilliant Orange when put under first a Shortwave U.V. lamp, and then a Longwave U.V. lamp. The bottom shelf of the "Fluorescent Mineral Display Case" is in the dark, on purpose, being the demonstration shelf for 'Glow-in-the-Dark' "Phosphorescent" minerals.

The fifteenth page of this Museum booklet is the back cover, and was designed to be seen by just turning over the booklet in the Museum while kneeling in front of the "Fluorescent Mineral Cave" in the Fluorescent "Participatory" Environment in the Museum, so you could identify any of the sixty-five specimens of the Fluorescent Minerals that you just turned the lights onto by having pressed a switch on the "Participatory Art" button pad. Underneath the half-page numbered drawing of the specimens of Fluorescent Minerals in the "Fluorescent Mineral Cave" there is a numbered list of the names, origins, and Fluorescent Colors of each specimen and a short description of this display.

In the 1950s and continuing for many years, a woman and her husband created some very early pieces of Art that applied this phenomenon of Fluorescence in minerals. Mr. and Mrs. Phillips lived in South Plainfield, New Jersey on top of a small mountain, and were collectors of Fluorescent Minerals from Franklin, New Jersey, "The Fluorescent Mineral Capitol of the World." They had the idea to use the fascinating phenomenon of these Fluorescent Minerals to do something creative, not just looking at these rocks, but to make simple pieces of Art with them. Mr. Frank Phillips rough crushed the Fluorescent Minerals with a sledge hammer, and then in the dark under Longwave and Shortwave Ultraviolet lamps the mineral fragments were tweezer-separated. From Franklin, the mineral Willemite was tweezer-separated into twenty shades of Fluorescent Green, as well as Mangano Calcite being separated into twelve shades of Fluorescent Red-Orange. Mrs. Eva Phillips then created the Fluorescent Mineral Artwork, first using a meat-tenderizer with which she further crushed the particles of Fluorescent Minerals into finer pieces. To make the actual pieces of Fluorescent Mineral Artwork Mrs. Eva Phillips first made pencil-outline drawings on simple canvas-board (canvas glued to cardboard). She then put common household "Elmer's Glue" on the area of the drawing she wanted Color, and finally applied the crushed Fluorescent Minerals to the glued area. This was done in the dark, of course, under separate Longwave and Shortwave Ultraviolet lamps. Two of Mr. and Mrs. Phillips' grandchildren visited the Museum during the last sixteen years, and told me some of the details of how their Grandmother made these Fluorescent Mineral Artworks, such as her technique of tying a rope around her dinning room table during the entire periods that she was creating these fragile Fluorescent Mineral Artworks, so nobody could disturb them. Mr. and Mrs. Phillips made these Fluorescent Mineral Artworks for years, into their retirement, and the late Mr. Ewald Gerstmann of the former "Gerstmann Museum" in Franklin, New Jersey told me "they did hundreds of small Artworks" - "they used to give them away." Before the "Gerstmann Museum" closed, the masterpiece of Mrs. Eva Phillips, "Peacocks" was on display. "Peacocks" is a large Fluorescent Mineral Artwork about a yard (meter) across, with two large Peacocks in a detailed landscape which took almost six months to make. In the "Electric Ladyland - the First Museum of Fluorescent Art" collection three of the ten pieces of Fluorescent Mineral Artwork on display are by Mrs. Eva Phillips. In one of the most fascinating demonstrations in the Museum, Mrs. Phillips' "Boats at Sea" is seen as three different pictures. Under the Longwave U.V. lamp the seascape is a Day scene, but when you turn on the Shortwave U.V. lamp, the same Day scene turns into a Night scene. Finally, when the seascape is seen under both the Longwave and Shortwave U.V. lamps, the way that almost all Fluorescent Mineral Artwork is intended to be seen, the picture bursts into brilliant Fluorescent Colors. I have seen a list of the Fluorescent Minerals Mrs. Eva Phillips used to create the multiple Colors she used during her years of making Fluorescent Mineral Artwork, and again, the simple Colors were made using the finely crushed particles of single Fluorescent Minerals, such as Red Fluorescing Mangano Calcite, Green Fluorescing Willemite, and non-Fluorescent Black Franklinite, all from Franklin, New Jersey. Yellow was made from the bright Scapolite (called the old name "Wernerite" by Mrs. Phillips) coming from Canada. "Bluish White" was made by Mrs. Phillips with pulverized Fluorite from Clay Center, Ohio, as well as her "Blue" sometimes coming from Calcite found in Bound Brook, New Jersey. Mrs. Phillips also created "Purple" out of Fluorite from Arizona, and she made mixed Colors as well, such as Orange-Yellow created by mixing together Yellow Scapolite and Red Mangano Calcite, and "Rose Pink" made with the combination of Red Mangano Calcite from Franklin mixed together with Blue Fluorescing Fluorite from Clay Center, Ohio. As a measure of her success, over the years of having limited communication with Mrs. Phillips' relatives, I've been told that Mrs. Phillips did have an exhibition of her Fluorescent Mineral Artworks in the "Smithsonian Institute" in Washington, D.C. during the 1976 Bicentennial celebrations.

Miera, "the Japanese Man," is the other person known for making these Fluorescent Mineral Artworks in northern New Jersey back to the 1950s. Very few details are known about this man, in fact during the 1990s in New Jersey they didn't even know his name anymore, but referred to him as simply "the Japanese Man." Fortunately, this "Japanese Man" signed three of his six Fluorescent Mineral Artworks in the Museum collection, and several different Japanese visitors could translate his signature as "Miera." He was supposed to have worked on these Fluorescent Mineral Artworks about the same time as Mrs. Phillips, but his style was much more professional than the few other people working in this obscure media, including his drawing, design, and execution. In Miera's work there are many combinations of Fluorescent Minerals that he used to achieve a wider variety of Colors than the few other 'Fluorescent Mineral Artists.' Many layers of glue and Fluorescent Minerals were applied on top of each other to realize a slight three-dimensional appearance to the pieces as well as very vivid, concentrated Colors. Miera's masterpiece is in the "Electric Ladyland - the First Museum of Fluorescent Art" collection, and is seen the last of these ten Fluorescent Mineral Artworks in the demonstration. This is a piece of Art that is hard to believe. It is a three-dimensional sculpture of a Japanese house and garden over a foot (30 cm) across, and almost that high, completely made out of crushed and tweezer-separated Fluorescent Minerals over fifty years ago. Miera worked on this masterpiece for six months, and it is supposed to be his final piece of Art, according to Mr. Richard Hauck of the "Sterling Hill Mining Museum" in Ogdensburg, New Jersey. One of the ten Fluorescent Mineral Artworks in the "Electric Ladyland" Museum collection was made by neither Mrs. Phillips or Miera, but by one of the miners who used to work in the Zinc mines of northern New Jersey. This miner's Fluorescent Mineral Artwork is an American Indian portrait made directly on a piece of plywood with just Green, Red, and non-Fluorescent Black, from the three most common minerals in Franklin, New Jersey, being Willemite, Mangano Calcite, and Franklinite, and is seen in the dark under just the Shortwave U.V. lamp, the only U.V. lamp which was used by the miners to find Zinc-containing Willemite. There were mines in northern New Jersey from the 1850s up until 1986, when the last operating mine in New Jersey "Sterling Hill Mine" closed and was turned into a Museum by Mr. Richard Hauck and his brother. Willemite, made up of a high Zinc content, which is the bright Green Fluorescent Mineral in all these Fluorescent Mineral Artworks, is the mineral that was primarily being mined for in New Jersey.

The author knows of very few other people who made Fluorescent Mineral Artwork, one person known through a photograph of a Fluorescent Mineral Artwork in Sterling Gleason's 1960 book "Ultraviolet Guide to Minerals," which was made by a doctor in New York. Another person who made this obscure Fluorescent Mineral Art was a woman who signed her Artwork "Colet" and made her Fluorescent Mineral Artwork on the West Coast in California during the 1960s. On all of the six Fluorescent Mineral Artworks by Colet seen by the author, she used much larger fragments of Fluorescent Minerals than Mrs. Phillips or Miera in her pieces of Art. All six of her Fluorescent Mineral Artworks were fairly small, all flowers, and all had delicate wooden frames. Colet also had a different method of working than Mrs. Phillips or Miera, and used printed magazine photos of flowers as a base onto which she then glued the larger particles of Fluorescent Minerals. In the 1990s there was also an Artist named John Zadik living in the New Jersey/Pennsylvania area who made small sculptures using Fluorescent Minerals in their natural state and created Art giving the impression of something like Fluorescent Japanese Rock Gardens.

Upon completion of the Fluorescent "Participatory" Environment, and preparing the half-ton of Fluorescent minerals, "Fluorescent Mineral Artworks" from decades ago, and countless other "Common (and not so common) Items That are Fluorescent" in display cases, we opened "Electric Ladyland - the First Museum of Fluorescent Art" on April 19, 1999, exactly twelve years after opening "Electric Lady" Art Gallery upstairs from the Museum on April 19, 1987.

Four months after the Museum opening I prepared a new series of paintings, which were naturally called "Thermal Expansion" paintings, because I wanted to create portable sections of what I had created in the Museum environment. Although it took seven years of work and an unimaginable amount of money to build the Fluorescent "Participatory" Environment in the Museum, Michèle and I rent the Art gallery and Museum space for the last twenty-nine years, we do not own it, so obviously this space and my Fluorescent "Participatory" Environment in the Museum will not be there forever. I made the first series of Fluorescent and Phosphorescent "Thermal Expansion" paintings in August, 1999, creating small and medium sized paintings in the traditional square and rectangular shapes to start. Four months after we opened "Electric Ladyland - the First Museum of Fluorescent Art" I started 'experimenting' with the "Thermal Expansion" series of paintings, which was nearly a never-ending journey, and which all began on the ceiling of the Museum Environment years before. The first series of "Thermal Expansion" paintings I made in August, 1999, and the last series of these paintings I made after returning with Michèle from the 2010 Kumbh Mela in Hardwar, India, which concluded the "Thermal Expansion" series and journey with the final painting "Thermal Expansion #447." Four-hundred and forty-seven experiments into a world of nearly infinite variables, which even when identified are nearly impossible to organize into a working, flowing progression that somehow miraculously results in a finished piece of Art. Even just identifying these endless variables involved with this process of painting took several years, and was only achieved by mistakes and retrials over and over again. For the first hundred or so "Thermal Expansion" paintings I had no idea how to control the endless variables involved in the creation of "Thermal Expansion" paintings, which resulted in many hair-raising sessions. For the very first August, 1999 "Thermal Expansion" series I began with the traditional rectangular and square shapes, which I added on top of each other in different

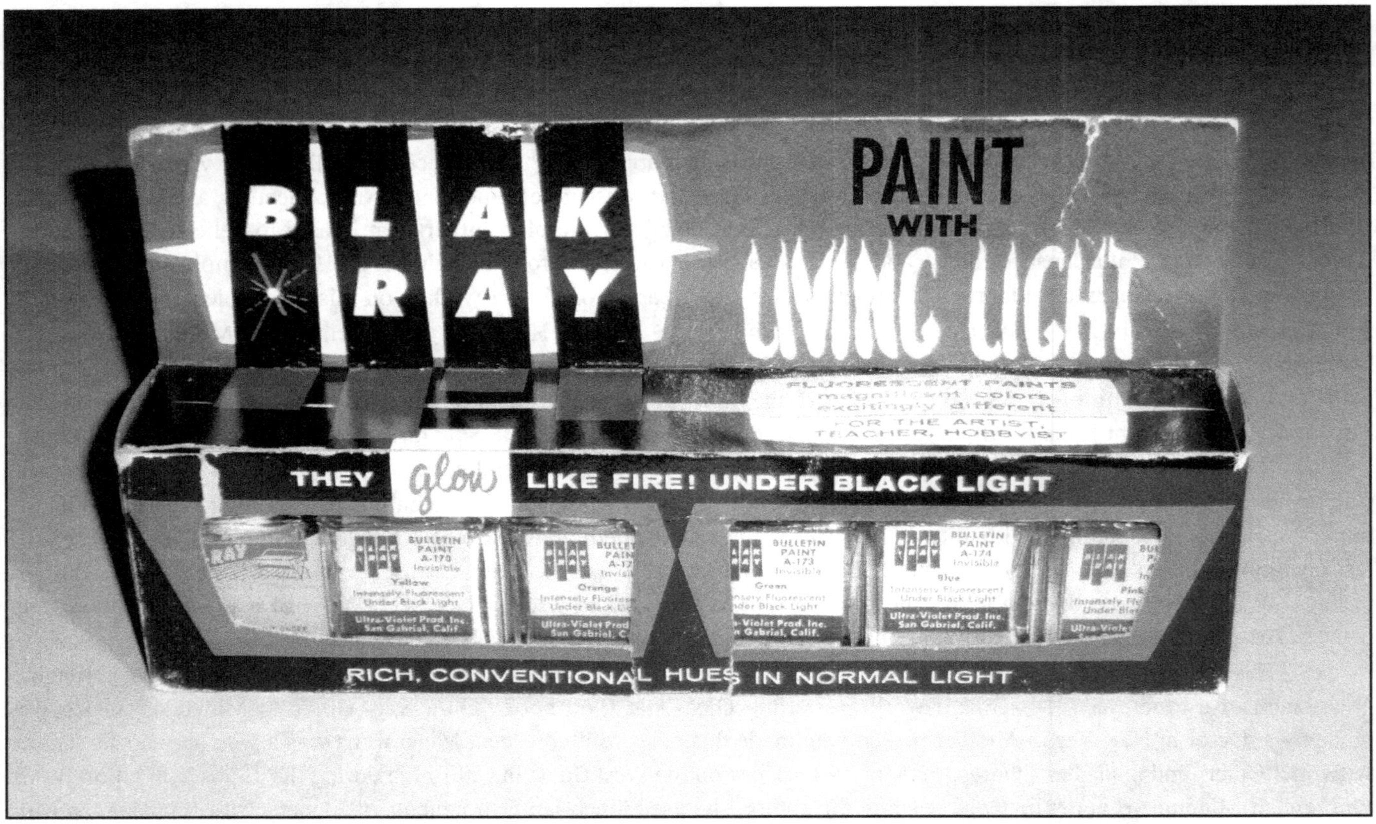

1950s "BLAK-RAY" "PAINT WITH LIVING LIGHT" Fluorescent Bulletin Paint set, "Ultra-Violet Products, Inc.," California

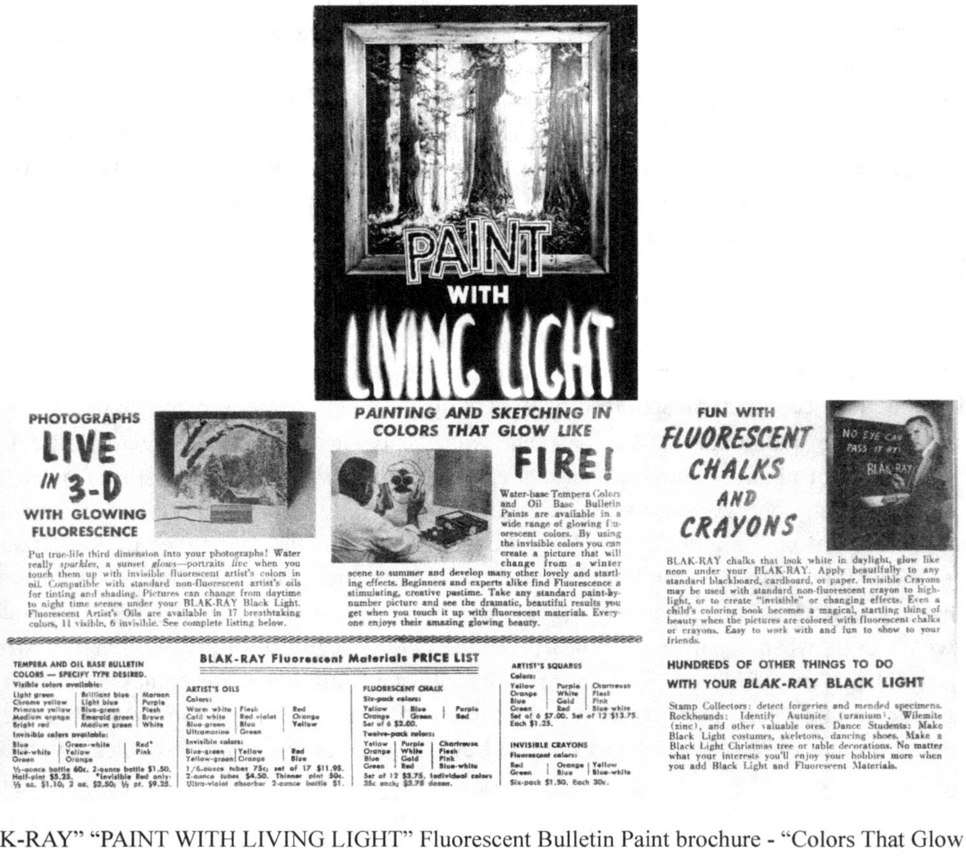

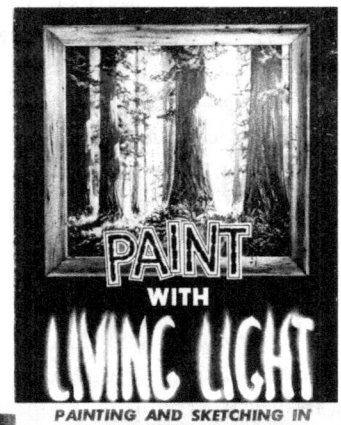

1950s "BLAK-RAY" "PAINT WITH LIVING LIGHT" Fluorescent Bulletin Paint brochure - "Colors That Glow Like Fire!"

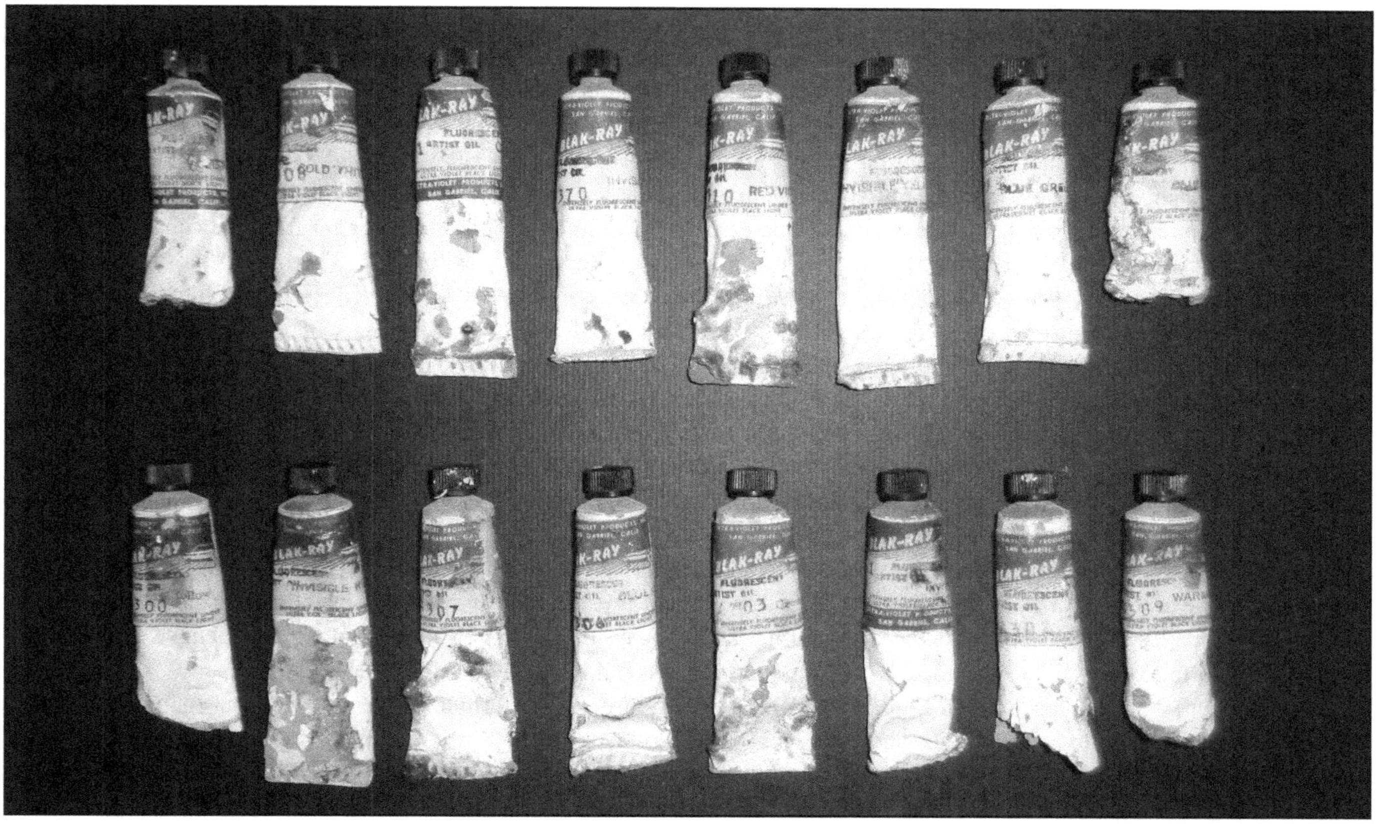

1950s "BLAK-RAY" Fluorescent Artist Oil Paint set - eight "Invisible" and eight "Visible" Colors, "Ultra-Violet Products, Inc."

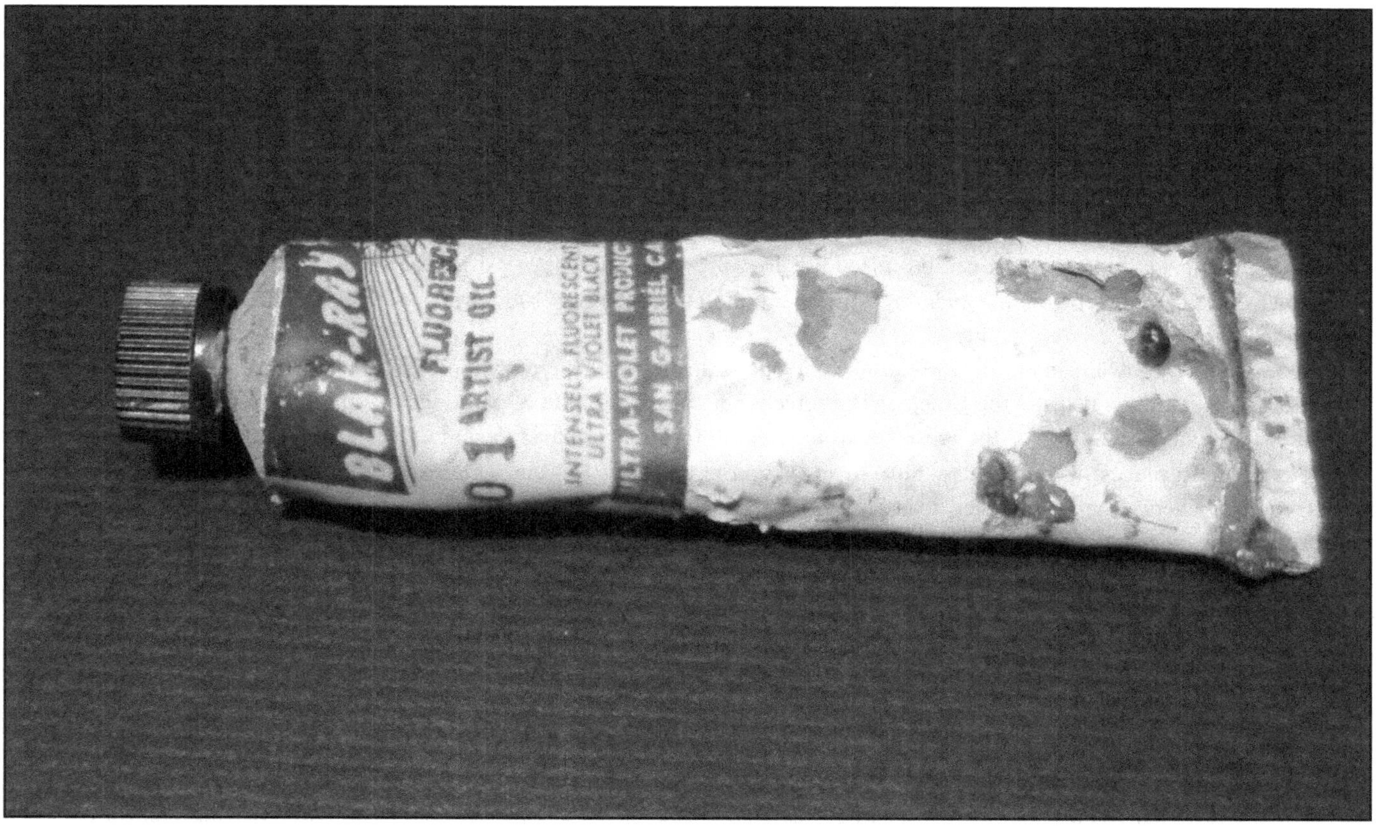

1950s "BLAK-RAY" Fluorescent Artist Oil Paint, "Ultra-Violet Products, Inc." Donated by Thomas S. Warren
"Electric Ladyand - the First Museum of Fluorescent Art" collection

sizes to create two different levels of surface. For the second series I had prepared long rectangular painting surfaces which I added texture to by attaching metal pieces to the upper level of the painting base. Coming back to the Gallery someone had thrown away the top of a wooden stool which was round, and this brought a natural selection of shape to all the following years of "Thermal Expansion" paintings, which were all made in a circular shape that represented more accurately the infinite celestial nature of the Art being created. In the past I had also experimented with circular paintings, and this shape is what I used for every one of the next approximately four-hundred and twenty "Thermal Expansion" paintings, with only one exception. The circular shape is natural as well as being essentially infinite - besides that, it is far from the conventionality of square or rectangular traditional paintings on canvas. During the early fascination with these "Thermal Expansion" paintings, in 2002 after making seven series of these paintings of which the last five series were exclusively circular, I found a quote from an American Indian holy man which went straight to the heart and soul after two solid years of making circular "Thermal Expansion" paintings. The Oglala Sioux holy man "Black Elk," who lived from 1863 to 1950, said that 'you notice that everything that Indians do is done in a circle,' which is because what Black Elk called the "Power of the World" 'works always in circles.' This holy man next enumerates the sky, Earth, stars, the wind, and even bird's nests being circular, as well as the cyclical cycles that make up the seasons, and finally the circular path of life itself, which Black Elk describes as being "a circle" beginning in "childhood" and again ending in "childhood." This Oglala Sioux holy man concludes with the statement that this cyclical nature is 'in everything which power moves.'

In the end I made 447 "Thermal Expansion" paintings in a total of twenty-eight "Series," beginning with the first Series of square two level works, and ending with large three or four layered 122 centimeter (four foot) wide circular works.

"Thermal Expansion" Series #2 was done during the final days of the show Michèle and I had in Geneva "Touten Fluo et Phospho," during which Michèle stayed in Switzerland until the end of the exhibition and I had returned to Amsterdam to open the Museum again. This "Touten Fluo et Phospho" exhibition of the year 2000 in Geneva was unforgettable, with the Fluorescent and Phosphorescent paintings and three-dimensional Artwork of both Michèle and myself exhibited under Black lights, as well as the creation of a large hand-sprayed Fluorescent painting on cotton on the floor of the Swiss gallery at night under Black lights in front of Swiss spectators and television cameras.

For the third "Thermal Expansion" Series of October, 2000 I decided to create only circular format paintings, which I called 'The Round Series.' The last painting of Series #2 was made on the discarded circular wooden stool top I found, and for this Series #3 I prepared seventeen round bases to paint on.

The next Series #4 of April, 2001 was the first real "Thermal Expansion" Sessions in which I felt more confident about what I was doing, with the actual series being primarily three very large "Thermal Expansion" paintings, the largest I had attempted. Four small and medium-sized paintings were also prepared for this series, and were made for the explicit purpose of 'practicing' on before beginning the 122 centimeter wide surfaces.

The fifth and sixth Series of "Thermal Expansion" paintings were done only one week apart, but during that one week the whole world changed. On September 9, 2001 I made the fifth Series of three paintings, and then two days later underneath a truly 'clear Blue sky' we were indeed promised the arrival of a "Brave New World." Five days after the world changed on September 11, 2001, I set up nine paintings in my studio/gallery under 1000 watts of Black lights and made "Thermal Expansion" #41-47.

Series #7-10 were made in 2002, and conclude with the initial realization that became the quest of the next 350 paintings: The Paintings became the <u>Cracks</u>. The 'cracks' in these multitude of paintings making up the "Thermal Expansion" series became the visual focus of the work, as well as being the first reason I became fascinated by, and continued to create hundreds of these pieces of Art. I saw an Astronomy program on "BBC" in which was explained the Cosmic Microwave Background of energy that is believed to be left over from the Big Bang, and through a new satellite the earliest complete image of the Universe was created. What this image revealed is very memorable, because it related directly to my series of "Thermal Expansion" paintings, being that the tiny 'cracks' in the image of the infant Universe eventually developed into everything that the Universe is made up of and all that we can see - in other words, "The Cracks became *Everything*." My notes for Series #9 end with "Exquisite cold weather mixture" for the Fluorescent paint of the "Thermal Expansion" Series. Even the room temperature and outside climate temperature dramatically effected the results of these "Thermal Expansion" paintings.

Two weeks after Series #9 I made the paintings "Thermal Expansion" #96-103 on October 19 and 20, 2002, which make up Series #10. After making a full one-hundred of these "Thermal Expansion" 'experiments' I finally reached a point with enough experience and experiments making these paintings, as well as identifying and having varying control over the limitless variables which make up this complicated, physically exhausting technique.

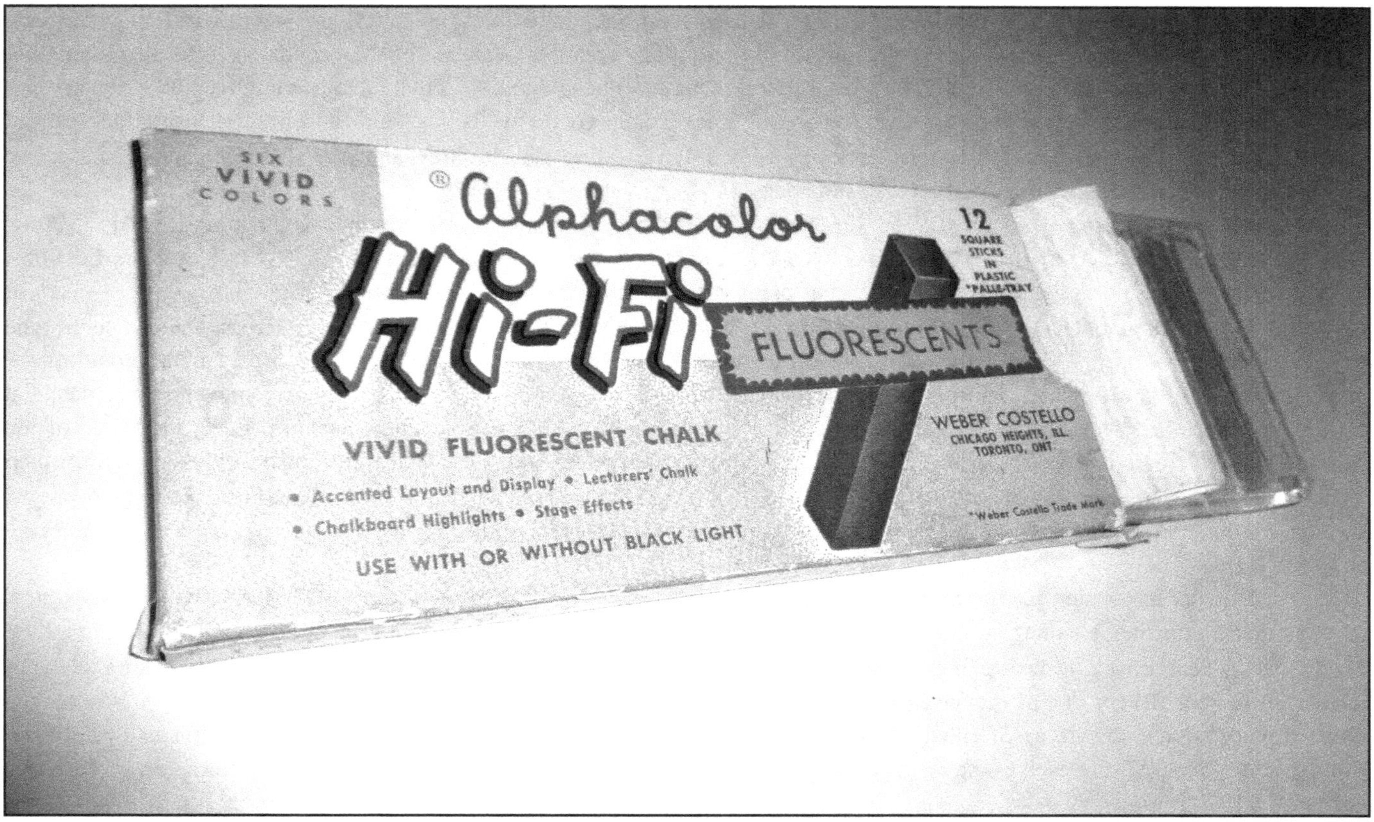

1940s-1950s "HI-FI"(!) "VIVID FLUORESCENT CHALK" set, "Alphacolor/Weber Costello," Toronto, Canada

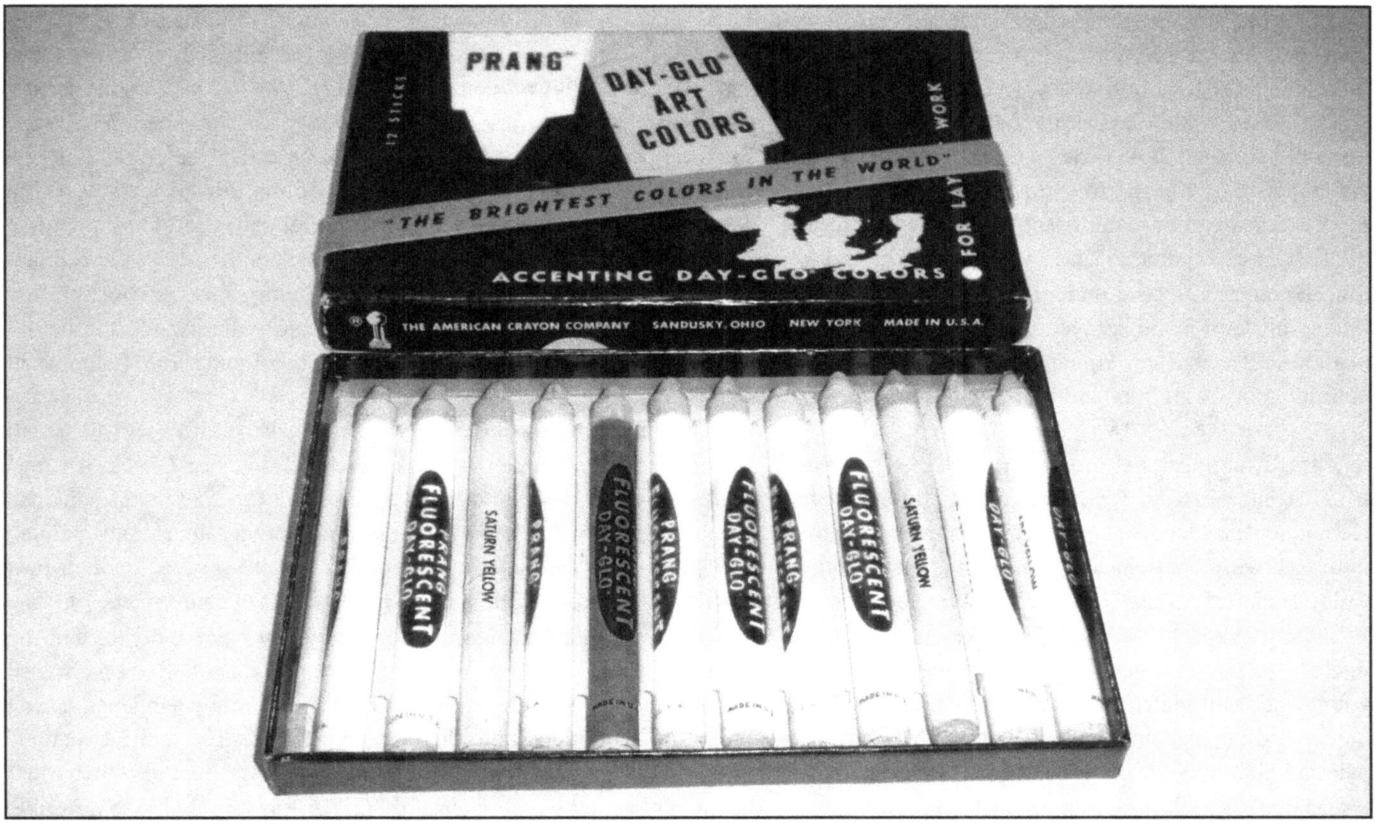

1950s-1960s "Prang" "Day-Glo Art Colors" Fluorescent Crayon set: "The Brightest Colors In The World," "The American Crayon Company"

In Series #11 of March 30 to April 3, 2003 I used nine pounds (4 kilos) of new Fluorescent and Phosphorescent pigments. While the cracks develop huge fractures and separations creating "islands" of the original surface of the painting 'floating' in the massive streams of endless Colors - Fluorescent and Phosphorescent - that have been pulled and stretched into bands of light, some very subtle mists of paint on top of other Colors create "veils" of Color and light. During the years of these "Thermal Expansion" paintings, I put Black paper under the paintings so the spray, and then flowing paint, would not be lost, totaling in 100s of these "paintings" on Black paper.

Thermal Expansion" paintings #155-176 I made during four Sessions in March and the beginning of April, 2004. During the three week Series #14 of September, 2004, I made thirty-one "Thermal Expansion" paintings over six Sessions, using 54.5 liters of Fluorescent and Phosphorescent paint which I mixed up over these weeks. The culmination of years of work and thought came out in the final painting of the Series, #207, which is about 110 centimeters across, and has about nine to ten liters of paint on it. Finally, the overall effect of totality - seemingly not a part, or at the most a small amount of the original surface of the finished painting is left still in it's original place - complete expansion and movement of the total painting surface. Of the entire 110 centimeter round painting, a tiny eight by two centimeter strip on the left side of the painting, and a strip on the right side of the painting about eight centimeters wide is all that is left intact of the original finished painting. There are more areas of veils of Colors pulled in streams over each other than there are areas of the finished sprayed surface - in other words, more "Cracks" than painting = the painting has become the "Cracks," which is what I had been trying to do for years.

"Thermal Expansion" Series #15 ("Thermal Expansion" #208-214) was made in May, 2005, during which I had a new pigment that is amazing, so amazing in fact it is what I called this series "The Blue Phosphorescent Session." For the first time I had "True Blue" Phosphorescent paint. This is very expensive - $40.00 for 100 grams, which makes 500 ml (half a quart) of total paint mixed. Every one of the seven paintings came out in the vein I've been moving towards the last year - to have a finished piece which is made up of mostly "Cracks," not the actual finished painted surface. The flowing streams of light and Colors - the "cracks" themselves have become the finished painting - these streams of flowing Colors form nearly by themselves.

Since I started painting I've been the most fascinated and intrigued by phenomenons in painting techniques that arrive at a finished piece which has no resemblance to 'human touch' and appears to be made by a form of energy resembling magic. The first real fascination I had with techniques of "Painting Magic" was in the 70s when I took swirls of paint and gently laid them out, or smeared them, onto canvas creating what I still call "Universes." I was still deeply fascinated by creating these tiny "Universes" and remember clearly Michèle's delight and similar intrigue when I showed her how to make them in 1986 during our first painting session together on Fagelstraat. The next phase was during the late 1980s when I stopped making the three-dimensional Box Series, and started to work 'flat' again on paper and wood. Working on large five meter paintings on wallpaper rolls, I began to spray paint by hand. The beginning of 1990 we were working on wood that I had prepared with a Fluorescent textured paint base, so when working under the Black lights the surface was brilliant already, before you applied the first drop of paint. These were the perfect surfaces to spray paint onto, because every drop was 'amplified' by the brilliant Fluorescent White base underneath it. I made three small paintings on wood/Fluorescent White textured surface for the first time using only hand-sprayed paint. The final work of this 1989 spraying series was the last major painting I made before beginning the "Mind-Arising Boxes," of which I made five for the next two years before beginning the Fluorescent "Participatory" Environment in the Museum.

For the next two years I hardly used the spraying technique at all in the 5 "Mind-Arising Boxes," except for small touches. The most spray of the five boxes is in the "Star Pool" of "The Garden of Enlightenment" in "The Dance of Life - Mind-Arising Box nr. 5." Next, creating the Fluorescent "Participatory" Environment in the Museum the "Thermal Expansion" technique developed. The earliest painting of the Museum Environment - the second and third preliminary areas that I painted in the Museum were made primarily with hand-sprayed paint. "The Reactor" interior is completely hand-sprayed with a seven Color gradation, going from Yellow-Orange on the floor, to Magenta-Purple at the top, with Cerise at the center-piece of "The Reactor." Next, "The Land Between Tick and Tock," having the center fractal-structure completely hand-sprayed, and the interior space - the stars - all hand-sprayed onto a flat Black background. These two preliminary areas were both then covered with plastic and sealed for years of construction. The chance discovery of the "Thermal Expansion" technique happened during the second major painting session in the Museum Environment and continued onto the large amount of "Thermal Expansion" painting that was subsequently done in the Environment for the next four years after I found the technique. "Thermal Expansion" went into a realm of such a heightened state of fascination and wonderment for me that it is impossible to describe. For the next four years much of the Environment was "Thermally Expanded." Most memorable are the "Rocks" - thirty 'rocks' that took me thirty days to "Thermally Expand" one-by-one. These 'Rocks' are where the real "Thermal Expansion" story began.

The most paintings I made in one Series was done in four Sessions between July and August, 2005, and in these four days I made the thirty-four "Thermal Expansion" paintings #215-248 of Series #16. In four all night Sessions "Thermal Expansion" #281-307 were painted, during the hottest July in recorded temperatures of Holland, so hot in fact that it caused my blender to seize up in the middle of mixing up the 60 liters of paint for the series.

Series #19 was during February and April, 2007, and for this double Session centering on Color Theory, I mixed up about 70 to 80 liters (18-21 gallons) of Fluorescent and Phosphorescent paint in two months. Michèle was in India during this series, and in less than three years we would return to India together for the 2010 Hardwar Kumbh Mela.

"Thermal Expansion" Series #21 was painted in two Sessions, and three weeks after was a short Series #22 of the six "Thermal Expansion" paintings #375-380. This series came fresh with alot of light and Yellow in the final pieces, including strong Phosphorescence, especially Strontium-Blue twelve hour pigment. The end of this series started the period I began taking 70 rolls of film with the used "Hasselblad 503" I could finally afford to buy that past December in New York. The sole purpose for buying this state-of-the-Art camera (which they brought to the Moon) was to take these 70 rolls of the finest quality photographs I could produce of the Fluorescent "Participatory" Environment in the Museum. 70 rolls of "Fuji Provia" slides came out better than I hoped they would - the optics in a "Hasselblad" are unsurpassed - period. Notes for this 2007 Series end with "In between all this I added another 3,000 words to my book, which I started in July: "Fluorescent Art and the Social Stigma of FLUOROPHOBIA."

In September, 2009 I made the last "Thermal Expansion" Series before returning to India for the 2010 Hardwar Kumbh Mela with Michèle. In two sessions "Thermal Expansion" #430-438 were painted, culminating in perhaps the most realized painting of the entire series, "Thermal Expansion" #438.

The trip to India for this 2010 Kumbh Mela in Hardwar was all it was supposed to be, complete with amazement, astonishment, shock, laughter and tears, rejoicing and despair, enlightenment, illness, dreams and nightmares - all happening simultaneously and continuously without end or even pause - life and death, creation and destruction - all happening simultaneously and continuously, as the Shiva Nataraja so divinely describes. This is India. It is nearly indescribable. Whether traveling continuously or staying only in one place, the experience in India is unique and a series of events and profound impressions each and every hour of which will stay with you in crystal clarity for the rest of your life. Extremely few experiences have ever had such truly life-changing and life-long effects on me, as well as resulting in a state of being eternally grateful for the "gratuitous grace" of these rare experiences of life. These few rare experiences in life are so truly profound that they also result in a state of being nearly unable to imagine what your life would be without having had such experiences, in addition to being nearly unable to remember what life was like before these pivotal all-encompassing changes and restructuring. Life, existence, and spirituality are all examined in a depth and with detail that is mind-boggling - again, simultaneously and continuously. These life-changing effects of such a journey to India are also created each and every time you have the experience - these experiences are the meaning of the word profound - they alter your life every time they happen. Very odd life after India - you feel genuinely disembodied. Almost nothing you ever experience in this life is as strong and life-changing as India.

At that time I had been thinking for the last few years about making some pieces dealing with Transparency, and the effects of Fluorescence and Phosphorescence when combined with layers of Transparent planes. I also thought for 4 years about what the Tibetan Monks inspired me with during the November, 2005 creation of the Holy Sand Mandala in Amsterdam.

This was a disembodied time, just back from the biggest gathering of humanity in history - 60,000,000 people! Hardwar is also only about the size of Soho. I clearly remember on the first afternoon the day we arrived back from India, coming back from the Gallery and asking Michèle if there had been an epidemic in Amsterdam, because fresh back from India to me it looked like a ghost town with empty streets and no people! In this disembodied atmosphere I made the final series of "Thermal Expansion" paintings, #439-448, in August, 2010 during three continuous Sessions. It could be imagined to be a moment of celebration, but after India, as usual, the cards have been reshuffled and values as well as achievements have been properly rebalanced with gained insight and perspective. Already in the middle of this last "Thermal Expansion" Series #28 the planning was going on for what I was going to do next, which involved the culmination of all I had been thinking about for the past years.

This next direction was based on two years of thinking about Transparency - the effect of Fluorescence and Phosphorescence when separated by transparency - as well as almost five years of thinking about what I was taught by the group of Tibetan monks during their creation of the Holy Sand Mandala "Kalachakra" in Amsterdam the end of 2005. The

Transparency and the movement of Fluorescent sand is what my thoughts combined into, and I began to plan what I had thought about so long - the advancement of "Participatory Art." Having years before distanced myself from traditional Art, such as a finished 'piece' of Art hung on a wall like a canvas and presented as such to the public, I began to design a piece that a person could not only 'Participate' with the creation of Art, as in the Fluorescent "Participatory" Environment in the Museum, but literally '*Create*' the piece of Art themselves. It became nearly immediately apparent that this would be a personal piece of Art, in which just a single person at a time could experience the creation of Art, not as with "Participatory Art" which can be experienced by a group of people simultaneously, as it is in the Museum Fluorescent "Participatory" Environment. I began to sketch new possible assemblages involving what was turning around in my head for years, transparency and Fluorescent sand. I began to imagine a configuration of these two essential elements into a piece of 'Art,' or at least what could be basically called a piece of 'Art,' but which would actually both represent - and be realized - as an Artistic 'tool:' something that would be both a piece of Art itself, and would also be a means of creating a piece of Art - simultaneously and continuously.

I began to meticulously construct the first "Participatory Fluorescent Box" in March and April, 2011. During the first week of raw construction on this first "Participatory Fluorescent Box" I was experimenting every night with the sand Colors decided upon. The construction of this first three-dimensional "Participatory Fluorescent Box" was a welcome anticipated change from years making essentially 'flat' circular "Thermal Expansion" paintings, but proved to be some of the most technical, precise work I ever attempted in my life. Pages of designs are left from this construction period, each covered with precise measurements to the millimeter.

After two months of severe construction I couldn't wait to be able to use this "Participatory Fluorescent Box," and was completely enraptured for hours by the subtle movements of Fluorescent Colors producing an intense vivid light. Very quickly I also took out my cameras and began to photograph the subtle Fluorescent combinations of Colors - each piece of 'Art' created by the viewer is as transient and short-lived as the formations of clouds moving across the sky, and obviously could only be captured and preserved by the eyes, or a camera. Almost immediately I also began taking video of the creation of the Art inside the "Participatory Fluorescent Box." The endless fascination of the creation infinitely in flux inside this "Participatory Fluorescent Box" is nearly impossible to describe, or to stop while you're doing it. After Michèle returned she was also fascinated by this "Participatory Fluorescent Box," and on April nineteenth during the Albert Hofmann celebration, I realized that the name I extended from the Fluorescent "Participatory" Environment in the Museum was not truly descriptive of this new "Participatory Fluorescent Box," because the interaction the viewer has with this new "Box" is not just "Participation" in the creation of Art, but the literal Creation of Art itself, so I coined a new term on that April 19, 2011: "Creativatory Art."

"Creativatory Art" is a natural organic extension of "Participatory Art," which is what I centered the Fluorescent "Participatory" Environment in "Electric Ladyland - the First Museum of Fluorescent Art" on, and which in turn was an extension of what I had experienced in the work of "Interactive Art" during the 1980s. "Interactive Art" was a form of expression/experience that offered much mental agility, but required none in any way. "Interactive Art" was often triggered by motion detection, so even a plastic bowling ball rolled into grand-scaled works of "Interactive Art" caused precisely the same action in the piece of Art as a living, intelligent Human being.

"Participatory Art" manifested itself in a three-dimensional environment which over 50,000 visitors have experienced since opening in 1999. "Participatory Art" offers the ability to participate with the creative process which forms a piece of Art, but admittedly has a reduced electrically-activated palette. It is something like what is explained to Museum visitors: completing the 'unfinished corner' of a nearly completed painting.

"Creativatory Art" begins with a blank 'surface,' and the person encountering this form of Art does not merely interact or even participate with the piece of Art, but literally - and physically - Creates the piece of Art themselves. Pure primary pigments emit vivid Color and create infinite patterns, further heightened with the addition of Phosphorescent pigment.

In October and November, 2011 I constructed the second Box, which would have an extended palette of three Colors, with the most important difference being that one of the Colors would be highly Phosphorescent and Fluorescent Blue. This not only extends the palette of Colors to create with inside this "Creativatory Fluorescent and Phosphorescent Box #2," but creates another dimension, because when the Black lights are switched off, the Fluorescent Blue sand Phosphoresces intensely an Aqua-Blue Color. This Blue Phosphorescent sand is one of the strongest Phosphorescent substances you can get, because it contains a rare element and will continue to Phosphoresce, or 'Glow-in-the-Dark,' for up to twelve solid hours, which is a little hard to believe, but quite accurate. When extending your search for Phosphorescent pigments to make paint by hand with, there are new Phosphorescent pigments which have been developed only within the last decades which are capable of unbelievable durations of Phosphorescence, such as five, twelve, or even twenty-four to thirty hours! These modern super-Phosphorescent pigments are not easy to find, and are so expensive that the pigment itself is sold priced by the gram. The majority of Phosphorescent pigments of the recent past have traditionally been produced with common, relatively cheap Sulphur as the 'activator,' or impurity, contained in tiny amounts inside the chemical mixture of the paint, which produces the cliché Green 'Glow-in-the-Dark' that most people know today. These super Phosphorescent new pigments (which are just as super-expensive) of the last decades are activated with trace amounts of the very expensive Rare-Earth elements Strontium, also used to make the Color Red in fireworks, as well as Europium.

In the middle of February, 2012 I walked for the first time on the Eglantiersgracht canal next to the Gallery which was literally frozen solid and I began the construction of the third and final "Creativatory Fluorescent and Phosphorescent Box #3." The final variation that was necessary to create in this study/series of "Creativatory Boxes" was to bring these brilliant Phosphorescent Colors into the foreground of the creation. The day I finished this "Creativatory Fluorescent and Phosphorescent Box #3" I photographed this incredibly Phosphorescent Blue glowing so brightly that it literally caused the digital photos from my Nikon to be over-exposed!

The subtle variations and alterations of the created three-dimensional images inside these three "Creativatory Art Boxes" are infinite. Obviously these endless variations of created visual data can be easily captured and preserved with a still camera, but with a video camera no nuances of the creation is lost. If I had a little more of a Yuppiezed fetish for modern technology I would have installed permanently a 'web-cam' video camera inside these "Creativatory Art Boxes," starting with the first one, but this 'constant communication/capturing' of the present day is outside of my acceptance. After photographing these "Creativatory Art Boxes" with three different digital cameras, including my Fujica 3-D camera, and then taking video of the creative process and the creations inside these Boxes, I used my Nikon digital camera to produce another level of imagery. I photographed closeups of the Fluorescent and Phosphorescent creations inside the "Creativatory Art Boxes" through the 'viewing window,' and then with the 'mini-projector' built-in to the front of my Nikon digital camera, I projected Color images of these closeups of the Fluorescent and Phosphorescent creations into the Box through the 'viewing window' onto a three-dimensional Fluorescent and Phosphorescent creation inside the Box, and proceeded to photograph this with a second digital camera. For exhibiting these "Creativatory Art Boxes," photographs of projected, Fluorescent and Phosphorescent Creativatory Art are to be mounted on all walls of the space, blown up to about three meters tall.

In the end I came to the realization during the summer of 2011 after making just the first "Creativatory Fluorescent Box," that I have become an Alchemist by creating the first "Creativatory Fluorescent Box" that March to April, 2011, because through that act of this creation I have manifested an opportunity for the average nearly brain-dead character to become - for the duration of their time using this piece of Art - an Artist. This seemingly impossible achievement of turning a Grey empty entity into an Artist capable of actually creating Art themselves acknowledges the achievement of the Transmutation of a common uninterested person into an Artist(!) In reality this achieved Transmutation is a greater - and a seemingly more impossible achievement - than even physically Transmuting one element like Tin into another completely different element like Gold!

In truth there could have been more exploration and variations in further "Creativatory Art Boxes," but although these three creations/"Creativatory" tools were incredible to build, they were just that: a built creation. I missed paint, more than any other point in the matter. Not only that, but for years before the building of the three "Creativatory Art Boxes," I had done 447 "Thermal Expansion" paintings/experiments, which, again, were incredible to create, but were also like making a combination of a painting and a science experiment. I wanted to paint again, and furthermore, I wanted to paint *free* again. The next series of Art I made was a complete departure from what I had been making with the three-dimensional "Creativatory Art Boxes," and back to 'flat' again. There was some unfinished, and even unexplored inspiration that went back to the late 1990s during the painting of the Fluorescent "Participatory" Environment in the Museum.

For the painting of the Fluorescent "Participatory" Environment in Electric Ladyland there were many studies and charts made that created extreme contrasts between large areas of complementary Fluorescent Colors, which is the major direction of my Art since the 1970s: "Vibrating Colors." I made charts with over twenty labelled and numbered Fluorescent paint Colors, which were then divided into two broad areas, the first half being based on a presence of Yellows, Oranges, and Reds in the Colors, which I thought of as the 'warm' Colors. The second half of this broad division of Fluorescent Colors to paint the Museum Environment are the 'cool' Fluorescent Colors, which are based on Magenta, not Yellows and Oranges. This was extremely important to my overall planning and painting of the Environment, because on the left side of the Environment while facing it, there is the brilliant "Skyline Caverns Pool" area that was painted with only all the 'warm' Fluorescent Colors of the palette, so from the vantage point of looking at the entire Fluorescent "Participatory" Environment while in front of it, the one element that continues throughout the Environment is the long "Spectrum Pole," and this was purposefully planned from the beginning to start on the left side of the Environment directly in front of, and juxtaposed to, the 'warm' "Skyline

Caverns Pool," so the first half of the "Spectrum Pole" on the left in front of the "Skyline Caverns Pool" was painted with only the 'cool' half of the Fluorescent palette which contains Magenta, making it stand out and apart from the 'warm' "Skyline Caverns Pool" area behind it. This was of such paramount importance to me, that all areas of the Fluorescent "Participatory" Environment were to be seen from in front of the Environment as Vibrating, separate areas of Colors, and not blend together with each other because of a similar Color palette. In direct planned contrast, the entire right half of the Fluorescent "Participatory" Environment was based on the 'cool' Magenta half of my Fluorescent palette, and in this way would also remain separate and vibrating with the second half of "The Spectrum Pole," which ends on the right side of the Environment with the 'warm' half of the palette, starting at Red, continuing through the Oranges, and then finishing with the brilliant "Flash" Yellow. The entire Fluorescent "Participatory" Environment was painted precisely in this way for the four years of Color application, creating a piece of Art which is based on, and stipulated by, the magical Vibration of Complementary Colors which have fascinated me since I was a child and have also been the true foundation of my Artistic oeuvre since 1977. As can be easily imagined, the method of a planned, stipulated palette of Fluorescent Colors dividing the entire Environment into the left 'warm' Colors and the right 'cool' Colors was not exactly what could be called completely 'free' painting, but based on this underlying theme of Color Vibration. One of the exceptions to these endless juxtaposed vibrating areas of Colors in the Environment was one of the only areas that would be not seen from the front vantage point facing the Museum Environment - the hidden back 'wall' area enclosing "The Reactor" on the left half. This, in the end, was an area that would not be seen from the facing point of the Environment, and also would not be seen immediately by viewers, and which became one of the only areas of the Environment in that I could do what I wanted(!) What this private obscure area of the Museum Environment became was a dynamic swirling vision of the Quantum world of "Electron displacement," and in the end is still one of my favorite areas of the Environment. Underlying sprayed and splashed Fluorescent hot Colors were covered over with denser Pthalocanine Blue than on the front two sections of the outside of "The Reactor," and then in a very inspired and altered state I cut abrasive sponges to 'pencil' size and rubbed overlapping orbits of swirling electrons into this painted area. Because of both it's curved organic shape, and it's placement on the hidden 'back wall' of "The Reactor," this magical section of the Museum Environment both fascinated and intrigued me since it's creation. More than a dozen years after I painted this area of 'Electron displacement' on the "The Reactor" the intrigue and mystery were still there, and after the 2010 Kumbh Mela in India, and also after I had finished the years of "Thermal Expansion" paintings, I began to think about creating something out of these many years of this 'back wall's' inspiration. It was during this period, while building the "Creativatory Art Boxes" that one of the most auspicious visits to the Museum occurred. On April 19, 2011 for the Albert Hofmann celebration a tall gentle man in his sixties comes into the Gallery with his wife and began to talk to me about the Museum. I ask them where they're from and he answers Oregon, to which I immediately reply 'Ken Kesey country.' To my great surprise, this gentle man then humbly and even softly tells me that they both knew Ken Kesey very well when he was alive, and in fact this man Phil Dietz then tells me that he not only knew Ken Kesey very well, but that he had been one of Kesey's "Merry Pranksters"(!) He explains to me (while I most probably was starring unblinkingly at him with my mouth open) that he wasn't one of the first "Merry Pranksters" who went across America in their "Day-Glo" school bus "Furthur" in 1964, but that he met Kesey and became one of the "Pranksters" about 1969. Phil Dietz then talks about some of the projects he was involved in with Ken Kesey, such as the theater and performances of "The Pranksters" up until the time of Kesey's passing in 2001, including the precious play written by Kesey and performed by himself, Phil Dietz, and the other "Merry Pranksters" during the 1990s: "Twister." In thanks for the experience in the Museum he had with his wife (who still works for the Kesey family yogurt business "Nancy" in Oregon), Phil Dietz talked to Kesey's son Zane, and had the DVD set "Twister" sent to me in Amsterdam. This is a twisting, turning journey which gives you the impression that while watching this play "Twister" you are actually looking directly into the mind of Ken Kesey, with the intact, cutting, exposing style he possessed coming to it's culmination in the 'sing-along' anthem of the "Twister" play: "Starvation, Starvation" (!) Jesus Christ, Kesey was a 1000% unique character and exposing Artist until the end. Anyway, all this explanatory background to come to the point of my inspiration from the back 'hidden' wall of "The Reactor," because after talking for an hour to Phil Dietz and his wife in the Museum, he told me that out of the entire Fluorescent "Participatory" Environment his favorite area which really intrigued him was the swirling dynamic painting of this hidden 'back wall' of "The Reactor!" That did it for me - in the middle of the "Creativatory Boxes" I already began planning the next series of paintings, which would be based on these dozen years of thought and inspiration from this "Electron displacement' on this back wall of "The Reactor."

      In September and October, 2012 I began this series of new paintings, and for the first time in years the dream of painting freely came true. Sixteen paintings were prepared, again based on the infinite circular form, and these paintings were then coated to create a textured underlying surface. The base I wanted for this series was the base that the inspirational

"Electron Displacement" swirls were made on the back wall of "The Reactor," pure Fluorescent White. On top of many base coats of acrylic White, many more coats of Fluorescent White were applied, creating a pure, rich base of dazzling Fluorescent White with it's beautiful tint of Blue. Then the inspiration for the 'forms' of Color subliminally came to me from my greatest master, Jackson Pollock, who close to the end of his life in search of a new direction after painting his most important Art, created a canvas which has always stayed in my mind, "Portrait and a Dream." This three and a half meter long Pollock mural of 1953 has fascinated me for decades, because although it is a complete statement, it is composed of two separate and nearly disjointed elements. Half of the Pollock canvas is the "Portrait," a loosely painted self-portrait created with great dynamism, while the other half is "the Dream," composed of even more dynamic applications of paint, and is visually linked to his most famous visionary "Action paintings" of the late 1940s, as well as his 'Black' action canvases of the early 1950s. This Pollock "Portrait and a Dream" became the subliminal inspiration for the base, underlying field of Color that I was going to paint first, and then when completely dry, Phthalo Blue was planned to be put on top of these forms of Color before being removed to create areas resembling what impossible-to-see electron orbits could be imagined to look like. The two forms of Jackson Pollock's painting were unconsciously mirrored in this series of paintings, creating a round form from the hand-sprayed hot Fluorescent Oranges, Reds, and Magentas. This sprayed round form of Color extends off the circular bases of the sixteen paintings and covers about half of the surface area. On the right side of these sixteen paintings I created what are essentially Fluorescent paintings inspired by Jackson Pollock composed of the hottest Fluorescent Colors in the spectrum extending the palette from the Magentas, Reds, and Oranges, to brilliant Orange-Yellows and Yellow. These paintings were something I've wanted to do for decades. With further inspiration from Jackson Pollock I used several different 'tools' and methods of dripping and spraying the Fluorescent paint, which I had experimented with while making the Fluorescent "Participatory" Environment in the Museum, especially on the top scalding hot area of "The Reactor." 'Turkey basters,' hollow plastic tubes, and other 'instruments' were used. What became very fascinating during this all night session of flinging two-meter long lines of Fluorescent Color onto this new series of sixteen round paintings, was the extension of these lines of Color onto several other paintings in close proximity, not just onto one painting at a time. Since 1987 almost everything I've painted has been done in my 'atelier,' which is in reality the back half of "Electric Lady" Art Gallery. The floor, walls, and all the exposed hung Artwork is covered with meters of Black plastic, creating a virtual plastic cocoon in which to paint, as well as the temporary 'wall' of a cotton curtain mounted permanently on the wall dividing the Gallery in half, effectively protecting all the finished Fluorescent Artwork on the three walls of the back half of the Gallery from paint flying or being atomized throughout the last twenty-nine years of painting sessions. Since the entire Gallery is a total of forty square meters (yards), the back half of the cocooned Gallery - and my 'Atelier' since 1987 - is obviously not a vast space. In this area of my 'Atelier' under ten thirty-six watt Black lights, I arranged all of the sixteen round vivid Fluorescent White paintings, each mounted and taped horizontally onto empty plastic paint pots together in this confined, intimate space. The plastic covered floor is prepared by covering it again with many pieces of large Black paper, for catching a portion of the flying, splashed, sprayed Fluorescent paint which misses the surface of paintings. With sixteen White wooden round paintings mounted horizontally, and ranging in size from over one meter down to about thirty centimeters, it not only made it hard to walk in between all these round paintings arranged nearly touching each other, but also created what appeared to be a glowing giant mushroom patch.

    As stated earlier, what I planned to do was to loosely and freely spray, and then fling onto these sixteen paintings what I envisioned to be just the base of this series of paintings, and would then when dry apply pure Phthalo Blue to the entire surface of all these paintings, on top of these Fluorescent painted areas before abrading the dense Blue off in swirling lines of electron orbits. Already during the actual session of spraying and throwing pure hot Fluorescent Colors onto these sixteen painting bases I began to realize that this was not going to happen as planned. The pure vivid hot Fluorescent Colors applied for hours were exquisite, and created patterns and textures I had waited decades to freely make, so obviously the thought of covering all this light up with non-Fluorescent very dense Phthalo Blue was almost horrifying(!) The space to maneuver around under ten Black lights between sixteen round paintings mounted horizontally taped to plastic paint pots was extremely limited - just enough to put my feet down between the sea of paintings in two little 'alley-ways.' This made it not only very intimate, but a perfect situation with the paintings nearly touching each other for the flung two-meter lines of Fluorescent paint to extend over sometimes two or three separate paintings. With sixteen paintings and flinging lines of Fluorescent paint every couple of seconds for several hours, the applied Fluorescent paint nearly approached a moire pattern. This flinging of all the hot Fluorescent Colors of the spectrum for several hours every few seconds onto these sixteen paintings left a finished dazzling array of Colors which were Fluorescing so intensely under ten Black lights that when they were just finished and the paint was still wet, I could see shimmering energy rising off this field of paintings, similar to waves of heat-dissipation rising off of scalding hot surfaces outside in the Sunlight(!) As I began to envision during the actual painting session, I could not imagine covering up all this pristine Fluorescent Color energy with non-Fluorescent dense semi-opaque Pthalocanine Blue to create the "Electron Displacement" Series of paintings that was my original intension, and in the end this did not happen. I did not want to cover up these fresh brilliant Fluorescent paintings with Phthalo Blue and swirling orbits of displaced electrons, but I also wanted to complete what I started out planning to do, so I decided to 'sacrifice' two of the sixteen completed paintings for the experiments with Phthalo Blue and "Electron Displacement" inspiration. During the second session a week after all the sprayed and flung areas of hot Fluorescent Colors on the series of sixteen paintings were thoroughly dry, I prepared one of these relatively small sized paintings of about a forty centimeter diameter to create an "Electron Displacement" painting like I originally intended to make with all sixteen paintings, again, like the 'back wall' of "The Reactor" in the Museum Environment. I held my breath and applied pure, nearly-opaque, dense, dark, "Liquitex" Phthalocyanine Blue onto this pristine array of hot Fluorescent Colors and let it begin to dry. Then I took sponges with an abrasive surface on one side, and cut them with scissors into different thicknesses, creating essentially sponge 'pencils' to 'draw' swirling electron orbits into the Phthalo Blue. This created a pattern of orbiting electrons with the underlying lines of hot Fluorescent Colors being revealed by the abrasion of the sponges, but on this first attempted painting I made the electron orbits too literal, and too much like a quantum mechanics diagram, so after the painting was 'completed' and I prepared myself for the second session and the second "Electron Displacement," upon looking at this first painting I decided to spray Fluorescent Yellow-Oranges directly onto the 'finished' painting of underlying Fluorescent Colors and Phthalo Blue electron orbits. This admittedly did not create what I originally intended, but did essentially save this first "Electron Displacement" painting. For the second of this "Electron Displacement" Sessions, I used a larger one of these sixteen prepared, sprayed and coated Fluorescent round paintings, about sixty centimeters across, and began in the same manor, with the dreaded application of this dense non-Fluorescent - almost Black - pure Phthalo Blue onto this next pristine field of pure hot Fluorescent Colors, and let it dry. After this thin, nearly opaque layer of Phthalo Blue was dry I began to 'draw' intersecting partial orbits directly into the dark Blue paint with pencil-shaped cut sections of abrasive sponges. The larger sized field of this second painting was necessary for creating intersecting orbits of electrons which created a naturalistic understandable image, not a 'science diagram' like the first attempted painting. Different thicknesses along with varying opacities of Phthalo Blue created a cross section of what I visualized: being at the center of an atom - the nucleus - and looking out at the swirling orbits of electrons flying past at varying distances.

After the fascination and the release of finally painting freely again after such a long period - years - of making Art which was made stipulated by an environment, or with contrasting juxtaposition of Colors in mind, I made a second series of "Portrait and a Dream" Pollock-inspired paintings. The first series of "Portrait and a Dream" paintings consisted of sixteen round paintings, which were of many varying sizes, the smallest being about thirty centimeters, and the largest painting of this series was about a meter (yard) across. The first of the two "Electron Displacement" paintings from this series was made on a medium sized base, which proved too small a surface to create the impression of swirling orbits of electrons, and then the second of these paintings was made on a medium-large base of about three-quarters of a meter wide, which proved to be the ideal size for creating the impression I wanted of being at the center nucleus of an atom and watching in the far distance of space, electrons whirling by in different circular orbits - similar to being on the Sun and watching the planets of the Solar system revolving past in their respective different orbits. This has intrigued me since I was a little boy - wondering which way the Earth was orbiting around the Sun from my perspective of being on the Earth. In the early 1990s I even wrote to the director of "Sky and Telescope" magazine and asked him precisely that question, to which he kindly replied that while we are looking at the sunset (which I wrote to him) from Earth, if you imagine the planet traveling in an orbit that is on a path towards roughly 5:00 on the face of a clock, then you can visualize our cosmic path through the Solar system.

The second series of "Portrait and a Dream" paintings in 2013 were also coated with vivid Fluorescent White paint on similar sized variations of circular wooden paintings, but the large painting for this second series is bigger than the first series, being a full 122 centimeters wide - the maximum size of sheets of plywood sold in Amsterdam. In addition to this large painting, there are also three paintings about three-quarters of a meter across, and then ten more paintings of diminishing sizes. The first series of "Portrait and a Dream" paintings were made with the intension of the two areas of sprayed and flung Fluorescent paint being only an *undercoat* of Colors that would be seen through different densities of Phthalo Blue, which I originally intended to coat every painting with before abrading 'electron orbits' into. For this second "Portrait and a Dream" series I finally intended that the sprayed and flung Fluorescent paint would be the painting, not an undercoat of Color, with the exception of just a single 'sacrificed' painting which would have Phthalo Blue totally applied to it before abrasion and creation of an "Electron Displacement" painting. For this second series of "Portrait and a Dream" paintings I also sprayed the left half of the paintings much more densely than the corresponding areas painted in the first series, as well as extending these circular areas of sprayed Fluorescent hot Colors further off of the round painting surfaces, which creates a greater sense of immersion into the image. The right side of the second series of "Portrait and a Dream" paintings was also much denser, with the flinging of Yellow, Oranges, Reds, and Magenta Fluorescent Colors lasting for several hours. Dense, overlaid lattices of straight lines in every hot Fluorescent paint of the spectrum created areas which are mesmerizing in their complexity. This right 'flung' side of these "Portrait and a Dream" paintings correspond to the right 'Portrait' on Jackson Pollock's original canvas, and this was my intent - to create a visual self-portrait of what I consider myself to be. The inspiration for these two series of "Portrait and a Dream" paintings is contained in two sentences from Jackson Pollock in which he profoundly states that with their "creation" an Artist must 'become totally intermingled.' Pollock further explains that an Artist must 'make painting' as well as their "act" of painting (what he considered "constant intervention") into what he plainly calls "reality."

During the final writing of this book, in 2014 and 2015 I made several sessions of a new series of Fluorescent and Phosphorescent paintings which are called "Light Impact." The first sessions of these circular "Light Impact" paintings evolved through what I've been thinking about after finishing the long series of four-hundred and forty-seven "Thermal Expansion" paintings, followed by several sessions of about thirty "Portrait and a Dream" circular Fluorescent paintings which were obviously inspired by Jackson Pollock, and which consisted of a third of the painted surface being a hand-sprayed area and the other two-thirds made up of a myriad of flung long lines of paint. Again, initially intended as just a base painting for what I first planned as "Electron Displacement" paintings, the flung lines of Fluorescent paint were extremely dynamic, but they were not, nor did they create, much more than flung lines of paint - there was not enough "magic" achieved only by hand, resulting in paintings that were not for me enough of a combination of intention together with creation brought about through energy. These new series of "Light Impact" paintings convey this "magic," as achieved with the "Thermal Expansion" series.

After the first series of these "Light Impact" paintings I continued the experiments into these paintings with a second series of paintings, culminating in a 122 centimeter wide circular "Light Impact #11." For eight hours I sprayed and then flung many liters of Fluorescent and Phosphorescent paint, until a myriad of brilliant Acid Yellow and Bengal Red flung lines of overlapping and intersecting paint began to create moire patterns.

I've been thinking for a long time about what is documented in this book, at least the last half of my life. I began writing this book when I was fifty years old and now I'm fifty-nine, which is more time than it took me to create "Electric Ladyland - the First Museum of Fluorescent Art" and it's Fluorescent "Participatory" Environment in the 1990s. I live in Amsterdam for thirty years with Michèle and am extremely thankful for it - I would choose to live nowhere else on the Earth. I am very grateful to the Dutch for letting me live the last half of my life in Amsterdam. The Dutch society is the only society I know of that has somehow mystically learned to live together with each other in relative *Harmony*. Imagine that! I have a Dutch friend for many years in Amsterdam named Benjamin who exemplifies what a person can hope to be.

Another Artist besides Jackson Pollock and Paul Gauguin, Vincent van Gogh, Michelangelo, Seurat, Monet (his late Waterlillies), and the original rebel Cezanne, who has inspire me deeply and have a lifelong influence on my Art is the "DaDa" Visionary master Marcel Duchamp. The entire concept which "Electric Ladyland - the First Museum of Fluorescent Art" was built on was realized by Duchamp in his masterpiece "Given: 1. The Waterfall 2. The Illuminating Gas" in the Philadelphia Museum of Art. Duchamp explains very lucidly that 'the viewer's Participation' is what the Artist described as this piece of Art's "integral element." Duchamp concludes this visionary statement with the fundamental point being that 'without the viewer's Reaction' this piece of Art "remains incomplete." Marcel Duchamp was truly a pivotal Artist, and has been an inspiration to my Art for decades, with his stance that in his "Precision Painting," which he referred to as 'an illustrative type of painting,' the piece of Art is created with the intention of not being conceived as an aesthetic end in itself, and also not being created for just the eyes of the viewer. Duchamp has been the father of what has been a school of Art called "Conceptual Art." In his "Green Box" of 1934 Duchamp created a whole new concept in his Art. The original ideas for what he had once called a "wedding" between "revelations" both 'Mental as well as Visual' was the formed concept in which he stipulated that the *ideas* which created a piece of Art are more important than the actual created visual realization. In the Philadelphia Museum of Art is the largest collection of Duchamp in the world, all contained in one large space and including both his masterpieces "The Bride Stripped Bare by Her Bachelors, Even" ('The Large Glass') and the installation "Given: 1. The Waterfall 2. The Illuminated Gas." When I finally met my long-lost descendent Victoria in 2006, I requested it to be in the Philadelphia Museum of Art, and to be photographed with her in front of the most well known painting by Duchamp, "Nude Descending a Staircase." I must also include in this list of the Artists who have most profoundly inspired me the Art of Kandinsky, for not only his first non-objective paintings, but also for his visionary book "Concerning the Spiritual in Art" in which he very accurately describes most museum visitors as the "Vulgar Herd."

What has not been included in this book until the end is the deep love the Artist writing has for these Fluorescent Colors. After washing Fluorescent Colors off my hands, feet, and every other part of my body for decades I finally decided five years ago during the writing of this book that I wanted these Fluorescent Colors to be a part of my skin permanently, so I bought all the necessary equipment and then proceeded to make by myself one Fluorescent Tattoo on each of my legs first, and then a larger Fluorescent Tattoo on my left forearm. The reason I made these three Fluorescent Tattoos myself is because it had become illegal to make Fluorescent Tattoos in parts of the world some years ago with the reason being that it had never been proven that Fluorescent Tattoo ink 'wasn't harmful,' but since I have been using Fluorescent substances for decades and have also mixed up thousands of liters of Fluorescent paint using powdered Fluorescent pigments which I have inhaled in this process also for decades, and since I am in good health now at almost sixty, still mixing up, breathing in, and painting with Fluorescent Colors, I am living proof of just how 'harmful' these Fluorescent Colors are. These Fluorescent Tattoos were common twenty years ago and made in Tattoo parlors everywhere, but at that time my feeling for the consciousness of the American Indians, many of whom did not permanently alter their bodies in any way for intentionally leaving this world as they had entered it, were stronger than wanting to have Fluorescent Colors a permanent part of my body. This Fluorescent Color permanently tattooed into my skin became more important to me than any American or Hindu Indian philosophies some years ago, so at the end of 2011 I ordered a full set of Fluorescent Tattoo inks, two different Colors of "Invisible" Fluorescent Tattoo inks, a tattoo gun, it's generator and all the necessary accessories, as well as a tiny Black light made to attach to the tattoo gun. This was all sent to my sister's house for my yearly U.S. visit, to which I arrived as usual late at night. The next morning at 7:00 AM I was up because I couldn't wait to tattoo myself with Fluorescent Ink! I opened up the large parcel and saw the brilliant set of Fluorescent Tattoo inks, but then got my first shock when I opened up the box containing what was labelled as a "Tattoo Gun," but which was to my surprise was just a collection of one-hundred rubber bands and undecipherable metal objects(!) Thankfully for the internet I could amazingly construct from what first appeared to be a box full of broken machine parts and rubber bands, a working Tattoo Gun! At 8:00 AM this same first morning in America in 2011 I began my first Fluorescent Tattoo, a relatively small "OM" on my left calf in two Colors, Fluorescent Red for the "OM" with a Fluorescent Orange outline. I did this freehand without a drawing or stencil application, just to see what it felt like to have a tattoo gun injecting ink rapidly into my skin. It had started as just a simple test, both to see if I could make a tattoo and also to see if I could bear the pain, but after about two minutes of relatively painless absolute fascination, I decided to continue right there and create my first Fluorescent Tattoo. The two Color Fluorescent "OM" took a couple of hours to make on my leg, and when my sister got home at 3:00 from work she was so amazed that she posted a picture on "Facebook" of my Fluorescent Tattoo under a Black light still bleeding!

    For my second Fluorescent Tattoo, which I would make two days later on my right calf, I prepared a stencil application of a molecular structure I have infinite respect for, and with the help of my sister Mary Jean Color-coded this molecular structure according to the spectrographic Color of each of it's constituent elements. Fluorescent Red, Blue, "Invisible" White, and Purple (substituted for the Black of carbon) were used to make my second Fluorescent Tattoo, which at a little over three inches (almost 9 cm) is twice the size of the first Fluorescent Tattoo I made on my left leg. After making these first two Fluorescent Tattoos, which included many straight lines in the molecular structure, I was confident I could make a

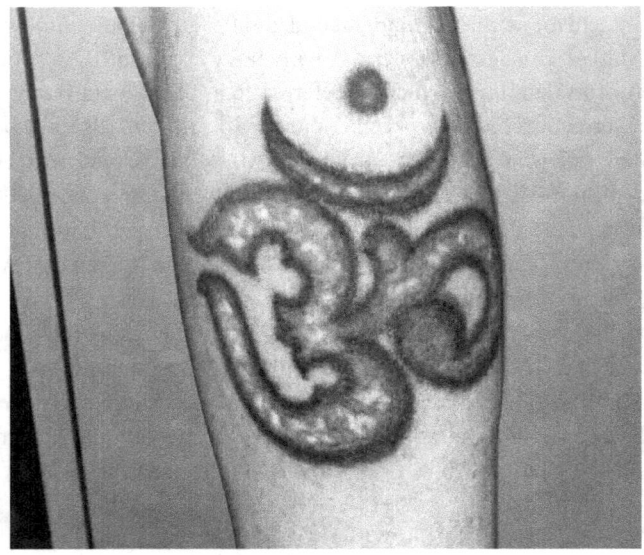 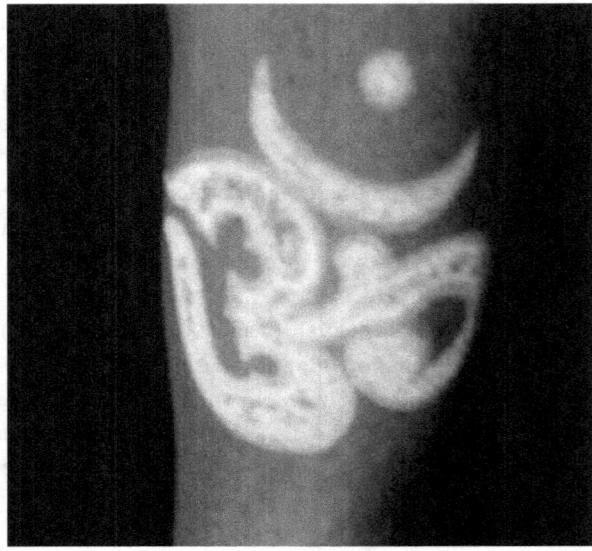

The author's third self-made Fluorescent Tattoo, December, 2011 (White light / Black light)

large multi-Colored intricate Fluorescent Tattoo on my left forearm. I had planned for this Fluorescent Tattoo still while in Amsterdam and made a copy to the size I wanted on my forearm of a silver "OM" that Moti, a Newar jeweler in Kathmandu who Michèle knows for many years had made for us when we were in Nepal in 1987. This intricate silver "OM" has hung in the doorway of "Electric Lady" Art Gallery ever since we returned from India and Nepal in 1988, until today. After preparing a transfer stencil of this "OM" to the size I wanted it on my left arm, three and a half inches tall (9 cm), I prepared the five hottest Fluorescent Tattoo Inks of the spectrum: Apricot-Yellow, Orange, Orange-Red, Red, and Magenta. Beginning with the intricate design on the interior of the "OM," I tattooed myself with Fluorescent Apricot-Orange, Orange, and Orange-Red. After several hours of creating this three-Color interior design of the "OM," I began a tick double outline of the "OM," first in Fluorescent Red and finally in Magenta. In total this five-Color Fluorescent "OM" Tattoo on my left forearm took me seven hours to complete, during which I made some digital photos and video of the process. In the end the most pain I had was not in my arm, but in the fingers of my right hand because the tattoo gun became increasingly hotter through the hours of constant vibrations, causing me to wrap several layers of cotton around it to relieve the heat on my fingers. This Fluorescent "OM" Tattoo on my arm came out like I had envisioned it, and was as soon as I returned to Amsterdam, the newest 'acquisition' to the Museum collection which has also been added since January, 2012 to the "Common Items that are Fluorescent" demonstration given to Museum visitors every day.

Another Artform I've experimented with six times since 2010 has been something that has fascinated me all my life: Glass-blowing(!) What I did was not actually glass-blowing but the forming of glass. With the help of a master Glass Artist, I could create six glass Shiva Lingas over the last six years in a glass-blowing atelier "Hot-Glass" of Asbury Park, New Jersey. Each December since 2010 (except 2012) for my yearly U.S. visit I've gone with my sister to make a six inch (10 cm) tall solid glass Shiva Linga containing the three primary Colors Red, Yellow, and Blue. You choose the Colors (which are not powdered pigments, but Colored crushed particles also made of glass) and with the help and instruction of a Glass Artist you manipulate molten sections of the glass form with heavy-duty huge iron 'tweezers,' through pinching, twisting, bending, and attaching together the glass form. It is infinitely fascinating, both the creation of the Glass Art as well as the viewing of it. In December, 2014 the Glass Artist who instructed me for my fourth glass Shiva Linga, and who is also named Nick, remembered me from one of the Shiva Lingas I made with him a few years before and had saved a piece of Fluorescent and Phosphorescent 'mineral' substance for me to incorporate into the top of the swirling Red, Yellow, and Blue forms of the Shiva Linga, making it a Luminous piece of Glass Art.

Very seldom indeed does a person witness unequivocal proof of what they have believed all their lives, and this unequivocal proof was directly witnessed by the current author during the closing of an exhibition of a truly Visionary Artist, Oskar Fischinger. A comprehensive retrospective of this Visionary Artist was held at the new "Eye Filmmuseum and Center for Visual Music" in Amsterdam from December, 2012 until March, 2013, which had ten of Fischinger's conceptual films being projected in the darkness of large galleries. This Oskar Fischinger retrospective was held in collaboration with Los Angeles' "Center for Visual Music." Oskar Fischinger is known as a pioneer in avant-garde abstract cinema and animated film, with this German-American filmmaker being influential in the historical development of animated films, today's ever-popular music videos, and even computer graphics. The retrospective of this Visionary Artist was appropriately entitled "Oskar Fischinger (1900-1967): Experiments in Cinematic Abstraction," with the exhibition in Amsterdam beginning with a large central focal point consisting of a projection of an early experimental film of the Artist, which could be today described as a combination of "Op Art" and "Psychedelia." The visitor has opened dark glass doors and walked into a dark room, which is the first room of the Fischinger exhibition, and at the center of this first space is one of the most visually captivating films of Fischinger's being projected in Black and White, the 1926 silent 35mm film "Spirals" ("Spiralen") which immediately set the tone of the entire oeuvre of the Artist. This was the entrance of the exhibition full in the face as you opened the doors to begin the show, just after walking past a sign to the public warning visitors that the projected movies of Fischinger could cause an epileptic seizure(!) The first impression of this Fischinger exhibition walking into a darkened room with "Spirals" being projected straight in front of you, was that the era of this Artist was during the 1960s, not forty years before that time period. In this first room of the Fischinger exhibition were several other monitors playing movies of early cinematic experiments of the Artist, along with photographs and explanations of his techniques such as the "Wax Experiments" of 1921-1926 which the Artist created with his infinitely intriguing "Wax Slicing Machine." A photo from 1922 of this mechanical filmmaking machine created by Oskar Fischinger shows the genius of the Artist, who prepared a block of wax made of many different Colors and marbleized forms. This block of prepared wax was placed into an upright massive iron structure and filmed frame-by-frame as the "Wax Slicing Machine" sliced the block of wax in this position, which made it look like a square painting on a wall. Although Fischinger shot these "Wax Experiments" on Black and White 35mm film stock, these films were also made with "tinted" Colors. The photographs, technical drawings, explanations, and viewing of these "Wax Experiments" in the first room of the Fischinger exhibition demonstrated the depth of the Artist who created these visions in the early 1920s. Fischinger is known to have had great respect for the Artists Paul Klee and Robert Delaunay, both visionary abstract Artists of that time period who continue to influence modern Artists up until the present day. The Artist who Oskar Fischinger is most often compared with is known as the first non-objective painter, Vassily Kandinsky, because Fischinger is now recognized as the first Artist who created non-objective abstract film, or as the introduction to the Amsterdam Fischinger exhibition worded it, a 'foremost pioneer' in cinematic abstraction and animation. By investigating devices such as the "Wax Slicing Machine" already in the 1920s, the Artist was called the "Wizard of Friedrichstrasse," and became famous for creating amongst the first music videos way back in 1930, as well as being known today as 'motion graphic's great-grandfather.' One of the lasting shocks of the exhibition is the fact that Fischinger dreamed up the very first full-length animation movie, which he then enthusiastically detailed to an associate, who then told Fischinger's dream to Walt Disney, who went ahead to produce the first full-length feature animated film, the world-famous "Fantasia!"

In 1936 Fischinger began to paint on canvas in California due to several reasons, including the lack of enthusiasm and funds for his abstract cinematic creations. Fischinger also knew the filmmaker and Dada Artist Man Ray who in 1940 had settled in California after leaving Paris, but mass society in the 1920s and 1930s even in California was still just getting used to "Impressionism." Amongst his inspirations in California during this period, Fischinger visited The Institute of Metaphysics several times a week in Los Angeles studying the Tantric mysticism of Tibet there, met Krishnamurti, and was exposed to the first non-objective painter Kandinsky. As well as creating oil paintings on canvas and glass, in 1947 possibly through the inspiration of Paul Klee, Fischinger created a film "Motion Painting No. 1" in which each and every brush stroke of Color in the creation of the painting was filmed as animation. Fischinger created this movie by the use of large transparent sheets of plastic which he painted and simultaneously filmed stroke by stroke. The finished canvas created by Fischinger was hung next to the HD projection of this film during the Amsterdam exhibition.

Another series of Oskar Fischinger's which truly defines the entire realm of Visionary Art was what he named "Stereo Paintings," and first exhibited during 1951 in Los Angeles. These "Stereo Paintings" were exhibited at Fischinger's solo show of 1953 in the San Francisco Museum of Art very prominently on the opening wall of the exhibition's entrance. This unique series of "Stereo Paintings" were often referred to by Fischinger as "Space paintings," because of their ability to create "space reality." "Stereopsis" was discovered in 1838, and after photography was invented during the mid-Nineteenth century the '3D' Stereo image became very popular, leading to a 1936 patent issued to Theodor V. Ionescu for 3D cinema, which was all brought to the masses by the 1940 bakelite "View-Master" marketed throughout America. In actual fact, the first 3D full-length feature film projected to the public was in Los Angeles, called "FOURSQUARE" in 1922. This series of the early 1950s "Stereo Paintings" or "Space Paintings" by Fischinger were intended by the Artist to be not just 3D paintings, but are imagery tools capable of manipulating a viewer's perception into creating a vision of a third painting manifesting itself through the controlled viewing of a juxtaposed pair of paintings. Identical to the first exhibition of Fischinger's "Stereo Paintings" in Los Angeles' Frank Perls Gallery of 1951 in which directions for viewing the "Stereo Paintings" were mounted on a wall, for the Amsterdam 2012-2013 exhibition the exact same directions by Fischinger were hung next to these works. Next to Fischinger's 1949 "Stereo Paintings" "Stereo No. 13" and "Circles in Circle (Stereo Painting)" exhibited in Amsterdam was Fischinger's original directions for creating this "Space reality" from his "Space Paintings," which carefully instructed the viewer to look towards the "Stereo Painting" while focusing on a single point in front of the face at arm's length in line with the "Stereo Painting." Fischinger continues, instructing the viewer to 'adjust their distance' until a point is reached where it distinctly gives the impression that the two juxtaposed paintings making up this "Stereo Painting" have physically moved away from each other, and have left in their wake a void between them in which an invisible magic third painting has appeared, with a greater 'brilliance' than the original two images. Fischinger then instructs the viewer to "observe" this "illusive" third painting with the "mind," which creates this "Space illusion." Having achieved this visual transcendence, the Artist informs the viewer that they will now be able to go 'wandering about' in this "space illusion" of the created third painting and be able to judge 'exact locations, positions, and distances between forms' with precise sharpness. These seemingly esoteric instructions were easily carried out during the Amsterdam exhibition, with Museum visitors standing for a few minutes in front of Fischinger's two "Stereo Paintings" at a distance of about ten feet (three meters), while focusing on their finger held at reading distance in direct line of sight towards the "Stereo Paintings." Magically, a third painting arises in the mind's eye that is indeed similar to a holographic image in it's sharpness, crystal clarity, and self-creation by the viewer. This comes from a Visionary Artist at the beginning of the 1950s, who turned to painting after being disgusted and forgotten by the growing film industry. This was the young Visionary Artist who excitedly told his visions in detail of a full-length animated feature film based on classical music to conductor Leopold Stokowski, who then proceeded to tell Fischinger's visions to Walt Disney, who had the finances to create just that: a full-length animated feature film, which, again, he named "Fantasia." To add infinite insult to obvious injury, the congenial Walt Disney hired Oskar Fischinger as a stock animator of "Cartoon Effects" for "Fantasia," paying the creator of the entire idea the princely sum of sixty dollars a week.

For a glimpse into the creative mind of Oskar Fischinger, there are detailed documentations of visits to the Artist's 'Color-Sound Animation Studio' during the mid-1930s in Berlin. Fischinger himself explains that along with classical production of animation in which drawings are filmed one-by-one in a built up sequence, the Artist used the "Gasparcolor System." This "Gasparcolor System" was capable of producing what was unbelievable during that age: between 6,000 and 7,000 different Color hues! Film shots were recorded using three Color filters precisely coordinated which produced three exposures of separate Colors. These three exposures of separate Colors were then recorded while played together, resulting in a finished Color film which was explained by Fischinger to 'exactly replicate' the original Colors. In this same 1934 interview Fischinger went on to explain that the ideas of his films are not developed through 'screenplays' or anything resembling classic filmmaking, but through pure "optical manipulation" of Color, light, movement, and sharpness, which the Artist defines as not coming from a classic "subject matter," but from materials and the pure image in the film itself, which Fischinger defines as his newly developed "optical art." In the catalogue for the Fischinger exhibition in Amsterdam it is stated that the Artist was "instrumental" in "Gasparcolor's" development, which was created by a Hungarian chemist Dr. Bela Gaspar. In 1933 during the "Congress for Color-Sound Research" in Hamburg, Fischinger projected publicity for "Gasparcolor" and then went on to create "Kreise" ("Circles") between 1933 and 1934, which was one of the first films made using this "Gasparcolor" technique, and was chosen as the cover image for this Amsterdam 2012-2013 Fischinger show's catalogue. In the end Dr. Gaspar left Nazi Germany and moved to Hollywood where his invention "Gasparcolor" was sold to and used by the famous industrial movie giant "Technicolor."

Oskar Fischinger worked with and was influenced by another visionary named Alexander Laszlo, a Hungarian genius who is known today as an Artist of "Color-Light Music." These two Artists worked together in Germany in 1926 and again in Hungary in the mid-1930s. In 1925 Laszlo presented in Kiel, Germany something completely new called "Farblichtmusik," literally translated as 'Color-Light Music,' in which the composer and pianist Laszlo played his original score of music accompanied to simultaneous Colored slide projections on a screen. Laszlo preformed this piece of 'Color-Light Music' for two years, during which the Artist collaborated with Oskar Fischinger in 1926, and on March seventh in Munich they worked together on a 'Color-Light Music' performance of Laszlo's. In the mid-1930s Fischinger began to realize with help from Laszlo's letters that the classic music he was using for his avant-garde films was out of place and "middle-class," so he changed his ideas and formed a music based on rhythmic and dynamic dance music, void of melody and composed of percussion instruments.

In mid-1937 Fischinger had moved to the United States and met a twenty-four year old visionary composer named John Cage, resulting in Cage working as an apprentice shortly on Fischinger's film "An Optical Poem." In 1943 Fischinger wrote to John Cage, realizing that the composer's music would be perfectly suited to his abstract films, but no further collaboration resulted. It is clear that Oskar Fischinger made a great impression on the young apprentice John Cage, as the visionary composer recalled often his meeting with Fischinger during which the Artist had spoken to his apprentice of the 'spirit which is inside of every object of the world,' and that the manner which to "draw forth" the sound of any object and liberate it's spirit was by simply 'brushing past' it.

In the end because of financial troubles and lack of public interest, both Laszlo and Fischinger's Artistic careers were derailed, with Laszlo spending the rest of his life as a composer and piano teacher, and with Fischinger making his last abstract film in 1947 and then changing his medium to paint on canvas and glass.

Developing his own sound fascinated Oskar Fischinger well into the 1950s, and began with the origin of "Electronic Music" which became popular during the 1950s and 1960s. "Electronic Music" had it's roots in early cinema's soundtracks in which "synthetic sound" was produced by physically manipulating the optical soundtrack already back in the 1920s. Sound was captured and then visually produced by a waveform on an optical soundtrack, so the creation of "synthetic sound" was achieved by simply scratching, drawing, or photographing directly onto this film-stock's optical soundtrack. By 1932 Fischinger had released" "Ornament Sound" made with this technique, and in 1948 the Artist built the "Synthetic Sound Machine" containing his "audio waveforms" printed onto celluloid strips fixed to glass plates held in a wooden frame. Photographs of the "Synthetic Sound Machine" as well as drawings for it's patent application reveal a design of genius and deep complexity.

Of the compositions Oskar Fischinger made on his "Synthetic Sound Machine" was a piece of abstract music based on Sibelus' "Valse Triste" used as the soundtrack for performances on what is considered Fischinger's masterpiece, his "Lumigraph." Oskar Fischinger filed a patent in 1950, which was received by the Artist in 1955, for a visionary conception and construction which he called the "Device for Producing Light Effects," and which became known as his "Lumigraph." This was a pioneering piece of not only "Interactive At," but more properly even an advancement into what was possibly the first concept of "Participatory Art," conceived by Fischinger decades before these concepts in Art were 'discovered' and named. The explanation of this piece of "Visionary Art" was provided by the Artist on his patent application of 1950, in which he simply describes "an instrument" that would have 'the capability to express artistic ideas through light.' 'Luminous effects in succession' could be produced by a performer on what Fischinger called in his notes, an instrument of "Color-Play." Fischinger clearly instructed that the performance on this "Lumigraph" would be played by "HAND" and that the "Player" would 'directly control' the created fantastic display of Color. This actual "Lumigraph" is described as a performance machine built into a wooden Black frame about five feet wide (1.7 meters), with the workings of the "Lumigraph" consisting of an assemblage of lights and Colored filters which emit Colored light through vertical slits built into the sides of the "Lumigraph." Pulleys and straps rotate a Color wheel containing the Colored filters in front of the lighting system, which produces an endless variation of Color combinations, and a White rubber sheet was stretched tight across the frame of the "Lumigraph" which was the actual "Playing area" for the "performer's" creation through movements of their hands on this stretched rubber sheet. These performances by individuals on Fischinger's "Lumigraph" were created solely with the hands pressing onto the flexible stretched rubber sheet, and were described by the Artist in his program notes as "Visual Color Symphonies." Two public performances by Oskar Fischinger are documented, the first being in January, 1951 at a theater in Los Angeles called "The Coronet Louvre," and the second Fischinger performance of a "Visual Color Symphony" on his "Lumigraph" was at the Beverly Hills Frank Perls Gallery in October, 1951, which is the same Art gallery in which Robert Mallary exhibited his early Fluorescent "Luminous Mobiles" under Black lights the next year in 1952. The contemporary 2012-2013 Fischinger Amsterdam exhibition catalogue correctly describes his "Lumigraph" as an 'early analog interactive instrument' to be used for public performances, and although the concept was clear to the Visionary Artist himself, the public during the beginning of the 1950s was many decades from comprehending this advanced concept of "Interactive Art." The beginning of the 1950s was a period in which "Abstract Expressionism" and Artists such as Jackson Pollock were still mystifying to the public (and in truth still very much are), so a performance of a "Visual Color Symphony" by Oskar Fischinger on his instrument the "Lumigraph" was literally decades before the public had any notion of such a concept, and who were subsequently described as being both 'mystified and amazed' at this concept which would take another thirty to forty years for the general public to even hear about. For example, the program notes for the two 1951 performances of "Visual Color Symphonies" by Oskar Fischinger describe not an Artist's "performance," but merely a comprehensible "demonstration." As all Visionary Artists, Fischinger envisioned this concept in Art and his "Color-Play Instrument" the "Lumigraph" as 'enriching visual arts' by being used for the commercial worlds of television and film production, as well as advertising, and also to be used therapeutically in hospitals and even in people's private homes for performances. Also like most visions of Visionary Artists, the intellectual scope of the creator is so far advanced from the average person in public that their visions are seen as nearly absurdities. Of course the visions of Fischinger were never realized during the early 1950s, with his "Lumigraph" performances in 1951 being held during an unenlightened, existential period of history only six years after the end of the Second world war, and of course Fischinger's invention the "Lumigraph" did not "enrich" or expand "visual art" worldwide as the Artist had imagined, because the concept was nearly incomprehensible to the public, as well as to most Artists, during that time period.

    The mechanical workings of Oskar Fischinger's "Lumigraph" can be more easily understood when studying both his drawings for the instrument's design and the clear mechanical drawings for the patent of this "Device For Producing Light Effects." Overhead and side-angle mechanical drawings clearly explain the design of the "Lumigraph," with pulleys and straps revolving a wheel on each side of the instrument which produce an endless variation of Colors. This Color show is projected behind the rubber sheet in front of the performer, and is unseen until this performer presses their hands into the large flexible White rubber sheet in front of them, which then causes this rubber sheet to move forward into the projected path of this endless flow of Colors.

    Oskar Fischinger performances on his "Lumigraph" were described in detail by the Artist's daughter Barbara, who in a 2007 interview explained that during the early 1950s her father would perform on his "Lumigraph" in his studio at home for visitors. It seems that it took two people to operate this "Device For Producing Light Effects," and Barbara Fischinger would be her father's assistant. The origin of the "Lumigraph" came from an experience the Artist had while entering a room in the dark in which a shaft of light was created by slightly opening a door, and that furthermore this shaft of light could be 'played' with and altered by simply varying the opening of the door. Barbara Fischinger describes her father then spending weeks in his studio before allowing his excited children and wife to see his first "Lumigraph" and to play it. The performances on the "Lumigraph" were accompanied by records that played light classical and other types of music which had 'strong movements' and a "definitive rhythm" for the performance. Visitors to Fischinger's studio would choose from his record collection and would then perform on the "Lumigraph" after the Artist played on it. Another precious memory from the Artist's daughter is that the neighborhood children would "beg" Fischinger to be allowed to play on his "Lumigraph," and that the Artist "loved" watching the children excitedly play on his Interactive Art instrument. It seems that Fischinger thought that children were spontaneous, free from concepts, and because of this they were the "most artistic" of all. It also seems that these Fischinger home performances on his "Lumigraph" were in unique settings as well, with his daughter describing shoveling dirt from beneath the deck in their backyard in West Hollywood to create one of three "studios," which Fischinger put this "Lumigraph" in. One studio was for film storage and constructed out of concrete, the large studio was for painting, and this third subterranean studio was for "Lumigraph" performances until 1956, when the Fischinger family moved to Laurel Canyon, California. In the large family room of their "Wonderland" house the Artist attached his "Lumigraph" to one wall and held performances. Behind the mounted "Lumigraph" was a space for the performers, where his daughter describes being instructed by her father to move the "Color wheels" consisting of glass panels that were long, thin, and covered with gels of the Colors Red, Blue, Green and Yellow. Sometimes the Artist would instruct his daughter to select a specific Color on the wheel, and sometimes he would tell her to quickly rotate the wheel to produce all the Colors. Fischinger's daughter also remembers her father being "intent" during his performances, with a concept of which Colors to be used for different movements of the accompanied soundtrack he had chosen, and a produced performance on his "Lumigraph" which left him "soaked" with sweat. It seems that sometimes Fischinger would hit the flexible latex screen during a performance, resulting in what his daughter remembers as a 'lovely explosion in rippling light.' Apparently Fischinger was very aware of his audience, and even had a series of three mirrors mounted so that he could literally see what part of his performance the audience was looking at, but his audience could not see him because the entire area of wallspace behind the "Lumigraph" was covered up with Black cloth and Fischinger himself was also dressed in Black. The closest that Oskar Fischinger's "Lumigraph" got to being exposed to a massive audience was when in the 1960s Andy Williams had the idea of featuring this Visionary Art instrument on his television special the "Andy Williams Show." Unfortunately the original "Lumigraph" was measured for light output by technicians who had come to Fischinger's house with Andy Williams, but there was not enough light to be filmed at that point in time for television broadcast.

    During the 1960s Oskar Fischinger's health deteriorated and he couldn't perform physically on his original "Lumigraph" anymore, so his son Conrad under the watchful eye of his father built a second larger "Lumigraph" that was operated through a foot pedal as well as being transportable. This second "Lumigraph" was featured in a science-fiction film of 1964 called "The Time Travelers," in which Fischinger's instrument was known as a "Love Machine," and was used in this future world that had a shortage of men by women who played the "Lumigraph" as an aphrodisiac. For this single large exposure to the public, Fischinger was awarded the sum of fifty dollars for the use of his masterpiece the "Lumigraph" in this movie "The Time Travelers," which was performed on by actors and actresses, not by Fischinger, and which the Artist's family made sure he had never seen or even read reviews of. After buying the very hard to find VHS of "The Time Travelers" from fifty years ago, it is easy to understand why Fischinger's family didn't want him to see the movie.

    The last time Oskar Fischinger performed in public with his "Lumigraph" was a celebrated event in 1953 at the "San Francisco Museum of Art" during which the Artist's masterpiece was included in a series of "Art in Cinema." The invitation card for this 1953 event describes Fischinger as a "Pioneer" in the synchronization of abstract film and music, and lists seven of the Artist's films from 1922 to 1948 which were screened before the two "Lumigraph" performances by Fischinger, the first accompanied by his own "synthetic sound," and the second performance was made with records playing. Oskar Fischinger's daughter also details a celebrated performance of the "Lumigraph" in 1996 at the Louvre in Paris for the "Poetique de la couleur" ('Poetry of Color') conference, during which Fischinger's wife Elfriede along with William Moritz performed on the "Lumigraph" to a large audience who were "charmed" at the Louvre. During the "Optische Poesie" show in Frankfurt during 1993, Fischinger's "Lumigraph" was performed on publicly by the Artist's wife, daughter, and William Moritz, and again in 2007 Barbara Fischinger performed on the first "Lumigraph" at the "Deutsches Filmmuseum" in Frankfurt, Germany. Fischinger's daughter also remembers playing the third "Lumigraph" in the "Goethe Institute" in Los Angeles. This third "Lumigraph" was constructed in 1969, after the Artist's death in 1967, and was also built by Fischinger's son Conrad because the gears connecting the four sides of the second "Lumigraph" were worn out and couldn't be replaced. This third "Lumigraph" had more light power, which enabled it to be filmed, was slightly smaller, and had an automated foot pedal to turn gears allowing it to be performed on by just one person. The original first "Lumigraph" was purchased in the late 1980s by the "Duetsches Filmmuseum" in Frankfurt, where Fischinger's daughter Barbara performed on it in 2007, and the second and third "Lumigraphs" remain in California. Barbara Fischinger also remembers a famous Laurel Canyon neighbor in Wonderland Park who met her father and who obviously must have been fascinated by performances on the "Lumigraph" by Oskar Fischinger, Timothy Leary(!)

In conclusion, Barbara Fischinger does not see her father's masterpiece the "Lumigraph" as a simple "Color Organ," but as an interactive light instrument, which she describes as being spontaneous as well as being an instrument that allows the performer to "create" directly as they play the instrument. Unfortunately none of the three "Lumigraphs" of Oskar Fischinger were exhibited during the 2012-2013 Fischinger show in Amsterdam, but there was a permanent video installation of the 16mm Color film made of Elfriede Fischinger playing the "Lumigraph" in 1969.

The event that occurred during the last day of the "Oskar Fischinger: Experiments in Cinematic Abstraction" exhibition in the "Eye Filmmuseum and Center for Visual Music" of Amsterdam, which went on from December 16, 2012 until March 17, 2013 - this event during the last moments of the last day of this exhibition on March seventeenth was an event that this Artist will never forget, and again, it was an event which undeniably proved what I have deeply believed all my life. It is indeed rare that a person witnesses before their eyes unequivocal proof of something so important to them, but such an event happened right before my eyes during the last moments of an exhibition which by itself made a profound impression on me. Taken directly from the single piece of paper I quickly scribbled on in the darkness of the last hall in this Amsterdam Fischinger exhibition: "On the closing day of the Oskar Fischinger exhibition in the "Eye" Filmmuseum in Amsterdam the full effects of visual dynamism and altering of consciousness - as well as physical brain waves - was witnessed by this author during the last hour of the show." To replicate the dramatic setting of this event, Michèle and I were speaking quietly in the final very large dark hall of the Oskar Fischinger exhibition about our impression of this incredible Visionary Artist. This was the fourth and final hall of the exhibition, in which five of Fischinger's Visionary full Color films were being projected on a huge scale simultaneously in this large space. The first hall of the exhibition was a direct projection of one of Fischinger's early and most dynamic films, "Spirals," which was immediately recognizable as the predecessor of Op Art. Each hall of this exhibition was dark and contained between three and eight Fischinger films being projected simultaneously, with the second hall being a long space with three large projections of early abstract Fischinger films in Black and White being played simultaneously next to each other. The third hall had three full Color Fischinger films also playing simultaneously on the three walls of this triangular hall, and this fourth and final hall of the Fischinger show, being larger than the first three halls combined, was the crescendo of what could be called a "visual experience." Upon entering the large dark forth hall there were two different "Stereo Paintings" by Fischinger on the wall with visitors starring at their fingers placed at arm's length in between themselves and one of these "Stereo Paintings," which as directed and explained, created a third floating image in mid-air before your eyes - like a magic hologram. Next to the pair of "Stereo Paintings" was a projection of a Color Fischinger film, and opposite this Color film being constantly projected was another screen in the middle of the dark hall with another Color film of Fischinger's being simultaneously and continuously played. At the same time, on the other half of this final hall of the Fischinger exhibition was the simultaneous projection of three more of Fischinger's Color films on just as large a scale as all of the other projected films in the exhibition, and at the final hall's exit were two benches in front of two small monitors playing very late Black and White examples of Fischinger's film work, one of which being the 1950s animation for an American children's cereal commercial for television. It was on these two benches - at the very end of the entire Oskar Fischinger exhibition - that this event occurred, which I will never forget for the rest of my life, and which in the end was the unforgettable and undeniable event that inspired the writing of this section on Oskar Fischinger. Again, directly from the single piece of paper I was scribbling on in the dark hall: "A man was sitting in front of two Black and White screens showing Oskar Fischinger's psychedelic animation - surrounded by a huge darkened hall of Fischinger's Color animation films - when all of a sudden he had a <u>FIT</u> - he fell from the bench onto the floor and was paralyzed on the left side for some minutes - he was crying out - "OH OH" - people gathered around him in the dark and I asked him if he was Epileptic - he was <u>Normal</u> and this never happened to him before(!) Hari Ram Ram - True 3D Sensurround Proof of the strength of the <u>Image</u>." As this all began, Michèle and I were speaking very low, discussing the impact of this 'Fischinger exhibition/ experience' in the semi-darkness of this final huge hall of the show when all of a sudden about ten meters (yards) in front of us one of the visitors sitting on the benches in front of the final two monitors at the exit of the exhibition space began to make a noise a little louder than speaking - "Uh, Uh" - what we thought was some young people fooling around, and we continued talking. Gradually over the course of like half a minute the volume of the visitor's "Uh, Uh" became louder and then he nearly started shouting "OH, OH!!" At this point Michèle and I were frozen solid and starring directly at this darkened silhouette of a man first sitting on this bench in the dark in front of the Fischinger animation monitors, and then before our eyes he fell in a horizontal position - like a beam of wood - to the floor of the exhibition hall from the bench while desperately screaming "OH, OH, OH!!!" I could literally fell the hair standing up on my neck as we both stood in shocked amazement at the spectacle unfolding before our eyes in the dark! Honestly my first thought was to take my 3D camera out and film this unique event, but compassion took over and I began to quickly walk with Michèle to this visitor of the Fischinger exhibition literally having a fit on the floor in front of us while desperately shouting! Again, I asked directly into his face on the floor if he was an Epileptic, who are well known to have their brain waves very easily disturbed and disrupted by extreme visual stimulation - like the Fischinger exhibition - but he said no, as a small crowd gathered around him writhing on the floor in the darkness of the Fischinger exhibition hall. The memory of this man lying on the floor with the wildest wide-opened eyes starring directly into the void will never fade. I suggested someone call an emergency number and send for an ambulance, but after several minutes this visitor who had been completely paralyzed on the left side of his body lying on the exhibition floor began to have feeling in his body again and could be helped off the floor and out of the darkened Fischinger exhibition hall through the exit door just some footsteps away, and to a chair in normal daylight right outside this exit. Michèle went with this visitor and the others, helping him get to a chair in normal lighting, without video being projected anywhere, then to a glass of water, while I scribbled frantically in the semi-darkness of this final hall of the exhibition on my single piece of paper documenting my immediate impression of this truly unforgettable experience we witnessed directly in front of us. As I wrote before, this event was nothing less than unequivocal, concrete three-dimensional proof of what I have personally known all my life, being that the strength and undeniable altering ability of the Image is not only mentally life-changing, but actually (as I asked Dr. Hofmann several times) is absolutely Physiological, with enough power to consequently throw a two meter tall man horizontally from his bench in the dark and cause him to shout "OH, OH!!" as he felt himself absolutely paralyzed on the entire left side of his body! This man was about thirty years old, was not Epileptic or sick in any way, and he told Michèle that nothing like that had every happened to him before in his life, but that he was tired from rehearsing the several previous days with an orchestra on his violin. Being an Artist my degree of compassion is real, but limited, and honestly I am eternally grateful for having witnessed such a proof through such an event, and my only regret is that I didn't preserve any video of this event. It's hard for people to believe that imagery - no matter how extreme or inexperienced to the viewer - could not only cause a person to have a physiological mental collapse - or something close to an Epileptic seizure - but could also physically paralyze a person! This strong man taller than me was thrown to the floor in a horizontal position - like a rag doll - and lay paralyzed throughout half of his body, giving the observer (myself) the convincing impression that he was about to leave his body in front of me right at that moment. Hari Om - as I wrote before I am eternally grateful to having been a direct witness to this great event, even the minute details of which I will surely never forget.

As the current author was completing the eighth year of writing this 'Black light history,' he was also direct witness to unequivocal proof of the impact of his Fluorescent Art. Three days ago during the 2015 Easter weekend with the Museum full and many visitors in the Fluorescent "Participatory" Environment, an English visitor about twenty years old walked down the entrance steps of the Museum, turned left, walked slowly into my Fluorescent "Participatory" Environment containing thirty-two cubic meters of extremely Fluorescent Color under one-thousand watts of Black light, and then in front of a crowd of Museum visitors he fell onto the floor of the Fluorescent Environment on his back with his eyes wide open - unconscious(!) He looked like Robert Kennedy on the floor with wide-opened staring eyes. I thought he was fooling around or something like that, but both his hands began shaking and he honestly scared the hell out of every Museum visitor (as well as myself). I quickly went to his side on the floor of the Fluorescent "Participatory" Environment and began speaking to him, trying to bring him back to life. After only about two minutes I could get him conscious again asking him questions, and then helped him off the floor and out of the environment to a cushion seat in the subdued light of the demonstration half of the Museum, which I put under the subterranean window to get him some fresh air. I ran upstairs to grab him a glass of water from the gallery, and he slowly came back. As he was sitting under the window getting fresh air and drinking the glass of water, and while still slightly shaking and recovering, I shook his hand and directly thanked him for the strongest reaction to my Fluorescent Art that I have ever seen(!) Although this Museum visitor's reaction was nothing compared to the near-seizure that Michèle and I witnessed during the closing of the Oskar Fischinger exhibition two years ago, it was without exception just like I told him = the strongest reaction to my Art that I have ever seen in my life, which I am also extremely thankful to have been witness to.

I have described the Fluorescent Artwork and inspiration from Michèle Delage, who I have shared the wonders of life with for the past thirty years, and who's eccentric, eclectic Fluorescent painting, collage, and sculpture has fascinated as well as inspired me for these last thirty years, and who is by far my favorite living Artist. Literally from the very first moment I saw Michèle in June, 1986, I have been transfixed. In Art, as equally in life itself, Michèle has an almost infinitely open mind, and in regards to Concepts of Art her vision is comparable for me to Artists such as Robert Rauschenberg and Marcel Duchamp.

Two other Artist's works have to be documented in this book as well, considering the dedication that went into their creations. The first is an Artist I know for about ten years in Philadelphia, who is a true character and has built for the last thirty years the "Philadelphia Magic Gardens." Isaiah Zagar created a huge environment which glimmers and sparkles as you walk through it's space. For decades he has been creating incredible Art installations around the city of Philadelphia, with the "Magic Gardens" being a multi-floored and open-air experience composed of countless collaged sections of mosaic, pieces of glass, metal found objects of every description, stone, mortar, plastic, and every other substance known to humanity - all interwoven with thousands of pieces of mirrors(!) In December, 2015, during my yearly visit to Isaiah Zagar and his incredible "Magic Gardens" something happened that was extraordinary (as well as being another prophetic example of "Qu'est-il arrive au miracle?" - 'What Happened to the Miracle?') It was a day of celebration first of all, because about the twentieth person after I entered the "Magic Gardens" was the much-anticipated 100,000th visitor. Sitting in the video room at the back of the museum with Isaiah Zagar and discussing our separate visits to the visionary "Palais Ideal" of Postman Cheval in south France, another visitor came in and sat down. Being all originally from Brooklyn, New York we began to talk together. This very common man was about sixty-five years old, in between Isaiah at seventy-five and myself at fifty-eight, and was well dressed in a suit with a yamaka on top of his very short snow-White hair. As we talked together, on the video in front of us flashed a photo of Isaiah Zagar in 1969 with long hair and a headband, which caused a reaction from this very straight sixty-five year old visitor that was necessary to include in this book. This heavyset White haired man wearing a traditional yamaka was the picture of a retired American, which made his comments all the more touching. He looked at Isaiah and myself and said in very soft, almost whispering words, with an obvious feeling of reverence, that he couldn't believe what had happened in contemporary times in regards to his own and everyone else's infinite visions during the 1960s Movement. He said, 'You know we all thought that the world was going to be changed *Forever* during the 1960s, that life was never going to be the same again after that period when the whole world and everybody's consciousnesses seemed to be radically converted to an understanding of personal 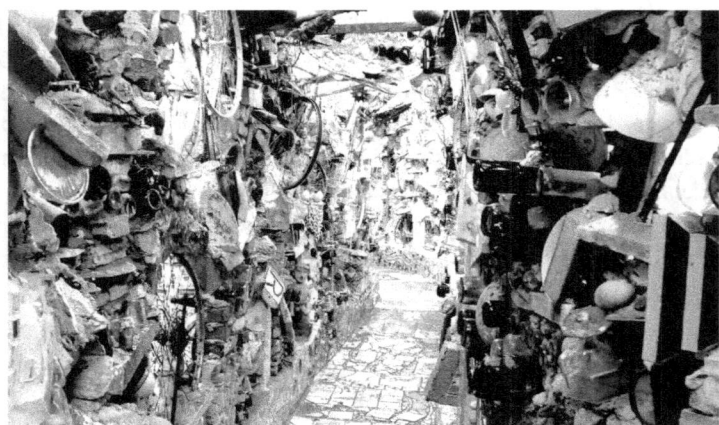 and social interaction, including the universe around us.' Nearly with tears in the eyes of this retirement-age American man, he looked around and concluded in soft tones of reverence, 'What Happened? We thought the world was going to be changed forever in the 1960s, but today it seems that life has gone back to nearly the same commercial life as all the time before the 1960s.' His emotional reaction touched me very deeply as he spoke in his soft voice, like he was in church or delving into something he not only respected, but also did not want others to hear him talking about. This sixty-five year old man became so emotional over the realization towards the end of his life that all the dreams of permanently changing the world to a better place, which was an integral part of the 1960s Movement - all of these dreams did not come true, and there in front of us he had to finally admit this to himself. Quite honestly, this heavyset, White haired, well dressed American man wearing a yamaka looked to be nearly on the verge of tears as he softly and slowly came to finally admit these truths to both himself, as well as to Isaiah and myself. I added in agreement my own observation, being that when you go through life today in 2015 and look around yourself - at this gentrified super-consumer sociological state of world society including all of it's facets, such as it's total lack of spirituality, it's fetish for wealth and social-standing, and even it's music, Art, and fashions - it's like the 1960s Movement *Never Even Happened!* Sure there have been minuscule changes to the world and to society after the 1960s Movement, but they are simply pitiful compared to the radical projected dreams of a completely changed world after the 1960s. Again, a parallel can easily be made between the projected dreams of a forever altered world after the 1960s - and the projected dreams of NASA at the end of the same period of the 1960s after Neil Armstrong had stepped on the Moon, when it was declared that space explorers would land on Mars by 1980(!)

The second Artist that must be included in this book is someone I heard about back in the 1970s in Art school - 'this Postman long ago who made an incredible sculpture environment by himself out of stone.' In September, 2015 Michèle and I finally made it to this 'incredible sculpture environment' we've talked about since 1986: The "Palais Ideal" of Facteur Ferdinand Cheval (Postman Ferdinand Cheval) in the mountains of Hauterieve, France. This 'incredible sculpture environment' I heard about in the 1970s in reality was inconceivably more amazing than I ever imagined! To begin with, the Artwork is immense - the size of a large two-story rectangular building - eighty-five feet (twenty-six meters) long and eight to ten meters (twenty-five to thirty feet) tall - all made by one man out of countless stones he carried every day in his wheelbarrow for miles, and cement.

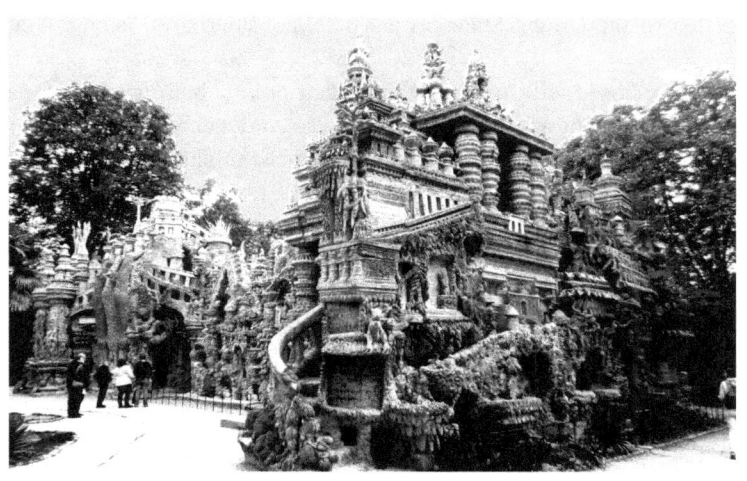

This amazing sculpture took Facteur Cheval thirty-three years to create (!) during which he used about four-thousand bags of cement. Cheval started the enormous sculpture/ environment at the age of forty-three in 1879, and worked on it continuously until 1912, when he was in his 70s. By his own account, Cheval wrote that the "Ideal Palace" took him more than nine-thousands days and sixty- five thousand hours of work to complete. After completing this incomparable "Palais Ideal" he worked on his sculpted tomb for eight more years until he was eighty-six years old! Cheval's sculpture has inspired many Artists since it's creation, including Picasso Max Ernst, Andre Derain, Jean Tinguely, and Larry Rivers, with it's surreal architecture and endless imagery sculpted in stone and mortar. A photograph of Cheval's "Palais Ideal" was also fittingly included in New York's Museum of Modern Art during it's 1936 exhibition "Fantastic Art, Dada, Surrealism." Even after hearing about it so long ago, the visit to Facteur Cheval's "Palais Ideal" far surpassed anything I ever imagined it could be.

Two museums must be included in this writing, which I visited many years apart from each other, which are totally opposite from each other, and correspondingly also made totally opposite impressions on me. The first is a sparkle of a memory from when I was in Art school in 1977 and went with other Artists of my painting class to one of the first "Museum of Holography" in the world down on Mercer Street across from the holy mandir "Pearl Paint" in New York's SOHO. Now for the last seventeen years many visitors have been surprised at the compact size of "Electric Ladyland - the First Museum of Fluorescent Art," but they would have been plum *shocked* if they would have walked into this "Museum of Holography" on Mercer Street in 1977! Without exaggeration in any way, you walked into a very small neon store, and at the very back of this very small neon store with a total space of maybe eight square yards (meters) - completely - was this "Museum of Holography!" As tiny as the space for this "Museum of Holography" was, the impact it made on myself and the other Art students was nothing less than life-changing. I am still there in the tiny back of this neon store in 1977 nearly hypnotized and staring unblinkingly at what must be described as nothing less than a magical apparition - with my mouth open as wide as my eyes along with every other Art student in the back of this dimly-lit neon store! There in front of us, as we crowded around it, was something not one of us had ever seen before: a tiny two-inch (5 cm) brilliant Green woman transparent, totally made of light - and dancing *Ballet!!* This magical mini-Ballerina made only of Green transparent light was dancing before a class of twenty-year old Art students standing in a circle around her - absolutely enraptured. I remember it as clear and with the same intensity as the first time I walked into that Black light 'Mod' clothing stand in the late 1960s! It was nothing less than being in the presence of, and witnessing, a *Miracle*! Again, this was in a museum which was just a little bigger than most people's closets. The other museum I must document was just the opposite of this "Museum of Holography," both in size and impression, and is the "American Visionary Art Museum" in the auspicious setting of Baltimore, Maryland. In 1999 after opening "Electric Ladyland - the First Museum of Fluorescent Art" a very special visitor came into the museum from Baltimore named Harry. This gentle man helped when it was needed most by commissioning a small Fluorescent environment from me. Harry also told me about the "American Visionary Art Museum" he had gone to in Baltimore and spoke of a special collection in this museum. Through emails I wrote to the director of acquisitions in this "AVAM," and surprisingly enough was invited by him to come to the museum that coming December when I would be in the states for two weeks, and show him examples of my Fluorescent Art. That December, 2000 I took the train down to Baltimore for my first (and only) visit there, having an appointment with this AVAM's directors of acquisitions. To be clarified first is what this Baltimore "American Visionary Art Museum" actually considers "Visionary Art," which consists in this multi-leveled modern museum exclusively of Artwork made by permanently institutionalized Autistic patients, the criminally insane, and prisoners permanently incarcerated for violent crimes. In the end, when the director of acquisitions came to meet me on my tour of the museum he was a short stocky

American man wearing a Red football shirt (numbers and all). He brought me up to his office, turned off the light, took one of my Fluorescent and Phosphorescent "Thermal Expansion" paintings I had brought from Amsterdam to show him, switched on the Black light I had also brought - and had nothing less than an absolutely blank look on his face(!) I knew immediately at that point I had just wasted $100.00 on a train ticket to Baltimore, and was not wrong. In the end this "American Visionary Art Museum" is a very good reflection of the United States as a whole, considering "Visionary" as nothing more than mentally disturbed.

This section on Art must be closed with two final important points, both to make a person partially realize that the creation process is the most important part of an Artist's life, and also to document some facts that must be known about Art and Artists. As an example of what the average person who is not an Artist thinks about the act of the creation of Art, as part of the commentary on a 2013 exhibition in London on "Ice Age Art," which showcased some of the earliest known creations of Art on Earth, the presenter asked what is probably the most common question pondered by non-Artists about this seemingly meaningless creation of Art: '*What* Makes People Do These Things??' As a partial response to this most-likely universal question of non-Artists, there is a tribe of Artists in India who's inner belief may serve to partially answer this question 'What Makes People Do These Things?' In Amehederbad, India there is this tribe of Artists going back generations who believe that it is not their choice or desire to make Art, and certainly nothing like their 'career' or 'occupation,' but that it is nothing less than their life's *Destiny* to make their paintings. For the average person who works, reproduces, and lives a normal life it is unimaginable what lengths the aspirations of a Human being can reach. Trying to imagine 'What Makes People Do These Things' is about as easy for the average person as trying to imagine flapping their arms and being able to fly over their house. An extremely definitive example of these lengths passion can drive a person to is embodied in an Italian who was the first person to record moving images on one of the fourteen Himalayan mountain peaks above 8,000 meters. In 1954, the year after Mt. Everest was climbed, the biggest expedition up to that point in time to climb a Himalaya peak numbered over seven-hundred people and was lead by an Italian team. This Italian team became the first to summit "K-2," the second highest mountain in the world, and also the first to take moving images from a peak over 8,000 meters. At the 8,611 meter peak of "K-2," in deadly temperatures averaging around forty degrees below zero, the lead climber Achille Compagnoni was operating the first movie camera ever brought above 8,000 meters, and to operate the camera to the best of his ability Compagnoni took off his gloves and filmed with bare hands. This first movie taken on a Himalayan mountain peak is in Color and is very good quality when viewed today over half a century later, which is because Compagnoni wanted to make the film to the best of his ability, and to accomplish this he decided to take off his mountaineering gloves at 8,611 meters and to film while operating the camera with his bare hands. Serving as a partial answer to this seemingly unfathomable question "What Makes People Do These Things?" his incredible desire to get this first movie footage above 8,000 meters initially caused frostbite, and then cost Achille Compagnoni two of his fingers.

Even though society in mass for the last forty years has never embraced or really accepted the Black light and Fluorescent Colors because of the associations these inventions had through particularly extreme periods of history during the last century, it must be admitted that the attitude of people about twenty or twenty-five years old has changed since 1987 when Michèle and I opened "Electric Lady" Art Gallery in Amsterdam. In 1987, and continuing nonstop for about another full decade, too many visitors would walk into the Art gallery which is totally comprised of Fluorescent paintings and Artwork and say 'Wow, back to the Sixties.' It took years for visitors to the Art gallery to stop saying that, and it wasn't, I realized after much contemplation as well as much conversation with Michèle, because the Fluorescent Artwork or anything else that later visitors saw in the Art gallery had changed - but it was because the visitors themselves had changed. By the year 1999 when Michèle and I opened "Electric Ladyland - the First Museum of Fluorescent Art" beneath the Art gallery, visitors who were twenty years old hadn't even been born until 1979, and had grown up in the 1990s. These visitors did not associate the Art gallery containing Fluorescent Artwork on all four walls under rows of Black lights with the "Sixties," because they weren't even born then - or any time soon after. Twenty or twenty-five year old visitors to the Art gallery and the Museum since the late 1990s do not immediately associate the Black light and Fluorescent Colors with the 1960s anymore, and it has thankfully at least for the younger unstigmatized people - gone back to the way it should be, with people appreciating the intensity of the Colors themselves - only - without too much sociological baggage attached.

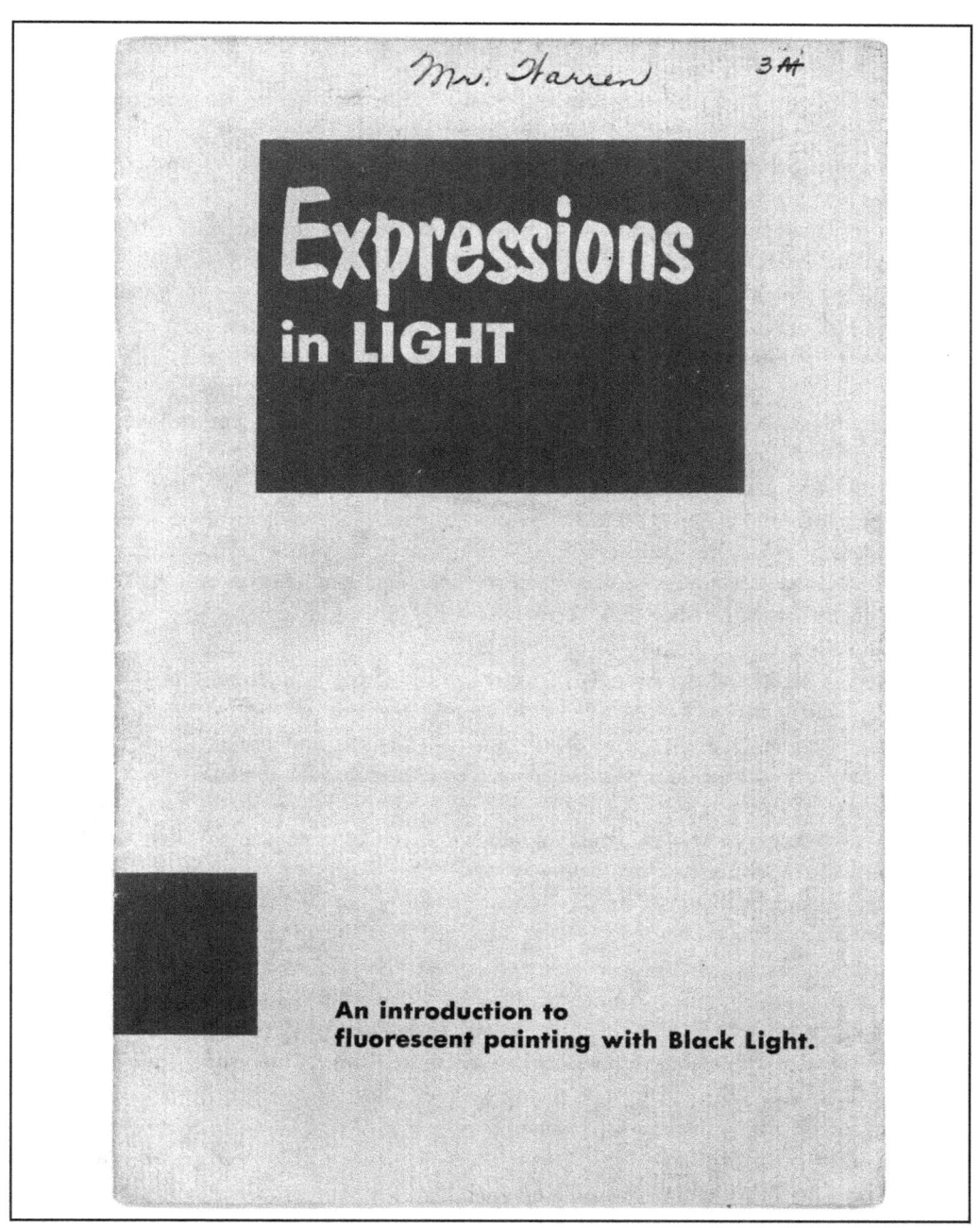

"Expressions in LIGHT: An Introduction to fluorescent painting with Black Light," Ultra-Violet Products, Inc. (1950s)

      For the conclusion of this long history of "Fluorophobia," during an era one and a half decades into the Twenty-first century when it is all too painfully clear that the dreams of the "Golden Age of Fluorescence: 1930s-1950s" which clearly and quite logically predicted that Fluorescent Colors would not only revolutionize the Art world, but would also revolutionize the entire world itself, did not in any shape, form, or way, actually happen. The era which dreamed about all Artists finally being able after countless millennia to paint with "Living Light" - Light-emitting paint - and in this way being able to not just *imitate* the light of nature in their Art, but being able to literally *reproduce* this light, did not in any way happen, nor is it predictable that this era's dreams of the world of Art being magically transformed by Fluorescent Color will come to be any time in the near-future. In the reality of today's stark existentialism, those dreams of the Art world being magically transformed by

Fluorescent Colors nearly overnight are about as far from reality as NASA's published, and just as logical, plans and endeavors for manned missions by 1980 landing on Mars(!)

To epitomize that "Golden Age of Fluorescence: 1930s-1950s" and all it's aspirations and nearly impossible-to-imagine planned dreams, a small, simple artifact directly transported from that era has been saved to purposefully be inserted at the end of this 'History of Fluorophobia' to confirm very lucidly that not only did these aspirations and planned dreams not come true, but that they are nearly absurd to even imagine today in 2016.

This small fourteen page booklet printed by what was the largest Black light producing company in the world, which was originally founded by Thomas S. Warren in 1932, is as precious as it is obviously old (on the cover is printed at the bottom "PRICE 25c"). Immediately recognizable is the 1950's design of the front cover of this four-and-a-half by eight-and-a-half inch (11.5 x 21.5 cm) booklet, with not only three lines of text printed in three different typefaces, but also the choice of typefaces used, especially the common 1950's "Dom Casual" font. The choice of Colors used for this sixty year old booklet on "fluorescent painting with Black Light" have disturbed me since I received this booklet through the mail twenty-five years ago from Thomas S. Warren, being Brown and Black printed on a just as miserable Tan paper, and then White paper with Brown and Black printed throughout the booklet's interior. The front cover has the title printed in a Brown box along with "T. Warren" written by hand in Black ink at the top of the cover, indicating that it was Thomas Warren's personal copy, and the back cover of this booklet has a Black and White photo of the "Ultra-Violet Products, Inc." factory along with a small description of the company. The inside of the front cover of this 1950s booklet begins with a quote from the Artist Laszlo Moholy-Nagy's "Vision In Motion" in which he stated quite accurately (and with poignant similarity to Vincent Van Gogh's quote about the 'future painter') that the 'future's visual work' will be created by what he envisioned as a "light painter." The introduction to "fluorescent painting with Black Light" follows on the inside cover under Moholy-Nagy's quote and retells the story of 'perception being governed by light' and the struggle of Artists 'endeavoring to interpret this natural light' using traditional non-Fluorescent pigments, which are very accurately described in the text of the introduction as being 'incapable for duplicating light,' 'only approximating light's true expression and quality,' and producing a mere 'imitation of nature's radiance.' The booklet's introduction concludes with the announcement that a "new dimension" was now available, which was made possible by the invention of the Fluorescent pigments used to create 'fluorescent paints, inks, crayons, and chalks' that for the first time allows an Artist to paint not only an 'imitation' of nature's light, but with actual "light itself!"

The first page of this booklet's interior text begins with the 'Cause of Fluorescence' being explained as the "emission" of light caused in some natural and synthetic substances through the energy of the "Ultra-Violet" spectrum, especially the part of the "Ultra-Violet" spectrum used to excite 'fluorescent paints and dyes' being "3650 Angstrom Units" known commonly today as "Longwave Ultraviolet" Black light of 366 nanometers. The enthusiasm so apparent universally in publications of this pioneering era is evident as the text continues, explaining graphically that what Fluorescent pigment essentially produces is a surface of "tiny lights" numbering in the "billions." Page four presents "FLUORESCENT MEDIA" and begins with the original choice of using "Visible" or "Invisible" Fluorescent pigments. "Visible" Fluorescent pigments today are referred to as "Daylight Fluorescent Colors," and are explained as being visible in the daylight as well as under Black lights, while "Invisible" Fluorescent pigments (mostly unknown in contemporary times) are explained as being White or even "off-White" in daylight and only producing their vivid Fluorescent Colors when put under a Black light. The five "Fluorescent Medias" described in the booklet are water-based quick drying Fluorescent "Blak-Ray" "Tempera Paints," which can be applied with a 'brush, air brush, or spray gun,' oil-based enamel Fluorescent "Blak-Ray" "Bulletin Paints" also advised to be applied with a brush, air brush, or spray gun,' as well as with a paint 'roller'(!) The next "Fluorescent Media" is listed as Fluorescent "Blak-Ray" "Artist Oils" being sold in 'standard' and 'large' size paint tubes, described as being the most "highly pigmented" of the Fluorescent Medias and to be used the same way as traditional Artist's Oil paints. The last two Fluorescent Medias listed are Fluorescent "Blak-Ray" "Chalks" being produced as "Invisible" Fluorescent Chalks having a White daylight appearance, of which there is a full set from the early 1950s on display in "Electric Ladyland - the First Museum of Fluorescent Art" with it's unbelievable "Use with the Black Light for *CHURCH GROUPS*" printed on it's box top. Last are the twelve "Invisible" Colors of Fluorescent "Blak-Ray" Wax Crayons also available during that time period so many years ago.

What is presented next in this booklet are the "Advantages" of painting with Fluorescent Color, beginning with the stated fact that the eye can see as many as ten times the amount of "shadings" between Colors when using Fluorescent pigments, as well as the three important advantages of using Fluorescent Colors, being listed as first "Contrast," then "Brightness," and finally "Motion." "Contrast" is described as being essential for "depth perception," and explained in this booklet through both the contrast of juxtaposed Colors in the Artwork itself, and the contrast produced by simply mounting a Fluorescent painting on a dark wall. "Brightness" is curiously explained with not an emphasis on the obvious brilliance of the

Fluorescent paints, but on the Fluorescent Artwork's 'relative brightness' in relation to it's presented "surroundings." Typical of the 1950s, and of it's Fluorescent pioneer Thomas S. Warren who wrote to me twenty-five years ago that Fluorescent paints should never be used pure, but used only toned down by adding non-Fluorescent White paint to them(!), it is clearly explained in this booklet produced and most likely written by Thomas S. Warren that Fluorescent Artwork should be displayed under conditions of "dim lighting" suitably found in "restaurants." "Motion" is next described as a "phenomenon" produced in Fluorescent Artwork through the illusion of Fluorescent Colors either 'coming forward' off the painted 'canvas,' or 'receding' into the background of the canvas. It is printed in italics that the 'glow' of Fluorescent Colors "accentuates" this motion phenomenon through the achievement of "increased depth" which is produced simply by the use of Fluorescent Color. Page six of this booklet extends the advantages of using Fluorescent paints to 'Color Mixing Secrets' and describes how mixing Fluorescent Colors differs from mixing traditional non-Fluorescent Colors. This antique booklet quite accurately explains the disadvantages of physically mixing Fluorescent Colors, which I have explained to visitors to the Gallery and to the Museum for the last twenty-nine years. Beginning with the fact that Fluorescent Colors actually create and emit "colored light," not just reflect light like all traditional Colors used since the beginning of time, it is accurately advised not to physically mix complementary Fluorescent Colors such as Yellow and Blue. What is not explained is that Fluorescent Colors are "Additive Colors," with similar reactions to mixing Colors of pure light, like spotlights used for stage performances, which when mixed together produce not Black but a Whitish Color. "Subtractive Colors" are all traditional Color pigments used since humans began painting caves, and just as traditionally all mix together to produce not a Whitish Color, but just the opposite of a Blackish Color. The accurate example given in this 1950s booklet is the mixture of Fluorescent Blue and Fluorescent Yellow, which every school child knows traditionally creates Green, but when using light-emitting Fluorescent Colors, Fluorescent Blue mixed with Fluorescent Yellow produces not traditional Green, but a pale unworldly pastel Color(!) Also explained is the mixture of non-complementary Colors, such as Fluorescent Yellow and Fluorescent Orange, which although produce a traditional Yellow-Orange, it is almost universally a pastel shade of the two separate intense Fluorescent pure Colors. For decades I rarely physically mix Fluorescent Colors, but achieve mixtures of pure Fluorescent Colors through the technique of "layering" these pure translucent Fluorescent Colors on top of each other. Next described in this 1950s booklet is the preferred method of Thomas Warren himself, as he wrote several times to me in the 1990s that an "accomplished artist" almost never uses pure Fluorescent Colors, but somehow toned down to an acceptable level of brilliance. It is clearly stated that pure Fluorescent Colors are only acceptable for use in "high-lighting," 'designing,' and "lettering," and furthermore that the method of painting with Fluorescent Colors in the past has "suffered" by the "frivolous application" of Fluorescent Colors used pure without their brilliant Colors toned down(!) It is further inaccurately and prejudicially stated in this 1950s booklet that what are labelled "Novel effects" produced by using pure un-toned Fluorescent Colors are for the eye 'too much to accept' because of the combination of both the "mass" of emitted pure light, and the 'lack of shadows.' Next, steps are advised to take the pure Colors of Fluorescent paints down to the level of traditional non-Fluorescent paints through the mixing of non-Fluorescent Color with Fluorescent Color(!) Not surprisingly the written example describes how to create a Fluorescent "Brown," advising to mix Fluorescent Orange or Yellow paints with non-Fluorescent traditional 'Ochres or Siennas.' This method, logic would strongly suggest, destroys the obviously disturbing brilliance of the pure Fluorescent Colors, and counter-productively produces a slightly Fluorescent Color not far from the traditional non-Fluorescent pigments used for all of history up until 1933 when Robert Switzer invented Fluorescent Colors. This is a method the current author has always been not only shocked by, but has been in total opposition to (and clearly remembers arguing with Thomas Warren about through written correspondence decades ago). The description as well as the advice for using Fluorescent Colors continues in this booklet with "Brushes," which are described as not being harmed by Fluorescent Colors, but good advice is given to clean Artist's brushes and inspect them under a Black light to make sure they are free of Color. The proper advice of painting Fluorescent Colors on top of a White "undercoating" follows, with further advice not to use an undercoating paint that contains the heavy metal lead, with similar heavy metals such as nickel and cobalt physically destroying or diminishing Fluorescence.

    The next advice in this booklet covers the "High Lighting" and the "Over Painting" of finished paintings, or even prints, with Fluorescent paint. Both "Visible" and "Invisible" Fluorescent paints are advised to be used for over-painting existing pieces of Art, with results described as a picture which would look very similar to the original finished Artwork, but would have a transformed 'unusual rendition' when put under a Black light. "Photographs" are the next subject of transformation presented, with advice to use Black and White photos retouched with "invisible" Fluorescent oil paint. The technique described is to use Fluorescent paint directly on top of large Black and White photo prints in the same manner that "photo-tinting" was done years ago. After retouching Black and White photos "sparingly" with Fluorescent "invisible" oil paint, similar to the last advice of "over-painting" finished paintings with Fluorescent Color, in the daylight these Black and

White photos will look the same as they did, but under a Black light they will be transformed into "unbelievable beauty" with Colors that are "breath taking." It is obvious what sort of transformations were in mind with these overpainting techniques advised in this section of the booklet, because on the facing page eight there is a very rudimentary Black and White illustration of a landscape painting in the daylight first containing a house covered in snow, and then underneath the daylight landscape is the same landscape typically transformed into a night scene complete with a half Moon in the night sky. The last advice of this booklet's section is a paragraph about 'Painting with a Black light,' in which it is first advised to set the studio's condition to similar lighting conditions that the painting will be displayed in the White light. For painting the same pieces of Art with Fluorescent Colors it is advised to not only obviously have a Black light, and to paint under it's "rays," but to also have a White light which could occasionally be switched on to compare the White light painting and the Black light "effects." It is further advised that the "Blak-Ray" Black light made by "Ultra-Violet products, Inc," should be the same which would be used to eventually display the finished piece of Fluorescent Art, and furthermore that the eventual positioning of the Black light for the completed painting should be identical to the positioning of the Black light used for painting the piece of Art.

One of the points that originally turned many Artists away from Fluorescent paint is the next proudly announced "Technique" not surprisingly from the businessman Thomas Warren's company "Ultra-Violet Products, Inc." in this 1950s booklet. This original gimmick used to first promote the use of Fluorescent Colors was the common effect of "Changing" a painting typically from Day into Night, but also used for many different "Change" effects. The son-in-law of Thomas Warren, Thomas Goff, who was not an Artist but an office worker for the Red-Cross, was also an early experimenter of this effect in the 1950s. Thomas Goff painted landscapes with traditional oil Colors, then added a layer of "Invisible" Fluorescent paint to create a painting which was "Autumn" in the daylight, and which would then transform itself into a dazzling Summer scene when the painting was put in the dark under a Black light, and finally would change a third time into a Winter scene with snow on the ground when a Shortwave Ultraviolet lamp was turned on. Thomas Goff also copied directly from the inventor of the first Longwave Ultraviolet "Black light" filter in 1903 Dr. Robert Wood, and made the transforming paintings "Chimp-Pansy" and "Crow-Cus" which need no explanation. Thomas Goff's final series of "Changing" Fluorescent paintings involved as much his 1950s state-of-mind as his karma, because he died whilst working on his last series "Blushing Brides," which display clearly the very limited 1950s imagination he had. This final series of "Changing" Fluorescent paintings by Thomas Goff were of women dressed in wedding gowns in the White light, then typically when put under a Black light were nude except for their underwear, and finally when the same paintings were put under a Shortwave Ultraviolet lamp, this series of "Blushing Brides" were reduced to Fluorescent Skeletons!

'Changing Effects' is the title of the following section in this 1950s booklet, and begins directly with the advice for use of the essential "Invisible" Fluorescent paint. "Numerous possibilities" are boasted of through the use of this "Invisible" Fluorescent paint overlaid on top of both "Visible" Fluorescent paints as well as "ordinary" paint. Further advice is given to use this "Invisible" Fluorescent paint on a plain White surface, so in the daylight the "invisible" scene painted with "invisible" Fluorescent paint would "Disappear," and in this way would create an Artwork containing 'two different scenes' painted over each other with two different paints, described as a 'concept that was entirely new.' This "concept" - or gimmick - is next hailed in this little booklet from sixty-five years ago with it's section not surprisingly entitled 'Changing From Night to Day.' The most common gimmicks of this advice are listed in order, with 'day to night changes' in Fluorescent paintings of course including campfires being lit up in the Black light which are obviously not lit up in the same hokey painting under the White light, the Moon itself could "come out" suddenly from a transformed night scene of a daylight landscape, or even the cosmic advice for "lamps" being lit up under the Black light in a painting which is just as obviously a daylight landscape in the White light. Directly stated next is that this type of Fluorescent "Changing" paintings were very applicable for decoration in "Restaurants," and furthermore that a "rheostat control" which was "motor-driven" should be used in these Restaurant decorations of "Changing" Fluorescent paintings so that a gradual change would occur on these "Changing" Fluorescent paintings over the course of five to ten minutes, further advising that this technique would 'increase the interest' of the "Fluorescent picture." Today there is still a successful Artist painting in exactly the same tradition of 'Changing paintings' from the 1950s, Gary Fenske.

Towards the end of this short 1950s booklet, on pages eleven and twelve is the section 'Drama, Depth, and Design,' which once more begins with the advice for creating "Changing" Fluorescent scenes with "Invisible" Fluorescent paints for both decorating the home and office. Advice is given for painting off-White "panel designs" of Green and Brown stems on walls, which would then burst into fully bloomed stems when a Black light was turned on, creating an "effect" for the home or office described as "truly remarkable." It is further advised that these "truly remarkable" home or office "effects" could be 'modern, abstract, or oriental.' Accompanying this section on 'Home Drama through the use of Fluorescent Colors' are miserable Brown and Black illustrations which not only reek of the 1950s era in both their design and execution, but are on nearly every page of this booklet. First explained is the technique of using Fluorescent Color and Black lights for "Stone Surfaces," and for which it is advised that Fluorescent paint could be applied to fireplaces, fountains, rock ponds, walls, or even patio floors, and either for use indoors or outside. It is proposed that "Invisible" Fluorescent paint be used along with large, concealed Black lights, with further advice to create "breathtaking beauty" given, including even the technique of the application of Fluorescent paint used for the 'Home's Stone Surfaces' being the long-loved "Spatter technique" which also needs no explanation. "Mobiles" that Fluoresce is the next section on 'Fluorescent Home Drama,' in which it is advised that in "modern homes" Mobiles were enjoying "increased popularity" both indoors and out of doors, and could create additionally a quality described as "un-attached floating" when made with Fluorescent paint and Black lights. "Glowing Decorations" follows 'Glowing Mobiles,' and gives further advice to coat ceramics or 'dresden type statues' with Fluorescent paint to be displayed "dramatically" under a Black light spotlight. 'Fluorescent Tempera paint' with a clear glaze is advised for coating the home's "Glowing Decorations," and in this way Fluorescent ceramic, plaster statues, or even "bric-a-brac" could be magically transformed into 'functional and interesting television lights.' Another idea to create a Fluorescent 'Dramatic Home' is given, with advice for painting the home's lamp bases with Fluorescent Color and then concealing a Black light in the lamp's shade. Two additional small sections of Fluorescent advice close this two page section on 'Fluorescent Homes,' the first with advice for creating Fluorescent "Mosaics" through the method of 'touching up' finished Mosaics with either invisible or visible Fluorescent paint, and the second being a personal favorite of Thomas S. Warren himself: "Christmas Decorations." It is stated that a "free bulletin" was available at that time explaining the use of 'prize-winning Fluorescent Christmas Decorations.'

The final two pages of this 1950s booklet 'Introduction into Painting with Fluorescent Colors and Black Light,' printed by the biggest manufacturer of Black lights at that time, "Ultra-Violet Products, Inc." and it's founder Thomas S. Warren, not surprisingly concludes with the section "Commercial Emphasis." Just as not surprisingly this final "Commercial Emphasis" begins not with Art itself, but with the spiritual endeavor of "Advertising." It is clearly stated in the very first sentence of this section that the Black light has been a big help to both small and large commercial 'advertisers.' The first advantage promoted is that with traditional large billboards of the past the light illuminating these billboards would also illuminate surrounding "undesirable objects" such as 'trees or construction areas,' but through the modern use of Fluorescent Color and Black lights, only the "advertisement itself" would be illuminated, and in this way concentrating the full attention of potential customers. For an even more efficient "attention getter" further advice is given in this "Advertising" section for using a combination of both Black lights and White lights on not only billboards, but also for "point-of-sale" advertising in which two different messages or images could be used on a single advertisement, that would then create a changing and moving Advertising image. This is all too clearly displayed in the "Invisible" Fluorescent "Beer Advertisement" from Thomas Warren's company in the 1950s displayed in the Museum. Advice is also given for extending the use of Fluorescent paint and Black lights to the areas of 'trade shows' or 'window displays' with the clear intention being to 'spotlight and create interest in the shown products.' "Visual Education" with the use of Fluorescent Colors and Black light follows "Advertising," and in this section it is advised for both 'industry and education.' To use these Fluorescent Colors and Black lights as a 'teaching tool,' advice is given for 'Artistic mastering of design layout, lettering, and Art work.' The section of "Visual Education" ends with an obscure explanation of spotlighting important parts or areas of a "Machine Tool" to "gain emphasis" with Fluorescent paint.

Again, not coming as a big shock, the *very last paragraph* in this "Ultra-Violet Products, Inc." Thomas S. Warren 1950s booklet is on Fluorescent "Paintings" and also "Murals." Don't get the wrong idea and begin thinking about Art in Galleries and Museums, because this last section on 'Fluorescent Paintings' starts directly with advice on using 'Fluorescent Paintings' in 'Restaurants, Homes, and Bars.' Not only is Fluorescent Art plainly labelled "Black art" in this same initial sentence of this booklet's final section, but it is also written that the 'largest commercial application' of "Black art" was for the aforementioned 'Restaurants, Homes, and Bars.' "Many" of which in this booklet are called "better restaurants" across America are next announced to have been "proud owners" of these Fluorescent paintings, that are explained to have been used best in "dimly lit" atmospheres in which the Fluorescent paintings glow alone would have been the only source of illumination used in these restaurants or bars. This booklet's last section ends with the promotional advice that once people had seen the Fluorescent painting's "effect," there is almost a "universal" desire to also own their own Fluorescent Mural or Painting and Black light as well.

As with a very large amount of artifacts and antiques of the era of the "Golden Age of Fluorescence: 1930s-1950s," many of the dreams, ideals, and just ordinary ideas for applications of the Black light and Fluorescent Colors are nearly impossible to imagine today in 2016 - "Use With the Black Light for: CHURCH GROUPS" (!!) is a perfect example of how dramatically and seemingly irreversibly the social outlook on Fluorescent Colors and Black lights have changed since that "Golden Age of Fluorescence" all those years ago.

The one-century history of the Back light and Fluorescent Colors could be realized clearly in a condensed form as in the beginning being introduced to the fascination of these vivid Colors Fluorescing under Black lights which were used in a small way for entertainment as well as Art, but actually beginning in a large way with the Industrial era of it's usage, especially it's massive use during the Second world war when millions of Black lights and an ocean of Fluorescent Colors were manufactured for, and used by, the military. After the Second world war ended many of the companies manufacturing Black lights and Fluorescent Colors couldn't sell anything anymore, so they began marketing these "Day-Glo" Colors and Black lights to children in the early 1950s (one of many good examples of this is the 1952 "BLACK LIGHT MAGIC" set "For Ages 8 - 15" on page 91). These children who were "Ages 8 - 15" during the 1950s grew up and many of them then became known as the "Hippies" ten years later during the 1960s.

Inspired by the predictions for the future by Sterling Gleason in his 1960 conclusion of "Ultraviolet Guide to Minerals," in which he envisions 'gigantic Ultraviolet lamps' to examine the universe around us with, the current author's visions are based more on Art than mineralogy. Imagining the future of Art intermingled with advances in technology is not a stretch of the imagination today, and in recent years the discovery of what is termed "Smart Dust" possibly contains this connectivity. "Smart Dust" is made with a specific nanostruture that gives it the unique ability to change Colors. Nano-sized pores carved into a wafer of Silicon-carbon gives this "Smart Dust" it's unique ability to change it's Color as a reaction to the pressure of different chemicals. Now imagine this "Smart Dust" being produced or ground fine enough to be used as the pigment for making paint! And further, imagine this "Smart Dust" being created to be Ultraviolet-reactive, or "Fluorescent," and also being used as a Fluorescent paint pigment containing the unique ability to change the Color of it's Fluorescence in the presence of different chemicals - I personally can't wait! It's almost enough to wish to live in the coming unimaginable future. Similar dreams are also becoming a reality with another very recent advancement in technology called "Claytronics," in which programmable matter can become any shape or any Color. This new technology "Claytronics" has been called a "3D Fax machine" because objects can be transmuted and replicated with different shapes and Colors.

A pigment available today can perhaps point a direction into the future of pigment possibilities, and it's known as "Thermochromic" paint. This amazing pigment changes Color when it's heated and, similar to Fluorescent Colors in their early days, this miraculous Thermochromism has been used mostly for commercial and industrial purposes, with limited use in Art. Thermochromic paint can make Color images appear, and then just as quickly disappear before your eyes in seconds, because this paint contains Liquid crystals which are made up of pin-shaped particles that are aligned randomly at room temperature, and this makes the surface of the paint opaque because light gets reflected off of it. When the same Colored Thermochromic paint is heated over eighty degrees (26 C) the pin-shaped particles within the Liquid crystal of the paint align themselves, and by doing so light can pass through the paint and the Color image under the Themochromic paint is suddenly clearly visible. When the temperature again drops under eighty degrees this 'invisible' Thermochromic paint is just as suddenly again opaque and back to the original Color of the Thermochromic paint that was applied on top of the Color image underneath it. Another cruder Thermochromic effect can be obtained with materials coated with "Leucodyes," which can only measure the extremes 'hot' and 'cold' and are unable to measure subtle variations in temperature changes that Thermochromic Liquid crystal technology can achieve. These "Leucodyes" are currently used even to make "Hypercolor" T-shirts that change Color when touched. Dreams like turning "Smart Dust" into a paint pigment capable of changing Colors are quickly becoming a reality during the current era. In 2009 researchers of the Oregon State University discovered the first new formula for an inorganic Blue Color in more than two-hundred years. The new Blue pigment is not only a different Blue Color than was ever made before, but it also has a unique quality that is a partial solution to the contemporary movement of much needed energy conservation. This new Blue inorganic pigment can be coated on houses and cars in the near future because the bonus property of this new Blue is that it reflects heat, keeping houses and cars cooler in the Sun than with other traditional paints. This Blue pigment is created not as a common liquid paint, but as a powder which is then used to coat objects. This new Blue was reported on in the February, 2013 "National Geographic" magazine, with details of the 2,350 degrees fahrenheit production of this stabile Blue pigment. This heat-resisting Blue paint discovered in Oregon State University is made with only the three simple ingredients of Manganese, Indium oxides, and Yttrium, yet amazingly not being a common "dye" composed of organic compounds used as the paint pigment, this new heat-resisting Blue pigment will never fade either. As can easily be imagined the small article in "National Geographic" ends with the news that both car and building manufacturers are crazy to get a various shade of this new Blue pigment to achieve the contemporary dream of lowering their product's "energy cost." Mas Subramanian, one of the materials chemists who discovered this new Blue pigment admits that White paint has the greatest efficiency for reflecting solar radiation, but White is not just difficult to keep looking good, it also doesn't look as beautiful as Blue does.

What is truly amazing is that a new extremely high-tech 'paint' has been recently invented specifically for the purpose of protecting Solar Probes in space from the heat of the Sun - and that this Twenty-first century space agency's 'paint' is made of the exact same pigment that the truly ancient human Art - Cave Paintings - were made with: Crushed Animal Bones! Crushed animal bones have been used for pigment not only for the earliest human Cave art, but also by Artists including Rembrandt for many centuries. This newly developed "ENBIO" "SolarBlack" 'paint' is to be used by space agencies for coating the essential heat shields on both Solar probes and Solar orbiters. This oldest human paint pigment - Crushed Animal Bones - is now used to coat heat shields on cutting-edge Twenty-first century spacecraft, because what was needed was a substance that can both absorb heat and then reemit as much as possible of this heat. This "ENBIO" "SolarBlack" is to be used as the outer layer of the heat shields, which is followed by many more layers underneath it composed of titanium and other substances. On the website of "ENBIO" the details of this "SolarBlack" are explained. This "SolarBlack" coating was developed specifically for the 2017 launch of the European Space Agency's Solar Orbiter, which will observe the Sun from a closer distance than has ever been attempted, so for the spacecraft's large heat shield of 3.1 by 2.4 meters a "next generation" heat resistance was needed. "ENBIO" collaborated with Airbus Defense & Space and ESA starting in 2011 to create this new "SolarBlack," which is not called a 'paint,' but a "CoBlast Skin." The "ENBIO" website not surprisingly does not announce that this high-tech "SolarBlack" is made out of primitive crushed animal bones, but states simply the identical chemical components as "calcium phosphate." Another newly developed 'paint' created for international space agencies is made not of organic crushed animal bones, but out of one of the most technologically advanced substances of the Twenty-first century: Carbon nanotubes. Both this 'paint' as well as the "SolarBlack" were demonstrated upon and explained in March, 2015 on "BBC's" "Stargazing Live 2015," with this new Carbon nanotube space agency 'paint' being the "Blackest Black" paint ever produced. This "Blackest Black" 'paint' can scatter light so efficiently that only ten-million-millionths of the light remains when instruments are coated with this new 'paint' compared to the amount of natural scattering of light. This new space agency 'paint' has been developed specifically to coat the extremely sensitive optical instruments also on Solar probes and Solar orbiters. This new "Blackest Black" spacecraft 'paint' is amazing, and when demonstrated upon it looks nearly like a magic trick. A wrinkled sheet of aluminum is coated at it's center with this "Blackest Black" 'paint,' and although the many folds of the uncoated wrinkled aluminum can be easily seen, the center area of the wrinkled aluminum sheet that is coated with the Carbon nanotube 'paint' amazingly looks like a "Black Hole" with not a wrinkle, fold, or sign of reflection visible.

Lucio Fontana, "Spatial Environment in Black Light"   (1948-1949)

The final well known Artist reviewed in this book who has created Fluorescent Art is one of the most respected of all these Artists covered here, Lucio Fontana. Not only was Lucio Fontana just the second documented Artist to create Fine Art with Fluorescent paint under Black lights in 1948 to 1949, just three or four years after John Ludlum used Fluorescent paint in Fine Art for the first time in 1945, but of special note to the Artist writing this book, this first Fluorescent Artwork that Fontana created in 1948 to 1949 was also the first time the concept of an "Environment" was used by an Artist. Appropriately included as "Conceptual Revolutions in Twentieth Century Art" by David Galenson, under the "1940s" section of his book it is explained that in 1946 Lucio Fontana began to regard all mediums of his Artwork from paintings and sculpture to architecture as "Spatial concepts." The direction Fontana had was to remove barriers between all the separated schools of Art and to bring forth the point that was important, being the 'mental concept' forming the Art. A new concept of space is what Galenson states was the intention of all the Art Fontana created.

Lucio Fontana (1899 - 1968) was Italian, born in Argentina to a father who was a sculptor, Luigi Fontana, and an Argentinean mother. Fontana lived from 1905 to 1922 in Milan, then returned to Argentina working for several years as a sculptor in the studio of his father. After opening his own studio Fontana exhibited in the city where he was born, Rosario de Santa Fé, Argentina, with young Artists of the city known as the group "Nexus" for their first exhibition. In 1928 Fontana enrolled in Accademia di Belle Arti di Brera for two years after returning to Milan. By 1930 Fontana had his first one man show at the Galleria Il Milione in Milan, and in 1935 the Artist joined the "Abstraction - Creation group" after going to Paris. In 1935 Fontana also began creating ceramic pieces of Art, initially which he had learned in Albisola, Italy, as well as near Paris at the Sèvres factory. Back in Milan the Artist became part of a group formed by expressionistic Artists known collectively as the "Corrente" in 1939. The next year Fontana moved back to Argentina, settling in Buenos Aires and in 1946 he founded the Academia de Altamira with a collection of his students. It was from this Academia that in 1946 the "Manifesto Blanco" group arose. The following year, 1947, the Artist again returns to Milan, collaborating with a group of philosophers and writers of the "Primo Manifesto dello Spazialism" ('The First Manifesto of Spatialism').

Lucio Fontana's Artwork "Ambiente spaziale a luce nera" ('Spatial Environment in Black light') exhibited in February, 1949 was the first piece of Art which introduced the concept of an "Environment" in Art. In "Lucio Fontana" by Sarah Whitfield this revolutionary concept in Art is detailed, beginning with the fact that this was the first "Environment" created by Fontana, and that it was only exhibited for a couple of days in February, 1949 in Milan's Galleria del Naviglio. The reader is lead through this first Art "Environment," entering into a small room and finding themselves confined in what appears to be an enclosed area so dark that it seems to envelop you. Above your head there are several large abstract sculptures floating, which are painted with Fluorescent Colors and suspended under "Wood's light" (Black light). It is explained that this "phosphorescent paint" which was used by Fontana on the sculptures couldn't be found in Italy yet, but in Buenos Aries it had already been used in 'Phosphorescent Ballets.' Two years previous to creating this Fluorescent Environment Fontana had been living in the country where he was born, in Buenos Aires. The sculptures of this Fluorescent Environment under Black lights in February, 1949 are described as being constructed out of paper maché, and the delicate nature of the material may add to the reasons why only one Environment of Fontana's survives today, even though he kept making Environments up until 1968. These Environments ("Ambiente") are known to have been made for exhibitions of his Art, and were put together by the Artist quickly before the show began. What was important to Fontana was the "ephemeral;" the Artist made these Environments to last at the most several weeks, and it could be possible that Fontana made these Environments based upon this very temporary existence. Entering into Fontana's 'Spatial Environment in Black light' exhibited in 1949 is described as an experience which few visitors would ever forget. The existing Color photographs of 'Spatial Environment in Black light' by Fontana are from a reconstruction of his original Environment, a 1976 replica which indicates the work to have been made "1948-1949." These vivid photographs show what appears to be seven individual Fluorescent abstract sculptures suspended from a gallery ceiling in the dark under Black lights. The forms of all the sculptures are organic, giving the impression of cellular life or DNA, with an outer wrinkled surface signatory of paper maché works. A large Fluorescent light Blue form extending arm-like structures in three directions, which is intersected at it's central point with a highly contrasting Fluorescent Red 's'-shaped form, is the largest piece of the Fluorescent sculpture/mobile group. Next to this central large Fluorescent Blue structure, the second largest form of the suspended group is of a more linear shape, and is brilliantly painted in contrasting Fluorescent Green and Orange-Red. Five or Six other smaller forms painted primarily Fluorescent Red or Magenta float at a little distance from the two central larger sculptural forms, and create a very spatial quality with the areas of empty darkness making up the separation.

Besides being the first Artist to introduce the concept of the "Environment" as an Artform in 1949, and being the second Artist to use Fluorescent paint and the Black light for Fine Art in 1948 to 1949, in this same year during the late 1940s the Visionary Artist Lucio Fontana was also the first Artist to imagine exhibiting Art on the Moon or on other celestial bodies after humanity has colonized space and migrated to the stars. Although it has been widely documented that John Plumer Ludlum was the first Artist to use Fluorescent paint for Fine Art in 1945, and although John Plumer Ludlum's Fluorescent masterpiece "Nativity" was the most expensive painting ever sold by a living Artist up until 1973, unfortunately both the Fluorescent master and his Fluorescent masterpiece have been lost to time and history forty-three years later, today in 2016. For both of these reasons the first Artist to have used Fluorescent paint in Fine Art who was internationally known, and who is still internationally known decades after his death, is Lucio Fontana. Just three or four years after John Ludlum used Fluorescent paint for the first time in Fine Art in 1945, in 1948 to 1949 Lucio Fontana created the first "Environment" in Fine Art, this "Spatial Environment in Black Light," an Environment in which Fontana used Fluorescent paint as well as installing a Black light in it.

In the recent 2011 MIT publication "Lucio Fontana: Between Utopia and Kitsch" the Twenty-first century contemporary traditional concept excluding the use of Fluorescent Color and Ultraviolet lamps in Fine Art is not only upheld, but it is also explicitly and vividly reconfirmed as well as culturally recemented by author Anthony White. The opinion of Anthony White, born in 1964, is very evident, both in the title of his book on Fontana, as well as throughout the text of his writing. White's book examines the life and oeuvre of Lucio Fontana, but here the period in which Fontana became the second documented Artist to have used Fluorescent paint and the Black light in Fine Art will be focused upon. In the forth chapter of "Lucio Fontana: Between Utopia and Kitsch" the decade of the 1940s is examined, with a separate section specifically written on Fontana's 1949 "Spatial Environment in Black Light." The author Anthony White's common contemporary prejudicial rejection of both Fluorescent Color and the Black light's use in Fine Art is extremely evident, and goes on to form the structure of his examination. The very first sentence of White's forth chapter covering Fontana's Art between 1940 and 1951, during which he went from 'Sculptures to Environment,' sets the prejudicial tone of the author's common opinion. White lists, with an obvious contemporary disapproval, that in the "environmental works" of Fontana from late in the 1940s and continuing into the early 1950s, "materials" were used by the Artist labelled by White as "flashy" and even *"low-culture"(!)* These both "low-culture" and "flashy" "materials" employed by Fontana are listed by Anthony White beginning with "fluorescent tubing," and then adding 'Fluorescent paint,' which is further cheapened by the author by incorrectly referring to Fluorescent paint using the very common terminology "glow-in-the-dark." In one swift blow (and just one sentence) the author manages to not only demean Fluorescent paint by labeling it with the most common cultural terminology "glow-in-the-dark," but also to describe Fluorescent paint incorrectly as "glow-in-the-dark," which is correctly termed Phosphorescent paint. Fluorescent paint does not "glow-in-the-dark," it converts the energy of the Black light through electron displacement to reemit the invisible Ultraviolet energy as visible Color - it Fluoresces. Phosphorescent paint not only glows under a Black light, but it stores some of the Ultraviolet energy and reemits it when the Black light is turned off - it Phosphoresces, or in common popular language, it "glows-in-the-dark." It's amazing that after the author so maliciously uses the term "low-culture," he himself stoops to using the "low-culture" term "glow-in-the-dark" for correctly termed Fluorescent paint. Of course the author also adds "ultraviolet light" to his first sentence in which he has listed "low-culture" and "flashy" "materials" used by Fontana to create his Art. The section in Anthony White's book centering on Fontana's 1949 "Spatial Environment in Black Light" examines this first Environment created as a piece of Art in detail. Lucio Fontana's "Spatial Environment in Black Light" was installed for a short time in February, 1949 in Milan at the "Galleria del Naviglio." White documents Fontana's 'Black Light Environment' of 1949, just four years after John Plumer Ludlum used Fluorescent paint in Fine Art for the first time, as "intersecting forms" of "papier-mache" which were brightly Colored with "polychrome" early "Fluorescent paint" and which were hanging from the gallery ceiling suspended in the dark. Being painted in Fluorescent Colors and suspended from the ceiling of Milan's "Galeria del Naviglio" under Black light (still called in 1949 "Wood's light") the conclusion by the author is that the "Spatial Environment in Black Light" by Fontana gave off what is labelled by White again using a very popular contemporary descriptive adjective concerning anything Black light or Fluorescent: an "eerie" glow. It is also explained by the author that there are no Color photographs in existence of Fontana's "Spatial Environment in Black Light," but in Fontana's own hand-painted Black and White photograph of the Environment (included in the book) the author describes "unusual coloration." This hand-painted photograph of "Spatial Environment in Black Light" is entitled "Black Environment," and illustrates a Violet space of varying tonal densities with at least three suspended organically shaped forms floating in this space and representing the three primary Colors by being coated in tones of Fluorescent Blues, Yellows, and Reds. The original Black and White photograph of "Spatial Environment in Black Light" is presented on the facing page to Fontana's hand-painted Color version of this Black and White photo, and the 1949 photo truly looks like an antiquated image from almost seventy years ago. Several curved organically shaped forms fill the space of this Environment suspended from the ceiling above the head, including a central large curved form in the shape roughly of a backwards "S." This large central form that Fontana has Colored Fluorescent Blue in his "Black Environment" painted photo contains a central circular area with an open center in which another much smaller organically shaped form also shaped like a backwards "S" has entered the circular opening and is there suspended vertically and perpendicular to the horizontal large central Fluorescent Blue form. This perpendicular smaller form which has entered the central open circular area of the major Fluorescent Blue form is indicated in Fontana's "Black Environment" painted photo as having been Fluorescent Red. The third major organically shaped form making up Fontana's "Spatial Environment in Black Light" looks in the Black and White photo of the Environment to be the highest of the organically shaped objects making up the piece, with this form looking very close to the ceiling and indicated by Fontana in his painted photo to have been Fluorescent Yellow. Although the original Black and White photo of "Spatial Environment in Black Light" is an antiquated image, it is still a precious document of the first recorded Environment to have been created as a piece of Art, and the photo reveals details of this Artwork by Fontana such as four wires attached to a central point above the center of the organically shaped forms, which suspended the papier-mache forms in place. It is also very easy to see in this 1949 Black and White photo that the entire area in which these organically shaped papier-mache Fluorescent forms were suspended - the Environment - was not entirely painted (or draped) in Black, but in fact the entire ceiling the forms were attached to, as well as the top half of one of the walls of the Environment were very lightly Colored and perhaps even White.

Although the author of "Lucio Fontana: Between Utopia and Kitsch" describes "Spatial Environment in Black Light" as having "unusual coloration," he also describes it's suspended forms creating for viewers a feeling of "webbing" or "clouds." The Ultraviolet light is described as causing the Fluorescent Colors used by Fontana to "emit light," and in this way they are 'diffused' into the surrounding space of the Environment. A viewer of the 1949 "Spatial Environment in Black Light" is quoted as feeling that the gallery was indeed "transformed" with 'Violet light, shadows, and suspended forms,' and that you entered into what he called a "pictorial environment." Reviewers of Fontana's "Spatial Environment in Black Light" wrote that "electric lights" caused the suspended forms of Fluorescent Colors to "vibrate" and created "unreal" as well as "fairytale hues." It was even written that Fontana's Environment created a utopian "new ecology" and 'represented life with forms and Colors more harmonious than reality.' Although there were also critics who wrote of nothing more than "black drapery" and "prehistoric bones," Fontana's Environment is described correctly by both the author and the majority of reviewers at the time of it's creation as being unprecedented and having the ability to transport viewers who entered physically into this piece of Art. The Black light in Fontana's "Spatial Environment in Black Light" caused viewers who entered into it to see their clothing glowing and emitting light, just like the Fluorescent paint coating the forms suspended above their heads making up the piece of Art were. Guido Balla wrote that this "Wood's light" (Black light) caused everything to be "livid," that viewers "became purple," and in those ways the viewer in Fontana's "Spatial Environment in Black Light" were "physically involved." At least somebody got the point. Contrary to these revelations, the author states that 'contemporary reviewers' felt the "modern lighting" used by Fontana - the Black light - related to an "unflattering" range of phenomenon referred to as "low-culture" and that this modern Black light 'evoked what is felt as banal, childish, and even the fraudulent.' One reviewer went so far as to write that the "Spatial Environment in Black Light" reminded one of having been produced by a 'Charlatan medium's seance.' Concluding the typical viewpoint of Fluorescent paint and Black light, some critics related Fontana's Environment to well-known 'decorations in bars or theatrical reviews,' while other critics wrote that Fluorescent paint had previously been used in Paris for the famous dancers of the "Folies-Bergère" and also in America for common "advertising purposes." It was also published that when entering Fontana's "Spatial Environment in Black Light" the viewer felt as though they had gone into either a 'macabre carnival booth' or into the office of a "Radiologist!" Lisa Ponti wrote that Fontana's Environment was the 'atomic age's first graffito,' and that it was also "grotesque." The author Anthony White's opinion is that Fontana's "grotesque" forms 'evoking exhumed fossils' prevented the feeling of "spirituality" for viewers of Fontana's "walk-in" Environment, and that by 'incorporating the spectator' into his Environment Fontana brought forth just the opposite, "materiality." In reference to the Black light installed in Fontana's Environment, White fortifies his viewpoint by claiming that through the participation of the viewer, who's clothing also glowed under the Black light of the Environment, their attention was centered on their "bodily presence" more than on the Artwork's "sculptural object." After having created a Fluorescent "Participatory" Environment which over 50,000 visitors have physically entered into for the last seventeen years in "Electric Ladyland - the First Museum of Fluorescent Art" and in which "walk-in" Environment visitors have also seen their clothing, teeth, eyes, and fingernails glowing under 1,000 watts of Black light, these physical distractions account for a mere fraction of visitors' experience in the Fluorescent "Participatory" Environment, so I must strongly disagree with author Anthony White also on this point. It is very easy for a writer to theorize with only their pens, but these are just theories, which many times do not apply in experienced reality. The author goes on in complete agreement with critics and restates that Fontana did explore "modern devices" including "low-culture" "nightclub decoration" as well as the "advertising spectacle," and in this way Fontana created an 'unworldly fairytale space.' Although White concedes that Fontana's "walk-in" Environment was capable of blurring a viewer's viewpoint in relation to the difference between 'material' and inanimate 'space,' the author's stated opinion is that Fontana 'cheapened his dream' by associating it with what Anthony White prejudicially labels very clearly the "commodity spectacle." Even though White admits that Fontana's "Spatial Environment in Black Light" had the ability of 'evoking wonder,' this 'wonder' that the Artist's Environment evoked is considered by the author to be both "fraudulent" and "ridiculous"(!) White restates his opinion that Fontana's combination of a "radical" Art form created together with "modern technology" failed to achieve the Artist's intention or ideal. Perhaps the author thinks that a new "radical" Art form should be created with 'ancient technology,' instead of what would be logical: "modern technology."

After pages of having a relatively negative attitude concerning Lucio Fontana's "Spatial Environment in Black Light," author Anthony White concludes his prejudicial text with the statement that with Fontana using "modern technology" incorporated into his Art it was a "perfectly amenable" comparison to nothing less than "political spectacle," with the author adding that the Artist as well as the viewer had to 'temper' their "technological optimism" with an "extreme" amount of "self-consciousness." The section on Fontana's "Spatial Environment in Black Light" is concluded by the Artist's memories and aged evaluation of his 1949 Environment, almost twenty years later in 1967, with the Artist explaining his motivation for choosing to use what is relabeled by White as "unusual materials." Fontana in 1967 reinforces his visionary dreams of Art by stating directly that the "Spatial Environment in Black Light" was a "sign" of what the Artist called "the void," and as being so 'ended the traditional Art gallery in which paintings were hung and sculptures were for sale.' In a totally Black Environment under the "Wood's light," the Fluorescent Colors created this "void," and evoked this emptiness for Fontana. The author of "Lucio Fontana: Between Utopia and Kitsch" typically reinterprets this visionary statement of the Artist, and 'tempered' with a contemporary arrogance as well as a contemporary negation of spirituality, proclaims with his all-knowing writing pen that this "strange effect" produced by Fontana of "emptiness" through his use of "low-culture" Fluorescent paint's "vapid radiance" created not a vision of what the author labels "paradise," but in White's contemporary Twenty-first century viewpoint, just the opposite, with the author describing Fontana's creation as 'macabre scientific technology.' Stooping to the oldest trick in the book on Fluorescence, the author directly compares Fluorescent paint's "eerie glow" under the Black light to the creation of "menace" in association with nothing less than both 'dead tissue of humans' and "toxic uranium"(!) Unbelievably, in this age, this truly text-book prototype of a "Fluorophobic" author Anthony White again restates criticism from three-quarters of a century ago when Polignoto likened Fontana's "Spatial Environment in Black Light" to 'an appointment in a Radiologist's office,' and then compares the experience of entering Fontana's Environment under a Black light with viewer's 'bodies turning Purple' as being what White calls an experience which was "unsettling," and in direct comparison to viewing their own body for the first time 'in an X-ray'(!) If Mr. White ever came into "Electric Ladyland - the First Museum of Fluorescent Art" he would have an embolism!

In his concluding statement on "Spatial Environment in Black Light" the author questions Fontana's interest in "modern technology" an adds an opinion about the "diabolical side" of the Twentieth century's "technological myths." Another viewpoint is added, which needs no explanation, in which Fontana is next compared to a naive native Indian in awe and amazement over the shining armour of the conquistadors. Finally a quote by the Artist himself, in which he describes his "Spatial Environment in Black Light" 'leaving the viewers in shock,' signifies for the author 'Fontana giving voice' to the underlying "sinister" beneath the "utopian possibilities" of 'modern technology.' After the "modern technology" of the Black light and Fluorescent Color, during the first years of the 1950s Fontana began huge installations of neon tubing looped into forms and suspended in architectural spaces, with the Artist describing a new Art that was based on both new techniques a well as new media, which Fontana lists as 'neon, the "Wood's light" [Black light], and the television' creating what this Visionary Artist called the "new aesthetics" of 'spaces' containing "light forms." Both the 1949 "Spatial Environment in Black Light" and the early 1950's neon sculptures were based on Fontana's desire to create a new Art using light and space, which led the Artist to what he is most known for, his famous years of "Hole" paintings. These series of "Hole" paintings began already while Fontana was working on his "Spatial Environment in Black Light," during which time he also created paintings he had punctured holes into. Author Anthony White explains that the many well-known series which Fontana punctured and called the "Holes" were created through the Artist's intention of 'connecting the Artworks together with space,' and that Fontana's "Spatial Environment in Black Light" was "closely connected" with his "Holes" paintings. The author links the 1949 Environment's ability to create what appeared to be both "solidified light" and also "luminous matter" through it's use of Fluorescent paint, to the early "Hole" paintings that had a lamp mounted behind them and projected light out of all the punctured holes in the painting, and in this way "connected" these "Hole" paintings to light as well as space.

For this author of "Lucio Fontana: Between Utopia and Kitsch" his contemporary Fluorophobic unacceptance of both Fluorescent Color and Ultraviolet lamps is evident throughout his writing. Concluding his chapter on Fontana's Artwork from 1940-1951, White restates his opinion, being that Fontana linked all the Environments he created with "decrepit forms" of culture by bringing attention to modern culture's aspects of the "fraudulent," the "outmoded," and the "commodified."

Again, 1949 was a pivotal year for Lucio Fontana, being the year that he created the first series of the paintings that he is still known for, the 'perforated' canvases which are referred to in Italian as the "Buchi" ('holes'). As explained previously, in February, 1949 Lucio Fontana introduced and created the first concept of the "Environment" as an Artform, which was the "Spatial Environment in Black Light," being an installation in the dark containing abstract sculptures painted in full Fluorescent Colors suspended from the ceiling under Black light. This first Fluorescent Environment exhibited briefly in 1949 led to further Environments by Fontana, including the 1951 Milano Triennale piece "Struttura al neon per la IX Triennale di Milano 51 A 1" which contained a neon light swirling above the head in an architectural space. Beginning to evolve his Art towards creations of "Installation" Art, or "Environments," Fontana justified his expansion by his opinion that "conventional" Art forms wouldn't exist for much longer because of the degree in which the Artist imagined the world would change through the new age of "space travel." Already in 1949, just four years after the end of the Second world war, and eight years before the "Space Age" even began with Sputnik's launch in 1957, Lucio Fontana was quoted as believing that when people live on the Moon the Art they will make will not be "conventional" paintings but "spatial art." In 1962 Fontana expanded upon his viewpoint, believing that 'one day' when humanity leaves the Earth in 'space ships' together with their conventional 'little paintings,' there will be no walls to hang them on. In 1963 Fontana was quoted with the idea that "future" humanity living in large "space stations" will have no need of either building 'capitals with columns,' or creating any forms of Art, because in his opinion, at that point in advancement the concept of Art as we know it "will end." Fontana realized that in this new future era of "space travel," the new form of Art he introduced in 1949, the "Installation," or Environment," was the only Art form which would still be considered "appropriate," because it was a new Art not connected to traditional or conventional Art of "the past," in the same way that "space travel" was something new and the beginning of a new era. Expanding upon his view of new "Spatial Art" being used in a future era of space travel, the Artist began to realize that this "Spatial Art" would have to be "integrated" with all the infinite expanse of "empty space," which led to the conclusion that there could exist no object created to adhere to these parameters he set for the future. The Artist began to understand that the only Artform which would exist as being "fully integrated" into the emptiness of space would be 'broadcast light from television.' Further realization by Fontana came to the point that this Artform of 'broadcast light' would both be formless, as well as having no fixed position, or "locality." The Artist's vision included creating Art of a truly "Global" scale, with exhibitions happening simultaneously across the world, through the transmission of forms to New York, Berlin, and Milan at the same time. Fontana's visions included the anticipation of "Spatial Art" being transmitted by "aeroplanes" and by "missiles," which are capable of circling Earth, floating out in space, or completely leaving the atmosphere of the Earth itself. What the Artist did after concluding that his visions of transmitted forms simultaneously across the world as a new form of "Spatial Art" could not be realized, was for the first time in his life as an Artist took up traditional painting on canvas. Although his turning to the most conventional form of Art, painting on canvas, was exactly the opposite of what he envisioned the "Spatial Art" of the future would be, going back to 1949 in both his quotes and his creations these paintings were not at all "conventional." Fontana's new early 1950s canvases were a full departure from conventional painting, with, again, the inclusion of punctures in the canvas, as well as lights which were installed behind these punctures canvases, and would then project light through the holes in his paintings out into the surrounding space, which adhered to his original concept of "Spatial Art" evolving into pure transmission of light. Eventually the Artist stopped using this transmission of light from behind the canvas, and through his paintings in the late 1950s and the 1960s of simply 'punctured' or 'slashed' canvases, these Artworks still defined "Spatial Art" through their presentation of space 'contained' in the Artwork. Fontana named these later punctured or slashed canvases "Spatial Concept: Expectations" because to the Artist they were the first forms in expectation of a new type of Art that would be created in the future. In reference to "Spatial Art" and to the new age of space travel, there was contained in this expectation a new future Artform which would be created, as explained in 1962 by the Artist in reference to the punctures in his paintings as being 'holes,' which were the first forms of sculpture in 'space.' During the 1960s Fontana expanded his viewpoint that space travel itself necessitated a new Artform to be created, which would include the technological advances that were beginning to rapidly develop, and which the Artist believed were the changes that would both cause traditional Art to be left behind, and a "new Language" of Art to be formed.

From 1963 to 1964 Fontana began a new type of painting with a series of thirty-eight canvases identical in their egg-like shape and height, entitled "Spatial Concept: The End of God." This series was made the height of the average male Italian in the 1960s, and were each painted with a single bright Color, such as bright Violet, Green, Pink, Red, White, or Black. The bright Orange canvas is punctured with hundreds of different size holes, immediately giving the first impression of the meteor-scarred surface of another planet. The standard height of 178 centimeters throughout the thirty-eight canvases created a relation to the viewer standing in front of the Artwork, as well as the similar egg-like shape of each canvas. The technique used by Fontana on this "Spatial Concept: The End of God" series was to puncture and cut into the canvas when his paint was still wet, so that as he physically punctured the wet canvas the holes would have a formed ridge around each one of them, making them appear to be impact craters, or as some critics suggest, inflicted wounds to the body. Fontana gave a hint at the direction of "Spatial Concepts: The End of God" in 1966, when he explained that the title did not refer to religion, but to the end of 'humanity imagining themselves to be God,' or the loss of the self in the vast void of emptiness, exemplified by not only space travel, but by a complete technological society (which the world today is currently immersed in).

In 1961 Lucio Fontana visited New York for an exhibition of his Artwork in the Martha Jackson Gallery, and in 1966 the Artist designed for theater, creating both costumes and opera stage sets for La Scala in Milan. The last paintings by Fontana before he died in 1968 were totally pure White, and during the last years of his life he created the Environment in which his last White canvases would be exhibited in the 1966 Venice Biennale. Fontana's final major exhibition was in 1968 when the Artist exhibited at the "Documenta" of Kassel, Germany.

In 2012 the Gagosian Gallery in New York held a major retrospective of the Artist's work entitled "Lucio Fontana: Ambienti Spaziali," which contained over one-hundred Artworks, as well as six of Fontana's "Spatial Environments" or "Ambienti spaziali." Fontana's first 1949 Installation "Spatial Environment in Black Light" was one of six of the Artist's Environments which were reconstructed for this 2012 exhibition in Chelsea, New York, and this first 'Black Light Environment' was explained by the Artist through a quote also mounted on Gagosian's wall, in which Fontana states that his new form of Art he exhibited as an Environment was 'not a painting or a sculpture,' but simply "luminous forms" which were floating "in space," creating what Fontana proclaims as 'emotional freedom for viewers.' The Installation that Fontana made for his last show, the exhibition "Documenta 4" in Germany, 1968, was also reconstructed in the Gagosian show of 2012, and is explained as a 'tiny labyrinth' which is cramped and under an illuminated ceiling, through which the viewer is led to a space which contains one slashed piece of pure White Art. This Installation is a key example of what curators of the Gagosian exhibition realize were early forerunners of the 1970's "Light and Space" Art. One of the curators of the 2012 Gagosian show knew Lucio Fontana in Italy, Germano Celant who was from Genoa. Celant was a young writer in his early twenties at the beginning of the 1960s when he met Fontana, and explains the reconstruction he helped to install in the Gagosian for the show as being an Environment which was very small, and done in Celant's hometown of Genoa. The year was 1967, and Celant describes this Environment as being installed in a "shop" which was on Genoa's beach. This small 1967 Fontana Environment is described as a 'narrow passage' which was blocked at the end by a Black hanging curtain. As the viewer went through the Black curtain there was entered a Black space inside which contained just a few small areas of Fluorescent paint glowing under Black lights. This brought the Artist to a full circle, which he began with the first "Environment" made as a form of Art in 1949, "Spatial Environment in Black Light," and which evolved to what he created as one of his final "Spatial Environments," this Genoa Black Light Environment with Fluorescent paint in 1967, the year before he died. Lucio Fontana was a truly Visionary Artist.

If the main reason that Fluorescent Color hasn't been accepted by the vast majority of contemporary Artists - or even Artists of the last three-quarters of a century since Fluorescent paint was invented in 1933 - is that Fluorescence was originally promoted and utilized as a choice of common advertising, nightclubs, and even 'war-time lighting' during the 1940s, it is then asked if Television and Video were not also mediums initially promoted and utilized for the common person, and not as Art mediums. The Television and Video are also deeply ingrained popular social media of the common person, but have in the last forty years become accepted as well as respected Art mediums. The question may then be asked if these two iconic popular mediums have been accepted as well as respected Art forms throughout the world, why has an exception been made for the universal unacceptance and disrespect for Fluorescent Art during the same period of time and up until the present day? Fluorescent paint and Black light became known as 'war-time lighting' after it's extensive use in the Second world war, sealing it's early fate as a paint not acceptable for Artists or for Fine Art because of it's connection with common culture - but what about Television and Video - these two mediums are even more ingrained in popular culture than 'war-time lighting,' but have been duly altered to their contemporary elevated status of mediums for Artists and Fine Art worldwide.

For the closing of this book on "the Social Stigma of Fluorophobia," the viewpoint of one of the only museum directors to have supported and even respected this dazzling, generally unaccepted invention of the Twentieth century - Fluorescent Colors - will be restated in all it's clarity. George D. Culler was the director of the San Francisco Museum of Art in 1961, and for the exhibition catalogue of one of the few successful Artists to have used Fluorescent paint, Richard Bowman, this director wrote a forward which still stands absolutely true today in 2016. As has been previously stated in this book, George D. Culler began his 'defense' of Fluorescent Colors with something the current author has dreamed about for many years, the imagined fantasy of going back in time to give a few pots of Fluorescent paint to the great Color masters of the past, such as Paul Gauguin(!) Culler wrote that he was "quite sure" that if Pierre Bonnard 'would have lived to see Fluorescent Colors, he surely would have been delighted to find these supercharged Colors,' and continues on to describe these new Fluorescent Colors as being not only comparable to light itself, but as being 'beyond any paint previously available for an Artist.' What George D. Culler closes his forward to Bowman's exhibition catalogue with is nothing less than prophetic, stating very clearly that what this director of the San Francisco Museum of Art could not understand was not the "technical properties" of Fluorescent Colors, but the human "reactions" to these brightest of all Colors that had ever been invented. Culler wrote that he could not figure out why 'in an age which allows almost anything, from the new synthetics to the actual trash of industrialized society' to be used by Artists to create their Art, it was "strange" to this 1961 museum director that a "strong exception" would be made, with the result being (still almost unchanged up until the present day) that these newly invented Fluorescent Colors which create the possibility of 'extending the range of Color's intensity' would be rejected by almost all Artists universally. In this rare questioning of the validity of Fluorescent Color's use in Fine Art, and it's almost immediate rejection by nearly all Artists, Culler goes on to very correctly further describe the main reason for Fluorescent Color's rejection by the Art world: *Tradition*. This very clear former director of the San Francisco Museum of Art further states that 'Judgements of what materials can be proper for making Art' are still based on tradition, and even by 1961 were becoming difficult to categorize. This point about 'almost anything' being acceptable for the creation of Art in 1961 is not only still valid in 2016, but is actually exponentially more valid today with the advent of "Transgenic Art" and "Bio Art" than it was when Culler wrote this fifty-five years ago.

The unacceptance and rejection of Fluorescent Color has roots in a much deeper aspect of human nature, closer to Shock and Fear than just common familiarity, which were both emotions brought about by the unnatural high intensity of the Fluorescent Color itself emitted through the invisible energy of the Ultraviolet lamp - as well as the time period of the 1960s Movement that these Fluorescent Colors and Black light are intrinsically and seemingly permanently associated with.

What must be made clear here in the conclusion of this long 'History of the Black Light' is the lack of resentment or ill feelings on the part of the Fluorescent Artist writing this 'Black Light History' towards mass society's unacceptance of the Black light and Fluorescent Colors, or towards the unacceptance of Fluorescent paint and the Black light for almost all Artists, Art galleries, and Museums throughout the world. As is explained to visitors in "Electric Ladyland - the First Museum of Fluorescent Art," a hundred years ago Claude Monet was a revolutionary Artist and even considered "Radical," which is most often met with a quizzical look from college-age visitors listening, who almost universally remember Monet being a pretty painting on their mother's Chocolate box - only. Almost universally, these Artists who were considered radical and who caused social scandal during their lives as Artists a century-plus ago, today have been absolutely accepted by society worldwide. Even the most unaccepted and rejected scandalous paintings of Gauguin's nude Tahitian teenagers have been today, a century later, elevated to the level of "icons" of culture in society worldwide. In actual fact a year ago in February, 2015 a painting of two Tahitian teenagers by Gauguin was sold to the Qatar Museums as the most expensive painting in history up to that date for almost $300,000,000.

The end result of banal society's acceptance after a full century-plus of what they call in general "Modern Art" is both not surprising, and nothing less than the creation of banality. Everything that this Grey-eyed visionless society touches and accepts universally is doomed towards the same shallow grave of banality evolving through familiarity. "The Mirror of Self-Reflection." It's like the touch of death from spiritually dead beings. This is what I personally have enjoyed not living through, a similar shallow grave for Fluorescent Colors and the Black light. Mass society has never truly accepted the Black light, and mass society has never truly accepted Fluorescent Colors. The prior chapter in this book described the rare Colorful characters who did not only accept - but actually embraced - the Black light and Fluorescent Colors, and obviously this small fringe of society has always, even today, made up the minority, which was even true during the height of the 1960s Movement. First the association of the Black light and Fluorescent Colors in it's infancy with the Second world war and it's description as "War-time Lighting," and then the association of Fluorescent Colors and the Black light with the 1960s "Psychedelic Movement" when the world found out about the Black light and Fluorescent Colors through the Hippies, created the title of this book: "The Social Stigma of FLUOROPHOBIA." If two sociological strikes against Fluorescent Colors and the Black light were not enough to create an unsurmountable stigma, then the third contemporary use of the Black light and Fluorescent Colors in the form of the "Green Fluorescent Protein" movement and it's offshoot "Transgenic Art" will help to complete the concretion of the "Social Stigma of Fluorophobia." But, like I wrote in the first sentence of this conclusion, the Fluorescent Artist writing this 'Black Light History' has no resentment towards society's unacceptance of Fluorescent Colors and the Black light, but amazingly just *gratitude* for their unacceptance of the Black light and Fluorescent Colors into their Grey, banal world. This universal rejection by society of the Black light and Fluorescent Colors has perpetuated the strength and radical standing of these brightest, wildest, and most disturbing of Colors by society's just-as-universal unacceptance - which has thankfully in no way resulted in it's familiarity. As the visionary Aldous Huxley wrote in 1959: 'Familiarity breeds Indifference.' Once the Color Red, simply being seen by a person, could excite the viewer and spiritually move them - this was a long time before Red was mass-produced on every soda can and package in the world, or as Aldous Huxley explains, before Red was mass-produced on square kilometers of linoleum. A similar obituary was thankfully not created by society for Fluorescent Black light Colors, because "Cola" was never made in soda cans that were Fluorescent Orange(!)

Today in 2016, go into any major Art Museum or even Art Gallery across the planet and you will have a hard time finding one drop of Fluorescent paint or one watt of Black light. Fluorescent paint and Black lights have been relegated to what even the first Artist to use Fluorescent paint in Fine Arts in 1945, John Ludlum, called towards the end of his life in the late 1980s, 'off-beat venues.' The unacceptance by society - or "Fluorophobia" - has not led to familiarity or to society's indifference towards Fluorescent Colors, but this unacceptance is what literally has produced the Black light and Fluorescent Color's durability and perpetual ability to awaken, or at least move, a Human being.

As Kahlil Gibran reminded us, "the lust" for what too many people sacrifice their lives for: "comfort" -
will "murder" your 'soul's passion' - and then will go on to "walk grinning" at the "funeral."
It does not take a great leap of the imagination to exchange the words "at the funeral" with "Today."

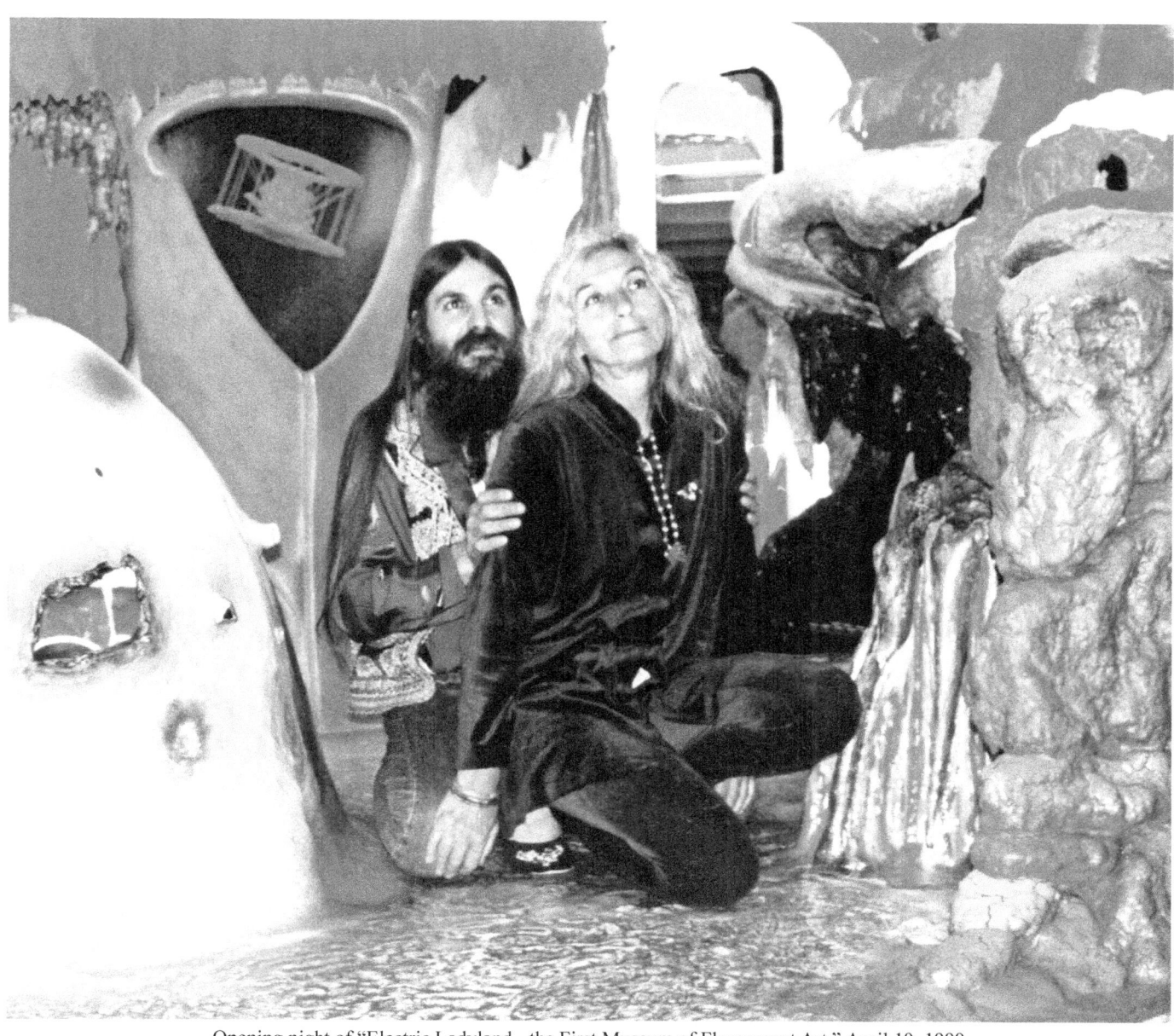
Opening night of "Electric Ladyland - the First Museum of Fluorescent Art," April 19, 1999

Photographs
©All Photographs Copyright Nick Padalino, 1999-2017

Front Cover: Gray common Fluorescent Minerals emitting vibrant Colors under Longwave and Shortwave Ultraviolet lamps

Back Cover: "Electric Ladyland - the First Museum of Fluorescent Art" - Fluorescent "Participatory" Environment

15   1984: The Sistine Chapel during restoration, showing a unrestored square Black section of Michelangelo's "Lunettes"

15   Ancient Greek fragment of a temple reveals it's original painted vivid Colors

42   Tibetan Monks create a "Kalachakra Sand Mandala," Amsterdam, 2005

42   Tibetan Monks create a "Kalachakra Sand Mandala," Amsterdam, 2005

68   1903: The "Spark Box" or "Iron Arc Lamp," one of the first Ultraviolet-producing mechanical device (close-up)

68   1903: The "Spark Box" or "Iron Arc Lamp," one of the first Ultraviolet-producing mechanical device

69   1915: The "Argon Bulb" or "Argon Glow Lamp" was the first Ultraviolet lamp sold to the public ("Electric Ladyland - the First Museum of Fluorescent Art" collection)

69   1920s: The "NICO Tube" was the first common tubular "Black light" or "Wood's Lamp" ("Electric Ladyland - the First Museum of Fluorescent Art" collection)

71   1920s: The "NICO Tube" was the first common tubular "Black light" or "Wood's Lamp" ("Electric Ladyland - the First Museum of Fluorescent Art" collection))

71   1930s: Professional Ultraviolet Lamp made with a wooden handle, including an electrical transformer and carrying case ("Electric Ladyland - the First Museum of Fluorescent Art" collection)

77   1930s "Stroblite" double-tube Black light with stand (("Electric Ladyland - the First Museum of Fluorescent Art" collection)

77   1930s Ultraviolet Germinology Lamp, "Bishop & Whalen Ultra-Violet Ray Equipment Co. Limited," Vancouver, B.C. ("Electric Ladyland - the First Museum of Fluorescent Art" collection)

79   1930s-1940s "FANTOM-FAST" Invisible Laundry-Marking Black light, "The National Marking Machine Co.," Ohio ("Electric Ladyland - the First Museum of Fluorescent Art" collection)

79   1930s Antique "Switzer Brothers, Inc." "Glo-Craft" Black light or "Blacklight" with a Bakelite handle ("Electric Ladyland - the First Museum of Fluorescent Art" collection)

81   1930s Checkoslovakian Ultraviolet Medical Lamp with wooden handle and wooden lamp flange ("Electric Ladyland - the First Museum of Fluorescent Art" collection)

81   1930s-1940s "Burton" Bakelite Ultraviolet Medical Lamp ("Burton" still produces a similar Ultraviolet Medical Lamp in 2016) ("Electric Ladyland - the First Museum of Fluorescent Art" collection)

83   1940s World War Two "Grimes Ultraviolet Cockpit Light" from the dashboard of a "B-17" Second World War Bomber ("Electric Ladyland - the First Museum of Fluorescent Art" collection)

83   1930s-1940s "Hampton Mfg." Ultraviolet "Metal Stress Detector" with a central magnifing glass for metal inspection ("Electric Ladyland - the First Museum of Fluorescent Art" collection)

87   1940s-1950s "Dye-Lite" 120 watt Ultraviolet Leak Detection Lamp with Fluorescent "Leak Detector" ("Electric Ladyland - the First Museum of Fluorescent Art" collection)

87   1930s-1940s "Ultra-Violet Products, Inc." "Blak-Ray" "BLF 6" "Long Wave Ultra-Violet Lamp" ("Electric Ladyland - the First Museum of Fluorescent Art" collection)

89   1953 "Blak-Ray" "Invisible Fluorescent Chalk Set," "Ultra-Violet Products, Inc.," San Gabriel, California ("Electric Ladyland - the First Museum of Fluorescent Art" collection)

89   **"Use With Black Light for: CHURCH GROUPS"** (!!)(1953)

91   1950s "ULTRAVIOLET SCIENCE and HOBBY SET - with MINERALITE LAMP," "Ultraviolet Products, Inc." ("Electric Ladyland - the First Museum of Fluorescent Art" collection)

91   1952 "BLACK LIGHT MAGIC" Set "For Ages 8-15" "Explore New Worlds - RIGHT AT HOME," Stroward, Inc. ("Electric Ladyland - the First Museum of Fluorescent Art" collection)

93   1930s-1940s "EXPERIMENTAL U.V. COLOR OUTFIT NO.4," "Stroblite Co., Inc.," New York ("Electric Ladyland - the First Museum of Fluorescent Art" collection)

93   1936 Fluorescent "RADIANT STROBLITE FABRICS" brochure, "Stroblite Co., Inc." ("Electric Ladyland - the First Museum of Fluorescent Art" collection)

95	1939 San Francisco World's Fair "Golden Gate International Exposition" "Treasure Island - Night and Day" fold-out souvenir ("Electric Ladyland - the First Museum of Fluorescent Art" collection)
121	1920s-1930s "Actinotherapy" Shortwave Ultraviolet "Miracle-Cure" Lamp: "Life-Lite" "Genuine Ultra-Violet Rays Lamp," Los Angeles, California ("Electric Ladyland - the First Museum of Fluorescent Art" collection)
121	1920s-1930s "Actinotherapy Goggles - Special for Ultra Violet Ray Treatment," "Portia/Solport Brothers Ltd.," London ("Electric Ladyland - the First Museum of Fluorescent Art" collection)
125	1922 "Actinotherapy" Shotwave Ultraviolet "Miracle-Cure" advertisement, "Vi-Rex Electric Co.," Chicago, U.S.A. ("Electric Ladyland - the First Museum of Fluorescent Art" collection)
133	1941-1942 Collection of "Conti-Glo BLACK LIGHT BEACON," "Conti-Glo Corporation," Cleveland, Ohio ("Electric Ladyland - the First Museum of Fluorescent Art" collection)
151	1940s-1950s "Ultraviolet Criminology Kit," "Fargo International," New Oxford, Pennsylvania ("Electric Ladyland - the First Museum of Fluorescent Art" collection)
151	1940s Invisible Fluorescent Fingerprinting Ultraviolet Unit and Ink Pad, "FLUOR-O-CHEK Invisible System" "Product Endorsement Fingerprinting Identification," "Blak-Ray Long Wave Ultra-Violet," "Ultra-Violet Products, Inc." California ("Electric Ladyland - the First Museum of Fluorescent Art" collection)
152	1942 Dodge automobile painted completely Fluorescent under Black lights(!)
183	1930s-1940s "Switzer Brothers, Inc." "Glo-Craft" "Model 70" 250 watt professional portable Black light Floodlight still in perfect working condition ("Electric Ladyand - the First Museum of Fluorescent Art" collection)
187	1930s-1940s "Conti-Glo" "Model 93" 100 watt professional portable Black light Spotlight still in perfect working condition ("Electric Ladyand - the First Museum of Fluorescent Art" collection)
191	1930s-1940s "Keese Engineering Company - The Shannon Line" 100 watt portable Black Light "Model 90STP," Hollywood, California ("Electric Ladyand - the First Museum of Fluorescent Art" collection)
193	1943-1950 Collection of "MINERALITE News Bulletin - for your life," "Ultra-Violet Products, Inc.," California ("Electric Ladyland - the First Museum of Fluorescent Art" collection)
195	1953: "VoGlo" "Invisible" and "Daylight" Fluorescent Paint Color sample swatch, "BLACK LIGHT CORP. of Northern California," San Francisco (containing the controversial 1950's Beige "FLESH" Color name) ("Electric Ladyland - the First Museum of Fluorescent Art" collection)
197	Fluorescent Mineral Viewing Box, "Electric Ladyland - the First Museum of Fluorescent Art," 1940s "Gisco Geophysical Instrument and Supply Company," Denver, Colorado - Originally used for Offshore Oil Drill-Core inspection ("Electric Ladyland - the First Museum of Fluorescent Art" collection)
197	1940s-1950s "MINERALITE" "Model M-14 Battery Operated Short Wave Ultraviolet," "Ultra-Violet Products, Inc." This is "The First Pocket-Size Transistor ULTRA-VIOLET LAMP" (("Electric Ladyland - the First Museum of Fluorescent Art" collection)
199	1938 "M-12" "MINERALITE," "Ultra-Violet Products, Inc.," the first portable Shortwave Ultraviolet lamp produced to prospect for Tungsten-containing Scheelite in the United States for the approaching Second World War ("Electric Ladyland - the First Museum of Fluorescent Art" collection)
199	1938 "M-12" "MINERALITE," "Ultra-Violet Products, Inc.," the first portable Shortwave Ultraviolet lamp produced to prospect for Tungsten-containing Scheelite in the United States for the approaching Second World War (top)
200	Fluorescent Mineral Viewing Box, "Electric Ladyland - the First Museum of Fluorescent Art" - Originally the top metal section is a 1940s "C-5" "Chromatoviewer" Longwave and Shortwave U.V. Medical Inspection Cabinet
212	"Common Items that are Fluorescent" Museum book, Nick Padalino, 1997
213	"FLUORESCENT FOOD and FLOWERS" Museum book, Nick Padalino and Michèle Delage, 2005
215	"FLUORESCENT FLOWERS" Museum book, Nick Padalino and Michèle Delage, 2005
217	"Electric Ladyland - the First Museum of Fluorescent Art" Museum book, Nick Padalino, 1999
217	"Fluorescence All Around Us" Museum book, Nick Padalino and Michèle Delage, 2005
229	**"Use With Black Light for: <u>CHURCH GROUPS"</u>** (!!)(1953) ("Electric Ladyland - the First Museum of Fluorescent Art" collection)
231	"Ultra-Violet Ray Carries Television Image," November, 1929 "Science and Invention" article on Television Invention ("Electric Ladyland - the First Museum of Fluorescent Art" collection)
246	1940s "Ultra-Violet Products Co.," Pasedena, California, Ultraviolet "Mineralite" Lamps convention booth "FLUORESCENT MINERALS" ("Electric Ladyland - the First Museum of Fluorescent Art" collection)

246	1950s "Ultra-Violet Products, INC.," Pasedena, California, Ultraviolet "BLAK-RAY" Lamps convention booth "SNEAK-A-PEEK!" ("Electric Ladyland - the First Museum of Fluorescent Art" collection)
253	1940s-1950s "Crocker" "DAY-GLO" Fluorescent "Coated Papers," sample booklet ("Electric Ladyland - the First Museum of Fluorescent Art" collection)
253	1940s-1950s "Kodak Fluorescent Water Colors" Fluorescent retouch set for photographs ("Electric Ladyland - the First Museum of Fluorescent Art" collection)
268	1950s "Invisible" Fluorescent Advertising counter-display
269	1950s "Invisible" Fluorescent Advertisement for "Acme Gold Label Beer," "Ultra-Violet Products, Inc." - WHITE LIGHT ("Electric Ladyland - the First Museum of Fluorescent Art" collection)
269	1950s "Invisible" Fluorescent Advertisement for "Acme Gold Label Beer," "Ultra-Violet Products, Inc." - BLACK LIGHT
270	1950s 30-watt Outdoor Black Light unit ("Electric Ladyland - the First Museum of Fluorescent Art" collection)
271	Thomas Warren's Black Light Christmas Show on his entire street Marengo Ave. in California every year from 1958 to 1966 ("Electric Ladyland - the First Museum of Fluorescent Art" collection)
271	Invitation to Thomas Warren's Black Light Christmas Show on Marengo Ave. in California every year from 1958 to 1966 ("Electric Ladyland - the First Museum of Fluorescent Art" collection)
275	John Plumer Ludlum (1906-1993) - the first Artist to use Fluorescent paint for Fine Art in 1945, "Spacial Fantasy #3" "Electric Ladyland - the First Museum of Fluorescent Art" collection
277	John Plumer Ludlum, "Ludlum Art Center" brochure, Tustin, California 1966-1993 (front) ("Electric Ladyland - the First Museum of Fluorescent Art" collection)
277	John Plumer Ludlum, "Ludlum Art Center" brochure, Tustin, California 1966-1993 (back) ("Electric Ladyland - the First Museum of Fluorescent Art" collection)
289	1944 "Black Light Spectacle" Poster ("Electric Ladyland - the First Museum of Fluorescent Art" collection)
290	1959: Booklets from the "Ultra-Violet MASTER SCIENCE LAB," "Ultra-Violet Products, Inc.," California ("Electric Ladyland - the First Museum of Fluorescent Art" collection)
290	1959: Booklets from the "Ultra-Violet MASTER SCIENCE LAB," "Ultra-Violet Products, Inc.," California ("Electric Ladyland - the First Museum of Fluorescent Art" collection)
291	1959 "Black Light MAGIC-GLO Kit" - "See The Invisible," "Black Light Eastern Corp.," Bayside, New York ("Electric Ladyland - the First Museum of Fluorescent Art" collection)
293	Antique Black Light Display Case, "Electric Ladyland - the First Museum of Fluorescent Art"
293	Antique Black Light Display Case, "Electric Ladyland - the First Museum of Fluorescent Art"
294	"the History of Fluorescent Art," Museum book, Nick Padalino, 1995
324	1964-1965 "New York World's Fair" Flag ("Electric Ladyland - the First Museum of Fluorescent Art" collection)
331	1960s "PSYCHEDELIC PAINTS" Set - "Poster Paint," Palmer's Paint Products Incorporated," Michigan ("Electric Ladyland - the First Museum of Fluorescent Art" collection)
331	1960s "PSYCHEDELIC PAINTS" Set - "Poster Paint" "HIPPIE ART - POSTERS - MODELS - FASHION ART"
333	1960s "DAY-GLO - First Name in Fluorescent Color" "Neon Red" Fluorescent oil paint, "Switzer Brothers, Inc.," Cleveland ("Electric Ladyland - the First Museum of Fluorescent Art" collection)
333	1960s "Luna Lite" "BLACKLIGHT" Poster lamp, with Fluorescent box - "Posters - Decorations - Crafts," New Mexico ("Electric Ladyland - the First Museum of Fluorescent Art" collection)
334	1930s-1940s "STROBLITE COMPANY-First in Fluorescence ... Since 1924," Fluorescent Paint Color sample swatch ("Electric Ladyland - the First Museum of Fluorescent Art" collection)
335	1968 "Stroblite Company, Inc. - First In Fluorescence ... Since 1924" brochure, "Magical Display Effects," New York (inside) ("Electric Ladyland - the First Museum of Fluorescent Art" collection)
335	1968 "Stroblite Company, Inc. - First In Fluorescent UV Color effects ... Since 1924" brochure, New York (outside)
337	1960s "HI-GLO Fluorescent Paint - For Things To Be Seen," "Pactra Industries, Inc.," Los Angeles ("Electric Ladyland - the First Museum of Fluorescent Art" collection)
337	1960s "BLAK-RAY Black Light Fluorescent Crayons," "Ultra-Violet Products, Inc.," San Gabriel, California ("Electric Ladyland - the First Museum of Fluorescent Art" collection)
339	"The Oracle of the City of San Francisco," Fluorescent cover of Black Light Poster Issue, Dec. 6, 1967-vol. 1, nr.8 ("Electric Ladyland - the First Museum of Fluorescent Art" collection)
339	"The Oracle of the City of San Francisco," Fluorescent poster in Black Light Poster Issue, Dec. 6, 1967, vol. 1, nr. 8 ("Electric Ladyland - the First Museum of Fluorescent Art" collection)
347	"Shiva Nataraja" statue from Hardwar, India in "Electric Ladyland - the First Museum of Fluoresent Art"
358	"Dr. Albert Hofmann in his study, July 21, 1998," Fluorescent bubble-jet computer print, ©Nick Padalino, 1998
358	Dr. Albert Hofmann in his study with the author, July 21, 1998
362	Hand-written dedication to Dr. Albert Hofmann from Aldous Huxley in "Island"
379	Transgenic Fluorescent "GLO-FISH" for sale in New Jersey(!)
456	"Richard Bowman: Paintings and Reflections, 1943-1961," 1961 San Francisco Museum of Art catalogue containing the historical front cover, which was the first time a piece of Art had been printed and published in Fluorescent Colors ("Electric Ladyland - the First Museum of Fluorescent Art" collection)

464	"Electric Lady Studios" built for Jimi Hendrix in 1970 (with original round facade)
465	The author in Jimi Hendrix's "Electric Lady Studios," "Studio A," January 21, 2002
465	"Electric Lady Studios," Color Control Panel with original Light Color-indicating labels written by Jimi Hendrix
467	Nick Padalino and Michèle Delage in "Electric Lady" Art Gallery, Amsterdam, 1990
467	"Electric Lady" Art Gallery, 2015
469	"Electric Ladyland - the First Museum of Fluorescent Art" Temporary Opening Exhibition, November 27 - December 12, 1992
471	Nick Padalino and Michèle Delage in "Electric Ladyland - the First Museum of Fluorescent Art" under construction, 1995
471	"Electric Ladyland - the First Museum of Fluorescent Art" Fluorescent "Participatory" Environment under construction, 1993
472	"Electric Ladyland - the First Museum of Fluorescent Art" Fluorescent "Participatory" Environment under construction, Session #2 - Mid-February to end April, 1993: "Initial Electric Ladyland Environment Construction."
473	"Electric Ladyland - the First Museum of Fluorescent Art" Fluorescent "Participatory" Environment under construction, 1993, Session #5 - February 22 to April 26, 1994: "The Unbelievable Session."
473	"Electric Ladyland - the First Museum of Fluorescent Art" Fluorescent "Participatory" Environment under construction, Session #5 - February 22 to April 26, 1994: "The Unbelievable Session." - the Stalagtites
474	"Electric Ladyland - the First Museum of Fluorescent Art" Fluorescent "Participatory" Environment under construction, Session #6 - July, 1994: "The Jupiter Collision." - Moving the "Hanuman Mountain"
474	"Electric Ladyland - the First Museum of Fluorescent Art" Fluorescent "Participatory" Environment under construction, Session #7 - September to November, 1994: "The Spaghetti-wire Lighting Session."
477	"Electric Ladyland - the First Museum of Fluorescent Art" Fluorescent "Participatory" Environment under construction, "Session #15a" - June 15, 1997: "Painting of 'The Draperies' with Michèle on my Fortieth Birthday."
479	Michèle Delage at 14,000 feet elevation (4,350 mtrs.) in Gaumukh, India - the Source of the Ganga, May, 1998
479	Nick Padalino and Michèle Delage at 14,000 feet (4,350 mtrs.) in Gaumukh, India - the Source of the Ganga, May, '98
481	The author giving possibly the First Fluorescent Mineral Demonstration in India at "The Santosh Puri Ashram," May, 1998
481	Nick Padalino and Michèle Delage - Fluorescent Mineral Demonstration in India at "The Santosh Puri Ashram," May, 2010
482	A brass Trishule and Damroe, with a marble Shiva Linga brought from Hardwar, India permanently mounted in "Electric Ladyand - the First Museum of Fluoresent Art," 1998
482	"Electric Ladyland - the First Museum of Fluorescent Art" Fluorescent "Participatory" Environment under construction, "Session #18a" - September, 1998: "Painting of 'The Bernadette Grotto' by Michèle."
484	Fluorescscent Mineral Artwork from the 1950s in New Jersey - Miera's masterpiece which took six months to create
484	Fluorescscent Mineral Artwork from the 1950s - "Electric Ladyland - the First Museum of Fluorescent Art" collection
485	"Electric Ladyland - the First Museum of Fluorescent Art" Fluorescent "Participatory" Environment under construction, "Session #20" - March 3 to April 1-2, 1999: "The Final Sessions." - The "Shiva Linga" and "Yoni"
485	"Electric Ladyland - the First Museum of Fluorescent Art" Fluorescent "Participatory" Environment under construction, "Session #20" - March 3 to April 1-2, 1999: "The Final Sessions." - One centimeter marble Shiva statue carved to order in India for the source of the Ganges River "Gaumukh" cave at the top-left of the "Shiva Linga"
488	"Electric Ladyland - the First Museum of Fluorescent Art" Opening Poster - April 19, 1999
489	Fluorescent "Participatory" Environment, "Electric Ladyand - the First Museum of Fluorescent Art"
489	"Participatory Art" in the Fluorescent "Participatory" Environment, "Electric Ladyland - the First Museum of Fluorescent Art"
492	1950s "BLAK-RAY" "PAINT WITH LIVING LIGHT" Fluorescent Bulletin Paint set, "Ultra-Violet Products, Inc.," California ("Electric Ladyland - the First Museum of Fluorescent Art" collection)
492	1950s "BLAK-RAY" "PAINT WITH LIVING LIGHT" Fluorescent Bulletin Paint brochure - "Colors That Glow Like Fire!" ("Electric Ladyland - the First Museum of Fluorescent Art" collection)
493	1950s "BLAK-RAY" Fluorescent Artist Oil Paint set - 8 "Invisible" and 8 "Visible" Colors, "Ultra-Violet Products, Inc." ("Electric Ladyland - the First Museum of Fluorescent Art" collection)
493	1950s "BLAK-RAY" Fluorescent Artist Oil Paint, "Ultra-Violet Products, Inc." Donated by Thomas S.Warren "Electric Ladyand - the First Museum of Fluorescent Art" collection
495	1940s-1950s "HI-FI"(!) "VIVID FLUORESCENT CHALK" set, "Alphacolor/Weber Costello," Toronto, Canada ("Electric Ladyland - the First Museum of Fluorescent Art" collection)
495	1950s-1960s "Prang" "Day-Glo Art Colors" Fluorescent Crayon set: "The Brightest Colors In The World," "The American Crayon Company" ("Electric Ladyland - the First Museum of Fluorescent Art" collection)
504	The author's third self-made Fluorescent Tattoo, December, 2011 (White light / Black light)
512	"Philadelphia Magic Gardens" Created by Isaiah Zagar
513	The "Palais Ideal" Created by Facteur Ferdinand Cheval
515	"Expressions in LIGHT: An Introduction to fluorescent painting with Black Light" Booklet, "Ultra-Violet Products, Inc." (1950s) ("Electric Ladyland - the First Museum of Fluorescent Art" collection)
529	Opening night of "Electric Ladyland - the First Museum of Fluorescent Art," April 19, 1999

References

Color
"The Principles of Harmony and Contrast of Colors and Their Applications to the Arts" M.E. Chevreul (1839, 1854, 1981)
"Theory of Colours" Johann Wolfgang von Goethe (1840, 1970)
"Grammar of Paintings and Design" Charles Blanc (1867)
"Purism" Le Corbusier (1920)
"Scientific American" magazine (October, 1934)
"Box Office" magazine (August 24, 1935)
"The Practical Application of Luminescence: Fluorescence - Phosphorescence - Black Light" Maurice Deribere (1938, 1955)
"Fluorescent Light and It's Applications - Including Location and Properties of Fluorescent Materials...A theoretical and practical Exposition of Fluorescence and Similar Phenomenon" H.C. Dake and Jack De Ment (1941)
"Black Light Beacon" "Conti-Glo" trade magazine (1941-1943)
"Mineralite Files" (numbers 1-5) "Ultra-Violet Products, Inc." trade magazine (1944-1945)
"Mineralite News Bulletin" (numbers 6-13) "Ultra-Violet Products, Inc." trade magazine (1945-1951)
"Handbook of Fluorescent Chemicals" Jack De Ment (1945)
"Fluorescent Gems" Jack De Ment (1947)
"Expressions in LIGHT: An Introduction to fluorescent painting with Black Light" "Ultra-Violet Products, Inc." (1950s)
"A History of Luminescence - From Earliest Times Until 1900" E. Newton Harvey (1957)
"Ultraviolet Guide To Minerals with Mineral Identification Charts" Sterling Gleason (1960)
"Fantasy Lighting for After Dark using Blak-Ray" "Ultraviolet Products, Inc." trade magazine (1960)
"Color: A Survey in Words and Pictures - from Ancient Mysticism to Modern Science" Faber Birren (1963)
"Carnival Under the Sea" Rene Catala (1964)
"Principles of Color - a review of past traditions and modern theories of color harmony" Faber Birren (1969)
"Nature's Hidden Rainbows: Fluorescent Minerals of Franklin, New Jersey" Robert Jones (1965)
"The Story of Fluorescence: An Explanation of Ultraviolet Fluorescence with Experiments and a Descriptive List of Fluorescent Minerals" "Raytech Industries, Inc." (1965)
"Rocks and Minerals: Radioactive & Fluorescent Minerals Ores, Metals Gems, Meteorites, Etc." Richard M. Pearl (1965)
"Infrared and Ultraviolet Photography" Eastman Kodak Company (1972)
"The Collectors Book of Fluorescent Minerals" Manuel A. Robbins (1983)
"The Henkel Glossary of Fluorescent Minerals" Journal of the Fluorescent Mineral Society (1989)
"The Story of Switzer Magic Day-Glo" Liesa Bing (1991)
"Fluorescent Rock Hunting" Carolyn Cory (1991)
"Fluorescence: Gems and Minerals Under Ultraviolet Light" Manuel A. Robbins (1994)
"Men in Black" J. Harvey (1996)
"Ultraviolet Light and Fluorescent Minerals: Understanding, Collecting and Displaying Fluorescent Minerals" Thomas S. Warren, Sterling Gleason, Richard C. Bostwick, Earl R. Verbeek (1999)
"Color and Meaning - Art, Science, and Symbolism" John Gage (1999)
"Chromophobia" David Batchelor (2000)
"Colors: the story of dyes and pigments" Francois Delamare and Bernard Guineau (2000)
"Bright Earth: Art and the invention of color" Philip Ball (2001)
"Color - A Natural History of the Palette" Victoria Finlay (2002)
"Something Out of Nothing: Marie Curie and Radium" Carla Killough McClafferty (2006)
"World of Fluorescent Minerals" Stuart Schneider (2006)
"The Day-Glo Brothers: The True Story of Bob and Joe Switzer's Bright Ideas and Brand-New Colors" Chris Barton (2009)
"Collecting Fluorescent Minerals" Stuart Schneider (2011)

Art
"Concerning the Spiritual in Art" Wassily Kandinsky (1912, 1977)
"The Letters of Vincent Van Gogh" (1914-)
"Dear Theo" Vincent Van Gogh (Edited by Irving Stone and Jean Stone) (1937-)

"Van Gogh in Arles" MET catalogue, Ronald Pickvance (1984)
"Robert Mallary's Luminous Mobiles" "Time" magazine (March 10, 1952)
"Richard Bowman: Paintings and Reflections, 1943-1961" San Francisco Museum of Art (1961)
"Richard Bowman: Forty Years of Abstract Painting" Harold Allen Parker (1986)
"John Ludlum's Fluorescent Masterpiece "Nativity" "Virtue" magazine (1977)
"The Agony and the Ecstasy: A Biographical Novel of Michelangelo" Irving Stone (1961)
"Michelangelo: The Complete Sculpture, Painting, Architecture" William E. Wallace (1998)
"Great Ages of Man; A History of the World's Cultures: Renaissance" John R. Hale (1965)
"Gauguin in the South Seas" Bengt Danielsson (1966)
"The Writings of a Savage" Edited by Daniel Guerin (1978)
"Noa Noa: The Tahitian Journal of Paul Gauguin" Paul Gauguin (1912, 1994)
"Gauguin: Catalogue Raisonne of the Paintings (1873-1888)" Daniel Wildenstein (2002)
"Seurat" Pierre Courthion (1968)
"Leonardo da Vinci's Advice to Artists" Leonardo da Vinci (1974)
"A Man and his Mountain: The life of Paul Cezanne" Hugh McLeave (1977)
"Monet's Years at Giverny: Beyond Impressionism" Metropolitan Museum of Art (1978)
"History of Modern Art: Painting, Sculpture, Architecture" H. H. Arnason (1977)
"Pollock Painting: Photographs by Hans Namuth" Edited by Barbara Rose (1978)
"Krasner/Pollock: A Working Relationship" Grey Art Gallery and Study Center (1981)
"Jackson Pollock: An American Saga" Steve Naifeh, Gregory White Smith (1989)
"Jackson Pollock" MOMA catalogue, Glenn Lowry and Pepe Karmel (2002)
"Joseph Cornell" Kynaston McShine (1980)
"Off the Wall: A Portrait of Robert Rauschenberg" Calvin Tompkins (1980)
"North American Indian Art" Peter T. Furst, Jill L. Furst (1984)
"Frank Stella: Paintings, 1958-1965: A Catalogue Raisonne" Lawrence Rubing, Robert Rosenblum, Frank Stella (1986)
"Hendrix: Setting the Record Straight" Edward E. Kramer, John McDermott (1992)
"Jimi Hendrix: Electric Gypsy" Caesar Glebbeek, Harry Shapiro (1995)
"The Wheel of Time, Sand Mandala: Visual Scripture of Tibetan Buddhism" Barry Bryant (1992)
"Peintures de sable des Indiens Navajo: la voie de la beaute" Sylvie Crossmant and Jean-Pierre Barou (1996)
"Dawn of Art: The Chauvet Cave (The Oldest Known Paintings in the World)" Jean-Marie Chauvet, Eliette Brunel Deschamps, Christian Hillaire (1996)
"The Eight Day: The Transgenic Art of Eduardo Kac" Edited by Sheilah Britton and Dan Collins (2003)
"Telepresence and bio art: networking humans, rabbits, and robots" Eduardo Kac (2005)
"Signs of Life: bio art and beyond" Edited by Eduardo Kac (2007)
"Marcel Duchamp, Etant donnes" Michael R. Taylor (2009)
"Out of the Kokoon" Henry Adams and Lawrence Waldman (2011)
"Lucio Fontana: Between Utopia and Kitsch" Anthony White (2011)
"Oskar Fischinger, 1900-1967: Experiments in Cinematic Abstraction" Edited by Cindy Keefer and Jaap Guldemond (2012)

Science
"Doctor Wood: Modern Wizard of the Laboratory - The Story of an American Small Boy Who Became the Most Daring and Original Experimental Physicist of Our Day - but Never Grew Up" William Seabrook (1941)
"Sensation and Perception: An integrated approach" Harvey Richard Schiffman (1976)
"A Brief History of Time: From the Big Bang to Black Holes" Stephen Hawking (1988)
"The Search for Infinity: Solving the Mysteries of the Universe" Gordon Fraser, Egil and Inge Sellevag, Stephen Hawking (1995)
"Aglow in the dark: the revolutionary science of biofluorescence" Vincent Pieribone and David F. Gruber (2005)
"Bioluminescence: Chemical Principles and Methods" Osamu Shimomura (2006)
"Cold Light: Creatures, Discoveries, and Inventions That Glow" Anita Sitarski (2007)
"The Elements: A Visual Exploration of Every Known Atom in the Universe" Theodore Gray (2009)

Culture

"The Prophet" Kahlil Gibran (1923)
"Steppenwolf" Hermann Hesse (1927)
"The Journey to the East" Hermann Hesse (1932)
"Magister Ludi: The Glass Bead Game" Hermann Hesse (1943)
"Strange News from Another Star" Hermann Hesse (1972)
"C.G. Jung and Herman Hesse - A Record of Two Friendships" Miguel Serrano (1966)
"Black Elk Speaks" John G. Neihardt (1932)
"Lost Horizons" James Hilton (1936)
"The Myth of Sisyphus" Albert Camus (1942)
"La Peste" Albert Camus (1947)
"Anthem" Ayn Rand (1953)
"The Iceman Cometh" Eugene O'Neill
"The Doors of Perception" Aldous Huxley (1954)
"Brave New World Revisited" Aldous Huxley (1959)
"Island" Aldous Huxley (1963)
"Literature and Science" Aldous Huxley (1963)
"This Timeless Moment: A Personal View of Aldous Huxley" Laura Archera Huxley (1968)
"Stranger in a Strange Land" Robert A. Heinlein (1961)
"One Flew Over the Cuckoo's Nest" Ken Kesey (1962)
"Garage Sale" Ken Kesey (1973)
"Demon Box" Ken Kesey (1986)
"The Further Inquiry" Ken Kesey (1990)
"The Hog Farm and Friends" Wavy Gravy (Hugh Nanton Romney), Ken Kesey (1974)
"On the Bus" Ken Babbs and Paul Perry (1990)
"Official Guide New York World's Fair: 1964/1965" Published by Time-Life Books (1964)
"The Psychedelic Review" Volumes 1-11 (1963-1971)
"The Electric Kool-Aid Acid Test" Tom Wolfe (1968)
"The Teachings of Don Juan: A Yaqui Way of Knowledge" Carlos Casteneda (1968)
"The Art of Dreaming" Carlos Casteneda (1993)
"Yanomamo - The Fierce People" Napoleon A. Chagnon (1968)
"Soma: Divine Mushroom of Immortality" R. Gordon Wasson (1969)
"The Road to Eleusis: Unveiling the Secret of the Mysteries" R. Gordon Wasson, Albert Hofmann, and Carl A.P. Ruck (1978, 2008)
"Persephone's Quest: Entheogens and the Origins of Religion" R. Gordon Wasson (1986)
"Lame Deer, Seeker of Visions: The Life of a Sioux Medicine Man" John (Fire) Lame Deer and Richard Erdoes (1972)
"Tales of Mystery and Imagination" Edgar Allen Poe (1976)
"Ancient Egypt - Discovering it's Splendors" National Geographic Society, Karl W. Butzer (1977)
"Plants of the Gods: Their Sacred, Healing, and Hallucinogenic Powers" R.E. Schultes, Albert Hofmann, and C. Ratsch (1979)
"LSD - My Problem Child" Dr. Albert Hofmann (1979)
"Insight Outlook" Dr. Albert Hofmann (1988)
"Sacred Mushrooms of the Goddess: Secrets of Eleusis" Carl A.P. Ruck (2006)
"Mystic Chemist: The Life of Albert Hofmann and His Discovery of LSD" Dieter Hagenbach and Lucius Werthmuller (2013)
"The Holy Mushroom: Evidence of Mushrooms in Judeo-Christianity" J.R. Irvin (2008)
"Fools Crow" James Welch (1986)
"The San Francisco Fair: Treasure Island, 1939-1940" Edited by Patricia F. Carpenter and Paul Totah (1989)
"Gateway to the Gods - Haridwar, Rishikesh, Yamunotri, Gangotri, Kedarnath, Badrinath" Reeta and Rupinder Khullar (2004)
"Kumbh Mela and the Sadhus: The Quest for Immortality" Badri Narain and Kedar Narain (2010)

Index

Aach, Herb   9, 450, 451, 452, 453, 454, 455
Adams, Henry   101, 104, 105, 110, 111, 115, 536
Alma-Tadema, Lawrence   22
Althammer, Jorgens   463
Anaximenes of Miletio   4, 51, 52, 53
Andrews, W.S.   70
Angelicus, Barthomeleus   4, 53
Anita Sitarski   54, 57, 536
Aristocris   41
Aristotle   3, 4, 20, 21, 30, 52, 53, 298, 306, 356, 389, 393, 395, 410, 414
Armleder, John   446
Arnason   37, 536
Aryabhata   41

Babaji Santosh Puri   278, 478, 482
Babbs, Ken   8, 324, 325, 537
Bacon, Francis   4, 55, 56, 110
Balduin, Christian Adolf   4, 62
Ball, Philip   3, 39, 40
Boltzmann, Ludwig   47
Bandinelli, Baccio   29
Barton, Chris   5, 75, 535
Baskerville, Charles   7, 247, 248, 317
Batchelor, David   3, 11, 31, 34, 535
Batman, Stephen   4, 53
"The Beatles"   310, 318, 350
Becquerel, Antoine   66, 220, 317
Becquerel, Edmond   66, 159, 206, 209, 247
Becquerel, Henri   4, 155, 159, 162, 192, 209
Benjamin   503
Beringer, Karl   25, 327, 332,
Beuys, Joseph   416, 417
Biehle, August   103, 108, 109, 111
Biehle, Mary   105
Bing, Liesa   73, 74, 204, 372, 535
Birren, Faber   3, 8, 35, 40, 352, 353, 354, 355, 356, 371, 535
"Black Elk"   494, 536
Blanc, Charles   3, 13, 17, 19, 20, 30, 32, 33, 35, 227, 261, 374, 413, 418, 428, 449, 485, 496, 521, 535
Blunt and Cowan   6, 122, 128
Boer, Nils   142, 295, 387
Boccioni, Umberto   46, 106
Bonnard, Pierre   456, 458, 459, 527
Borofsky, Jonathan   9, 446
Bosch, Hieronymus   325, 371, 410
Bostwick, Richard   228, 315, 483, 535
Bottoni, Domenico   4, 62, 63
Bowman, Richard   9, 450, 451, 455, 456, 457, 458, 459, 460, 461, 527, 533
Boyle, Robert   4, 56, 57, 61, 222, 389, 393, 395, 428
Brand, Hennig   4, 54, 61, 62
Brand, Stewart   420
Brewster, Sir David Gabriel   4, 65, 202, 234, 316, 317
Britton and Collins   9, 324, 536
Brown, Richard O.   409
Brunelleschi   28
Burroughs, William   345
Byler, William   5, 67, 98, 99, 118

Caravaggio, Michelangelo   14, 424
Carson, Rachel   439, 440
Casciarola, Vincenzo   4, 50, 51, 53, 54, 55, 56, 62, 188, 316, 320
Cassady, Neal   323, 325
Casteneda, Carlos   330, 537
Cellini   4, 29, 54
Cennini   29
Cezanne, Paul   25, 32, 33, 34, 35, 39, 40, 103, 503, 536

Chalfie, Martin   7, 9, 48, 321, 386, 392, 393, 395, 401, 405, 408, 409,
Chagall, Marc   416
Charles Francois de Cisterney du Fay   4, 63
Cheval, Facteur Ferdinand   512, 513, 534
Chevreul, Michel Eugene   3, 30, 33, 35, 36, 40, 119, 321, 463, 535
Cicero   345
Clarke, Arthur C.   8, 327
Cohen, Dr. Sidney   100, 338
"Colet"   315, 491
Compagnoni, Achille   514
Culler, George D.   456, 459, 527
Curie, Marie   153, 154, 155, 157, 158, 159, 160, 161, 162, 163, 164, 165, 166, 220, 261, 535
Curie, Pierre   99, 155, 157, 159, 160, 161, 162, 166

Dake, H.C.   63, 70, 85, 86, 96, 149, 184, 201, 102, 211, 230, 232, 233, 234, 247, 248, 257, 258, 310, 535
Dali Lama   43
Dali, Salvador   97, 371, 374, 415
David, Jacques Louis   340
"davidkremers"   425
DaVinci, Leonardo   16, 29, 33, 37, 116, 322, 353, 378, 417, 424, 463, 536
Davy, Humphrey   8, 127, 144, 244, 329,
de Boeck, Felix   9, 450
Delacroix, Eugene   39, 113, 425
Delage, Michèle   1, 38, 39, 213, 215, 217, 467, 471, 479, 481, 512, 532, 533, 534,
Delaunay, Sonia and Robert   13, 25, 40, 103, 278, 371, 506
DeMent, Jack   6, 7, 63, 70, 85, 86, 96, 149, 184, 202, 211, 219, 233, 244, 247, 248, 257, 258, 310, 311
Deribere, Maurice   7, 67, 99, 243, 244, 245, 247, 249, 250, 251, 252, 254, 255, 256, 257, 258, 259, 260, 261, 262, 263, 535
DeSantis, Michael   107, 110
Descartes, Rene   4, 56, 61, 410, 414, 426
Dieter and Rosie   463
Dietz, Phil   324, 500, 501
"Dig Space"   463
Ditko, Steve   462
Donatello   28
Dorgeles, Ronald   414, 415, 417
Dubois, Raphael   61, 393
Duchamp, Marcel   8, 103, 351, 352, 404, 412, 415, 417, 503, 504, 512, 536
Dumollard, Remi   409

Edison, Thomas E.   7, 116, 128, 155, 247
Eidelberg, Tal   380
Einstein, Albert   47, 165, 203, 317, 338, 348, 378, 437, 438, 441, 469
Emperor Wu   52
Evans, Anthony   381, 382, 383

Father Bourzes   4, 63
Fenske, Gary   261, 284, 285, 518
Finlay, Victoria   3, 37, 38, 535
Finsen, Nils Ryberg   6, 128, 129, 130, 132
Fischinger, Oskar   9, 506, 507, 508, 509, 510, 511, 536
"Fluorescent Preacher Hofmann"   92, 208, 229
Fontana, Lucio   9, 450, 521, 522, 523, 524, 525, 526, 527
Forbes, Dick   80
Foster, Dan   359, 470
Francois Delamare and Bernard Furneua   3, 32, 535
Franklin, Benjamin   1, 4, 50, 64, 66, 186, 393

Galileo   4, 41, 54
Galvani, Luigi   411
Gandhi, Maneka   437
Garcia, Jerry   323, 370, 474
Garramone, Joseph   108
Gaspar, Dr. Bela   507
Gauguin, Paul   3, 25, 28, 32, 39, 40, 45, 49, 102, 103, 135, 137, 278, 320, 370, 371, 401, 404, 436, 456, 503, 527, 528, 536
Gell, Sir William   22
Gerstmann, Ewald   64, 189, 316, 490
Gesner, Conrad   4, 53
Gessert, George   9, 415, 416, 417, 418, 419

Ghiberti, Lorenzo   28, 29
Kahlil Girban   528
Gibson, John   22
Giesecke   318
Ginsberg, Alan   7, 248, 323, 326, 345
Giotto   28
Gleason, Sterling   6, 7, 188, 189, 190, 192, 247, 296, 311, 312, 313, 314, 315, 316, 317, 318, 350, 491, 520, 535
Goethe   3, 4, 17, 19, 21, 30, 31, 32, 35, 50, 51, 54, 64, 272, 356, 374, 454, 510, 535
Goff, Thomas   36, 261, 315, 518
Goldstein, Howard   463
Gray, Delmar   5, 74, 75, 76, 78, 80, 82
Grimes, Warren   5, 82, 83, 84, 88, 90, 268, 531
Grinspoon and Bakalar   8, 329
Grove, Sam   463
Grunfeld, Thomas   425
Guggenheim, Peggy   457

Harvey, E. Newton   3, 32, 51, 65, 202, 205, 210, 216, 218, 243, 249, 288, 390, 393, 394, 535, 536
Heffter, Arthur   8, 330, 332
Hendrix, Jimi   112, 264, 318, 321, 322, 359, 360, 396, 463, 464, 465, 470, 472, 533, 536
Henri, Robert   101, 103
Heracledes   41
Herman von Helmholtz   35
Herschel, Sir John   4, 65
Herschel, William   4, 63, 119, 127, 234
Hesse, Hermann   8, 25, 324, 326, 327, 330, 332, 334, 336, 350, 351, 371, 536
Hirst, Damien   27
Hittorff, J.I.   22
Hofmann, Dr. Albert   8, 297, 298, 302, 304, 306, 328, 338, 340, 341, 343, 344, 345, 346, 358, 359, 360, 361, 362, 363, 365, 366, 369, 370, 482, 533, 537
Hofmann, Dunot   4
Hooke, Robert   4, 61, 63
Huxley, Aldous   8, 18, 19, 336, 347, 348, 349, 350, 351, 362, 365, 528, 533, 557

Ingres   22, 40

Jacapo da Pontormo   16
Jean-Jacques Dortus de Mairan   4, 63
Jicha, Joseph   105, 107, 108, 109
Jobs, Steve   369
John "Fancy Free"   463
Johnson, Professor Frank   390, 393
Jung, Carl   25, 148, 332, 336, 354, 356, 371, 482, 536

Kac, Eduardo   9, 48, 320, 321, 404, 405, 406, 407, 408, 409, 410, 411, 412, 413, 414, 415, 416, 417, 420, 421, 422, 423, 425, 426, 427, 536
Kandinsky, Wassily   39, 103, 424, 425, 506, 535
Kaplan, Phillip   105, 106, 107, 115, 385
Kaprow, Allen   351
Dr. Kellogg   27, 97
Kenn., Jake   90, 91
Kennedy, Robert   338, 511
Kerouac, Jack   325, 326, 327
Kesey, Ken   7, 8, 100, 107, 139, 310, 323, 324, 325, 326, 327, 328, 332, 338, 350, 352, 372, 373, 374, 420, 469, 500, 501, 537
Kipling, Rudyard   371
Kircher, Athanasius   4, 56, 57, 63, 390
Kish, Daniel   357, 359
Klee, Paul   8, 25, 327, 336, 459, 506
Knutsson, Anders   461
Koons, Jeff   27, 404
Kosa, Victor   148
Krasner, Lee   45, 464, 536
Kromeyer   6
Kuch, Dr. Richard   5, 118
Kunz, Dr. George F.   7, 225, 247, 248, 315, 317

Lackner, Frank   143, 150
Leary, Timothy   242, 323, 326, 327, 365, 510
Le Bon, M. Gustave   66

Le Corbusier   3, 17, 19, 20, 30, 33, 34, 35, 535
Leeteg, Edgar   137
Lennon, John   40, 318
Leverrenz   239
Lewin, Lewis   8, 330, 332
Licetus, Fortunius   4, 55
Livius, Titus   4, 52
Lorand, Dr. Arnold   5, 120, 122
Luce, Henry and Claire   298, 338,
Lucie-Smith, Edward   424, 425
Luckiesh, M.   5, 118, 119, 120
Ludlum, John Plumer   7, 9, 114, 261, 274, 275, 276, 277, 278, 279, 280, 281, 282, 283, 284, 285, 286, 287, 288, 448, 449, 450, 451, 455, 458, 487, 521, 522, 523, 528, 533
Lukyanov, Sergey   8, 48, 397, 398
Lumière, Auguste and Louis   154

Madame Haoguo   53
Malek, Rajesh   359
Malevich, Kazimir   416
Mallary, Robert   9, 448, 449, 450, 508
Manetti   28
Martialis, Marcus Valerius   4, 53
Martin, John   475
Matisse, Pierre   39, 107, 103
Matz, Mikhail   397, 398, 401
Maxwell, James Clark   127
Dr. Mellanby   123
Mendoza, Ceyetano Garcia   305
Mercipinetti   7, 261
Michaux, Henri   371
Michelangelo Buonarroti   14, 15, 16, 17, 24, 28, 29, 30, 33, 37, 97, 100, 463, 503, 531, 536, 539
Miera   315, 483, 484, 488, 490, 491, 534
Millson, H.E.   226, 227, 228
Miro, Joan   25, 458
Moellmann, Carl   80, 84, 101, 102, 103, 105, 106, 107, 11, 112, 116
Monardes, Nicolas   4, 53, 56, 57
Mondrian, Piet   457
Monet, Claude   27, 39, 46, 103, 453, 460, 476, 503, 528, 536
"Mountain Girl"   8, 327, 328
Munsell, Albert   35

Napoleon   37, 106, 362, 537
Newsome, Don   228
Newton, Sir Isaac   3, 4, 13, 22, 35, 40, 56, 63, 320, 353,
Nichols, Mayme   104, 105

Oppenheimer, Robert   295
Orell, Marc   463
Orwell, George   22, 38, 310,
Osmond, Dr. Humphrey   8, 304, 336, 348, 349

Padalino, Christine and Nick   223, 315, 469
Padalino, Mary Jean   47, 184, 185, 265, 504, 505
Padalino, Nick   1, 2, 212, 213, 215, 217, 294, 358, 467, 471, 479, 481, 532, 533, 534
Padalino, Tony   468
Panceri, Paolo   393
Perry, Charles   8, 325, 326
Phillips, Eva   315, 487, 490
Picasso, Pablo   103, 114, 274, 281, 283, 286, 371, 414, 415, 425, 446, 458, 513
Piero di Cosimo   28
Pissarro, Camille   35
Plato   3, 20, 30, 298, 306, 340, 344, 345
Pliny the Elder   3, 4, 20, 21, 29, 52, 53, 58, 390, 393, 395
Plot, Robert   4, 20, 62
Plotinus   20
Plutarch   21
Poe, Edgar Allen   319, 537
Pollock, Jackson   3, 45, 46, 404, 457, 464, 476, 501, 502, 503, 508, 536

Priestly, Joseph   8, 329
Puri, Mandakini   480

Qianlong Emperor   30
Qin Shi Huang Di   23
Quattlebaum, W.D.   233
Quieheille, Toni   462

Rand, Ayn   47, 294, 537
Rand, John Goffe   36
Raphael   28, 60, 103,
Rauschenburg, Robert   351
Rembrandt   37, 39, 103, 520
Renoir, Auguste   39
Rhead and Evans   97, 98
Richardson, Allen   304, 305, 307, 308, 309, 345
Rigby, Bruce   30, 463
Riley, Charles A.   20
Riley, Janis   469
Rinkel, Dr. Max   297, 336
Ritter, Wilhelm   4, 50, 51, 64, 119, 126, 127, 321, 454
Robbins, Manuel   189, 239, 314, 535
Rodin, Auguste   12, 60, 154, 155
Roget   329
Rohault   4, 61
Dr. Rollier   130
Romita, John   462
Rood, Ogden Nichola   35
Rosenquist, James   9, 450
Rouhier, Alexander   332
Dr. Russell and Dr. Russell   126
Ruck, Carl A.P.   7, 298, 306, 338, 340, 341, 342, 343, 344, 345, 346, 537

Sabrina, Dona Maria   305, 306, 307, 308, 309, 340, 345
Dr. Sampurnanand   7, 299, 300, 301
Sam., Drey   92
Schatten, Gerald   398
Scheele, Carl Wilhelm   4, 119, 237
Schneider, Start   314, 535
Schutes, Richard E.   8, 345
Sebern, Roy   325, 327, 352
Serusier, Paul   40
Seurat, Georges   32, 33, 39, 40, 280, 503, 536
Shannon, John Thompson   5, 72, 74, 78, 99, 142, 145, 150, 168, 191, 237, 458, 532
Shelly, Mary   410, 411, 417
Dr. Shilipi   468
Shimomura, Osamu   7, 8, 9, 53, 55, 321, 386, 388, 390, 391, 392, 393, 394, 395, 397, 401, 405, 536
Siqueiros, David Alfaro   448
Smith, Leonard S.J.   78, 80
Schneider, Stuart   314, 535
Sommer, William   101, 102, 103, 104, 105, 106, 107, 108, 111
Sonfist, Alan   415
Soubirous, Bernadette   478, 482, 534
Spath, Ernst   8, 332
Srnec, Jiri   462
"Stelarc"   427, 428
Steichen, Edward   416, 426
Steiner, Rudolph   438, 439
Stella, Frank   9, 447, 448, 450,
Stern, Bert   374, 375
Steves, Rick   90
Stokes, Sir George Gabriel   4, 50, 64, 65, 66, 202, 203, 208, 209, 256, 317, 367, 470, 487
Stoll, Dr. Werner   297
Stoll, Rolf   108, 109
Strobl, Alexander   5, 72, 73, 74, 76, 77, 86, 93, 96, 98, 100, 334, 335, 531, 533
Stuart and Revett   21
Subramanian, Mas   520
Swan, Joseph   106, 127, 128

"The Switzer Brothers"   5, 73, 74, 75, 76, 82, 102, 111, 112, 115, 116, 117, 134, 145, 150, 153, 166, 180, 196, 204, 226, 227, 255, 267, 272, 274, 372, 373
Switzer, Joseph   5, 76, 80, 86, 115, 116, 117, 179, 192, 227, 255, 274, 450, 453
Switzer, Robert   1, 5, 67, 72, 73, 74, 75, 78, 80, 84, 86, 99, 110, 111, 117, 145, 169, 180, 192, 204, 236, 249, 273, 274, 276, 285, 372, 373, 377, 448, 450, 460, 487, 517

Tachard, Pere Guy   4, 62
Taylor, Marv   282, 283, 284, 285, 286, 288
"The Beatles"   310, 318, 350
Thomson, Sir J.J.   128
Thumpah and Angie   462
Tsai, H.J.   396
Tsien, Roger   8, 9, 400, 401, 402, 405
Tullet, Herve   8, 378
Turner   30, 39

Uccello   29

Van Dyck   39, 103
Vasari   28, 29
Venter, Dr. Craig   8, 383, 384, 385
Verri, Dr. Geovanni   12, 13
Victoria   503
Vigliante, Anthony   100
Vigliante, Virginia   223, 315, 318, 469
Vincent Pieribone and David Gruber   65, 536
Vincent Van Gogh   28, 32, 33, 39, 40, 49, 103, 132, 278, 417, 463, 464, 503, 516, 535

Waalwijk, Aja   512
Warhol, Andy   20, 373, 375, 415, 446, 451, 454
Warshawsky   102, 103
Warren, Thomas S.   72, 86, 88, 90, 114, 149, 175, 184, 189, 192, 194, 196, 204, 208, 226, 228, 230, 232, 236, 237, 261, 270, 271, 296, 297, 311, 312, 314, 315, 483, 487, 490, 493, 516, 517, 518, 519, 533, 534, 535, 541
Wasson, R. Gordon   7, 8, 298, 299, 301, 303, 304, 305, 306, 307, 308, 309, 310, 338, 340, 341, 344, 345, 346, 361, 365, 537
Wells, H.G.   410, 428
White, Anthony   522, 523, 524, 525
Wiedemann, Eilhardt   393
Wimmer, Karl Helmut   285
Wolfe, Tom   8, 100, 325, 326, 327, 328, 332, 372, 537
Wood, Dr. Robert   5, 11, 67, 72, 86, 118, 138, 189, 207, 243, 256, 318, 518

Zagar, Isaiah   512, 534
Zanotti, Francesco Mario   4, 63
Ziegfeld, Florenz   11, 72, 74, 78, 142, 156, 243, 262, 272, 278
Zimmer, Dr. Marc   8, 9, 386, 388, 389, 390, 391, 395, 396, 398, 399, 400, 404, 407, 408, 409, 421
Zorach, William   103
Zucchi, Nicola   4, 54, 56, 63

www.ingramcontent.com/pod-product-compliance
Lightning Source LLC
Chambersburg PA
CBHW082318220526
45470CB00008B/2351